S0-AVU-675

"Not long after I learned to read, I would grip the flashlight in my teeth and stay awake late into the night scouring my parent's copy of the 3rd edition of *Freedom of the Hills*. I studied the mystifying aid climbing techniques and the challenging navigation skills, subjects I eventually mastered. But what this book captured, what it meant, what it hinted at that was so crucial to my fascination with mountaineering was this: Freedom, itself, was the most important thing. Freedom to explore who I am. Freedom afforded by learned skills to explore any mountain wilderness. Freedom to move, to climb. It's what still drives me today."

—Steve House

"The paradox is that, with a half century behind it, *Freedom* just grows better and better. Would that the aging process do as well for those of us who savor the wisdom within! Freedom is truly the Everest of mountaineering texts and a great preparation for a life wandering among high hills, including the big one itself."

—Tom Hornbein

"Growing up in Southern California in the 1960s, I couldn't find anyone who shared my passion to learn how to climb. So I bought an ice axe, crampons, and *Freedom of the Hills* and still remember being on a snow slope with axe in one hand, book in the other, trying to teach myself how to self-arrest. It worked: I'm still around and still climbing."

—Rick Ridgeway

"My *Mountaineering: The Freedom of the Hills* is not just a book. To open my copy, a 5th edition, worn and frayed and with many vital passages underscored and noted by my pen, is to open a memory into what was certainly the most charged moment of my life, those teenage years hurtling forward and upward toward the vertical world that has come to not only represent my reason for living, but be the foundation for my values, education, and understanding of this world. I know I'm not alone. For many generations of climbers, *The Freedom of the Hills* is more than just a book. It's a passport to a rare and wild place."

—Andrew Bisharat

"I have never felt more alive than when adventuring in remote mountains, dependent on a rope, a rack, and the partner that's got my back... *Freedom of the Hills*, risk's best friend, is that partner."

—Timmy O'Neill

"As chief guide for Rainier Mountaineering for over 30 years, I have trained hundreds of new guides. And *The Freedom of the Hills* is the required textbook for their basic training on Mount Rainier. The new edition is even more valuable than ever. Thanks for the good work!"

—Lou Whittaker

"My first exploration of *Freedom of the Hills* took place in the late 1960s when I was barely a teenager, but was passionate about climbing Northwest volcanoes and whatever else I could get under my cramponed feet. What I remember most were the how-to illustrations, which entertained while they taught and made learning a pleasure."

—John Harlin III

"The 2nd edition of *Freedom of the Hills* (as well as pictures of Bonatti in an old REI catalog) jump-started my climbing education. The manual's content has kept pace with the evolution of the sport and should be considered mandatory reading for every mountain climber. This truly remarkable resource has no equal in any language."

—Mark Twight

"I've taught climbing on the world's great mountains for 25 years, and so it is humbling to realize how much I can still learn from simply sitting in a chair and reading *Freedom of the Hills*. But the game keeps changing, with new technologies and new techniques, and *Freedom* does a remarkable job of staying not just current, but on the cutting edge. Turning on new climbers to this resource is one of the best things I can do to prepare them for life in the big hills."

—Dave Hahn

"If the mountains are my church, then *Freedom* is my bible. From my early 5.4 leads more than 25 years ago to present day, it has served me well as a base for exploring every facet of the mountains. As a very young climber I read it cover to cover, then dug through it again and again for nuggets of wisdom. I still do."

—Will Gadd

"I purchased my first copy of *The Freedom of the Hills* in 1976 and consumed it several times, well before I ever set foot in the mountains. Through the years, my well-worn copy became my guide and reference for the art of mountaineering. I would highly recommend this book as a 'must have' for any aspiring mountaineer's library."

—Ed Viesturs

MOUNTAINEERING

The Freedom of the Hills

8th EDITION

50th anniversary

MOUNTAINEERING

The Freedom of the Hills

Edited by Ronald C. Eng

THE MOUNTAINEERS BOOKS
is the nonprofit publishing arm of The Mountaineers, an organization founded in 1906 and dedicated to the exploration, preservation, and enjoyment of outdoor and wilderness areas.

1001 SW Klickitat Way, Suite 201, Seattle, WA 98134

First edition 1960. Second edition 1967. Third edition 1974. Fourth edition 1982. Fifth edition 1992. Sixth edition 1997. Seventh edition 2003. Eighth edition 2010.

Manufactured in the United States of America

Developmental Editor: Julie Van Pelt
Copy Editor: Kris Fulsaas
Cover and Book Design: Heidi Smets
Layout: Marge Mueller, Gray Mouse Graphics
Illustrators: Dennis Arneson; Andrea Arneson; Jim Hays; Electronic Illustrators Group; Marge Mueller, Gray-Mouse Graphics; Ani Rucki; Ramona Hammerly
Front cover photograph: *Climber on Fox Glacier, Westland National Park, Southern Alps, New Zealand* (photo by Colin Monteath/maxximages.com)
Spine photograph: *Ice climber on vertical ice in Ouray Ice Park near Ouray, Colorado.* ©Sergio Ballivian/Aurora Photos
Back cover photograph: *Climbers on the Salbitnadel, Göscheneralp, Switzerland.* ©Christof Sonderegger
Frontispiece: *Two climbers on glacier in Bugaboo National Park, British Columbia, Canada.* ©Kennan Harvey/Aurora Photos
Page 6: *North Rim of the Black Canyon of the Gunnison National Park, Colorado.* ©Kennan Harvey/Aurora Photos
Pages 12–13: *Tents at Kahiltna Glacier airstrip camp on Mount Denali, Alaska.* ©Craig Rowley
Pages 132–33: *Climbers on the West Buttress of Mount Denali, Alaska.* ©Craig Rowley
Pages 209–10: *Simon Tappin on* Fitz-In, *Huntman's Leap, Pembroke, Wales.* ©Simon Carter/Onsight Photography
Pages 318–39: *Abby Watkins on* Half 'n' Half, *Haffner Creek, British Columbia, Canada.* ©Simon Carter, Onsight Photography
Pages 472–73: *Karstens Ridge, Mount Denali, Alaska.* ©Craig Rowley
Pages 530–31: Nieves penitentes *between the West Col and Panch Pokhari Lakes, Nepal.* ©Craig Rowley
Page 562: *Crossing a stream below Amphu Laptsa Pass in the Khumbu region of Nepal.* ©Craig Rowley

Trademarks and brand names used in this book: Alien; Allen wrench; ATC Guide; Avalung II; Band-Aid; Block Roll; Bug; Camalot; Camalot C3; Camalot C4; Cinch; Clean Mountain Can; Cordura; Curve Hex; DeLorme Topo USA; Diamox; Dyneema; Earthmate PN; Eddy; Ensolite; EpiPen; eTrex; Fat Cam; Friend; Gamow bag; Ghost; Google Earth; Gore-Tex; Green Trails Maps; Grigri; Hexentric; Hybrid Alien; Kevlar; Leave No Trace; Link Cam; Masonite; Mini Traxion; Molefoam; Moleskin; National Geographic TOPO!; National Geographic TOPO USA; Oregon series GPS; Panoramio; Parsol 1789; Pecker; Perlon; Phillips; Pro Traxion; Pyramid; Reverso^3; Revolving Carabiner; RURP; SAM; Screamer; 2nd Skin; Spectra; Stairmaster; Steri-Strip; Stopper; Sum; Talon; Technical Friend; Teflon; TerraServer-USA; Tricam; Triton series GPS; Tuber II; Tyvek; Valley Giant cams; Velcro; Vibram; Wag Bag; Waste Case; WD-40; Web-o-lette; Z nailer

Selected text in Chapter 4 was adapted from *The Outdoor Athlete* (2009) by Courtenay Schurman and Doug Schurman with permission from Human Kinetics, Champaign, IL.

Library of Congress Cataloging-in-Publication Data

Mountaineering : the freedom of the hills / edited by Ronald C. Eng and Julie Van Pelt. —8th ed.
p. cm.
ISBN 978-1-59485-137-7 (hardcover) — ISBN 978-1-59485-138-4 (trade paper) —ISBN 978-1-59485-408-8 (e-book)
1. Mountaineering. 2. Rock climbing. 3. Snow and ice climbing. I. Eng, Ronald C. II. Van Pelt, Julie.
GV200.M688 2010
796.52'2—dc22

2010015099

ISBN (cloth): 978-1-59485-137-7
ISBN (paper): 978-1-59485-138-4
ISBN (ebook): 978-1-59485-408-8

 Printed on 100% recycled, 30% PCW paper

CONTENTS

PREFACE

"The quest of the mountaineer, in simplest terms, is for the freedom of the hills...."
—*The first line of the first edition*

Mountaineering: The Freedom of the Hills is used by recreational and professional climbers throughout the world. It is an essential reference for both the beginner and for the experienced mountaineer. As a comprehensive textbook of mountaineering, it has few peers. For the novice climber, *Freedom* provides an encyclopedic and accessible source book. The various editions of this book have been translated into ten languages.

The eighth edition commemorates the fiftieth anniversary of the publication of the first edition in 1960. Each chapter has been reviewed, revised, and—where necessary—expanded. These revisions reflect the rapid changes in mountaineering, including the development of new techniques and the introduction of improved equipment. In this edition we continue to emphasize the responsibility we assume as climbers to practice good stewardship and to use minimum impact techniques in order to leave no trace of our passage.

SCOPE OF THE BOOK

As in previous editions, the eighth edition of *Freedom* provides sound and clear coverage of the current concepts, techniques, and problems involved in the pursuit of mountaineering, and provides a fundamental understanding of each topic covered. In addition to presenting information for the novice, much of the material in this book can help experienced climbers review and improve their skills. Coverage of some topics, such as rock climbing, ice climbing, and aid climbing, is detailed enough to be useful to readers with specific interests in those topics.

Freedom is not intended, however, to be exhaustive; some climbing disciplines are not comprehensively addressed in these pages. Gym and sport climbing, for example—making use of artificial climbing walls or fixed-protection routes at developed climbing areas—are increasingly popular. Although many techniques related to both disciplines are interchangeable with those of mountain and rock climbing, there are differences. Those interested solely in gym or sport climbing should also consult specialized texts.

Mountaineering cannot be learned just by studying a book. However, books can be important as a source of information and as a complement to good instruction. *Freedom* was originally written as a textbook for students and instructors participating in organized climbing courses. The learning environment that is found in a climbing course taught by competent instructors is essential for beginning climbers.

Of necessity, climbing requires continual awareness of the situation and environment at hand. Varying conditions, routes, and individual abilities all mean that the techniques used and decisions made must be based on the particular circumstances. To any situation, the individual climber and climbing team must apply their knowledge, skills, and experience and then make their own judgments. To reflect this process, *Freedom* presents a variety of widely used techniques and practices, and then outlines both their advantages and limitations. Material is presented not as dogma or the definitive word but as the basis for making sound judgments. To climb safely, climbers must realize that mountaineering is a problem-solving process and cannot be viewed as a rote application of techniques.

The type of climbing described in *Freedom* is frequently experienced (and, most people would say, best experienced) in the wilderness. Wilderness mountaineers take responsibility for helping to preserve the wilderness environment for present and future generations. The preservation of wilderness is crucial to protecting the health of our ecosystem.

ORIGINS OF THE BOOK

A synopsis of *Freedom*'s evolution presents a capsule history of The Mountaineers. From its beginnings, *Freedom* has been the product of the concerted effort of a team of members. For each edition, the team of contributors has sprung forth from across the organization's membership.

When The Mountaineers was founded in 1906, one of its major purposes was to explore and study the mountains, forests, and watercourses of the Northwest. The journey to the mountain summit was a long and difficult one, and it required a variety of skills. With the knowledge gained from mastering these skills, the competence that came from their practice, and the experience developed through climbing mountains, more than a few climbers acquired the exhilarating freedom of the hills.

Freedom's direction and emphasis originated from the nature of climbing in the Pacific Northwest. The wild and complex character of the mountains in this region, with their abundance of snow and glaciers throughout the year, furthered the mountaineering challenge. Access was inherently difficult. There were few roads, the terrain was rugged, and the initial explorations were themselves expeditions, often requiring the assistance of Native American guides.

As interest in mountaineering in the region grew, so did a tradition of tutelage. Increasingly, experienced climbers took novices under their wings to pass on their knowledge and skills. The Mountaineers formalized that exchange by developing a series of climbing courses.

Initially various climbing texts were used, but it became obvious that none of them were ideal for the region. *Freedom* has grown out of more than a century of teaching mountaineering and conducting climbs in the Northwest and throughout the world.

The first edition of *Freedom* was published in 1960 (the work had begun in 1955), with an eight-person editorial committee coordinating the efforts of more than 75 contributors. Harvey Manning was the chief editor and was primarily responsible for establishing the scope of the book. It was his idea to add the distinctive subtitle "The Freedom of the Hills." The first edition of *Freedom* included 430 pages, 134 illustrations and 16 black and white plates organized into 22 chapters. In comparison, this 50th anniversary edition is 600 pages, 424 illustrations, and 21 black and white photos organized into 27 chapters.

LEGACY OF THE PRECEDING EDITIONS

Isaac Newton wrote, "If I have seen further, it is by standing upon the shoulders of giants." The previous editions of *Freedom* represent a tradition of compiling, sorting, and integrating the knowledge, techniques, opinions, and advice of a large number of practicing climbers. Students, both in training sessions and on climbs, have always been a pivotal sounding board and testing ground. Each new edition has been carefully built on the foundation of the preceding editions.

Prior to publication of the first edition of *Freedom* in 1960, The Mountaineers climbing courses had used a number of European textbooks, particularly Geoffrey Winthrop Young's classic *Mountain Craft*. However, these books did not cover the various subjects unique and important to American and Pacific Northwest mountaineering. To fill in the gaps, course lecturers prepared outlines, which they distributed to students. These outlines were first fleshed out and compiled as the *Climber's Notebook*, and subsequently published as the *Mountaineers Handbook*. By 1955, the tools and techniques had changed so drastically, and the climbing courses had become so much more complex, that a new and more comprehensive textbook was needed.

The first edition editorial committee included Harvey Manning (chair), John R. Hazle, Carl Henrikson, Nancy Bickford Miller, Thomas Miller, Franz Mohling, Rowland Tabor, and Lesley Stark Tabor. A substantial portion of the then relatively small Puget Sound climbing community participated—some 75 were writers of the preliminary, revised, advanced, semifinal, and final chapter drafts, and an additional one to two hundred were reviewers, planners, illustrators, typists, proofreaders, financiers, promoters, retailers, warehousemen, and shipping clerks. In fact, there were few Mountaineers climbers who did not have some involvement with the book. Those donating their time and effort were rewarded by their accomplishment, and those donating their money were repaid from the success of the book. *Freedom* became the first title published by the now very productive Mountaineers Books.

The second edition revision committee included John M. Davis (chair), Tom Hallstaff, Max Hollenbeck, Jim Mitchell, Roger Neubauer, and Howard Stansbury. Work on the second edition, which was published in 1967, began in 1964. Even though much of the first edition was retained, the task force was, again, of impressive proportions, numbering several dozen writers and uncounted reviewers and helpers. Members of the first committee, notably John R. Hazle, Tom Miller, and Harvey Manning, provided continuity to the effort. As with the first edition, Harvey Manning once again edited the entire text and supervised production.

The third edition revision committee, which was formed in 1971, included Sam Fry (chair), Fred Hart, Sean Rice, Jim Sanford, and Howard Stansbury. Initially, a planning committee analyzed the previous edition and set guidelines for its revision. Once again, a large number of climbers contributed to individual chapters; the reviewing, revising, editing, and collation of chapters and sections were a true community effort. Peggy Ferber edited the entire book, which was published in 1974.

The fourth edition revision committee included Ed Peters (chair), Roger Andersen, Dave Anthony, Dave Enfield, Lee Helser, Robert Swanson, and John Young. The fourth edition of *Freedom*, which was published in 1982, involved a major revision and included complete rewrites of many chapters, most notably the entire section on ice and snow. A team of hundreds was guided by the revision committee. A large number of climbers submitted comments to the committee. Small teams of writers prepared a series of drafts for review by the technical editors. In addition to the substantial contribution such writers made, many others provided valuable help through critiques of subsequent and final drafts not only for technical accuracy and consistency but also for readability and comprehension.

The fifth edition revision committee, which was chaired first by Paul Gauthier and later by Myrna Plum, included section coordinators Marty Lentz, Margaret Miller, Judy Ramberg, and Craig Rowley, and editorial coordinator Ben Arp. Work on the fifth edition began in late 1987. The fifth edition involved another major revision and was published in 1992. Content was brought up-to-date and the layout and illustrations were made more contemporary and readable. Professional editor and writer Don Graydon blended the volunteers' efforts into a consistent and readable style.

The sixth edition revision committee included Kurt Hanson (chair), Jo Backus, Marcia Hanson, Tom Hodgman, Myrna Plum, and Myron Young. Don Heck coordinated the illustrations. Don Graydon again edited the text. The committee began work in the autumn of 1994 and the sixth edition was published in 1997. Three new chapters were added: "Mountain Geology," "The Cycle of Snow," and "Mountain Weather."

The seventh edition revision committee included Steven M. Cox (chair), Ron Eng, Jeremy Larson, Myrna Plum, Cebe Wallace, John Wick, and John Wickham. Preparation of the illustrative material was overseen by Jeff Bowman and Debra Wick. Kris Fulsaas edited the text. Planning for the seventh edition began in autumn of 2000 and it was published in 2003. It included a new chapter, "Waterfall Ice and Mixed Climbing," and new illustrations.

THE EIGHTH EDITION

What sets *Freedom* apart from other climbing texts is the process by which its content is prepared. The contributors are all climbers who regularly use and teach the information and techniques about which they write in this book. The collaborative effort distills the knowledge and experience of the many contributors into a cohesive whole. Although only one or two individuals have responsibility for preparing the initial draft of a chapter, the other contributors review and share their opinions on the material.

Planning for the eighth edition began in autumn of 2008. The Mountaineers Board of Trustees appointed Ronald C. Eng to lead the effort to develop the new edition. Comments and suggestions were then gathered from experienced climbers throughout the world. The eighth edition revision committee, which also included Jeff Bowman, Peter Clitherow, Dale Flynn, Gretchen Lentz, Mike Maude, Mindy Roberts, and John Wick, first met in November 2008.

Part I, Outdoor Fundamentals, was overseen by Peter Clitherow. Individual chapters were written by: Susan Wright Geiger, "First Steps"; Bill Deters, "Clothing and Equipment"; Satu Muldrow, "Camping and Food"; Courtenay Schurman, "Physical Conditioning"; Bob Burns and John Bell, "Navigation"; Peter Clitherow, "Wilderness Travel"; Steve Payne, "Leave No Trace"; and Peter Clitherow, "Stewardship and Access."

Part II, Climbing Fundamentals, was overseen by Dale Flynn. Individual chapters were written by: Joe Dumelin, "Basic Safety System"; Phil Kelley, "Belaying"; and Steve Biem, "Rappeling."

Part III, Rock Climbing, was overseen by Mindy Roberts. Individual chapters were written by: Sunny Remington and Gary Yngve, "Alpine Rock Climbing Technique"; Doug Souliere and Mindy Roberts, "Rock Protection"; Jim Gawel and David Moore, "Leading on Rock"; and Holly Beck and Jeff Bowman, "Aid and Big Wall Climbing."

Part IV, Snow, Ice, and Alpine Climbing, was overseen by Mike Maude. Individual chapters were written by: Jim Nelson and Randy Nelson, "Snow Travel and Climbing"; Peter Clitherow, "Glacier Travel and Crevasse Rescue"; Mike Maude and Anita Cech, "Alpine Ice Climbing" and "Waterfall Ice and Mixed Climbing"; and Grace Parker, "Expedition Climbing."

Part V, Emergency Prevention and Response, was overseen by John Wick. Individual chapters were written by: Don Goodman and Cebe Wallace, "Leadership"; John Ohlson, "Safety: How to Stay Alive"; Gretchen Lentz, M.D., and Geoff Ferguson, M.D., "First Aid"; and Doug Sanders, Jeff Bowman, and Ron Eng, "Alpine Search and Rescue."

Part VI, The Mountain Environment, was overseen by Gretchen Lentz. Individual chapters were written by: Scott Babcock, "Mountain Geology"; Sue Ferguson, "The Cycle of Snow"; and Jeff Renner, "Mountain Weather."

Preparation of the illustrative material was overseen by Jeff Bowman.

Laura Martin, Steve Cox, and Dave Shema provided additional valuable input. The staff of The Mountaineers Books also contributed their time and talents, particularly project editor Mary Metz, freelance editors Julie Van Pelt and Kris Fulsaas, and illustrators Marge Mueller and Dennis Arneson.

A NOTE ABOUT SAFETY

Safety is an important concern in all outdoor activities. No book can alert you to every hazard or anticipate the limitations of the reader. The descriptions of techniques and procedures in this book are intended to provide general information. Nothing substitutes for formal instruction, constant practice, and experience. When you follow any of the procedures described here, you assume responsibility for your own safety. Use this book as a general guide to further information. Under normal conditions, excursions into the backcountry require attention to traffic, road and trail conditions, weather, terrain, the capabilities of your party, and other factors. Keeping informed on current conditions and exercising common sense are the keys to a safe, enjoyable outing.

Political conditions may add to the risks of travel in other countries in ways that this book cannot predict. When you travel, you assume this risk and should keep informed of political developments that may make safe travel difficult or impossible.

—*The Mountaineers Books*

PART I

OUTDOOR FUNDAMENTALS

TECHNICAL KNOWLEDGE AND SKILLS • PHYSICAL PREPARATION • MENTAL PREPARATION • JUDGMENT AND EXPERIENCE • CARING FOR THE WILDERNESS—LEAVE NO TRACE • PRESERVING WILDERNESS • A CLIMBING CODE • GAINING THE FREEDOM OF THE HILLS

Chapter 1 FIRST STEPS

Mountaineering is many things. It is climbing, panoramic views, and wilderness experience. For many, it is the fulfillment of childhood dreams; for others, an opportunity to grow in the face of difficulty. In the mountains await adventure and mystery and lifetime bonds with climbing partners. The challenge of mountaineering offers you a chance to learn about yourself by venturing beyond the confines of the modern world.

To be sure, you will also find risk and hardship, but despite the difficulties sometimes faced—or maybe because of them—mountaineering can provide a sense of tranquility and spiritual communion found nowhere else. In the words of British climber George Leigh Mallory, "What we get from this adventure is just sheer joy."

But before you find joy or freedom in the hills, you must prepare for the mountains by learning technical, physical, mental, and emotional skills. Just as you must take a first step in order to climb a mountain, you must also take first steps to become a mountaineer. And though becoming skilled in the mountains is a process that continues as long as you spend time there, you have to begin somewhere. This book can serve as your guide and reference in acquiring those skills and, as such, your passport to the freedom of the hills. This chapter starts you along the path to learning the techniques needed for safe and skilled mountain travel.

TECHNICAL KNOWLEDGE AND SKILLS

To travel safely and enjoyably in the mountains, you need skills. You need to know what clothing, basic equipment, and food to bring into the backcountry and how to overnight safely. You need to know how to cover long distances while relying on only what you carry in your pack, navigating without trails or signs. You need technical climbing skills, including belaying (the technique of securing your rope partner in case of a fall) and rappeling (using the rope to descend), to competently scale and descend the mountains you reach. And you must have the specific skills for the terrain you choose—whether it is rock, snow, ice, or glacier. Although mountaineers always strive to minimize risks to themselves and others, mountain travel can never be completely predictable. For that reason, every mountaineer should be trained in safety, wilderness first aid, and rescue.

PHYSICAL PREPARATION

Mountaineering is a physically demanding activity. Nearly every type of climbing has become increasingly athletic, especially at the higher levels of difficulty. Climbers today accomplish feats that were once considered impossible. In rock, ice, and high-altitude climbing, new standards are set regularly. Limits are being pushed not only on the way up peaks, but also on the way down. Steep routes once considered difficult or impossible to ascend are now also descended on skis and snowboards. Among the changes to the landscape of climbing, notable are the advances and increasing popularity of steep ice climbing and "mixed" climbs, those that include a combination of frozen water and rock. Although most people appreciate such extreme achievements from the sidelines, higher standards at the extreme performance levels of climbing often result in higher standards at all levels.

Whatever your skill level and aspiration, good physical conditioning is critically important. The stronger you are, the better prepared you will be to face the challenges of climbing mountains, whether your outing goes as expected or includes unexpected difficulties. You will have a wider choice of mountains to climb, and you will be more likely to enjoy trips rather than to simply endure them. More important, the safety of the whole party may hinge on the strength—or weakness—of one member.

MENTAL PREPARATION

Just as important as physical conditioning is mental attitude, which often determines success or failure in mountaineering. The ability to keep a clear, calm mind helps in everything from deciding whether to stay home due to a weather forecast to pushing through a difficult technical climbing move or rescuing a climbing partner after a crevasse fall. Mountaineers need to be positive, realistic, and honest with themselves. A can-do attitude may turn into dangerous overconfidence if it is not tempered with a realistic appraisal of the circumstances and environment.

Many a veteran mountaineer says the greatest challenges are mental. Perhaps this is one of mountaineering's greatest appeals: While seeking the freedom of the hills, we come face to face with ourselves.

JUDGMENT AND EXPERIENCE

As important as mental preparation and attitude is the ability to solve problems and make good decisions. Sound judgment, perhaps a mountaineer's most valued and prized skill, develops from integrating knowledge with experience. This book outlines equipment and techniques ranging from the basic to the advanced, but the goal of every mountaineer is determining how best to use that learning to answer the sometimes unpredictable challenges faced in the mountains.

Much of what mountaineers need are coping skills and problem-solving skills—the ability to deal with external factors such as adverse weather, long hikes, and mountain accidents, as well as internal factors including fear, exhaustion, and desire. As climbers experience challenging situations, they become better decision makers, gaining judgment and experience that can help them in the future.

However, mountaineering tends to provide many novel situations that require careful judgment rather than automatic responses. Although you may use past experience to make decisions in the mountains, you will almost certainly never face the same situation twice. To be sure, this creates the potential for tragedy, but this uncertainty also holds the allure and challenge of mountaineering.

The same can be said of many situations that involve risk, challenge, and accomplishment. As Helen Keller observed in 1957 in *The Open Door*, "Security is mostly a superstition. It does not exist in nature, nor do the children of men as a whole experience it. Avoiding danger is no safer in the long run than outright exposure. Life is either a daring adventure, or nothing."

CARING FOR THE WILDERNESS—LEAVE NO TRACE

The mountaineering skills in this book are tools that allow you to visit remote areas of the world. If you use these skills to answer the call of wild vistas, remember that the beauty of wilderness frequently becomes its undoing by attracting visitors—leaving the landscape touched by human hands and eventually less than wild.

People are consuming wilderness at an alarming rate—using it, managing it, and changing it irreparably. For this reason, The Mountaineers and many other outdoor enthusiasts have adopted a set of principles and ethics referred to as Leave No Trace.

The mountains do not exist for our amusement. They owe us nothing, and they ask nothing of us. Hudson Stuck, a member of the first team to ascend Mount McKinley, fervently described this attitude in *The Ascent of Denali*: The summit party felt they had been granted "a privileged communion with the high places of the earth." As mountaineers traveling in the wilderness, our minimum charge for this privilege is to leave the hills as we found them, with no sign of our passing.

PRESERVING WILDERNESS

The privileges we enjoy in the mountains bring the responsibility not only to leave no trace but also to help preserve these environments we love. The facts of mountaineering life today include permit systems that limit access to the backcountry, environmental restoration projects, legislative alerts, clashes among competing interest groups, and closures of roads, trails, and entire climbing areas. In addition to being vigilant in treading softly in the mountains, mountaineers must now speak loudly in support of wilderness preservation, access, and sensitive use of our wild lands. We can no longer assume that we will have access to explore the vertical realms of our planet. In addition to being mountaineers, climbers, and adventurers, we must be active wilderness advocates if we want to continue to enjoy what was once taken for granted.

A CLIMBING CODE

Many years ago, The Mountaineers devised a set of guidelines to help people conduct themselves safely in the mountains. Based on careful observation of the habits of skilled climbers and a thoughtful analysis of accidents, those guidelines have served well not only for climbers but, with slight adaptation, for all wilderness travelers. (See Climbing Code sidebar.)

This Climbing Code is not meant to be a step-by-step formula for reaching summits or avoiding danger but, rather, a set of guidelines for encouraging safe mountaineering. It is recommended especially for beginners, who have not yet developed the necessary judgment that comes from years of experience. Experienced mountaineers often modify these guidelines in practice, making judgments based on an understanding of the risk as well as the skill to help control that risk.

Climbers sometimes question the need for such standards in a sport notable for the absence of formal rules. However, many serious accidents could have been avoided or minimized if these simple principles had been followed. This Climbing Code is built on the premise that mountaineers want a high probability for safety and success, even in risk-filled or doubtful situations, and that they want an adequate margin of safety in case they have misjudged their circumstances.

GAINING THE FREEDOM OF THE HILLS

"Freedom of the hills" is a concept that combines the simple joy of being in the mountains with the skill, equipment, and strength to travel without harm to ourselves, others, or the environment. The hills do not offer this freedom freely—only on trade. What you must offer in this trade is training, preparation, and desire.

We live in an age in which a conscious choice is required to avoid civilization with all of its technologies and conveniences. Particularly in the modern digital world, we are often accessible by phone or email every minute of every day. With the right equipment, this can be true anywhere on the planet. Although you do not have to leave these things behind to go to the mountains, for those who want to step out of—if only briefly—this mechanized, digitized world, the mountains beckon. They offer a place of richness and communion with the natural world that is now the exception rather than the rule.

Mountaineering takes place in an environment indifferent to human needs, and not everyone is willing to pay the price for its intense physical and spiritual rewards. But those who dream of climbing mountains can use this book to follow that dream. And if you learn to climb safely and skillfully, body and spirit in tune with the wilderness, you too can heed the inspiration of John Muir. "Climb the mountains," he told us, "and get their good tidings. Nature's peace will flow into you as sunshine flows into trees. The winds will blow their own freshness into you and the storms their energy, while cares will drop off like autumn leaves." As Muir wrote in *Our National Parks*, "Walk quietly in any direction and taste the freedom of the mountaineer."

CLIMBING CODE

- Leave the trip itinerary with a responsible person.
- Carry the necessary clothing, food, and equipment.
- A climbing party of three is the minimum, unless adequate prearranged support is available. On glaciers, a minimum of two rope teams is recommended.
- Rope up on all exposed places and for all glacier travel. Anchor all belays.
- Keep the party together, and obey the leader or majority rule.
- Never climb beyond your ability and knowledge.
- Never let judgment be overruled by desire when choosing the route or deciding whether to turn back.
- Follow the precepts of sound mountaineering as set forth in books of recognized merit.
- Behave at all times in a manner that reflects favorably upon mountaineering, including adherence to Leave No Trace principles.

Chapter 2
CLOTHING AND EQUIPMENT

Packing for a wilderness trip is a question of take it or leave it. With thousands of choices available in outdoor clothing and equipment, it is no longer a question of how to find what is needed but, rather, of limiting the load to the items necessary to keep you safe, dry, and comfortable. The idea is to carry what is needed and leave the rest at home. More clothing and equipment may make you more comfortable, but the extra weight may also limit how far, fast, or high you can go.

To strike a balance between too much and too little, monitor what you take on a trip. After each trip, determine what you used, what was genuinely needed for a margin of safety, and what items were unnecessary. When buying equipment, go for lightweight, low-bulk alternatives if the reduction does not jeopardize the item's performance or durability.

If you are new to mountaineering, you will not have the experience yet to know what will work best, so do not buy all the basic gear right away. Take it one trip at a time, one purchase at a time. New climbers tend to buy for extremes they seldom encounter. Wait until you have garnered enough experience to make intelligent decisions before spending money on clothing, boots, or packs. Rent, borrow, or improvise during early outings. Get advice by talking to seasoned climbers, by window-shopping at outdoor stores, and by reading mountaineering magazines. The "latest and greatest" product is not always best overall. The best items for a person's intended use are not necessarily the most costly. However, the cheapest gear is often not the most economical; with experience, you might discover that certain gear features and attributes justify a higher cost, and as a result you might replace cheaper gear with what you really want and need.

This chapter provides information on basic and

essential wilderness gear. Additional gear for overnight trips, such as stoves, cookware, sleeping bags and pads, and tents, is covered in Chapter 3, Camping and Food. This chapter includes guidelines on what constitutes good equipment, and though it will not advise which brands to purchase, it will help you select high-quality items among the many choices.

CLOTHING

Clothing helps a person stay comfortable by creating a thin insulating layer of air next to the skin. The enemies of comfort—precipitation, wind, heat, and cold—work against this protective air layer.

"Comfort" is usually a relative term for mountaineers. Inclement weather often forces climbers to endure conditions that deteriorate far below most people's concept of comfort. In climbing, the key to maintaining relative comfort is to stay dry—or, when wet, to stay warm and get dry quickly.

Mountaineering clothing serves a much greater purpose than comfort. In the wilderness, safety is a primary concern. When venturing into remote territory, climbers lose the option of quickly dashing back to civilization to escape foul weather. Instead, they must deal with difficult conditions for however long those conditions last.

Prolonged periods of dampness, even in moderately cool temperatures, can cause the body's core temperature to fall. Failure to protect yourself from wind exposes you to the accelerated drop in temperature known as the windchill effect (see Appendix B, Windchill Temperature Index). For many unfortunate individuals, substandard clothing has led to hypothermia—a dangerous, uncontrolled drop in body temperature that is a frequent cause of death in the mountains (see Chapter 23, First Aid, for more on hypothermia). Carefully select your clothing system to assure your survival during sustained exposure to cold and wet conditions.

Conversely, the clothing system must also protect you from overheating on hot days and prevent excessive sweating, which can dampen clothing from within and lead to severe dehydration. Ventilation, breathability, and sun protection are additional key considerations (see Appendix C, Heat Index).

At outdoor equipment stores, an overwhelming variety of garments, high-tech fabrics, features, and brand names all proclaim superior performance. With the dazzling matrix of high-tech gear vying for purchase, assembling a clothing system for the first time can be a daunting and confusing task. When shopping for clothing, ask questions and read tags to help make informed decisions. Evaluate garments for their functionality and versatility: Will they work when wet? Do they have a wide comfort range? In addition to cost, consider durability, fit, versatility, and reliability. Clothing for other outdoor activities may be suitable for climbing also.

Keep in mind that no single garment or fabric is ideal for all climbers or all situations. One climber may select a clothing system markedly different from that chosen by another with a different body structure or metabolism. Nor will an individual climber always use exactly the same clothing system on every outing. Different clothing may be worn depending on the season and type of activity. Personal preference plays a significant role. The best way to select an outdoor wardrobe is to gain experience and judgment by trial and error, sticking with the clothing strategies that provide the most comfort.

If you are new to wilderness travel, it is probably best to start out carrying what seems like more than enough layers to keep warm and dry. Delete items from your pack only when there is no doubt that it is possible to survive without them, regardless of the conditions. Try to minimize the weight of your clothing, but not at the expense of safety. Before heading out to the peaks, get a weather forecast and think ahead about what temperatures and conditions might be encountered, then pack accordingly.

LAYERING

Optimize the effectiveness and versatility of clothing by wearing a system of layers. Layering makes it easier to adapt to fluctuating temperatures and conditions in the mountains. The goal of layering is to keep your body temperature comfortable at all times, with the least clothing weight and bulk possible. This often means frequent adjustments. Most experienced mountaineers eventually develop a basic system of a few very select garments of high functionality, which they use in combination, depending on conditions and personal preferences, for most of their mountaineering activities. The base layer may change, more or less insulation might be carried, perhaps a different outer garment, or something new to try out—but the basic layering system has withstood the test of time and the latest fad in high-tech sportswear. This basic outdoor clothing system consists of three types of layers: a layer next to the skin, insulating layers, and an outer shell layer.

Layer next to the skin. The base layer should allow perspiration to pass away from your skin, keeping it dry. This wicking process can be vital to keeping you warm, because wet garments in contact with the skin can cause far more heat loss than dry ones.

Insulating layers. The insulating layers should trap warm air next to your body. The thicker the layer of trapped air, the warmer you will be. Although they are not as efficient as a single, monolithic block of "dead" air (as in a down parka, for example), several light, loosely fitting layers can trap a lot of insulating air in and between each other, and such an arrangement is very adjustable.

Shell layer. The outer layer should provide protection from wind and precipitation.

CHOOSING FABRICS

Clothing suitable for the outdoors is made from a great variety of fabrics, each with its particular advantages and drawbacks. Various qualities of outdoor fabrics are detailed in the following sections and summarized in Table 2-1.

Natural Fibers

In the early days of mountaineering, natural-fiber clothing was all that was available. Although they can work well, most natural fibers readily absorb water. This is usually (but not always) a disadvantage.

Cotton. Comfortable to wear when dry, cotton loses its insulating qualities when wet, absorbs many times its weight in water, and generally takes a long time to dry. Because of these characteristics, it is dangerous to rely on cotton for warmth. Cotton plays a common role in many hypothermia tragedies. In hot weather, however, cotton ventilates and cools well, and it can provide good sun protection. Wear a wet cotton T-shirt on a hot day, and the evaporating water will cool you off.

Wool. Far less absorbent than cotton, wool holds less water when wet and requires less heat to dry. When wet, wool does not collapse as much as cotton; thus, it retains much of its dead-air space and works well as an insulating layer. This noncollapsing feature also makes wool a great material for socks. The main drawbacks of wool are its relatively heavy weight and its bulkiness. Wool garments vary in their processing—the lighter the processing (that is, the closer the wool resembles raw wool), the better the garment will shed water. Wool can feel scratchy, but some types (such as merino) are very soft and comfortable next to the skin. Some people prefer to wear wool, which has greater absorbency than synthetics, next to the skin. Wool does not melt when exposed to heat from a stove, and it creates more friction than other fibers when the person wearing it is sliding on steep snow—a real plus for self-arrest.

Synthetic Fibers

Synthetic fibers and fabrics have largely replaced natural fibers in mountaineering clothing. Many synthetic fibers are hydrophobic, which means they tend not to absorb moisture. Garments made of synthetic fibers will absorb some moisture, but only in the spaces between the fibers rather than inside the individual fibers themselves. When such a garment is wet, most of this moisture can be wrung out; the rest evaporates quickly.

Polyesters and polypropylene. These fabrics are good at wicking perspiration, so they are well suited for use next to the skin. They are not absorbent, however, so depending on how a garment made from them interacts with the next layer, it may not completely dry the skin. Polypropylene underwear performs well but may be somewhat scratchy and may retain odor after several wearings. Polyesters have largely replaced polypropylene for underwear, offering a softer feel against the skin and less odor retention.

The packaging for different types of synthetic underwear commonly displays fancy-sounding brand names. It is easy to become confused trying to compare them. Often, brand names merely refer to different fabric treatments, and different-looking garments may actually be quite similar. Reading the garment tags and consulting a salesperson can help you to sort through the confusion.

In addition to use against the skin, polypropylene and polyesters work well as insulating layers. Long underwear is available in a number of different weights. Or consider jackets and pants of different weaves, such as thick and fluffy polyester pile or fleece. Although generally lightweight, most fleece and pile garments by themselves offer only fair wind resistance and can be bulky.

Nylon. This synthetic is manufactured in many, many forms, making it one of the world's most versatile materials. In outdoor clothing, nylon fabrics find their main uses in shell garments. Characteristics vary widely from one style of nylon to another. Some nylons provide good wind resistance, others feel slick or soft, but virtually all are known for strength and durability. One shortcoming is that, unless treated, many nylons absorb water and may dry fairly slowly.

When two or more fibers are blended together,

the resulting fabric's characteristics are somewhere in between those of the materials used. For example, underwear that is 80 percent polyester and 20 percent spandex provides more stretchiness but less wicking than plain polyester.

Waterproof-Breathable Fabrics

Rain parkas and rain pants are generally made of nylon or nylon blends. Since nylon itself is not waterproof, rain garments derive their waterproofness from a number of different fabrication methods and/or treatments applied to the fabric. Much research and development continues in this area.

Waterproof-nonbreathable coating. The simplest method is to cover the nylon garment with a waterproof-nonbreathable coating, such as polyurethane. Such coatings are lightweight and relatively inexpensive, but often they are not very resistant to abrasion or mildew. Although such coatings keep rain out, they also seal sweat and water vapor in. If you are working hard, the sweat generated can dampen your insulating layers. Think of a cup of hot coffee. If a lid is put on top, water from the coffee's steam will condense on the inside of the lid. In a way, your body is like that coffee: If your sweat does not have a way to escape through the clothing, you will get wet.

Waterproof-breathable coating. These coatings were designed to reduce the problem of sealing water in as well as out. Applied to the inside of a nylon shell, the coatings have billions of microscopic pores per square inch. Because moisture vapor from the skin is emitted in the form of individual water molecules that are much smaller than droplets of rain, the holes in the waterproof-breathable coating are large enough to let

TABLE 2-1. FABRIC COMPARISONS

FABRIC	ADVANTAGES	DISADVANTAGES	USES
Cotton	Good in hot weather. Breathes well. Comfortable when dry.	Highly absorbent; dries slowly. Loses insulating qualities when wet. Inappropriate for cool or wet conditions.	Sun protection, bandannas, hats, T-shirts.
Wool	More abrasion- and wind-resistant than many synthetics. Retains insulating qualities when wet. High friction on snow, ice. Does not melt with high heat.	Heavier; absorbs more water and dries less quickly than most synthetics. Can be bulky.	Skin layers, insulating, and outer layers (sweaters, shirts, pants), hats, gloves, socks.
Polyester or polypropylene	Most types absorb little water. Retains insulating qualities when wet. Lightweight.	Some types retain odors. Not wind resistant. Can be bulky. Melts with high heat.	Many different forms. Skin layers (underwear, T-shirts) Insulating layers (pile, fleece), hats, gloves, socks.
Nylon	Strong, durable, lightweight. Good wind- and abrasion resistance.	Fairly absorbent if not treated. May dry slowly. Slippery. Melts with high heat.	Outer layers (parkas, wind garments, rain pants, overmitts), hats, vapor-barrier socks.
Stretch or woven nylon blend	Versatile. Stretchy, durable, fairly insulative and wind resistant. Usually dries quickly. Wide comfort range.	Some types dry slowly. May snag. May be expensive.	Skin layers, light outer or midlayer (pants, shirts).

vapor escape but too small for raindrops to get in. The coating breathes somewhat while staying waterproof. Unsurprisingly, coatings such as these are more expensive to apply than regular coatings; therefore, garments treated with them cost more. Like much mountaineering equipment, waterproof-breathable coatings go by a variety of brand names, and often it is necessary to talk to a salesperson to understand what to purchase.

Laminated waterproof-breathable membrane. These membranes—Gore-Tex is the best known—are perforated with microscopic pores, like a waterproof-breathable coating. Membranes work on the same theory as such coatings but are instead fabricated as a separate layer inside the nylon shell. These garments typically are even more expensive than those with waterproof-breathable coatings. Both can have a long functional life if they are cared for properly (see "Care of waterproof-breathable fabrics," below).

Although the waterproof-breathable fabrics are a marked improvement over nonbreathable coated nylons, they are not perfect. A person who is working hard can exceed the garment's ability to pass water vapor, and sweat will condense inside the shell. Once in liquid form, the sweat can no longer escape through the garment, and the original problem is back again. The water repellency of the outer fabric is also a factor; if water does not bead up, it coats the exterior, greatly reducing the fabric's ability to breathe. Most waterproof-breathable fabrics work reasonably well at being waterproof, but designs can vary considerably in their ventilation, depending on construction techniques and features such as zippered vents under the arms or in the torso. Extra ventilation often commands a higher price.

Care of waterproof-breathable fabrics. Waterproof-breathable shells—whether they have a coating or a laminated membrane—depend on relatively delicate components in order to function. Do not expect even the most expensive rain parka to last for long if it is abused. Many experienced mountaineers use less expensive wind shirts or shells for most activities, keeping their waterproof-breathable shells in the pack until they are really needed.

Dirt and sweat can clog and contaminate fabric pores, reducing breathability. Keeping the shell clean helps it to function at its full capability. Certain types of detergents can break down shell elements, so read the tags and follow the manufacturer's recommended washing and drying procedures.

It is usually not a good idea to toss a parka in the washer after every use. The churning motion of a washing machine will gradually remove the shell's water-repellent finish.

Water-repellent finishes are applied in order to make rainwater bead up on the shell surface. When water no longer beads on the surface, the shell can be restored somewhat by putting it through a gentle cycle in the dryer or by ironing it. Follow the manufacturer's instructions, especially before treatment with a spray-on or wash-in agent.

Insulating Fills

Down. High-quality goose down is the warmest, lightest, most compressible, and most luxurious insulating fill available. It packs small yet quickly regains its loft—and therefore its warmth—when unpacked. High-quality goose down has 700 to 850-plus fill power. This means that an ounce of down, uncompressed, expands to fill 700 or 850-plus cubic inches (382 or 464-plus cubic centimeters per gram). Down's low weight-to-warmth ratio makes it very popular for cold-weather jackets and especially for sleeping bags. Good down is expensive yet has a much longer useful life than other insulating fills. Unfortunately, down loses all its insulating value when wet and is almost impossible to dry in damp conditions. Down must be protected from moisture.

Synthetic fill. Unlike down, synthetic fills do not collapse when wet, so they provide more reliable insulation in damper climates. Heavier and less compressible than down, they are also less expensive and more easily cleaned. Compared to down, synthetic fills cannot withstand as many compression cycles (stuffing and unstuffing), which means that they lose their loft and insulative properties more quickly than down. Again, brand names for these fillings can be confusing, so read the tags to figure out what the product really is.

PUTTING THE CLOTHING SYSTEM TOGETHER

Armed with knowledge of outdoor fabric characteristics and the strategy of layering, you can assemble an effective mountaineering clothing system. Figure 2-1 shows typical examples of how the various articles in a complete clothing system can be mixed and matched to function over a wide spectrum of weather conditions. The exact items chosen will vary significantly from climber to climber. The goal is to make the system comprehensive and versatile. Following are some specific guidelines for each clothing layer.

Layer Next to the Skin

Long underwear. Protection from cold begins with appropriate long underwear. Wicking fabrics made of polypropylene and polyesters are very popular for this purpose; some climbers prefer wool, and wool garments of the latest generation are softer, more comfortable, and less prone to shrinkage than the wool of old. Dark-colored long underwear absorbs more heat and dries more quickly in sunlight. Light colors are better on hot days, when long underwear may be worn alone as protection from sunburn or insects.

For rock climbing, spandex-blended polyester tights are occasionally used instead of long underwear because their stretchiness permits fuller range of motion. They are generally not as warm as polyester underwear. Lightweight nylon or stretch-woven nylon pants or knickers are also used alone against the skin; these can be very versatile.

T-shirts and shorts. Although T-shirts, shorts, underwear, and sports bras do not in themselves constitute a "layer," they need to perform as part of the total clothing system (fig. 2-1a).

For hot weather, a cotton T-shirt or tank top may suffice, although long sleeves provide more sun and insect protection. But for cooler mountain climates, cotton is a poor choice. On a moderately cool and breezy day, a cotton T-shirt can become soaked with sweat during an ascent of a steep hill, and you can get a deep chill when stopping for a break. Less-absorbent fabrics are much better than cotton for most situations. Warm-weather shirts should be light-colored for coolness and moderately baggy for good ventilation. Some garments are made of fabric that has been rated with an ultraviolet protection factor (UPF). Tight weave and dark color typically provide more sun protection, and these garments are designed to provide maximum coverage and ventilation.

Ventilation and durability are key requirements for shorts. A loose-fitting pair of nylon shorts, perhaps fitted with an integral mesh brief, can work well. Cotton shorts are far less versatile. A popular clothing combination for mild conditions is lightweight polyester long underwear under a pair of nylon shorts (fig. 2-1b). Lightweight nylon pants with zip-off legs that convert to shorts are also very popular and versatile.

Insulating Layers

For cold weather, more insulating layers are needed. Upper-body layers can include more long underwear, wool or synthetic shirts, fleece sweaters and vests, or down- or synthetic-filled jackets (fig. 2-1c). For the legs, choose long underwear or pants made of wool, blends,

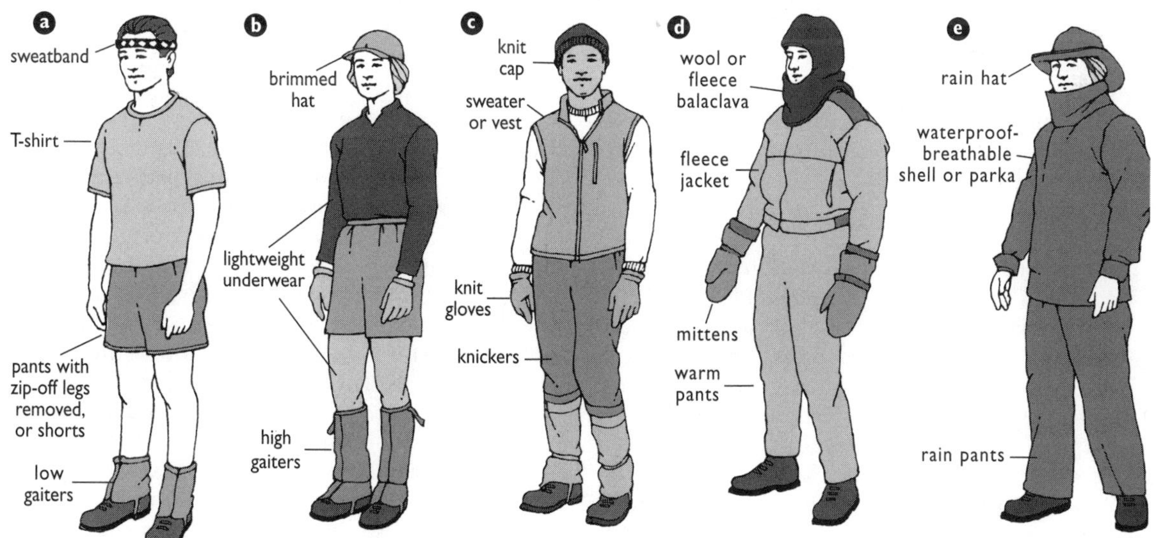

Fig. 2-1. Typical examples of clothing layering systems: a, hiking in warm weather; b, hiking in cool weather; c, cool weather in camp; d, cold weather in camp; e, rainy or windy weather.

stretch-woven nylon, or fleece. One-piece insulating garments are sometimes used in very cold weather. There are many choices; the main objective is retaining warmth when wet. Do not depend on cotton for insulation.

Shirts and sweaters. These should be long in the torso so they tuck into or pull over the waist of the pants. Gaps between the pants and upper-body layer(s) let valuable heat escape. Turtleneck underwear and sweaters can provide significant warmth with little extra weight.

Insulating pants. These should be loose fitting or stretchy for freedom of movement and made of a closely woven fabric with a hard finish for resistance to wind and abrasion (fig. 2-1d). Wool and wool-synthetic blends work well. Fleece pants, while lighter, are not as abrasion- or wind-resistant by themselves. Look for pants with reinforced seats and knees and with full-length side zippers that make it possible to put the pants on while you are wearing boots, crampons, skis, or snowshoes.

Knickers. Some climbers prefer knee-length knickers and gaiters (see "Footgear," below) instead of full-length pants for freer movement and better ventilation; wearing knickers and gaiters can also avoid pant legs getting saturated from contact with snow or dew.

Belay parka. In very cold weather, a belay parka can make life better. This is a simply cut insulated jacket, sized to fit over everything. It is worn by the belayer of a climbing team, who is comparatively stationary while the other member of the rope team climbs—the garment helps keep the belayer warm and therefore attentive. Good features include an integral hood, thick (very compressible) insulation, and lightweight, water-resistant shell material. Ideally it will fit both members of the rope team.

Shell Layer

The ideal shell is uninsulated, windproof, completely waterproof, and completely breathable. There is no single garment that can achieve all these objectives, but there are various strategies that come close.

One strategy is to have a single, multifunctional, waterproof-breathable shell layer for both parka and pants. If this single shell layer provides sufficient breathability, it may be the best way to go.

Many climbers carry two shell layers: a light, breathable layer of wind gear and a light set of raingear, either breathable or (occasionally) not. With these systems, the wind gear is worn in cool, windy, and even lightly drizzling conditions and for periods of heavy exertion, whereas the more expensive shell is worn for slower periods or in heavier rain. This two-shell strategy can be cheaper, and the wind gear allows much better ventilation. But a nonbreathing layer (if used) will be more uncomfortable than waterproof-breathable raingear, and bringing two shell layers adds weight.

Rain parkas. These come in different styles. Standard parkas feature full front zippers and are easier to ventilate; anoraks (pullover parkas without full front zippers) are preferred by some climbers as lighter, less bulky, and more windproof (fig. 2-1e). When shopping for a rain parka of either style, look for the same qualities whether or not the fabric breathes (see the "What to Look for in a Rain Parka" sidebar).

Rain pants. These should have full-length zippers so they can be added or removed over boots, crampons, skis, or snowshoes. Because rain pants tend to be worn less often than parkas (often a good set of gaiters is enough) and they can be ruined by bushwhacking through brush or glissading down snow, choosing a nonbreathable pair of rain pants can save money.

Some climbers, especially in cold conditions, use waterproof-breathable bib pants held up with suspenders as a lower-body shell layer. Some bibs contain insulating fills and are best suited to extreme-cold-weather expeditions. They are considerably warmer than rain pants because they cover much of the torso and keep snow from entering around your waistline, but they are too warm for most summer uses. One-piece suits are also used by some—they are the warmest but least-versatile option.

Hard and soft shells. Waterproof garments made from coated fabrics or that have a laminated membrane are classed as hard shells to distinguish them from soft shells. Soft-shell garments are composed of two- or four-way stretch-woven fabrics. These garments feature very tight weaves and water-repellent treatments and have been specifically designed to maximize both water resistance and breathability. Soft shells tend to be lighter and more comfortable than hard shells. The stretch-woven fabric allows the garments to be more flexible, so they tend to fit and to drape better. But compared to hard shells, soft shells are less water- and wind-resistant. Soft shells are, however, much more breathable and are well suited for any conditions except for the most extreme weather. A soft shell makes a good first shell layer that can be covered by a more water-resistant hard shell if conditions worsen.

WHAT TO LOOK FOR IN A RAIN PARKA

- **A size large enough** to allow for additional layers of clothing underneath without compressing insulation or restricting movement
- **A hood** with a brim, neck flap, and good drawstrings to keep water from dribbling down your face and neck. The hood should be sized to accommodate a climbing helmet but should not impair peripheral vision.
- **Adjustable openings** at the front, waist, underarms, sides, and cuffs that can be opened up for ventilation or shut tight
- **Zippers** with large, durable teeth and good flaps that keep the zipper dry but still allow ventilation. Some zippers are waterproof.
- **A design that does not interfere** with a climbing harness or belaying
- **Well-bonded, tape-sealed seams**
- **Pockets** that are easily accessible with gloved hands and with a pack on. Pockets should also have water-resistant closures.
- **A length that extends** well below the waistline of pants and a drawstring at the waist so the torso can be sealed off
- **Sleeves that cover the wrists.** Snaps, elastic, or hook-and-loop fasteners (such as Velcro) should keep the sleeve in place at the wrist.

Headgear

The old adage says, "If your feet are cold, put on a hat." A person's head accounts for approximately 10 percent of the body's surface area, and without insulation it can account for a significant amount of heat loss. As the body gets cold, it reduces blood flow to the arms and legs in an attempt to warm more vital areas. Putting on a hat helps to reduce heat loss.

Climbers often carry several different types of hats in order to quickly adapt to changing temperatures. To prevent the misfortune of having a hat blow off and sail over a cliff, some choose headgear with a strap or leash (security cord) or sew them onto headgear.

Warm insulating caps come in wool, polypropylene, or polyester fleece. Balaclavas are versatile insulators because they can cover both your face and neck or can be rolled up to allow ventilation of the collar area. Consider carrying two insulating hats; an extra hat provides almost as much warmth as an extra sweater while weighing much less. Sometimes a thin hat is worn beneath a climbing helmet in cold weather.

A rain hat is useful, because it provides more ventilation and is often more comfortable than a parka hood. Some rain hats are available in waterproof-breathable fabrics, allowing further ventilation.

Sun-protection hats, with wide brims or protective shades draping over your neck and ears, are popular for glacier climbs. A baseball cap with a bandanna pinned on or worn under it can accomplish the same purpose. A bill helps shade your eyes and keep rain and snow off glasses.

Gloves and Mittens

Activities such as handling wet rope or scrambling on wet rock can saturate gloves or mittens, even in dry weather. Fingers are perhaps the most difficult part of the body to keep warm because of the body's tendency to sacrifice blood flow to the extremities when cold. Unfortunately, this altered blood flow can inhibit tasks that involve the fingers—such as pulling zippers and tying knots—which may slow a climbing party's progress at the very time when they need to move fast to find shelter from the cold.

It can take considerable experience to wisely choose the mittens and gloves that work best for each individual. Selection usually entails a compromise between dexterity and warmth. In general, bulk means increased warmth and reduced dexterity. The more technical a climb, the more significant the compromise.

The layering concept for clothing also applies to hands. The first layer may be a light pair of gloves; additional layers are usually mittens. Mittens are warmer than gloves because they allow fingers to share warmth. A layered system of thin glove liners topped with mittens and/or overmitts usually works well, as long as it does not constrict circulation.

As with other insulating garments, mittens and gloves must be made of fabrics that retain warmth when wet. Suitable gloves and mittens come in synthetics, wool-synthetic blends, or all wool.

Overmitts are the shell layer for hands. A nonslip coating on the palm will improve your grip on snow and ice tools. The overmitt cuff should overlap the parka sleeve some 4 to 6 inches (10 to 15 centimeters), and elastic or hook-and-loop (Velcro) closures can cinch the overmitt around your forearm.

Attach security cords to mittens and overmitts. It is

well worth the effort when you need to pull off your mittens to climb rock or apply sunscreen.

In camp, wearing glove liners or fingerless gloves inside mittens can permit good dexterity for delicate chores without exposing bare skin. Be aware that many synthetics can melt in the heat from a stove. Even so, in very cold temperatures—around 0 degrees Fahrenheit (minus 18 degrees Celsius)—it is important to keep fingers from freezing to metal, and glove liners are better for this than fingerless gloves. But when you are rock climbing in cold weather and it is not desirable to add a layer of fabric between your fingers and the rock, fingerless gloves are best. Some climbers carry several pairs of liners, changing them when they become wet and cold.

Leather gloves are often worn for rope handling such as rappeling or belaying, providing a better grip and preventing rope burns in the event of a fall. They provide no insulation when wet, and they dry slowly.

FOOTGEAR

A climber's feet are the means for reaching the objective, so they need especially good gear. Footgear includes boots, socks, and gaiters—and sometimes additional footwear for other situations.

BOOTS

A good alpine climbing boot is a compromise between performance and suitability for the range of conditions likely to be encountered during an outing: No single boot type or design will do everything well. The rigidity of the boot's sole, the stiffness and support provided by the upper, and how the sole and upper interact in use are the characteristics that matter most. A general mountaineering boot must strike a balance of being tough enough to withstand being scraped on rocks and stiff and solid enough for kicking steps in hard snow and wearing crampons, yet comfortable enough for the approach hike. In a single day of climbing, boots may have to contend with trails, mud, streams, gravel, brush, scree, hard snow, steep rock, and ice.

Historically, mountaineering boots were made of heavy sewn leather. Efforts to reduce costs and weight while improving performance brought the advent of alternative materials and construction methods. The "classic" leather boot, while still respected for its versatility, is less common today, having been joined by new designs: boots with plastic-composite shells, fabric panels, waterproof linings, integral gaiters, and so on. Although boots themselves are changing, the many jobs they need to do have not.

Leather Boots

The classic leather mountaineering boot (fig. 2-2) evolved from the uses to which it was put; it has most or all of the following features:

- **High upper** (5½ to 7½ inches/14 to 19 centimeters) to support and protect the ankle in rough terrain
- **Vibram-type lug sole** for traction on slippery vegetation, mud, and snow
- **Welt** (the joint between the upper and the sole)
- **Rubber rand** sealing the sole to the upper, to aid in waterproofing and to simplify boot maintenance
- **A fairly stiff shank** (metal or plastic stiffener built into the boot sole)
- **A minimum number of seams**, to minimize places water can leak through
- **A gusseted or bellows tongue**, to keep water from easily entering the boot
- **Reinforced toe and heel**, with double- or triple-layered leather, to provide durability and protection
- **Hard toe counter** (interior stiffener) to protect the foot, reduce compression caused by crampon straps, and facilitate step-kicking in hard snow
- **Heel counter** (interior stiffener) to increase foot stability and facilitate plunge-stepping down steep snow slopes
- **Top that opens wide** so the boot can be put on easily even when it is wet or frozen

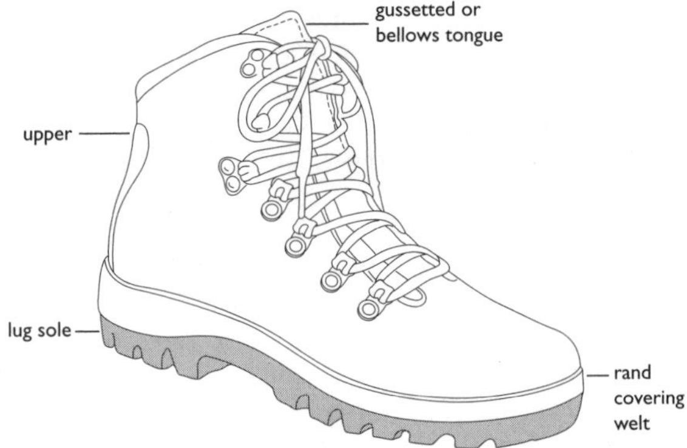

Fig. 2-2. Classic leather mountaineering boot.

Leather-and-Fabric Boots

Advances in boot technology have led to boots that incorporate synthetic fabric panels that partially replace leather. Some (not all) may be suitable for climbing. Leather-and-fabric boots (fig. 2-3) may provide a number of advantages over all-leather boots, including these:

- Reduced weight
- Improved comfort and shorter break-in time
- Faster drying time
- Lower cost

However, leather-and-fabric boots may have significant drawbacks compared with all-leather boots:

- Less stability on difficult off-trail terrain
- Less waterproofness
- Less durability
- Insufficient weight or stiffness for step-kicking in firm snow or for wearing with crampons

If you are considering leather-and-fabric boots for climbing, here are some things to look for: Check that the uppers are high and rigid enough for good ankle support, that stiff counters wrap the heel and toe, and that abrasion areas are reinforced. If the boot is very flexible, it will not edge well or be suitable for crampons. A distinct heel is desirable, especially on snow.

Some leather-and-fabric boots feature Gore-Tex liners, which can help keep feet drier in wet conditions. Gore-Tex is no panacea for boots, however: The membrane is hard to keep clean and can degrade from dirt and sweat. It also adds cost, and it may make feet more uncomfortable during hot weather.

Plastic Composite Boots

Plastic composite boots (fig. 2-4) consist of hard synthetic outer shells with inner insulating boots. They were originally designed for ski mountaineering, cold-weather expeditions, and serious ice climbing but have since found a much wider market among those interested in snow and glacier routes.

The synthetic shells of these boots are usually quite stiff, which makes them good for use with crampons or snowshoes. They permit straps and bindings to be cinched tightly without impairing circulation in the feet. They provide solid support for edging and kicking steps.

Being truly waterproof, plastic composite boots are great in wet conditions. The inner insulating boot remains free of snowmelt and keeps feet warm. In camp, the inner boot can be removed and warmed, which helps in drying out perspiration. Unfortunately, the very factors that make plastic boots ideal for snow and ice (rigidity, waterproofness, and warmth) make them a poor choice for general trail use.

The Right Choice

The best choice of boot depends on how it will be used and is generally a compromise between the boot's walking comfort and its technical capability (see the "Specialized Footwear" sidebar).

For trails and easy snow or rock routes, boots with moderately stiff soles and uppers provide enough support while being acceptably flexible and comfortable. Both leather and leather-and-fabric boots can work well

Fig. 2-3. Lightweight leather and fabric boots.

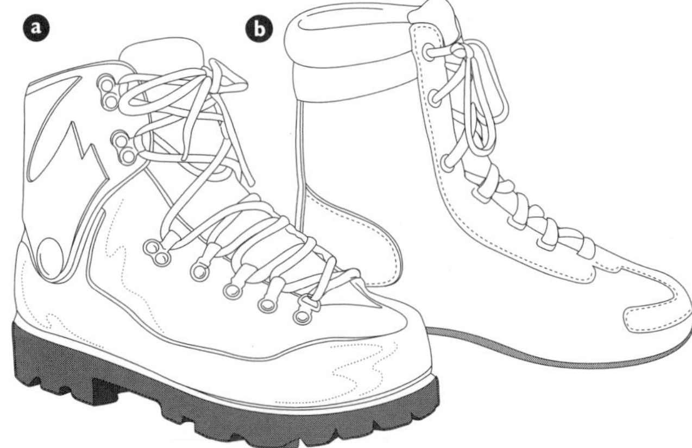

Fig. 2-4. Plastic mountaineering boot: a, waterproof shell; b, insulating inner boot.

for these applications, provided their soles and uppers are reasonably firm.

For technical alpine rock climbing, a stiffer boot is desirable for its edging capabilities. Flexible boots (fig. 2-5a and b), while sometimes used on technical rock, are usually a poor substitute for rock shoes. (For information on rock shoes, see Chapter 12, Alpine Rock Climbing Technique.) Stiffer boots can make walking less comfortable, but they greatly reduce leg fatigue when a climber is standing on small rock nubbins. Look for boots stiff enough to permit edging on narrow rock ledges with either side of the boot (fig. 2-5c) or with the toe (fig. 2-5d).

For traveling on hard snow, a highly flexible boot is a disadvantage. It takes a stout boot to kick good steps or plunge-step with confidence. Snowshoe and (especially) crampon bindings may not stay on if a boot is too flexible.

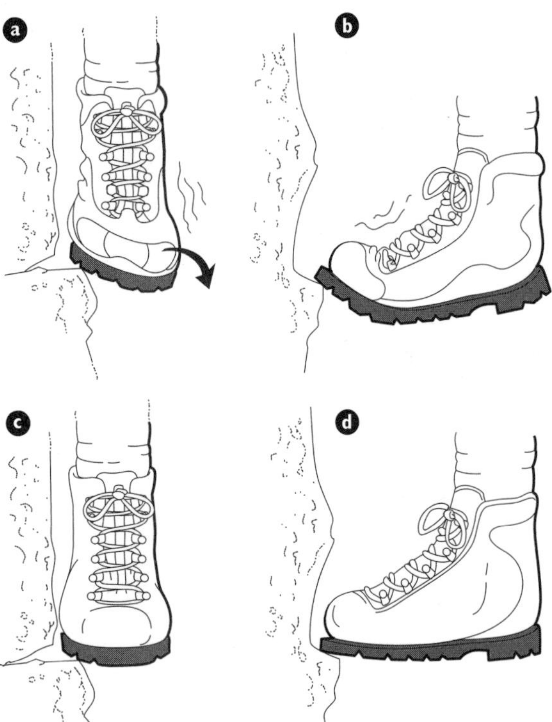

Fig. 2-5. The stiffness of a boot affects its technical capability—stiffer boots edge better, flexible boots "smear" better: a and b, flexible backpacking boots bend more, requiring more contact with a hold to support well; c and d, stiff mountaineering boots edge well on small holds.

SPECIALIZED FOOTWEAR

Depending on the trip, a climber may wear one kind of boot for the approach hike, another type of footwear in camp, and yet another climbing. If additional footgear is affordable and you are willing to carry the extra weight, consider these options:

- **Lightweight, flexible trail shoes** for easy approaches are less likely to cause blisters and less fatiguing to wear than leather boots; however, they may not provide the support needed when you are carrying a heavy pack, especially on rough ground or descents.
- **Running shoes, tennis shoes, sandals, or neoprene socks or booties** for comfort in camp also give boots and feet a chance to dry; they can also be used for stream crossings.
- **Insulated booties and/or fleece socks** for warmer lounging and sleeping are great in camp.
- **Rock climbing shoes for technical rock** (see Chapter 12, Alpine Rock Climbing Technique) are lightweight and compact.
- **Insulated overboots** for extremely cold weather are also good for use at high altitude.

Ice climbing demands an even higher level of boot support, and very stiff soles and uppers are desirable. Plastic composite boots or extremely stiff leather boots are generally best (see Chapter 18, Alpine Ice Climbing).

The Proper Fit

No matter what the boot's design or materials are, fit is critical. Try on several makes and styles. Some brands are available in multiple widths; others offer both men's and women's models—so shop around.

When heading to the stores to compare boots, take along the socks that you will wear on a climb, as well as any orthotic devices, custom insoles (see the "Insoles" sidebar), or other inserts that you will use. Most people's feet swell during the course of the day, so consider shopping in the evening when your feet are at their largest.

After lacing up the boots in the store, try standing on a narrow edge or rocking side to side to test their stability. Stand and walk in the boots for several minutes, with a heavy pack on if possible, to allow the boots and your feet to get used to each other. Then note whether the boots have any uncomfortable seams or creases or whether they pinch anywhere. In boots that fit properly, your heels will feel firmly anchored in place while your toes will have plenty of room to wiggle and will not jam against the toe box when you press your foot forward. Try standing on a downward incline for a critical test of toe space. Kick something solid—your toes should not hit the front of the boot.

Boots that are too tight will constrict circulation, which causes cold feet and increases chance of frostbite. Either too-tight or excessively loose boots can cause blisters. Given the choice between boots that are a bit too big and ones that are a bit too small, go with the larger boots. The space can be filled somewhat with thicker socks or insoles.

Plastic composite boots need to fit well from the start because their rigid shell will not conform to your feet as much as the lining of a leather or leather-and-fabric boot will. Be especially careful that boots intended for use in extreme cold and/or high altitudes do not constrict your feet and impede circulation.

Boot Care

With proper care, good boots can last many years. Keep the boots clean and dry when not in use. Avoid exposing boots to high temperatures, because heat can damage leather, linings, and adhesives. During an outing, water can seep into boots through the uppers and seams. Waterproofing agents can help limit the entry of water. Waterproofing is a process that needs to be repeated regularly.

Before waterproofing, boots must be clean and dry. Clean them with a mild soap, such as saddle soap, that will not damage the leather. Use a stiff brush to remove grit. It is difficult to remove every speck of dirt, so waterproofing usually does not last as long on used boots as on new. With plastic composite boots, remove the inner boots after use and allow them to dry. Shake and/or wipe out any debris in the shells to prevent abrasion and excessive wear.

Of the several types of boot waterproofing products available, the appropriate type for a pair of boots depends on the boots' construction, so follow the manufacturer's recommendations. Apply the appropriate product to the boots frequently to keep your feet dry, again following the manufacturer's instructions.

SOCKS

Socks cushion and insulate the feet and reduce friction between the boot and the foot. Socks made of wool or synthetic materials can perform these functions; those made of cotton cannot. Cotton socks will saturate, collapse, and stick to the feet, softening the skin and leading to blisters.

Socks should absorb perspiration. Because boots do not breathe appreciably, the sweat generated by the feet collects and builds up until the boots are removed. Synthetic sock materials (including polyesters, nylon, and acrylic) dry faster than wool but may be more compressible. Too much compressibility can reduce cushioning and affect the fit of the boots.

Many climbers wear two pairs of socks. Next to the skin, a thin liner sock transports perspiration away from the foot and stays somewhat dry in the process. The outer sock is thicker and rougher in order to absorb the moisture passing through the inner sock and to cushion against the boot lining. Others prefer a single medium- or heavy-weight wool or synthetic sock.

Of course, there are many exceptions. Rock climbers want flexible rock shoes to fit like skin, and so they wear no socks or one thin pair. Hikers using trail shoes on a warm day may keep feet cooler by wearing a single pair of socks, whereas winter climbers may wear three pairs of socks inside oversize boots. Whatever the strategy, keep your toes free enough to wiggle; an additional pair of socks will not improve warmth if they constrict circulation.

Before donning socks, consider protecting your feet at places prone to blisters, such as the back of the heel, with athletic tape, duct tape, or moleskin (soft, adhesive-backed padding). This is especially valuable when breaking in new boots or early in the climbing season before your feet have toughened up. Another blister fighter is foot powder sprinkled on your feet, on socks, and in the boots.

Waterproof-breathable Gore-Tex socks can improve comfort in wet conditions. Worn over an inner pair of standard socks, the Gore-Tex socks function much like

INSOLES

Adding insoles to the inside of boots provides extra insulation and cushioning. Synthetic insoles are nonabsorbent, do not become matted when damp, and may have a loose structure that helps ventilate the foot. Insoles made of felt, leather, or lambskin all absorb moisture and must be removed when drying boots.

boots with Gore-Tex liners, while providing a higher and snugger cuff.

In very cold weather, a vapor-barrier sock may be worn between two main sock layers. Vapor-barrier socks are nonbreathing, which may seem at first to be contradictory to clothing strategies outlined earlier in this chapter. However, think of the example of the hot coffee in the cup: Although putting the lid on the cup keeps the moisture trapped inside, it also keeps the coffee hotter. Vapor-barrier socks apply the same principle to feet: Your feet get damp, but they lose less heat and so stay warmer. Vapor-barrier socks are best suited for extremely cold conditions, when they can reduce the danger of frostbite. However, if the internal moisture is allowed to continue for too long, the serious condition of immersion foot can develop (see Chapter 23, First Aid). If you use vapor-barrier socks, dry your feet thoroughly at least once each day.

GAITERS

During an outing, water, snow, and debris can get into boots over their cuff. Gaiters are used to seal the boundary between pant legs and boot tops. Climbers often carry gaiters in both summer and winter, because rain, dew, mud, and snow provide year-round opportunities for water to saturate pant legs, socks, and boots.

Short gaiters (fig. 2-6a), extending 5 or 6 inches (12 or 15 centimeters) above the top of the boots, are adequate for keeping corn snow and debris out of boots in summer. The deep snows of winter, however, usually call for standard gaiters (fig. 2-6b) that extend up to the knee. Supergaiters (fig. 2-6c) completely cover the boot from the welt up, leaving the lug soles exposed; insulation built into supergaiters covers the boots for added warmth.

The portion of any gaiter covering the boot should be made of a heavy-duty fabric coated with some type of water repellent. Some gaiters may feature an additional waterproof membrane inside the heavy-duty fabric. The fabric covering your calf should be breathable or waterproof-breathable, to allow perspiration to escape.

Gaiters are usually held closed with snaps, zippers, or hook-and-loop fasteners (such as Velcro); Velcro offers the easiest fastening in cold weather. If you select gaiters with zippers, be sure the teeth are heavy-duty. A flap that closes over the zipper with snaps or Velcro protects it from damage and can keep the gaiter closed and functional even if the zipper fails. A drawstring at the top of the gaiter keeps it from sliding down. A snug fit around the calf helps prevent crampon points from catching on the gaiters.

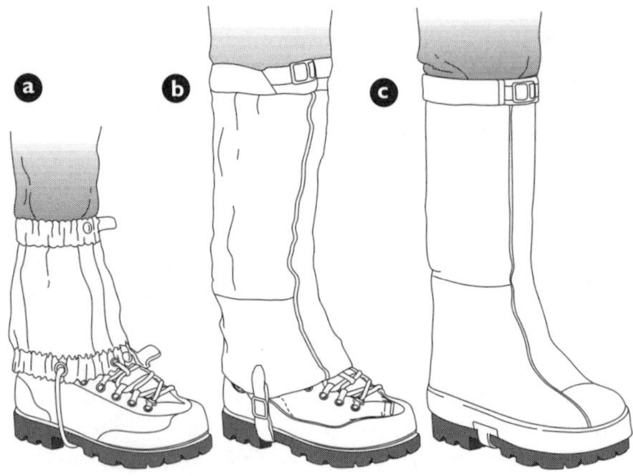

Fig. 2-6. Gaiters: a, short; b, full length; c, supergaiters.

A close fit all around the boot is essential to prevent snow from entering under the gaiter, especially when you are plunge-stepping during descents. A cord, lace, strap, or shock cord runs under the foot to help the gaiter hug the boot. The part under the foot will wear out during the life of the gaiter, so look for designs allowing easy replacement. Neoprene straps work well in snow but wear quickly on rock, whereas cord survives rock better but can ball up with snow.

PACKS

Climbers usually own at least two packs: a day pack to hold enough for a single-day climb, and a full-size backpack to carry gear for camping in the backcountry. All packs should allow the weight to be carried close to your body and the load to be centered over your hips and legs (see Figure 2-8).

INTERNAL-FRAME VERSUS EXTERNAL-FRAME PACKS

Internal-frame packs (fig. 2-7a and b) are by far the most popular packs among climbers and ski mountaineers. A rigid frame within the pack helps it maintain its shape and hug your back, assisting you in keeping balanced while climbing or skiing. When you wear such a pack, weight is carried relatively low on your body, an advantage for maintaining balance. The body-hugging nature of internal-frame packs can make them somewhat uncomfortable in hot weather.

The volume of most internal-frame packs can be easily adjusted with compression straps, a significant advantage for climbing. A full-size pack can be used on the approach and then emptied of tent and sleeping bag at camp and transformed into a compact summit pack. The clean, narrow profile of internal-frame packs

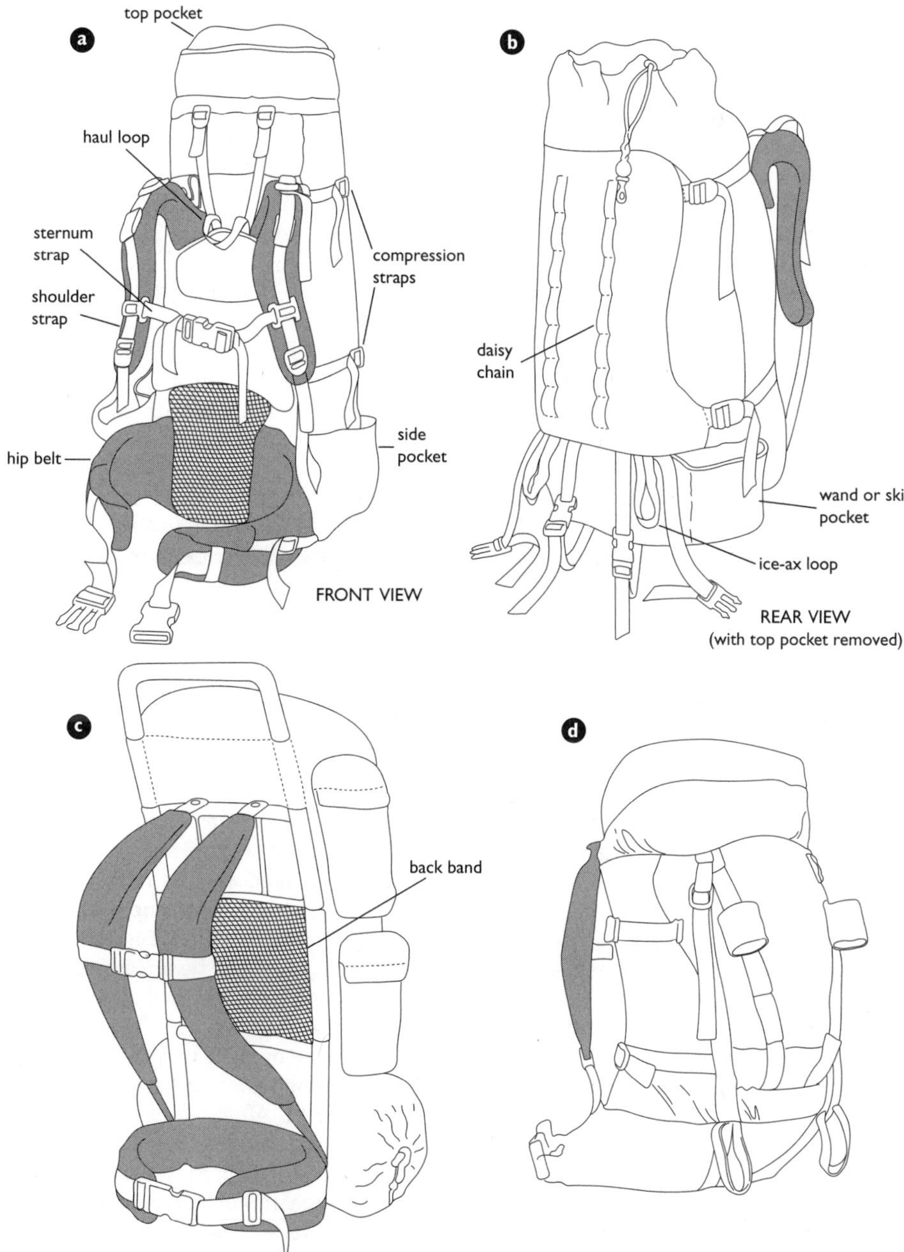

Fig. 2-7. Typical packs: a and b, large internal-frame pack; c, large external-frame pack; d, medium-size day pack.

allows them to be taken through heavy brush or hauled up rock pitches with a minimum of snags.

External-frame packs (fig. 2-7c), once the primary type of pack in use, now see only limited service with mountaineers. The pack contents are suspended from a ladderlike frame, which is held away from your back by taut nylon back bands. External-frame packs provide some advantages with very heavy or awkward loads and provide better ventilation. Some climbers use them for long, easy approaches, carrying a day pack (fig. 2-7d) inside for the summit day. But external frames are mainly limited to open trail use. They tend to shift without warning on uneven terrain and may catch on brush or in tight quarters. It is also difficult to glissade or self-arrest on snow while wearing an external-frame pack.

BUYING AN INTERNAL-FRAME PACK

Before shopping for a full-size internal-frame pack, decide what capacity is right for how it will be used. Overnight trips typically require packs of around 3,000 to 5,000 cubic inches (50 to 80 liters) capable of carrying about 30 to 55 pounds (13 to 25 kilograms), depending on the demands of the climb. Longer trips and winter climbs require more volume; expedition climbs can demand even more. (For special considerations in buying day packs, see the next section.)

The most important objective in choosing a pack is to find one that fits your body. The pack's adjustment range must be compatible with the length of your back. Some packs adjust to a wide range of body sizes; others do not. Virtually no individual backpack provides a good fit for everyone, so do not place faith in endorsements from acquaintances or outdoor equipment magazines or websites. Try on various packs and make your own decision (see the "Questions to Consider When Choosing a Pack" sidebar).

Do not be in a hurry when fitting a pack. Load it up, as you would on an actual climb; bring personal gear to the store. Without a typical load, you cannot tell how the pack rides or if the adjustments provide a good fit.

Before putting the pack on, loosen all the adjustment straps, and once the pack is on tighten up the straps in the order recommended by the salesperson

ULTRALIGHT TRAVEL

Light is right.

—alpinist John Bouchard

The ultralight concept is as much a philosophy of mountain travel as it is a specific set of gear recommendations. It is the antithesis of the style used by the huge Himalayan expeditions of the middle part of the twentieth century. Those efforts typically involved hundreds of porters, tons of equipment, and the veritable siege of a peak. On such expeditions, climbing style was completely subjugated to the success of the project—if an ice pitch could not be climbed, a ladder was used.

In contrast, the ultralight concept espouses two principal considerations: First, consider each item of gear and select the lightest version available, and second, take only the minimum amount of gear consistent with your chosen degree of commitment. The ultralight approach recognizes that the circumstances encountered on an outing can limit what can be accomplished—for example, prudent mountaineers turn back when faced with inclement weather or unanticipated technical difficulties, and this is even more true of ultralighters, who carry minimal gear and so have less margin for error.

There have, of course, been ultralight devotees for as long as there have been mountaineers. Indeed, the Sourdough Expedition party made their final push to the north summit of Denali in 1910 with no more than doughnuts, hot chocolate, and homemade crampons—and a spruce flagpole! The movement toward ultralight was perhaps first popularized by Yosemite climber Ray Jardine in the 1990s; the idea is to use multipurpose, lightweight gear and clothing in place of ever-increasing technically sophisticated equipment.

For mountain travel, less weight may mean a more enjoyable trip. For many technical routes, climbing light means climbing faster and, consequently, more safely (see Chapter 12, Alpine Rock Climbing Technique, for further discussion). Free soloing a technical climbing route—that is, climbing without a rope—could be considered the ultimate expression of the ultralight concept; however, the consequences of mistakes or accidents in such circumstances would be dire.

QUESTIONS TO CONSIDER WHEN CHOOSING A PACK

- **How is the suspension system designed?** Does it look durable, or does it look as though it could fail at weak spots?
- **How sturdy is the pack's stitching?**
- **Does the pack rely on zippers** to retain the contents? If the zippers fail, can the pack still be used?
- **How convenient is it** to store, arrange, and access gear in the pack?
- **Does the pack provide a means of carrying special items** such as crampons, skis, snowshoes, shovels, and wands?
- **Does the pack have haul loops and ice-ax loops?**
- **Are there compression straps** to reduce the pack's volume and prevent the load from shifting during climbing or skiing?
- **Is there a means of increasing the pack's capacity** for extended trips, such as an expandable snow collar with a floating top pocket or separate side-pocket accessories?
- **Does the pack have a sternum strap** to help prevent the pack from shifting on difficult terrain?
- **Does the pack have a smooth profile,** or will it get tangled up during bushwhacks through heavy brush or get hung up if it is hauled up a steep face?

or the pack instruction manual. Check in a mirror, or ask someone to check, to see if the frame correctly follows the curve of your back. If it does not, check whether the stays or frame can be bent to improve the fit. Some frames are made of composite materials that cannot be reshaped. The shoulder straps should attach to the pack about 2 or 3 inches (5 to 7.5 centimeters) below the crest of your shoulders and leave little or no gap behind your back.

Once the pack is adjusted, check your head clearance. Is it possible to look up without hitting the back of your head against the pack? Is it possible to look up while wearing a helmet? Next, check for adequate padding wherever the pack touches your body. Pay particular attention to the thickness and quality of padding used in the shoulder straps and hip belt. The hip belt should be substantial; its padding should cover your hip bones by good margins. For proper load transfer to your hips, ensure that the hip belt wraps directly onto the top of your hip bones, not around the sides of your hip bones or around your waist.

BUYING A DAY PACK

Day packs for climbing (see Figure 2-7d) usually have volumes of between 1,800 and 2,500 cubic inches (30 to 40 liters), enough to carry 20 to 30 pounds (9 to 14 kilograms). A large selection of day packs is on the market, varying over a wide spectrum of sturdiness. Some are designed without rigid frames or padded hip belts and may be too flimsy for serious climbing. Keep in mind that climbers carry heavy items such as rope, helmet, climbing gear, and ice ax in or on a day pack. Seek a pack with a sturdy internal frame and a hip belt that is at least 2 inches (5 centimeters) wide at the buckle and 4 inches (10 centimeters) wide where it covers the hips. Eliminate day packs that lack climbing features such as ice-ax loops, haul loops, crampon carriers, or compression straps.

Most of the features that are considered in choosing a full-size pack are applicable to day packs. Does the pack offer a sternum strap, compression straps, sturdy stitching, convenient storage and access, and a smooth profile? Try on and compare day packs as thoroughly as you would a full-size backpack.

TIPS ON PACKING

Strategically loading items in a pack can dramatically influence a climber's speed, endurance, and enjoyment of an outing. Generally, climbers will feel best if they can concentrate the load on their hips and avoid loading their back and shoulders.

Pack heavy items as close to your back as possible and center them in the pack to lower your center of gravity, allowing you to keep your balance more easily (fig. 2-8).

Along with arranging items in the pack for optimum weight distribution, organize them for quick access. The gear that will be needed most often should be carried close at hand. Articles such as gloves, hats, sunglasses, maps, and insect repellent are ideally carried in side and top pockets, jacket pockets, or a fanny pack that is worn on the abdomen in combination with the main pack. Adjusting and readjusting the backpack during use will help reduce soreness and fatigue.

Determine a strategy to keep pack contents dry in rainy weather, because even packs constructed from waterproof materials are not necessarily waterproof. Water can leak through seams, zippers, pockets, the top opening, and places where the coating has worn

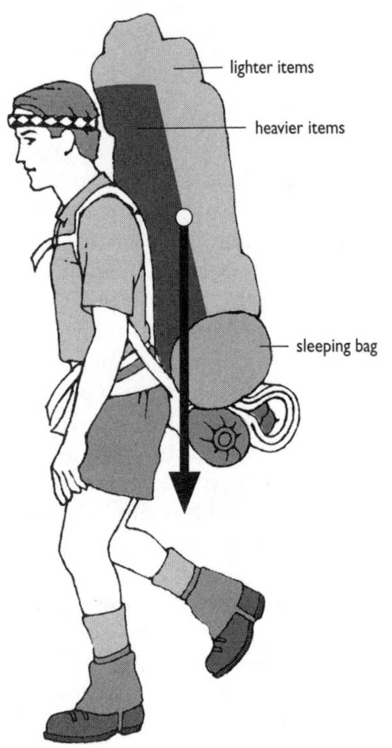

Fig. 2-8. Loading heavier items closer to the center of the back improves balance and endurance. The large black arrow shows approximate center of gravity and weight distribution.

off. Individual plastic bags or waterproof stuff sacks can help protect pack contents, especially when it is necessary to set up or break camp in the rain. Waterproof pack covers are available as accessories. Some climbers use a large plastic trash bag as a waterproof liner inside their pack.

ESSENTIAL EQUIPMENT—A SYSTEMS APPROACH

Certain equipment deserves space in every pack. A climber will not need every item on every trip, but essential equipment can be a lifesaver in an emergency.

Exactly how much equipment "insurance" should be carried is a matter of healthy debate (as mentioned in "Ultralight Travel," above). Some respected minimalists argue that weighing down a pack with such items causes people to climb slower, making it more likely they will get caught by a storm or nightfall and be forced to bivouac. "Go fast and light. Carry bivy gear, and you will bivy," they argue. The other side of this debate is that, even when climbers are not slowed by the extra weight of bivy gear, they still may be forced to bivouac. Will the party be safe?

The majority of climbers take along carefully selected items to survive the unexpected. They sacrifice some speed but argue that they will be around tomorrow to attempt again what they failed to climb today. The best-known list, first developed in the 1930s, became known as the Ten Essentials.

THE TEN ESSENTIALS

The point of the Ten Essentials list has always been to help answer two basic questions: First, can you respond positively to an accident or emergency? Second, can you safely spend a night—or more—out? The Ten Essentials has evolved from a list of individual items to a list of functional systems that satisfy certain needs. As shown in Table 2-2, the classic list has been expanded to include hydration and emergency shelter. The systems are discussed in more detail below.

1. Navigation

Climbers must carry the tools and possess the skills required to know where they are and how to get to their objective and back. Always carry a detailed topographic map of the area you are visiting, and place it in a protective case or plastic covering. Always carry a compass. Climbers may also choose to carry other navigational tools, such as an altimeter or global positioning system (GPS) receiver; additional aids include route markers, route descriptions, and other types of maps or photos. Know how to use map and compass and other navigation aids—refer to Chapter 5, Navigation, for more information. Route markers (such as glacier wands) should be removed after use to leave no trace. If you are separated from your party, a whistle can be a simple but reliable signaling device.

2. Sun Protection

Carry and wear sunglasses, sunscreen for the lips and skin, and clothing for sun protection.

Sunglasses. In alpine country, sunglasses are critical. The eyes are particularly vulnerable to radiation, and the corneas of unprotected eyes can be easily burned before any discomfort is felt, resulting in the excruciatingly painful condition known as snow blindness. Ultraviolet

TABLE 2-2. THE TEN ESSENTIALS

Ten Essentials: A Systems Approach	Ten Essentials: The Classic List
1. Navigation	1. Map 2. Compass
2. Sun protection	3. Sunglasses and sunscreen
3. Insulation (extra clothing)	4. Extra clothing
4. Illumination	5. Headlamp or flashlight
5. First-aid supplies	6. First-aid supplies
6. Fire	7. Firestarter 8. Matches
7. Repair kit and tools, including knife	9. Knife
8. Nutrition (extra food)	10. Extra food
9. Hydration (extra water)	
10. Emergency shelter	

rays can penetrate cloud layers, so do not let cloudy conditions fool you into leaving your eyes unprotected. It is advisable to wear sunglasses whenever you would wear sunscreen, and both are especially necessary on snow, ice, and water and at high altitudes.

Sunglasses should filter 95 percent to 100 percent of the ultraviolet light. They should also be tinted so that only a fraction of the visible light is transmitted through the lens to the eyes. For glacier glasses, a lens should allow 5 percent to 10 percent visible light transmission. Look in a mirror when trying on sunglasses: If your eyes can easily be seen, the lenses are too light. Lens tints should be gray or brown for the truest color; yellow provides better contrast in overcast or foggy conditions.

There is little proof that infrared rays (heat-carrying rays) harm your eyes unless you look directly at the sun, but any product that filters out a high percentage of infrared, as most sunglasses do, gives added eye protection insurance.

The frames of sunglasses should have side shields that reduce the light reaching your eyes, yet allow adequate ventilation to prevent fogging. Problems with fogging can be reduced by using an antifog lens-cleaning product.

Groups should carry at least one pair of spare sunglasses in case a pair is lost or forgotten. If no spare is available, eye protection can be improvised by cutting small slits in an eye cover made of cardboard or cloth.

Many climbers who need corrective lenses prefer using contact lenses instead of eyeglasses. Contacts may improve visual acuity, plus they do not slide down your nose, do not get water spots, and do allow the use of nonprescription sunglasses. Contacts have some problems, however. Blowing dust, sweat, and sunscreen can irritate your eyes. Backcountry conditions make it difficult to clean and maintain contacts. Eyeglasses protect your eyes better than contacts. Whether you choose contacts or eyeglasses, if you depend on corrective lenses, always carry a backup, such as a spare pair of eyeglasses or prescription sunglasses or goggles.

Sunscreen. Skin products containing sunscreen are also vital to climbers' well-being in the mountains. Although individuals vary widely in natural pigmentation and the amount of screening their skin requires, the penalty for underestimating the protection needed is so severe, including the possibility of skin cancer, that skin must always be protected.

While climbing, use a sunscreen that blocks both ultraviolet A (UVA) and ultraviolet B (UVB) rays. UVA rays are the primary preventable cause of skin cancer; UVB rays primarily cause sunburn. To protect skin from UV rays, use a sunscreen with a sun protection factor (SPF) of at least 15. The SPF number means that the sunscreen is formulated to permit you to stay in the sun that many times longer than if no protection was applied, with the same effect. For example, wearing a sunscreen rated SPF 15 allows you to stay in the sun 15 times longer than if you were not wearing any sunscreen. To protect skin from UVA rays, use a sunscreen that contains zinc oxide, titanium dioxide, or avobenzone (sometimes listed as Parsol 1789). Titanium oxide also blocks UVB and short-wave UVA rays. Manufacturers often use it in combination with zinc oxide.

All sunscreens are limited by their ability to remain on the skin while you are sweating. Some sunscreens are advertised as waterproof and will protect longer than regular products, but regardless of the claims on the label, reapply the sunscreen frequently.

Apply sunscreen to all exposed skin, including the undersides of your chin and nose and the insides of nostrils and ears. Even if you are wearing a hat, apply sunscreen to all exposed parts of your face and neck to protect against reflection from snow or water. Apply sunscreens half an hour before exposure to sun, because they usually take time to start working.

Clothing offers more sun protection than sunscreen. Long underwear or wind garments are frequently worn on sunny glacier climbs. The discomfort of long underwear, even under blazing conditions, is often considered a minor nuisance compared to the hassle of regularly smearing on sunscreen. Some UPF-rated garments (see "Putting the Clothing System Together," above) designed to maximize ventilation are meant for use in hot weather.

Lips burn, too, and require protection to prevent peeling and blisters. Sunblocks that resist washing, sweating, and licking are available. Reapply lip protection frequently, especially after eating or drinking.

Also see Chapter 23, First Aid, for information on sunburn and snow blindness.

3. Insulation (Extra Clothing)

How much extra clothing is necessary for an emergency? The basic climbing outfit (garments used during the active portion of a climb) includes inner and outer socks, boots, underwear, pants, shirt, sweater or fleece jacket, hat, mittens or gloves, and raingear. The term "extra clothing" refers to additional layers that would be needed to survive the long, inactive hours of an unplanned bivouac. Extra clothing should be selected according to the season. Ask this question: What is needed to survive the worst conditions that could realistically be encountered on this trip?

An extra layer of long underwear can add much warmth while adding little weight to a pack. It is also wise to pack an extra hat or balaclava, because they provide more warmth for their weight than any other article of clothing. For your feet, bring an extra pair of heavy socks; for your hands, an extra pair of polyester or fleece mitts. For winter and expedition climbing in severe conditions, bring more insulation for your torso as well as insulated overpants for your legs.

4. Illumination

Even if the climbing party plans to return to their cars before dark, it is essential to carry a headlamp or flashlight, just in case. Batteries and bulbs do not last forever, so carry spares.

Lights vary greatly in their brightness. In general, brighter illumination consumes more battery power. The highest-powered lights require more weight in batteries to last long enough for several hours of use. Technological improvements continue to make lights and batteries more efficient—xenon or halogen bulbs, brighter light-emitting diodes (LEDs), and better rechargeable batteries are examples. LEDs in particular have become very popular for their light weight, efficiency, and durability. Some lights combine LEDs with xenon or other high-powered illumination for versatility.

Headlamps. Few climbers carry anything besides headlamps, which allow freedom of both hands and, thus, are so much more convenient than flashlights. Lights are important enough and temperamental enough to make it worthwhile to invest only in quality equipment. At a minimum, get a light that is at least moisture-proof (designed to keep out rain). Waterproof lights often merit their extra expense, because they function reliably in any weather and the contacts or batteries are less likely to corrode in storage.

All lights need durable switches that cannot turn on accidentally in the pack, a common and serious problem. Switches tucked away in a recessed cavity are excellent. So are rotating switches in which the body of the light must be twisted a half turn. If it looks as though a light switch could be tripped accidentally, guard against this danger by taping the switch closed, removing the bulb, or reversing the batteries.

Adjustable beam is an excellent feature available on some lights. Wide floodlighting is good for chores close at hand; concentrated spotlighting assists in viewing objects far away, making it possible to see farther than with a brighter light lacking this feature.

Make sure the spare bulbs and batteries you carry still work and fit the light.

Alkaline batteries. The most commonly available general-purpose batteries, alkaline batteries pack more energy than cheaper lead-zinc batteries. The major problems with alkalines are that voltage (hence, brightness) drops significantly as they discharge, and their life is drastically shortened by cold temperatures: They operate at only 10 percent to 20 percent efficiency at

0 degrees Fahrenheit (minus 18 degrees Celsius). Also, they tend to be heavy and are difficult to recycle or dispose of properly.

Lithium batteries. For longer life and lighter weight, lithium batteries are available, though at a higher price. Voltage remains almost constant over their charge, and efficiency at 0 degrees Fahrenheit is nearly the same as at room temperature. Lithium batteries may have twice the voltage of their same-sized counterparts, so make sure they are compatible with the light you are using. Again, recycling or disposal of spent batteries is a concern.

Rechargeable batteries. Today's rechargeable batteries are better than ever. The once-common nickel-cadmium types function well in cold conditions but do not store as much energy as alkaline or lithium batteries and are difficult to dispose of properly. Much "greener" and more efficient alternatives are available in nickel-metal hydride (Ni-MH) and lithium-ion technologies, which pack more energy and hold their charges longer in storage. Some (not all) perform better in cold temperatures, others less so—check specifications carefully. A popular option is to use suitable rechargeables for the main batteries and lithium or alkaline batteries as spares.

5. First-Aid Supplies

Carry and know how to use a first-aid kit, but do not let a first-aid kit give you a false sense of security. The best course of action is to always take the steps necessary to avoid injury or sickness in the first place.

Getting mountaineering-oriented first aid (MOFA) training or wilderness first responder (WFR) training is very worthwhile. Most first-aid training is aimed at situations in urban or industrial settings where trained personnel will respond quickly. In the mountains, trained response may be hours—even days—away.

The first-aid kit should be compact and sturdy, with the contents wrapped in waterproof packaging. Commercial first-aid kits are widely available, though most are inadequate. At a minimum, a first-aid kit should include gauze pads in various sizes, roller gauze, small adhesive bandages, butterfly bandages, triangular bandages, battle dressing (or Carlisle bandage), adhesive tape, scissors, cleansers or soap, latex gloves, and paper and pencil. Carry enough bandages and gauze to absorb a significant quantity of blood.

Consider the length and nature of a particular trip in deciding whether to add to the basics of the first-aid kit. If the party will be traveling on a glacier, for example, tree branches will not be available for improvised splints, so a wire ladder splint would be extremely valuable in the event of a fracture. For a climbing expedition, consider bringing appropriate prescription medicines. See Chapter 23, First Aid, for details on a basic first-aid kit for one person.

6. Fire

Carry the means to start and sustain an emergency fire. Most climbers carry a butane lighter or two instead of matches in a waterproof container. Either must be absolutely reliable. Firestarters are indispensable for igniting wet wood quickly to make an emergency campfire. Common firestarters include candles, chemical heat tabs, and canned heat. On a high-altitude snow or glacier climb, where firewood is nonexistent, it is advisable to carry a stove as an additional emergency heat and water source (see Chapter 3, Camping and Food, for information concerning stoves).

7. Repair Kit and Tools (Including Knife)

Knives are so useful in first aid, food preparation, repairs, and climbing that every party member needs to carry one. Leashes to prevent loss are common. Other tools (pliers, screwdriver, awl, scissors) can be part of a knife or pocket tool or can be carried separately—perhaps even as part of a group kit. Other useful repair items are shoelaces, safety pins, needle and thread, wire, duct tape, nylon fabric repair tape, cable ties, plastic buckles, cordage, webbing, and replacement parts for equipment such as tent, tent poles, stove, crampons, snowshoes, and skis.

8. Nutrition (Extra Food)

For shorter trips, a one-day supply of extra food is a reasonable emergency stockpile in case foul weather, faulty navigation, injury, or other reasons delay the planned return. An expedition or long trek may require more. The food should require no cooking, be easily digestible, and store well for long periods. A combination of jerky, nuts, candy, granola, and dried fruit works well. If a stove is carried, cocoa, dried soup, and tea can be added. There are many possibilities. Some climbers only half-jokingly point out that pemmican bars and U.S. Army meals ready to eat (MRE) packs serve well as emergency rations because no one is tempted to eat them except in an emergency.

9. Hydration (Extra Water)

Carry sufficient water and have the skills and tools

required for obtaining and purifying additional water. Always carry at least one water bottle or collapsible water sack. Widemouthed containers are easier to refill. An accessory pocket makes it possible to carry a water bottle on a pack hip-belt for easy access. Some water sacks (hydration bladders) designed to be stored in the pack feature a plastic hose and valve that allow drinking without slowing your pace.

Before starting on the trail, fill water containers from a reliable source, such as from a tap at home. In most environments you need to have the ability to treat—by filtering, using purification chemicals, or boiling—additional water that is encountered. In cold environments, a stove, fuel, pot, and lighter are needed to melt snow for additional water.

Daily water consumption varies greatly. Two quarts (liters) daily is a reasonable minimum; in hot weather or at high altitudes, 6 quarts may not be enough. In dry environments, carry even more water. Plan for enough water to accommodate additional requirements due to heat, cold, altitude, exertion, or emergency. (See "Water" in Chapter 3, Camping and Food, for more information.)

10. Emergency Shelter

If the climbing party is not carrying a tent (see Chapter 3, Camping and Food), carry some sort of extra shelter (in addition to a rain shell) from rain and wind, such as a plastic tube tent or a jumbo plastic trash bag. Another possibility is a reflective emergency blanket, which can also be used in administering first aid to an injured or hypothermic person.

Carry an insulated sleeping pad (see Chapter 3, Camping and Food) to reduce heat loss while sitting or lying on snow.

Even on day trips, some climbers carry a bivy sack as part of their survival gear, and they partially compensate for the extra weight by going a little lighter on their insulating clothing layers. Others rely on their regular gear. A bivy sack protects insulating clothing layers from the weather, minimizes the effects of wind, and traps much of the heat escaping from your body inside its cocoon. (See "Shelter" in Chapter 3, Camping and Food, for details on bivy sacks.)

OTHER IMPORTANT ITEMS

There are, of course, many items in addition to the Ten Essentials that are useful for climbing. Every climber has a personal opinion about what items are necessary. With experience, all climbers develop their own preferences. However, regardless of the "essentials" an individual climber selects or does not select, it is always essential to engage the brain while mountain climbing. Think ahead. Take time periodically to envision scenarios of possible accidents and unexpected circumstances. What would you do in those situations? What equipment would be necessary in order to be prepared? What risks are you willing to accept?

Ice Ax

An ice ax is indispensable on snowfields and glaciers and is very useful on snow-covered alpine trails. An ice ax is a versatile tool, coming in handy for traveling in steep heather, scree, or brush; for crossing streams; and for digging sanitation holes. (For details on ice axes and their uses, see Chapter 6, Wilderness Travel, and Chapter 16, Snow Travel and Climbing.)

Insect Repellent

The wilderness is an occasional home for people, but it is the permanent habitat of insects and other arthropod pests. Some of them—mosquitoes, biting flies, no-see-um gnats, blackflies, ticks, chiggers—want to feast on the human body. For winter trips or for snow climbs any time of year, insect repellent may be unnecessary; for a low-elevation summer approach, thwarting mosquitoes may be essential.

One way to protect yourself from voracious insects is with heavy clothing, including gloves and head nets in really buggy areas. In hot weather, long shirts and pants made of netting may prove worthwhile. If it is too hot to wear much clothing, insect repellents are a good alternative.

Repellents with N,N-diethyl-metatoluamide (DEET) claim to be effective against all the principal biting insects but really perform best against mosquitoes. One application of a repellent with a high concentration of DEET will keep mosquitoes from biting for several hours, though they will still hover about annoyingly. Mosquito repellents come in liquid, cream, spray, and stick form and are available in various strengths.

Be aware that DEET is a potent toxin. It can also dissolve plastics and synthetic fabrics. There are less-toxic alternatives such as citronella and even clothing made of fabrics containing pyrethrins, which are natural insecticides extracted from chrysanthemum, but test these alternatives out first and make sure they work for you. In many situations, DEET is the only effective solution.

TABLE 2-3. SAMPLE EQUIPMENT LIST

Items in brackets [ ] are optional, depending on personal preference and the nature of the trip. Items with an asterisk (*) can be shared by the group. See various other chapters for details on some of the gear on this list.

ALL TRIPS

Ten Essentials

1. Navigation
2. Sun protection
3. Insulation (extra clothing)
4. Illumination
5. First-aid supplies
6. Fire
7. Repair kit and tools (including knife)
8. Nutrition (extra food)
9. Hydration (extra water)
10. Emergency shelter

Clothing

Boots
Socks (inner and outer)
[T-shirt or tank top]
[Shorts]
Long underwear (top and bottom)
Insulating shirts, sweaters, or jackets (synthetic or wool)
Insulating pants (synthetic or wool)
Rain parka
[Wind-resistant jacket]
Rain pants
[Wind pants]
Insulating hats (synthetic or wool)
[Rain hat]
[Sun-protection hat]
[Balaclava]
Mittens
Gloves
[Glove liners]
[Overmitts]
[Gaiters]
[Stream-crossing footwear]
[Waterproof-breathable socks]

Other

Day pack
Toilet paper
[Signaling device: whistle, cell phone, etc.]
[Insect repellent]
[Spare eyeglasses]
[Cup]
[Moleskin]
[Nylon cord]
[Altimeter]
[GPS]
[Camera and batteries]
[Binoculars]
[Bandannas]
[Ice ax]
[Helmet]

ADDITIONAL ITEMS FOR OVERNIGHT TRIPS

Internal- or external-frame pack
Sleeping bag and stuff sack
Sleeping pad
*Tent, tarp, or bivy sack
*Ground cloth
*Food
*Water container
*Repair kit
*Stove, fuel, and accessories
*Pots (and cleaning pad)
Spoon
[Fork]
[Bowl]
[Toiletries]
[Alarm clock or alarm watch]
[Camp clothing]
[Camp footwear]
[Pack cover]
[Candle lantern]

ADDITIONAL GEAR FOR ROCK CLIMBS

Helmet
Seat harness
Carabiners
Runners
Belay-rappel device
Leather belay gloves
Prusik slings
*Climbing rope
*Rack: chocks, cams, etc.
*Chock pick
[Rock climbing shoes]
[Chalk]
[Daisy chain]
[Athletic tape]

ADDITIONAL GEAR FOR SNOW, GLACIER, OR WINTER CLIMBS

Ice ax
Crampons
Carabiners
Seat harness
Chest sling or harness
Prusik slings
Rescue pulley
[Belay-rappel device]
*Climbing rope
*Spare sunglasses
Additional warm clothing, such as mittens, mitten shells, socks, balaclava, insulated parka, insulated bib pants, long underwear
*Snow shovel
*Group first-aid kit
[Plastic boots]
[Runners]
[Supergaiters]
[Snowshoes or skis]
[Avalanche transceiver]
*[Avalanche probe]
*[Flukes, pickets, ice screws]
*[Wands]
*[Snow saw]
[Handwarmer]
[Thermos bottle]

DEET is not very effective at repelling biting flies. Products with ethyl-hexanediol and dimethyl phthalate are much more effective against blackflies, deer flies, and gnats. Unfortunately, fly repellents do not do much to ward off mosquitoes.

Ticks are a potential health hazard because they can carry Lyme disease, Rocky Mountain spotted fever, or other diseases. In tick country, especially when thrashing through brush, check your clothing and hair frequently during the day, and give your clothes and body a thorough inspection at night.

Signaling Devices

Whistles, avalanche transceivers, radios, and cell phones may be lifesavers in some situations but useless in others. Because all signal devices are unreliable or ineffectual under certain circumstances, they should never be carried with absolute faith that they will actually transmit an emergency message. Bring signaling devices on a climb if it is decided that they are worth the burden of carrying them, but never depend on them to get the party out of a jam. Successful climbers prepare for the wilderness and act safely to minimize the chance they will ever need to send an emergency signal.

Whistle. Though limited in its scope, a whistle is probably the most reliable signaling device that can be carried. A whistle's shrill, penetrating blast greatly exceeds the range of the human voice and can serve as a crude means of communication in situations in which shouts for help cannot be heard—such as being trapped in a crevasse or becoming separated from the party in fog, darkness, or thick forest. Whistles prove much more useful if a climbing party designates certain signals before the trip, such as one sound of the whistle for "Where are you?"; two for "I'm here and OK"; and three for "Help!"

Avalanche transceiver. Snow climbs, especially during winter, can require carrying an avalanche transceiver, used to locate a buried victim of a snow slide. (See Chapter 16, Snow Travel and Climbing, for detailed instructions on using avalanche transceivers.)

Handheld radio. On an expedition, handheld radios can greatly ease communication between climbing partners or between a climbing party and base camp, and they could save critical hours in getting help for an injured person. A handheld radio may be worth its weight on some climbs. Ranger stations or logging operations may monitor specific channels, although their policies vary from region to region. Radios are by no means foolproof; their range is limited, and in rugged terrain a peak or ridge can easily block transmission.

Wireless telephone (cell phone). Cell (or mobile) phones have become common, and they can dramatically shorten the time it takes to summon rescuers. They are also useful for telling people back home that the party will be late but is not in trouble and thus can forestall unnecessary rescue efforts. Understanding the limits of cell phones (and the availability of rescue) is as important as understanding their usefulness: the batteries can deplete; cell phones are unable to transmit or receive in many mountain locations; a rescue may not be possible due to weather conditions or availability of rescuers. Cell phones should be viewed as an adjunct to, not a substitute for, self-reliance. No party should set out ill prepared, inadequately equipped, or attempting a route beyond the ability of its members with the notion that they can just call for help if needed. They will imperil themselves and the rescuers who may try to bail them out.

EQUIPMENT CHECKLIST

Whether you are experienced or not, it is easy to forget an important item in the rush to get ready for the next trip. Seasoned climbers have learned that using a checklist is the only sure way to avoid an oversight. The list in Table 2-3 is a good foundation for formulating a personal checklist. Add to or subtract from this list as necessary; then get in the habit of checking your own list before each trip.

PREPARING FOR THE FREEDOM OF THE HILLS

When you go into the wilderness, you should carry what you need and leave the rest at home. Achieving that balance takes knowledge and good judgment. Understanding the basics of clothing and equipment will help you decide what you really need to be safe and comfortable in the mountains. This is only the beginning of your discovery of the freedom of the hills. The next chapter, Camping and Food, will further expand your horizons.

SHELTER • SELECTING THE CAMPSITE • SNOW AND WINTER CAMPING • THE SLEEPING SYSTEM • STOVES • WATER • FOOD • "IT'S JUST CAMPING"

Chapter 3
CAMPING AND FOOD

Spending nights out in a beautiful alpine environment is one of the delights of mountaineering. Mastering the arts of camping and alpine cooking only enhances the experience. Setting up a temporary home in the wild can be quick work, yet can provide cozy shelter, a warm bed, and good food. When it is time to move on, the best camps leave no trace.

SHELTER

Choosing a shelter depends on each climber's situation and preference.

Tents are the most common and versatile mountain shelter. They are relatively easy to set up, usually in 10 minutes or less; they provide privacy; they are rainproof and a refuge from wind or sun; they are usable in almost any terrain; and often they are roomy enough for both you and your gear. Tents usually are the first choice for shelter above timberline and for glacier camps, for winter camping, in moderate winds, and in bear and/or mosquito country.

Tarps are a lightweight alternative to tents, and they can be used in conjunction with bivy sacks to provide effective shelter from rain and sun. The term "bivy" comes from bivouac, a French word meaning "temporary encampment." Bivy sacks can be used as lightweight emergency shelters or carried as primary bare-minimum shelters for light traveling.

TENTS

Tent selection is a calculation of trade-offs between protection (sturdiness), weight, comfort, and price. The choice depends on how and where the tent will be used and on personal preferences (see the "Questions to Consider When Choosing a Tent" sidebar).

Moisture Strategies

Tents must serve two competing functions in managing moisture. They need to keep out as much moisture as possible from the external environment, while at the same time venting as much moisture as possible from the interior. One person exhales a substantial amount of water overnight. If the tent were completely waterproof, this water vapor would drench sleeping bags and leave puddles on the floor. Therefore the tent must "breathe."

Tent floors are coated nylon, and most tents have a sill—an extension of the floor up the sides of the tent. A higher sill gives more protection from rain blown in under the fly. It also reduces the amount of breathable fabric and can become an area of gathering condensation.

The floor and sill can be separate pieces connected by a bound seam or can be one continuous piece of fabric, commonly known as a bathtub floor. Bathtub floors give better protection from groundwater but are not easily replaced if the floor wears out before the upper part of the tent.

Many tents come with floors and flies seam-taped at the factory to keep the water from passing through. If a tent is not factory taped, then a sealing compound must be applied to all exposed seams to prevent leakage.

Double-wall tents. Double-wall construction usually solves the dilemma of a waterproof yet breathable tent. The inner wall, suspended away from the outer wall, is breathable: It is not waterproof, so it allows exhaled moisture and perspiration to pass through to the outside. The outer layer is a detachable waterproof rain fly that keeps rain off the tent's inner wall and also collects the moisture from inside the tent, which then evaporates into the air flowing between the two layers. The rain fly must not touch the inner walls, because where it touches, water will leak through the inner wall. The fly of a mountaineering tent should come fairly close to the ground, covering the tent and entryway, shedding wind-driven rain.

Single-wall tents. Just one layer of waterproof-breathable fabric, usually consisting of three layers laminated together, composes a single-wall tent. An outer layer of nylon provides strength and protects the middle membrane layer. The middle membrane keeps water and rain out but allows warm vapors from inside to escape. The inner layer is a fuzzy, blotterlike facing that holds excess moisture.

The great advantage of a single-wall tent is its light weight, typically about 5 pounds (2.3 kilograms) for a two-person tent. They are also quieter in high winds because there is no outer fly to flap against the tent walls. The major disadvantages of single-wall tents are that they are quite expensive and they sometimes collect moisture on the inside during warm, wet weather. The membrane works best when outside temperatures are several degrees cooler than inside. This temperature differential pushes the moist air out through the breathable tent walls.

QUESTIONS TO CONSIDER WHEN CHOOSING A TENT

- Can it be set up easily and without help?
- Is it easy to get in and out of the door(s)?
- Is there enough head and foot room?
- How much of the occupants' gear will fit inside?
- Does it match the intended use? For example, three- versus four-season; room for two, three, or more climbers, etc.
- Is everything included that is needed to use the tent, such as stakes, poles, fly, seam sealer, instructions, and stuff sacks?

Three- and Four-Season Tents

Tents for mountaineering are either three-season tents (nonwinter use) or four-season tents (used for all situations, including snow camping).

Three-season tents. The side or top panels of many three-season tents are made with see-through netting, providing ventilation, bug protection, and lower weight. However, blowing snow can come in through the netting. Three-season tents tend to be lighter in weight and construction. These tents are adequate for mountaineering in a wide variety of conditions from late spring to early fall, and they can be ideal for weeklong traverses on which weight must be kept to a minimum.

Four-season tents. Usually heavier, more costly, and built to withstand winter conditions of high winds and snow loading, four-season tents have stronger poles (higher-strength aluminum or carbon fiber, rather than fiberglass) and more-durable reinforcing. The doors, windows, and vents have solid panels that zip as near to closed as desired (keeping ventilation requirements in mind), and the fly extends close to ground level all the way around. Four-season tents usually have at least three poles, with greater emphasis on guylines (cords attached to the tent and staked out to brace it). Some manufacturers also supply an internal guyline kit to augment the external guylines, but climbers can set up their own internal guys as well. Usually the tent shape is some variation on the dome.

Tent Shapes

Designers shape tents to maximize usable interior space, load-bearing strength, and ability to withstand high winds, while at the same time minimizing a tent's weight. A great tent must be easy to pitch and disassemble but very tenacious when storms attempt to take it down.

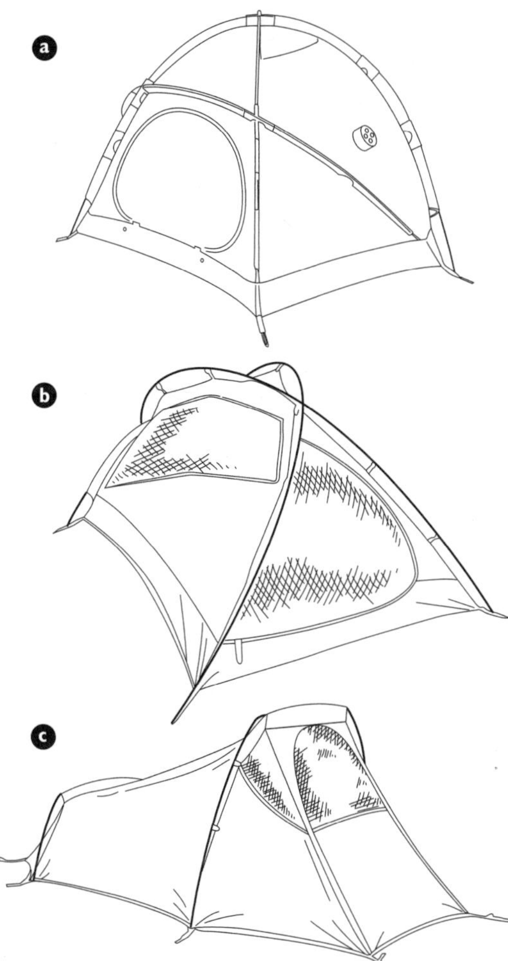

Fig. 3-1. Tent designs (shown without rain flies): a, dome tent; b, wedge tent; c, hoop-style tent.

Dome. The freestanding dome tent (fig. 3-1a) is usually round or hexagonal in shape, with several poles crisscrossing over it so it needs no stakes to hold its shape. A person can pick it up and move it but still must stake it down and attach it to guylines so it will not blow away. The possibility of the tent blowing away is a real danger in a heavy storm or when the tent is unoccupied.

Wedge. The wedge tent (fig. 3-1b) uses two crisscrossed poles as a frame and is relatively freestanding. It is less rigid than the dome and needs guylines to hold its shape in high winds.

Hoop. The two- or three-hoop tunnel tent (fig. 3-1c), usually not freestanding, offers efficient use of space and is good at shedding wind.

Comparing these designs, a freestanding tent is much easier to assemble and move to the best location than a tent that must be staked down before it will hold its shape. The hoop and wedge designs are typically lighter for a given volume.

Tent Size

Two-person. The most popular tent size for mountaineering is the two-person because it offers the greatest flexibility in weight and choice of campsite. For a group, it is generally more versatile; for example, bringing two two-person tents rather than one four-person tent offers more options. Many two-person tents handle three people in a pinch, yet are light enough to be used by one person. The tent will be warmer, however, with more than one occupant.

Larger. Some three- and four-person tents are light enough to be carried by two people who crave luxurious living (or two large people who crave adequate space). Larger tents, especially those high enough to stand in, are big morale boosters during an expedition or long storm but are burdens to carry. Before you set out, distribute the tent parts (tent, fly, poles and stakes, etc.) among the party to share the weight of carrying it.

Features

A good mountaineering tent keeps out most of the rain and snow as climbers get in and out. Manufacturers offer many different features, such as extra doors, interior pockets, gear loops, tunnels, alcoves, vestibules, and hoods. Of course, most extra features add weight and cost. A mountaineer cannot enjoy that nice extra door

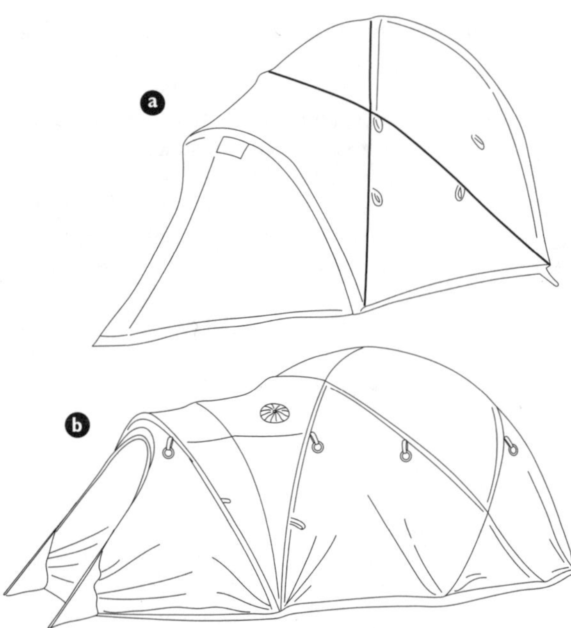

Fig. 3-2. Dome tent vestibule styles: a, tent with three-season rain fly and vestibule; b, tent with four-season or mountaineering rain fly and tunnel-style vestibule.

or vestibule without first paying for it and then carrying it up to high camp.

Vestibules. Four-season tents, and some three-season models, commonly include a protruding floorless protected area known as a vestibule (fig. 3-2a). Some expedition rain flies come with their own poles for extending the vestibule area farther (fig. 3-2b). Vestibules help shelter the entrance and provide more room for storing gear and boots, dressing, and cooking. In foul weather, cooking in the tent vestibule is an art to be appreciated (but be very careful—see "Safety" under "Stoves," later in this chapter). Some four-season tents provide two vestibules, allowing for specialization (for example, cooking in one, boot storage in the other).

Vents. A tent needs vents located toward the ceiling that can open, allowing warm, moist air (which rises) to escape. Mosquito netting allows air to flow freely when the doors are unzipped and will keep out rodents and reptiles as well as flies and mosquitoes (see Figure 3-1b and c).

Color. Tent color is a matter of personal taste. Warm tent colors such as yellow, orange, and red are cheerier if the party is stuck inside, and they make it easier to spot camp on the way back from a summit. On the other hand, subdued hues blend into the landscape. One color may be an eyesore; the other may camouflage the camp too well, making it hard to find.

Knowing what you prefer will be difficult until you go out a few times and establish some form of basecamp routine. If possible, rent a tent and try it out before purchasing.

Anchoring the Tent

Bring stakes designed to handle the terrain. In forest duff, short plastic or wire stakes, such as those that come with most tents, are just fine. In rocky alpine terrain, metal skewer-type stakes (fig. 3-3a) or sturdier plastic T-shaped stakes (fig. 3-3b) may be required. In sand or snow, a broader surface area on the stake will help (fig. 3-3c).

Anchoring a tent in snow requires more attention. Stakes simply driven into the snow in the normal fashion will pull out in heavy wind and melt out during the day. Snowshoes, ice axes, skis, and ski poles can make solid anchors but cannot be used for anything else while they are holding down the tent. For extra security, tie the tent to a tree if there is one nearby.

The best snow anchors are deadman anchors (fig. 3-4). These can be stakes, stuff sacks packed with snow, metal plates called flukes made specifically for this purpose (see "Snow Anchors" in Chapter 16, Snow Travel and Climbing), or even rocks. First, tie the deadman to the tent guyline, or form a loop in the line and slip the deadman into it. Dig a T-shaped trench at least

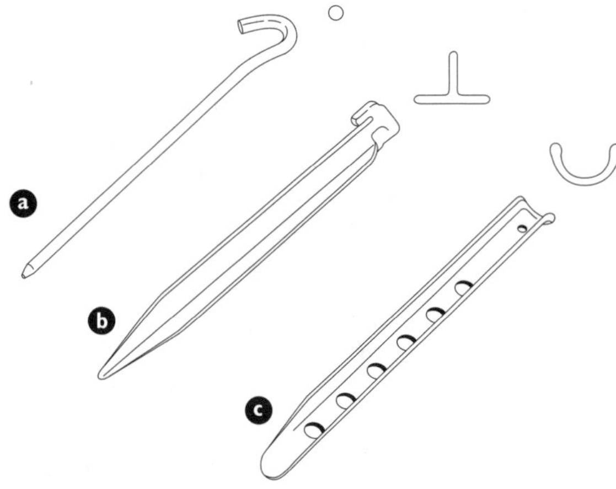

Fig. 3-3. Tent stakes: a, skewer; b, T-shaped ; c, snow or sand stake (note cross sections of profiles at right).

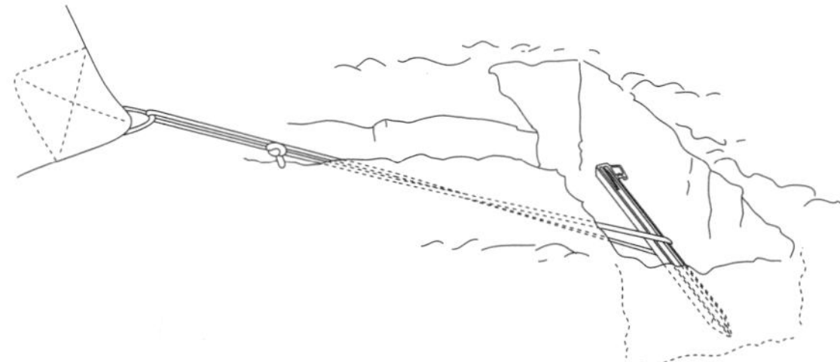

Fig. 3-4. Deadman anchor: Dig a T-shaped trench about 12 inches deep, fasten the tent's guyline around the anchor, and place it in the trench's crossbar. Pull the line taut to tension the tent. Backfill the trench and stomp to compact the snow over the anchor.

12 inches (30 centimeters) deep, with the long leg of the T facing the tent. Put the deadman into the trench in the crossbar of the T, then pull the line taut, backfill the trench, and stamp down the snow.

A couple of tensioning methods keep the guylines taut. One way is to buy small plastic or metal tensioners that slide up and down the line to make adjustments (fig. 3-5a and b). Another is to use a taut-line hitch (fig. 3-5c).

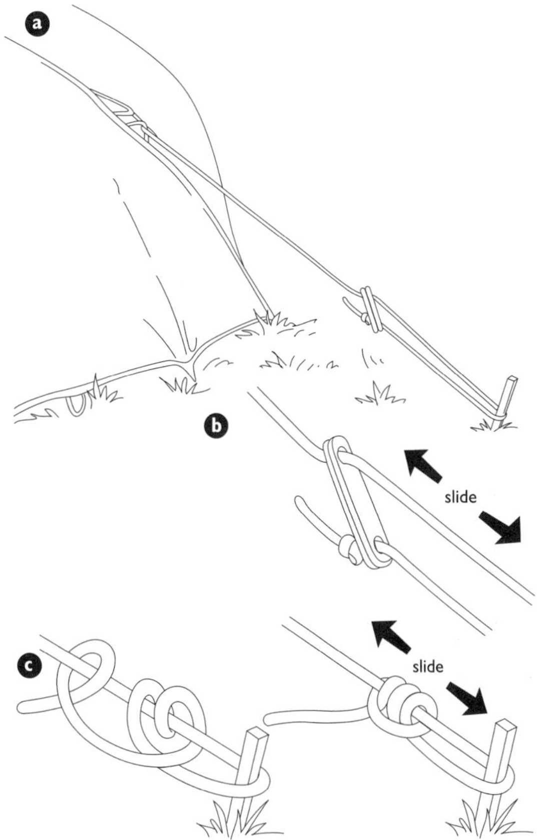

Fig. 3-5. Tensioning guylines: a, guyline with a tensioner device; b, close-up view of a tensioner; c, taut-line hitch.

Tent Setup, Care, and Cleaning

When setting up or taking down a tent, push poles through the tent sleeves rather than pulling them. Pulling can separate the pole sections and lead to snagging of sleeve fabric on the section ends. A tent goes up quickly and easily if two or three members of the party know exactly who does what: who holds the tent to keep it from blowing away, who threads poles through the sleeves, who pushes the poles toward the threader, etc.

To protect the tent floor from water, dirt, and abrasion, discourage wearing boots inside the tent. A small whisk broom and camp towel or sponge help keep the floor clean. When not on an ultralightweight trip, bring a tarp or ground cloth to set underneath the tent to protect the floor from abrasion (tuck in the sides so the ground cloth does not channel in rainwater). Some manufacturers offer a tent "footprint" ground cloth shaped for the tent. You can also make your own ground cloth from synthetic polyethylene fiber fabrics (such as Tyvek) or another lightweight and durable material.

A tent gives more years of good service if it is carefully cleaned and air-dried after each trip. To clean a tent, hose it off or wash it with mild soap and water. Scrub stains with a sponge. Spot-clean any tree sap. Do not put the tent in a washer or dryer.

High temperatures and prolonged exposure to sun damage tent material, so do not leave the tent set up for unnecessary periods of time. The damage from ultraviolet light can ruin a rain fly in a single season of prolonged exposure. Do not touch tent fabric just after applying insect repellent to yourself; the chemicals can ruin fabric coatings.

TARPS

A tarp—lightweight and low cost—may offer adequate shelter from all but extreme weather in lowland forests and among subalpine trees. Compared to a tent, a tarp gives less protection from heat loss and wind and none at all from insects or rodents. A tarp also requires ingenuity

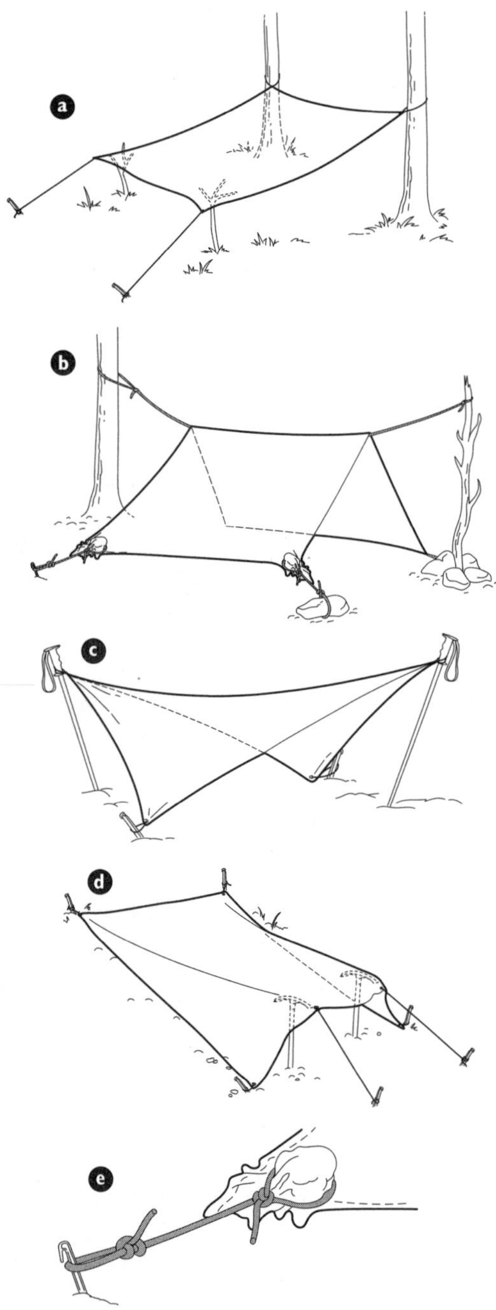

Fig. 3-6. Improvised tarp shelters: a, using two trees and two sticks; b, A-frame using two trees; c, shaped tarp with two short poles; d, using two ice axes; e, tying off corners on a tarp that has no grommets or tie-off loops.

and some cooperation from the landscape to set up (fig. 3-6a and b). It may be a poor choice above timberline unless poles, such as ice axes or ski poles, are brought along (fig. 3-6c and d). A tarp shelter can be very helpful as a cooking and eating area in camp during inclement weather. Do not wrap yourself (with or without a sleeping bag) in a tarp as if it were a blanket, because perspiration will condense inside the waterproof material.

Plastic tarps are inexpensive but do not hold up very well. Coated nylon tarps are stronger and usually very lightweight. Many come with reinforced grommets on the sides and corners for easy rigging. If a tarp lacks grommets, sew on loops of fabric such as nylon or twill tape. Alternatively, just tie off each corner around a small cone or pebble from the campsite (fig. 3-6e). Take along some lightweight cord, and perhaps a few light stakes, to string the tarp up.

Some manufacturers offer lightweight, floorless nylon tents. They are not simply flat sheets but have a tailored shape and usually at least one pole. Similarly, the rain fly of some double-wall tents can be set up without the tent, serving as a freestanding, lightweight shelter.

BIVY SACKS

The bivy sack is a lightweight alternative to a tent—and an acquired taste. It is a large fabric envelope with a zipper entrance at one end, sometimes with zippered mosquito netting. Bivy sacks provide the moisture-management functions of a tent—keeping out external moisture while venting internal water vapor. The bottom is usually waterproof coated nylon; the upper is of a waterproof-breathable material. Styles vary from spartan sacks (fig. 3-7a) weighing scarcely 1 pound (about 0.4 kilogram) to minitents that may be staked out and have a hoop to keep the fabric off the sleeper's face (fig. 3-7b). The sack is designed for one person, two in an emergency.

A bivy sack can be used alone or carried as only an emergency shelter. The common practice, however, is to put a sleeping bag inside and an insulating pad beneath. Putting the insulating pad inside the bivy sack is a matter of personal preference that requires a sack large enough to accommodate the pad. A bivy sack increases the insulation provided by a sleeping bag (and the insulating pad, if it is inside the sack), making it a nice addition in snow shelters.

In very cold conditions, the bivy sack must be large enough to allow the sleeping bag to loft fully. In mild conditions, a bivy sack, in combination with a tarp set up over it, offers good protection at less weight than

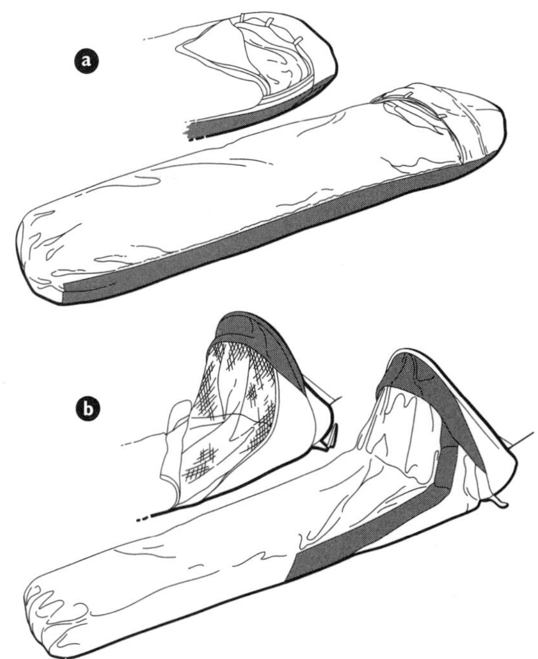

Fig. 3-7. Bivy sacks: a, lightweight; b, hoop style.

most tents. In wet conditions, a bivy sack inside a tent will keep the sleeping bag dry no matter how damp the tent. Make sure all seams are sealed before taking the bivy sack out on an adventure.

SELECTING THE CAMPSITE

The ideal campsite is comfortable, with plenty of great views, a nearby water source, and flat space for tents and cooking. Some places have it all, but usually selecting a campsite involves a trade-off. Climbers may walk right past an idyllic spot in the forest in favor of a cramped mountain ledge that puts them closer to the summit.

Wind is a big consideration in choosing a campsite, and mountaineers learn to think about windbreak shelter. In most areas, prevailing winds tend to come from a particular direction. A ridge-top camp will be very exposed should a strong wind develop. A notch or low point on a ridge is the windiest of all. Alpine breezes can be capricious. An afternoon breeze blowing upslope may reverse at night as heavy, chilled air rolls downslope from the snowfields above. Cold air, heavier than warm air, flows downward during settled weather, following valleys and collecting in depressions. Thus, there is often a chill breeze down a creek or dry wash and a pool of cold air in a basin. Night air is often several degrees cooler near a river or lake than on the knolls above.

Consider wind direction when pitching a tent. Pitching camp on the lee (downwind) side of a clump of trees or rocks is often best. Facing the tent door into the wind in good weather will distend the tent and minimize flapping. In stormy conditions, pitch the tent with the rear toward the wind so rain and snow will not be blown inside whenever the door is unzipped.

Consider how changes in temperature or weather may affect the campsite. For example, avoid camping in gullies or creek beds, which are susceptible to flash floods during a thunderstorm. Consider the potential for a rise in water level if you are camping near a river or stream. The braided rivers in the Alaskan interior, for example, often rise considerably during the day due to increased glacier runoff as the day warms up. In winter or in the high country, make sure the tent is clear of any potential avalanche path.

LEAVE NO TRACE

Environmental impact is of paramount importance in campsite selection. The more human traffic there is and the more fragile the setting, the more careful you must be (see the "A Few Cardinal Rules for Clean Camping" sidebar). Chapter 7, Leave No Trace, discusses campsite selection in detail. Here, briefly, are campsite options,

A FEW CARDINAL RULES FOR CLEAN CAMPING

1. Camp in established campsites whenever possible.
2. Dispose of human waste properly, away from water, trails, and campsites (see Chapter 7, Leave No Trace).
3. Use a camp stove instead of building a fire.
4. Wash well away from campsites and water sources.
5. Leave flowers, rocks, and other natural features undisturbed.
6. Do not feed the wildlife. This keeps wildlife healthy and self-reliant, limiting the likelihood of encounters between wild animals and humans.
7. Pack out all garbage, including litter left by others.

listed from best to worst in terms of minimizing damage to the environment:

Best choice:	Established, fully impacted site Snow
Good choice:	Rock slab Sandy, gravelly, or dirt flat Duff in deep forest
Poor choice:	Grass-covered meadow Plant-covered meadow above timberline
Worst choice:	Waterfront along lakes and streams

IN BEAR COUNTRY

Learn to recognize the "game trails"—faint trails that appear and disappear through the terrain—that large animals are most likely to amble on, and never set up camp on a game trail. Sleep in a tent rather than out in the open. Large animals such as bears and cougars are not known to attack parties of four or more persons, so this may be a useful minimum group size for extended trips in wilder areas—if everyone stays together.

In treeless bear country, set up camp in a triangle configuration (fig. 3-8) that is at least 100 yards (90 meters) on each side: one point of the triangle that has good visibility in all directions is the cooking and eating area; at another point of the triangle, set up storage of food, camp kitchen items (stove, pots, pans, scrubber, etc.), and any other items with an aroma (such as toothpaste, deodorant, lotions, and used feminine-hygiene products); at the third point of the triangle, upwind from the other two points, establish the tent site.

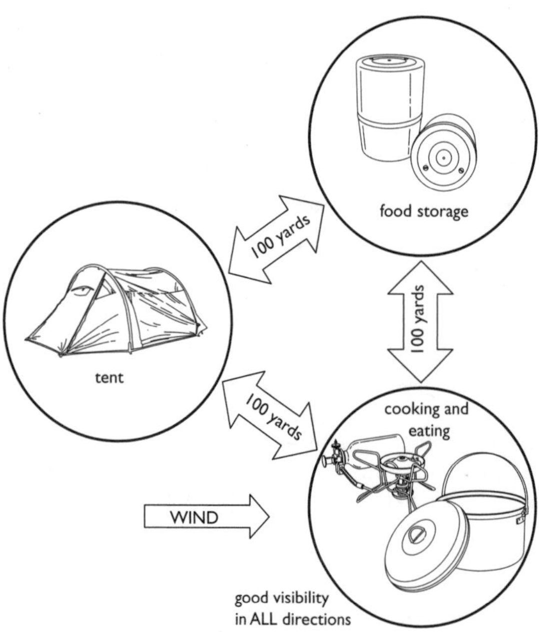

Fig. 3-8. Campsite triangle for bear habitat.

SNOW AND WINTER CAMPING

For winter camping, a good shelter, proper insulation, and the skills to stay dry are essential. Tents are the preferred choice when weather conditions are changing, with temperatures near the freezing point; in terrain with low amounts of snow; on short trips; or when camp must be set up quickly. If the sun is out at midday, the inside of a tent can be 40 or 50 degrees Fahrenheit (22 to 28 degrees Celsius) warmer than the outside air, making it a great place for drying out sleeping bags and clothing. More exotic snow shelters such as snow caves and igloos require more time, effort, and skill but may be stronger, more spacious, and even warmer in very cold weather.

TOOLS

A mountaineering snow shovel is essential for preparing tent platforms, digging emergency shelters, excavating climbers from avalanche debris, and sometimes even clearing climbing routes. In winter, every member of the party should carry a shovel. For summer snow camping, take one shovel per tent or rope team, with a minimum of two shovels per party.

Look for a lightweight shovel with a compact sectional or telescoping handle and a sturdy blade. Blades are made of metal (aluminum is common) or strong plastic. Some mountaineers prefer a metal blade because it is better for chopping into icy snow. The blade may be scoop-shaped (fig. 3-9a and b), which makes it easier to move large volumes of snow, or relatively straight-bladed (fig. 3-9c), which makes cutting easier. A D-shaped handle (see Figure 3-9c) or L- or T-shaped handle (see Figures 3-9a and b) can provide leverage and a firm grip.

A snow saw (fig. 3-9d) is the best tool for cutting blocks to make an igloo, a snow trench, or a wind-blocking snow wall around your tent (see Figure 3-10).

TENTS IN WINTER

Locate a winter camp away from hazards such as crevasses, avalanche paths, and cornices. Observe the local wind patterns: A rock-hard or sculpted snow surface indicates frequent wind, whereas an area with loose, powdery snow indicates a lee slope where wind-transported snow is deposited. An area deep in powdery snow may be protected from wind, but the tent may frequently have to be cleared of snow.

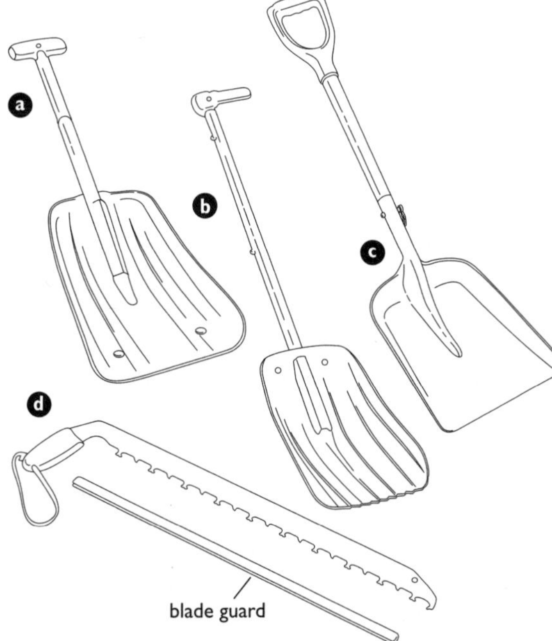

Fig. 3-9. Snow tools: a, scoop-style shovel with T-shaped handle; b, scoop-style shovel with L-shaped handle; c, straight-blade shovel with D-shaped handle; d, snow saw with detachable blade guard.

Select a flat spot. Establish a tent platform by compacting an area large enough to hold the tent and to allow for movement around it to check guylines or clear snow. A straight-bladed shovel works well to flatten the tent site. Tromping around on it with snowshoes will compact the surface. A ski does a great job of grading it. Flatten and smooth the tent platform thoroughly to keep occupants from sliding downslope during the night and to get rid of uncomfortable lumps. This is especially important when staying in one location for several nights, because the features will be cast in ice after the first night, and the platform will become rock hard. If the site is slightly off level, sleep with your head toward the high side. Use deadman anchors (see Figure 3-4) attached to long guylines to secure the tent in snow.

After erecting the tent, dig a pit about 1 foot (30 centimeters) deep in front of the tent door (fig. 3-10). Climbers can sit comfortably in the doorway of the tent with their feet in this pit while putting on boots and gaiters. Put the cook stove on the snow directly across from the pit. In bad weather, the pit is a convenient, wind-protected location for the stove, allowing climbers to wiggle forward in their sleeping bags and just reach out to cook. The tent vestibule can be erected over the pit.

Build snow walls around the tent if the site is exposed to the wind (see Figure 3-10). Blocks cut by a snow saw or straight-bladed snow shovel make the easiest, quickest walls. Simply shoveling snow into a pile can

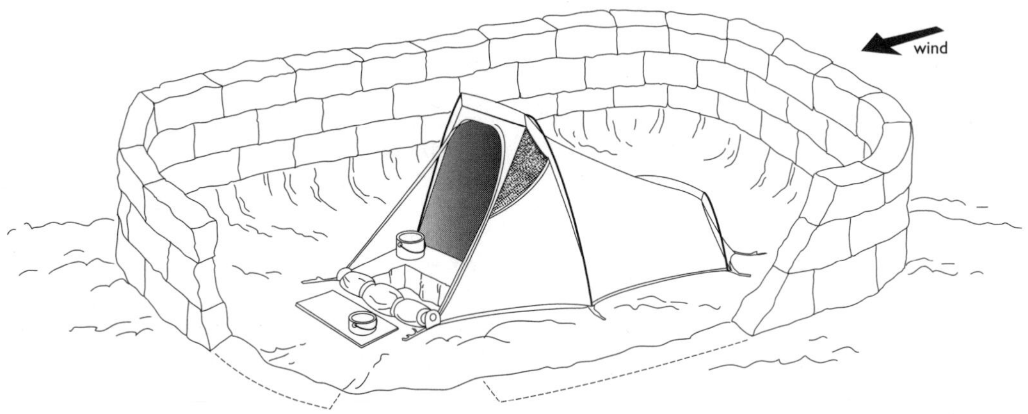

Fig. 3-10. Typical winter camp: snow walls and a tent placed with its door downwind and a small kitchen area off the vestibule.

make a wall, but a rounded pile is a less effective windbreak. The walls should be 3 to 6 feet (1 to 2 meters) high to deflect wind away from the tent. Keep the walls as far from the tent as they are high: for example, a 3-foot-high wall should be 3 feet away from the tent, because wind will quickly deposit snow on the leeward side of the wall.

During a storm, party members will periodically have to clear snow away from the tent. In most storms, the problem is not the snow falling from the sky, but the snow carried in by the wind. Snow deposits develop on the leeward side of tents and snow walls. Even a partially buried tent poses the risk of asphyxiation, especially if someone is cooking inside. Snow can also pile up and load the tent with enough weight to break the poles and bring the whole structure down. Shake the tent walls regularly and shovel out around the tent, taking care to remove snow from below the lower edge of the fly so air can flow between the fly and tent. Be careful not to cut the tent with the shovel; nylon slices easily when tensioned by a snow load. In a severe or prolonged storm, a tent may begin to disappear into the hole created by neighboring snowdrifts, making it necessary to move the tent up to the new snow surface.

A number of special items are useful for winter camping. Each tent should have a small whisk broom to sweep snow from boots, packs, clothing, and the tent. A sponge is useful for cleaning up food and water spills and removing condensation from interior walls. A candle lantern is a cheery addition during long nights near the winter solstice. For a larger community tent, a gas lantern can repay its price in weight and bother by adding tremendous brightness and warmth.

Some house rules can help make tent-bound hours more pleasant. With a small tent, packs may have to be outside. Most four-season tents have vestibules to store gear under cover. Brush off all snow thoroughly before bringing packs inside. It often helps to have one person enter the tent first to lay sleeping pads and organize gear. House rules may also dictate that boots be taken off outside, brushed free of snow, and placed in a waterproof boot bag inside the tent. Boots can bring in snow or tear holes in the tent floor. Plastic boots are best for winter camping, because the shells can be left covered outside or in the vestibule, while the liners can come inside to keep from freezing. Use stuff sacks or a large tent sack to reduce clutter and protect personal gear. Put the next day's dry clothing inside your sleeping bag or in a waterproof plastic sack so it does not get wet from tent condensation.

Sleeping bags offer not only warmth and comfort but also an opportunity to dry out gear. Put boot liners, gloves, and socks in the bag before you go to sleep, and they will be dry and warm in the morning. Do not attempt to dry large items of clothing by wearing them to bed; they will just make you and the bag wet and cold. In extreme cold, put boots inside an oversize stuff sack and place them inside or next to the sleeping bag to prevent them from freezing. To prevent a water bottle from freezing overnight, seal it tightly and place inside the sleeping bag.

SNOW SHELTERS

When the temperature drops or winter storms bring strong winds and heavy snowfall, seasoned mountaineers often prefer to sleep in a snow shelter rather than a tent. A snow cave or an igloo takes more time to build, but either is more secure than a tent and warmer in cold weather. Newcomers to snow camping are surprised at what a warm, comfortable, and beautiful experience a snow shelter can be. The interior of a properly built snow cave will be at least 32 degrees Fahrenheit (0 degrees Celsius) no matter what is going on outside, and when a few warm climbers pile in, it gets even warmer. As snow accumulates during a storm, the snow shelter becomes even sturdier, whereas a tent requires continual snow removal to protect the structure and its occupants. Snow shelters make sense on extended winter trips, when the construction time can be offset by staying in it for several nights.

Construction time and effort are the major drawbacks of snow shelters. Among the different types, snow trenches are relatively quick to complete, snow caves take more time to build, and igloos require the most time. Snow shelters require no special equipment other than a mountaineering snow shovel and perhaps a snow saw to cut blocks—but they do require skill. Practice before committing to a trip that relies on snow shelters. See the "Emergency Snow Shelters" sidebar for other options.

Dripping water is a potential problem in any snow shelter. The occupants' body heat warms the air, which rises to the ceiling, resulting in some melting. If the ceiling is smooth, most of the meltwater will absorb into the snow. But little spikes and bumps will become dripping points, so take the time to smooth the inner walls. Finally, do not cook inside the snow shelter; the ventilation may be inadequate, making carbon monoxide poisoning likely.

Snow Trench

A snow trench can take only a half hour to build, making it suitable for bivouac use as well as for spartan one- or two-person quarters. It is the simplest structure to build out of snow blocks sawed with a snow saw. Unlike a snow cave, a trench does not require particular terrain features; it is appropriate for the flats or on an avalanche-safe slope. The snow must be deep enough that the completed trench floor still sits in snow.

To build a snow trench, establish an initial cut line 6 to 7 feet (about 2 meters) long with either a straight-blade shovel or a snow saw (fig. 3-11a). Dig a narrow trench along this cut line by using the snow saw or shovel to quarry snow blocks about 1 to 1.5 feet (40 centimeters) thick by 2 feet (60 centimeters) wide by 3 feet (90 centimeters) long (fig. 3-11b). The blocks can be created as part of the process of removing snow for the trench, or they can be quarried nearby. Set each snow block aside carefully when it is removed from the quarry—they will form the roof of the trench.

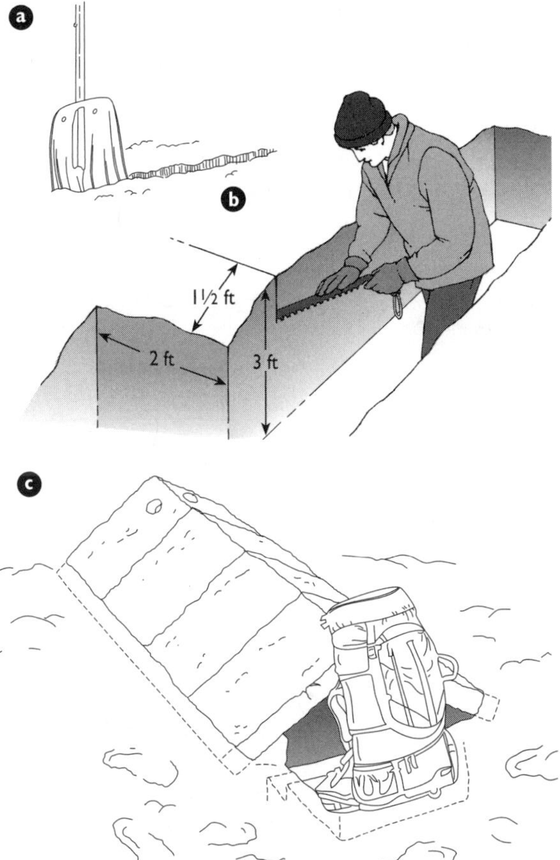

Fig. 3-11. Building a snow trench: a, establish initial cut line with straight-blade shovel; b, quarry snow blocks 1.5 feet thick by 2 feet wide by 3 feet long; c, build an A-frame roof with snow blocks, enlarge interior, and provide ventilation hole in roof.

Once the trench area is large enough—2 feet (60 centimeters) wide by 6.5 feet (2 meters) long by 3 feet (90 centimeters) deep for one person—roof the trench, A-frame style, with the snow blocks (fig. 3-11c). Close off the back with another snow block. When the A-frame roof is in place, crawl underneath it into the trench and enlarge the interior down and out to accommodate the intended number of occupants. Build steps leading down into the trench. Provide a ventilation hole in the roof. Use loose snow to caulk any gaps between roof blocks and around the back. Smooth out any bumps or irregularities in the ceiling so meltwater will run down the blocks to the sides rather than dripping on the occupants. Cover most of the entrance with a pack covered by a plastic bag, but leave some space for ventilation. Cook outside of the trench.

A more basic, emergency snow trench shelter can be built by digging a trench some 4 to 6 feet (1.2 to 2 meters) deep and large enough for the party to sleep in. Stretch a tarp over the top and weigh the edges down with snow (fig. 3-12). On a flat site, provide some slope to the tarp by building up the snow on one side of the trench. This quick shelter works moderately well in wind or rain, but a heavy snowfall can collapse the roof. As with all snow shelters, the smaller the trench, the easier it is to keep warm.

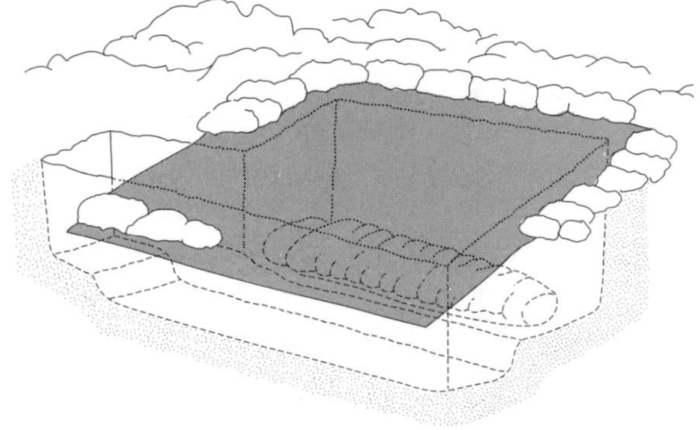

Fig. 3-12. Basic snow trench roofed with a tarp.

Snow Cave

Snow caves are most suitable in locations where climbers can burrow into a substantially snow-covered hillside. The snow must be deep enough to leave about 2 feet (60 centimeters) of ceiling thickness. A strong and stable cave also requires somewhat firm (consolidated) snow. Several people can shelter in one snow cave.

A well-built cave dug in firm snow is a very secure structure. However, if the outside temperature is warming toward freezing, a tent or tree shelter may be a better choice. The impact of a collapsed snow-cave roof can cause serious injury to anyone struck by it.

Find a short—7 feet (2.1 meters) minimum—snowdrift or 30- to 40-degree slope that is clear of any potential avalanche hazard (fig. 3-13a). It is easier to dig the cave into a steep slope than a gentle slope. The snow must be deep enough that you will not hit ground before you finish excavating the entire cave. Dig an entry that is 1.5 feet (0.5 meter) wide and 5 feet (1.5 meters) high (fig. 3-13b), and dig it into the slope about 3 feet (1 meter) deep. Then create a temporary construction-debris exit slot by digging a waist-high platform centered on the entryway, forming a T that is 4 feet (1.2 meters) wide by 1.5 feet (0.5 meter) high (fig. 3-13c). Develop this platform so that it forms a horizontal slot extending into the slope, allowing for easy snow removal from the interior of the cave. Shovel snow out through the horizontal slot; a second person, working outside, can clear the snow away.

Create the main room of the cave by digging inward from the entry and expanding the room to the front, sides, and upward—all directions except down (fig. 3-13d). Keep digging until all the snow within easy reach has been excavated. Extend the original entry hallway another 2 feet (60 centimeters) into the slope (fig. 3-13e), permitting the excavator to get farther into the cave to continue excavating outward and upward. Now it should be nearly possible to stand inside. Continue to excavate, now out of the wind; when enough snow has been cleared to allow the excavator to sit up on the main

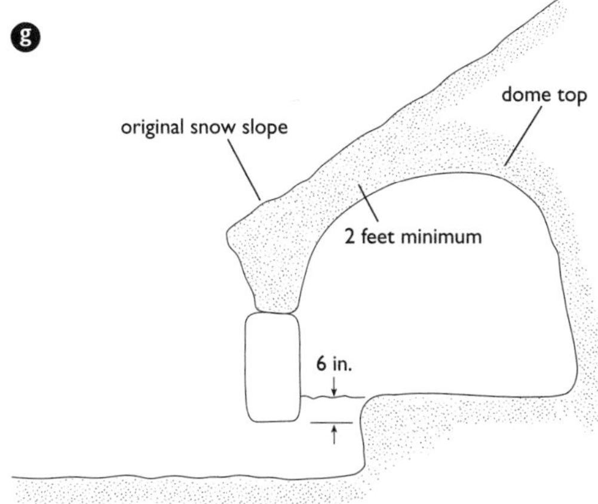

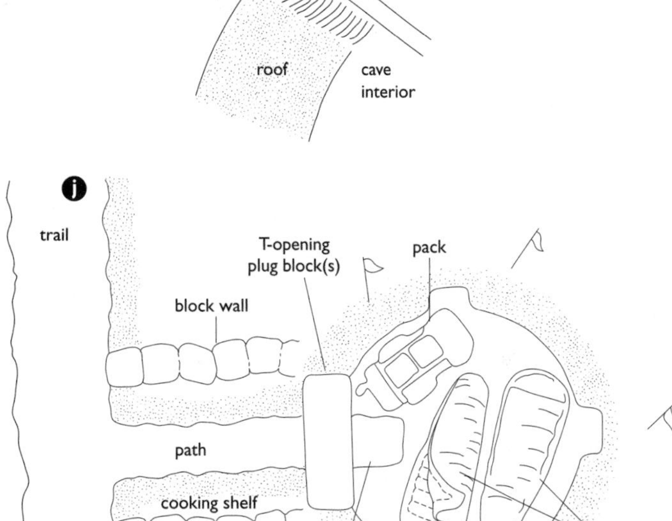

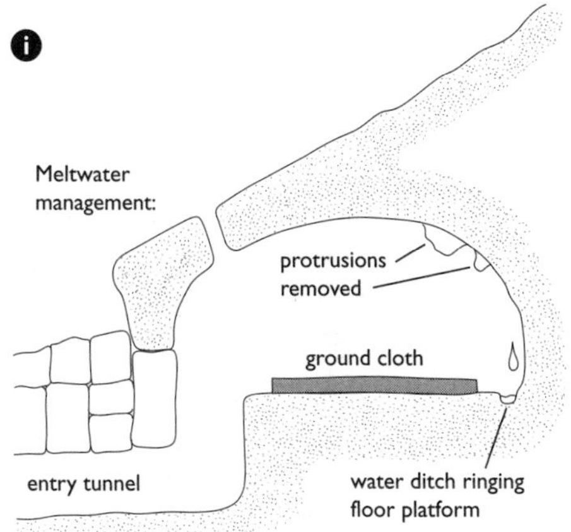

Fig. 3-13. Building a snow cave:
a. Choose location
b. Dig entry
c. Dig T-shaped slot
d. Dig inward, expanding up, left, and right
e. Expand to desired size
f. Fill in T-shaped slot
g. Snow cave cross section
h. Create ventilation holes
i. Smooth ceiling and dig meltwater ditch
j. Mark cave perimeter and erect wind blocks
k. Create storage alcoves and deepen entryway

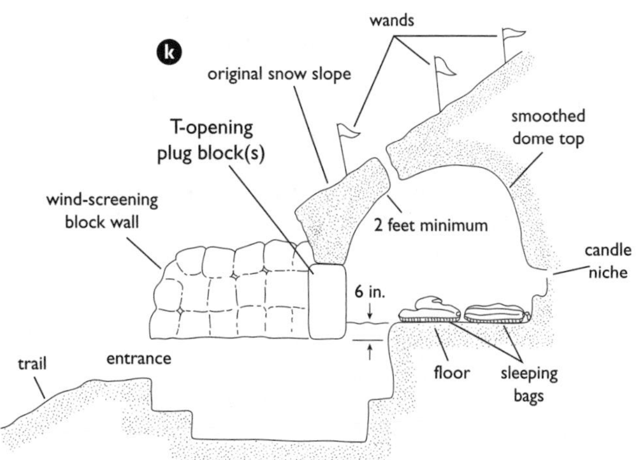

cave floor, another person can enter and help continue to expand the cave in all directions except downward.

Excavate until the inside dimensions are about 5 feet (1.5 meters) from front to back by 7 feet (2.1 meters) wide and 3.5 feet (1 meter) high, a comfortable minimum for two people. Make the cave larger for more occupants, but remember that a small cave is warmer than a large one. Keep a minimum of 2 feet (60 centimeters) of firm snow on the slope above the cave ceiling (see Figure 3-13g) to provide enough strength to keep the roof from collapsing. Avoid building a flat ceiling. The more dome-shaped the contour, the stronger the ceiling.

Fill in the temporary horizontal slot with snow blocks (fig. 3-13f); one large block or two smaller blocks leaning against each other may be sufficient. Caulk any spaces around the blocks with snow. The top of the completed entrance tunnel should be at least 6 inches (15 centimeters) lower than the cave floor, keeping warm air in the cave and cold drafts out (fig. 3-13g). Use snow blocks to build a wind-screening wall on either side of the entry path.

Poke a pair of ski-pole-basket-size ventilation holes through the cave ceiling from the inside out (fig. 3-13h) to prevent asphyxiation. If it gets too warm inside, enlarge these holes. Do not use a camp stove inside the cave—cook outside at the entrance, in open air.

Smooth the domed ceiling of the cave's interior so that it is free of any bumps or protrusions (fig. 3-13i); this way, melting water will flow down the walls of the cave instead of dripping from bumps onto the occupants. Scratch a small ditch all around the base of the wall to channel any meltwater away from the floor. Place a ground sheet on the floor—clear of the meltwater ditch—to help keep things dry and to prevent equipment loss. Keep stormy weather out by putting a small tarp or a pack (inside a plastic bag) over the entrance, but leave an opening for ventilation air to flow in. Mark the outside area around the cave with bamboo wands (fig. 3-13j), so that someone does not inadvertently walk onto the roof.

Customize the inside of the cave by digging small alcoves into the walls to store boots, stove, and cooking utensils or to hold candles for illuminating the cave at night (fig. 3-13k). Digging the entrance tunnel deeper under the wind-screening snow blocks will make entry easier. Entrance-area seats, a cooking platform, and other personal touches make the cave a snow home. Collapse the snow cave when you leave the area so that it is not hazardous for others.

Igloo

Igloo construction takes more time and skill than other types of snow shelters. Temperatures must be reliably frigid for this shelter to be practical, around 28 degrees Fahrenheit (minus 2 degrees Celsius) or below. Any warmer, and it is likely to melt and collapse. If conditions are right, igloos are undeniably fun to build and use.

Begin by finding a good location clear of any potential avalanche path and in close proximity to a good quarry area for sawing snow blocks. Wind-packed snow is easiest to work with; if the snow seems too loose and powdery, tromp the quarry area down and let it set up (consolidate) for 30 minutes before beginning to saw. Use a snow saw; a straight-bladed snow shovel will also work, though not as well. Saw blocks about 2.5 feet (75 centimeters) long by 1.5 feet (45 centimeters) wide by 1 foot (30 centimeters) thick (fig. 3-14a). Heavier snow requires smaller blocks. If the blocks' snow quality is inadequate and they fall apart when moved, abandon plans for building an igloo and construct a different type of shelter.

Compact the igloo's base by walking over the area on snowshoes, then put the first three blocks in place, cutting an angle contouring down the top of these three blocks to create a ramp that begins the spiral that will force subsequent layers ever upward and inward (fig. 3-14b). Bevel the bottom and mating edge of each block so the wall tilts inward at the properly increasing angle, spiraling upward (fig. 3-14c). Start this inward

EMERGENCY SNOW SHELTERS

Winter travelers should know how to build quick snow shelters for emergency situations, such as being unexpectedly out overnight on a day trip without tents. With a little improvisation, natural features can convert into snow hideaways for an unplanned bivouac. Such shelters occur under logs, along riverbanks, or in the pits or wells formed when the limbs of large conifer trees deflect snow from the tree trunks. For a tree-well shelter, enlarge the natural hole around the trunk and roof it with any available covering, such as ice blocks, tree limbs, an emergency space blanket, or a tarp. Boughs and bark can provide insulation and support. Do not cut live boughs unless it is a life-or-death emergency.

tilt immediately, so that the igloo does not get so tall that the top cannot be reached to cap it.

Set each block firmly and hold it in place until the next block in the spiral is set and the cracks caulked with loose snow. One person works inside, shaping and setting the blocks and caulking. Others work outside, sawing and carrying blocks and caulking the outside. Although the igloo in Figure 3-13d shows alternating vertical seams between blocks, the seams may be either staggered or aligned.

Cap the igloo's apex, then excavate into the floor from outside, digging down below the igloo wall and inward to create a tunnel entrance for the igloo (fig. 3-14e). As with a snow cave, the igloo's entrance ceiling should be at least 6 inches (15 centimeters)

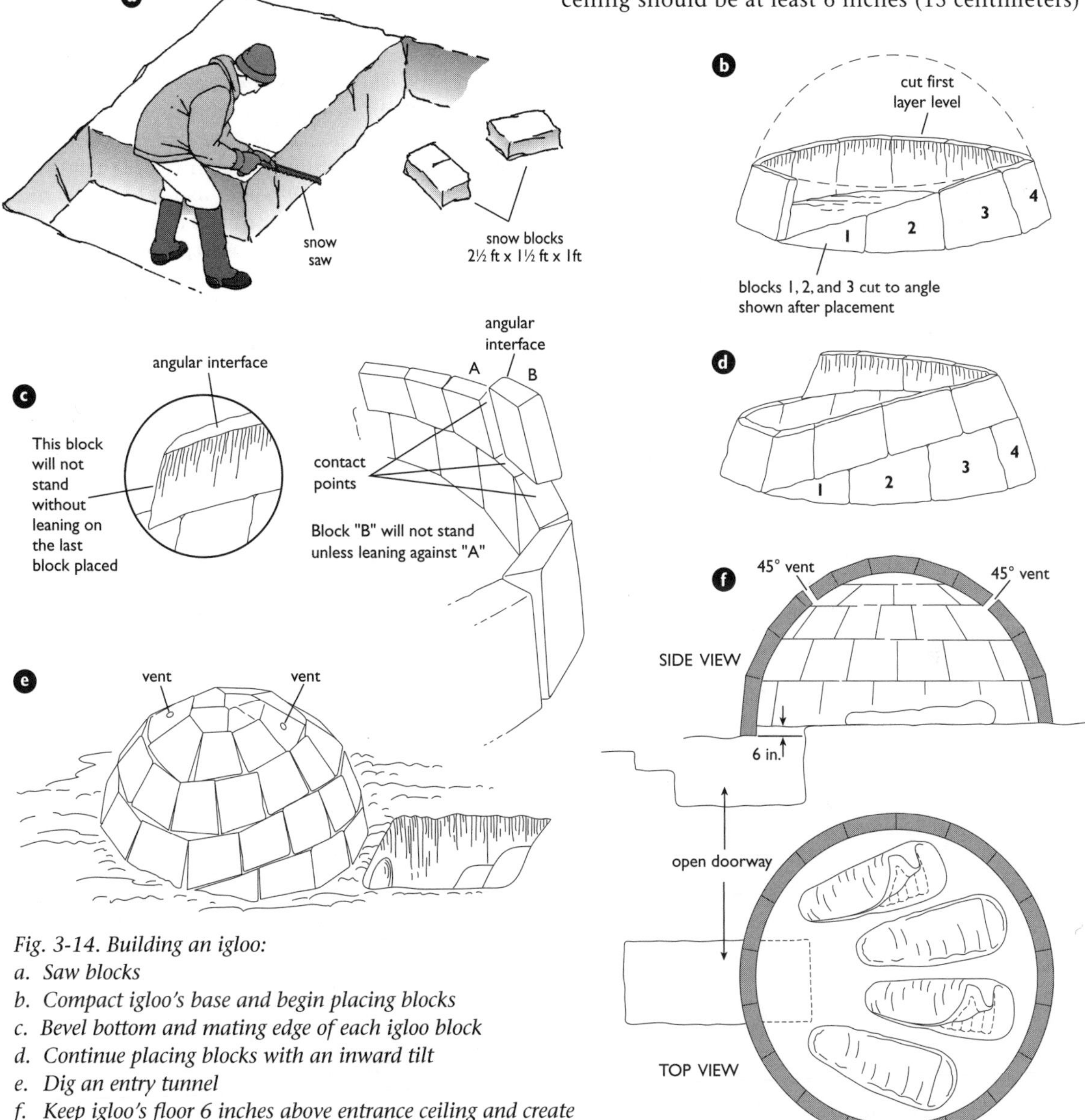

Fig. 3-14. Building an igloo:
a. Saw blocks
b. Compact igloo's base and begin placing blocks
c. Bevel bottom and mating edge of each igloo block
d. Continue placing blocks with an inward tilt
e. Dig an entry tunnel
f. Keep igloo's floor 6 inches above entrance ceiling and create ventilation holes

below the level of the floor (fig. 3-14f). Place ventilation holes at 45-degree angles in at least two spots in the igloo roof (fig. 3-14f).

THE SLEEPING SYSTEM

Sleeping bags and ground insulation are the components that ensure a warm, comfortable overnight in the wilderness.

SLEEPING BAGS

For most climbers, a sleeping bag is the critical component to their outdoor sleeping system. A good sleeping bag fits your body, retains body heat, is light and compressible, and often ensures that a climber actually gets sleep. For mountaineering, nothing beats the efficient design of the mummy bag.

A sleeping bag's fill material traps an insulating layer of air between the climber's warm body and the external cooler air, keeping a climber warm. A sleeping bag's efficiency depends on the type, amount, and loft (thickness) of this insulating fill, as well as the bag's style and fit to your body.

Insulation

The two types of insulation for mountaineering sleeping bags are goose down and synthetic fibers. Each type has its own advantages and disadvantages. See Chapter 2, Clothing and Equipment, for a discussion of insulating fill material.

Cover Materials

Several types of cover materials are commonly used to make the outside shells of mountaineering sleeping bags. The most popular are laminated or waterproof-breathable-coated fabrics, microfibers, and nylon.

Laminated or waterproof-breathable-coated fabrics. These will keep water out while allowing moisture vapor to escape. These fabrics are expensive but advantageous in damp environments such as the inside of a snow cave, tent, or bivy sack. They are especially desirable with a down bag. The laminate process is complex, and occasionally the fabric will delaminate or wear excessively over time and extended use.

Microfibers. These shells are constructed of very tightly woven nylons or polyesters with a very high thread count. These shells offer water repellency with greater breathability than that of coated or laminated fabrics. Some microfiber fabrics are further treated with polymers such as silicone, which increase their water resistance and durability. Microfibers are lighter and more compressible than coated and laminated fabrics.

Nylon. Sleeping-bag shells made of nylon are the very lightest, most compressible, and most breathable fabrics available. Unfortunately, they offer the least protection against condensation in the tent and moisture in the outside environment.

Features and Components

The features and components of a sleeping bag improve efficiency and ventilation (fig. 3-15). A good hood surrounds your head, retaining precious heat, while leaving your face uncovered for respiration. A collar seals around your neck to further retain heat inside the main body of the bag. Long zippers make it easy to get in and out of the bag and help ventilate excess heat if the bag gets too warm. Some designs offer complementary left- and right-hand zippers so that two bags can zip together. A half- or three-quarter-length zipper saves weight and bulk but loses flexibility in ventilation. A draft tube on the inside of the bag running along the length of the zipper helps to seal out cold air.

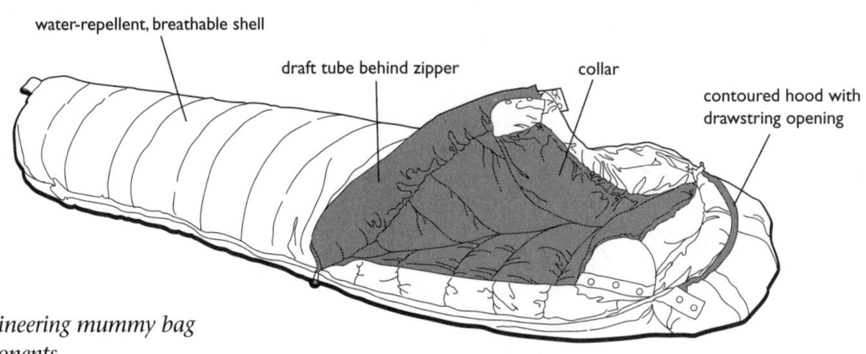

Fig. 3-15. Mountaineering mummy bag features and components.

Accessories

Some manufacturers make washable sleeping-bag liners, which add a few degrees of warmth by trapping heat close to the body. A liner also keeps body oils from soiling the bag's interior and insulation. A liner is especially handy while you are on an extended trip where washing the sleeping bag is difficult or impractical. Bag liners do add weight and bulk.

Vapor barrier liners (VBLs) are constructed of a nonbreathable, totally waterproof coated nylon; you sleep inside the VBL inside the sleeping bag. They make the bag warmer by reducing evaporative heat loss. VBLs also reduce the amount of moisture in the insulation; in arctic environments, this cuts down ice buildup within the sleeping bag's insulation. Despite the advantages, many climbers find VBLs awkward and clammy. Before committing to using VBL on a big climbing trip, try using one.

Most sleeping bags come with a stuff sack and a breathable storage sack, which should be used to store the bag between trips. Most stuff sacks are not completely waterproof, so in wet conditions, wrap the stuffed sleeping bag in a plastic bag before putting it into the pack, or use a waterproof compression sack.

Fit

Your sleeping bag must fit your body. Too wide, and it will be drafty, cold, and unnecessarily heavy. Too tight, and it will be uncomfortably snug and your body will compress the insulation from the inside, making the bag colder. Too short, and the insulation in the footbox and hood will be compressed, making the bag colder.

Sleeping-bag designs come in a variety of widths and lengths for different body shapes, so get the size that fits you best. Size the bag a little longer for winter camping or expedition use; the extra room can be used for drying small items such as wet gloves, socks, and boot liners.

Rating Systems

Manufacturers give their bags a minimum temperature rating or comfort range. Rating systems are only rough guidelines. The ratings mean different things to different companies, and they are not meant to compare bags from different companies.

Many factors dictate how warm or cold you will be in a particular bag. Personal metabolism, level of hydration or fatigue, ambient air temperature, and ground insulation all affect warmth (see the "Tips on Staying Warm" sidebar). Remember that a sleeping bag does not warm the person who is inside it; you warm the bag with your body heat. The insulation and cover material only serve to reduce heat loss.

Specialty Bags

Some climbers prefer to go as light as possible, sacrificing a little comfort to gain an advantage in lighter weight. Half- or three-quarter-length bags are available, and when used in conjunction with an insulating jacket, they can be adequate for temperatures down to just below freezing.

Care and Cleaning

A sleeping bag is a serious investment, and with a little care it will last for many years. Always follow the manufacturer's recommendations. The company that made the bag knows the best way to care for it. That said, here are a few techniques to make a sleeping bag last a long time.

Storage. Always store the bag fully lofted. Only keep the bag in a compression stuff sack for a short period of time, such as while it is in the pack or during travel.

Protection from soiling. Consider using a removable liner to protect the bag's interior from body oils, especially on long trips.

Cleaning. Spot-clean soiled areas with soap specified by the manufacturer. Any bag will need to be laundered over time. Never dry-clean a sleeping bag. Wash the bag with mild soap on the gentle cycle in a large washing machine. Run the bag through the rinse cycle several times to remove all soap. Dry the bag in a large clothes dryer under medium heat. Remove the bag occasionally and break up clumps of down, or throw in a tennis ball during the last few drying cycles. Make sure the bag is completely dry by squeezing the insulation and feeling for moisture. Washing and drying a bag takes several hours. Some outdoor repair shops specialize in laundering sleeping bags.

GROUND INSULATION

The starting point for a comfortable night in the outdoors is a good piece of insulation under the sleeping bag. In summer or winter, whether you are in a tent or out under the stars, a sleeping pad reduces the amount of heat you lose to the ground or snow. If you are forced to sleep without a pad, use extra clothing, your pack, the climbing rope, or your boots for padding and insulation.

Materials

Closed-cell foam. A thin pad of closed-cell foam provides good lightweight insulation. Textured designs in closed-cell pads give them a softer sleeping surface, lower weight, and an increased ability to trap air, resulting in greater thermal efficiency.

Air mattress. By itself, an air mattress is comfortably soft but provides no insulation. In fact, the air in the mattress convects heat away from the body by internal air circulation—not a good choice for climbers. If you choose to use an air mattress, remember that if it fails, you are left with no insulation.

Open-cell foam. Avoid uncovered pads of open-cell foam; these are bulky, and they absorb water like the sponges they are, making them inadequate for snow camping.

Self-inflating or inflatable pad. The self-inflating or inflatable pad is made of open-cell foam enclosed in an airtight, waterproof envelope. This type of pad combines the insulation of foam with the softness of an air mattress, which is very popular and effective.

Size

Insulation pads come in a variety of lengths, but the 4-foot (1.2-meter) length is usually adequate for general mountaineering; you can use a smaller sit pad or items of gear to pad and insulate feet and legs. When camping on snow or in winter or arctic environments, use a 4-foot self-inflating pad on top of a full-length closed-cell foam pad for greater insulation. For example, in winter in the Cascades, use a ⅜-inch-thick, full-length closed-cell foam pad and an ultralight, three-quarter-length self-inflating pad; or on Denali, use a ½ -inch-thick, full-length closed-cell foam pad and a "regular" three-quarter-length self-inflating pad.

STOVES

Stoves are better than campfires for backcountry travel because they are faster, cleaner, and more convenient; they will operate under almost any conditions; and they have minimal impact on the environment. In choosing a stove for mountaineering use, consider its weight (very important), the altitude and temperature where it will be used, fuel availability, ease of operation, and reliability. The stove should be easy to operate and maintain and should work even in cold, wet, windy conditions. It must have a high heat output to melt snow quickly and stability to avoid tipping. For travel in remote areas, choose a stove that accepts a variety of fuels. Read the operating instructions and ask questions before making a purchase.

Types

Mountaineering stoves require pressurized fuel so that the fuel will flow at a sufficient rate to support a hot flame at the burner. Some stoves use a fuel cartridge; others use a refillable liquid-fuel reservoir. Different fuels are suitable for these two types of stoves; see "Stove Fuels" and Table 3-1 for a summary of each fuel's advantages and disadvantages.

Fuel cartridge. A cartridge stove (fig. 3-16a, c, f, and g) requires no pumping to maintain pressure during operation, because the fuel cartridge is already fully pressurized, but when the cartridge is nearly empty, the pressure is too low for adequate heat output. This causes a brief gap in cooking, while the stove cools enough to allow you to disconnect the cartridge from the burner, pack it (for carrying out with the trash), and then connect a new cartridge. Cartridge stoves use pressurized butane, propane, isobutane gas, or a blend of these fuels.

Refillable liquid-fuel reservoir. Stoves with refillable liquid-fuel reservoirs can have either a tank under the burner (fig. 3-16b) or a separate fuel bottle connected to the burner by a rigid pipe or flexible hose (fig. 3-16d and e). You must pump the reservoir up to operating pressure each time you use the stove. You must maintain the operating pressure by periodically pumping by hand to regain full heat output. Stoves with refillable liquid-fuel reservoirs typically use white gas or kerosene.

Weight

Mountaineering stoves typically weigh 1 to 1.5 pounds (about 0.4 to 0.5 kilogram); for a short trip, there is little weight difference between using a cartridge stove and using a stove with a refillable tank or bottle. For long trips, refillable liquid-fuel stoves are better. The fuel can be purchased and carried in bulk, and there are no empty cartridges to carry out.

Stability

Stoves with a fuel cartridge or tank directly beneath and attached to the burner assembly (see Figure 3-16a, b, and c) tend to be more vulnerable to tipping over than stoves with a fuel cartridge or bottle set off to the side of the burner assembly (see Figure 3-16d, e, and f). The exception to this general rule is the hanging stove, a specialized mountaineering stove in which the entire stove and pot hang as an integral unit from a chain

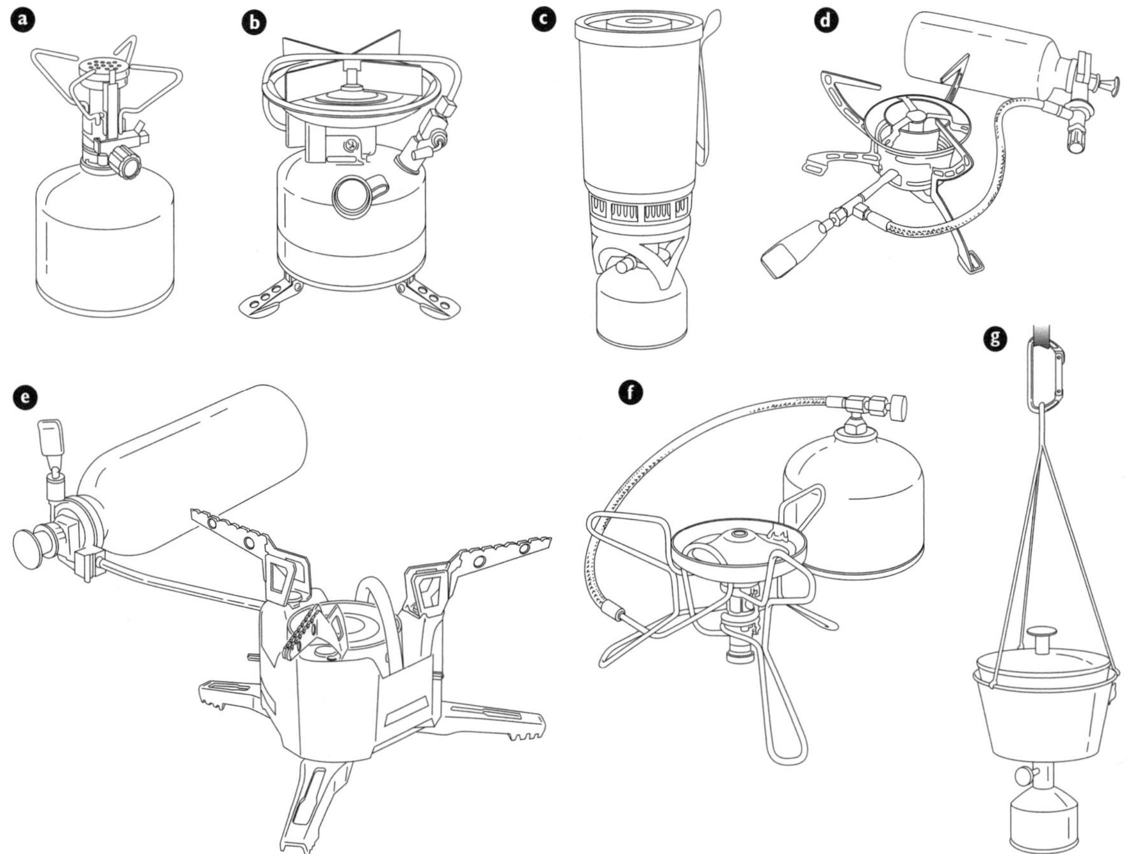

Fig. 3-16. Types of mountaineering stoves: a, cartridge stove; b, white gas stove with integral fuel tank; c, cartridge stove with integrated pot; d, white gas stove using fuel bottle as tank; e, multifuel stove using fuel bottle as tank; f, cartridge stove with flexible hose; g, hanging cartridge stove and cook pot.

or wire (see Figure 3-16g). Hanging stoves typically use pressurized fuel cartridges. They are primarily used for big wall climbing and at high camp on expeditions.

Operation

A stove ignites (or starts) when a spark or flame is applied to vaporized fuel at the burner. Some stoves have an integrated ignition device as a convenience; with most stoves, you must use matches or a lighter. With fuel cartridge stoves, the fuel is already vaporized, so starting the stove is a simple matter of turning the regulating valve and lighting the released fuel. In contrast, a stove with a refillable liquid-fuel reservoir requires priming to convert the released liquid fuel to a vapor before the stove will operate efficiently.

A common method of priming is to preheat the stove by burning a small amount of liquid fuel in a priming cup to heat the region surrounding the supply line's jet. When the flame from the priming process wanes but is not quite gone, open the fuel regulator valve to start fuel vaporizing at the supply line's jet, which ignites from the residual priming-cup flame. This is a simple process but requires practice at home (see the "Common Priming Mistakes" sidebar).

Stoves can fail, and will, often at the most inopportune time. In windy, dusty conditions, debris can clog the jet and cause unexpected stove failure. Read the manufacturer's instructions and learn how to make emergency field repairs on your stove before you leave home.

To assure trouble-free operation, clean the stove

COMMON PRIMING MISTAKES

- Using too much fuel initially in the priming cup prolongs the process and wastes fuel.
- Opening the regulator valve too soon causes a potentially dangerous flare-up.
- Opening the regulator valve too late leaves the stove to sputter out.

regularly and rebuild it periodically, replacing seals and pump cups.

ACCESSORIES

Mountaineering stoves typically burn about an hour on 8 ounces (250 milliliters) of fuel and will boil 1 quart (liter) of water in four to eight minutes at sea level. Wind can increase that time to as much as 25 minutes, or even prevent boiling altogether. For fuel efficiency, keep a lid on the cook pot and use a windscreen to shield the flame and to prevent heat from blowing away. Some stoves come with a windscreen made of a flexible sheet of aluminum, which fits around the burner like a curtain (fig. 3-17a). However, do not use this type of screen with stoves that have integral fuel tanks, because too much heat will reflect back onto the fuel tank, dangerously overheating it. Some cartridge stoves integrate the burner and the windscreen, avoiding any assembly (see Figure 3-16c). With any type of stove, it is safe to improvise a windscreen using pot lids, metal plates, or small rock walls.

A heat exchanger (fig. 3-17b) keeps even more heat around the stove and pot. These devices can be heavy, but on longer trips they may save enough fuel to make up for their weight. A few stove designs incorporate pots with nonburning insulating covers, which can improve boiling times and fuel efficiency (see Figure 3-16c).

Some stoves have a flame-control valve to allow simmering. Stoves that boil water fast often do not simmer well. To reduce heat for slower cooking on any stove, put a metal lid or plate between the pot and burner.

For snow camping, bring along a small, foil-wrapped platform of thin plywood, Masonite, or even cardboard to support the stove and keep it off the snow. If using white gas (likely in cold conditions), insulate the fuel bottle in a thick sock for better fuel performance.

STOVE FUELS

Fuel consumption depends on trip conditions, how the party plans to cook, and water supplies. For instance, cup-cooking (see "Food" later in this chapter) takes less

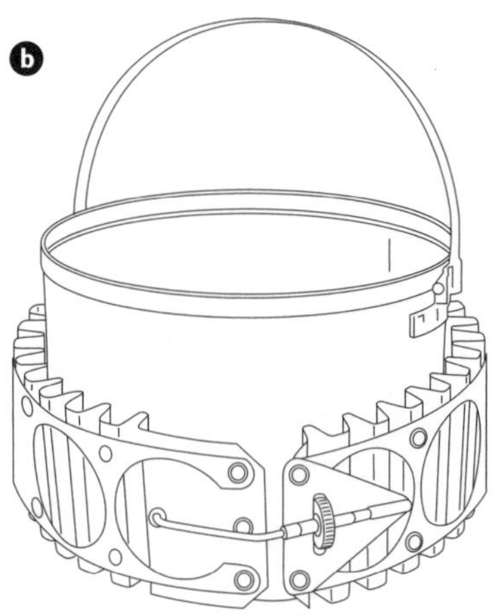

Fig. 3-17. Stove accessories: a, windscreen; b, heat exchanger.

fuel than cooking meals on a stove. Melting snow takes at least twice as much fuel as simply heating water. Keep notes on fuel consumption under various circumstances; experience will provide guidelines on how much fuel is needed for various types of trips. A minimum is 4 ounces (125 milliliters) per person per day, if the party is neither melting snow nor doing elaborate cooking. If two people are sharing a stove, they will want at least 8 ounces (250 milliliters) of fuel for an overnight trip. Consider taking an extra fuel reserve on extended trips in remote areas. Table 3-1 summarizes the pros and cons of common stove fuels.

TABLE 3-1. COMPARISON OF STOVE FUELS

Fuel	Advantages	Disadvantages	Best For
LIQUID FUELS			
White gas	High heat output. Spills evaporate quickly. Readily available in North America. Can use for priming.	Priming required. Spills very flammable. Self-pressurized models must be insulated from cold or snow.	Cooking in any conditions, temperature, or altitude.
Kerosene	High heat output. Spilled fuel will not ignite readily. Available worldwide. Does not burn clean; jet requires periodic cleaning.	Not suitable for priming. Spills do not evaporate readily, leaving a residue.	International expeditions on which fuel availability is unknown.
Alcohol	None.	Lowest heat output (slow cooking time).	Sometimes used in small emergency stoves. Poor choice for mountaineering.
COMPRESSED-GAS CANISTER FUELS			
Butane	No priming or pumping required. Immediate maximum heat output. Full flame control, down to simmer. Maintenance-free. Stove units are super lightweight. No-spill fuel container. Readily available in North America and Europe.	Lower heat output than white gas or kerosene. On long trips, pressurized fuel cartridges are heavier and bulkier than liquid fuels. Must pack out disposable canister. Fuel cartridges expensive. Fuel does not burn efficiently below freezing. No way to know amount of remaining fuel. Not as widely available as white gas and kerosene.	Short, light trips in temperatures above freezing. Good at high altitudes if temperatures are above freezing.
Blended fuels (butane-propane, sometimes with isobutane added)	All the advantages of butane, plus somewhat better cold-weather performance than straight butane.	Same as butane, except fuel burns somewhat more efficiently below freezing.	Same as butane.
Isobutane	All the advantages of butane, plus works well below freezing.	Same as butane, except fuel works well below freezing.	Short trips under any conditions.

White gas. The most popular mountaineering stove fuel in North America is white gas. It burns hotter than butane and is excellent for melting large amounts of snow, boiling water, or heating food quickly. Unlike kerosene, white gas is its own priming agent. Use only refined or white gasoline prepared for pressurized stoves; do not use automotive gasoline, whether leaded or unleaded. The correct fuel is safer and is less likely to clog jets, build up excess pressure, or emit toxic fumes. Spilled white gas evaporates readily, with little odor, but is very flammable.

Kerosene. Less volatile than white gas, kerosene is therefore safer to transport and store. Because the fuel does not burn hot enough to prime the burner, kerosene stoves require priming with white gas, alcohol, lighter fluid, or priming paste. If not adequately primed, the stove will burn with a sooty yellow flame, giving off smoke and carbon. When it burns efficiently, a kerosene stove has a high heat output, at least equal to that of white gas.

Butane. Butane or butane-propane cartridge stoves are the most convenient—easy to light, good flame control, immediate maximum heat output, and no chance of fuel spills. As the valve opens, the pressure in the canister forces fuel out, eliminating both priming and pumping. Standard butane stoves do not function well at temperatures below freezing. The disposable cartridges are not refillable. There is no way to tell how much is left in a partially used cartridge, so owners of these stoves often carry a spare cartridge just in case. Some cartridges cannot be changed until they are completely empty. Never change a cartridge in the tent or near any flame because residual fuel in spent canisters is a fire hazard.

Isobutane. Isobutane comes in canisters as butane fuel does and shares all the conveniences and inconveniences of butane, but it performs better at high altitude and subfreezing temperatures.

Solid fuels. Candles and canned heat are solid fuels that serve primarily as firestarters. They are lightweight and cheap but provide limited heat. Carry solid fuels for emergency use, along with a metal cup for heating small amounts of water.

STOVE AND FUEL STORAGE

Carry extra white gas or kerosene in a metal bottle specifically designed for fuel storage, with a screw top and rubber gasket. Plainly mark the fuel container to distinguish it from other containers, such as water bottles, and stow it in a place where any leaks will not contaminate food.

Leave about 1 inch (2–3 centimeters) of air space in the stove's fuel reservoir, rather than filling it to the brim, to prevent excessive pressure buildup. At the end of the season, put the stove into storage and remember to empty the fuel bottle. After storage, test the stove at home before using it again in the field.

SAFETY

Tents have been blown up, equipment has burned, and people have been injured by careless stove use. Before lighting a stove, check fuel lines, valves, and connections for leaks. Let the stove cool completely before changing cartridges or adding liquid fuel. Change pressurized fuel cartridges, and fill and start liquid-fuel stoves, outside the tent and away from other open flames.

Do not cook inside the tent unless it is so windy that the stove will not operate outside or so cold that the cook risks hypothermia. The risks range from the relatively minor one of spilling pots onto sleeping bags to the deadly dangers of tent fires or carbon monoxide poisoning.

If it is absolutely necessary to cook inside a tent, follow these safety rules:

1. Light the stove outside or near a tent opening so it can be tossed away from the tent if it flares; bring the stove inside only after it is running smoothly.
2. Cook near the tent door or in the vestibule, for better ventilation and so the stove can be thrown outside quickly in an emergency.
3. Provide plenty of ventilation. This is critical because carbon monoxide is colorless and odorless; humans cannot detect it. Better to err on the conservative side by cooling off the tent with too large a ventilation hole rather than risk carbon monoxide poisoning with too small an opening.

WATER

During the sedentary activities of everyday life, mild dehydration simply causes discomfort in the form of thirst. With the sustained exertion of mountaineering, however, fluid loss may cause fatigue, disorientation, and headaches. Dehydration becomes debilitating more quickly than you might expect. It is a factor in a number of mountain maladies, including acute mountain sickness. (See Chapter 23, First Aid, for more information on dehydration, acute mountain sickness, and other health hazards.)

Drink more water than usual, perhaps 2 to 3 extra quarts (liters), during the 24-hour period before a climb to boost your strength and endurance. Additionally, it is wise to drink a generous quantity of water, more than feels necessary, immediately before beginning the climb. Your skin and lungs can release large amounts of moisture into cold, dry, high-altitude mountain air. Do not wait until you are thirsty to drink; thirst is a sign that dehydration is already in progress. A better indicator of adequate hydration is lightly colored or colorless urine. At high elevations, dehydration can contribute to nausea that, ironically, reduces the desire to take in fluids.

Keep water handy. Have a bottle within easy reach inside your pack or in a pouch on the hip belt. Some climbers use a bladder device carried in their pack, with a tube clipped to the shoulder strap for convenient sipping.

A well-balanced diet replaces most electrolytes that are lost during heavy sweating. In hot weather or on extended heavy-exertion trips, however, climbers may need to consider electrolyte replacement. Sports drinks may be useful, but not everyone can tolerate them. Diluting sports drinks or drinking additional water afterward makes them easier to digest. Try them at home before relying on them in the mountains.

WATER SOURCES

Water can be scarce in the mountains. Some climbs have abundant streams and snowfields to replenish water supplies, but often the high peaks are bone dry or frozen solid, and the only water available is what climbers carry with them.

On one-day climbs, the usual source is simply the tap at home. For most people, 1.5 to 3 quarts (liters) of water is enough. Take more than what you think is necessary. During a tough three-day climb, each person might drink 6 quarts while hiking and climbing, plus another 5 quarts in camp. That is too much to carry, so supplies must be replenished from lakes, streams, and snow.

When the only water source along the trail is snow, pack it inside a water bottle and place the bottle on the outside of your pack to melt it and prevent any condensation from getting your pack's contents wet. Start with a bit of water in the bottle to hasten the melting time; stow the bottle on the sunny side of your pack.

Try catching the drips from overhanging eaves of melting snow. Or find a tongue of snow that is slowly melting into a trickle, dredge a depression below, let the water clear, and channel the resulting puddle into a container.

When the only water source near camp is snow, set out pots of snow to melt if there is both sun and enough time. Otherwise, melt snow in a pot on the stove, although this takes time and uses up cooking fuel. Either way, get the snow from a "drinking-snow" pit, well away from the designated toilet and cleaning areas. Collect the snow in small, pot-size chunks rather than as loose snow in order to make stoking the melting pot simpler and neater. Always have a little water already in the pot when starting to melt snow on the stove; oddly, the pot can burn if it contains only dry snow. If you are cooking in the tent vestibule, collect snow in a sack before bringing it inside.

Just before bedtime, melt enough snow to fill all water bottles and cooking pots so that there is enough to rehydrate during the night and refill bottles again in the morning.

PATHOGENS IN WATER

In the old days, there were few joys as supreme as drinking pure, refreshing alpine water right from the source. Nowadays, even in remote areas, animal or human waste can contaminate water. Even snow is suspect. Fresh-fallen snow is as pure as can be, but human and animal waste can contaminate snow, and microscopic organisms can survive freezing temperatures. The tainted snow melts, trickling and percolating its way to cross-contaminate other snow a long distance away. Purify melted snow just as if it were any other water source.

Treat water to guard against the three types of waterborne pathogens: viruses, bacteria, and large parasites.

Viruses. Most often, viruses are present in tropical waters. Hepatitis A (infectious hepatitis) is an example of a virus-caused disease that can be contracted by drinking contaminated water. Although wilderness waters in North America are usually free of viruses, it never hurts to treat against them. Viruses are easily killed with chemical treatment but are too tiny to be removed by most filters. Boiling kills viruses.

Bacteria. Mountain waters contain a wide range of types and sizes of bacteria. Common harmful waterborne bacteria include *Salmonella* (incubation period 12–36 hours), *Campylobacter jejuni* (incubation three to five days), and *Escherichia coli* (incubation 24–72 hours).

TABLE 3-2. WATER TREATMENT METHODS

Method	Effectiveness	Advantages	Disadvantages
Boiling	Very effective against all pathogens.	Most effective method.	Slow and inconvenient. Requires additional fuel, which adds weight to pack. Leaves flat taste to water.
Iodine	Very effective against bacteria and viruses. Effective against *Giardia*, but requires soak time. Not effective against *Cyclosporum*.	Lightweight and compact. Can be combined with filtration to protect against all pathogens. Inexpensive.	Slow (one hour for cold water or water cloudy with sediment). Disagreeable taste unless cleared afterward with vitamin C. Not to be used by persons with allergy to iodine or active thyroid disease. Not to be used as the sole method of purification.
Chlorine	Very effective against bacteria and viruses. Effective against *Giardia*, but requires soak time. Not effective against *Cryptosporidium* or *Cyclosporum*.	Lightweight and compact. Can be combined with filtration to protect against all pathogens. Inexpensive.	Waiting time. Disagreeable taste. Not to be used as the sole method of purification.
Chlorine dioxide	Effective against all pathogens. Lightweight and compact. Can be combined with filtration to more effectively protect against all pathogens.	Taste of water not altered significantly.	Waiting time.
Filtering	Very effective against large parasites. Effectiveness against bacteria varies, depending on filter's pore size. Not effective against viruses.	Quick. Taste of water not altered significantly.	Expensive. May be bulky or heavy. May clog or break. (River water carrying glacial silt definitely will clog the filter.) Do not use as the sole method of purification.

In some parts of the world, water may contain bacteria that cause severe illnesses such as cholera, dysentery, and typhoid. Like viruses, most bacteria can be effectively killed with chemicals. Bacteria are larger than viruses, and so they can be removed with the proper filters. Boiling kills all bacteria.

Parasites. Larger parasites are protozoa, amoebas, tapeworms, and flatworms. The protozoa *Giardia lamblia* and *Cryptosporidium parvum* ("crypto") are major health concerns for alpine travelers. Both are common in backcountry waters worldwide, including all of North America. The illnesses caused by these parasites—giardiasis and cryptosporidiosis, respectively—take 2 to 20 days to manifest themselves, with symptoms that include intense nausea, diarrhea, stomach cramps, fever, headaches, flatulence, and belches that reek like rotten eggs. Some of these parasites have tough cell walls that are resistant to chemical treatment. Because of their larger size, they can be filtered out, and boiling kills them.

A very small parasite, *Cyclosporum sp.*, commonly contaminates surface water in Nepal during spring and summer, and it is found increasingly in other areas, including North America. Halogen chemicals, such as chlorine or iodine, do not kill it, but boiling does; a filter with a small-enough pore size (see the next section) will also remove it.

WATER PURIFICATION

The principal methods of water purification are boiling, chemical treatment (iodine or chlorine), and filtering. No single method is the best for every situation, and the only guaranteed method is boiling. See the summary in Table 3-2. Water containing a lot of sediment should be strained through a cloth, paper coffee filter, or paper towel before being disinfected or pumped through a water filter.

Boiling

Boiling is the surefire method of water purification. Boiling kills all waterborne pathogens. Simply bring the water to a rolling boil and maintain the boil for one minute, regardless of elevation.

Chemical Disinfecting

Iodine. Treatment with iodine is effective against most bacteria and all likely viruses, but it is not reliable as the sole method of purification. It does not work against the parasites *Cryptosporidium* or *Cyclosporum*, which are highly resistant to halogens such as iodine and chlorine. Iodine is effective against *Giardia lamblia*, although a soak time is required for penetrating the parasite's cyst walls. The time can be as much as one hour for frigid water from a glacial stream. The usual procedure is to drop iodine tablets or solution into the water in a bottle. Avoid dipping the drinking bottle directly into a stream because the threaded top may become contaminated. Do slosh a bit of the treated water onto the threads around the bottle's top and the cap. Iodine imparts a mildly disagreeable taste. Adding vitamin C (50 milligrams per quart/liter), in tablet form or in powdered drink mix, will eliminate the iodine taste. Vitamin C will also stop iodine's germicidal action, so add it to water only after the soak time is complete.

Chlorine. The common disinfectant chlorine is perhaps not the best choice for climbers. It is not the most effective treatment for *Giardia* cysts, and it definitely is unreliable for attacking *Cryptosporidium*. Chlorine gives water an unpleasant taste and odor, although adding peroxide (after disinfection is complete) will eliminate it.

Chlorine dioxide. Water-treatment kits using chlorine dioxide are another choice. The chlorine dioxide is mixed with phosphoric acid five minutes before use, which releases oxygen to produce the disinfectant effect. The treated water is ready after a 15- to 30-minute wait period. This chemical appears to be effective against *Cryptosporidium* and *Giardia* as well as against other pathogens.

Filtering

Water filters work wonderfully well against protozoa and bacteria but are not effective against viruses. Removal

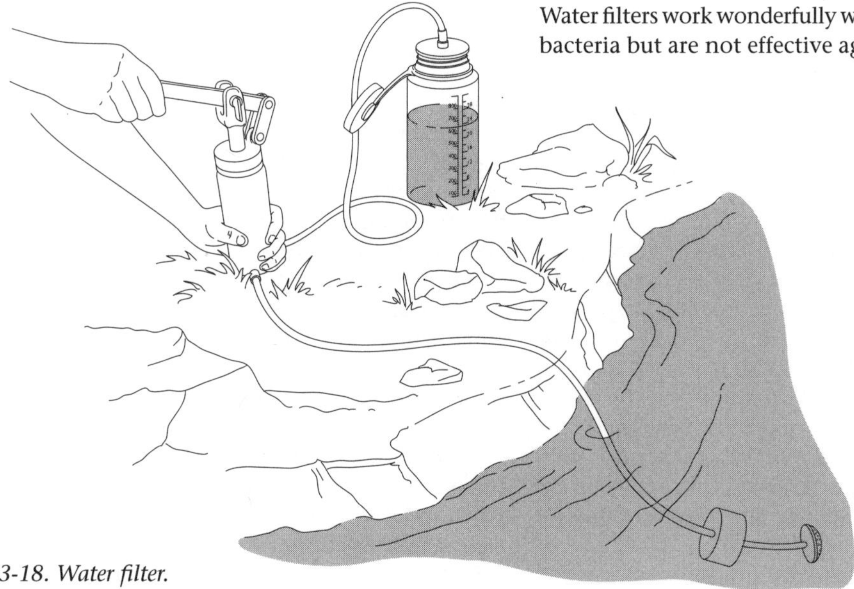

Fig. 3-18. Water filter.

of bacteria depends on the filter's pore size and rating. Manufacturers describe filter pore size in various ways. Look for information on the package stating that the "absolute" pore size is 0.4 micron or less.

Water filters (fig. 3-18), though expensive, are relatively quick and easy to use compared with other purification methods. To guard against viruses, treat the water with iodine before pumping it through the filter. Some filters feature an integral iodine chamber designed to do this for you. Others come with an integral charcoal element that removes iodine and its taste. Aside from special features, look for a compact, lightweight filter that is easy to use, clean, and maintain. Specifically, make sure that it can be field-maintained, including cleaning a clogged filter in the field.

Ultraviolet Purification

A battery-operated ultraviolet water purifier can kill most all bacteria, viruses, and protozoa, some in just a minute of ultraviolet exposure. Research the specifications of all such purifiers to see which pathogens they work against. These purifiers can be fast and effective, but they depend on batteries, which can die. It may be prudent to start each trip with a fresh set or to bring a spare set. A solar charger is an alternative backup system.

SANITATION

Use only purified water for dishwashing and brushing teeth. Always wash your hands well before preparing or handling food. If it is impractical to wash your hands, clean up with waterless hand-sanitizer gel (which kills germs by dehydrating them) or unscented antibacterial baby wipes.

FOOD

A well-rested, well-hydrated, and well-fed climber is less likely to experience difficulties from exertion, heat, cold, or illness. Mountaineering is a strenuous and demanding activity, so your body needs a variety of foods to provide sufficient carbohydrates, protein, and fats. With planning, it is possible to choose foods that keep well, are lightweight, and meet all nutritional needs. The longer the mountaineering trip, the more the menu must provide variety and complexity. And the food must taste good, or no one will eat it. If fueling your body quickly and simply is the first aim of alpine cuisine, enjoying your meals is a worthy secondary goal.

Energy expenditure on a climb can go as high as 6,000 calories per day, possibly even higher for larger folks. In comparison, most people require only about 1,500 to 2,500 calories per day when living a sedentary life. Adequate caloric intake is essential for climbers. Determine what food intake plan is best, depending on the demands of the trip and your own size, weight, metabolic rate, and level of conditioning. Never engage in calorie restriction (dieting) during a mountaineering trip, for this will interfere with performance and stamina, possibly putting extra demands on others. Put the weight-loss diet on hold until the trip is over.

TABLE 3-3. CALORIC PROPORTIONS FOR GENERAL MOUNTAINEERING

Food Source	Percentage of Daily Calories
Carbohydrates	50 to 70 percent
Proteins	15 to 25 percent
Fats	15 to 25 percent

COMPOSITION OF FOODS

Each of the three basic food components—carbohydrates (sugars and starches), proteins, and fats—provides energy, and each must be supplied in approximately the right proportion for the human body to function well. For general mountaineering, try to consume total calories in the range of proportions shown in Table 3-3 (compare with Table 20-1 in Chapter 20, Expedition Climbing).

Carbohydrates. The easiest food for the body to convert into energy, carbohydrates should constitute most of the calories. Think of carbohydrates as the main "fuel food" to keep your body functioning most efficiently. Good sources of carbohydrate starches include whole grains, rice, potatoes, cereals, pasta, bread, crackers, and granola bars. Sugars can be supplied not only by honey or granulated sugar but also by fruits (fresh or dried), jam, hot cocoa, sport gels, and drink mixes.

Proteins. The daily requirement for proteins, which are also important, is nearly constant regardless of type or level of activity. The body cannot store proteins, so once the protein requirement is met, the excess is either converted to energy or stored as fat. High-protein foods include cheese, peanut butter, nuts, dried meat, canned or vacuum-packed meats and fish, beans, tofu, powdered milk and eggs, and foil-packaged meals containing meat or cheese.

Fats. Because fats pack more than twice as many

calories per gram as proteins or carbohydrates, they are an important energy source. Fats are digested more slowly than carbohydrates or proteins, so they help keep you satisfied longer. This is useful, for example, for staying warm on cold nights. Fats occur naturally in small amounts in vegetables, grains, and beans, and when these are combined with fish, red meat, or poultry, the body's requirements for fat are easily met. High-fat foods include butter, margarine, peanut butter, nuts, salami, beef jerky, sardines, oils, eggs, seeds, and cheese.

The better a climber's condition, the more efficiently food and water will provide energy during heavy exercise. Many people find that foods high in fat are more difficult to digest during strenuous exercise. Eat mainly carbohydrates during the day; replenish calorie stores by adding fats and proteins to the evening meal. Cold-weather mountaineers stay warmer at night if they have a bedtime snack high in slower-burning food fuel.

To fuel working muscles, maintain a steady all-day carbohydrate and water intake beginning one to two hours into the climb. The carbohydrate source can be solid food or a prepared beverage. Some climbers like to use a "high-performance" sports drink, an option for replacing water, carbohydrates, and electrolytes simultaneously. Try these preparations at home, however, before relying on them in the mountains. Some people react to particular brands with bloating; these drinks may be easier to tolerate if diluted or taken with additional water.

FOOD PLANNING

As a rough guideline, provide 2 pounds (0.9 kilograms) of food per person per day.

On very short trips, climbers can carry sandwiches, fresh fruits and vegetables, and just about anything else. Taking only cold, ready-to-eat food saves the weight of stove, fuel, and cook pots, a good idea for lightweight bivouacs. In nasty weather, this approach allows you to bundle directly into the tent without the hassle of cooking. Use firm bread, rolls, or bagels for a sandwich that won't get squished. Leave out mayonnaise and other ingredients that spoil readily.

For trips of two or three days—or longer, if base camp is close to the road—any food from the grocery store is fair game.

For longer trips, food planning becomes more complicated and food weight more critical. Freeze-dried food is compact, lightweight, and easy to prepare but is relatively expensive. Outdoor stores carry a large selection of freeze-dried foods, including main courses, potatoes, vegetables, soups, breakfasts, and desserts. Some require little or no cooking; just add hot water, let it soak for a while, and eat from the package. Others are less easily reconstituted and require cooking in a pot.

With access to a food dehydrator, climbers can enjoy a more varied menu at substantial savings. Simple and nutritious mountaineering foods can be made from dried fruits, vegetables, and meat. Dehydrate thin slices of fruits and vegetables—some particularly tasty choices are bell peppers, carrots, summer squash, apples, pears, oranges, steamed yams, and blueberries. The dehydrated produce can be eaten as is or added as an ingredient to a cooked dish. Fruit leather is easy to prepare with a dehydrator. Dry a good spaghetti sauce to serve with angel-hair pasta (which is thin and cooks quickly). Many dehydrated foods simply require soaking.

Vacuum sealing provides even more variety. Dehydrate the food first, then seal it. This process removes all air from the food package, reducing spoilage. Vacuum-sealing machines are expensive, but the results can be worthwhile, especially for extended trips.

For a Group

Because meals are social events, climbing groups often plan all food together. A good menu boosts morale. A carefully planned, shared menu can reduce the overall food weight carried by each person. Another common arrangement is to leave breakfast and lunch to each individual, with only dinner, the most complicated meal of the day, as a group effort.

Group meals can be planned by the group or by a chosen individual. The usual process is this:

1. Canvass the group members for food preferences and dislikes; one person may be a vegetarian, another may refuse to eat freeze-dried entrées.
2. Write down a menu.
3. Discuss the menu with the group.
4. Compile an ingredients list.
5. Go shopping.
6. Package the food (see the next section) for backpacking it in to camp.

The ideal number of people in a cooking group is two to three per stove, four maximum. Beyond that, group efficiency is outweighed by the complexities of large pots, small stoves, and increased cooking times.

For High Altitudes

High-camp cooking is more difficult because conditions can be harsh and cooking times are long. At higher altitudes, the atmospheric pressure decreases, and water—in its liquid form—does not keep getting hotter once it has reached its boiling point. Consequently, water boils at lower and lower temperatures (as shown in Table 3-4), and cooking takes longer at higher altitudes. For every decrease of about 10 degrees Fahrenheit (5 degrees Celsius) in boiling temperature, cooking time doubles. The most suitable foods are those that require only warming, such as canned chicken and instant rice. The additional weight of fuel required for long cooking times is another argument for simple menus and precooked foods.

The rigors of rapid ascent to higher altitudes also require special attention to the choice of food. Many climbers fall victim to symptoms of mountain sickness, ranging from a slight malaise to vomiting and severe headaches. Under these conditions, food becomes more difficult to digest because the stomach and lungs are competing for the same blood supply. Climbers must continue to eat and drink, whatever the effort, because the loss of energy from a lack of food or water will only reinforce the debilitating effects of reduced oxygen. Keeping well hydrated is essential. To cope with this aversion to food, eat light and eat often; also, emphasize carbohydrate foods, which are easiest to digest. Fatty foods can be particularly unappealing to some climbers at altitude. Spicy foods also are sometimes unappetizing. Trial and error will determine what foods your body can tolerate.

TABLE 3-4. BOILING POINT OF WATER

Elevation	Temperature	Cooking Time Increase (relative to sea level = 1)
In feet (meters)	**°Fahrenheit (°Celsius)**	
Sea level (0)	212° (100°)	1.0
5,000 (1,525)	203° (95°)	1.9
10,000 (3,050)	194° (90°)	3.8
15,000 (4,575)	185° (85°)	7.2
20,000 (6,100)	176° (80°)	13.0

PACKAGING THE FOOD

Most grocery-store food packages are too bulky and heavy for wilderness trips, and the entire contents may be more than needed. A small kitchen scale is useful for precise planning and packaging. Repack food in resealable plastic bags, sealable plastic packets, or other containers. Enclose identifying labels and cooking instructions, or write this information on the outside of the bag with a permanent marker. Ingredient or meal packages can be placed inside larger bags labeled in broad categories, such as "breakfast," "dinner," or "drinks."

MENU SUGGESTIONS

Try out various menu items and food combinations on day hikes or short outings before taking them on an extended trip in the mountains.

Breakfasts

For many people, breakfast is the worst meal of the day for culinary adventures, so emphasize comforting and familiar foods.

For a fast start, prepackage a standard meal before the trip. A single bag can contain a prepared cold cereal such as granola with raisins or other fruit, plus powdered milk. Stir in water—cold or hot—and breakfast is ready. Other quick breakfast options are instant or quick-cooking oatmeal with powdered milk; bakery items; dried fruits and meat; nuts; fruit bars and energy bars; and dehydrated applesauce. Try to include some protein along with carbohydrates.

Hot drinks are a pleasant addition to a breakfast. Common choices are instant cocoa, coffee, malted milk, mocha, tea, powdered eggnog, and instant breakfast drinks. Fruit-flavored drinks include instant hot cider and flavored gelatin.

On a rest day, when an early start is not required, prepare a full-scale breakfast, with such items as hash browns, omelets, scrambled eggs, bacon bits, or pancakes with syrup (made by adding hot water to brown sugar or syrup crystals). Bring a small plastic container of vegetable oil when planning this type of cooking.

Lunches and Snacks

During a climb, lunch begins shortly after breakfast and continues throughout the day. Eat small amounts, and eat often. At least half of a climber's daily food allotment should be for lunch and snacks. A good munching staple is GORP (originally, "good old raisins and peanuts"), a mixture that can contain peanuts, small candies such as chocolate chips, raisins, and other dehydrated fruits. One handful makes a snack; several make a meal. Granola is another option, with its mixture of grains, honey or sugar, and bits of fruit and nuts. GORP and granola are available in a variety of mixes at many food stores, or make your own. Other popular snack items are fruit leather, candy bars, energy bars, and dried fruits.

To encourage rehydration, mountaineers often enjoy mixing up a flavored beverage such as lemonade or fruit punch at lunch. In cold weather, fill a light thermos with hot water at breakfast, and enjoy a cup of instant soup at lunch. A basic lunch can include any of the following:

Proteins. Sources include canned or vacuum-sealed meats and fish, beef jerky, dry salami, meat spreads, hummus (available in powdered form and reconstituted with cold water), cheese, nuts, and seeds (sunflower and others). Because these foods also contain fats, they are more suited for extended lunch breaks rather than brief rest stops. On trips longer than a weekend, any cheese should be firm and relatively low in water content. By the second half of a weeklong trip, most cheeses will transform into a messy, rubbery mass oozing oil.

Starches. Carbohydrates include whole-grain breads, bagels, pita bread, granola and other cereals, firm crackers, brown-rice cakes, chips, pretzels, and granola bars.

Sweets. Some treats are cookies, chocolate, candy bars, hard candy, muffins, pastries, jam, and honey.

Fruits. Sources include fresh fruit, fruit leather, and dried fruits such as raisins, figs, and apples.

Vegetables. Some vegetables that travel well are fresh carrot or celery sticks, sliced sweet peppers, or dehydrated vegetables.

Dinners

The evening meal should have it all: it should be nourishing and delicious, yet easy and quick to prepare. To supplement liquid intake, include some items that take a lot of water, such as soup, hot cider, tea, fruit drink, cocoa, or hot fruit-flavored gelatin. A cup of soup makes a quick and satisfying first course while you are preparing the main course. A hearty soup can also serve as the main course. Good choices include miso, minestrone, bean, beef barley, lentil, chili, or chicken. Add to the menu instant potatoes, dehydrated vegetables, rice, crackers, cheese, or bread, and the meal is complete.

One-pot meals with a carbohydrate base of pasta, rice, beans, potatoes, or grains are easy and nutritious. To ensure adequate protein, fat, and flavor, add other ingredients such as canned, pouched, or dried chicken, beef, or fish; sausage; freeze-dried vegetables or fruits; margarine; or a dehydrated soup or sauce mix. Outdoor stores carry a variety of freeze-dried entrées that are nutritionally balanced and easy to prepare, but they're costly. Prepackaged dishes from the grocery store—such as spaghetti, noodle dishes, rice mixes, ramen noodles, and instant salads—are also good, easy, and less expensive.

Freeze-dried vegetables add variety to the meal. Prepare them as side dishes, or add to soups or stews. Freeze-dried cooked beans or processed soy products in powdered or textured forms (texturized vegetable protein, or TVP) are excellent, low-cost protein additions. Natural-food stores often have a wide selection of these ingredients.

Margarine, which keeps better than butter on long trips, improves the flavor of many foods and is available in liquid form or in small tubs. For seasonings, try salt, pepper, herbs, garlic, chili powder, bacon bits, curry powder, dehydrated onions, grated Parmesan cheese, hot sauce, or soy sauce.

Dessert choices include cookies, candy, no-bake cheesecake, applesauce, cooked dried fruit, instant pudding, and freeze-dried ice cream. Dessert time, accompanied by a cup of hot tea, can provide a pleasant backdrop to group talk about the next day's itinerary and a decision on who will provide the morning wake-up call.

Cup-cooking. For the evening meal, cup-cooking works well and simplifies cleanup. Cup-cooking is particularly nice in winter or foul-weather camping when cleanup is a nasty chore. Use the cook pot only to boil water. Pack food that requires no cooking—only the addition of boiling water—and reconstitute it in a drinking cup. Be sure to select items that do not need a long soak time, or the meal will be cold before it is ready to eat. Start with some instant soup. The main course can be based on a starchy food (instant mashed potatoes, instant rice, or couscous) with added protein, vegetables, and condiments. Or use a freeze-dried entrée that can be rehydrated in its own packaging. Follow with a dessert of instant applesauce or instant pudding, and end with hot tea or hot cider. The only items to wash up are the spoon and cup; the cook pot remains clean.

PROTECTING FOOD FROM ANIMALS

Bears, rodents, raccoons, ravens, and other animals can smell food and will tear or gnaw through plastic bags, stuff sacks, and even packs to get at it. Do not leave food inside the tent at night or when leaving camp for an extended period. Ravens and jays can peck through mesh tent windows; weasels can fiddle with zippers skillfully enough to enter the tent; other animals simply rip or chew through the fabric, taking food, making a mess, and damaging a costly tent.

The traditional solution is to hang a nylon stuff sack or pack from a tree limb that is 12 feet (3–4 meters) off the ground, with the food bag at least 4 feet (1.2 meters) from the tree trunk. Attach a small, heavy object (such as a fist-sized rock) to a long cord and, holding on to the free end of the cord, toss the rock over the tree limb. Attach a food bag to one end of this cord and raise the food bag as high as possible, then secure the haul line to the tree trunk. Two food bags connected by a short cord can be counterbalanced on either side of the limb.

An improved version is the "bear wire," suspending the food bag(s) on a tight line strung 12 feet from the ground between two trees that are at least 8 feet (2.5 meters) apart, but this is difficult to rig (fig. 3-19). Land managers may set up steel-wire high lines or poles in popular camping areas. Use them if they are available; they are sure signs that local wildlife is able to get into campers' food.

Whatever method you use, begin food-storage preparations well before nightfall, so you have plenty of visibility for setting up the system safely.

Animals are clever at outwitting campers' efforts to keep food off-limits. They will sometimes gnaw through the cord suspending a food bag, dropping it to the ground. Dexterous critters such as bears and raccoons have been observed perched on a tree limb, hauling a food bag up "hand over hand."

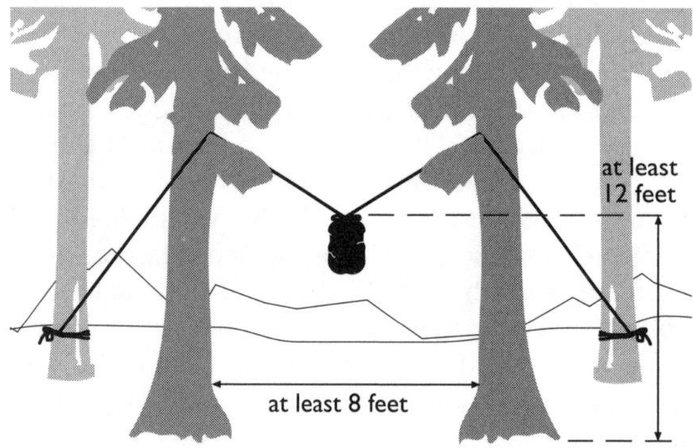

Fig. 3-19. The bear wire. Suspend a food bag on a line 12 feet from the ground between two trees at least 8 feet apart.

Managers of numerous wilderness areas in the western United States find that the use of special bear-resistant, unbreakable plastic food containers (see Figure 3-8) is a more effective technique than the traditional hanging food bag. The containers are bulky, however, and are heavier than nylon or plastic sacks. In places with significant bear populations, land managers often loan these containers, perhaps for a small rental fee. Some areas require them. In treeless terrain, triple-bag anything with an odor attractive to bears—including deodorant and toothpaste—and pack it into a bear-resistant container.

Hiding a food cache in the wilderness is generally a poor practice that is prohibited in some areas. Animals can get into an improperly protected cache and leave a big mess, which will only draw more animals, which then get in the habit of seeking people out for food. If a large predator, such as a bear or cougar, becomes habituated to people's campsites as a food source, the animal may become a nuisance and eventually a dangerous "problem" animal that requires removal from the area.

When storing food to protect it from animals, include such odorous items as toothbrushes, toothpaste, and sweet-smelling lotions. Package garbage—including used feminine-hygiene products—separately and store it with food to keep it away from animals.

FOOD HANDLING IN BEAR COUNTRY

For meal preparation, go to the food storage site and collect just the items for that meal, then pack other items back in animal-resistant storage immediately. Bring the necessary items to the cooking and eating site. Maintain a lookout during cooking and eating. Have a small pair of binoculars handy for checking suspected bear sightings. If a bear is ambling toward the group, quickly pack up the food.

At the end of the meal, wash up well with unscented soap to remove food odors from people, clothes, and equipment. Dispose of cleaning water downwind from the campsite and well away from water sources (see Chapter 7, Leave No Trace). Return all the cooking equipment and leftover food to the food storage site. Do not keep any food in the tent, and avoid bringing clothes with food stains or cooking odors into the tent. Do not sleep in a shelter that smells like food.

UTENSILS FOR COOKING AND EATING

On a superlight trip with just cold food, fingers are the only utensils needed. (Wash hands before preparing food or eating, or at least use a hand-sanitizing gel.) Making dinner with the cup-cooking method described in "Menu Suggestions," above, requires only a cup and spoon per person, plus one cook pot for each group of three or four.

On less spartan trips, bring one pot for cooking, another for boiling water, and light, unbreakable bowls for eating. Alpine cook sets come in aluminum, stainless steel, and titanium (fig. 3-20a and b). Aluminum, which is light and relatively inexpensive, is the most common. Stainless steel is strong and easy to clean but heavy. Titanium is light and strong but very expensive. A very large water pot is useful for melting snow. A wide pot is more stable than a tall, narrow one and also more efficient, because it catches all of the stove's flame. Be sure all pots have bails or handles, or bring a small metal pot lifter (fig. 3-20f). Tight-fitting pot lids conserve heat.

Insulated cups (fig. 3-20d) are popular; a sipping lid keeps the contents warm and prevents spills. Cups, spoons, and bowls (fig. 3-20c, e, and g) come in the same materials as cook sets and also in strong, light polycarbonate plastic. Some cooking pans have a nonstick coating for easy cleaning, but require plastic or silicone utensils to avoid scratching the coating. A small silicone spatula is useful for cooking and efficiently getting food out of the pan, whether for eating or cleaning up. Bring a small plastic scrub pad and a synthetic-fabric pack towel for cleaning.

Many specialized pieces of kitchenware are available for camp cooking, such as bake ovens, Dutch ovens, pressure cookers, and espresso makers. These generally do not accompany mountaineers on a climb; they make their appearance on car camping, kayaking, or other expeditions when their weight is not a hindrance.

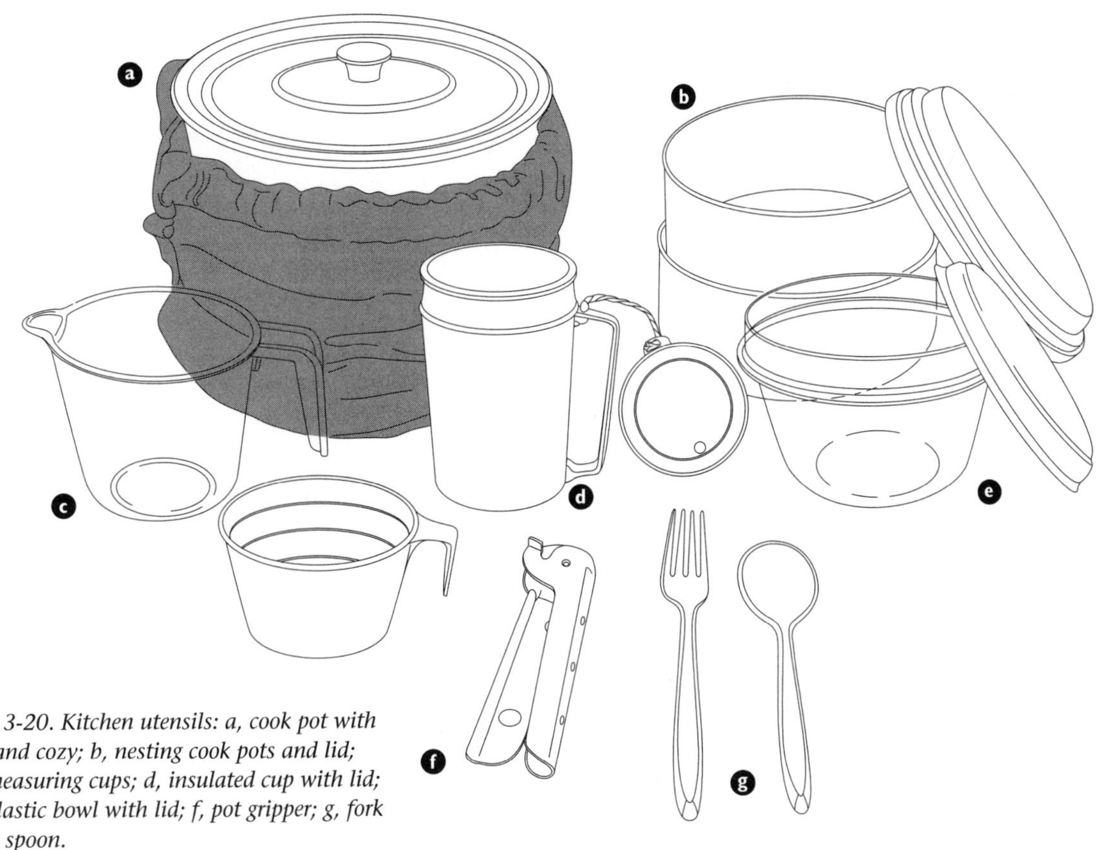

Fig. 3-20. Kitchen utensils: a, cook pot with lid and cozy; b, nesting cook pots and lid; c, measuring cups; d, insulated cup with lid; e, plastic bowl with lid; f, pot gripper; g, fork and spoon.

TIPS ON STAYING WARM

- **Eat well and stay hydrated**; this boosts metabolism.
- **Use proper ground insulation** to separate your body from the cold earth and snow.
- **Dress and undress inside the sleeping bag**. Sleep in a next-to-skin layer. Avoid wearing tight clothing that may reduce circulation and prevent radiated heat from entering the bag's insulation.
- **Keep a hat or balaclava handy**, and wear dry socks to bed.
- **Augment loft** by placing an insulated jacket on top of the sleeping bag. If possible, shift the down in the sleeping bag to the top side, increasing the loft on top.
- **Place a leak-proof bottle of hot liquid in the bag**.
- **Increase metabolism** by drinking and eating if you wake up cold.
- **Use a pee bottle** so that you can remain in the warm tent when nature calls.

"IT'S JUST CAMPING"

Pioneer American alpinist Paul Petzoldt said, in an interview about climbing in the Himalaya and Karakoram, "It's just camping." His point was that technical climbing skills are less important than the ability to survive and even less so than the resourcefulness necessary to be at home and comfortable in the high mountains.

Camping skills are the basis upon which all the more technical mountaineering skills rely. Once climbers develop and hone the skills to stay in the mountains, they will have the confidence to venture further. They will begin to understand what it means to have the freedom of the hills.

GOAL SETTING • MOUNTAINEERING FITNESS COMPONENTS • FUNDAMENTAL TRAINING CONCEPTS • TRAINING GUIDELINES • BUILDING BLOCKS OF AN ANNUAL TRAINING PROGRAM • ANATOMY OF AN ANNUAL TRAINING PROGRAM • SAMPLE NOVICE MOUNTAINEERING PROGRAM • BEYOND TRAINING: RECOVERY

Chapter 4
PHYSICAL CONDITIONING

An appropriate mountaineering conditioning program includes a proper blend of aerobic and anaerobic cardiovascular training, strength training, flexibility training, skill development, cross training, and adequate rest and recovery based on fundamental training concepts.

Many mountaineers dedicate an hour or two each day to conditioning, reserving weekends for longer outings in the mountains. The best way to train for a certain activity is to participate in the activity itself. However, when you cannot do a specific mountaineering activity, numerous other training options can help you prepare optimally. Guidelines follow for developing a systematic conditioning program to optimize training time and to get you out in the mountains happily, safely, and well prepared.

GOAL SETTING

To begin the journey toward mountaineering fitness, first develop an understanding of what fitness means for you. This chapter defines mountaineering fitness as the full-body conditioning needed to comfortably perform necessary movements in the mountains while maintaining a reserve of strength and stamina for any unforeseen challenges.

Before designing a suitable training program, ascertain your end goal and what it will take to get there. First, set some targeted goals that are SMART:

- **S**pecific
- **M**easurable
- **A**ction-oriented
- **R**ealistic
- **T**ime-stamped

A SMART goal might look like this: "Climb Mount X by Y route in three days by the end of the coming summer, through a workout program that includes five weekly workouts and, every other week, a 6- to 8-mile (9.7- to 12.9-kilometer) hike gaining 3,000 feet (914 meters) of elevation, gradually increasing pack weight by 3 to 5 pounds (1.35 to 2.25 kilograms) per outing." Including all the SMART elements makes the goal more attainable than a vague desire to "get fit for mountaineering."

MOUNTAINEERING FITNESS COMPONENTS

The level of fitness required for a beginning level one-day rock climb will differ significantly from that needed for an advanced two-day ice climb. Both programs will look vastly different compared to that of someone training for a three-week-long high-altitude alpine expedition. With an end goal in mind, you can turn to what you need to do to prepare.

CARDIOVASCULAR TRAINING

Cardiovascular endurance is the body's ability to perform any repetitive activity for an extended length of time. During cardiovascular work, the body uses large muscle groups simultaneously, either aerobically or anaerobically. A strong cardiovascular base is a prerequisite for all aspects of mountaineering.

Aerobic exercise. Any cardiovascular activity that requires a significant amount of oxygen for sustained effort and can be categorized as being short (two to eight minutes), medium (eight to thirty minutes), or long (30-plus minutes) is considered aerobic exercise. When compared with anaerobic activities, aerobic activities are performed for longer durations and at lower intensities.

To start earnest preparation for mountaineering, you should be able to complete a 5-mile (8-kilometer) round-trip hike with roughly a 13-pound (5.9-kilogram) pack, ascending and descending 2,000 feet (610 meters), in less than two and a half hours. In addition to having such baseline hiking capability, you should build up to doing four to six cardiovascular workouts per week (depending on your objective) as you approach your goal.

Whereas some of these workouts should be in the mountains or at least have an uphill emphasis, most can be done near your home. Examples of suitable cardiovascular training options include inclined treadmills, elliptical cross-training machines, stair machines, revolving stair climbers, hiking, hill walking, snowshoeing, cross-country skiing, step aerobics, and road and trail running. All of these activities load the spine and legs as required in mountaineering. Biking, paddling, and swimming can be included in the off-season as rehabilitative alternatives, as needed to enable continuity of training or as supplemental cross-training alternatives (see "Cross Training," below).

Anaerobic exercise. Near-maximal cardiovascular training that reaches a person's upper aerobic training zone and beyond (65 percent to 95 percent of your maximum heart rate, or MHR) is called anaerobic exercise. In simplest terms, you are working anaerobically when you are starting to gasp for air. Such training involves working at heart rates higher than are sustainable during aerobic sessions. This kind of training prepares you for when you need a sudden burst of energy to respond to emergencies in the mountains or to link a series of powerful moves together on a climbing wall. Anaerobic training helps increase leg turnover rate so you can build speed. Activities that once made you breathless will feel easier and more comfortable. Examples of anaerobic training include stair climbing (walking sets of stairs while wearing a pack), hill wind sprints (running uphill without a pack), and *fartlek* (random speed burst) training, with or without a pack.

Cardiovascular endurance assessment. To periodically assess your own cardiovascular fitness, choose a favorite nearby hiking route that is snow-free year-round and use it as a test piece every two or three weeks. Each time you do it, try to increase the difficulty in some way, either by adding weight to your pack (no more than 10 percent per week, or 3 to 5 pounds/1.35 to 2.25 kilograms per outing) or by completing the hike in a shorter amount of time, either of which indicates increased cardiovascular endurance.

An easy way to add several pounds of weight is to fill several 2-quart (liter) bottles with water. In early season, to save wear and tear on your joints on the descent, simply dump the water at the top without leaving any trace. As you near your objective, however, be sure that you can carry down what you carry up. If you struggle with breathlessness while carrying a light pack, concentrate on developing endurance during your weekly training sessions; if your legs feel heavy as soon as you start to increase pack weight, focus on increasing your strength.

STRENGTH TRAINING

Strength training is crucial to success in mountaineering: It gives you the power and force to withstand both predictable and unforeseen challenges in the mountains. Strength training prevents injuries by helping your body adapt to overloading, providing muscle balance, improving performance, and enhancing body composition. Strive to be stronger than you think will ever be necessary; the extra training will put you exactly where you need to be when you factor in the endurance aspect of mountaineering.

Mountaineers benefit from strong upper-back, core, and leg muscles; solid balance and agility; and flexibility in the calves, knees, torso, and ankles. Rock and ice climbers benefit from strong and balanced upper-body muscles as well. Include full-body strength training year-round so you can maintain a baseline level of strength and then build as needed at appropriate times.

During the preseason, use single-limb (unilateral) free-weight exercises to correct any weaknesses in your legs and hips. Focus particularly on achieving the full range of motion you might encounter on alpine outings. Exercises such as static lunges, one-legged dead lifts, step-ups, and step-downs ensure that your legs and hips are evenly balanced and doing equal work.

One-legged dead lift. To develop stability in the ankles, hips, and feet, as well as strengthen the entire leg, gluteals, and lower back, do the one-legged dead lift. Stand balanced on one leg, holding a dumbbell in each hand (fig. 4-1a)—or in only one hand. Hinge forward at the hips with as much or as little knee bend as desired, and reach the dumbbell(s) to the floor, keeping the other foot lifted but near the floor in case you need to touch it down for balance (fig. 4-1b). Then exhale and return to a fully upright position. Do six to fifteen repetitions on your nondominant leg and repeat on your dominant leg for the same number of repetitions. Complete two to three sets per leg.

Reverse step-up. To effectively strengthen the quadriceps for downhill hiking and climbing, do the reverse step-up. Use a 6- to 12-inch (15- to 30-centimeter) step and minimize lateral knee movement. Stand on the step with your toes turned out 5 degrees and light dumbbells in each hand. Slowly step off the step as though walking down stairs and stepping lightly on eggshells (fig. 4-2a). Slowly reverse the movement, starting on your toes and using your leg on the step to lift yourself back up (fig. 4-2b). Keep your knee tracking directly over the middle toe, not collapsed toward the midline of your body. Each reverse step-up should last

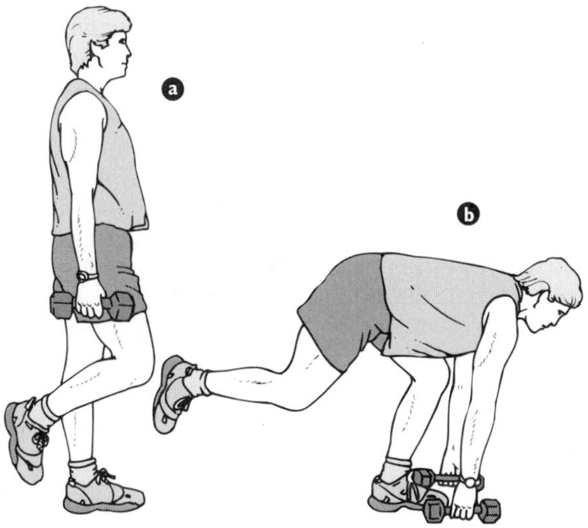

Fig. 4-1. One-legged dead lift: a, stand balanced on one leg, holding dumbbells; b, hinge forward at the hips, reaching dumbbells to the floor, then exhale and return to upright position.

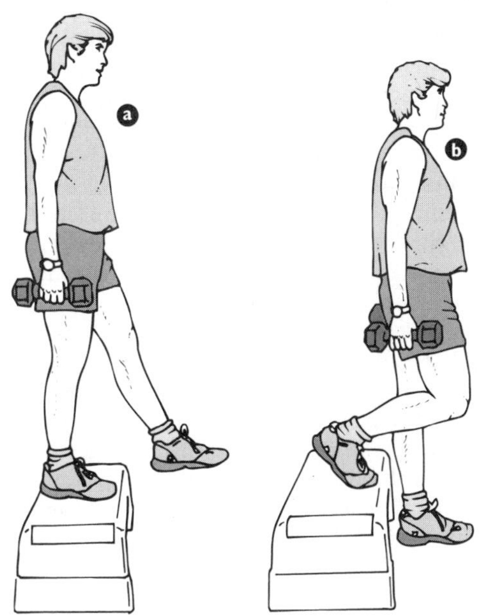

Fig. 4-2. Reverse step-up: a, slowly step off step as though walking down stairs; b, slowly reverse the movement, starting on toes and using the leg on the step to lift yourself back up. Keep the knee tracking directly over the middle toe.

two to three seconds. Do six to fifteen repetitions on your nondominant leg and repeat on your dominant leg for the same number of repetitions. Complete two to three sets per leg.

Many of these exercises can be performed at home using bodyweight initially, then a loaded pack as your balance improves and strength increases. Since your calves will take the brunt of the load whenever you are on steep terrain, include straight-leg variations of calf exercises—see *The Outdoor Athlete* by Courtenay and Doug Schurman (listed in Appendix D, Supplementary Resources).

After you have established good muscle balance and core integrity and stability, incorporate full-body, bilateral (two-limbed) full range of motion exercises, including variations on the squat, dead lift, bench press, pull-up, and row (or horizontal pulling movement), among others. Train each arm or leg to do the same amount of work without any hidden compensation, so you can confidently increase the weights used in order to build additional strength.

Because of the dynamic and unpredictable nature of performing self-arrests with an ice ax, be sure you have full range of motion in your shoulders, as well as good strength and joint integrity throughout your chest, shoulders, and core. Pull-ups, push-ups, and core exercises enable you to get into position rapidly and hold your ice ax in place on icy slopes while you fight to stop yourself from sliding. Training options that help increase strength and strength endurance include training with free weights, uphill training, sled dragging, weighted pack work, training with body resistance and bands, bouldering, and hang board training.

Try to anticipate which muscles your outdoor activities will demand, then match your training exercises to those anticipated movements. For example, if you know you will be snowshoeing on an approach for a winter mountaineering outing, develop strength endurance in your hip flexors for repeated high steps. Add ankle weights or ski boots to short anaerobic uphill or strength workouts. Do not, however, add ankle weights to long endurance workouts, as they can alter your natural stride, not to mention cause overuse injury. If you know you are weak on overhanging movements, develop your core and grip by training your abdominals, obliques, forearms, and fingers in addition to the larger muscle groups in your upper body.

Use your cardiovascular test piece as a guideline for refining your strength training program. If your ankles become tired whenever you hike on uneven terrain, add unilateral balance exercises or include a short weekly training session either walking on gravel or sand or traversing slopes, to help get your ankles used to such terrain. If your quadriceps muscles are sore following a particularly steep outing, increase the number of reverse step-ups, front squats (a variation that involves holding the weight in front of the body rather than behind the neck), or lunge sets you do to strengthen the fronts of your thighs. As you add pack weight, if you find your shoulders and neck getting tired, add exercises for your trapezius muscles, such as upright rows (pulling a weight up toward your chin) or shrugs. By tracking such challenges on your conditioning hikes, you can determine what areas are weak and need additional strength training focus.

FLEXIBILITY TRAINING

Flexibility refers to the active range of motion of muscles about a particular joint. Done properly, stretching can promote flexibility and can also help prevent discomfort after strenuous workouts. It can help with changes in body alignment (such as during weight gain or loss), with injury recovery, and with correcting faulty biomechanics.

Experiencing minor stiffness when starting a new training routine is normal, but you can prevent delayed-onset muscle soreness (DOMS) to some degree by stretching. DOMS occurs most often after workouts that stress the body with the eccentric, or lowering phase, of an exercise, such as extended downward travel with a heavy pack, downhill trail running, or bouldering that requires you to drop repeatedly onto your feet. Whenever you start exercising or return to training following time off, you may experience mild pain, soreness, stiffness, and joint aches unless you ease back into your routine by using lower intensity, weight, duration, and volume.

Frog stretch. An excellent lower-body mountaineering and climbing stretch is the frog stretch (fig. 4-3). With your feet slightly wider than shoulder width apart, sink into a full squat, keeping your heels on the floor and leaning your torso slightly forward. Press your elbows against your knees to increase the hip and inner-thigh stretch. Hold for 30 to 60 seconds.

SKILL DEVELOPMENT

Skill refers to technique and mastery of coordination. Skilled mountaineers are precise with their move-

Fig. 4-3. Frog stretch: Keeping heels on the floor and leaning torso slightly forward, squat down as low as comfortable and press elbows against knees to open up hips.

ments and use less energy completing an activity when compared with their less-skilled counterparts. A novice climbing four days a week may risk overtraining, whereas a highly conditioned climber will be able to perform the movements with far less exertion and strain and may be able to climb at the same or higher frequency without overdoing it.

Experienced mountaineers have a sense of when to back off of intensity or frequency and to work instead on less-taxing but equally important skills. Skilled mountaineers also are more comfortable and confident in situations that could cause novice climbers to panic, make mistakes, have poor judgment, or suffer from accidents that might lead to injury. Skill can be successfully developed by putting into practice all the techniques discussed in the rest of this book and getting appropriate training as needed.

CROSS TRAINING

The final component to consider when conditioning for mountaineering is cross training. Cross training simply means doing supplemental physical activities not directly related to your sport. At higher skill levels, cross training recruits muscle groups in different patterns and provides psychological and physiological breaks from excessive repetition. It provides body and muscle balance for sports such as rock and ice climbing that involve high repetition using small muscle groups. While cross training may not relate directly to sport performance, keeping your joints healthy and preventing overtraining does relate directly to long-term performance.

Cross training for the climber may involve horizontal pulling movements or rowing training to balance out the dominant vertical component of the sport. A cross training activity commonly seen in many mountaineering programs is cycling; this seated sport does not load the spine as mountaineering does, but it provides nonimpact cardiovascular training that is gentler on the legs than the high-impact activity of running—and it also gets athletes outdoors.

FUNDAMENTAL TRAINING CONCEPTS

Once you understand the training components that are involved in mountaineering conditioning, you can start to manipulate them according to FITT parameters:

- **F**requency (how often you exercise)
- **I**ntensity (how hard you exercise)
- **T**ime (how long you exercise—duration)
- **T**ype (what exercise modes you do)

Together, these four elements constitute your training load, or stress. A person who trains for a one-day beginner rock climb has a low workload (low frequency, low intensity, low duration); the advanced high-altitude mountaineer who is getting ready for an alpine expedition will have a very high workload (high frequency, low to high intensity, low to high duration). The greater the workload, the more creative and carefully designed the program needs to be, with sufficient rest and recovery days, in order to prevent both physical and psychological burnout.

Frequency. How often you train depends on your current fitness level, your end goal, and your desired level of achievement. According to the American College of Sports Medicine and the American Heart Association, a suitable fitness program for average healthy adults includes three to five aerobic workouts per week of 20 or more minutes each and activities that maintain or increase muscular strength and endurance for a minimum of two nonconsecutive days a week.

Mountaineering is a strenuous activity that requires far more training than what an average healthy adult needs. As you progress to more demanding alpine goals, the frequency of your cardiovascular, sport-specific, and strength training workouts will increase, and your workouts will vary in intensity and duration.

Intensity. How hard your workouts are describes their intensity. The optimum cardiovascular intensity for fitness improvement is 65 percent to 95 percent of your maximum heart rate (MHR). Most of your preseason workouts should be at a low intensity; gradually build your cardiovascular endurance (in other words, increase duration first) before adding high-intensity anaerobic workouts.

Strength training should also start with low-intensity workouts. Work with lighter weights for a moderate number of repetitions (for example, sets of eight to ten repetitions), especially if you are relatively new to strength training. Next, progress to increasing strength by performing more sets with heavier weights and fewer reps. As you peak for your goal, focus on building strength endurance by using lighter weights and completing more repetitions. Table 4-1 indicates how strength sets and repetitions vary according to what phase of training you are in.

Time. Cardiovascular and strength workouts range in length according to your end goals, training cycle, and exercise type. To see improvements in cardiovascular conditioning, start with aerobic exercise in your aerobic training zone (65 percent to 85 percent of your maximum heart rate, or MHR) for at least 15 to 20 minutes per session and work up to gradually including anaerobic sessions as well. A strength workout as short as eight to ten minutes can provide some benefits, although a typical strength workout ranges from 20 to 60 minutes, depending on the frequency of the strength training.

Type. Workouts vary according to the specific cardiovascular exercises and strength exercises they encompass. Exercise selection depends on individual preference, location (climate and terrain), season, and sport. Choices may vary significantly from one athlete to the next: A rock or ice climber may spend more time at indoor climbing gyms and focus on upper-body and core training in the off-season, while a high-altitude alpine climber may opt for backpacking trips year-round and focus on core and lower-body conditioning exercises in the off-season. Supplemental cross training outside of the chosen sport provides rest and recovery, as well as additional training stimulus for the cardiovascular and musculoskeletal systems.

TRAINING GUIDELINES

In addition to properly manipulating the four FITT parameters, also adhere to the following guidelines.

Train specifically. Match your cardiovascular modes as closely as possible to the primary movements of your sport. Train at similar intensities to those you expect to encounter in the mountains. Sometimes it is difficult to train by practicing your sport—ice climbing is challenging in a warm winter, rock climbing is difficult in the middle of the city, and high-altitude trekking may be hard to do regularly when you live at sea level. Sometimes it is beneficial to include cross training for rehabilitation or injury prevention.

For most of your training, however, choose comparable activities that work the muscle groups in the same ways your sport works them. While non-spinal-loading cardiovascular activities (such as biking, rowing, and swimming) may be included for cross-training purposes in a well-rounded program, spinal-loading choices such as hill climbing with a pack, stair climbing, using inclined cardiovascular machines (for example,

TABLE 4-1. SAMPLE PERIODIZATION OF YEAR-ROUND STRENGTH TRAINING

Preseason			In-season	Postseason	Off-season
Early	Middle	Late			
Lower volume, moderate weights with moderate repetitions	Moderate volume, heavy weights with fewer repetitions, focusing on strength	High volume, light weights with high repetitions, focusing on strength, endurance	Maintain, with moderate volume, weight, and repetitions	Correct imbalances developed from sport-specific activities	Train weak muscles; add unilateral exercises

Source: Courtenay Schurman and Doug Schurman, The Outdoor Athlete

elliptical trainer, treadmill, StairMaster, or step mill) with a pack, and trail running should be the dominant cardiovascular choices for mountaineering.

Train functionally. Keep your exercise selection functional, choosing exercises that integrate as many muscle groups as possible rather than training the body in isolation. Working with free weights provides far greater benefits compared with training on weight machines. Training with free weights requires you to balance weight and to coordinate in all three dimensions; such training loads your spine similarly to when you are hiking on a trail, snowshoeing, skiing, traversing a slope, or standing on a rock ledge.

Increase gradually. Increase training volume by no more than 5 percent to 15 percent at any given time. If you start with 20-minute workouts, add two minutes to subsequent cardiovascular sessions. This suggested progression is based on the amount of musculature a training activity uses, its impact on joints, and the relative support a type of exercise provides for the body. Activities that rely heavily on smaller upper-body musculature or rigorous full-body movements (for example, cross-country skiing or technical climbing) should increase by no more than 5 percent at a time. High-impact activities that use large muscles (such as trail running or telemark skiing) should increase by no more than 10 percent at a time. Low-impact activities (for example, hiking or scrambling) or seated, supported activities (such as biking) should stay under 15 percent.

Include adequate recovery time. High-intensity workouts need more recovery time. Endurance days may be done at low intensities, but if you add pack resistance or hilly terrain, follow such workouts with a recovery day. Low-intensity recovery cross-training exercises may include walking, swimming, dancing, easy flat biking, yoga, or yard work. Such light days help you avoid overtraining by allowing tired muscles to rest before they perform again. As you grow older, you may need additional recovery time, as well as more overall training time to reach your goal.

BUILDING BLOCKS OF AN ANNUAL TRAINING PROGRAM

In order to develop a conditioning program that will support your end goal—whether that is completing a basic climbing program, going on your first ice climb, or reaching the summit of a remote peak—start with the end date for achieving your goal and work backward. In many cases, registering for a climb or making a deposit on a trip will give you a deadline that would be hard to change. There may also be a short window of opportunity for a given climb, such as for ice climbing in most parts of the world. Once you have a firm date in mind, break the time between your end goal and your starting point into distinct training blocks. Table 4-2 illustrates how you might divide an entire year into training blocks.

Each block of time will have a different objective. The *preseason* can last as long as one to six months and encompasses three phases itself. In the *early phase of preseason training*, your goal is to establish a solid foundation, or baseline, on which the rest of your training builds. Frequency, intensity, and duration for both cardiovascular training and strength training will probably be fairly low.

In the *middle phase of preseason training*, as you focus on increasing cardiovascular endurance, frequency

TABLE 4-2. TRAINING BLOCKS AND GOALS

Preseason			In-season	Off-season
Early	Middle	Late		
Establish baseline	Increase cardiovascular endurance and build strength	Enhance mental toughness and stamina; peak and taper	Maintain performance level	Focus on imbalances developed from sport-specific activities. Prioritize training of weak muscles

Source: Courtenay Schurman and Doug Schurman, The Outdoor Athlete

and duration of cardiovascular exercise will gradually increase while intensity remains low. Focus on building strength specific to your chosen activity, with increased intensity (more weight, fewer repetitions, more sets) for strength exercises.

In the *late phase of preseason training*, your focus shifts to enhancing mental toughness and increasing stamina, adding intensity to one or two weekly anaerobic sessions, adding pack weight and distance to your long weekend conditioning hikes, and training for more strength endurance (lighter weight, higher repetitions) as you approach in-season. At the end of this last preseason phase, peak and taper for your objective, whether this is the start of a climbing season or a single alpine climb.

In-season is when you might make trips to the mountains as frequently as several times a month. This period encompassing a series of climbs or trips is generally in the summer (though ice climbing would be in the winter).

The *postseason* lasts for two to four weeks immediately following the completion of your in-season events.

The *off-season* is the time that remains between postseason and preseason, generally several months, unless you participate in multiple sports or multiple seasons of climbing (for instance, winter ice and summer rock climbing).

If you are training for a very first easy mountaineering outing, the early preseason phase of your program may last only one to two weeks, with two to three weeks in both the middle and late preseason phases. If you are a more experienced mountaineer or you are working toward challenging goals that require more than half a year of training, you may spend a month in each training block and cycle several times through the preseason phase of training, alternating between a middle-preseason strength-building phase and a late-preseason endurance-building phase, separating each phase with a week of active recovery. No matter your goal, each phase in your program will have a different focus, so your daily workouts need to reflect that focus.

ANATOMY OF AN ANNUAL TRAINING PROGRAM

For the northern-hemisphere mountaineer who typically climbs most during the late spring and summer, preseason is January to April, in-season is May to September, postseason is October, and off-season is November and December. This will, of course, vary somewhat depending on where you do most of your mountaineering. For the winter ice climber, preseason is generally September to November, in-season is December to February, postseason is March to April, and off-season is May to August. Summer alpine ice climbing peaks in late August and September and more closely resembles the rock climbing calendar, offset by roughly two months.

Preseason. Include unilateral strength exercises for balance and agility. Introduce pack carrying and other sport-specific training at somewhat reduced intensities from those of the previous fall, and build up to your goal weight and distance. Increase training volume by 10 percent or less per week.

In-season. Participate in as many trips, climbs, or events as desired, and schedule suitable recovery time following outings. Shift your training focus to maintenance. That means completing full-body strength training once or twice a week, weekly anaerobic training whenever appropriate for upcoming high-altitude trips or high-intensity outings or contests, and several aerobic training sessions to allow maintenance of all components of training while allowing for adequate recovery between outings.

If you climb both summer rock and winter ice, you can take one to two weeks of off-season between the end of summer rock climbing and the beginning of preparation for winter ice climbing, and again following the last ice climb before resuming rock climbing preparation in spring. In such cases, you will have two seasons to prepare for and smaller lead-in times for each sport. However, participating in both sports will help you maintain a baseline of climbing strength and flexibility so that your preseason training does not have to be as extensive.

Off-season. After an intense season of mountaineering, your body needs a break. The postseason includes shorter aerobic workouts, reduced pack weights, and cross-training workouts unrelated to your summer activity. The goal in this phase is to rest, both physically and mentally. Many climbers shift to winter-season training after several weeks of reduced intensity to get ready for snow sports such as snowshoeing, cross-country skiing, downhill skiing, or, for some, winter ice climbing.

The off-season is the ideal time to evaluate what worked well in your training program from the previous season. Include strength-training sessions that address any muscle imbalances you may have developed or identified over the summer. Add flexibility

TABLE 4-3. PERIODIZATION FOR SIX-WEEK NOVICE MOUNTAINEERING PROGRAM

Week	Day 1	Day 2	Day 3	Day 4	Day 5	Weekend (1 day)
BUILD STRENGTH						
1	40 minutes aerobic 75%–85% MHR*; 30 minutes strength	60 minutes aerobic 65%–75% MHR*, with 15-pound (6.8 kg) pack	Off	60 minutes aerobic 65%-75% MHR*, no pack	30 minutes full-body, sport-specific strength	2,300 feet (701 m) gain, 5–6 miles (8–9.7 km) round-trip, with 13-pound (5.9 kg) pack
2	40 minutes aerobic 75%–85% MHR*; 30 minutes strength	60 minutes aerobic 65%–75% MHR*, with 17-pound (7.7 kg) pack	Off	65 minutes aerobic 65%–75% MHR*, no pack	30 minutes full-body, sport-specific strength	2,600 feet (792 m) gain, 5–6 miles (8–9.7 km) round-trip, with 16-pound (7.3 kg) pack
3	45 minutes aerobic 75%–85% MHR*; 40 minutes strength	30 minutes uphill or stairs intervals, with 20-pound (9.1 kg) pack	Off	70 minutes aerobic 65%–75% MHR*, no pack	45 minutes full-body, sport-specific strength	2,600 feet (792 m) gain, 5–6 miles (8–9.7 km) round-trip, with 19-pound (8.6 kg) pack
BUILD STAMINA						
4	45 minutes aerobic 75%–85% MHR*; 45 minutes strength	35 minutes uphill or stairs intervals, with 22-pound (10 kg) pack	Off	60 minutes aerobic 70%–75% MHR*, next level resistance, no pack	45 minutes full-body, sport-specific strength	2,900 feet (884 m) gain, 6–8 miles (9.7–12.9 km) round-trip, with 19-pound (8.6 kg) pack
5	45 minutes aerobic 75%–85% MHR*; 45 minutes strength	40 minutes uphill or stairs intervals, with 25-pound (11.3 kg) pack	Off	65 minutes aerobic 70%–75% MHR*, no pack	45 minutes full-body, sport-specific strength	2,900 feet (884 m) gain, 6–8 miles (9.7–12.9 km) round-trip, with 23-pound (10.4 kg) pack
6	60 minutes recovery (easy) aerobic 65% MHR*	30 minutes 75%–85% MHR* aerobic; 45 minutes strength	Off	45 minutes aerobic 65% MHR*, no pack	Off	3,200 feet (975 m) gain, 7 miles (11.3 km) round-trip, with 20-pound (9.1 kg) pack

* MHR = maximum heart rate

Source: Courtenay Schurman and Doug Schurman, The Outdoor Athlete

training if you have any residual stiffness that might have stemmed from a season of repetitive movement or overuse. Intensity and duration of workouts should remain low, but frequency of training may increase once you are fully recovered from the season. If you participate in winter ice climbing as well, add focus on calf, core, and forearm training specific to swinging ice axes overhead for longer periods of time.

SAMPLE NOVICE MOUNTAINEERING PROGRAM

When you assemble your goals and exercise preferences, evaluate your skill level, and combine all the fitness components and training parameters, you will have a personalized training program that will work uniquely for you. Your program will look different from anyone else's based on your body type and size, your goals, your age, and your social environment. A single program cannot possibly work for every mountaineer.

Table 4-3 illustrates a single example of how all the variables might fit together into a complete six-week program to attain the goal of a 7-mile (11.3-kilometer) outing with a 20-pound (9.1-kilogram) pack covering an elevation gain and loss of 3,200 feet (975 meters). The progression shows how to gradually transition from baseline hiking of 5 miles (8 kilometers) round-trip, 2,000 feet (610 meters) elevation gain, carrying a 13-pound (5.9-kilogram) pack to steeper terrain by increasing elevation gain by 300 to 500 feet (91 to 152 meters) per outing and gradually increasing pack weight to 20 pounds (9.1 kilograms). Types of cardiovascular exercise and specific strength movements would then be chosen to fit personal preference, lifestyle factors, and individual body needs. Note that in the fifth week the recommendation is to carry slightly more weight but at the same time to cover less mileage and gain less elevation than the target goal one week later. This is an example of how to exceed your goal in some way in order to be more physically prepared for your end objective.

BEYOND TRAINING: RECOVERY

All the hard training in the world will mean nothing unless you give your body the recovery time it needs to repair damage, replenish muscle glycogen stores, and prepare to work hard again. High-intensity cardiovascular and strength workouts require more recovery time than endurance or recovery workouts need. While endurance days (that is, aerobic workouts lasting over an hour) are done at lower intensities, as soon as you add pack resistance or hilly terrain, you also need to insert a rest day, unless your plan calls for back-to-back training in preparation for a multiday trip. Recovery days at lower intensity (less than 65 percent maximum heart rate) might include cross-training exercises such as walking, swimming, dancing, easy flat biking, yoga, or yard work. Such easy days help you avoid strain by allowing tired muscles to rest before they perform again. Mountaineers over the age of 50 may need even more recovery time as well as overall training time to achieve a particular goal.

Pay close attention to your body. As you warm up for your workouts, if you feel like you are still tired or sore from a previous workout or climb, reduce the intensity or complete a shorter workout than scheduled. If your finger or elbow tendons are tender to the touch following a hard climb or workout, add some cross training to allow for adequate recovery. Place strength-training sessions or highly demanding rock or ice climbs at least 48 hours apart so that the targeted muscles, tendons, and ligaments can recover before they are stressed again. If you anticipate multiple days of climbing, try to alternate days of higher-intensity workloads (or carries, in the case of expeditions) with those of lower-intensity workloads (or "climb high, sleep low," in the case of high-altitude expeditions). Tendons and ligaments take longer than muscles to adjust to increased workloads. They also take an infuriating amount of time to heal once they are injured.

Although it is difficult for most mountaineers to take time off from a favorite activity, it is better to let your body heal completely before resuming; otherwise, an acute irritation may turn into a chronic injury that requires much longer time away from your sport. Knowing that you have done the physical training necessary to succeed will empower you to face challenges or worst-case scenarios not only in your activity but also in daily life. The first step toward achieving your mountaineering goals is acquiring the knowledge about proper physical conditioning parameters and guidelines needed to get you there; execution of the appropriate workouts is all up to you.

TRIP PREPARATION • THE MAP • THE COMPASS • THE CLINOMETER • THE ALTIMETER • THE GLOBAL POSITIONING SYSTEM • ORIENTATION BY INSTRUMENT • NAVIGATION BY INSTRUMENT • LOST • FINDING THE FREEDOM OF THE HILLS

Chapter 5 NAVIGATION

"Where am I?" "How far is it to the summit?" "How can I find my way back?" These are three of the most frequently asked questions in mountaineering, and this chapter shows you how to find the answers.

First, a few definitions are in order: *Orientation* is the science of determining your exact position on the earth. It requires mastery of map and compass, plus the ability to use an altimeter and perhaps a global positioning system (GPS) receiver.

Navigation is the science of determining the location of your objective and of staying pointed in the right direction all the way from the starting point to the destination. Like orientation, navigation requires use of a map and compass as well as other instruments and techniques. Navigation is a required skill for all wilderness travelers.

Routefinding is the art of selecting and following the best path appropriate for the abilities and equipment of the climbing party. In selecting the best path to your objective, you may travel on trails partway and cross-country where trails do not lead to where you want to go. The latter activity, wilderness routefinding, is covered in more detail in Chapter 6, Wilderness Travel, but understanding it requires a solid foundation in the orientation, navigation, and routefinding skills described in this chapter.

TRIP PREPARATION

Routefinding—selecting the best path to your objective—begins at home. Consult guidebooks for critical information and seek out other climbers who have made the trip. Useful details are also packed into maps of all sorts. See "Gather Route Information" in Chapter 6, Wilderness Travel, for suggestions on researching a route.

Before even shouldering a pack, have a mental image of the route to the planned climb. Using the information gained from guidebooks or other climbers, plot the route out on the topographic map for the climb. Drawing on your experience, and from all the sources of information about the climb, make the terrain work in your favor.

To avoid brush, try not to follow watercourses or drainages; select ridges rather than hillsides and gullies. Clear-cuts are also often full of slash or brushy second-growth trees. A rock-slide area can be a feasible route—providing the climber watches carefully for new rockfall. One problem in planning the route, however, is that a rock-slide area may look the same on a map as an avalanche gully, which can be an avalanche hazard in winter and spring and choked with brush in summer and fall. If information sources are not helpful, only a firsthand look can clear up this question.

The most straightforward return route is often the same as the route going in. If the plan is to come back a different way, you also need to do careful advance preparation for that route.

THE MAP

No mountaineer should travel without a map and the skill to translate its shorthand into information about details on the route. A number of different types of maps are available:

Relief maps. Terrain is shown in three dimensions on relief maps with various shades of green, gray, and brown, plus terrain sketching and raised surfaces. These maps help in visualizing the ups and downs of the landscape and have some value in trip planning.

Land management and recreation maps. Because recreation maps are updated frequently, they are very useful for current details on roads, trails, ranger stations, and other human constructions. They usually show only a two-dimensional (flat) relationship of natural features, without the contour lines that indicate the shape of the land. These maps, published by the U.S. Forest Service and other government agencies and by timber companies, are suitable for trip planning.

Climbers' sketch maps. Often called climbers' topos, climbers' sketch maps are not topographic maps but are generally crudely drawn, two-dimensional sketches that usually make up in specialized route detail what they lack in draftsmanship. Such drawings can be effective supplements to other map and guidebook information.

Guidebook maps. Some guidebook maps are merely sketches, whereas others are accurate interpretations of topographic maps. They vary greatly in quality but generally contain useful details on roads, trails, and climbing routes.

Topographic maps. Essential to off-trail travel, topos are the best of all for climbers. They depict topography—the shape of the earth's surface—by showing contour lines that represent constant elevations above sea level. These maps are produced in many countries. Some are produced by government agencies; others are printed by private companies, with special emphasis on trails and other recreational features. Perhaps the most familiar of topographic maps in the United States are those produced by the U.S. Geological Survey (USGS). In some areas of the United States, private companies produce maps based on USGS topographic maps but updated with more recent trail and road details, and sometimes they combine sections of USGS maps. These maps are often useful supplements to standard topographic maps. Topographic maps may also be obtained using computer software, such as National Geographic's TOPO! and DeLorme's Topo USA, and on several websites (see Appendix D, Supplementary Resources).

Aerial and satellite photographs. Though not technically maps, aerial and satellite photographs can be of significant help in researching climbing routes. The photos are generally taken from an elevated position above the ground, such as from an aircraft or satellite. Google Earth and TerraServer-USA are two websites that have these kinds of images (see Appendix D).

HOW TO READ A TOPOGRAPHIC MAP

Topographic maps are essential to wilderness travel, and mountaineers must be able to glean as much information from them as possible. Understanding topo features such as latitude and longitude, scale, colors, and contour lines is a crucial navigation skill.

Latitude and Longitude

Because Earth is a sphere, the distance around it—whether from east to west or from north to south—can be divided into 360 units called degrees (the same as for a circle). A measurement east or west around the globe is called longitude; a measurement north or south is called latitude. Longitude is measured 180 degrees east and 180 degrees west, starting at the north–south line (meridian) that goes through Greenwich, England. Latitude is measured 90 degrees north and 90 degrees south, starting from the equator. This system allows each place on the planet to have a unique set of coordinates. For example,

New York City is situated at 74 degrees west longitude and 41 degrees north latitude.

Each degree is divided into 60 units called minutes, and each minute is further subdivided into 60 seconds—just as for units of time. On a map, a latitude of 47 degrees, 52 minutes, 30 seconds north is written like this: 47°52'30"N.

Another way of identifying a point on a map is with the Universal Transverse Mercator (UTM) coordinate system. This system, very useful when using a global positioning system (GPS) receiver, is discussed in "Orientation Using GPS," near the end of this chapter.

One type of USGS topographic map commonly used by mountaineers covers an area of 7.5 minutes (that is, ⅛ degree) of latitude by 7.5 minutes of longitude. These maps are known as the 7.5-minute series. An older type of USGS map covers an area of 15 minutes (that is, ¼ degree) of latitude by 15 minutes of longitude. These maps are part of what is called the 15-minute series.

Scale

The scale of a map is a ratio between measurements on the map and measurements in the real world. A common way to state the scale is to compare a map measurement with a ground measurement (for example, 1 inch equals 1 mile) or to give a specific mathematical ratio (for example, 1:24,000). The scale is usually shown graphically at the bottom of a map (fig. 5-1).

In the USGS 7.5-minute series, the scale is 1:24,000, or roughly 2.5 inches to the mile (4.2 centimeters to the kilometer). The map's north–south extent is about 9 miles (14 kilometers), while its east–west extent varies from about 6 miles (9 kilometers) in the north to about 8 miles (13 kilometers) in the south. (The east–west span of maps decreases as one moves north, due to the fact that the lines of longitude converge as they get closer to the North Pole.) In the older 15-minute series, the scale is 1:62,500, or about 1 inch to the mile (1.6 centimeters to the kilometer), and each map covers four times the area of the 7.5-minute maps. If they have a choice, mountaineers prefer the 7.5-minute maps because of their greater detail.

The 7.5-minute map is now the standard for the United States, except for Alaska. The 15-minute maps have been phased out by the USGS for the other 49 states, though some private companies still produce them (such as Green Trails Maps for the mountainous regions of Washington and Oregon). For Alaska only, the standard scale is 1:63,360, or exactly 1 inch to the mile. These cover an area of 15 minutes in the north–south dimension. The east–west dimension of these maps varies from 20 to 36 minutes, depending on the location.

Each topographic map is referred to as a quadrangle (or quad) and covers an area bounded on the north and south by latitude lines that differ by an amount equal to the map series (such as 7.5 minutes or 15 minutes) and on the east and west by longitude lines that differ by the same amount (again, except for Alaska). Each quadrangle is given the name of a prominent topographic or human feature of the area: for example, USGS Glacier Peak East.

What the Colors Mean

Most topographic maps use colors to differentiate features. On a USGS topographic map, colors have very specific meanings:

Red. Major roads and survey information, such as section lines, are shown in red; sections are 1-square-mile (2.6-square-kilometer) areas.

Blue. Rivers, lakes, springs, waterfalls, and other water-related features are shown in blue.

Black. Minor roads, trails, railroads, buildings, benchmarks, latitude and longitude lines, UTM coordinates and lines, and other features not part of the natural environment are shown in black.

Green. Areas of heavy forest are shown in green. Solid green indicates a forested area; mottled green indicates scrub vegetation. A lack of green does not mean that an area is devoid of vegetation, but simply that any growth is too small or scattered to show on the map. Do not be surprised if a small, narrow gully with no green color on the map turns out to be an avalanche gully choked with impassable brush in the summer and fall, with significant avalanche hazard in the winter and spring.

Brown. Contour lines and elevations are shown in brown, except on glaciers and permanent snowfields.

Purple. Partial revision of an existing map is shown in purple.

White. The color of the paper on which the map is printed; it can have a variety of meanings, depending on the terrain:

White with blue contour lines. A glacier or permanent snowfield is shown as white; the contour lines and edges of glaciers and permanent snowfields are shown in blue.

White with brown contour lines. Any "dry" area without substantial forest, such as a high alpine area, a clear-cut, a rock slide, an avalanche gully, or a meadow,

Fig. 5-1. Photograph of a mountainous area; keyed features are also represented on the accompanying topographic map.

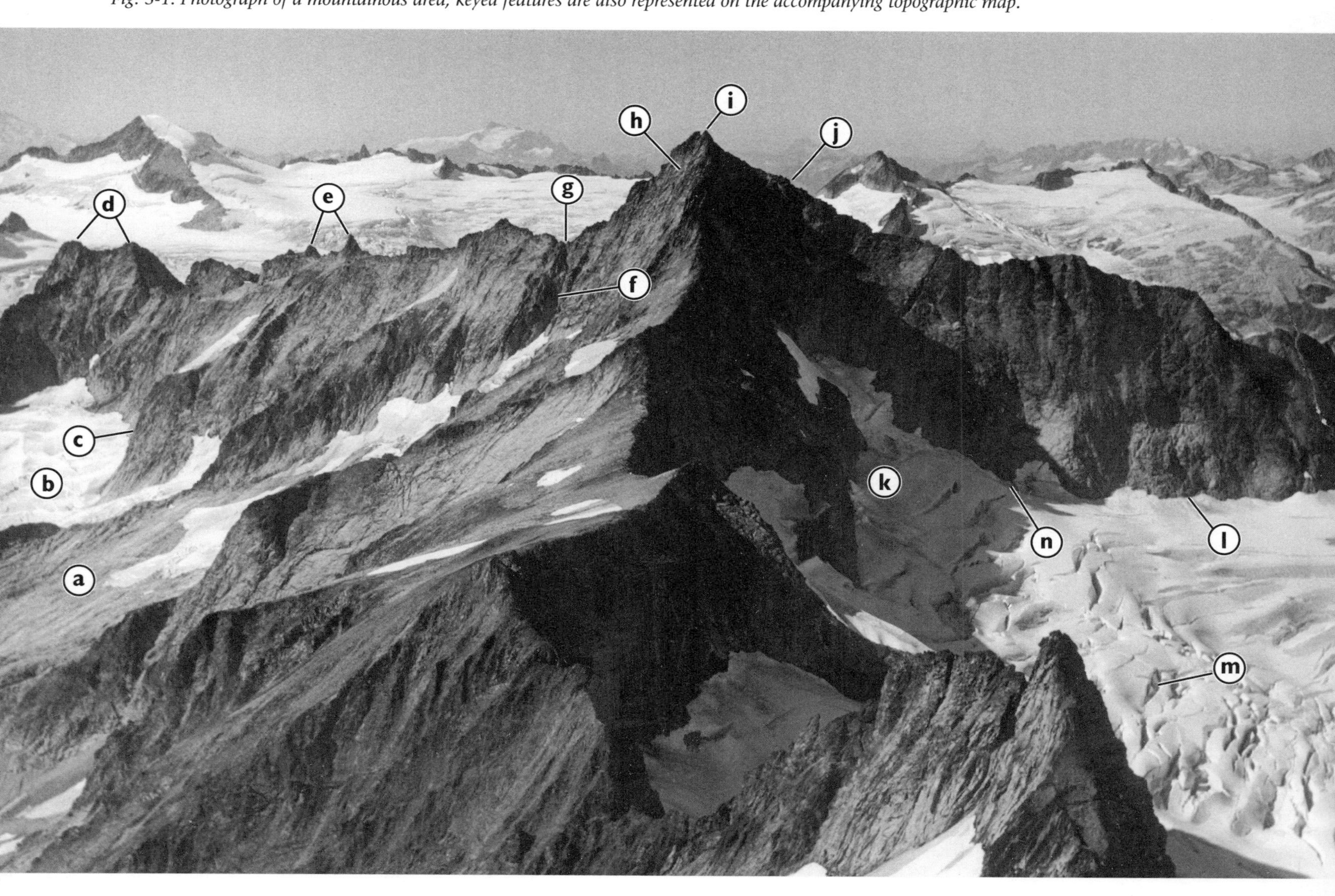

KEY

a. Basin: moderate slope, camp spots
b. Snow or ice line: dashed line ends on cliffs, rock
c. Buttress: change in features of wall may provide approach to ridge
d. Twin summits
e. Gendarmes, aiguilles, or pinnacles
f. Gully or couloir
g. Saddle, pass, or col
h. Rock face
i. Summit: highest point on map
j. Ridge or arête
k. East slope: note shadows and ice accumulation
l. Moat
m. Crevasses: indicated by irregular contours, not smooth as near buttress, c, above
n. Bergschrund: not seen on map but possibility inferred when rock and snow are steep
o. Photo taken from above this spot, looking in direction of arrow

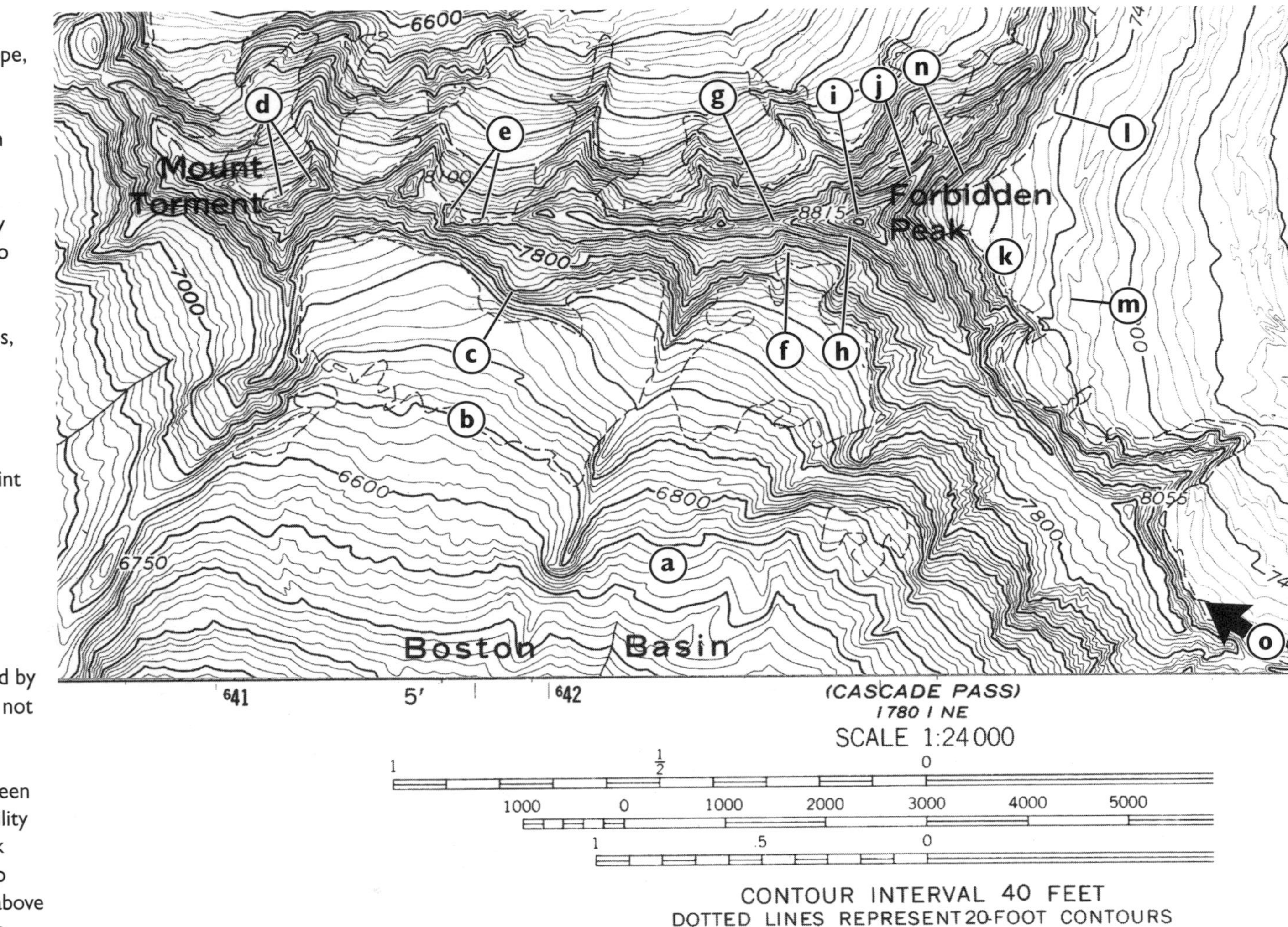

is shown in white with brown contour lines. Study the map for other clues.

Contour Lines

The heart of a topographic map is its overlay of contour lines, each line indicating a constant elevation as it follows the shape of the landscape. A map's contour interval is the difference in elevation between two adjacent contour lines. In mountainous areas, this interval is often 40 feet (12 meters) on 7.5-minute maps and 80 feet (24 meters) on 15-minute maps. Every fifth contour line is printed darker than the other lines and is labeled periodically with the elevation. On metric maps, a contour interval of 5, 10, or 20 meters (16, 33, or 66 feet) is usually used.

One of the most important bits of information a topographic map reveals is whether the route will be uphill or downhill. If the route crosses lines of increasingly higher elevation, it is going uphill. If it crosses lines of decreasing elevation, the route is downhill. Flat or sidehill travel is indicated by a route that crosses no lines, remaining within a single contour interval.

This is only the start of the picture that contour lines paint of an actual route. They also show cliffs, summits, passes, and other features (see Figure 5-2). Climbers get better and better at interpreting these lines by comparing actual terrain with its representation on the map (see Figure 5-1). The goal is that someday you will be able to glance at a topographic map and have a sharp mental image of just what the actual place will look like. The following gives the main features depicted by contour lines:

Flat areas. No contour lines at all, or contour lines very far apart (fig. 5-2a), indicate flat areas.

Gentle slopes. Widely spaced contour lines (fig. 5-2b; see also Figure 5-1a) indicate gentle slopes.

Steep slopes. Closely spaced contour lines (fig. 5-2c; see also Figure 5-1k) indicate steep slopes.

Cliffs. Contour lines extremely close together or touching (fig. 5-2d; see also Figure 5-1h) indicate cliffs.

Valleys, ravines, gullies, and couloirs. Contour lines in a pattern of Us pointing uphill show gentle, rounded valleys or gullies; Vs, sharp valleys or gullies (fig. 5-2e; see also Figure 5-1f). The Us or Vs point in the direction of higher elevation.

Ridges or spurs. Contour lines in a pattern of Us pointing downhill show gentle, rounded ridges; Vs, sharp ridges (fig. 5-2f; see also Figure 5-1j). The Us or Vs point in the direction of lower elevation.

Peaks or summits. Concentric patterns of contour lines show peaks, with the summit the innermost and highest ring (fig. 5-2g; see also Figure 5-1d and i). Peaks may also be indicated by Xs, elevations, benchmarks (BMs), or a triangle symbol.

Cirques or bowls. Patterns of contour lines forming a semicircle, rising from a low spot in the center of the partial circle, show a natural amphitheater at the head of a valley (fig. 5-2h).

Saddles, passes, or cols. An hourglass shape, with higher contour lines on each side, indicates a low point on a ridge (fig. 5-2i; see also Figure 5-1g).

Other Map Information

The margin of a USGS topographic map holds important information, such as date of publication and revision, names of maps of adjacent areas, the contour interval, and the map scale. The margin also gives the area's magnetic declination (discussed later in this chapter), which is the difference between true north and magnetic north.

Topographic maps have certain limitations. They do not show all the terrain features that you actually see on a route, because there is a limit to what can be jammed onto a map without reducing it to an unreadable clutter. If a feature is not at least as high as the contour interval, it may not be shown, so if you are navigating with a map that has a 40-foot contour interval, a 30-foot cliff may come as a surprise to you.

Check the date of the map because topographic maps are not revised very often, so information on forests, declination, roads, and other features could be out of date. A forest may have been logged or a road either extended or closed since the last map revision. Although topographic maps are essential to wilderness travel, they must be supplemented with information from visitors to the area, Forest Service or Park Service rangers, guidebooks, and other maps. Note changes on the map as they are encountered.

Sometimes a trip runs through portions of two or more maps. You can fold adjoining maps at the edges and bring them together, or you can create a customized map by cutting out the pertinent areas and splicing them with tape. Include plenty of territory so that there is a good overview of the entire trip, including the surrounding area. Computer programs can create customized maps, but these maps are limited by printer quality and paper size.

Maps—precious objects that they are—deserve tender care in the wild. Some custom maps can be obtained or printed on waterproof paper that makes it easier to care

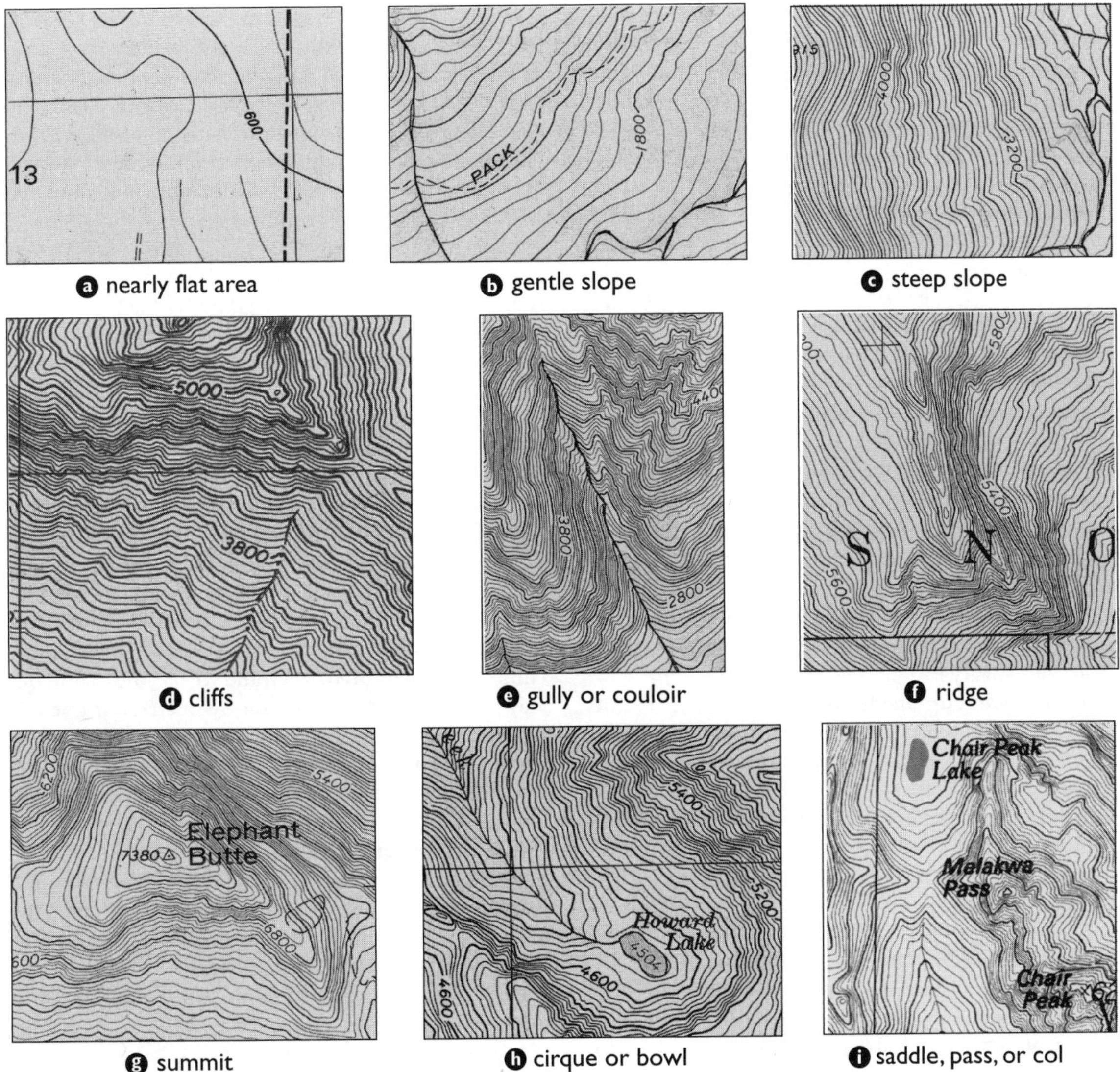

ⓐ nearly flat area ⓑ gentle slope ⓒ steep slope ⓓ cliffs ⓔ gully or couloir ⓕ ridge ⓖ summit ⓗ cirque or bowl ⓘ saddle, pass, or col

Fig. 5-2. Contour lines showing basic topographic features.

for them under wet conditions that can easily destroy ordinary maps. A map can also be kept in a plastic bag or a map case. On the trip, carry the map in a clothing pocket or some other easily accessible place so you do not have to take off your pack to reach it.

ROUTEFINDING WITH A MAP

Most orientation, navigation, and routefinding with a map is done by simply looking at the surroundings and comparing them with the map, before, during, and after a trip.

Before the Trip

Before the trip, make some navigational preparations with the map, such as identifying handrails, baselines, and possible routefinding problems.

Handrails. Any linear feature on a map that parallels the direction of travel is a handrail, which helps you to stay on route. The handrail should be within frequent sight of the route, so it can serve as an aid to navigation. Features that can be used as handrails from time to time during a trip include roads, trails, powerlines, railroad tracks, fences, borders of fields and meadows, valleys, streams, cliff bands, ridges, lakeshores, and the edges of marshes.

Baselines. A long, unmistakable line that always lies in the same direction from you, no matter where you are during your trip—a baseline—provides another map technique that can help you find the way home if you have gone offtrack. During trip planning, pick out a baseline on the map. It does not have to be something visible during the trip; you just have to know that it is there, in a consistent direction from you. A baseline (sometimes called a catch line) can be a road, the shore of a large lake, a river, a trail, a powerline, or any other feature that is at least as long as the climbing area. If the shore of a large, distant lake always lies west of the climbing area, heading west at any time will be sure to get you to this identifiable landmark. Heading toward this baseline may not be the fastest way to travel to the destination, but it may save you from being truly lost.

Routefinding problems. Before the trip, also anticipate specific routefinding problems. For example, if the route traverses a glacier or any large, featureless area such as a snowfield, consider carrying route-marking wands. (Chapter 16, Snow Travel and Climbing, explains the construction and use of wands.) Identify any escape routes that can be used in case of sudden bad weather or other setbacks.

During the Trip

Get off on the right foot by making sure that everyone in the climbing party understands the route and the route plan. Gather the party around the map, taking time to discuss the route and make contingency plans in case the party gets separated. On the map, point out where the party is, and correlate your surroundings with what is shown on the piece of paper in front of everyone. The route plan should include a detailed explanation of how the party will navigate to and from the objective.

Relate surroundings to the map. Along the way, everyone needs to keep relating the terrain to the map. Ignorance is definitely not bliss for any daydreaming climber who does not pay attention to the territory and then gets separated from the party. Whenever a new landmark appears, connect it with the map. At every chance—at a pass, at a clearing, or through a break in the clouds—update your fix on the group's exact position. Keeping track of position this way makes it easy to plan each succeeding leg of the trip, and it will help to prevent climbers from getting lost. It also may turn climbers into expert map interpreters, because they will know what a specific valley or ridge looks like compared with its representation on the map.

Look ahead to the return trip. The route always looks amazingly different on the way back. Avoid surprises and confusion by glancing back over your shoulder from time to time on the way in to see what the route should look like on the return. If you cannot keep track of it all, jot down times, elevations, landmarks, and so on in a notebook. A few cryptic words—"7,600, hit ridge"—can save a lot of grief on the descent. It will remind you that when the party has dropped to 7,600 feet, it is time to leave the ridge and start down the slope.

Think about the route. Your brain is your most valuable navigational tool. As the party heads upward, ask yourself questions: "How will we recognize this important spot on our return?" "What will we do if the climb leader is injured?" "Would we be able to find our way out in a whiteout or if snow covered our tracks?" "Should we be using wands or other route-marking methods right now?" Ask the questions as you go, and act on the answers. Each person in the party should know the route, the route plan, and how to get back.

Mark the route if necessary. At times, it may be best to mark the route going in so that it can be found again on the way out. This situation can arise when the route is over snowfields or glaciers during changeable weather, when the route is in heavy forest, or when fog or nightfall threatens to hide landmarks. On snow, climbers use wands to mark the path. In the forest, plastic surveyors' tape is sometimes tied to branches to show the route, but its use is discouraged due to its blight and permanence. From an ecological standpoint, unbleached toilet paper is the best marker, because it will disintegrate during the next rainfall. Use toilet paper if good weather is assured. If not, use crepe paper in thin rolls. It will survive an approaching storm but will disintegrate over the winter.

One commandment is needed here: Remove your markers. Markers are litter, and mountaineers never, ever litter. If there is any chance you will not come back the same way and will not be able to remove the markers, be especially sure to use paper markers.

Cairns—piles of rocks used as markers—appear here and there, sometimes dotting an entire route and at other times signaling the point where a route changes direction. These heaps of rock are another imposition on the landscape, and they can create confusion for any traveler but the one who put them together—so do not build them. If there comes a time when you must build a cairn, then do so, but tear it down on your way out. The rule is different for existing cairns. Let them be, on the assumption that someone, perhaps even land managers, may be depending on them.

Keep oriented. As the trip goes on, it may be helpful to mark the party's progress on the map. Keep yourself oriented so that at any time you can point out your actual position to within 0.5 mile (about 1 kilometer) on the map.

Monitor rate of travel. Part of navigation is having a sense of the party's speed. Given all the variables, will it take the party one hour to travel 2 miles (3.2 kilometers), or will it take two hours to travel 1 mile (1.6 kilometers)? The answer is rather important if it is 3:00 PM and base camp is still 5 miles (8 kilometers) away. After enough trips into the wilds, climbers are good at estimating wilderness speeds (see the "Typical Speeds for an Average Party" sidebar, noting that there will be much variation).

In heavy brush, the rate of travel can drop to a third or even a quarter of what it would be on a good trail. At high altitudes, the rate of travel will also greatly decrease, perhaps down to as little as 100 feet (30 meters) of elevation gain per hour.

With a watch and a notebook (or a good memory), monitor the rate of progress on any outing. Always make sure to note the time of starting from the trailhead. Also note the times at which identifiable streams, ridges, trail junctions, and other points along the route are reached.

Experienced climbers regularly assess their party's progress and compare it with trip plans. Make estimates—and reestimates—of what time the party will reach the summit or other destination, as well as what time the party will get back to base camp or the trailhead. If it begins to look as though the party could become trapped in tricky terrain after dark, the group may decide to change its plans and bivouac in a safe place or call it a day and return home.

TYPICAL SPEEDS FOR AN AVERAGE PARTY

- **On a gentle trail, with a day pack**: 2 to 3 miles per hour (3 to 5 kilometers per hour)
- **Up a steep trail, with a full overnight pack**: 1 to 2 miles per hour (2 to 3 kilometers per hour)
- **Traveling cross-country up a moderate slope, with a day pack**: 1,000 feet (300 meters) of elevation gain per hour
- **Traveling cross-country up a moderate slope, with a full overnight pack**: 500 feet (150 meters) of elevation gain per hour

On Technical Portions of the Climb

When the going gets tough, the tough forget about navigation and start worrying about the next foothold—but you should keep the map and other route information handy for use during occasional rests. On rock climbs, do not let the mechanics of technical climbing overwhelm your need to stay on route.

On the Summit

Here is a golden opportunity to rest, relax, and enjoy—and to learn more about the area and about map reading by comparing the actual view with the way it looks on the map.

The summit is the place to make final plans for the descent, which often leads to many more routefinding errors than on the ascent. Repeat the trailhead get-together by discussing the route plan and emergency strategies with everyone. Stress the importance of keeping the party together on the descent, when some climbers will want to race ahead while others lag behind.

During the Descent

The descent is a time for extra caution while climbers fight to keep fatigue and inattention at bay. As on the ascent, everyone needs to maintain a good sense of the route and how it relates to the map. Stay together, do not rush, and be even more careful if the party is taking a descent route that is different from the ascent route.

Imagine that your climbing team is almost back to the car after a tough 12-hour climb. The party follows a compass bearing directly back to the logging road but cannot see the car, because the group has gotten off route by a few degrees. The car is either to the left or the right, and perhaps around a bend, so you may have to guess which way to go. It is a bad ending to a good day if the car is to the right of your route and the party goes left. It will be even worse if the car is parked at the end of the road and a routefinding error takes the party beyond that point and on and on through the woods (fig. 5-3a).

Intentional offset. This situation gave rise to the intentional offset, also called "aiming off" (fig. 5-3b). If you fear you might get into this kind of trouble, just travel in a direction that is intentionally offset some amount (say, 20 to 30 degrees) to the right or the left of where you really want to be. When you hit the road (or the river, the ridge, or whatever), there will be no doubt about which way to turn.

After the Climb

Back home, write a description of the route and of any problems, mistakes, or unusual features; do it while the details are fresh in your mind. Imagine what you would like to know if you were about to make the climb for the first time, so you will be ready with the right answers when another climber asks about it. If a guidebook or a map was confusing or wrong, take time to write to the publisher.

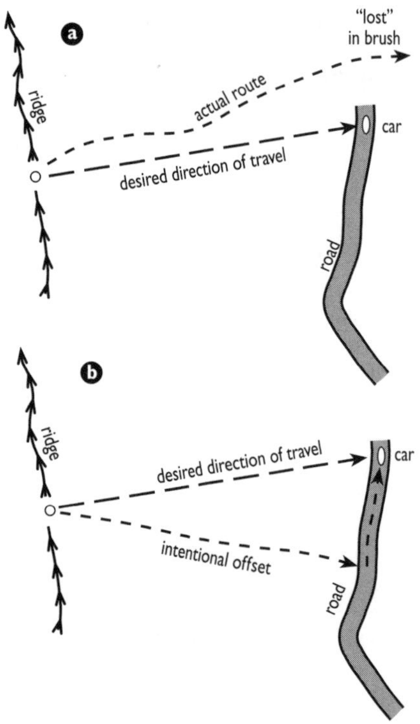

Fig. 5-3. Navigating to a specific point on a line: a, inevitable minor errors can sometimes have disastrous consequences; b, to avoid such problems, follow a course with an intentional offset.

THE COMPASS

A compass is essentially a magnetized needle that responds to the earth's magnetic field. Compass makers have added a few things to this basic unit in order to make it easier to use. But stripped to the core, there is just that needle, aligned with the earth's magnetism, and from that you can figure out any direction. These are the basic features (fig. 5-4a) of a mountaineering compass:

- **A freely rotating magnetic needle.** One end of the magnetic needle is a different color from the other so it is easy to tell which end is pointing north.
- **A circular rotating housing for the needle.** The housing is filled with a fluid that dampens (reduces) the vibrations of the needle, making readings more accurate.
- **A dial around the circumference of the housing.** The dial should be graduated clockwise in degrees from 0 to 360, in increments of no more than 2 degrees.
- **An orienting arrow and a set of parallel meridian lines.** The meridian lines and orienting arrow are in a fixed position beneath the needle; they are essential for using map and compass together.
- **An index line.** Read and set bearings with the index line.
- **A transparent, rectangular base plate for the entire unit.** The base plate includes a direction-of-travel line (sometimes with an arrow at one end) to point toward the objective. The longer the base plate, the easier it is to get an accurate reading.

The following are optional features (fig. 5-4b) available on some mountaineering compasses:

- **An adjustable declination arrow.** The declination arrow is well worth the added cost because it is such an easy, dependable way to correct for magnetic declination.
- **A sighting mirror.** The mirror provides another way to improve accuracy. (This feature is also helpful in applying sunscreen and for emergency signaling.)

- **A ruler.** Use the ruler, calibrated in inches or millimeters, for measuring distances on a map.
- **A clinometer.** Use the clinometer to measure the angle of a slope. It can help resolve arguments over the steepness of slopes, and it can determine whether you are on the higher of two summits.
- **A magnifying glass.** Use the magnifier (not shown in Figure 5-4b) to help read closely spaced contour lines.

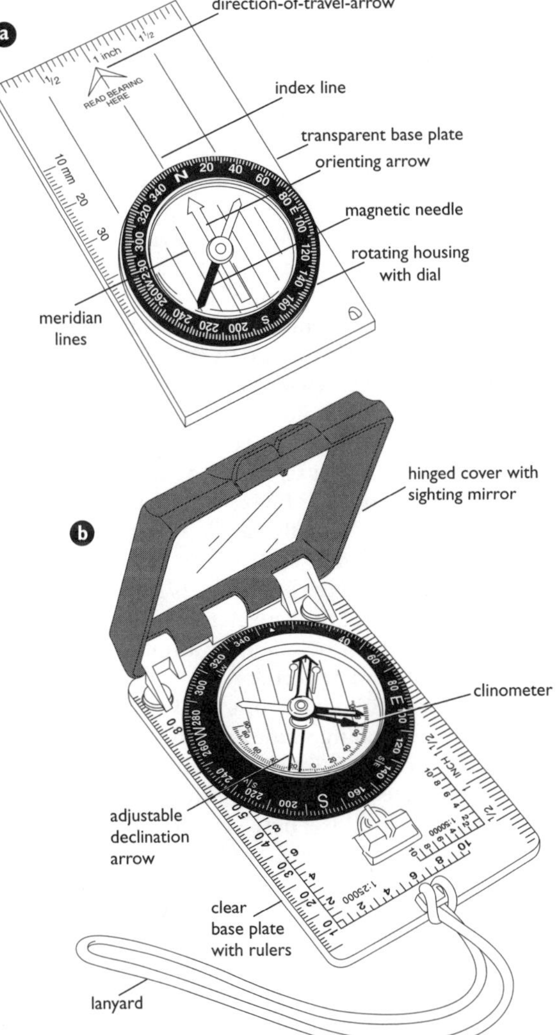

Fig. 5-4. Features of mountaineering compasses: a, essential features; b, useful optional features.

Some compasses have an adjustable declination arrow but no mirror. Such compasses are midway in price between the basic compass of Figure 5-4a and the full-featured compass of Figure 5-4b. These compasses offer a good compromise for someone who prefers the adjustable declination feature but does not want to pay for the added cost of the mirror.

Most compasses have a lanyard—a piece of string a foot or so long for attaching the compass to a belt, jacket, or pack. It is not a good idea to put the lanyard around your neck; this can be an unsafe practice, particularly when you are doing any technical climbing.

Small, round, cheap compasses without base plates are not suitable for mountaineering, because they cannot be used for precise work with a map.

BEARINGS

A bearing is the direction from one place to another, measured in degrees of angle with respect to an accepted reference line. This reference is the line to true north.

The round dial of a compass is divided into 360 degrees. North is at 0 degrees (the same as 360 degrees), East is at 90 degrees, South is at 180 degrees, and West is at 270 degrees (fig. 5-5).

The compass is used for two basic tasks regarding bearings:

1. **Taking bearings (also called measuring bearings).** Taking a bearing means measuring the direction from one point to another, either on a map or on the ground.
2. **Plotting bearings (also called following bearings).** Plotting a bearing means setting a specified bearing on the compass and then plotting out, or following, the direction where that bearing points, either on a map or on the ground.

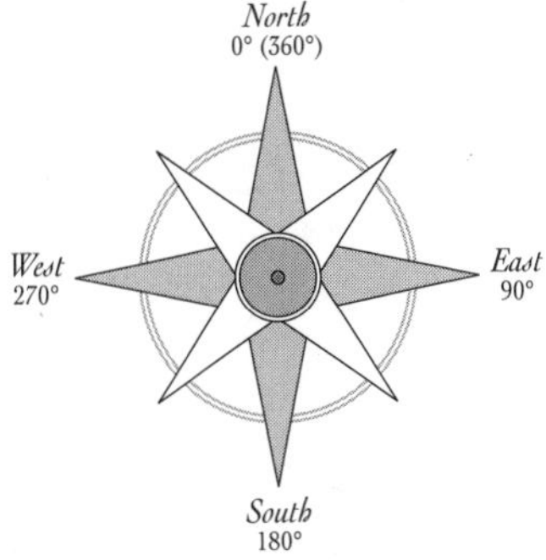

Fig. 5-5. Cardinal directions and corresponding degrees on the compass.

Bearings on the Map

The compass is used as a protractor to both measure and plot bearings on a map. Magnetic north and magnetic declination have nothing to do with these operations. Therefore, never make any use of the magnetic needle when you are taking or plotting bearings on a map. (The only time the magnetic needle is used on the map is whenever you choose to orient the map to true north, which is explained in "Orientation by Instrument," later in this chapter. But there is no need to orient the map to measure or plot bearings.)

Taking (measuring) a bearing on the map. Place the compass on the map, with one long edge of the base plate running directly between two points of interest. While measuring the bearing from point A to point B, make sure that the direction-of-travel line is pointing in the same direction as from A to B (fig. 5-6).

Then turn the rotating housing until its set of meridian lines is parallel to the north–south lines on the map. If the map does not have north–south lines, just draw some in, parallel to the edge of the map and at intervals of 1 or 2 inches (3 to 5 centimeters). Be sure the orienting arrow that turns with the meridian lines is pointing to the top of the map, to north. If the arrow is pointed toward the bottom, the reading will be 180 degrees off. (In Figure 5-6, the magnetic needle has been omitted to provide a better view of the meridian lines.)

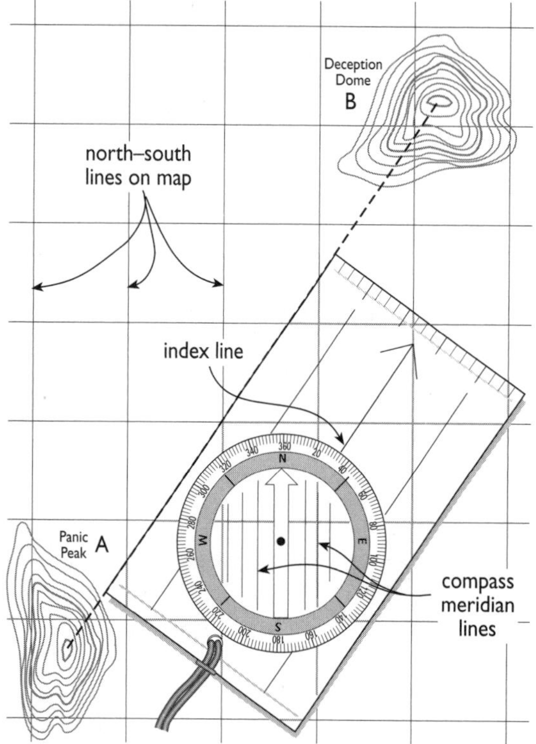

Fig. 5-6. Taking a bearing on a map with the compass as a protractor (magnetic needle omitted for clarity).

Now read the number on the dial that intersects with the index line. This is the bearing from point A to point B. In the example shown in Figure 5-6, the bearing from point A, Panic Peak, to point B, Deception Dome, is 34 degrees.

Plotting (following) a bearing on the map. To follow a bearing, you must start with a known bearing. Where does that bearing come from? From an actual landscape compass reading. In a hypothetical example, a friend returns from a trip, disgusted at himself for having left his camera somewhere along the trail. During a rest stop, he had taken some pictures of Mount Magnificent. At the same time, he had taken a bearing on Mount Magnificent and found it to be 130 degrees. That is all you need to know. You are heading into that same area next week, so get out the Mount Magnificent quadrangle, and here is what you do to follow the bearing he took.

First, set the bearing of 130 degrees at the compass index line (fig. 5-7). Next, place the compass on the map, one long edge of the base plate touching the summit of Mount Magnificent. Now rotate the entire compass (not just the housing) until the meridian lines are parallel with the map's north–south lines, and make sure the edge of the base plate is still touching the summit. Ensure that the orienting arrow points to the top of the map, toward north.

Now you can follow the line made by the edge of the base plate, heading in the opposite direction from the direction-of-travel line, because the original bearing was measured toward the mountain. Where the line crosses the trail is where your friend's camera is (or was).

Bearings in the Field

All bearings in the field are based on where the magnetic needle points, so now that needle gets to do its job. The first two examples below, for the sake of simplicity, ignore the effects of magnetic declination, which is covered in the next section. Imagine you are taking the bearings in New Orleans, Louisiana, where declination is negligible at this time.

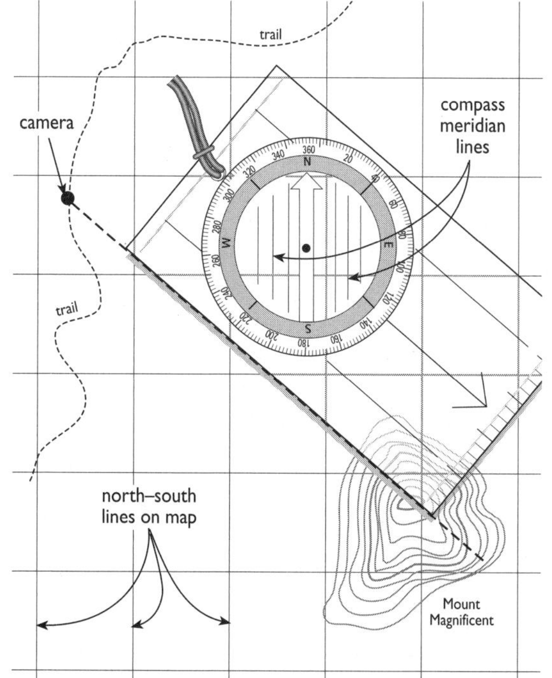

Fig. 5-7. Plotting a bearing on a map with the compass as a protractor (magnetic needle omitted for clarity).

Taking (measuring) a bearing in the field. Hold the compass in front of you and point the direction-of-travel line at the object whose bearing you want to find (fig. 5-8). Next, rotate the compass housing until the pointed end of the orienting arrow is aligned with the north-seeking end of the magnetic needle. Now, read the bearing on the dial where it intersects the index line—270 degrees in Figure 5-8.

If the compass has no sighting mirror, hold the compass at or near arm's length and at or near waist level. With a sighting mirror, fold the mirror back at about a 45-degree angle and hold the compass at eye level with the sight pointing at the object. Observe the magnetic needle and the orienting arrow in the mirror while rotating the housing to align the needle and the arrow.

In either case, hold the compass level. Keep it away from ferrous metal objects, which can easily deflect the magnetic needle.

Plotting (following) a bearing in the field. Simply reverse the process used to take a bearing in the field. Start by rotating the compass housing until a desired bearing, say 270 degrees (due west), is set at the index

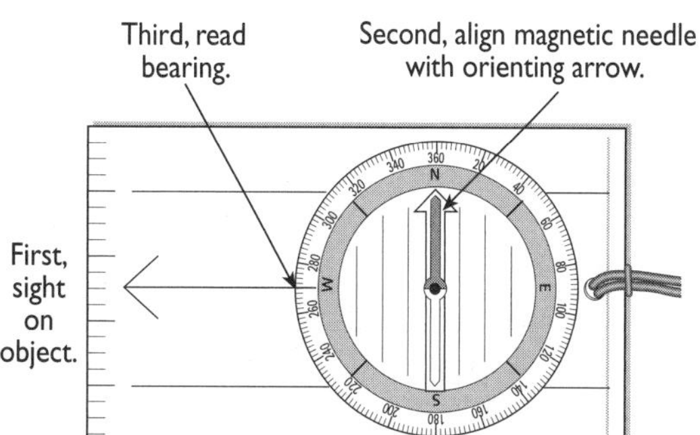

Fig. 5-8. Taking a compass bearing in the field in an area with zero declination.

line (see Figure 5-8). Hold the compass level in front of you, and then turn your entire body (including your feet) until the north-seeking end of the magnetic needle is aligned with the pointed end of the orienting arrow. The direction-of-travel line is now pointing due west.

MAGNETIC DECLINATION

A compass needle is attracted to magnetic north, whereas most maps are oriented to a different point on the earth: the geographic North Pole (true north). This difference between the direction to true north and the direction to magnetic north is called magnetic declination. It is usually expressed in degrees east or west of true north. A simple compass adjustment or modification is necessary to correct for magnetic declination.

The line connecting all points where true north aligns with magnetic north is called the agonic line, or the line of zero declination. In the United States, this runs from Minnesota to Louisiana (fig. 5-9). In areas west of the line of zero declination, the magnetic needle points somewhere to the east of true north, so these areas are said to have east declination. It works just the opposite east of the line of zero declination, where the magnetic needle points somewhere to the west of true north; these areas have west declination.

Adjusting Bearings for Magnetic Declination

Consider a traveler in central Utah, where the declination is 12 degrees east (fig. 5-10a). The true bearing is a measurement of the angle between the line to true north and the line to the objective. The magnetic needle, however, is pulled toward magnetic north, not true north. So instead it measures the angle between the line to magnetic north and the line to the objective.

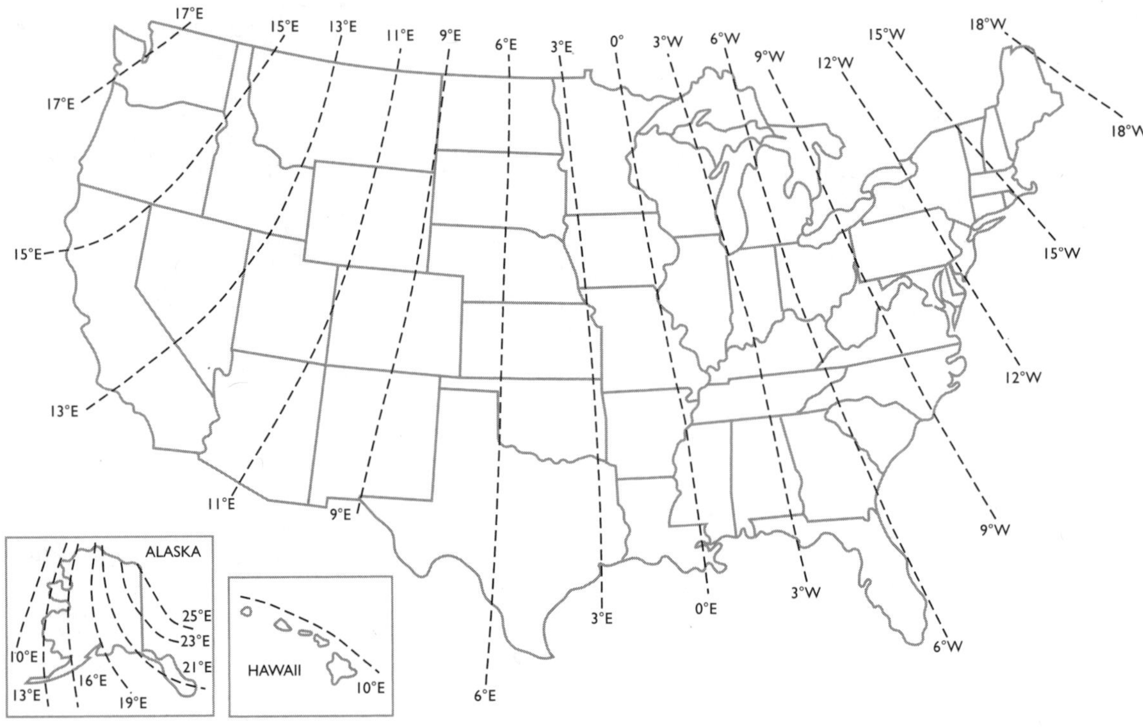

Fig. 5-9. Magnetic declination in the United States in 2010.

This "magnetic bearing" is 12 degrees less than the true bearing. To get the true bearing, it is possible to add 12 degrees to the magnetic bearing (though easier ways are described later in this section).

Travelers in all areas west of the zero declination line, as in the Utah example above, could add the declination to the magnetic bearing. In the Rocky Mountains of Colorado, for example, about 10 degrees would be added. In western Washington State, it is about 17 degrees.

East of the zero-declination line, the declination can be subtracted from the magnetic bearing. In Vermont, for example, the magnetic bearing is 15 degrees greater than the true bearing (fig. 5-10b). Subtracting the declination of 15 degrees gives a wilderness traveler in Vermont the true bearing.

Adjustable declination arrow. Adjusting for magnetic declination is all very simple in theory but can be confusing in practice, and the wilderness is no place for mental arithmetic that can have potentially serious consequences. A more practical way to handle the minor complication of declination is to pay somewhat more for a compass and get one with an adjustable declination arrow (as shown in Figure 5-4b) instead of a fixed orienting arrow (as shown in Figure 5-4a). The declination arrow can easily be set for any declination by following the instructions supplied with the compass. Then the bearing at the index line will automatically be the true bearing, and there will be no need for concern about a declination error.

Customized declination arrow. On compasses without adjustable declination arrows, the same effect can be achieved by sticking a thin strip of tape to the bottom of the rotating housing to serve as a customized declination arrow. Trim the tape to a point, with the point aimed directly at the specific declination for the intended climbing area.

In Utah, the taped declination arrow must point at 12 degrees east (clockwise) from the 360-degree point (marked N for north) on the rotating compass dial (fig. 5-11a). In Vermont, the declination arrow must point at 15 degrees west (counterclockwise) from the 360-degree point on the dial (fig. 5-11b). In western

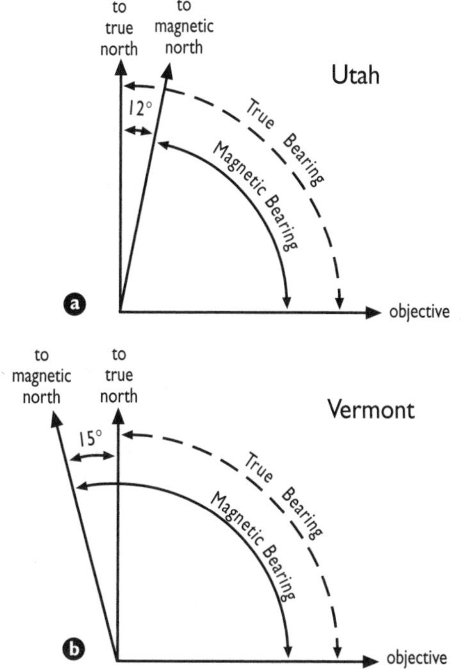

Fig. 5-10. Magnetic and true bearings: a, in Utah (east declination); b, in Vermont (west declination).

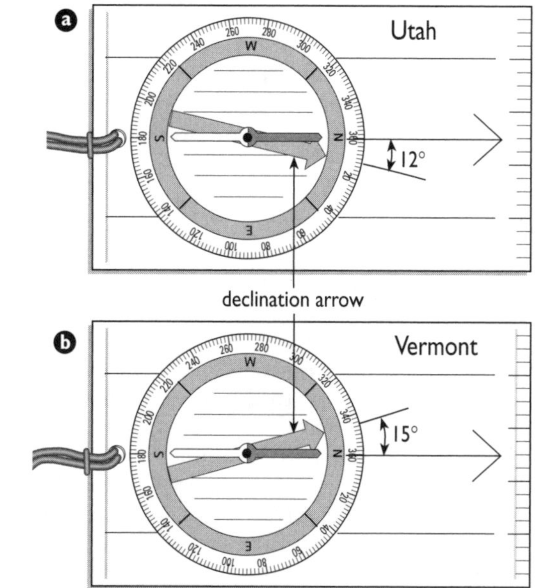

Fig. 5-11. Compass declination corrections: a, for an area west of the zero-declination line (Utah); b, for an area east of the zero-declination line (Vermont).

Washington State, the declination arrow must point at 17 degrees east (clockwise) from 360 degrees.

Taking or following bearings in the field. To take or to follow a bearing (that has been adjusted for magnetic declination) in the field, follow exactly the same procedure used in the earlier examples from New Orleans, where the declination is near zero. The only difference is that you align the magnetic needle with the declination arrow instead of with the orienting arrow.

Note: From here on, this chapter assumes you are using a compass with a declination arrow—either an adjustable arrow or a taped arrow that has been added. For all bearings in the field, align the needle with this declination arrow. Unless otherwise stated, all bearings referred to are true bearings, not magnetic.

Changes in Magnetic Declination

Declination changes with time, by as much as 0.5 degree per year in some parts of the United States (this is because the molten magnetic material in the earth's core is continually moving). Declination is shown on all USGS topographic maps, but since these are not updated very frequently, the declination shown on maps is usually somewhat out of date. The map in Figure 5-9 shows the declination for the year 2010 and will be fairly accurate for most parts of the United States until about 2015. Some websites can be used to find the current magnetic declination for any location on Earth: the Geological Survey of Canada calculator at the National Resources Canada (NRC) site, for example, and the U.S. National Oceanographic and Atmospheric Administration's (NOAA) National Geophysical Data Center site (see Appendix D, Supplementary Resources).

As an example of declination change, a USGS map of the Snoqualmie Pass area of Washington State dated 1989 gave a declination of 19°30'E. Another map of the same area dated 2003 gave a declination of 18°10'E. Using the NOAA website for December 31, 2009, gives a declination of 16°42'E and shows it decreasing by 10 minutes per year.

Declination change varies widely throughout the world. In Washington, D.C., declination is not changing at all. In northeast Alaska it is changing by as much as 1 degree every two years. In Washington State, the change is about 1 degree every six years. In Colorado, it is about 1 degree every eight years.

(These values can be found on the NOAA website.) From these examples, it should be clear that the declination on maps more than a few years old should not be trusted; it is important to find the latest declination information to prevent errors in navigation by compass.

COMPASS DIP

The magnetic needle of the compass is affected by not only the horizontal direction of the earth's magnetic field but also its vertical pull. The closer you get to the magnetic North Pole, the more the north-seeking end of the needle tends to point downward. At the magnetic equator, the needle is level; at the magnetic South Pole, the north-seeking end of the needle tries to point upward. This phenomenon is referred to as the compass dip.

To compensate for this effect, most compass manufacturers purposely introduce a slight imbalance to the magnetic needles of their compasses, so that their dip is negligible for the geographic area where they will be used. However, if you buy a compass in the northern hemisphere—say, in North America or Europe—and then try to use it in the southern hemisphere—say, in New Zealand or Chile—the difference in dip may be enough to introduce errors in compass readings or even make it impossible to use. For this reason, if you bring your compass to a faraway place, as soon as you get to the country you are visiting, first try out your compass in an urban area to make sure it works properly before you head out into the wilderness. If your compass is adversely affected by dip, you may have to buy a new compass in the general area where you are traveling. Most compasses sold anywhere in the world are compensated for dip in that particular zone.

Some compass manufacturers produce compasses that are not affected by dip. Some such compasses have the term "global" in their names or a notation on the package that the compass is corrected for dip anywhere in the world. If you intend to go on worldwide climbing expeditions, you might consider such a compass.

Another way of ensuring that dip will not be a problem is to buy a compass ahead of time that is properly compensated for dip in the area you intend to visit. Some retail stores and mail-order companies have or can order compasses compensated for whatever zone you will be visiting. Doing this in advance of a visit ensures that you will not have a problem with compass dip on your climb.

PRACTICING WITH THE COMPASS

Before counting on your compass skills in the wilderness, test them where you live (see the "Map and Compass Checklist" sidebar). The best place to practice is someplace where you already know all the answers, such

MAP AND COMPASS CHECKLIST

Do you have the hang of using map and compass? Run through the whole procedure once more. Check off each step as you do it. And remember the following:

- Never use the magnetic needle or the declination arrow when measuring or plotting bearings on the map.
- When taking or following a bearing in the field, always align the pointed end of the declination arrow with the north-seeking end of the magnetic needle.

Taking (Measuring) a Bearing on a Map

1. Place the compass on the map, with the edge of the base plate joining the two points of interest.
2. Rotate the housing to align the compass meridian lines with the north–south lines on the map.
3. Read the bearing at the index line.

Plotting (Following) a Bearing on a Map

1. Set the desired bearing at the index line.
2. Place the compass on the map, with the edge of the base plate on the feature from which you wish to plot a bearing.
3. Turn the entire compass to align the meridian lines with the map's north–south lines. The edge of the base plate is the bearing line.

Taking (Measuring) a Bearing in the Field

1. Hold the compass level in front of you and point the direction-of-travel line at the desired object.
2. Rotate the housing to align the declination arrow with the magnetic needle.
3. Read the bearing at the index line.

Plotting (Following) a Bearing in the Field

1. Set the desired bearing at the index line.
2. Hold the compass level in front of you and turn your entire body until the magnetic needle is aligned with the declination arrow.
3. Travel in the direction shown by the direction-of-travel line.

as a street intersection where the roads run north–south and east–west.

Take a bearing in a direction you know to be east. When the direction-of-travel line or arrow is pointed at something that you know is due east of you and the declination arrow is lined up with the magnetic needle, the number on the dial that intersects with the index line should be within a few degrees of 90. Repeat for the other cardinal directions: south, west, and north.

Then do the reverse: Pretend you do not know which way is west. Set 270 degrees (west) at the index line and hold the compass in front of you as you turn your entire body until the needle is again aligned with the declination arrow. The direction-of-travel line should now point west. Does it? Repeat for the other cardinal directions. This set of exercises will help develop skill and self-confidence at compass reading and also is a way to check the accuracy of the compass.

Look for chances to practice in the mountains. A good place is any known location—such as a summit or a lakeshore—from which you can see identifiable landmarks. Take bearings as time permits, plot them on the map, and see how close the result is to your actual location.

CAUTIONS ABOUT COMPASS USE

It should be evident by now that there is a big difference between using a compass for working with a map and using a compass for fieldwork. When measuring and plotting bearings on a map, ignore the compass needle; just align the meridian lines on the compass housing with the north–south lines on the map. In the field, however, you must use the magnetic needle.

The presence of nearby metal can interfere with a compass reading. Ferrous objects—iron, steel, and other materials with magnetic properties—will deflect the magnetic needle and produce false readings, as will a battery-powered watch that is within a few inches of a compass. Keep the compass away from belt buckles, ice axes, and other metal objects. If a compass reading does not seem to make sense, check whether it is being affected by nearby metal.

Keep your wits about you when you are pointing the declination arrow and the direction-of-travel line. If either is pointed backward—an easy thing to do—the reading will be 180 degrees off. If the bearing is north, the compass will say it is south. Remember that the north-seeking end of the magnetic needle must be aligned with the pointed end of the declination arrow and that the direction-of-travel line must point from you to the objective, not the reverse.

There is yet another way to introduce a 180-degree error in a compass reading: by aligning the compass meridian lines with the north–south lines on a map but pointing the rotating housing backward. The way to avoid this is to check that "N" on the compass dial is pointing to north on the map.

If you are in doubt, trust the compass. The compass, correctly used, is almost always right, whereas your contrary judgment may be clouded by fatigue, confusion, or hurry. If you get a nonsensical reading, check to see that you are not making one of those 180-degree errors. If not, and if there is no metal in sight, verify the reading with other members of the party. If they get the same answer, trust the compass over hunches, blind guesses, and intuition.

THE CLINOMETER

The clinometer is a tool used to measure angles; it is a feature of some compasses (see Figure 5-4b). The clinometer consists of a small needle (not the magnetic needle), which points downward due to gravity, and a numbered scale along the inside of the compass housing (which may also be the scale used for declination adjustment).

To use the clinometer, rotate the compass housing to either 90 degrees or 270 degrees at the index line. Then hold the compass on edge so that the clinometer needle swings free and points down toward the numbered scale. With the compass held level in this way (that is, with the direction-of-travel line held level), the clinometer should read zero. Tilting the compass up or down will cause the clinometer needle to point to the number of degrees upward or downward. There are two ways to use a clinometer:

Angle to a distant object. The first way to use a clinometer is to measure the angle to a distant object. For example, suppose you are at the summit of a peak; you see another peak of nearly the same elevation, and you wonder if you are on the higher of the two summits. To find out, hold the compass on its side, with its long edge pointing toward the other peak. Then sight along the long edge of the base plate toward the other peak. Steady the compass on a rock or other stable object, if possible. Tap the compass lightly to overcome any friction in the mechanism, and ask a companion to look at the clinometer needle to see if it indicates an upward or a downward angle toward the other peak. If the angle is upward, then the other peak is higher than you are.

Angle of a slope. The clinometer can also be used to find the angle of a slope. Set the compass to 90 degrees or 270 degrees at the index line, and lay the long edge of the compass on the slope, along the axis from the slope's lowest to highest point; then read the angle of slope on the clinometer scale. Due to variations in a slope over small distances, it is best to place an ice ax, ski pole, or other long object on the slope along the axis from its lowest to highest point, and then place the long edge of the compass on this object to get a better idea of the average slope. The presence of metal, such as an ice ax or ski pole shaft, will affect the magnetic needle but not the clinometer needle, which is only affected by gravity.

THE ALTIMETER

An altimeter, like a compass, provides one simple piece of information that forms the basis for a tremendous amount of vital detail. A compass points the direction to magnetic north from where you are standing; an altimeter gives the elevation where you are standing. By monitoring the elevation and checking it against the topographic map, mountaineers can keep track of their progress, pinpoint their location, and find the way to critical junctions in the route. Every climbing party should have an altimeter.

An altimeter is basically a modified barometer. Both instruments measure air pressure (the weight of air). A barometer indicates air pressure, whereas an altimeter reads in feet or meters above sea level—which is made possible because air pressure decreases at a predictable rate with increasing altitude.

The most popular mountaineering altimeter is the digital type (fig. 5-12a and b), usually combined with a watch and worn on the wrist (fig. 5-12b). The digital wristwatch altimeter has a number of advantages over the analog type (fig. 5-12c). Some digital altimeters display additional information, such as the temperature and the rate of change in altitude gain or loss. Because most climbers wear a watch anyway, this type of altimeter is helpful because it combines two functions in one piece of equipment. The altimeter worn on the wrist is also more convenient to use than one kept in a pocket or pack. Some GPS receivers have internal altimeters that also display the altitude based on barometric pressure.

A disadvantage of the digital type is that it requires a battery—which can die. In addition, the liquid-crystal display (LCD) usually goes blank at temperatures below about 0 degrees Fahrenheit (minus 18 degrees Celsius), making it essential to keep the instrument relatively warm. To keep your altimeter watch from getting banged up on the rock when you are starting a technical pitch, it is a good idea to remove it from your wrist and attach it to a pack strap or put it in a pocket or your pack.

The analog altimeter has the advantages of being a simpler instrument than a digital one, requiring no battery, and working at temperatures well below zero. To read an analog altimeter, hold it level in the palm of one hand. Look directly down on the needle, your eyes at least 12 inches or so (30 centimeters) above it, to reduce errors due to viewing angle. Tap it lightly several times to overcome any slight friction in the mechanism, and then take a reading.

Fig. 5-12. Typical altimeters: a, digital pocket type; b, digital wristwatch type; c, analog pocket type.

The accuracy of an altimeter depends on the weather, because a change in weather is generally accompanied by a change in air pressure, which can cause an error in the altimeter reading. A change in barometric pressure of 1 inch of mercury corresponds to a change in altitude reading of roughly 1,000 feet (10 millibars of barometric pressure corresponds to 100 meters of altitude). If a climber is in camp during a day on which the air pressure increases by 0.2 inch (7 millibars)—for example, from 30.0 to 30.2 inches (1,016 to 1,023 millibars), the altimeter will show a reading about 200 feet (60 meters) less than it did at the beginning of the day, even though the climber has remained at the same place. If the climber had gone out on a climb during that same day, the elevation readings would likewise be about 200 feet too low. During periods of unstable weather, the indicated elevation may change by as much as 500 feet (150 meters) in one day even though the actual elevation has remained the same. Even during apparently stable conditions, an erroneous indicated change in elevation of 100 feet (30 meters) per day is not uncommon.

Because of the strong influence of weather on an altimeter's accuracy, do not trust the instrument until it is first set at a location of known elevation. Then it is important while traveling to check the reading whenever another point of known elevation is reached so you can reset it if necessary, or at least be aware of the error.

HOW ALTIMETERS AID MOUNTAINEERS

Altimeters can help in calculating the rate of ascent, in determining exact location, and in predicting weather.

Calculating Rate of Ascent

The altimeter helps mountaineers decide whether to continue a climb or to turn back, by letting them calculate their rate of ascent. For example, during a climb a party has been keeping an hourly check on time and elevation. The party gained only 500 feet (150 meters) in the past hour, compared with 1,000 feet (300 meters) in the first hour. The summit is at an elevation of 8,400 feet (2,560 meters), and an altimeter reading shows the party is now at 6,400 feet (1,950 meters). So the climbers can predict that if they maintain their present ascent rate, it will take roughly four more hours to reach the summit. Take that information, courtesy of the altimeter, combine it with a look at the weather, the time of day, and the condition of the party members, and the group has the data on which to base a sound decision about whether to proceed with the climb or turn back.

Navigating

An altimeter also can help determine exactly where you are. If you are climbing a ridge or hiking up a trail shown on the map, but you do not know your exact position along the ridge or trail, check the altimeter for the elevation. Your likely location is where the ridge or trail reaches that contour line on the map.

Another way to ask the altimeter where a climbing party is located is to start with a compass bearing to a summit or some other known feature. Find that peak on the map, and plot the bearing line from the mountain back toward the climbing party. The group now knows it must be somewhere along that line—but where? Take an altimeter reading and find out the elevation. The party's likely location is where the compass bearing line crosses a contour line at that elevation on the map.

Navigation gets easier with the aid of an altimeter. If you top a convenient couloir at 9,400 feet (2,870 meters) and gain the summit ridge, make a note of that elevation. On the way back, descend the ridge to that elevation to easily find the couloir again.

Last but not least, an altimeter may reveal whether you are on the real summit when the visibility is too poor to be able to tell by looking around.

Predicting Weather

The altimeter can help in predicting weather. The readings on an altimeter and on a barometer operate in opposition to each other. When one goes up, the other goes down. An altimeter reading showing an increase in elevation when no actual elevation change has taken place (such as at camp overnight) means a falling barometer, which often predicts deteriorating weather. A decreasing altimeter reading, on the other hand, means increasing barometric pressure and improving weather. This is an oversimplification, of course, because weather forecasting is complicated by the wind, local weather peculiarities, and the rate of barometric pressure change. (See Chapter 27, Mountain Weather, for more information on interpreting barometric change.)

Some digital wristwatch altimeters can be adjusted to read barometric pressure instead of altitude, but keep in mind that changes in barometric pressure are useful in assessing the weather only when the readings are taken at a constant elevation (such as in camp). Using

5

the altimeter as a barometer while climbing will give readings that are influenced not only by changes in the weather but also by changes in elevation while climbing. This can lead to erroneous conclusions regarding barometric pressure.

CAUTIONS ABOUT ALTIMETER USE

Because even the most precise and costly altimeters are strongly affected by the weather, do not be misled into trusting them to accuracy greater than is possible. A typical high-quality altimeter may have a resolution—the smallest marked division (of an analog instrument) or the smallest indicated change (of a digital altimeter)—of 3 feet (1 meter). This does not mean that the altimeter will always be that close to the truth; changes in weather could easily throw the reading off by hundreds of feet.

An altimeter expands and contracts due to variations in its temperature, causing changes in the indicated elevation. Try to keep the temperature of an altimeter as constant as possible. Body heat will usually accomplish this with a wristwatch altimeter, particularly if you wear it under a parka when the outside temperature is low. Keep the temperature of an analog altimeter relatively constant by carrying it in a pocket rather than in your pack.

In temperature-compensated altimeters, a bimetallic element adjusts for the effect of temperature when there is no actual change in elevation. The element counterbalances the effect on other parts of the instrument. When you are gaining or losing elevation, however, this adjustment sometimes is not enough, resulting in errors even in altimeters that are temperature-compensated.

Get to know your own altimeter, use it often, check it at every opportunity, and note differences of information between it and the map. You will soon know just what accuracy to expect, and your altimeter will then be a dependable aid to roving the wilds.

THE GLOBAL POSITIONING SYSTEM

The U.S. Department of Defense has placed a system of satellites in orbit around the earth. Small handheld global positioning system (GPS) receivers (fig. 5-13) can pick up the signals from these satellites and give the user's position and altitude to within about 50 feet (15 meters). Most GPS receivers cost from about $100 to $500 and have a variety of features that allow them to store and later recall specific positions (called landmarks or waypoints), determine the compass bearing and the distance between waypoints, and plot out routes comprising a series of waypoints from one position to another.

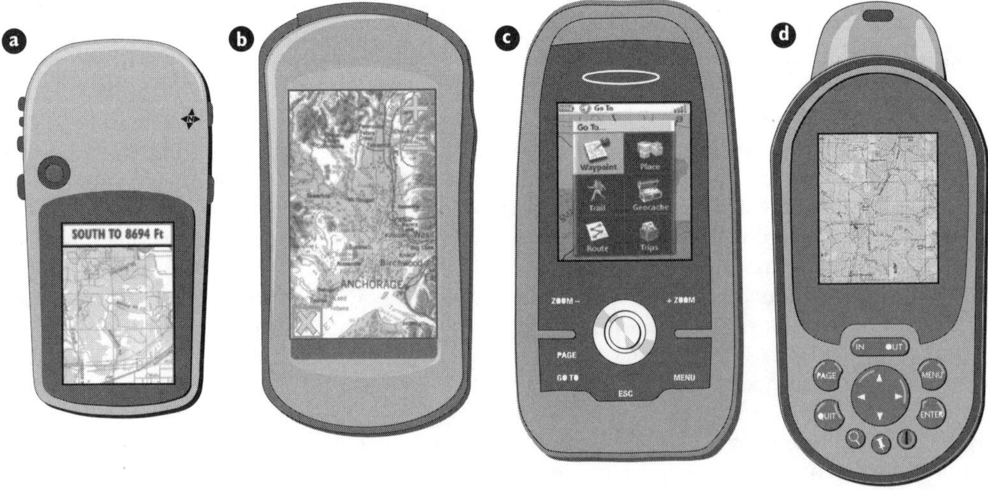

Fig. 5-13. GPS receivers: a, Garmin eTrex series; b, Garmin Oregon series; c, Magellan Triton series; d, DeLorme Earthmate PN series.

WHAT TO LOOK FOR IN A GPS RECEIVER

Before deciding which receiver to buy, talk to friends and acquaintances who already have GPS receivers to learn about their features, ease of operation, ability to work in challenging terrain, water resistance, and other attributes. If possible, borrow a receiver and try it out to learn if it is the receiver for you. If you intend to use it in a cold climate, pay particular attention to the operating temperature limitations stated in the specifications. Some GPS receivers operate reliably down to only freezing; others work down to as low as about 0 degrees Fahrenheit (minus 18 degrees Celsius).

Make sure your chosen GPS receiver can make use of the UTM coordinate system described in "Navigation by Instrument," later in this chapter. Some receivers can make use of additional satellites that are part of the Federal Aviation Administration's Wide Area Augmentation System (WAAS). This can sometimes increase GPS accuracy to as close as 10 feet (3 meters).

Another useful option available on some GPS receivers is built-in map capability: Topographic maps can be uploaded into the receiver from a computer or may be preloaded by the receiver manufacturer, depending on the type of receiver.

To get the most benefit from a GPS receiver, be sure to read its instruction manual carefully and master all of its features. In addition, several good books and useful websites are available that explain GPS in greater detail (see Appendix D, Supplementary Resources).

GETTING STARTED WITH GPS

Start by thoroughly reading the instruction manual and getting totally familiar with your receiver before using it in the wilderness.

The first step is to initialize the receiver to establish your approximate position, using a menu-driven set of commands. Then select which units to use (miles or kilometers, feet or meters, magnetic or true bearings, etc.) and—very important—select the datum to agree with the datum for the topographic map of the area. Many GPS receivers use a default datum called "WGS84" (World Geodetic System 1984), whereas many U.S. topographic maps use the 1927 North American Datum (NAD27) for horizontal position. The difference in position between these two datums can be as much as 1,000 feet (300 meters), so it is essential to do this prior to trying to using a GPS receiver with a map.

Try the GPS receiver out around home, in city parks, and on trail hikes before taking it on a climb. Talk with friends or acquaintances familiar with GPS use to obtain helpful hints.

USING A GPS RECEIVER IN MOUNTAINEERING

This section is intended to give you a general understanding of how to apply GPS usage to mountaineering situations. Below is only one example of how a GPS receiver can help in mountaineering situations. Several more applications are given in "Orientation by Instrument" and "Navigation by Instrument," later in this chapter.

The first rule of using a GPS receiver is to not become dependent on it. The receiver is a delicate battery-powered electronic device that can fail or whose batteries may give out. Always carry a topographic map and a magnetic compass, even if the GPS receiver has topographic map capability. In addition, carry route-marking materials such as flagging and wands, regardless of whether you have a GPS receiver. Some GPS receivers have built-in electronic compasses, which also depend on battery power. These can lose accuracy over time or if the batteries are replaced, requiring occasional recalibrating. For all these reasons, no GPS receiver is a substitute for an ordinary magnetic compass or paper maps. Never rely solely on the GPS receiver.

Here's an example of using a GPS receiver on a climb: Use the receiver along with a compass in order to be sure you can get back to your starting point. At the trailhead or campsite, or wherever your climb starts, turn the receiver on to establish your GPS position. This usually takes several minutes. Save this position as a waypoint, giving it a unique name if desired. Then turn off the receiver to save battery power, and pack it away carefully to protect it from harm while you are climbing. At crucial locations along the route to the objective, again turn on the receiver and establish additional waypoints. Once you are at the destination or turnaround point, use the receiver to find the distance and compass bearing from one waypoint to another to get back to the starting point. Then turn off the receiver and use the compass to travel to the next waypoint.

With some GPS receiver models, if you leave the receiver on during the entire trip, you can later download the tracks and waypoints to map software such as TOPO! and TOPO USA, and then you can see the entire route on the screen of your computer. In particularly challenging navigational situations, or if you wish to make a track of your route for possible future use, you may want to leave the receiver on for extended periods of time, to use the receiver's backtrack feature. If you do this, find a way to attach the receiver or its case to your pack strap to avoid having to hold it in your hand. (You might prefer to use that hand for climbing or for holding an ice ax or a ski pole.) Start each trip with a fresh set of batteries, and avoid becoming totally dependent on the GPS receiver.

LIMITATIONS OF GPS RECEIVERS

Most GPS receivers cannot determine direction, so a compass is required to use the GPS in the wilderness. The GPS receiver can tell the straight-line route from one point to another but has no way of indicating if there is a river, a lake, or a cliff along this route. For this reason, you still must use a topographic map, even if you also have a GPS receiver. The GPS receiver is not a substitute for a map and compass or the ability to use them.

Most GPS receivers will not work at temperatures much below freezing, and battery life is limited to 15 to 30 hours, depending on the model. Lithium batteries are helpful in extending cold-weather battery life.

GPS receivers must track signals from at least four satellites to provide trustworthy position information. If the satellite signals are blocked by heavy forest cover, cliffs, or canyons, this is often not possible. When a GPS receiver is not able to pick up signals from the four satellites it needs in order to provide a three-dimensional position, it sacrifices altitude information in favor of horizontal position. Some receivers indicate that this is happening by displaying a "2D" message or icon to tell you that it is operating in a two-dimensional mode. Other receivers may merely display a "frozen" altitude display if this occurs. In either case, always note whether you are getting a two-dimensional position. If so, then be aware of the fact that the GPS receiver's horizontal position may be significantly in error as well, particularly if you are thousands of feet above sea level. Under such less-than-ideal conditions, horizontal position errors of 1,000 feet (300 meters) or more are possible.

ORIENTATION BY INSTRUMENT

The goal of orientation is to determine that precise point on the earth where you are standing. That position can then be represented by a mere dot on the map, which is known as the point position. There are two less specific levels of orientation. One is called line position: The party knows it is along a certain line on a map—such as a river, a trail, or a bearing or elevation line—but does not know where it is along the line. The least specific is area position: The party knows the general area it is in, but that is about it.

POINT POSITION

The primary objective of orientation is to find out your exact point position. Figuring out exactly where you are is usually relatively simple: Just look around and compare what you see with what is on the map. Sometimes this is not accurate enough, or there is just nothing much nearby to identify on the map. The usual solution then is to get out the compass and try to take bearings on some landscape features. This is an example of orientation by instrument.

With point position known, there is no question about where you are, and you can use that knowledge in identifying on the map any major feature visible on the landscape. You can also identify on the landscape any visible feature shown on the map.

For example, climbers on the summit of Forbidden Peak know their point position: at the top of Forbidden Peak. (Refer back to the topographic map in Figure 5-1.) The climbers see an unknown mountain and want to know what it is. They take a bearing and get 275 degrees. They plot 275 degrees from Forbidden Peak on their topographic map, and it passes through Mount Torment. They conclude that the unknown mountain is Mount Torment.

In reverse, if the climbers know from the map that they are in the vicinity of Mount Torment and want to identify which mountain it is from where they are atop Forbidden Peak, they must do the map work first. They can measure the bearing on the map from Forbidden to Mount Torment and come up with 275 degrees. Keeping 275 at the index line on the compass, they turn the compass until the magnetic needle is aligned with the declination arrow. The direction-of-travel line then points to Mount Torment.

Finding Point Position from a Known Line Position

With line position known, the goal is to determine point position. When climbers know they are on a trail, ridge, or some other identifiable line, they need only one more trustworthy piece of information. For example, they are on Unsavory Ridge (fig. 5-14)—but exactly where? Off in the distance to the southwest is Mount Majestic. A

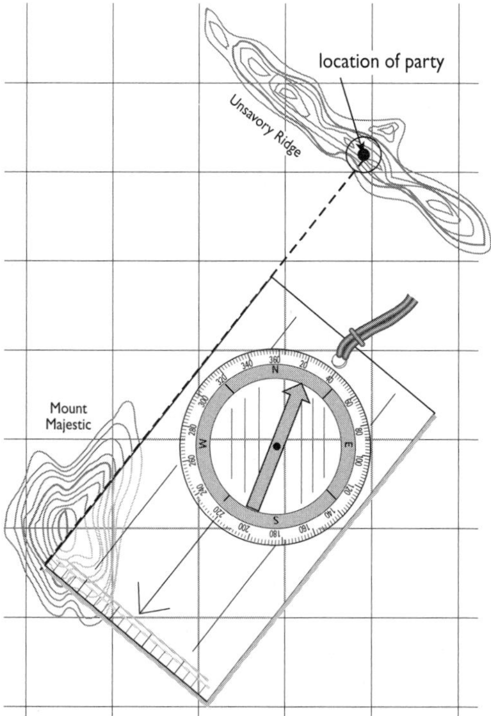

Fig. 5-14. Orientation from a known line position to determine point position (magnetic needle omitted for clarity).

bearing on Majestic reads 220 degrees. Plot 220 degrees from Mount Majestic on the map. Run this line back toward Unsavory Ridge, and where it intersects the ridge is the point position where the climbers are.

Finding Point Position from a Known Area Position

Suppose a climbing party knows only its area position: the general area of Fantastic Crags (fig. 5-15). They want to determine line position and then, from that, point position. To move from knowing area position to knowing point position, two trustworthy pieces of information are needed.

Climbers may be able to use bearings on two visible features. Suppose you take a bearing on Fantastic Peak and get a reading of 38 degrees. You plot a line on the map, through Fantastic Peak, at 38 degrees. You know you must be somewhere on that bearing line, so you now have line position. You can also see Unsavory Spire. A bearing on the spire shows 130 degrees. You plot a second line on the map, through Unsavory Spire, at 130 degrees. The two bearing lines intersect, and that shows your point position. The closer an angle of intersection is to 90 degrees, the more accurate the point position will be.

Use every scrap of information at your disposal, but be sure your conclusions agree with common sense. If you take bearings on Fantastic Peak and Unsavory Spire and find that the two lines on the map intersect in a river, but you are on a high point of land, something is wrong. Try again. Try to take a bearing on another landmark and plot it. If the lines intersect at a map location with no similarity to the terrain where you are, there might be some magnetic anomaly in the rocks, or you may have an inaccurate map. And who knows? Maybe those peaks are not really Fantastic and Unsavory in the first place.

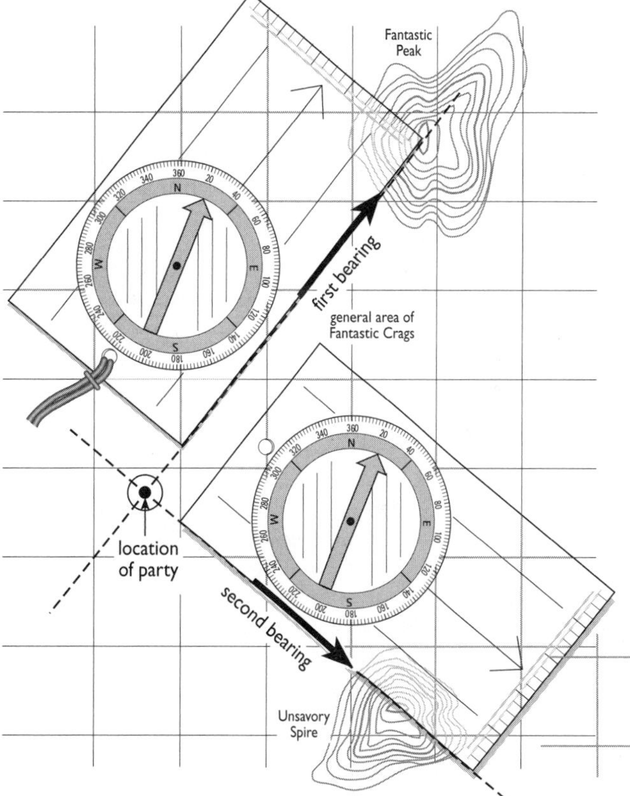

Fig. 5-15. Orientation from a known area position to determine point position (magnetic needle omitted for clarity).

Finding Line Position from a Known Area Position

When the area position is known and there is just one visible feature to take a bearing on, the compass cannot provide anything more than line position. That can be a big help, though. If the climbers are in the general vicinity of Fantastic River, then they can plot a bearing line from the one feature to the river; they then know they are near where the bearing line intersects the river. Perhaps from a study of the map, the climbers can then figure out just exactly where they are. They can also read the altimeter and see on the map where the bearing line intersects the contour line for that elevation.

ORIENTING A MAP

During a trip it sometimes helps to hold the map so that north on the map is pointed in the actual direction of true north. This is known as orienting the map, a good way to gain a better feel of the relationship between the map and the countryside.

It is a simple process (fig. 5-16). Set 0 or 360 degrees at the index line of the compass, and place the compass on the map near its lower-left corner. Put the edge of the compass' base plate along the left edge of the map, with the direction-of-travel line pointing toward north on the map. Then turn the map and compass together until the north-seeking end of the compass needle is aligned with the pointed end of the declination arrow of the compass. The map is now oriented to the scene before you. (Map orientation can give a general feel for the area but cannot replace the more precise methods of orientation covered above.)

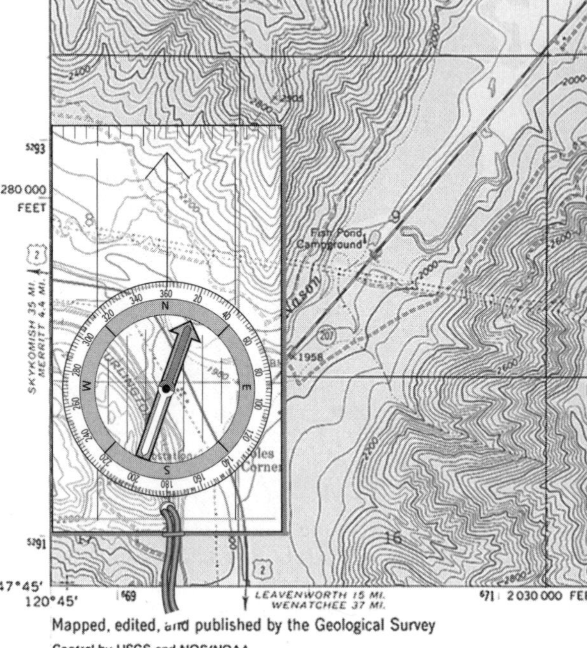

Fig. 5-16. Using the compass to orient a map.

ORIENTATION USING GPS

Suppose a climbing party wants to identify its point position on a topo map. Take out the GPS receiver, turn it on, and let it acquire a good, stable 3-D position. The receiver is probably reading latitude-longitude, the usual default coordinate system. For mountaineering use, however, a much easier system to use is the Universal Transverse Mercator (UTM). The UTM system is a grid of north–south and east–west lines at intervals of 1,000 meters (3,281 feet or 0.62 mile). This is far more precise than the latitude-longitude system, because USGS maps identify latitude and longitude coordinates only every 2.5 minutes—approximately 2 to 3 miles (3 to 4 kilometers). Using the receiver's setup screen, the climbers should be able to change the coordinate system from latitude-longitude to UTM. They can then correlate the UTM numbers on the receiver's screen with the UTM grid on the map. Without using a scale or a ruler, climbers can usually eyeball their position to within about 100 meters (328 feet), which is often close enough to get to within sight of an objective. If greater accuracy is desired, use the "meters" scale at the bottom of the map.

For example, suppose you are climbing Glacier Peak and clouds obscure all visibility. You reach a summit but are not sure whether it is Glacier Peak. You turn on your GPS receiver and let it acquire a position. The UTM numbers on the screen of your GPS receiver are as follows:

10 6 40 612E
53 29 491N

The top number is called the easting, which is the number of meters east of a reference line for your area. The "10" is the UTM zone number, which can be found in the lower-left corner of your USGS topographic map. The numbers "6 40 612E" indicate that your position is 640,612 meters east of the reference line for your area. Along the top edge of the map, you can find the number

"6 40 000mE" (fig. 5-17). This is the full easting (except for zone number). To the right of this is the number 6 41. This is a partial easting, with the "000" meters omitted. You can see that the number "10 6 40 612E" on the screen of the GPS receiver is approximately six-tenths of the way between 6 40 000 and 6 41 000. Your east–west position is therefore about six-tenths of the way between the 6 40 000 and the 6 41 lines.

Along the left edge of the map is the number "53 31 000mN." This is the full northing, which indicates that this point is 5,331,000 meters north of the equator. Below this is a line labeled "53 30" and another labeled "53 29." These are partial northings, with the "000" meters omitted. The lower number displayed on the GPS receiver screen in this example is 53 29 491N. This is a horizontal line about halfway between 53 29 and 53 30. The point where the easting and northing lines intersect is your point position. Finding this point in Figure 5-17 shows that you are on Disappointment Peak, not Glacier Peak.

The internal topographic map capability of some GPS receivers can be useful in quickly identifying your location, but the maps can be difficult to interpret because receivers' screens are small. Such internal maps are therefore useful supplements to conventional paper maps but cannot replace them.

NAVIGATION BY INSTRUMENT

Getting from point A to point B is usually just a matter of keeping an eye on the landscape and watching where you are going, helped by an occasional glance at the map. However, if your current objective is out of sight, take compass in hand, set a bearing, and follow the direction-of-travel line as it guides you to the goal. This is navigation by instrument.

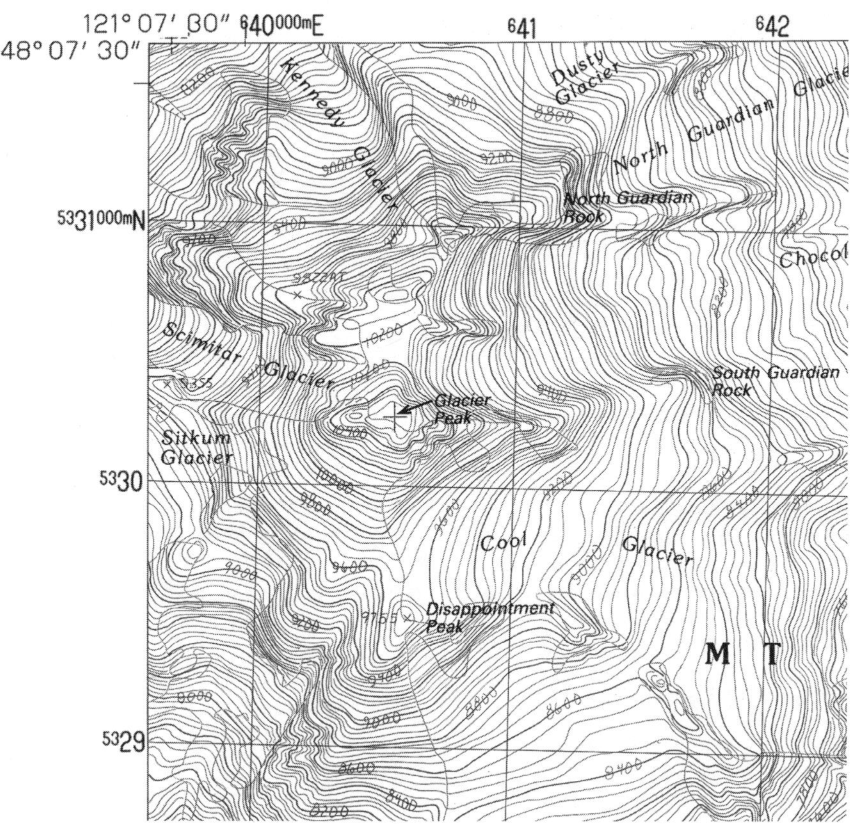

Fig. 5-17. Example of orientation using a GPS receiver with a topo map.

Navigation by instrument is sometimes the only practical method for finding your way. It also serves as a supplement to other methods and as a way of verifying that you are on the right track. Again, use common sense and question a compass bearing that defies reason. (For example, is the declination arrow pointing the wrong way, sending you 180 degrees off course?)

USING MAP AND COMPASS

The most common situation requiring instrument navigation comes when the route is unclear because the topography is featureless or because landmarks are obscured by forest or fog. In this case, the climbers know exactly where they are and where they want to go, and they can identify on the map both their current position and their destination. Simply measure the bearing to the objective on the map and then follow that bearing.

Suppose you measure a bearing of 285 degrees on the map (fig. 5-18a). Read this bearing at the index line and leave it set there as is (fig. 5-18b). Then hold the compass out in front of you as you rotate your body until the north-seeking end of the magnetic needle is aligned with the pointed end of the declination arrow. The direction-of-travel line now points to the objective (fig. 5-18c). Start walking in that direction.

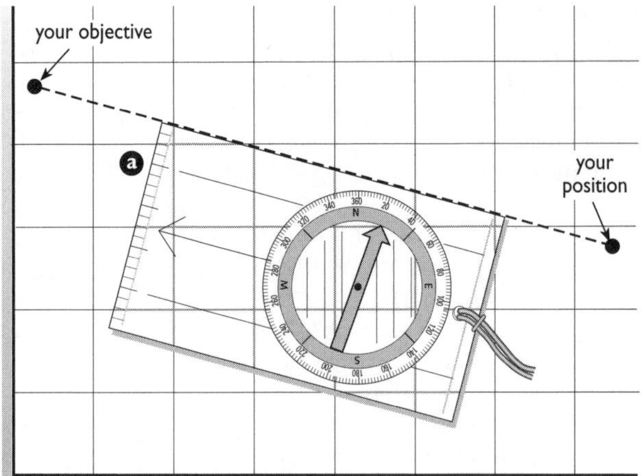

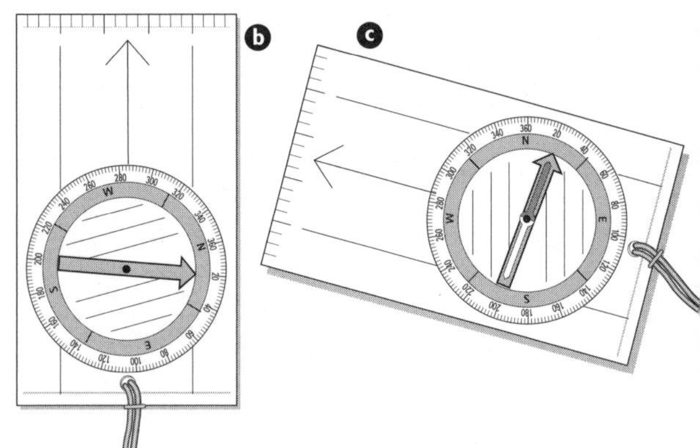

Fig. 5-18. Navigation using the map and compass: a, measuring the bearing on the map from your position to your destination; b, bearing at index line; c, following the bearing (on a and b, magnetic needle omitted for clarity).

USING COMPASS ALONE

Navigators of air and ocean often travel by instrument alone; so can climbers. For example, if you are scrambling toward a pass and clouds begin to obscure it, take a quick compass bearing on the pass. Then follow the bearing, compass in hand if desired. It is not even necessary to note the numerical bearing; just align the magnetic needle with the declination arrow and keep it aligned, and follow the direction-of-travel line.

Likewise, if you are heading into a valley where fog or forest will hide the mountain that is the goal, take a bearing on the peak before dropping into the valley (fig. 5-19). Then navigate by compass through the valley. This method becomes more reliable if two or more people travel together with compass in hand, checking one another's work.

USING INTERMEDIATE OBJECTIVES

The technique of intermediate objectives is handy for those frustrating times when you try to stay exactly on a compass bearing but keep getting diverted by obstructions such as cliffs, dense brush, or crevasses. Sight past the obstruction to a tree, a rock, or another object that is exactly on the bearing line between your position and the principal objective (fig. 5-20a). This is the intermediate objective. Now scramble over to the tree or rock by whatever route is easiest. When you get there, you can be confident that you are still on the correct route. The technique is useful even when there is no obstruction. Moving from one intermediate objective to another means it is possible to put the compass away for those stretches, rather than having to check it every few steps.

Sometimes on snow, on glaciers, or in fog, there are no natural intermediate objectives, just an undifferentiated white landscape. A similar situation can occur in

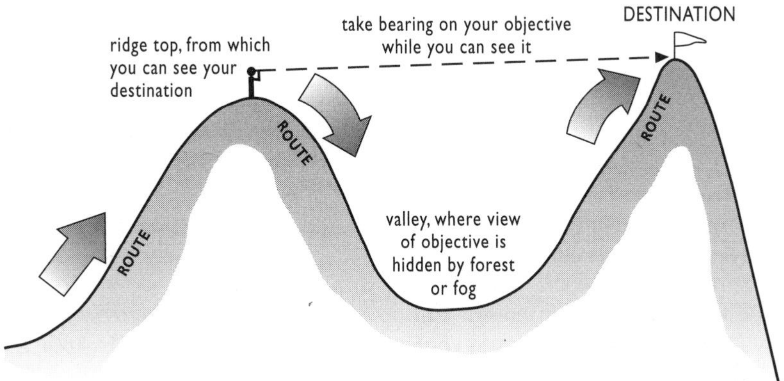

Fig. 5-19. Following a compass bearing when the view of the objective is obscured by forest or fog.

a forest, where all the trees may look the same. Then another member of the party can serve as the intermediate objective (fig. 5-20b). Send that person out to near the limit of visibility or past the obstruction. Wave the party member left or right until the person is directly on the bearing line. That person can then improve the accuracy of the route by taking a back bearing on you. (For a back bearing, keep the same bearing set at the index line, but align the south-seeking end of the magnetic needle with the pointed end of the declination arrow.) The combination of a bearing and a back bearing tends to counteract any compass error.

USING GPS

Suppose a climbing party can identify its desired destination on the map but cannot actually see it in the field. They can read the UTM position of the destination off the map and then enter it into the GPS receiver's memory as a waypoint.

Going back to the Glacier Peak example shown in Figure 5-17, suppose you wish to find a route to the summit of Glacier Peak. You can see that this point is about halfway between the eastings of 6 40 000 and 6 41 000, so you could estimate the easting as 10 6 40 500 (the zone number is 10 in this example). You can also see that the summit is about three-tenths of the way between the northings of 53 30 000 and 53 31 000, so you can estimate the full northing to be 53 30 300N. You can now enter these coordinates into the GPS receiver by simply turning it on and entering the UTM coordinates of 10 6 40 500E and 53 30 300N. You can then name the waypoint (for example, "GLPEAK") and save it.

Once you have entered your destination into the GPS receiver's memory, let it acquire a position. Then ask it

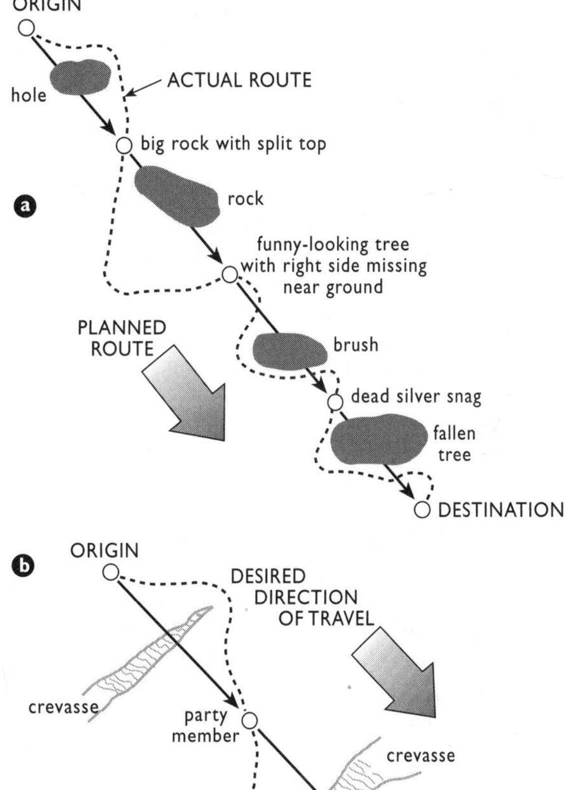

Fig. 5-20. Using intermediate objectives: a, in a forest; b, on a glacier.

to "Go To" the name of the new waypoint ("GLPEAK" in this example), and the receiver will tell you the distance and compass bearing from wherever you are to the summit of Glacier Peak. Then set this bearing on your magnetic compass, turn off the GPS receiver and put it away, and follow the compass bearing until you arrive at Glacier Peak.

What if you get off route due to a crevasse or other obstruction? After passing the obstruction, again turn on the GPS receiver, acquire a position, and again ask it to "Go To" the waypoint that is your destination. The receiver will then tell you the new distance and compass bearing to your destination. Set the new bearing on your compass and follow it to your destination.

LOST

Why do people get lost? Some travel without a map because the route seems obvious. Some people trust their own instincts over the compass. Others do not bother with the map homework that can start them off with a good mental picture of the area. Some do not pay enough attention to the route on the way in to be able to find it on the way out. Some rely on the skill of their climbing partner, who may be in the process of getting them lost. Some do not take the time to think about where they are going because they are in a hurry. They miss junctions or wander off on game trails. They charge mindlessly ahead despite deteriorating weather and visibility or fatigue.

Good navigators are never truly lost—but, having learned humility through years of experience, they always carry enough food, clothing, and bivouac gear to get them through a few days of temporary confusion.

WHAT IF YOUR PARTY IS LOST?

The first rule if your party is lost is to stop. Avoid the temptation to plunge hopefully on. Try to determine where the party is. If that does not work, figure out the last time when the party did know its exact location. If that spot is fairly close, within an hour or so, retrace your steps and get back on route. But if that spot is hours back, the party might instead decide to head toward the baseline they established when they started out. If the party tires or darkness falls before finding its way out, bivouac for the night.

Groups of two or more rarely become dangerously lost, even if they have no wilderness experience. The real danger comes to an individual who is separated from the rest of the party. For this reason, always try to keep everyone together, and assign a rear guard to keep track of any stragglers.

WHAT IF YOU ARE LOST ALONE?

The first rule if you are lost alone is, again, to stop. Look for other members of the party, shout, and listen for answering shouts. Blow your whistle. If the only answer is silence, sit down, regain your calm, and combat terror with reason.

Once you have calmed down, start doing the right things. Look at the map in an attempt to determine your location, and plan a route home in case you do not connect with the other climbers. Mark your location with a cairn or other objects, and then scout in all directions, each time returning to the marked position. Well before dark, prepare for the night by finding water and shelter. Go to an open area so that you can be seen from the air. Spread out some brightly colored clothing or other material to give searchers something to see. Staying busy will raise your spirits; try singing for something to do and to give searchers something to hear.

The odds are that you will be reunited with your group by morning. If not, fight panic. After a night alone, you may decide to hike out to a baseline feature picked out before the trip—a ridge, stream, or highway. If the terrain is too difficult for you to travel alone, it might be better to concentrate on letting yourself be found. It is easier for rescuers to find a lost climber who stays in one place in the open and shouts periodically than one who thrashes on in hysterical hope, one step ahead of the rescue party.

FINDING THE FREEDOM OF THE HILLS

The mountains await those who have learned the skills of orientation, navigation, and routefinding. In large part, navigation is the subject of this entire book because it is so essential to all off-trail adventure.

In medieval times, the greatest honor a visitor could receive was the rights of a citizen and the freedom of the city, sometimes even today symbolized by presenting a guest with the "keys to the city." For the modern alpine traveler, navigation is the key to wandering at will through valleys and meadows, up cliffs and over glaciers, earning the rights of a citizen in a magical land, a mountaineer with the freedom of the hills.

WILDERNESS ROUTEFINDING • APPROACH OBSERVATIONS • WALKING • TRAIL FINDING • SHARING THE WILDERNESS WITH ANIMALS • NEGOTIATING DIFFICULT TERRAIN • READY FOR THE WILDERNESS

Chapter 6
WILDERNESS TRAVEL

Climbing the mountain is one thing; getting from the trailhead to the mountain is another. Wilderness travel is the art of getting there—along trails, around brush, across rock, over snow, and across streams. If you learn the skills of wilderness travel, you open the gateway to the summits.

WILDERNESS ROUTEFINDING

Wilderness routefinding is the art of working out an efficient route from trailhead to summit that is within the abilities of the climbing party. Intuition and luck play a role, but it takes skill and experience to surmount the hazards and hurdles between here and there. Aside from orientation and navigation skills described in Chapter 5, Navigation, climbers rely on their ability to interpret trail, rock, snow, and weather conditions before and during the climb, to skillfully travel over different terrain, and to comprehend the clues that the wilderness offers as they go.

GATHER ROUTE INFORMATION

The more information you gather ahead of time, the better your judgment is later on. Take time to research the geology and climate of the area the party will be climbing in, especially if the party frequents the area. Each mountain range has its own peculiarities that affect routefinding. Mountaineers familiar with the Canadian Rockies, accustomed to broad valleys and open forests, will need to learn new rules to contend with the heavily vegetated, narrow canyons of British Columbia's Coast Range. The Pacific Northwest mountaineer used to deep snow at 4,000 feet (1,200 meters) in June will discover drastically different June conditions in the California Sierras.

Guidebooks offer detailed climb descriptions, including information on the climbing route, the estimated time necessary to complete it, elevation gain, distance, and so forth. But be aware that guidebooks become outdated; one bad winter can completely alter an approach. Make sure to have the latest edition, and take a look at two or three different guidebooks. Publications that cover other aspects of the area—its skiing, hiking, geology, and history—also will have something to offer as the party plans its trip.

Check online resources for weather forecasts, snow conditions, and Forest Service and Park Service information. Climbers who have made the trip can describe landmarks, hazards, and routefinding difficulties. Check climbers' message boards covering the area of the climb. Exercise some judgment when using these types of computer sources, though; there is variable accountability on the Internet, and it can be difficult to gauge the credibility of those posting advice there.

Useful details are packed into maps of all sorts: Forest Service maps, road maps, aerial maps, climbers' sketch maps, and topographic maps. For a trip into an area that is especially unfamiliar to you, more preparation is needed. This might include scouting into the area, observations from vantage points, or study of oblique aerial photos. Forest Service or Park Service rangers can usually provide information on road and trail conditions. The most popular climbing areas may even have designated climbing rangers who are in the mountains regularly and can give informed and current reports. Some of the digital sources of topographic maps referenced in Chapter 5, Navigation, can even provide invaluable three-dimensional views of portions of maps from various vantages (see the Chapter 5 section of Appendix D, Supplementary Resources).

Some of the best route details come out of conversations with locals. The person pouring coffee in the local cafe may be a veteran climber of the area. Ask about trails that do not appear on the maps, snow conditions, and the best places to ford streams.

Always consider the season and the amount of snowfall in a given year when preparing for a climb. Early in the season, avalanche danger may be high on steep slopes, especially if there is a heavy accumulation of snow from the winter before. Late in the season, or following a warm winter with low snowfall, a slope that is usually covered in snow may be exposed talus.

Finally, do not let outdated information ruin a trip. Check beforehand with the appropriate agencies about roads and trails, especially closures, and about climbing routes and regulations, permits, and camping requirements.

LEARN FROM EXPERIENCE

There is no substitute for firsthand experience. Climb with seasoned mountaineers, watch their techniques, and ask questions. The more familiar you are with the wilderness, the greater your freedom to find your own way.

APPROACH OBSERVATIONS

Climb with your eyes. Continually study the mountain for climbing routes. A distant view can reveal patterns of ridges, cliffs, snowfields, and glaciers, as well as the degree of incline. At closer range, details of fault lines, bands of cliffs, and crevasse fields appear. Look for clues of routes: ridges with lower incline than the faces they divide; cracks, ledges, and chimneys leading up or across the faces; snowfields or glaciers offering easy or predictable pitches. Look for climbable sections and link them together. With experience comes a good eye for what you know you can climb.

If the approach skirts the base of the mountain, try to view the peak from various perspectives. Even moderate slopes can appear steep when you look at them head on. A system of ledges indistinguishable against background cliffs may show clearly from another angle or as shadows cross the mountain.

The presence of snow sometimes promises a modest angle and easy climbing, because snow does not last long on slopes of greater than 50 degrees. Snow and shrubs that appear on distant rock faces often turn out to be "sidewalks" with smaller ledges between. However, snow can be deceptive. What appear to be snowfields high on the mountain may be ice. Deep, high-angle couloirs often retain snow or ice year-round, especially when shaded.

WATCH FOR HAZARDS

Stay alert to climbing hazards. Study snowfields and icefalls for avalanche danger and cliffs for signs of possible rockfall. Snowfields reveal recent rockfall by the appearance of dirty snow or rock-filled craters. If the route goes through avalanche and rockfall territory, travel in the cold hours of night or very early morning, before the sun melts the ice that bonds precariously perched boulders and ice towers. Move through such places quickly. Take rest breaks before or after danger zones, and when you enter them, try not to get caught behind slower parties. If possible, avoid these areas in heavy rain. Also watch for changing weather conditions (see Chapter 27, Mountain Weather).

Keep evaluating hazards and looking for continuous routes. If the route begins to look questionable, search for alternatives and make decisions as early as possible.

THINK ABOUT THE RETURN

Always consider the descent while making the approach. What is easy going up is not necessarily easy going down, nor is it easy to find. Look back frequently, take notes, take GPS and altimeter readings, and, if necessary, mark the route. (For additional information, see Chapter 5, Navigation; Chapter 7, Leave No Trace; and Chapter 16, Snow Travel and Climbing.)

The approach is also a time for looking ahead to the end of the day. Consider where the party has to be by dark and whether it will be safe to travel by headlamp if necessary. Keep an eye out for emergency campsites, water supplies, and anything else that might make the return trip easier and safer.

WALKING

Reaching the summit often involves more walking than climbing. Walking skill is as important as any other that climbers learn.

Before hitting the trail, stretch your legs, hips, back, and shoulders. Drink some water. Consider taping or putting moleskin on areas prone to blisters. Take time to get a good fit of your pack and boots to avoid aches and pains—and frequent stops—later on.

Prepare for stops before starting. Use your pack's outside pockets for items that will be needed repeatedly throughout the day, such as snacks, water, jacket, hat, gloves, gaiters, sunglasses, and headlamp. Not only will it be easy for you to reach these items, but other members of the party can also reach them, without your needing to remove your pack or even reduce the pace. Strap your ice ax and trekking poles to the outside of your pack so they are readily available for rough terrain. The ice ax will be very useful, even before snow line.

PACE

Setting the right pace from the start ensures a happier, stronger day of climbing. The most common mistake is walking too fast, perhaps out of concern for the long miles ahead or from a desire to perform well with companions. Why get worn out on the first mile of a 10-mile (16-kilometer) approach if the whole day is available? You are going too fast if you cannot sustain your pace hour after hour, or if you cannot converse without losing your breath. Take your time and enjoy yourself (see the "Hiking with the Group" sidebar).

The other mistake is walking too slowly. This only prolongs the hike and leaves less time to negotiate the more technical portions of the trip. If you are walking slowly due to fatigue, remember that the body has considerable reserves. Muscles may ache but still have 10 miles left in them. A degree of discomfort is inevitable; walking too fast or too slow only creates additional fatigue.

At the start, walk slowly to allow your body to warm up. Before you start to sweat, take a break and remove some clothing. Increase the pace, and accept the pain as your body works harder to experience its second wind. Physiologically, your heartbeat and circulation increase, and muscles loosen. As endorphins kick in and the feelings of physical stress subside, you feel strong and happy.

Vary the pace depending on the trail. Plod slowly and methodically up steep hills. As the grade lessens, pick up the tempo. Eventually you will find a natural pace that adapts to pack weight, terrain, weather, and other conditions.

The pace will inevitably slow late in the day as fatigue sets in. Adrenaline may fuel short bursts of exertion, but there is no "third wind."

THE REST STEP

Slow and steady is a pace that gains the summit. On steep slopes, in snow, and at high altitudes, the rest step controls your pace and reduces fatigue. Use this technique instead of frequent rest stops whenever legs or lungs need to recuperate. The rest step is simple but subtle; practice it.

The essence of the technique is to end every step with a momentary but complete stop, giving your leg muscles a rest. Swing one foot forward for the next step. Stand upright and exhale while letting your rear leg support your entire body weight (fig. 6-1a). Straighten your rear leg so that you are supported by bone, not muscle. Feel the weight sink into your bones and foot. Now completely relax and soften the muscles of your forward leg, especially the thigh. This momentary rest, no matter how brief, refreshes the muscle. Then take a breath and swing your rear foot forward for the next step (fig. 6-1b), and repeat the rest step for your other leg (fig. 6-1c).

Synchronize breathing with leg movements. Typically, take a new breath with each step. Inhale and take a step up; exhale while pausing and letting your front

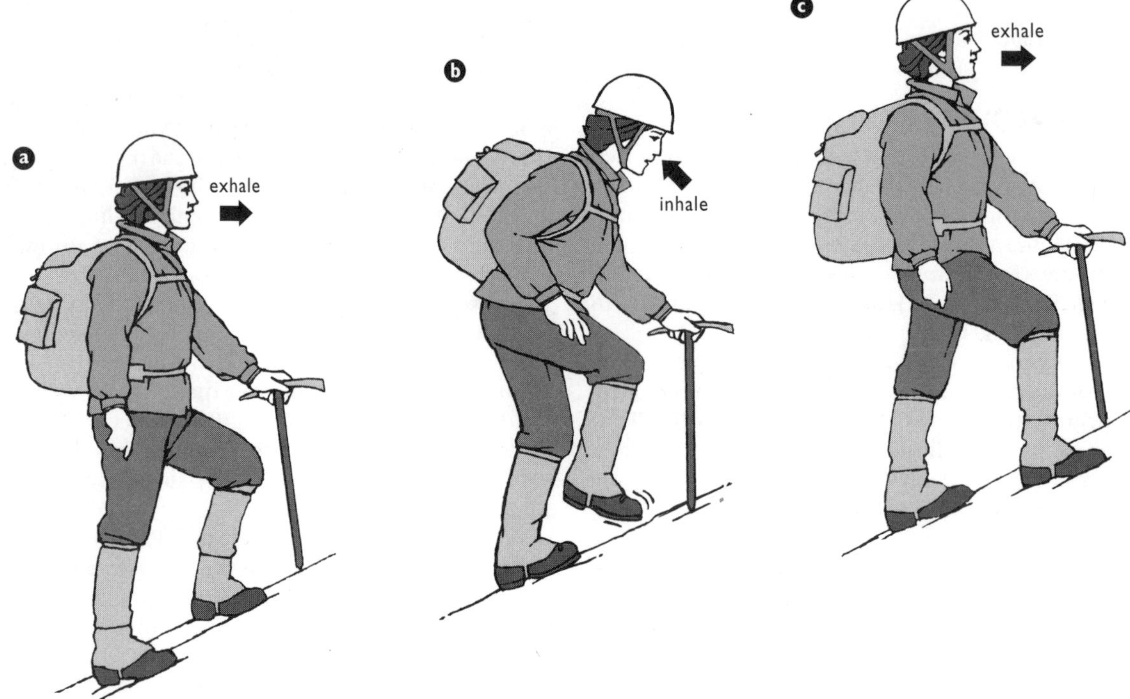

Fig. 6-1. The rest step: a, stand with entire body weight on right leg and exhale, completely relaxing left leg; b, inhale and step forward with right leg, shifting weight to left leg; c, place entire body weight on left leg and exhale, completely relaxing right leg.

leg rest as your rear leg supports your weight. Keep repeating the sequence. Many experienced climbers find a tune they run over in their head to keep a comfortable rhythm. The number of breaths per step depends on the difficulty of the work and your level of fatigue. At high altitudes, climbers sometimes take three or four deep breaths before each step up.

The rest step requires patience. The monotony of the pace can undermine morale, especially when you are following another climber up a snowfield and there is no routefinding or step kicking to occupy your thoughts. Play an upbeat tune in your head. Trust the technique to chew up the miles, even when the summit seems to recede.

RESTS

Rests allow your body to recover from strenuous activity and to maintain an efficient pace. Take rests only when necessary; otherwise, keep moving. Numerous unnecessary stops can turn a 10-hour day into a 15-hour day, affecting group morale or even the team's chance of reaching a summit.

During the first half hour, stop to allow the group to readjust bootlaces and pack straps, add or take off layers of clothing, stretch warmed-up muscles, etc.

Take short breathers—once every one to one and a half hours—during the early part of the day, while bodies are fresh. Rest in a standing or semireclining position, leaning against a tree or hillside to remove pack weight from your shoulders. Take deep breaths, and have a bite to eat and something to drink. Stay hydrated—always drink at every stop.

Remember to declare regular party separations (toilet stops), especially out of courtesy to the person who may be too shy to express the need. However, in order to minimize your impact on the mountains, your first toilet stop should be at the last available restroom facility found at or before the trailhead.

Later in the day, fatigue may demand more complete relaxation, and the party can take a full rest every two hours or so. Look for a place with advantages, such as water or convenient slopes for removing packs and enjoying a view. Stretch muscles and put on additional clothing to avoid stiffness and chilling. Remove extra clothing before starting out again in order to prevent another stop a few minutes down the trail.

DOWNHILL

Walking downhill is a mixed blessing. The pace quickens without increasing fatigue; however, climbers may feel pain long after the day is over. When you walk downhill, your body and pack weight drop abruptly on your legs, knees, and feet. Toes jam forward. Jolts travel up your spine and jar your entire body.

Avoid a host of injuries—including blisters, knee cartilage damage, sore toes, blackened toenails, headaches, and back pain—just by using a few of the following tricks:

- Trim toenails close before starting out.
- Tighten laces—especially on the upper part of the boot—to reduce movement inside the boot and avoid jamming toes.
- Bend the knees with each step to cushion the shock.
- Place each foot lightly, as if it were already sore.
- Use ski or trekking poles to reduce the load on the knees and to provide additional stability.
- Maintain a measured pace that is slower than the one urged by gravity.
- Use an ice ax for balance or a brake when necessary. The ice ax is not just for snow. It is also helpful in steep meadow, forest, and heather. (To learn ice ax techniques, see Chapter 16, Snow Travel and Climbing.)

SIDEHILL

The ups and downs of climbing are far preferable to the torments of cross-country sidehilling (traversing). Walking across the side of a slope twists your ankles, contorts your hips, and undermines balance. If possible, abandon a sidehill and drop down into a brush-free valley or go up onto a rounded ridge. If traversing is unavoidable, look for rocks, animal trails, and the ground just above clumps of grass or heather to provide flat spots of relief. Switchback often to avoid ankle strain.

HIKING WITH THE GROUP

Walking with others involves certain considerations that help make travel more efficient and enjoyable:

- **Set a pace that makes good time but does not burn out slower climbers.** Adjust the party's pace so that slower climbers do not fall far behind. Do not allow anyone to travel alone, either last or first. Give the last person time to catch up with the party at rest stops—and time to rest once that person gets there.
- **Try putting the slowest person in front to set the pace.** This helps keep the group together and may motivate a slow hiker to set a faster pace than usual.
- **Redistribute group gear to people who are full of energy.**
- **Stay three to five paces behind the person ahead.** Give the climber—as well as that person's ice ax—some space.
- **Stay close to the group.** Do not lose contact with other hikers or make them continually wait for you or wonder how far ahead you are.
- **Step off the trail when you stop.**
- **Ask permission to pass,** and pick a good spot to do so.
- **Mind the person behind you when grabbing branches.** Before releasing branches, look back and call out "Branch."
- **Be courteous when meeting an oncoming party.** Traditionally, the party heading downhill steps aside to let the ascending climbers continue upward without breaking pace. However, in steep terrain or if the descending party is larger, the climbers moving uphill may step aside and take a few breaths. When meeting pack animals, move aside and stand on the downhill side of the trail; speak quietly and make no sudden movements. People on mountain bikes should always yield to those on foot.
- **Select gathering points for the party** during long approaches and descents where routefinding is not a concern. This allows party members to find their natural pace within smaller groups. Regroup at trail junctions and difficult stream crossings. Ask the most experienced members to take front and rear positions.
- **Be cheerful and helpful.** Be someone you would want to hike with.

TRAIL FINDING

For a wilderness traveler, a trail is any visible route, no matter how ragged, that efficiently gets the party where they want to go. The goal is to find the easiest route using the tools at hand: awareness of the terrain, navigational skills, weather conditions, and tips from guidebooks and experts.

Even in popular areas with heavy foot traffic and signage, keep alert to find and stay on the trail. Missing a turnoff is easy when a sign is gone or where logging, erosion, avalanche, or rockfall obliterates the trail. On an established forest trail in deep snow, saw-cut log ends peeking through may be the only indication of a trail's location.

Old blazes cut in tree trunks, or ribbon tied to branches, often mark the trail through a forest. Rock cairns (piles of rocks placed along the route as markers where the path is not obvious) may show the way above timberline. These pointers may be unreliable. A tiny cairn or a wisp of ribbon may indicate nothing more than a lost climber, a route to an alternate destination, or an old route since obstructed by rockfall.

The trick is to stay on the trail until the inevitable moment it disappears or until it becomes necessary to head off-trail in order to go in the right direction. Choose a course that a trail would follow if there were a trail. Trail builders look for the easiest way to go. Do as they do.

SHARING THE WILDERNESS WITH ANIMALS

Alpine wildlife is fascinating and often charming, but the birds and animals should be enjoyed from a distance and not disturbed. When you encounter animals on the route, move slowly and allow them plenty of time to drift away. Try to pass on their downhill side; typically they head uphill to escape. Give them plenty of elbow room. An animal rushing from a close encounter with a human is in danger of stress or injury; if it has too many of these encounters, it may feel forced to abandon its home grounds for poorer terrain.

BEARS

In bear country, stay out of the "personal space" of bears. Try not to surprise them. Whenever possible, go around brushy ravines with poor visibility rather than through them, even if it makes the route considerably longer. Make plenty of noise in unavoidable lower-visibility areas to warn animals of your approach.

If the climbing party surprises a bear or cougar, do not turn and run. Running may elicit a chase response in the large predator, and bears and cougars are very fast runners. Instead, stand your ground, face the animal, talk, and slowly edge away at a walk while still facing the animal. (See Appendix D, Supplementary Resources, for specific information about handling animal encounters.)

NEGOTIATING DIFFICULT TERRAIN

The biggest barriers on the way to a mountaintop often appear before snow line.

BRUSH

Brush thrives in young forests or in wet, low altitude, subalpine areas that have few trees. A river that frequently changes course prevents large-tree growth and permits brush to thrive. In gullies swept by winter avalanches, the shrubs simply bend undamaged under the snow and flourish in spring and summer. Brush can be a backcountry horror, making for difficult, dangerous travel. Downward-slanting vine maple and alder are slippery. Brush obscures the peril of cliffs, boulders, and ravines. Brush snares ropes and ice-ax picks. The best policy is to avoid brush. Try the following techniques:

- **Use trails as much as possible.** Five miles (8 kilometers) of trail may be less work and take less time than 1 mile (1.6 kilometers) of brush.
- **Travel when snow covers brush.** Some valleys are easy going in the spring when it is possible to walk on snow, but they are almost impossible in summer when it is necessary to burrow through the brush.
- **Avoid avalanche tracks.** Avalanches are less frequent on southern or western slopes in the northern hemisphere. When you are climbing a valley wall, stay in the trees between avalanche tracks.
- **Aim for the big trees,** where brush is thinner. Mature forests block sunlight and stifle brush growth.
- **Travel on talus, scree, or snow remnants** rather than in adjacent thickets.
- **Look for game trails.** Animals generally follow the path of least resistance. Take care not to startle large animals in heavy brush.
- **Travel on ridges and ridge spurs.** They may be

dry and brushless, whereas creek bottoms and valley floors are often choked with vegetation.
- **Scout both sides of a stream** for the route with the least amount of bushwhacking.
- **Consider going into the stream channel** if the route parallels a stream. Wading may be necessary, but the streambed can be an easier tunnel through the brush. Dry streambeds are often ideal. Take care in deep canyons, where waterfalls and fallen trees interrupt a stream.
- **Take a high route.** Climb directly to timberline or a ridge top.
- **Go up to the base of side bluffs.** There is often an open, flattened corridor next to the rock.

TALUS, SCREE, AND BOULDERS

Mountain peaks constantly crumble, dropping rock fragments that pile up below as talus, scree, and boulders. Most of the rubble pours from gullies and spreads out in alluvial fans that often merge into one another, forming a broad band of broken rock between valley greenery and the peaks. These fans can alternate in vertical strips with forest. Talus consists of the larger fragments, usually big enough to step on individually. Scree is smaller—from the size of coarse sand up to a couple inches across—and may flow a bit around your feet when you step on it. When even larger rocks fall off cliff faces, they form boulder fields.

Talus slopes build gradually over the ages. On the oldest slopes, soil fills the spaces between the rocks, locking them together to create smooth pathways. Talus can be loose on volcanoes and younger mountains, where vegetation has not filled in the spaces. Even large rocks can roll. Try for a route where the rock is lichen-covered, which indicates that the rock has remained in place for a long time.

Slopes of talus, scree, and boulders can either help or hinder a climber. Most offer handy, brush-free pathways to the mountains. Some are loose and dangerous, with sharp-edged rock that can cause injury.

Move nimbly on talus, ready to leap away if a rock shifts underfoot. Use your eyes and plan four or five steps ahead. Take care on wet talus.

Facing the exposure while descending talus, scree, or boulders can be intimidating. Climbers may hesitate or move slowly. This can be dangerous. Move in short, quick steps, and know where the next step is, to be ready to quickly get off a moving rock and avoid injury. Trekking poles or an ice ax are helpful, as long as they are always in front of you.

Loose scree can make going uphill a slow-motion torment, with each step lost as your foot settles in. Stepping on or just above a larger rock in scree can pry or wedge it out. However, descents can be fun. It may be possible to move down the scree in a sliding stride something like cross-country skiing or plunge-stepping down snow. Ice axes are helpful; the technique on scree is similar to that on snow (see Chapter 16, Snow Travel and Climbing). Nonetheless, be aware that scree can sometimes consist of only a thin, ball bearing–size cover over large rocks. If there is vegetation on the slope, avoid setting off scree slides that can damage the plants.

Although riding a scree slope can be fun, bits of rock can work their way into your boots and cause discomfort when you reach talus or a downward trail. Wear gaiters, even in the summer, just for scree.

Boulder fields can be pleasant alternatives to being tortured by scree slopes, but they have their own dangers. Normally, fallen boulders form a steep slope beneath the cliff they detached from—the steepest slope that such boulders can pile up in is called the angle of repose. The boulders landing on even steeper slopes tend to fall off unless stabilized by vegetation. The most commonly traveled routes up boulder fields are usually quite stable, since foot traffic has gradually shifted the riskiest boulders to more stable places. Beware the unfrequented boulder field—where there are no boot marks on the boulder moss, for instance.

Sometimes the route ascends a steep gully filled with a mix of boulders embedded in talus and scree—this is a classic scenario for party-induced rockfall. Disturbing one key stone on a glacial moraine or a talus slope can set off a rock avalanche.

MINIMIZE BRUSH HASSLES

Some skirmishes with brush are inevitable; here are some tips for dealing with it:

- Choose the shortest route across the brushy area.
- Look for animal trails through the brush.
- Use fallen trees with long, straight trunks as elevated walkways.
- Push and pull the bushes apart, sometimes by stepping on lower limbs and lifting and clinging to higher ones to make a passageway.
- Use hardy shrubs as handholds on steep terrain.

Safety dictates traveling outside the fall line of climbers above and below you if possible. If you are in a narrow gully where this is not possible, tread gently and be ready to shout "Rock! Rock!" if a stone dislodges. Keep the party close together so a rock set off by one climber cannot gain dangerous momentum before reaching others (fig. 6-2a). Consider permitting just one climber, or small groups keeping closely together, to move at a time while the rest of the part remains in protected spots (fig. 6-2b).

Party-induced rockfall is by no means the only hazard of loose gullies. Even rainfall can set off smaller or bigger rockfall. Other times, rockfall may be set off by a different climbing party out of sight. Overall, rockfall is one of the most common causes of mountain accidents, so beware!

SNOW

Snow can be a blessing in wilderness travel, especially if climbers study weather and snow conditions before the climb. Many peaks are best climbed early in the season when consolidated snow covers talus, brush, and logging

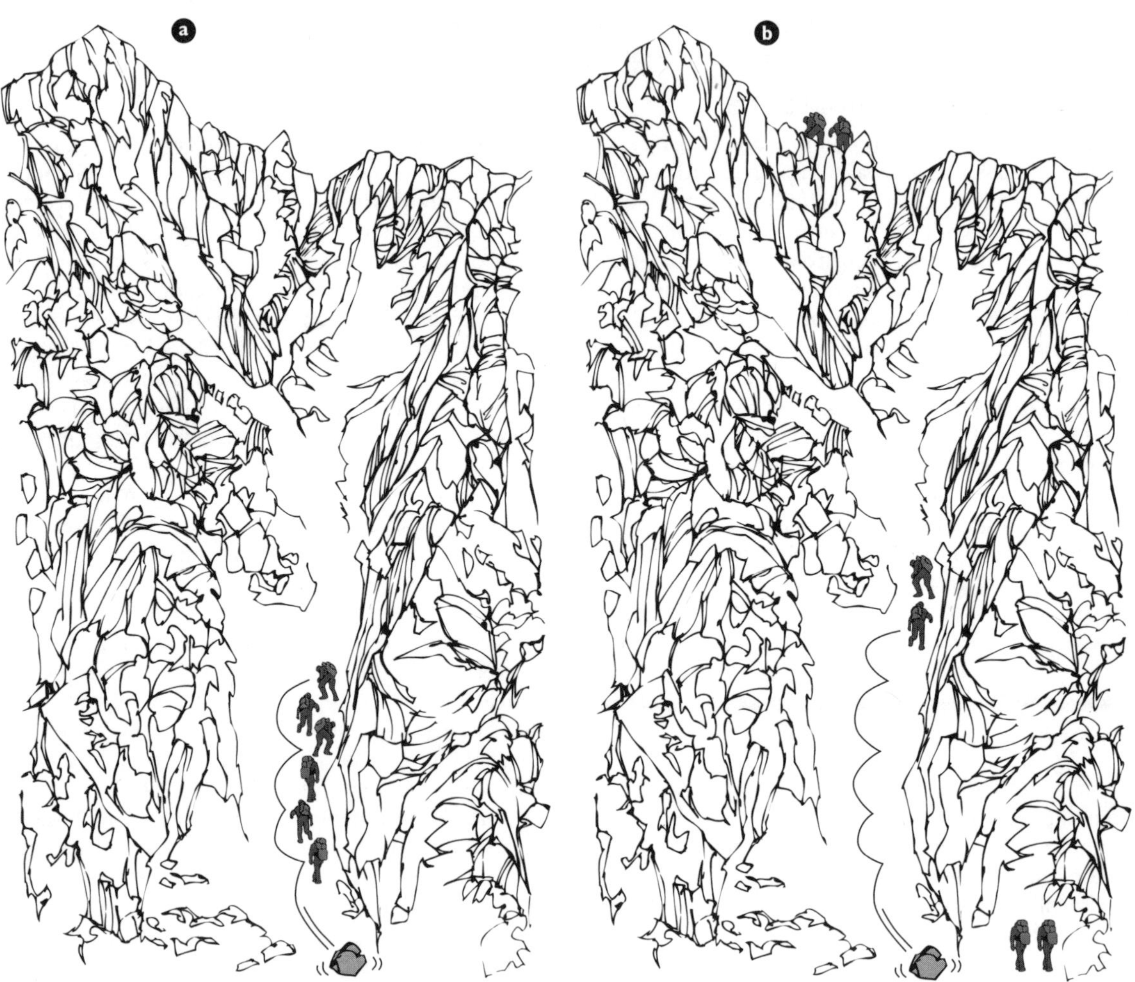

Fig. 6-2. Traveling safely on loose rock: a, climbers stay close together so a dislodged rock does not gain dangerous momentum before reaching the climbers below; b, climbers ascend in pairs or small groups out of one another's fall line, so a dislodged rock harmlessly passes the climbers below.

slash. Snow bridges provide easy access over streams.

However, in a different season or with less-than-ideal snow conditions, snow can be a curse. Trails are lost under snow or are washed out by avalanche or heavy thaw. Thin snow is unstable. And, given the time of day, the pace, or changing weather conditions, a party may encounter different snow conditions on the approach, the climb, and the descent.

If there is snow on the approach, watch for visible terrain features, because they may indicate thin or melting snow. The snow next to logs and boulders often covers holes and soft spots called moats, which occur when the snow partially melts away from the wood and the rock. A moat is common around trees where lower limbs keep the snow from filling in. Probe with an ice ax to avoid likely trouble spots, step wide off logs and rocks, and stay away from treetops poking above the snow. If the snow is thin on a talus slope, there can be large voids under the snow that are easy to punch through. Go slow on talus on the return trip if the snow is thin.

Streams will melt the underside of a snow bridge until it can no longer support your weight. To guard against a dunking, watch for depressions in the snow and variations in color or texture, and listen for sounds of running water. Water emerging at the foot of a snowfield indicates the existence, and perhaps the size, of a cavity beneath the snow. Probe for thin spots with your ice ax.

With experience, you will recognize both the advantages and dangers of snow and learn to use the medium to make wilderness travel easier and more enjoyable. See Chapter 16, Snow Travel and Climbing, and Chapter 26, The Cycle of Snow, for more information.

RIVERS AND STREAMS

When your objective lies on the far side of a sizable river or stream, crossing it is a major factor in route selection. Crossings can consume huge amounts of time and energy, and they can be the most dangerous part of the trip.

Finding the Crossing

Try to get a distant, overall view of the river and scope out crossing possibilities. This can be more useful than a hundred close looks from the riverbank. When a distant view is impossible or unhelpful, the party may be stuck with either thrashing through the river-bottom brush looking for a way across or traversing the slopes high above the river in hopes of a sure crossing.

The surrounding landscape indicates the options. In a deep forest, there is a good chance of finding easy passage on a large log or logjam, even over wide rivers. Higher in the mountains, foot logs are harder to come by, especially if the river frequently changes course and prevents the growth of large trees near its channel.

If it is necessary to wade across, find the widest part of the river. The narrows may be the shortest way, but they are also the deepest, swiftest, and most dangerous. If snowmelt feeds a river, its flow is at a minimum in the early morning. Sometimes a party may camp overnight to take advantage of this morning low water.

Making the Crossing

Unfasten the hip belt and sternum straps of your pack before you try any stream crossing that may require swimming in case of a fall. It is necessary to be able to remove your pack in a hurry.

Logs. A foot log is a great way across. If the log is thin, slippery, or steeply inclined, use a trekking pole (or poles), an ice ax, a stick, crampons, or a tightly stretched hand line (see below) to help with balance, traction, and support. Sit down and scoot across if that helps.

Boulder hopping. Boulders offer another way across. Before you cross, mentally rehearse the entire sequence of leaps. Safety lies in smooth and steady progress over stones that may be too slippery and unsteady for you to stop on for more than an instant. Use an ice ax or trekking pole(s) for additional balance.

Wading. If you are wading, try to keep your gear dry. If the water is placid and the stones rounded, put your boots in your pack while you wade across. In tougher conditions, wear your boots, but put your socks and insoles in the pack; on the far side, drain your boots and replace the dry insoles and socks. In deeper crossings, consider removing your pants or other clothing. Loose clothing increases the drag from the water, but it also reduces chilling and may permit a longer crossing.

If you are trying to cross where the water is deep but not swift, cross with the least force against your body by angling downstream at about the same speed as the current. However, the best way to cross is to face upstream, lean into the current, and stab an ice ax, trekking pole, or stout stick upstream for a third point of support. Your leading foot probes for solid placement on the shifting river bottom, your following foot advances, and you thrust the ax or pole into a new position.

Swift water is easy to underestimate. With one false step, you can be pushed under and dashed against rocks and logs or sent bouncing along in white water. Water is dangerous whenever it boils above your knee. A swift stream flowing only shin deep can boil up against your knees. Knee-deep water may boil above your waist and give a disconcerting sensation of buoyancy. Frothy water, containing a great deal of air, is wet enough to drown in but may not be dense enough to float the human body. Streams fed by glaciers present an added difficulty because their bottoms are hidden by milky water from glacier-milled rock flour.

Team crossing. Two or more travelers can cross together, taking turns securing each other as one person moves to a solid new stance. Team crossing with a pole is another method. Team members enter the water, each grasping the pole, which is parallel to the flow of the stream. The upstream member breaks the force of the current. Anyone who slips hangs onto the pole while the others keep the pole steady.

Hand lines. A hand line for small streams can be helpful. Angle the line downstream so that if any climbers lose their footing, they will be swept to shore. If a nylon climbing rope is the only option available, consider the rope stretch. Always use appropriate anchors (see Chapter 10, Belaying).

Using ropes for stream crossings in deep, swift water can be hazardous. If someone is belayed across the river, there is a possibility that the crossing person can be held by the belay but trapped underwater. Consider belaying the pack, however. If anyone falls, they can shed their pack and it will not get swept away.

Falling In

If you are swept downstream by a swift current, the safest position is on your back with your feet pointed downstream; backstroke to steer. This position vastly improves your chances for survival with minimal injuries. Be alert. If you approach a "strainer" (small dam or collection of debris), switch quickly to normal headfirst swimming. Swim furiously to stay high in the water and get on top of the debris. The strainer may be your route ashore.

If falling off a log into the water seems imminent, try to fall off on the downstream side to avoid getting swept under the log.

If a member of the party falls in, those on shore can try to reach out with a pole, ice ax, or branch. It may be possible to throw out a floating object, such as an inflated water bag. Make a realistic evaluation of the danger to yourself before you decide to go into the stream to attempt a hands-on rescue.

READY FOR THE WILDERNESS

Traveling in the wilderness is like wandering in a foreign country. The unfamiliarity of a place is the attraction, yet it also limits the journey. Preparation is essential, and nothing rivals the knowledge gained from personal experience.

Immerse yourself in the wilderness again and again; study it like a new language. Use all five senses to master the "vocabulary" of the terrain. Some of your best moments will come when you discover your ability to respond well to what it asks of you.

With fluency comes the freedom to roam, and with that freedom comes responsibility. The next chapter discusses ways to keep the wild places wild for those who travel after us, so they too can experience the exhilaration of discovery.

PLANNING ACHIEVES MORE THAN A SUMMIT • TRAVEL AND CAMP ON DURABLE SURFACES • USE STOVES, NOT CAMPFIRES • DISPOSE OF WASTE PROPERLY • CLEANING UP • DO NOT DISTURB • RESPECTING THE FREEDOM OF THE HILLS

Chapter 7
LEAVE NO TRACE

Mountaineers seek the uncharted way, the trail less traveled, and a summit to stand on. We recognize that the wilderness we seek is a resource that we must protect.

Most mountaineers have seen the consequences of overuse, carelessness, and thoughtlessness in the backcountry. Today's mountaineers need to be conscientious visitors who have developed the requisite knowledge and skills to preserve and protect the fragile natural resources they explore. Climbers not only set the example for appropriate wilderness behavior but are frequently the educators who help other backcountry users accept individual responsibility.

Over the past 40 years, there has been an ethical evolution in climbing, beginning with the first chocks used to replace rock-deforming pitons. Early educational efforts and publications emphasized basic messages, such as "leave only footprints" and "pack it in, pack it out." Through experience and research, mountaineers have expanded the skills and techniques that are applied in the backcountry so that all visitors can truly leave no trace of their visit.

In 1994, the Leave No Trace Center for Outdoor Ethics was established as a nonprofit educational organization to promote a consistent set of minimum-impact guidelines, now referred to as Leave No Trace.

This chapter's Leave No Trace guidelines can be applied to and adapted for any outdoor pursuit, location, and circumstance, as witnessed by worldwide adoption and adaptation for a variety of recreational activities on land and water. Leave No Trace is as basic and essential to mountaineering as technical climbing skills, first aid, and navigation. Like any skill, Leave No Trace techniques do take practice and judgment, but with each trip, all mountaineers can enhance their knowledge and refine their skills so that their wilderness visits are neither seen nor felt by others.

PLANNING ACHIEVES MORE THAN A SUMMIT

If there is one common objective among backcountry visitors, it is to find solitude—a sense that you are alone—perhaps experiencing the perceived joy of being the first, even when this is not the case. This is a challenging objective, especially when you are visiting a popular destination. But with planning, visitors can achieve that sense of having their small, personal space. If climbers cannot actually be alone, they can at least create the sense, for themselves and others, of being first or being alone in the wilderness.

BE REALISTIC AND RESPONSIBLE

Start by defining the expectations and capabilities of the group. A party that stretches itself to the limit, and perhaps gets into trouble, will no longer care about the principles of Leave No Trace. If rescuers must be called, safety comes first, regardless of environmental damage. Realistic planning can often prevent desperate situations in the first place.

Discuss trip expectations with party members so that everyone agrees to employ Leave No Trace techniques. Help them understand what that means for the area the group plans to visit.

If the party is new to Leave No Trace principles, use established trails and campsites at first. The group might encounter more people, but everyone gains valuable experience. Use hardened trails until the Leave No Trace techniques are mastered. Be willing to modify plans or the route if fragile conditions or sensitive circumstances are discovered. Books frequently direct people to the most popular summits, vistas, and crags. Consider the less-popular destinations, where visitor impacts can be spread out and visitors can find more solitude and wildlife.

THINK SMALL

Limit the size of the group. Outdoor trips are often social events, but keeping groups smaller enhances the sense of solitude for the party and other visitors. If local land managers have a party size limit, consider making your group even smaller. Ask yourself, "What is the minimum group needed for safety?"

CONSIDER CONDITIONS

A little research goes a long way. Route descriptions from fellow climbers are a start, but dig deeper. Contact the land management agency responsible for the area you plan to visit, so that the group can make decisions about when and where to go and the Leave No Trace techniques that should be applied. Inquire about these considerations:

- Permits and camping regulations
- Frequency of use. When it is practical, schedule the trip when conditions will cause less impact, perhaps selecting a weekday rather than a weekend for popular destinations.
- Hiking or climbing difficulties or recommendations
- Waste disposal preferences. Are backcountry outhouses or toilets available, or should the group pack out its waste?
- Fragile or sensitive areas, including flora, fauna, or geology
- Soil conditions and moisture level

ELIMINATE EXCESS PACKAGING

The more packaging you carry, the greater the chance that something will be left in the backcountry. Eliminate unnecessary food packages, wraps, twist ties, and covers. This not only reduces the potential for littering but also saves weight and space. Repackage food in reusable containers or resealable bags. See the "Gearing Up to Leave No Trace" sidebar for more gear suggestions. Plan meals so you take only the amount of food necessary, except for emergency rations. Leftovers should be eaten later or carried out, not buried or burned.

GEARING UP TO LEAVE NO TRACE

- **Thoughtful selection of clothing and equipment** is an important part of Leave No Trace. Stoves and adequate clothing eliminate the need for fires.
- **A large, collapsible water container** reduces the number of trips to water sources.
- **A plastic scrubber** eliminates the need to use sand or grass to clean cooking utensils.
- **A small, lightweight trowel** or ice ax aids proper waste disposal.
- **Waterproof footwear and gaiters** make it possible to stay on the trail even where it is wet and muddy.
- **Earth tones,** instead of "hot" colors, for tents, packs, and clothing reduce the sense of overcrowding.
- **Carry a pair of sandals** or lightweight, soft-soled shoes to wear around camp. Heavy, lug-soled boots are hard on soil and vegetation.
- **Use a sleeping pad.** Cutting tree boughs for bedding has long been unacceptable.

TRAVEL AND CAMP ON DURABLE SURFACES

Whenever possible, stay on established trails and use established campsites. As climbers move off trail into pristine environments, Leave No Trace knowledge and skills become even more critical.

Trails are wilderness highways. Like the roads people drive on, trails that are designed properly can withstand high foot traffic, channel users through fragile areas, and prevent water flow and soil erosion. Trailside signs (fig. 7-1) urge hikers to stay on trails.

TRAIL USE

- **Always use and stay on trails where they exist.**
- **Stay within the established tread,** even if it is muddy or rutted, to protect trailside vegetation and prevent unnecessary widening of trails. Hike single file.
- **Never cut switchbacks**—doing so does not save a significant amount of time, but it does take more energy, increase chance of injury, kill plant roots, and create unsightly, eroded gullies.
- **Travel on snow when possible.** Take extra care when traveling through the fragile transition zone between dirt and snow where the soil is saturated with water, especially during spring and late fall.
- **Pick up scraps of litter** left by others and put them in a plastic bag in your pocket. Carry a large garbage bag to haul out larger materials, especially on the trip back out.
- **Perform light and safe trail maintenance** when storm debris or small rocks are encountered.
- **Select resilient areas for rest breaks.** Move off and away from the trail to remain unobtrusive to fellow hikers. If this is not possible due to fragile or dense vegetation, find a wide spot in the trail.
- **Yield to hikers coming uphill by finding a durable spot and stepping aside,** whether you are traveling up- or downhill; this sets a better example than standard trail etiquette, which suggests stepping off the trail. Otherwise, many hikers encountered will attempt to keep moving by stepping off the trail and trampling the vegetation.
- **Take care along stream banks to avoid erosion.**

Fig. 7-1. Actual trailside sign at Mount Rainier National Park.

OFF TRAIL

- **Keep a slow enough pace** to be aware of your surroundings and to plan a low-impact route.
- **Spread the party out for off-trail travel,** unlike trail travel, with each member taking a separate path, especially in fragile meadows. The exception is where there is an established climbers trail to use.
- **Look for durable surfaces** such as bare ground (patches between vegetation, wildlife trails), rock (bedrock, talus, scree, stream gravel), and sedge grasses. Avoid tromping on woody or herbaceous vegetation, such as heather and partridgefoot.
- **Take extra care in transition areas** between dirt and snow where the soil is water-saturated during spring and late fall.
- **Leave trailless areas free of cairns and flagging** unless those markers are already there. Never carve trees. Let the next party have its own routefinding adventure. If you need to mark the route, remove the markers on the way back down.

CAMPSITES

Look for previously used, hardened sites. Resist the temptation to use a less-disturbed site because it has a better view or is closer to a water source. (See Table 7-1 for guidelines in choosing campsites.)

If a pristine site is all that is available, stay only a night or two and then find another location. If you have a choice between a pristine spot and a new, slightly impacted campsite, the better choice could be the pristine site if you carefully apply Leave No Trace guidelines. Although this may be contrary to first instinct, it allows a slightly impacted area to recover from use. In pristine sites, observe these recommendations:

- **Avoid grouping tents together.**
- **Disperse toilet sites and vary walkways** so that no single path gets so trampled that the vegetation cannot recover.
- **Find a spot with a slight natural slope** so that water will not pool beneath your tent and tempt you to dig a trench.
- **Never level a site, remove leaves and needles, or dig trenches.**

When selecting a campsite, apply the 200-foot rule (about 75 paces): Camp at least 200 feet (60 meters) away from water, trails, and people. Land managers may allow use of already hardened sites even though they are close to water. If so, go ahead and use them, but do not create a new site in the same vicinity. In a pristine area, enhance the sense of solitude for yourself and others by choosing an out-of-the-way site or one with good natural screening.

Try to use established mountaineering bivy sites or high camps. Moving alpine rocks may kill fragile plants that take many years to grow. Build new sites or

TABLE 7-1. WILDERNESS CAMPSITE OPTIONS

Best to Worst Campsite Option	Reasons to Select or Not Select This Campsite
1. Established, fully impacted campsite	A hardened site cannot be impacted further, as long as it is not enlarged or manipulated in any way. Use existing rocks and logs instead of moving more in.
2. Snow	Snow will melt and show no sign of use, but avoid the area if vegetation or soil is showing. Before leaving, break down snow structures and make the site as natural-looking as possible.
3. Rock slab	Solid rock resists most damaging effects except fire scars.
4. Sand, dirt, or gravelly flat	Most signs of human presence can be swept away.
5. Duff in deep forest	Duff and other decaying matter are only lightly impacted by campers' presence.
6. Grass-covered meadow	A meadow covered by tents for a week can have its entire growing season wiped out. Move a long-term camp every few days to reduce the harm to any one spot. The higher the meadow, the more sensitive it is to trampling.
7. Plant-covered meadow above timberline	Alpine plants grow very slowly, and woody plants are more sensitive to impact than grasses. Heather, for example, has only a couple of months at timberline to bloom, seed, and add a fraction of an inch of growth for the year. Alpine plants could take many years to recover from the damage of a brief encampment.
8. Waterfront along lakes and streams	Waterside plant life is delicate, and water pollution is a growing problem as more people head into the backcountry.

improve existing ones only when absolutely necessary. Then select rocks that disturb the least possible amount of vegetation.

Keep track of gear and maintain a tidy camp so that equipment and food are not lost or forgotten. Leave the site in better condition than you found it. Pristine sites require a little extra effort; cover used areas with native materials, brushing out footprints and fluffing up matted grass.

USE STOVES, NOT CAMPFIRES

Today's climbers use lightweight stoves rather than campfires. Stoves do not consume wild materials and do not fill the mountain air with smoke. In addition, they are faster, cleaner and more convenient, and work in just about any weather conditions. There is a certain romance to campfires, but they result in trampled terrain, unwanted social trails, and denuded trees and shrubs, robbing an area of biological material and wildlife habitat. Campfire rings and blackened rocks and trees are blemishes that last for decades.

Since circumstances can make a campfire enticing, learn to identify the conditions needed to create a safe campfire where they are permitted. Use existing fire rings. Carry a fire pan or learn how to make and break down a Leave No Trace mound fire (see the Leave No Trace website, listed in Appendix D, Supplementary Resources). Only use dry sticks found on the ground that can be broken by hand. Burn wood to ash, and scatter cooled ashes so there is no visual evidence.

DISPOSE OF WASTE PROPERLY

Mountaineers generally travel in harsh environments—alpine, desert, arctic—where waste breaks down slowly or not at all. Improper waste disposal is unhealthy and creates unsightly and unpleasant discoveries. Whenever possible, use an outhouse or wait until returning from the backcountry. Granted, these are not always practical options, so go into the backcountry prepared for healthy, safe, and thoughtful waste disposal. Everyone's health is dependent on vigilant personal hygiene. Wash your hands frequently, away from camp and water sources, or use quick-dry liquid disinfectant.

THE FUNDAMENTALS

Apply the 200-foot (60-meter) rule to take care of your business well away from watercourses, trails, campsites, and gathering areas. Urinate on bare ground or rocks—not on vegetation—in random locations. The salt in urine attracts animals that might damage plants. On snow or ice, concentrate urine at designated locations in camp or at rest stops rather than creating a proliferation of pee holes. Cover yellow snow. On steep rock or ice faces, wait until you reach a place where urine can be streamed away from the climbing route. In tents or on long routes, some climbers use a pee bottle to collect urine for later disposal.

Instead of toilet paper, consider using natural materials such as river rock, conifer cones, broad leaves (being careful to recognize and use safe vegetation), or snow. If you use toilet paper, use neutral-colored and non-scented. Avoid the fire hazard of burning toilet paper; instead, pack it out.

The two acceptable and time-tested methods for ethical and safe waste disposal are cat-hole burial and packing it out.

CAT-HOLE BURIAL

The cat hole is most suited to lower elevations where there is a deep layer of organic soil. Find a suitable, thoughtful location. Here's a rule of thumb: If it is easy for you to reach, it will be easy for others too. Challenge yourself to avoid concentrating waste. When you find a good location, use a trowel or ice ax to remove a top layer, or divot, about 4 to 6 inches (10 to 15 centimeters) in diameter, and set it aside. Dig the hole no more than 8 inches (20 centimeters) deep—deeper than forest litter and duff, but not deeper than the humus—for faster decomposition (fig. 7-2). After making your deposit, fill the hole with loose soil. Using a stick or trowel, mix the waste with some soil, then replace the divot. Tamp the soil and distribute area vegetation to create a natural appearance.

In thin mineral soil, on rocks of high alpine areas, or

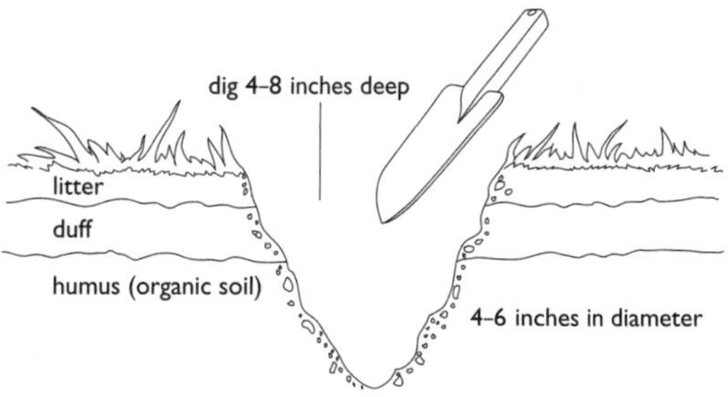

Fig. 7-2. Cat-hole burial.

in desert canyon country—all places where the waste will not readily break down—burying solid waste is not recommended. Although it is possible to hide waste by burying it, its decomposition is doubtful. The cat hole is not suitable in snow, either, unless mineral soil can be found underneath it, possibly in a tree well.

PACKING WASTE AND MATERIALS OUT

Mountaineers are already accustomed to packing out used toilet paper and personal hygiene products (bandages, sanitary napkins, tampons). Increasingly, climbers must be prepared to pack out feces as well. Packing out waste is the preferred practice on popular glacier routes, in alpine areas with thin mineral soils, in desert country, on steep rock and ice routes, including big wall climbs, on arctic tundra, and for winter travel.

Double-Bag

Two resealable plastic bags, stored in a stuff sack or a garbage bag, work effectively and safely. Like a dog owner walking a pet, put the inner bag over your hand like a glove, then scoop up the solid waste. Then turn the bag inside out to envelop the waste, seal the bag, place it inside the second bag, and seal or tie it. You can reduce odor in the first bag by placing a 2-inch-square (5-centimeter-square) sponge saturated with ammonia in it or by adding some chlorinated lime, cat-box filler, or chemical gelling treatments.

Commercially available waste alleviation and gelling kits such as the Wag Bag use a double degradable plastic bag system approved for deposit in landfills, with the inner bag containing powder that gels waste and neutralizes odors. In some wilderness areas, land managers hand out ready-made basic double-bag sets, gelling kits, or other supplies, such as a cardboard sheet for initial deposit of waste and a paper bag with cat-box filler inside in which to bag the cardboard sheet. Be aware of the options available to you and promoted by the area you are visiting, especially since land managers may provide collection containers for you to deposit your waste in if you use their preferred method.

Container Options

Most backcountry travelers will want some kind of sturdy container in which to store the double bags used to initially collect waste. This container could be as simple as an old stuff sack, or you could use a watertight dry bag (such as those used on river trips) carried inside or outside your backpack or sturdy commercially available products, all of which can be reused. Commercial varieties include products designed for big wall climbers, such as the Metolius Waste Case, which is made out of haul-bag material and has sturdy haul straps sewn on to allow for secure hauling of the container below the haul bag. Another sturdy commercially made product is the Clean Mountain Can, designed for use on Denali, which contains waste in a hard-sided cylinder, has a large capacity, and can be used as a toilet. You can fashion your own container using the many types of light, durable, watertight plastic containers that are available.

These waste-disposal options are only as good as they are thoughtfully employed. There are no easy answers to the question of proper waste disposal. Increasingly, at popular climbing and mountaineering routes, land managers provide specially marked collection bins for human waste. Usually, however, it will be up to you to dispose of waste properly after you have finished a trip. Do not simply put waste in a garbage can. Waste in paper bags may go into RV dump stations or front-country restrooms of the type that get pumped out. Paper or plastic bags should not go into pit toilets, flush toilets, or composting toilets. Waste in plastic bags should be emptied into a flush toilet, then the bag should be washed before it is thrown into the garbage. Be sure to wash your hands after handling waste.

CREVASSE BURIAL IN REMOTE AREAS

For remote, expedition glacier travel, waste disposal in crevasses has been an accepted practice. Check with the responsible land management agency, if one exists. Where crevasse disposal is acceptable, solid waste is collected in a biodegradable plastic bag and then thrown into a deep crevasse, away from the climbing route, after the party breaks camp. This practice could be on the cusp of change as distant routes gain popularity. The waste might not be ground up by the moving ice, as once was thought, and may lead to polluted snow that can cause gastrointestinal illnesses in other travelers.

CLEANING UP

If climbers can carry full food containers and packaging into the wilderness, they can carry them out empty—and maybe carry a little more out besides. In a pocket, carry a small resealable plastic bag to hold bits of litter you pick up from the trail. Take an extra heavy-duty plastic bag to carry out all your trash and anything else you find, no matter who left it. Never bury or burn garbage or dump it in outhouses.

WASHING

For all types of cleaning and washing, always apply the 200-foot (60-meter) rule. Hot water cleans dishes just fine without soap. If you really want soap, use a biodegradable product and keep it off plants. Dispose of cleaning water downwind from the campsite and well away from water sources. Dig a small cat hole for wastewater, straining food scraps out first; pack these out like other garbage. Or fling the wastewater out in an arc with a fast, sweeping motion, which disperses the water in fine droplets. Carry out any leftover food.

Use different standards of cleanliness in the wilderness than at home—it is not practical to shower and wash your hair every day. If you do need to wash yourself or your clothing, either do without soap or use a biodegradable soap in very small quantities. Try new products that clean without water. Never wash directly in a water source. Take a pot of water 200 feet away from water sources, trails, campsites, etc.; wash, rinse, and dispose of the water 200 feet away as well. If you applied sunscreen or insect repellent, follow the 200-foot rule to wash yourself off before jumping into a lake or stream. These chemicals and oils can cause harm to aquatic plants and wildlife and will leave an oily surface film.

DO NOT DISTURB

The Leave No Trace ethic goes beyond eliminating litter and waste. Learn to pass through the wilderness in a way that literally leaves no trace of your passage.

LEAVE WHAT YOU FIND

Established campsites should be used and left as found, if not better. Do not bring saws, hatchets, and nails into the wilderness. Existing, legal fire rings can be left alone rather than dismantled, because it is likely that someone will create a fire ring again and blacken more rocks. If a campsite has an excessive number of seats, tables, or fire rings, thoughtfully disperse logs and rocks.

Avoid disturbing vegetation or rocks on a climbing route. Look at, draw, or photograph wilderness flora rather than picking or collecting. Do not touch or remove fossils you may discover. Leave untouched any area with evidence of archaeological or historic artifacts, such as those left by prehistoric or native populations. Report findings to land managers. Do not climb, and never bolt, near indigenous rock artwork.

RESPECT WILDLIFE

Never feed wildlife. Animals will eat what is given to them or left behind, which can threaten an animal's health. Some animals will store human food for winter use, only to have it turn moldy and inedible. People enjoy feeding chipmunks and birds, but this makes these creatures dependent on humans, and since you likely will not be around to feed them in winter, this could lead to their death. Carry a resealable plastic bag to clean up even the smallest specks of food at trail stops and campsites.

Watch for nesting birds, especially raptors, on rock routes so as not to disturb them. Check with land managers for nesting seasons and closures. If you do encounter nesting birds, back off or take another route.

Even the best-behaved pet can disturb wildlife. The mere presence of a dog can cause wild animals to flee, using up energy and exposing themselves to predators. This is especially harmful in winter when their energy reserves are low and must be carefully conserved. Consider leaving pets at home. If you do bring a pet into the wilderness, do so only where permitted. Pets must be leashed at all times. Use the 200-foot (60-meter) rule for dog waste, too, and bury it in a cat hole or pack it out in a poop bag.

BE CONSIDERATE OF OTHER VISITORS

Most people go into the wilderness to be alone or with just a few companions. Mountaineers can contribute to the wilderness experience of others by camping away from them, respecting their privacy, traveling through their space only if necessary, and keeping voices and other sounds to a minimum.

Enjoy the sounds of the wilderness. You will return to your daily routine, and the urban sounds that go with it, soon enough. Recorded music may be desired on long expeditions, but for most backcountry trips, MP3 players and other audio devices and cell phones can be distracting and unpleasant. Check with trip companions before you take any of these along. If you do, wear earphones. If you insist on making a summit call, find a space away from others.

MINIMIZE CLIMBING IMPACTS

- **Use natural-color webbing at rappel points.** Every time you place a rappel sling, remove and pack out at least one old sling, if not more.
- **Try to adjust loose rocks** to make them stable on an alpine climb, rather than just pushing them off. At popular sport climbing crags, however, it is better to remove loose rocks because of the danger they pose in crowded areas.
- **Break down snow structures** before you leave, to reduce visual impact and inadvertent safety hazards.
- **Avoid setting up new, permanent fixed anchors and rappel points** or reinforcing existing ones, unless it is necessary for safety.
- **Never chip holds or alter the rock structure** for climbing purposes. Use as little chalk as possible.
- **Avoid the damaging practice of using pitons;** hammerless nuts, cams, and other pieces of protection have largely eliminated the need for pitons. Pitons are appropriate for winter climbing, when cracks are filled with ice, and for aid climbing.
- **Bolts should be considered only when no other protection is possible** and when they are needed to provide a margin of safety. Because bolts are permanent, think carefully before deciding to place one.
- **Follow the local practices and rules** at climbing crags. In one area, the local climbers may use only camouflaged bolt hangers (painted so that they are not shiny); in another area, the bolting of new routes may be illegal.
- **Cleaning new routes of vegetation should be done for safety,** not aesthetic reasons.
- **Learn about and respect the customs and culture** of the area in which you are traveling. Pack in stove fuel rather than despoiling these areas in the search for firewood. Just as you would at areas closer to home, pack your garbage out.

RESPECTING THE FREEDOM OF THE HILLS

As mountaineers, we do our part to protect and preserve the wild country we explore by applying Leave No Trace principles, using good judgment, and educating others. There is no more positive way to help ensure continued access, unfettered by restrictions and excessive rules and regulations. When we enter the backcountry, we are active stewards and contribute to the lasting protection of wild resources for ourselves and future generations.

Chapter 8
STEWARDSHIP AND ACCESS

Perhaps because of their unique relationship with the mountains, climbers have long been at the forefront of protecting wild places around the globe. John Muir, a leading conservationist of the nineteenth century, was a climber, as was David Brower, a leading conservationist of the twentieth century.

The tradition of climbers working to protect wild places continues today. On every continent, climbers act as stewards of the mountains, taking on actions as small as packing out their own refuse and as large as fighting large-scale development that threatens the places mountaineers love.

As more and more people turn to the mountains, such stewardship becomes ever more important. The "freedom of the hills" is not absolute. To a great extent, outdoor exploration is subject to restriction by the persons or entities in control of the land where mountaineers climb.

Maintaining access to wild places depends on minimizing the actual and potential conflicts between mountaineering and the interests of those who control the land. Although practicing good stewardship should rightfully be considered the moral obligation of every climber, it is also the key to minimizing access conflicts.

ACCESS PROBLEMS

Environmental impacts and aesthetics can lead to access restrictions; religious or historical significance can also give rise to restricted access to a climbing area. In addition, fees and regulations can affect access to climbing areas.

ENVIRONMENTAL IMPACTS

Stewardship starts with the natural environments that attract mountaineers in the first place. Alpine ecosystems are typically fragile and highly affected by human impact. Vegetation is delicate and shallow rooted. Human waste is particularly slow to decompose in the ice and rock zone, and it can become a problem on popular routes and at bivouac or camping areas. If a single climber fails to utilize Leave No Trace principles, the damage may be visible for months or years.

Cliff environments often have their own unique features. Cliffs may host nesting raptors, serve as home to bat colonies, and support highly specialized (and sometimes very rare) plant communities. Because cliffs may create their own microclimates and provide conditions that are either drier or wetter than the surrounding area, the tops and bases of cliffs may feature plant and wildlife concentrations unique to an area. Climber impacts can occur both on the cliff faces themselves (through wildlife disturbance and passive or active devegetation) and at cliff tops and bottoms (often in the form of erosion and ground-cover loss associated with concentrated foot travel and groups gathering).

In addition to affecting the environment, these impacts can result in access restrictions when the impacts conflict directly with laws intended to protect habitat for endangered species, create conflict with another user group, or reach a level that is unacceptable under the management mandate of the entity controlling the land. This "acceptable level" of impact may vary greatly depending on who manages the land. The same impacts that are acceptable in a park that is being managed for recreation may be unacceptable in an area managed specifically for habitat preservation.

To avoid such access problems, every climber should adhere to the principles discussed in Chapter 7, Leave No Trace. In practical terms, this means adjusting climbing practices in relation to whatever constitutes a "trace" where you are climbing. What constitutes a "trace" may be different at a popular roadside crag than at a remote alpine area. Climbers should strive to minimize their impacts everywhere, and they should go to even greater lengths in wilderness and environmentally sensitive areas. Become familiar with who or what agency manages your climbing destinations, and learn the rules that govern use of those areas.

CULTURAL IMPACTS

In addition to environmental conflicts, cultural resource conflicts may also give rise to access concerns. Local cultural populations, including native and religious groups, have sought access restrictions for mountaineers, rock climbers, and trekkers in various locations around the world, based on the religious or historic significance attached to natural features.

The issues are complex when climbing intersects with religious beliefs that attach significance to a climbing objective. Whether you choose to forego an ascent out of respect for another's religious considerations is a personal matter. However, at a minimum, become knowledgeable of the local customs, religious and otherwise, that may be impacted when you are climbing at an area outside your own cultural background, and make decisions with full awareness of the consequences of your actions.

Good stewardship requires leaving artifacts and rock art (petroglyphs and pictographs) undisturbed and free from contact. (Oil from a human hand can adversely affect the pigments associated with rock art.)

> *I felt then that [this] was another special place. A place where climbers lived who cared for it, and knew it well enough to say that the yellow rock was more brittle than the red, or that there are hidden holds inside that crack, or that the number of condors is on the up, that the boulder in the next valley gives good shelter, or at what time exactly does the sun shine on that face of the mountain. Simple shared knowledge. That which we have of our home rocks.*
>
> —*Paul Pritchard,* Deep Play

AESTHETIC IMPACTS

Certain climbing practices have also led to access issues. The use of fixed gear such as bolts, in situ pitons, and rappel slings has been at the center of a number of conflicts. Some of this conflict is a matter of aesthetics: A high density of bolts on a cliff or rappel anchors that stand out at a distance can offend the sensibilities of certain climbers and nonclimbers alike. Some of this conflict can be traced to some people's philosophic opposition to the notion of drilling bolt holes or leaving slings on a cliff, even if the objective impact is minimal. The use of hand-drying chalk by rock climbers has also created some access issues, particularly where chalk residue on holds visually contrasts sharply with the surrounding rock or is not removed by weathering.

> *We are entering a new era of climbing, an era that may well be characterized by incredible advances in equipment, by the overcoming of great difficulties, with even greater technological wizardry, and by the rendering of the mountains to a low, though democratic, mean.*
>
> *Or it could be the start of more spiritual climbing, where we assault the mountains with less equipment and with more awareness, more experience and more courage.*
>
> —*Yvon Chouinard, "Coonyard Mouths Off,"* Ascent *(1972)*

FEES AND RESTRICTIONS

Restrictions and fees applicable to all recreational users can also affect climbing access. For instance, one land management agency has established "solitude criteria" for designated wilderness areas. These criteria prescribe the number of human encounters a visitor should experience in a day in order to maintain a "wilderness experience." Such wilderness areas often include mountainous regions.

Access fees, climbing fees, and permit fees, particularly in Asia, create an economic barrier for some mountaineers. These fees are sometimes used for stewardship by land management agencies, and sometimes they are chiefly governmental revenue devices.

PRESERVING ACCESS

As people who endeavor to enjoy the freedom of the hills, all climbers are at the center of at least some of these access issues and can have an impact on preserving access.

THROUGH FORMAL CHANNELS

Certain issues, such as the appropriateness of solitude criteria and use fees, are purely legal or political questions. Regardless of whether you favor or oppose such measures, individual influence over such issues is largely obtained through a formal process rather than by how individual climbers conduct themselves while climbing. You are a stakeholder in the political process, and your influence will be proportional to your level of involvement in that process.

THROUGH STEWARDSHIP

Each individual's conduct while climbing can make a profound difference regarding most other access problems. Maintaining access to wild places, as pointed out earlier in this chapter, depends on minimizing the actual and potential conflicts between climbing and the interests of those who control the land. To the extent that each person's climbing is in harmony with the management of an area, each mountaineer will help ensure access for all climbers. To accomplish this, constantly look to become an active steward of the places where you climb.

Stewardship can be as simple as picking up someone else's litter, decaying slings, and abandoned fixed lines. Taken to a greater length, stewardship can help transform an area through trail building and revegetation projects.

8

THROUGH ACTIVE MEMBERSHIP

An easy way to influence access policies and practice stewardship is to support organizations and groups that are active in access issues. In North America, organizations such as The Mountaineers, the American Alpine Club, the Alpine Club of Canada, and particularly the Access Fund are active in access issues and stewardship projects. This activity includes working with agencies that are developing management plans for climbing, assisting in tailoring site-specific closures to protect critical resources (such as seasonal restrictions for nesting raptors), and providing grants for land acquisition, trail building, trailhead maintenance, and other conservation projects, as well as scientific studies related to climbing impacts. Finally, local and regional climbing organizations have been formed at a number of areas to address access issues close to home.

THE FUTURE OF MOUNTAINEERING

Mountaineers, by their very nature, pursue unconfined exploration. This fact can pose challenges for those who control the land. As more people continue to join the climbing ranks, it is increasingly incumbent on all climbers to minimize their impacts and maximize their stewardship of the land and watercourses they travel. By doing so, they and the generations of mountaineers who follow can continue to enjoy the freedom of the hills.

PART II

CLIMBING FUNDAMENTALS

ROPES • KNOTS, BENDS, AND HITCHES • HELMETS • HARNESSES • RUNNERS • CARABINERS • KEEPING THE SAFETY NET STRONG

Chapter 9
BASIC SAFETY SYSTEM

The rope symbolizes climbing and the climber's dependence on another person. The rope protects you when the difficulty of a pitch or an unexpected occurrence—a broken hold or collapsing snow bridge—causes you to fall.

However, the rope alone cannot safeguard you. Instead, it is a critical component in a safety system that includes knots for specialized tasks, the harness that attaches you to the rope, the loops of webbing (known as runners) used to connect the rope to rock, snow, or ice, and the carabiners that join the various parts of the climbing system. The mechanical components of this safety system are the topics of this chapter.

ROPES

Originally, climbers used ropes made of natural fibers (manila and sisal), but these ropes were not reliable for holding severe falls. The development of nylon ropes during World War II forever changed climbing. Nylon climbing ropes are lightweight and very strong, capable of bearing a load of more than two tons. They also have the remarkable quality of elasticity, which is the critical component in the rope's ability to protect a climber in a fall. Rather than bringing a falling climber to an abrupt, jolting stop, nylon ropes stretch and dynamically dissipate much of the energy generated by the fall, thereby reducing the forces associated with the fall.

Early nylon ropes were of "laid" or "twisted" construction. They were composed of many tiny nylon filaments bunched into three or four major strands that were then twisted together to form the rope. Gradually, twisted nylon ropes were replaced by kernmantle ropes designed specifically for climbing. Today's kernmantle ropes (fig. 9-1) are composed of a core of braided or parallel nylon filaments encased in a smooth, woven sheath of nylon. Kernmantle rope maintains the advantages of nylon but minimizes the problems associated with twisted ropes—stiffness, friction, and excessive elasticity. Kernmantle ropes are now the only climbing ropes approved by the Union Internationale des

Fig. 9-1. Construction of a kernmantle rope.

Associations d'Alpinisme (UIAA), the internationally recognized authority in setting standards for climbing equipment, and the Comité Européen de Normalisation (CEN), the European group responsible for creating and maintaining equipment standards.

VARIETIES OF CLIMBING ROPE

Climbing ropes are available in a great variety of diameters, lengths, and characteristics. Any rope used for climbing should have the manufacturer's label, a UIAA or CEN rating, and specifications such as length, diameter, stretch or impact force, and fall rating. Because the rating organizations are both European, rope measurements universally use the metric system; in this book, English measurements (inches, feet, and so on) are occasionally given in parentheses as well.

Dynamic. Kernmantle ropes designed for climbing are termed "dynamic" ropes. Dynamic ropes achieve low-impact forces by stretching under the force of the fall. One of the most important considerations when looking at rope specifications is the impact force—generally, lower is better. Using a rope with a lower impact force means that a climber's fall will be stopped less abruptly (a "softer catch") and less force will be imparted onto the fallen climber, the belayer, and the anchor system.

Dynamic ropes come in a variety of diameters that are acceptable for technical climbing. Table 9-1 illustrates some typical ropes and their common uses. Smaller-diameter dynamic ropes (down to about 8 millimeters) are typically used in pairs as part of either a twin- or double-rope system (see Chapter 14, Leading on Rock). These small-diameter rope systems rely on the elastic properties of both ropes to protect the climber and must be used as a pair.

Dynamic ropes also come in a variety of lengths. Useful lengths range from 30 meters to 70 meters. Although 60 meters (200 feet) is the most common length for all-around recreational climbing, a climber might want to choose a rope that is either shorter or longer, for a variety of reasons. Rope weight, the nature and length of the route, and the ability to rappel safely are some things to consider when selecting a rope's length.

Static. In contrast to dynamic ropes, static ropes, nylon slings, and cord do not stretch, and a fall of even a few feet can generate impact forces severe enough to cause failure of the anchor system or severe injury to the climber.

Climbers use no-stretch or very low-stretch ropes for purposes other than protecting the lead climber, including cave exploring or rescue work, as fixed line on expedition-style climbs, or sometimes as the haul line during aid climbing. Although static ropes often

TABLE 9-1. SOME TYPICAL ROPES AND THEIR COMMON USES

Diameter	Type	Common Use
8 mm	static	Fixed lines on expedition-style climbs
8 mm	dynamic	As part of a twin-rope system for rock and ice climbing
9 mm	dynamic	As part of a double-rope system for rock and ice climbing or as a lightweight single rope for simple glacier travel
10 mm	dynamic	Lightweight single rope for rock and ice climbing and glacier travel
10.5 mm	dynamic	Moderate-weight single rope for rock and ice climbing and glacier travel
11 mm	dynamic	More durable single rope for rock and ice climbing and glacier travel
12 mm	static	Caving and rescue (not for climbing)

are sold at climbing stores, these ropes should never be used for lead climbing, which requires the impact-absorbing qualities of a dynamic rope.

Colors of Ropes

Ropes are manufactured with different patterns and colors woven into the sheath. Some ropes have a few inches of contrasting color or a change in color or pattern at the midpoint to make it easy to find the middle of the rope. Others have distinctively colored ends so that it is easier for the climber to visually determine that the end of the rope is being reached while belaying or rappeling. If a climb calls for two ropes, it is useful to use different colors to assist in distinguishing between them when belaying or rappeling. The UIAA warns against marking a rope with any substance that has not been specifically approved by the rope manufacturer.

Water-Repellent Ropes

Wet ropes, in addition to being unpleasant to handle and heavy to carry, can freeze and become very difficult to manage. Equally important, studies show that wet ropes hold fewer falls and have about 30 percent less strength than the same ropes when they are dry.

Rope manufacturers treat some of their ropes with either a silicone-based coating or synthetic fluorine-containing resin coating (such as Teflon) to make them more water-repellent and therefore stronger in wet conditions. The "dry rope" treatment improves the abrasion resistance of the rope and also reduces friction of the rope as it runs through carabiners. Dry ropes usually cost about 15 percent more than untreated ropes.

PERFORMANCE TESTS

The UIAA and CEN test equipment to determine which gear meets their standards. Because climbing is a sport in which equipment failure can be fatal, it is wise to purchase equipment that has earned UIAA and/or CEN approval.

In its rope tests, the UIAA checks the strength of the single ropes used in most climbing—which generally measure between 9.4 and 11 millimeters in diameter—and also the thinner ropes used in double-rope climbing. To receive UIAA approval, a rope must survive a required minimum number of falls. The tests measure the impact force of the rope, which determines the stress of the fall on the climber's body and on the pieces of protection.

The UIAA also applies static tension tests to determine how much the ropes elongate under load. Approved ropes do not stretch by more than a specified percentage.

ROPE CARE

A rope protects your life and must be treated with care.

Preventing Damage to the Rope

Stepping on a rope is a common form of abuse that grinds sharp particles into and through the sheath. Over time, the particles act like tiny knives that slice the rope's nylon filaments. When you are wearing crampons, you must be doubly careful about keeping off the rope, because a misstep could damage the rope. Crampons may damage the core of a rope without leaving any visible gash on the sheath.

Protect the rope from contact with chemicals (especially acids) or other compounds that might damage the rope. For example, parking lot surfaces or dark, dank corners of a car trunk or basement may harbor substances that could damage a rope.

Washing and Drying

Follow the manufacturer's recommendations for care. Most ropes should be washed frequently with tepid water and mild soap, although some manufacturers recommend against using detergents on water-repellent ropes. The rope's water-repellent finish can also be replaced with aftermarket products made for that purpose. A rope can be washed by hand in a bathtub or in a front-loading washing machine (ropes can get caught under the agitator in a top-loading machine). Rinse the rope several times in clean water and then hang it to dry, out of direct sunlight.

Storing

Before storing any rope, be sure it is completely dry. Remove all knots, coil the rope loosely, and store it in a cool, dry area away from sunlight, heat, chemicals, petroleum products, and acids.

Retiring a Rope

Examine your rope's sheath to get the best picture of the rope's overall condition. Inspect your ropes frequently, particularly after a fall, to ensure that the sheath is clean, that there are no abraded or soft spots in the rope, and that the ends are properly fused and not fraying or unraveling. If a crampon wound, excessive abrasion, rockfall, or a sharp edge leaves the sheath looking tattered, the

THE LIFE OF A ROPE

Following are some general guidelines to help you decide when to retire your ropes:

- A rope used daily should be retired within a year.
- A rope used on most weekends should give about two years of service.
- An occasionally used rope should be retired after about four years (nylon deteriorates over time).

rope's integrity should be seriously questioned. If the core of the rope is visible, it is time to retire the rope.

It is harder to decide when to retire the rope if it does not contain any obvious soft spots or scars in the sheath. The rope's actual condition depends on many factors, including frequency of use, the care it has received, the number of falls it has endured, and how old it is.

After a severe fall, it may be wise to replace a rope, particularly if any segment of the rope feels mushy or flat. A new rope may be certified to take five UIAA falls, but in your decision whether to retire the rope, consider the rope's history and other factors affecting its condition. The guidelines for rope replacement (see "The Life of a Rope" sidebar) assume that the rope is kept properly cleaned and stored.

COILING THE ROPE

For carrying or storing, the rope is normally coiled, most commonly in the mountaineers coil or the butterfly coil. Most climbers prefer one coil or the other, but knowing both is useful.

Mountaineers coil. When the rope is carried over a pack, the mountaineers coil is advantageous. Coil the rope, leaving a couple of feet at one end and doubling back the other end, then bring the long end through the coil (fig. 9-2a). Wrap the coil several times, securing the doubled-back end (fig. 9-2b). Bring the long end down through the loop of the doubled-back end and pull the doubled-back end tight (fig. 9-2c), then tie the long end to the doubled-back end in a square knot (fig. 9-2d). See the next section for knot tying. When it is being uncoiled, the mountaineers coil easily develops twists that are difficult and time-consuming to remove.

Butterfly coil. Usually faster to coil and uncoil, the butterfly coil does not kink the rope, and can be tied snugly to your body if you are not wearing a pack. Coil the rope, leaving both ends long, and bend the coil into a horseshoe shape (fig. 9-3a). You can coil the rope by finding the middle and coiling two strands at a time, starting from the middle, or by coiling one strand back and forth. Gather the two loose ends together and wrap them around the middle of the coil several times (fig. 9-3b). Bring a loop of the loose ends through the loop at the top of the coil (fig. 9-3c), pulling enough through to form a good-sized loop. Then bring the rest of the loose ends through this good-sized loop (fig. 9-3d), drawing the loose ends all the way through (fig. 9-3e). To tie the butterfly coil to your body, place the coil against your back and draw a loose end over each shoulder and around your back, crossing them over the coil and bringing them around your waist; tie them together in front (fig. 9-3f).

Flaking the rope out. Whatever coil method you choose, it is important to uncoil the rope carefully

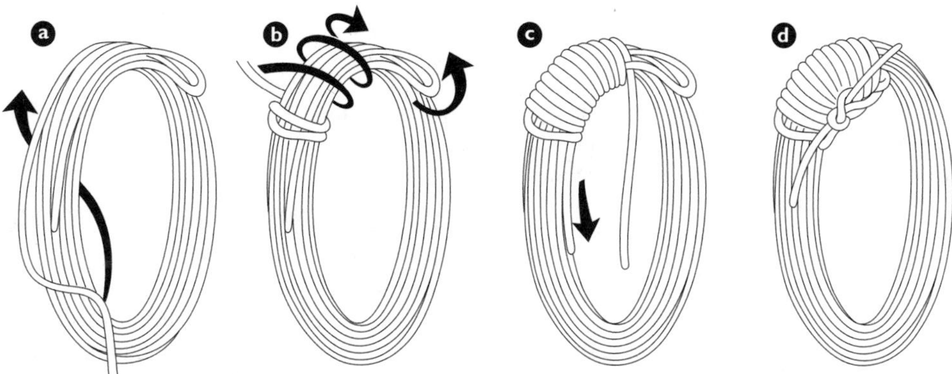

Fig. 9-2. Mountaineers coil: a, bring long end through coil near doubled-back other end; b, wrap coil several times; c, bring long end through loop of doubled-back end; d, pull loop tight and tie square knot to secure.

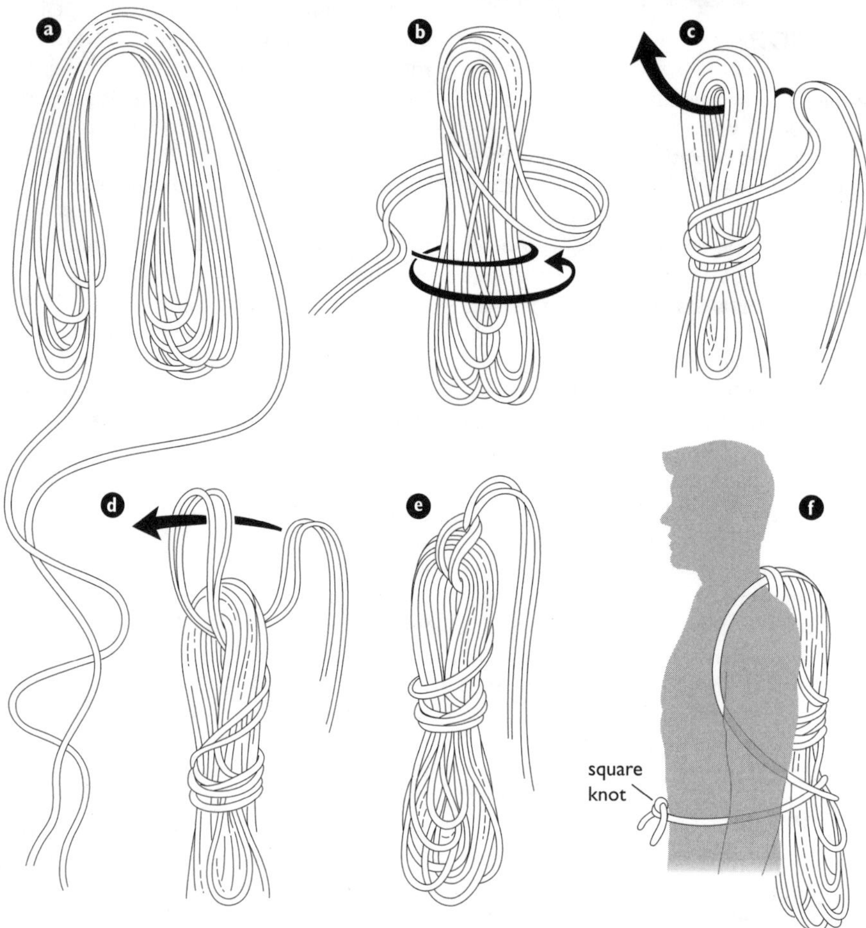

Fig. 9-3. Butterfly coil: a, form coil into horseshoe shape; b, wrap both loose ends around the middle several times; c, bring loop of loose ends through upper loop of coil; d, bring loose ends through loop of loose ends; e, bring loose ends all the way through and cinch; f, put a loose end over each shoulder, around behind the back, and over the coiled rope, then bring each end forward around the waist and tie together with a square knot.

before you use it, to minimize the chance of coils balling up into a tangle. Do not just drop the coils and start pulling on one end, which may create a tangled mess. Untie the cinch knot and then uncoil the rope, one loop at a time, into a pile, a procedure known as "flaking the rope out." It is always a good practice to flake out the rope before each belay to avoid the possibility of having a knot or tangle appear during the belay process.

Rope bags and tarps. Alternatives to coiling the rope include rope bags and tarps. Both can protect a rope during transport. The tarp, unfolded, also helps protect a rope from the ground. The bags and tarps add weight and cost, but for certain situations, such as sport climbing, they are worth it.

KNOTS, BENDS, AND HITCHES

Knots allow you to use the rope for many special purposes. Knots let you tie in to the rope, anchor to the mountain, tie two ropes together for long rappels, use slings to climb the rope itself, and much more. In common usage, the word "knot" is often used generically to refer either to a knot, a bend, or a hitch. But, properly speaking, they are different from each other.

A knot refers to material tied on itself; a bend refers to a joining of material ends; a hitch refers to material tied around a solid object. In this book, the word "knot" is often used in its all-inclusive sense.

Climbers rely most heavily on a dozen or so basic knots, bends, and hitches. Practice these knots until tying them is second nature. In some cases, more than one knot can perform a particular task, and the knot chosen is a matter of personal preference. Some knots may be preferred over others because they have a smaller effect on the overall strength of the rope, as shown in Table 9-2. Others may be chosen because they are easier to tie or are less likely to come apart in use.

Regardless of the knot you use, some terms and techniques are common to all knot tying. The end of the rope that is not being actively used is called the standing end; the other end is called the loose end. A 180-degree bend in the rope is called a bight; a loop is formed when the rope is curled around in 360 degrees so that both ends of the loop join or overlap. A double knot is a knot tied in a pair of ropes or in a doubled portion of one rope.

Regardless of its type, tie a knot neatly, keeping the separate strands of the knot parallel and free of twists. Tightly cinch every knot by pulling on each loose strand, and tie off loose ends with an overhand knot. Always tie knots in perfect form so that it becomes easy to recognize a properly tied knot. It is also important to develop the habit of routinely inspecting your own knots and those of your climbing partners, particularly before beginning a pitch or a rappel.

As a general rule, keep knots away from points of greatest stress, sharp edges and corners, friction, and abrasion.

BASIC KNOTS

Basic knots are used to tie in to harnesses, to tie ropes together for rappel, to tie slings, and for anchoring and rescue procedures.

Overhand Knot

The overhand knot (fig. 9-4a) is frequently used to secure loose rope ends after another knot has been tied. For instance, the overhand knot can be used to secure rope ends after tying a square knot (fig. 9-4b) or a rewoven figure eight (fig. 9-4c). To tie the overhand knot, pass the loose end of the rope through a bight of rope.

9

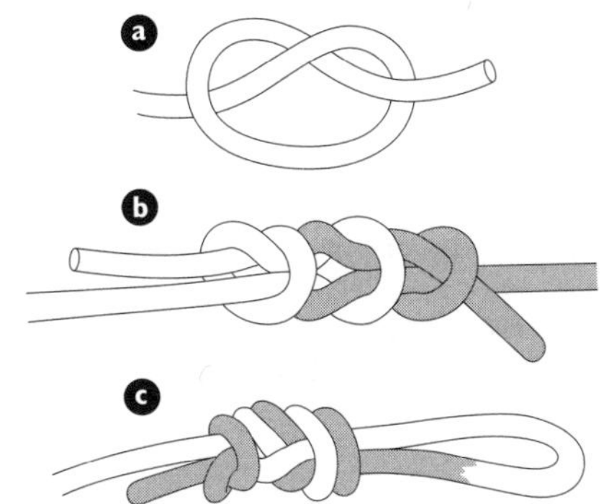

Fig. 9-4. Overhand knot: a, tying an overhand knot; b, overhand knots backing up both sides of a square knot; c, overhand knot backing up a rewoven figure eight.

TABLE 9-2. RELATIVE REDUCTION IN BREAKING STRENGTH OF SINGLE KERNMANTLE ROPE AT KNOT

Knot	Reduction in Breaking Strength	Knot	Reduction in Breaking Strength
Bowline	26–45 percent	Figure eight on a bight	23–34 percent
Butterfly knot	28–39 percent	Girth hitch	25–40 percent
Clove hitch	25–40 percent	Overhand loop	32–42 percent
Double fisherman's bend	20–35 percent	Square knot	53–57 percent
Figure eight bend	25–30 percent	Water knot (ring bend)	30–40 percent

Source: Clyde Soles, The Outdoor Knots Book

Offset Overhand Bend

The offset overhand bend (fig. 9-5) is useful as a rappel knot in icy conditions or for rappels where the knot might catch when the rappel rope is retrieved. The knot is tied using the loose ends of two ropes to set up a double-rope rappel.

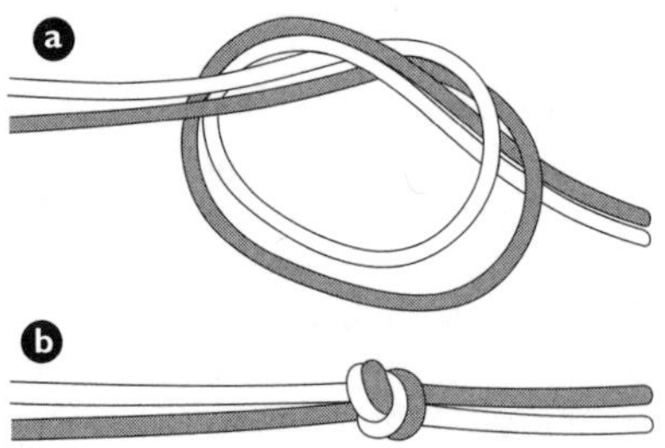

Fig. 9-5. Offset overhand bend: a, tie an overhand knot in two strands of rope; b, pull all four strands tight.

Overhand Loop

The overhand loop is often used for creating leg loops in accessory cord as part of a Texas-prusik system (described in Chapter 17, Glacier Travel and Crevasse Rescue) or to make a loop in a doubled rope or a length of webbing. The basic overhand knot is tied using a bight in the rope instead of a loose end (fig. 9-6).

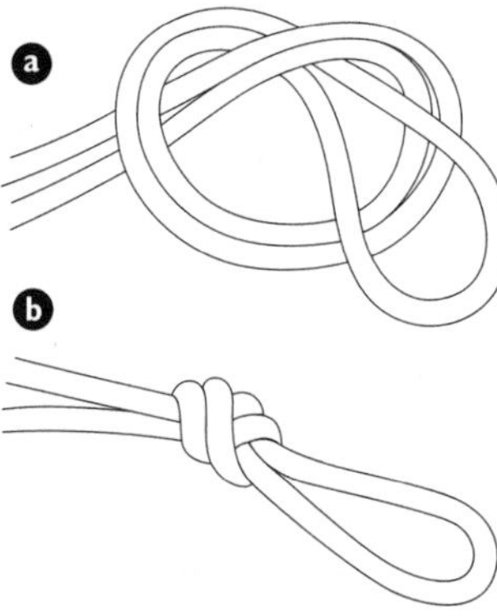

Fig. 9-6. Overhand knot on a bight: a, tie an overhand knot in a bight of rope or cord; b, dress and pull all strands tight.

Water Knot (Ring Bend)

The water knot (fig. 9-7), also known as the ring bend, is frequently used to tie a length of tubular webbing into a runner (see "Runners" later in this chapter). A water knot can work loose over time, so it is important to cinch

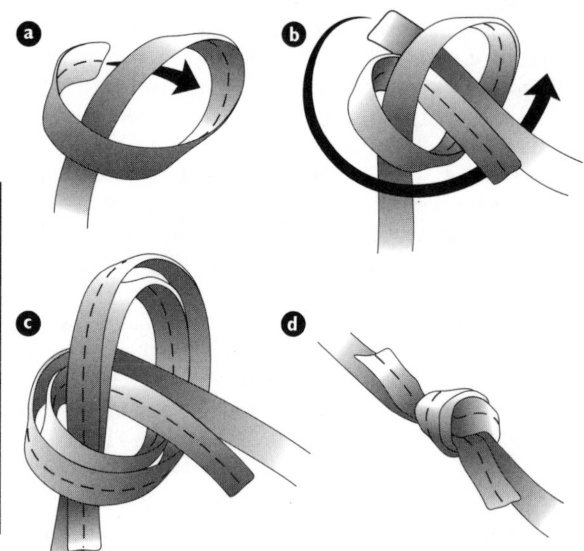

Fig. 9-7. Water knot (ring bend): a, draw a loose end through a bight of webbing; b, bring other loose end through the bight, around the first end, and under itself; c, draw ends well through knot so 2- to 3-inch tails extend; d, pull all four strands tight.

the knot by pulling each of the four strands tight and to make the tails of the knot at least 2 to 3 inches (5 to 7.5 centimeters) long. Check water knots often and retie any that have worked loose or that have short tails.

Square Knot

The square knot (fig. 9-8) can be used as a rappel knot (finished with overhand knots on both rope ends), and it is often used to finish off a coil of rope.

Fisherman's Bend

The fisherman's bend (fig. 9-9) is used to join two ropes together. Overlap a loose end of each rope and tie each end in an overhand knot around the other rope's standing end. For climbing purposes, however, this knot has been replaced to a large degree by the double fisherman's bend. The fisherman's bend is shown here primarily to provide a clearer understanding of the double fisherman's bend.

Double Fisherman's Bend

The double fisherman's bend (fig. 9-10), also known as the grapevine knot, is a very secure knot for tying the ends of two ropes together for a rappel or for tying

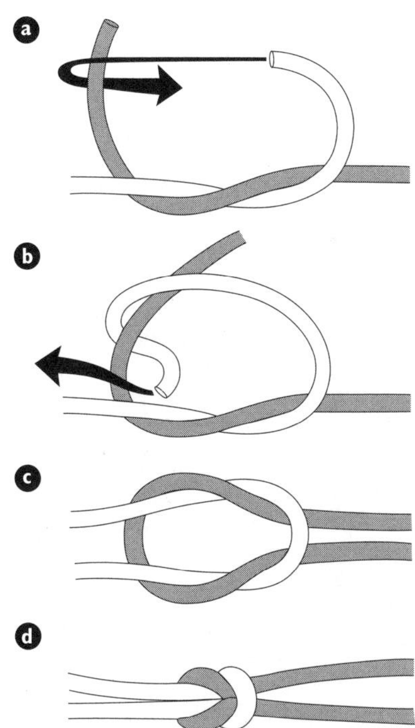

Fig. 9-8. Square knot: a, cross two loose ends over each other and bring one end up and around the other; b, bring end through their loop; c, dress all four strands; d, pull all four strands tight.

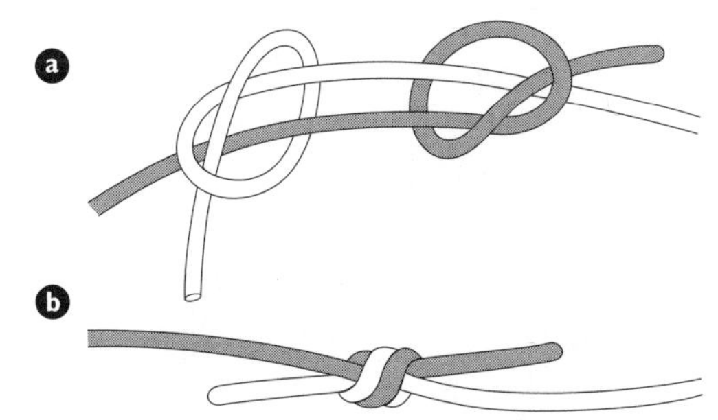

Fig. 9-9. Fisherman's bend: a, overlap a loose end of each rope, and tie each end in an overhand knot around the other rope's standing end; b, pull all four strands tight.

secure loops in round cords. Start as for the fisherman's bend, but pass each loose end twice around the other rope's standing end before tying the overhand knot, pulling the ends through both their loops.

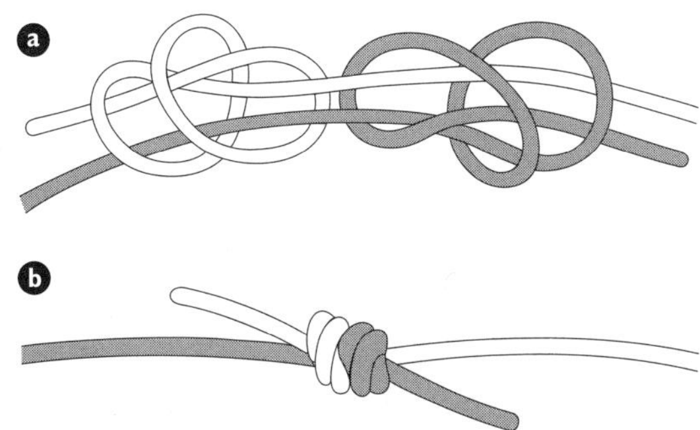

Fig. 9-10. Double fisherman's bend: a, pass each loose end twice around the other rope's standing end and then tie an overhand knot; b, pull all four strands tight.

Triple Fisherman's Bend

This is similar to the double fisherman's bend, but the loose end goes around the other rope's standing end three times instead of twice. The triple fisherman's is preferred when low-friction materials such as Spectra cord are joined together.

Figure Eight on a Bight

The figure eight on a bight (fig. 9-11) is a strong knot that can be readily untied after being under a load.

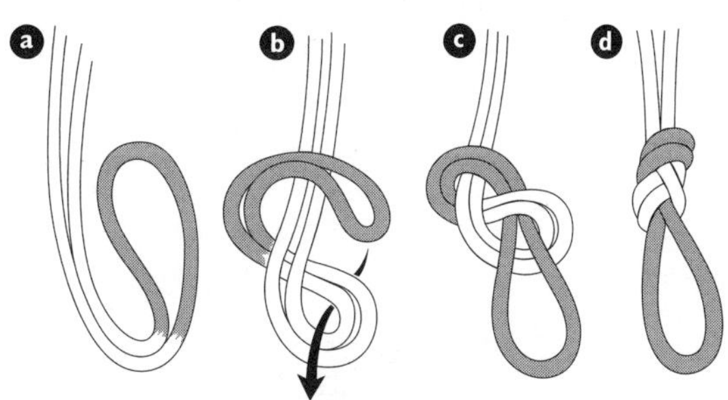

Fig. 9-11. Figure eight on a bight: a, bring a bight back parallel to the standing ends; b, bring bight under and then over the ends, forming an 8, then bring the bight down through the bottom loop of the 8; c, dress the strands; d, pull all four strands tight.

Rewoven Figure Eight

The rewoven figure eight (fig. 9-12) is an excellent knot for tying in to a seat harness at the end of the rope. The rewoven figure eight is finished off by tying an overhand knot in the loose end of the rope. This knot also can be used to connect a rope to an anchor.

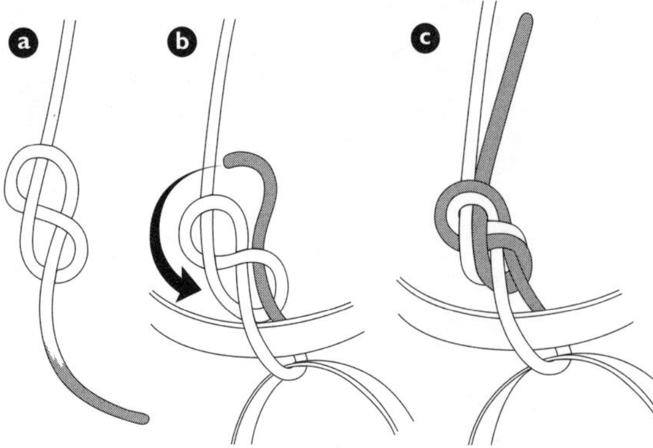

Fig. 9-12. Rewoven figure eight: a, tie a figure eight; b, double the loose end back and retrace the 8 so the loose end is parallel to the standing end; c, pull both the ends and the end loop tight.

Figure Eight Bend

The figure eight bend may be used to join two ropes together for rappeling or to create a cordelette or equalette used in building anchors (see Chapter 10, Belaying). Tie a figure eight in the loose end of one rope (fig. 9-13a). Use the loose end of the other rope to retrace the 8, going toward the standing end of the first rope (fig. 9-13b, c, and d). (Caution: Do not accidentally tie an offset figure eight bend by holding the two loose ends parallel and tying a figure eight with the two strands. This is very dangerous to use for a rappel.) After being weighted, the figure eight bend is easier to untie than the double fisherman's bend.

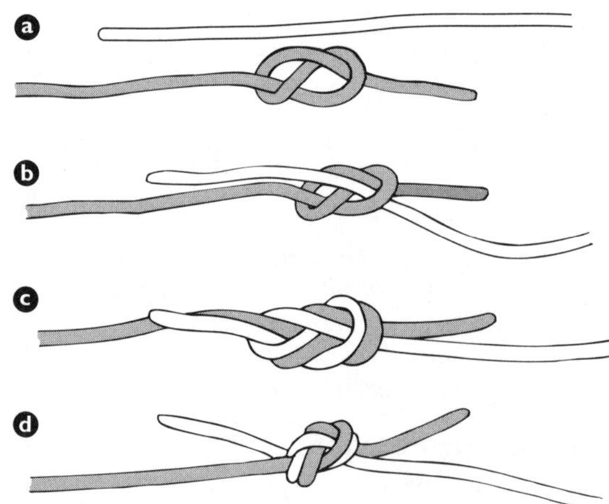

Fig. 9-13. Figure eight bend: a, tie a figure eight in the loose end of one rope; b and c, retrace the 8 using the other rope's loose end; d, tighten all four strands.

Single Bowline

The single bowline (fig. 9-14a) makes a loop at the end of the climbing rope that will not slip, and it can secure the rope around a tree or other anchor. The loose end of the rope should come out on the inside of the bowline's loop (fig. 9-14b) because the knot is much weaker if the loose end finishes on the outside of the loop. Tie off the loose end with an overhand knot (fig. 9-14c and d).

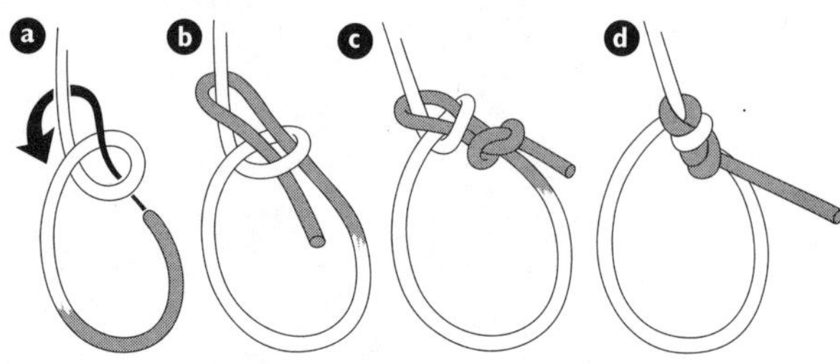

Fig. 9-14. Single bowline: a, make a loop and pass the loose end of the rope under and through it, then around the back of the standing end; b, bring the loose end back through the loop; c, pull ends tight and tie an overhand knot; d, dressed and backed-up knot.

Double Bowline

The middle climber on a three-person rope can tie the double bowline (fig. 9-15a) to the seat harness. Secure the resulting end loop with an overhand knot or a locking carabiner (fig. 9-15b); the carabiner makes a cleaner finish and a smaller knot.

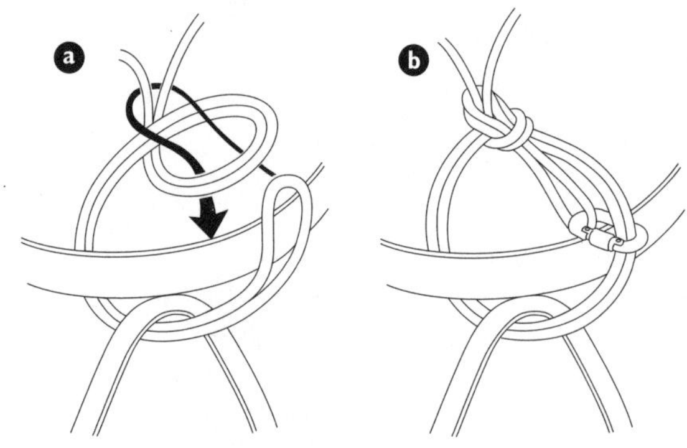

Fig. 9-15. Double bowline: a, tie a bowline on a bight; b, secure end loop with a locking carabiner.

Single Bowline with a Yosemite Finish

The single bowline with a Yosemite finish (fig. 9-16a) is the same as a single bowline, except that the loose end retraces the rope until it is parallel with the standing end (fig. 9-16b and c). This knot is easy to untie after it has been loaded, making it a good choice for a top-roping tie-in.

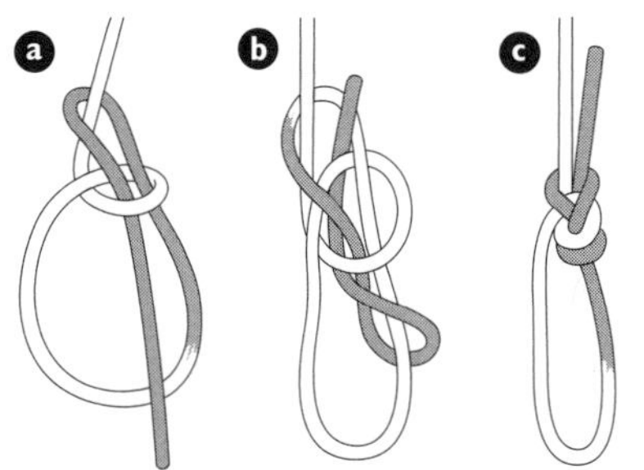

Fig. 9-16. Single bowline with a Yosemite finish: a, tie a single bowline, keeping the knot loose; b, bring the loose end under and over the rope and under the entire knot, then up through the bowline's topmost loop; c, pull all four strands tight.

Butterfly Knot

The useful characteristic of the butterfly knot (fig. 9-17) is that it can sustain a pull on either end of the rope or the loop and not come undone. A connection to this knot is made with a locking carabiner through the loop.

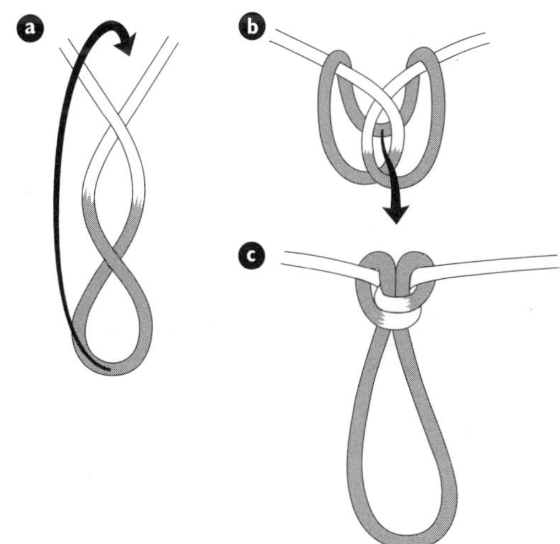

Fig. 9-17. Butterfly knot: a, form a double loop; b, pull the lower loop over and then back up through upper loop; c, pull loop and both strands tight.

Clove Hitch

The clove hitch (fig. 9-18a and b) is a quick knot for clipping in to a locking carabiner (fig. 9-18c) attached to an anchor (fig. 9-18d). The main advantage of the clove hitch is that the knot makes it easy to adjust the length of the rope between the belayer and the anchor without unclipping the rope from the carabiner.

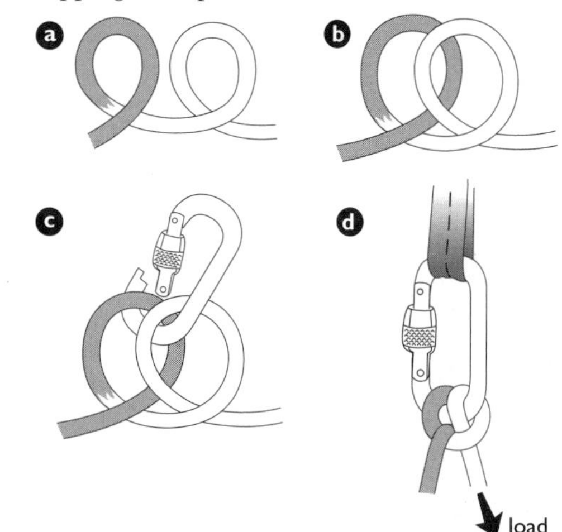

Fig. 9-18. Clove hitch: a, form two bights side by side; b, bring left-hand bight behind the other; c, clip a locking carabiner through both bights; d, pull both ends tight.

Girth Hitch

The girth hitch (fig. 9-19a) is a simple knot that can serve a variety of purposes, such as attaching webbing to a natural anchor or to a pack's haul loop (fig. 9-19b). It can also be used to tie off a short-driven piton (see Figure 13-9 in Chapter 13, Rock Protection).

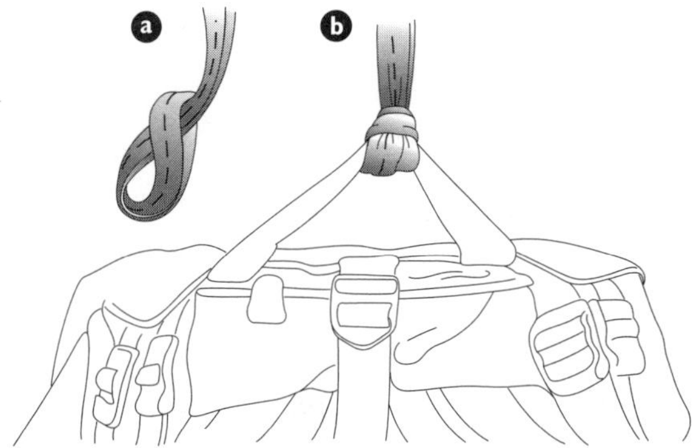

Fig. 9-19. Girth hitch: a, pull both ends through a bight; b, girth hitch tied around a pack's haul loop.

Overhand Slipknot

The overhand slipknot (fig. 9-20a and b) is another simple knot. It may be used to attach a tie-off loop (see "Runners," below) or one end of a personal anchor (see "Personal Anchors," below) to a carabiner. The overhand slipknot has the added benefit of immobilizing a runner's knot or a sewn bar tack on the carabiner (fig. 9-20c). Like the girth hitch, it can also be used to cinch a runner to a rock feature or to tie off a short-driven piton.

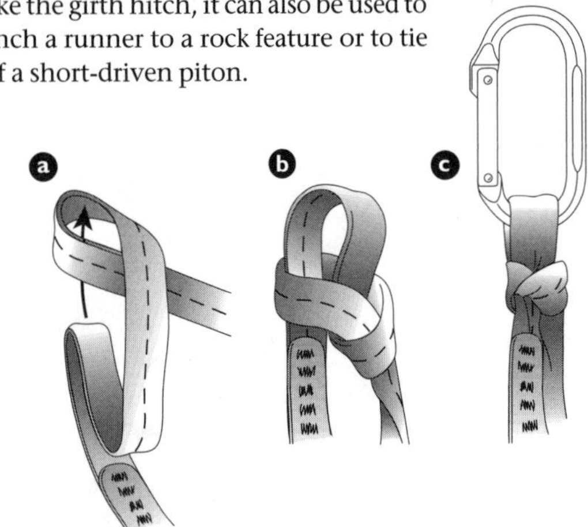

Fig. 9-20. Overhand slipknot: a, make a loop, then bring a bight up through the loop; b, draw loop closed to tie off bight; c, clip bight into a carabiner and pull both ends tight.

Mule Knot

The mule knot is used to temporarily tie off a belay to a fallen climber so both hands may be safely used to set up an anchor and free oneself from the climbing rope (see "Escaping the Belay" in Chapter 10). When belaying with a device, wherein the braking hand is pulling back, pull a bight of rope through the locking carabiner on your harness (fig. 9-21a). Pull the bight behind the loaded strand of rope going to the fallen climber and twist to form a loop. Then fold another bight of rope over the loaded strand and push it through the loop (fig. 9-21b). Remove any slack and pull the knot tight by pulling on the upper strand (fig. 9-21c); the result is called a device-mule. Back up the device-mule with an overhand knot (fig. 9-21d).

When using a munter hitch belay (this hitch is described below), hold the fallen weight with the braking hand and make a loop in the rope on the same side as the braking hand. With the other hand, pull some slack rope behind the loaded strand of rope going to the climber and make a bight (fig. 9-22a). Fold the bight over the rope and push it through the loop. Tighten the knot by pulling on the upper strand (fig 9-22b). Pull additional slack through the mule knot as needed by

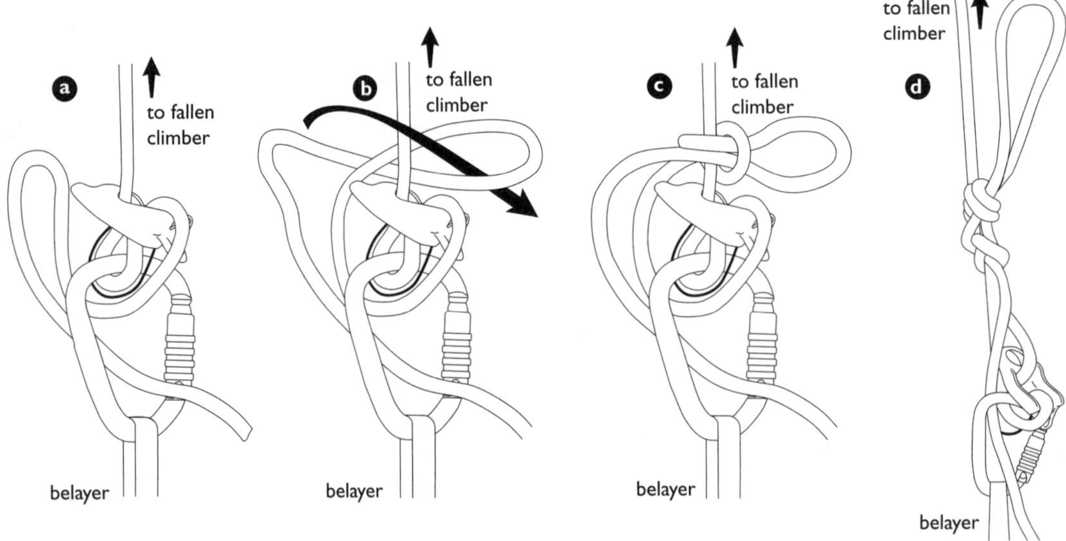

Fig. 9-21. Mule knot with belay device (device-mule): a, pull a bight of rope through the locking carabiner; b, pull the bight behind the loaded strand and form a loop, then fold another bight over the front of the loaded strand and push it through the loop; c, remove slack and tighten knot by pulling on the upper strand; d, back up with an overhand knot, pulling on the lower strand if more rope is needed.

pulling on the lower strand; the result is a munter-mule. Back up the munter-mule with an overhand knot around the climbing rope (fig. 9-22c).

The mule knot also is a useful temporary tie-off when stopping during a rappel.

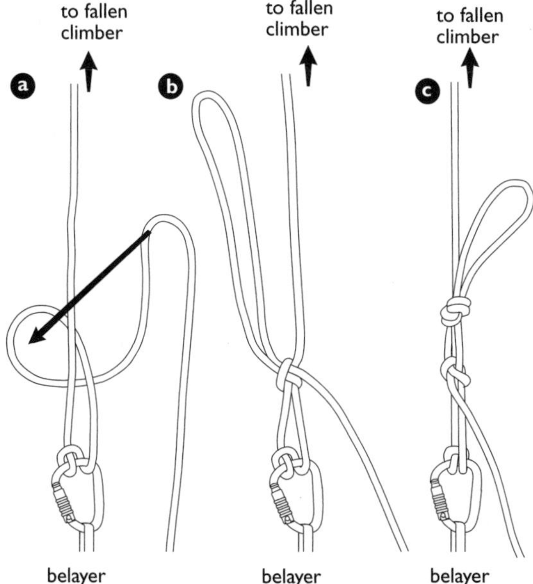

Fig. 9-22. Mule knot with munter hitch (munter-mule): a, make a loop under the loaded strand, then take a bight and fold it around the loaded strand and through the loop; b, tighten the knot by pulling on the upper strand; c, back up with an overhand knot, pulling on the lower strand if more rope is needed.

FRICTION HITCHES

Friction hitches are a quick and simple way to set up a system for ascending or descending a climbing rope without the use of mechanical ascenders or for backing up a rappel. Hitches grip the climbing rope when weight is placed on them but are free to move when the weight is released. The best-known friction hitch is the prusik, but others, such as the bachmann and the klemheist, are also useful.

Prusik Hitch

The prusik hitch requires a girth hitch (fig. 9-23a) and a few wraps of accessory cord around the climbing rope (fig. 9-23b and c). For use on a climbing rope, a tie-off loop of 5- to 7-millimeter accessory cord, for example, is wrapped two (fig. 9-23d) or three (fig. 9-23e) times around the rope. Icy ropes, thinner-diameter ropes, or heavy loads require more wraps of the hitch to ensure sufficient friction to hold the load.

To create the necessary friction, the cord must be smaller in diameter than the climbing rope; the greater the difference in diameter, the better the hitch grips. However, very small-diameter cords make the prusik hitch more difficult to manipulate than do cords of larger diameter. Experiment to see which diameter of cord works best. Webbing is usually not used for prusik hitches because it may not hold.

By attaching two slings to a climbing rope with prusik hitches, you can ascend or descend the climbing rope. Chapter 17, Glacier Travel and Crevasse Rescue, explains the Texas-prusik method of ascending the rope using prusiks.

The prusik hitch is also used as part of the rescue systems needed to raise and lower people and equipment during rescues. These systems are also described in Chapter 17.

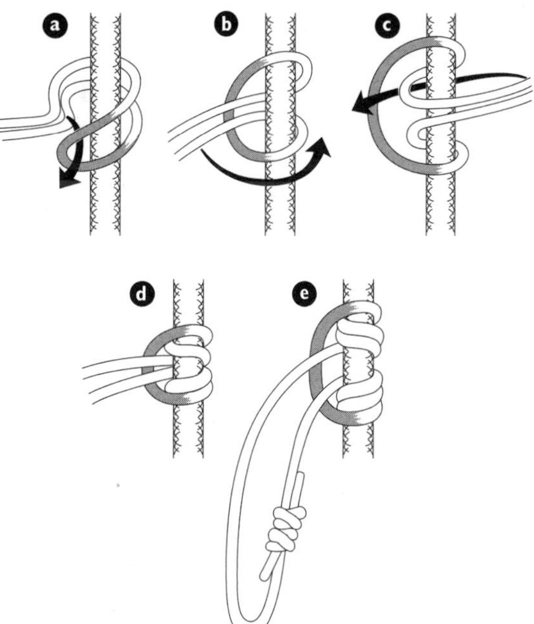

Fig. 9-23. Prusik hitch: a, girth-hitch cord around rope; b, bring loose ends of cord around the rope and under cord; c, wrap loose ends around rope again; d, two-wrap prusik hitch; e, three-wrap prusik hitch.

9

Bachmann Hitch

The bachmann hitch is used for the same purposes as a prusik hitch. The bachmann hitch is tied around a carabiner (fig. 9-24a) and the climbing rope (fig. 9-24b and c), making it much easier to loosen and slide than a prusik. The bachmann hitch has the virtue of sometimes being "self-tending" (it will feed rope in the non-load-bearing direction without requiring you to actively manipulate it) when the climbing rope is passing through it.

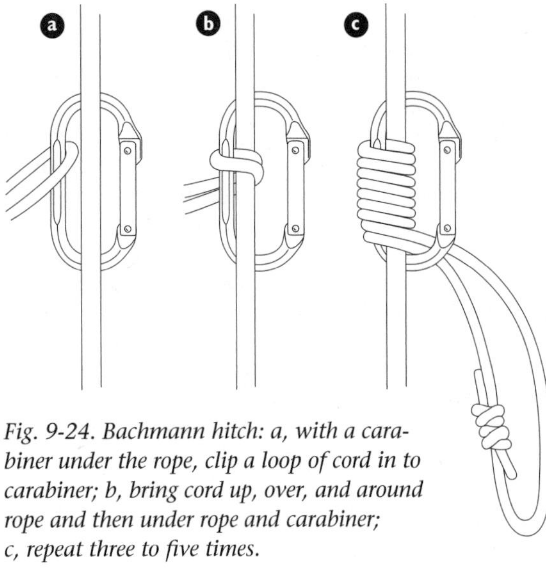

Fig. 9-24. Bachmann hitch: a, with a carabiner under the rope, clip a loop of cord in to carabiner; b, bring cord up, over, and around rope and then under rope and carabiner; c, repeat three to five times.

Klemheist Hitch

The klemheist hitch is another alternative to the prusik, with the advantage that it can be made from either accessory cord or webbing, which may become important if you are caught with an ample supply of webbing but little cord.

A tied loop of cord or webbing is wound around the main rope in a spiral and then threaded through the loop created by the top wrap of the cord or webbing (fig. 9-25a). Pull down to create the basic klemheist (fig. 9-25b), which can be clipped to a carabiner (fig. 9-25c). The tied-off klemheist (fig. 9-25d) is less likely to jam and easier to loosen and slide than the basic klemheist. The klemheist can also be tied around a carabiner (fig. 9-25e), which then provides a good handhold on the rope.

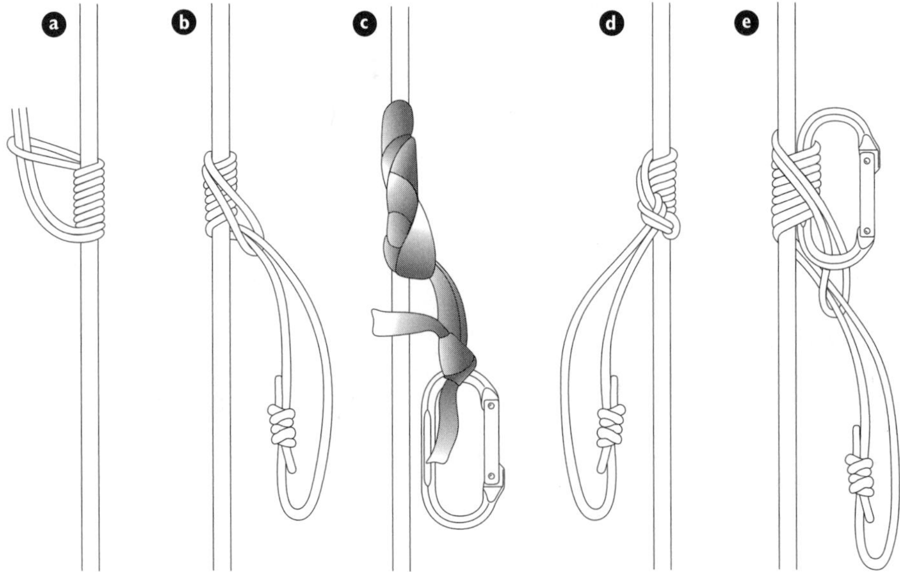

Fig. 9-25. Klemheist hitch: a, wrap a loop of cord around the rope five times and draw loose ends through the end loop; b, pull ends down; c, klemheist hitch tied using webbing and clipped to a carabiner; d, klemheist hitch tied off—bring ends up, then under and over the loop, forming a new loop, and then down through this loop, pulling the ends tight; e, klemheist tied around a carabiner.

Autoblock Hitch

The autoblock hitch is similar to the klemheist but should be made only with accessory cord, not webbing. One end of the cord is girth-hitched to the harness leg loop. The cord is then wrapped three or more times around the rope to provide friction, and the free end of the loop is secured to the leg loop with a carabiner. The autoblock is often used as a self-belay during rappels (See Figure 11-20 in Chapter 11, Rappeling). If using an extended harness during a rappel, then both ends of the autoblock would be clipped directly into the harness carabiner.

Munter Hitch

The munter hitch is very easy to set up and use, but it feeds rope effectively only if used on a large pear-shaped or HMS locking carabiner. The munter is a simple hitch in the rope (fig. 9-26a) that is clipped in to a carabiner (fig. 9-26b) to create friction (fig. 9-26c).

It is an excellent method of belaying a leader or lowering a climber, because the hitch is reversible (the rope can be fed out of the carabiner, or the rope can be pulled back in through the carabiner) and the knot provides sufficient friction for the belayer to stop a falling or lowering climber by holding the braking end of the rope. The munter hitch can also provide the necessary rope friction for rappeling, though it puts more twist in the rope than other rappel methods. Even if you prefer to use a specialized belay device, this hitch is worth knowing as a backup if you lose or forget your belay device.

The munter hitch is known by a variety of names: the friction hitch, Italian hitch, half ring bend, carabiner hitch, running R, half-mast belay, backhanded hitch, and UIAA method. It was introduced in Europe in 1973 as the *halbmastwurf sicherung* ("half clove-hitch belay"), abbreviated as HMS.

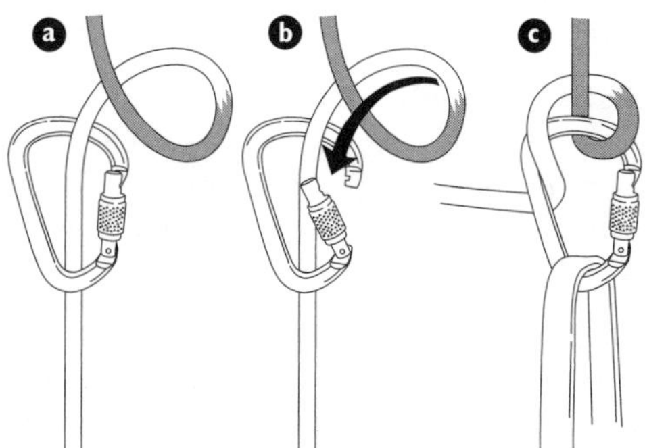

Fig. 9-26. The munter hitch: a, draw rope up through carabiner and form a bight; b, clip carabiner through bight; c, pull ends in opposite directions.

HELMETS

Climbing helmets help protect your head from rockfall and from gear dropped by climbers above you. Helmets also protect you from the many ways in which you can suddenly impact hard surfaces such as rock or ice: a fall to the ground, a leader fall that swings you into a wall, or a quick move upward against a sharp outcropping. However, keep in mind that no helmet can protect you from all possible impacts.

Modern climbing helmets are lightweight, ventilated, and available in many designs (fig. 9-27). Buy a climbing helmet with the UIAA and/or CEN mark, which ensures minimum standards of impact resistance. Shell materials may be plastic, fiberglass, and/or carbon fiber. The suspension system may be a system of strapping, which keeps the helmet shell from coming into contact with

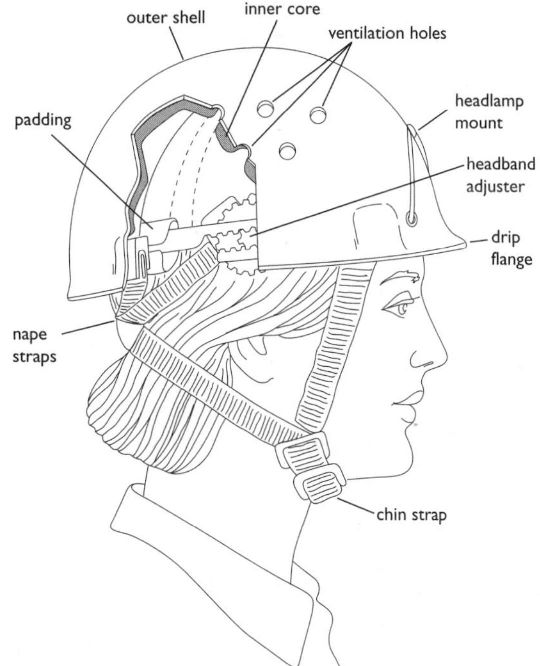

Fig. 9-27. Climbing helmet features; generally, no individual helmet will come with all these features.

9

your head during impact, or a polystyrene core designed to shatter upon severe impact, absorbing force. This latter design must be replaced after an impact. It is recommended that any helmet be replaced as soon as possible after a significant impact: Any time you take a hard hit and think to yourself, "I would have been seriously hurt if not for my helmet," then it is probably time to get a new one. Make sure that a headlamp can be attached securely to the helmet.

Choose a helmet that fits well and can be adjusted to fit your bare head whether or not you are wearing a hat or balaclava. Fit is very individual because normal skull shapes and sizes vary. Make sure you wear the helmet so it is forward (fig. 9-28a), which helps protect your forehead and frontal lobe, rather than tipped back (fig. 9-28b).

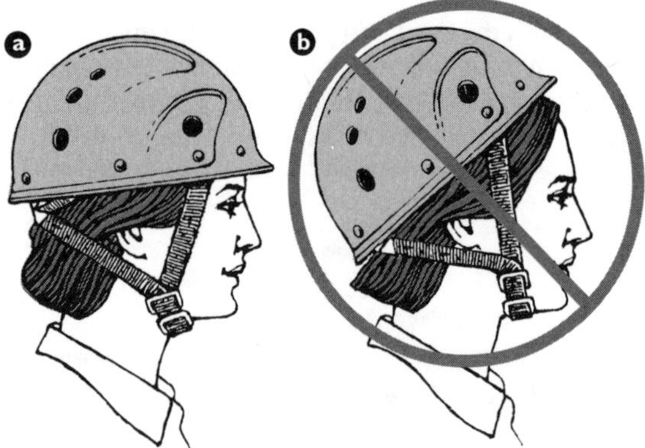

Fig. 9-28. Wearing a helmet: a, proper; b, improper, leaving forehead exposed to rockfall and icefall.

Climbing helmets have a limited life span. Even with limited use, they should be retired no later than ten years after the date of manufacture (stamped on some brands). Even with ultraviolet inhibitors, the plastic materials in the helmets are vulnerable to ultraviolet radiation from sunlight, which causes them to weaken. Frequent climbers may want to cut the time they use a helmet in half (if not more). A helmet should be retired when it has been dented, cracked, or damaged—including the straps. Helmets can be damaged and still not show obvious wear and tear.

To maximize the life of your helmet, protect it from banging against hard surfaces, which makes it vulnerable to chipping and cracking, whether it is hanging from your pack or sitting in the trunk of your car. And follow these steps each time before storing it:

- Test to see that the chin buckle is in good working order.
- Check the webbing (near the ears). Is it in good shape and free from frays and tears?
- Make sure the foam casing is secure inside the helmet's shell.

HARNESSES

In the early days of climbing, the climbing rope was looped around a climber's waist several times and tied in to the rope with a bowline on a coil. That practice is no longer considered safe because long falls onto waist loops can severely injure a climber's back and ribs. Additionally, falls that left the climber hanging, such as a fall into a crevasse or over the lip of an overhang, could cause the rope to ride up and constrict the climber's diaphragm, leading to suffocation. Improvising leg loops and attaching them to the whole coil can help prevent injury, but the bowline on a coil is best avoided except for emergencies.

Today, climbers tie the rope in to a harness designed to distribute the force of a fall over a larger percentage of the climber's body. A climber at either end of a climbing rope ties in to the harness with a knot such as the rewoven figure eight (see Figure 9-12). A climber in the middle of a rope usually ties in to the harness with a double rewoven figure eight or a double bowline (see Figure 9-15).

Harnesses deteriorate over time; they should be inspected often and replaced with the same frequency as a climbing rope. The bowline on a coil remains an option for emergency use if no harness or harness material is available, but an improvised diaper sling (see below) would be a better choice.

SEAT HARNESSES

With properly fitted leg loops, a seat harness rides snugly above your hip bones yet transfers the force of a fall over your entire pelvis. It also provides a comfortable seat during rappeling.

Manufactured Seat Harness

Several features are particularly desirable in a mountaineering seat harness (fig. 9-29). Adjustable leg loops maintain a snug fit no matter how few or how many layers of clothing you are wearing. A padded waist belt and leg loops can provide additional comfort, particularly if you will be hanging for any length of time. Leg loops that can

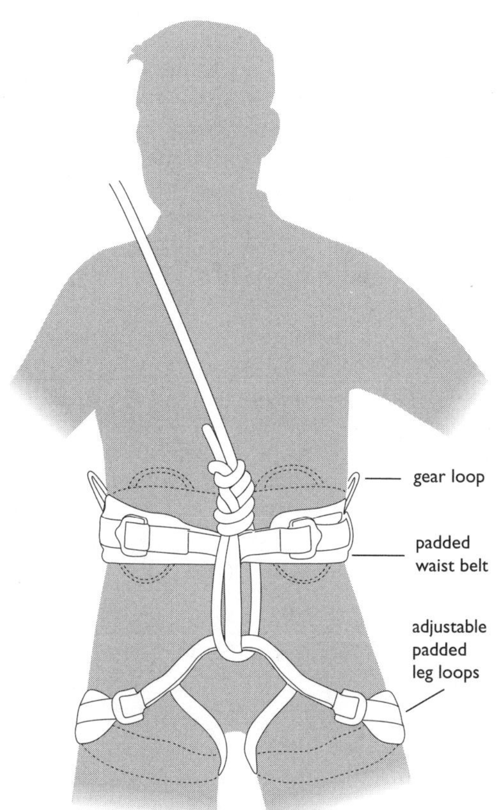

Fig. 9-29. Seat harness with common features.

be unbuckled permit toilet calls without your having to remove the harness or untie from the rope. Having the waist buckle located toward one side helps avoid conflict with the rope tie-in or with the locking carabiner that is attached to the harness for use in belaying and rappelling. Gear loops are desirable for carrying carabiners and other pieces of climbing gear.

Before buying a harness, try it on to be sure the harness fits properly over your climbing clothes. With the profusion of harness styles on the market, you must consult each manufacturer's instructions to learn how to safely wear and tie in to that particular harness. Printed instructions accompany any new harness, and they also are usually sewn inside the waist belt. For most harnesses, you must pass the waist strap back over and through the main buckle a second time for safety. Be sure at least 2 to 3 inches (about 5 centimeters) of strap extends beyond the buckle after you reweave the strap.

Diaper Sling

In an emergency, a diaper sling may be improvised as a harness. The diaper sling takes about 10 feet (3 meters) of webbing tied in a large loop. With the loop behind your back, pull each end around your sides to your stomach (fig. 9-30a). Bring one piece of the webbing loop down from behind your back and between your legs, then up to your stomach to meet the other two loop ends (fig. 9-30b). Clip them together in front with two opposite and opposed carabiners (see Figure 9-37a) or a locking carabiner (fig. 9-30c). The diaper sling may also be clipped to a safety loop made of webbing tied around your waist.

9

A description of how to build a homemade seat harness can be found in a book for professional rescuers: *Technical Rescue Riggers Guide*, by Rick Lipke (see Appendix D, Supplemental Resources). The homemade seat harness is not a substitute for the effective reliability of a modern commercial harness, but the knowledge of how to build one could be useful in an emergency if the requisite amount of tubular webbing is available.

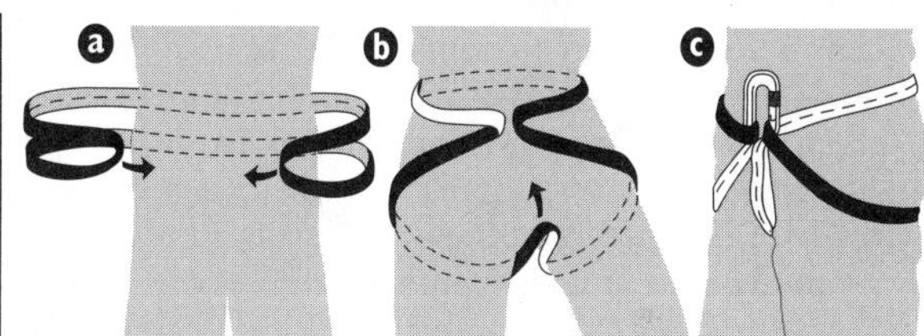

Fig. 9-30. Diaper sling: a, bring large loop around waist from the back; b, bring one piece of loop behind back down through the legs and up; c, clip all three parts together.

Personal Anchors

Many climbers use a personal anchor, or leash, and attach themselves to belay and rappel anchors while they set up and tear down the belay, the rappel, and/or the anchor. Use a runner, usually double length (see "Runners," below), and girth-hitch one end to the seat harness, following the same path with the runner as you would to tie the climbing rope to your harness. Add a locking carabiner to the other end of the runner for connecting to the anchor.

When not in use, the personal anchor can be wrapped around the waist and clipped to the seat harness or otherwise neatly stowed on the seat harness. Commercial personal anchors are available that are made of a series of full-strength loops, so the system can be shortened and lengthened.

Daisy chains are sometimes used as personal anchors, but they are dangerous if used incorrectly. They are made for aid climbing (see Chapter 15, Aid and Big Wall Climbing), and the stitches of the sewn links are rated for body weight only. If you cross-clip only a sewn link (that is, clip in to the anchor through two loops of the daisy chain), a fall can break the relatively weak bar tacks separating the loops and completely detach the climber from the anchor. The result can be catastrophic failure.

CHEST HARNESS

A chest harness helps keep you upright after a fall or while ascending a rope using prusiks or mechanical ascenders. Following a fall, you simply clip the climbing rope through the carabiner of the chest harness, which provides stability and assists you in staying upright. The chest harness will deliver some of the force of a fall to your chest, which is more easily injured than your pelvis (where the force is directed by a seat harness). Thus, a rope is not usually clipped in to the chest harness during rock climbing or general mountaineering. The rope is sometimes clipped in to the chest harness during glacier travel, though some climbers prefer to leave the rope unclipped until a crevasse fall actually occurs (see Chapter 17, Glacier Travel and Crevasse Rescue).

A chest harness may be purchased or is readily improvised with a long loop of webbing (a long runner). One popular design depends on a carabiner to bring the ends of the harness together at your chest. To make a carabiner chest harness, start with 9.5 feet (2.9 meters) of 1-inch tubular webbing. Use a distinctive color of webbing to distinguish the chest harness from other double-length runners (see the next section, "Runners"). Tie the webbing into a loop with a water knot; adjust the size of the webbing loop to fit comfortably. Give the loop a half twist to create two temporary loops, and push one arm all the way through each loop. Lift the runner over your head and let it drop against your back, with the crossed portion at your back (fig. 9-31a); then pull the two sides together in front and clip with a carabiner at your chest (fig. 9-31b). Keep the knot in front of you and out of the way of the carabiner.

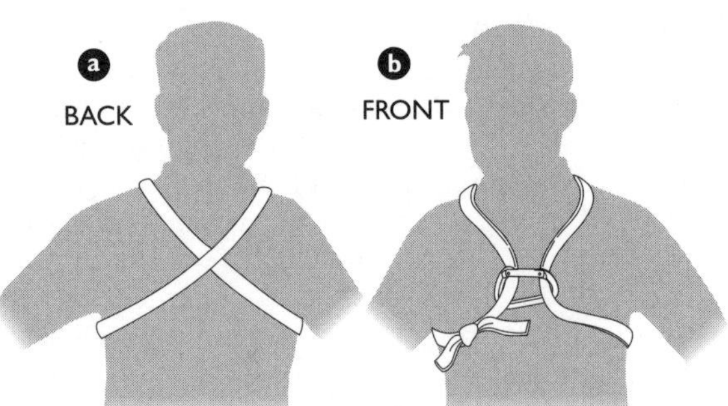

Fig. 9-31. Carabiner chest harness: a, form two loops in a runner by twisting it across the back; b, clip the two loops together at the chest with a carabiner.

BODY HARNESS

Full-body harnesses, which incorporate both a chest and a seat harness, have a higher tie-in point (fig. 9-32). This reduces the chance of your flipping over backward during a fall. Because a body harness distributes the force of a fall throughout the trunk of your body, there may be less danger of lower-back injury.

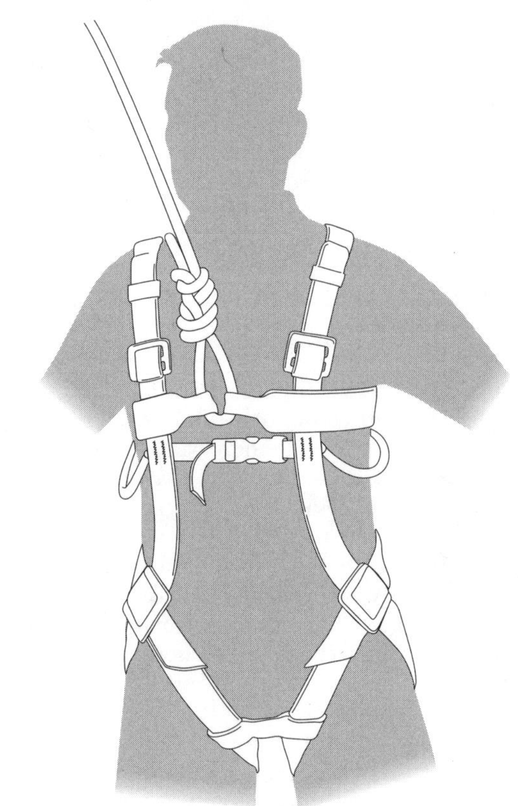

Fig. 9-32. Full-body harness.

Although in some circumstances body harnesses may be safer, they have not found popular favor in mountaineering. They are more expensive and restrictive and make it hard to add or remove clothing. Instead, most climbers use a seat harness and then improvise a chest harness when one is warranted, such as when climbing with a heavy pack, crossing glaciers, or aid climbing under large overhangs. Full-body harnesses are necessary for children whose hips are not yet fully developed.

RUNNERS

Loops of tubular webbing or round accessory cord, called runners or slings, are among the simplest pieces of climbing equipment and among the most useful. (Note that flat webbing differs from tubular webbing: Flat webbing is used for things like pack straps, while tubular webbing—so-called even though it lies flat—is used in climbing-specific applications.) Runners are a critical link in climbing systems. Standard single runners require 5.5 feet (1.7 meters) of webbing or cord. Double-length runners require 9.5 feet (2.9 meters) of webbing or cord. Triple-length runners require 15 feet (4.6 meters) of webbing or cord. After being tied into loops, the standard lengths become 2 feet (0.6 meter), 4 feet (1.2 meters), and 6 feet (1.8 meters) for single-, double-, and triple-length runners, respectively. A beginning climber should own many single runners, a few doubles, and a triple.

To help you quickly identify the different lengths, it is useful to use single runners of one color of webbing, double runners of another color, and triple runners of a third color. For a tied webbing runner, it is useful to write your initials and the date the runner was made on one of the tails of the water knot. Identifying the runner and its age helps in deciding when to retire it. Runners should be retired regularly, using the same considerations as for retiring a rope or harness (see those sections above).

It is very important to remember that webbing and accessory cord do not have dynamic characteristics. If they are used without a dynamic rope, a fall of even a few feet can impart catastrophic force onto the anchor system and climber (see Chapter 10, Belaying, for forces on anchors).

Sewn. You can purchase high-strength, presewn runners (fig. 9-33a) at climbing stores. Sewn runners come in various lengths: 4-inch (10-centimeter), 6-inch (15-centimeter), 12-inch (30-centimeter, called half-length), 2-foot (0.6-meter, called single-length), 4-foot (1.2-meter, called double-length), 6-foot (1.8 meter, called triple-length), and also in sizes between the standard half-, single-, double-, and triple-length runners. Some runners are specially sewn into preformed quickdraws, typically 4 to 8 inches long, and have carabiners attached at each end (fig. 9-33b). Sewn runners also come in a variety of widths, with 9/16, 11/16, and 1-inch (1.4-, 1.7-, and 2.5-centimeter) widths the most common.

Runners are often made from Dyneema and Spectra, high-performance polyethylene fibers that are stronger, more durable, and less susceptible to ultraviolet deterioration than nylon. However, these materials have a lower melting temperature and lower friction, which can affect their use in friction hitches. Sewn runners are generally stronger, usually lighter, and less bulky than tied runners. Using a sewn runner also eliminates the possibility of the knot untying, a concern with tied runners.

Tied. Runners can also be made by tying a loop in 9/16- to 1-inch tubular webbing or in 8- to 9-millimeter Perlon accessory cord. A runner made of webbing is typically tied with a water knot to make the loop (fig. 9-33c). Avoid putting twists into the runner while tying it. A cord runner is typically tied with either a double fisherman's bend (see Figure 9-10) or a triple fisherman's bend, required for Spectra or aramid-fiber (Kevlar) cord. Tails on tied runners should be 2–3 inches (5–8 centimeters) long. If the webbing or cord is cut to make the runner, the ends must be melted with a small flame to keep the ends from unraveling.

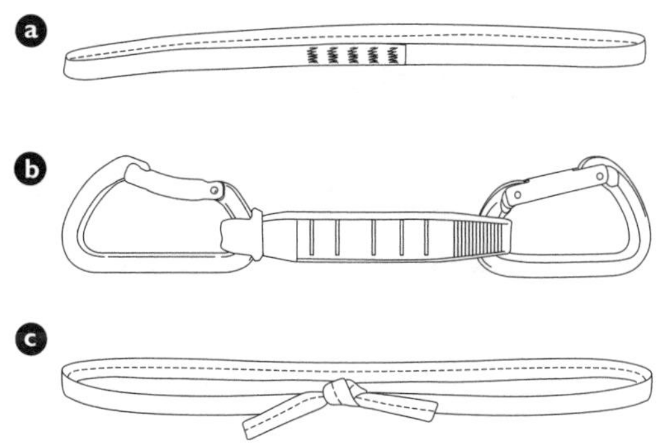

Fig. 9-33. Runners made of webbing: a, sewn runner; b, sewn quickdraw with two carabiners; c, tied runner.

Tied runners have several advantages over commercially sewn runners. Tied runners are inexpensive to make, can be untied and threaded around trees and natural chockstones (rocks firmly lodged in cracks), and can be untied and retied with another runner to create longer runners.

Tie-off loops. Also called hero loops, tie-off loops are short runners usually made of 5- to 8-millimeter cord tied (fig. 9-34a) or ½- to ⅝-inch webbing sewn or tied (fig. 9-34b) into a loop. The length of the loop depends on its intended use. They are commonly used for tying off belays (Chapter 10, Belaying), for self-belay during a rappel (Chapter 11, Rappeling), in aid climbing (Chapter 15, Aid and Big Wall Climbing), and in crevasse rescue (Chapter 17, Glacier Travel and Crevasse Rescue).

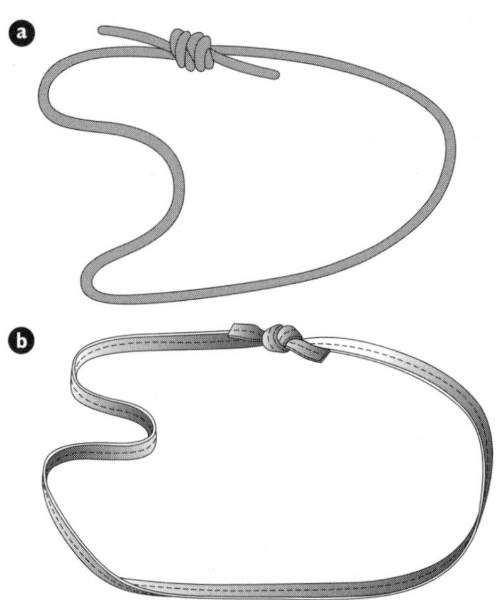

Fig. 9-34. Tie-off loops: a, double fisherman's bend in cord; b, water knot in webbing.

Load-limiting runners. A climber can effectively limit the maximum impact on individual protection placements by using a load-limiting device (such as the Yates Gear Screamer). A load-limiting runner consists of a sewn runner with a series of weaker bar tacks (fig. 9-35a), usually encased in a sheath (fig. 9-35b); the bar tacks fail at a specific impact force, which reduces high loads, while the runner retains full strength if fully extended (fig. 9-35c).

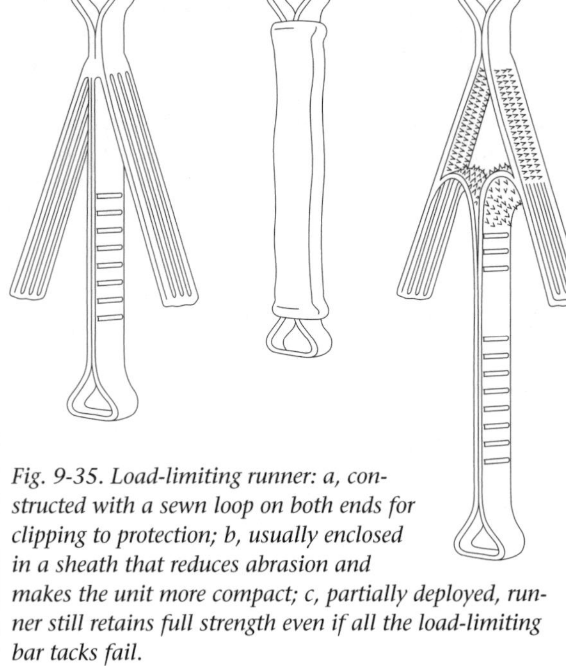

Fig. 9-35. Load-limiting runner: a, constructed with a sewn loop on both ends for clipping to protection; b, usually enclosed in a sheath that reduces abrasion and makes the unit more compact; c, partially deployed, runner still retains full strength even if all the load-limiting bar tacks fail.

CARABINERS

Carabiners are another versatile and indispensable climbing tool used for belaying, rappeling, prusiking, clipping in to safety anchors, securing the rope to points of protection, and numerous other tasks.

SHAPES AND STYLES

Carabiners come in many sizes and shapes. Ovals (fig. 9-36a) were once very popular for general mountaineering because their symmetry makes them good for many purposes. D carabiners (fig. 9-36b) also offer a good general-purpose shape, but they are stronger than ovals because more of the load is transferred to the long axis and away from the gate, the typical point of failure for a carabiner. Offset Ds (fig. 9-36c) have the strength advantage of standard Ds, but the offset D's gate opens wider, making it easier to clip in awkward situations. Bent-gate carabiners (fig. 9-36d) facilitate clipping and allow climbers to quickly clip and unclip the carabiners from the feel of the gates alone; they are often used in quickdraws for sport climbing.

Traditionally, the gate of a carabiner connects to the rest of the frame through a latch that creates a hook

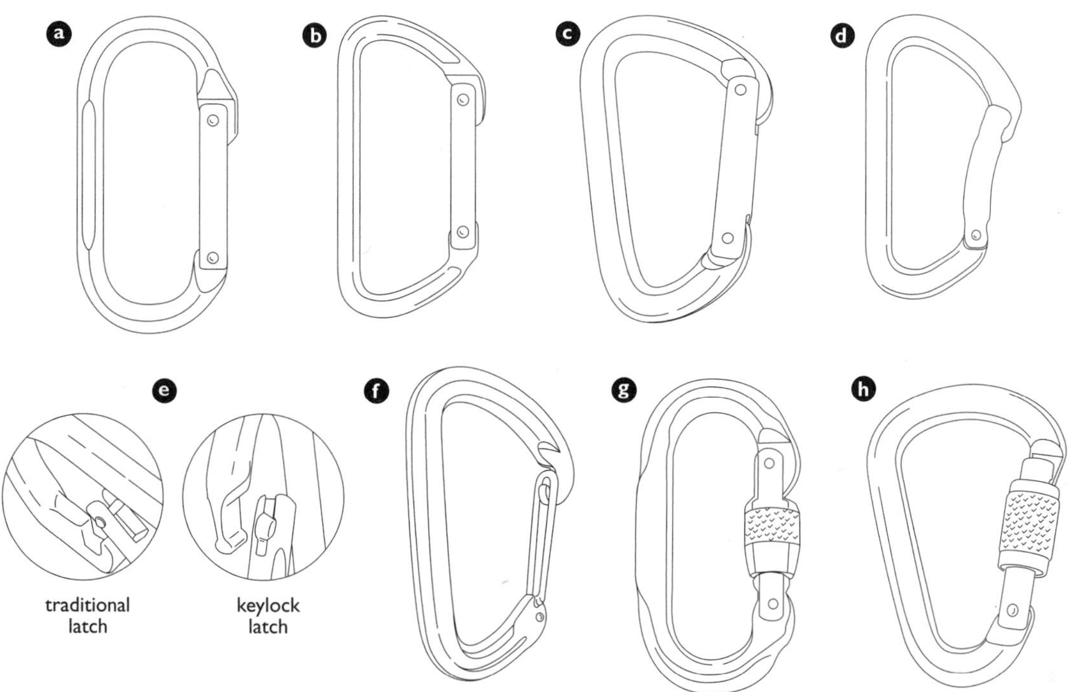

Fig. 9-36. Carabiners: a, oval carabiner; b, standard D carabiner; c, offset D carabiner; d, bent-gate carabiner; e, traditional latch and newer keylock latch ; f, wire-gate carabiner; g, standard locking carabiner; h, pear-shaped locking carabiner.

toward the inside of the carabiner. Because this latch's hook can interfere with unclipping ropes or slings, several models of carabiner now use a keylock connection that doesn't use a hook (fig. 9-36e).

With a trend toward lighter and stronger gear, wire-gate carabiners have become very common (fig. 9-36f). They provide a strong gate at a reduced weight, and they are less prone to freezing. Some studies also indicate that wire-gate carabiners are less prone to gate fluttering, which can occur when a rope passes quickly through a carabiner during a leader fall.

Some carabiners are made from bars with cross sections that are oval, T-shaped or cross-shaped, or wedge-shaped—as opposed to round—in order to save weight.

Locking carabiners. With a sleeve that screws over one end of the gate to minimize accidental opening, locking carabiners (fig. 9-36g) provide a wider margin of safety for rappeling, belaying, or clipping in to anchors. Some locking carabiners have a spring that automatically positions the sleeve, rather than the climber having to screw it down, whenever the gate is closed. Regardless of the carabiner's particular locking mechanism, always check to make sure that the carabiner is properly locked. Test it manually before relying on it.

Pear-shaped locking carabiners, also called HMS carabiners (fig. 9-36h), are much larger at the gate-opening end than at the hinge end; they are ideal for belaying with the munter hitch (see Figure 9-26). They are also a good choice for use in conjunction with the seat harness. The extra cost and weight of pear-shaped locking carabiners is justified by the increased ease of loading and managing all the ropes, knots, cords, and runners that are used at the seat harness' anchor point.

Two regular carabiners can be substituted for a locking carabiner, but only if they are joined correctly. Align the gate side of each carabiner with the spine side of the other, so their gates are on opposite sides. The gate-opening ends should face the same direction (fig. 9-37a), so the two gates open toward—or opposed to—each other. This opposite and opposed configuration helps prevent the carabiners from being

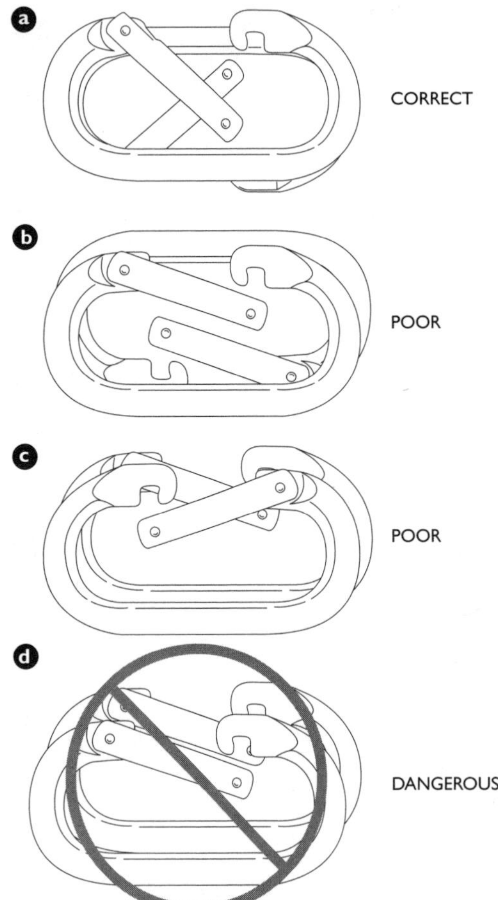

Fig. 9-37. Substituting double oval carabiners for a locking carabiner: a, gates are on opposite sides and the same ends, so they are opposite and opposed (correct); b, gates are on opposite sides and ends, so they are opposite and parallel (poor); c, gates are on the same sides and opposite ends, so they are parallel and opposed (poor); d, gates are on the same sides and ends, so they are doubly parallel (dangerous).

forced open and accidentally unclipping. You can check that the carabiners are in the proper configuration by opening both gates at the same time; in profile, the gates should appear to cross, forming an X.

USE AND CARE

A few basic rules apply to the use and care of all carabiners. Always make sure the force on a carabiner falls on the spine side, and be especially careful that the gate does not receive the load.

Check the carabiner gates occasionally. A gate should open easily, even when the carabiner is loaded, and the gate should have good side-to-side rigidity when open.

A dirty gate can be cleaned by applying a solvent or lubricant (lightweight oil, citrus solvent, or products such as WD-40) to the hinge, working the hinge until it operates smoothly again, and then dipping the carabiner in boiling water for about 20 seconds to remove the cleaning agent.

Finally, remember that a carabiner that has fallen off a cliff onto a hard surface may have suffered invisible damage and should be retired.

KEEPING THE SAFETY NET STRONG

Avoid using any critical climbing equipment if its history is not personally known to you. Ropes, harnesses, runners, and carabiners, as well as protection pieces (see Chapter 13, Rock Protection) and belay devices (see Chapter 10, Belaying), are all vital links in your chain of protection. Secondhand equipment, whether found or passed along without an account of its use, increases the possibility of a weak link in the chain protecting the lives of you and your climbing partner.

Knowing your equipment and knowing how to use it are essential for safe climbing. But the most important part of the basic safety system is you. There is no substitute for common sense, judgment, and a sense of awareness to keep you safe in a climbing environment.

HOW BELAYS ARE USED IN CLIMBING • APPLYING BRAKING FORCE TO THE ROPE • ANCHORS • BELAY POSITION AND STANCE • ROPE HANDLING • COMMUNICATION • OTHER BELAY TECHNIQUES • SECURING THE FREEDOM OF THE HILLS

Chapter 10 BELAYING

Belaying is a fundamental technique for climbing safely, a system of using a rope to stop a fall if one should occur. Belaying can safely control the enormous energy that a falling climber generates, but it takes practice to do well and requires an understanding of its underlying principles.

In its simplest form, a belay consists of nothing more than a rope that runs from a climber to another person—the belayer—who is ready to stop a fall. Three things are necessary to make the system work:

1. A method of applying a stopping force to the rope
2. A stance with an anchor strong enough to resist the pull of the fall
3. A skilled belayer

There are different ways to apply this stopping force, a variety of stances, and many methods of setting up and tying in to a belay anchor (a secure point to which the rest of the system is attached). This chapter introduces the principal techniques and major options of belaying so that you can choose the methods that work best in your own climbing.

HOW BELAYS ARE USED IN CLIMBING

Before explaining the details of belay setups and procedures, it is helpful to start with a general understanding of how belays are used on a climb. For simplicity, picture just the essentials of a belay. There are two climbers, each tied in to an end of the climbing rope, forming a rope team (fig. 10-1). As one climbs, the other belays. The belayer is connected to an anchor, a point of secure attachment to the terrain using rock, snow, ice, or trees. As the climber ascends, the belayer pays out or takes in rope, ready to apply a stopping force to the rope in case the climber falls. A belayer may also be called upon to hold the climber stationary under tension or to lower the climber.

Being the belayer is a demanding and important task that is often awkward, of long duration, and boring, yet also requires constant vigilance for the safety of the climber. The belayer's job is much easier if the belayer is able to find a comfortable spot on which to establish a secure position.

Belay setups are usually established on the ground or on a ledge that provides reasonable comfort and the possibility of solid anchors. One climber takes the lead and, belayed from below, moves up the route to the next desirable spot and sets up a new belay. The distance between belays is known as a pitch or a lead. The length of each pitch is usually determined by rope length and the location of a convenient spot to establish the next belay. For more on this subject, see "Leading and Following," below.

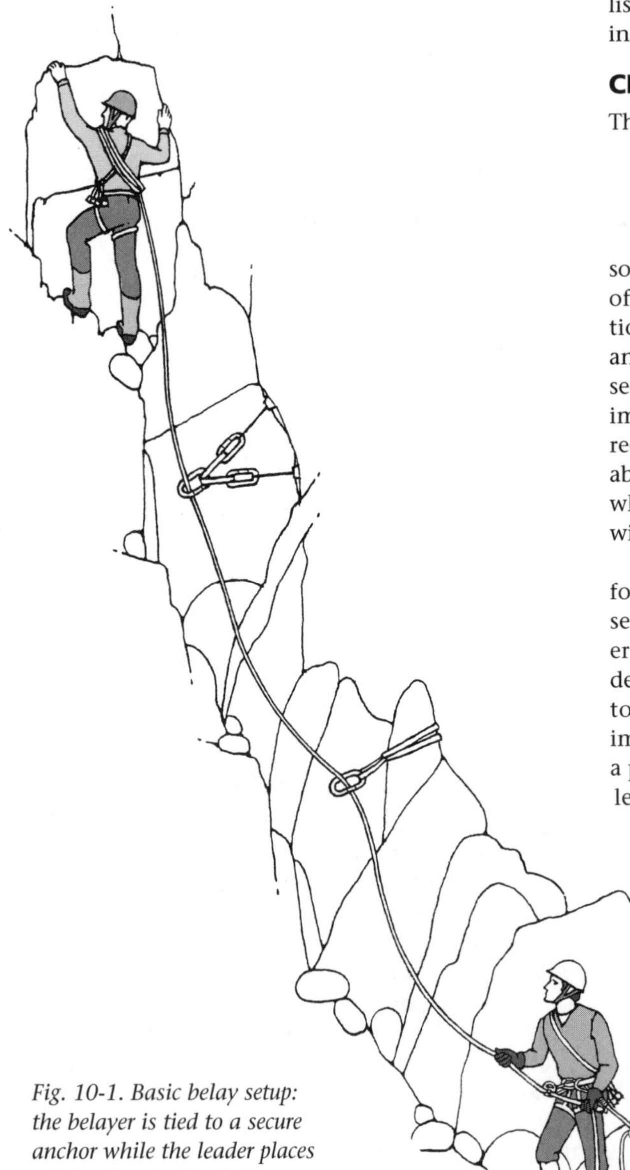

Fig. 10-1. Basic belay setup: the belayer is tied to a secure anchor while the leader places points of protection between them.

CHOOSING A BELAY SPOT

The belay location should have three attributes:

1. Good placement for anchors
2. Safe position
3. Reasonable comfort

When choosing a belay position, always look for solid anchors. Critical to a safe belay, solid anchors are of paramount concern. When selecting a belay location, be aware of the possibility of rockfall or icefall, and pick a stance that will provide some shelter if this seems a likely hazard. If a belay location is exposed to imminent danger from rockfall or icefall, safety may require moving the belay to a location with less desirable anchors. Additionally, it is useful to find a position where climbing partners can see and/or communicate with each other.

Many factors ultimately determine the best choice for a belay spot. Longer leads are more efficient, so if several good belay ledges are available, climbers generally pick the highest one. However, the leader may decide to stop and set up the next belay early in order to mitigate the problem of rope drag (friction that impedes the rope's travel). A leader may also shorten a pitch because a comfortable stance at a partial rope length is of greater advantage than pushing the lead as far as possible. Perhaps a difficult section may lie ahead, and the lead climber, feeling too tired or unsure of personal leading ability, may want to end a pitch early so that the other climber can take over the lead.

LEADING AND FOLLOWING

On multipitch routes, climbers commonly alternate, or "swing," leads so that in turn they belay at the top of every pitch they lead, which allows a rest before following the next pitch. In other cases, climbers may lead in blocks, with one person taking a number of leads before trading off. This can be more efficient: Less time is spent in changeovers, and one climber can become immersed in the rhythm of leading. Also, if a team consists of climbers of different skill levels, one partner may assume all or most of the leading duties for increased safety or speed.

The climber belayed from above, known as the follower, or "second," can climb aggressively, confident that any fall will be held easily by the belayer and will be very short, typically involving little more than stretching of the rope. It is a different matter for the leader of a pitch, who is belayed from below and will drop some distance before the rope begins to stop the fall.

To reduce the distance of a potential fall, the leader must rely on intermediate points of protection (see Chapter 14, Leading on Rock) that he or she sets in the rock or ice on the way up. The leader attaches the rope to the protection and continues the ascent. Now the length of a fall is limited to twice the distance that the leader is above the highest piece of protection, plus some rope stretch, belayer movement, rope slippage, and whatever slack was already in the rope. These factors are examined in detail later in this chapter, showing how the actions of the rope team influence each climber, as well as the possible implications in the event of a fall.

HOLDING A FALL

When considering the effects of a fall, climbers get used to thinking in terms of force, rather than weight, because force expresses not only a climber's weight but also the energy that climbers and anchors are subjected to in the event of a fall. This notion of force should be a familiar one from experiences in everyday life.

Static force. Imagine that a 10-pound (4.5-kilogram) object is attached to a rope; then imagine grasping the rope a few feet from the object in order to hold the object up off the floor. Gravity exerts a downward force on the object while you exert an equal and opposite force to hold it up. This force that gravity exerts on an object is commonly referred to as weight. The force you exert to hold the object up is a static force.

Impact force. Now imagine this variation. While holding your arm still and gripping the rope tightly, have someone lift up the object and then drop it. Gravity will cause the object to fall with an acceleration rate of 32 feet (9.8 meters) per second for every second it falls. When the rope you are holding arrests the object's fall, the sudden impact force generated will be much greater than the force of the object's weight when you were merely holding the object up against gravity. Catching the weight of this falling object obviously involves much higher forces than holding this weight statically, because the amount of energy generated in a fall goes up dramatically as the falling object accelerates. Similarly, holding the weight of a stationary climber involves relatively small forces, but a falling climber quickly generates much greater energy.

Impact forces are rated in kilonewtons (kN). One kilonewton of force is about equal to 225 pounds (102 kilograms) of static weight—remember, weight is a measure of force. The human body cannot tolerate more than about 12 kilonewtons, which is equivalent to 2,700 pounds (1,225 kilograms)—or roughly 15 times the weight of the human body—for a brief instant without risk of severe injury.

Stopping distance. The force required to catch an object also depends on how quickly its fall is arrested. It takes less resistance to stop the weight if the rope is allowed to slip a bit, but then the fall lasts longer. Stopping a fall as quickly as possible may prevent the falling climber from hitting something, such as a ledge; however, stopping a fall with a rope too suddenly would subject every component of the system—including the falling climber—to dangerously high impact forces. There needs to be some way to safely absorb the energy generated by the falling climber.

Benefits of dynamic rope. Because modern belay devices limit rope slippage, something else must provide that soft catch. That something is rope stretch. Modern dynamic climbing ropes prevent dangerously high impact forces by elongating under load to absorb energy. In the days of hemp ropes, the golden rule of belaying was "the rope must run." That was because the rope had neither the strength to withstand high impact forces nor the shock absorption to avoid injuring the climber. The only safe way to stop a fall was by making the belay dynamic, allowing some rope to slip through the belay to make a soft catch. This worked, but not without problems; it was difficult to learn, and the friction of the running rope could badly burn a belayer.

For a rope to be safe for leading, an activity in which falls are to be expected, it must be an approved dynamic climbing rope (see "The Standard Drop-Test Fall for Dynamic Ropes" sidebar). Static ropes, webbing slings, and accessory cord, while fine for rappeling, constructing anchors, or other uses, do not stretch enough to safely catch a fall. Look at manufacturers' specifications for climbing ropes. They are rated not by strength

10

but by impact force and number of falls held. This is because the rope does more than simply not break under the impact of a falling climber; it also stretches to absorb the energy of multiple falls.

The beauty of dynamic climbing ropes is that, by limiting the impact force of a fall, less force is exerted throughout the system. As a result, the anchor is subjected to lower stresses, the falling leader receives a softer catch, and the belayer has an easier task holding the fall.

Fall factor. Impact forces generated by falls onto dynamic ropes are determined by both the length of the fall and how much dynamic rope is available to absorb the energy of that fall—together, these determine the fall factor, defined as the length of the fall divided by the length of rope fallen on. Fall factor, not length of fall, determines the impact force that will be generated in the event of a fall. This is written mathematically as follows:

length of fall ÷ length of rope fallen on = fall factor

In any normal climbing situation, a fall factor of 2.0 is the highest a climber could ever encounter, because this would mean falling exactly twice the length of the rope that the climber has run out. For example, assume that two climbers are on a smooth vertical face with no ledges or other hazards to hit in a fall. If the leader falls from 10 feet (3 meters) above the belay without any protection, there would have been 10 feet of rope played out. That climber would end up 10 feet below the belay stance, having fallen 20 feet (6 meters) on 10 feet of rope. Applying this example to the fall factor formula above looks like this:

20-foot fall ÷ 10 feet of rope = fall factor of 2.0

This would be a fall factor of 2.0, also stated as a factor 2 fall. Such a fall would generate the maximum impact on anchors and climbers, creating a hazardous situation. If there is any slack in the rope, intermediate points of protection, rope slippage, or movement of the belayer, the fall factor would always be less than 2.0. When more rope is played out, falls of a similar length will generate much lower impact forces, putting less stress on the system. That same 20-foot fall on a 100-foot (30-meter) section of rope would still involve an exciting bit of air time, but the catch would be quite gentle by comparison:

20-foot fall ÷ 100 feet of rope = fall factor of 0.2

Lower fall factors always mean lower impact forces because there is more rope relative to the length of fall.

THE STANDARD DROP-TEST FALL FOR DYNAMIC ROPES

In the standard UIAA-CEN single dynamic rope drop-test fall, an 80-kilogram (176-pound) mass affixed to a solid fixed anchor is dropped 5 meters (16⅓ feet) on a 2.8-meter (9¹⁄₁₆-foot) section of rope running over a 1-centimeter (⅓-inch) steel bar. To pass the test, a rope must withstand at least five standard drops and not exceed a 12 kN impact force on the first drop. This maximum 12 kN figure is derived from studies showing that the human body could briefly withstand 15 times its weight when dropped. Maximum impact forces for current single ropes usually range between 8.5 and 10.5 kN. Be aware that as a rope ages it loses some of its ability to absorb energy. A frequently used rope may generate considerably higher forces than the figures for new test ropes (see "Rope Care" in Chapter 9, Basic Safety System).

By design, the standard drop test produces a fall that would be considered severe in normal climbing situations. First, in most real-life situations, any belay is, to a certain extent, a dynamic belay. Rope slippage, belayer movement, and friction of the rope against rock and through carabiners all serve to dissipate force. The standard drop test is not a dynamic belay; the rope absorbs virtually all of the impact force of the fall. Additionally, the standard drop-test fall is set up with a high fall factor. In the UIAA-CEN standard drop test, the fall factor is calculated like this:

5-meter fall ÷ 2.8 meters of rope = fall factor of 1.78

This tests the rope's properties to ensure that it will absorb the impact force generated by a severe fall without subjecting the system to excessively high loads. While the maximum fall factor of 2.0 could be encountered under normal climbing circumstances, such high-factor falls are uncommon enough that 1.78 is an acceptable and more realistic figure.

It is important to realize that any fall of the same factor will generate the same impact force. Take the 5-meter UIAA-CEN drop-test fall described in the sidebar and multiply it by 5; now it is a 25-meter (82-foot) fall on 14 meters (46 feet) of rope, but the fall factor remains the same: 1.78. The fall is much longer (and clearly riskier for the falling climber), but because the amount of rope available to absorb shock is also greater, the amount of impact force that the belay system is subjected to remains the same.

PROTECTING THE LEADER

Understanding fall factor and how it determines impact forces is fundamental to safe leading. As described in "Leading and Following," above, the leader places intermediate points of protection to reduce potential fall length, and a leader fall is at least twice the distance between the climber and the last placement of protection. As described in "Holding a Fall," above, the impact forces are highest when a fall occurs on a relatively short section of rope. It is important to recognize that the most severe strain on the belay system and anchor may occur just as a leader starts up a pitch, should the leader happen to fall before any intermediate anchors have been placed to limit the distance of that fall.

Therefore, climbers should always establish a solid first placement as soon as possible after starting a new lead. This not only will reduce the chance for a high-factor fall but will also establish the direction from which the force of a leader fall will come (see "Judging the Direction of Fall Forces" in Chapter 14, Leading on Rock). Chapter 14 goes into further detail about how these principles are applied; understanding the dynamics involved will help you make more sense of how belaying protects the leader.

APPLYING BRAKING FORCE TO THE ROPE

Climbing belays must be able to resist the large forces generated in a fall. With the dynamic climbing rope acting as the shock absorber in the system, the belayer's job is to quickly stop the rope from running. Any additional rope that runs through the belay system as the fall is caught has two related effects: softening the impact forces, and lengthening the distance fallen. Occasionally the belayer may want to deliberately provide a more dynamic belay—for instance, if protection is suspected to be weak—but there is always the trade-off of a longer fall, with increased possibility of the lead climber hitting a ledge or other hazard.

In any belay method, the rope from the climber goes around or through some friction-producing element—such as a belay device, a munter hitch on a carabiner, the camming action of a self-braking belay device, or the belayer's hips—and then to the belayer's braking hand. Except for some self-braking devices (see "Types of Belay Devices," below), the braking hand gripping the rope produces the initial force.

Because everything starts with the braking force applied by the belayer's grip, it is important to consider the factors that affect the generation of this force. Grip strength varies considerably from one person to another, with the average being somewhere around 50 pounds (23 kilograms—in other words, 0.2 kilonewtons). This likely becomes reduced when the belayer is substantially fatigued or positioned awkwardly. Ropes that are thinner, as is the current trend, are more difficult to grip, and reduced friction, as found with wet, icy, or (possibly) dry-treated ropes, will lower braking force to some degree. Conversely, as ropes age they develop a rougher sheath with higher friction and therefore can be easier to grip. In all cases, grip strength alone is not sufficient to stop a fall.

Instead, climbers rely on a mechanical means of increasing this force. Arresting force is greatly enhanced by the friction-producing element, commonly a belay device, to stop the falling climber. The belay device or braking method is the essential means by which the limited force of the belayer's grip strength can control the large impact forces generated in a fall.

Stopping a fall is accomplished by assuming the braking (or arrest) position (fig. 10-2a) and, gripping the rope tightly with the braking hand, pulling back on the free end of the rope (fig. 10-2b). This action must be practiced and learned well so that it becomes automatic; immediately going into arrest position as soon as a fall is sensed is the best way to stop a fall.

Wearing gloves while belaying is very important but often overlooked. Belayers accustomed only to gym climbing or single-pitch sport climbs may be unaware of the increased potential for loss of belay control that occurs with higher-factor falls. Studies show that in more severe falls, a significant amount of rope will run through the system and at a certain point will burn the belay hand to the extent that involuntary reflexes will cause the belayer to let go of the rope, losing control.

Leather gloves protect your hands from friction

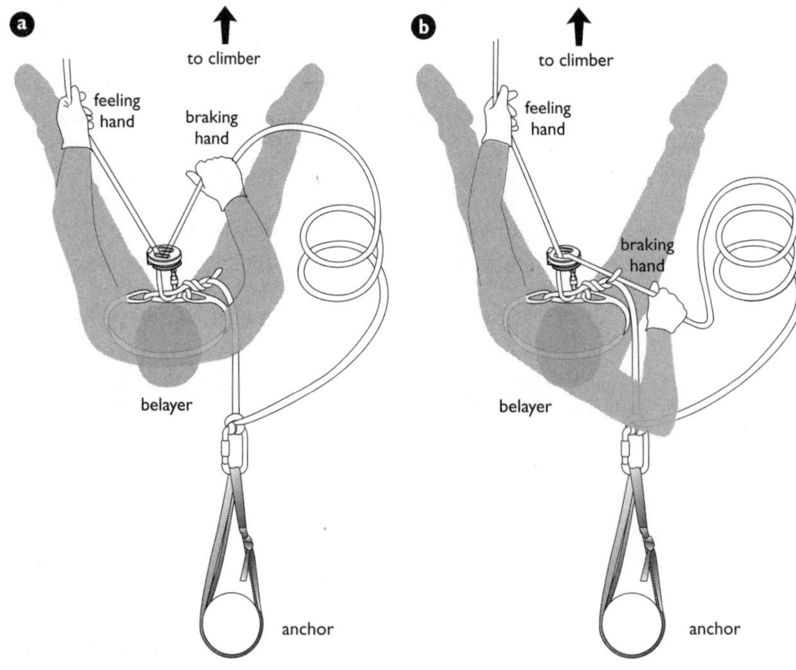

Fig. 10-2. Braking position: a, the belayer is anchored and ready to belay a climber; b, to arrest a fall, the belayer pulls back on the free end of the rope.

burns in the case of rope slippage and, despite some disadvantages, are worth getting used to wearing. The material of the gloves should be rough enough to add some friction to the system, essentially increasing your grip strength. Some climbers dislike the fact that gloves may interfere with dexterity and tend to leave their hands damp and soft, which is undesirable for climbing rock.

The most important thing for all belayers to do is to perfect whichever belay method they use. Having one method that you can absolutely count on is the first priority; after that, learning other methods for versatility is valuable and quite worthwhile.

BELAYING TECHNIQUE

The belayer's hand that holds the rope coming from the climber is known as the feeling hand and is used to pay the rope in and out. The other hand, known as the braking hand, must never let go of its grip on the rope, remaining ready to catch a fall at any time.

It is important to maintain the correct tension on the rope, preventing excess slack, anticipating the climber's movements and needs, letting out rope as the climber moves up or clips in to protection, or taking rope in as needed. Practice until you learn to quickly take in or let out rope with the feeling hand as required while never removing the braking hand from the rope.

Taking in the rope. A specific sequence of hand motions is used to take in the rope. With both hands on the rope, start with the braking hand close to your body and the feeling hand extended (fig. 10-3a), then pull in the rope using both hands by moving the feeling hand toward your body and pulling away from your body with the braking hand (fig. 10-3b). Then slide the feeling hand forward beyond the braking hand and grasp both strands of rope with the feeling hand (fig. 10-3c). Finally, slide the braking hand back toward your body (fig. 10-3d); then let the feeling hand drop the braking-hand strand of the rope, repeat the sequence of hand motions as often as needed to take in the appropriate amount of rope. The braking hand must never leave the rope.

Letting out the rope. It is easy and intuitive to let out the rope. With the feeling hand, pull the rope away from your body while using the braking hand to help feed the rope. Again, the braking hand must never leave the rope.

USING BELAY DEVICES

When properly used, most belay devices multiply the friction and grip strength of the braking hand by passing the rope through an aperture, wrapping it around a post, and passing it back out through the aperture. This configuration provides a wrap, or bend, in the rope to assist in producing a stopping force. The post is usually a locking carabiner or part of the belay device itself. There is no automatic clamping effect with most belay devices. The belayer's braking hand is the initial, and critical, source of friction; without the braking hand on the rope, there is no belay.

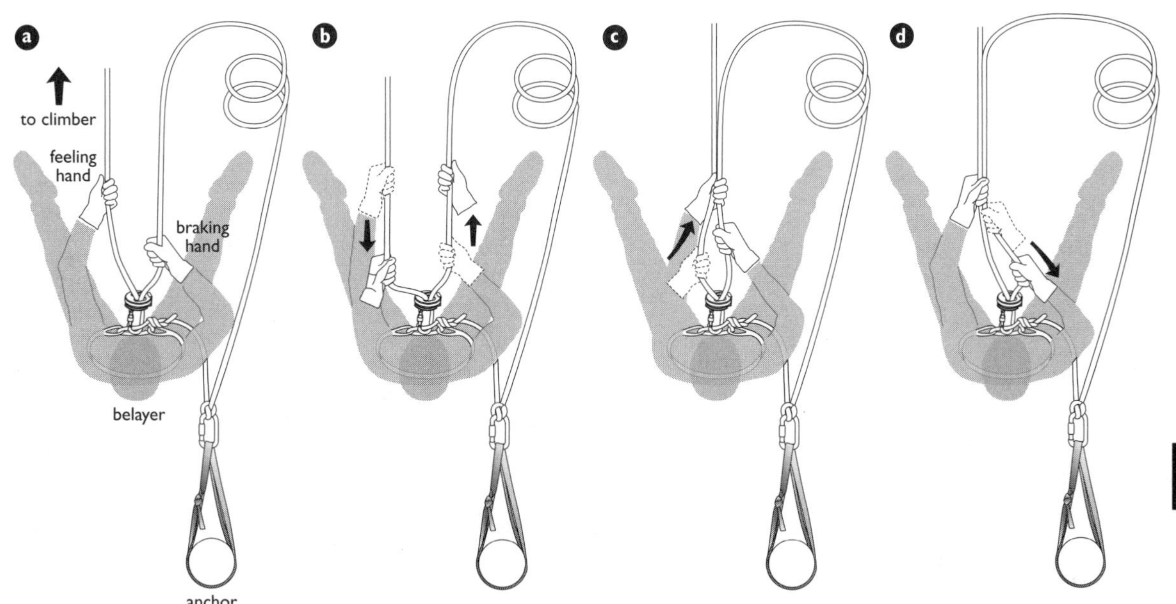

Fig. 10-3. Hand motions for taking in rope, with the braking hand never leaving the rope: a, start with the feeling hand extended and the braking hand close to the body; b, pull in the rope with the feeling hand while pulling the rope through the belay device and away from the body with the braking hand; c, extend the feeling hand past the braking hand and grasp both strands of the rope with the feeling hand; d, slide the braking hand back toward the body and release the braking hand's strand of the rope from the feeling hand.

The total braking force exerted on the rope during the arrest of a fall depends on three things: the total degree of bend produced in the rope created by the belay device, as well as the rope's inherent resistance to bending and deforming; the friction generated as the rope runs over the surfaces of the belay device; and the force exerted by the belayer's grip. Fortunately, despite the variations in the strength of belayers' grips, modern belay devices work well enough that when they are properly used, adequate stopping force can be generated even with modest grip strength.

To stop a fall, the belayer pulls back on the free end of the rope to create a difference in angle of at least 90 degrees between the rope entering the belay device (from the climber) and the rope leaving it (toward the brake hand). This angle of separation between the two strands of the rope (fig. 10-4) is critical to the strength of the belay. Figure 10-4 shows how the braking force is increased as the braking hand pulls the rope farther back to increase the angle of separation from 90 degrees toward 180 degrees. Nothing must be in the way of the braking hand or elbow when the belayer goes into the braking position; also, this critical task must not require an unnatural body twist or motion.

One of the simplest and most convenient belay methods is to clip a belay device into a locking carabiner on the harness, typically to a sewn belay loop. It is important to follow the manufacturer's instructions for clipping in properly, as to do otherwise loads the harness in ways it was not designed for and may lead to failure. This section describes the use of belay devices when they are attached to the seat harness. "Belay Position and Stance," later in this chapter, addresses considerations for belaying off the seat harness versus belaying directly off the anchor.

Types of Belay Devices

There are many popular belay devices. When using any belay device, always read and follow the manufacturer's instructions carefully; be certain that you fully understand these instructions and that the device is properly rigged each time you use it.

Aperture devices. Aperture belay devices simply provide an opening through which a bight (loop) of rope is

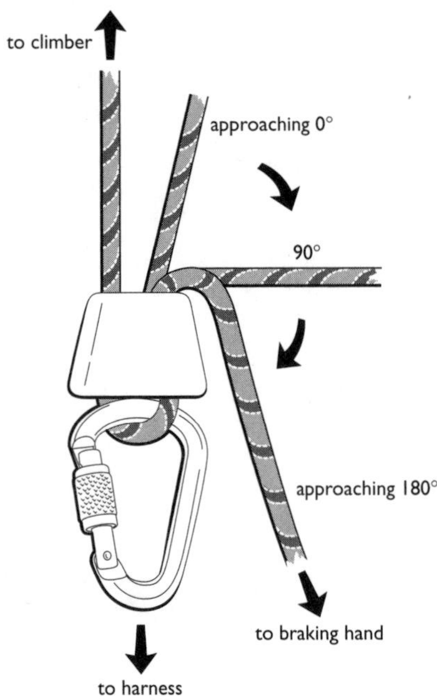

Fig. 10-4. Angle of separation between the two rope strands. With the angle of separation approaching 0 degrees, little friction is produced, and the belayer can easily pay rope in or out as required. As the angle of separation increases to greater than 90 degrees, more friction is generated. At the maximum angle of separation of 180 degrees, enough friction is generated to control the force of a fall.

pushed and then clipped in to the locking carabiner on the seat harness (fig. 10-5a). In most current versions, the device is a cone-shaped or somewhat square tube (fig. 10-5b; the Lowe Tuber II, ATC, DMM Bug, Trango Pyramid, etc., are examples of such devices). Plates and tubes must be kept from sliding down the rope and out of reach. Most of these devices include a wire loop that is clipped in to the locking carabiner on the seat harness (see Figure 10-5b). The connection to the harness must be long enough so that it does not interfere with belaying in any direction.

Many current aperture devices have a higher- and a lower-force mode. The higher-force mode is usually achieved by adding V slots and/or ridges to one side of the aperture; rigging the device so that the rope going to the brake hand is pulled into the narrower V slot increases the braking force. This may be useful, especially when using thinner ropes, or in situations wherein a belayer is much smaller than the climber.

Figure eight devices were originally designed for rappeling, not belaying, but some figure eight devices can serve both functions. If the hole in the small end of the figure eight is the size of the hole in a typical aperture device, the figure eight can be used just like an aperture device by feeding a bight of rope through this hole and into a locking carabiner (fig. 10-5c). This is the preferred method for using a figure eight as a belay device; other methods have enough disadvantages that they are best not used. Make certain that the figure eight device is intended for belaying use by the manufacturer; many are not.

Self-braking belay devices. Numerous manufacturers make belay devices that function differently from the common aperture devices in that they are self-braking or have a self-braking mode, as in the Petzl Reverso[3] (fig. 10-6a). Though these devices are self-braking, their manufacturers caution that safe use still requires an attentive belayer's hand on the rope to tend the rope and initiate the braking action. In common usage, the term "self-braking" is often used interchangeably with "self-locking," "autolocking," or "mechanical-assisting." There can be significant differences between self-braking belay devices, but they basically divide into two classes of devices: spring-loaded cam-style belay devices and multifunction aperture-style belay devices.

Spring-loaded self-braking belay devices. The Petzl Grigri, Trango Cinch, Edelrid Eddy, and Faders Sum are specialized self-braking belay devices that feed rope smoothly as the belayer pays rope in or out, but the sudden acceleration of the rope in a fall causes an internal cam to lock down on the rope, creating a braking force that is not dependent on resistance from the belayer's grip (fig. 10-6b). Popular for gym, sport, and aid climbing, they have definite advantages when used properly. For example, they enable a smaller, lighter belayer to confidently arrest and hold even heavy partners or to stop long falls. All current models have a release mechanism that allows controlled rappeling or lowering of a top-roped climber. Accidents have happened due to improper application of the lowering action, so it is very important to follow all of the manufacturer's instructions.

Because these devices depend on proper functioning of internal mechanisms, they may not work with all rope diameters. These devices have a tendency to lock up when the lead climber makes a sudden move up or when rope is fed too quickly. It is extremely important that the user carefully follow manufactur-

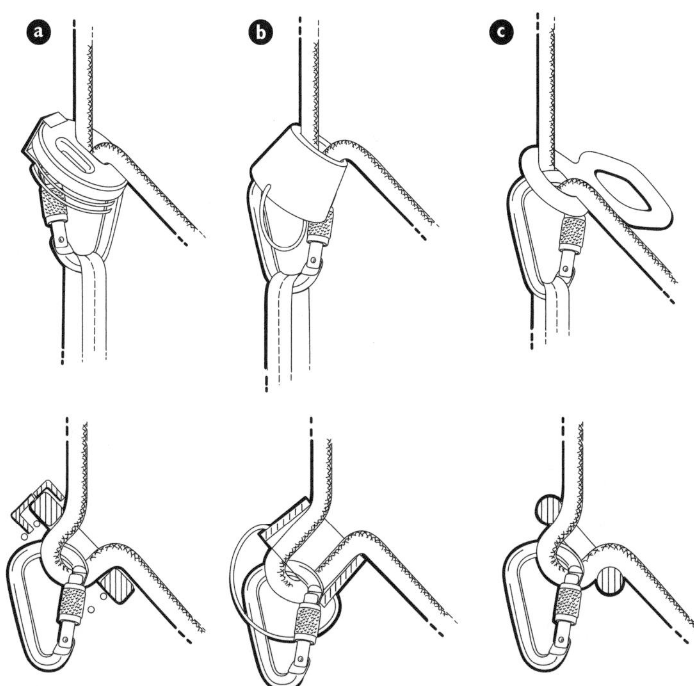

Fig. 10-5. Aperture belay devices; the top illustrations show the external view and the bottom illustrations show a cutaway view to reveal the rope path: a, slot or guide plate; b, tube type; c, figure eight in aperture configuration.

er's instructions and test proper setup each time the device is rigged. Disadvantages include weight and bulk. They also may work poorly with wet or icy ropes, which makes them largely unsuitable for mountaineering despite other advantages. Note that those who have used self-braking devices exclusively may not be aware of the greater demands required of other belay methods and devices.

Multifunction aperture-style self-braking belay devices. A number of self-braking devices are designed to function in the same way as a standard aperture device and also have an alternative rigging mode that provides a secure means of belaying one or two followers directly off an anchor. The original guide plate (see Figure 10-5a) works this way, but it has been largely replaced by multifunction devices like the Petzl Reverso[3] (see Figure 10-6a), Black Diamond ATC Guide, and Kong Ghost. These devices look similar to other aperture devices and may be used off the harness in the same way as a standard aperture device. In self-braking mode, the device is connected directly to the anchor with a locking carabiner while the rope runs over itself and through a second locking carabiner. When rigged this way, the rope can easily be pulled in by the belayer. But when the climber's strand is loaded, as in a fall, the rope locks down on itself. Follow the manufacturer's instructions to safely use these devices.

Pay particular attention if these devices are to be used with small-diameter ropes; the self-braking characteristics of these devices may not function in certain configurations or circumstances when used with ropes of less than 10 millimeters. Refer to the manufacturer's instructions before using self-braking belay devices on small-diameter ropes.

Also be aware that, in self-braking mode, these multifunction aperture-style self-braking devices do lock up under load, so they do not function as effective lowering devices, which is a drawback. Additionally, if the belayed climber falls and is unable to unload the device, the belayer must have a way to unlock it. Many of the newer devices have a hole specifically for attaching a cord or carabiner to release a locked device to lower a fallen climber. Otherwise, it would be necessary to rig a raising system to the rope and take the climber's weight off the device to unlock it.

Special Considerations in Using Belay Devices

When a climber using a belay device is facing away from the belay anchor, the tie-in to the anchor should be on the braking-hand side. This way, body rotation under the force of a fall will assist, rather than hinder, the belayer. When facing toward the anchor (usually when belaying a leader), the belayer's braking hand should be opposite the side where the leader would likely drop in case of a fall before the first protection is put in place. For example, if the climber leads up and to the right, so that in an unprotected leader fall the climber would fall past the belayer on the right, the braking hand should be the belayer's left hand.

Another choice the belayer must make when using a belay device is whether to have the braking hand in the

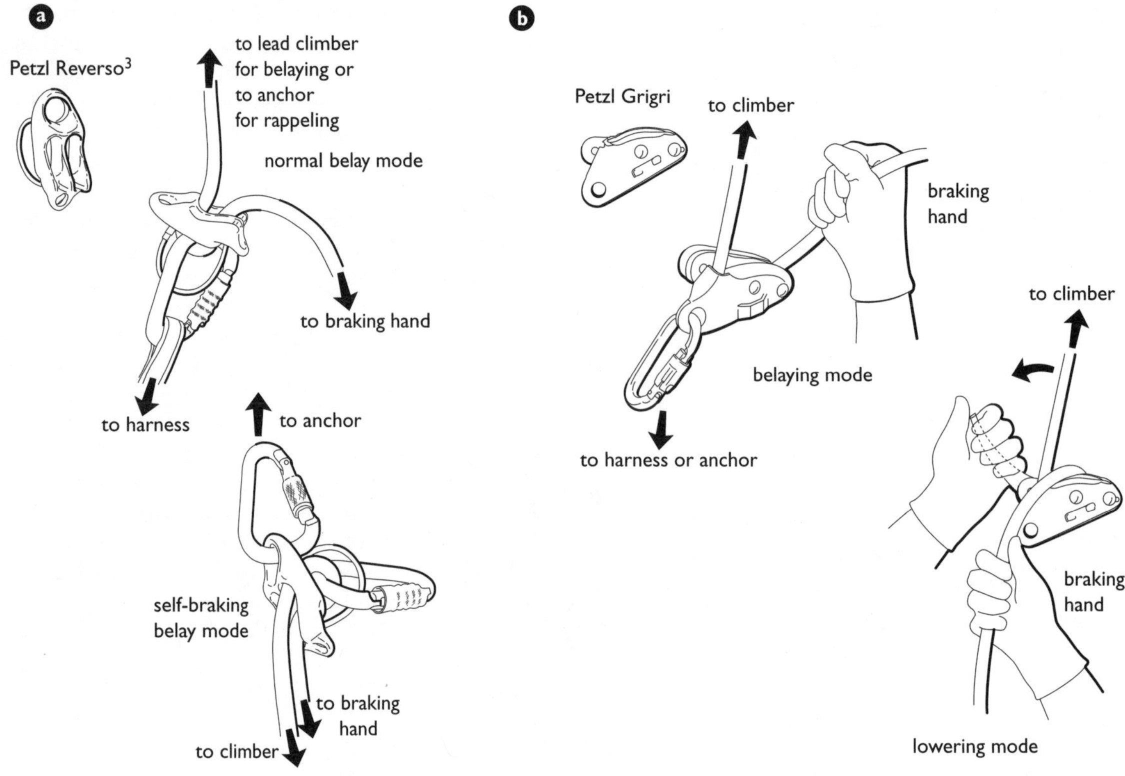

Fig. 10-6. Self-braking belay devices: a, Petzl Reverso³; b, Petzl Grigri.

palm-up or the palm-down position. In the palm-down position (fig. 10-7a), the hand motions for taking in rope are somewhat more awkward and put more strain on the upper arm. However, in the palm-down position, the grip on the rope in the braking position is more natural and grip strength is probably higher. But when the belayer in the palm-down position suddenly goes into the braking position, the tendency is to slap the closed hand up against the hip, possibly hitting the thumb against any equipment carried on the gear loops of the seat harness. This can be a problem even when wearing gloves. The palm-up position (fig. 10-7b), although somewhat weaker than palm-down, usually makes rope management less awkward while still maintaining adequate grip strength. Beginning belayers should practice belaying and catching falls with both hand positions in order to decide which works best for them.

When taking in or letting out slack with an aperture device (whether a plate type or a tube type), keep the ropes strictly parallel; otherwise, the rope will pull the device up against the carabiner, and braking will begin. Eventually the technique becomes automatic.

Like any piece of critical climbing equipment made of metal, a belay device that is dropped a significant distance should be retired because hidden damage may have occurred, weakening the device.

Performance Differences Among Belay Devices

Belay devices vary significantly in the amount of friction they produce in routine rope handling and in arresting a fall. Tests indicate that not all devices will easily stop a catastrophic factor 2.0 fall, and those who plan on climbing difficult multipitch routes are advised to seek out a belay method with higher braking properties. Occasionally a device or method that generates less friction is desirable when a party needs to travel more quickly or when a more dynamic belay is better due to relatively weak anchors.

Different devices also vary in how easily they perform

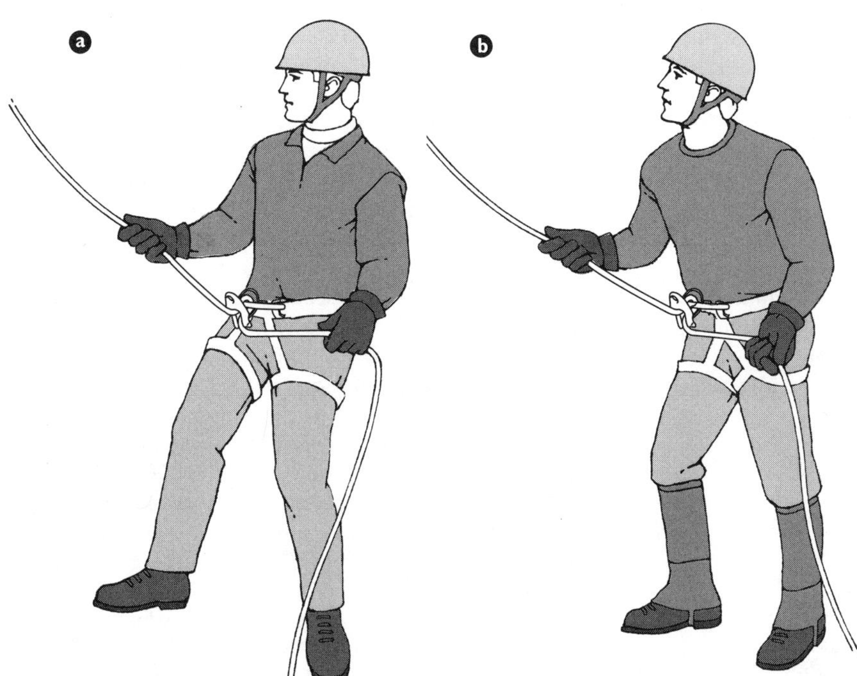

Fig. 10-7. Hand positions for belaying (anchor omitted for clarity): a, palm-down position has stronger grip but is more awkward for paying rope in or out while belaying; b, palm-up position is somewhat weaker but more natural and comfortable when managing rope.

the tasks of holding the climber stationary under tension or lowering the climber to a ledge. Devices that require the least force to hold the climber's weight are generally less smooth in taking in rope and lowering the climber. The differences in how smoothly different aperture devices work for lowering and feeding rope are difficult to quantify, and they vary widely with different rope, carabiner, and device combinations.

Belay devices are frequently used for rappeling (see Chapter 11, Rappeling). Plates and tubes can produce a jerky ride that may put undesirable impact loads on the rappel anchor, a grave concern when circumstances do not allow for ideal rappel anchors. Figure eights are the smoothest for rappeling, but figure eights put twists in the rope, later producing snarls in the coils.

All belay devices come with manufacturer's instructions. Always read these carefully and follow them.

USING THE MUNTER HITCH

The munter hitch is a very effective method of belaying that uses only the rope, a specialized carabiner, and a hitch to provide the friction necessary to stop a fall. The munter hitch should be attached to the carabiner so the rope to the belayer's braking hand is closest to the solid spine of the carabiner and so the rope to the climber is closest to the locked gate. This reduces the possibility of the rope running across the carabiner's locking mechanism and either unlocking the carabiner or being damaged.

Efficient belaying with a munter hitch requires an HMS-type (pear-shaped) carabiner with an opening large enough to allow the hitch to feed through smoothly. As a result of its configuration, the hitch multiplies the effect of the braking hand with friction created by the rope being wrapped on itself and around the HMS carabiner.

The munter hitch is unique in that it is the only traditional belay method that provides sufficient friction regardless of the angle at which the braking end of the rope is held. With most belay devices, maximum friction is generated when the brake-hand strand of the rope is held at an angle of 180 degrees from the strand of rope attached to the climber. In contrast, the munter hitch, because of the way it wraps around the HMS carabiner, actually generates more friction when both strands of the rope are aligned (fig. 10-8). Furthermore, in absolute terms, the munter hitch generates more friction than most other belay devices regardless of the angle at which the braking strand of the rope is held. This higher friction can mean a quicker stop to a severe fall.

Because no special braking position is required, the munter hitch has an advantage over most belay devices in that if a fall takes a belayer by surprise, the hitch will function even if the belayer does no more than firmly grip the rope. Rope handling with the munter hitch is quick and easy, making it an ideal method when climbers are moving rapidly over easy ground. As with a belay device, the belayer can choose to belay with the brake hand palm up or palm down. With the munter hitch, the palm-up position (as in Figure 10-7b) has the advantages of making rope management less awkward and being a more natural—and therefore stronger—braking position when the munter hitch is in the position of greatest friction (see Figure 10-8). The palm-down position (as in Figure 10-7a) is more awkward both for rope management and for braking. Finally, because no specialized equipment other than an HMS carabiner is required, the munter hitch provides a ready backup belay method if a belay device is lost.

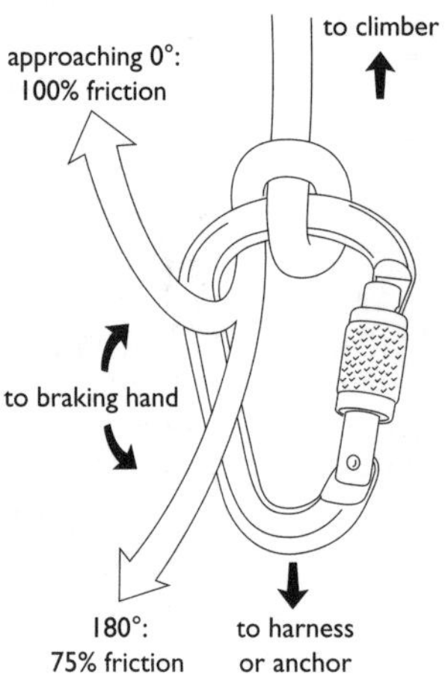

Fig. 10-8. The munter hitch provides sufficient friction for belaying regardless of the angle between the ropes entering and leaving it.

The munter hitch has some drawbacks as well as advantages. It can kink the rope more than other belay methods, but this can be minimized by allowing the rope to feed freely unless needed to arrest a fall. To unkink the rope, shake it out while it is hanging free. After a big fall, the outermost layer of the rope's sheath may be glazed—which is only cosmetic; this glazing, which also occurs to some degree with mechanical devices, wears off with use. The munter hitch is not preferred for rappeling because it twists the rope.

USING THE HIP BELAY

The hip belay (also called the body belay) is a belay method in which the rope is wrapped around the belayer's body to generate enough friction to stop a climber's fall. The belayer connects to a solid anchor and assumes a stable stance facing the direction of an anticipated pull on the rope. The rope from the climber is passed around the belayer's back and sides just below the top of the hips (fig. 10-9a). To arrest a fall, grip the rope tightly with the braking hand and assume the braking (or arrest) position—braking arm pulled across the stomach (fig. 10-9b). This action must be practiced and learned well so that it becomes automatic; immediately going into arrest position as soon as a fall is sensed is the best way to stop a fall. The braking position increases the amount of friction-producing wrap of the rope around the body, thereby increasing the stopping force.

The hip belay, once the standard for high-angle climbing, has significant disadvantages; therefore few climbers use it as their primary method of belaying.

Because the force of a fall is dissipated as friction against the belayer's body, a belayer stopping a severe fall can suffer serious rope burns. Protective clothes are required to prevent this. Even fairly minor leader falls can melt and severely damage expensive synthetic garments. If a belayer is burned badly enough, the belayer could drop a falling climber. Because the belayer's hands provide a greater proportion of friction in the hip belay than in other methods, gloves are essential to protect the hands from burns. A tighter grip causes less-severe burns because faster stops and less rope slippage generate less heat. Another problem with the hip belay is that if the climbing rope runs over the anchor attachment during a fall, the anchor attachment may be burned.

Because the hip belay requires more time to attain braking position and generates less braking force than any other method, more rope slippage generally occurs and the climber usually falls farther. If the belay stance fails, it is much more likely that the belayer will lose control of the rope than with other methods. In summary, all elements of the hip belay must come together to make it work effectively during a long, hard fall.

Despite its drawbacks as a general-purpose belay method, the hip belay does have advantages that make it worth learning, if only for special purposes, especially snow and ice climbing (see Chapter 16, Snow Travel and Climbing, and Chapter 18, Alpine Ice Climbing).

With the hip belay, the belayer can take in rope much faster than with other methods, and the hip belay can be set up quickly with a minimum of equipment. It is probably most useful when belaying a fast-moving

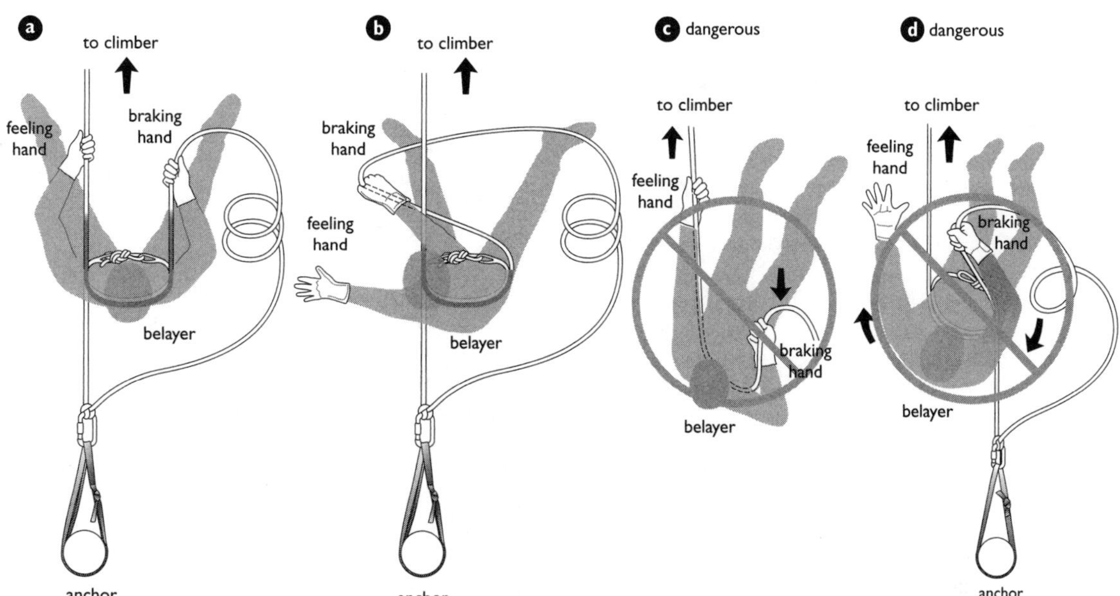

Fig. 10-9. The hip or body belay: a, the belayer is anchored and ready to arrest a fall—the rope goes from the braking hand around the back (to produce friction), and to the climber; b, the braking position—with the braking arm extended across the stomach to create additional friction; c, if the elbow of the braking hand is not straightened before braking begins, then the braking arm may be pulled into a helpless position (dangerous); d, having the anchor attachment on the same side as the braking hand can allow the hip belay to unwrap (dangerous).

10

partner over moderate terrain. A common and efficient practice is to use a simple hip belay to bring a following climber up a relatively easy pitch and then switch to another method when this climber leads the next pitch. Assuming the belayer and climbing partner do not let slack develop and there is no possibility of a pendulum fall (in which the climber swings toward the fall line, creating larger forces), the hip belay method has little risk when belaying a second in this manner.

The hip belay can also be useful for belaying on snow, where it may be desirable to have a more dynamic belay because anchors are absent or suspect. Also, if climbers have lost or forgotten their belay device and do not have the right kind of carabiner for a munter hitch, there may be no choice but to use the hip belay.

Special Considerations in Using the Hip Belay

When using the hip belay, you must keep a number of special considerations in mind.

To catch a fall with this method, straighten the elbow of the braking arm before you begin to grip hard. Then bring the braking arm across in front of your body (see Figure 10-9b), to increase the amount of wrap for maximum friction. The natural reaction is to grip the rope first, but this may pull the braking arm into a helpless position (fig. 10-9c), requiring you to let go and grasp the rope again. An optimal braking position can only be learned with practice, ideally with actual weights being dropped and held.

When you are attaching to the anchor, rig the connection to the side opposite the braking hand (again, see Figure 10-9b). Note that this is different from tying in for belaying with a mechanical device. If the braking hand and anchor rope are on the same side of your body (fig. 10-9d), the force of a fall can partly unwrap the rope from around your body, decreasing both friction and stability.

Another precaution is to clip a control carabiner on your seat harness (fig. 10-10). The carabiner goes in front, or on the same side as the rope coming from the climber, but well forward of your hip bone. Clipping the rope in to this carabiner keeps the rope where it is needed (at your hip), counteracts body rotation, and adds friction to the system.

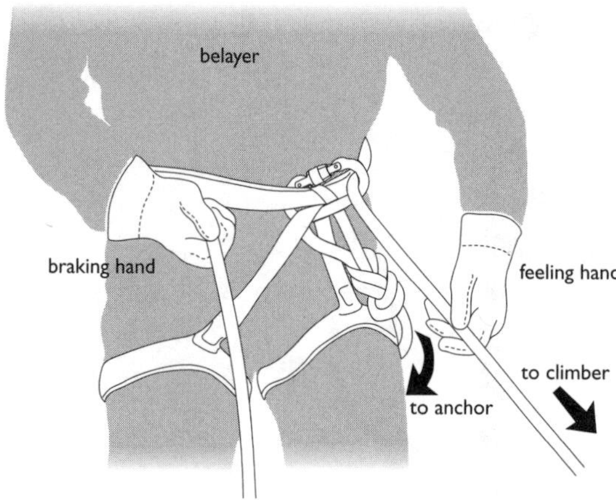

Fig. 10-10. A control carabiner on the harness helps keep the hip belay from unwrapping.

Be aware of any potential direction of pull from a fallen climber, and take advantage of a stable stance and the anchor attachment to keep you and the climbing rope from being pulled out of position, causing loss of control of the belay. Wrapping the rope around your back and above the anchor attachment will prevent the rope from being pulled below your seat. If the pull will come from above with no possibility of a downward pull, wrap the rope around your back and below the anchor attachment to prevent it from being pulled over your head.

CHOOSING A BELAY METHOD

It might seem that the choice of a general-purpose belay method would be a simple matter of choosing the method that exerts the most stopping force. However, even if two belay methods differ significantly in the maximum stopping force that they can exert, there will be little practical difference between them for most falls that a belayer will have to hold. For most falls, the force the belayer is able to exert will be enough to control the fall regardless of the belay method.

The choice between different belay methods matters in the case of a high-factor fall on steep terrain, with little or nothing to produce friction other than the belay; in this situation, the belay method can mean the difference between the rope running and not running. These types of falls are the critical ones, wherein there is little margin for error.

If the rope starts to run while the belayer is holding a fall, the climber will fall that much farther than if the fall were held with no run-through. A longer fall is generally undesirable and potentially dangerous. However, in any protected leader fall, it is important to consider that the maximum force on the top piece of protection is one and a half to two times as high as the maximum force on the climber—in a high-factor fall on vertical rock, the maximum force on the climber can easily be 1,500 pounds (6.7 kilonewtons). If the protection fails under this force, the climber will definitely fall farther. To reduce this force on the protection, some belayers choose a relatively weak method of belaying, one that will let the rope start to run at a lower force to lessen the likelihood of the protection failing.

The leader can also effectively limit the maximum impact on individual protection placements by using a load-limiting runner (see "Runners" in Chapter 9, Basic Safety System). The leader may clip in to a suspect placement with one of these devices without compromising overall belay strength. During a fall, a force greater than the runner's activation point (usually 2 kilonewtons) will start to tear the weak bar tacks. As the total energy of the fall increases, more of the weak bar tacks on a load-limiting runner will fail and can reduce by 3 to 8 kilonewtons the peak load that the fall imposes on the placement.

COMPARING BELAY DEVICES AND METHODS

When selecting a general-purpose belay device or method, research available performance information and consider the following factors:

- Which device or method will hold a fall with minimum force exerted?
- Which device or method allows for easy paying out and taking in of the rope?
- Which device or method makes it easy to lower a climber?
- Which device or method can most effectively double as a rappel device?

Occasionally, figures are published that state the force at which a rope will start to run for certain belay devices or methods. Any UIAA-approved belaying device or method provides adequate braking force for most falls if used correctly. Proficiency with a device or method is critical irrespective of the differing performance characteristics.

ANCHORS

Secure anchors are vital. Climbers should remind themselves, as they acquire more experience, that the moment when they will have to stop an extreme leader fall cannot be anticipated. And when it happens, the anchor must hold, or the climbers—leader and belayer both—will suffer a catastrophic fall. The word "anchor" refers to a whole system. An anchor can be composed of many components and one or more anchor points: It may include natural features, fixed protection pieces, removable protection pieces, runners, carabiners, and the climbing rope itself.

SELECTING AN ANCHOR

This section gives a few tips on selecting good anchors for belays, but for full details on finding and using natural features and on setting artificial anchors on rock, snow, and ice, study Chapter 13, Rock Protection; Chapter 14, Leading on Rock; Chapter 16, Snow Travel and Climbing; and Chapter 18, Alpine Ice Climbing. Also, see Appendix D, Supplementary Resources.

When selecting belay anchors, always consider every possible direction from which a force may load the anchors. Belaying a follower usually results in a downward pull, but leader falls belayed from below generate substantial upward forces, and traversing pitches exert strong lateral loads. Make sure the belay anchors will withstand a pull from any conceivable fall.

Natural Anchors

A large natural feature, such as a live, good-sized, well-rooted tree or a pillar of sound rock, can make an ideal anchor.

Trees and large bushes provide the most obvious anchors. Do not trust a tree or shrub that is loose or appears weak or brittle. Carefully evaluate tree anchors near or on cliff faces; these trees may be shallow-rooted and not as solid as they appear. Test all trees by pushing against them with one foot. Attaching to an unquestionably stout tree branch rather than low on the trunk helps limit the rope's contact with the ground, reducing abrasion on the rope and reducing the risk of rockfall. However, connecting to a branch rather than the trunk puts more leverage on the tree, increasing the danger that the tree could be uprooted. Be cautious about using a bush as an anchor. If you use one, consider placing an additional anchor or two for safety. Also be careful using trees and bushes in very cold weather, when they can become brittle.

Rock features—horns, columns, rock tunnels such as those formed by the contact point between two boulders, large and flat-bottomed boulders—are commonly used as anchors. Note that it is easy to overestimate the stability of large boulders. As important as size is the shape of the boulder's bottom, the shape of the socket it is sitting in or the angle of the slope it is on, and the ratio of its height to width. Imagine the hidden undersurface and the block's center of gravity: Will it pull over under a big load? Test it gently at first so you do not send it over the edge. Occasionally, climbers have to set up a belay at a jumble of large boulders, where some are resting on others. A boulder underneath other large boulders might be quite solid but can be difficult to assess even with careful checking.

Any rock feature used as an anchor should be checked for fracture lines, which may be subtle and difficult to judge, such as at the base of a rock horn or near the edge of a crack. When using protection in a crack for an anchor, check to see whether one side of the crack may actually be a detachable block or movable flake; a crack has to widen only a fraction of an inch under the force of a fall for the protection to pull out.

Always evaluate the probable strength and stability of a rock feature or chockstone prior to using it as an anchor. Place a sling on a rock feature well below the feature's center of gravity to reduce the chance of it tipping or dislodging. If there is any question about a natural anchor, test it before gear is attached, never after the rope or the belayer is hooked in. (See also "Natural Protection" in Chapter 13, Rock Protection.)

Fixed Anchors

Artificial (manufactured) anchors include bolts and pitons that, once set, are usually left "fixed" permanently in place. On established routes, climbers may encounter previously placed bolts and pitons; in unknown alpine terrain, some climbers carry pitons and a hammer to set anchors. Bolts are permanent pieces of artificial protection, driven into a hole that has been drilled into the rock. Bolt hangers, which may or may not be permanent, allow carabiners to be attached to bolts (see Figure 13-6 in Chapter 13, Rock Protection). Pitons are metal spikes pounded into cracks. The blade of the piton is driven into the crack; the eye is the point of attachment for a carabiner (see Figure 13-8 in Chapter 13, Rock Protection). Climbers may also encounter other fixed pieces—hardware such as nuts, hexes, and so forth, which are normally removable protection that became fixed

SRENE ANCHOR SYSTEMS

A simple yet highly effective set of principles to follow when evaluating anchor systems goes by the acronym **SRENE**. This means that any anchor system should fulfill these requirements:

- **S**olid. Each individual component should be solid to the greatest extent feasible.
- **R**edundant. Always use redundant components in setting up an anchor; two solid anchor points are considered an absolute minimum, and then only if they are really bombproof, but three or more are preferable.
- **E**qualized. Use a rigging method that tries to equally distribute the load between the various individual anchor points, which greatly increases the reliability of each part of the system.
- **N**o **E**xtension. Eliminate the possibility that failure of one component in the anchor system will cause the anchor to suddenly extend, which would cause subsequent shock loading and generate dangerously high impact forces on the remaining components.

when someone could not remove them. On rock climbing topo maps, bolts and fixed pitons are often shown as "x" and "fp," respectively (see Figure 14-3 in Chapter 14, Leading on Rock).

Fixed pieces that have been left in place by previous climbers must be evaluated for safety. Bolts and fixed pitons are often solid if of recent vintage, but older placements are notoriously difficult to assess (see "Fixed Protection" in Chapter 13, Rock Protection). Old ¼-inch bolts are no longer the accepted standard and should not be trusted.

Many popular routes now feature fixed anchors at belay stations; commonly these consist of two or more bolts, sometimes connected with a short section of chain.

Removable Anchors

Where natural features or fixed protection are not available, climbers build anchors and remove them as they complete a pitch (see Chapters 13, Rock Protection, and 14, Leading on Rock, for rock anchors; Chapter 16, Snow Travel and Climbing, for snow anchors; and Chapter 18, Alpine Ice Climbing, for ice anchors). Climbers may encounter removable pieces left behind on routes by others. Removable hardware that has been left in place must be evaluated for safety. Perhaps it was left because the climbers could not remove it, or perhaps a party descended the route and had to leave it.

TYING IN TO THE ANCHOR

The connection between the harness and the anchor—whether a tie-in or a clip-in—should be separate from and independent of the carabiner connected to the belay device. The best way for the belayer to connect to the anchor is to tie in with the climbing rope itself, using the first few feet of rope as it comes from its tie-in at the belayer's harness. This ensures that there will be a dynamic link between the belayer and anchor because the rope itself is dynamic.

Climbers often connect to the anchor using runners or their personal anchors. Although this may save time and keeps the maximum amount of rope available for climbing longer pitches, there are hazards associated with this practice. Many runners and personal anchors are made of materials such as Spectra that do not react dynamically under load. If a climber is any distance above the anchor and falls, the climber may experience a high-factor fall, and even short falls on these static materials can generate extremely high impact forces. Despite their high strength, such runners, as well as carabiners, have failed under these circumstances. If using a personal anchor, beware of climbing above the anchor. Additionally, if a climber is using a daisy chain as a personal anchor and clips in to the anchor through two loops of the daisy chain, a fall can break the relatively weak bar tacks separating the loops and completely detach the climber from the anchor.

To tie directly in to the anchor with the climbing rope, a couple of different knots may be used. First, establish a solid anchor, then use clove hitches or a figure eight on a bight in the climbing rope to connect the rope to the anchor points with carabiners. The figure eight is strong, stable, and easy to untie. The clove hitch has the advantage of being adjustable after it is tied and is a quick, versatile way to connect a belayer to the anchor. When connecting to an anchor, use one locking carabiner or two regular carabiners with the gates opposite and opposed (see Figure 9-37 in Chapter 9, Basic Safety System). Avoid chaining carabiners in succession, because they can twist, which weakens them and can open a gate.

Redundancy requires employing multiple anchor placements for belaying—commonly, two or three that will hold a downward pull and one that will hold an upward pull. The upward-pull and downward-pull placements are not necessarily separate: a multidirectional placement (such as a bolt, tree, or well-placed cam) may serve as one of the downward-pull components and also as the upward-pull component. When constructing an anchor using chocks, a common arrangement is to create a multidirectional placement with a pair of opposing chocks (see "Opposition Placement" in Chapter 13, Rock Protection). Redundancy is not achieved by backing up a strong placement with a weak one. Substandard placements may be equalized to create one acceptable anchor point, but always try to create the strongest individual placements available when building a belay anchor.

Equalizing the load among the multiple anchor placements is important, as the peak loads created in a fall can exceed the expected strength of individual anchor components, and this is especially vital if one of the components is suspected to be weak. There are a number of different ways to rig multiple anchor points, and many considerations affect the choice among them.

One technique is to tie in separately with the climbing rope to a series of anchor points, using clove hitches for their adjustability (fig. 10-11a). This method, although quick and simple, has several drawbacks. If a serious fall occurs, all the impact is imposed on a single anchor point; the other placements come into play only if the first one fails. Although the force that goes to the second piece should be less than that on the first (because some of the energy of the fall has been

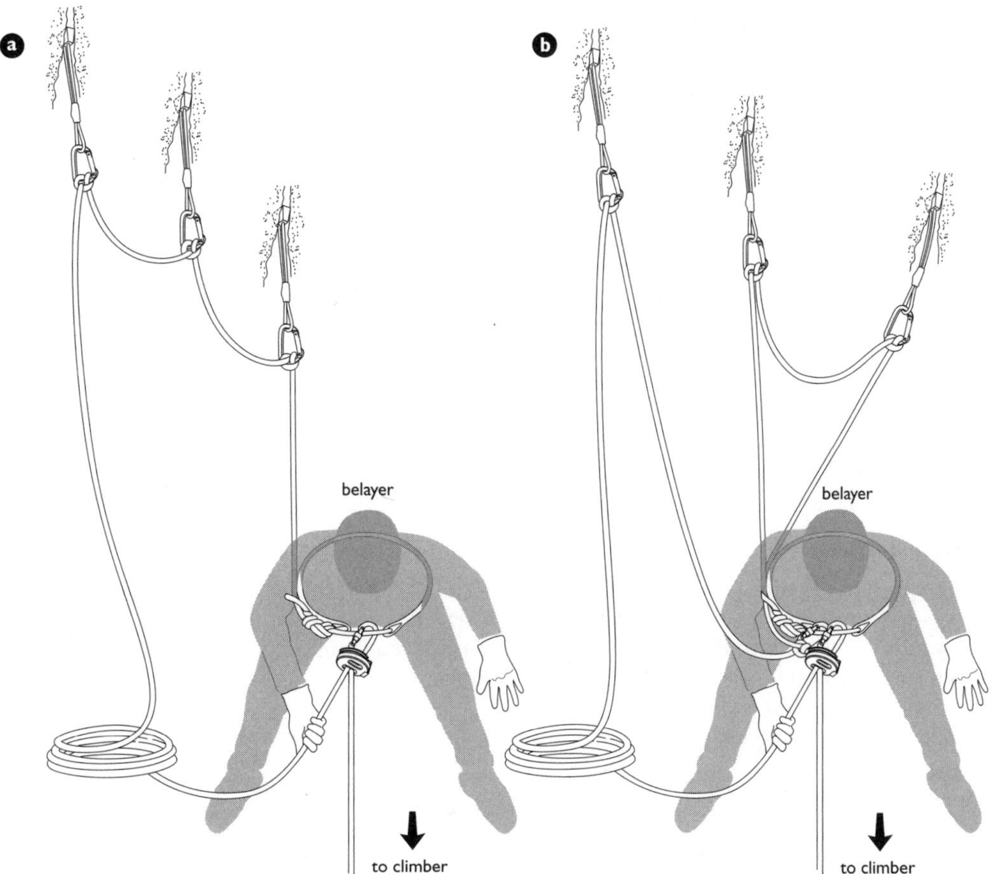

Fig. 10-11. Tying in to several anchor points with a series of clove hitches: a, only one of these anchor points holds weight at any given time; b, weight is distributed among all these anchor points.

absorbed), it may still be considerable. And as each anchor placement fails, the belayer may suddenly drop some distance and lose control of the belay. Successive loading of the remaining anchor components risks a catastrophic cascade of anchor component failures.

It is far better to use a method that distributes the load among two or more anchor placements. Properly done, this shares the load more or less equally between the various anchor points, significantly reducing the force on any one and increasing reliability of the belay. This could be done by tying sections of rope between the seat harness and each anchor carabiner with clove hitches (fig. 10-11b). By adjusting the clove hitches to snug up the strand to each carabiner, the force of a fall will be shared by the multiple placements, and if one fails, minimal extension results before the others come into play. However, this method uses a lot of rope and is somewhat cumbersome to set up; therefore, it is not often used. Preferred methods of equalizing the load among multiple anchor points are discussed in the next section.

Sometimes climbers will want to belay from a stance that is some distance from the anchor. Once the belayer is set in the stance, precise adjustment is impossible if the tie-in knot to the anchor is out of reach from the stance. A solution is to tie in with a knot on only the seat harness. Take the rope—after it has run from the harness and simply been clipped through the anchor carabiner—and tie it to a carabiner on the seat harness (fig. 10-12). Use a clove hitch so the tension on the rope between belayer and the anchor can easily be adjusted. This method avoids much fussing around and moving back and forth from anchor to stance, but it does use up additional rope.

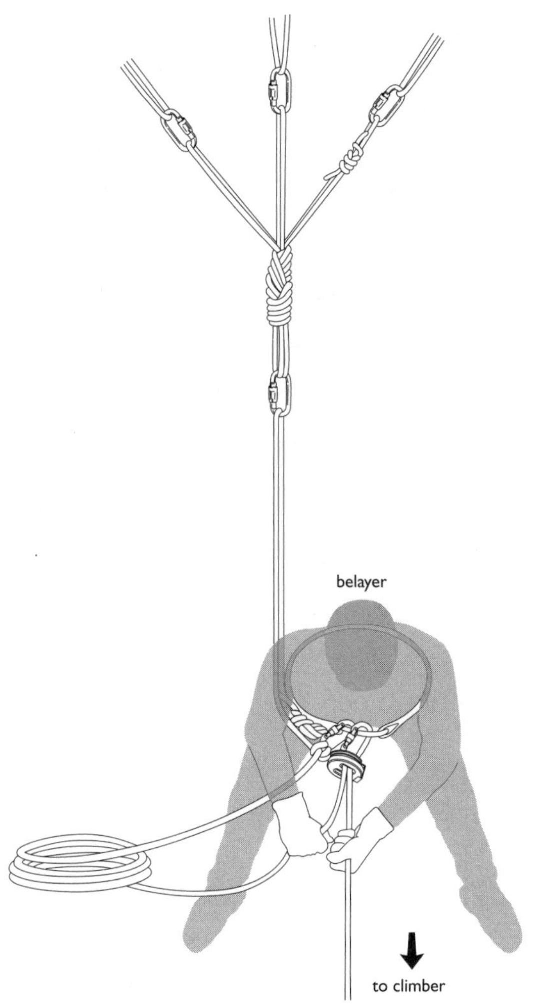

Fig. 10-12. Tying the climbing rope to a locking carabiner on the belayer's harness with a clove hitch allows convenient adjustment of the belayer's distance from the anchor.

EQUALIZING ANCHORS

Most ways of equalizing the load on multiple anchor points make use of runners or loops of accessory cord; they can be roughly divided into two methods: static equalization and self-equalization. In reality, no practical system achieves true equalization, and the various methods commonly used have advantages and disadvantages. Sources conflict about which method is best, so it is not possible to state that any one choice is preferable. It is important to understand the variables involved, knowing how anchors function in different situations, and to make informed decisions about how best to construct anchors in various configurations. Ultimately, any multipart anchor is only as good as its individual components, and safety depends on skillful placement of individual pieces.

Static Equalization (Runners and Cordelettes)

A simple method of static equalization consists of two independent anchor placements with separate runners attached to each, with the two free ends clipped together with a carabiner at the bottom of the V (fig. 10-13). This will seldom achieve effective equalization, except under ideal circumstances, and should not be counted on to do so.

Another popular kind of static equalization uses a cordelette—a long runner of about 18 feet (5.5 meters), usually made using 7- to 8-millimeter nylon accessory cord—or small-diameter, high-strength cords made of a material such as Spectra or Dyneema.

The small-diameter, high-strength cords are popular due to their low weight and bulk, but they have disadvantages. Polyethylene materials like Spectra and Dyneema have lower melting points than that of nylon, making it critical that they not be subjected to a loaded rope running over them. Test data show that with knotting and repeated flexing, most of these materials weaken much faster than nylon, which means that their strength in use may actually be lower than 7-millimeter nylon cord. The smaller-diameter, high-strength cords are also more expensive than nylon ones and may have to be replaced more frequently as they lose strength with use. Perhaps most significantly, the high-strength cords have low stretch, and analysis of separate anchor loads shows that this leads to poorer load distribution than with nylon. Everything considered, 7-millimeter nylon cord probably combines the best properties of strength, elongation, and long service life. If you do use the smaller-diameter, high-strength cords, keep in mind that the cordelette must be tied using a triple fisherman's bend because of the material's lower friction.

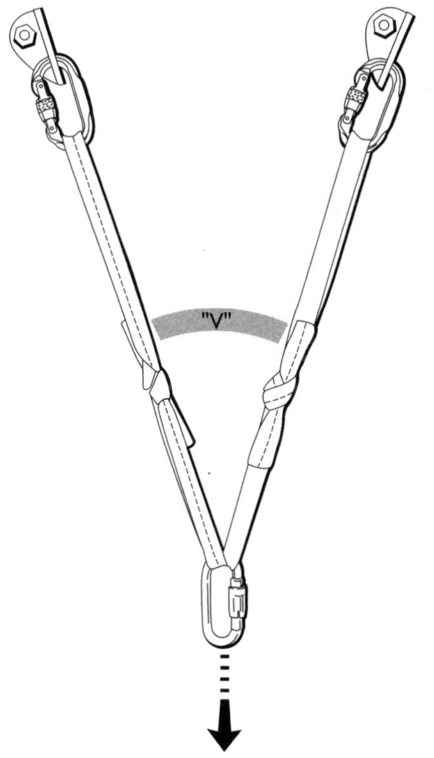

Fig. 10-13. Simple static equalization: The length of the runners must be sized accurately to evenly distribute the load. The angle "V" formed by the runners should always be less than 90 degrees, or the load on individual anchor points increases (see Figure 10-17).

Webbing cordelettes, called Web-o-lettes, are also available. They are made of ½-inch (12-millimeter) nylon-Dyneema webbing with a carabiner loop sewn into each end. They are stronger and lighter than tied cordelettes, they are easy to set up, and they function much like tied cordelettes.

To equalize three anchor points, clip the cordelette in to each anchor point's carabiner and pull down the top segments between the anchor points (fig. 10-14a). Join them with the bottom part of the cordelette by gripping the three loops (fig. 10-14b) and connecting a locking carabiner to all three loops. Shift the carabiner around while squeezing the strands together to even out the tension in all strands as best you can. Then, while pulling in the predicted direction of force, tie all three segments together into an overhand or figure eight bend (fig. 10-14c). Pull on the carabiner at the end loop to make sure all legs are weighted. Either knot is acceptable; the overhand requires less cord than the figure eight, but it will be much harder to untie if it is heavily loaded. The end loop created by this knot, often called a power point, will be the main attachment point to the belay anchor. Additional connections, such as a second climber clipping in on arrival at the belay stance, can be made into a "shelf" consisting of the strands above the power point (clip a carabiner to one strand coming from each of the anchor points); these are strong enough for loads not expected to approach those generated by a leader fall. This can simplify clipping to or unclipping from a loaded anchor and can avoid much clutter and confusion. Equalization with a cordelette can also be done with either more or fewer than three anchor points.

Load testing of cordelettes shows that the ideal, even distribution of forces is not usually achieved using this setup. Even under ideal circumstances, with three anchor placements symmetrically arranged, the middle

10

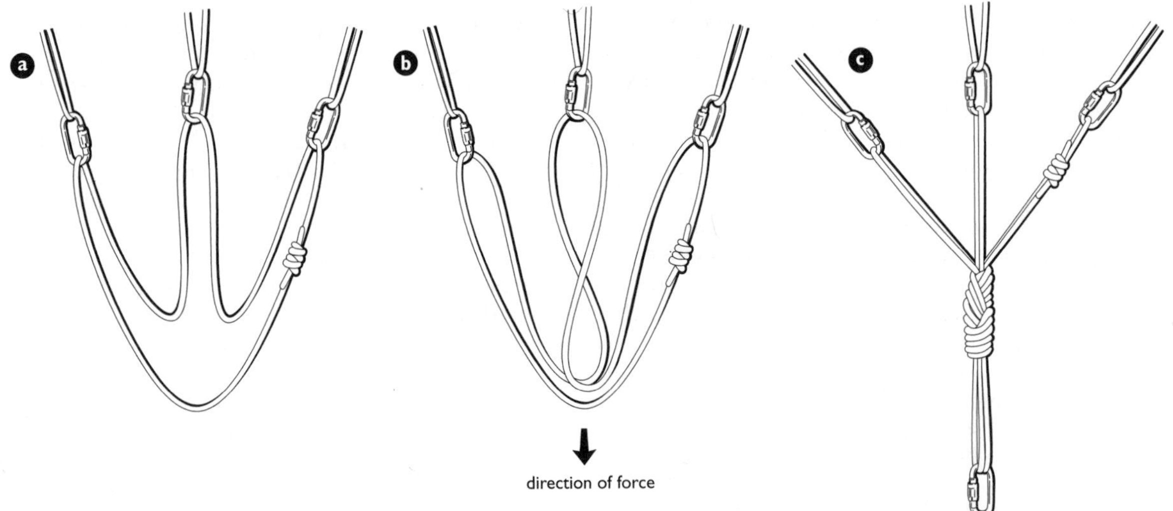

Fig. 10-14. Static equalization with cordelette: a, clip cordelette in to three anchor points and pull the top segments between the anchor points down; b, grasp all three segments together and clip a carabiner in to the loops; c, tie all three segments together into an overhand or figure eight knot.

leg may be subjected to twice the load of the two side legs. Asymmetrical configurations tend to primarily load the two legs closest to the direction of pull. As the lengths of the different legs become more uneven, as is common when rigging an anchor in a vertical crack, the lowest leg is subjected to much higher loads than the longer legs. These differences are due to greater elongation that occurs with longer sections of cord. The effects of uneven rigging configurations can be reduced by extending the individual placements with low-stretch runners to equalize the length of the elastic cordelette legs. Any slack in a leg of the cordelette means that it supports negligible weight and is not equalized.

Self-Equalization (Sliding X and Equalette)

Self-equalization is intended to react to changing load direction and to distribute any force equally among all the anchor components. There are two primary methods.

Sliding X. Two-point equalizing is the simplest example of self-equalization. Clip a runner in to the two anchor carabiners; grasp the top part of the runner between the two anchor points and put a half twist in it, making an X and forming a loop (fig. 10-15a); then clip the loop and the bottom part of the runner together with a carabiner. The rope gets tied to this carabiner (fig. 10-15b). It is absolutely essential to put the loop in the runner rather than just clipping the top and bottom of the runner with the carabiner into which the rope is tied. Otherwise, if one anchor point fails, the runner will simply slip through this carabiner, leaving the rope completely unanchored.

This method, known as the "sliding X," depends on the carabiner attachment sliding freely to self-equalize as the direction of pull changes. Studies of how well this system works are contradictory, with some recommending the sliding X and claiming that it functions quite well in most circumstances and with others recommending against its use. Care should be taken in rigging this system to minimize friction between the sliding carabiner and the X; it is likely that some poor results have been due to avoidable binding effects. It appears that the new, thinner sewn runners work better with this method than bulky 9⁄16-inch or wider webbing. Using larger-diameter carabiners also reduces friction.

With a longer runner, the sliding X can work well to equalize more than two anchor points. This method violates the No Extension principle (see the "SRENE Anchor Systems" sidebar) unless shorter slings or limiter knots are tied in the runner (fig. 10-15c). Without such limiter knots, if one anchor point fails, there will be extension of the runner as the load transfers to the one remaining anchor point. This risks failure of the second anchor point and potential loss of control of the belay.

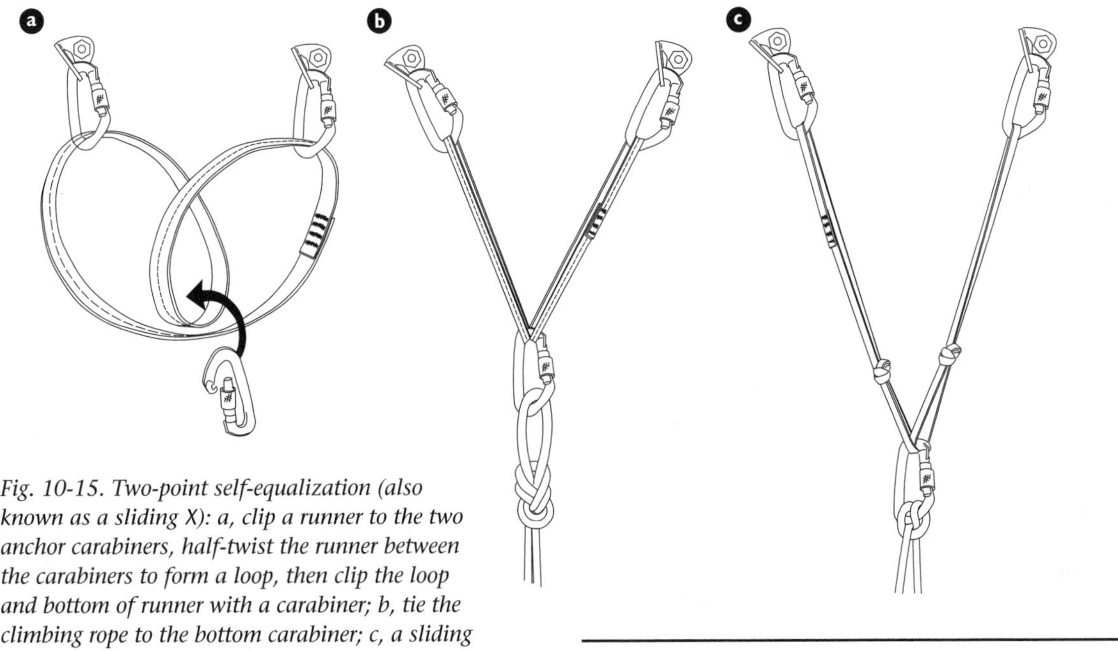

Fig. 10-15. Two-point self-equalization (also known as a sliding X): a, clip a runner to the two anchor carabiners, half-twist the runner between the carabiners to form a loop, then clip the loop and bottom of runner with a carabiner; b, tie the climbing rope to the bottom carabiner; c, a sliding X with limiter knots to minimize extension of runner should one anchor point fail.

Equalettes. The equalette was developed to overcome the disadvantages of friction and elongation associated with the sliding X and the potentially poor equalization of a cordelette. It combines elements from both the sliding X and the cordelette.

Equalettes are normally constructed from 20 feet (6 meters) of 7-millimeter nylon or smaller-diameter, high-strength cord. Tie the cord into a loop with a double or triple fisherman's bend, as appropriate to the material. Grab a bight to form a four-stranded U, with the fisherman's bend offset from the center of the U by about 18 inches (45 centimeters), then tie overhand limiter knots on either side of the U to create a section about 10 inches (25 centimeters) long. You now have a loop about 8 feet (2.5 meters) long consisting of an isolated center section and two longer side loops (fig. 10-16). To build a multipoint anchor using the equalette, estimate the most likely direction that the force of a fall will come from, and orient the central section toward that pull, just as is done when tying a power point in a cordelette anchor system.

Now connect both of the side loops to one or more anchor components. Various configurations are possible using one or more anchor elements per side,

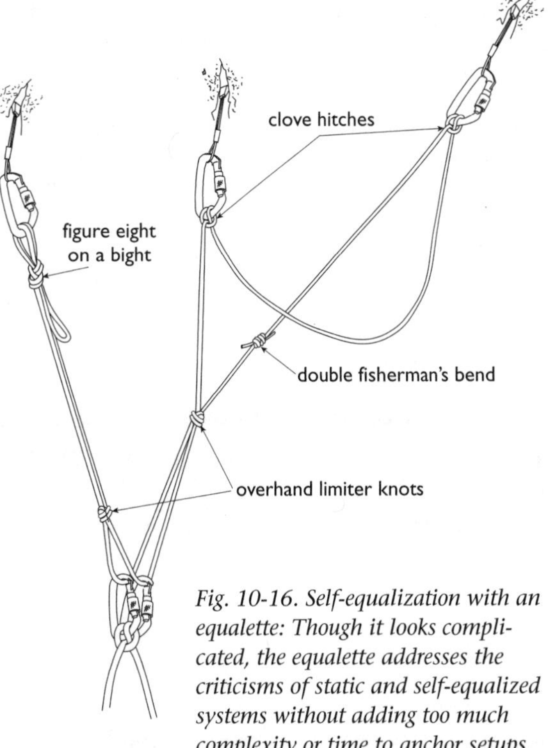

Fig. 10-16. Self-equalization with an equalette: Though it looks complicated, the equalette addresses the criticisms of static and self-equalized systems without adding too much complexity or time to anchor setups.

equalized with combinations of clove hitches, sliding Xs, and so on. Once the anchor is constructed, clip in to the equalette, preferably using one locking carabiner for each of the two central strands. If using one carabiner, be sure to put a half twist and loop in one of the strands just as with the sliding X, to prevent complete disconnection if one side of the equalette were to fail.

In action, this method is designed to self-equalize; the tie-in can redirect itself and maintain load distribution to both sides if the direction of pull changes. If one leg were to completely fail, the limiter knots would keep extension to a reasonable minimum. Though seeming rather complicated at first, the equalette addresses the criticisms of static and self-equalized systems, and it need not add too much complexity or time to anchor setups.

Choosing an Equalization Method

A common factor affecting both static equalization and self-equalization must be clearly understood. How well an equalization setup reduces the pull on each individual anchor placement depends on the angle formed by the runner or runners coming together. The smaller the angle, the less force each anchor point will be subjected to (fig. 10-17a). As the angle increases, each anchor point experiences an increasing force (fig. 10-17b). For example, when the angle is 90 degrees in a two-piece setup (fig. 10-17c), each piece will take 71 percent of the force downward at the point of attachment (see Table 10-1). When the angle is greater than 120 degrees (fig. 10-17d), each of the two placements will actually be subjected to a greater force than if equalization was not even used.

A rigging system sometimes used at bolt anchors consists of a single runner (or multiple runners) simply clipped in to two anchor points and the carabiner into which the rope is tied. When loaded, the runner forms

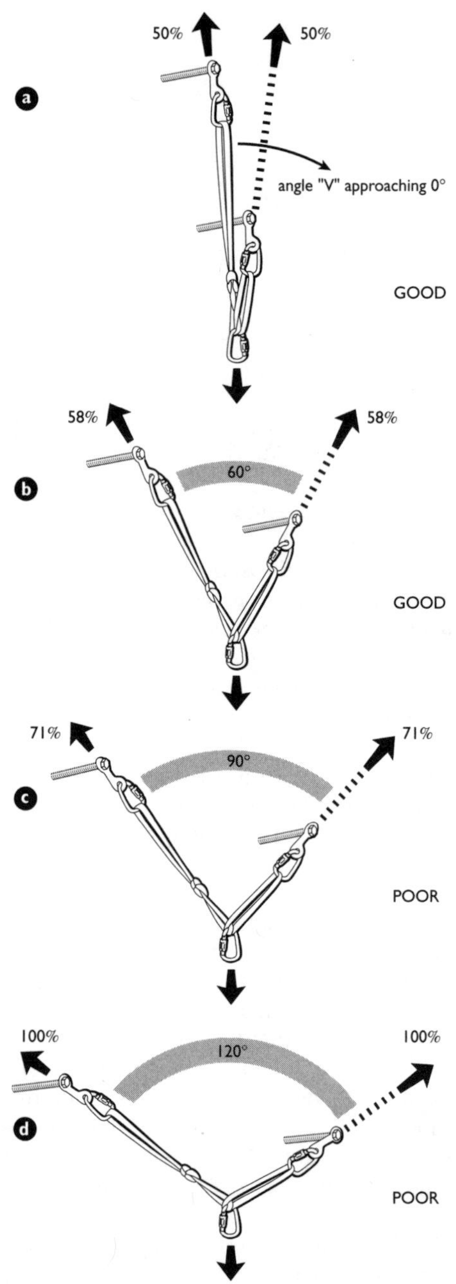

Fig. 10-17. Two-point anchor equalized with tied runners: a, the angle V where two runners meet approaches 0 degrees; b and c, as the angle V increases, the load on each anchor point increases; d, load exceeds 100 percent on each anchor point as the angle becomes greater than 120 degrees.

TABLE 10-1. FORCE ON EACH OF TWO EQUALIZED ANCHORS

Angle	Force on Each Anchor
0°	50%
60°	58%
90°	71%
120°	100%
150°	193%
170°	573%

a triangle between the three points, apparently equalizing the load on both bolts. In fact, with this rigging system, forces on the bolts are multiplied because the top of the triangle acts like a 180-degree angle between the two pieces. This creates forces many times more than the downward pull. Avoid using this rigging system. If you find such a configuration, it is best to replace it with a properly equalized configuration as shown in Figure 10-13.

Now consider a simple two-point static equalized anchor. If the vertical line representing the direction of force of a downward pull bisects the angle at the V, the load will be equalized (fig. 10-18a). If the vertical line representing the direction of force of a downward pull does not bisect the V but instead forms two unequal angles within the V, more of the load will be on the anchor point that is closer to parallel to the direction of force (fig. 10-18b), because the point of attachment does not move. Therefore, to get approximate equalization, two things must be done correctly. First, the direction of force must be accurately predicted. Second, the two runners must be sized just right for an equal distribution of force. You can achieve static equalization without the need to tie or retie any runners if you use a cordelette and can estimate the direction of pull correctly, tying the knot while pulling the rope in that direction.

The need to equalize the load and the need to have a relatively small angle at the V tend to work against each other. The smaller the angle, the more any wrong guess about the direction of force will load the anchor placements differently. A further difficulty is that the direction of force may be difficult to predict. For instance, if a climber is leading out on a traverse and falls before placing any protection, the fall may be downward, or it may be to the side if the rope runs over a block near the point of fall. When a belayer's guess on direction of force is so wrong that all the force of a fall initially goes onto one anchor point, static "equalization" is no equalization at all; it is no different from simply tying separately into two anchors. In fact, many anchor arrangements that are intended to achieve equalization may fail to do so in an actual fall because it is difficult to predict the direction of force with the necessary precision. This practical limitation on the effectiveness of equalization underscores the importance of placing multiple, solid, redundant anchor placements.

10

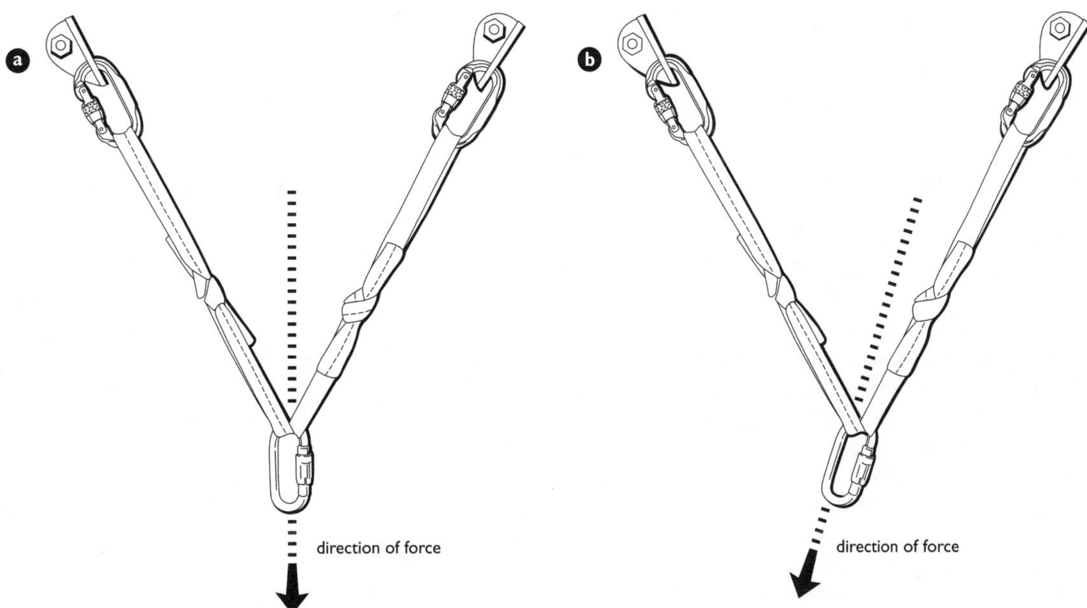

Fig. 10-18. Static equalization: a, line representing direction of force bisects the angle, so the load on the two anchor points is equal; b, direction of force is to one side, so the load on the right-hand anchor point is greater than on the left-hand anchor point.

Intelligent use of equalization principles depends on finding suitable anchor placements close together. Anchor placements must be sufficiently close to each other to make equalization feasible without an unacceptably large angle at the V, which would magnify rather than reduce forces on the placements. Inferior anchor placements should not be used in lieu of solid placements merely because the more solid placements cannot be equalized. You must always exercise judgment in determining the best anchor arrangement. Most of the time, the best arrangement involves an equalized anchor—but not always.

In climbing, especially for an element as critical as the belay anchor, no system is best in all situations, and rigid adherence to any one method can lead to trouble. It is highly recommended that beginning climbers consult different sources, become familiar with the underlying principles, practice several methods, and be ready to respond flexibly to a variety of situations. Despite the complexity and real risks associated with belay anchors, outright failure is rare, and the systems appear to be robust despite not meeting ideal standards.

Fig. 10-19. Belaying directly from the anchor with a munter hitch.

BELAY POSITION AND STANCE

When belaying a leader with an aperture device or munter hitch, belay directly off of the seat harness. This position puts the belayer's hands and arms in the correct position to manage the rope and to apply braking force the instant a fall occurs. When belaying a follower, there is also the choice of belaying directly off of the anchor if using either the munter hitch (fig. 10-19), a multifunction aperture-style self-braking belay device in self-braking mode, or a spring-loaded self-braking belay device (see "Using Belay Devices" and "Using the Munter Hitch," above). A munter-hitch belay works well with the brake hand either above or below the hitch (as shown in Figure 10-19), but an aperture-style self-braking device in normal belay mode (as shown in Figure 10-6a) will not work when rigged directly off the anchor. You must be able to achieve a minimum of 90 degrees of separation between the load and braking strands of the rope (as shown in Figure 10-4); often, this minimum angle cannot be reached when belaying directly off the anchor with an aperture device.

An advantage of belaying from the anchor is that the belayer is not subject to the forces created by a fall and is less likely to be injured or to lose control of the belay. Furthermore, when using a self-braking device, the belayer can manage tasks such as eating, drinking, and adjusting clothing layers without putting the follower at great risk. Given the benefits to belaying from the anchor, this method is becoming more popular with the introduction of more types of self-braking devices. The issues of stance and position discussed in this section are hardly concerns when you are belaying from the anchor.

A small advantage of belaying from the body is that the movement of the belayer under the force of a fall introduces a dynamic element that somewhat reduces the forces on the protection and on the falling climber's body. Some climbers believe that a significant advantage of belaying from the body is the ability to adopt a stance so strong that little or no force goes onto the anchor—and the anchor essentially becomes a backup. This often makes sense when belaying a follower with little possibility of a serious pendulum fall or of significant slack in the rope; with a good stance, little, if any, force may go onto the anchor.

Although reducing loads on the anchor seems to make good sense, it is unreasonable to expect any stance to withstand the kind of force that would cause an adequate belay anchor to fail. In any situation in which an extreme leader fall or a serious pendulum fall is a possibility, it is impossible for the belayer to protect the anchor by maintaining a stance; whatever force goes onto the belayer is likely to go largely undiminished onto the anchor.

Because any stance is unlikely to be able to withstand the force of a severe fall, belays should be set up with the assumption that in such a fall, the belayer will be pulled into a position in a direct line between the anchor and the first piece of protection placed by the fallen climber. One way to keep this in mind when setting up belays is to remember the **ABC**s: Severe forces will result in a pull in a direct line between the **A**nchor, **B**elayer, and **Cl**imber's line of travel (fig. 10-20a). If the

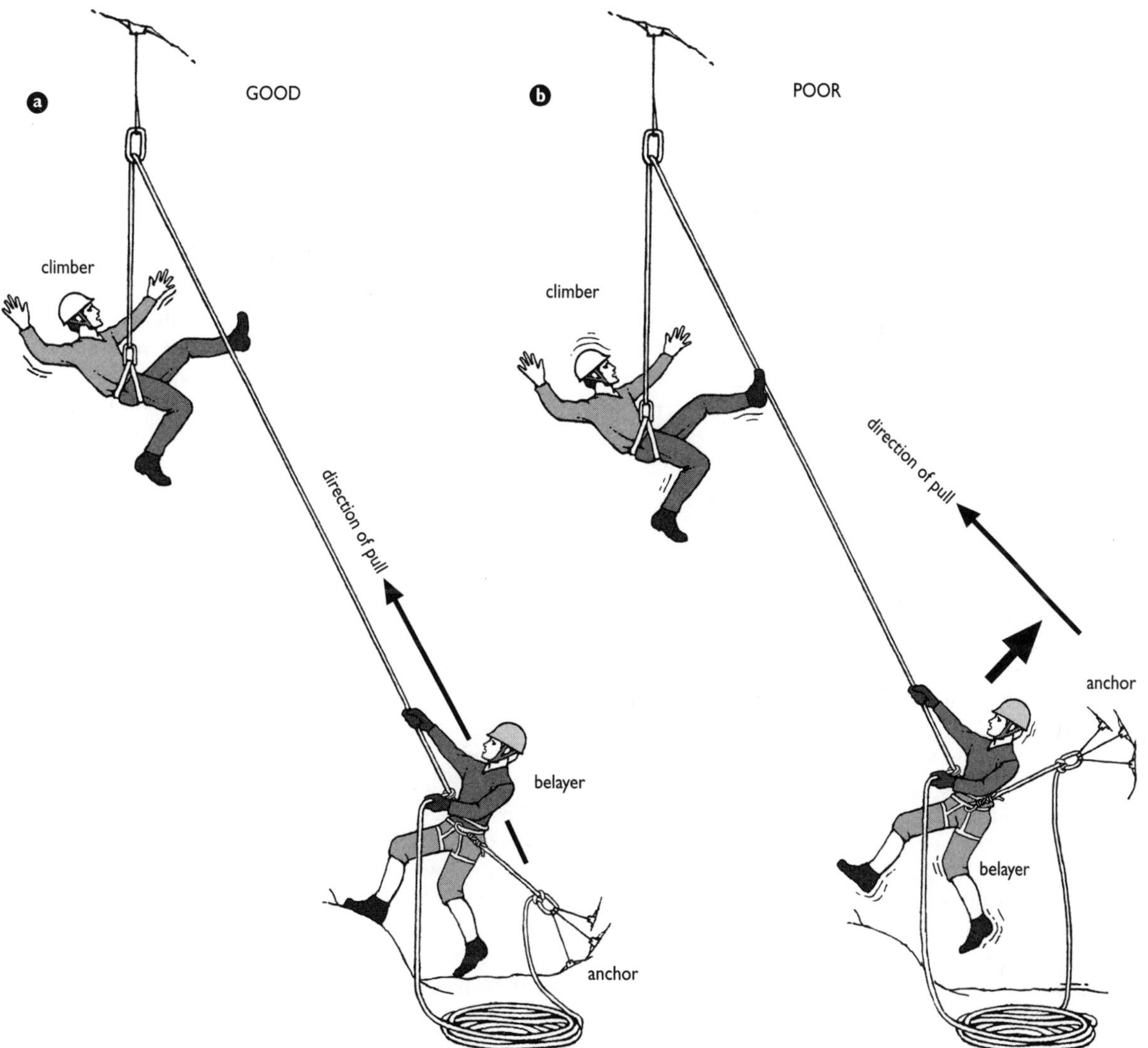

Fig. 10-20. The **A***nchor-***B***elayer-***Cl***imber load axis: a, the belayer is in a direct line between the anchor and the direction of pull, and the load is transferred directly to the anchor; b, the belayer is positioned away from the load axis and gets pulled from the belay stance.*

belayer is in a position other than along this load axis, the belayer will be pulled, sometimes violently, in the direction of this axis (fig. 10-20b). The force of even a moderate fall can take belayers by surprise, and those who find themselves pulled out of position risk injury or loss of control of the belay.

Earlier in this chapter, the "Protecting the Leader" section recommends that the lead climber place a secure point of protection soon after starting a new lead, to reduce the fall factor and establish a predictable direction from which the force of a leader fall will come. The importance of knowing the direction from which a shock load will come becomes apparent when you apply the ABC principles.

FACING IN OR FACING OUT

When belaying a follower off of the harness, it is common to face out, usually with the anchor at your back as you look down to watch for your climbing partner coming up.

An alternative that works especially well when in a hanging or semihanging stance on multipitch routes is to face in toward the anchor while you are hanging in the seat harness. Pass the rope through a directional carabiner (a carabiner acting to direct the rope) that is attached to the anchor and then to the climber below. In this setup, the force from a fall will always come from the directional carabiner rather than from the climber directly onto the belayer. If a separate piece of protection is used for the directional carabiner (fig. 10-21a), then a first solid placement is already established as the climber begins the next lead (fig. 10-21b). This establishes the load direction and reduces the potential fall factor for the first moves. A directional carabiner should never be clipped in to one piece of a multipart anchor because a fall would load just one piece and would not be distributed across the equalized anchor.

When belaying a leader, there are many advantages to facing in to the mountain. Facing in usually allows you to watch your partner climb, enabling you to anticipate movements and to pay out or take in rope more efficiently. It may also be possible to figure out how to get past some of the difficult sections when it is time for you to climb if you have seen where your partner had difficulty or found a good solution to a problem. You are better able to take cover from rockfall. And you are in the best position to see a leader fall start, so you can quickly brace and go into the braking position. Being able to see a leader fall begin is a particular advantage when the first piece of protection is low and the force of the fall would tend to pull you into the rock.

These advantages of facing in are lost when you are belaying in an alcove with a roof or bulge overhead that prevents you from watching your partner and when the first piece of protection is directly above you. In this situation, you are no worse off facing out when it comes to holding a protected leader fall, and you are probably in a much better position to hold an unprotected leader fall because you are not in danger of being spun around.

POSITION AND ANCHOR

When belaying off the seat harness, the belayer's position relative to the anchor is a fairly straightforward matter: Tie in as closely as feasible to the anchor, with no slack, to avoid shock-loading the anchor system or being pulled off the stance by a severe fall. When belaying a follower, this tie-in needs to hold only a downward pull. But in the event of a leader fall, you cannot be sure whether the force will be upward (most likely) or downward (unlikely but potentially dangerous).

Consider an upward pull first. In a severe fall, you may be jerked sharply upward for a couple of feet, especially if you are much lighter than your partner. This can cause you to lose control and can result in injury if you are yanked up against an obstruction. It can even result in the downward-pull anchor placements pulling out if they are not multidirectional, leaving you and your partner both hanging from the top piece of protection. Your sudden upward movement actually can reduce the force that is put on the top piece of protection—but it is still probably best to avoid such a surprising jolt by maintaining a fairly tight tie-in to an upward-pull anchor placement somewhat below your waist. A standing, rather than a sitting, position is best for this tie-in.

Now consider an unprotected leader fall wherein the force is downward. In a standing belay of a leader, it is very common to see a belayer with a fairly long attachment to an anchor at about waist height or lower. This belayer is not prepared to stop an unprotected leader fall. If the belayer is standing on a ledge and the partner falls past the belayer, the downward force builds quickly beyond the point that the belay stance can hold. The belayer would then be pulled violently off the ledge or driven sharply down onto it, with almost certain loss of control of the belay and probable injuries. To prevent this possibility, you need to be tightly attached to an anchor above your waist level so that you cannot be pulled down more than a few inches. (It might also be a good idea to adopt a sitting stance or to belay directly off the anchor in circumstances wherein a solid anchor above waist level is not available.)

In deciding on a belay position in relation to the belay anchor, think through the possibilities of what could go wrong given varying positions and potential falls. Try to plan for worst-case scenarios and make sure that a bad fall would be caught by the belay anchor before you would be pulled off your stance, which entails the very real possibility of losing control of the belay.

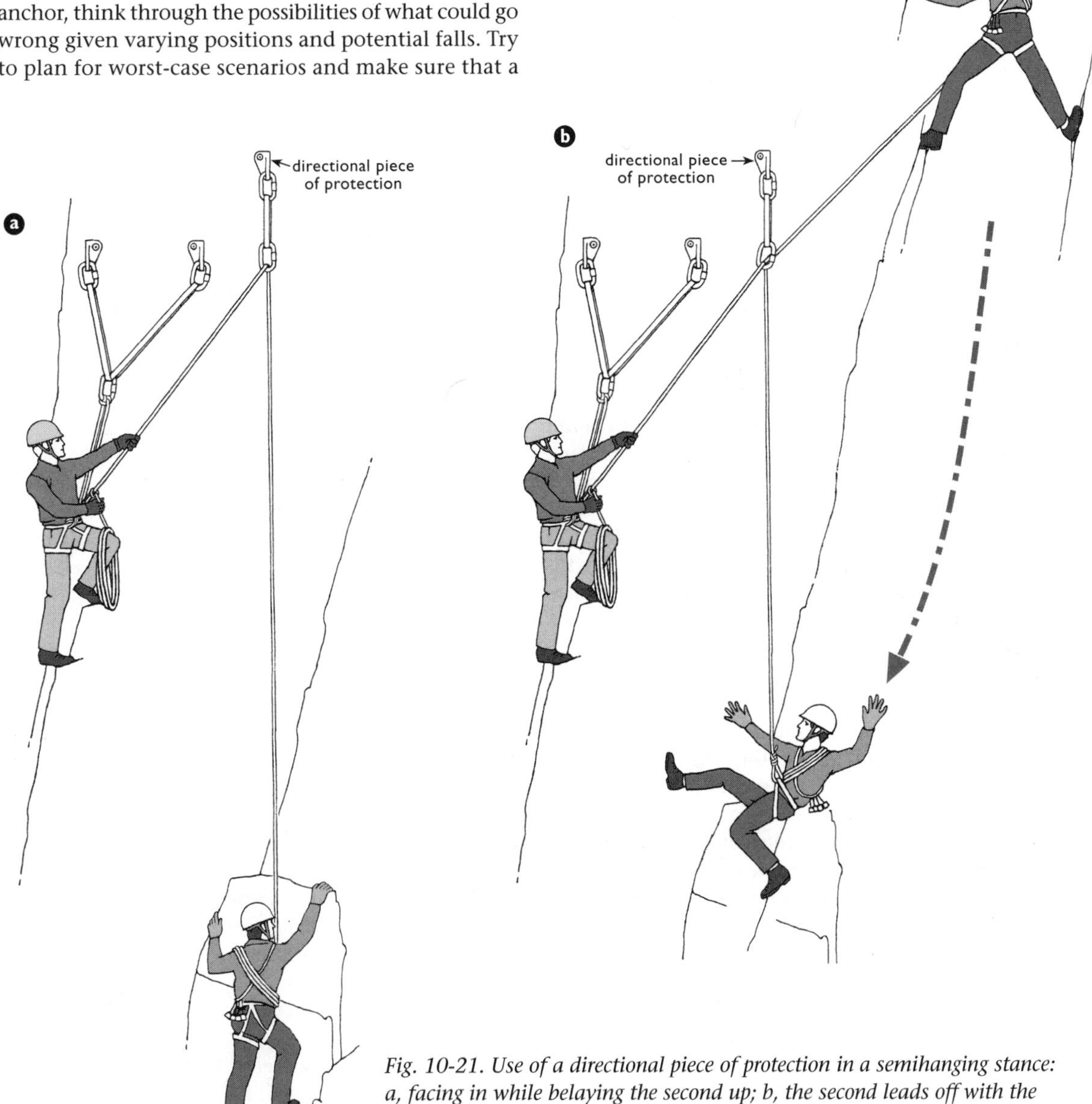

Fig. 10-21. Use of a directional piece of protection in a semihanging stance: a, facing in while belaying the second up; b, the second leads off with the directional piece of protection also establishing the first placement—fall factor is reduced, and load direction is predictable.

ROPE HANDLING

When belaying the leader, never let the rope get taut, because that would impede the climber's next move. An alert belayer keeps just a hint of slack and responds immediately to the leader's advance by paying out more rope. Any friction applied by the belayer is multiplied, so if the leader tells you that rope drag is a problem, keep about a foot or so of slack in the rope and do everything possible to eliminate any pull. If the climber falls when there is a lot of friction in the system, you may actually be unsure whether a fall took place. If it is impossible to communicate with the climber, you can find out by letting out a few inches of rope. If the same tension remains, then you are probably holding the climber's weight.

Ideally, when belaying a follower, there is no slack in the rope. At the same time, the rope should not be taut, which would affect the climber's movement and balance.

An especially acute problem with slack can occur when you are belaying someone who is leading out on a traverse with a significant distance between you and the first piece of protection. Because of the weight of the rope, any attempt you make to keep only a little slack will exert a potentially dangerous pull on the climber, so it is natural to have quite a lot of slack. This extra slack cannot always be avoided, but it is important for both belayer and climber to realize that it can greatly increase the length of a fall. Only a few feet beyond the last protection, the leader could be facing a fall of, say, 15 feet (5 meters) because of the slack.

When you are belaying a follower up to the belay position, pile or drape the rope neatly. Do not let loops hang down the pitch. If the entire pile must be moved, it is tempting to pick it up, but this can easily produce snarls later. It is best to flake out or repile the entire rope twice, so that the leader's end is on top. If the belay ledge is too small for a pile of rope, or if a hanging belay is being used, coil the rope back and forth across the belayer's anchor tie-in. If the follower leads the next pitch, the belayer simply reverses the coils and pays out the rope to the new leader.

In general, you can take in more rope with each pull by leaning forward or bending over. Occasionally when you are belaying a follower, rope drag is so great that it is almost impossible to pull the rope in by hand in the usual way. Here is a technique that works when you are belaying in a sitting position, though it is extremely slow: Bend forward and simultaneously pull the rope through the belay device (this is easy, because you are not actually pulling the rope up yet). Then, gripping the rope tightly, in the braking position if necessary, lean back. This pulls the rope up a few inches; you are using your upper body, not your arms, to pull the rope. Then repeat the process. Once the climber is past enough bends or obstructions, rope drag will decrease and you can revert to normal rope handling.

To minimize falling distance, leaders preparing to make difficult moves often place protection well above their harness tie-in and clip in before moving up. The leader will need some additional slack, and the direction of rope movement will reverse twice. While you are belaying the leader and letting out rope, you will suddenly be taking in slack as the climber moves up to the protection, and then you will be letting it out again as the climber moves past the protection and puts renewed pull on the rope. These switches call for extra attention, especially because this tends to happen at the most difficult spots. To review the basic hand movements of belaying, go back to "Belaying Technique," earlier in this chapter.

COMMUNICATION

As climber and belayer get farther apart and begin to have difficulty hearing each other, stick exclusively to a set of short commands designed to express essential climbing communications (see Table 10-2). Combining these commands with explanations or justifications makes them harder to recognize and defeats their purpose. Use the commands alone. They have been chosen to produce a distinctive pattern. When the belayer is a long way from the climbing partner, shout as loudly as possible and space out each syllable, using very big spaces if there are echoes. In a crowded area, clearly preface commands with your partner's name to avoid confusion about who is being safely belayed, lowered, etc.

Three problems are common at or near the end of each pitch, when hearing each other is most difficult. First, when you are calling out to tell the leader how much rope remains in the coils, the first syllable is often lost, and if normal word order is used, the leader hears only "—ty feet." Instead, invert the word order and pronounce each digit separately: "Feet: . . . three . . . zero" for 30 feet. The leader will pause upon the first word and have a better chance of understanding the remainder. Second, when the leader completes a pitch and

TABLE 10-2. BASIC VOICE COMMANDS USED BY CLIMBERS

Who Says It	Command	What It Means
Follower:	"That's me."	You have pulled up all the slack in the rope and are now tugging on my body; do not pull any more.
Climber:	"On belay?"	Do you have me on belay?
Belayer:	"Belay on."	I am belaying you.
Climber:	"Climbing."	I am, or will resume, moving up.
Belayer:	"Climb."	Response to "Climbing."
Climber:	"Slack."	Give me some slack in the rope and leave it out until I call "Climbing." (To indicate how much slack is needed, the command is "Slack X feet," with X being the amount.)
Climber:	"Up rope" (usually to upper belayer).	There is slack in the rope; pull it in.
Climber:	"Tension" (usually to upper belayer).	Take up all slack and hold my weight. (Should be used sparingly by beginners, to avoid overdependence on rope. Say "Watch me" instead.)
Climber:	"Falling!"	Assume your braking position and brace for a pull on the rope.
Belayer:	"Halfway."	About half of the rope remains.
Leader:	"How much rope?"	What length of rope remains?
Belayer:	"Feet . . . four . . . zero."	Forty feet of rope remains; find a belay soon (best used when 20 to 50 feet [6 to 15 meters] remain).
Leader:	"Off belay."	I am secure and no longer need your belay. Take it apart and prepare to follow the pitch.
Leader:	"Take!"	I expect to weight the rope. Take up the slack and apply braking force to hold me.
Anyone:	"OK."	I heard you.
Follower:	"Belay off" (after taking apart the belay).	You may pull in all the slack and remaining coils when you are ready.
Anyone:	"Rock! Ice!" (Very loudly, immediately, and repeatedly until falling object stops; mandatory.)	Falling objects. Take cover immediately. (Looking up to see approaching danger is a normal reaction, but it risks serious head injuries.)
Anyone:	"Rope."	A rappel rope is about to be thrown down by another party. Look up or take cover.
Climbers also use some discretionary voice commands, depending on local custom or prior arrangement with a climbing partner. These are examples; many variations are used:		
Leader:	"Clipping."	Prepare to give slack so I can clip this protection.
Leader:	"Pro in" or "Clipped in."	I have just clipped in to the first protection. (Or, I have clipped in to protection located above my harness tie-in, so the direction of rope movement will reverse twice as I move up through a difficult spot.)
Climber:	"Protection" or "Cleaning."	I am placing or cleaning protection and will not move up for a while.
Climber:	"Good belay" or "Watch me."	I anticipate a fall or difficult move.
Climber:	"On top."	I have passed the difficulty.

calls "Off belay," do not respond with "Belay off" to indicate that you heard. Instead use "OK." "Belay off" means that you have taken apart the belay and the rope coils are ready to be pulled up, and you are not ready to shout that command for a while yet. Third, avoid the impatient question "On belay?" unless an inordinate amount of time has passed. Often the leader, at work setting up anchors, is out of earshot anyway.

Verbal communication often becomes impossible because of wind or obstructions. In such cases, commands are sometimes transmitted by rope pulls, but there is no universal system for this. Because of rope stretch at the end of long leads, it is necessary to greatly exaggerate the pulls. A simple tug will seldom be felt at the other end. Take in all slack and, for each signal, reach far out along the rope and pull the rope as taut as possible, holding it tight for a while before releasing the tension. If there is much friction, pulls may not be distinguishable from normal rope movements. The most common rope-pull commands correspond to the number of syllables in their verbal equivalents: One pull from the follower means "Slack," two means "Up rope," and three from the belayer above means "Belay on."

Whistle blasts are a good alternative when rope tugs are ineffective, as often is the case with rope drag. Many climbers now use family radio system (FRS) radios to maintain communication, but they are an additional piece of equipment to rely on. It is advised to have the basics of rope or whistle signals worked out in advance, in case of a radio failure.

OTHER BELAY TECHNIQUES

A few special situations are related to belaying: escaping the belay in the event of an injured partner, self-belaying for solo climbing, and belaying a sport climb.

ESCAPING THE BELAY

At least one aspect of belaying most climbers hope they will never have to use is tying off and escaping the belay in order to help an injured partner. If a climbing partner is seriously injured and other climbers are nearby, it is usually best to let them help while you continue to belay. By staying in place, you could also help in raising or lowering the victim if needed. But if two climbers are alone, it may be necessary to tie off the climbing rope to remove yourself from the belay system, so you can investigate, help your partner, or go for help.

In escaping the belay, you eventually want to have the load connected directly to the anchor. It is very helpful to do this with a releasable knot, usually a munter-mule knot (see "Knots, Bends, and Hitches" in Chapter 9, Basic Safety System). The munter hitch may be used to lower the injured climber, or if a raising system is going to be used, it can serve as a backup belay on the climber.

If you are belaying directly off the anchor using a munter hitch, you need only prevent the rope from sliding through the belay. Tie off the munter hitch with a mule knot and back it up with an overhand knot. You can now take the braking hand off the rope and the load will be held. Then back up the munter-mule to the anchor with a figure eight on a bight, which is connected to the anchor with a carabiner. Leave just enough slack in this backup to disassemble the belay later on.

If you are using a belay device or munter hitch attached to your seat harness, the first step is to tie off the belay with a mule knot backed up with an overhand knot (fig. 10-22a). The load is now on the belayer's harness, and the belayer's hands are both free. Now attach a cord tie-off loop to the climber's end of the rope with a prusik hitch, and connect this loop to a locking carabiner. Attach this locking carabiner to the loose rope coming from the belayer tie-in at the anchor; connect the carabiner and rope with a munter hitch, tied off with a mule knot (a munter-mule) and backed up with an overhand knot (fig. 10-22b). Untie the first overhand knot backup and mule knot (from the belay setup on the harness), and slowly transfer the load to the tie-off loop using the belay device (fig. 10-22c). Finally, connect the rope to the anchor with a figure eight on a bight as a backup, leaving just enough slack to disassemble the belay, and disconnect the belay device from the system (fig. 10-22d).

There is another way to tie off a belay, but without the releasable knot. Tie a cord tie-off loop to the fallen climber's end of the rope with a prusik hitch. Attach the tie-off loop to the anchor using runners and carabiners. Slide the prusik hitch as far down the rope toward the fallen climber and away from the anchor as possible, and slowly release the belay to load the prusik hitch. Once the prusik hitch is loaded, connect the rope to the anchor with a figure eight on a bight as a backup, leaving just enough slack to remove the rope from the belay device, and then disconnect the belay device from the system (fig. 10-23). The big

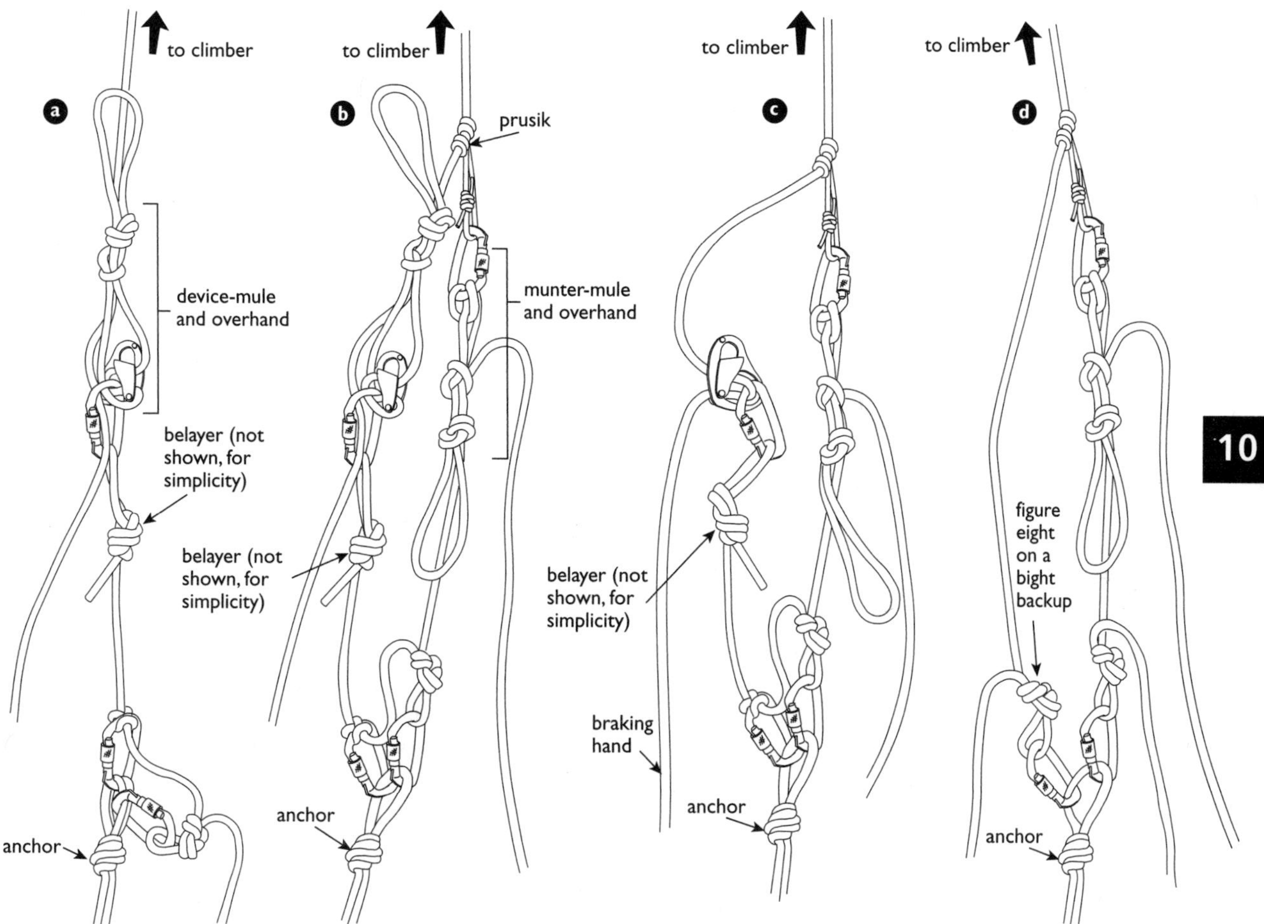

Fig. 10-22. Escaping the belay: a, tie off belay device with mule knot (device-mule) backed up with an overhand knot; b, attach a tie-off loop to the rope with a prusik hitch and clip a locking carabiner to the loop, then attach the carabiner to the rope from the anchor with a munter-mule and overhand knot backup; c, untie the first overhand backup and device-mule, and slowly transfer load to the tie-off loop using the belay device; d, as a backup, connect the rope from the fallen climber to the anchor with a figure eight on a bight, and then remove the belay device.

disadvantage of this simple method is that the prusik hitch cannot be unweighted easily.

SELF-BELAYED SOLO CLIMBING

Self-belay devices, which allow roped solo climbing, have been available for some time. They are worn by the climber, and they work like a ratchet, sliding up the rope during the climb but not down it in a fall. To lead a pitch, the rope is first anchored at the bottom, and you place protection while ascending. Then you anchor the rope at the top and rappel. Finally, you remove the bottom anchor and climb the pitch a second time, retrieving the protection while ascending again.

This is not just another belaying alternative to be chosen on occasion. It is a different form of climbing, requiring a commitment to relearn many fundamentals. Compared to a belay by a live partner, the self-belay's shortcomings are inevitable. Read the manufacturer's literature carefully, and practice in a safe situation. In evaluating the self-belay device, ask some questions: Is the

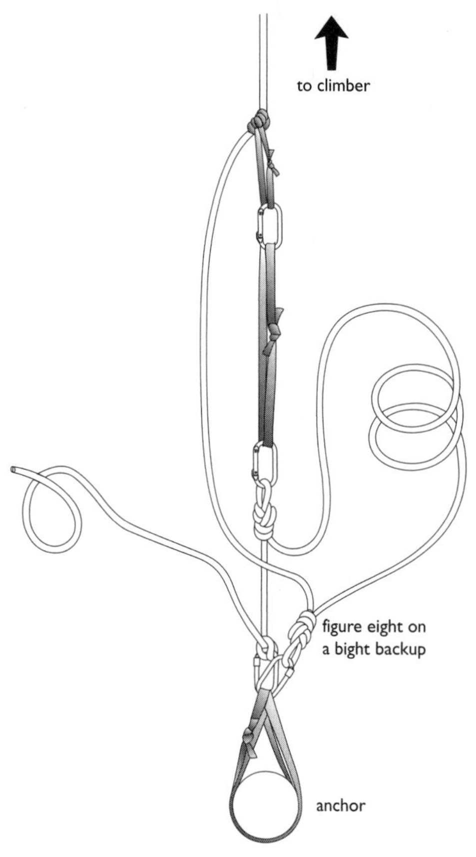

Fig. 10-23. Belay escape with the prusik hitch attached to the anchor: Once the prusik hitch is loaded, connect the rope to the anchor with a figure eight on a bight as a backup.

belay static? Does it work if I fall in a horizontal or head-down position? When I am climbing, does the rope feed automatically, without producing extra slack or drag, especially at the top of a pitch or on a traverse? Can I clip in to protection above waist level without trouble?

BELAYING IN SPORT CLIMBING

Much climbing today takes place on artificial rock and manufactured climbing walls, in gyms or outdoors, and on short routes in rock climbing areas. Often, sport climbs are top-roped; when led, they are usually protected by clipping in to bolts. Although in these instances the general principles of belaying are the same as in other climbing environments, some characteristic features and problems in sport climbing are worth separate discussion.

The sport climbing environment, which usually seems less threatening than that of longer, multipitch climbs, can induce complacency. It is important to keep in mind that the risk of serious injury always exists, and a thorough understanding and application of safe climbing principles is the best way to prevent accidents.

Typically, when a sport pitch is being top-roped, the belayer stands at the bottom, with the rope running up through a preplaced top anchor and back down to the climber, who then ascends while the belayer takes in rope. At the top of the climb, the climber signals for the belayer to hold the climber by saying "Take." The belayer can then lower the climber to the ground. This technique is not typically used in alpine climbing. The belayer often is not anchored; there is often nothing to anchor to, and even when there is, anchoring may seem too fussy and time-consuming.

Belaying without an anchor can cause problems. If you are belaying and standing well away from the rock or off to one side, the force of a fall—even a top-roped fall—can pull you sharply into or along the wall. You may be injured or lose control of the belay, and the climber's fall will certainly be lengthened—perhaps enough to allow the climber to hit a ledge or the ground. When considering what kind of force could have this effect, remember that the peak impact force, even with a top rope, is significantly greater than the climbing partner's weight; remember also that pendulum falls create even greater forces. If belaying without an anchor, it is usually best to be positioned as nearly as possible directly beneath the top anchor. Even then, if the belayer is considerably lighter than the climber, the belayer could be lifted upward by the force of a fall. This movement is not always serious, but it does provide a reason to use a belay device, such as a Grigri, that is very unlikely to result in loss of control of the belay.

The problems of unanchored belaying can be even more serious when the pitch is being led instead of top-roped. If the bolts are in a straight line and a fall is taken low on the pitch—after the first or second bolt—the force on the belayer can be considerable. In this situation, stand as close as possible under the first bolt. If your climbing partner is much heavier than you, insist on being tightly anchored.

An occasional practice in top-roping areas is to run the rope through a runner on the anchor, rather than through carabiners, and then have several people take turns climbing the pitch. This is extremely dangerous because the friction generated by lowering a climber will weaken the runner very quickly, creating a risk of anchor failure.

A number of sport climbing accidents have occurred when a climber was lowered from the top anchors on too short a rope. In multipitch climbing, two climbers are typically tied in to either end of the rope, but in sport climbing, this is often not so. In this case, if the rope runs out while the climber is being lowered with the end unsecured, the result is a ground fall for the climber. Make sure that the rope is long enough to safely lower the climber all the way to the ground or, better yet, tie a figure eight backup knot in the end of the rope.

Remember that even in seemingly benign climbing environments—with everyone having fun, pushing their limits, taking a lot of falls without getting a scratch—all the basic climbing hazards remain, requiring constant attention to safety.

SECURING THE FREEDOM OF THE HILLS

Belaying and anchor setup are the fundamental skills of the technical climber. Practice belaying often, with both your right hand and your left hand as the braking hand. Study and practice anchor techniques. There are many different ways of anchoring yourself, but ideally the anchor system should be **SRENE**: **S**olid, **R**edundant, **E**qualized, and providing **N**o **E**xtension.

Being proficient with belay technique and anchor setup will help you become a good climbing partner. These methods are also related to skills required for rappeling; once you become proficient in them, you will have more confidence when it comes time to rappel. Overall, solid skills in belaying and anchor setup will help you secure the freedom of the hills.

THE RAPPEL SYSTEM • RAPPEL ANCHORS • THE ROPE • RAPPEL METHOD • RAPPEL TECHNIQUE • MULTIPLE RAPPELS • SAFETY BACKUPS • RETRIEVING THE RAPPEL ROPE(S) • EXPERIENCING THE FREEDOM OF THE HILLS

Chapter 11
RAPPELING

Rappeling, the technique of descending a rope by using friction to safely control the rate of descent, is indispensable to technical climbing in the mountains. Unfortunately, rappeling is also one of the more dangerous techniques employed by climbers, because it is often so easy and routine that the inherent risks may be forgotten or ignored. Proper rappeling technique, learned thoroughly and employed carefully, allows for a safe descent of almost any climbing pitch. In fact, rappeling is often the only way to get down some rock or ice faces.

When rappeling a steep cliff, you depend entirely on the strength of the anchors securing the rope, the rope itself, and proper technique. If any element of the rappel system fails, the result will likely be catastrophic. Unlike the belay system, which is called upon only if a fall occurs, the rappel system is necessarily called upon to absorb the forces exerted by the rappel each and every time it is used. Consequently, there is never room for error in the setup or use of the rappel system.

Coming down from a climb, you may have a choice between rappeling and down-climbing. Sometimes rappeling is the fastest and safest way to descend, but many times it is not. One of the hidden shortcomings of rappeling is that it can waste considerable time in the hands of the inexperienced. Think through the options available, considering the terrain, the weather, the time available, and the strength and experience of the party. If you elect to rappel, do it safely and efficiently.

THE RAPPEL SYSTEM

A rappel system has four basic elements: an anchor, a rope, a rappel method for applying friction to the rope, and the person rappeling (fig. 11-1). Each element is

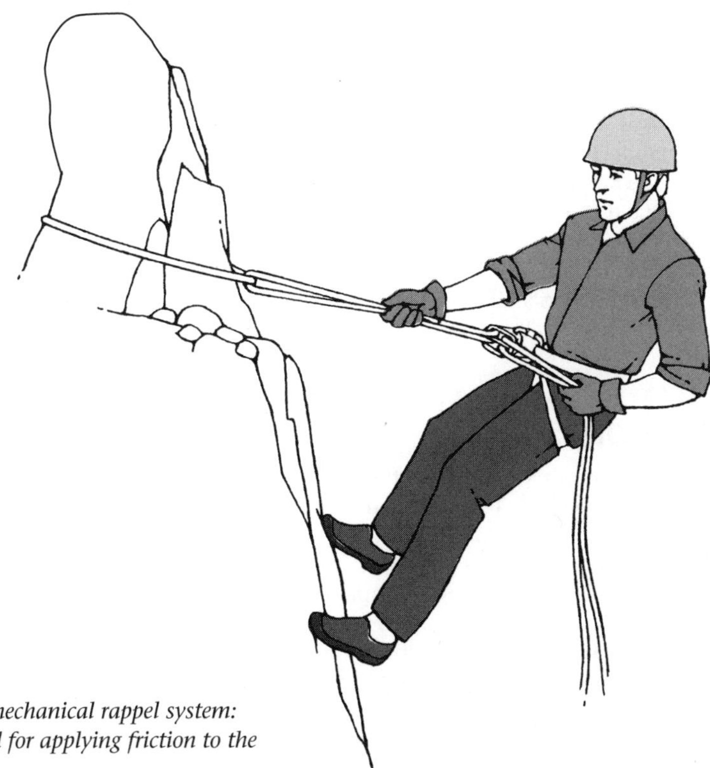

Fig. 11-1. Components of mechanical rappel system: anchor, rope, rappel method for applying friction to the rope, and rappeler.

equally important. Always remember all four of the rappel elements—even when you are cold, tired, hungry, and racing to beat the darkness—and check and double-check that every element is in place, functioning properly, and connected together to make an integrated system. Each of these elements is briefly described below, followed by expanded sections in the rest of this chapter. The integrated rappeling system must be understood thoroughly and practiced properly at every rappel to ensure a safe descent.

Rappel anchor. The first element of the rappel system is the anchor—the point on the mountain to which the rest of the system is attached. The anchor must be carefully selected for strength and reliability. Once the rappel has begun, a safe descent depends entirely on the anchor, and returning to the anchor to make adjustments can be problematic, if not impossible.

Rope. The second element of the rappel system is the rope. The midpoint of the rope is looped through the anchor, with the two ends hanging down the descent route. You descend this doubled rope and retrieve it from below by pulling on one end.

Short rappels can be handled with just one rope. Longer rappels need the extra length of two ropes tied together, with an offset overhand bend, figure eight bend, or double fisherman's bend. The knot joining the ropes should be placed near the anchor, with the two equal-length ends hanging down the route. Ropes of different diameters can be joined in a two rope-rappel—for example, an 11-millimeter rope paired with a 9-millimeter rope.

On rare occasions, you might use a single-strand rappel, in which the rope is simply tied at one end to the anchor.

Rappel method. The third element of the system is the method you use to apply friction to the rope to control your rate of descent while at the same time remaining firmly attached to the rope. There are two methods for applying this friction.

In mechanical rappel systems, the doubled rope passes through a friction device attached to your seat harness.

In nonmechanical systems, you wrap the rope around your body to provide the necessary friction.

In either case, the braking hand grasps the rope to

control the amount of friction and the rate of descent. Be vigilant regarding unaccustomed circumstances—such as a new, smaller-diameter, stiffer, or icy rope, heavier pack, etc.—because friction can vary greatly.

Rappeler. The final and most variable element in the rappel system is the rappeler. You must use proper technique both to attach into the rappel system and to descend safely. Individual circumstances such as your attitude, your level of fatigue and anxiety, poor weather, impending darkness, rockfall, icefall, and your level of skill and training potentially affect the safety of the rappel.

RAPPEL ANCHORS

A rappel anchor attaches the rappel system to the rock, snow, or ice that will be descended. The rappel anchor must be solid enough to support your full weight as well as absorb any additional forces that may occur, such as the dynamic force of a sudden stop during the rappel. Set up the anchor as near to the edge of the rappel route as possible while ensuring a solid and safe anchor. This affords the longest possible rappel. It also makes it easier to pull the rope down from below after the rappel and often reduces the danger of rockfall during retrieval of the rope.

When looking for an anchor, think about possible effects on the rope. Consider any sharp edges that might damage or sever the rope as it is loaded. Locate the anchor to minimize chances of the rope being pulled into a constricting slot or otherwise hanging up when it is retrieved from below. Check the position of the rope over the edge of the rappel route as the first rappeler finishes rappeling. If the rope moves near or into a slot on the surface that could cause it to jam upon retrieval, consider relocating the anchor. In winter conditions, be cautious of the rope cutting into snow or ice and freezing in place.

Either natural anchors or artificial (manufactured) anchors serve as suitable rappel anchors (see "Selecting an Anchor" in Chapter 10, Belaying). This chapter principally discusses rappel anchors for use on rock. See Chapter 13, Rock Protection, for details on placing removable protection in rock, using natural features, and clipping bolted anchors. For information on anchors for use in snow and ice, see the sections on anchors in Chapter 16, Snow Travel and Climbing; Chapter 18, Alpine Ice Climbing; and Chapter 19, Waterfall Ice and Mixed Climbing.

On popular climbs, established rappel anchors have slings and rappel rings left behind from prior rappels; these remnants need to be closely scrutinized for wear and damage. If the slings are not equipped with a rappel ring or carabiner, they may no longer be safe because rappel ropes have been pulled through them on previous rappels, which generates friction that may have weakened the sling's nylon webbing. Nylon slings also suffer damage from ultraviolet light, and older slings will feel noticeably dry and less supple from ultraviolet damage. However, nylon may be seriously weakened by ultraviolet exposure without visible effects. Therefore, always carefully evaluate slings at an established rappel anchor. Sometimes so many slings compose an anchor that total failure of every sling is unlikely. Still, a prudent rappeler might cut out a few of the oldest slings and add a new one before attaching the rope. If using more than one sling, make them of equal length to help distribute the load. (Pack out the old slings.)

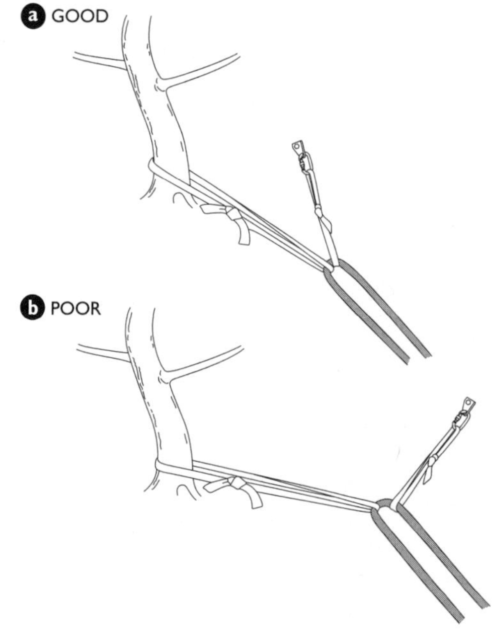

Fig. 11-2. The most common method of attaching the rappel rope to multiple anchors, with a separate sling attached to each of two anchors and meeting at the rappel rope: a, a narrow angle between slings is best; b, when the angle between slings is too wide, the load on each anchor point increases.

When using two anchor points to support the rappel, the most common method is to run a separate sling from each point, with the slings meeting at the rappel rope. Try to adjust the slings so the force is the same on each anchor point. For the strongest setup, keep the angle between the two slings narrow (fig. 11-2). See Chapter 10, Belaying, for methods of equalizing anchor points.

Keep this in mind about anchors: When you are climbing and belaying, you build strong and redundant anchors just in case you fall. You never really stress the anchor (or the belay) unless someone falls. But when you rappel, your life hangs on the weight-loaded anchor from start to finish. It is essential to build rappel anchors that are **SRENE**: **S**olid, **R**edundant, **E**qualized, and with **N**o **E**xtension (see the "SRENE Anchor Systems" sidebar in Chapter 10, Belaying).

NATURAL ANCHORS

Often the best natural anchor is a living, good-sized, well-rooted tree (see "Natural Anchors" in Chapter 10, Belaying). The rope usually goes through a runner attached to the anchor (fig. 11-3a). The rope could be looped directly around a tree without the use of a sling (fig. 11-3b), but this causes rope abrasion damage, soils the rope with tree resins, makes it harder to retrieve the rope, and, if done enough times, can kill the tree. Attaching a runner to an unquestionably stout tree branch rather than low on the trunk helps make it easier to retrieve the rope and reduces the risk of rockfall. However, connecting to a branch rather than the trunk puts more leverage on the tree.

If there is any question about a natural anchor, test whether it can support the weight of the heaviest rappeler and still provide a large safety margin in case a rappeler puts extra force on the anchor by stopping quickly. Test the anchor before rappel gear is attached, never after the rope or the rappeler is hooked in. Back up any suspect anchor for the initial rappelers. The final rappeler may remove the backup or leave it in place.

If you are using a runner looped around a rock horn for an anchor (fig. 11-4a), take care to determine the angle of force on the horn. Guard against the dire possibility that the runner could ride up and off the horn during a rappel (fig. 11-4b).

You might use a single anchor point if it is an unquestionably solid, dependable natural anchor. But if you have any doubts, add another equalizing feature or two to the anchor (see "Equalizing Multiple Anchors" in Chapter 10, Belaying).

11

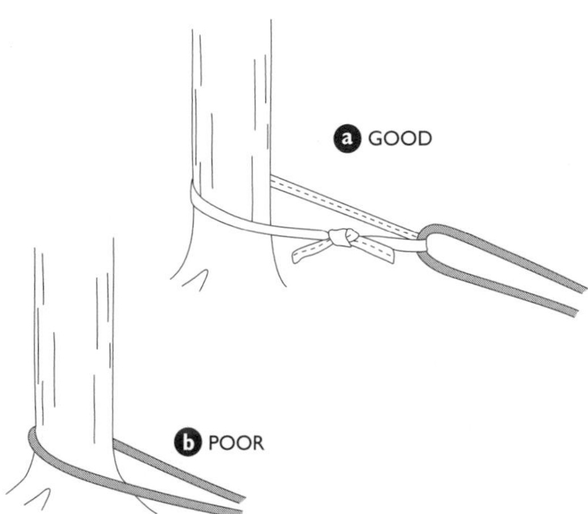

Fig. 11-3. A tree as a natural rappel anchor: a, rappel rope through a sling tied around a tree (good); b, rappel rope looped directly around tree (poor).

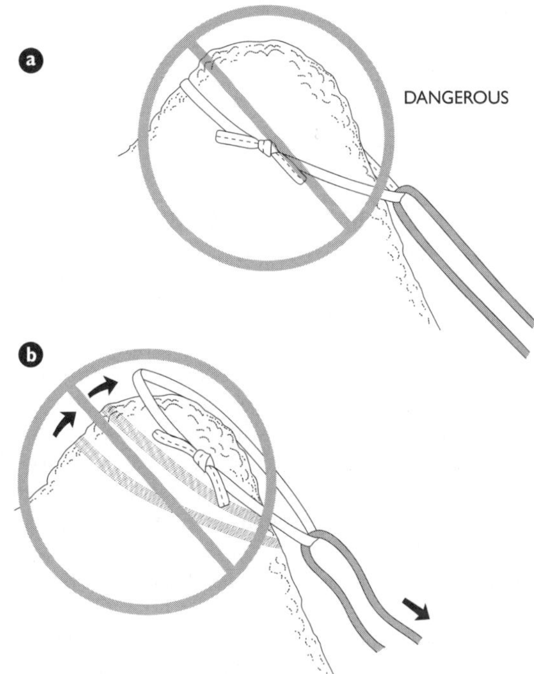

Fig. 11-4. A rock horn as a natural rappel anchor: a, a dangerous runner placement; b, runner can ride up and off rock horn.

ARTIFICIAL ANCHORS

As a rule, when using artificial (manufactured) fixed or removable protection for an anchor, use two or more anchor points and equalize the load between them.

In unknown alpine terrain, some climbers carry pitons and a hammer to set protection. The most common artificial rappel anchors are bolts or pitons that have been left in place by previous climbers. These must be evaluated for safety just as they would if they were being used for belaying or for protection while climbing.

Removable protection such as chocks—nuts, hexes, and so forth—are usually used only if no good alternative is available, but it is better to use and leave behind some equipment than to rely upon a shaky rock horn. Be suspicious of chocks found already in place, perhaps left behind by climbers who were not able to work them loose. Also beware of old slings attached to such chocks, which may no longer be safe. Sometimes an abandoned chock may be used like a natural chockstone—by looping a runner directly around it and making no use whatsoever of the sling attached to the old chock.

THE ROPE

Before setting up the rappel, run through the entire length of the rope to check that no cuts, fraying, or other damage occurred during the climb or a previous rappel.

ATTACHING THE ROPE TO THE ANCHOR

To prepare the rope for rappeling, attach it to the anchor, whether created from a natural feature or manufactured equipment. In the simplest case, suspend the midpoint of the rope from one or more runners or slings that have been attached to the anchor (as shown in Figures 11-1, 11-2a, and 11-3a). Some rappelers prefer to use two slings instead of one, for added security.

One rope. If you are using just one rope, put one end of the rope through the slings and pull it through until the rope's midpoint is reached. Take care not to create friction between the rope and slings, because heat generated by friction may dangerously weaken the slings. As an alternative, tie the slings around the midpoint of the rope before attaching them to the anchor. If you are carrying sewn runners for climbing, bring along some 9⁄16-inch webbing to use in tying rappel slings.

Rappel rings. To eliminate the risk of damage from friction both when setting the rappel and when retrieving the rope, attach the rope to the anchor sling(s) with a rappel ring. Rappel or descending rings are simply continuous aluminum or titanium rings, about 1½ inches (3 centimeters) in diameter, made for rappeling. Thread the rappel sling(s) through the ring, and then thread the rope through the ring (fig. 11-5a), to prevent direct contact between the rope and the anchor sling(s) and also the dangerous friction of a pulled rope on nylon slings. Older, welded rappel rings should not be trusted.

The descending ring does add another possible point of failure. Some climbers insist on two rings, even if both are nonwelded. An alternative is a single ring backed up by a non-weight-bearing sling from the anchor through the rope, ready to hold the rope in case the ring fails (fig. 11-5b). Carabiners can be used in place of rappel rings but, of course, they must then be left behind.

Two ropes. For longer rappels, join two ropes together: Put one end of a rope through the anchor and tie it to the other rope with an offset overhand bend (leaving tails of 12 to 16 inches / 40 to 60 centimeters), with a figure eight bend, or with a double fisherman's bend. The offset overhand bend is less likely to catch

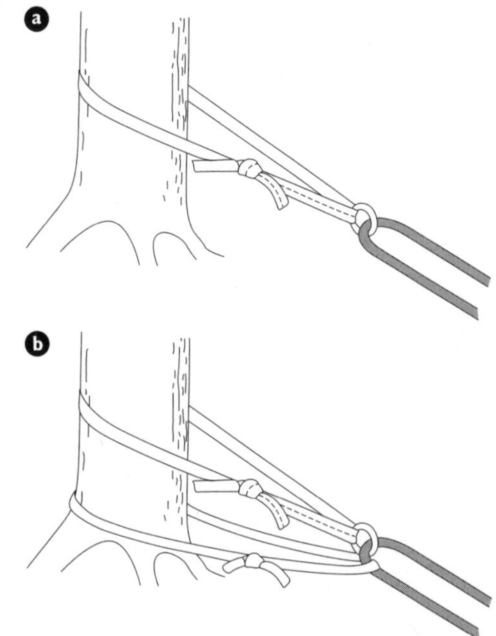

Fig. 11-5. Rappel rope attached to anchor through descending ring: a, single ring; b, single ring with backup sling.

on edges (fig. 11-6) and hang up during rope retrieval. You can back up the first offset overhand bend with a second one. Do not expand an offset overhand bend into an offset figure eight bend: The latter has been known to fail during rappels. A figure eight bend, on the other hand, works fine with a rappel and is relatively easy to untie after being loaded. The double fisherman's bend is a very secure way to join two ropes but can be very difficult to untie after being loaded. The "Knots, Hitches, and Bends" section in Chapter 9, Basic Safety System, describes all of these knots.

Slings. If the anchor is a rock feature, bolts, or pitons, always attach slings to the anchor, then run the rappel rope through the slings. Never put the rope directly around the rock or through the eye of the bolt hanger or piton, because friction may make it impossible to pull the rope back down from below or may damage the rope. When attaching the rope to the anchor, note which end of the rope will be pulled for retrieval. For help with single-rope rappels, some ropes are manufactured with a contrasting color or pattern that distinctly changes at the midpoint as a visual aid to help with pulling the correct strand down and in centering the rope at the anchor. Note that trimming either or both ends of the rope may change its length such that the color or pattern change no longer marks the true midpoint.

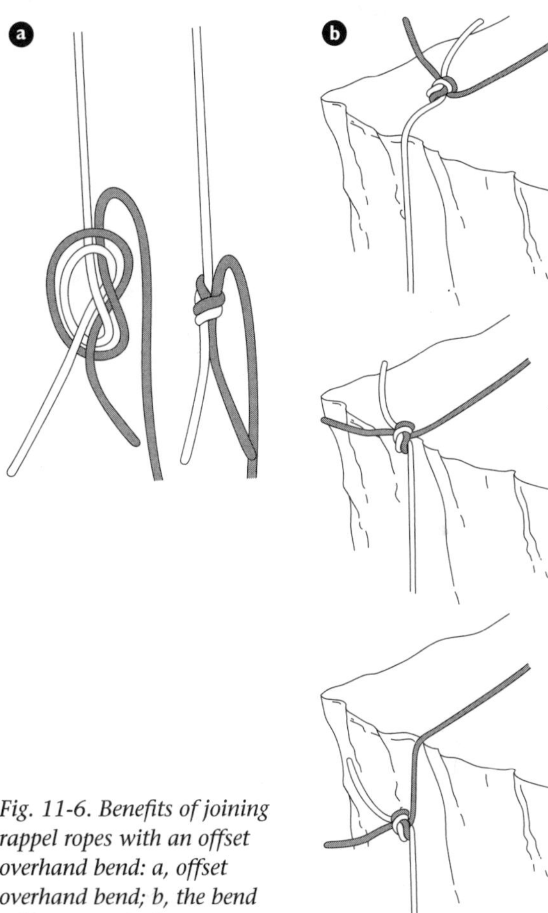

Fig. 11-6. Benefits of joining rappel ropes with an offset overhand bend: a, offset overhand bend; b, the bend will rotate, which prevents the knot from catching on an edge.

When using two ropes, try to use ropes of two different colors if possible. If the rope lies with one strand against the rock and the other strand on top of the first, friction will impede retrieval, and it may be possible to pull only the strand closest to the rock. When using two ropes, place the knot joining them below the anchor, toward the strand to be pulled (fig. 11-7a)—otherwise, the rope may pinch between the rock and the end of the rope being pulled, and retrieval may not be possible (fig. 11-7b).

Keep the point of connection between the rappel anchor sling and the rope away from the edge of the rock, snow, or ice of the rappel route to help prevent binding and abrasion (fig. 11-8).

THROWING DOWN THE ROPE

After looping the rappel rope at its midpoint through an anchor, prepare the rope for tossing it down the rappel route. There are several methods for tossing, or lowering, the rope down the rappel route. With any method, the goal is to reduce rope snags and tangling as well as the risk of losing the rope.

The following sequence uses four butterfly coils (see "Coiling the Rope" in Chapter 9, Basic Safety System). Some climbers make only two, rather than four, coils for the sake of speed and efficiency.

1. Tie backup knots at the ends of the rope if desired (see "Safety Backups" later in this chapter).
2. Beginning from the rappel sling, coil each half of the rope separately into two butterfly coils, creating a total of four butterfly coils, two on each side of the anchor.
3. Tie an overhand knot on a bight of rope near the midpoint and clip it to the anchor with a carabiner to prevent the disaster of losing the rope when the coils are tossed.

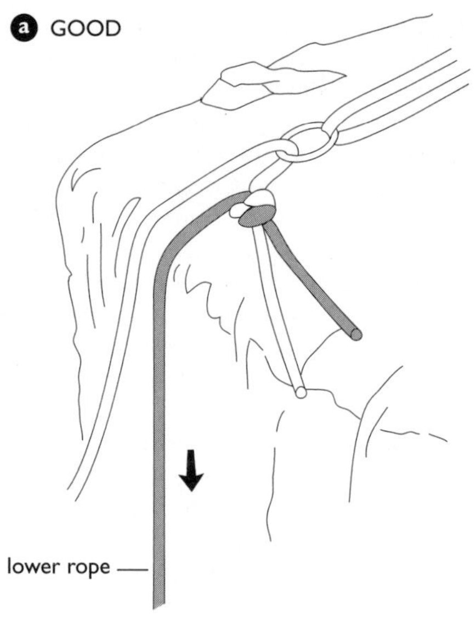

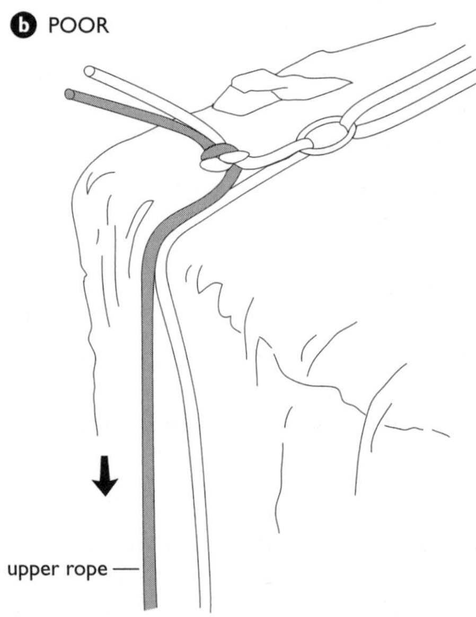

Fig. 11-7. Knot placement with two-rope rappel: a, on lower rope, with the knot in the lower rope, the rope can be retrieved without getting stuck; b, with the knot on the upper rope, the lower rope can be pinched tight (between the rock and the upper rope) when you try to retrieve the rope.

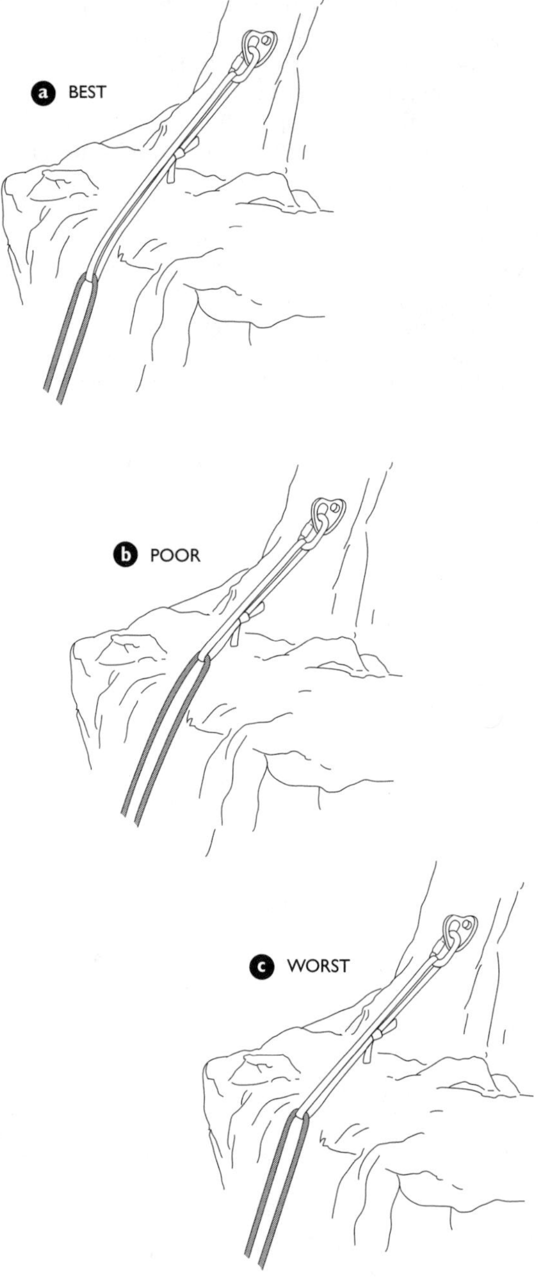

Fig. 11-8. The point of connection between the rappel sling and the rappel rope: a, rope free to move and clear of rock (best); b, rope will not bind but will still abrade (poor); c, rope will bind and abrade against rock (worst).

4. Be sure to attach yourself to an anchor before you stand at the edge of the route to toss the rope. Use a personal anchor to secure yourself, preferably with a locking carabiner (see "Personal Anchors" in Chapter 9, Basic Safety System).
5. Before making the toss, alert others below by shouting "Rope!" Some rappelers shout the word two times to give anyone below a little time to respond or to watch out for the rope. Others shout just once but wait a moment for any response.
6. Evaluate the wind and terrain before throwing the coils out. Be sure to compensate for any significant wind. Avoid throwing the coils onto snags, pinch points, or sharp edges below.
7. Start on one side of the anchor by tossing the coil nearest the anchor out and down the route, then the rope-end coil. Repeat for the other half of the rope (fig. 11-9).
8. After all the coils have been tossed, remove the carabiner and bight, leaving the rope in the anchor sling.

If the rope tangles or hangs up on the rappel route below, it is usually best to pull it back up, recoil it, and toss it again. Sometimes, however, it is possible to just free the rope during the rappel.

In some circumstances—for instance, in a high wind—it is hard to get a perfect toss. One of the more experienced rappelers in the party can rappel down to just above the first problem, stop, recoil the strands below that point, toss them again, and continue the rappel. ("Rappel Technique" later in this chapter explains how to stop in midrappel.)

Instead of throwing the rope, some rappelers feed it out as they rappel. This works particularly well in adverse conditions. One method is to simply feed the rope out of a pack or rope bag during the descent. Another option is to fashion the rope coil into a "saddlebag": Girth-hitch a single-length runner to the harness wherever it is convenient. Cradle the butterfly

Fig. 11-9. Throwing down the rope: Climber is tied in to a personal anchor for safety while working near the edge; rope is clipped to rappel anchor with a bight near the middle to prevent losing it. Toss the coil nearest the anchor first, then the rope-end coil.

coils in the runner next to the harness, and clip the other end of the runner to the harness with a carabiner. The butterfly coil should be oriented so that it feeds freely as the climber rappels. When either feeding rope out of a rope bag or using this saddlebag method, the rappeler may need to actively tend the rope to get it to feed out properly during the rappel.

KEEPING ROPE LENGTHS EQUAL

Both strands of the rappel rope must either touch the next stance or hang equally. If not, one end may pull through the rappel device before you reach a stance at the end of the rappel. Should this occur, you would fall out of the system. Watch for the potential problems discussed below. Backup knots at the ends of the rope are recommended (see "Safety Backups" later in this chapter).

When you are using two ropes of unequal diameters, take extra care to monitor the length of each strand during the rappel. The differing diameters and elastic characteristics of the ropes may cause one rope to advance through the rappel device more quickly than the other, thereby altering the relative lengths of the rope strands. It is also possible for the knot joining ropes of unequal diameter to "creep" away from the anchor, again resulting in differing lengths for the separate strands of rope. Place the knot on the side of the anchor with the rope that is most likely to slide; usually this is the smaller-diameter rope.

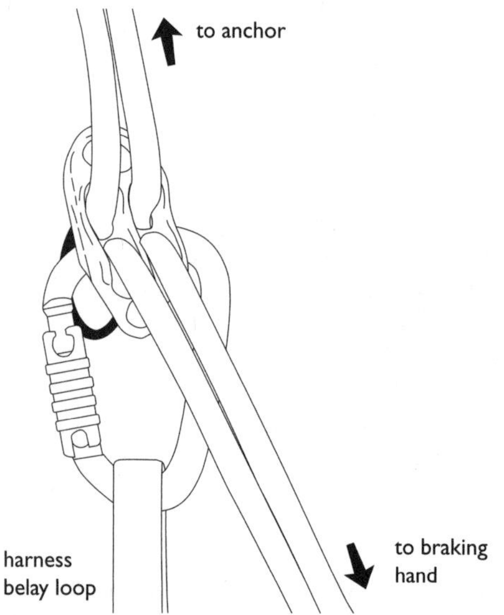

Fig. 11-10. Setting up an aperture-style device for rappeling.

Also, be aware that ropes that are nominally of equal length, even from the same manufacturer, are often actually of different lengths.

RAPPEL METHOD

Once the rappel anchor and the rope are set up, you need a method of attaching into the rope and applying friction to it to control your rappel. Typically, a mechanical device provides a secure means of attachment, but methods of wrapping into the rope may also be used.

MECHANICAL RAPPEL DEVICES

Many rappelers use a system consisting of their climbing harness and a belay-rappel device as their principal rappeling method. All of the devices operate in essentially the same manner: by applying varying degrees of friction to the rope. (With some belay devices, the rope does not feed through the device smoothly on rappel. Some devices may also easily heat up. Before using any new device, closely read and follow the manufacturer's instructions.)

The two free strands of rope at the anchor are inserted into your rappel device, which is then clipped with a locking carabiner to your harness, in much the same way as for belaying. During the rappel, the bends in the rope through the device and around the locking carabiner apply friction, magnifying the force exerted by your braking hand (fig. 11-10). Your braking hand, which holds both strands of rope below the device (see Figure 11-1), provides a controlled descent through a combination of variations in grip and hand position. The rappel device and the braking hand together control the speed of descent and allow you to completely halt the descent at any time.

At the top of the rappel, the weight of the rope hanging below the device adds friction, making it easier to control the rate of descent near the top of a rappel than at the bottom. This is especially so on very steep or overhanging rappels on which most of the rope hangs free. But no matter how little grip strength may be required to control the descent, the braking hand must never leave the rope. The other hand—the guiding, or uphill, hand—may slide freely along the rope to help maintain balance. With some setups, wrapping the rope partly around your back further increases friction.

Rappeling with a mechanical system requires a harness (see Chapter 9, Basic Safety System). Never rappel with just a waist loop, which is a simple loop of

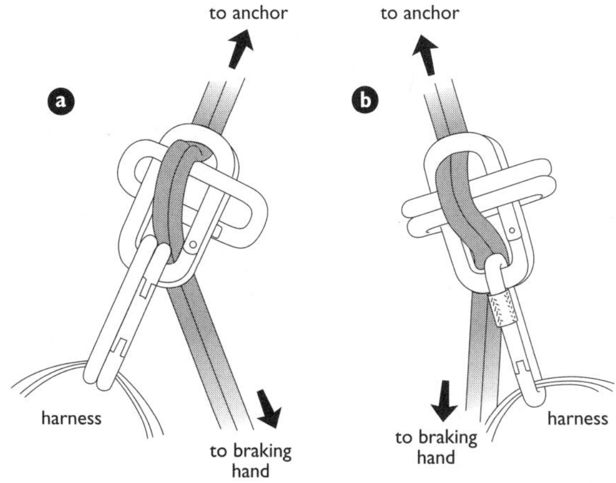

Fig. 11-11. Carabiner brake system: a, with two opposite and opposed carabiners at the harness and one carabiner clipped across the outer (opposite and opposed) carabiner pair; b, with one locking carabiner at the harness and two carabiners clipped across the outer (opposite and opposed) carabiner pair in order to provide greater friction.

webbing tied around your waist—it can constrict your diaphragm enough to cause you to lose consciousness. In an emergency, an improvised diaper sling may be used for rappeling, even though it would not ordinarily be used for climbing (see "Diaper Sling" in Chapter 9, Basic Safety System).

Carabiner Brake Method

The carabiner brake method for rappeling is somewhat complex to set up but has the virtue of not requiring any special equipment—just carabiners. All climbers should know how to use the carabiner brake method, even if they normally use a specialized rappel device. It is a great backup if you forget or lose your rappel device. The carabiner brake system works best with oval carabiners but can also be managed with D-shaped carabiners (see Chapter 9, Basic Safety System).

To create the carabiner brake setup, start by attaching one locking or two regular carabiners to your seat harness. Because a harness carabiner could be subjected to a twisting or side load, two carabiners or a locking carabiner should be used. If you are using two regular carabiners, position the gates to keep them from being forced open and accidentally unclipping. The correct position (called opposite and opposed) is with the gates on opposing sides, forming an X when they are opened at the same time (see Figure 9-37a in Chapter 9, Basic Safety System).

Next, clip another pair of carabiners—here, a pair is required and a single locking carabiner will not suffice—to the harness carabiner(s), also with the gates opposite and opposed. Then, if possible, face the anchor. Lift a bight of the rappel ropes through the outer carabiner pair, from the bottom. Take yet another carabiner and clip it across the outer carabiner pair, beneath the bight of rope, so its gate is facing away from the rope loop. The rope then runs across an outer edge (not the gate!) of this final carabiner, known as the braking carabiner (fig. 11-11a).

One braking carabiner provides enough friction for most rappels on ropes that are 10 to 11 millimeters in diameter. A second braking carabiner (fig. 11-11b) or even a third might be used for thinner ropes, heavy climbers, heavy packs, or steep or overhanging rappels. Two carabiner brakes in a series generate additional friction, if needed. The ropes must always run over the solid side of the braking carabiners, never across the gate.

Watch for a couple of things in setting up the carabiner brake system. First, it may not be convenient to face the anchor as you insert the bight of rappel rope into the carabiner brake; in this case, a possible mistake is to put the rope into the system backward, as if you were preparing to rappel "uphill" toward the anchor.

Second, the weight of the rope hanging down the cliff may make it very difficult to pull the bight of rope up through the outer pair of carabiners and hold it while clipping in the braking carabiner. It helps to get that weight off the system. Pulling up some slack rope and throwing a couple of wraps around your leg to take the weight solves this problem. Alternatively, pull the loop of rope through the carabiners, but make it extra large and lay it over your shoulder while you are clipping in the braking carabiner; then drop the downhill strands back through the system so the brake remains close to the anchor.

Other Mechanical Systems

Figure eight. A popular special device for rappeling has been the figure eight device (fig. 11-12a). It is simpler to set up and requires less force to control than the carabiner brake method.

Keep in mind its disadvantages. It means carrying an extra piece of equipment, and most figure eights are relatively heavy. If it is lost or forgotten, another rappel method must be used. Most figure eights require

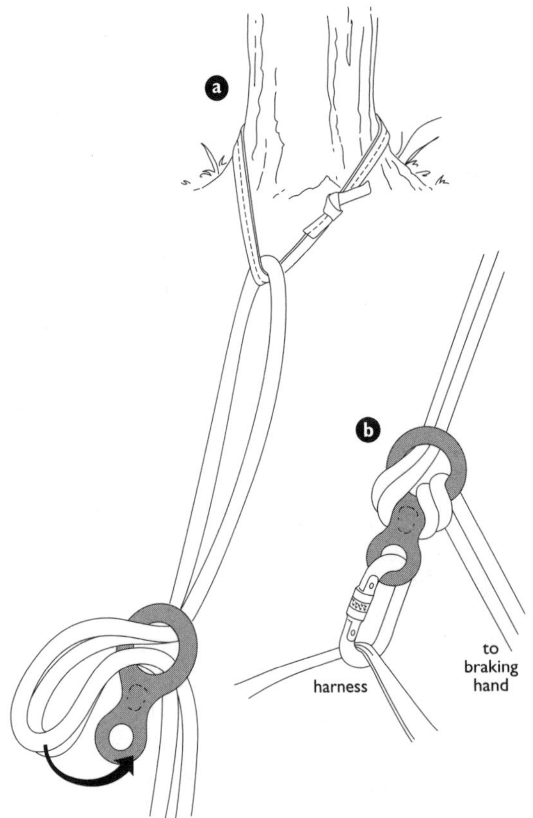

Fig. 11-12. Attaching a figure eight device for use in rappeling: a, pull a bight of the doubled rope through larger hole in figure eight device, then pull lower part of device through the bight and pull the rope snug; b, attach locking carabiner to figure eight rappel device's smaller hole and then to harness.

a locking carabiner to be attached to the harness (fig. 11-12b) and do not provide the option of using doubled carabiners. And the figure eight puts some twists in the rope. The figure eight was designed for rappeling, though some climbers use the device in one of several possible configurations for belaying (see Chapter 10, Belaying).

Munter hitch. The same hitch that is used for belaying can also be used for rappeling (see Chapter 10, Belaying). It is probably worthwhile to learn as insurance because it requires only a locking carabiner. Though it is easy to set up and very safe, it puts significantly more twists in the rope than do other methods.

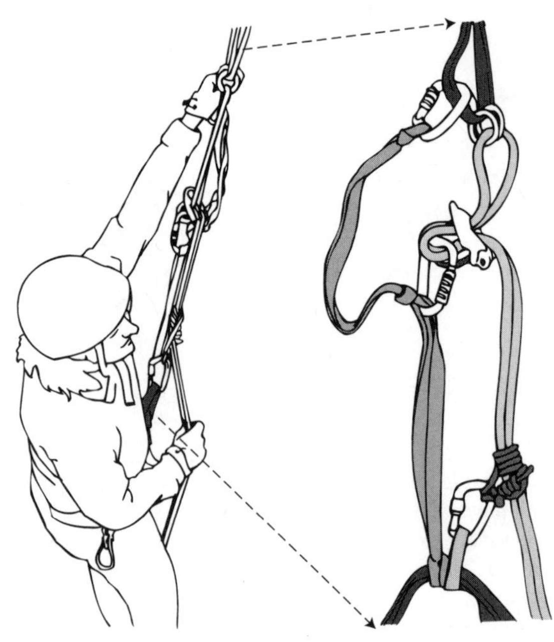

Fig. 11-13. Rappel extension (double-length runner clipped in the middle to the rappel device) with integrated personal anchor (carabiner in climber's left hand, the outer half of the rappel extension) and autoblock (wrapped around rappel rope and both ends clipped to harness carabiner).

RAPPEL EXTENSION

When rappeling, many climbers extend the rappel device connection to their harness with a personal anchor so that the rappel device rides higher on the rappel rope and in front of the chest (fig. 11-13). This gives several advantages: The rappeler can comfortably use either hand (or both hands) to brake the rappel and can add—and manage—a superior autoblock (see "Safety Backups" later in this chapter); both ends of the autoblock can be clipped in to the harness carabiner, which is the best place to support weight; the autoblock cannot run against the rappel device (which can cause the autoblock to fail); and the personal anchor is readily available for clipping to anchors. The disadvantage is that this technique introduces one more piece into the rappel system—the runner used for the extension.

To create the extension, use a double-length runner (for example, made of 9⁄16-inch webbing). Tie an overhand knot in the middle of the runner to create two equal loops. Girth-hitch the loop without the knot (or bar tacks) to the harness, around both the waist belt and the leg loop attachment. A locking carabiner at the far end of the two-loop runner serves as the personal anchor (a slipknot at the end keeps the carabiner in place); a locking carabiner in the middle of the runner serves as the attachment for the rappel device. To add an autoblock, attach both ends directly to the harness carabiner instead of to the leg loop of the harness, using a slipknot to keep the autoblock cord immobilized in the carabiner (see "Safety Backups" later in this chapter). When the personal-anchor component is not in use, simply clip its locking carabiner to your harness and out of the way.

NONMECHANICAL METHODS

Two traditional rappel methods use no hardware whatsoever to create friction on the rope. Instead, the rope is simply wrapped around parts of your body.

Dulfersitz. A simple, all-purpose method, the *dulfersitz* should be mastered by every rappeler in the event that a harness or carabiners are not available. Face the anchor and step into the *dulfersitz* by straddling the rope. Bring it from behind you and around one hip, up across your chest, over the opposite shoulder, and then down your back to be held by the braking hand (the downhill hand) on the same side as your wrapped hip (fig. 11-14). Your other hand is the guiding hand to hold the rope above and to assist you in staying upright.

Fig. 11-14. The dulfersitz*: a nonmechanical rappel method.*

The *dulfersitz* has a number of drawbacks compared with mechanical rappel systems. It can unwrap from your leg, especially on high-angle rappels, though it helps to keep your wrapped leg slightly lower than your other leg. Stay under careful control and try to pad your body underneath the path of the rope, because rope friction around your hip and across your shoulder can be painful, especially on steep rappels. Turning up your collar protects your neck. If you are wearing a pack, the *dulfersitz* is even more awkward. The *dulfersitz* is used in modern climbing only when there is no reasonable alternative or for short and easy, low-angle rappels to save the trouble of putting a seat harness back on.

Arm rappel. Though the arm rappel is not used much, it is occasionally helpful for quick descent of a low-angle slope. Lay the rappel rope behind your back, under your armpits, and wrap it once around each arm (fig. 11-15). Be sure the rope does not run over any exposed flesh; it will get surprisingly hot. Control the rate of descent

Fig. 11-15. The arm rappel: another nonmechanical rappel method.

with your hand grip. For an arm rappel with a pack, be sure the rope goes around your pack rather than on top of or underneath it.

RAPPEL TECHNIQUE

When a party reaches a rappel point, typically the first rappeler is one of the more-experienced members of the group. On the rappel, this first rappeler will usually fix any tangles or problems with the rope and clear the anchor area and route of debris that might be dislodged onto subsequent rappelers or others below.

Use the four elements of the rappel system—anchor, rope, rappel method, and rappeler—as a mental checklist to prepare for each rappel.

1. **Anchor.** Start by ensuring that the anchor is solid and dependable.
2. **Rope.** Ensure that the rope was inspected during the rappel setup for cuts, fraying, or other damage, which might have occurred during climbing or on prior rappels. Then check that the rope is properly threaded through the anchor, that it is not tangled or knotted, and that it will not load dangerously over a sharp edge or suffer abrasion damage against the rock, snow, or ice. If you are using two ropes, check the knot joining them.
3. **Rappel method.** Check your own attachment to the rope, through the rappeling device or other setup. Partners should also independently check each other's setups at each rappel. Be sure the harness is fastened properly. Pay special attention to the brake system: Are both ropes threaded through the device and around the locking carabiner correctly? Is the locking carabiner attached to the harness properly and locked? Which hand will be the braking hand? Does the braking hand have a secure grasp on the rope? If you are using a carabiner brake system, are the gates of carabiner pairs correctly opposite and opposed? Are the ropes threaded in the correct direction, so as not to rappel "uphill" and jam the system? Are any self-belay or safety backup methods properly set up and functioning?
4. **Rappeler.** Think through the entire rappel. Make a mind's-eye check of the setup, the descent, and the finish at the next stance. Check the backup knots; check that the rope will pull; ensure that both strands are properly attached through the rappel device; check which rope to pull. It is advisable to wear gloves. Look for and secure things that can get caught in the system, such as long hair, loose clothing, pack straps, or helmet chin straps. Be mentally prepared for a safe rappel, and anticipate any challenges that might occur during the rappel.

When you are ready to go, face the anchor with your back to the descent route, firmly gripping the free-hanging strands of the rappel rope with the braking hand. With the nonbraking hand, detach your personal anchor sling from the rappel anchor.

GETTING STARTED

Just before descending, shout "On rappel!" to warn others that a rappel has begun.

Now comes the most nerve-wracking part of many rappels. To gain stability, your legs must be nearly perpendicular to the slope. Therefore, at the very brink of a precipice, you must lean backward, out over the edge (fig. 11-16). If the terrain allows it, you may ease the transition by down-climbing several feet before leaning out and weighting the rope to start the rappel (fig. 11-17). Take up any slack between you and the anchor before leaning out or weighting the rope.

Fig. 11-16. Starting rappel from a high anchor.

Fig. 11-17. Down-climbing to get below a low anchor before starting rappel.

You may be able to sit or crouch on the edge of the rappel ledge (fig. 11-18a) and wiggle gently off (fig. 11-18b), simultaneously turning inward to face the slope (fig. 11-18c). This technique is particularly useful when you are starting the rappel above an overhang or when the anchor is located lower than your harness when you are standing on the rappel edge.

MAKING THE RAPPEL

Three things that must be considered during the rappel are position, speed, and movement.

Position

While you are descending, your body position should be stable: feet shoulder-width apart, knees flexed, body at a comfortable angle to the slope and facing a little toward the braking hand for a view of the route. Common beginners' mistakes include keeping your feet too close together and failing to lean back far enough. Some go to the other extreme and lean too far back, increasing their chance of flipping over. If anything should happen, such as tipping over or losing your

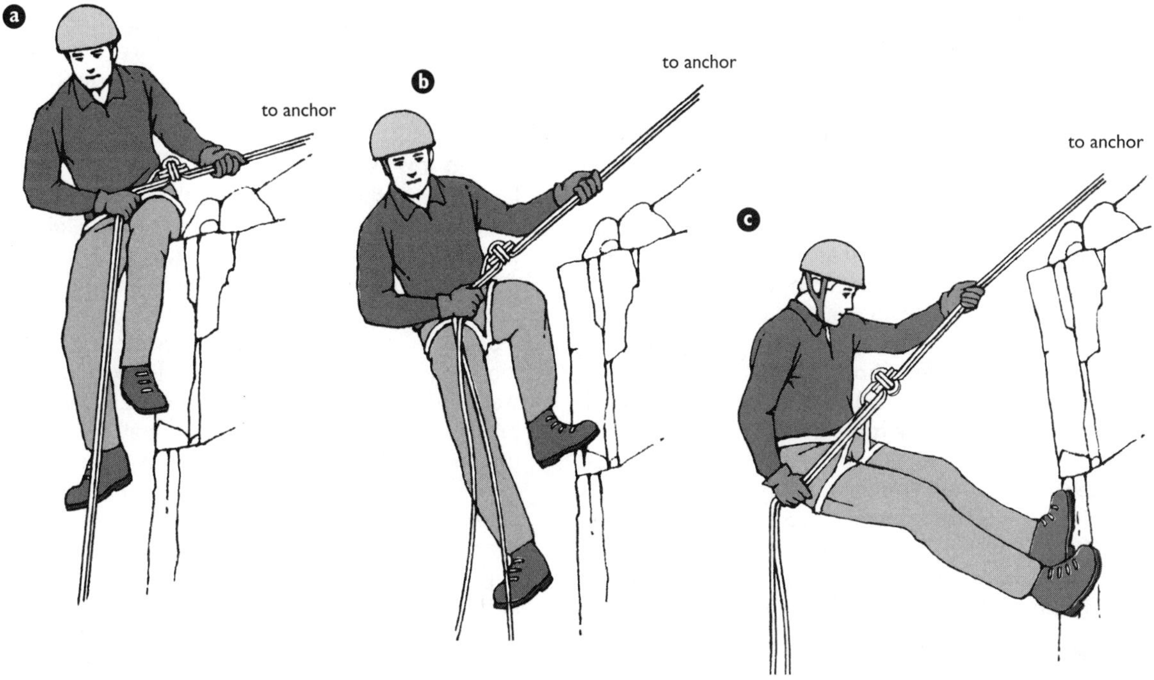

Fig. 11-18. Starting a rappel from a steep ledge and a low anchor: a, sitting down on the ledge; b, squirming off to get started; c, turning inward to face the slope.

POTENTIAL PROBLEMS WHEN RAPPELING

LOOSE ROCK. Use extreme caution when you are rappeling a face with loose or rotten rock. The danger is that rock may be knocked loose either by you, as you descend, or by the rope itself. The loose rock could injure you or damage the rope. Another danger is that the next rappeler could knock rocks down on you. Take care to position yourself in a safe area until the entire party has rappeled.

OVERHANGS. It is easy to swing into the face below the overhang, smashing your hands and feet. There is also the risk of jamming the brake system on the lip of the overhang. A couple of methods assist in making the difficult transition from above the lip of an overhang to below it.

One method is to bend deeply at your knees with your feet at the uppermost edge of the overhang, then release enough braking tension to slip down 3 or 4 feet (about 1 meter) at once and then lock off the rappel with sudden braking action, which halts further acceleration once past the lip of the overhang. The abrupt halt and resulting bounce stress the rappel system, but this helps reduce both the chance of a swing into the face below and of jamming the brake system on the lip.

Another method is to place your feet on the lip of the overhang and then lower your waist down below your feet. Then "walk" your feet, while they are still above your waist, down the underside of the overhang until, once you are below the lip, the rope above makes contact with the rock face above.

Below an overhang, you will dangle free on the rope. Assume a sitting position, use the guiding hand on the rope above to remain upright, and continue steadily downward. Often you will slowly spin as twists in the rope unwind.

PENDULUMS. Sometimes reaching the next rappel stance requires you to move at an angle to the fall line, walking down the face diagonally instead of moving straight down. If a slip occurs, you will swing on the rappel rope back toward the fall line in what could be a nasty pendulum fall. Also, after such a fall, it may be difficult to get reestablished on the proper rappel course without climbing back up the rope with prusik slings or mechanical devices. To avoid this potentially dangerous situation, try to rappel down the fall line as much as possible.

LOOSE ENDS. Clothing, long hair, pack straps, chin straps from a helmet, and just about anything with a loose end all have the potential to get pulled into the braking system. Keep a knife handy to cut foreign material out of the system, but be extremely careful with a sharp knife around rope, especially a rope under tension that is supporting you.

ROPE TANGLES. If the rope gets tangled or jammed during your descent, the problem must be corrected before you rappel past it. Stop at the last convenient ledge above the area, or stop with a leg wrap (see "Stopping in Midrappel"). Pull the rope up, correct the problem, then throw it down again. Sometimes there is a simple solution; for instance, when you are rappeling down blank slabs, tangles often may be shaken out as they are encountered.

JAMMED RAPPEL DEVICE. If the rappel brake system jams on something (such as a shirt) despite your precautions, it can most likely be freed by unweighting it. First, free your hands by using your backup autoblock, prusik, or leg wraps. Next, unweight the brake system by either standing on a ledge or tying a prusik hitch above your brake system and chaining slings together until they are long enough to stand in. In the worst case, you might even Texas-prusik some distance up the rappel ropes (see Chapter 17, Glacier Travel and Crevasse Rescue, for information on the Texas prusik). Then, if you are able to free the jammed material, cut it away from the brake system, taking care not to nick the rope. A prusik tie-off loop, three or four slings, and a knife should always be on hand.

footing, it is absolutely critical to remember to hold onto the rope with the braking hand. If the braking hand releases its grip, you will quickly accelerate out of control. Once an awkward situation has stabilized, work on getting reestablished against the rock, in the basic position shown in Figure 11-18c.

Some climbers prefer to brake with both hands. With two hands, use an alternating, hand-over-hand, shuffle-brake motion to feed the rope through the rappel device. Some climbers might feel safer with two hands on the brake, while others will feel more secure with a nonbraking hand high on the rope, to help keep them upright and to fend off any hazards (see the "Potential Problems When Rappeling" sidebar). Either way, what is imperative is that one hand remain on the rope and braking at all times.

Speed and Movement

Move slowly and steadily, with no bounces or leaps. Feed the rope slowly and steadily into the rappel system, avoiding stops and jerks. Higher rappel speeds put more heat and stress on the rappel system. Also, it is important to go slowly and steadily to avoid shock-loading the anchor. A sudden stop during a rapid descent subjects the anchor to a dynamic load and a great deal of additional force.

STOPPING IN MIDRAPPEL

If you need to stop partway down a rappel, you can secure the rope in a couple of ways, described below. Some rappel or belay devices have other ways to stop the rope in the device; consult the manufacturer's instructions or obtain reliable instruction on their use.

Leg Wrap

The first method is to wrap the rope two or three times around one leg (fig. 11-19). The friction of the wrap, increased by the weight of the rope hanging below the wrap, is usually enough to halt further descent. Keep the braking hand on the rope while passing the rope behind your back, and use the guiding hand to assist with wrapping the rope around your leg. Keep the braking hand in position until the wraps are completed and tested. For even more friction, tuck a bight of the loose end of the rope under all the leg wraps. If the wraps are not tight, you will slip a few feet as the wraps tighten. To continue the descent, be sure to reestablish the braking hand before releasing the leg wraps. On steep rappels,

Fig. 11-19. Leg wrap: stopping "hands free" midrappel with the rope wrapped around one leg.

simply remove your foot and leg from contact with the rock and shake the wraps off while holding the rope with the braking hand.

Autoblock or Prusik

A second way to stop in midrappel is to employ your safety backup—either an autoblock or a prusik (see "Safety Backups" later in this chapter).

Mule Knot

Another method is to use a mule knot to tie off the rappel, just like tying off a belay (see "Mule Knot" and Figures 9-21 and 9-22 in Chapter 9, Basic Safety System).

FINISHING THE RAPPEL

Near the end of the rappel, it becomes much easier to feed rope through the rappel device because the extra friction caused by the weight of the rope below you is now considerably less.

The amount of rope stretch, particularly on a two-rope rappel, may be surprising. Be aware of this stretch factor as the rope is cleared from the rappel device after

11

you complete the rappel. If you let go of the rappel rope, it could contract to its normal length and suddenly be up out of reach. Better to end the rappel *near* the end of the rope rather than at the very end of it.

Near the end of the rope, be sure to find a good place to stop the rappel. Establish a good stance and anchor in before clearing the rope from the rappel device. In establishing a secure stance, consider the possibility of rockfall and icefall, and attempt to be out of the way of the next person coming down.

Shouting "Off rappel!" lets those above know that you have safely completed the rappel and are detached from the rope, so the next person can begin the rappel.

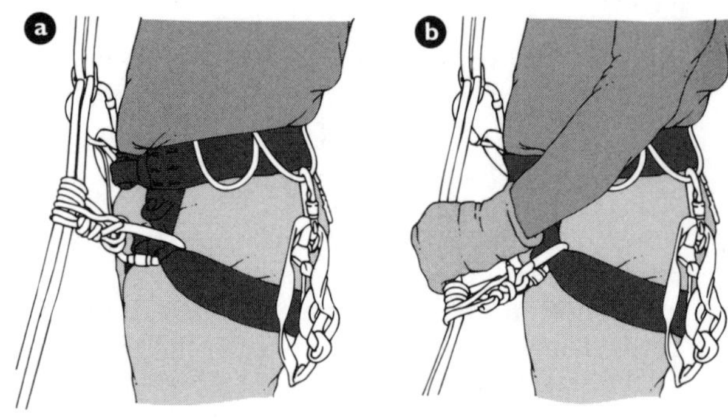

Fig. 11-20. Self-belay autoblock on rappel: a, with an aperture-style device setup; b, tend the friction hitch by manually sliding it down along the rope.

MULTIPLE RAPPELS

A descent route often involves a series of rappels. These multiple rappels, especially in alpine terrain, present special problems and require maximum efficiency to keep the party on the move.

As a party moves through a series of rappels, the first person down each pitch usually carries gear for setting up the next rappel, after finding a secure stance, establishing an anchor, and attaching to it out of the path of icefall and rockfall. Gain more efficiency by moving ropes from preceding rappels down the current rappel as soon as practicable; with these ropes, prepare the next rappel while the remaining party members complete the current rappel. More experienced climbers in a party can take turns being first and last. It is best for beginners to be somewhere in the middle of the rotation so that assistance is available at each end of each rappel.

UNKNOWN TERRAIN

The trickiest of multiple rappels is one into the unknown, down an unfamiliar route. Avoid this kind of multiple rappel if possible. If an unfamiliar rappel is necessary, take time to check out the possible rappel lines as carefully as time and terrain permit. Sometimes it is possible before a climb to find a photo of the rappel route. Bring it along for reference. Keep in mind that the first couple of rappels down an unfamiliar route may, for better or worse, commit the party to the route entirely.

If the bottom of an unfamiliar rappel pitch cannot be seen, the first person down must be prepared to climb back up in case the rappel hangs free at the end of the rope before there is a good stance. This rappeler should carry prusik slings or mechanical ascenders for ascending the rope.

Rappeling down unfamiliar terrain brings an increased risk of getting the rope hung up. Minimize the problem by down-climbing as much of the route as possible, instead of rappeling. Also, consider rappels using just one rope, even if two ropes are available. Although this increases the number of rappels and the time spent descending, one rope is easier to retrieve and is less likely to hang up than two. If one rope does hang up, the second rope is available to protect a climb back up to free the stuck rope. You may then carefully climb back down or establish an intermediate rappel where the hang-up occurred.

Although it is efficient to gain the maximum distance from each rappel, do not bypass a good rappel anchor spot even well away from the end of the rope if there are doubts about finding a good place farther down.

SAFETY BACKUPS

Belay methods and backup knots at the end of rappel ropes can enhance the safety of a rappel. In addition, they add security to particularly risky or unnerving rappels and may save the life of a rappeler hit by rockfall. They also help beginners gain confidence in rappeling.

SELF-BELAY WITH AN AUTOBLOCK OR PRUSIK

Tying a friction hitch (either an autoblock or a prusik) below the rappel device, clipped to a harness leg loop, enables you to stop without gripping the ropes. These self-belay hitches will grip the rope and halt your descent any time you do not actively tend them.

To make a self-belay autoblock, use a sewn runner of 9⁄16- or 1-inch webbing, or use 7-millimeter accessory cord for a tie-off loop (see "Runners" in Chapter 9, Basic Safety System). Attach the runner or loop to the seat-harness leg loop with a carabiner (or a girth hitch); wrap the loop around both strands of the rappel rope(s) below the rappel device—typically, three wraps provide enough (but not too much) friction; then clip the end of the runner or loop to the seat-harness leg loop with the same carabiner (fig. 11-20a). Alternatively, tie the tie-off loop to both strands of the rappel rope(s) with a prusik hitch below the rappel device and clip the free end of the loop to the harness leg loop.

In general, the autoblock is easier than the prusik to release once it has been loaded. For both the autoblock and the prusik, the runner or loop must be short enough that the hitch cannot either jam the rappel device or be tended by the rappel device (which could result in failure of the hitch to hold). The autoblock can also fail if the seat harness somehow gets positioned below the autoblock.

If the braking hand releases the rope—for instance, as the result of rockfall—a self-belay friction hitch can prevent you from accelerating out of control. Reestablish the braking hand and tend the self-belay hitch by manually sliding it down along the rope to allow the descent to resume (fig. 11-20b).

These hitches require some testing and adjustment before each rappel in order to establish the runner or loop's proper length (so the hitch does not hang up in the rappel device) and the proper amount of friction (adjusted by the number of wraps) to accommodate your weight, rappel device, comfort, and any other individual considerations.

FIREMAN'S BELAY

A person standing below a rappeler can easily control the rappeler's movement or stop it altogether—thus providing an effective belay—simply by pulling down on the rappel rope(s), which puts friction on the brake system (fig. 11-21). To safeguard the rappeler with this method, the person at the bottom simply holds the rope strands loosely, ready to pull them tight the instant the rappeler has difficulty.

Fig. 11-21. Fireman's belay: rappel halted by a climber below, who is pulling down on the ends of the rope.

BACKUP KNOTS

Even very experienced rappelers have inadvertently rappeled off the end of their ropes with tragic results. When you use a rappel device, put a large knot, such as a figure eight, in the ends of the rope or tie the ends together to reduce this danger. If you add knots, do not rely blindly on them; knots might come untied, and in any case, you must keep an eye on the ends of the rope to plan where to stop. Knots may jam in the rappel device if, at the end of the rappel, you try to rappel all the way through the

11

end of the rope. Backup knots can also cause a problem before a rappel begins by jamming in the rock and hanging up when the ropes are tossed.

TOP BELAY

The rappeler can also be protected by a belay from above with a separate rope. If the belayer uses a separate anchor, the rappeler is safe from even a total failure of the rappel anchor. A top belay may be used for beginners, for climbers with minor injuries, and for the first person descending on a suspect anchor. The belays are too time-consuming for routine use because they drastically increase a party's descent time.

RETRIEVING THE RAPPEL ROPE(S)

Successfully retrieving the rope(s) after a rappel depends on some important steps before the last rappeler starts down the rope. Just one frightening experience with a stuck rappel rope guarantees that these precautions will always be taken.

FINAL PRECAUTIONS

With two ropes joined at the anchor, it is critical to know which rope to pull on from below when the rappel is completed. Pull the wrong one, and the knot will jam in the rappel sling. In some parties, the final two rappelers say out loud which rope is to be pulled, as an aid to remembering which is which, before they begin their rappels.

The last rappeler should take a good final look at the rope(s) and the rappel sling to see that everything is in order and that the rope(s) will not catch on the sling or the rock, snow, or ice. Before the last person starts down, a person at the bottom should pull on the proper strand to check that it pulls freely. The rappeler above should confirm that the connecting knot in a two-rope rappel can be pulled free of the edge and that the rope does not bind on itself when pulled (see Figures 11-6 and 11-7).

On a two-rope rappel, the last person who starts down may want to stop at the first convenient ledge and pull enough of the rope down so that the connecting knot is clear of the edge. This helps take some of the uncertainty out of the difficult business of recovering a long rappel rope. However, it also shortens one rope end, so be sure you still have enough rope to reach the next rappel stance safely.

The last rappeler has the main responsibility for spotting any retrieval problems. This last person can get twists out of the rope(s) by keeping one finger of the braking hand between the strands throughout the descent. The same purpose is served by splitting the two strands through a carabiner on your harness, just uphill of the braking hand.

PULLING THE ROPE(S) DOWN

With the last rappeler down, it is time to retrieve the rope(s). First, take out any visible twists and remove any safety knots in the ends of the strands. Then give the proper strand a slow, steady pull. As the pulled strand starts to travel freely, yell "Rope!" to warn of falling rope. Others should take shelter to stay out of the way of falling rope, rocks, or other debris. With proper preparation, the rope(s) should pull free.

Rope Jams

A jammed rappel rope may be a serious problem, perhaps even stranding a party on a descent that requires further rappels. If the rope hangs up, either before or after the end clears the anchor, try flipping the rope with whipping and circular motions before attempting any extreme pulling. Often a change in angle, back from the face or to the right or left, can free the rope. Sometimes pulling on the other end of the rope (if it is still in reach) can free the rope. Be alert and cautious when pulling a stuck rope; as it springs free, it may be accompanied by rock- or icefall.

If both ends of the rope(s) are still in reach when the hang-up occurs, it is possible to safely prusik up both strands (see "The Texas Prusik" in Chapter 17, Glacier Travel and Crevasse Rescue, for one ascending method on a free-hanging rope), clear the jam, and rappel back down. Tie in to the rope at frequent intervals to back up the prusiks. If all else fails and only one rope end can be reached, it may be necessary to climb up and free the rope(s). If the route up is not too difficult to climb, several increasingly poor options are possible, depending on the situation:

1. If enough rope is available from the other strand, belay the climb up.
2. If not enough rope is available from the other strand, lead up the climb with a self-belay by anchoring the available rope and placing conventional protection in conjunction with a prusik ascent. If the rope suddenly pulls free from above, the hope is that the combination of

the prusik attachment, the periodic protection, and the anchor will limit the length of the fall.

3. If no belay is possible, and if the party cannot proceed without the rope, a final resort is to attempt the desperate and very dangerous tactic of ascending the stuck rope with prusik slings or mechanical ascenders. The extreme danger of climbing an unsecured rope must be weighed against the consequences of remaining stranded until another rope is available. Again, if it is possible to place protection during the ascent, attach the rope with clove hitches; perhaps the consequences of the rope pulling free from above might be mitigated.

EXPERIENCING THE FREEDOM OF THE HILLS

Rappeling is one of the activities central to climbing, and if you learn it thoroughly and employ it carefully, it is safe and works well. Take care to avoid complacency. Rappeling is one of the essential, specialized techniques that enables climbers to experience the freedom of the hills.

PART III

ROCK CLIMBING

TYPES OF ROCK CLIMBING • GEAR • CLIMBING EFFICIENTLY • FACE CLIMBING • CRACK CLIMBING • OTHER CLIMBING TECHNIQUES • STYLE AND ETHICS

Chapter 12
ALPINE ROCK CLIMBING TECHNIQUE

Alpine rock climbing can range from moderate routes only a few hours from the trailhead to multiday climbs in remote settings. Rock climbing gives you the kinesthetic pleasure of movement combined with the challenge of solving a three-dimensional puzzle on intriguing landforms.

This chapter focuses on the basic and intermediate-level rock climbing skills needed in the mountains. For those interested in a sport climbing emphasis, see Appendix D, Supplementary Resources, for several excellent texts on techniques more suited to that environment.

Note: When rock climbing on technical terrain, you should always be on belay. However, to more clearly show body positions involved in different climbing techniques, the illustrations in this chapter omit components of the basic safety system such as ropes, harnesses, and protection.

TYPES OF ROCK CLIMBING

Technical climbing begins when anchored belays are needed for the party's safety. Free climbing is simply climbing using your own physical ability to move over the rock via handholds and footholds, with the rope and protection used only for safety. This is contrasted with aid climbing, which involves the use of artificial aids to make upward progress such as protection placed in the rock for use as hand- and footholds. Climbers use aid technique (see Chapter 15, Aid and Big Wall Climbing) if the rock does not offer enough natural features or if the route is too hard for their skill level. Big wall climbing means climbing on—what else?—a large, sheer wall, which usually requires extensive aid, but frequently these wall routes include sections of free climbing. Ascents of big walls typically take longer than one day, usually including either a hanging bivouac or ledge bivouac as well as sack hauling. Solo climbing is, of course, climbing by yourself, but it usually refers to unroped climbing (called free soloing); you can also rope-solo a route, using gear, and so self-belay on a solo free or aid climb.

Nontechnical climbs, or scrambles, occur on second-, third-, or even fourth-class terrain (see Appendix A, Rating Systems). Note that "third classing" a climb also means to do it unroped. A climb is rated by its most difficult portion. On a long route, portions may be considerably easier, perhaps even second class. Depending on the skills and experience of the climbers and the condition of the routes, some easier sections may be climbed unroped, walked while coiled short (see "Climbing in Coils" in Chapter 14, Leading on Rock), or climbed with a running belay (using a technique called simul-climbing; see Chapter 14). This compromise of safety is often made to gain the speed necessary to climb a longer route in a shorter period of time with less gear. For experts, these easier sections may be as hard as mid-fifth class, despite the potential for fatal consequences should one fall.

Although experienced climbers occasionally free-solo a route, all unroped climbing is risky. The risk depends on not only how likely you are to fall but what the consequences of a fall would be. Is the rock loose? Is it raining, which makes the rock slippery? Could you be hit by rockfall—or by a climber above you falling—and thereby be knocked off the holds? Is the ground 10 feet (3 meters) below or several hundred feet? Fatal falls have occurred on third-class terrain as well as on 5.12 routes.

Sport climbing and crag climbing are two types of free climbing that refer to technical rock climbs close to roads and civilization that do not require alpine skills. To the mountaineer who climbs distant peaks in the wilderness, sport and crag climbing might be viewed as ways to practice the technical, physical, and mental aspects of rock climbing in a less remote, relatively lower-risk environment—for example, where help is usually more accessible in the event of an accident.

In contrast to a traditional climb, or trad climb, in which you place and remove rock protection, sport climbing involves routes where bolts have been previously drilled into the rock face for protection. The emphasis is on pushing your physical limits in terms of gymnastic ability, physical strength, and endurance. Therefore, in most instances, these climbs are bolted so that falls taken while on lead should be safe. For more information on sport climbing, refer to books in Appendix D, Supplementary Resources, and seek out instruction for training in the proper techniques for falling while on lead, belaying a climber on lead who is expected to fall, and assessing the safety of falling on a given route.

Crag climbs generally require placement of traditional rock protection in cracks in the rock face. However, entire routes or sections of routes with extensive face climbing and little opportunity for traditional protection placements may be bolted. Lead falls taken on bolts or traditional rock gear while crag climbing are not necessarily safe; carefully assess each route's risk compared to the level of risk you are willing to accept and the likelihood of falling, compounded by the consequences of such a fall. Crag routes vary widely in length, ranging from one to more than fifteen pitches. Some have bolts for belay and rappel anchors, whereas others require that climbers build an anchor for belaying or that they walk or scramble down for the descent.

Alpine rock climbing refers to routes farther from civilization that require many of the technical, physical, and mental aspects of rock climbing involved in sport and crag climbing, in addition to alpine routefinding or glacier climbing skills and equipment. Alpine routes are almost never bolted.

Of course, all these categories have some overlap. For example, some multi-pitch bolted climbs are in somewhat remote areas.

GEAR

Ropes and harnesses are covered in Chapter 9, Basic Safety System; protection hardware is covered in Chapter 13, Rock Protection.

FOOTWEAR

On rock climbs of moderate difficulty, the same mountain boots you wear on the approach generally work well for the actual climbing. (For more information on mountain boots, see Chapter 2, Clothing and Equipment.) When the climbing is more difficult, specialized footwear—rock shoes (fig. 12-1a, b, and c)—gives a significant advantage. Most rock shoes have flexible uppers, plus smooth, flexible soles and rands of sticky rubber. These soles create excellent friction when weighted on rock, allowing purchase on angles and nubbins that can amaze the beginning climber. Most alpine rock climbers use rock shoes if the technical difficulty is rated 5.6 or 5.7 or higher.

On a climb that is a carryover—climbers do not go back to their starting point or base camp on the way down—using rock shoes on the route means climbing with the weight and bulk of mountain boots in their pack. If the climbing includes patches of snow or ice between the rock sections, wearing mountain boots for the entire route avoids time-consuming breaks for changing footwear. Some advanced climbers climb through short sections of snow with rock shoes, or one climber leads the rock pitches in rock shoes and the other climber leads the mixed pitches of rock, snow, and ice in boots. For difficult rock climbing, especially narrow cracks, the better purchase and thinner profile afforded by rock shoes may make for safer and faster climbing. The choice of footwear and pack is personal and depends on the route. Climbing often in mountain boots makes your footwork more precise, and you will have an advantage when you do use rock shoes.

Approach shoes (fig. 12-1d) are a compromise between mountain boots and rock shoes. These are useful when the approach is snow free, and they can be worn on the climb itself if the route is of moderate difficulty. To avoid the burden of carrying boots on a sustained rock climb, some experienced climbers strap crampons onto running shoes for short snow crossings, such as a small pocket glacier.

In choosing an appropriate pair of rock shoes, the confusing array at outdoor stores can be daunting. Remember that climbing technique is far more important than the shoes! Specifically, until you have mastered the techniques necessary to climb at the 5.10 or 5.11 level and beyond, the choice of rock shoe will not likely make a significant difference. That said, here are some useful guidelines on rock-shoe selection.

Stiff-soled, more cambered shoes are better at edging (see Figure 12-1b); flexible shoes are better at frictioning or smearing (see "Footholds," later in this chapter). Shoes with laces, such as in Figure 12-1a and b (as opposed to laceless slippers, in Figure 12-1c), and higher tops that cover the anklebones (as in Figure 12-1a and c) offer protection when jamming feet in cracks. If a climber is restricted to owning only one pair of rock shoes, a pair with all-around characteristics is best.

Good fit is paramount. Rock shoes should fit snugly, to allow dexterity and a good sense of the rock's features, yet not so tightly as to cause pain. Rock shoes should be comfortable enough to wear for an all-day climb. Unlike sport and crag climbers at local crags, alpine rock climbers do not have the luxury of taking their shoes off after each 40-foot (12-meter) pitch. Some makes of rock shoes are sized for wider or narrower feet than others; try on different styles to find

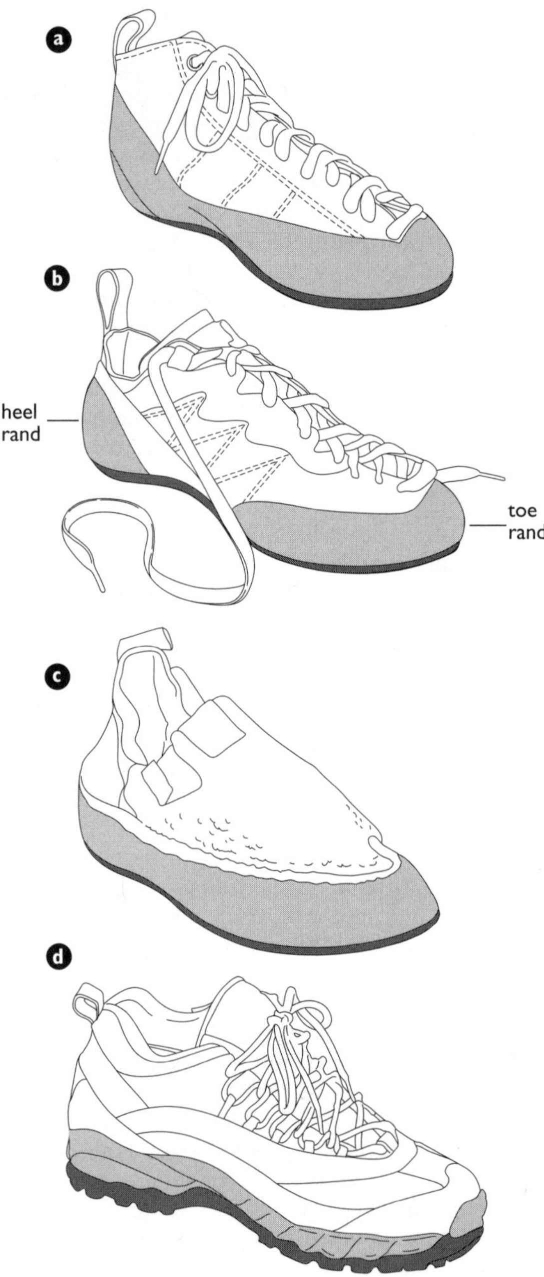

Fig. 12-1. Rock shoes: a, all-around shoe; b, more specialized edging shoe; c, slipper; d, combined approach and climbing shoe.

what fits. A thin pair of liner socks add comfort and a little warmth, a bonus when climbing is done in chilly conditions. Some climbers have a pair of "alpine rock shoes" sized to fit over their mountain-boot socks. All rock shoes stretch somewhat, usually only a quarter to a half size in width and much less in length. Leather shoes stretch more than synthetic shoes. Lined shoes stretch the least.

Rock-shoe rubber oxidizes and hardens over time; try a brisk scrubbing with a wire brush to expose a new, stickier layer. If holes develop in the rubber, rock shoes can often be resoled. This is significantly less expensive than buying a new pair.

CLOTHING

Alpine rock climbing clothing must be comfortable, allow free range of movement, and handle changing weather conditions. For general information on alpine clothing, see Chapter 2, Clothing and Equipment.

Remove rings, bracelets, and watches before climbing rock, because they will probably get scratched at the least; at the worst, they may catch in a crack and damage your hands. A stuck ring can cause serious injury, even amputation of the finger.

TAPE

Athletic tape can be used to protect hands from abrasive rock when crack climbing. Tape is advisable for those learning crack techniques, for those climbing more difficult cracks (especially on rock that has many sharp crystals), or for those who have occupations where raw hands could be a hazard (such as health care or food service). Some climbers feel that tape around their fingers helps protect finger tendons.

12

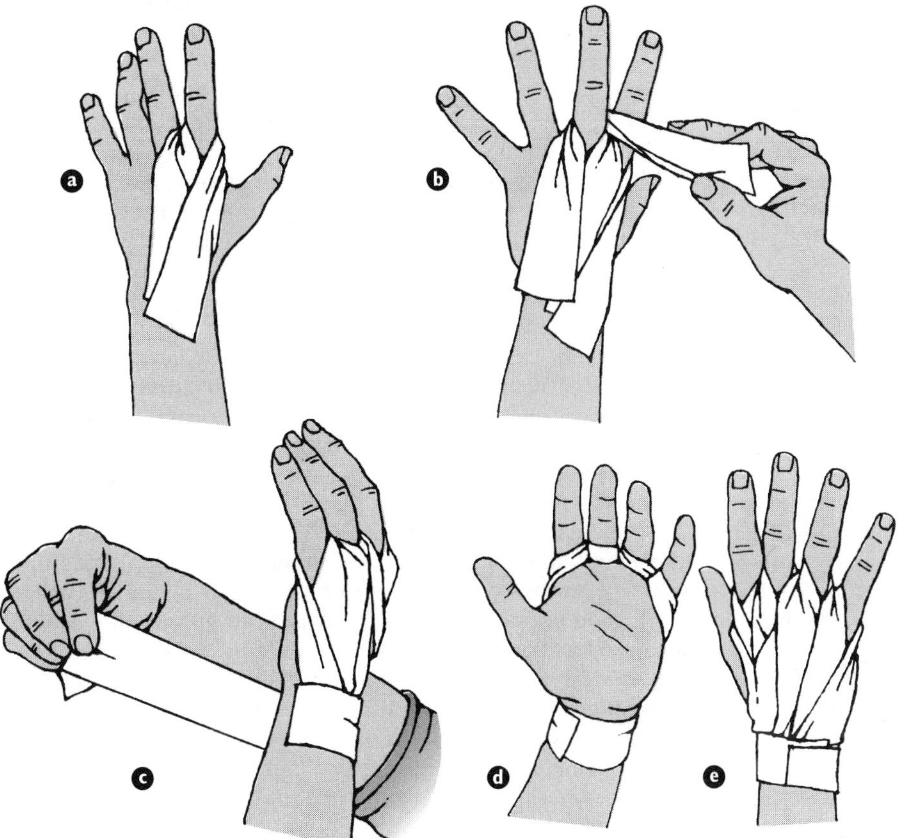

Fig. 12-2. Hand taped for climbing: a, wrap tape around first finger; b, wrap tape around remaining fingers; c, wrap wrist; d, palm is mostly left open; e, back of hand and knuckles are protected.

Taping methods vary; see Figure 12-2 for a method that leaves the palm untaped, to ensure sensitivity during face holds. When taping your hands, flex them so that when you later make a fist or hand jam the tape will not be too tight. After climbing, you can often cut off your tape "gloves" and save them for later use.

CHALK

Gymnastic chalk can improve your grip, especially in hot weather, by absorbing sweat. Chalk is available as loose powder and as a crushable block, either of which is usually carried in a chalk bag. Chalk is also available contained inside mesh balls (often refillable) that allow smaller amounts of chalk to sift out and thus minimize spillage.

Chalk marks tend to identify the holds that are used, thus making a climber's moves obvious and minimizing the adventure for the next climber. Excess chalk on holds makes them slippery.

CLIMBING EFFICIENTLY

Efficient technique makes alpine rock climbing more enjoyable. It enables you to climb with as much speed as is reasonable, without exhaustion. Climbers need to have enough strength for the approach and the climb itself, as well as the descent and the hike back out. Good technique combines balance, footwork, and handwork with the minimum expenditure of strength. Climbing efficiently also requires proficiency with technical gear by both the leader and follower (described in Chapters 13, Rock Protection, and 14, Leading on Rock). All of this comes with time and practice.

Rock climbing may appear to require great arm strength. It is true that strength may get climbers up certain rock sections if they have no technique, but they will also burn out quickly. On some rock features, strength alone will not work; technique is necessary. The best of both worlds combines technique with good physical training in strength, power, and endurance (see Chapter 4, Physical Conditioning; Eric Hörst's *How to Climb 5.12*, is a also a good resource for physical training, listed in Appendix D, Supplementary Resources). Following are some general guidelines about technique that apply to climbing any type of rock, whether a face or a crack.

FOCUS ON SPEED AND SAFETY

Speed is often an important part of safety on an alpine rock climb. Less time climbing means less time exposed to rockfall and changing weather, as well as more time to solve routefinding problems, deal with injury, get off the mountain before dark, or handle any number of possible risks inherent in the alpine environment. However, reasonable caution must not be sacrificed to speed. Practice on shorter, easier routes and move to more difficult, longer routes as your efficiency improves.

Aim to move smoothly over the rock, set up belays, exchange gear, and manage the rope with a minimum of wasted time. Alpine rock climbing often necessitates carrying a pack, and choices regarding packs are route-dependent and personal. Pack enough gear to do the climb and survive unexpected situations, but be spartan. Depending on the situation, for speed and safety, both climbers in a climbing team may choose to carry similar packs, or the follower might carry either the only pack or the larger one.

Keep small snacks and water readily accessible for sipping water at a belay and nibbling on a snack in a few seconds. Many a climber has "bonked" up high: gotten dangerously tired and slow from inadequate nutrition during the day. Be aware of your own—as well as your partner's—food and water intakes and energy level.

The size of the climbing party and the number of rope teams affect overall trip speed. The more rope teams there are, the longer it will take for the entire party to finish, all else being equal.

CLIMB WITH YOUR EYES

Observe the rock. See where the holds are—the edges, the cracks—before even setting foot on the rock. Obviously, specifics of the entire pitch cannot be visually memorized beforehand, but it is possible to get an overall idea.

Look off to the side as well as up and down while climbing, to continually check where the holds are and will be in relation to your hands and feet. Many choices of holds are available on easy to moderate routes; look around and do not let tunnel vision stop you from seeing them. Because the number of available holds decreases as the difficulty increases, a calm attitude helps on even more difficult terrain. (Arno Ilgner's book *The Rock Warrior's Way: Mental Training for Climbers* discusses the mental aspects of climbing in detail; see Appendix D, Supplementary Resources.)

Tune in to how your balance feels as you move in a deliberate, smooth, and fluid manner. Much of successful climbing results from a relaxed yet alert mind.

USE FOOTWORK

Footwork and balance are the foundations of rock climbing. Good footwork gives a climber good balance and requires less exertion than handwork. Leg muscles are larger and stronger than arm muscles, and therefore they provide the most efficient use of muscle power. That is why climbers are frequently told to climb with their feet.

Look for footholds that are comfortably spaced. Shorter steps take less energy than longer, higher steps, and you will stay in balance more easily. However, steps too close together take up more time per foot of upward progress.

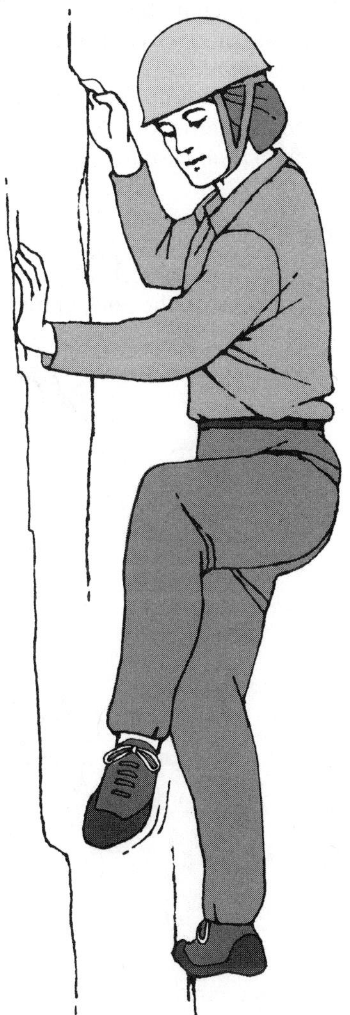

Fig. 12-3. Three-point suspension: Keep three body points weighted on the rock at all times; here, hands and right foot provide secure stance while left foot is moved to a higher hold.

Stand erect over your feet—this keeps your body weight centered over your feet, and the resulting down-pressure helps keep your feet on the holds. Anxious climbers tend to hug or lean into the rock, but this just tends to push their feet off the rock because the pressure is out, not down.

Try to walk up the rock from foothold to foothold, as if you were going up a ladder—use your hands merely for balance. When you raise a foot toward the next foothold, eye the hold and aim precisely for it. Once your foot is set in place, commit to the hold and leave your foot there. Adjust your balance to the new position by shifting your hips over the new hold. Continue transferring your weight through your leg down to that foot. Complete the move: Stand up by using your leg muscles to push your body up.

MAINTAIN THREE POINTS OF CONTACT

When you begin to learn rock climbing, keep three body points (any combination of hands and feet) weighted on the rock at all times (fig. 12-3). This can be two hands and one foot, or one hand and two feet. Keep your balance over your feet until you release a hold to move for the next one. This is an especially useful approach when testing a hold for looseness without weighting it because it allows you to balance securely on three holds while testing the new one.

Be aware of where your center of gravity is—directly over your feet is usually the most stable stance. Moving your center of gravity over a new foot- or handhold causes your weight to shift to that new hold.

On more difficult climbs, it is not always possible to keep three body points in contact with the rock. There may be only one or two sound holds, so use your body position to maintain a delicate balance over those holds. Regardless of the number of points you have in contact, however, the same principle of balance applies: Keep your weight over your holds.

CHECK FOR LOOSE HOLDS

Loose rock can be all too common in the mountains. Many loose holds are obvious, but be alert for those that are not. Look for fracture lines and loose rocks (fig. 12-4a). Gently nudge any suspect hold, or give it a push with the heel of your hand (fig. 12-4b). A

Fig. 12-4. Looking for loose holds: a, visually inspect the route for loose rocks (circled); b, if loose rock cannot be avoided, use extra caution in that area and test holds before using them.

hollow-sounding rock is usually loose. Make sure your testing does not actually dislodge the rock! If loose rock cannot be avoided, move with extra care and deliberation. Sometimes a loose hand- or foothold can be used if you carefully push downward and in on it while weighting it—but be careful.

FACE CLIMBING

Face climbing is simply climbing by using the various features on the surface of a rock face, as contrasted with climbing the cracks that may split a face. A particular hold may be used in a variety of ways by feet and hands as the climber moves up the rock. Face climbing also includes the ascent of nearly featureless slabs, using friction and balance (fig. 12-5).

HANDHOLDS

Handholds can be used for balance, to help climbers raise themselves by pulling up on the hold, or for providing

Fig. 12-5. Face climbing uses friction and balance when holds are minimal.

various forms of counterpressure. Handholds that are at about head height are best because they do not demand a tiring overreach.

Handholds offer maximum security when all the fingers are used. Keeping fingers close together provides a stronger grip on the hold (fig. 12-6a). The most common handhold is the cling hold (fig. 12-6a and b). Large cling holds (see Figure 12-6a) allow the entire hand to be cupped over the hold; smaller variations (see Figure 12-6b) may allow room for only fingertips. If the hold is not large enough for all the fingers to be placed on it, at least curl the other ones, which permits the fingers in use to get the most force from the muscle and tendon system (fig. 12-6c). When using cling holds, be careful not to overstress fingers and cause injury by using holds that are too difficult or small for your technique level.

Because climbers depend mainly on their legs for upward progress, handholds are sometimes used only for balance. The pinch grip (fig. 12-6d) is a handhold that may allow climbers to maintain a balanced stance on good footholds long enough to shake out their free arm and to reach for a higher, more secure handhold or to place protection.

As holds become smaller, different techniques are needed. For example, with fingers holding onto a tiny ledge, for additional strength climbers may use the thumb in opposition on a minor wrinkle (fig. 12-6e) or in a ring grip, where the thumb pressing against the index finger adds strength (fig. 12-6f). On a narrow hold or a small pocket in the rock, climbers can use one or two fingers in a pocket grip (fig. 12-6g). On a very narrow hold, climbers can stack fingers on top of each other to increase pressure on the hold (fig. 12-6h).

Handholds that are at about head height are ideal if it is necessary to hang straight-armed for a rest (fig. 12-7), which is less tiring than hanging from bent arms. You can lower your center of gravity by bending your knees or leaning out away from the rock. When you are able, hang an arm down and shake it out for a brief recovery before climbing again.

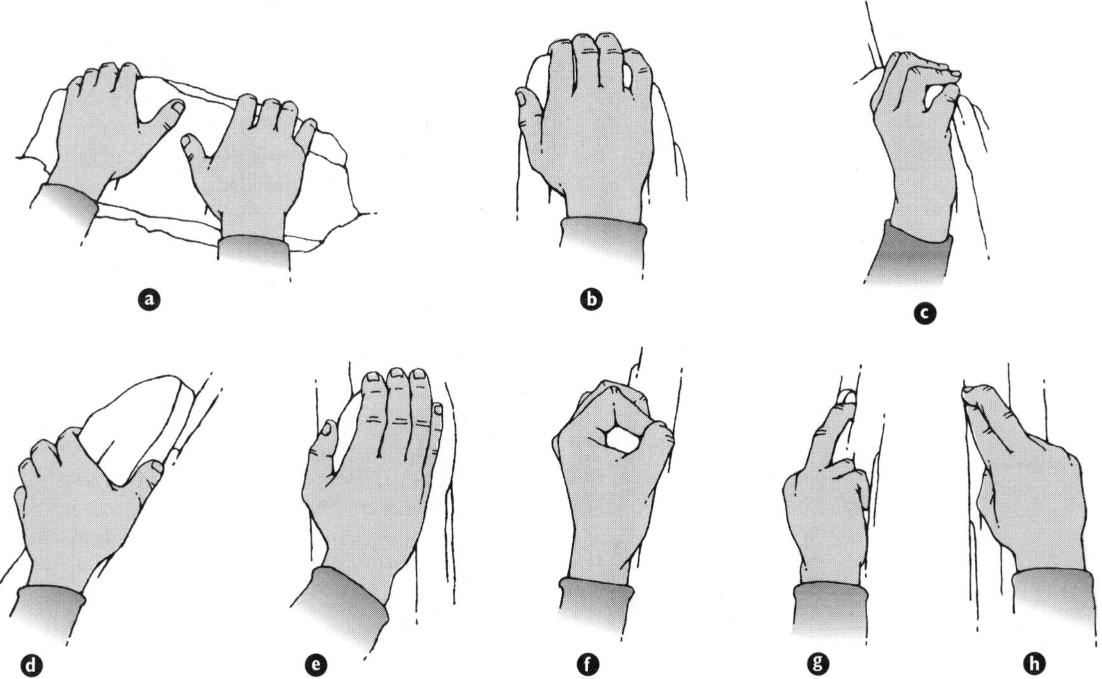

Fig. 12-6. Handholds: a, large cling hold with fingers close together; b, smaller cling hold with an open grip; c, cling grip on a smaller hold (more stressful on finger joints); d, pinch grip; e, thumb used in opposition to other fingers; f, ring grip; g, pocket grip; h, stacked fingers.

Fig. 12-7. "Resting" an outstretched arm while hanging on a straight arm.

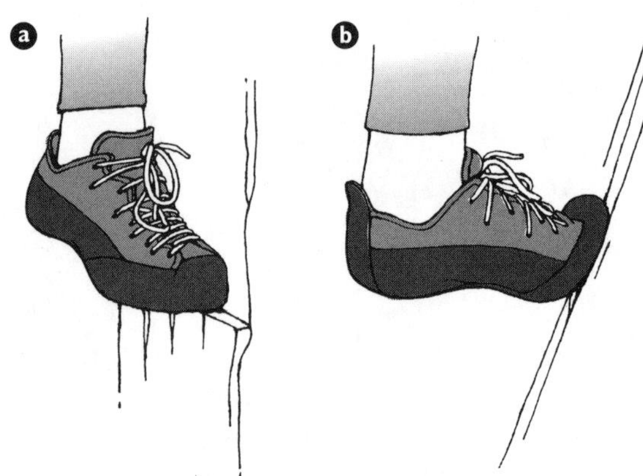

Fig. 12-8. Footholds: a, edging; b, smearing.

FOOTHOLDS

Climbers use most footholds by employing one of two techniques: edging and smearing. On many holds, either technique will work, and the one to use depends on personal preference and the stiffness of the climber's footwear. A third technique, foot jamming, is covered in "Crack Climbing," later in this chapter.

When edging, the climber weights the edge of the shoe sole over the hold (fig. 12-8a). Either the inside or outside edge is used, but the inside is usually preferred for greater ease and security. The ideal point of contact may vary, but generally it is between the ball of the foot and the end of the big toe. Keeping the heel higher than the toes provides greater precision but is more tiring. Using the toe of a boot or rock shoe on a hold (toeing in) is also very tiring. With practice, climbers become proficient using progressively smaller footholds.

In smearing, the foot points uphill, with the sole of the shoe "smeared" over the hold (fig. 12-8b). Smearing works best with rock shoes or flexible boots. On lower-angle rock, climbers may not need to use an actual hold but only to achieve enough friction between sole and rock. On steeper terrain, smear the front of the foot over a hold, and see how even tiny irregularities in the rock can provide significant friction and security.

In using footholds, make the best use of the direction of force on the hold. Flexing the ankle may increase the surface area of contact between sole and rock, giving maximum holding power. Leaning away from the rock creates inward as well as downward force on the hold, increasing security.

When using large footholds, called buckets, place only as much of the foot as necessary on the hold (fig. 12-9a). Putting a foot too far into the bucket can sometimes force the lower leg outward, making for an out-of-balance stance (fig. 12-9b).

Avoid placing knees on a hold, because knees are susceptible to injury and offer little stability. Nevertheless, even experienced climbers may on rare occasions use a knee hold to avoid an especially high or awkward step. The main considerations are to avoid injury from pebbles and sharp crystals and to avoid becoming trapped on your knees, unable to rise beneath a bulge or roof.

Fatigue, often aggravated by anxiety, can lead to troublesome spastic contractions of the leg muscles, jocularly known among climbers as "sewing-machine" or "Elvis" legs. The best way to stop it is to relax your mind, remember to breathe, and change your leg

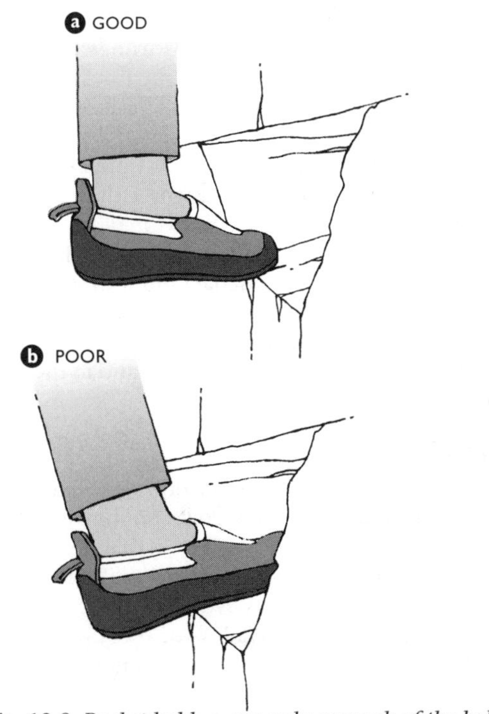

Fig. 12-9. Bucket hold: a, use only as much of the hold as needed (good); b, a foot too far into a bucket can force lower leg outward (poor).

position, either by moving on to the next hold, lowering your heel, or straightening your leg.

Friction or slab climbing requires liberal use of smearing (also called frictioning) moves. Balance and footwork are the keys to success, and the primary technique is smearing with the feet.

Remember to flex the ankle (lowering the heel) and to keep weight directly over the ball of the foot for maximum friction between rock and sole (fig. 12-10a). Avoid leaning into the slope with your body, which causes the feet to slide down (fig. 12-10b). Instead, keep your weight over the feet, bending at the waist to allow the hands to touch the rock and pushing the hips and buttocks away.

Take short steps to maintain balance with your weight over your feet. Look for the small edges, rough spots, or changes in angle that provide the best foot placements. Sometimes climbers actually have to feel with their hands or feet to find the irregularities.

Other techniques can also be useful on friction slabs. Face holds and cracks may be intermittently available for hands or feet. On small edges or irregularities, use down-pressure (see next page) with fingertips, thumb, or the heel of the hand. A lieback (see later in this chapter) with one hand might be possible using tiny edges. Look for an opportunity for stemming (see later in this chapter), which could mean a chance to rest.

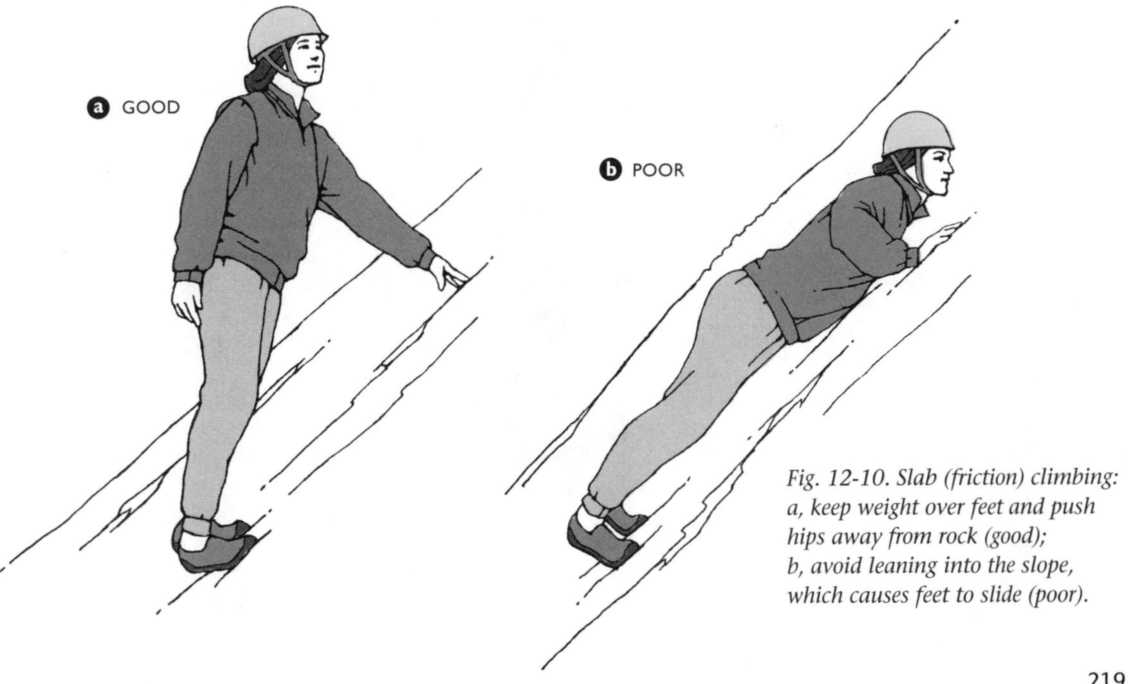

Fig. 12-10. Slab (friction) climbing: a, keep weight over feet and push hips away from rock (good); b, avoid leaning into the slope, which causes feet to slide (poor).

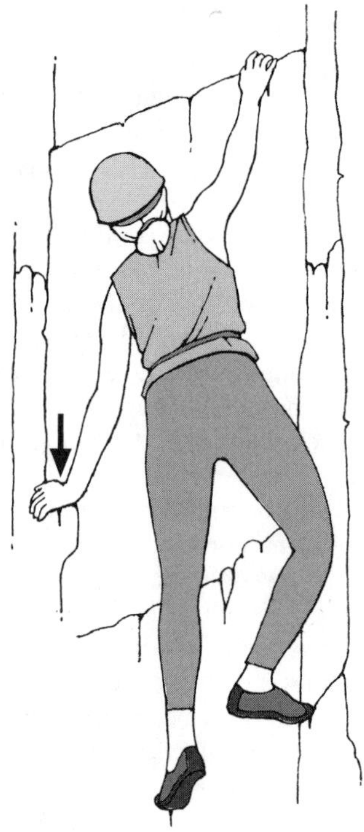

Fig. 12-11. Down-pressure using left hand.

DOWN-PRESSURE

For the down-pressure technique, place fingertips or the palm, side, or heel of the hand on the hold and press down (fig. 12-11). Pressing down with the thumb can be useful on very small holds.

Holds are often used as cling holds from below and then as down-pressure holds as the climber moves above them. Down-pressure holds may be used by themselves or in combination with other holds, such as in counterforce with a lieback hold or as part of a stemming move. With arm extended and elbow locked, climbers can balance one-handed on a down-pressure hold as they move the other hand to the next hold.

MANTEL

The mantel is a specific use of the down-pressure technique. It lets climbers use hand down-pressure to permit their feet to get up onto the same hold that their hands are using when no useful handholds are available higher.

The classic mantel is easiest if the ledge is about chest high (fig. 12-12a). Walk your feet up the rock (fig. 12-12b) until you can place both hands flat on the

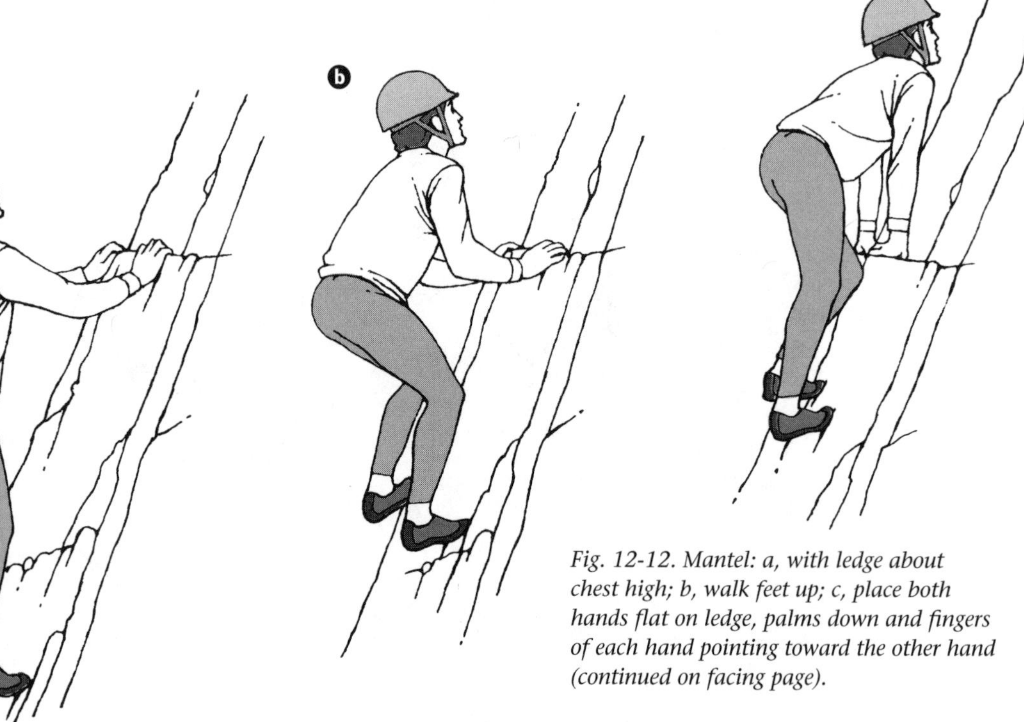

Fig. 12-12. Mantel: a, with ledge about chest high; b, walk feet up; c, place both hands flat on ledge, palms down and fingers of each hand pointing toward the other hand (continued on facing page).

ledge, palms down, with the fingers of each hand pointing toward the other hand. Then raise your body up onto stiffened arms (fig. 12-12c). Continue to walk your feet up the rock or, if you can, spring up from a good foothold, lift one foot up onto the ledge (fig. 12-12d), and stand up, reaching for the next handholds for balance (fig. 12-12e).

This basic mantel, however, is not always possible, because a ledge is often higher, smaller, or steeper than a climber might wish. If the ledge is narrow, it may be possible to use the heel of the hand, with the fingers pointed down. If the ledge is over your head, use it first as a cling hold and then convert to a down-pressure hold as you move upward. If the ledge is not big enough for both hands, mantel on just one arm while the other hand makes use of any available hold, or perhaps just balances against the rock. Do not forget to leave room for your foot.

Avoid using knees on a mantel because it may be difficult to get off them and back on your feet, especially if the rock above is steep or overhanging. Sometimes in midmantel it is possible to reach up to a handhold to help as you begin standing up.

COUNTERFORCE

Counterforce plays a part in many of the climbing maneuvers described in this chapter. Counterforce is the use of pressure in opposing directions to help keep the climber in place. For instance, place both hands in a vertical crack and pull in opposite directions on the sides of the crack—a pulling-apart action (fig. 12-13a)—to create outward pressure. Or pull in on widely spaced

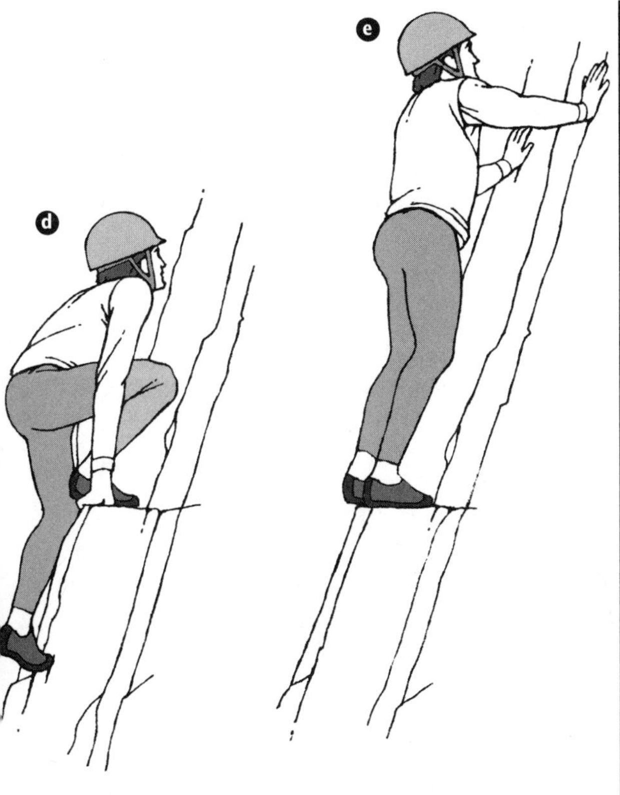

Fig. 12-12. Continued from facing page; d, place one foot on ledge; e, stand up and reach for next handholds.

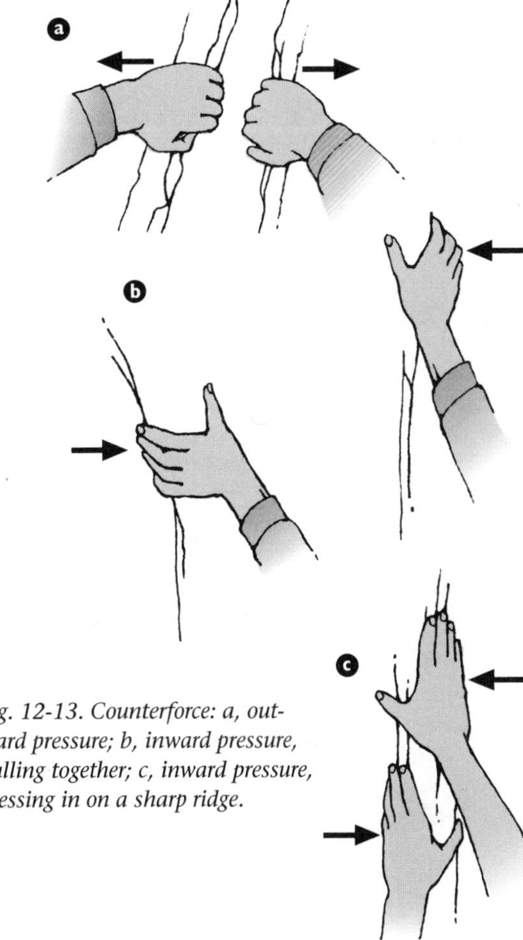

Fig. 12-13. Counterforce: a, outward pressure; b, inward pressure, pulling together; c, inward pressure, pressing in on a sharp ridge.

12

holds—a pulling-together action (fig. 12-13b)—or press in on both sides of a sharp ridge (fig. 12-13c) to create inward pressure. The hands can also be used in counterforce to the feet, as in the undercling (see below).

Stemming

Stemming is a valuable counterforce technique that lets climbers support themselves between two spots on the rock that might be of little or no use alone. It often provides a method of climbing steep rock where no holds are apparent, simply by pressing in opposing directions with the feet or with a hand and a foot.

The classic use of stemming is in climbing a rock chimney. It also comes into play in climbing a dihedral (also called an open book), where two walls meet in an approximately right-angled inside corner. One foot presses against one wall of the chimney or dihedral, while the other foot or an opposing hand pushes against the other wall (fig. 12-14a).

Stemming may also open an avenue of ascent on a steep face, where climbers can press one foot against a slight protrusion while the other foot or a hand gives opposing pressure against another wrinkle (also known as a rugosity) in the rock (fig. 12-14b).

Undercling

In the undercling, your hands (palms up) pull outward beneath a flake or lip of rock while your body leans out and your feet push against rock (fig. 12-15). Your arms pull while your feet push, creating a counterforce. Try to keep your arms extended. Both hands can undercling at the same time, or one hand can undercling while the other uses a different type of hold.

An undercling hold may have multiple uses. For example, from below a rock flake, climbers can hold its bottom edge in a pinch grip and then convert to an undercling as they move up to the flake.

Liebacking

The classic lieback technique, another form of counterforce, uses hands pulling and feet pushing in opposition as the climber moves upward in shuffling movements (fig. 12-16a). It is used to climb a crack in a corner, a crack

Fig. 12-14. Stemming: a, across a chimney; b, on a steep face.

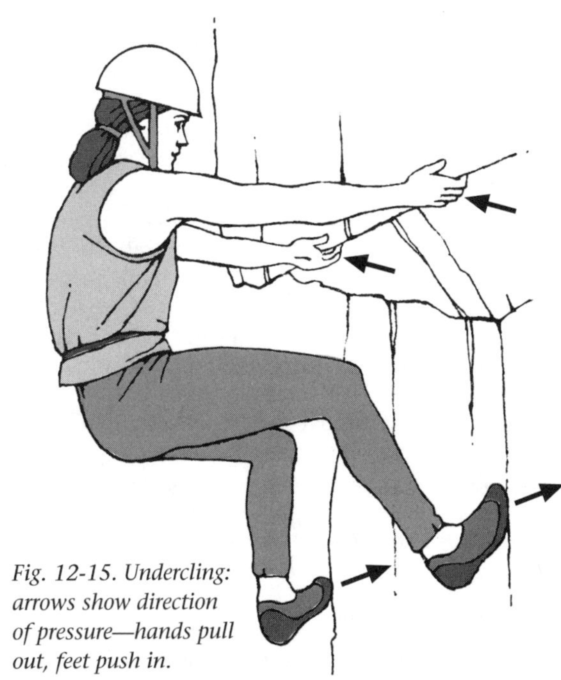

Fig. 12-15. Undercling: arrows show direction of pressure—hands pull out, feet push in.

with one edge offset beyond the other, or along the edge of a flake. Grasp one edge of the crack with both hands and lean back and to the side, away from the crack, on straightened arms. At the same time, push your feet against the opposite wall of the crack. Keep your arms extended to minimize muscle stress. Keep your feet high enough to maintain friction on the rock, but not so high that it is too strenuous. As always, feel for your body's balance and adjust accordingly. This is a strenuous technique, and it is difficult to place protection when liebacking.

The lieback can be used along with other holds as the rock allows. Climbers can lieback on a single handhold in combination with other holds or use one hand and foot in a lieback while using face holds for the opposite hand and foot (fig. 12-16b).

When using the lieback technique, a climber's body may have a tendency to swing sideways out of balance toward the crack, in what is known as the "barn-door" effect, which usually results in a fall. To avoid the barn-door effect, do not apply too much pressure with the leg closest to the rock.

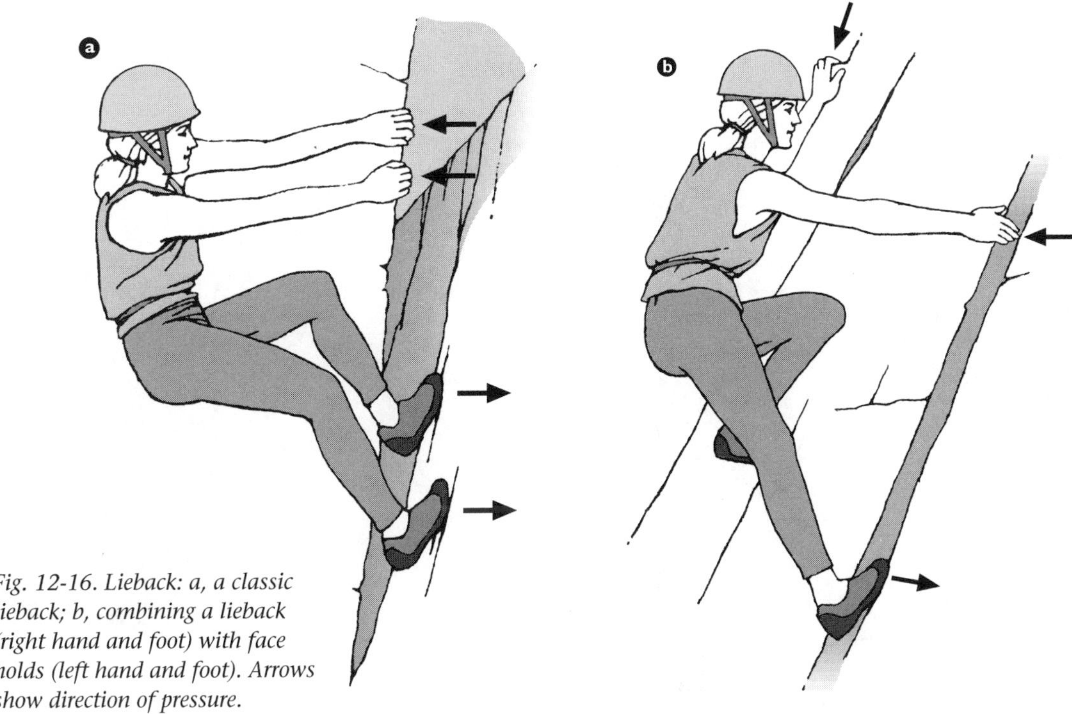

Fig. 12-16. Lieback: a, a classic lieback; b, combining a lieback (right hand and foot) with face holds (left hand and foot). Arrows show direction of pressure.

COUNTERBALANCE

Counterbalance, or flagging, is not a specific type of move but, rather, a concept that can be used in all kinds of climbing. It is the principle of distributing your body weight in a way that maintains your balance. This means selecting holds that do the best job of keeping your body in balance. But it also sometimes means putting a hand or foot in a particular location, even if no hold is available there, in order to provide counterbalance to the rest of your body (fig. 12-17a). Your hips and shoulders also come into play as you move them to provide counterbalance. Flagging is useful because it enables climbers to extend their reach (fig. 12-17b).

LONG REACHES

Several techniques can be used when the next available handhold is a long reach away or even out of reach. First, make the most of available holds. Move as high as possible on existing holds. Stand on your toes, but remember that this is strenuous and can contribute to sewing-machine leg if you continue too long. Sometimes a longer reach is possible by standing on the outside edge of a boot, which tends to turn the body somewhat sideways to the rock. The longest reach possible is with the hand that is opposite the foot you are standing on.

Another option is to consider quick intermediate moves, using holds that are marginal but can be used just long enough to allow the climber to scamper up to the next good hold. This leads to using a dynamic move (or dyno): a lunge or simply a quick move before you lose your balance. The time to grab the next-higher handhold while making a dynamic move is at the "dead point": the apex of the arc of movement when your body is weightless for a fraction of a second before it begins to fall. Movement is most efficient at that point.

Make a dynamic move only after calculating and accepting the consequences of failure. If a dynamic move fails, a fall is likely. Do not make a dynamic move out of desperation. Ensure beforehand that the protection is secure and that a fall onto the protection will not result in hitting a ledge or the ground.

EXCHANGING PLACEMENTS

Sometimes a climber needs to move one foot onto a small hold already occupied by the other foot or one

Fig. 12-17. Two examples of counterbalance, which enables an extended reach: a, the left foot is flagged to the side to provide counterbalance; b, the left foot is flagged behind the right for counterbalance.

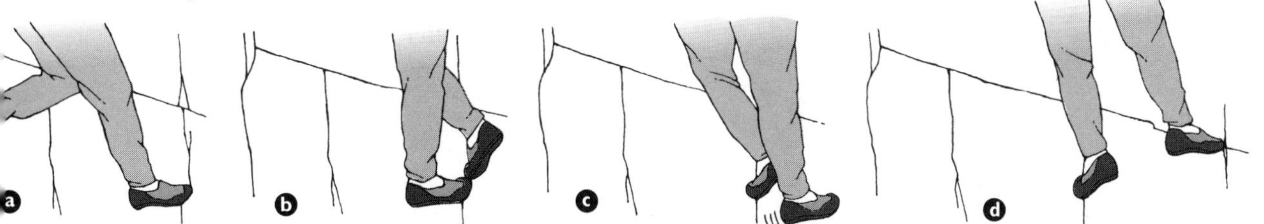

Fig. 12-18. Using a crossover to exchange foot placements on a small hold: a, right foot is on a hold; b, left foot crosses in front of the right; c, left foot is on the hold while right foot readies for next hold; d, right foot is on next hold.

hand onto a hold being used by the other hand. Either move can be made several different ways. This is known as matching.

To exchange a foot placement, make an intermediate move using a poorer, even marginal, hold to get the one foot off the good hold long enough for the other one to take it over. Or hop off the hold while replacing one foot with the other. Or try sharing the hold by matching feet, moving one foot to the very edge of the hold to make enough room for the other.

The crossover (fig. 12-18), is another technique in which one foot is crossed in front of the other (fig. 12-18b) to occupy a small spot on the hold while the first foot is moved off that hold (fig. 12-18c) to another (fig. 12-18d).

An intermediate move can be made to trade hands, much as might be done in exchanging feet. Place both hands on the same hold, one on top of the other, or if space is limited, try picking up the fingers of one hand, one finger at a time, and replacing them with the fingers of the other hand. The crossover technique also is occasionally useful.

CRACK CLIMBING

Many climbing routes follow the natural lines of cracks in the rock. Cracks have the advantage of offering handholds and footholds virtually anywhere along their length, as well as protection opportunities (see Chapter 13, Rock Protection). Some climbers seem to find crack climbing technique more difficult to develop than face climbing technique. Perhaps this is because even easy crack climbs demand a higher proportion of technique to strength than do face climbs. Crack climbing is also very individualized, based on the size of each climber's hands and fingers. A crack climb that is easy for one climber may be more difficult for others with smaller hands, for example, or vice versa. Because of the individualized nature of crack climbing, experiment with what works for you; as with face climbing, balance and continued practice are the keys to success. That said, the following crack climbing techniques are essential tools.

JAMMING

Jamming is the basic technique of crack climbing. To jam, place a hand or foot into a crack, then turn the foot or flex the hand so that it is snugly in contact with both sides of the crack. This wedging must be secure enough that the hand or foot will not come out when weighted. Look for constrictions in the crack, and place hand and foot jams just above these constrictions. When learning to crack climb, it is a good idea to try weighting jams as a test—while remaining balanced on the other points of contact—before actually trying to move up on the jams.

Cracks may be climbed with a pure jamming technique, with both feet and hands using jams, or in combination with other types of holds. While moving up on a jam, maintain the jammed position by using downpressure. Of course, there is nothing to stop a climber from also using any nearby face holds (fig. 12-19).

The following technique descriptions are basic guidelines that may be adapted to the varying size and configuration of the particular crack a climber is on. With practice, climbers become more adept at selecting the appropriate technique to apply in a given situation.

Hand-Sized Cracks

The easiest crack to master is the hand-sized crack. As the name implies, climbers insert their entire hand into the crack—relax the hand when you insert it, and then expand it so that it becomes stuck in the crack. Different ways to increase hand width include tucking the thumb

Fig. 12-19. Combining jamming (with the hands) in a crack with face climbing.

across the palm so that the lower "meaty" part of the hand catches on the walls of the crack, as well as cupping the hand as needed (fig. 12-20a). To increase pressure against the walls, climbers sometimes tuck their thumb across the palm, especially in wider cracks (fig. 12-20b). The hold can often be improved by bending the wrist so the hand points into the crack rather than straight up and down.

The hand jam is done either thumb up or thumb down. Thumb up (the bottom hand in fig. 12-20c; see also Figure 12-20a and b) often is easiest and most comfortable for a vertical crack, and it allows climbers to reach higher in vertical cracks. The thumb-up configuration is most secure when the climber's body leans to the same side as the hand that is jammed.

The thumb-down technique (the top hand in fig. 12-20c; fig. 12-20d) may allow for a more secure jam when the thumbs-up technique feels insecure. However, it is not possible to reach as high with this jam in a vertical crack, resulting in more hand jams and more energy expended. Because the hand can be twisted for better adhesion, climbers can lean in any direction off this jam. Climbers use a combination of thumbs up and thumbs down, especially in diagonal cracks, where it is often useful to jam the upper hand thumb down and the lower hand thumb up (see Figure 12-20c).

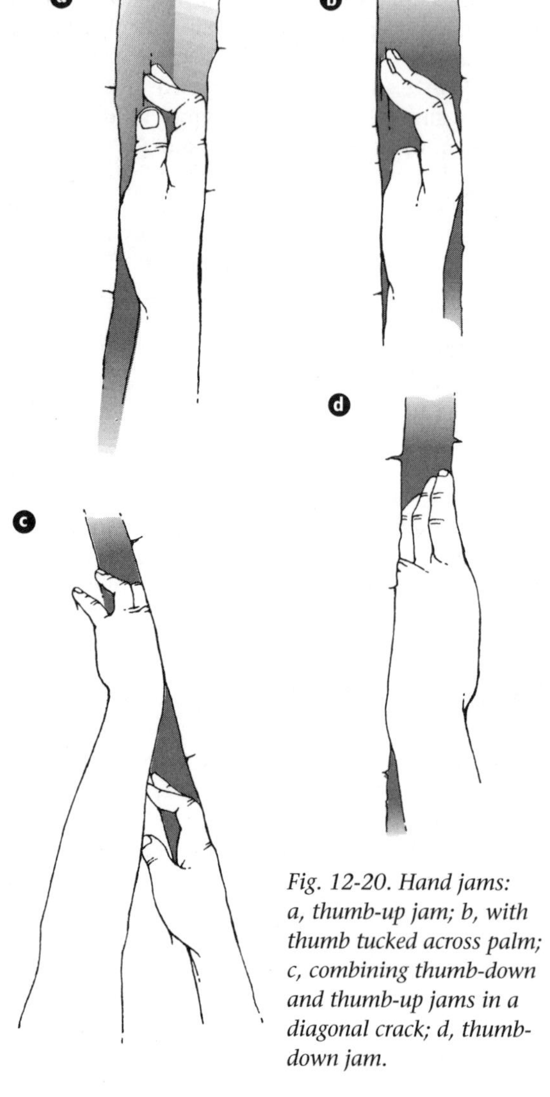

Fig. 12-20. Hand jams: a, thumb-up jam; b, with thumb tucked across palm; c, combining thumb-down and thumb-up jams in a diagonal crack; d, thumb-down jam.

With hand jams, climbers must keep alert to the effect of their elbow and body position on the security of the hold. As they move up, they may have to rotate their shoulder or trunk to keep sufficient torque and downward pressure to maintain the jam. Direction of force should be pulling down, not out of the crack. In general, keep the forearm parallel to the crack while climbing.

In dealing with hand jams, climbers encounter variants at both ends of the size scale: thinner cracks that will not admit an entire hand but are larger than finger cracks, up to wider cracks that are not quite large enough for a fist jam but require extra hand twisting to create enough expansion for a secure jam. The size of a climber's hand is a major factor in determining the appropriate technique and the degree of difficulty of any particular crack.

Hand-sized cracks are good for foot jamming too, and it is generally possible to wedge a shoe in as far as the ball of the foot. Insert a foot sideways, with the sole facing the side of the crack, and then twist it up to jam (fig. 12-21a). Avoid twisting the foot so securely that it gets stuck.

Fist-Sized Cracks

In a crack that is too wide for a hand jam, climbers can insert a fist. The thumb may be inside or outside the fist, depending on which provides the best fit. The palm may face either the back of the crack (fig. 12-22a) or the front (fig. 12-22b); if a full fist jam cannot be done, try turning the hand slightly to the side to do an oblique fist jam (fig. 12-22c and d). Flexing the muscles in the fist can expand it slightly to help fit the crack. Fist jams are often painful, but they can be very useful. For the most secure hold, try to find a constriction in the crack and jam the fist above it. If the crack is too wide for a hand but too small for a fist, it is often possible to shove an entire forearm into the crack and flex it for purchase.

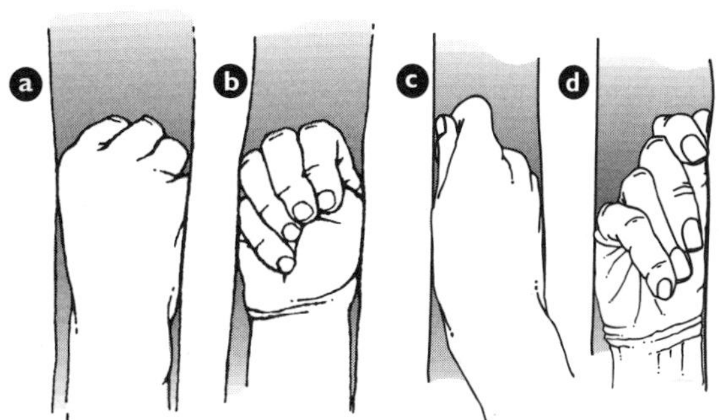

Fig. 12-22. Fist jams: a, palm facing in; b, palm facing out; c, oblique facing in; d, oblique facing out.

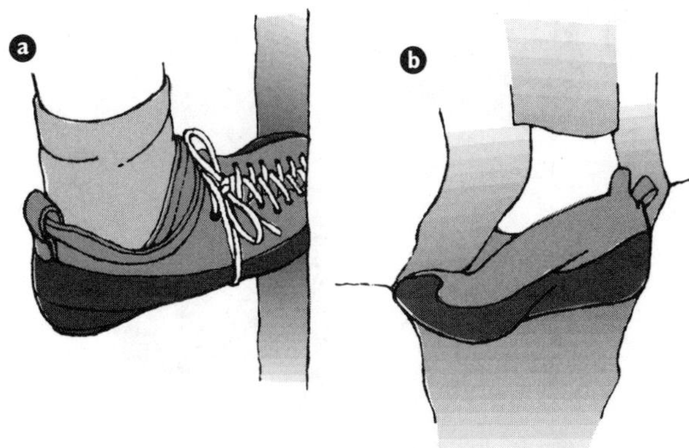

Fig. 12-21. Foot jams: a, foot jam in a hand-sized crack; b, heel and toe jam in an off-width crack.

Fist-sized cracks can generally accept an entire foot. As with hand-sized cracks, insert a foot sideways, sole facing the side of the crack, and rotate the foot to jam it securely in place. In even wider cracks, it is possible to jam a foot diagonally or heel to toe (see Figure 12-21b).

Finger-Sized Cracks

Finger jams make it possible to climb some of the narrowest cracks, where a climber may be able to insert only one or more fingers or perhaps just the fingertips. Finger jams are commonly done with the thumb down. Slip the fingers into the crack and twist the hand to lock the fingers in place (fig. 12-23a). Climbers get added strength by stacking fingers and also by pressing their thumb against their index finger in a ring jam (fig. 12-23b and c).

In slightly wider cracks, try a thumb lock, also called a thumb cam (fig. 12-23d). Place an up-pointing thumb in the crack, the thumb pad against one side of the crack and a knuckle against the other. Slide the tip of the index finger tightly down over the first joint of the thumb to create the lock.

The pinkie jam is done with a thumb up (fig. 12-23e and f). Put a little finger in a crack and stack the other fingers on top (fingertips down, nails up). In slightly larger cracks, it may be possible to wedge the heel of a hand and its smaller fingers into a crack that is not quite wide enough for a full hand jam. The weight here is borne by the heel of the hand.

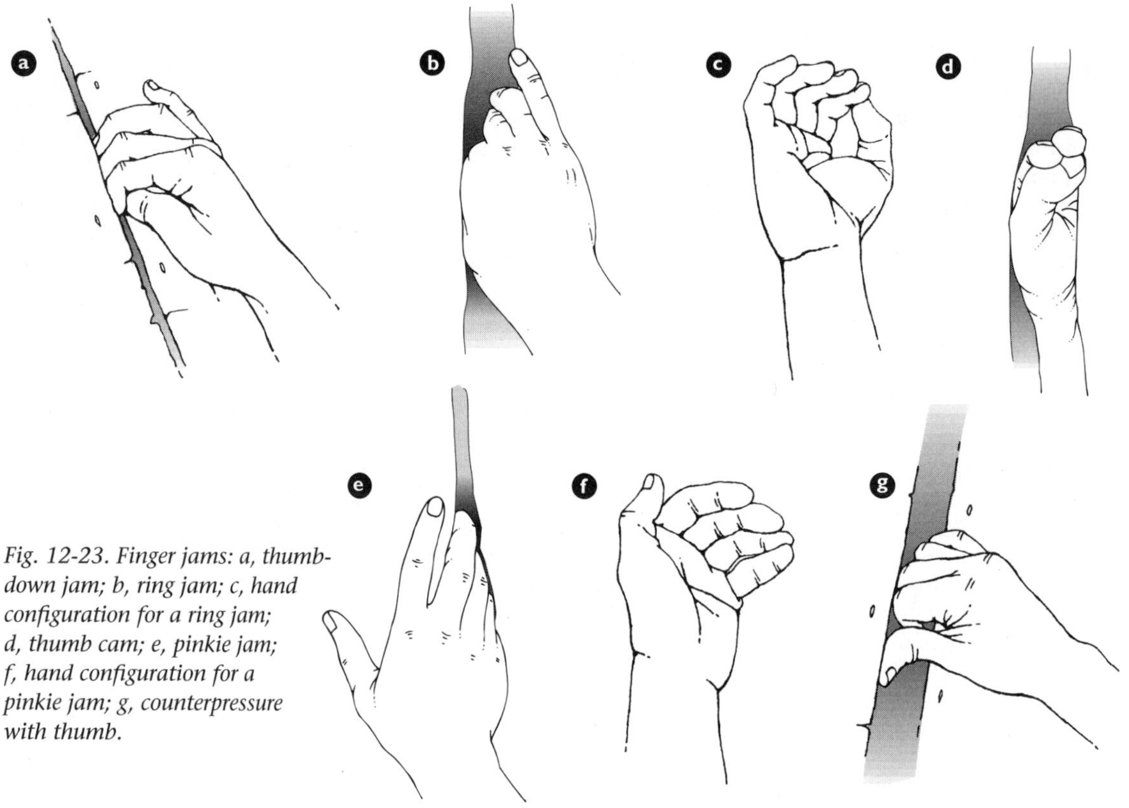

Fig. 12-23. Finger jams: a, thumb-down jam; b, ring jam; c, hand configuration for a ring jam; d, thumb cam; e, pinkie jam; f, hand configuration for a pinkie jam; g, counterpressure with thumb.

For another variation done with thumb down, use the counterpressure of a thumb pushing against one side of the crack and the fingers pushing against the other (fig. 12-23g).

Finger-sized cracks are not big enough to accept a climber's foot, but there is often room for toes. Wedge toes into a crack by turning the foot sideways—usually with the inside of the ankle up—inserting toes in the crack and then twisting the foot to jam it (fig. 12-24a). Climbers also wedge their toes into a steep inside corner with a smearing technique, keeping their heel lower than their toes and putting pressure down and in to keep their toes in place (fig. 12-24b). Using smearing and friction for the feet also works well when climbing a finger-sized crack.

CHIMNEYS

A chimney is any crack big enough to climb inside, ranging in size from those that will barely admit a climber's body (squeeze chimneys) to those that a climber's body can barely span.

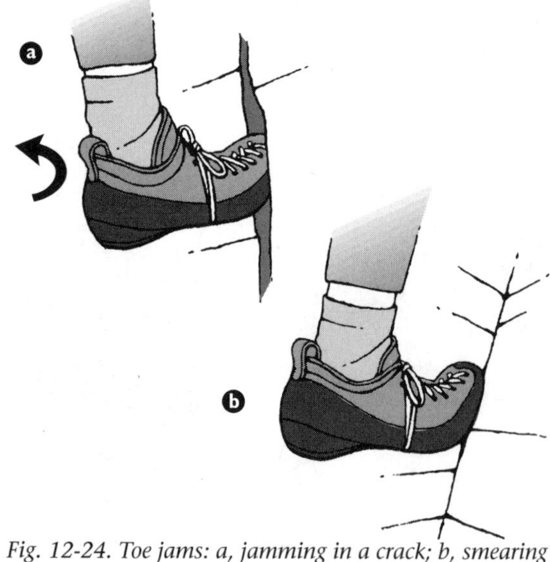

Fig. 12-24. Toe jams: a, jamming in a crack; b, smearing in a corner.

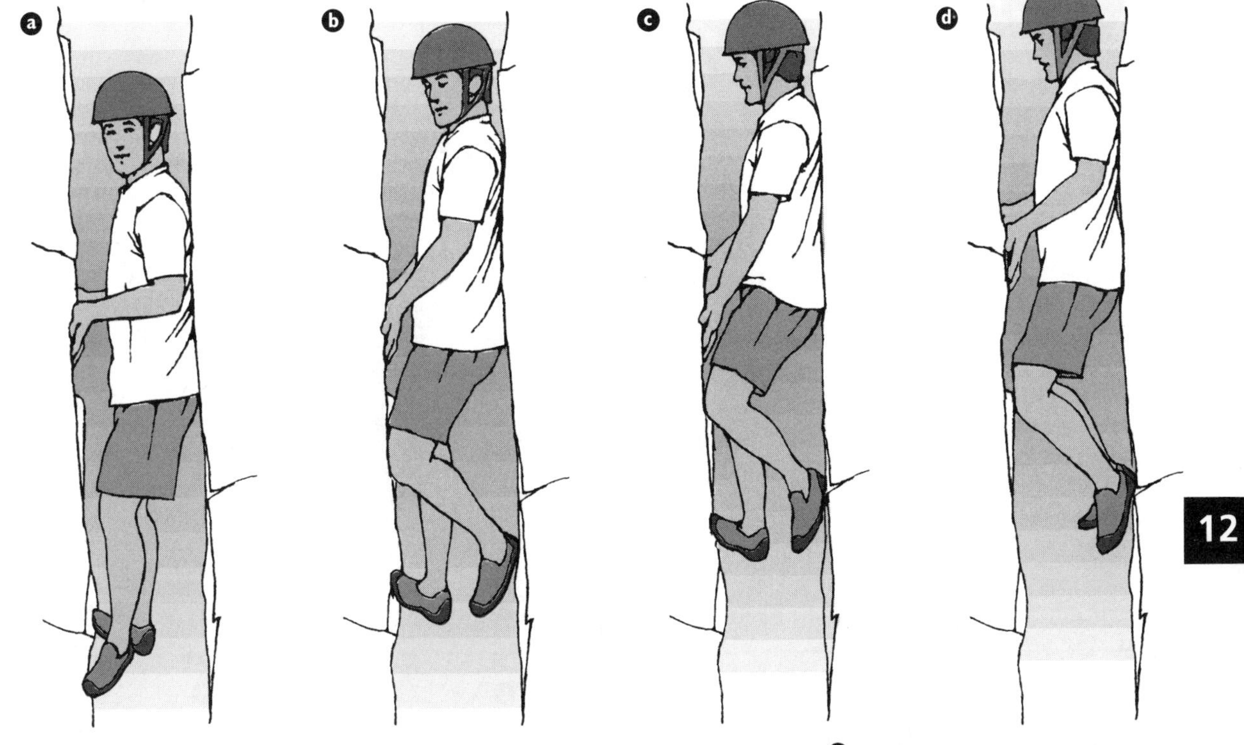

Fig. 12-25. Chimney technique in a squeeze chimney: a, wedge whole body into chimney; b, press foot and knee against opposite sides; c, squirm up; d, begin another sequence; e, stacking feet.

The basic principle is to span the chimney with the body, using counterforce to keep from falling. Depending on the width of the crack, either face one side of the chimney or face directly into or out of the chimney. The best body position and technique to use depend on the situation, the climber's size, and whether the climber is wearing a pack. Which direction to face may depend on what holds are available outside the chimney and what the best way will be to climb out of it.

In squeeze chimneys, wedge the body in whatever way works best (fig. 12-25a and d) and squirm upward (fig. 12-25b). Look for handholds on the outside edge or inside the chimney. Arm bars and chicken wings (see "Off-Width Cracks," below) may be useful. It is helpful, sometimes, to press a foot and knee of one or both legs, for example, against opposite sides of the chimney (fig. 12-25c). Try stacking both feet in a T configuration, with one foot placed parallel to one side of the rock and the other placed perpendicular to it, jammed between the first foot and the opposite wall (fig. 12-25e). Climbing squeeze chimneys can be very strenuous.

A crack that is somewhat wider than a squeeze chimney has some more room to maneuver. Press the back and feet against one side of the chimney as the knees and hands push against the other side (fig. 12-26a). Move upward by squirming. Or try a sequence of wedging the upper body while raising feet and knees and then wedging them and raising the upper body.

A wide chimney calls for stemming technique, in which a climber faces directly into or out of the chimney (fig. 12-26b). Counterforce is applied between the right hand and foot on one side of the chimney and

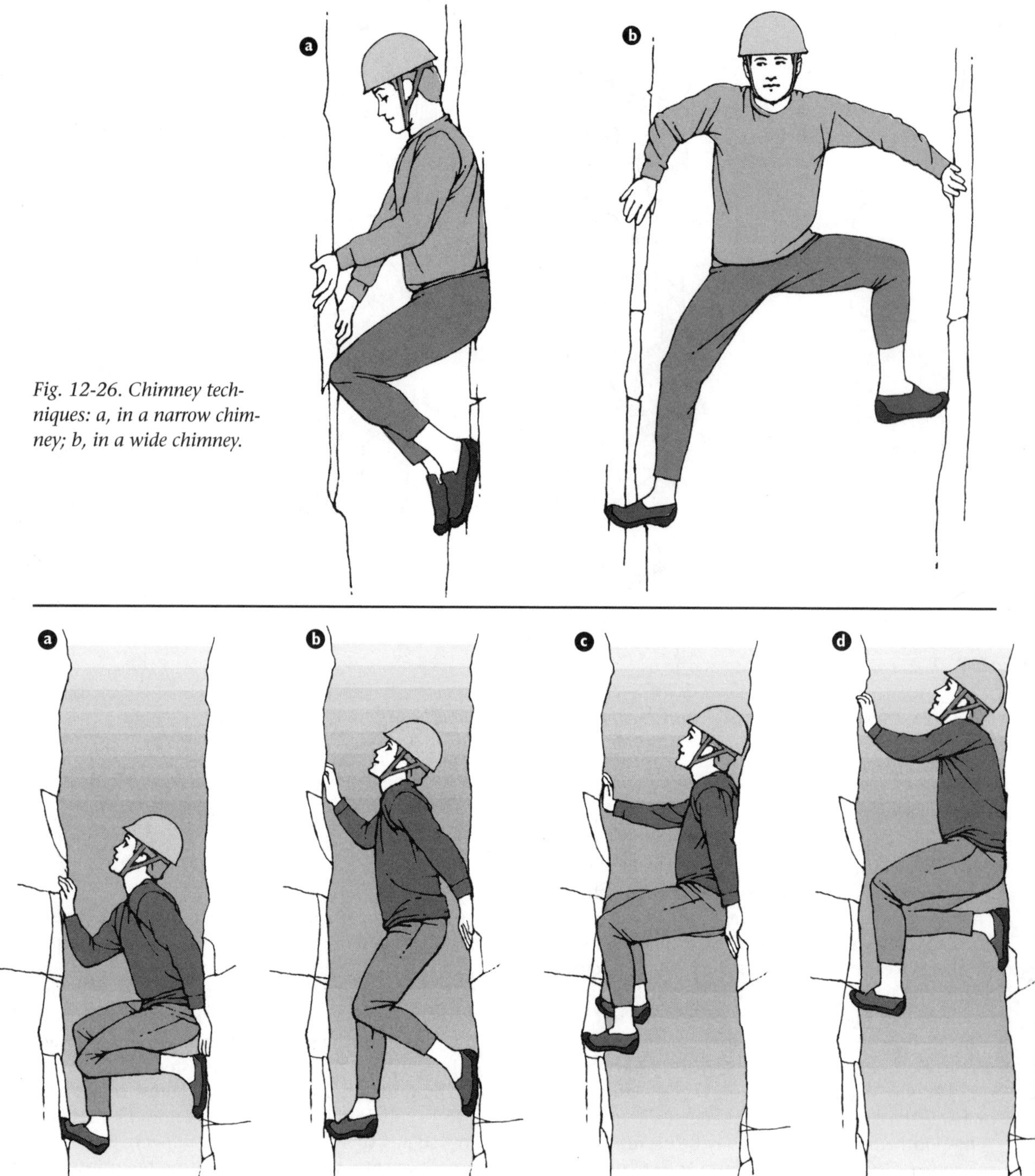

Fig. 12-26. Chimney techniques: a, in a narrow chimney; b, in a wide chimney.

Fig. 12-27. Chimney techniques in a moderate-width chimney: a, using counterforce between hands and between feet; b, moving up; c, using counterforce between buttocks and feet; d, beginning the sequence again.

the left hand and foot on the other side. Press down as well as against the sides, especially if there are holds on the sides of the chimney. Ascend either by alternately moving arms and legs or by moving each leg and then each arm.

In a moderate-width chimney, perhaps 3 feet (1 meter) wide, again face one wall of the chimney, with your back to the other (see Figure 12-27a). For the upper body, your hands may push against one wall in counterforce to your back pressed against the other, or the counterforce may be between your hands on opposing walls (see Figure 12-27b). For your lower body, your feet may push against one wall in counterforce to your buttocks against the other (see Figure 12-27c), or the counterforce may be between your two feet (see Figure 12-27d).

To climb a moderate-width chimney, use the following sequence: Start with your back toward one wall. Press one foot against each wall and one hand against each wall (fig. 12-27a). Move upward by straightening your legs and then reestablishing hand positions (fig. 12-27b). Immediately bring your back leg across to the same side as the forward leg (fig. 12-27c). Then swing your forward leg across to the back position (fig. 12-27d). Now move upward again by straightening your legs.

Beware of getting too far inside a chimney. Although psychologically it may feel more secure, climbers can get lodged deep inside and find it difficult to move back out. There is a better chance of finding useful handholds and footholds near the outside of the chimney.

Climbing deep inside the chimney also can make it harder to exit at the top. The transition from the top of the chimney to other types of climbing is often a challenge that may require extra thought and creativity.

Chimney technique may be useful in places that do not look like classic chimneys. It can be used to climb dihedrals (fig. 12-28) or short, wide sections of otherwise narrower cracks. Knee pads can be very useful when climbing routes with extensive chimney sections.

OFF-WIDTH CRACKS

Climbers have figured out ways to jam their arms, shoulders, hips, knees, and just about anything else into the difficult and awkward features known as off-width cracks. They are "off-width" because they are too wide for hand or fist jams but too narrow to admit the entire body for chimneying.

Fig. 12-28. Chimney techniques in a dihedral.

The basic off-width technique calls for standing sideways to the crack and inserting one full side of the body into it. When confronted by an off-width crack, first decide which side of the body to put inside the crack. This depends on several things, such as holds in the crack or on the face, the direction in which the crack leans, and whether it flares larger in places.

After settling on which side to use,put the inside leg inside the crack to form a leg bar, usually with counterpressure between foot and knee or foot and hip. This foot is often placed in a heel-toe jam (fig. 12-29). The outside foot also is inside the crack in a heel-toe jam. Try to keep heels above toes (for better friction) and turned into the crack (to allow the outside knee to turn out).

A primary body-jam technique is the arm bar. With your body sideways to the crack, insert one arm fully into the crack, with the elbow and the back of the upper arm on one side of the crack giving counterpressure to the heel of the hand on the other side (fig. 12-30a). Get

Fig. 12-29. Climbing an off-width crack: counterpressure between hip or knee and foot, plus heel-toe jams.

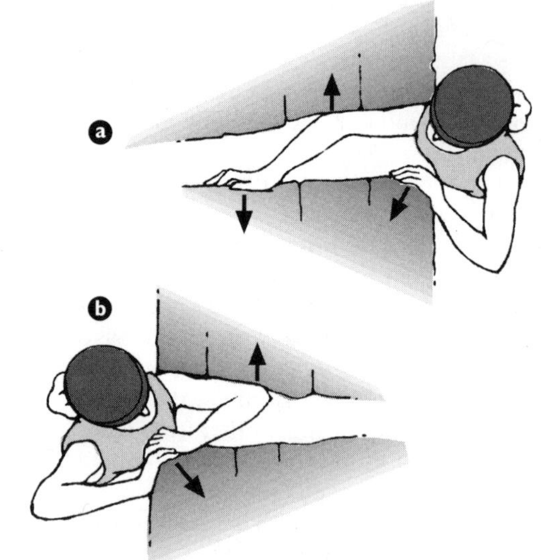

Fig. 12-30. Off-width climbing techniques: a, arm bar; b, chicken wing.

the shoulder in as far as possible, and have the arm bar extend diagonally down from the shoulder.

For chicken-winging, a variation of the arm bar, fold an arm back at the elbow before inserting it in the crack, and press the palm against the opposite side in counterforce to the shoulder (fig. 12-30b).

In either the arm bar or the chicken wing, use the outside arm to provide down-pressure to help hold you in the crack, or bring it across the front of your chest and push it against the opposite side of the crack, elbow out.

You are now wedged securely in the crack. To climb, move the outside leg upward to establish a higher heel-toe jam. When this jam is set, stand up on it. Then reestablish the inside leg bar and arm bar (or chicken wing), and reposition the outside arm. This again wedges your body in the crack. You are now ready to move the outside leg upward again to establish a yet higher heel-toe jam. Continue repeating this procedure.

Climbers may use their outside foot occasionally on face holds, but watch out for the tendency for these outside footholds to pull you out of the crack.

For especially awkward crack sizes, climbers may have to stack hand jams (the butterfly technique) or fist jams in the crack, or jam with the knee. A specialized technique, Leavittation (named after Yosemite climber Randy Leavitt), is used to climb an overhanging off-width.

Many alpine climbs have short sections of off-width cracks, but some climbs with long, strenuous off-widths have a cultlike following. For these, specialized rock protection (such as Big Bros; see Chapter 13, Rock Protection) and extra clothing and padding to protect the skin are a must. Online resources go into detail about specialized crack climbing (see Appendix D, Supplementary Resources).

COMBINING CRACK AND FACE CLIMBING TECHNIQUES

Cracks also may be climbed with a pure lieback technique or by liebacking with one arm in combination with face holds for the other hand (fig. 12-31). This may result in a kind of stemming action.

Dihedrals may be climbed by using various combinations, such as hands jammed in a crack splitting the

Fig. 12-31. Liebacking combined with face holds.

Fig. 12-32. Climbing a dihedral using stemming and hand jams.

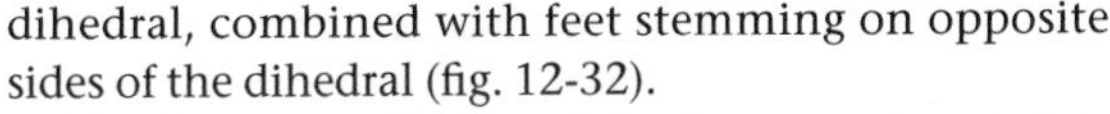

dihedral, combined with feet stemming on opposite sides of the dihedral (fig. 12-32).

Climbers may find useful edges or other holds hidden within cracks—on the sides or even at the back of wide cracks. Horizontal cracks can also be used as cling holds.

OTHER CLIMBING TECHNIQUES

Features such as overhangs, roofs, horizontal or diagonal sequences, and ledges challenge climbers to employ a variety of techniques.

NEGOTIATING OVERHANGS AND ROOFS

To climb overhangs and roofs, remember the main points for any climbing: Stay in balance and conserve strength. Identify handholds for moving up and over the bulge. Make the most of footholds by keeping feet high and hips low to help press weight against the footholds (fig. 12-33). In some situations, it means pressing hips into the rock, with the back arched, to keep weight over feet while poised under an overhang.

Fig. 12-33. Climbing an overhanging route: Keep feet high, hips low.

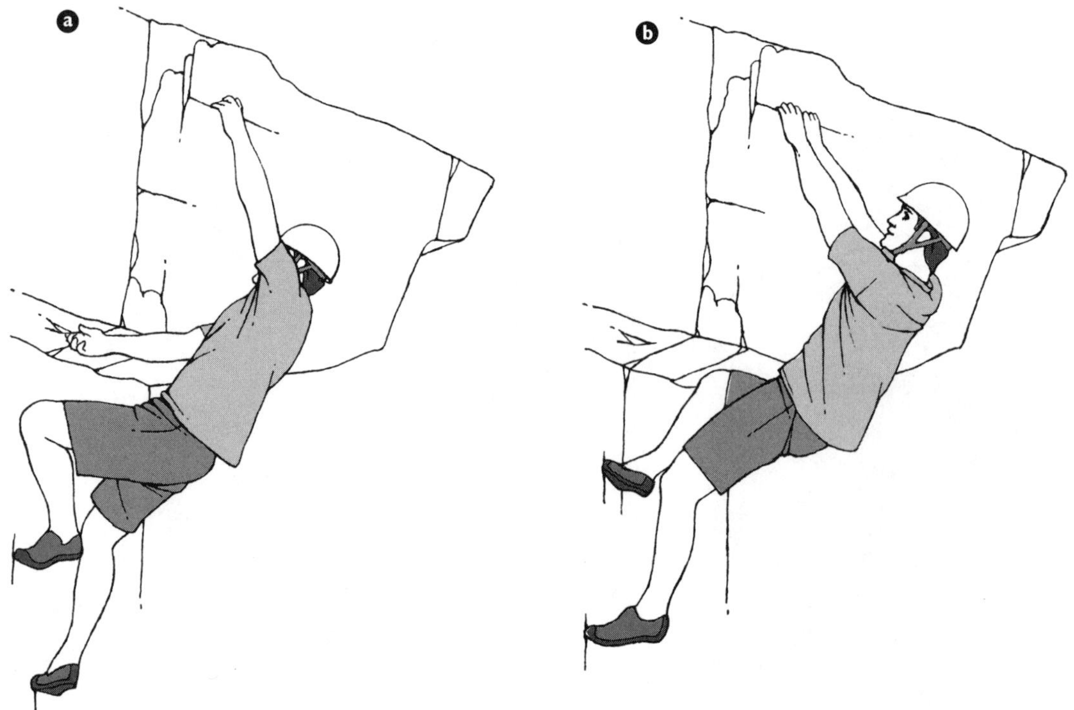

Fig. 12-34. Climbing over a roof: a, lean out on an outstretched arm to locate a hold above the roof, keeping hips close to the rock and feet weighted; b, both hands above the roof, with arms straight (continued on facing page).

To conserve strength, weight the feet as much as possible, even when negotiating a roof (fig. 12-34a). Keep arms straight while raising the feet (fig. 12-34b). Avoid hanging on bent arms, because this position will quickly exhaust arm strength. Push your body up with the legs rather than pulling with the arms (fig. 12-34c). Move quickly to minimize the time spent in these strenuous positions. Occasionally it may be necessary to rise up on the feet while making a dynamic reach to a handhold. Another trick is to throw one foot up onto a ledge while pushing with the other foot and pulling with the arms to swing up onto the top foot (fig. 12-34d).

TRAVERSING

Traversing—going sideways across a section of rock—calls for a wide variety of climbing techniques. The main ones are side clings, liebacks, and stemming. Good balance and being aware of your center of gravity are especially important during traverses.

Usually climbers face into the rock when traversing, their feet pointed away from each other (fig. 12-35a). Commonly climbers shuffle their hands and feet sideways, although it can be very useful to exchange one hand for the other, or one foot for the other, on a single hold. Climbers may occasionally cross one foot behind the other to reach the next hold, or cross one hand over the other (fig. 12-35b and c).

A hand traverse is necessary when footholds are marginal or nonexistent. The hands grip a series of holds or shuffle along an edge, while the feet provide a counterforce by pushing against the rock, as in a lieback or undercling (fig. 12-36a). Keep feet high and the center of gravity low so feet are pushed into the rock. Cross one hand over the other (fig. 12-36b). Again, keep arms straight to conserve arm strength and to let the legs do as much of the work as possible.

EXITING ONTO LEDGES

When approaching a ledge, continue to walk the feet up the rock, and then use down-pressure with hands

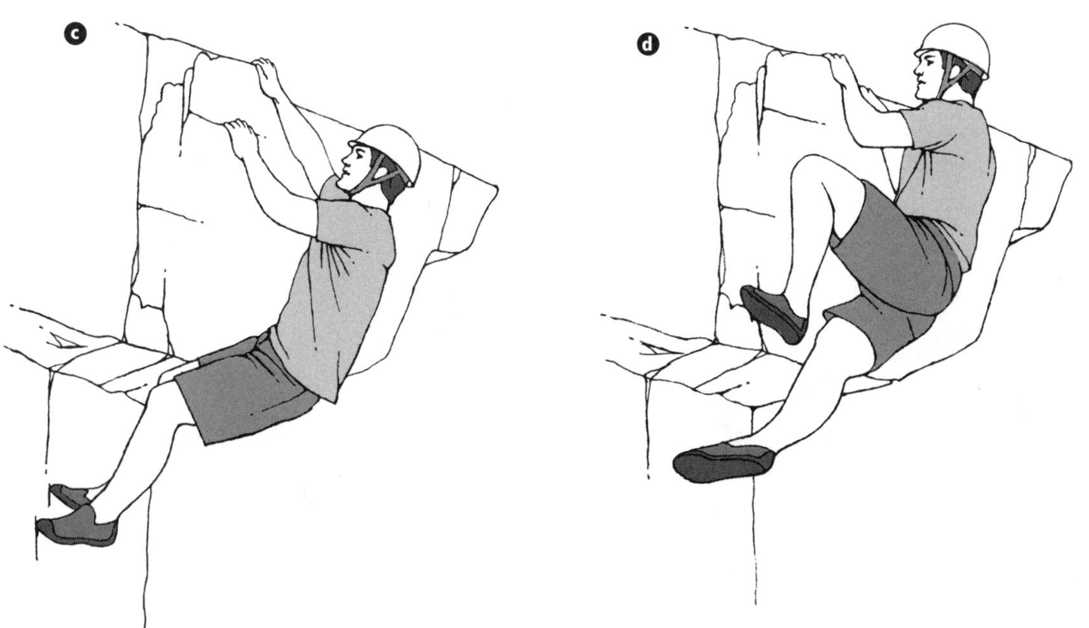

Fig. 12-34. Continued from facing page; c, feet are high, pushing against the rock; d, finally, bring one foot up and begin to pull over the roof.

Fig. 12-35. Traversing a steep face (an advanced technique): a, start the sequence with right foot on a hold in the direction of the traverse; b, twisting the body, reach through with the left hand; c, move the right hand to a new hold.

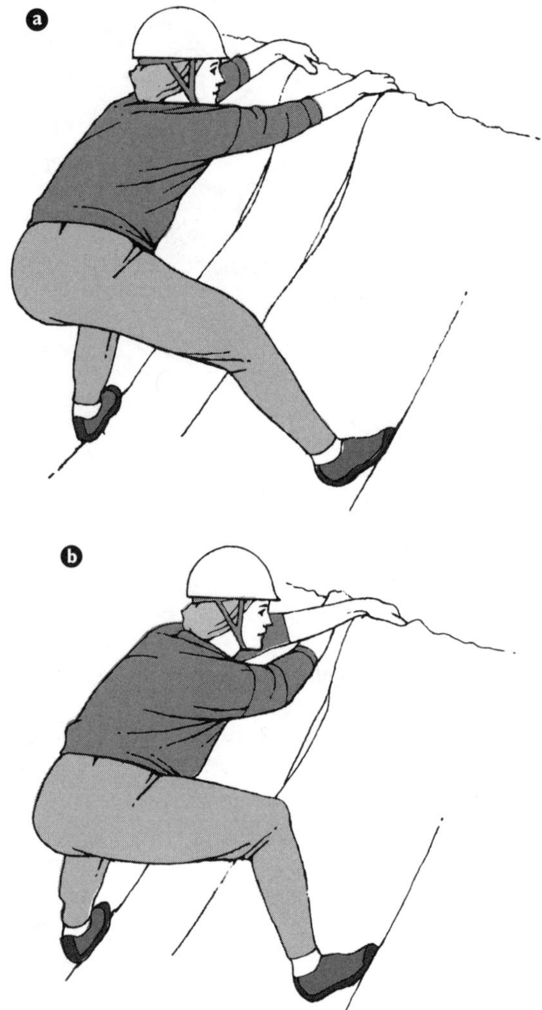

Fig. 12-36. Hand traverse: a, push feet against rock, providing counterforce; b, cross one hand over the other.

Fig. 12-37. Exiting onto a ledge: a, keep hands close to lip of ledge and step up; b, reaching too far forward with hands causes feet to lose their hold.

near the edge of the ledge. A classic mantel is often an excellent exit move (fig. 12-37a). Avoid the temptation to reach forward and pull yourself onto the ledge; this may throw you off balance and also make it impossible to keep an eye on the footholds (fig. 12-37b).

DOWN-CLIMBING

Efficient down-climbing is useful on many alpine climbs. Down-climbing is sometimes faster, safer, or easier than rappeling, and it may provide another retreat option when necessary.

Holds are harder to see when down-climbing than when climbing upward. The steeper the face, the harder the holds are to see. It is difficult to test holds without committing to them.

On low-angle rock, face outward for the best ability to see the route when down-climbing (fig. 12-38a).

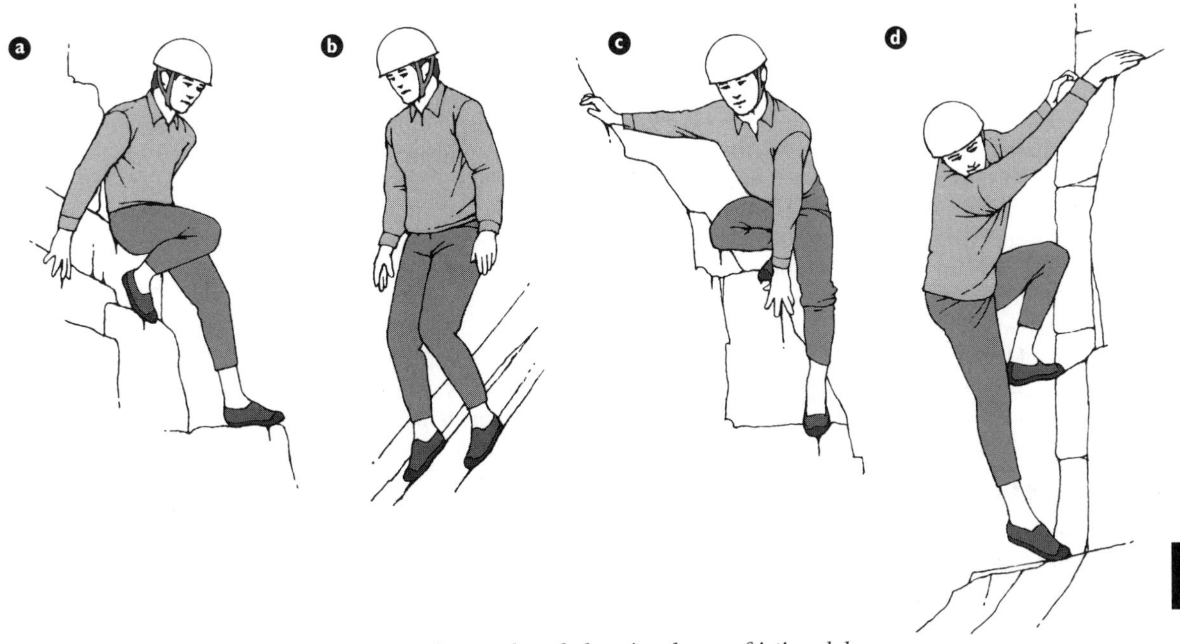

Fig. 12-38. Down-climbing: a, facing out on low-angle rock; b, going down a friction slab; c, facing sideways on steeper rock; d, facing in on steep rock.

Keep hands low and use down-pressure holds whenever possible. Keep your weight over your feet to maximize friction, especially when going down slabs. It may help to keep your center of gravity low, with knees well bent (fig. 12-38b). As the rock steepens, turn sideways, leaning away from the rock for better ability to see the route (fig. 12-38c). If the angle gets even steeper, face into the rock (fig. 12-38d).

STYLE AND ETHICS

Climbers debate endlessly over which styles are fair and which are less than sporting and over which practices are harmful to the environment and which are not. Climbers soon discover that getting to the end of the pitch or the top of the peak is not the only goal—another is getting there in a way that feels right, that respects the rock, and that tests a climber's skill and resolve. These are matters of style and ethics.

The terms "style" and "ethics" are sometimes used interchangeably by climbers, but *style* is generally an individual attribute, while *ethics* pertains to overall application of the pursuit. In other words, style refers to each climber's personal mode of climbing; for example, is it fair to say you have led a first ascent if you first climbed the route on a top rope? Ethics pertain to issues concerning preservation of the rock itself.

DIVERSITY OF STYLES

Styles change and attitudes evolve, but the core of the debate on climbing styles is about how to maintain the challenge of climber against rock and how to play the game in a way that fairly tests the climber.

Climbers adhering to traditional style prefer to climb each route strictly from the ground up, with no help from such aids as top ropes or pre-placed protection such as bolts. New routes are explored and protected only on lead. This type of climbing characterizes rock climbing in the alpine setting, but it is also found at many popular crags.

Climbers following the European-influenced sport climbing style are more likely to find other techniques acceptable as well. This can include inspecting the route on rappel before trying to lead it from below. It can also mean cleaning the route (removing protection placed by the lead climber or by another climber) and perhaps pre-placing protection on rappel. Routes may be climbed with multiple falls, by resting on the rope while checking out the next move (hangdogging), or by rehearsing moves with the help of a top rope. These techniques have made it possible to climb harder and harder routes with the climber assuming less risk.

Often, alpine climbers, due to the commitment and remoteness of climbs, will pull on gear or stand on a sling to climb through a hard section with greater speed and safety. Just as alpine climbers can improve their technique by cross-training with sport climbing, they will also benefit from a knowledge of aid climbing. (See Chapter 15, Aid and Big Wall Climbing.)

A particular climbing area may lend itself more to one style than another because of the type of rock, the difficulty of the routes, or the prevailing style among the local climbers. In the world of climbing, there is room for a diversity of styles, and most climbers experience a variety of them.

ETHICS AND THE ROCK

The subject of ethics has to do with respecting the rock and every person's chance to use it. Unlike climbing style, ethics involves personal decisions that do affect others' experience and enjoyment. This includes the sticky question of the manner in which bolts are placed on a route. Are bolts that are placed on rappel different from—less "ethical" than—bolts placed on the lead? Some climbers may argue that bolts placed while on rappel rob others of the chance to try the route from the ground up, and such bolts are often placed at less-convenient places than bolts would be if they were placed on a ground-up ascent. But other climbers may say that placing the bolts on rappel gives them a chance at a route that otherwise would be unclimbable at the present time.

Each area has its own tradition of what styles and ethics are acceptable. Visiting climbers should observe the local standards, which are usually described in local guidebooks, as well as any land management regulations. Sometimes locals may disagree among themselves. This book does not try to resolve issues of style and ethics, but there is general agreement on a couple of principles.

Preservation of the rock is paramount. Chipping the rock to create new holds is unacceptable and destroys a natural feature—and who knows? It may be climbed someday as it is. Although bolt-protected routes are common in many areas, bolting should not be indiscriminate. In the mountains or other wilderness areas, away from concentrated centers of rock climbing, it is particularly important to preserve the environment for those who follow. If possible, stick to clean climbing, using only removable gear for protection. (See Chapter 13, Rock Protection, for more on this.)

It is almost never justifiable to add a bolt to an existing route (retro-bolting). If you feel you cannot safely climb the route as it is, do not try it. Retro-bolting usually occurs when a consensus of local climbers agree that more bolts should be placed to promote safety and enjoyment. This may occur with the agreement of the first ascensionists.

There should be no objection to replacement of an old bolt with a newer, stronger one at an established belay or rappel point, provided you have the necessary skills and experience.

COURTESY

Climbers should keep others in mind when they are out climbing. If a climbing party is moving up a multipitch route at a pace that is much slower than that of the people behind them, the first group should let the following party pass at a safe spot, such as a belay ledge. Passing can be awkward or dangerous on some longer, harder routes, so a party traveling more slowly than the norm for such a route may leave many frustrated climbers waiting for several hours or having to retreat.

Beware of tackling climbs that are beyond your personal abilities. Try climbs at your limit on the crags rather than in the mountains. If inexperience gets a climbing party in trouble in the mountains, they may involve other climbers in a time-consuming and dangerous rescue of their party. Come prepared to handle the possibilities inherent in the chosen climb. Aim to be self-reliant within your climbing party and capable of self-rescue. This competence will add to climbers' confidence and enjoyment of the alpine environment.

CONNECTING THE ROPE TO PROTECTION • NATURAL PROTECTION • FIXED PROTECTION • REMOVABLE PROTECTION • ROCK PROTECTION ETIQUETTE • BUILDING SKILLS

Chapter 13
ROCK PROTECTION

The "rack and rope" are, collectively, the rock climber's protection. The rope connects two climbers—one leading a pitch while the other belays. Protection, or "pro," connects them both to the rock face. The belayer is connected to an anchor that can be natural, such as trees, or formed from several pieces of protection. To limit a fall, the climber on lead places protection from the rack (the collection of gear used for protection) periodically while climbing.

The quality and location of the protection that the lead climber places largely determine the consequences of a potential fall. If a climber falls while leading, the length of the fall will be about twice the distance between the climber and the last point of protection, plus rope stretch (fig. 13-1). If the last piece placed pulls out, the fall increases in length by double the distance to the next piece that holds. Skill both in selecting good locations for protection and in actually making the placement makes for far safer climbers.

CONNECTING THE ROPE TO PROTECTION

Carabiners and runners (fig. 13-2a) are the tools you use to connect the climbing rope to protection. The carabiner should almost always be used in the down-and-out position: the gate should point down and away from the rock surface (fig. 13-2b). This position lessens the chance of accidental (and potentially disastrous) opening of the carabiner gate during a fall. The rope itself should be clipped in so that it runs freely through the carabiner in the direction of travel (fig. 13-2c): the rope should travel from the rock surface upward through the carabiner and then out toward the climber. If the route does not take the climber straight upward, the rope exits the carabiner on one side or the other; it should exit on the side opposite from the gate. This minimizes the chance that the rope will twist across the gate and open it during a fall.

Runners serve to lengthen the distance between the point of protection and the rope. This helps to isolate

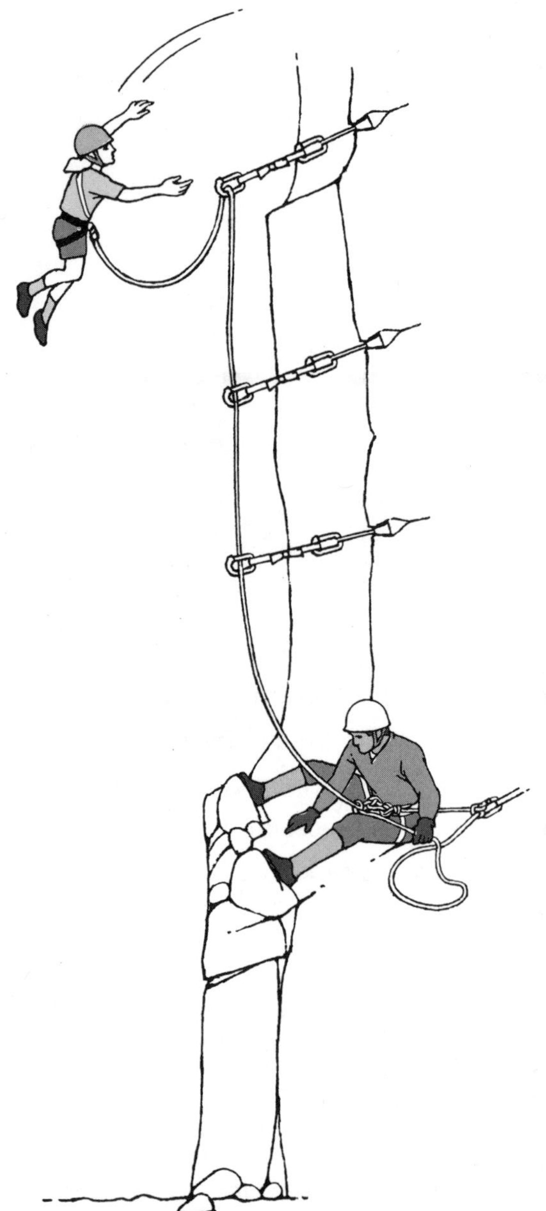

Fig. 13-1. Leader fall with intermediate points of protection in place.

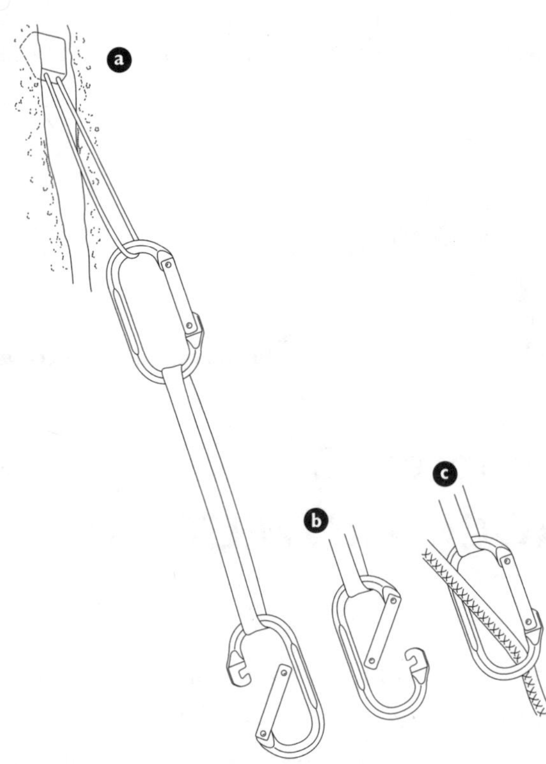

Fig. 13-2. Correct down-and-out positioning of a carabiner: a, clip the carabiner in a downward direction; b, then rotate it out and away from the rock (gate opening is now down and facing out from rock); c, rope clipped through carabiner in direction of travel.

rope movement from the protection, keeping protection from wiggling or "walking" from its intended placement, and also helps to minimize friction or rope drag on the climbing rope by allowing it to run in more of a straight line. Runners can connect directly to natural protection (fig. 13-3a, b, and c) or, rarely, to preexisting fixed protection (such as that shown in Figure 13-8) without the use of an intervening carabiner.

NATURAL PROTECTION

Trees and rock features can provide excellent protection, conserve gear, and offer a quicker alternative than a gear placement, but carefully evaluate them for stability and strength. "Test before you trust" is a good rule. Be wary of rock that is brittle, vegetation that is poorly rooted, and other suggestions of weakness. An error in judgment could result not only in failed protection but also in a rock or tree crashing down upon the climber, the belayer, or other parties on the route.

Trees and large bushes provide the most obvious points of attachment but do not trust a dead, brittle,

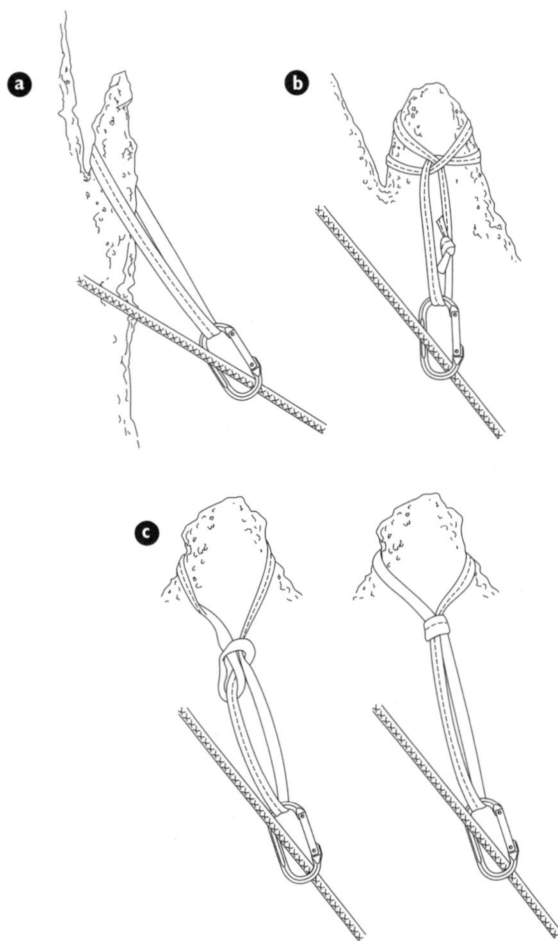

Fig. 13-3. Attaching the rope to a rock feature: a, using one runner and one carabiner to link a point of natural protection with the rope; b, securing a runner to a rock horn with a clove hitch; c, slinging a horn with a slipknot on a runner, with the dressed slipknot shown at right.

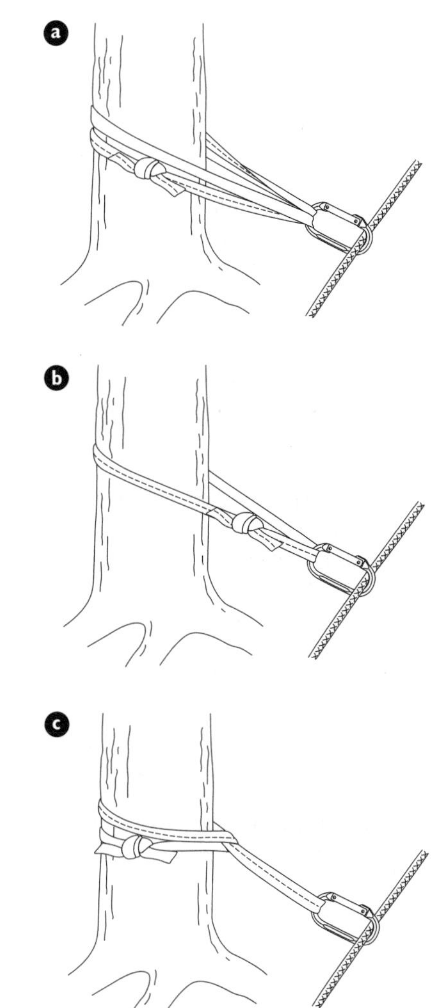

Fig. 13-4. Attaching a runner to a tree trunk: a, looped around the trunk, the ends clipped together with a carabiner; b, retied around trunk; c, girth-hitched around trunk.

weak, or loose tree or shrub. Look for a healthy trunk with live branches and a solid root system. If there is any question, test smaller trees by pushing against them with one foot. Runners commonly are looped around the base of the trunk, with the ends clipped together with a carabiner (fig. 13-4a). You can also untie a runner and then retie it around the trunk (fig. 13-4b). A third method is to use a girth hitch (fig. 13-4c). The runner usually should be as close to the roots as possible, although with a strong tree the runner may be placed higher if necessary. Often a double runner or longer is needed.

Rock features—horns, columns, rock tunnels, chockstones, large and flat-bottomed boulders—are other common forms of natural protection. In evaluating a rock feature, consider its relative hardness, how crumbly it is, and whether it is firmly attached to the rock around it. Attempt to move the rock, being careful not to pull it loose. Whack it a few times with a hand or fist. Beware of hollow sounds or brittleness.

13

Horns (also called knobs or chicken heads, depending on their shape and size) are the most common type of natural rock protection. If there is any question about rock horns, test them by pushing against them with one foot. To attach to a rock horn, a runner can be looped over the horn and clipped in to the rope (see Figure 13-3a), but it may be pulled off the horn by rope movement. Use a clove hitch (see Figure 13-3b) or slipknot (see Figure 13-3c) to tighten the runner around the horn to help prevent it from slipping off. The slipknot can be tied easily with one hand and requires less sling material than a girth hitch or clove hitch.

To attach to a rock column or chockstone or through a rock tunnel, first thread a runner around the feature, then connect the ends with a carabiner (fig. 13-5). Alternatively, secure the runner to the rock feature with a girth hitch or untie the runner and retie it after threading it through the point of protection.

Extra care should be taken when using freestanding boulders. They should not move or rock when tested. Consider not just the size but the shape of the boulder, what it rests on, and changing conditions such as snow or ice. Avoid any feature with a rounded bottom or that narrows at the base, as well as features that rest on gravel, sand, or downsloping ledges. Sling boulders around the base. Keep the pulling point low to minimize leverage.

Natural protection used for anchors on popular routes often accumulates slings as parties rappel from a route and leave them behind. Do not trust these slings with your life without inspecting and testing their strength. Sunlight, weather, and age can degrade them.

See "Natural Anchors" in Chapter 10, Belaying, for related information about selecting natural anchors.

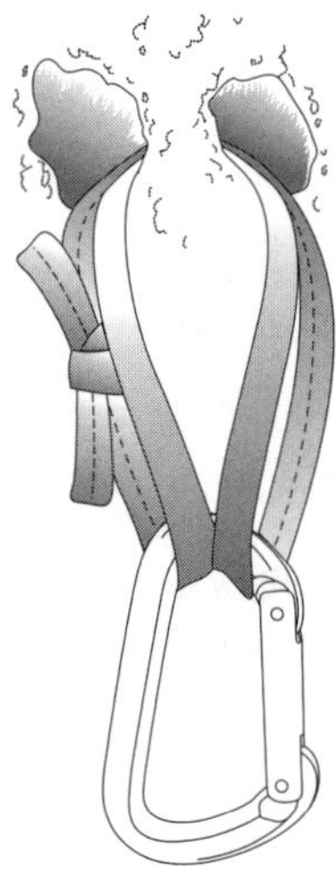

Fig. 13-5. Attaching a runner to a rock tunnel.

FIXED PROTECTION

On established routes, climbers may encounter previously placed bolts and pitons (see also "Fixed Anchors" in Chapter 10, Belaying). Climbers also may encounter removable protection that became fixed when someone could not remove it. On rock climbing topo maps (see Figure 14-3 in Chapter 14, Leading on Rock), bolts and fixed pitons are often shown as "x" and "fp," respectively.

BOLTS

Bolts are most commonly seen in sport climbing areas, but they may also be found on traditional or aid climbing routes. Bolt hangers allow carabiners to be attached to bolts (fig. 13-6a and b). Chains are sometimes found at sport climbing anchors (fig. 13-6c) to facilitate rappeling.

A well-placed bolt will last for years, but age and weather can compromise it. Be especially wary of ¼-inch bolts, which were placed primarily in the 1960s and 1970s. Bolts measuring ⅜ to ½ inch in diameter have been used since the mid-1980s and are now the standard. Standard metric bolts are 10, 12, and 14 millimeters in diameter.

Visually check both the bolt and its hanger for signs of weakness, especially for cracks, excessive corrosion, or brittleness. A rust streak below the bolt indicates metal wear. Do not trust an old sheet-metal-style hanger with heavy rust. Test whether the bolt is securely anchored into the rock by clipping in to the bolt hanger with a carabiner and trying to pull the bolt around or out. Any bolt that can be moved in any direction, however slightly, is probably not trustworthy. Avoid banging on the bolt, which weakens it. Back up any suspect bolt with another point of protection wherever possible.

If the bolt and its placement seem solid, use a carabiner to clip a runner to the bolt hanger. At a fixed anchor with chains hanging from the bolt hanger, clip the bolt hanger if at all possible to free up the links for rappels (see Figure 13-6c). Some carabiners may not fit through the upper links.

Bolts without hangers can be reliable protection. If

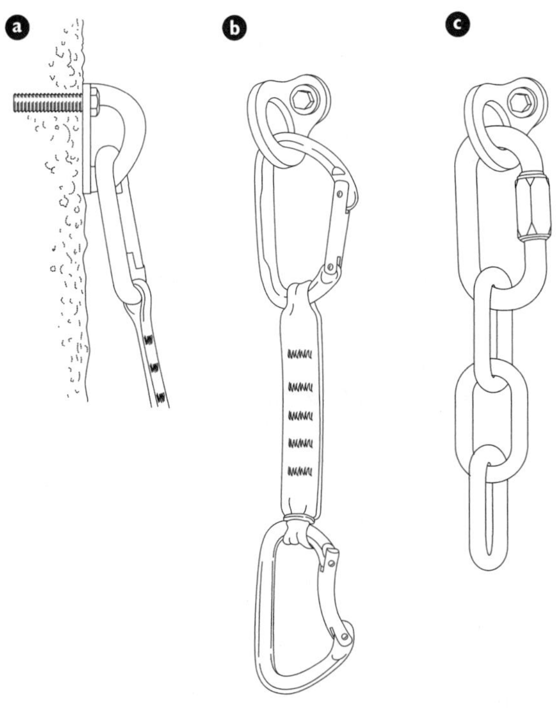

Fig. 13-6. Bolt and bolt hanger with a carabiner clipped in to the hanger: a, from the side; b, from the front; c, bolt hanger with quick link and chains.

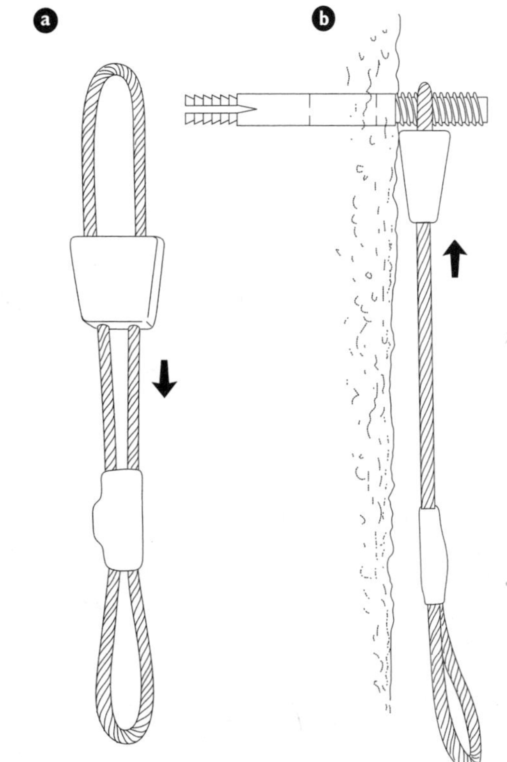

Fig. 13-7. Placing a wired chock on a hangerless bolt: a, create a loop by sliding the chock down its wires; b, slide the chock up its wires to form a noose around the bolt.

you anticipate hangerless bolts, carry extra hangers and nuts. If a bolt has no hanger, a last-resort solution is to slide a chock down its wire (fig. 13-7a), slip the upper wire around the bolt stud, and snug the chock against the bolt (fig. 13-7b). Use a runner attached to the lower end of the chock wire. The wire stopper may lever off if a nut is not added to the bolt.

PITONS

Pitons were commonly used in mountaineering through the 1970s but are rarely used today, because placing and removing them scars the rock. However, many pitons remain as fixed placements on various routes.

Pitons, even more than bolts, are vulnerable to weathering. Years of melt-freeze cycles widen cracks in the rock and loosen pitons. Examine pitons closely for signs of corrosion or weakness, and examine the cracks they are in for deterioration. Heavy use, failed attempts at removal, and falls on a piton can lead to cracks in the metal around the eye or other damage.

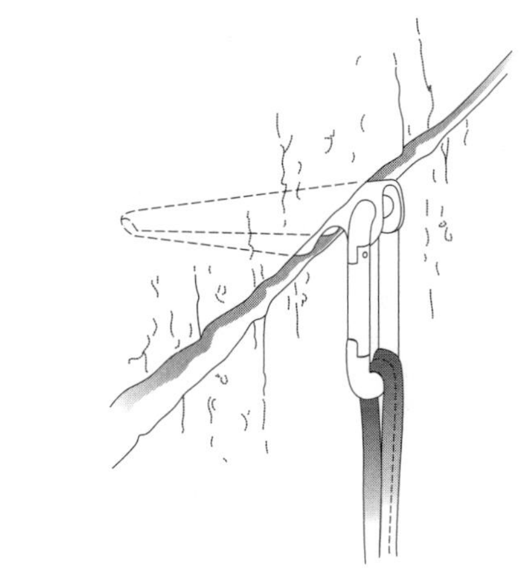

Fig. 13-8. Piton driven into rock: carabiner (with runner attached) clipped through piton's eye.

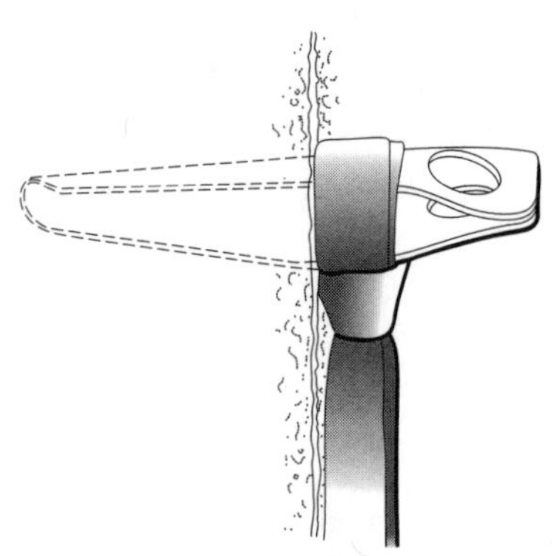

Fig. 13-9. Partially driven piton, with a runner girth-hitched to it close to the rock to reduce the leverage.

Ideally the piton was driven in all the way, with its eye close to the rock and the piton perpendicular to the likely direction of pull (fig. 13-8). If the piton appears strong, secure, and in good condition, clip a carabiner (with runner attached) through the eye of the piton. Place the carabiner so that under a load it will not be levered against the rock.

If a piton is driven in only partially but otherwise is secure, try to hammer it in. Use a runner to tie the piton off next to the rock with a girth hitch, clove hitch, or slipknot (fig. 13-9) to reduce the leverage on the piton under the impact of a fall. Thoroughly inspect the setup, especially noting whether the piton has sharp edges that could cut the runner. Do not rely on this setup if there is better protection available.

OTHER FIXED PIECES

Removable protection may be abandoned when a party is unable to remove it. Do not trust removable gear that someone else placed. When these "fixed" pieces are encountered, examine them carefully and consider that the party may have abandoned it as the oldest piece on the rack that they were retiring anyway.

In addition to examining the gear and the rock where the piece is placed, note whether the sling attached to the chock appears to be worn or damaged. Because of these chocks' questionable integrity, consider them primarily as backup protection.

REMOVABLE PROTECTION

Removable protection includes the various types of artificial protection other than bolts and pitons. Removable protection generally consists of a metal device that can be secured into the rock, with a sling for use in linking the metal piece to the rope. Removable protection must be placed in high-quality rock to maximize strength.

For environmental reasons, using removable protection is preferred to placing new pitons or bolts because it leaves no scars on the rock.

Removable protection generally falls into one of two categories: without moving parts (passive) or with moving parts (active). Passive removable protection pieces, also known as chocks, are made from a single piece of metal and a connecting sling or cable. A typical placement is into a constriction in a crack. Shapes can vary from a tapered wedge, often called a nut or stopper (see Figure 13-10), to a deformed hexagonal tube, often called a hex (see Figure 13-11), to the more unusually shaped passive camming pieces such as the Tricam (also

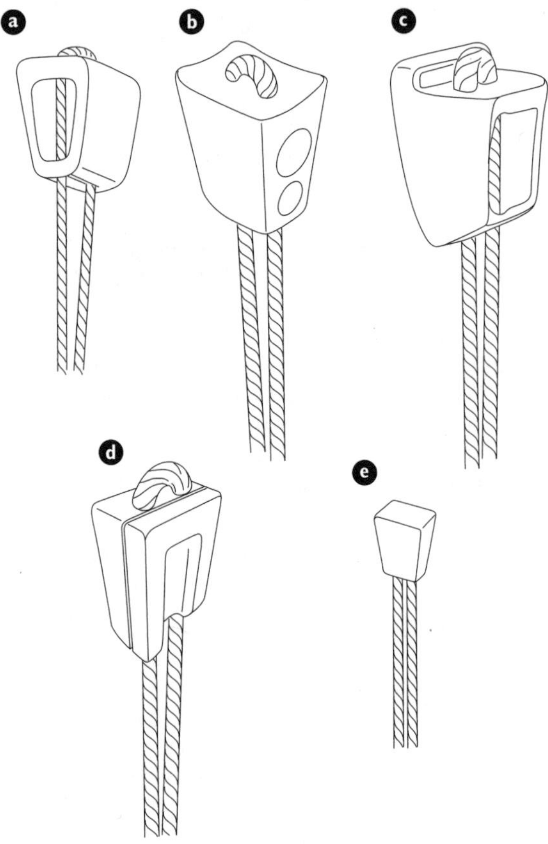

Fig. 13-10. Passive wedging chocks: a, stopper; b, curved nut; c, wall nut; d, offset nut; e, micronut.

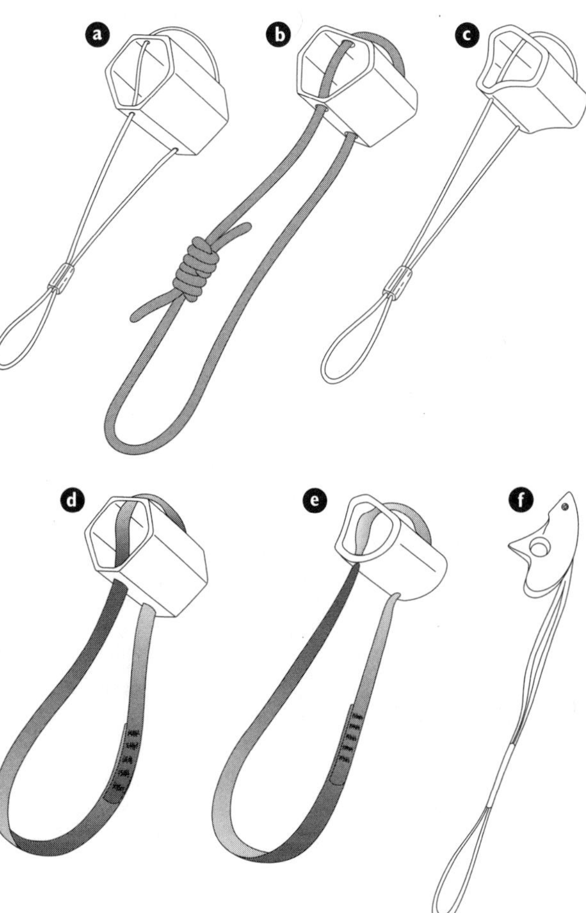

Fig. 13-11. Passive camming chocks: a, wired hex; b, hex slung with high-strength cord; c, wired curved hex; d, hex slung with high-strength webbing; e, curved hex slung with high-strength webbing; f, Tricam.

see Figure 13-11) that can be used in a torquing orientation, with counterforce exerted between the piece's point and its curved side.

Tube chocks, often called Big Bros (see Figure 13-13) do have movable parts—they telescope out to a desired size—but they are passively placed much like a hex or a Tricam.

Spring-loaded camming devices (SLCDs), which are commonly called cams, are active devices that use spring mechanisms to allow portions of the device to cam against opposite walls of a crack (see Figure 13-14). Loading the device increases the pressure against the rock. Triggers on the device retract the parts, allowing insertion and removal.

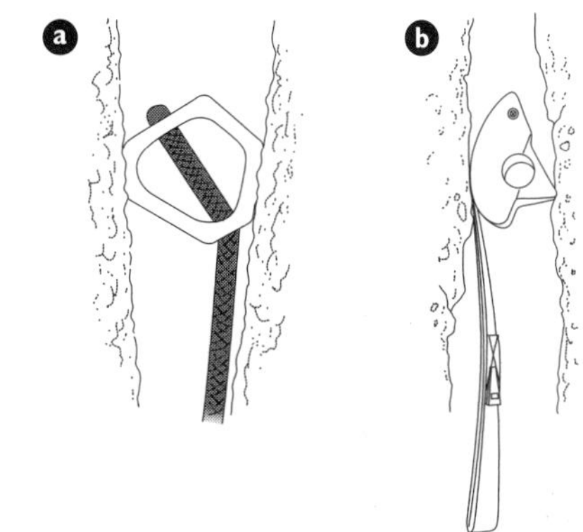

Fig. 13-12. Passive camming chocks in a vertical crack: a, Hexentric; b, Tricam.

Multiple chock shapes fit multiple rock cracks, but chocks are strongest when the most metal is in contact with the rock. Chocks have a primary placement direction, but many chocks also are designed for multiple placement options to maximize adaptability. Manufacturers rate the breaking strength of gear, and in general bigger chocks have higher breaking strength.

PASSIVE REMOVABLE PROTECTION

Passive wedging chocks come in a wide variety of shapes and sizes, but most have a generally wedge-shaped appearance (see Figure 13-10). They are called by many names, from brand names such as Stoppers to simply wired nuts or wedges.

These chocks are narrower at the base than at the top (fig. 13-10a), which lets them slip down into a constriction. Variations include chocks with flat faces, chocks with curved faces (fig. 13-10b), chocks with more-curved faces (fig. 13-10c), and chocks with notches or grooves in the faces (fig. 13-10d) and sides that may be parallel or offset.

Some of the smallest wedging-type chocks, referred to as micronuts, are designed for very thin cracks and for aid climbing (fig. 13-10e). Manufacturers construct the nuts with softer metals so that the rock will bite into them better than it will into standard aluminum chocks, but this also makes micronuts less durable, with breaking strength not much more than body weight. The thinness of the micronut's cable makes it more prone to damage from normal use. Inspect the

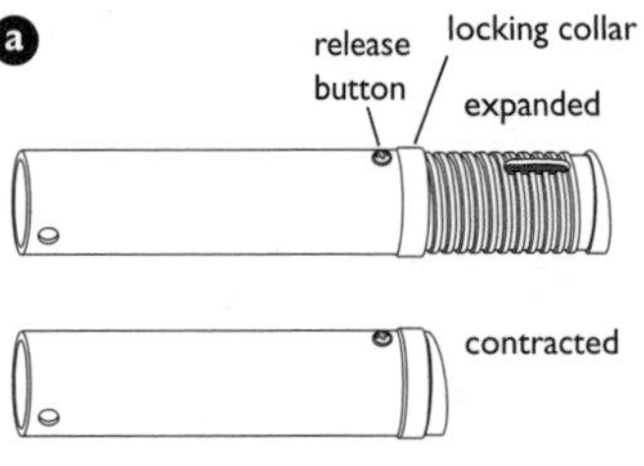

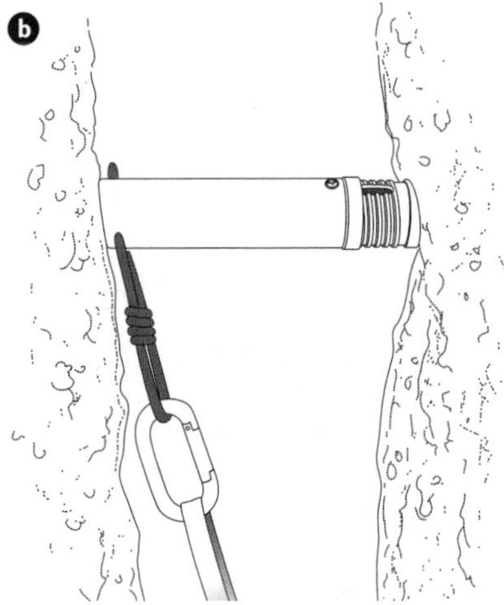

Fig. 13-13. Spring-loaded tube chock: a, contracted and expanded; b, correctly placed in a vertical crack, where it acts as a passive cam.

micronut and cable often for nicks and other signs of wear, and retire it if there is any cable damage.

Hexentrics and other similar chocks take their name from their hexagonal shape (fig. 13-11a through e). Each pair of opposing sides on a hex is a different distance apart, permitting three different placement options per piece. The off-center sling creates the camming action (fig. 13-12a), or the piece can be wedged in a constriction. More rounded versions of the hex work on the same principles. Some hex-shaped chocks come with wire cables or sewn runners, and others come with holes through which cord must be threaded (see Figure 13-11b).

Tricams have curved rails along one side opposite from a point, or stinger, on the other side (fig. 13-11f). Camming action is produced by running the sling between the curved side rails and setting the stinger in a small depression or irregularity in the crack (fig. 13-12b); the load on the sling rotates the device into the rock with a camlike action. Tricams also can be used as passive devices simply set into a constriction (see Figure 13-20b), particularly those that narrow sharply.

Another device that acts as a passive cam (even though it is spring loaded) is the Big Bro, a tube chock with a spring-loaded inner sleeve that telescopes out to bridge a crack when a release button is pressed (fig. 13-13a). The extended sleeve is then locked into place by spinning the collar down snugly against the outer tube. The sling is attached at one side so a torquing action adds to stability when loaded (fig. 13-13b). Tube chocks are specialized for wide parallel cracks (off-widths).

Most wedge-shaped chocks and some hex-shaped chocks are slung with wire cable, which is much stronger than cord or webbing of the same size. The stiffness of the wire cable sometimes aids in placing the chock. Other chocks have sewn slings of cord, nylon webbing, or high-strength materials such as Spectra. A few are available without slings, and the climber must tie them. The sling material should be rated for climbing forces and should be twice as long as the desired sling length, plus about 12 inches (30 centimeters) for the knot and 1-inch (2.5-centimeter) tails—or 28 to 32 inches (71 to 81 centimeters) of material to make a loop 8 to 10 inches (20 to 25 centimeters) long. Due to the greater stiffness and lower friction of Spectra and other high-strength materials, a triple fisherman's bend is recommended for tying the sling (see Figure 13-11b). Inspect cables and slings regularly for damage, and follow manufacturer's instructions for replacing or repairing them.

ACTIVE REMOVABLE PROTECTION

Spring-loaded protection devices expand the limits of free climbing by providing protection that can be placed easily with one hand and that can adapt to a variety of cracks.

Spring-Loaded Camming Devices (SLCDs or Cams)

The first spring-loaded cams, called Friends, were introduced in the mid-1970s. Now SLCDs are manufactured in a wide size range and with multiple designs (see Figure 13-14).

The basic design has four blades—called a four-cam

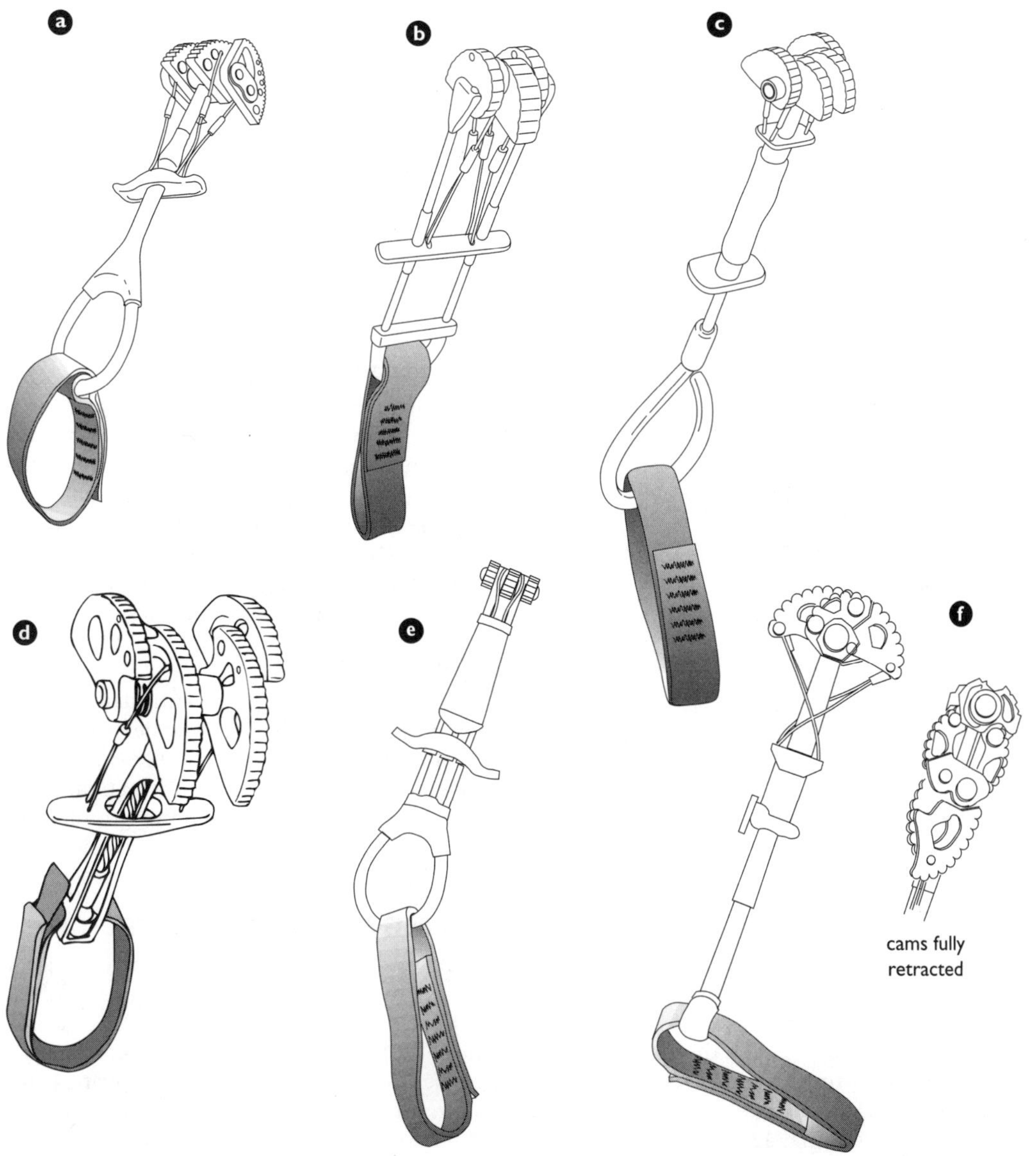

Fig. 13-14. Spring-loaded camming devices (SLCDs): a, Camalot C4; b, Metolius three-cam unit (TCU); c, Alien; d, Technical Friend; e, Camalot C3; f, Omega Pacific Link Cam.

unit—that rotate from one or two axles, connected to a trigger mechanism on a stem. When the trigger is pulled, the blades retract, narrowing the profile of the device for placement in a crack or pocket (fig. 13-15b). When the trigger is released, the blades open up against the sides of the rock (fig. 13-15b).

The cams move independently of each other, permitting each to rotate to the point needed for maximum contact with the rock. This movement sets the device in place. If you fall, the stem is pulled downward or

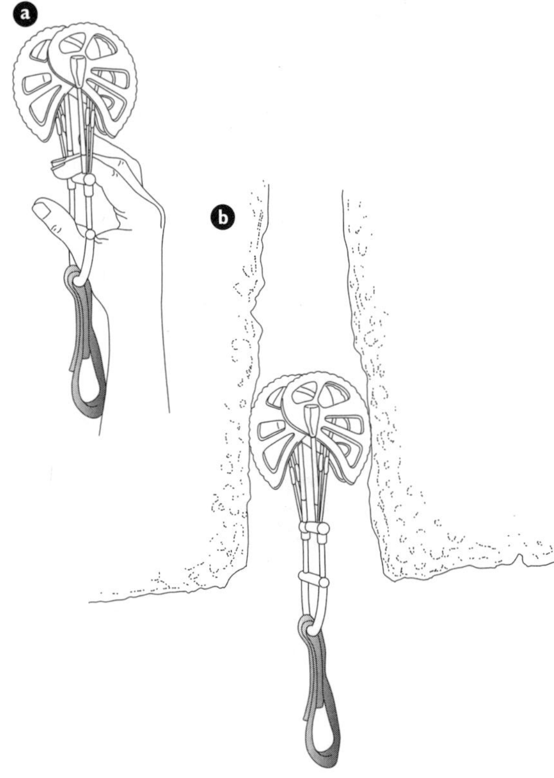

Fig. 13-15. Spring-loaded camming device (SLCD): a, retracted; b, correctly placed in a vertically oriented crack.

outward, increasing the camming action and increasing the outward pressure of the cams on the rock.

Variations of SLCDs include double-axle cams that can be used in the totally open position—called Camalots (fig. 13-14a is a C4)—and those that cannot; specialized cams that fit into narrower placements (side to side) such as three-cam units (fig. 13-14b; called TCUs) and Aliens (fig. 13-14c), as well as two-cam units (not shown); cams with rigid stems or flexible stems; specialized cams designed to hold better in sandstone—called Fat Cams; cams with different trigger designs; specialized cams, such as the Hybrid Alien, designed for flaring cracks; lightweight cams that cover wide ranges (fig. 13-14d is a Technical Friend); cams for small cracks (fig. 13-14e is a C3); and extended-range cams (fig. 13-14f) that maximize the range of a single piece of gear. Some manufacturers indicate the optimum camming range with colored dots.

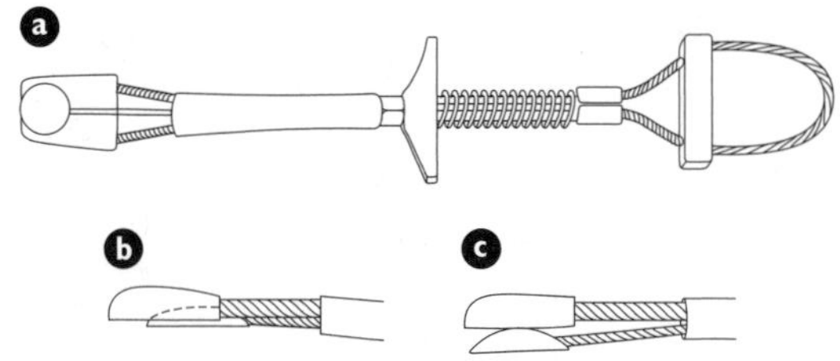

Fig. 13-16. Spring-loaded wedging device: a, Camp USA ball nut; b, contracted; c, expanded.

Spring-Loaded Wedges

Spring-loaded wedges (fig. 13-16a) use a small sliding piece to expand the profile of the chock after it is placed in a crack. To place the wedge, first retract the smaller piece by pulling back on the spring-loaded trigger, thereby narrowing the profile of the chock so it can be inserted into a thin crack (fig. 13-16b). Then release the trigger, permitting the smaller piece to press up between the larger piece and the rock, filling in the gap and increasing the area of the chock that is in contact with the rock (fig. 13-16c).

Spring-loaded wedges work particularly well in small, parallel-sided cracks where other devices may be difficult or impossible to place. But, like micronuts, these chocks have less holding power than larger wedges because of the smaller surface area gripping the rock and because the spring may allow some movement—or "walking"—within the crack after placement.

PLACING REMOVABLE PROTECTION

Placing solid protection is both art and science. Developing an eye for good placement sites, and then placing the right piece into the right place securely and efficiently, are two skills that require practice to perfect (see the "General Considerations in Placing Removable Protection" sidebar).

Good placements start with good rock; in poor rock even apparently good placements may not hold a fall at all. In good rock look for constrictions in a crack, irregularities in crack surfaces, and prominences behind a flake. A good site for protection placement has solid rock sides—free of vegetation, dirt, or deteriorating rock. Avoid crystals or irregularities that may not be bonded strongly to the surrounding rock. Check for loose blocks or flakes by shaking or hitting the rock with your fist; if the rock moves or sounds hollow, look for a better spot.

The next consideration is the type of protection to use. Wedges work best when placed behind constrictions in a vertically oriented crack. Hexes or Tricams work well in horizontal cracks and behind small irregularities in cracks or flakes where it may be difficult or impossible to position wedges. Tricams often are the only pieces that will work in shallow, flaring pockets.

SLCDs are easier to place, but they are relatively heavy and expensive, and placement integrity can be more difficult to evaluate. However, SLCDs often work in parallel-sided or slightly flaring cracks where it is difficult or impossible to get anything else to hold.

More than one type of device may work in a given spot. Make a choice based on ease of placement and what may be needed later on the pitch. Ration the pieces that will be needed higher up.

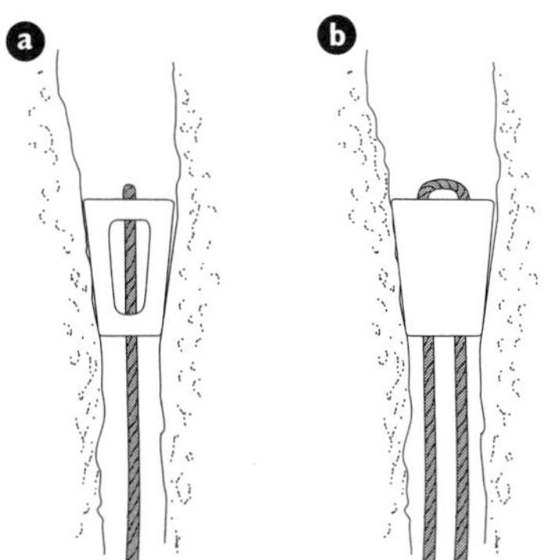

Fig. 13-18. Placement of passive wedging chocks: a, wide sides are in contact with the rock, a stronger placement; b, ends are in contact with the rock, a weaker placement.

Placing Passive Wedges

The basic procedure for placing passive wedges is quite simple: Find a crack with a constriction at some point, place an appropriate piece of protection above the constriction (fig. 13-17a), slide it into place (fig. 13-17b), and pull down on the sling to set the chock firmly in position (fig. 13-17c). Slot the chock completely into the crack, with as much of the chock surface as possible contacting the rock. Use your fingers to set the piece in the best spot, although sometimes threading the cable behind a protrusion is the best option.

The best choice of chock for any given placement is whichever size and shape offers the best fit. As a general rule, greater contact between chock and rock means a stronger placement. Therefore, larger chocks generally are stronger than smaller ones, and wide-side placements (fig. 13-18a) generally are stronger than end placements (fig. 13-18b and 13-19b); however, the fit is most important. Micronuts must be placed especially carefully and have excellent contact with the rock, given their low strength.

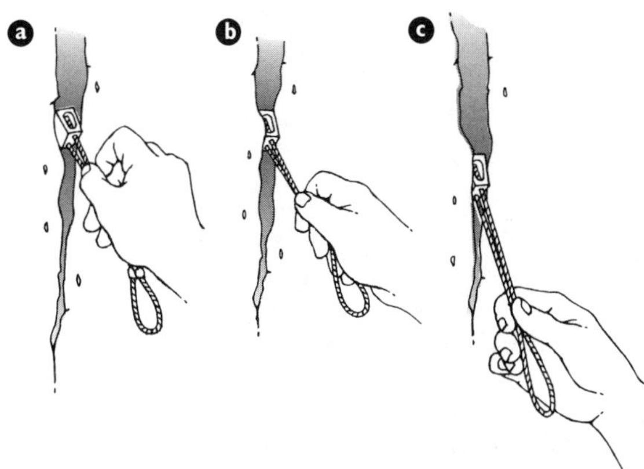

Fig. 13-17. Placing a passive wedge: a, place wedge into crack above constriction; b, slide it into place; c, tug on chock sling to set it.

Evaluate chock placements from multiple directions if possible. Even if the front looks good, the back may not be in contact with the rock. If it looks doubtful from other angles, find a better place or piece. Carefully evaluate the potential effects of rope drag and the direction of loading in the event of a fall. In vertical cracks, setting a chock with a downward pull usually keeps the chock in place, although the rope may pull sideways or upward. In horizontal cracks, chocks will be pulled outward. Climbers can also place two chocks to equalize or oppose for greater security (techniques discussed in "Opposition Placement" and "Equalizing Protection," later in this chapter).

Placing Hexes and Tricams

In addition to being used as a chock in a constriction, a hex or a Tricam also is designed to cam under load. In parallel-sided cracks, this feature must be used for the placement to work. A good placement is tight enough to have good contact with the rock and to avoid being displaced by the rope, yet positioned to allow camming action under load.

In vertical cracks, the piece will be more secure if it is placed just above a constriction or irregularity in the

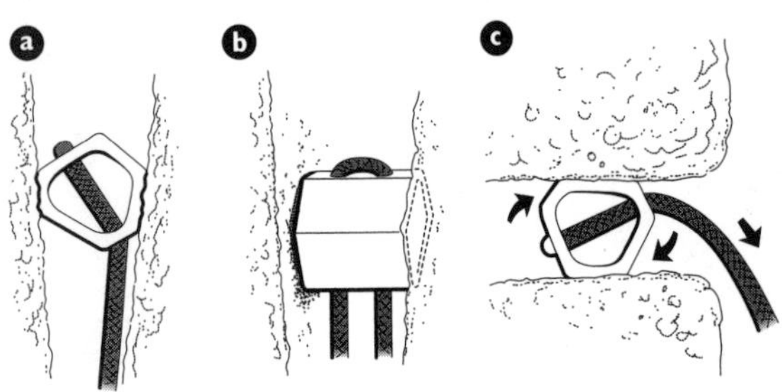

Fig. 13-19. *Placements of a hex: a, in a vertical crack as a passive cam; b, sideways in a vertical crack as a passive wedging chock; c, in a horizontal crack as a passive cam.*

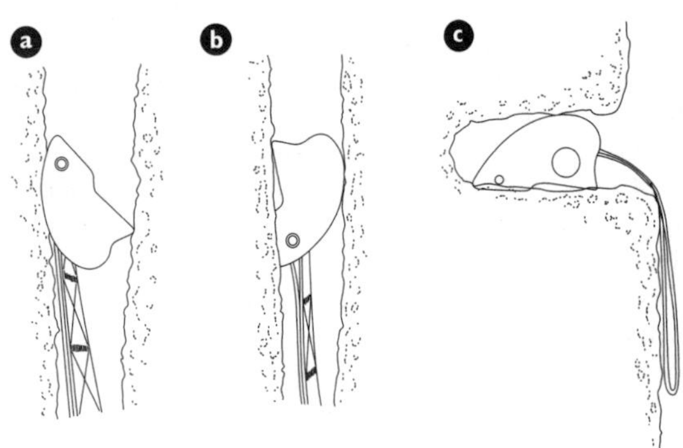

Fig. 13-20. *Placements of the Tricam: a, in a vertical crack, as a passive cam; b, in a vertical crack, as a passive wedging chock; c, in a horizontal crack, as a passive cam.*

crack and if it is oriented so that the camming action pulls it more tightly against any irregularity (fig. 13-19a and fig. 13-20a).

In horizontal cracks, the piece should be placed so that the downward or outward pull of a fall would maximize camming action. Hexes should be positioned so that the sling exits the crack closer to the roof than to the floor (fig. 13-19c) to maximize camming action. Tricams should be placed to optimize overall fit, and the sling and rails can be either down or up (Figure 13-20c shows rails and sling up).

Placing Spring-Loaded Camming Devices

An SLCD can be placed very quickly. It is the device of choice for parallel-sided cracks that lack the constrictions

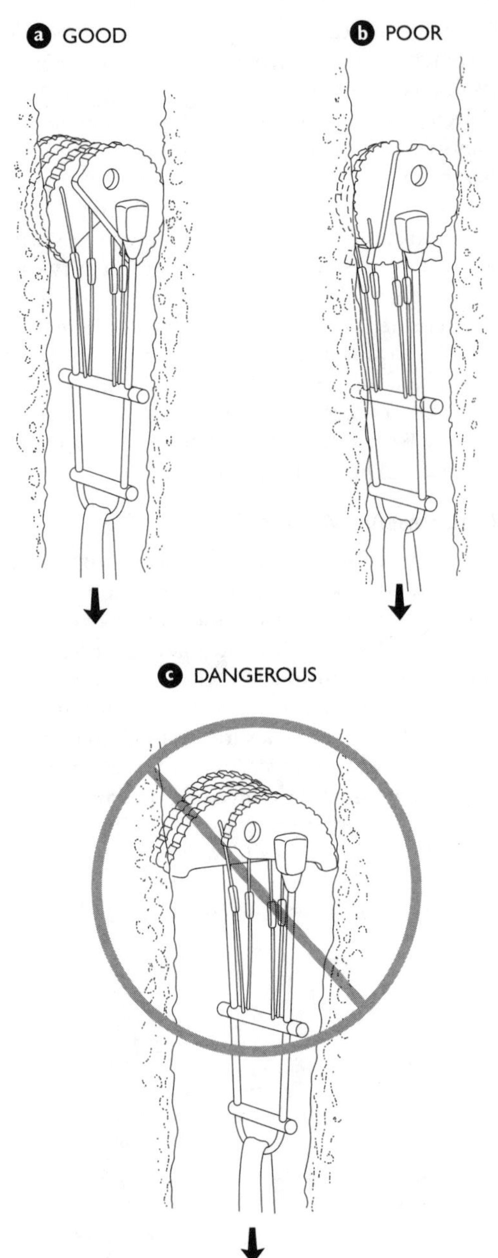

Fig. 13-21. *Placement of spring-loaded camming devices (SLCDs): a, cams expanded to midpoint—stem in likely direction of pull (good); b, cams are over-retracted—hard to remove (poor); c, cams are overexpanded—failure likely (dangerous).*

TIPS FOR PLACING SLCDS

- **Be aware that the device may become jammed** in the crack and impossible to remove if the cams are fully retracted in the placement (see Figure 13-21b).
- **Do not overexpand the cams** since little camming action can then occur (see Figure 13-21c) and the device would be more likely to pull loose during a fall.
- **Remember SLCDs can be pulled out by a hard fall in soft rock,** such as sandstone or limestone, even when they are placed properly.
- **Be certain all cams contact the rock** so the placement is stable.
- **Place SLCDs with their stems pointing in the direction of pull from a fall.**
- **Make a careful placement and use a suitable runner** to minimize "walking": Rope movement can cause the entire piece to "walk," moving it either deeper into or out of the crack, jeopardizing stability of the placement.
- **In a horizontal crack,** place a three-cam unit's side with two cams on the bottom for best stability. **In vertical cracks,** place the two cams on whichever side provides the best fit in the crack.
- **Carry a few SLCDs and ration them carefully,** because of the added weight per piece compared with nuts, even though SLCDs work well when chocks do not.

or irregularities needed for passive chocks. It also can be used in slightly flaring cracks and in cracks under roofs where other chocks may be difficult to place or questionable to use.

Within their given range, the three or four individual cams in the device will adjust to the width and irregularities of the crack as the trigger is released. The stem of the device must be pointed in the likely direction of pull during a fall to provide maximum strength and to help keep it from being pulled out of position (fig. 13-21). SLCDs work best in harder rock such as granite rather than sandstone and in cracks with relatively even sides.

When placed well (see the "Tips for Placing SLCDs" sidebar), SLCDs can protect against somewhat multidirectional loads, and climbers may use these to decrease chances of the zipper effect (see Chapter 14, Leading on Rock). After clipping a runner to the SLCD and rope, wiggle the rope and make sure the SLCD does not walk back in the crack.

If the SLCD being used has a solid stem rather than a flexible one, make sure that the stem will not be forced against the edge of the crack during a fall, since that could cause the stem to bend or break. This is especially important in horizontal or near-horizontal cracks, where the stem hangs out over the edge of the crack. A flexible-stem device is more reliable in this situation (fig. 13-22a). If a solid-stem device must be used, then place a loop through one of the holes in the stem (fig. 13-22b) so the force of a fall will be less likely to break the stem.

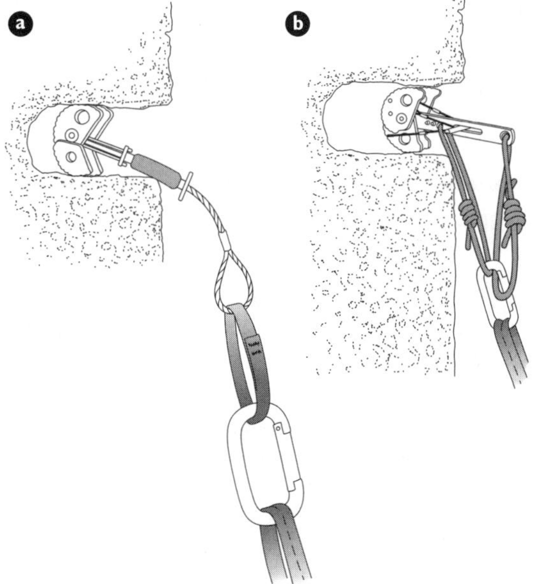

Fig. 13-22. Spring-loaded camming device (SLCD) placement in a horizontal crack: a, flexible cable stem can bend and adjust to the direction of pull; b, a tie-off loop can reduce the danger of solid-stem breakage.

Placing Spring-Loaded Wedges

Spring-loaded wedging chocks can be used almost anywhere that a passive wedge would be used, but they really come into their own in thin cracks, including parallel-sided cracks (fig. 13-23).

13

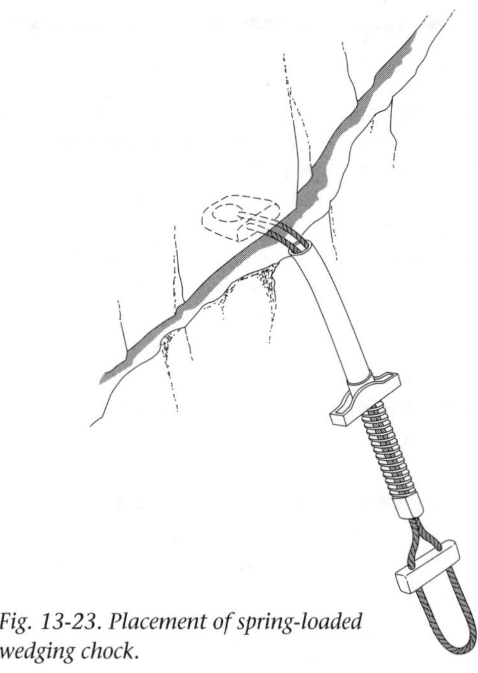

Fig. 13-23. Placement of spring-loaded wedging chock.

In placing spring-loaded wedges, select just the right size for the crack, because the placement size range for any one of these devices is quite narrow. They are susceptible to being pulled out of place by rope movement, so attach a runner to the piece. As with any piece of protection, place the device so it is strongest in the direction of the force of a potential fall.

OPPOSITION PLACEMENT

Sometimes a second chock must be placed in order to keep the initial one in position, such as the first placement on a pitch to avoid the zipper effect (see Chapter 14, Leading on Rock). Single placements can sometimes be dislodged by sideways or upward pulls on the rope as the lead climber advances, because of changes in the direction of the route (see Figure 14-10 in Chapter 14).

To form an opposition placement, place two pieces that will pull toward each other when linked. Use carabiners with slings to link the chocks. Ideally the chocks should be held together under a slight tension. Use clove hitches to tie a runner between the carabiners on the chock slings, then cinch up the runner; the climbing

GENERAL CONSIDERATIONS IN PLACING REMOVABLE PROTECTION

- **Select high-quality rock** and avoid rock that crumbles or flakes.
- **Learn to estimate the right chock size and shape** for a particular placement. Use your hands to size the crack to the equipment. The better your estimate, the more efficient the placement.
- **Often, cams or hexes are best in parallel cracks,** while offset cams or Tricams are best in flaring cracks. Chocks with slings or flexible stems are best in horizontal cracks.
- **Use your fingers to place the piece** just where you want it. Avoid dragging the chock blindly through a crack and hoping it catches.
- **Reinforce doubtful pieces** with another chock, use a load-limiting runner to decrease forces on the piece, or find a better placement.
- **Remember the climber who will be following** behind you and removing the protection. Make your placements secure, but also try to make them reasonably easy to remove and within reach of a shorter follower.
- **Let your follower know if an intricate series of moves was necessary** to place the piece, if possible, so your follower can reverse the moves and return your gear.
- **Avoid shallow placements** where chocks can easily pull out of the crack, but avoid very deep placements that are hard for the follower to retrieve.
- **Recheck the chock after it is placed.** Look to see that it is in good contact with the rock. Give the piece a strong tug in the direction of pull to set the piece and test the reliability of the placement.
- **Clip a runner between the chock and the rope** to minimize the effect of rope movement on the piece. An adequate length of runner not only prevents pulling on the piece but also helps prevent rope drag (see Chapter 14, Leading on Rock).
- **Use a cam or oppositional chocks as the first placement** to avoid the zipper effect caused by an outward or upward pull in a fall (see "Opposition Placement").

rope may then be clipped to the long loop of the runner (fig. 13-24a). Or just clove-hitch the runner to the upper carabiner, which tensions the lower carabiner, and clip the climbing rope to the runner (fig. 13-24b).

EQUALIZING PROTECTION

A leader who is faced with a hard move or questionable protection may decide to place two pieces of protection close together. If one piece fails, the other remains as a backup.

Another option is to equalize the load over two protection points, subjecting each to only a portion of the total force. (For equalizing protection to establish an anchor, see Chapter 10, Belaying.)

Equalizing the forces between two points of protection can be accomplished with one hand and requires only one runner. First clip the runner in to both chocks. Twist one length of the runner in the middle, and pull it down to meet the other side of the runner. Then simply clip an extra carabiner through both, with the rope attached to this carabiner (see Figure 10-15 in Chapter 10, Belaying). If one chock later pulls out, the twist in the runner will slide down and catch around the carabiner, but some extension will occur. Do not clip the carabiner across, rather than through, the twisted runner because the entire setup will then fail if one chock comes loose.

STACKING

If nothing on a rack will accommodate the crack in which protection must be placed, the advanced technique called stacking can sometimes help. Place two passive wedges in opposition, with the larger one on top (fig. 13-25). A downward pull on the larger chock causes it to wedge between one side of the crack and one side of the other chock. Seat the larger chock with a firm tug before using it, and connect it to the rope in the usual way. Use a runner to clip the smaller chock in to the wire of the larger chock or another runner to keep the smaller chock from becoming a flying missile when it is

13

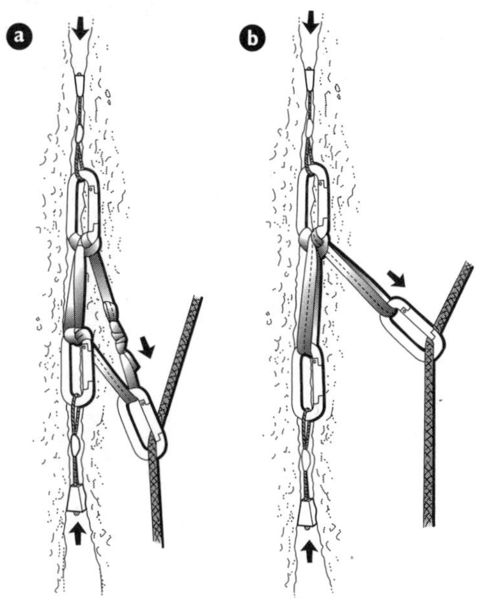

Fig. 13-24. Opposing chocks in a vertically oriented crack: a, connected by a runner secured with clove hitches to each chock's carabiner; b, connected by a runner clove-hitched to the upper chock's carabiner, which tensions the lower carabiner.

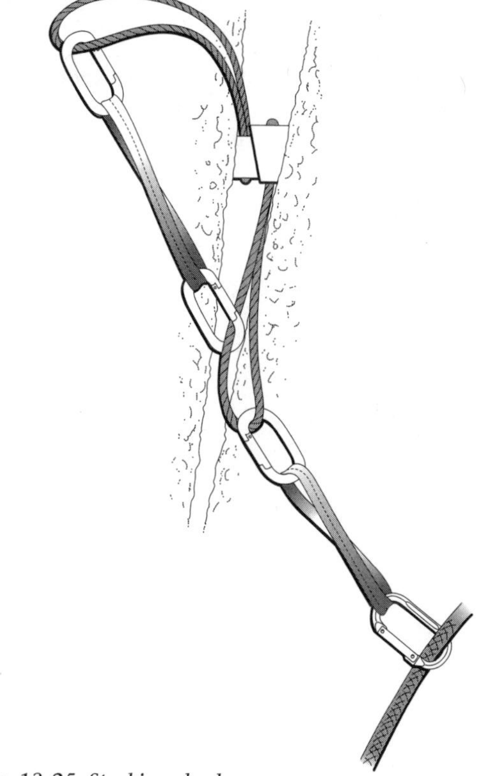

Fig. 13-25. Stacking chocks.

removed by the follower or if it comes loose in a fall. Use only chocks that seat well against one another; otherwise, stacking is not effective.

REMOVING PROTECTION

Removable pro can be easy to place but sometimes difficult to remove, whether for the leader who wants to choose a different piece for a crack other than the one just placed or for the follower cleaning the pitch. A chock pick is a specialized tool to assist in removing protection (see Figure 14-4 in Chapter 14, Leading on Rock). Chock picks often are racked separately on the harness, sometimes with retractable cord to avoid losing them if dropped. Chock picks can be used to apply force underneath a stubborn piece to push it up and to reverse how it was placed. In a narrow crack, the pick can be used to grab the cable at the top of a wedge and pull it out from above.

ROCK PROTECTION ETIQUETTE

Chapter 12, Alpine Rock Climbing Technique, discusses the issue of ethics in placing protection. Specifically, many climbing areas expressly forbid placing or even replacing bolts, and it is each climber's responsibility to understand the rules before installing a bolt. Some land managers request that climbers receive permission before placing or replacing bolts. Common practice for sport climbing routes is for the first ascensionist to place the only bolts.

Popular routes where natural features such as trees and horns are common rappel stations often collect slings that are used by various parties over time. If climbers find damaged slings, they should cut the slings off and remove them from the route.

Many climbing areas encourage the use of natural-colored bolts and slings for those that are left on routes, to address aesthetic concerns of nonclimbing visitors.

BUILDING SKILLS

The way to become proficient at placing protection is very simple: practice. First, practice by placing protection while standing on the ground. When following as a second, observe closely how the leader places protection. Practice placing pieces while climbing on a top rope. When you believe you are ready to try leading, start on an easy pitch that you have already climbed as a second or while top-roped. Place more pieces than are needed, just for the practice. Do not be discouraged if the first time turns out to be harder than it looks. Bring along a knowledgeable, experienced climber as your second—it is a great way to get valuable feedback. Just keep at it, and soon you will be the one giving advice.

LEADING ON NONTECHNICAL TERRAIN • LEADING TECHNICAL CLIMBS • LEADING ON ROCK, STEP BY STEP • PERSONAL RESPONSIBILITY

Chapter 14
LEADING ON ROCK

Leading on rock requires the complementary skills of both the leader and the belayer. The lead climber determines the route ahead, places protection for the pitch, and sets up the next belay station. The belayer monitors the leader, feeds the rope, anticipates the leader's need for tension or slack, and passes on needed information to the leader (remaining rope length, route descriptions, etc.). Although the leader in some ways incurs additional risk while on the "sharp end of the rope," the belayer and leader both play a critical role in making each pitch safe and successful.

Imagine two climbers high on a rock face. One is on lead, climbing up a crack, belayed by rope through numerous points of protection by a partner anchored to a ledge below.

The leader gives a sharp yank to the stopper he just placed in the crack. Grasping the rope tied to his harness, he pulls it up and clips it in to the protection. His belayer yells up to him "Halfway!" to indicate that he has reached the midpoint on the rope. He exhales deeply, switches hands in the crack, and shakes out his arm before raising his eyes to study the route ahead.

He sees that the thin splitter crack continues up steeply, with a few uneven pockets where a hand jam appears solid. From his rack, he readies a cam he feels would be ideal for placement when he reaches the most promising pocket several moves up. He mentally rehearses his moves, then resumes climbing.

Leading on rock requires merging climbing skill and psychological readiness. How do climbers decide whether they are ready? Others, especially more

Fig. 14-1. A hand line offers limited protection for an unroped party.

experienced climbers, can help assess someone's skills. However, only the individual climber can assess personal mental preparation, so each must search deeply within. Prepare by practicing and gaining confidence with placing rock protection, building anchors, belaying, learning how to manage the rope, and understanding fall forces. Work on rock technique, a methodology of gear selection and placement, and routefinding. Use every pitch you follow as an opportunity to observe and learn. Experience helps refine judgment.

LEADING ON NONTECHNICAL TERRAIN

A climbing party may travel unroped or unbelayed over third-class and fourth-class rock, each person climbing in balance and maintaining three points of contact with the rock. If the risks of the climb escalate beyond the party's comfort level, the leader has several options for using a rope to help minimize danger, short of full belayed climbing.

HAND LINE

A fixed hand line can be set up for members of an unroped party on less technical but exposed terrain to save the time it would take to belay multiple party members. The leader can either be belayed up or can scramble up this section, bringing along the loose end of the rope and placing protection along the way, if warranted. At the top, the leader anchors the rope, taking care not to place the rope under tension over sharp edges. The other climbers then move through this section, either holding on to this hand line or preparing to grab it if needed. Alternatively, if they are wearing harnesses, they can clip in to the line with a carabiner attached to a runner from their harness, or they can clip a carabiner directly from their harness in to a sling attached to the line with a prusik hitch (fig. 14-1). The rope may also be anchored at the start of this section to make it easier to prusik—that is, to move along the rope using the climbers' prusik slings tied to the rope, or to safeguard a traverse. The last climber breaks down the hand line while ascending, possibly on belay or while prusiking up the hand line.

RUNNING BELAY

The running belay, also known as simul-climbing, is another useful option when a team is climbing together over relatively easy terrain but is still roped together (fig. 14-2). Roped climbing teams normally consist of only two people. To establish a running belay, the lead climber simply clips the rope in to some rock protection that she places at appropriate intervals. At least two pieces of protection should be in place, clipped in to the rope between the leader and the follower at all times. The follower climbs simultaneously with the leader (hence the term "simul-climbing"), removing any protection that he passes. If one climber takes a fall, the rope will remain linked to the protection—and the weight of the other climber will naturally arrest the fall at some point.

If a party decides to use a running belay, the climbers must decide how much rope to leave between the leader and follower. Having more rope out has the advantage of absorbing more force should a fall occur, but it also increases the potential for the rope to snag on blocky or bushy terrain, and it can make communication between the leader and follower more difficult. When the situation calls for it, a Kiwi coil (see Chapter 17, Glacier Travel and Crevasse Rescue) can be used to shorten the rope to the appropriate length.

The running belay is less secure than belayed climbing but considerably safer than no protection at all.

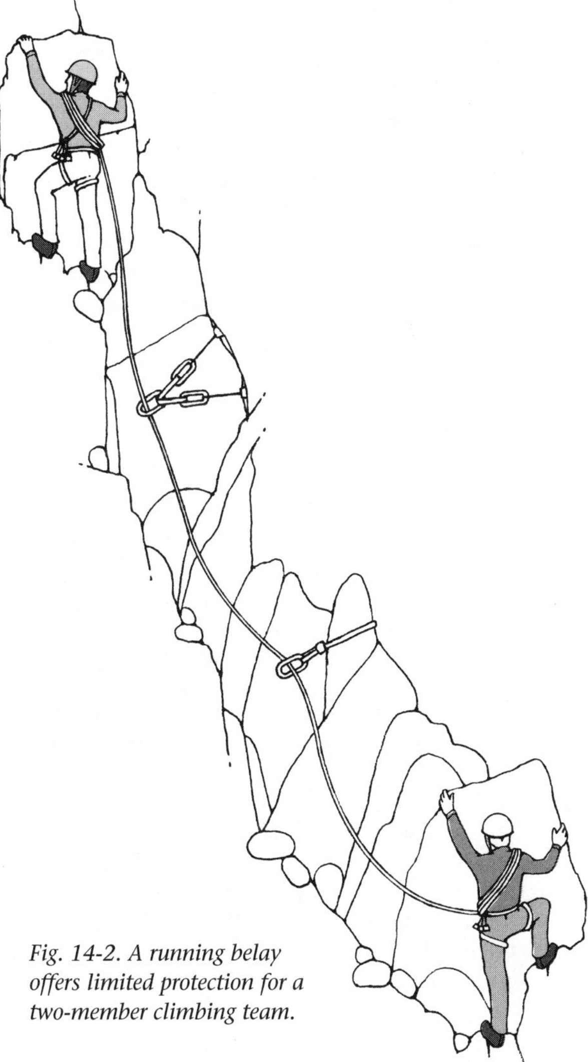

Fig. 14-2. A running belay offers limited protection for a two-member climbing team.

Given the advantages and disadvantages of this technique, the decision to simul-climb should be made carefully, weighing the potential risks and benefits for the given party and the specific situation. Important factors to consider include both the skill and comfort level of the climbing party, the degree of time pressure experienced during the climb, the likelihood of falling, and the degree of exposure or consequences of falling in the given situation. The lead climber needs to be sensitive to the skill level of the follower and should be ready to set up an anchored belay if the follower needs that degree of security. An anchored belay would also need to be set up if the lead climber runs out of protection while simul-climbing, so that the follower can either transfer gear back to the leader or can switch leads and continue the running belay.

CLIMBING IN COILS

Sometimes, between sections of more technical terrain where running or fixed belays are used, climbers coil most of the rope between them, leaving themselves tied in and with about 10–16 feet (3–5 meters) of climbing rope separating them. This is called "climbing in coils." Climbers coil the extra rope over their shoulders and tie in short to a locking carabiner attached to their harness (the adapted Kiwi coil is one method).

This method can increase efficiency, saving time because climbers can forgo untying from the rope and packing it up in between more technical pitches. Also, by climbing closely together, climbers can minimize rope-induced rockfall.

LEADING TECHNICAL CLIMBS

Technical rock climbing begins when anchored belays are needed for the party's safety. In this scenario, each pitch will be led and belayed. The leader accepts more risk than the second, who is belayed from above and does not have to worry about falling more than a very short distance. An aspiring leader should learn the mechanics of leading while climbing well below his or her actual climbing ability. It may sound obvious, but always be sure your climbing ability is consistent with the route you decide to lead. For example, you may be good at face climbing but have trouble with cracks; in that case, if a route requires crack climbing, make sure that it is within your crack climbing ability.

Steep, bolt-protected sport climbing routes can be relatively safe places to attempt leading hard moves.

An overhanging 5.11 route can be safer to lead than a 5.7 climb of ledges if the only risk in a fall off the former is hitting air. When transitioning from sport climbing to alpine rock climbing, be conservative in estimating your climbing abilities. The extra time and additional skills required for setting protection can substantially increase the difficulty of a trad climb compared to a bolted sport climb of the same rating. In addition, your climbing will be greatly affected by carrying a pack and wearing mountain boots. On a long, remote alpine climb, even if the actual rating of the climb is relatively easy, the consequences of a fall can be great. Evaluate routes in terms of potential risk and your ability to manage the consequences of a fall, and be conservative in choosing an alpine route and gear.

CHOOSING THE RACK

The collection of gear used for protection is called the rack. Each climbing team prepares just one rack, which is carried by whoever is leading. While climbing each pitch, the leader places some of the individual pieces of protection from the rack; the follower removes these and carries them up while climbing. At the top of the pitch, the rack is reorganized, and the leader takes the gear needed for protecting the next pitch.

The decision about what to bring is determined by the climb and each climber's comfort level. If the selected climb is in an area covered by a guidebook, check the book for general information such as the type of rock and what a "standard rack" for that area contains. The climbing route topo (fig. 14-3) for the selected climb, if there is one, may show the width of cracks, the amount of fixed or natural protection, the length and direction of each pitch, the difficulty of each section and the overall climb, and perhaps even the precise sizes of the pieces of protection needed. Particularly on commonly climbed routes, more detailed information regarding the specific protection needed can sometimes be found online in climbing trip reports or climbing community blogs or websites.

If the selected climb is in a remote area, usually not as much information is available. Take too big a rack, and the extra weight and equipment can impede the climbing. Take too little protection or the wrong pieces, and the team may not have what it needs to safely climb the route. Research the climb by consulting several guidebooks or talking with other climbers who have done the route, as well as by checking any relevant resources on the Internet.

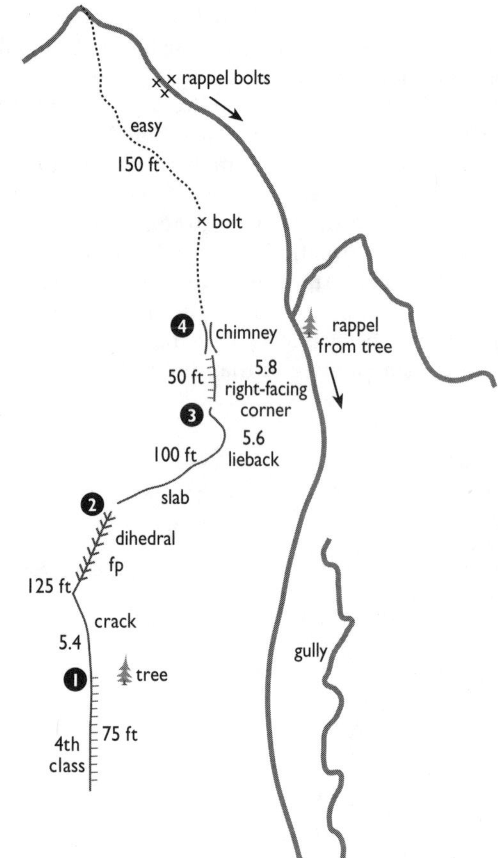

Fig. 14-3. A typical climbing route topo.

A typical rack includes a selection of passive chocks (nuts and hexes, for example), spring-loaded camming devices (SLCDs or cams), carabiners, and runners. The specific selection of protection varies with each route. A long, thin crack might dictate small wired nuts and some small cams. A wide crack may require the largest cams, hexes, or tube chocks. A long, parallel hand crack may require multiple 2-inch (5-centimeter) cams. Many cases are less clear-cut, requiring a full range of sizes. The "standard rack" is difficult to define narrowly, since different climbs call for different types and sizes of protection; in addition, individual climbers often have their own "pet pieces" of gear that they never leave home without. However, as an example, a rack that will accommodate a large number of traditional alpine climbs in Washington State's Cascade Mountains and beyond is generally defined as one that includes gear up to 2 or 3 inches (5 to 7.6 centimeters), consisting of at least a full set of nuts, some additional chocks (such as hexes and Tricams), and a set of cams ranging from small to medium-sized.

The pieces of protection typically connect to the rope with two nonlocking carabiners and a runner or quickdraw. Locking carabiners can be used instead if the gate is in a position where it could be forced open during a fall (by striking the rock). Carry a few extra carabiners as insurance against running short of them. The ideal runner at any protection point will be just long enough to help the rope stay in as straight a line as possible. A runner that is longer than necessary lengthens a fall, and one that is shorter than necessary causes rope drag. Quickdraws may work well for a straight-up climb. A zigzag line, roofs, or turns on the pitch require longer runners. Additional runners may be needed for belay anchors, unanticipated protection placements, and rappel slings. Especially on alpine climbs and any routes that deviate from a direct vertical line, it is recommended to bring several longer slings (multiple singles and at least a few doubles), as quickdraws will be insufficient. Slings are inexpensive and light, and they can be shortened and used as quickdraws for straight pitches (see Figure 14-7). The importance of bringing and using sufficiently long runners for reducing or preventing rope drag cannot be overemphasized (see Figure 14-10), yet failing to do so is a common mistake made by novice leaders.

The chock pick, a thin metal tool designed to help extract pieces of protection (fig. 14-4), is carried by each climber to use when following a pitch; if a team is swinging leads, both climbers will take turns following. Also known as a cleaning tool or a nut tool, the chock pick can help the follower retrieve pieces of protection that do not come out easily. It is also recommended that climbers carry this tool when leading, since occasionally the leader may need it to reset or replace a piece of protection in order to take advantage of a more secure placement.

In addition to carrying gear for protection, carabiners, runners, and a chock pick, a rock climber also carries a few other important pieces of equipment. These include a belay device, material for building belay anchors (in other words, a cordelette, equalette, and/or webbing for equalizing anchor points—see Chapter 10, Belaying), a tie-off loop (a short loop of accessory cord for emergency prusiking, tying off a climber after a fall, or a rappel backup—see Chapters 9, Basic Safety System, 10, Belaying, and 11, Rappeling), at least one rappel ring, a pocketknife for removal of old slings (or for emergencies), and perhaps chalk for keeping hands dry. Overall equipment choices, which are influenced by the setting and the type and length of the rock climb, warrant careful consideration and planning.

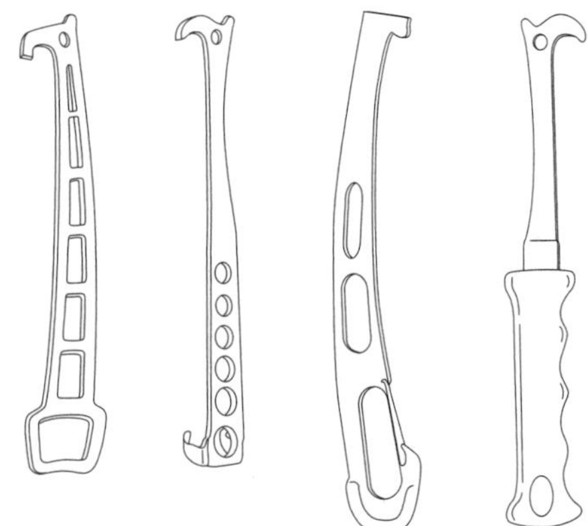

Fig. 14-4. Cleaning tools (chock picks).

14

OTHER IMPORTANT ITEMS

Particularly for multipitch routes that the climbing party is not intimately familiar with, it is also a good idea for the party to bring along a route description, topo, and/or notes to help with routefinding. Packs (of varying sizes, depending on the route and the speed of the climbing party) are often carried by at least one member of the climbing team for many alpine climbs or for traditional crag climbs in which the party does not plan to return to the base of the climb. Depending on conditions and the comfort level and skill of the individual climbers, various types of footwear may be chosen for the approach and the climb itself. Mountaineering boots (from very lightweight to heavyweight) or lightweight approach shoes are typically used for the approach (and sometimes on the climb itself as well). Climbing shoes (see Figure 12-1 in Chapter 12, Alpine Rock Climbing Technique) are generally the preferred choice when leading technical routes, especially for climbs of higher relative difficulty and virtually all cragging and sport climbs.

HOW TO RACK

The ideal racking method permits the leader to place protection efficiently and to climb smoothly despite carrying the gear; it also allows easy transfers between climbers for swinging leads. Keeping the hardware away from the rock makes the gear more readily available. For instance, when you are climbing an inside corner with your left side in, it is easier to have the rack hang from your left shoulder and under your right arm. No racking method is perfect, but several are commonly used, alone or in combination.

Group passive pieces and small cams together on a single carabiner. When organizing gear for the rack, it generally works best to group several passive pieces of protection (nuts, hexes, and Tricams) on a single carabiner (see Figure 14-6). For example, most climbers group a partial or full set of nuts together on a single carabiner. If a large number of nuts are included in the rack, or if there are doubles in certain sizes, sometimes the set of nuts will be divided into smaller and larger sizes, and a couple of carabiners will be used. The same method is often used for small cams as well.

This strategy reduces the number of carabiners needed for carrying these pieces, and this method can make climbing easier because it results in a less-bulky rack with better weight distribution. This technique also facilitates more efficient gear placement for these types of pieces. To choose the best piece for a placement, unclip the carabiner of gear for that size range and hold the whole batch of pieces up to the placement, eyeing each piece for fit. Then unclip the carabiner from the chosen piece, place the chock or cam, and return the carabiner and unused pieces to the gear sling.

With this method, climbers usually have two carabiners pre-attached to several runners or quickdraws because the placed protection lacks a carabiner (remember that one carabiner attaches to the protection and the other carabiner attaches to the rope; see Figure 13-2 in Chapter 13, Rock Protection). Although this method of racking may increase somewhat the risk of dropping gear, since more gear is handled every time a piece is placed, many climbers feel that this disadvantage is far outweighed by the increased ease of climbing offered.

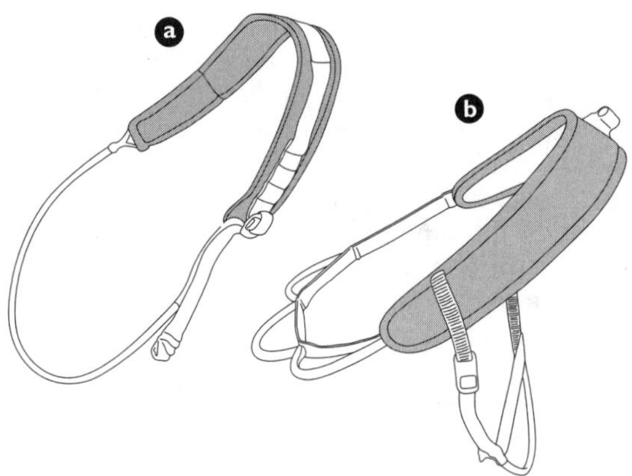

Fig. 14-5. Commercial gear slings: a, basic padded gear sling; b, partitioned gear sling.

Place other pieces of protection on separate carabiners. In contrast to passive pieces and small cams, most climbers prefer racking medium-sized to large cams and other active pieces such as tube chocks on separate carabiners (see Figure 14-6). By design, active protection including cams (at least medium-sized to large units) cover a wider range of sizes than passive pieces such as nuts or hexes. With experience, it is easier to spot the single right cam for a given placement than it is to identify a single nut that is the right size in a given situation.

Arranging medium-sized to large cams on separate carabiners is often preferred, as it is usually easier to gauge the correct size of cam for larger cracks without trying multiple pieces to find the right one. Racking in this way results in faster placement and less awkward juggling of multiple large pieces of protection on the same carabiner. After placing the appropriate cam in the rock, the leader can simply clip the cam's pre-attached carabiner to a runner, then the runner's carabiner to the rope.

WHERE TO RACK GEAR

After deciding how many pieces to place on the carabiners in the rack, the next question to answer is where a climber will rack the gear. The three most common options are on a gear sling, on the climbing harness, or on a combination of the two. A padded gear sling from a climbing shop may be the most comfortable choice, but a single-length runner can also be used. Commercial gear slings (fig. 14-5a) are also available with partitions (fig. 14-5b).

Rack gear on a sling. Climbers racking protection on a gear sling (fig. 14-6a) place it over one shoulder and under the opposite arm (see Figure 14-6c). This method of racking has the advantage of smooth gear transfers when switching leads, since the entire rack can be passed from the belayer to the leader at once. The primary disadvantage of this method is that having the entire rack over the shoulder can make the climber feel a bit top-heavy, and, at least with nonpartitioned slings, the weight of the rack can shift quite a bit when the leader is climbing.

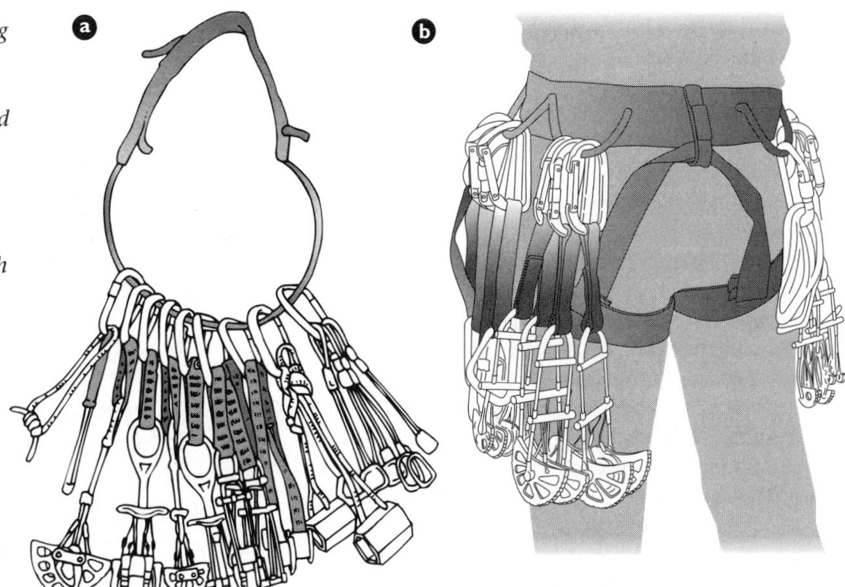

Fig. 14-6. Examples of racking methods: a, pieces of protection racked on a gear sling; b, pieces of protection attached to gear loops on the seat harness; c, hybrid method in which gear is racked on both a gear sling and the harness, and one or more double-length runners are also looped over one shoulder.

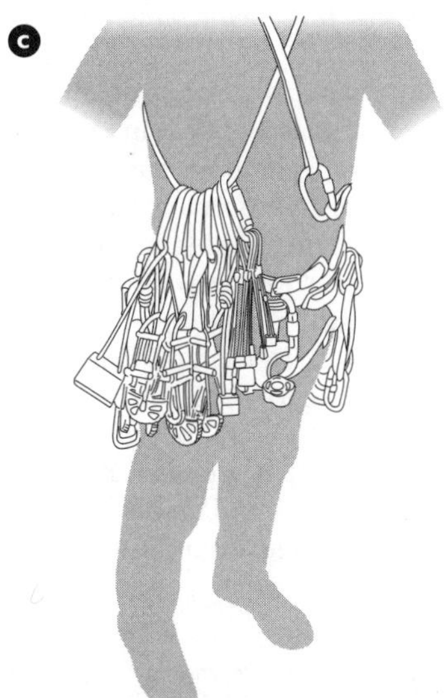

Rack gear on the climbing harness gear loops. Using the gear loops on the climbing harness to rack gear (fig. 14-6b) evenly distributes the weight of the rack on the climber's waist, and the different types of protection can be separated (although the latter can also be done with a partitioned gear sling).

Transfer of gear at belays can take longer with this method of racking, since gear must be transferred from multiple gear loops rather than a single gear sling. However, for experienced climbers, this time difference is likely to be nominal. When using this method, be sure the gear does not hang down so far that it interferes with climbing footwork. Also, on many climbs, it is a good idea to rack runners and/or quickdraws and carabiners on both sides of the harness for easy access when clipping the rope in to protection.

Rack gear on both the harness and a gear sling. Perhaps the most common method of racking is a hybrid of these two systems (fig. 14-6c). For example, a climber could place all the pieces of protection on a sling over the shoulder but place runners and carabiners on the harness. Conversely, a climber could place the protection on the harness, with runners and carabiners on a sling. Or a climber could place some gear on a sling and some on the harness.

Whatever method is used, rack the protection in a systematic order so that a particular piece can be found in a hurry. The usual order is to start at the front with the smallest wired chocks and work back with larger pieces. For each carabiner clipped to the rack, use the same orientation so that each one unclips in exactly the same way. For example, all the gates of the carabiners should be facing the same way—either in or out, but not both.

Particularly for climbers who are relatively inexperienced at swinging leads or transferring gear at belays, it is recommended that climbing partners agree beforehand on using one racking technique; otherwise, much precious time may be lost in re-racking at each belay when climbers are swinging leads.

OTHER RACKING CONSIDERATIONS

Runners need to be racked as well. Quickdraws can be racked on the harness or on a sling. Climbers can carry single-length runners over one shoulder, but if a number of them are carried, it can be difficult to retrieve just one from the tangle. Climbers can carry a single-length runner quickdraw-style by attaching two carabiners to it and putting one carabiner through the other (fig. 14-7a), then clipping the resulting loop (fig. 14-7b) and straightening it (fig. 14-7c). This style is also called an alpine draw; clip one carabiner to protection (fig. 14-7d). Such runners can be quickly extended by unclipping all but a single strand from one carabiner (fig. 14-7e) and then pulling this carabiner until the runner is fully extended (fig. 14-7f). Climbers can carry double-length runners looped over a shoulder and connected with a carabiner (see Figure 14-6c). Alternatively, climbers can chain the runner (fig. 14-8) before attaching it to the harness; when it is needed, pull or shake it out to remove the loops. Climbers can also fold a double- or triple-length runner several times and tie it in an overhand or figure eight knot, then clip it to the harness.

When climbing with a pack, put it on first, then the rack. When carrying double-length and single-length runners over one shoulder (or both shoulders), put the single-length runners on top so that the doubles can be removed without displacing the singles.

Carry cordelette (or other anchor-equalizing cord or webbing), chock pick, and belay device on the harness gear loops so that they are easily accessible. Other gear such as a pocketknife and tie-off loop can be clipped to the harness or carried around the neck so they are out of the way but accessible.

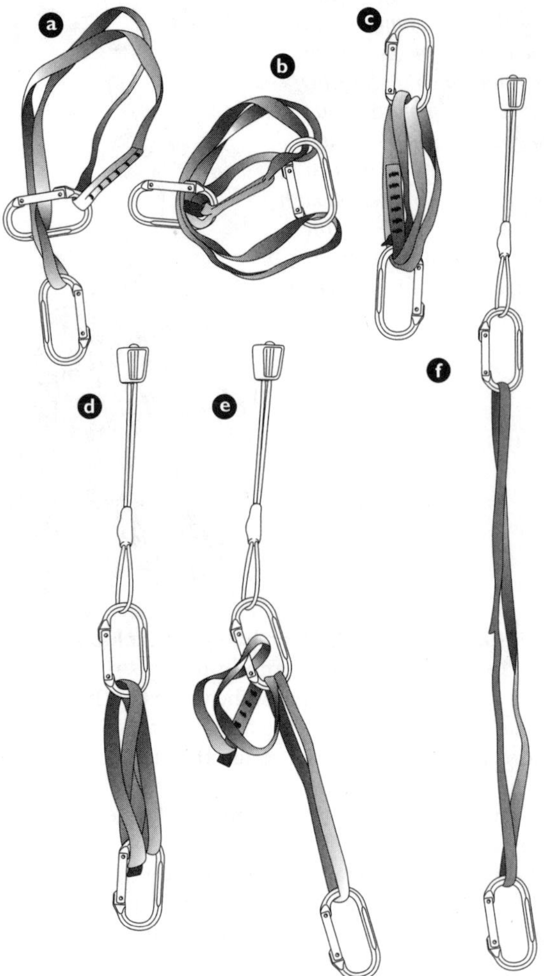

Fig. 14-7. Racking and extending a single-length runner quickdraw-style (also known as an alpine draw): a, clip two carabiners to a single-length runner and pass one carabiner through the other; b, clip the first carabiner back in to the newly formed loop; c, straighten the loops; d, clip the protection to one carabiner; e, unclip that carabiner from all but the uppermost loop; f, straighten and extend the runner.

LEADING ON ROCK, STEP BY STEP

Whether leading the next pitch or the next climb, it is imperative to plan the route, evaluate rope and rack requirements, and know the descent. Leading is a complex business. Beginners usually need an apprenticeship, moving behind seasoned climbers before they can safely "take the sharp end of the rope" (lead). Never take the lead if you do not feel ready, and do not pressure others into leading. Keep the art of leading exciting, challenging, satisfying, and safe—as it ought to be.

PLANNING THE ROUTE

Planning a route begins with background research at home. Look for climb descriptions in printed guidebooks and online climbers' blogs. Talk to others who have climbed the route before. For alpine climbs, obtain needed maps for the approach, and check weather

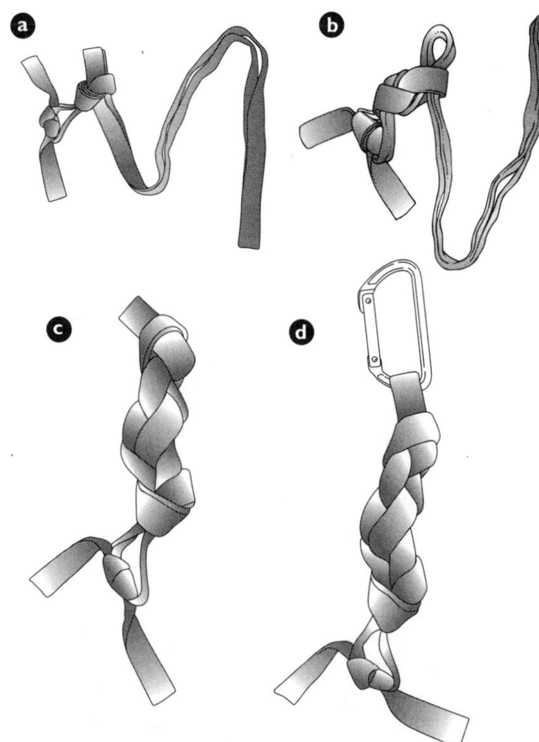

Fig. 14-8. Chaining a long runner: a, form a slipknot; b, pull runner through the loop formed by the slipknot; c, repeat this process until the runner is chained; d, attach the final loop to a carabiner to carry it and to ensure it does not unravel.

and avalanche conditions for the dates being considered (see Chapters 5, Navigation, and 27, Mountain Weather). The skill required depends on the location and nature of the climb as well as potential difficulties that might be encountered on the approach and descent.

Routefinding can be as easy as following a guidebook picture with a climbing route topo or simply following a line of bolts on a crag; but it can also be as difficult as a multiday, off-trail approach and ambiguous technical climb with a vague route description. Routefinding on alpine routes or some long crag routes can be complex. Longer routes often are less clearly defined. The guidebook description may be sketchy: "Ascend northeast buttress for several hundred feet of moderate climbing." The descent may be complicated and vaguely described.

For any climb, confirm the descent and—if it is not obvious—perhaps check with others who have done the route. Decide whether boots are needed for the descent. Make sure the rope is long enough for rappels.

ON THE WAY IN

Once on the way, study the route on the approach if possible; often the best view of a climbing route is at a distance from the start of the climb. Look for major features that the line of ascent might follow, such as crack systems, dihedrals, chimneys, or areas of broken rock. Note areas of small trees or bushes that could indicate belay ledges or rappel anchors. Identify landmarks that, when they are reached, will help determine the party's position on the route. For this kind of planning, the climbers' eyes will tell them what the topographical map cannot.

Watch out for deceptively tempting lines that lead to poor-quality rock, broad roofs, blank walls, or false summits. These may not be visible once the party is on the climb and, if they climb these features in error, they may dead-end after several pitches.

Develop a plan for the line of ascent, but keep likely alternatives in mind. Continue planning the routefinding as the actual climb begins, looking for more local features and landmarks. Seek out natural lines to follow when leading the route. Form a tentative plan for each pitch, perhaps including a place for the first piece of protection and a spot for the next belay station. Do not hesitate to look around the corner for easier route alternatives that may not be visible from below.

When faced with a choice between pitches of varying difficulty, consider the rest of the climb. Two moderate pitches are better than an easy pitch followed by one beyond the party's ability (see the "Questions to Ask Before Leading a Pitch" sidebar).

On the way up, keep track of retreat possibilities in case the climb is aborted, and study, to the extent possible, the party's planned descent route. Rain, lightning, unexpected wind or cold, injury, or illness may make it prudent to retreat from the route. As the climb progresses, evaluate changing route conditions, the weather, and the climbing party. Know the party's alternative responses to any changes, weighing all resources. Consider whether the party is equipped to deal with an unplanned bivy while on the climb. Know descent or escape routes in case they are needed. See Part 5, Emergency Prevention and Response.

PROTECTING THE LEAD

Placing protection every few feet requires a big rack and eats up time. Placing very little protection at all greatly increases the risk of a long leader fall and potential injury. Learning the appropriate balance requires practice and sound judgment. Climbers certainly should protect moves they expect to be hard. Always space the protection to avoid potential falls that are excessively long or dangerous. Protection above a move provides the safety of a top rope. In deciding when to place another piece of protection, keep in mind the quality of the placements already made. Consider how to minimize dangerous rope drag, which is exacerbated by changing rope angles through protection and around rock corners, and how to take the fall factor into account (see Chapter 10, Belaying).

SELECTING AND MAKING A PLACEMENT

The perfect placement is a combination of a crack sized and shaped ideally for placing protection with a comfortable stance from which to place it, located right at the next hard move—but two out of three is not bad either. When on the sharp end of the rope, avoid making difficult moves far away from the last protection. Place protection right before and after a hard move.

Chapter 13, Rock Protection, details types of protection and good placements. Consider the stability of the rock when placing protection. Look, listen, and feel for the soundness of the rock by hitting suspect rock with the heel of a hand. Beware of expanding flakes and hollow-sounding or crumbling rock. Remember that a protection placement is only as solid as the rock into which it is placed.

To place protection, find a stance that is secure enough that you can release one hand, because you must be able to make the placement and then clip in to it without falling or seriously tiring. When possible, take advantage of natural protection—a tree, bush, rock tunnel, or horn—because it can be easy to use and is often multidirectional, and doing so can save on gear. The leader must be able to quickly place and clip sound protection with either hand, whether the carabiner gate faces left (fig. 14-9a and b) or right (fig. 14-9c and d), to make the lead safer. Clipping inefficiently and incorrectly is a common and potentially dangerous mistake made by new leaders. An especially common mistake among novice leaders is back-clipping, that is the leader's end of the rope is clipped so that it travels *behind*—rather than in front of—the carabiner to which it is clipped (fig. 14-9f) as the leader ascends above this piece of protection. A consequence of back-clipping is the rope accidentally opening the carabiner gate (fig. 14-9g and h) during a leader fall. Study diagrams on correct clipping technique (fig. 14-9e), and then practice clipping with either hand until the process is fluid and fast.

Suppose that as a leader you are faced with a choice between two or more possible placements. Ask these questions:

- Which placement combines the best fit with stability in the direction(s) of pull?

QUESTIONS TO ASK BEFORE LEADING A PITCH

- **How long and hard is the pitch?**
- **Can the leader see the general path of the pitch** and where the next anchor will be?
- **What is the nature and location of the crux** (most difficult move of the pitch)?
- **What sizes, types, and amount of protection** will be needed?
- **How much other gear,** including carabiners and runners, will be needed to protect the lead?
- **What gear will be needed to build the anchor at the end of the pitch?**
- **What climbing techniques will be used?** Liebacking? Chimneying? Jamming? As a result, on what side should the climber rack?
- **Does the leader want the belayer to shout out how much rope is left while climbing** (calling out "halfway," "20 feet," or "feet . . . two . . . zero")?
- **Can the belayer and leader hear each other throughout the climb?** If not, do they have rope signals? Radios?
- **How will a fall affect the belay?** Could the leader drop past the belayer in a fall? Is the belayer well secured for any pull from a potential leader fall?
- **Where and how will the first piece of protection be placed?** Will it minimize the fall factor and minimize the chance of setting off the zipper effect? (See "The Zipper Effect" later in this chapter.)

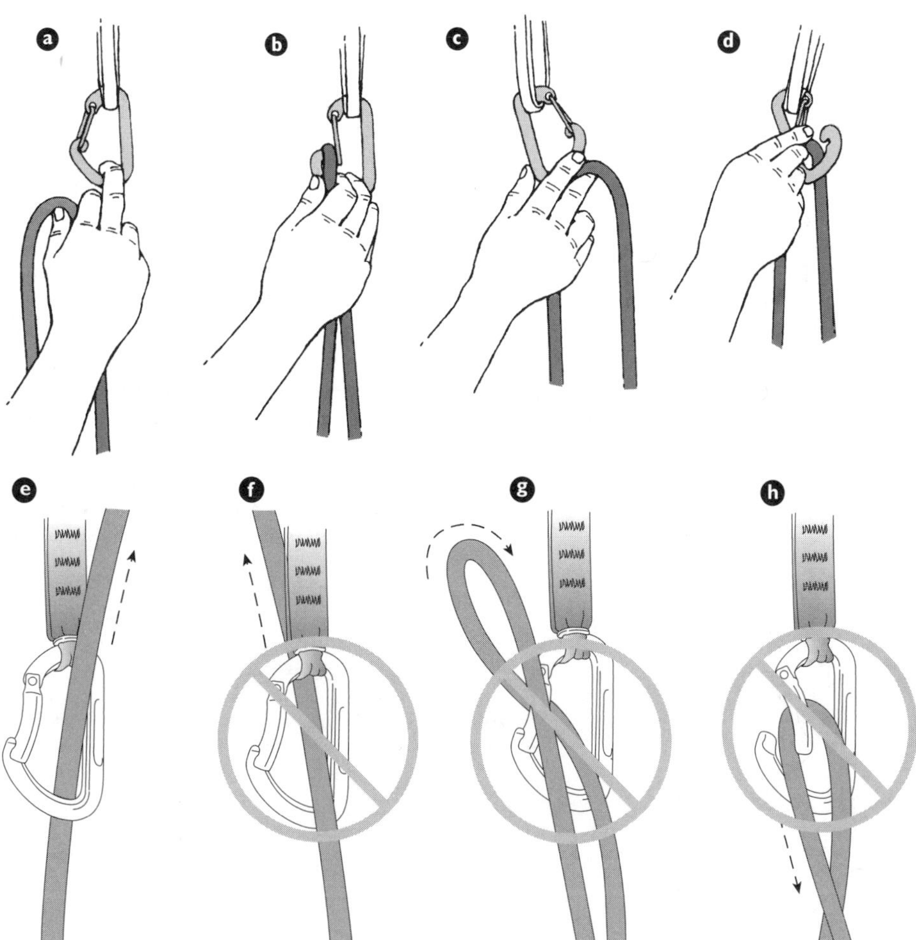

Fig. 14-9. Clipping technique: a and b, gate facing left, right hand; c and d, gate facing right, right hand; e, correctly clipped carabiner; f, rope is back-clipped (dangerous); g and h, back-clipping causes carabiner gate to open in a fall.

- Which placement will be stronger?
- What size chocks or cams should be conserved for use higher on the pitch or at the anchor?
- Which placement will be easier for the second to remove?
- Will one placement interfere with a needed foothold or handhold?
- Which placement will minimize rope drag?

If the unfortunate choice is between questionable protection and none at all, by all means place something, but also plan to place additional protection as soon as possible. Placing and equalizing two pieces can also help (see Chapter 13, Rock Protection). Do not let such placement give a sense of false security, however. Do not trust obviously bad protection.

Suppose the leader faces a hard move without any apparent protection. Restudy the rock for some less obvious way of protecting the move. Evaluate whether there is a movement sequence or rock feature not seen at the outset. The options are these:

- Protect the move after all, and then resume climbing.
- Go ahead and attempt the move without good protection.
- Down-climb and see if the belayer will lead the pitch.
- Find an easier line to climb.
- Consider retreating from the climb.

After studying the situation and evaluating the consequences of a fall, carefully and calmly weigh the options, and then decide on the course of action that seems best.

DETERMINING THE LENGTH OF THE PITCH

The length of a given pitch is dictated by several factors. On most sport climbs and many single-pitch traditional crag climbs, the end of a pitch is clearly indicated by the presence of bolt anchors and/or chains, and the pitch is often short enough that the leader can be lowered back to the ground by the belayer. On other traditional crag climbs and most alpine rock climbs, the pitches are more variable in length and may be considerably more ambiguous, since they are often not marked with bolted belay anchors but instead utilize natural anchors or require the leader to construct gear anchors. This latter type of route requires more routefinding and discretion by the leader.

The maximum length of a pitch can never exceed the length of the rope, which typically ranges from 50 to 70 meters, with 60 meters being the most commonly used rope length for most rock climbs. However, in many cases, the ideal pitch length will be less than the full length of the rope, often considerably less. The key point here is that the leader should be prepared to do pitches of varying lengths, depending on the circumstances. Avoid the temptation to make every pitch a full-rope-length pitch, which can result in slower, rather than faster, climbing, especially when it causes rope drag or the need to down-climb to a more secure belay location that a leader passed up.

When determining pitch length, use any available information from route descriptions and topos. Beyond this, seek out and use good belay spots (in other words,

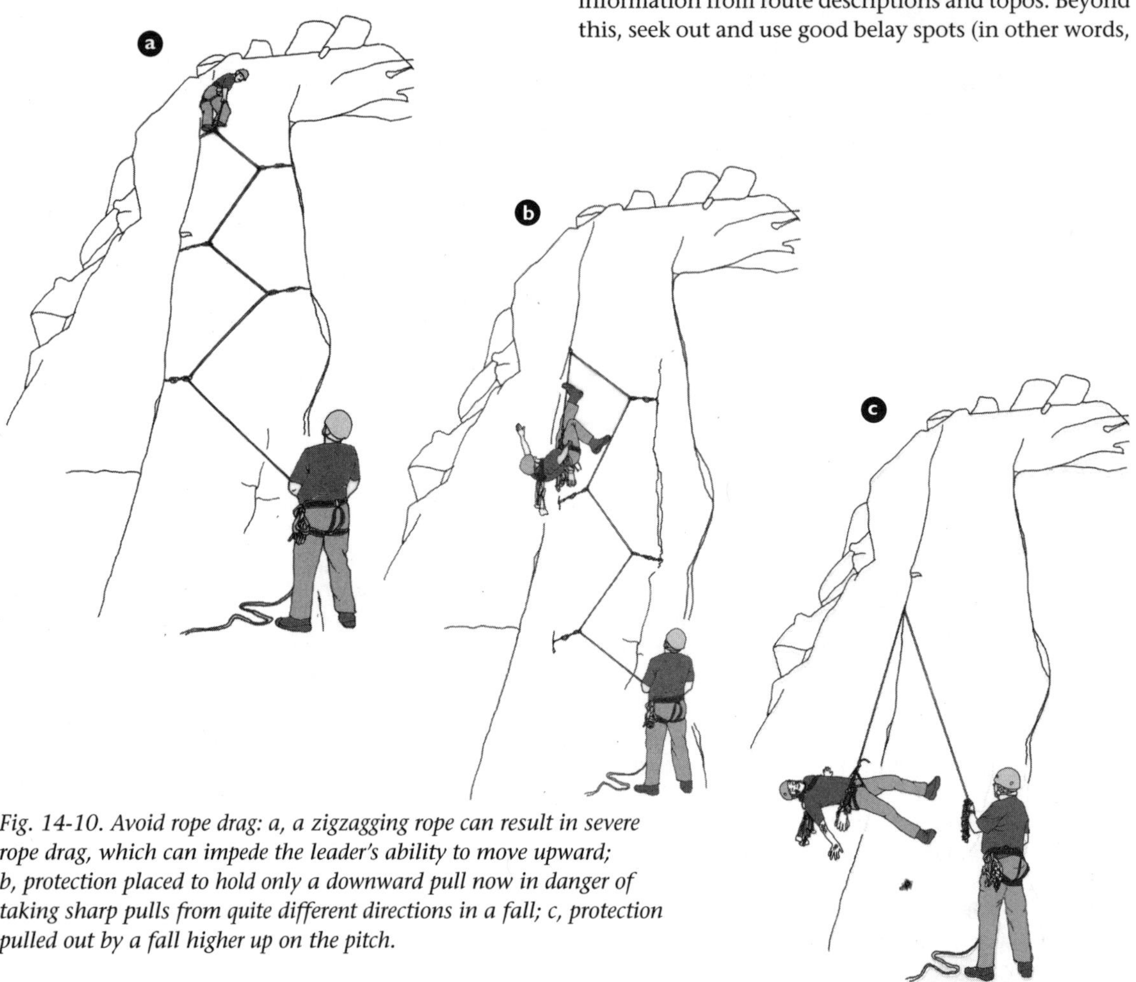

Fig. 14-10. Avoid rope drag: a, a zigzagging rope can result in severe rope drag, which can impede the leader's ability to move upward; b, protection placed to hold only a downward pull now in danger of taking sharp pulls from quite different directions in a fall; c, protection pulled out by a fall higher up on the pitch.

when in doubt about the best pitch length, do not pass up a great location to set up a belay anchor), try to maintain communication (particularly in windy conditions, long pitches can significantly compromise communication with a climbing partner), and work to prevent or minimize rope drag. If rope drag becomes a problem, seek out a good belay spot sooner rather than later.

JUDGING THE DIRECTION OF FALL FORCES

The leader must anticipate the direction of forces on the protection in order to make placements, but this judgment must take into account the entire climbing system. A protection point may seem solid for a fall when it is placed, but later it could pop out when the system causes pulls in directions not initially anticipated.

A zigzagging climbing rope causes severe directional forces as well as rope drag that, at its worst, can immobilize the leader (fig. 14-10a). Pieces of protection that may have been placed to hold only a downward pull may now be in danger of taking sharp pulls from quite different directions in case of a fall. In catching a fall, the rope loads and straightens from the belayer up to the highest protection point and then back down to the falling climber (fig. 14-10b). When the protection has been placed in a zigzag, pieces can be pulled sideways or upward by the tightening rope. If protection is placed for only a downward pull, it can be pulled out by falls higher up the pitch (fig. 14-10c).

During a fall, the top piece of protection is loaded with high forces: the force of the falling climber, plus the force of the belayer holding the fallen climber, minus friction forces in the system between the fallen climber and belayer (fig. 14-11).

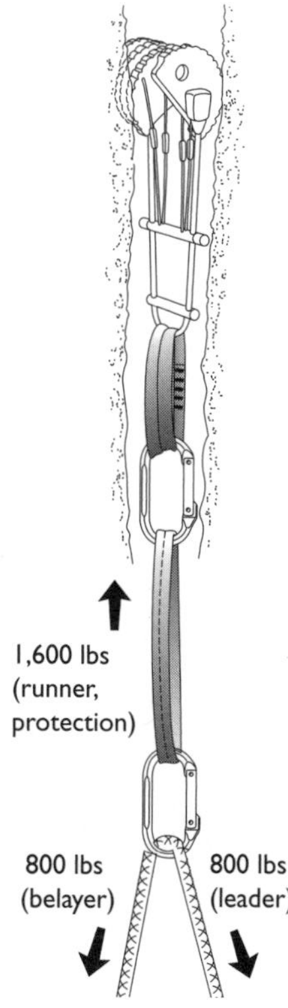

Fig. 14-11. The combined force on the top protection placement during a fall.

All protection placements should be solid, but consider backing up protection before hard moves if the placements afforded are less than ideal. Protection that allows the rope to follow in a straight line helps preserve the integrity of the system and minimizes rope drag. Extend protection with runners where needed. Rope drag not only can immobilize the climber, but it also decreases the rope's ability to absorb forces in case of a fall by effectively increasing the fall factor (see Chapter 10, Belaying). Make placements multidirectional when a bend in the climbing line must be made—use natural protection, opposing chocks, or cams that can safely rotate with minimal walking (see "Opposition Placement" in Chapter 13, Rock Protection). Or consider placing the belay on the other side of the bend.

The Zipper Effect

The full-scale zipper effect is a dramatic demonstration of the importance of anticipating force directions. The zipper effect occurs most readily where the belay is established away from the base of the pitch (fig. 14-12a) or where the rope zigzags up the route (see Figure 14-10). Again, as the rope loads during a leader fall, the bottom chock can have a tremendous outward pull placed on it. If it pulls out, the next piece becomes subject to the outward pull. Each in turn could fail, causing the line of chocks to be yanked out one by one as the "zipper" opens from the bottom up (as in Figure 14-12a). Overhangs and sharp traverses also have the potential to zipper.

Prevent the zipper effect by making the suspect placements multidirectional through the use of opposing chocks, cams, or natural protection (fig. 14-12b) and by eliminating the potential for outward pull by extending pieces with runners. The belayer could also reduce outward pull by belaying closer to the base of the route (see Figure 14-12b).

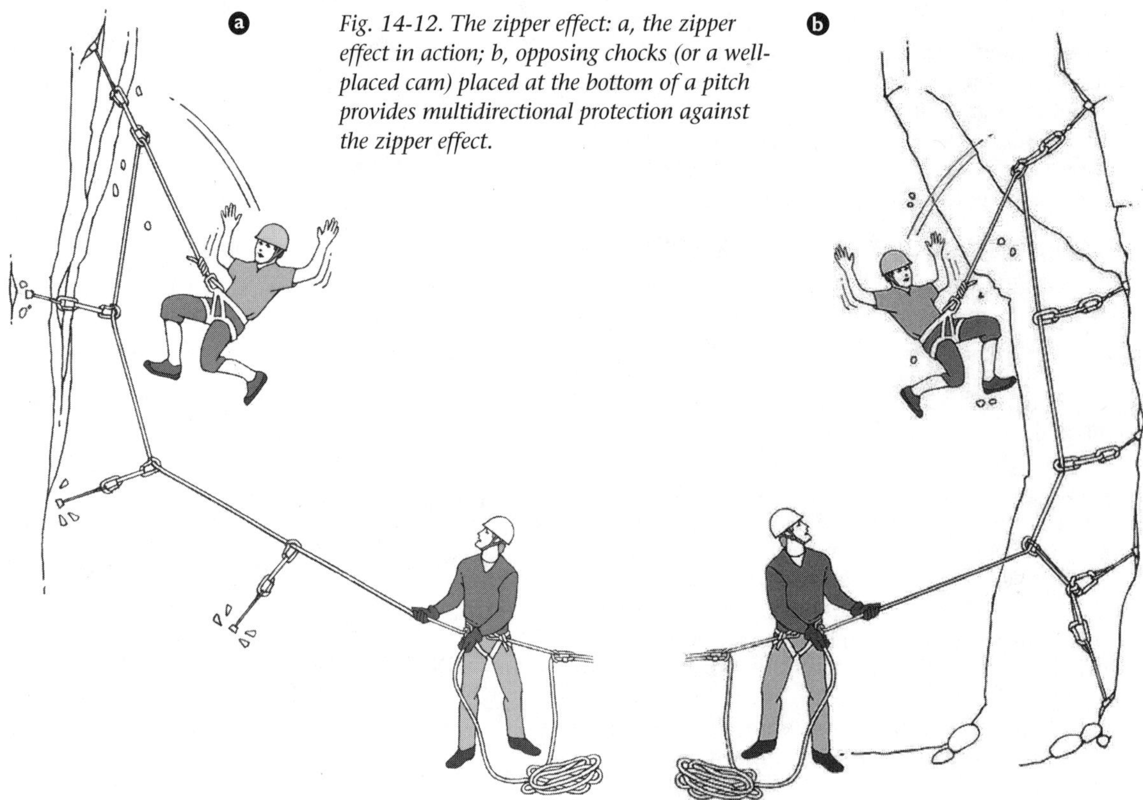

Fig. 14-12. The zipper effect: a, the zipper effect in action; b, opposing chocks (or a well-placed cam) placed at the bottom of a pitch provides multidirectional protection against the zipper effect.

PROTECTING SPECIAL SITUATIONS

Leading on overhangs or traverses requires special considerations.

Overhangs

Keep the rope running as free of an overhang as possible. Extend the rope with runners in order to reduce rope drag (fig. 14-13a), prevent dangerous fall forces such as the zipper effect, and keep the rope from being cut by the edge of the overhang (fig. 14-13b). On small overhangs, leaning out and placing protection above it may be the most effective strategy.

Traverses

When leading a traverse, be sure to place protection both before and after a hard move (fig. 14-14a). This guards not only the leader but also the follower from the possibility of a long pendulum fall (fig. 14-14b). In addition to the danger of injury, that kind of fall could leave the second in a tough spot, off route and with no easy way back.

When leading a diagonal or traversing section, keep in mind the effect each placement could have on the second climber. Put yourself in the second's shoes and ask, "Would I like some protection here?" If so, place it. Asking this question will help you avoid a common and potentially dangerous mistake made by beginning leaders: neglecting to adequately protect the follower on a traverse.

If the party has the necessary equipment and it seems prudent, consider belaying the second with an extra rope, which may help protect against a long pendulum fall and provide better protection than using the leader's rope. If the party is using double-rope technique (described later in this chapter), do not clip in both ropes during the traverse, so that the follower can receive a belay from above on the free rope.

CLIPPING BOLTS AND OTHER PROTECTION

The carabiner clipped to a bolt hanger should normally have its gate facing away from the subsequent direction

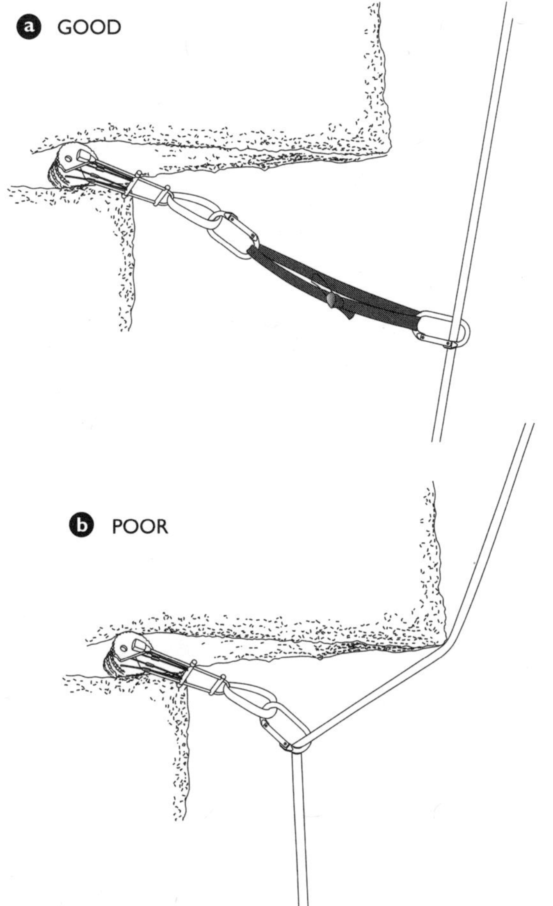

Fig. 14-13. Placements under overhangs: a, rope running free of the overhang (good); b, bends cause rope drag, and rope could be cut by rock edge during a fall (poor).

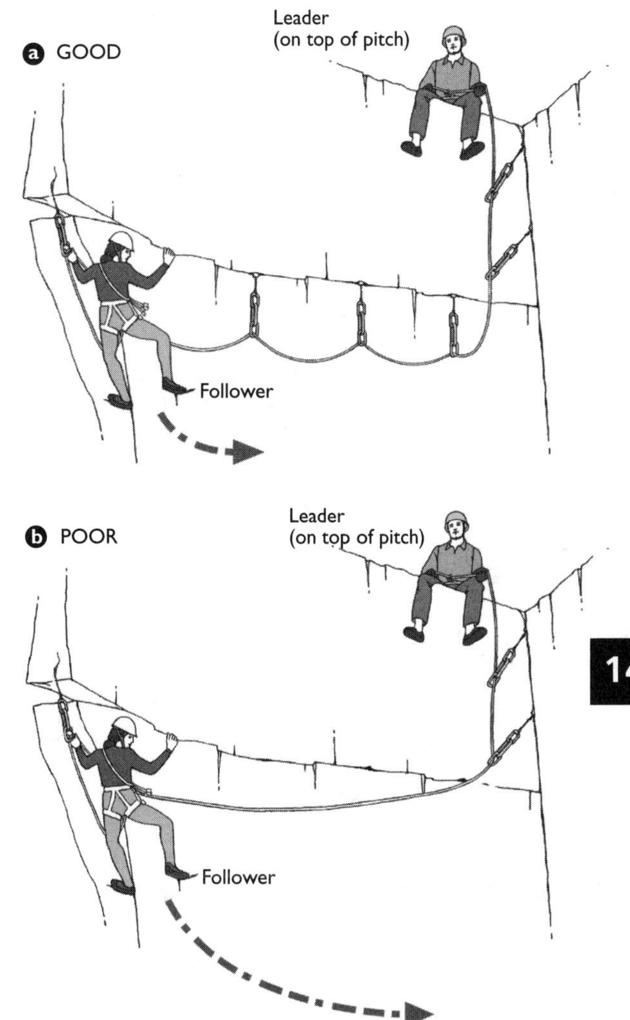

Fig. 14-14. Protecting a traverse: a, placing protection both before and after a hard move on a traverse reduces potential for a long pendulum fall (good); b, the second climber faces a long pendulum in case of a fall because of inadequate protection (poor).

of travel of the leader (fig. 14-15a and b). Otherwise, the carabiner may rotate or slide in such a way that the gate makes direct contact with the bolt hanger (fig. 14-15c). In the case of a sudden fall, the gate can then open and potentially come unclipped by striking the bolt hanger. However, not all carabiners and bolt hangers are alike, so the leader should evaluate each circumstance with that in mind, with the goal of trying to safeguard against situations in which the gate of a carabiner could come unclipped when sudden force is applied.

The same basic principle applies when clipping in to pieces of protection other than bolts. Avoid placing a carabiner in a position wherein the gate could open if it strikes the rock or any other contact point.

Similarly, the gate of the carabiner clipped in to the rope should always face the opposite direction that the rope is traveling. If the climb proceeds to the right after a protection point, the gate of the lower carabiner clipped to the rope should face left (as in Figure 14-15a). If the climb proceeds to the left, the gate should face right. If

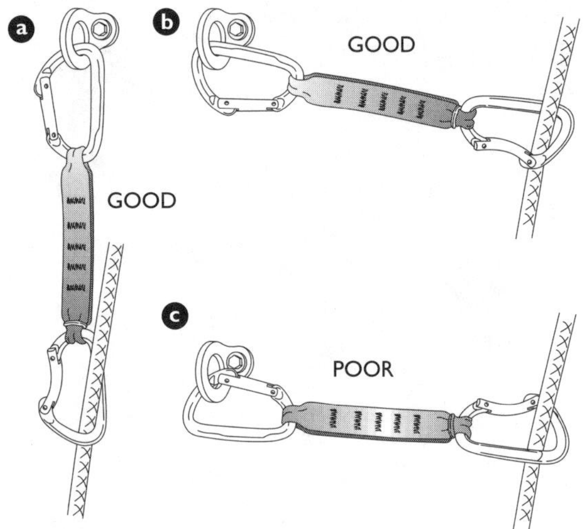

Fig. 14-15. Clipping a carabiner in to a bolt hanger: a and b, gates face opposite direction of climb that goes up and right and are not in danger of unclipping (good); c, gates face wrong direction and are in danger of unclipping (poor).

this principle is not followed, there is an increased risk that the rope could travel over the gate if a fall occurs and open up the carabiner, causing the rope to become unclipped. When the climb travels straight up from the last protection point, the gate can be facing either left or right.

ARRIVING AT THE NEXT BELAY

At the top of the pitch, clip in to a solid anchor before signaling "off belay." Add additional pieces as needed to form a multidirectional belay anchor (see Chapter 10, Belaying). Make sure the anchor secures the leader against being pulled from the stance by the second.

Think through the belay sequence before settling in so that it is clear which hand to use for the braking hand and where to flake the rope while belaying up the second. Keep the belay system simple. Strive for straight, easily traceable lines from the anchor points to you. Effective rope management techniques are critical to a safe belay, especially when at a hanging or sloping belay stance (fig. 14-16). The most common method is for the belayer to flake or stack the rope neatly on the rope or runner that connects him to the belay anchor; alternatively, devices such as rope hooks or rope buckets specifically made for this purpose can be used.

Never lay belay devices, gloves, carabiners, or other items on the ground. If an item is not in use, keep it attached to yourself or to an anchor. Have only one item, such as the rope, a chock, or a carabiner, in hand at a time. The moment an item is no longer needed for whatever you are doing, reattach it to yourself or an anchor. Unattached objects are easily knocked or blown off the belay ledge.

Take off your pack and rack and attach them to an anchor, but keep them within easy reach. That way, you will be more comfortable while belaying the second.

When the belayer is settled in, haul up the slack rope until it is taut. The second should yell, "That's me." After placing the second on belay, yell, "On belay." See Chapter 10, Belaying, for a full set of climbing commands.

Fig. 14-16. Multidirectional belay anchor at the top of a pitch. Careful and clean rope management, shown here at a sloping belay stance, is a critical skill for leaders.

CLEANING A PITCH

The climber who follows the leader should climb as quickly and efficiently as possible after being put on belay (see the "Tips to Save Time and Energy as the Second" sidebar). While ascending, the second climber cleans the pitch: removes the protection from the rock in an orderly way, organizes it, and efficiently transfers it to the belayer at the end of the pitch.

The second can minimize the risk of dropping gear by using a careful cleaning procedure, which may depend on the method used to rack the hardware. Consider a typical placement consisting of chock-carabiner-runner-carabiner-rope. The following procedure is an efficient way to clean gear that minimizes the risk of dropping gear:

1. First remove the chock from the rock.
2. Holding the carabiner that is clipped to the chock, clip the carabiner-chock combination directly to the gear sling or harness gear loop.
3. Then unclip the carabiner-chock combination from the runner.
4. Next, loop the runner over your head, unclip the runner-carabiner combination from the rope, and rotate the carabiner-runner combination so that it is under one arm.
5. Continue climbing to the next piece of protection, and repeat.

If the placement uses a quickdraw instead of a runner, follow this procedure:

1. First remove the chock from the rock.
2. Next, clip the carabiner that connects the chock and quickdraw in to the racking sling.
3. Last, unclip the quickdraw's other carabiner from the rope.

In general, cleaning from rock to the rope is best. This keeps the pieces clipped to something at all times, and there is little possibility of dropping any gear. In any racking procedure, minimizing the handling of unattached gear also lessens the risk of dropping it.

TRANSFERRING EQUIPMENT AT THE TOP OF A PITCH

The first thing the second climber needs to do when arriving at a belay station—before being taken off belay—is to clip in to the belay anchor. If the climbers are swinging leads, then the belayer need not remove the rope from the belay device but can back it up with an overhand or figure eight on a bight. If they are not swinging leads, the climbers have to trade places, with the follower taking over the belay to free up the leader to lead the next pitch. In either case, if the second is neat, organized, and efficient in cleaning the pitch, the transfer of gear at the belay station should go quickly,

TIPS TO SAVE TIME AND ENERGY AS THE SECOND

- **Start preparing to climb as soon as the leader is off belay.** When it is safe to do so, begin breaking down the belay station (but always stay clipped in to at least one anchor until the leader has you on belay).
- **Put the pack on before anything else.** If you are already carrying climbing hardware on a gear sling, put it on next. Plan where to put the gear that you clean, whether on the gear sling, the harness, or another sling.
- **Give the area a last look to make sure nothing is left behind.** Then, once you are on belay, yell, "Climbing!" and start out.
- **Remove each chock by reversing the way of how it was placed.** A Stopper slotted down and behind a constriction should be removed by pushing it back away from the constriction and up.
- **Be persistent but careful.** Use the chock pick to tap on a stubborn wedge or hex-shaped chock to loosen it, taking care to avoid hitting the wires; then lift the chock out gently. Prying and tugging often only tightens or wedges the chock more and can damage the wires. Use a loose rock or other object, if available, to tap on the end of the chock pick.
- **Sometimes chock picks can retract the triggers of cams** that have "walked" back into a crack, so that their trigger cannot be retracted with your fingers. Or use the wires of two Stoppers to snare the trigger device to retract the cams.
- **Consider asking your belayer for tension** and put your weight on the rope, freeing your hands to work on removing a chock that refuses to budge.
- **As a final option, simply abandon protection if necessary.** Too much time and effort can be wasted on a piece of protection that is not going to come out.

whether the original leader transfers the rest of the rack to the second, who will now lead, or the second transfers the cleaned pieces back to the leader's rack.

Follow this sequence remembering that both climbers always stay anchored to the rock.

1. First, reconstruct the rack. Clip the cleaned pieces to the rack, whether the original leader or the new leader has it. Be careful not to drop any gear.
2. Then hand the removed runners and/or quickdraws over to whoever will lead.
3. If either climber is wearing a pack, it can be removed and clipped in to the anchor.
4. If the original leader plans to lead the next pitch, reflake the rope so that the second's end of the rope is on the bottom and the leader's end is on top; the second should then settle into the belay position.

Swinging leads is more efficient but requires both climbers to be competent at leading. The new leader shoulders the reconstructed rack and then racks the runners according to the climbers' chosen system. The new leader rechecks and adjusts the rack to ensure that everything is ready for the next pitch. A look at the route description may be in order. At the very least, the leader should examine the next pitch and have a sense for the general line to be traveled. The leader is placed on belay and then unclips from the anchor, and the climbing resumes.

CLIMBING WITH A PARTY OF THREE

Most rock climbing is done in pairs, but occasionally a party has three climbers. A three-person team generally is more awkward and less efficient than a two-person team. However, it has an advantage of an extra person available for hauling, rescue, etc. A team of three is faster than two teams of two. Two ropes are required unless the pitches are extremely short.

Using two ropes sequentially. In a team of three, the leader climbs with one rope while the second belays and the third remains anchored at the belay station. At the top of the pitch, the leader sets up a belay and brings up the second, who is belayed by the first rope and has the second rope either clipped with a locking carabiner to the harness' back haul loop or tied in at the front of the harness; the second rope will be used by the third climber. If the pitch follows a straight line up, the second can clean the pitch; remember, a top belay is very safe, and if a fall occurs, the climber falls only a very short distance. If the pitch includes some traversing, some or all of the protection should stay in place for the third climber to help prevent a pendulum fall. In this situation, the second climber unclips each piece of protection from the first rope and clips the protection to the second rope. Once the second climber is at the top of the pitch, the first rope is now completely at the top belay, and the second rope is put on belay to bring up the third climber. When the third climber reaches the top of the pitch, the climbers then may decide to swing leads, with the third climber leading the next pitch using the second rope. For the second to lead, the ropes will need to be retied and perhaps restacked.

Using two ropes simultaneously. Another way to climb with three is for the leader to tie in to both ropes while the second and third climbers each tie in to one of the ropes. Double or twin ropes can be used for this method instead of two larger-diameter single ropes (see the next section), if desired. The leader then climbs the pitch, belayed on both ropes. The belay can be provided by one belayer with two ropes in one device (preferable) or by two belayers with one rope per belayer. At the top of the pitch, the leader sets up a belay station. Then the leader can either belay one follower at a time or bring both up together, one slightly ahead of the other, making sure to leave sufficient space between the climbers so that they will not collide in the case of a fall by the higher climber. Several belay devices available on the market work well for belaying two climbers at a time (see self-braking belay devices in Chapter 10, Belaying). This technique takes more rope management, but this way three climbers can ascend nearly as fast as two. When using this strategy, it is simplest for the original leader to remain on lead throughout the climb. With the additional rope and climber involved in a three-person team, belay stations can be more confusing and messy. Each of the three climbers must remain securely anchored when not climbing.

DOUBLE- AND TWIN-ROPE TECHNIQUES

Most of this book describes climbing situations in which a single rope is usually used. However, climbers can opt for one of the methods that use two smaller-diameter ropes: double-rope technique or twin-rope technique.

Double-Rope Technique

The double-rope technique uses two ropes that serve as independent belay lines. Each rope is referred to as a "half rope," is approved by the UIAA and/or CEN for such use, and is marked by a "½" on the end of the rope.

Half ropes are usually 8 to 9 millimeters in diameter. The leader clips each rope in to its own protection on the way up, and the belayer manages the ropes separately. Most belay devices with two slots can be used, but some are specially designed for use with double ropes. See the manufacturer's guidelines for more details on the approved use of different devices.

Although this technique is more complicated than using a single rope, it does offer some advantages. Rope friction can be greatly reduced, falls can be shorter, two ropes are less likely than one to be severed by rockfall or sharp edges, and two ropes are available for rappel. The technique is widely used by European climbers, by ice climbers, and by an increasing number of climbers everywhere to increase protection on highly technical routes. The ropes should be different colors to allow for clear communication about which rope needs slack or tension.

The double-rope technique offers great advantages when the route meanders. With a series of zigzag placements, one rope can be clipped in to the pieces on the left and one rope in to those on the right, allowing the ropes to remain relatively straight, in roughly parallel lines that do not cross (fig. 14-17a), thereby preventing rope drag (fig. 14-17b). When both ropes are clipped to the same protection placement, each rope is attached using a separate carabiner.

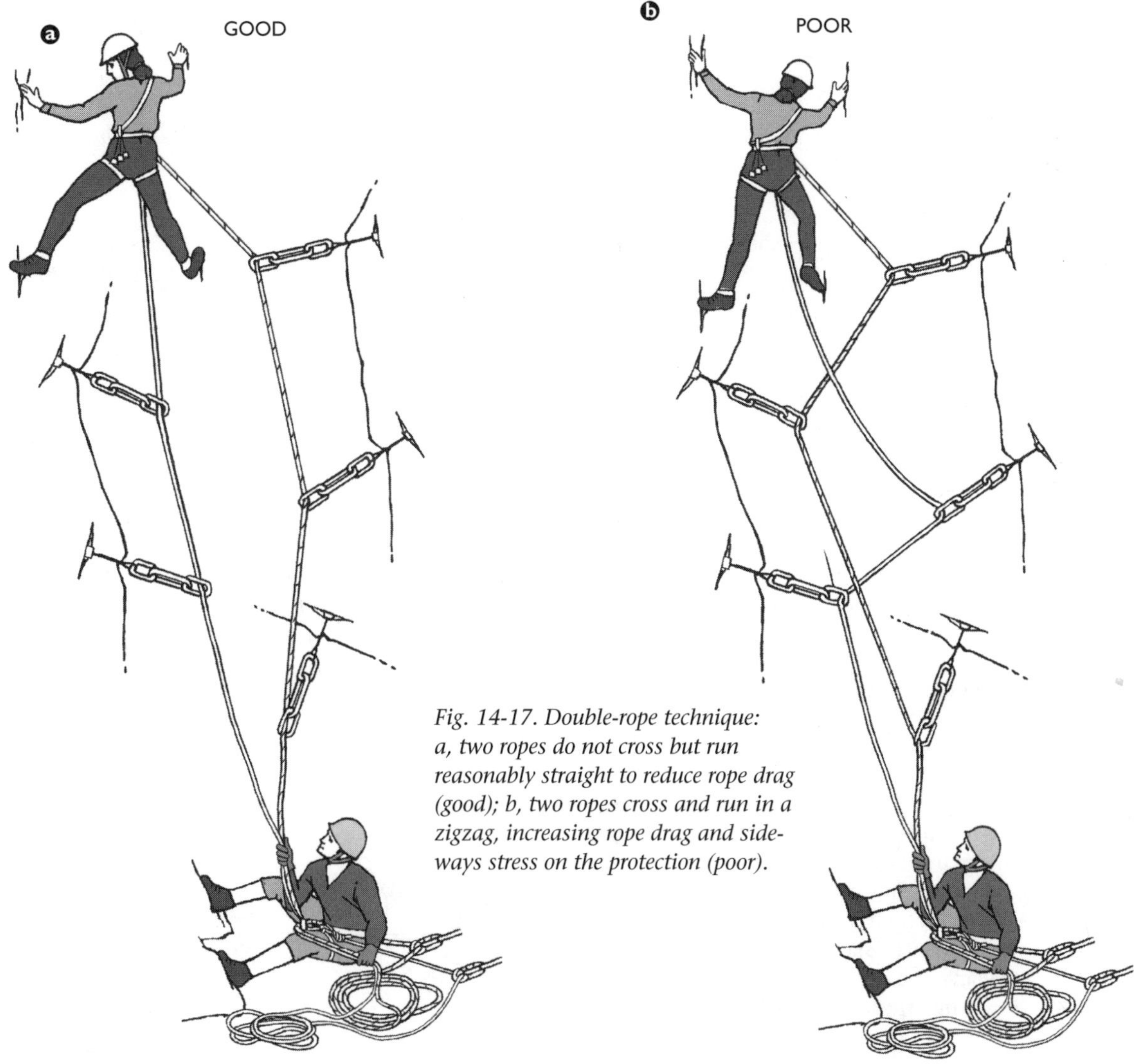

Fig. 14-17. Double-rope technique: a, two ropes do not cross but run reasonably straight to reduce rope drag (good); b, two ropes cross and run in a zigzag, increasing rope drag and sideways stress on the protection (poor).

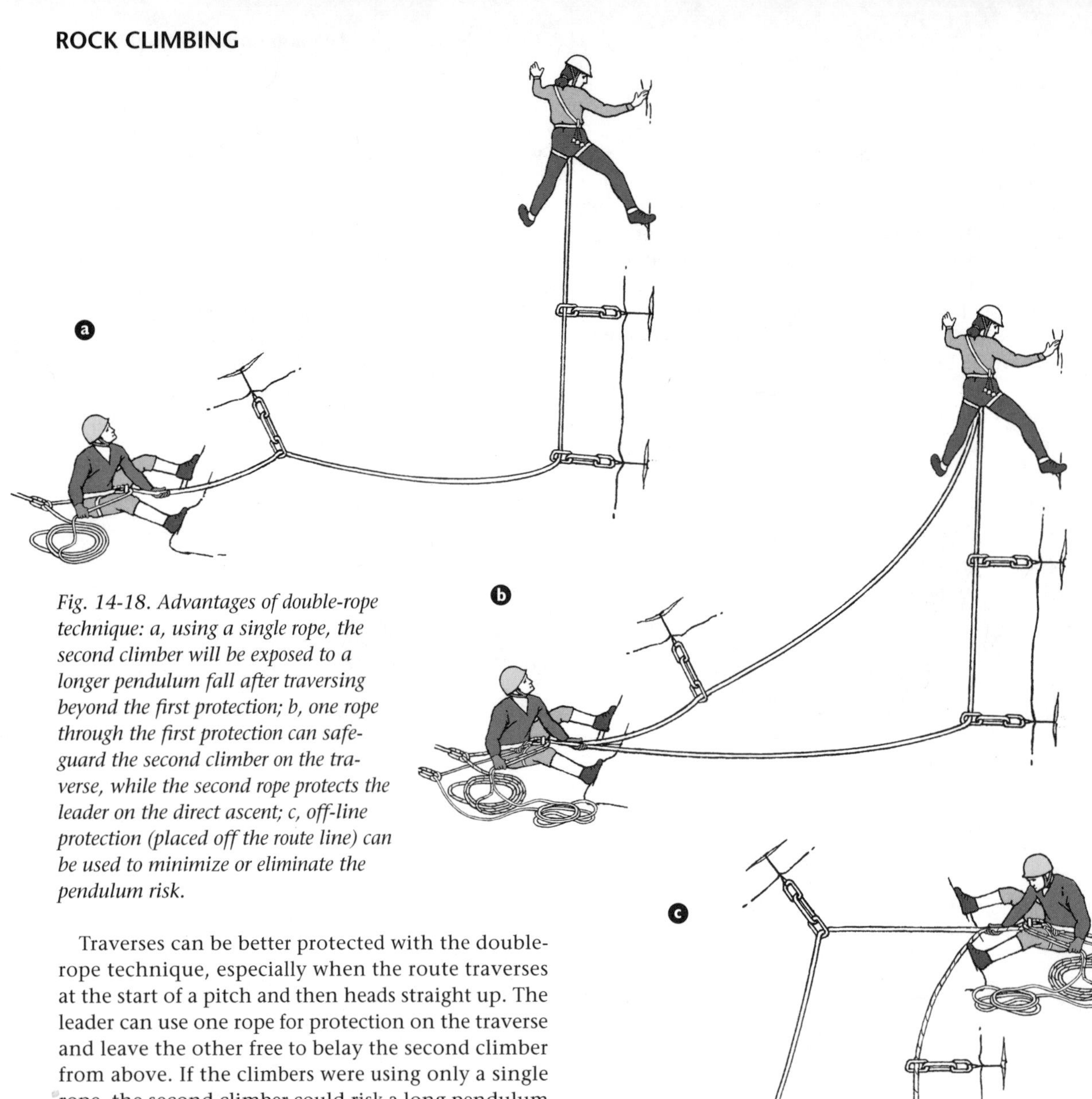

Fig. 14-18. Advantages of double-rope technique: a, using a single rope, the second climber will be exposed to a longer pendulum fall after traversing beyond the first protection; b, one rope through the first protection can safeguard the second climber on the traverse, while the second rope protects the leader on the direct ascent; c, off-line protection (placed off the route line) can be used to minimize or eliminate the pendulum risk.

Traverses can be better protected with the double-rope technique, especially when the route traverses at the start of a pitch and then heads straight up. The leader can use one rope for protection on the traverse and leave the other free to belay the second climber from above. If the climbers were using only a single rope, the second climber could risk a long pendulum fall (fig. 14-18a). But with double ropes, the belay on the free rope can minimize or prevent a long pendulum (fig. 14-18b and c).

Another major advantage of the double-rope technique is that it reduces the worries of the leader who is straining to clip in to the next piece of protection. In single-rope climbing, the rope is slack as the leader pulls up a big length to clip in to the next placement, but with a double rope, the slack for clipping is provided on one rope, and the other rope is held snug by the belayer. Thus, when the leader is clipping in to a newly placed piece of protection, a potential fall is shorter.

One disadvantage is that the belayer's job is more complex, handling the movements of two ropes at the same time—often letting out slack on one rope while taking it in on the other. Also, the two ropes weigh and cost more than a single rope or twin ropes. Another drawback is that the technique requires more practice for both leader and belayer than does single-rope technique.

However, many climbers find that on long, challenging, and complex rock pitches, the advantages of double ropes greatly outweigh the disadvantages.

Twin-Rope Technique

UIAA- and/or CEN-approved twin ropes are generally 7.5 to 8.5 millimeters in diameter, and they are not rated for use as single ropes. The ends of the rope are marked with a symbol of two overlapping circles.

The twin-rope technique shares some characteristics with the single-rope technique and some with the double-rope technique. Two ropes are used, but they are each clipped in to the same piece of protection, as a single larger-diameter rope would be (fig. 14-19).

The twin ropes together absorb more energy and can withstand more falls than a single rope. Though twin ropes are smaller-diameter, severing both at one time is less likely than severing one larger-diameter rope. Plus, two ropes are available for double-rope rappels.

A disadvantage is that the thinner the rope, the more likely it is to tangle. Also, together, twin ropes weigh and cost more than a single rope. Another disadvantage is that the technique lacks the specific advantages of the double-rope system on meandering routes, traverses, and shorter falls. As with double-rope technique, the belayer has to deal with two ropes, but separate management of each rope is greatly lessened.

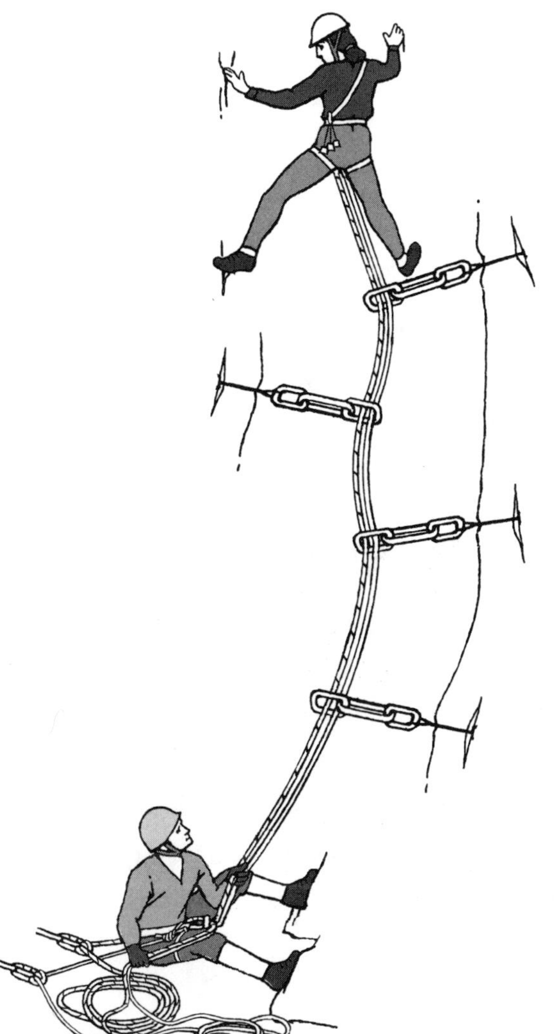

Fig. 14-19. Twin-rope technique: two small-diameter ropes are used as one, with both attached to each protection placement.

PERSONAL RESPONSIBILITY

Leading on rock is a serious commitment. Climbers face decisions in which a poor choice may be fatal. It is impossible to have a complete set of rules that cover every situation. Memorized dogma will not ensure safety. Accurately evaluating the risks of climbing requires instead a fundamental understanding of the risks of the environment and the consequences of each climber's own actions. Base your decisions and actions not on superficial rules but rather on the knowledge gained through study and experience.

CLEAN AID CLIMBING • USES OF AID CLIMBING • AID CLIMBING EQUIPMENT • AID PLACEMENTS • BASIC AID TECHNIQUES • SECONDING • CHANGING LEADS • BIG WALL MULTIDAY TECHNIQUES • THE SPIRIT OF AID CLIMBING

Chapter 15
AID AND BIG WALL CLIMBING

Aid climbing is the technique of using gear to support your weight as you climb. It can be as simple as pulling on a quickdraw or as complex as climbing an entire multiday route with your weight suspended from gear you have placed. Aid climbing is an intricate and personal art, and everyone who participates does it somewhat differently.

Historically, nearly all rock climbs included piton placements and aid climbing, and many classic free climbs enjoyed today were first established as aid climbs. Pioneers such as Fred Beckey, Royal Robbins, Allen Steck, and Layton Kor relied heavily on aid climbing to achieve historic first ascents.

As free climbing skills continue to rise, climbers are freeing many routes originally climbed with aid. But despite the rise in free climbing standards, there will always be tempting routes that are more difficult still—and so devoid of natural features—that a climber will need some of the aid climbing skills described in this chapter. And, whereas today's elite climbers may be able to free an aid route at a high standard of free climbing, the average climber will likely still perform aid climbing to complete these routes in the historical style.

Skills in aid climbing can also help overcome unexpected difficulties during normal free climbing. Aid techniques can provide a way to move safely up or down when bad weather or an accident puts a climbing party in jeopardy. Many routes have short sections of very difficult climbing or poor rock that may be negotiated by aid climbing to gain access to excellent free climbing or a summit. Finally, aid climbing techniques give climbers access to the vertical world of the big walls, such as El Capitan in Yosemite National Park, California, that inspire the dreams of so many climbers around the world.

Aid climbing requires skill, judgment, and a lot of practice. To learn both the basics and the many tricks of aid climbing, work with an experienced partner, and climb often.

CLEAN AID CLIMBING

Aid climbing takes a lot of gear, but it does not need to damage the rock. Traditionally, aid climbing involved hammering in pitons of various sizes, and in the early development of climbing, the entire rack for a climb consisted exclusively of pitons. Both placing and removing pitons permanently damages the rock and over time creates scars and ever-widening placements. On popular routes, tiny cracks sometimes evolve into finger or hand cracks after generations of climbers force them to accept pitons. Today, with chocks, spring-loaded camming devices, hooks, and other gear available, climbers have a better chance of climbing aid routes "clean."

A clean placement is one made without using a hammer. Clean placements can also almost always be removed without defacing the rock, leaving no trace of the party's ascent. Nailing in placements with a hammer is more time consuming for both leader and follower than making clean placements, so climbing clean not only benefits the rock and the state of the route for future parties, but it can speed the ascent of the team.

Because the first ascent party may have left fixed protection such as bolts, pitons (see "Fixed Protection," in Chapter 13, Rock Protection), or copperheads, a clean ascent of an aid route often entails using fixed gear while also carrying some pitons, copperheads, and other nailing hardware in case fixed gear has been removed or is no longer usable. Thus, most clean ascents rely on some protection that earlier parties placed with a hammer and left in place.

Aid and big wall climbers almost always bring a hammer, even if they intend to climb clean, as it is a critical tool used for a wide range of functions in aid climbing. A hammer can be essential in removing clean gear that has been weighted. Some climbers enjoy the challenge of hammerless climbing—climbing with no hammer available on the route—on established aid routes with known fixed gear or even on new routes. The clean and hammerless styles of climbing present an additional level of commitment, and climbers choosing these styles should accept the possibility of retreat.

USES OF AID CLIMBING

Aid climbing can be roughly categorized based on the extent of its use on a particular climb. See Appendix A, Rating Systems, for information on the various grades of difficulty in aid climbing.

Alpine climbing. When ascending a route in the alpine environment, climbing without weighting any gear is usually the climber's goal. However, the climber may use aid techniques and equipment to overcome short, blank, or extremely difficult sections of a route that otherwise can be free climbed. This type of climbing often requires little or no specialized aid equipment; usually climbers just use the free climbing gear they have along. This could include pulling on gear, stepping in a sling, or even creating a makeshift aider or two from slings to get through a section. Sometimes pulling on gear is intentionally done to speed progress and minimize exposure to objective hazards or other risks in the mountains. Some routes have one pitch of aid climbing (or a relatively small number of aid pitches on the overall route), allowing an otherwise free line to be ascended. Packs may be hauled on a difficult pitch, or climbers may perform a pendulum swing to reach the next section of free climbing.

Aid may also be used on alpine climbs for extended distances and with aid-specific equipment, although aid- and free climbing techniques may be interspersed. Long one-day climbs may involve fixing the initial pitches on a preceding day: putting up ropes and leaving them in place so they can be climbed with mechanical ascenders (a technique called jugging) to reach the previous day's high point and complete the route on a second day.

Big wall aid climbing. Ascents of big walls typically take longer than one day to complete, even if the initial pitches are fixed. These climbs usually involve a bivouac and require hauling techniques. With the proliferation of speed climbing techniques, some big walls that originally took many days to ascend are now being climbed in a day by expert climbers. Many big wall climbs require aid on every pitch, and wall climbers typically have many items of aid-specific equipment.

AID CLIMBING EQUIPMENT

This section discusses the range of equipment used in aid climbing, building on all the gear and techniques described in Chapter 13, Rock Protection, and Chapter 14, Leading on Rock. Unique to aid climbing is the use of gear that is designed only for the body weight of the climber. All technical equipment for free climbing is designed to protect the climbers in the event of a fall and to withstand the high forces generated. In aid climbing, certain equipment is used that is designed only for upward progress on the climb, and this equipment is not expected or rated to catch a fall.

BASIC EQUIPMENT FOR AID CLIMBING

Aid climbing relies heavily on standard free climbing equipment. Aid climbers may simply need more of it. The following gear used in free climbing is also used in aid climbing, with some differences in uses at times, as discussed below.

Chocks and Camming Devices

The same chocks and spring-loaded camming devices (SLCDs, or cams) used in free climbing are used on aid climbs. Some SLCDs, like the Camalot and the Alien, feature a large clip-in point on the unit itself in addition to the sling sewn onto the SLCD (see Figure 13-14 in Chapter 13, Rock Protection). This makes it possible to clip an etrier (a webbing ladder used in aid climbing) directly to the piece of protection, which is a higher and more convenient clip-in point than the SLCD's sewn sling. This allows the climber to make fewer placements overall by getting as high as possible in etriers on each SLCD placement. When selecting SLCDs for aid climbing, it may be desirable to give preference to these types of units.

Some SLCDs fit better than others into flaring pin scars (rock that has been damaged by placement and removal of pitons). Aliens are preferred by many aid climbers for pin-scar placements. Hybrid Aliens, also called offset Aliens, with cams of different sizes on each side of the unit, work so well that they have eliminated the need to hammer piton placements on many pitches.

It is often helpful to mix many brands and styles of chocks and SLCDs on the rack when aid climbing, because sometimes the perfect SLCD for the crack being climbed will be in between the sizes made by one manufacturer. In that case, a different brand of SLCD that is slightly different in size may fit the crack better.

Carabiners

Aid climbing employs many carabiners! The more organized and efficient the climbers are, especially at anchor building and organization of gear inside the haul bag, the fewer carabiners needed. Carabiners are used to rack protection, to sling protection (see "Slings," below), to build anchors, to clip the haul bag to the haul line, to clip critical gear to gear loops inside the haul bag, to attach etriers, daisy chains, and ascenders—and for many other purposes.

Traditionally, aid climbers preferred oval carabiners for the entire rack because of the "biner shift" phenomenon. Biner shift occurs after a climber clips one carabiner to another so that a piece of protection can be weighted while the climber stands in etriers, and then a carabiner shifts, making a sound like gear popping. In the context of aid climbing, this can be a terrifying false alarm of an imminent fall. However, the modern techniques of clipping directly in to the aid protection with the etrier, instead of putting a sling on the protection and clipping in to that sling's carabiner, and the use of oval keylock carabiners on both etriers, eliminate biner shift most of the time. As a result, there is no longer a special emphasis on oval carabiners, so most aid climbers now carry lighter wire-gate carabiners as much as possible to reduce the overall weight of the aid rack. One common method is to use wire-gate carabiners for protection and slings and to carry conventional-gate carabiners, including many locking carabiners, for anchors. Aid racks are especially heavy on the climb's descent, so saving weight using modern lightweight and wire-gate carabiners pays off.

Small and Offset Nuts

Aid racks include small micronuts that are even more specialized than those for typical free climbing racks. These tapered nuts are often used instead of thin pitons or in pin scars, but they may not be as strong.

Two general styles of micronuts are available. The first is a smaller version of the classic tapered Stopper. The other style has both horizontal and vertical taper and is referred to as an offset nut (see Figure 13-10d and e in Chapter 13, Rock Protection). These offset nuts are more secure in flaring cracks and pin scars. Offset nuts are also made in larger sizes than micronuts and are very useful, possibly indispensible, when climbing walls with pin scars.

The heads of small nuts are made from aluminum, brass, or stainless steel. The rock bites into aluminum or brass, and so these materials tend to hold better in marginal placements, but steel nuts are less likely to deform and fail if a fall is taken on one of them. Small and offset nuts can be difficult or impossible to remove after they have been weighted by the aid climber. The heads of the smallest nuts are very small, and the cable blocks the area a climber would normally hit with a chock pick. Using a hammer and funkness device (see "Universal Aid-Specific Equipment," below) is often the only way to remove nuts once they have been weighted.

Ropes

The tough duty of aid climbing usually requires a 10- to 11-millimeter kernmantle lead rope, 60 meters (approximately 200 feet) long. The haul line is typically a second lead rope or a 10-millimeter static line. If the route entails long pendulum swings or other unusual problems, a third rope may be needed—either another kernmantle rope or another static line. When selecting a rope, keep in mind its resistance to abrasion and edge cutting, because of the typically rough terrain and demands associated with aid climbing. See "Ropes" in Chapter 9, Basic Safety System.

Examine ropes often, and consider retiring aid ropes earlier than a free climbing rope might be retired. Jugging, rappeling, and hauling put extreme wear on ropes. Climbers trust their life to the rope when using ascenders to jug a fixed line, so they do not want to worry about whether they waited too long before retiring it.

Slings

Carry single-length slings for establishing anchors, extending placements to reduce rope drag, and other normal rock climbing uses. Single-length slings are the most useful because they can easily be carried over the shoulder; they can also be carried like quickdraws and easily extended to full length after the first half is clipped to the placement (see Figure 14-7 in Chapter 14, Leading on Rock).

Load-limiting runners, such as the Yates Screamer, are sometimes used to climb above placements of questionable strength. In a fall, the slings limit the shock delivered to the protection (see Figure 9-35 in Chapter 9, Basic Safety System).

Cordelettes and other sling materials used to create anchors for free climbing are equally useful for aid climbing. Cordelettes are popular for anchors on big walls, because multiple anchor points are usually employed. See Chapters 9, Basic Safety System, and 10, Belaying, for more information on slings and cordelettes.

Self-Braking Belay Device

Certain self-braking belay devices, such as the Petzl Grigri, have special uses in aid climbing. While aid routes can be climbed without these devices, these multipurpose tools are helpful in many tricky situations encountered in aid climbing. (See Figure 10-6b in Chapter 10, Belaying, pictures the Grigri.) During long belays, for example, a Grigri can help you manage the rope while accomplishing other tasks such as managing the haul line, eating, drinking, and even relieving yourself. The Grigri is also helpful as a backup when following, it can be used during hauling, it can substitute as a mechanical ascender if one is dropped, it allows superior control when rappeling on a single line—and it serves many other helpful purposes on an aid climb.

Helmet

A helmet is absolutely essential for aid climbing (see Chapter 9, Basic Safety System). Steep terrain, large racks (which make the climber top-heavy), and the dynamics of a popped placement tend to send aid climbers into headfirst falls. Other hazards include rockfall, dropped gear, roofs, and other climbers. If used properly, a chest harness may keep the climber upright if the rope draws taut prior to contacting the rock, but this in no way replaces the need for head protection.

Gloves

Over and above their value for belaying and rappeling, leather gloves are critical for hauling. Gloves protect the climber's hands while jugging and removing protection. Aid climbing is very hard on gloves, and they need to be replaced often. Leather gardening gloves can be used, with the fingertips cut off just slightly. Tape makes a great reinforcement on the cut edge to keep cut fingertips from unraveling (fig. 15-1).

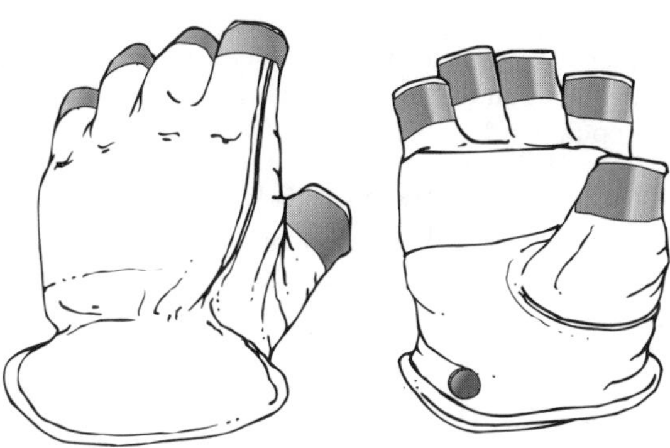

Fig. 15-1. Leather gloves with cutoff fingers, reinforced with tape, and with holes cut as a clip-in point.

Shoes

If the route involves only a small amount of aid, normal rock shoes perform best. If sustained aid climbing is anticipated, shoes or boots with greater sole rigidity provide a better working platform and more comfort. Sticky rubber approach shoes are very popular for aid climbing, including on big walls. They provide arch support and good torsional rigidity for aid climbing yet have a flexible toe and a soft friction rubber sole for good free climbing capabilities.

Eye Protection

It is important both for leaders and followers to protect their eyes from debris when cleaning out cracks, when using a hammer, and from equipment or other hazards that could come loose or contact the face. Sunglasses typically provide adequate protection. However, consider photosensitive or changeable lenses so that eye protection can be comfortably worn when it is not sunny or when climbing in the shade.

Knife

Just as in free climbing, a sharp knife is required equipment on the harness. Climbers often must remove webbing or cord in order to be able to clip a carabiner to a piece of fixed protection, to replace the worn webbing with new webbing, or simply to remove unnecessary old fixed slings from the rock to help keep the climb pristine for other climbers. Given the heavy loads involved in aid climbing, unexpected situations can occur wherein a sling or cord has to be cut in order to free a load or fix an error. For example, if a climber accidentally tied in a haul bag on a docking cord with a nonreleasable knot, the only way to free the bag might be to cut that docking cord (see "Big Wall Multiday Techniques," later in this chapter). A knife comes in handy for repairing or making homemade gear during a multiday climb and for many other purposes.

UNIVERSAL AID-SPECIFIC EQUIPMENT

In addition to equipment normally used in free climbing, aid climbers need a selection of gear that is used both for clean aid climbing and for aid that may involve placing pitons.

Etriers (Aiders)

Webbing ladders, also called aiders, allow the climber to step up from one placement to the next when the aiders are clipped to a chock, SLCD, or other aid piece. When making or buying aiders, consider their intended use. For alpine climbs, minimize weight by using a single lightweight pair of aiders. For most aid climbing, five-step or six-step aiders sewn from 1-inch (2.5-centimeter) webbing are standard (fig. 15-2a and b). They are used, usually in pairs, in leapfrog fashion as the climber ascends. Aiders should be long enough to allow the climber to reach the bottom step of the higher ladder when testing aid placements from a comfortable stance on the lower ladder. More difficult aid routes usually require six-step ladders, because there may be longer distances between placement options and because down-climbing to the lower piece is more common.

The basic aid sequence (see "The Basic Sequence," later in this chapter) uses two aiders. However, some aid climbers use four aiders, permanently set up in pairs. A third method is to use two aiders but to have a spare

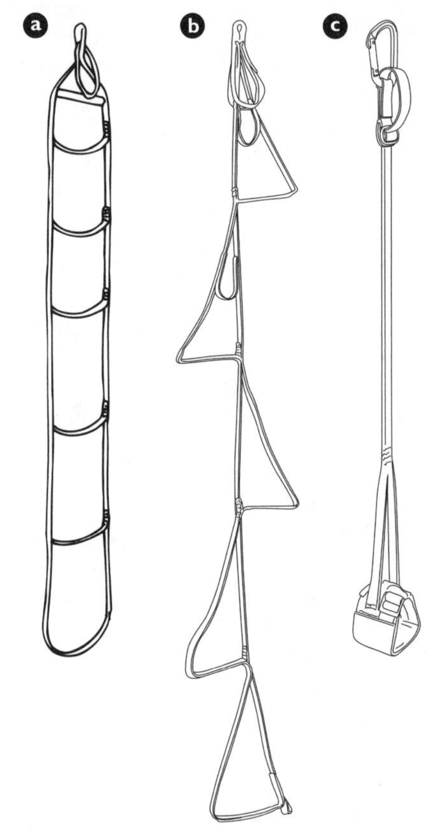

Fig. 15-2. Types of etriers: a, ladder style; b, offset-step style; c, adjustable.

third aider available, possibly loose on the harness, for occasional tricky sequences. The use of more than two aiders is popular on more difficult aid routes, but ultimately, the number of aiders used depends on personal preference.

Other aider systems that have been developed have become quite popular. An adjustable type of aider (fig. 15-2c) tends to be lighter and is especially well suited for quick adjustment for optimal jugging. Most climbers use adjustable aiders as follower gear only. Other different aider systems include the "Russian aider" system, which completely diverges from the ladder design: It instead uses a system of slings with small metal rings and a knee strap, which is equipped with hooks that allow the climber to "hook" the aider and stand suspended in the rings. However, the ladder-type system remains the most commonly used and most commercially available.

Daisy Chains

Traditional daisy chains are sewn slings with multiple loops (fig. 15-3a)—formed by stitching—every 3 to 6 inches (8 to 15 centimeters). Daisy chains are used as tethers to keep new placements and aiders attached to the lead climber; they are an integral part of the jugging setup. A daisy chain should, when attached to the harness, reach at least as far as the climber's raised hand. Typical daisy chains are 45 to 55 inches (115 to 140 centimeters) long. Longer daisy chains are helpful for difficult aid routes, because they permit the climber to down-climb longer distances below a piece, which allows for adequate testing (see the "The Basic Sequence," later in this chapter). The sewn loops are used to shorten the daisy chain when it is used in the jugging mode. This shortening must be done in accordance with the manufacturer's guidelines.

Usually two daisy chains are carried, one for the left-side aider and one for the right-side aider. One end of each daisy chain is girth-hitched to the climbing harness while the other end is attached to the appropriate aider with a carabiner, preferably a dedicated oval key-lock carabiner. Connecting the aider to the daisy chain prevents the loss of an aider if it is dropped or if a placement fails, and the daisy chain also provides a convenient method for resting on a placement by using a fifi hook (see below). Adjustable daisy straps (fig. 15-3b), a new tether option for the modern aid climber, are an alternative to the classic daisy chain, and they have special features outside of their use as a tether (see below).

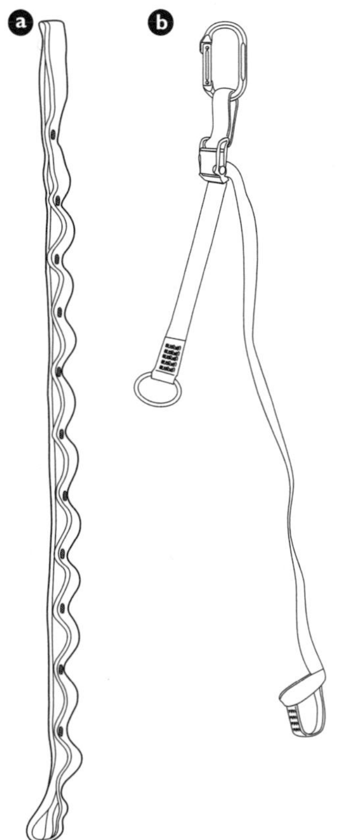

Fig. 15-3. Daisy chains: a, loop-style daisy chain; b, adjustable daisy strap.

Adjustable daisy straps must also be used in accordance with the manufacturer's guidelines. Some designs are sturdier and more reliable than others.

Fifi Hooks

A fifi hook (fig. 15-4a) can be a critical part of the basic aid sequence. Attached to the harness, it is used to hook in to a placement and to hold the climber's body weight. Using a fifi hook or an adjustable daisy strap is important in order to conserve energy and to aid climb steep routes, including roofs. A fifi hook allows climbers to rest on placements, which is more efficient than holding their weight with body tension or with their arms and legs. The fifi hook also provides helpful countertension when used to hook a piece at waist level while climbing above it to top-step (see Figure 15-20) or to make difficult reaches above protection, such as on overhangs.

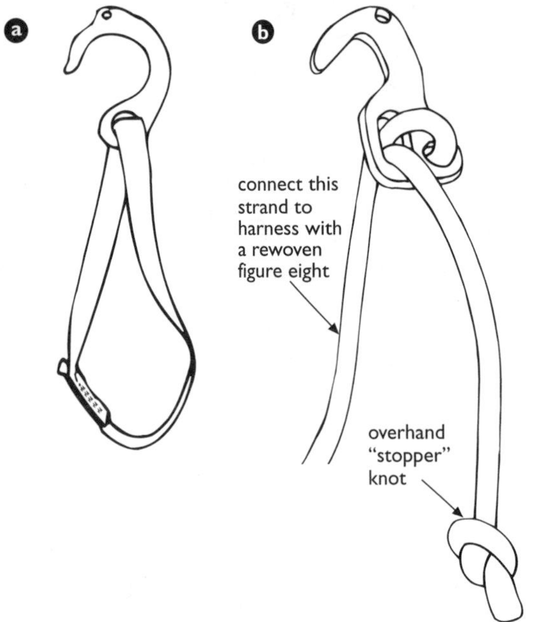

Fig. 15-4. Fifi hooks: a, classic style; b, adjustable.

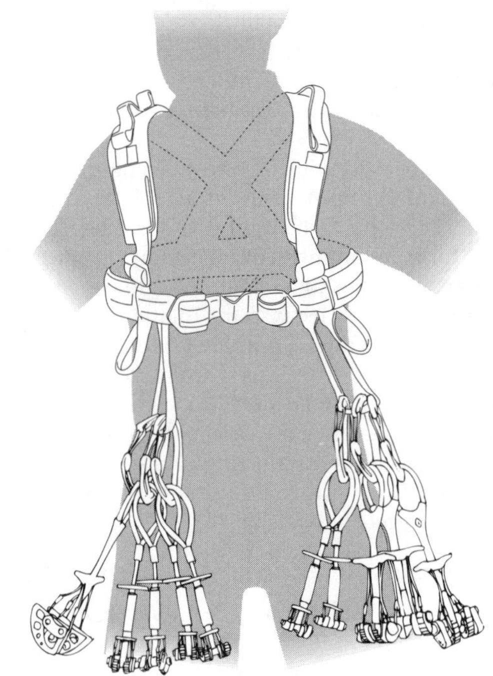

Fig. 15-5. Double gear sling with racked SLCDs.

The classic fifi hook is girth-hitched to the harness with a sling that reaches 2 to 4 inches (5 to 10 centimeters) away from the harness after the girth hitch is tied. An adjustable fifi hook (fig. 15-4b) is rigged with slippery 6-millimeter accessory cord and is tied in to the harness on one end with this cord, typically with a rewoven figure eight knot. The adjustable fifi hook can be placed higher away from the harness initially than the classic fifi hook, and then the distance can be shortened as needed by pulling on the cord.

An adjustable daisy strap (see "Daisy Chains," above) can be used in place of an adjustable fifi hook. Some climbers use two traditional daisy chains as tethers to attach their aiders to their harness and one adjustable daisy strap to rest on pieces.

Double Gear Sling

A double gear sling distributes the weight of the hardware with equipment slings on both sides of the body (fig. 15-5). It improves balance and comfort, and it reduces neck strain caused by the single bearing point of a traditional free climbing gear sling. A double gear sling can also serve as a chest harness, if it is designed for this use, when the climber is jugging up a rope or to keep the climber upright during a fall. Racking methods vary widely, but given the weight and volume of gear carried on aid climbs, double gear slings are standard equipment.

Aid-Specific Harness

Harnesses made specifically for aid climbing are not required, but they typically feature an extrawide belt and larger leg loops, and on some harnesses, both belt and leg loops have padding. Most such harnesses also feature a hammer holster. Some have other special features, including wider, extra-strong belay loops. All these features help ease the pain of continuous days in the harness during big wall climbs.

Knee Pads

A climber's knees are regularly in contact with the rock during low-angle aid climbing and during hauling, so wearing knee pads protects them. Knee pads should be comfortable and allow good circulation.

Belay Seat

A belay seat is a great creature comfort during hanging belays. *Warning:* Never let the belay seat be the sole means of attaching to an anchor. Clip in from the harness to the anchor with the climbing rope as usual, and attach the belay seat to any secure point with its own carabiner. Belay seats can be purchased, or climbers can make their own out of wood, a little padding, and some slings.

Mechanical Ascenders

When aid climbing was pioneered, ascending fixed ropes was always done with prusik hitches. Mechanical ascenders—often referred to as "jugs" or "jumars" (fig. 15-6)—are stronger, safer, faster, and less tiring; they have generally replaced the prusik hitch for ascending a fixed line. The devices are also very helpful for hauling bags up big walls.

All ascenders employ a cam, allowing them to slide freely in one direction on a rope but to grip tightly when pulled in the opposite direction. Ascenders also have a trigger or locking mechanism to keep them from accidentally coming off the rope. Some triggers are difficult to release, decreasing the chance of accidental removal but making it harder to get them off when the climber wants to remove them. They are designed for use by a specific hand, either left or right, and when using two, climbers carry one for each hand. (See "Using Ascenders," later in this chapter.)

In addition to the main opening at the bottom of the ascender which is used as the primary attachment point, additional carabiner holes at the top and the bottom of the ascender come in handy for a number of purposes.

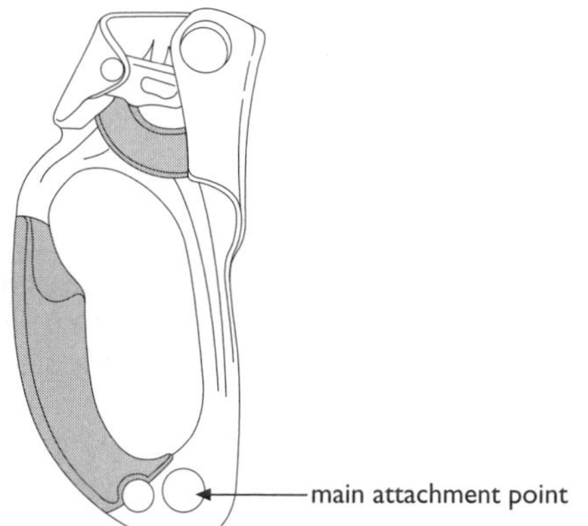

Fig. 15-6. Handled mechanical ascender for left hand (right-hand ascender is a mirror image): The rope passes through the vertical passage near the top; carabiner holes at top and bottom are used for a number of purposes.

Big Wall Hammers

The big wall hammer (see Figure 15-7) is a basic aid tool that has a flat striking surface for cleaning and driving pitons and a blunt pick for prying out protection, cleaning dirty cracks, and placing malleable pieces. A carabiner hole in the head is useful for cleaning pieces (see "Cleaning," later in this chapter).

A sling is attached to the handle of the hammer to prevent the climber from losing the hammer if it is dropped; the sling should allow full arm extension when the hammer is used. Be sure to check the sling regularly for wear. It is a good idea to holster the hammer whenever it is not in use, to keep it secure and to allow quick access; a commercial holster can be added to the harness.

Funkness Device

A funkness device (fig. 15-7) is a metal sling made from cable, with loops on each end for clipping carabiners. The device is used as a static sling to assist in cleaning pieces; it is helpful for removing pins and also chocks that have been weighted by the leader. One carabiner is clipped to the piece that needs to be removed, and the other carabiner is connected to the hammer; then the climber jerks upward and outward with the hammer to remove the wedged piece. In order to withstand the inevitable beating, carabiners used with a funkness device should be conventional (not wire-gate) carabiners. The carabiners should fit comfortably in the holes in the hammers being used so that the funkness device can

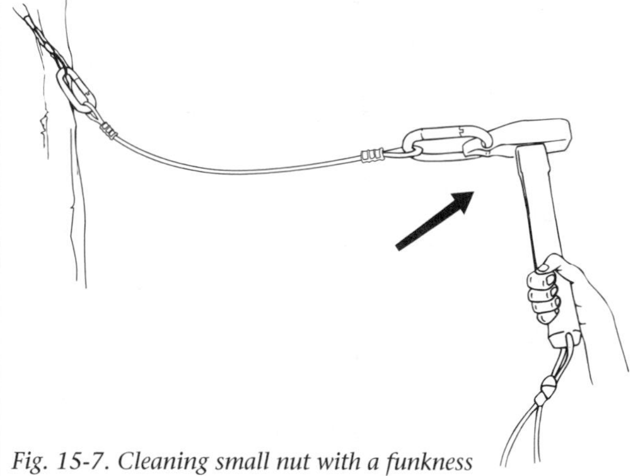

Fig. 15-7. Cleaning small nut with a funkness device and hammer.

15

be easily clipped to the hammer and also have adequate freedom of movement while in use.

Tie-off Loops

Tie-off loops are carried in a variety of sizes and strengths. Sizes range from 4 to 8 inches (10 to 20 centimeters) long when tied. The loops are made either of full-strength webbing—meaning the webbing has a strength rating expected to arrest a fall—or of thinner ½-inch webbing that is meant for body weight only. Climbers often purchase sewn full-strength tie-off loops to avoid having a knot on these small slings, but they typically tie their own body-weight tie-off loops.

Body-weight tie-off loops are very inexpensive to create, which makes them attractive for leaving behind on a route, girth-hitched to fixed gear, for example, often for the purpose of lowering off of a fixed piece when following a pitch. Body-weight tie-off loops are also used to prevent the loss of stacked pieces (described in "Piton Placement," later in this chapter).

Full-strength tie-off loops are used on a placement expected to hold a fall. These loops might be used through the head of a fixed piton if the eye would not accommodate a carabiner, when tying off partially driven pins (see Figure 13-9 in Chapter 13, Rock Protection), or as a makeshift quickdraw if the leader runs out of gear.

Hooks

Hooks (sometimes called standard hooks, with the advent of camming hooks—see below) come in many shapes; they are commonly used to grip ledges or small holes. Hooks are typically made of chromium molybdenum steel for strength and curved for stability. Hooks are used for body weight only and by their nature are almost never left behind as protection (see "Hook Placement and Use," later in this chapter).

Attach a sling to a hook by feeding a tie-off loop through from the front until the knot jams (see Figure 15-8b). The sling should hang from the rock side of the hook, with the knot on the other side. This puts the line of force next to the rock, eliminates rotation of the tip of the hook off the rock feature, and keeps the knot out of the way, allowing the hook to rest against the wall. Hooks are often slung with ½-inch tie-off webbing.

Many different sizes and types of hooks can be useful on a big wall. Some popular models, no longer commercially available, are still considered critical gear for certain types of ascents and popular routes. (This creates a sourcing challenge for aspiring aid climbers.) In general, for most routes consider carrying at least one basic hook (fig. 15-8a), one bat hook (fig. 15-8b), and one large hook (fig. 15-8c). One model, the Talon, features three differently shaped hooks (fig. 15-8d). Because the two extra hooks can serve as "legs," this hook can be the best fit for some features. It is a good idea to carry two of each type of hook on longer aid routes, in case the same type of hook is needed two times in a row or in case a hook is dropped.

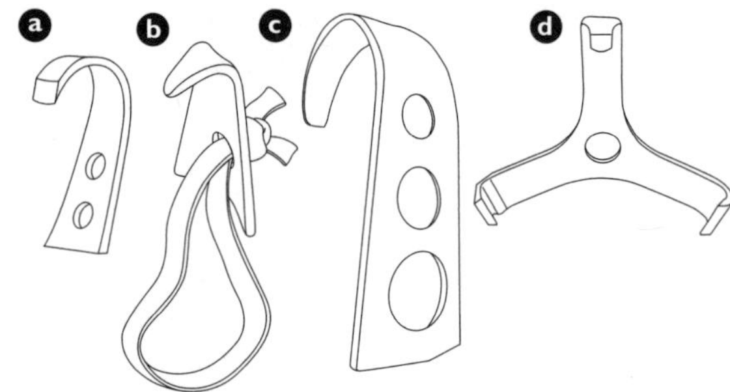

Fig. 15-8. Standard hook types: a, basic; b, bat hook; c, large hook; d, Talon.

Greater stability can be achieved on some placements if the tip of the hook is filed to a point that can be set into small holes drilled at the back of tiny ledges. Bat hooks are used almost exclusively in shallow, ¼-inch (6-millimeter) holes that have been drilled for their use.

There are additional variations on the hooks shown here, as well as many more shapes and sizes not shown.

Camming Hooks

Camming hooks (also called cam hooks) can be used in any crack that is at least as wide as the thickness of the metal and no wider than the width across the hook's tip. Often, a cam hook can be used to avoid placing a pin, especially in scars made by wedge pitons (Lost Arrows). Cam hooks have different tip widths and "arm" lengths (fig. 15-9a), which produce different leverage on the rock features. Too much leverage may bite into the rock or expand a flake, whereas too little leverage may make the placement insecure. Narrow cam hooks tend to have higher leverage (fig. 15-9b and c); wider cam hooks tend to have lower leverage. Cam hooks can be used in leapfrog style to advance quickly on relatively easy terrain.

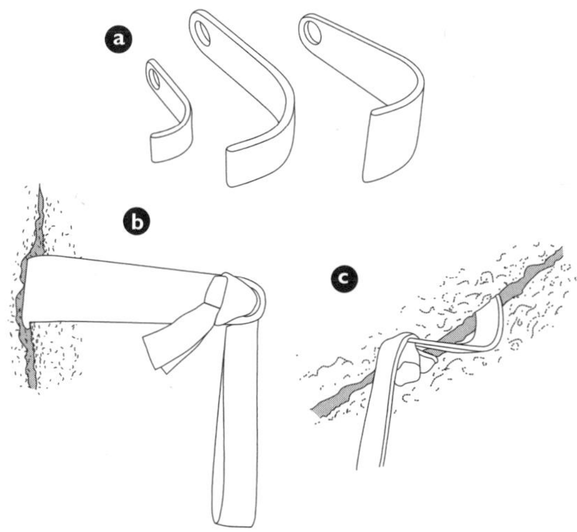

Fig. 15-9. Cam hooks: a, typical cam hook sizes; small, medium, large; b, cam hook placement in vertical crack; c, cam hook upside down under a roof.

Rivet Hangers

Rivet hangers are used to attach to bolt studs and rivets (which are basically shallowly driven ¼-inch bolts with a wide head).

Wire hangers (fig. 15-10a and b) are loops of wire ⅛-inch or 3⁄32-inch in diameter, with a slider to cinch the wire tight. Small nuts with wire slings can be used in a similar manner, with the chock itself acting as the slider to tighten the wire against the bolt stud (see Figure 13-7 in Chapter 13, Rock Protection); however, because chocks have a longer wire loop than wire hangers do, they do not provide as much elevation gain. Wire hangers primarily assist with upward progress and may not catch a fall, and rivets are generally considered body weight protection only, so use careful judgment when relying on them as protection.

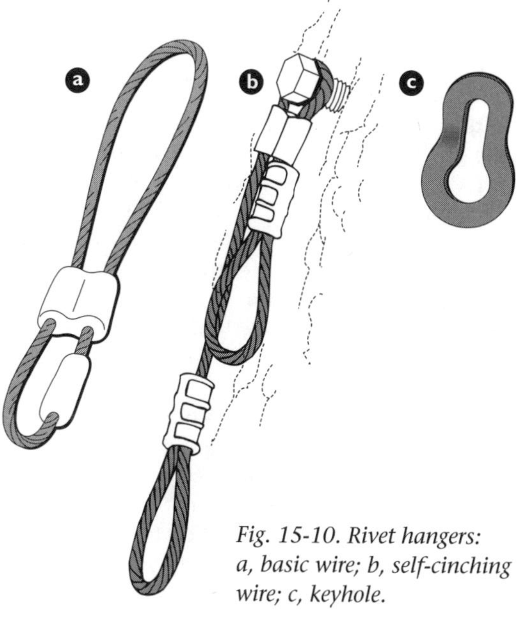

Fig. 15-10. Rivet hangers: a, basic wire; b, self-cinching wire; c, keyhole.

Regular and keyhole hangers are rivet hangers made from shaped pieces of metal (fig. 15-10c). They are useful especially for belay anchors and for fixed bolts that have no hangers. Keyhole hangers have the metal between the bolt hole and the carabiner hole filed out to allow placement over rivets and buttonhead bolts. When a regular or keyhole hanger is placed over a good bolt, it is considered protection that would arrest a fall. It is also wise to carry a few loose nuts for bolts and rivets without hangers.

IRON HARDWARE AND BOLTS

The full range of aid climbing techniques can be mastered only with knowledge of pitons, malleable hardware, and bolts.

Pitons

Modern pitons—also called pins—are made of hardened chromium molybdenum steel or other suitable alloys such as titanium alloys. Rather than molding to cracks the way the malleable pitons of old did, they force the crack to their form. To fit the diverse cracks encountered on rock walls, pitons vary tremendously in size and shape.

Realized Ultimate Reality Piton. The RURP is the smallest piton, a postage-stamp-sized, hatchet-shaped pin (fig. 15-11a) used in incipient cracks. It will usually support only body weight.

Birdbeaks. Also called beaks and commonly known by the brand name Peckers, birdbeaks (fig. 15-11b) range from those similar to RURPs in size to larger units that fit in placements similar to those for knifeblades or even wedge pitons. Beaks are particularly strong when they can be placed so that the long nose of the beak creates camming action inside the crack, which often makes them a more secure choice than knifeblades. In an excellent beak placement, the nose of the beak goes back into the crack away from the climber and also angles down into the crack toward the ground, so that when removing the beak, the follower must nail

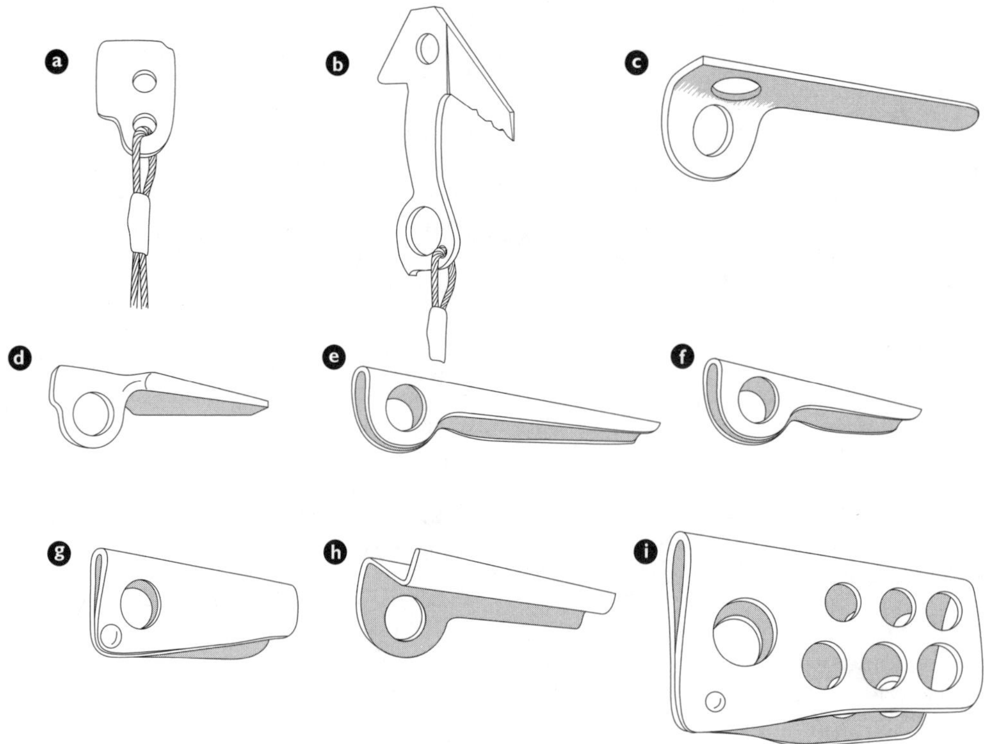

Fig. 15-11. Piton (pin) types: a, Realized Ultimate Reality Piton (RURP); b, Pecker; c, knifeblade; d, Lost Arrow; e, angle; f, sawed-off angle; g, large angle, sawed off; h, Leeper Z; i, bong.

it not only up and down, as with a typical piton (see "Seconding," below), but also outward toward the follower. Thus, beaks can be especially difficult to clean. It is common to damage the cable on the beak when cleaning, so take care and consider backing up the cable with webbing.

Knifeblades. Also called blades, knifeblades are long and thin and have two eyes—one at the end of the blade and a second in the offset portion of the pin (fig. 15-11c). They come in different lengths, in thicknesses ranging from ⅛ to 3⁄16 inch (3 to 4 millimeters). They are commonly used to fit cracks that are too thin for tiny nuts. Many routes have plenty of fixed blades in place, but their use has become less common because beaks tend to be more secure in cracks of the same size.

Wedge pitons. Known commonly by the brand name Lost Arrows, wedge pitons have a single eye centered and set perpendicular to the end of the pin (fig. 15-11d). These are commonly used; they come in several lengths, in thicknesses ranging from 5⁄32 to 9⁄32 inch (4 to 8 millimeters). They are very good in horizontal cracks.

Angles. Pitons formed into a V shape are called angles (fig. 15-11e, f, and g). The V varies in height from ½ to 1½ inches (12 to 38 millimeters). The strength of these pitons is derived from the metal's resistance to bending and spreading. Angles are commonly used in angle pin scars, since oftentimes nothing else will fit in a pin scar except a pin. Otherwise, a crack large enough to accept an angle will normally accept clean climbing equipment if the crack has never been used for pin placements.

Leeper Z pitons. The Leeper Z piton has a Z-shaped profile (fig. 15-11h), as opposed to the V profile of an angle. These pitons often make very solid placements and work well for pin stacking (see "Stacking and Nesting," later in this chapter). Sawed-off Leeper Z pins (discussed below) can work well in angle scars.

Bongs. Bongs are large angle pitons, varying from

2 to 6 inches (5 to 15 centimeters) wide (fig. 15-11i). SLCDs and other large gear options have generally replaced the need for bongs.

Sawed-off pitons. Pitons with a few inches cut off the end are useful for shallow placements. These sawed-off pitons are handy for protection on routes that have been heavily climbed using pitons, which leaves shallow pin scars. Sawed-off angles (see Figure 15-11f and g) of widths from ¾ to 1½ inches (19 to 38 millimeters) are the most common sawed-off pins.

Malleable Hardware

Generally called copperheads (even when not made of copper), or just heads, malleable hardware is designed to hold weight by melding the soft head of the piece to the irregularities of the rock, such as a small constriction or corner. The security of heads varies greatly, and it is difficult to gauge the strength of a copperhead when placed, making them last-resort equipment, generally capable of holding only body weight, although they may hold falls.

Copperheads. Copperheads have a sleeve, called a ferrule, of copper or aluminum swaged to one end of a short cable that has a loop at the other end (fig. 15-12a). They are placed by pounding the relatively soft metal end into an irregularity in the rock. Copper forms well and is more durable than aluminum; aluminum copperheads are not as strong but are more malleable, and because of that, they are generally easier to place correctly. Aluminum is the best choice for most placements; copper is generally best used only for the smallest copperheads.

Circleheads. Circleheads consist of a wire loop with one or more copper or aluminum ferrules swaged on the loop (fig. 15-12b), one of which is pounded into the rock in the same manner as a copperhead. They are used in horizontal cracks, overhead placements, and other applications wherein the symmetry of the wire loop's attachment point is preferable to a regular head because of the anticipated direction of pull.

Bolts

Chapter 13, Rock Protection, includes a section on the use of existing bolts found on climbing routes. Proper bolt placement is a special skill, beyond the scope of this book. Bolt placement is best left to the skill and judgment of very experienced climbers.

BIG WALL EQUIPMENT

Climbers undertaking a big wall have other specialized equipment needs to consider. Safeguard important equipment taken on a big wall climb by using tie-in loops or lanyards to attach anything that might be dropped. Bring gear that will get the party through the worst possible weather, because there is not likely to be any easy way to retreat. Be sure all equipment is durable, and

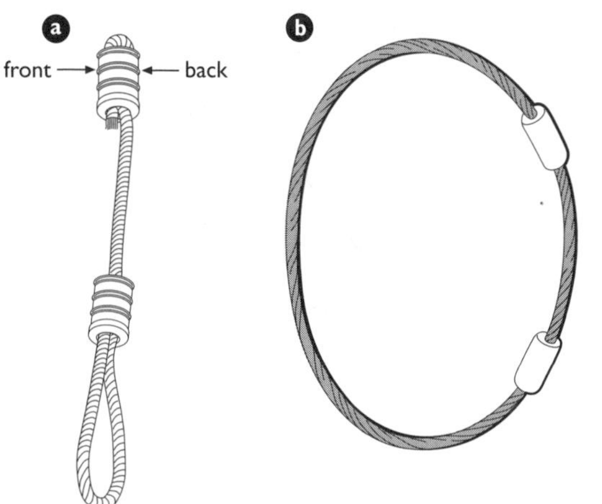

Fig. 15-12. Malleable hardware types: a, copperhead; b, circlehead.

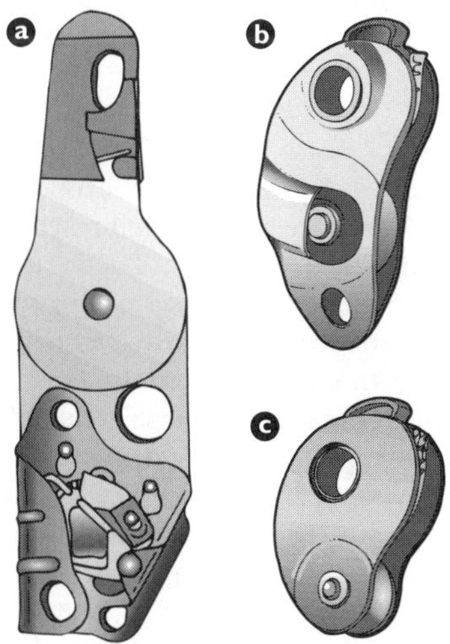

Fig. 15-13. Hauling devices (or haulers): a, Kong Block Roll; b, Petzl Pro Traxion; c, Petzl Mini Traxion.

consider reinforcing equipment—with duct tape, when applicable—such as water bottles, portaledges, haul bags, and other items that can be protected from failure with some preventive maintenance.

Pulleys and Hauling Devices

Pulleys are necessary to ease the chore of hauling. They receive much abuse, so they must be durable. Pulleys with bearings and larger wheels operate more smoothly. Pulleys with self-locking cams, also called haulers or hauling devices, are especially useful for extensive hauling (fig. 15-13). It is a good idea to carry simple pulleys for setting up mechanical advantage during a haul or for using in rescue situations (see Chapter 24, Alpine Search and Rescue).

Haul Bags

Haul bags carry clothing, water, food, sleeping bags, and other climbing and nonclimbing paraphernalia (fig. 15-14a). A good haul bag has adequate cargo capacity, a solid haul suspension, durable fabric, no snag points, and a removable backpacking harness system. A knot protector helps protect the knot connecting the haul bag to the haul line and may reduce snagging problems during hauling. An effective knot protector can be readily fashioned from the top of a 2-liter plastic bottle and some cord (fig. 15-14b). Before leaving the ground, equip your haul bag with a docking cord, typically 20 feet (7 meters) of 8-millimeter cord. Attach the cord directly to the primary haul strap of the haul bag with a rewoven figure eight.

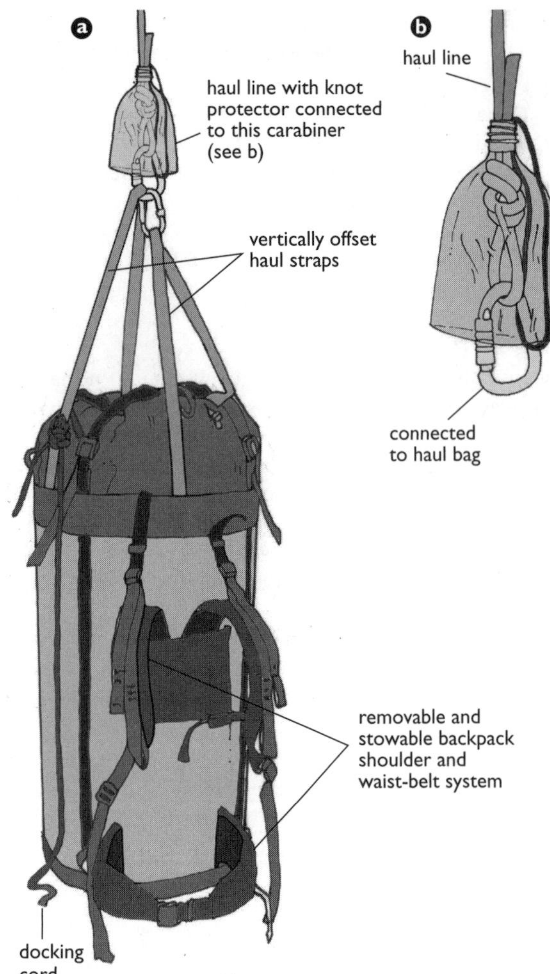

Fig. 15-14. Haul bag: a, features include solid haul suspension and removable backpacking harness system; b, protecting the knot.

Cheater Sticks

Cheater sticks allow climbers to clip the rope or an aider in to a piece of hardware beyond their reach. The most important reason to carry some kind of cheater stick on a big wall is for use in down-aiding (making placements and clipping the rope in to them while rappeling) in the event of a retreat through steep terrain. If a fixed placement is missing, broken, or otherwise not usable, using a cheater stick to reach another placement provides a viable option to placing new pitons, copperheads, or bolts.

A tent pole or hiking stick can be fashioned into a cheater stick in an emergency by taping on a carabiner with duct tape or climbing tape. Cheater sticks as simple as a quickdraw reinforced and taped to be rigid may be mandatory for shorter climbers, especially when the gear is fixed and intermediate placements are not available.

Duct Tape

On big walls, duct tape is indispensable for climbing, equipment repair, and gear protection. Duct tape can be stuck to the rock to pad sharp edges in order to protect the rope. Duct tape is also used to tape down hooks, to tape the edges of hangerless bolts to prevent rivet hangers from sliding off, to tape rivet hangers to the aider carabiner to extend the climber's reach to a rivet, or to tape the chock pick or hammer (or both) to aiders, hooks, or protection to reach an especially high placement. Small-diameter rolls can be slung with cord and carried on the harness when leading. Duct tape is also commonly used to repair gear and to fashion homemade aid-specific equipment.

Portaledges

A climber's sleeping platform, called a portaledge (fig. 15-15), is a lightweight cot that allows climbers to sleep reasonably well on a big wall without reaching a natural ledge. Portaledges can be folded up and hauled with the haul bag. They can also be equipped with a rain fly to provide protection in a storm. Portaledges and rain-fly styles vary, and some rain flies are more suitable for big storms than others. An alternative to a portaledge is a hammock, which is significantly lighter and more uncomfortable. As with belay seats, when using portaledges or hammocks, climbers must always be anchored to the rock.

Waste Containers

On big wall ascents, waste containers must be carried to haul human waste, and they are typically attached to and hauled below the haul bag. When using these containers on a big wall, it is very important that the haul straps on the container are reliable and attached securely, so the container will not detach during the ascent. Such detachments not only leave the team without an appropriate waste container, but they leave waste on the rock or at the base and can injure parties below. While homemade containers may survive the rigors of a big wall, commercial containers specifically designed for big wall climbing, such as the Metolius Waste Case, tend to be more reliable when hauled. Outer containers are usually used in combination with internal packaging of the waste. (See Chapter 7, Leave No Trace.) It should go without saying that it is never appropriate to toss waste off the cliff during an ascent.

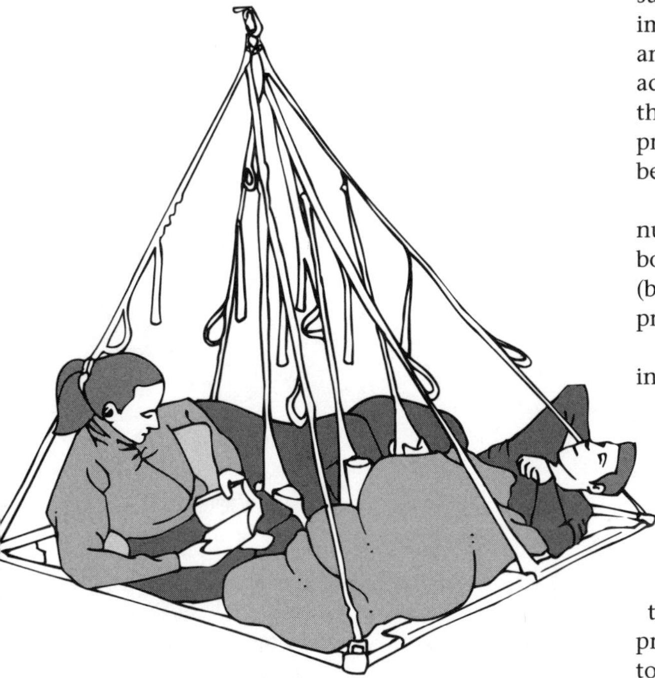

Fig. 15-15. Portaledge.

AID PLACEMENTS

The general rule for aid climbing is to place each aid piece as high as possible. For example, making most placements at 4-foot (1.2-meter) intervals rather than at 3-foot (0.9-meter) intervals over the course of a 160-foot (approximately 50-meter) pitch saves more than 10 placements and much time.

Most of the techniques for placing free climbing protection apply to aid climbing; however, unlike free climbing, some aid climbing placements are generally suitable to hold only body weight, not fall forces. It is important to keep in mind good basic protection skills and free climbing concepts and to leave protection at adequate intervals. Also, always keep in mind that if the follower will be jugging, the leader needs to leave protection close enough together that the follower will be able to clean the placements.

Using a solid cam-hook placement rather than a nut or piton placement can save considerable time for both leader (placement is much simpler) and follower (because there is nothing to clean), but this provides no protection against the consequences of a fall.

Placing nuts during an aid climb is similar to placing them on a free climb, but because aid nuts take the weight of the lead climber, and because they may be smaller than the chock pick, they can be difficult to remove. Consider using nuts only for protection and not weighting nuts for upward progress if possible.

Evaluate fixed pins, bolts, and other fixed gear before using them (see Chapter 13, Rock Protection). Clip a carabiner directly to fixed gear left as protection whenever possible rather than clipping in to old fixed slings that might be attached to the fixed gear. For example, cut old slings from piton eyes when

15

necessary so that the piton eye can accept a carabiner. If for some reason a carabiner will not fit in the eye—because the pin is bent or is too close to an obstruction, or because fixed webbing cannot be removed from the eye—thread a full-strength tie-off loop through the eye and then either girth-hitch it or clip the two ends of the tie-off loop with a carabiner.

PITON PLACEMENT

A properly sized pin can be placed one-half to two-thirds of the way by hand; the remainder of the pin is then hammered in place. Select the correct pin to fit the crack. Do not try to make the crack fit the pin; this practice causes needless destruction of the rock. A sound piton rings with a higher-pitched ping with each strike of the hammer. After the pin is driven, bounce-test the piece (see "The Basic Sequence," later in this chapter). Well-placed pins or fixed pins can flex when weighted, but they should not shift. Knowing just how much to hammer a piton is a matter of touch and experience. Excessive hammering wastes energy, makes it harder for the second to remove the piton, and needlessly damages the rock. Underdriving a piton, however, increases the risk of it pulling out. If several pins are underdriven, the failure of one could result in a long fall as the series of pins zippers out. Here are additional guidelines for the sound placement of pitons:

- **Hand-placement of pitons** eliminates further damage to the rock.
- **Try to determine what type of pin was previously placed** and how it was placed, since most piton placements now occur in pin scars, in order to use the scar in the same manner.
- **Place pins in wider portions of a crack,** in the way chocks are placed. If the crack is thinner below and above the pin, the pin will be supported when it has to take your weight (fig. 15-16a).
- **Add a full-strength tie-off loop** to the piton if the piton's position causes the connecting carabiner to extend over an edge, to prevent cross loading the carabiner across its sides (fig. 15-16b).
- **Keep the three points of the V in contact with the rock** when placing angles (fig. 15-16c). The back (the point of the V) must always be in contact with one wall, while the edges (the two tips of the V) are in contact with the opposing wall. In a horizontal crack, put the back of the angle up and the edges down.

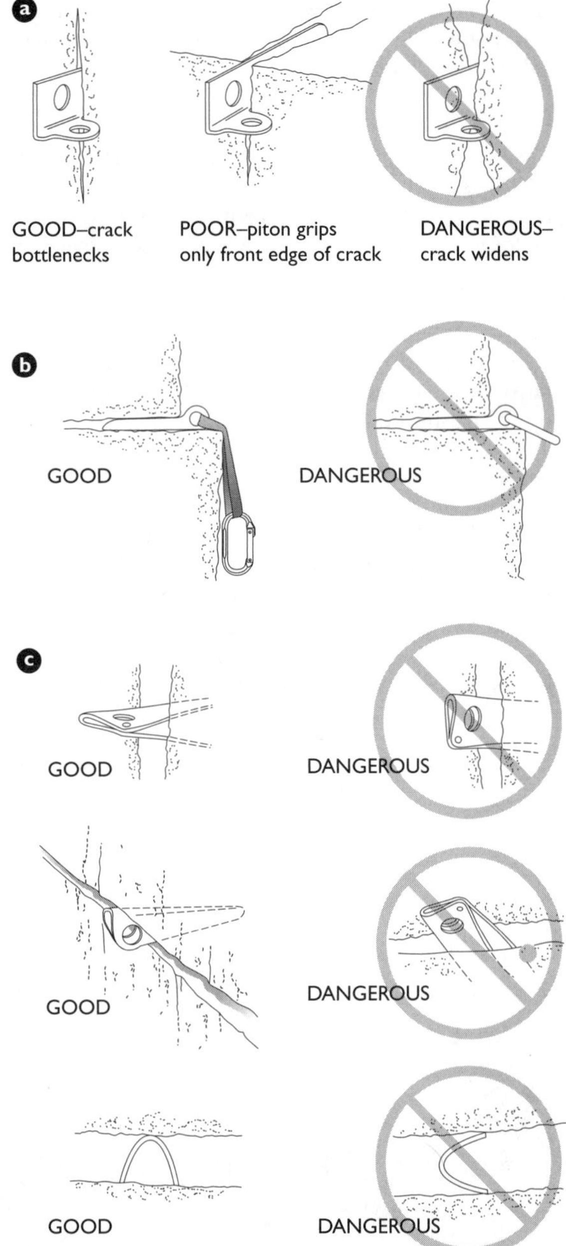

Fig. 15-16. Piton placements: a, placements are best if crack constricts above and below piton; b, safely extending a piton to avoid cross-loading the carabiner; c, angle piton placements should have all three points in contact with the rock.

- **Stop hammering when a pin bottoms out in a crack** (that is, cannot be driven in all the way). The piton must be tied off around the shaft at the point where it emerges from the rock. A tie-off loop connected with an overhand slipknot, girth-hitched or clove-hitched to the pin, supports the climber's weight and reduces levering action (see Figure 13-9 in Chapter 13, Rock Protection). Loop a longer sling (or a second carabiner) through the eye of the pin and clip it in to the tie-off loop or its carabiner. This "keeper sling" does not bear weight but will catch the pin if it pops out.

STACKING

When no single pin, chock, or SLCD fits the crack at hand, aid climbers get very creative. Whether a climber has run out of proper-sized pieces or is facing a beat-out, pod-shaped pin scar, it is time to improvise by driving in two or more pins together, known as "stacking." This can be done many different ways, depending on the size of the crack and the pins available.

Blades are stacked back to back and are usually driven together. If a third blade is necessary, the first two are inserted by hand, and then the third is driven in between them. Leeper Z pitons are especially useful for stacking, and Lost Arrows can also be stacked, either back to back or with a shorter arrow on top of a longer arrow.

There is some disagreement about the best way to stack angles. Some climbers stack them by keeping the spines of both angles against each other and the edges of each piton into the rock, but any combination will work. Try to avoid stacking angles by simply placing one over the other, because these may be very hard to separate once they are removed.

When pins are stacked, girth-hitch the pins together with a tie-off loop. It is typical to clip in to only one pin directly, or if the eyes of the stacked pins are blocked, it may be necessary to clip directly to the tie-off loop. In either case, using a tie-off loop ensures that if the stacked pins fail, you will not lose the pins that have not been clipped directly in to the rope.

HOOK PLACEMENT AND USE

To place a hook, set the hook on the ledge, flake, or hole where it will be used. When learning, try several hooks to see which one sits most securely in the feature. Move the hook around to try to find the most secure positioning by feel, and if the hooked feature can be seen, visually inspect the quality of the placement as well. Hooks can sometimes be placed on top of a fixed copperhead that has lost its wire (called a "dead head").

After selecting the hook and placement position, clip an aider and daisy chain to the hook. Test all hooks before applying full body weight (or gently "ooze" body weight onto the hook if it is off to the side or otherwise cannot be tested). Climbers usually start very low in their aiders so that their weight and stance are well below the hook before they move up one step at a time. Climbers should avoid standing with their face directly in front of the hook because it could pop out with a good deal of force. Once the climber's weight is on the hook in one aider (or one pair), it can be helpful to fifi in (in other words, to hook in to the aider's carabiner and hang your body weight), just as with other pieces of protection. Always keep constant downward pressure on the hook when standing in the aiders, especially when moving up in the aiders and switching weight from one foot to the other.

Cam hooks should be placed in the crack or pocket in a fashion that will make the hook bind up and rotate to cause a camming force on the rock. These placements rely on the force created by the torque (camming action) of the hook into the rock. With practice, cam hooks can be placed in many seemingly unlikely positions and orientations. The tighter the cam hook fits into the crack (the closer the width of the metal sheet is to the width of the crack), the more secure the placement and the less potential there is to do any damage to the rock. A cam hook can be hit once with a hammer to increase the security when needed. Sometimes a hammer is needed to remove a cam hook, even when it has only been body weighted. Climbers generally agree that cam hooks should not be used in certain rock, such as sandstone, because they may damage the rock with their camming action.

MALLEABLE PLACEMENTS

Because climbers often cannot tell how secure the placements of malleable heads are, and because such heads damage the rock, do not use them except where other protection just will not work. Heads are used like any other aid piece but have an inescapable weakness: Inspection cannot guarantee that the head has been molded to the rock. Some heads may hold a short fall, others will support body weight only, and others might fail. All malleable-head placements are suspect, and acceptance of this fact is inherent in their use.

Assuming that there is an adequate selection of heads

available for the route, use the largest head that the rock feature will best accommodate. Gently bounce-test all head placements (see "The Basic Sequence," below), whether placed by you or a previous party. Do not get impatient when placing heads—spend as much time as needed for the placement to be as good as possible. Consider using load-limiting runners on heads, since a well-placed head may arrest a fall.

Copperheads and circleheads take more practice to place than other types of aid gear, and placing them requires some specialized tools. The hammer pick works for setting ("pasting") large heads, but small heads require a striking tool such as a blunt chisel, a punch, or, in a pinch, a Lost Arrow or chock pick. Using a striking tool reduces the likelihood of a missed hit, which causes undue damage to the rock (fig. 15-17).

Before placing a head, examine it carefully. Note that, starting with the clip-in loop, the cable comes up through the "back" of the head, does a 180-degree turn, and ends at the bottom of the "front" of the head (see Figure 15-12a). Make sure the back of the head is placed against the rock, with the frayed ends of the cut cable, which is the front of the head, visible, in order to minimize the cable's outward bending movement on the cable and also to protect the cable when the head is being pasted.

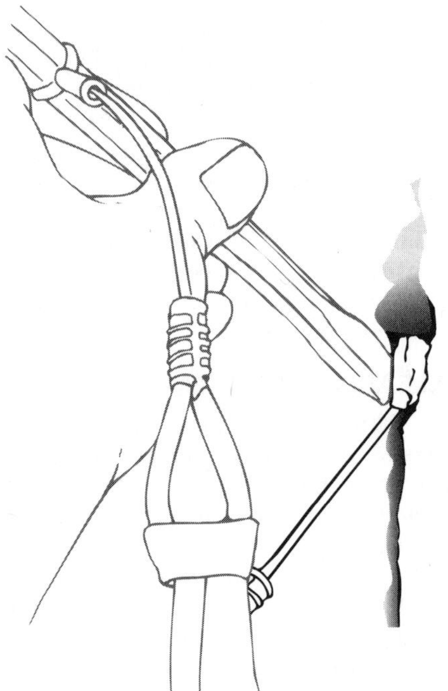

Fig. 15-17. Placing a copperhead with a chisel.

Think of the head as being like a chock inserted in a placement that is not quite able to accept a chock, possibly due to the placement being shallow. Look for a placement that is tapered downward or at least has parallel sides. Practice head placement on the ground, perhaps in some boulders or other nonclimbable rock, to gain experience before placing heads on an established climbing route.

Follow these steps when placing a head:

1. Warm up the head by hitting it on every surface with the hammer. If needed, carefully shape the head slightly to match the intended placement by rotating the head while hitting it gently, approximately 10–20 times.
2. Place the head by positioning it similarly to a chock—in a narrowing portion of a flare or seam, making sure to orient the head correctly: with the back of the head placed against the rock.
3. Seat the head into the rock, using a punch to hit it perhaps four to five times, over the entire head. At this point, the goal is simply for the head to stay in place in the constriction during additional pasting without the climber having to hold on to it.
4. Pound the head in, possibly using a chisel to make many angled strokes that form an X pattern on the head or by simply hitting the head repeatedly enough times to weld the head into the placement. Take care to not hit and damage the rock or the cable of the head. Hit the head all over—top, middle, and bottom. If the head rocks while being hit on its top or bottom, go back to hitting the middle of the head. If the metal starts separating from the cable, stop hitting, to avoid overpasting the head.
5. Paste the head on its edges by setting the chisel or punch right on the edge of the head and pounding both sides to "pin" the head.
6. "Pin" the head on the top and bottom with special care; this is the area of the head that often gets the best "bite" in the rock.
7. Gently bounce-test the head before committing your weight to ensure that it will hold. However, overaggressive bounce-testing can pull a good head placement, so try to generate only about twice the force of the body weight to be held (see "The Basic Sequence," below).

BASIC AID TECHNIQUES

Before starting to lead any aid pitch, study the terrain and make a plan. Plan what gear the leader will need and what the second can carry. Figure out how to minimize rope drag. Spot any obstructions that might create hauling problems. Decide whether to save aid pieces of certain sizes for the end of the pitch.

RACKING

Racking varies greatly with personal style, just as in free climbing (see Chapter 14, Leading on Rock). It is common on aid routes to have more than one SLCD on each racking carabiner. Wire-gate carabiners are preferred for racking SLCDs because they are lighter.

A recommended racking system is to clip the loops on the SLCD to the carabiner, instead of clipping the SLCD in with the sewn sling, as is done in free climbing. Face the gate of the carabiner out and away from the harness, with the opening of the gate at the bottom of the carabiner. This allows the climber to open the carabiner by flicking the SLCD against the carabiner gate, removing just one SLCD from the carabiner and with one hand. When racking multiple SLCDs on one carabiner, consider mixing sizes so that if one carabiner full of SLCDs is dropped, all of the pieces of that size are not lost. (Figure 15-5 shows how SLCDs are typically racked.)

Consider racking half of the SLCDs, nuts, pins, and slings of each size on each side of your body so that all sizes of gear are available from both sides. Typically, gear is racked from small to large or large to small. Some climbers rack all their slings on their seat harness and all their protection on their chest harness. Making "two-packs" of slings reduces the amount of space the slings take up on the harness (fig. 15-18a). Or rack single slings over a shoulder.

It is helpful to rack pitons on oval carabiners, because they allow pieces to nest better (fig. 15-18b); specialized oval wire-gate carabiners weigh less. Do not overload a carabiner to the point that gear is lost because the equipment cannot be accessed easily enough. Alternate the direction of angles and Lost Arrows for better racking on the carabiner. Consider racking nuts and hooks onto traditional latch-style carabiners (see Figure 9-36e), which have a hook that makes it that much harder for the nuts or hooks to accidentally come off of the carabiner. Free carabiners are often racked as "footballs" in groups of five or seven carabiners, depending on the climber's preference (fig 15-18c).

Often it is useful for the leader to have a chock pick

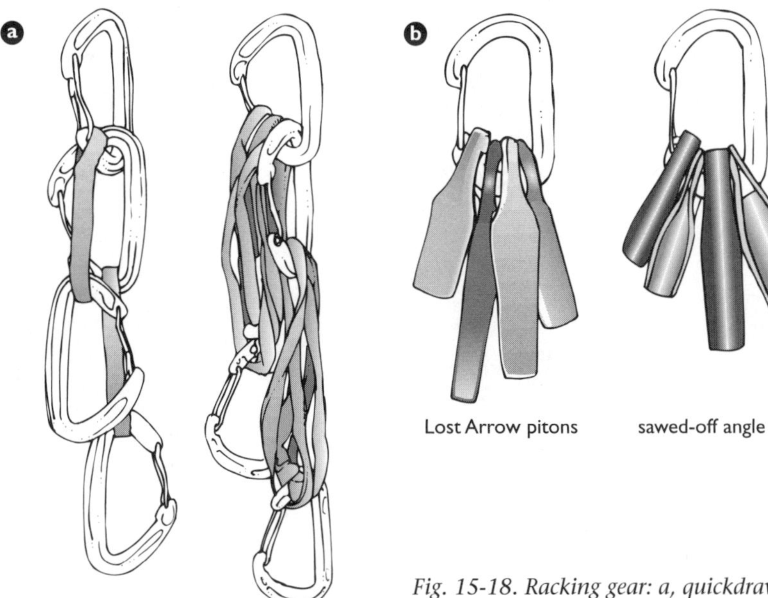

Fig. 15-18. Racking gear: a, quickdraw and alpine draw "two-packs"; b, pitons nested on oval wire-gate carabiners; c, carabiners racked in "footballs."

for removing unsettled placements and for cleaning out grass and dirt from cracks. Finally, check that the hammer, if one is being carried, is accessible, with its sling untangled.

THE BASIC SEQUENCE

The basic aid sequence is the same whether the leader is starting from the ground, from a comfortable free stance, or from the top step of the aiders. The following basic sequence assumes that the climber is using two aiders (see also the "Tips for Leading Aid Pitches" sidebar):

1. Look at and feel the terrain above, and select an aid piece to place at the highest suitable spot within reach (fig. 15-19a).
2. Place the piece and visually inspect it if possible. Clip the free aider and daisy-chain combination in to the new piece with its dedicated oval key-lock carabiner (fig. 15-19b).
3. Bounce-test the new piece in the typical sequence: (a) Tug down firmly one or more times on the aider with a hand; (b) place a foot in the aider and give a few solid, down-forcing "kicks" with that foot (keep all your weight supported on the previous piece during this first leg test); (c) transfer about half of your weight to the new piece and give a few more vigorous hops (keep a hand on the aider of the previous piece and the other foot in that aider so that you can hold yourself upright and on the previous piece should the new piece fail during this step; if possible, stay fified in to the previous piece); and (d) transfer all of your weight to the new piece and give more vigorous bounces (fig. 15-19c).

If the new piece is questionable, is not intended for more than body weight, or is behind an expanding feature, some climbers may decide

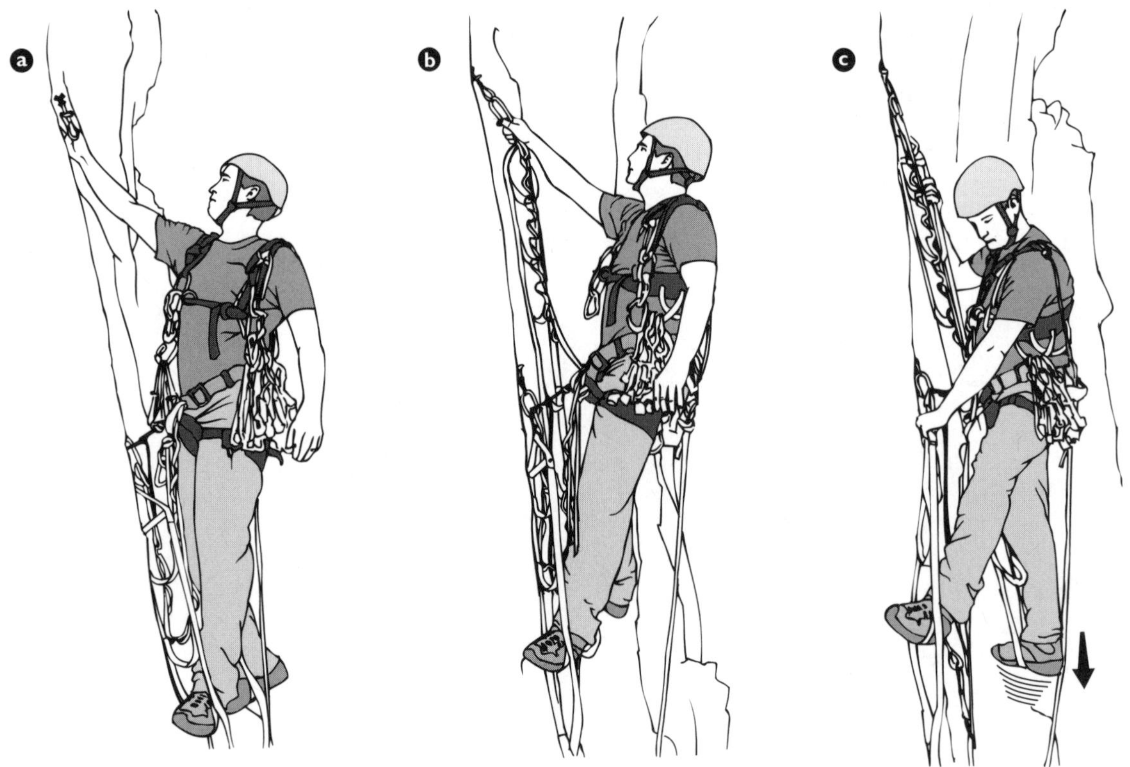

Fig. 15-19. The basic aid sequence (some equipment omitted for clarity): a, select piece of protection; b, place protection, then clip aider-daisy to it; c, bounce-test the protection (continued on facing page).

to avoid aggressive bounce-testing. Instead, (a) hand-set the placement (if appropriate) with a firm tug, and (b) simply "ooze" onto the new placement, applying your weight as gradually and smoothly as possible.

Some climbers rely on their experience and knowledge of the specific rock type to set good placements and forgo anything more than hand-setting the placement. Others believe that the only safe climbing method is vigorous bounce-testing. Warn the belayer when you are about to test or move onto a dubious placement.

4. Once your weight is committed to the new placement, fifi in to the piece with the fifi hook, or clip in the adjustable daisy strap, and rest (fig. 15-19d). If not using an adjustable fifi hook or an adjustable daisy, climb up to the second or third steps in the aiders at this point in order to fifi in to the new piece. With a classic fifi hook, it is also possible to fifi in to one of the traditional daisy chain loops.
5. While resting on the new piece, reach back to the previous piece. If clipping this piece for protection, add a carabiner, quickdraw, or sling and clip in the rope. Then remove the aider and daisy-chain combination (fig. 15-19e) and clip the oval keylock carabiner of this aider and daisy-chain combination in to the oval keylock carabiner of the higher aider (fig. 15-19f). If removing this lower piece, rerack the piece.

Fig. 15-19. Continued from facing page; d, shift weight to protection and rest on fifi hook; e, clip rope to previous piece of protection and remove lower aider-daisy; f, clip this second aider-daisy to first, higher aider-daisy and prepare to climb high in aiders and repeat the sequence.

6. Climb as high as possible in the aiders, possibly to the second or top steps, moving or adjusting the fifi or adjustable daisy while advancing higher (as shown in Figure 15-19f). Resist the temptation to look for placements until you have climbed as high as you plan to climb in the aiders. This helps ensure that you do not get distracted by lower placement possibilities and increases efficiency of piece selection.
7. Repeat the process starting with step 1.

TOP-STEPPING

Moving onto the top step of the aiders can be unnerving, but being able to do so greatly improves the efficiency of aid climbing. The process is simple on low-angle rock, where the top steps are used like any other foothold and the climber's hands provide balance. Sometimes it is faster and less fatiguing to make multiple placements from steps lower than the top step, such as on very steep terrain or when aiding deep inside awkward cracks and corners. On such terrain, climbers may find that they can move faster by always placing from the second step. However, the ideal is to top-step as much as possible.

Vertical and overhanging rock can make top-stepping difficult because the climber's center of gravity moves away from the rock and above the point where the aiders are clipped to the aid placement. If the rock offers any features, use hands or an intermediate placement as a handhold to provide balance. If the rock is blank and the placement suitable, keep your weight on your feet while standing up and applying tension to the fifi hook or adjustable daisy strap between the harness and the aid placement. That tension provides the means of balancing yourself (fig. 15-20). If using a classic fifi, an alternative method is to clip a quickdraw in to the piece and use it as a handhold, pulling upward on the quickdraw with one hand and making the next placement with the other hand.

RESTING

Do not wear yourself out. Climb in a relaxed fashion, taking rests as often as necessary to conserve strength or to plot the next series of moves. The best way to rest is to immediately clip in to a new tested piece with a fifi hook or adjustable daisy strap. Rest by fully weighting the fifi or adjustable daisy, freeing your feet completely before using the aiders to move up on the piece. This also allows you to switch feet between aiders as needed, to reach sideways to attach aiders to a new piece, or to execute whatever change of direction the next move may

TIPS FOR LEADING AID PITCHES

- **Minimize rope drag,** which can become a problem, as in free climbing. Consider each aid placement carefully, and extend slings when necessary to keep the rope running straight. In addition, if the follower will ascend the lead line using ascenders, pay attention to how the rope runs over edges, and set protection and slings so that the rope does not rub over sharp edges. If necessary, pad edges, usually with duct tape.
- **Think strategically while climbing** about what pieces can be left and what pieces should be removed as you go, known as back-cleaning, for reuse later on the pitch. Some pitches will require a large number of pieces of the same size, or the leader may have only one or two of certain critical pieces, so these pieces will have to be back-cleaned often.
- **Consider when to clip the rope,** which depends on personal preference and on the quality of the lower and higher pieces of protection (which has a direct relationship to the aid rating of the pitch). Some climbers prefer to clip the rope in to the lower placement before completing the final bounce-testing or before committing full weight on the new placement, so that if the new placement fails, the leader will not take a fall onto the lower piece caught only by the daisy chain and not the rope. Other climbers use bounce-testing to ensure that the new higher piece will hold their weight long enough for them to reach down and clip the rope to the lower piece. Generally, climbers do not want to pull up rope in order to clip, as this increases the length of a potential fall. However, the more suspect the new higher piece, the more likely that the climber will clip the current piece as protection prior to moving onto the higher piece, rather than after moving onto the higher piece, as in the basic sequence. When climbing pitches that are rated A1 or C1, generally follow the basic sequence.

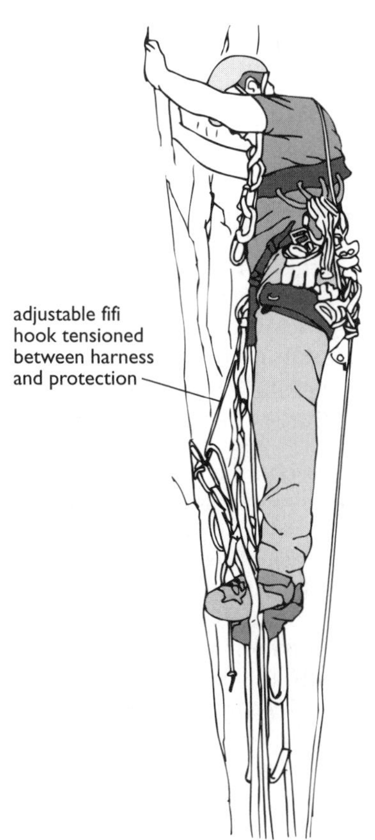

Fig. 15-20. Top-stepping.

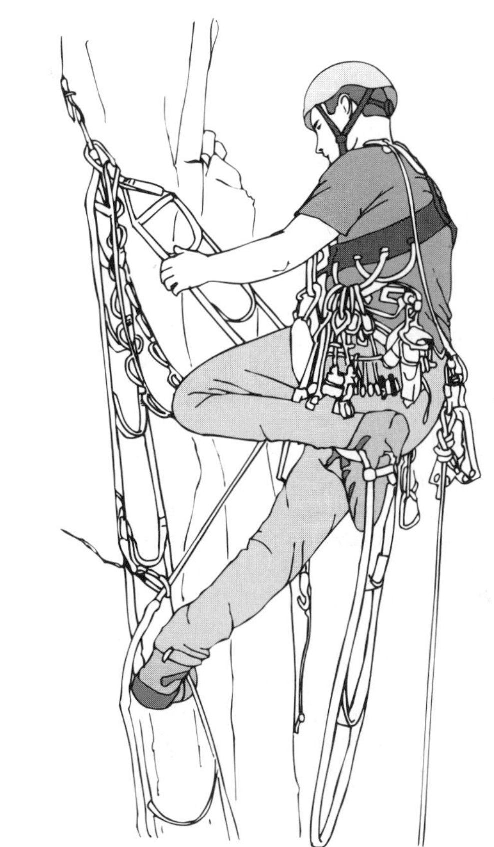

Fig. 15-21. Rest position.

require. As you advance upward on pieces, move your classic fifi up or pull in your adjustable fifi or adjustable daisy, resting on this equipment as much as possible.

If not using a fifi hook or adjustable daisy, or if on lower-angle terrain, try this rest technique: With each foot in separate aiders and one foot one step below the other, bend the knee of the higher leg and bring that foot under you. Most of your weight now rests over the bent leg. The outstretched leg takes minimal weight but maintains balance (fig. 15-21).

Another way to rest is to ask the belayer for tension and to rest on the climbing rope once it has been clipped in to the supporting piece. This is not an efficient method, however, due to stretch in the rope and the need for verbal communication.

Finally, relaxing stances can often be found in the aiders. Generally, the greatest stability is obtained by standing with heels together and toes spread apart against the rock. The heels-together position can be very helpful when standing high in the aiders and stretching up to make a difficult placement.

SWITCHING BETWEEN AID AND FREE CLIMBING

Stowing and deploying aiders as well as free climbing with aid gear, a large rack, and a haul line are some of the difficulties in switching between aid and free climbing. Weighting the first piece on aid after free climbing can be scary if the last piece of protection is far away or untested.

From Free to Aid

Switching from free climbing to aid climbing is the easier transition because as long as the climb accepts rock protection, it is easy to switch to aid at any time by simply calling for tension or clipping the belay loop directly in to a piece. If the climber has been free climbing because the rock did not accept protection, the last piece may be far below. Either way, test the first aid piece carefully, especially with the first visual inspection and tests prior to weighting the piece. If using aiders to aid climb the section, release the aiders and daisy chains, which could already be rigged on the harness, and move into the basic aid sequence (see "The Basic Sequence," above). This is easy if the climber has anticipated changing to aid, but if the climber is not expecting to use aid and suddenly needs it, problems arise. When in this bind, improvise aiders by interconnecting several slings and then aid climb over the blank area.

From Aid to Free

A climber may wish to transition from aid to free climbing when encountering a section that cannot be aided (face climbing with no rock protection available) or when the climbing becomes easy enough that free climbing is faster and more efficient than aid climbing. Two methods are commonly used to switch to free climbing:

On easier or low-angle terrain, it is often possible to move out of the aiders and onto the rock with all your weight on your hands and feet and still reach back to unclip the aiders to bring them along. If the transition occurs at a ledge or stance, simply clip aiders and daisy chains to the harness gear loops and start free climbing. Make sure that the aid equipment will not hinder your movement when free climbing.

When the aid climbing is steep just before the transition to free climbing, the preferred technique is to clip a single or double runner to the last piece of aid protection. Then stand in the sling, using this sling as an improvised aider. Remove the aiders and stow them on the harness. This enables the climber to make free climbing moves and not have to reach down to retrieve the aiders. If moving from a hook to free climbing, simply pull up on the aiders from the first free moves, and the hook and the aider should release.

TENSION TRAVERSES AND PENDULUM SWINGS

Tension traverses and pendulum swings are used to traverse horizontally across unaidable territory into a new crack system. First ascentionists use these techniques to avoid placing bolt ladders to reach the new system.

The main difference between a tension traverse and a pendulum is that a pendulum requires the climber to run across the face in order to reach the new system, while during a tension traverse the climber does not run but uses friction on small holds to work hands and feet sideways. Both pendulums and tension traverses can be difficult, and they pose special problems for the second climber.

For both methods, the leader starts by placing a solid piece of protection at the top of the planned traverse and clipping the rope in to this protection, or clipping in to fixed gear at this point. Usually the equipment used for the tension or pendulum point cannot be retrieved, unless it is possible to come back to it from above, so these points on most routes are equipped with fixed gear. Climbers might use a locking carabiner on a tension or pendulum point for extra security.

During a tension traverse, after clipping in the rope, the leader takes tension from the belayer and starts to move toward the new crack system, using hands and feet to move across the rock (fig. 15-22a). Some tension traverses require climbers to achieve a sideways or even nearly upside down position as they move. Often during tension traverses, leaders will call for more slack as they make progress during the traverse. Keep good communication with the belayer, with clear "Lower me," "Stop," or "Hold" commands. Once the final destination is reached, the leader may need to call for slack so that the tension ceases and climbing can continue in the new crack.

For a pendulum, the leader clips in to the pendulum point with the rope and has the belayer take tension. Then the leader calls for a lower. The belayer lowers the leader until there is enough rope out for the leader to run back and forth across the rock and swing into the new crack system (fig. 15-22b).

When being lowered by the belayer, it is better to be lowered too little than too much, because if you are too low, it may be very difficult to correct the error. Stop early and try the pendulum. While running back and forth across the rock, start slow and increase speed on each back and forth. Stay in control to avoid spinning and hitting the rock. If you find yourself too low and cannot correct the error, an easy method to adjust a pendulum point is to attach a mechanical ascender to an aider and daisy chain combination and ascend the rope until back to the desired height. Then, with your weight hanging from one or both ascenders, complete the pendulum.

Some pendulums and traverses are difficult due to length, angle of the face, or other factors. Climbers may want to attach an SLCD to their aider so that they

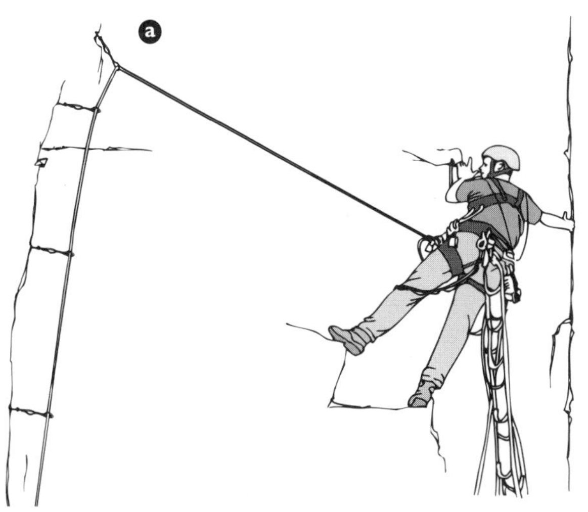

Fig. 15-22. Leading: a, tension traverse; b, pendulum.

can jam this piece into the new crack very quickly. If a climber has barely reached the new crack but has managed to bury the right piece into it, the piece and the daisy chain will catch the climber's weight before he or she swings back into the old plumb line.

Once in the new crack system, climb as high as safety allows before clipping the rope in to aid pieces for protection. The higher a climber gets before placing protection, the easier it is for the belayer, who will second the pendulum (see "Seconding Pendulums," later in this chapter). A Grigri is helpful for the belayer to use for pendulums and tension traverses because it allows the belayer to hold the leader in the exact position required to complete a pendulum, and in a tension traverse, it allows for a precise belay and perfect amount of tension as called for by the leader.

OVERHANGS AND ROOFS

Overhangs and roofs can appear intimidating but often are easier than they look to aid through, especially because fixed gear tends to be prevalent in roofs. Keep ascenders handy, because if a piece pulls out and you end up hanging, ascenders may be needed to climb back up to the last secure piece.

Under a steep overhanging wall or a roof, it may not be possible to place your feet against the rock. In this situation, start by hanging as far below the piece as possible and in the low steps on the aiders. To move up and reach the next placement, use the fifi hook or adjustable daisy strap to hang from the harness rather than trying to stand with your full weight in the aiders. After making the new placement, test it and clip in an aider, then step into the lowest possible step and fifi in.

When climbing very steep overhangs, placements will probably be made close together. Be careful not to remove gear during these sections, because the follower will need more gear to stay in place in order to successfully clean the pitch. Or consider back-cleaning the entire section to allow the second to simply ascend the fixed line.

As an overhang becomes horizontal, it will actually become easier to aid because the climber can stand fully erect in the aiders under the roof, possibly in the bottom steps, and aid sideways through the horizontal crack system.

Despite the difference in balance, for aiding over a roof climbers use the same sequence as described in "The Basic Sequence," above. Reach up and over the roof to find the next placement. It may be necessary to feel the placement without getting a good visual inspection. When first moving onto the aider clipped to the piece above the roof, it may be difficult to pull yourself up to the piece and over the roof. Stepping into the lowest step on the aider and standing up in that aider can help you get started. Then, with an adjustable fifi or an adjustable daisy, it should be possible to fifi in to the piece above the roof.

Rope drag is a common side effect of overhangs. Try not to give in to the temptation to put long slings on these placements, because it will make cleaning very difficult for the follower. Some climbers pull along a second belay rope and start climbing on it after clearing the lip of the overhang, although this technique is not common.

Finally, try to relax when working out moves over a big roof. Have confidence in your pieces. Clutching at them will not keep them in place but will drain your strength.

ESTABLISHING BELAYS

Upon reaching the end of a pitch, the leader must establish an anchor. Many routes have bolts at the end of the pitch, but climbers may have to place their own gear. If hauling, you will typically set up an anchor with two main power points (see "Equalizing Anchors" in Chapter 10, Belaying)—one for fixing the lead line and supporting the weight and safety of the climbers, and one for the haul system. Carefully consider which side to put the lead line on versus the haul system. Generally, try to keep the haul system in a straight line and position the haul anchor out of the path of the route so that the follower does not have to push past the haul bag(s). Other considerations in selecting the location of the lead-line and haul-system anchors are the quality of the protection and the weight of the haul bag(s). With these considerations in mind, the leader sets up an anchor upon completing the pitch (fig. 15-23a).

Lead-line anchor. Attach the lead line to the lead-line anchor first (fig. 15-23b). To do this, call for slack, pull up several armfuls of rope, and fix the line for the follower. Typically the rope is fixed by clove-hitching it to a carabiner that is clipped to a solid piece of protection already used in the anchor, preferably a bolt. Use a clove hitch so that it can be easily untied after being weighted. Then back up this clove hitch with a figure eight on a bight. Clip this figure eight to the power point of the lead-line anchor. Make sure that there is enough rope between this figure eight and the leader building the anchor to allow the leader to perform the haul. As soon as the lead line is fixed with the clove hitch and backed up, the leader calls down to the follower that the lead line is fixed. This also tells the follower that the leader is off belay (or "off belay" may be called separately).

The follower immediately attaches to the lead line with ascenders and a backup, removes most of the anchor from the lower station, and unties the backup knot in the haul line (fig. 15-23c). The only pieces that the follower will leave in place until the haul starts are those directly weighted by the haul-bag docking cord.

Fig. 15-23. Establishing a belay: a, leader builds anchor; b, leader fixes lead line (continued on facing page).

Fig 15-23. Continued from facing page; c, second attaches to lead line and begins dismantling lower anchor; d, leader sets up the hauling system while second prepares to jug and clean; e, second releases haul bag; f, leader hauls while second jugs and cleans.

This ensures that the follower will be ready to ascend as soon as the haul bag leaves the station.

Haul-system anchor. After fixing the lead line and while the second is preparing to jug and clean, the leader sets up the haul system (fig. 15-23d; also see "Hauling," later in this chapter). When setting up the haul-system anchor, the leader may use one of the points in the lead-line anchor as part of the haul anchor. This creates a backup for both of the anchors. As part of the hauling sequence, the follower releases the haul bag from the lower anchor so that the leader can haul (fig. 15-23e), then removes any pieces that the haul bag was directly weighting, and finally ascends the fixed lead line.

As the leader hauls, he stacks the haul line neatly so that it is ready to go for the next lead (fig. 15-23f). After the hauling is completed (or after the climbing rope is fixed, if the leader is not hauling), establish the belay seat, get comfortable, and prepare to exchange leads. Sort the rack, organize the ropes, prepare the belay system, and so forth.

TYROLEAN TRAVERSES

Tyrolean traverses may be used to move between two rock features, such as a main wall and a detached pinnacle. They are also useful for crossing rivers and other spans. Ropes are strung between points on each side of the span, allowing climbers to traverse through the air, attached to the rope. As an example, the instructions that follow are for a Tyrolean traverse between a main wall and a detached pinnacle, such as the Lost Arrow Spire in Yosemite National Park, California, and then back to a new location on the main wall.

1. After setting up a bombproof anchor on the main wall—one that can take both a horizontal and a vertical pull—connect one end of a single-strand rappel line to this anchor. Rappel this rope to the saddle between the main wall and the detached pinnacle, passing a knot if two ropes are needed. Note that the rappel line must be at least twice the distance of the span between the main wall and the detached pinnacle.
2. Climb the pinnacle using an additional climbing rope if needed. The follower brings up the free end of the rappel line if it was not used as the climbing rope (consider tying in to this line to avoid dropping it).
3. Once both climbers are atop the pinnacle, pull the rappel line (which becomes the traverse line) tight against the anchor on the main wall and fix this rope to the pinnacle anchor. Feed the free end of the traverse line through the anchor just as would be done to set up a rappel (if using two ropes, untying and retying is best). Note that after the traverse, the equipment used for the pinnacle anchor cannot be recovered. If using the free end of the rappel line to initiate the traverse (see step 4, below), consider fixing the second rope to the pinnacle anchor for redundancy and to avoid passing a knot on the rappel.
4. The first climber connects to the traverse rope and takes the free end of the traverse line with him or her (consider tying in to the end to ensure that it is not dropped). Depending on the terrain, span distance, elevation difference, rope stretch, and tension in the traverse line, a short lower-out, rappel, down-jugging, or down-prusiking may be necessary to start the traverse and prevent the climber from careening away from the detached pillar at an uncontrolled speed. Often, the first climber may rappel on the free end of the traverse line to initiate the traverse. Do not attach a rappel device to the tensioned traverse rope to initiate the traverse, because this device will likely become tensioned and stuck near the midpoint of the traverse.

If the traverse line is mostly horizontal or if the destination is higher than the starting point, many methods can be used to cross the span on the traverse line: using a Mini Traxion and one ascender (fig. 15-24a); using two ascenders (fig. 15-24b); or using a combination of pulleys, carabiners, and prusik hitches. In this case, attach the traversing gear prior to starting the traverse, and only a short rappel or lower-out likely would be required.

However, if the destination is lower than the starting point, a rappel will likely be required for the entire traverse for all climbers, and ascending equipment would be needed only for the final few feet and could be attached when needed. In this case, climbers would attach themselves to the traverse line with a locking carabiner or a pulley and locking carabiner. They would rappel on a separate line while suspended from the traverse line. Plan ahead to ensure that adequate equipment and lines are available to safely perform the traverse.

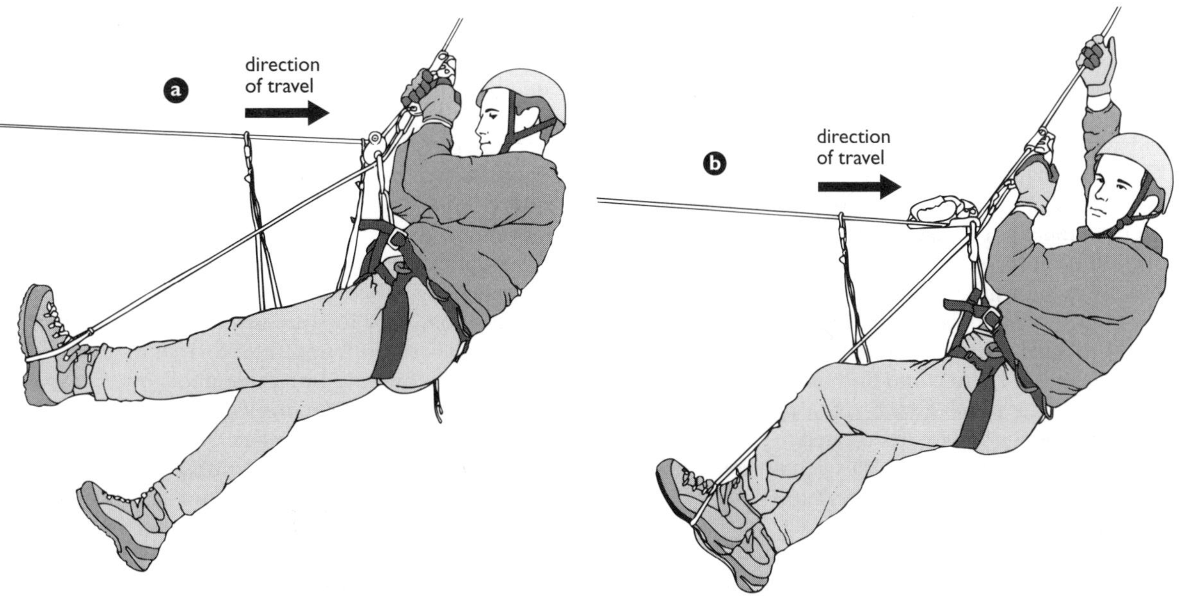

Fig. 15-24. Tyrolean traverse setups: a, using Petzl Mini Traxion and one ascender; b, using two ascenders.

5. After the first climber traverses from the pinnacle back to a new location on the main wall, the second climber unfixes the first rope from the pinnacle anchor, ensuring that the rope is threaded through the anchor and, if two ropes are used, taking note of the correct rope to pull when the traverse is complete, just as when preparing a double-rope rappel. Then the first climber tightens and fixes the free end of the traverse line in to the new anchor at the new location on the main wall.
6. The second climber sets up for the traverse using the system of choice (see steps 4 and 5, above) and if two ropes are used, selects the strand of traverse rope without a knot so that no knot pass is required on the traverse.
7. Once both climbers are at the new location on the main wall, they untie the ends of the traverse line from the main wall anchor and pull the appropriate rope, if two ropes are used, taking care that the ends of the lines do not tangle.

SECONDING

On short sections of aid, the second climber usually follows the same sequence as the leader, except that the second is belayed from above. The second might use aiders for following a short section of aid, clipping these aiders to the protection left by the leader, or the second might just pull on the protection left by the leader and use the rock for counterpressure or stances. The follower's technique depends on how steep and smooth the short section of aid is that is being followed.

Long sections of aid call for a different strategy. The leader fixes the lead line to the anchor, and the second uses mechanical ascenders to ascend the fixed climbing rope and also cleans the protection left by the leader. If the team is hauling a bag, the second must release the bag for hauling before leaving the lower anchor. If the bag hangs up along the way, the follower can help to free it.

USING ASCENDERS

Each ascender (left and right) should have a dedicated locking carabiner. Smaller oval or D-shaped carabiners with a regular locking gate (not an auto-locking gate) are usually most convenient. When ascenders are not in use, they reside on the harness or gear sling on their dedicated locking carabiner.

When preparing to follow a pitch, attach the locking carabiner to each aider and daisy-chain combination. The ascender is always clipped in to the end of the daisy chain rather than in to one of its loops. Lock the carabiner to ensure that the ascender will stay attached to the daisy chain and aider, primarily to ensure that the attachment to the daisy chain is secure before weighting

15

it. Place the ascender for the climber's dominant hand above the other ascender on the rope (fig. 15-25a).

For most ascending, shorten the overall length of the daisy chain for the upper ascender. The amount that this daisy chain is shortened varies based on the steepness of the pitch and may change many times during an individual pitch. In general, the upper daisy chain should be adjusted so that it draws tight prior to or exactly at full arm extension.

To shorten the daisy chain, first place the ascender at approximately full arm extension. Pull up the daisy chain from the harness and find the loop that touches the locking carabiner attached to the ascender. Use a free carabiner (usually the dedicated oval keylock carabiner belonging to the aider–daisy-chain combination) to attach this loop of the daisy chain directly to the locking carabiner. This method of shortening the daisy chain allows the climber to change the length of the daisy during the pitch without opening the locking carabiner (fig. 15-25b). Experiment with jugging with the daisy chain shortened to different lengths to find what is most comfortable and efficient. It is not necessary to shorten the daisy chain for the nondominant hand. Another option is to use an adjustable daisy strap.

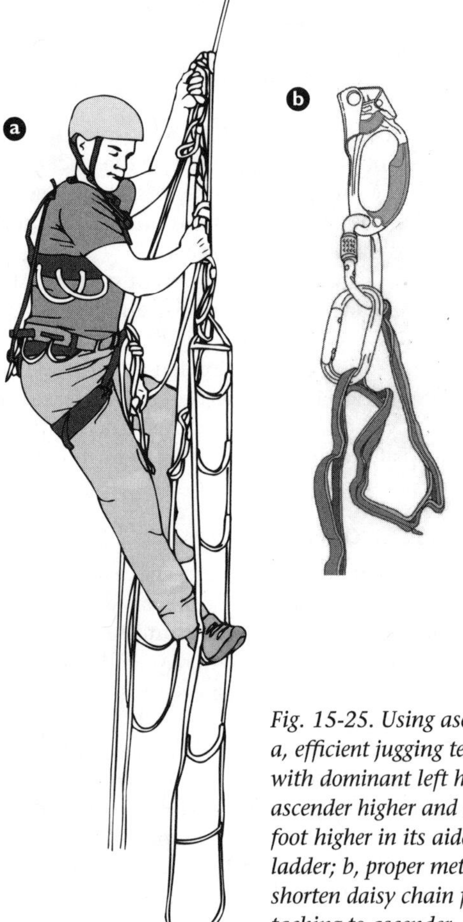

Fig. 15-25. Using ascenders: a, efficient jugging technique, with dominant left hand's ascender higher and right foot higher in its aider's ladder; b, proper method to shorten daisy chain for attaching to ascender.

When jugging, offset your feet in the aider steps: If the left hand is dominant and that ascender is higher, and if the left foot is in the fifth step, the right foot should be in the fourth step; this way, the feet are at roughly the same height, which is an efficient jugging technique.

When moving up the ascenders, the upper ascender will move easily while you stand with your weight on the lower ascender and aider, but the lower ascender may be more difficult to advance because there is no weight below that ascender. Resist the temptation to hold or pull down on the rope below the lower ascender in order to be able to move it up. Although this works, it is an inefficient and inadequate technique for covering long distances. Instead, practice "thumbing"—using your thumb to slightly open the cam on the lower ascender so that it will move upward. Most ascenders will open with thumbing without risk of opening fully and unattaching from the fixed line. Thumbing is very efficient, and it may be necessary to do it on every stroke.

Ascending Steep Terrain

When ascending very steep terrain, rather than fully weighting the aiders during the entire ascending process, the climber should drastically shorten the upper daisy chain, probably to about the third loop from the harness, and rest body weight directly on the upper ascender after moving it up. In this sequence, move up the upper ascender and then rest with all your weight by hanging in the harness from the ascender. Move up the lower ascender, stand up, and push up the upper ascender a few feet and hang again. Other variations of this technique exist, so climbers should experiment to find out what works best for them.

Backing Up Ascenders

As a rule, do not untie from the end of the climbing rope while ascending. Remaining tied in serves as a backup in case both ascenders fail. To further decrease the likelihood of a long fall, periodically "tie in short," using the climbing rope as the backup (as discussed below), or otherwise provide a backup on the rope below the ascenders. Tying in short or providing a backup below the ascenders is an easy precaution that has saved lives. Conversely, mistakes in attaching and backing up ascenders have led to many deaths.

As the second ascends, an ever-lengthening loop of climbing rope forms below the ascender, making for a long fall if the ascenders fail. A backup shortens this potential fall. One way to achieve this backup is to attach the Grigri directly below the ascenders. This not only provides a backup but also allows the Grigri to be employed in other simple and extremely efficient techniques for following pitches and cleaning gear (for example, the Grigri lower-out method, described below).

To use the climbing rope as the backup, stop periodically and tie any knot, such as an overhand, just below the ascenders, and clip the loop in to the harness with a locking carabiner. Repeat this procedure as often as necessary to shorten the fall potential. Keep in mind that the ascenders are most likely to come off on a traverse and less likely to come off on simple jugging up a straight line. Most climbers using this method keep all the loops clipped in to their harness until they reach the anchor.

Often while jugging, the climber may choose to remove the upper ascender from the rope and place it above a piece of protection that is still weighted. It is prudent to tie in short or make sure to use a backup method before removing the upper ascender.

Other Precautions While Ascending

Other precautions should be taken while ascending. First, carry a spare prusik sling just in case an ascender fails or is dropped. A Grigri is a much more effective and efficient lower ascender than a prusik, so this is the first backup to an ascender. And, as in all climbing, beware of sharp edges. Jugging places the rope under tension, and sharp edges can cut it. Ascend as smoothly as possible to minimize any sawing action on the rope running over an edge.

ROPE MANAGEMENT

Rope management while following is critical, especially when high winds or "rope-eating" cracks may foul or snag the rope. Popular methods of managing the rope include clipping a rope bag to some part of the harness, such as a leg loop, and stuffing the rope hanging below the ascenders into the rope bag while the climber is ascending; clipping in backup loops (see "Backing Up Ascenders," above) or making coils of the rope and clipping them to the harness. Leaving the rope hanging for the entire pitch can work when the pitch is overhanging or when there is otherwise little risk of the rope hanging up. When the rope is hanging, eventually this weight makes moving the lower ascender easier as the climber ascends, and thumbing is not required.

CLEANING

Efficiency in aid climbing is directly linked to organization. While ascending and cleaning a pitch, the follower should take the extra time to rerack the equipment for leading, including reracking single slings into quickdraws. This makes belay transitions go faster. Keep

TIPS FOR CLEANING PINS

1. **First, tap the pin lightly** to get an idea of how much it moves initially. While pins may need to be hit many times in order to remove them, attaching any kind of carabiner to the pin too early makes it harder to hit and slow to clean. For all pins except sawed-off angles, it should be possible to move the pin before the sling is attached. But be careful! If the pin flies out with no sling attached, the pin will probably be lost forever.
2. **Attach either a carabiner with a sling or the funkness device,** once the pin is loosened or, for sawed-off angles, before hitting at all. Clip one end to the pin and one end to yourself, possibly to the aider or daisy chain. Continue to hit the pin back and forth until it comes out. Try not to hit the funkness-device carabiner, because it can break. Use one hand to hold the carabiner to the side while you make blows. It might be a good idea to use the pick side of the hammer when the funkness device is attached. For sawed-off angles, err on the side of putting the sling on early, because they do not visibly move much from side to side, and it is hard to know when they are ready to come out.
3. **Try clipping the free end of the funkness device to the hammer** if the pin does not come out with back-and-forth hits. Then "funk" on the pin by making a big jerk out and up with the hammer and then another separate "funk" with a jerk out and down. "Funk" the pin multiple times, as needed, up and down to loosen it. Sometimes funking straight out away from the rock is helpful, especially with angles.

specialized cleaning gear handy, including the chock pick and funkness device.

When cleaning a pin, first hit it back and forth or up and down, along the axis of the crack. For pins placed in vertical cracks, try to favor the upward hits, which can create future nut placements. See also the "Tips for Cleaning Pins" sidebar.

SECONDING TRAVERSES AND OVERHANGS

Seconding traverses when aid climbing can be both strenuous and technical. Some of the most common and useful methods are described below. These basic methods can often be applied to overhangs as well.

Re-aiding

When traversing horizontally, it may be more efficient to aid climb across the traverse, using aiders, as if leading (called re-aiding). Aiding in this fashion, the second can self-belay by attaching ascenders to the harness with slings and sliding the ascenders along the climbing rope. Make sure to back yourself up to the lead rope or tie in short from time to time.

Seconding Short and/or Diagonal Traverses

The second can cross short traverses and sections of pitches that are more diagonal than horizontal by using normal jugging techniques. The closer to horizontal the traverse is, the less efficient this technique becomes, because at each piece there is a small lower-out of just a few feet. Two main techniques can be used to second a short diagonal traverse with normal jugging techniques, rather than re-aiding as described above:

Grigri lower-out method. The first technique is very easy and requires a Grigri. Jug up to the piece you plan to pass, moving both ascenders as close to the piece as possible (fig. 15-26a). Then bring the Grigri up under the lower ascender and rest all weight onto the Grigri (fig. 15-26b). Remove the top ascender and place it above the piece, and then repeat with the lower ascender (fig. 15-26c). Then open the handle of the Grigri and feed out rope, lowering yourself onto the ascenders and daisy chains (fig. 15-26d). Reestablish your weight in the aiders and reach back to clean the piece (fig. 15-26e).

Alternate method without a Grigri. The alternate method is a little trickier, but it works if the climber does not have a Grigri. When approaching a piece of

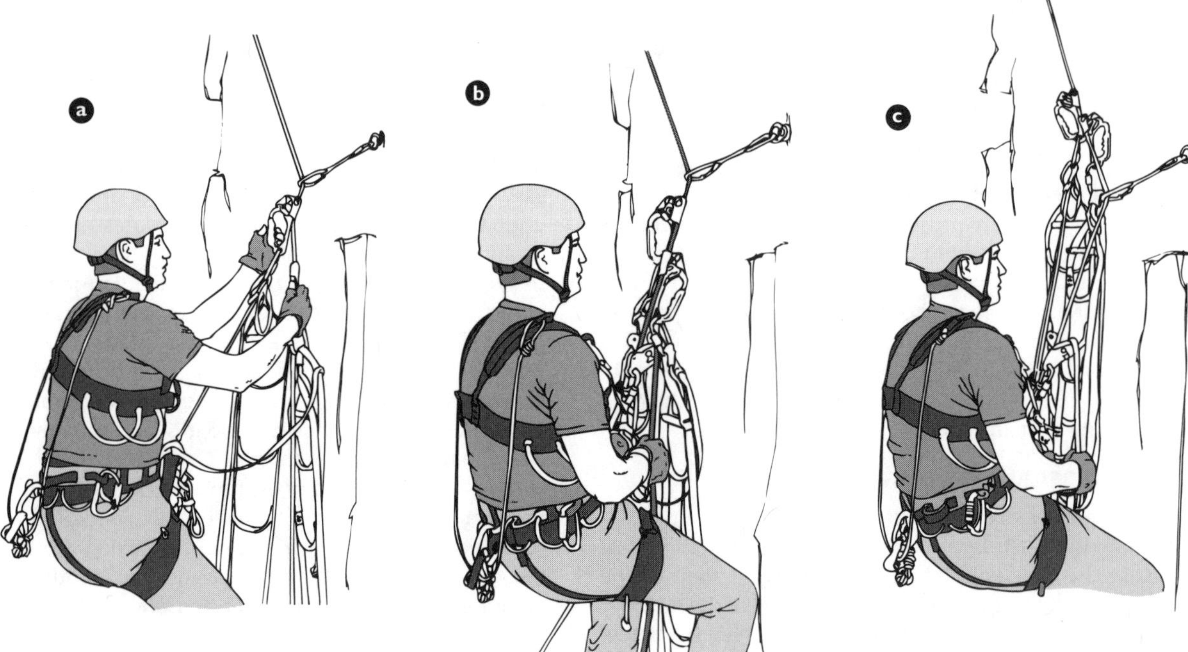

Fig. 15-26. Grigri lower-out method: a, move ascenders to just below protection; b, bring Grigri below lower ascender and transfer weight to it: c, remove ascenders—upper first, then lower—and reinstall above protection (continued on facing page).

protection, leave the lower ascender some distance below the piece, about an arm's length or so, depending on the steepness of the terrain and the distance to and position of the next piece. With your weight on the lower ascender, remove the upper ascender and attach it as far as possible above the currently weighted piece. Then transfer your weight to the upper ascender; this will pull the lower ascender up toward the piece. If you have allowed enough space, the ascender will not jam into the carabiner of the piece, and it will be possible to remove the piece and move up the lower ascender.

Seconding Longer and/or Horizontal Traverses

The best way to follow longer traverses and horizontal traverses is often to do a lower-out, using the methods described below in "Seconding Tension Traverses and Pendulum Swings." If the leader has left some kind of piece that is suitable to lower off of and then cleans all of the traversing pieces, the second can lower from the beginning of the traverse to the next piece left by the leader. This method is often faster than other methods of following a traverse, but the decision on whether or not to use this method is largely up to the leader, who has to make the decision at the time that he protects the pitch.

SECONDING TENSION TRAVERSES AND PENDULUM SWINGS

The best method for seconding a tension traverse or pendulum swing depends on the length of the pendulum and the ropes available. As described in "Tension Traverses and Pendulum Swings," earlier in this chapter, the pendulum point is usually fixed and is often a carabiner, rappel ring, or a piece (or pieces) of webbing. If the leader climbs a long distance without leaving gear, expecting the second to lower off to reach the new plumb line, the leader should ensure that there is adequate fixed gear left for the second to lower off of. This method of seconding pendulums is often called a lower-out.

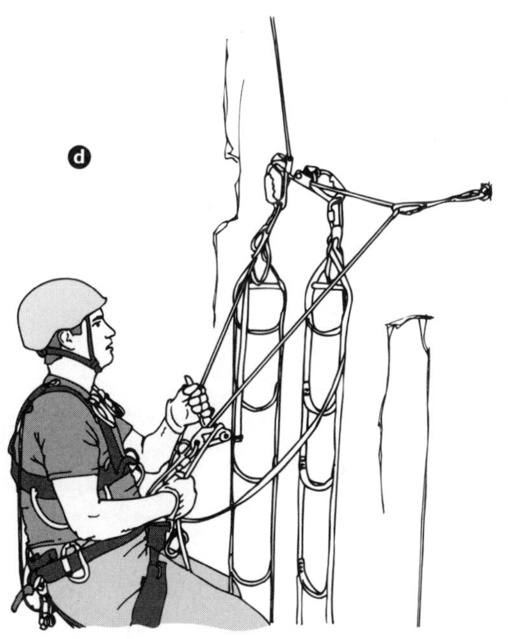

Fig. 15-26. Continued from facing page; d, lower with Grigri until weight is transferred to ascenders in new plumb line; e, clean the piece.

Short Pendulum Swings and Tension Traverses

One clever and useful method of accomplishing a lower-out is shown in Figure 15-27. The follower stays tied in to the climbing rope during the entire sequence, making this a safe and preferable method. This method requires the available rope to be four times as long as the distance to be traveled.

1. Jug up to the fixed point. If possible, fifi in to something without blocking the opening of the lower-out point (fig. 15-27a). Often, the leader will leave protection, such as a quickdraw clipped to a fixed pin, that is totally separate from the lower-out point itself, which could be fixed webbing tied to the pin. This webbing is not clipped in to anything, so clipping in to the quickdraw with a fifi or adjustable daisy does not block the lower-out point from being rigged and loaded. Or, if using a Grigri as a backup, hold your weight on the Grigri.
2. Clip a carabiner to the belay loop on your harness. Then find the end of the rope that is tied in to the harness. Take this rope out to about arm's length from the harness tie-in knot and make a bend in it. Push this bight of rope through the lower-out point, and then bring the bight back toward the harness (fig. 15-27b).
3. Clip the bight in to the carabiner attached to the belay loop. Pulling on the free end that comes out of the lower-out point, cinch yourself up and hold your weight on the climbing rope through the lower-out point (fig. 15-27c). This allows you to remove the quickdraw or other protection from the fixed pin, retrieving all of the team's gear before lowering out. Two additional optional steps are (1) clipping a carabiner around the rope and through the top hole of either (or both) ascender(s), to ensure that the ascender stays on the rope (see figure 15-28), and (2) shortening the daisy chain on the upper ascender to reduce the overall lower-out distance.
4. To lower out, let the rope feed through your hand

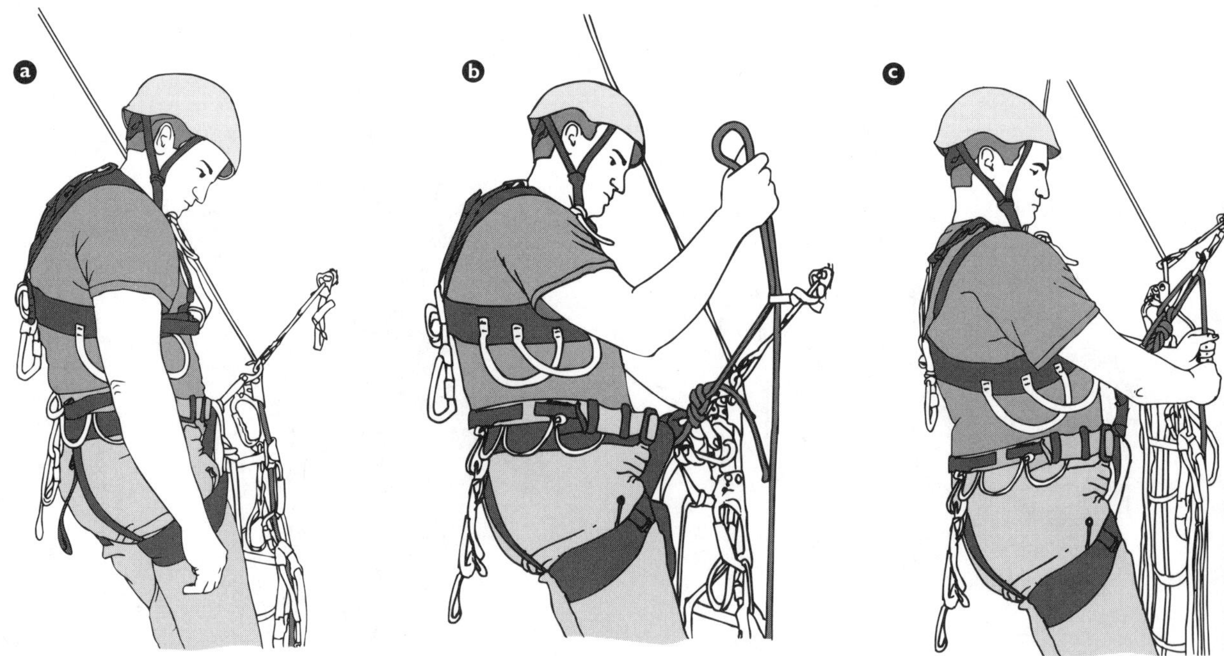

Fig. 15-27. Lower-out method for seconding short pendulum or traverse: a, jug until ascenders are just below protection at lower-out point, then fifi to protection (here, a quickdraw); b, clip a carabiner to harness belay loop, then pull a bight of rope through lower-out point; c, clip bight to harness belay loop and transfer weight to rope (continued on facing page).

(fig. 15-27d). At first, there will be considerable friction, but be diligent as you lower yourself to avoid dropping the rope and lowering too fast. As your weight comes onto the ascenders in the new plumb line, continue to feed rope through the lower-out system.

5. Once you have all your weight on the ascenders in the new plumb line, unclip the bight of rope from the carabiner on the harness belay loop. Pull the ends of the rope so that the bight of rope that was clipped to the harness gets pulled through the lower-out point (fig. 15-27e). The rope has now been freed.

Sometimes short pendulum swings can be seconded without actually lowering out, especially when the terrain is not steep. The follower moves up to the piece and finds a stance or a nearby crack or feature to hold on to, which takes the climber's weight off of the piece to be cleaned. Then the follower removes the piece and, with anticipation of a swing, lets go without lowering out, swinging into the new plumb line while hanging from the ascenders and daisy chains. When used with good judgment, this technique, sometimes called the "Rudy," can be a safe and fast way of following a low-angle short pendulum swing.

Long Pendulum Swings and Tension Traverses

The lower-out method discussed above requires the follower to have the available rope be four times as long as the distance to be spanned, so it works well for seconding short pendulum swings and tension traverses. For long lower-outs, or when this length of rope is not available to the follower, a different method that involves untying from the climbing rope must be used. Since it is preferable to stay tied in to the climbing rope, this technique is used only when the above technique is not possible. For this method, the follower must have the available rope be twice as long as the distance to be spanned.

1. After the leader indicates that the lead line is fixed, the follower prepares to untie from the climbing rope. Before untying, the follower makes sure

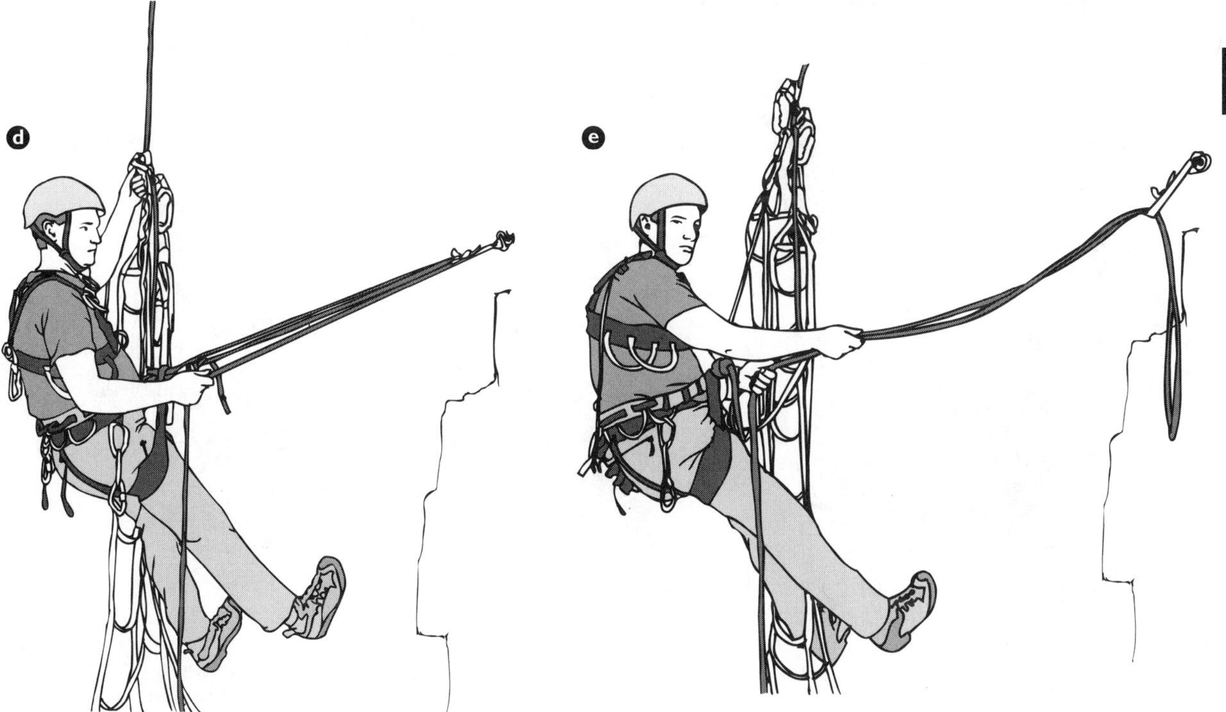

Fig. 15-27. Continued from facing page; d, feed the rope through the harness carabiner until ascenders are weighted; e, unclip the bight of rope from the harness and pull it through the lower-out point.

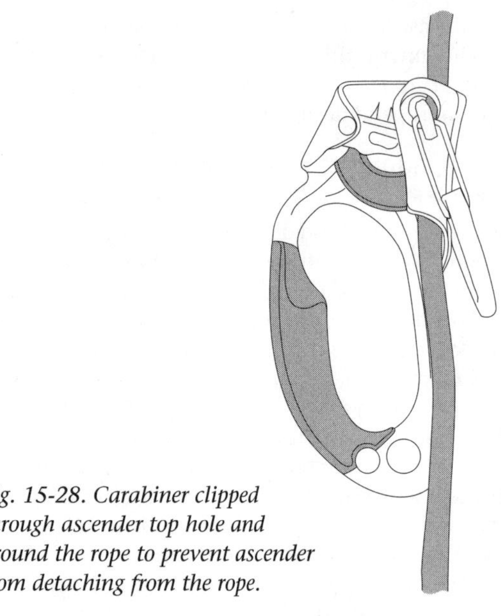

Fig. 15-28. Carabiner clipped through ascender top hole and around the rope to prevent ascender from detaching from the rope.

that he or she is attached to the anchor with at least two points of protection, such as the daisy chains. Pull up a bight of rope and tie in short to the harness. Check and double-check the attachment points, then untie from the lead line (fig. 15-29a).

2. Thread the end of the lead line through the lower-out point. For large lower-outs on established routes, the lower-out point should be fixed and is likely to be a sturdy metal rappel ring. Feed the entire length of the rope through the ring (fig. 15-29b).
3. Put yourself on rappel on the tail of the rope. Clip both of the ascenders to the lead line and shorten the daisy chains (fig. 15-29c) (optional). It is possible to make the lower-out much shorter by pushing the ascenders up the rope as high as possible. If desired, use a Grigri below the ascenders on the end of the rope that goes to the leader, for another backup. Consider clipping a carabiner through the hole of the ascender and around the rope, for one or both ascenders (see Figure 15-28).
4. Rappel the pendulum (fig. 15-29d).

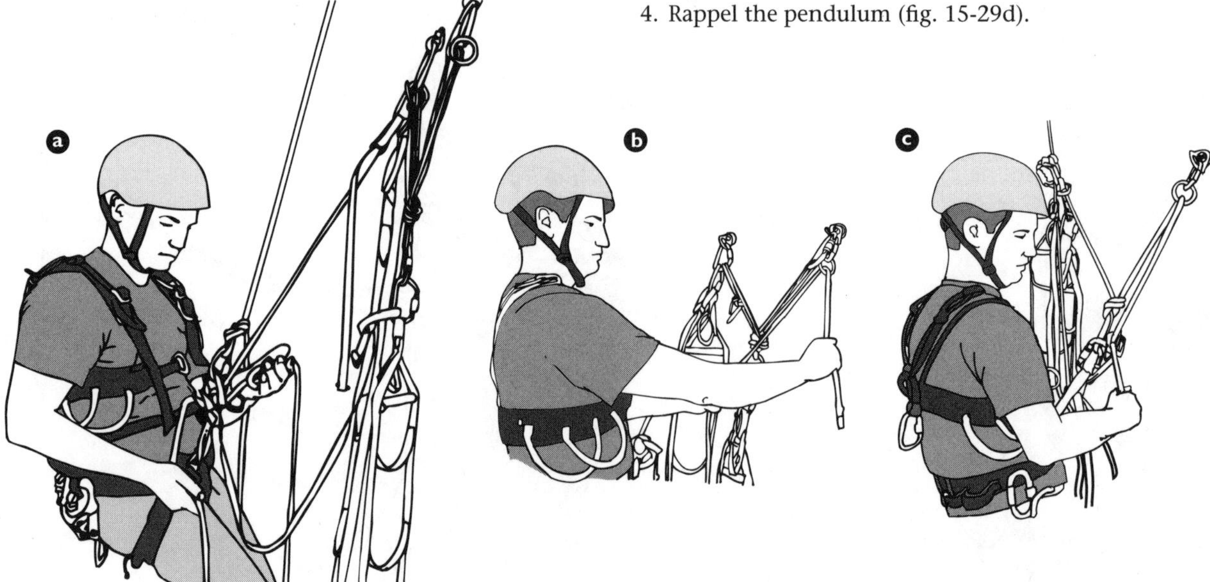

Fig. 15-29. Seconding a long pendulum: a, tie in short, attach daisy chains to two points of protection, then untie from the rope; b, feed the free end of the rope through the lower-out point (here, a metal rappel ring clipped to fixed protection; c, rig rappel device, then attach both ascenders to rope (continued on facing page).

5. Once all weight is on the ascenders in the new plumb line, remove the rappel device and pull the end of the rope through the lower-out point (fig. 15-29e). The rope has now been freed. Tie back in to the end of the rope before continuing to follow the pitch.

CHANGING LEADS

Unorganized belay stations can become a rat's nest of tangled ropes, twisted slings, and assorted hardware. Basic organization keeps the belay station manageable and the team functioning efficiently. The following methods improve organization of the belay station:

- **Use ropes of a different color** when possible, to easily differentiate them.
- **Always stack the haul line** while hauling the bag, using rest intervals to stack the haul line in a rope bag or on a sling. After hauling, organize what remains of the rack and put it all on one side of your body or on a sling on the anchor so that the second can rerack for the next pitch without the leader's help, freeing the leader for other chores after the second arrives.
- **Plan where the second will come up,** and have a locking carabiner ready to clip the second in to the anchor, or ask the second for one as soon as she arrives. This allows the second to safely and quickly anchor in.
- **Focus on the needs of the new leader** when the second arrives. Get the weight of the lead rope off of the second as soon as possible. While the second reracks, pull up the lead line and restack it if necessary. Put the new leader on belay immediately, even if that climber is not ready to lead. Find out what the new leader needs in order to leave, and facilitate that. Accept from the new leader any gear not wanted for the next pitch, and offer food or water.
- **For a smooth belay transition,** all team members should at all times be doing some chore to advance the team, until the leader starts out on the next pitch. If you are the next belayer, try not to eat, drink, adjust your clothing, or take care of yourself when the new leader is at the belay. These needs should be taken care of after you

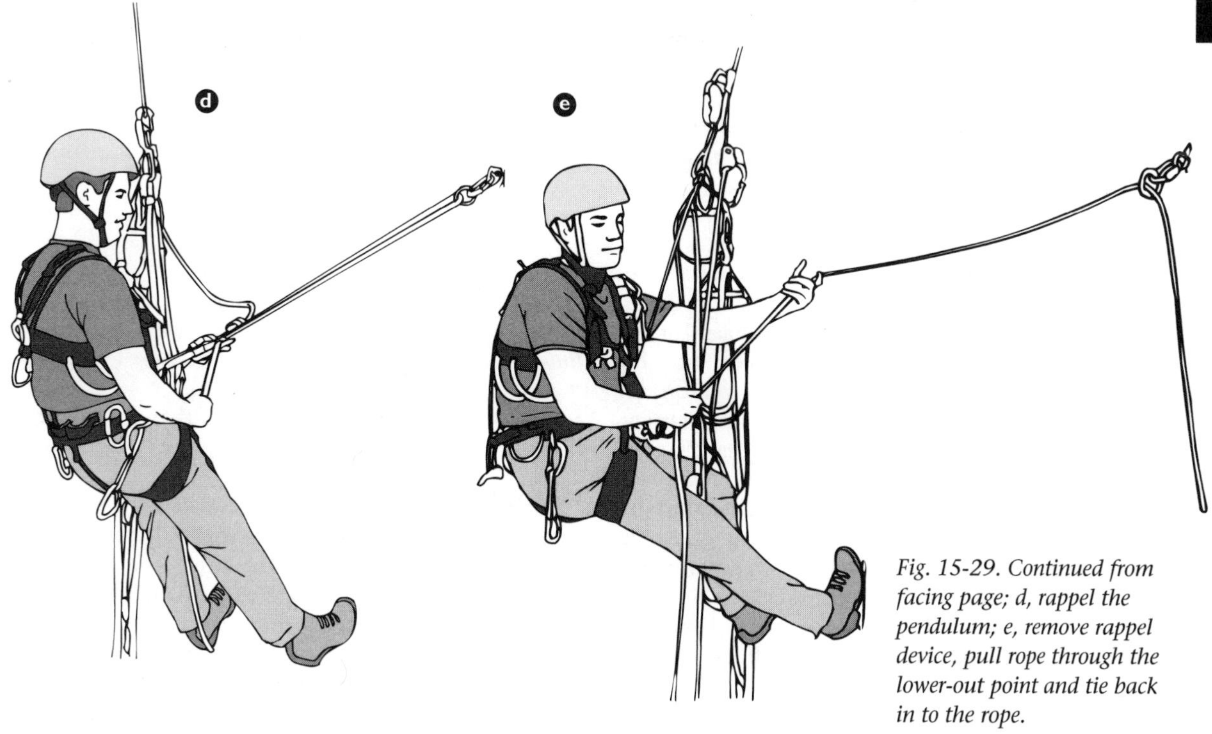

Fig. 15-29. Continued from facing page; d, rappel the pendulum; e, remove rappel device, pull rope through the lower-out point and tie back in to the rope.

finish hauling and before the follower arrives, or while the new leader heads out on the next pitch. Watch the new leader attentively until he or she places protection on the new pitch. Then consider your needs while belaying the leader farther.

BIG WALL MULTIDAY TECHNIQUES

For some climbers, only the reward of a big Grade VI wall could entice them to pick up jumars and aiders and undertake the process of aid climbing. Big wall climbing is sometimes referred to as vertical backpacking, because the big wall climber hauls heavy bags with water, food, and camping supplies and typically covers ground very slowly, compared to free climbing. Big walls are hard work, with endless chores of rope stacking, bag hauling, and ascending. Efficiency, organization, and proper conditioning are critical to success.

Big walls also call for a high degree of mental composure. Inexperienced wall climbers easily find themselves the victim of heightened fears brought on by prolonged and severe exposure. Climbers who are new to the game can perhaps soothe their fears by realizing that techniques for dealing with major walls are much the same as those needed for smaller climbs. Concentrate on the problem at hand, and work away at the objective one move at a time.

Guidebooks and other climbers are helpful sources of information in preparing for a big wall. Beware, however, of overdependence on climbing route topos and equipment lists. Routes do change over time, especially if pins are used regularly.

Solid, efficient aid technique is a prerequisite for completing a major wall within the time constraints dictated by reasonable food and water supplies. For success on the big walls, develop competence in hoisting heavy haul bags up a route and in living comfortably in a vertical world for days at a time. Amazing journeys to seldom-visited places amid a sweeping sea of granite await those who accept this adventure.

(*Note:* the anchor setup and hauling diagrams in this chapter assume anchors that include one or more bolts properly installed in good rock, which is the situation most likely encountered on well traveled aid routes. In the event that climbers must construct their own anchors, they should carefully evaluate the strength of each piece of protection used in the anchor and consider fixing the lead line or attaching the haul device to the power point of the anchor rather than directly to one point of protection.)

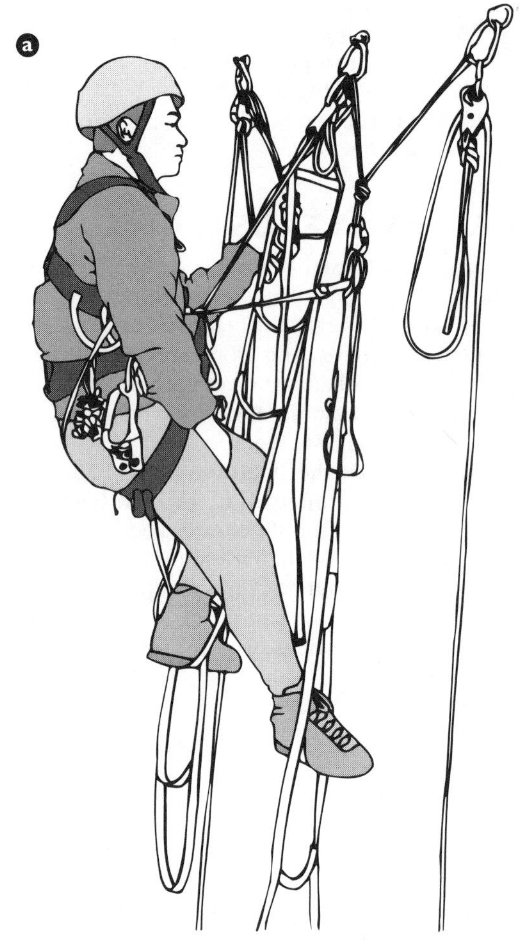

Fig. 15-30. Hauling: a, install haul rope in hauling device, then pull up and stack rope until rope is taut (continued on facing page).

HAULING

After the leader anchors in and fixes the climbing rope for the second, he or she begins hauling:

1. Load the hauling device with the haul line: Tie an overhand knot on a bight in the end of the haul line and attach this to the locking carabiner on the hauling device. Clip this hauling device to the haul anchor. Prepare a sling or rope bag to stack

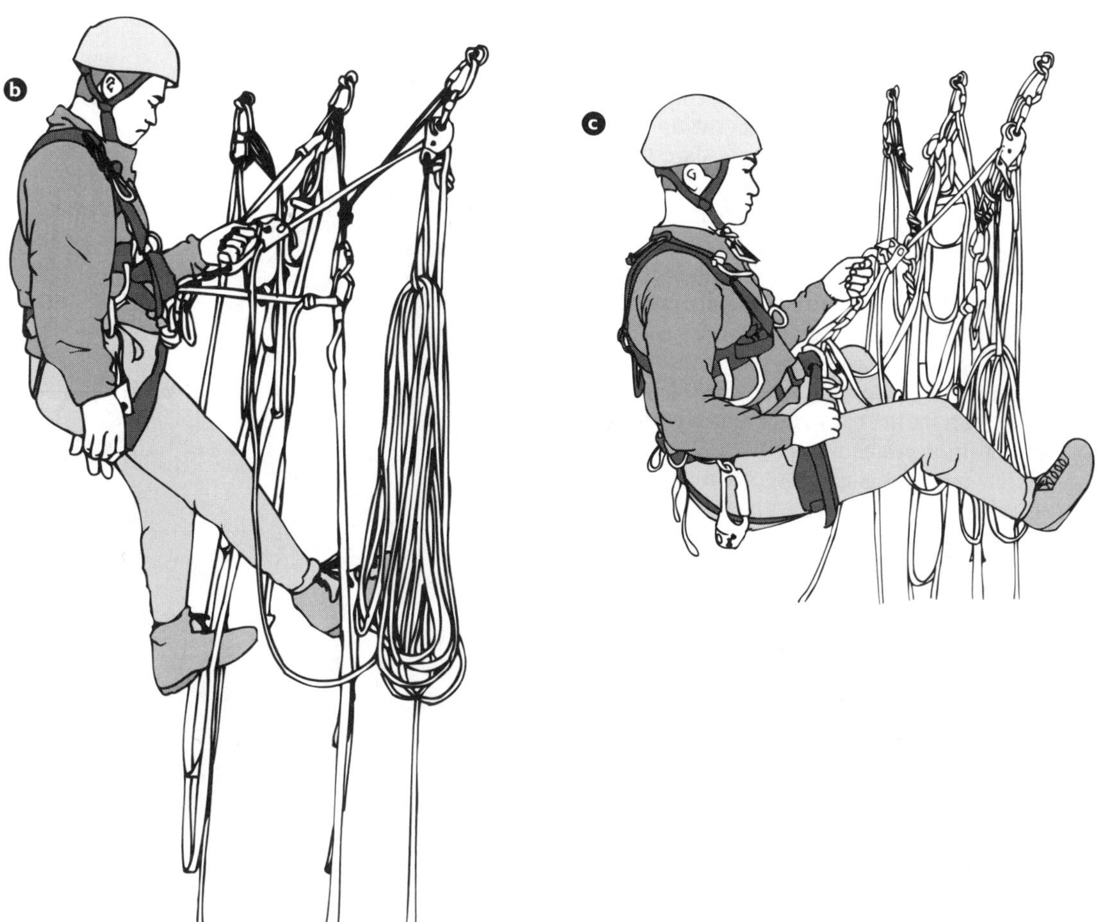

Fig. 15-30. Continued from facing page; b, use one ascender (clipped to harness belay loop) to haul rope until haul bag is lifted from lower anchor; c, haul away after the second releases the haul bag from the lower anchor.

the haul line into while hauling (fig. 15-30a). Pull up all the slack in the haul line, through the device, until the line comes tight. Your follower should then call out "That's the bag."

If not using a hauling device, set up a haul system with a pulley and an ascender. Run the haul line through a regular pulley and clip the end of the haul line to the locking carabiner on this pulley. Clip this pulley to the haul anchor. Attach an upside-down ascender to the haul line on the haul-bag side of the pulley. Clip the upside-down ascender in to the anchor. It may be helpful to use a short sling, such as a full-strength tie-off loop, to extend the ascender so that it is positioned directly below the pulley on the anchor system.

2. Connect one ascender to the belay loop on the harness and lock the carabiner. Attach this ascender to the haul line on the slack side of the rope coming out of the hauling device or pulley. Do a small amount of hauling, just a few inches at a time, as described in step 3 below, to unweight the bags off of the lower anchor (fig. 15-30b). Then the follower can free the haul bag from the anchor and call out "Bags are free, haul away."
3. Begin the regular hauling process: Push back from the wall using your legs and palms to raise the haul bag. For heavy bags, it may be necessary

to also pull up with one hand on the weighted haul line (fig. 15-30c). When you stop hauling, the cam in the hauling device or upside-down ascender acts as a brake to prevent the haul bag from slipping backward. A little slack is needed in the climbing rope between yourself and the anchor to allow hauling movement.

You can also haul by allowing slack of 6 to 8 feet (2 to 3 meters) between you and the anchor. Then walk down the wall 6 to 8 feet until the anchor rope tightens. Climb back to your original position by jugging, possibly with one aider and daisy chain on an ascender and with one Grigri. Repeat the process. This method works best with lighter bags, since a heavy bag cannot be "walked" up the wall.

A similar method is also used if two people are needed to lift a very heavy bag. The leader can stay at the anchor station and haul the bag normally, while the follower can attach his ascenders on the pulling side of the haul rope, about 6 to 8 feet below the leader. As the leader hauls, the follower hangs on the haul line to provide counterweight and walks down the wall while the leader hauls. The follower must jug periodically to prevent his tie-in to the anchor from becoming tight. Regardless of which method the team uses, the climbers should always connect themselves to the anchor with the climbing rope.

Once the leader has completed the haul, the haul bag must be "docked" in order to attach it to the wall and free the haul line for the next pitch. First, stop hauling before the knot in the haul line that attaches the haul rope to the top of the haul bag reaches the pulley. Then select a spot in the anchor to dock the bag, and attach a carabiner to this location. Pull the docking cord up from the top of the haul bag and tie the cord to the carabiner as close to the haul bag as possible, using a load-releasing hitch such as a munter-mule (see Figure 9-22 in Chapter 9, Basic Safety System). Back up the hitch with another knot in the docking cord (fig. 15-31a).

Then do a minihaul on the hauling system, raising the bag just an inch or so to release the cam on the hauling device or upside-down ascender to the open position. Unlock the hauling device or upside-down ascender so that the haul bag can be lowered and then carefully lower the bag, using your weight and the ascender clipped to the harness belay loop, so that the bag rests on the docking cord (fig. 15-31b).

It may be necessary to reengage the cam on the hauling device or upside-down ascender and repeat this minihaul process one or more additional times before the bag's weight completely rests on the docking cord, allowing the leader to fully disengage and remove the hauling device or upside-down ascender. With the bag free from the hauling system, also tie the haul line from the bag in to the anchor with a figure eight on a bight as a backup (fig. 15-31c) in case the docking cord should fail.

Dock the bag as high as possible on the anchor, so that less height is lost during the dock and so that the bag can be accessed during the belay. If there is time, the leader could now restack the haul line so that the free end of the haul line is stacked on top. Or, more

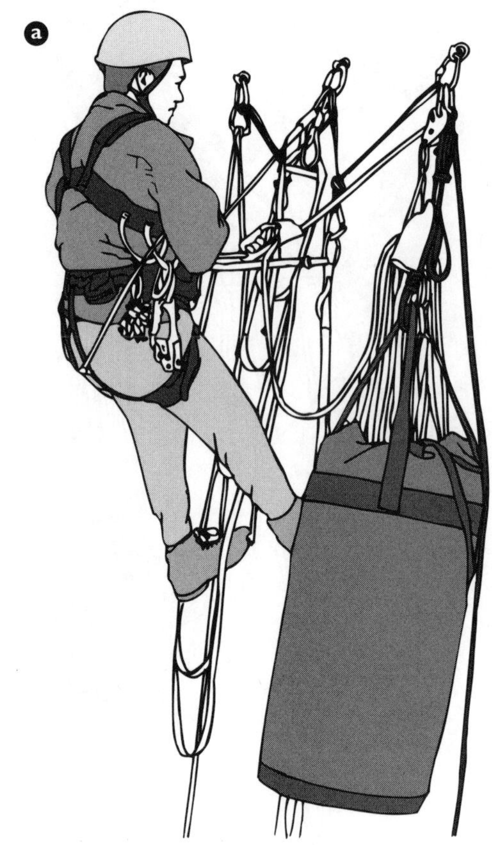

Fig. 15-31. Docking the haul bag: a, attach the haul bag's docking cord to the anchor with a munter-mule and an overhand backup (continued on facing page).

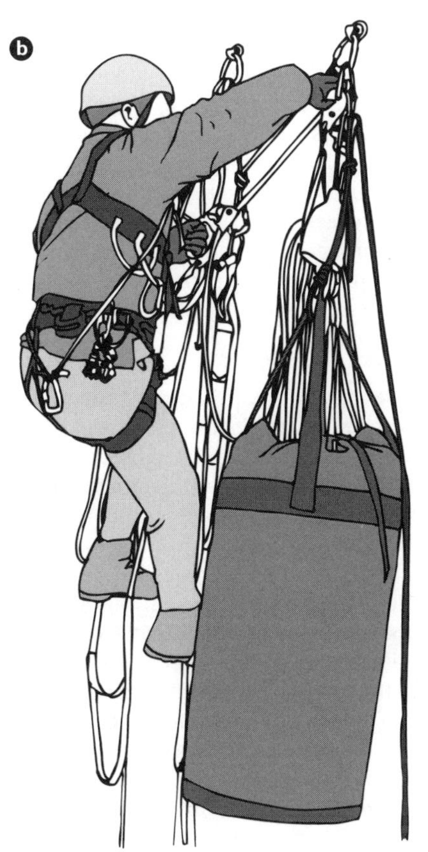

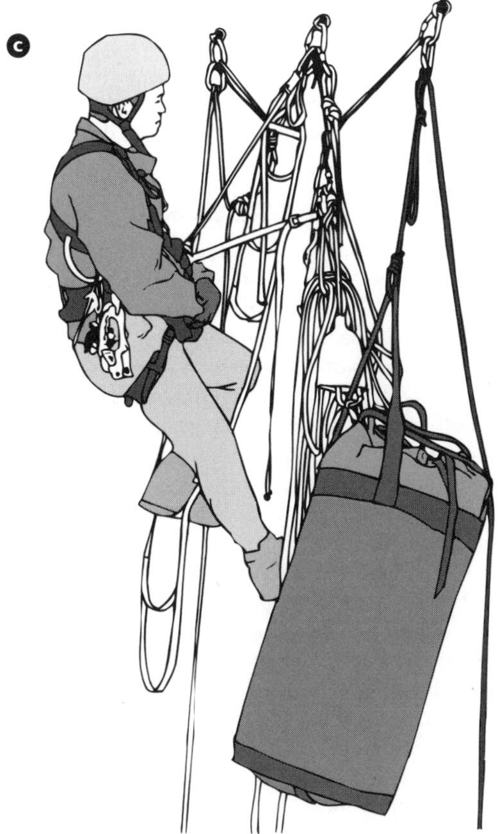

Fig 15-31. Continued from facing page; b, haul enough to release the hauling device and lower the haul bag onto its docking cord; c, remove the rope from the hauling device and back up the docking cord by tying a figure eight on a bight in the haul rope.

efficiently, just feed the haul line as it is while the leader is aiding the next pitch.

FIXING PITCHES

On long aid climbs, climbers often "fix" pitches: put up ropes and leave them in place so they can be climbed quickly with mechanical ascenders the following morning to reach the previous day's high point. Climbers frequently fix one or two pitches above the ground or beyond the bivouac site, and at the high point they leave gear that is not needed for the bivouac. The lower end of each fixed rope is attached to the anchor of the previous pitch.

When fixing pitches, take care to protect the rope from sharp edges or abrupt contours by using duct tape or other material to cover the sharp feature. Intermediate anchor points, if available, should be used; they reduce rope stretch and direct the rope toward the direction of travel. Intermediate anchor points can also be used to redirect the rope around abrasion points.

RETREATING

Before a major aid climb, plan retreat lines in case of bad weather, an accident, or another emergency. Locate other easily reached routes that offer a speedier descent or fixed retreat lines.

If there is no retreat route, consider carrying a bolt kit for emergencies, to allow placement of rappel anchors.

Also, as each pitch is climbed, consider how to descend it. On major walls, rescues may be slow and difficult, if they are possible at all. It may be up to the climbing team to get back down in an emergency. Rappeling the route for retreat with haul bags can be difficult, so practice this skill.

LIVING IN THE VERTICAL WORLD

Living for days on a vertical wall of rock brings some intriguing problems. Once gear is dropped, for instance, it is gone for good. All vital items must have clip-in loops and should be clipped in when not in use or not in the haul bag. Handoffs of gear between partners must be done with care, and "Got it" is a phrase used frequently so that both partners are sure when gear is secure during a handoff. Consider bringing duplicates of key items, such as knives for opening canned food, communication devices, an extra aider or two for the team, etc.

Learn about the gear so that it can be used confidently. Get acquainted with unfamiliar items, such as portaledges or hammocks, beforehand, preferably by testing them out in a hanging environment.

Big wall climbers must carry all their water with them. Each climber generally needs a minimum of 1 gallon (almost 4 liters) per day. For hot weather, especially if the route gets a lot of sun, carry even more. Often, climbers choose to bring food, such as canned food, with high water content; since water must be hauled anyway, the weight of this food is not a consideration. Canned soups, stews, fish, and fruit are favorite big wall fare. Bringing food that requires water to prepare demands accurate planning, since running out of water is bad, but running out of water when it is needed in order to eat is even worse. Some climbers boil water on the wall, especially those who enjoy daily hot drinks. Stoves and cooking accessories must be usable in a hanging environment, and they add weight to the haul bag.

Waste disposal poses another challenge. Do not toss garbage down the wall. Haul it up and off the climb. Keep all bivouac sites clean and sanitary, with no sign of your passing. Use a waste container to pack out human waste. Whenever feasible, pack out garbage left behind by others, to leave the wall in better condition than you found it.

Generally, synthetic sleeping bags and clothing are the best choices for a big wall because they retain their insulating properties when wet. Inflatable pads are more compact and, thus, easier to pack in the haul bag, and they are warmer to sleep on in the portaledge. Just as in camping on the ground, consider backing up an inflatable pad with a closed-cell foam pad, in case the inflatable pad fails. Some climbers use foam pads to help pad the haul bag, but on the first days of a climb these are all but impossible to remove from the haul bag and then repack. The best plan is to always bring a bivy sack, no matter the weather forecast. Your sleeping bag can be stored in its bivy sack, and neither needs to be stuffed into stuff sacks—they provide great padding in the haul bag.

Consider that the air temperature, both day and night, may cool significantly during the ascent of a big wall, so bring extra clothing. Some clothing can be shared, such as a large insulated belay jacket. Consider the chore of hauling when selecting layers and try to wear clothing that will protect the skin from being rubbed by the harness.

Organization on the wall goes beyond climbing gear to include the items in the haul bag. Knowing the location of every item and having it accessible when needed will speed the climb and ensure that climbers can address their needs and any emergencies in a timely manner. Stuff sacks, often of different colors and sizes for identification, help greatly with organization inside the haul bag. Break up critical items, such as food for a long wall, into multiple bags to reduce the impact on the team if a bag is dropped. Use bags strong enough to stand up to wear and tear on the wall, and consider using bags with sewn-on full-strength webbing for clipping in to the wall. It is smart to know where storm gear, the first-aid kit, and human waste kits are located and to pack these items where they can be accessed quickly.

DESCENDING

After completing a major wall, climbers need to get their gear back down. Usually, they must hike or rappel off of the route with all their gear packed in haul bags. Before packing the haul bag, consider whether ropes need to be left accessible for rappeling; if rappeling, set aside all personal gear needed on the rappels before packing the bags.

Haul bags can be tossed off of walls and packed in such a way that all gear arrives intact, but this technique requires special training from an experienced tosser, as well as an improvised parachute for the haul bag. There are no guarantees that the bags will land where intended, and in some places this practice is illegal. Furthermore, many climbers have discovered that their gear has been stolen by the time they get back down. The safest, stress-free bet is to do the hard work of humping out all the gear.

Before packing the haul bag, make sure that the backpack harness is attached, or it will be necessary to unload the bag and pack it again to get the harness system attached.

Pack haul bags with the heaviest items on the bottom for the hike out. Attempt to fill all the small spaces in the bag while packing it from the bottom up so that the bag is packed compactly. Sleeping bags, bivy sacks, and clothing make good space fillers. Consider loading climbing gear into the haul bag loose, unclipping carabiners from protection and unclipping all gear from gear slings, to allow the bag to be packed much more compactly. A compact, tightly packed haul bag can be safely carried off a difficult descent much easier than a floppy, top-heavy tall haul bag. If the team has carried multiple bags, consider packing the smaller bag(s) with the heavier items and making any larger haul bags a little lighter to compensate for carrying a tall, bulky load.

As is true for all long climbs, the hike out can be a dangerous time, because the climbers are exhausted from the effort expended on the climb. Take your time, watch your step, and double-check your systems when rappeling or performing other technical maneuvers.

THE SPIRIT OF AID CLIMBING

Aid climbing offers high adventure in exchange for perseverance and hard work. The pioneers of rock climbing developed aid climbing to open up the vertical world and its fabulous summits, including legendary walls such as El Capitan and Half Dome in Yosemite National Park. In following the path of aid climbing's pioneers, you will reach locations visited by relatively few climbers and can imagine the great vision and dedication required by the first ascensionists to establish these routes.

Aid routes require technical skill in placing gear and boldness to climb thin cracks and steep walls while relying on the proper use of equipment. Keep aid climbing adventurous by resisting the temptation to alter established routes by adding bolts, drilling holes of any kind, nailing pitons, and even leaving behind excess fixed gear. Clean up routes when climbing them by removing old and tired fixed slings, and in general try to leave the route in better condition than you found it. Always practice Leave No Trace ethics on the wall. The rewards of all alpine trips are great, but most likely, your memories of long, multiday wall routes will stand out in a lifetime of climbing as unique and special experiences.

PART IV

SNOW, ICE, AND ALPINE CLIMBING

EQUIPMENT • TECHNIQUES OF SNOW CLIMBING • ROPED SNOW CLIMBING TECHNIQUES • ROUTEFINDING ON SNOW • AVALANCHE SAFETY • AVALANCHE RESCUE • SAFE SNOW TRAVEL

Chapter 16
SNOW TRAVEL AND CLIMBING

Climbing in snow is fundamental to mountaineering. Snow is magical stuff, cloaking the landscape in a sparkling mantle. Gently falling snowflakes can be a balm to the human spirit, an aesthetic delight. But technically, snow is rather dryly defined as "a consolidated mass of water crystals." It is the degree of consolidation that is significant to the climber.

Snow falls in a variety of forms ranging from tiny crystals to coarse pellets. Initially the snowpack can consist of up to 90 percent air by volume. Once the snow is on the ground, a cyclic process of melting and freezing begins. Even though a snow climber might be literally walking on air, climbing on snow is not to be taken lightly. The snow becomes increasingly dense as the air is displaced. Ultimately, the density of glacial ice can be the same as that of ice formed directly from water. See Chapter 26, The Cycle of Snow, for more about snow.

Snow displays a broad spectrum of physical characteristics, and the distinction between hard snow and ice is rather arbitrary. Snow climbing is described in this chapter, whereas ice climbing techniques are discussed in Chapter 18, Alpine Ice Climbing, and Chapter 19, Waterfall Ice and Mixed Climbing, but note that the techniques overlap with no distinct separation.

Climbers travel in a world that is affected by snow on two very different scales. On a rather grand scale, snow—in the form of glaciers—sculpts the terrain. On a more human scale, snow often is the climbers' landscape, largely determining how and where they can travel.

Snow travel is trickier than trail hiking or rock climbing. A rock face is essentially unchanging, whereas the snowpack undergoes rapid changes. Depending on the degree of consolidation, snow can present a widely variable surface: seemingly insubstantial and bottomless unconsolidated powder, a consistently firm and resilient surface, or rock-hard alpine ice. A snowpack that appears to be firm can under certain conditions suddenly collapse and flow (avalanche) and then quickly set as hard as concrete. Safe snow travel requires judgment based on experience.

During a single season, a snowfield may start as a dusting of snow over a brushy slope, progress to a bowlful of powder ready to avalanche, then change to a solid surface offering firm footing, and finally revert back to scattered snow patches. In the course of a day, snow can change from a firm surface in the morning to slush in the afternoon.

Snow can facilitate travel, making climbs easier by providing a pathway over brush and other obstacles on the approach hike and reducing the danger of loose rock on the ascent. But snow conditions also affect decisions on routefinding and climbing technique. Should the climbing party hike up the comfortable, snow-covered valley bottom or on the ridge crest away from avalanche hazard? Should climbers go for easy step-kicking up the sunny slope or the more labor-intensive climb on the firmer, more stable snow of the shaded hillside? Is it safer to travel roped or unroped? The changeable nature of snow requires climbers to be flexible in choosing their mode of travel, and to be ready to use snowshoes, skis, or crampons.

EQUIPMENT

Ice axes and crampons are at the top of the list of basic snow climbing equipment. Snowshoes, skis, and ski poles are other important snow-travel aids, as are wands and shovels. Snow climbers must also construct anchors in snow (snow protection equipment is discussed in "Snow Anchors" later in this chapter).

ICE AX

The ice ax, or *piolet,* and skill in it's use allow climbers to venture onto all forms of snow and ice, enjoying a greater variety of mountain terrain during all seasons of the year. Selecting an ice ax means choosing between features designed for specific uses. A long ax is suitable for cross-country travel and scrambling, in which it is used as a cane and to provide security in low-angle climbing. However, on steeper slopes, a shorter ax is better. Axes designed for ice climbing have even shorter shafts and specialized features including the shape of pick and adze and the placement of teeth. (Ice tools are discussed in Chapter 18, Alpine Ice Climbing.)

Weight is another consideration. The adage "light is right" should not be taken too far. Be sure to select an ax that is designed for general mountaineering. Some very light axes are meant for only light use—that is, ski mountaineering or trekking. Ice axes that meet the Comité Européen de Normalisation (CEN) standards for general mountaineering (see Chapter 9, Basic Safety System) are designated by a "B." At the other extreme, technical ice axes tend to be heavier (and more expensive) than general mountaineering axes. Tools that meet the CEN standards for technical mountaineering are designated by a "T." Ice axes designated with a "T" rating meet higher strength requirements than "B"-rated axes.

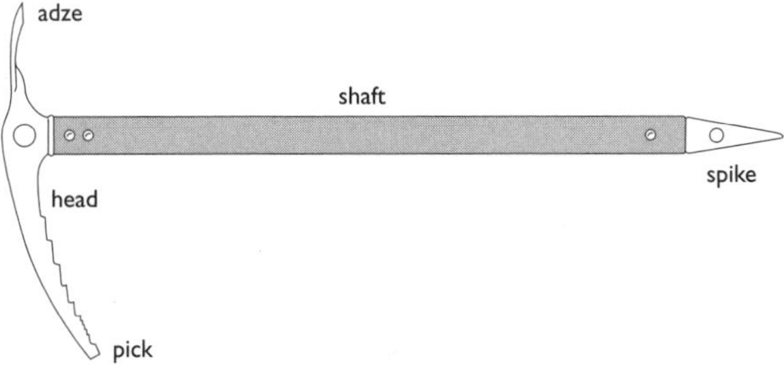

Fig. 16-1. Parts of an ice ax.

Parts of the Ice Ax

16

Head. The head of an ice ax—the pick and the adze (fig. 16-1)—is typically made of steel alloy. The hole in the ax head, the carabiner hole, is used by most climbers to attach the ice-ax leash.

Pick. The pick is curved or drooped (fig. 16-2a), a design that provides better hooking action in snow or ice, enabling the ax to dig in when climbers are trying to stop themselves (self-arrest) after a fall. A moderate hooking angle of 65 to 70 degrees relative to the shaft is typical of general mountaineering axes (fig. 16-2b). A sharper angle of 55 to 60 degrees is better for technical ice climbing (fig. 16-2c); the more acutely angled pick holds better in ice and snow, and it coincides with the arc of the tool head as it is swung.

The pick teeth provide grip in ice and hard snow. Ice axes designed for general mountaineering typically have aggressive teeth only at the end of the pick, as shown in Figure 16-2a and b. Picks of ice axes and tools designed for technical climbing typically have teeth along the entire length, as shown in Figure 16-2c.

The end of the pick may have clearance that is termed positive (fig. 16-3a), neutral, or negative (fig. 16-3b).

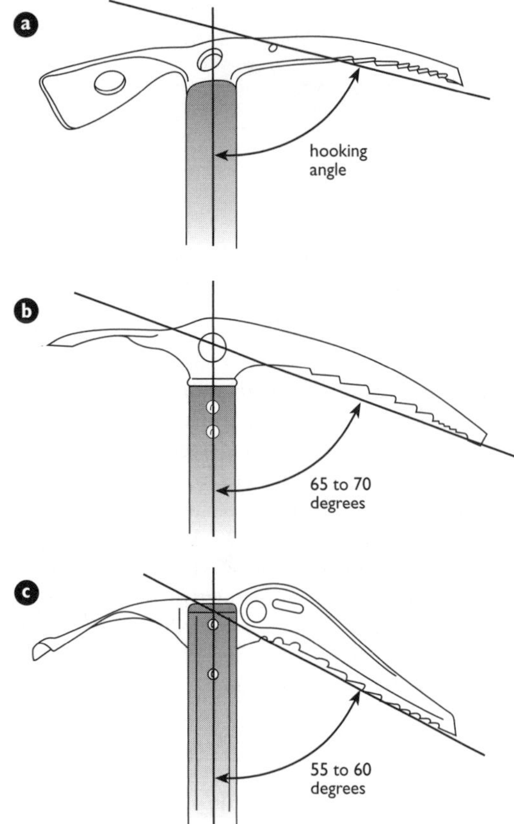

Fig. 16-2. Ice-ax pick shapes and teeth patterns: a and b, for general mountaineering; c, for technical ice climbing.

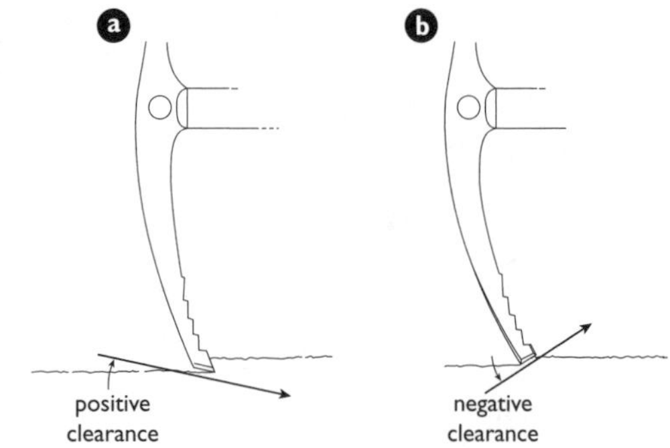

Fig. 16-3. Ice-ax clearance: a, positive; b, negative.

The clearance is determined by comparing the angle of the pick tip relative to the axis of the shaft. In theory, the degree of clearance affects how the ax performs in self-arrest. A pick with positive clearance should penetrate more readily; a pick with negative clearance would tend to skate on ice or hard snow. However, the clearance actually makes little difference: Self-arrest is almost impossible on ice, and in softer snow the pick will dig in, regardless what type of clearance it has. In any case, clearance can always be modified by using a hand file.

Adze. The adze is used mainly to cut steps in hard snow or ice. The flat top of the adze also provides a firm, comfortable platform for a hand when the climber is using the self-belay grasp (see "Techniques of Snow Climbing," later in this chapter). Most adzes for general mountaineering are relatively flat and straight-edged with sharp corners (see Figure 16-2a). This is the best all-around design for cutting steps.

Shaft. Ice-ax shafts (see Figure 16-1) are made of aluminum or a composite material—fiberglass, Kevlar, or carbon filament—or a combination of these. Such materials are much stronger and more durable than wood, which they have replaced.

Some shafts are covered at least partly by a rubber material, which gives climbers a better grip and, hence, better control of the ax, and it also dampens vibrations and increases a climber's control in planting the pick. If the ax shaft lacks a rubber grip, wrap the shaft with athletic grip tape (for example, bicycle handlebar tape) or wear gloves with leather or rubberized palms. However, the friction of any shaft covering may impede the ax from readily penetrating the snow when it is being used for a boot-ax belay, for probing, or for self-belay.

Spike. The spike—the metal tip of the ax (see Figure 16-1)—should be sharp enough to readily penetrate snow and ice. Using the ice ax for balance on rocky trails and talus slopes dulls the spike (see "Ice-Ax Maintenance and Safety," below).

Ice-Ax Length

Ice axes (which are described only in metric units) range in length from 40 to 90 centimeters (16 to 35 inches)—still much shorter than the 5-foot (1.5-meter) alpenstocks used by the alpine pioneers. The shortest axes are for technical ice climbing; the longest ones are for tall mountaineers using the ax as a cane on easy terrain.

The optimal length for an ice ax depends more on how the climber intends to use it than on the climber's height. For general mountaineering, a 70-centimeter ax is the best choice for the majority of climbers. This length offers the best compromise of balance and appropriate length for use on steep snow slopes.

Axes less than 60 centimeters long are technical ice climbing tools, excellent for placements on very steep slopes. However, these ice tools are not as good for self-arrest; the shorter shafts offer less leverage, and many of the technical pick designs do not lend themselves to the self-arrest technique. A 70-centimeter ax is the longest that is generally useful for technical ice climbing. Thus, a length of 60 to 70 centimeters works well in most alpine situations, wherein climbing is on moderately steep snow slopes and the ax is being used for self-belay and self-arrest. Longer axes are better for cross-country travel and scrambling, for snow anchors, and for probing for cornices and crevasses.

Ice-Ax Leash

The ice-ax leash provides a sure way to attach the ice ax to the climber's wrist or harness. A leash is valuable insurance on crevassed glaciers or long, steep slopes where losing an ax would leave a climber without a principal safety tool and put climbers below in danger from the runaway ax. A leash also allows climbers to let the ice ax hang free while they make a move or two on the occasional rock they encounter during a snow climb.

There are two schools of thought regarding the use of an ice-ax leash during snow travel that requires using self-belay technique. Most climbers use a leash so that the ice ax is secure against loss. Others, however, believe that a flailing ice ax, hanging by the leash from the wrist of a climber who has lost his grip on the shaft, is a potential threat during a fall. Ultimately, it is a judgment call.

The leash typically consists of a piece of accessory cord or webbing attached to the carabiner hole in the ice ax head. A vast array of commercially manufactured leashes are available, or a leash can be made using either 5- or 6-millimeter Perlon accessory cord or ½- to l-inch tubular webbing. Tie the ends of the material together with a suitable knot to create a sling, girth-hitch the sling through the carabiner hole, then tie an overhand knot to form a wrist loop.

The length of a leash can vary. Short leashes (fig. 16-4a) are favored by those using ice axes for basic snow and glacier travel. The short leash is easy to use and allows climbers to regain control of the ice ax quickly during a fall. During an uncontrolled fall in which a climber loses his grip on the ax, an ax on a short leash will not flail around as much as one on a longer leash.

However,the majority of climbers prefer a longer leash (fig. 16-4b). When shifting the ax from one hand to the other while changing direction up a snow slope, a climber with a long leash does not need to switch the leash from wrist to wrist. A long leash can be chained to a runner clipped to the seat harness, so that the ax can be used as a personal anchor. The long leash also makes the ax more versatile for climbing steep snow or ice. A long leash is usually about as long as the ax shaft, and if it is adjusted correctly, it will reduce arm fatigue during step-cutting and ice climbing. With one hand through the wrist loop, the climber should be able to grasp the end of the shaft near the spike.

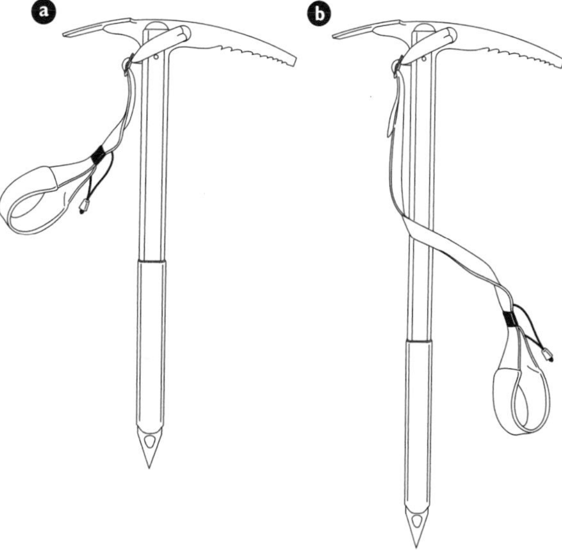

Fig. 16-4. Ice-ax leashes attached through hole in head of ax: a, short; b, long.

Ice-Ax Maintenance and Safety

Ice axes require very little special care. Before each use, inspect the shaft for deep dents that might weaken it to the point of failure under load (but do not worry about minor nicks and scratches). After each climb, clean mud and dirt off the ax. Use a combination of solvents (such as a lubricating and penetrating oil) and abrasives (scouring pads or a soft ski hone—a soft synthetic block with embedded abrasive) to remove any rust.

Check the pick, adze, and spike regularly for sharpness. To sharpen, use a hand file, not a power-driven grinding wheel. High-speed grinding can overheat the metal and change the temper, diminishing the strength of the metal.

Guards are available to cover the sharp edges and points of the pick, adze, and spike.

CRAMPONS

Crampons are a set of metal spikes that strap on over boots to penetrate hard snow and ice where boot soles cannot gain sufficient traction (see the "History of Crampons" sidebar). When should crampons be worn? There is no steadfast rule. Make this decision based on individual skill and experience, as well as personal assessment of conditions. If it seems best to wear crampons, put them on.

Choosing among the different crampon designs involves a trade-off between features that are essential for general alpine use and those designed for technical ice climbing (see the "Questions to Consider When Selecting Crampons" sidebar).

Crampon Points

The early-model 10-point crampon was eclipsed in the 1930s by the addition of two forward-slanting or "front" points, which created the 12-point crampon. The front points reduced the need for step-cutting and permitted front-pointing up steep snow and ice (see Chapter 18, Alpine Ice Climbing). Currently, crampons designed for general mountaineering include both 12-point and lighter 10-point models, but all have front points.

Most crampons are made from chromium molybdenum steel, an extremely strong, lightweight alloy. However, some models are fabricated from aircraft-grade aluminum alloys, which are lighter than steel but also much softer, and these may not stand up to the rigors of rock underfoot. Snow and ice routes often include short sections of rock that are climbed wearing crampons. Most crampons are able to take the punishment, but very much travel on rock will dull the points.

The relative angles and orientation of the first two rows of points determine the best use for a set of crampons. When the first row (front points) is drooped and the second row (secondary points) is angled toward the front of the crampon (fig. 16-5a), the crampons are better suited for ice climbing (front-pointing) than for general mountaineering. This configuration allows easier engagement of the secondary points when front-pointing, which greatly reduces calf strain (see Chapter 18, Alpine Ice Climbing). In contrast, downward-angled secondary points (fig. 16-5b) facilitate a more ergonomic walking motion on moderate terrain.

Front points can also be either horizontally (fig. 16-5c) or vertically oriented (fig. 16-5d). Vertically oriented front points, whose height is greater than their width, are designed for technical ice climbing. Their shape mimics that of an ice-ax pick. They are well suited for penetration into hard water ice, but in softer alpine ice and snow, they are prone to shearing through unless

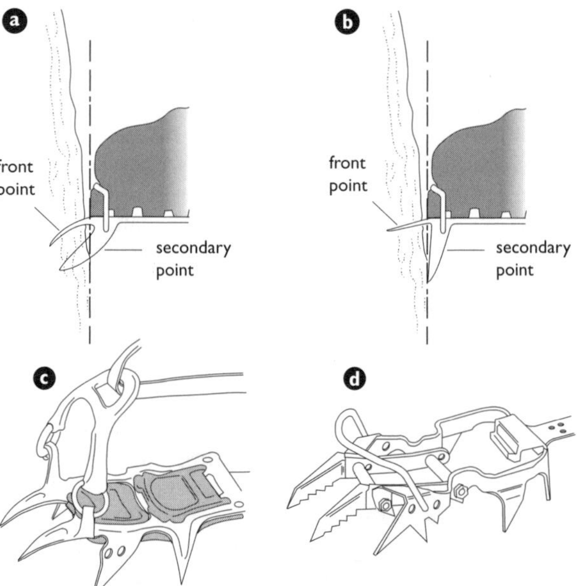

Fig. 16-5. Angle of first two rows of points: a, out from toe of boot best suited for front-pointing; b, downward-angled secondary points best suited for general mountaineering; c, horizontal front points best suited for general mountaineering; d, vertical front points best suited for technical ice climbing.

QUESTIONS TO CONSIDER WHEN SELECTING CRAMPONS

When shopping for crampons, ask the following questions:

- What type of crampon is appropriate for your intended activity?
- What terrain is the crampon designed for?
- How will you know when the crampons fit your boots?
- Which attachment system is best for your needs?

HISTORY OF CRAMPONS

Crampons are an ancient tool, invented more than 2,000 years ago. Early inhabitants of the Caucasus region wore leather sandals soled with spiked iron plates to travel on snow and ice. Celtic miners used iron foot spikes as early as 2,700 years ago. Medieval alpine shepherds wore three-point crampons—horseshoe-shaped frames bearing three sharp spikes.

At the end of the 19th century, the four-point crampon was state of the art. Then in 1908, Oscar Eckenstein created the 10-point crampon. Many alpinists thought the gadgets were an unsporting advantage. However, these crampons relieved climbers of the tremendous tedium of cutting steps and opened up a vast array of unclimbed snow and ice faces. In 1932 Laurent Grivel added two front points, creating the 12-point crampon, which was specifically designed for climbing steep hard snow and ice. They have evolved into the crampons that are essential for mountaineering today.

they are deeply set. In contrast, horizontally oriented front points, with height that is less than their width, are designed for the alpine ice and snow conditions encountered in most general mountaineering situations. They provide a larger surface area and therefore are more stable in softer snow.

Hinged, Semirigid, and Rigid Crampons

Mountaineering crampons can be categorized into three types: hinged, semirigid, and rigid.

Hinged. Crampons designed for general mountaineering are hinged (fig. 16-6a). They fit a wide variety of mountaineering boots, are light, and flex with the natural rocking action of walking. Attached to a stiff boot, hinged crampons perform nearly as well for ice climbing as rigid crampons because the boot provides the stable platform, although there may be more vibration than with a stiffer crampon.

Semirigid. Crampons that are semirigid are designed for both general mountaineering and technical ice climbing (fig. 16-6b). They have some flex, which creates some give with a fairly stiff-soled boot. Semirigid crampons are designed with either horizontally or vertically oriented front points. Some semirigid crampons are designed so that with a reconfiguration of the linking bar, the crampon can be converted to a more ergonomic flexible walking mode, compatible with a flexible boot. They can then be readjusted for any technical front-pointing that may lie ahead.

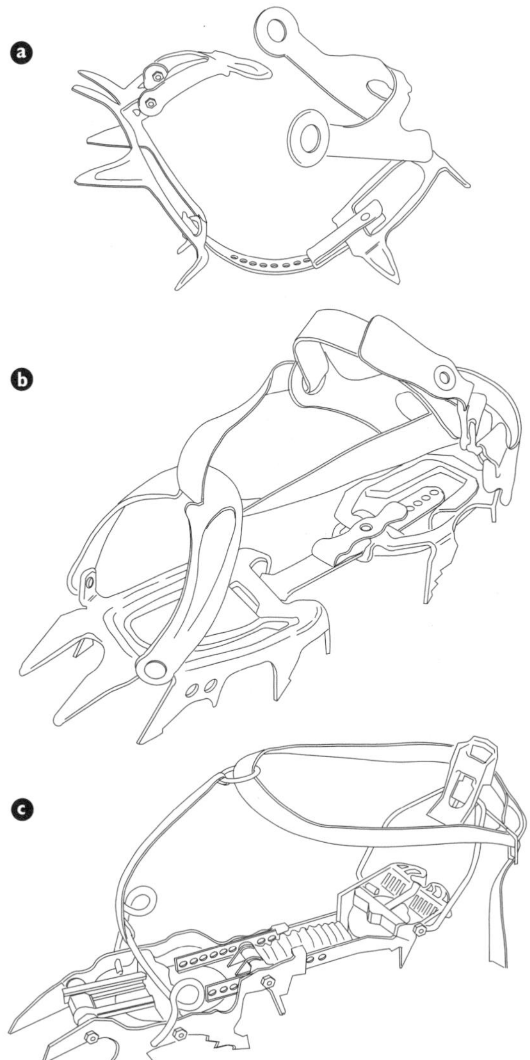

Fig. 16-6. Types of crampons: a, hinged; b, semirigid; c, rigid.

Rigid. Crampons designed for technical ice climbing are rigid (fig. 16-6c). They vibrate less than hinged crampons when they are kicked into the ice, and their stiffness provides more support, which helps climbers to conserve energy. Most rigid crampons require a very stiff boot, because a flexible boot is likely to flex out of the attachment system, causing the crampon to pop off. Rigid crampons are generally more awkward when climbers are traveling on flat or rocky terrain, where some flexibility is desired, and they are typically the heaviest of all crampon types.

Crampon Attachment

Three main crampon attachment systems are available: strap or universal, clip-on (also referred to as "automatic"), and hybrid. In general, hinged crampons work best with strap systems and flexible boots. Rigid crampons work best with clip-on systems and very stiff boots. Semirigid crampons work best with hybrid attachment systems—a combination of a rear clip and straps over the front of the boot—and fairly stiff boots. Ultimately, the choice of crampon attachment system is largely dictated by the attachment platform that the boot provides.

Straps. Modern strap or universal bindings (fig. 16-7a) are much easier and faster to use than the original strap systems. If climbers plan to do a wide variety of climbing and scrambling over a range of terrain (trail, rock, and snow), this binding type will provide secure and fast attachment with the widest selection of footwear (fig. 16-7b). These are excellent bindings for use with a mountaineering boot covered by an insulating overboot.

Clip-on. With clip-on bindings, the crampons attach to the boot with a wire toe bail and a heel clip or lever (fig. 16-7c). These systems are fast and easy to use. With clip-on bindings, the fit of the crampon to the boot is much more critical than with crampons that strap on. In order to fit securely, the boot must have pronounced grooves at both the heel and toe. When the crampon is sized correctly, the heel clip should decisively "snap" into place, forcing the wire toe bail firmly into the boot toe groove. Clip-on bindings typically include a safety strap wrapped around the ankle to secure the cram-

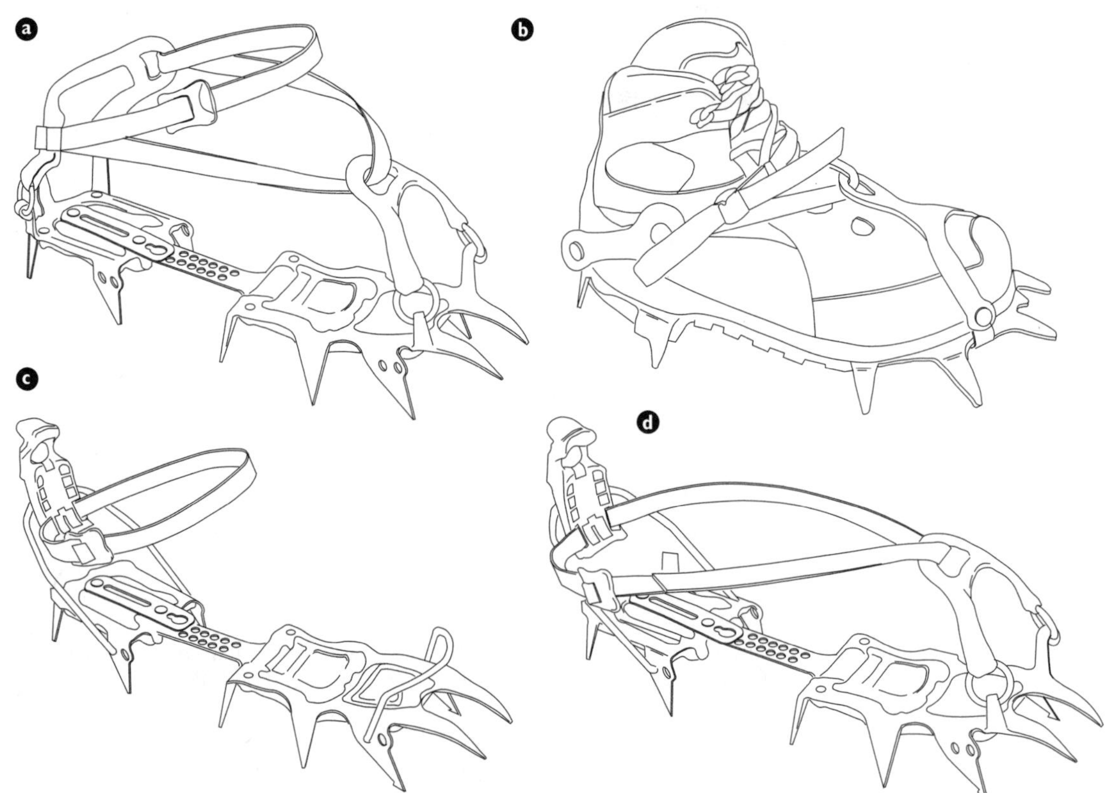

Fig. 16-7. Systems for attaching crampons to boots: a, strap or universal; b, light hiking boot with universal binding and flexible crampon; c, clip-on; d, hybrid.

pon if it pops off the boot. Some clip-on bindings also include a metal strap attached to the toe bail. The safety strap is threaded through the metal strap to prevent the crampon from popping off the boot.

Hybrid. Hybrid bindings feature toe straps combined with a heel clip (fig. 16-7d). These bindings are popular because they work well on boots that have a pronounced heel groove but lack a toe groove. As with clip-on bindings, the heel clip should decisively "snap" into place, forcing the boot into the front attachment posts.

Crampon Fit

It is critical that crampons fit boots perfectly. When purchasing crampons, bring the boots to the shop for a proper crampon fitting (see the "Tips for Fitting Crampons" sidebar). If the crampons will be used on more than one pair of boots, check the fit on all pairs. Be sure to purchase crampons that match the intended usage.

Practice putting on the crampons while in the comfort of home. There will be plenty of opportunity to put them on under less-ideal conditions: by feel in dim light or in the limited illumination of a headlamp, fumbling with cold, numbed fingers.

Crampon Maintenance and Safety

Regular simple maintenance is required to keep crampons safe and dependable (see the "Crampon Safety Rules" sidebar). After every climb, clean and dry the crampons and inspect them for wear. Repair or replace worn straps, nuts, bolts, and screws. Check the points: For ice climbing, maintaining sharp points is essential, but for most snow climbing and classic mountaineering, it is best not to have sharp points. File down burrs, rough edges, and very sharp points with a small file. Brand-new crampons frequently come with razor-sharp points (fig. 16-8a) and will almost always require a bit of maintenance or tuning before use (fig. 16-8b). If crampon points are overly dull, a file can also be used to sharpen them. Also check alignment of the points—splayed points make the crampons less efficient at penetrating snow and ice and more likely to slash pants, gaiters, and legs. It is probably best to retire a pair of crampons whose points have been badly bent or overly filed.

In soft, sticky snow, crampons can accumulate a growing buildup of snow. This ball of snow can interfere with the crampon points' penetration and be dangerous, particularly where sticky snow overlays an icy base. To minimize this hazard, climbers can use manufactured antiballing plates—plastic, rubber, or vinyl sheets that fit on to the bottom of the crampon (fig. 16-9). Alternatively, climbers can wrap the bottom of the crampon with duct tape. When soft, sticky snow

TIPS FOR FITTING CRAMPONS

- Clip-on bindings grip the boot at toe and heel, so the boot's welt is especially important. Clip-on bindings require well-defined grooves at the toe and heel on plastic and very stiff leather boots.
- The front crampon points should protrude ¾ to 1 inch (2 to 2.5 centimeters) beyond the toe of the boot.
- Be sure to wear supergaiters when fitting the crampons if the gaiters have a rubber rand that fits around the rand and instep of the boot.
- Crampons must be fitted with the overboots on, as with supergaiters, if overboots will be worn to help insulate feet from the cold and snow in very cold conditions. Make sure any attachment straps are long enough.

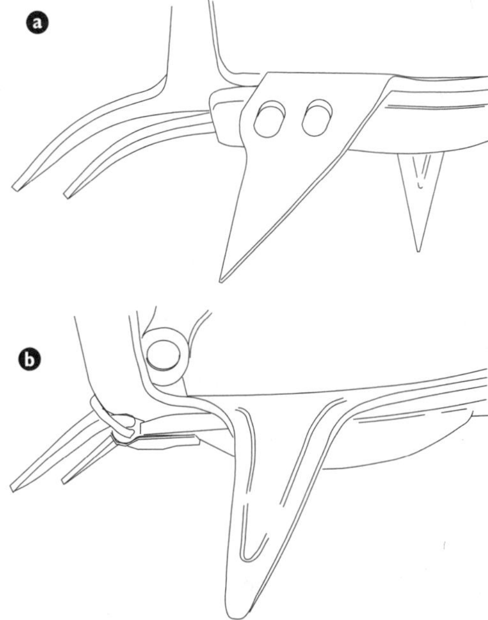

Fig. 16-8. How to finish crampon points: a, very sharp (new); b, rounded off (after filing).

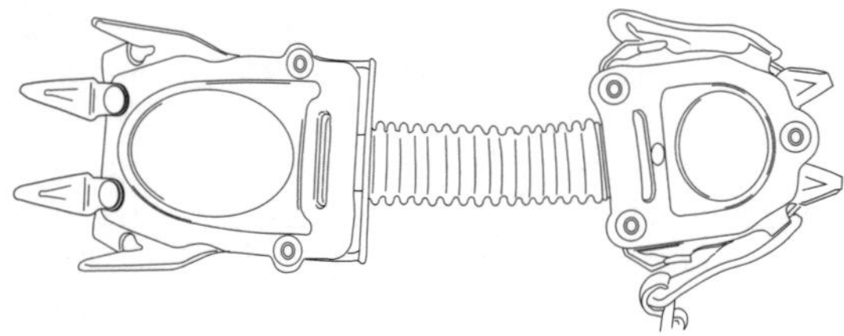

Fig. 16-9. Crampon with anti-balling plates.

is encountered, consider whether crampons are really needed. It may be safer to proceed without them.

Instep and Approach Crampons

Small instep crampons with four or six points are designed for crossing an occasional short snowfield. Because these crampons have no points at the heel or toe, they are not suitable for mountaineering and can be dangerous on steep snow or ice.

Approach crampons are flexible, full-length plates that typically have eight points. Approach crampons are designed for use on moderate terrain, and they also are not suitable for mountaineering.

Instep and approach crampons are not a substitute for 10- or 12-point mountaineering crampons.

WANDS

Mountaineers often use wands to mark their route so they will be able to retrace their path during inclement weather. Wands may also be used to indicate potential danger. Two wands forming an X indicate a known danger, such as a weak snow bridge. Wands can also be used to mark the boundaries of safe areas for unroped walking at camp and the location of buried supplies (caches).

Wands are available commercially, but climbers usually make their own, using green-stained bamboo garden stakes, topped with a colored duct-tape flag (fig. 16-10). Wands vary in length from 30 to 48 inches (76 to 122 centimeters). If the wand is less than 30 inches, the flag may not be seen easily; if longer than 48 inches, the wands are awkward to carry in pack compression straps.

Mark the party's wands with its initials and the date to be certain that the party is retracing its own path, not another's. Insert the wands firmly into the snow, planting them deeply enough to compensate for melting or high winds. Place them so that they indicate the direction of travel, using any one of a number of ways to do this. Use long wands in winter, when they have to be inserted deeper in soft snow and when heavy snowfall can bury them. Retrieve wands on the descent.

SKI POLES

Ski poles are not only used for skiing. Ski or trekking poles can be used whether climbers are traveling by foot, snowshoes, or skis. Poles are better than an ice ax for balance when climbers are carrying heavy packs over level or low-angle snow, slippery ground, or scree or when they are crossing a stream or boulder field. Poles also can take some of the weight off the lower body. And the basket at the bottom keeps the poles from penetrating

CRAMPON SAFETY RULES

In the mountains, climbers can follow a few rules to protect themselves, their gear, and their climbing companions from sharp crampon points:

- Use a crampon pouch or a set of rubber point protectors when carrying crampons.
- Always bring the tools needed to adjust the crampons, as well as any necessary spare parts.
- While climbing, step deliberately to avoid snagging pants or gaiters, gashing a leg, or stepping on the rope.
- Be careful not to snag gear hanging low from gear loops on the climbing harness; avoid having slings hang below the thigh.

Fig. 16-10. Construction of a wand with a duct-tape flag.

too deeply into soft snow, which ice axes do unless they are fitted with a special snow basket.

Some ski and trekking poles have features helpful to the mountaineer. Adjustable poles enable climbers to set the length to suit the conditions or the terrain; on a traverse, the uphill pole can be set to a length shorter than the downhill pole. These poles can be fully compressed for easy packing. Adjustable poles require more maintenance; after each trip, disassemble, clean, and dry them.

Poles with removable baskets can serve as probes for crevasses when their baskets are removed. Some poles are made so that a pair can be fastened together to form a serviceable avalanche probe. However, this is a poor substitute for a commercial avalanche probe.

Some ski poles can be fitted with a special self-arrest grip that has a plastic or metal-tipped pick, but on technical terrain this definitely is not a substitute for an ice ax.

SNOWSHOES

Snowshoes are a traditional aid for snow travel, and their design has been updated into smaller, lighter models. Modern designs include models consisting of tubular metal frames with lightweight, durable decking materials (fig. 16-11), as well as plastic composite models. Modern bindings are easy to use and are more stable than older models. Snowshoes include cramponlike, toothed metal plates designed to improve traction on hard snow; many models also include serrated heel and/or side plates that decrease side-to-side slippage.

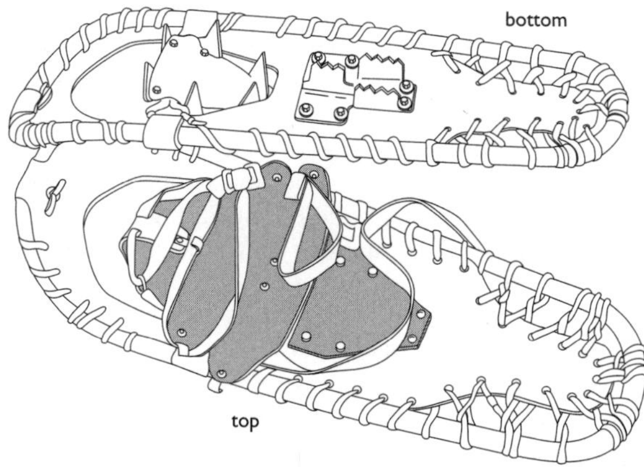

Fig. 16-11. Snowshoes for winter mountaineering: tubular aluminum frame, polyurethane deck, aluminum cleats, and nylon straps.

Snowshoes permit efficient travel in soft snow, where otherwise hikers laboriously posthole (sink deeply with each step). Snowshoes can be used to kick steps uphill. Although travel on snowshoes may be slower than travel on skis, snowshoes can be used in brushy or rocky terrain where skis would be awkward, and they are often more practical than skis when climbers are carrying heavy packs. If the climbing party includes some people who are not very good on skis, it is much less frustrating and more efficient for the group to travel on snowshoes. Snowshoe bindings can be used with almost any footwear, whereas most ski bindings require specialized boots.

SKIS

Nordic and mountaineering skis fitted with climbing skins provide a convenient mode of travel in the mountains. The traditional Nordic ski binding leaves the heel free and is worn with a special boot (fig. 16-12a); the free heel allows the Nordic skier to use the telemark turn for downhill travel. Depending on the design and purpose of the skis and boots, they may be used for cross-country, touring, or telemark skiing. Ski mountaineering has traditionally used a randonée binding that also leaves the heel free for uphill travel, but the heel can be locked down for standard alpine downhill technique (fig. 16-12b). Special randonée or alpine touring boots are designed for use with mountaineering skis; because of the strength and stability of the modern plastic telemark double boot, it is common for the telemark skier to simply link turns using the same parallel skiing techniques that the randonée skier employs. Some bindings can accommodate plastic mountaineering boots, but there is a significant loss of skiing performance. Telemark equipment is still evolving, and a new binding design may solve some of the last remaining issues—such as boot flex and ease of climbing—inherent in the older telemark binding design, which have been less of a problem in the randonée-style binding.

The past decade has seen a marked evolution and rapid development of both randonée and telemark ski gear for ski mountaineering. The traditional ski mountaineer has used a wider, heavier ski (sometimes called a randonée ski) that was closer to a traditional alpine (downhill) ski (see Figure 16-12b). In fact, randonée and telemark skis are now often the exact make and model, differing only in the types of bindings used. Both modern types of skis are quite wide compared to the older alpine gear, especially the older Nordic gear.

Fig. 16-12. Ski equipment for mountaineering: a, Nordic ski boot and three-pin binding; b, randonée boot and binding; c, climbing skins for skis.

And both modern types are highly shaped, often with modified tips and tails for ease and stability of turning during the descent. Nordic, telemark, and randonée skis all permit climbers to travel the backcountry. Climbing skins (strips of rough-textured material) that can be attached temporarily to the bottom of the skis provide traction for uphill travel (fig. 16-12c).

Climbers who are not accomplished skiers may find that the disadvantages of using skis in the backcountry outweigh the advantages. When the skis must be carried, they are awkward and heavy. Wearing skis complicates self-arrest. Skis can be awkward on rocky or forested slopes, and skiing can be difficult when climbers are carrying heavy packs. Every party member must have similar skiing ability for the group to keep a steady pace. This is especially true for roped glacier travel.

Skis can be faster for basic snow travel, and they can provide a way to reach areas that are otherwise not accessible. Skis offer a bonus for glacier travel: They distribute the climber's weight over a larger area and may decrease the chance of breaking through snow bridges. Skis can also come in handy for rescue work, because they can be converted into a makeshift stretcher or sled.

Backcountry skiing is a complex activity, with special techniques and equipment. For detailed information, see Appendix D, Supplementary Resources.

SHOVEL

A broad-bladed shovel is both a tool and a safety device for the snow traveler. A shovel is a necessity for uncovering an avalanche victim. Shovels are also used for constructing snow shelters and tent platforms, and they have even been used as climbing tools to ascend particularly snowy routes. Keep a mountaineering snow shovel readily available.

A good shovel (see Figure 3-9a and b in Chapter 3, Camping and Food) has a blade large enough to move snow efficiently and a handle long enough for good leverage but short enough for use in a confined area: 2 to 3 feet (60 to 90 centimeters) long. Some shovels feature extendable and/or detachable handles. Another desirable feature is a blade that can be rotated perpendicular to the handle and locked so that the shovel can be used as a trenching tool. A D-shaped grip on the handle can make shoveling more comfortable. Some models have a hollow handle, inside which climbers can carry a snow saw or avalanche probe.

In dry, powdery snow, a plastic-bladed shovel provides a good compromise of weight to strength.

However, metal-bladed shovels are much stiffer and therefore better for chopping through hard snow or avalanche debris. The edge of a shovel blade (whether metal or plastic) can be sharpened with a file.

TECHNIQUES OF SNOW CLIMBING

The first priority of snow travel is to avoid a slip or fall, but if climbers do slip on snow, they must know how to regain control as quickly as possible. Travel on steep alpine snow slopes is dangerous unless climbers have an ice ax and crampons—and the skill to use them.

To determine how to travel on steep alpine snow safely, ask the following questions: Is the snow good for self-belay, or is it too hard for the ice-ax shaft to be placed securely? Will crampons be helpful or a hindrance? What are the climbers' levels of experience and skill? Is everyone comfortable with the particular situation? Are climbers wearing heavy overnight packs?

Relying on self-belay or self-arrest (both discussed later in this chapter) should be considered adequate only for very experienced climbers. Understanding the limits of self-belay and self-arrest, combined with assessing the runout, are crucial considerations.

ASSESSING RUNOUT

Because a falling climber's acceleration rate on a 30-degree snow slope can approach that of free-falling, it is very important to always be aware of a snow slope's runout. Are there rocks, crevasses, a moat, a bergschrund, or cliffs below (fig. 16-13)? Constantly assessing and being aware of runout is the first thing to consider when deciding what techniques and equipment to use for travel on snow slopes.

If the runout is dangerous or unknown, careful consideration should always be given to how to proceed. Is a belay with anchor and rope required? If a belay is deemed necessary and there is not time, skill, or equipment for a solid belay, turning around is advised.

USING THE ICE AX

The ice ax, an inherently simple tool, has many uses. Below the snow line, it can serve as a walking cane or be used to help climbers brake when they are going downhill. But its main role is in snow and ice travel, wherein it is a balance aid, a tool to prevent a fall, and a tool to stop a fall. The ice ax is also used in a variety of ways to make a snow anchor.

Fig. 16-13. Assessing runout: rocks below a snow slope make a dangerous runout.

How to Carry an Ice Ax

Always carry an ice ax carefully. Be aware of what its sharp points and edges can do to you and others in the climbing party.

When the ax is not needed, carry it on your pack. Slip it down through the pack ice-ax loop, flip the shaft up, and strap it to the pack (fig. 16-14a). Keep guards on the pick, adze, and spike. To carry the ax in one hand, grasp the shaft with the spike forward and the pick down to avoid jabbing the person behind you (fig. 16-14b).

When travel on snow alternates briefly with areas of rocks or steep brush, where both hands need to be free, slide the ax diagonally between your back and the pack (fig. 16-14c). Place the spike down and the pick between the two shoulder straps, clear of your neck and

16

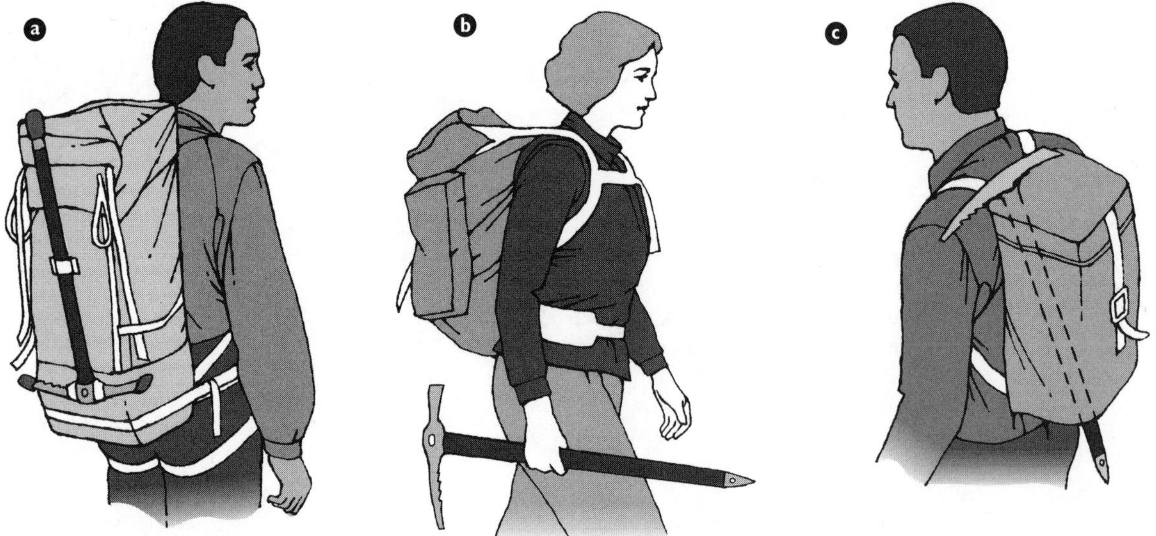

Fig. 16-14. Carrying an ice ax: a, attached to a pack by an ice-ax loop and strap, with guards on the pick, adze, and spike; b, in the hand while walking, with spike forward and pick down; c, temporarily between back and pack.

pointing in the same general direction as the angle of the shaft. In this position, the ax can be stowed and retrieved quickly.

How to Grasp an Ice Ax

There are two ways to grasp an ice ax. Conditions determine which grasp is best at any moment.

Self-arrest grasp. Place your thumb under the adze and your palm and fingers over the pick, near the top of the shaft (fig. 16-15a). While climbing, point the adze forward. The self-arrest grasp puts climbers in position to go directly into arrest in case of a fall (see "Self-Arrest," below).

Self-belay grasp. Rest your palm on top of the adze and wrap your thumb and index finger under the pick (fig. 16-15b). While climbing, point the pick forward. The self-belay grasp provides a firmer anchor and may keep climbers from slipping in the first place (see "Self-Belay,"below).

When using the self-belay grasp, the climber must be able to instantly change to a self-arrest grasp in case of a slip. Grab the shaft of the ax, momentarily loosen your grip on the head, and rotate the head 180 degrees into the self-arrest grasp. This takes practice. If a climber lacks the skill to shift from the self-belay grasp to the self-arrest grasp, it is safer to do self-belays while holding the ax head in the self-arrest grasp.

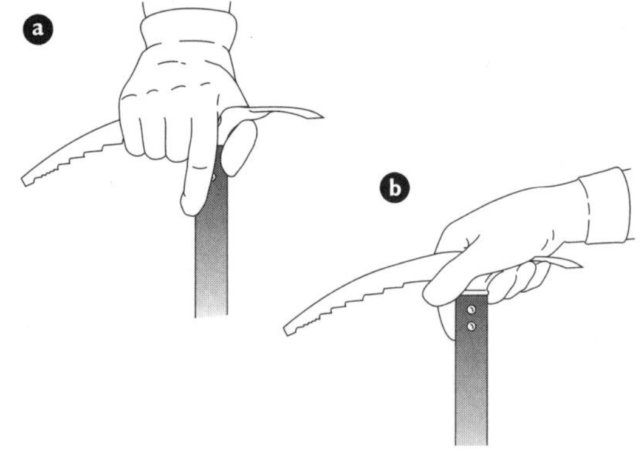

Fig. 16-15. Grasping an ice ax: a, self-arrest grip; b, self-belay grip.

Some climbers simply choose to use the self-arrest grasp at all times. Others prefer the comfort of the self-belay but shift to the self-arrest grasp whenever they feel there is a significant danger of slipping.

USING CRAMPONS

Crampons are generally considered essential when conditions are icy, but they can also be useful on snow, even soft snow. For ice, a bit of crampon technique is usually necessary (see "Climbing with Crampons" in Chapter 18, Alpine Ice Climbing). For snow, simply use the same techniques as would be used without crampons (step-kicking, combined with balance and use of an ice ax, all described in this chapter), but the crampon points improve traction and security.

Learn how and when to use crampons. Ask these questions: Are crampons helpful? Do they make walking on snow easier and more efficient? Does the slope have a dangerous or unknown runout? (If yes, then crampons should always be considered.) What footwear is being worn? (Rigid-sole boots kick steps much better than softer, more flexible boots; crampons should be considered more often with softer, more flexible footwear because many crampon designs will add stiffness to the boots.)

One reason for not wearing crampons is the increased potential for tripping in them or even being injured by their sharp points. Learning to walk in crampons without tripping takes practice, and injury from sharp points can be reduced with proper crampon maintenance (see "Crampon Safety and Maintenance," above).

Another reason not to use crampons is if snow is balling up underfoot. Snow can stick to the underside of the metal crampon frame, packing into a ball that completely voids the effectiveness of the crampon points. Fresh snow combined with warm temperatures can create conditions that even antiballing plates cannot overcome. Such conditions can be particularly challenging. Sometimes the snow may be hard under the softer fresh snow, requiring crampon use even when the snow sticks to them. These conditions with or without crampons require great care, and they will certainly slow progress. If the decision is made to wear crampons, then knocking the stuck snow free with an ice ax may be necessary, sometimes with every step.

ASCENDING SNOW

Climbing up snow slopes takes a set of special skills. Different techniques come into play, depending on the slope's hardness or steepness. The direction of ascent can be either direct or diagonal.

Climbing in Balance

Although climbers need to be proficient at ice-ax self-arrest, it is important to make every effort not to have to use it. Climb in balance to avoid falling. Climbing in balance means moving from one position of balance to another, avoiding any prolonged stance in an out-of-balance position.

On a diagonal uphill route, a climber is in a position of balance when the inside (uphill side) foot is in front of and above the outside (downhill side) foot, because body weight is evenly distributed between both feet (see Figure 16-16a). When the outside foot is forward, the climber is out of balance because the trailing inside leg, which is not fully

16

Fig. 16-16. Ascending a snow slope, diagonally, in balance: a, placing the ice ax from a position of balance; b, advancing one step into an out-of-balance position; c, advancing another step back into a position of balance.

extended and therefore cannot make use of the skeletal structure to minimize muscular effort, is nonetheless bearing most of the body's weight (see Figure 16-16b).

The diagonal ascent is a two-step sequence: from a position of balance through an out-of-balance position and back to a position of balance. From the position of balance, place the ax above and ahead of you into the snow in the self-belay position (fig. 16-16a). Move up one step, bringing your outside (downhill) foot in front of your inside (uphill) foot, which puts you out of balance (fig. 16-16b). Then move up another step, putting your inside foot in front of your outside foot, which puts you back in a position of balance (fig. 16-16c). Then reposition the ice ax. Keep your weight over your feet and avoid leaning into the slope. Keep the ax on your uphill side.

If a climber is heading straight up the fall line, there is no longer an uphill or downhill reference for arms and legs. Just carry the ax in whichever hand feels comfortable, and climb in a steady, controlled manner. Regardless of the direction of travel, place the ax firmly before each move to provide self-belay protection.

The Rest Step

Climbing a long, featureless snow slope can give a frustrating sensation of getting nowhere. Few landmarks help measure progress. Novice climbers try a dash-and-gasp pace in an attempt to rush the objective. But the only way to the top of the slope is to find a pace that can be maintained—and then maintain it. The solution is the rest step, a technique that conserves energy as it moves the climber methodically forward. Use the rest step whenever legs or lungs need a bit of recuperation between steps. At lower elevations, it is usually leg muscles that require a break; at higher elevations, lungs need the pause. See Chapter 6, Wilderness Travel, for a description of the rest step.

Step-kicking

Step-kicking creates a path of upward steps with the best possible footing and the least expenditure of energy. Climbers move in single file up the steps, improving them as they go. The head of the line has the hardest job: kicking fresh steps and looking for the safest route up the slope.

The most efficient kick to use for creating snow steps is to swing your leg and allow its own weight and momentum to provide the impact, with little muscular effort. This works well in soft snow. Harder snow requires more effort, and the steps may be smaller and less secure.

An average climber needs steps deep enough to place the ball of the foot when going straight up and at least half of the boot on a diagonal ascent. Steps that are kicked level or tilted slightly into the slope are more secure. The less space there is on a step, the more important it is that the step be angled into the slope.

When kicking steps, keep other climbers in the party in mind. They can follow up your staircase if the steps are spaced evenly and somewhat close together. Make allowance for climbers with shorter legs.

Followers improve the steps as they climb. The follower must kick into the step, because simply walking onto the existing platform is not secure. In compact snow, drive your toe in and deepen the step. In soft snow, bring your boot down onto the step, compacting the snow and making the step stronger.

Switch leads occasionally to share the heavy work. The leader can step aside and fall in at the end of the line. (The related skills of step-cutting and cramponing are discussed in Chapter 18, Alpine Ice Climbing.)

Direct Ascent

Speed is a consideration on a long snow climb, and a direct ascent is a good choice if climbers face bad weather, avalanche or rockfall danger, poor bivouac conditions, or a difficult descent. Ice-ax technique varies according to snow conditions and steepness.

Cane position. On a slope of a low or moderate angle, climb with the ax in the cane position: holding it in one hand by the head (by whatever grasp is preferable) and using it for balance (fig. 16-17). Continue in the cane position as the snow gets steeper, as long as it feels secure. Setting the ax firmly before each move provides a self-belay.

Stake position. As the snow gets steeper, climbers may choose to switch to the two-handed stake position (fig. 16-18). Before moving upward, use both hands to plant the ax as far as it will go into the snow. Then continue to grasp it with both hands on the head, or with one hand on the head and one on the shaft. This position is useful on steeper soft snow.

Horizontal position. The horizontal position is effective on steep, hard snow covered with a soft layer. Hold the ax with both hands, one in the self-arrest grasp on the head and the other near the spike end of the shaft. Jab the ax horizontally into the snow above you, the pick down and the shaft at a right angle to your

Fig. 16-17. Direct ascent with ice ax in cane position.

Fig. 16-18. Direct ascent with ice ax in stake position.

body (fig. 16-19). This jabs the pick into the harder base while the shaft gets some purchase in the softer surface snow.

Diagonal Ascent

When time and weather conditions permit, climbers may prefer a longer diagonal ascent, switchbacking up moderately angled slopes. In marginal conditions, a diagonal route may be more difficult because of the work of kicking numerous edged, traversing steps in hard snow. Again, ice-ax technique varies according to snow conditions and steepness.

Cane position. The ax works fine in this position on moderate slopes (see Figure 16-17). As the slope gets steeper, the cane position becomes awkward.

Cross-body position. Hold the ax perpendicular to the angle of the slope, one hand grasping the head and the other holding the spike end of the shaft, and jab the spike into the snow (fig. 16-20). The ax crosses diagonally in front of you, the pick pointing away from your body. The shaft should bear your weight, while the hand on the head of the ax stabilizes the ax.

Changing directions. Diagonal ascents often mean

Fig. 16-19. Direct ascent with ice ax in horizontal position.

Fig. 16-20. Diagonal ascent with ice ax in cross-body position.

making changes in direction, or switchbacking. The sequence of steps for a safe change in direction on a diagonal route, whether the ax is in the cane position or the cross-body position, is this:

1. Start from a position of balance, with your inside (uphill) foot in front of and above your outside (downhill) foot. Jab the ax shaft straight down into the snow at a spot as directly above your location as possible.
2. Move your outside foot forward, bringing you into the out-of-balance position (fig. 16-21a). Grasp the head of the ax with both hands. Continue holding onto the head with both hands while moving into a stance facing uphill, turning your inside foot toward the new direction of travel and ending with your feet in a splayed position (fig. 16-21b).
3. Kick steps into the slope if your splayed feet feel unstable.
4. Turn your body toward the new direction of travel, returning to a position of balance by placing your new uphill foot in front of and above your new outside (downhill) foot (fig. 16-21c).

In the cane position, your new uphill hand now grasps the ax head (as in Figure 16-21c). In the cross-body position, the hands holding the head and the shaft are now reversed.

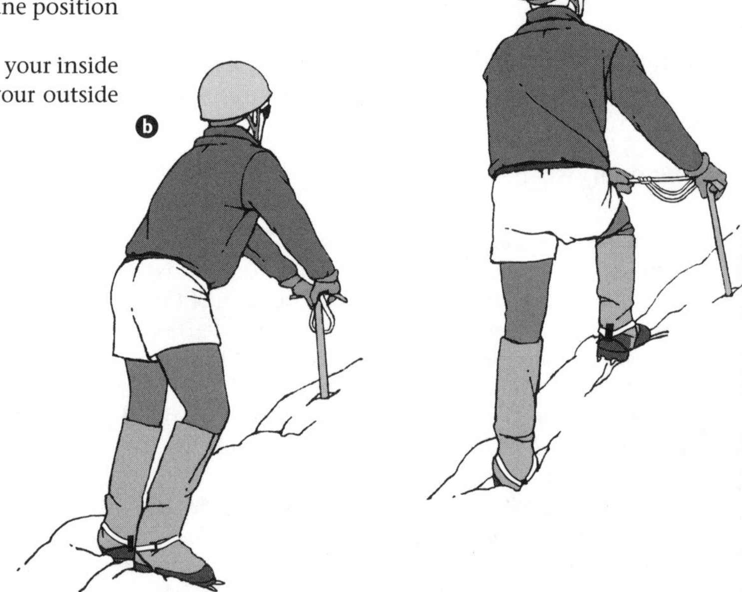

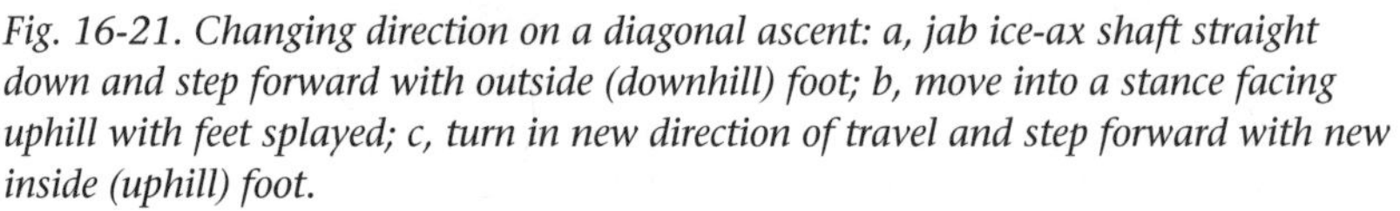

Fig. 16-21. Changing direction on a diagonal ascent: a, jab ice-ax shaft straight down and step forward with outside (downhill) foot; b, move into a stance facing uphill with feet splayed; c, turn in new direction of travel and step forward with new inside (uphill) foot.

Traversing

Long horizontal traverses that neither gain nor lose elevation are best avoided. This "sidehill gouging" is fine on soft snow at low and moderate angles, although it is not as comfortable or as efficient as a diagonal route. If it is necessary to traverse over hard or steep snow, face directly into the slope and kick straight into it for the most secure steps.

DESCENDING SNOW

One mark of a skillful snow climber is the ability to go downhill efficiently and confidently. Descending snow is frequently more challenging than ascending the same slope. Due to gravity and momentum, it is easier to slip while descending than while ascending. Many otherwise competent and aggressive climbers blanch at the prospect of going forward down a steep, exposed snow gully. To move down, place the ax down low, which provides a less-comfortable stance and handhold than on the way up. Master the following descent techniques to help conquer any uneasiness about downhill travel.

Facing Out (Plunge-stepping)

When descending, determine technique mainly by the same factors as when ascending: the hardness and angle of the snow. In soft snow on a moderate slope, simply face outward and walk down. With harder snow or a steeper angle, use the plunge step.

The plunge step is a confident, aggressive move. Face outward, step assertively away from the slope, and land solidly on your heel with your straightened leg vertical, transferring weight solidly to the new position (fig. 16-22a). Avoid leaning back into the slope, which can result in less-secure steps or perhaps an unplanned glissade. Keep knees slightly bent, not locked, and lean forward to maintain balance. How much the knees are bent depends on the angle of the slope (the steeper the slope, the greater the bend) and the firmness of the surface (the harder the snow, the greater the bend). Plunge-stepping can be secure with steps that hold only the heel of the boot, but most climbers do not trust steps shallower than that.

When plunge-stepping, maintain a steady rhythm, almost like marching. This helps maintain balance. Once a comfortable rhythm is found, do not stop. Plunge-stepping in a stop-and-start fashion can cause climbers to lose their balance.

When plunge-stepping, hold the ice ax in one hand in either the self-arrest or self-belay grasp, with the spike close to the surface of the snow, well forward and

16

Fig. 16-22. Facing out (plunge-stepping): a, on moderate slope; b, with self-belay on steeper slope.

ready to plant in the snow (see Figure 16-22a). Spread out your other arm and move it for balance. Some climbers hold the ax in both hands in the full self-arrest position—one hand on the head, the other near the end of the shaft—but this allows less arm movement for maintaining balance.

An aggressive stride creates a deep step. Take care in deep, soft snow not to plunge so deeply that your legs get stuck and you fall forward, injuring yourself. If the snow is too hard or steep for plunge-stepping, descend in a crouched position, planting the ax as low as possible in a self-belay with each step (fig. 16-22b).

Facing In (Backing Down)

While generally slower than facing out, backing down is usually more comfortable and secure. Try to plunge the shaft of the ice ax as low on the slope as is comfortable before stepping down (fig. 16-23). If the snow is too firm for a solid shaft placement, the pick of the ax (placed low) can be used for support while the climber steps down. Remember that leaning into the slope does not put your body in a good position of balance. Try to keep your weight centered over your feet as much as possible.

Fig. 16-23. Facing in (backing down): place ax low on the slope and don't lean in toward the slope.

Glissading

Glissading is the fastest, easiest, and most exhilarating way down many snow slopes if climbers are on foot. On slopes where speed can be controlled, it is an efficient alternative to walking or plunge-stepping.

Glissading can be hazardous. Do not glissade in crevassed terrain. Glissade only when a safe runout is close enough that if a slide goes out of control, the climber will not be injured before reaching it. Unless the climbing party can see the entire descent route, the first person down must use extreme caution and stop frequently to look ahead. The biggest risk is losing control at such a high speed that self-arrest is not possible. This is most likely to happen on the best glissading slope: one with firm snow.

Before glissading, remove crampons and stow them and other hardware in the pack. Crampon points can catch in the snow and send climbers tumbling. Wear rain pants to keep dry. Wear gloves to protect hands from the abrasive snow.

Always maintain control of the ice ax. If an ice-ax leash is worn, climbers risk injury from a flailing ax if it is knocked loose from their grip. If a leash is not used, climbers risk losing their ax.

Effective glissading requires a smooth blend of several techniques. Climbers who lack finesse in the standing glissade (see below) often use a combination: breaking into a plunge step to control speed, stepping off in a new direction rather than making a ski-style turn, and skating to maintain momentum as the slope angle lessens.

Sometimes in soft snow, a glissader accidentally sets off a mass of surface snow, which slides down the slope with the glissader aboard. These are small avalanches, known as avalanche cushions. The trick is to decide whether the avalanche cushion is safe to ride or is about to become a serious avalanche. If the moving snow is more than a few inches deep, self-arrest will not work because the ice-ax pick cannot penetrate to the stable layer below. Sometimes climbers can drive the spike deep enough to slow the glissade, although probably not deep enough to stop themselves. Unless a climber is sure the cushion is safe and the glissade speed is under control, get off. Roll sideways out of the path of the moving snow and then self-arrest.

Of the three methods of glissading—the sitting glissade, the standing glissade, and the crouching glissade—the one to use depends on snow and slope conditions, the appearance of the runout, and the climber's mastery of the techniques.

Sitting glissade. This works on soft snow on which climbers would bog down if they tried a standing glissade. Sit erect in the snow, bend the knees, and plant boot soles flat along the snow surface (fig. 16-24a). Hold the ice ax in self-arrest position while glissading downhill. To maintain control, run the spike of the ax like a rudder along the snow on one side of you. Keep both hands on the ax. Put pressure on the spike to reduce speed and to thwart any tendency to pivot the ice-ax head downward.

The standard posture, with knees bent and feet flat, also reduces speed. This posture is good when the snow is crusted or firmly consolidated, pitted with icy ruts or small suncups (hollows melted by the sun), or dotted with rocks or shrubs. It provides more stability and control than having legs straight out in front and helps minimize wear and tear on a climber's bottom.

To stop, use the spike to slow down, then dig in your heels—but not at high speed, or a somersault may be the result. For an emergency stop, roll over, and self-arrest.

Turns are almost impossible in a sitting glissade. The best way to get around an obstruction is to stop, walk sideways to a point that is not directly above the obstacle, and glissade again.

Standing glissade. The most maneuverable technique is the standing glissade, and it saves clothes from getting wet and abraded. This glissade is similar to downhill skiing. Crouch slightly over your feet, bend the knees, and spread out your arms (fig. 16-24b). Feet, which provide stability, can be spread out or placed together, with one foot slightly forward to improve stability and prevent nosedives. Bring the feet closer together and lean forward over them to increase speed.

To slow down and stop, stand up and dig in your heels, turn feet sideways and dig their edges into the slope, or crouch and drag the ice-ax spike as in the crouching glissade (see below).

It is also possible to perform a turn similar to skiing by rotating your shoulders, upper body, and knees in the direction of the turn and rolling your knees and ankles in the same direction to rock your feet onto boot edges.

The standing glissade is most effective on a firm base with a softer layer on top. The softer the snow, the steeper the slope needs to be to maintain speed. It is possible to do a standing glissade down slopes of harder snow, but these are usually slopes of lower angles with a safe runout. It is possible to skate slopes of very low angles if the snow is firm.

Changes in the snow texture are tricky. If a climber hits softer, slower snow, the head and torso will suddenly outpace the legs, so move one boot forward for stability. If a climber hits harder, faster snow or ice below the surface, lean well forward to prevent a slip. Keep the glissade speed under control by regular braking and traversing.

Fig. 16-24. Glissades: a, sitting; b, standing; c, crouching.

Crouching glissade. The crouching glissade is slower than a standing glissade and easier to learn. From the standing glissade position, simply lean back, hold the ice ax in the self-arrest position to one side of your body,

16

and drag the spike in the snow (fig. 16-24c). Because it uses three points of contact, it is also more stable. However, it is more difficult to turn and to control the glissade speed.

STOPPING A FALL: SELF-BELAY AND SELF-ARREST

Wear gloves on snow slopes; hard snow is quite abrasive, and sliding unprotected over its surface can cause hands to lose their grip on the ice ax.

Self-Belay

Self-belay can keep a simple slip or misstep on a snow slope from turning into a serious fall. To self-belay, be sure both feet are secure, then jam the spike and shaft of the ice ax straight down into the snow (fig. 16-25a). Continue to grip the head of the ax with your uphill hand while moving forward. (Use either the self-belay grasp or the self-arrest grasp to perform self-belay.) Take a step or two, pull out the ax, and replant it. For self-belay to work, the shaft must be placed deep enough in firm snow to hold your full weight.

If you slip, keep one hand on the head of the ax and grab hold of the shaft at the surface of the snow with your other hand (fig. 16-25b). The key to successful self-belay is to grab the shaft right next to the surface, so that you pull against the buried shaft. Your hand on the head of the ax minimizes the risk of levering the ax out (fig. 16-25c).

If self-belay fails and you begin an uncontrolled slide down the slope, you must immediately self-arrest.

Self-Arrest

Preventing a fall is a primary goal while climbing, but if climbers do fall, their life may depend on self-arrest skills. Self-arrest technique holds a climber's fall or the fall of a rope mate. During glacier travel, self-arrest stops the rest of the team from sliding into a crevasse (discussed in Chapter 17, Glacier Travel and Crevasse Rescue). For climbers who practice and master self-arrest, steep alpine snow slopes become highways to the summit.

The goal of self-arrest is to stop safely in a secure and stable position. The last panel of Figures 16-26, 16-28, and 16-29 illustrate the completion of a successful self-arrest: lying face down in the snow with the ice ax beneath you. Here is how to do it:

- **Hold the ax in a solid grip.** Place one hand in the self-arrest grasp, with your thumb under the adze and fingers over the pick (see Figure 16-15a), and

Fig. 16-25. The self-belay: a, climbing; b, falling; c, recovering.

your other hand on the shaft just above the spike.

- **Press the pick into the snow just above your shoulder.** Place the adze near the angle formed by your neck and shoulder. This is crucial. Sufficient force cannot be exerted on the pick if the adze is not in the proper position.
- **Place the shaft across your chest diagonally.** Hold the spike end close to the hip that is opposite the ax head. Grip the shaft near the spike end to prevent that hand from acting as a pivot point around which the spike can swing to jab your thigh. (A short ax is held the same way, although the spike will not reach the opposite hip.)
- **Press your chest and shoulder down on the ice-ax shaft.** Successful self-arrest relies on your body weight falling and pressing on the ax,

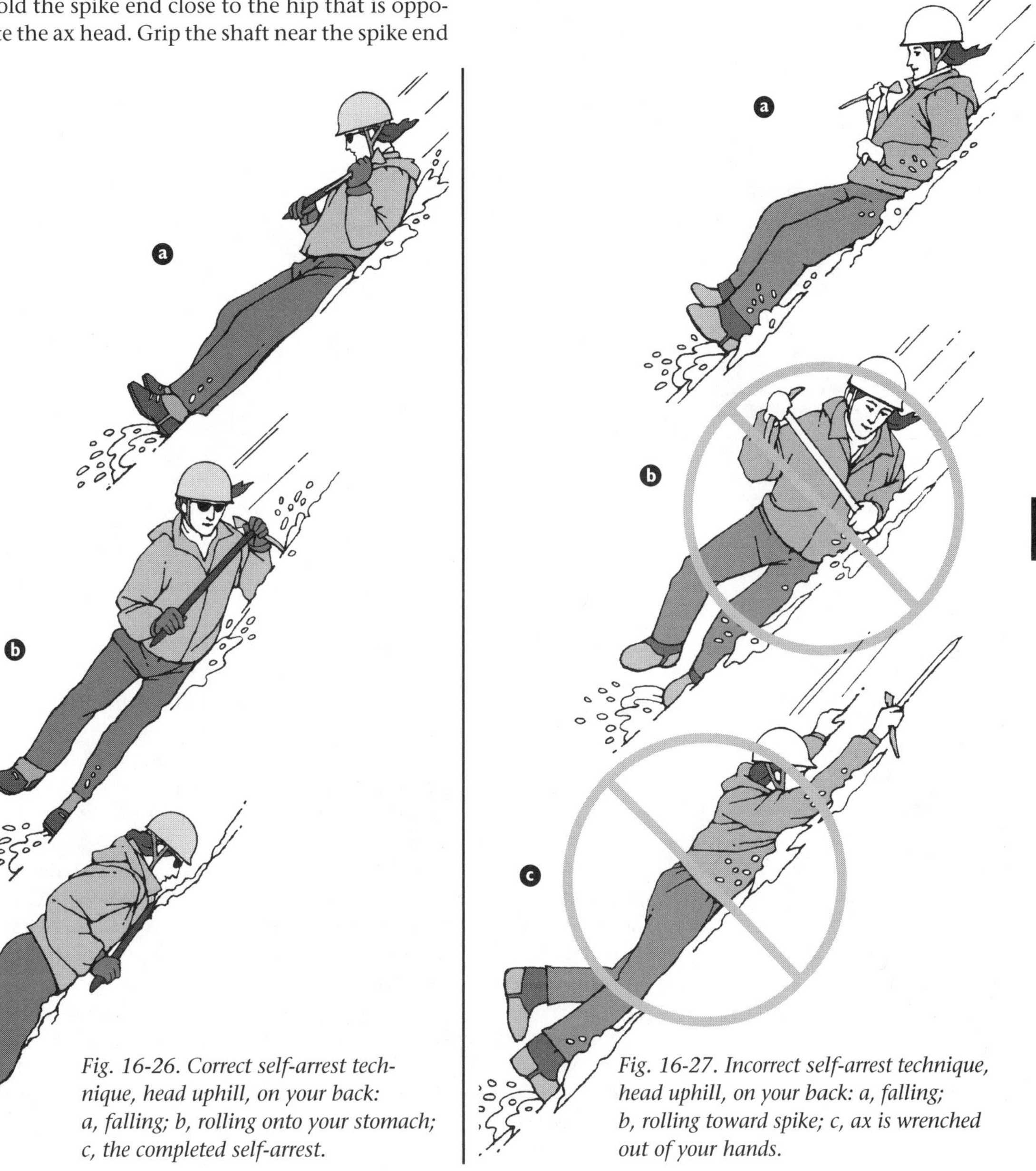

Fig. 16-26. Correct self-arrest technique, head uphill, on your back: a, falling; b, rolling onto your stomach; c, the completed self-arrest.

Fig. 16-27. Incorrect self-arrest technique, head uphill, on your back: a, falling; b, rolling toward spike; c, ax is wrenched out of your hands.

16

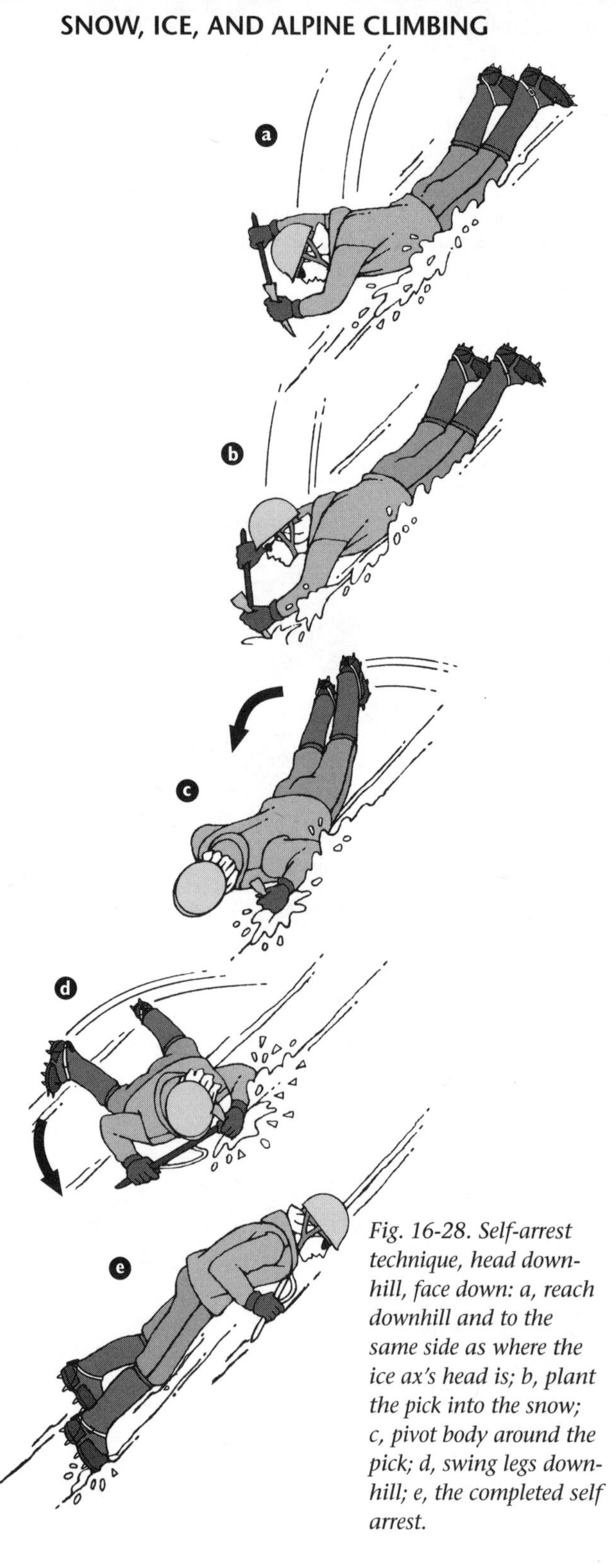

Fig. 16-28. Self-arrest technique, head downhill, face down: a, reach downhill and to the same side as where the ice ax's head is; b, plant the pick into the snow; c, pivot body around the pick; d, swing legs downhill; e, the completed self arrest.

rather than just arm strength driving the ax into the snow.

- **Keep your head face down.** Place the brim of your helmet in contact with the slope. This position prevents shoulders and chest from lifting up and keeps weight over the adze.
- **Place your face in the snow.** Your nose should be touching the snow.
- **Arch your spine slightly away from the snow.** This places the bulk of your weight on the ax head and on your toes or knees, which are the points that dig into the snow to force a stop. Pull up on the spike end of the shaft, which starts the arch and rolls your weight toward your shoulder by the ax head.
- **Bend your knees slightly.** Place them against the surface to slow the fall in soft snow. On harder surfaces, where knees have little stopping power, they help stabilize your body position.
- **Keep your legs stiff and spread apart, toes digging in.** If wearing crampons, dig in with knees and keep toes off the snow.

Self-arrest technique depends on the position the climber is in after a fall. A fallen climber will be sliding in one of four positions: head uphill or head downhill and, in either case, face down or on the back.

If a climber is falling, the immediate goal is to get the body into the only effective self-arrest position: head uphill, feet downhill, and face pressed into the snow. The first move toward that goal is to grasp the ax with both hands, one hand on the ax head in the self-arrest grasp and the other hand at the base of the shaft. The next moves depend on what position the climber is in while falling.

Head uphill, face down. This is already the self-arrest position. All the climber has to do is get the pick pressed into the snow and body over the ax shaft, ending in a secure self-arrest.

Head uphill, on your back. Falling with your head uphill, on your back (fig. 16-26a and fig. 16-27a), is not much more difficult to self-arrest than the face-down position (see Figure 16-28). Roll toward the head of the ax and aggressively plant the pick into the snow at your side while rolling over onto your stomach (fig. 16-26b). Roll in the direction of the ax head (fig. 16-26c). Beware of rolling toward the spike, which can jam the spike in the snow before the pick (fig. 16-27b) and wrench the ax from your hands (fig. 16-27c).

Head downhill, face down. Self-arrest from a headfirst fall is more difficult because you must first swing your feet downhill. In this face-down predicament, reach downhill and off to the ax-head side (fig. 16-28a) and get the pick into the snow (fig. 16-28b) to serve as a pivot to swing your body around (fig. 16-28c). Work to swing your legs around (fig. 16-28d) so they are pointing downhill (fig. 16-28e). Never jab the spike into the snow and pivot on that end of the ax. That will bring the pick and adze of the ax across your slide path and on a collision course with your chest and face.

Head downhill, on your back. Again, self-arrest from a headfirst fall is more difficult because you must first swing your feet downhill. In this face-up predicament, hold the ax across your torso and aggressively jab the pick into the snow (fig. 16-29a), then twist and roll toward it (fig. 16-29b). Once again, the pick placed to the side serves as a pivot point. Planting the pick will not bring you around to the final self-arrest position. Work at rolling your chest toward the ax head (fig. 16-29c) while you work your legs to swing around and point downhill (fig. 16-29d). A sitting-up motion helps the roll.

Practice self-arrest in all positions on increasingly steeper slopes and hard snow above a safe runout. Practice with a full pack. The key to success is to get quickly into the arrest position and dig in. During practice, leave the ice-ax leash off your wrist so there is less chance of the ax striking you if you lose control of it. Cover or pad the adze and spike to minimize chances of injury. Whereas crampons are often worn on snow slopes where self-arrest may be necessary, crampons should never be worn when practicing self-arrest.

The effectiveness of the self-arrest depends on the climber's reaction time, the steepness and length of the slope, and snow conditions.

On steep or slippery slopes. When the slope is too steep or slippery, even the best technique will not stop a slide. Acceleration on hard snow, on even a modest snow slope, can be so rapid that the first instant of the fall is the whole story: The climber rockets into the air and crashes back to the unyielding surface with stunning impact, losing uphill-downhill orientation.

On hard or loose snow. Arrest on hard snow is difficult, if not impossible, but always give it a try, even if on belay. In loose snow, the pick may not be able to reach compact snow, making the usual self-arrest useless. The best brakes in this case are feet and knees and elbows, widely spaced and deeply pressed into the snow. If the initial efforts at self-arrest are unsuccessful, do not give

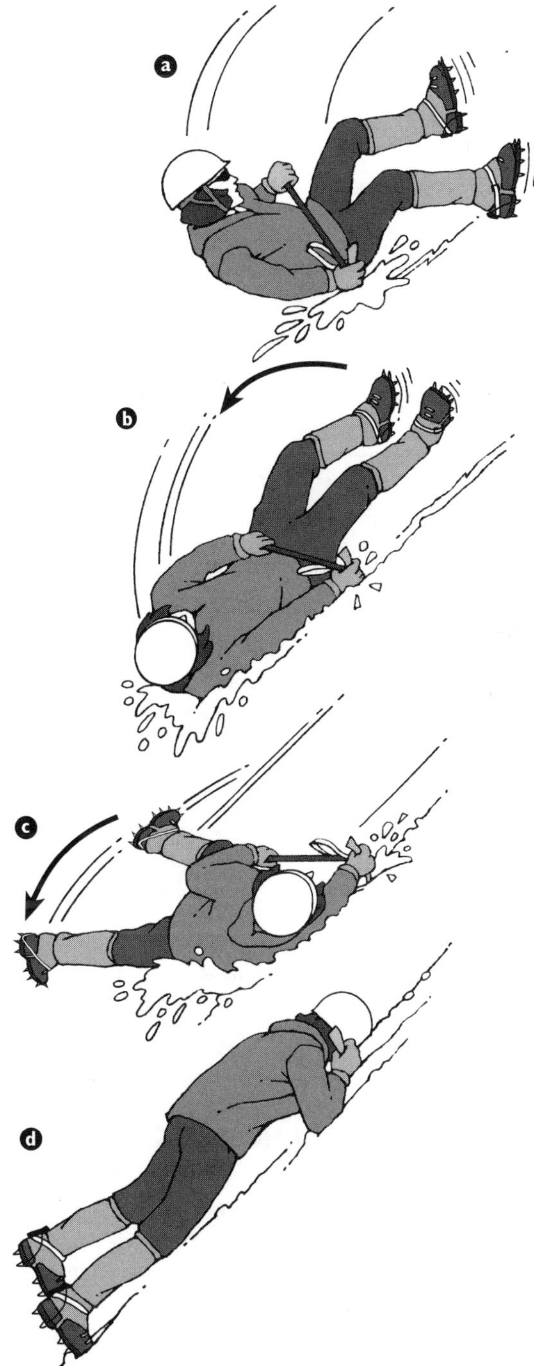

Fig. 16-29. Self-arrest technique, head downhill, on your back: a, plant the pick; b, twist and roll toward pick; c, swing legs downhill and roll chest toward pick; d, the completed self-arrest.

16

up. Keep fighting. Even if you do not stop, the attempt itself may slow the fall and help prevent rolling, tumbling, and bouncing. It may also help keep you sliding feet first, the best position if you end up hitting rocks or trees. If roped to other climbers, anything a falling climber can do to slow a fall increases the chance that their self-arrests or belays will hold.

Without an ax. If you lose your ice ax in a fall, use hands, elbows, knees, and boots to dig into the snow slope, using positioning similar to what would be used if you still had the ax. Try to clasp hands together against the slope so that snow is accumulated in them and creates more friction.

Times when self-arrest should not be trusted include when a slope seems too fast or the runout too dangerous, or when members of the climbing party doubt their strength or skill. If this is the case, back off, look for another route, or rope up and put in protection. (See "Roped Snow Climbing Techniques," below.)

Crampons and Self-Arrest

It has traditionally been taught that wearing crampons when trying to self-arrest may not be a good idea, because they can catch and flip a climber over backward or even break an ankle. This is especially true if the snow is hard or icy. Unfortunately, if climbers are on a slope where self-arrest may be necessary, there is a good chance they will want to be wearing crampons. This is also especially true if the snow is hard or icy.

The important thing is to stop yourself. Crampons may actually help in executing a self-arrest in many snow conditions by providing more traction than boots alone. If on an icy slope with a dangerous runout, a belay of some type is generally recommended instead of relying on self-arrest.

ROPED SNOW CLIMBING TECHNIQUES

On a glacier, teams rope up for protection from hidden crevasses. On a nonglaciated snow slope, the decision is not so clear-cut, and climbers have to weigh several options:

The party can climb unroped, relying on each individual to stop a personal fall. They may decide to travel roped together but unbelayed, which offers some security for a weaker climber and gets the rope set up in case no convenient rope-up place exists later. Or the party may decide to travel roped together and to use belays, because route conditions or the climbers' abilities dictate this level of protection.

The risks of roping up are not trivial. One climber can fall and pull the entire rope team off the mountain. Risk of avalanche and rockfall exposure is also higher and the party will move more slowly.

OPTIONS FOR ROPED TEAM PROTECTION

If the climbing party decides it is safer overall to rope up, several different ways allow a party to match the type of rope protection to climbing conditions and climbers' strengths.

Team Arrest (Roped but Unbelayed)

Team arrest depends on individual climbers to stop their own falls and to provide backup in case someone else falls. Relying on team arrest as the ultimate team security makes sense only in certain situations, such as on a low- or moderate-angle glacier or snow slope. The proficient members of the rope team can save a less-skilled climber from a dangerous slide.

On steeper, harder slopes, the party has to decide which option is safest: continuing to rely on team arrest, using anchors for protection, or unroping and letting each climber go it alone.

To increase the odds that team arrest will work on a snow slope, use the following procedures:

- **Carry a few feet of slack rope coiled in your hand if any climbers are below you.** If a climber falls, drop the loose rope, which allows an extra instant before the rope is loaded; use this moment to get the ice ax into self-arrest position and to brace before the falling climber's weight impacts the rope. However, if too much slack is carried, the distance that your rope mates will slide before you stop them is increased, heightening the danger to your teammates and you.
- **Put the weakest climber on the downhill end of the rope.** As a rule, the least-skilled climber should be last on the rope while ascending and first on the rope while descending. This puts the climber most likely to fall in a position where a fall will be less serious: below the other climbers, where the impact will be quickly felt along the rope.
- **Climb on a shortened rope.** This technique is best for a two-person rope team. A climbing pair that uses only a portion of the rope reduces the sliding distance and the tug from the fall if

one partner falls. To shorten the rope, wind as many coils as necessary until the desired length remains. Then use a loop of the climbing rope to tie an overhand knot through the coils, and clip the loop in to your harness with a locking carabiner. Carry the coils over one shoulder and under the opposite arm (fig. 16-30). If more than two climbers are on the rope, the middle climber or climbers should take coils in the direction of the leader. See "Special Rescue Situations" in Chapter 17, Glacier Travel and Crevasse Rescue, for a description and illustration (Figure 17-24) of a similar technique, called the adapted Kiwi coil.

- **Climb in separate parallel tracks.** This is another option that is best for a two-person rope team. The climbers are abreast of each other, separated by the rope. A falling climber will pendulum down, putting force on the rope to the side of and below the partner. The tug on the rope will be less than if the climber fell from high above. Also, the friction of the rope as it pendulums across the snow will absorb some of the force. On ascents where kicking two sets of steps would be a waste of time and energy, this style may be impractical, but on ascents of harder snow and on descents, it can be good.
- **Handle the rope properly.** Keep the rope on the downhill side of the team so that there is less chance of stepping on it. Hold the rope in your downhill hand, in a short loop. You can then take in or let out the rope, adjusting to the pace of the person ahead of or the person behind you, rather than getting into a tug-of-war.
- **Observe your rope mates' pace and position and adjust and prepare accordingly.** When the rope goes taut, it may be hung up on the snow, or your rope mates may be in a delicate situation in which any additional tug on the rope could yank them off their feet.
- **Yell "Falling!" whenever any climber falls.** All rope partners can self-arrest and avoid getting pulled off their feet.

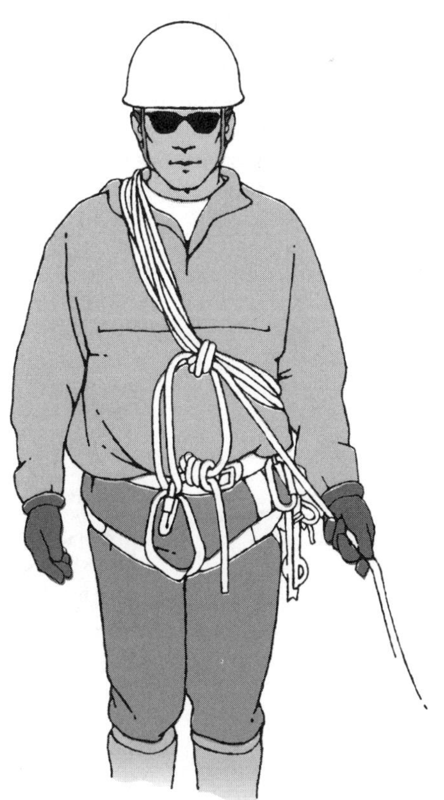

Fig. 16-30. Climbing on a shortened rope (prusiks omitted for clarity).

Running Belays

Roped climbers can move together on snow with the help of running belays. This technique saves time over regular belayed climbing but still allows for protection. Running belays, which are also useful in rock climbing, ice climbing, and alpine climbing, are discussed in Chapters 14, Leading on Rock, and 18, Alpine Ice Climbing.

The running belay offers an intermediate level of protection, somewhere between team arrest and fixed belays. The running belay helps when a successful team arrest is improbable but fixed belays are impractical. For example, running protection may do the job on long snow faces and couloirs.

To place running belays, the leader puts in pieces of snow protection when necessary and uses a carabiner to clip the rope in to each one. (For more information on snow anchors, see the next section.) All members of the rope team continue to climb at the same time, just as in unbelayed travel, except that now there is protection in the snow that will be likely to stop a fall (fig. 16-31). To pass each running belay point, when the middle climbers reach an anchor, they unclip the rope that is in front of them from the carabiner attached to the protection, then clip the rope that is behind them to the carabiner. The last climber on the rope removes each piece of protection.

Combination Protection Techniques

Long snow routes usually demand fast travel to reach the summit. Climbers often use a combination of roped and unroped travel, mostly unbelayed. They rely primarily on team arrest or running protection, and some sections of the climb will warrant unroped travel. Belays are typically used on steeper, harder snow or when climbers are tired or hurt. The option of turning around is always worth considering (see the "Decision Making for Roped Snow Travel" sidebar). The party can select a new route, choose another destination, or just head home.

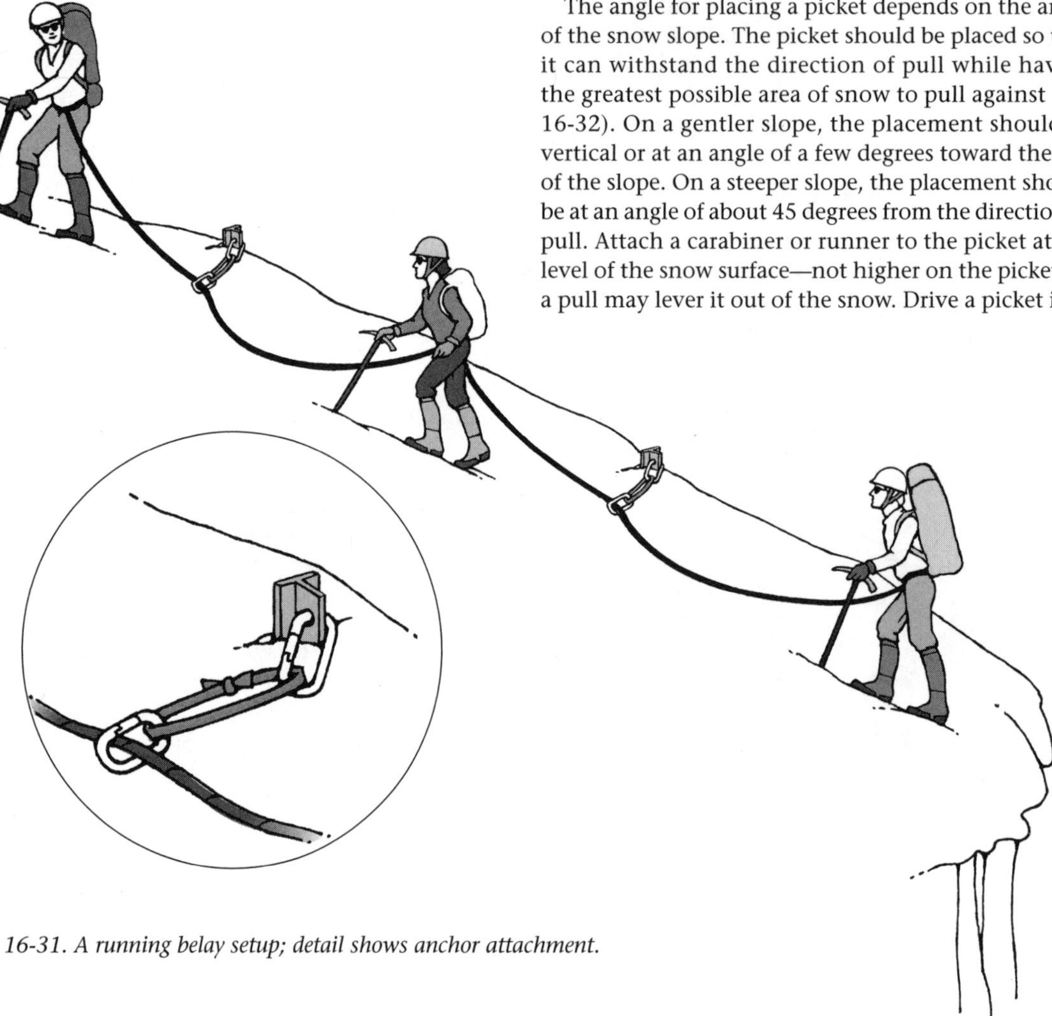

Fig. 16-31. A running belay setup; detail shows anchor attachment.

SNOW ANCHORS

Snow anchors provide protection and secure rappels and belays. The strength of a snow anchor placement depends on the strength of the snow. The greater the area of snow the anchor pulls against and the firmer the snow, the stronger the anchor. Ultimately, the strength of snow anchors depends greatly on proper placement and snow conditions. Common snow anchors are pickets, deadman anchors, flukes, and bollards.

Picket

A picket is a stake driven into the snow as an anchor. Aluminum pickets are available in lengths ranging from 18 to 36 inches (46 to 91 centimeters) and in different styles, including round or oval tubes and angled or T-section stakes.

The angle for placing a picket depends on the angle of the snow slope. The picket should be placed so that it can withstand the direction of pull while having the greatest possible area of snow to pull against (fig. 16-32). On a gentler slope, the placement should be vertical or at an angle of a few degrees toward the top of the slope. On a steeper slope, the placement should be at an angle of about 45 degrees from the direction of pull. Attach a carabiner or runner to the picket at the level of the snow surface—not higher on the picket, or a pull may lever it out of the snow. Drive a picket into

DECISION MAKING FOR ROPED SNOW TRAVEL

A team always ropes up on glaciers, but on snow or mixed terrain the climbing team has a few considerations:

1. Is each member of the party able to use self-belay or self-arrest? If the answer is yes, the party can continue unroped.
2. Can the team stop all falls by roping up and relying on team arrest? If so, rope up and continue climbing unbelayed.
3. Can the team use some form of belay (running or fixed) that will provide adequate protection? If so, begin belaying.
4. Should the party turn around, or should the team proceed unroped and assume the risks?

the snow with a rock, the side of an ice ax, or an ice hammer. An ice ax or ice tool can also serve as a makeshift picket.

A picket works best in firm, hard snow. If the snow is too soft, use the picket as a deadman (see below). Make sure the picket is not pulling out of the snow and that there are no visible cracks in the snow in the area against which the picket exerts force.

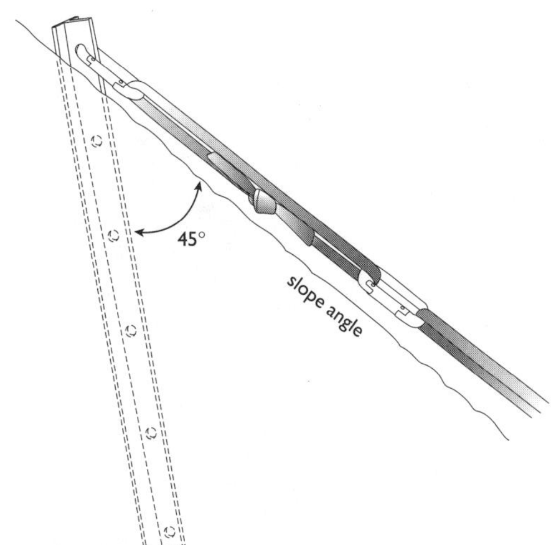

Fig. 16-32. The angle of picket placement varies with the steepness of the slope.

Inspect a picket after every use. Every member of a rope team using a running belay should check the picket as they pass it.

Deadman

A deadman anchor is any object buried in the snow as a point of attachment for the rope. Ice axes, ice tools, and pickets can be used as deadman anchors. Here are the steps to build a deadman:

1. Dig a trench as long as the item being used and perpendicular to the load.
2. Girth-hitch a runner to the item at its midpoint and place the item in the trench. To prevent the runner from sliding off the ends, use a carabiner. For a picket, clip a carabiner to the picket's midpoint and to the runner (fig. 16-33a). For an ice

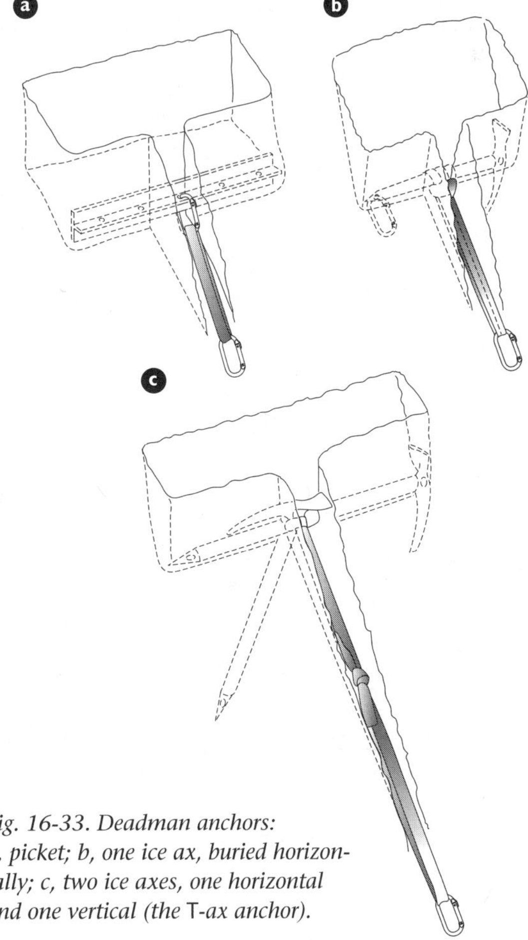

Fig. 16-33. Deadman anchors: a, picket; b, one ice ax, buried horizontally; c, two ice axes, one horizontal and one vertical (the T*-ax anchor).*

16

ax or ice tool, clip a carabiner to the hole at the spike end (fig. 16-33b).

3. Cut a slot in the snow that is as deep as the trench, to allow the runner to lie in the direction of pull. If this slot is shallower than the trench, there will be an upward pull on the anchor.
4. Cover everything with snow except the tail of the runner. Stamp down on everything to compact and strengthen the snow.
5. Clip in to the end of the runner.

If the snow is soft, increase the strength of the deadman placement by increasing the area of snow it pulls against; do this by using a larger object. Try using a pack, a pair of skis, or a long, large stuff sack tightly filled with snow. Do not use ski or trekking poles—they are not strong enough.

In a variation of the buried-ax deadman anchor, place a second ax vertically behind the horizontal ax (fig. 16-33c). In this variation, called the T-ax anchor, girth-hitch a runner to the vertical ax and run the shaft of the horizontal ax through the runner.

As with all snow anchors, inspect a deadman after every use. Look for cracks and bulges in the snow above the buried item.

Snow Fluke

The snow fluke is a specially shaped aluminum plate with a metal cable attached (fig. 16-34a). A buried fluke should be angled back about 40 degrees from the direction of pull (fig. 16-34b). Dig a slot in the snow to permit the cable to be pulled in as direct a line as possible.

In theory, the snow fluke serves as a dynamic anchor, planing deeper into the snow when it takes a load. In practice, a fluke may behave in more complicated ways, even coming out if its top is tipped too far forward (fig. 16-34c) or backward or if the load is not in a direct line (fig. 16-34d), such as to the side rather than straight out.

Flukes work best in moist, heavy snow. They are less reliable with snow layers of varying density: If the fluke or its cable travels down into the snow and hits a harder layer, the fluke could be deflected and pull out. Nor do flukes do well in dry, unconsolidated snow.

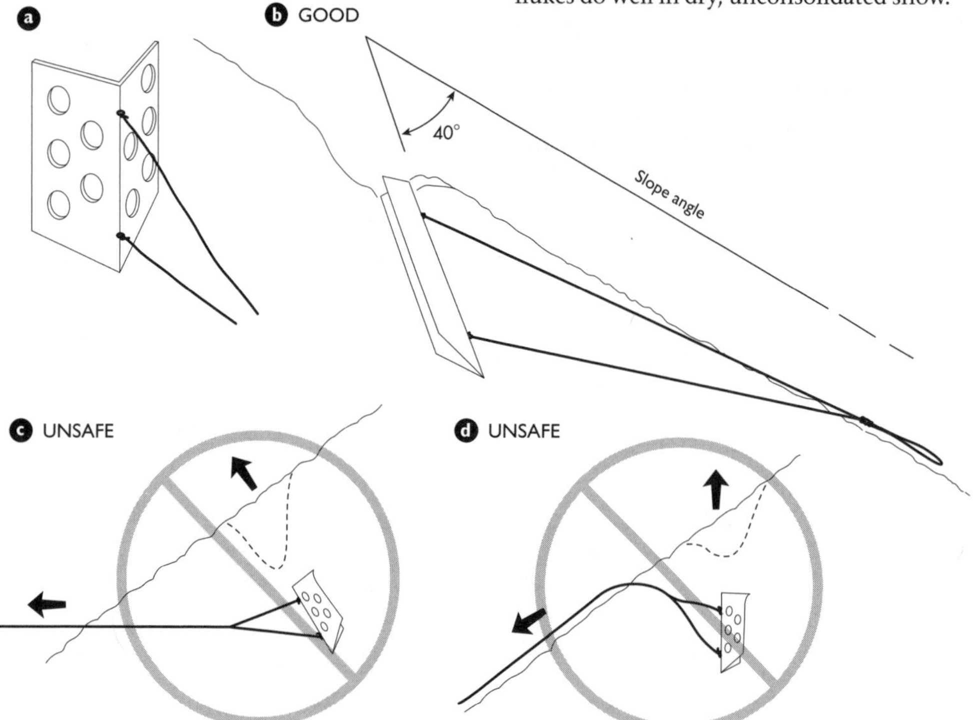

Fig. 16-34. Snow flukes: a, typical snow fluke; b, correct angle for fluke placement; c, incorrect placement (unsafe), not angled back sufficiently; d, incorrect placement (unsafe), no slot for cable.

Snow Bollard

A snow bollard is a mound carved out of snow. When rigged with rope or webbing, bollards can provide strong, reliable snow anchors (fig. 16-35a). However, building bollards can be time consuming.

Create the mound by making a horseshoe-shaped trench in the snow, with the open end of the horseshoe pointing downhill (fig. 16-35b). In hard snow, chop out the trench using the adze of an ice ax; in soft snow, stamp out a trench or dig one. The trench should be 6 to 8 inches (15 to 20 centimeters) wide and 12 to 18 inches (30 to 45 centimeters) deep (fig. 16-35c). In hard snow, the mound should be at least 3 feet (1 meter) in diameter, and in soft snow it should be up to 10 feet (3 meters).

The bollard should not be in an oval teardrop shape in which the legs of the trench come together. This configuration results in a weaker anchor by not taking advantage of the entire snow slope in front of the mound.

During construction, assess the snow in the trench for changes in consistency or weak layers that could allow the rope or webbing to cut through the mound.

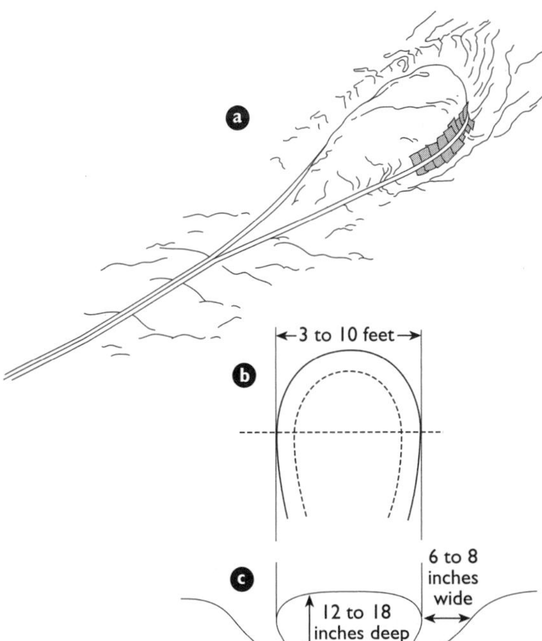

Fig. 16-35. Snow bollard: a, in a rappel setup; b, viewed from above; c, cross section.

Webbing is less likely than rope to saw into the mound. Avoid pulling on the rope or webbing after it is placed. Ice axes planted vertically at the shoulders of the trench prevent rope or webbing from cutting in. Pad the rear and sides of the mound with packs, clothing, or foam pads. Inspect the bollard for damage after each use.

Multiple Anchors

Multiple anchors are safest. They can be placed one behind the other to provide backup and absorb any remaining force (fig. 16-36a), or they can be placed independently and connected to share the load (fig. 16-36b). Keep the anchors several feet apart so they do not share any localized weaknesses in the snow. Inspect every anchor after each use. (More details and illustrations on joining multiple anchors are found in "Equalizing Anchors" in Chapter 10, Belaying, and in "Equalizing Protection" in Chapter 13, Rock Protection.)

BELAYING ON SNOW

When climbing on snow, climbers give quicker and less-formal belays using an ice ax, or they set up belays using established snow anchors. No matter what the belaying technique, every snow belay should be as secure and dynamic as possible to help limit the force on the anchor. The hip belay can provide a more gradual, dynamic belay than do belay devices, but it takes more practice to execute correctly (see "Using the Hip Belay" in Chapter 10). Plan your stance so your body takes the force, which is dissipated as much as possible by the belay. The dynamic, shock-absorbing quality of climbing rope also helps to minimize chances of an abrupt stop to a fall.

Set up a belay close to the climbing difficulties. To belay the lead climber, get out of the line of fire by setting up the belay stance to one side of the fall line. If the leader is heading up on a diagonal, get outside any point where that climber's route can cross directly above you. On a ridge crest, it is not always possible to predict a fall line and plan a belay in advance. If a rope mate slips off one side of the ridge, the best tactic may actually be to jump off the opposite side, with the rope running over the ridge and thus saving both climbers.

Carabiner–ice ax belay. Also called the stomper belay, the carabiner–ice ax belay provides better security than a boot-ax belay (see below), with easier rope handling. One good thing about the carabiner–ice ax belay is that the force of a fall pulls the belayer more firmly into the stance.

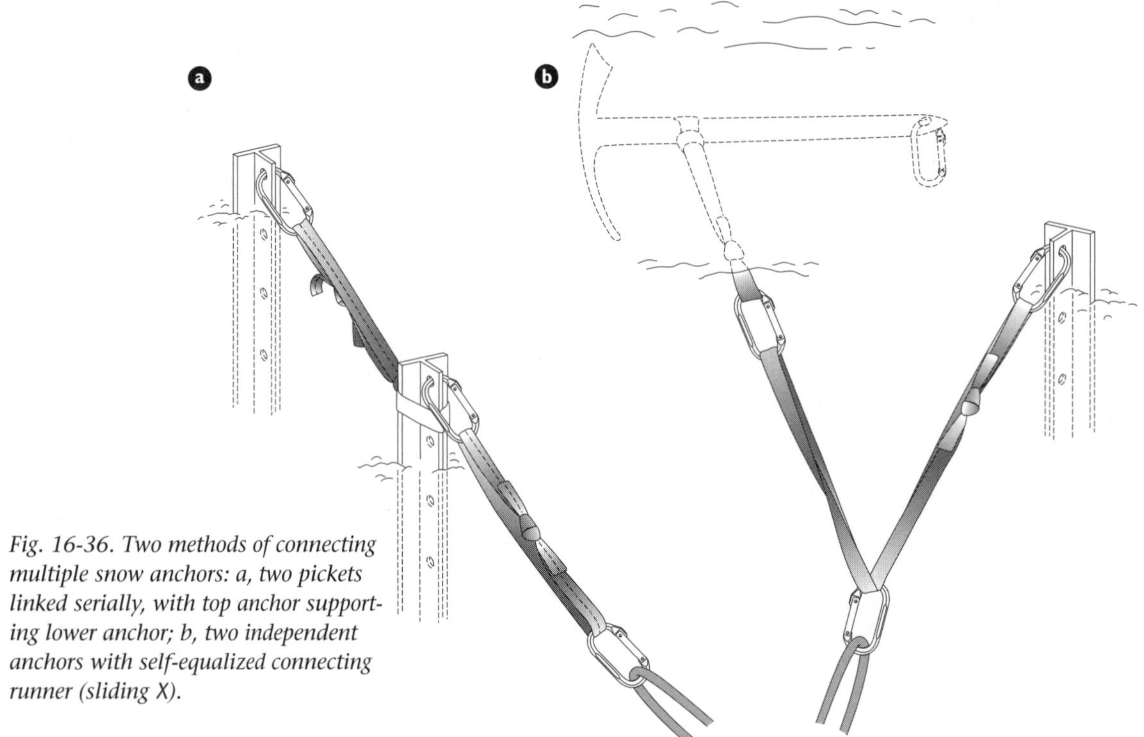

Fig. 16-36. Two methods of connecting multiple snow anchors: a, two pickets linked serially, with top anchor supporting lower anchor; b, two independent anchors with self-equalized connecting runner (sliding X).

To set it up, plant the ax as deeply as possible, the pick perpendicular to the fall line. Girth-hitch a very short sling to the ax shaft at the surface of the snow, and clip a carabiner to the sling (fig. 16-37a). Stand at a right angle to the fall line, facing the same side as the climber's route. Brace the ax with your uphill boot, standing atop the sling but leaving the carabiner exposed (fig. 16-37b). Keep crampons off the sling. The rope runs from the potential direction of pull up through the carabiner and then around the back of your waist and into your uphill (braking) hand.

Boot-ax belay. The boot-ax belay is a fast and easy way to provide protection as a rope team moves up together. The boot-ax belay, a form of dynamic belay, cannot hold the force of a high fall from above the belay, and because of the belayer's hunched-over stance, rope management is difficult. The boot-ax belay may be used when protecting a rope mate who is probing a cornice or crevasse edge or when providing a top belay. With practice, this belay can be set up in a matter of seconds with a jab of the ice ax and a quick sweep of the rope around the shaft near the head, then in front of your ankle (fig. 16-38a and b).

Belay devices and munter hitch. Belay devices and the munter hitch used in conjunction with a snow anchor provide a very secure belay on snow. The belayer may be standing, sitting, or belaying directly off of the anchor, depending on a number of factors (see "Belay Position and Stance" in Chapter 10, Belaying). Consider belaying directly off of the anchor only when multiple anchor points are used. Standing and belaying from the harness or belaying directly from the anchor permits the belayer to get into a drier, more comfortable position. These belays are easy to set up and operate even with wet or icy ropes.

Sitting hip belay. Used with a snow anchor, the sitting hip belay is dynamic and secure on snow. It does have its drawbacks. The sitting belayer may face the prospect of a cold, wet assignment, and the belay can be difficult to work if the rope is frozen.

To set up the belay, stamp or chop a seat in the snow as well as a platform to brace each boot against. Put down a pack, foam pad, or other material as insulation from the snow, and then settle into a standard hip belay, with legs outstretched and stiffened (fig. 16-39). (See "Using the Hip Belay" in Chapter 10, Belaying.)

Fig. 16-37. Carabiner–ice ax belay: a, girth-hitch a short runner to ax and clip carabiner to it; b, plant ax, stand on runner, and run rope up through carabiner and around waist.

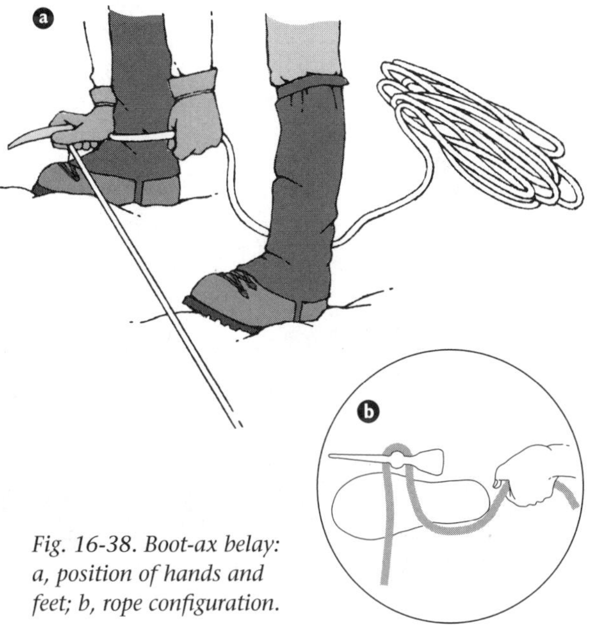

Fig. 16-38. Boot-ax belay: a, position of hands and feet; b, rope configuration.

Fig. 16-39. Sitting hip belay.

ROUTEFINDING ON SNOW

Snow can provide passage over some frustrating obstacles, including tundra, talus, brush, streams, and logging debris. At its best it provides a smooth, uniform surface and a straight shot up the mountain.

At its worst, snow can be too soft to support your weight, or it can be hard and dangerously slick. It can obscure trails, cairns, ridge crests, and other guideposts to the route, especially above tree line. Dangers often lie beneath the surface: moats, creeks, or glacier crevasses hidden by a thin snow cover. Unstable snow slopes may avalanche.

Minimize the frustrations and dangers of snow travel by studying the medium. See Chapter 26, The Cycle of Snow, for information on snow formation, types of snow, and the creation of glaciers. Learn how seasonal weather patterns affect snow accumulation and avalanche conditions. Hone navigation skills. Make the snow work for you: read the snow surface and terrain features to determine a safe, efficient route.

ROUTEFINDING AIDS

A good routefinder uses a variety of tools, including map, compass, altimeter (see Chapter 5, Navigation, for details on use of these as well as GPS receivers), wands, the sun, and other visual landmarks. Wands are used to mark the return route, but they can also mark points of danger (such as moats and crevasses) and changes in direction.

Fig. 16-40. Alpine terrain features.

a. Horn or aiguille
b. Ridge
c. Rock arête
d. Cornice
e. Glacier basin
f. Seracs
g. Fallen seracs
h. Icefall
i. Glacier
j. Crevasses
k. Lateral moraine
l. Snout
m. Moraine lake
n. Terminal moraine
o. Glacial runoff
p. Erratic blocks
q. Rock band
r. Shoulder
s. Col
t. Couloir or gully
u. Hanging glacier
v. Bergschrund
w. Buttress
x. Cirque or bowl
y. Headwall
z. Flutings
aa. Ice wall
bb. Summit
cc. Ice arête
dd. Towers or gendarmes
ee. Avalanche chute
ff. Avalanche debris
gg. Snowfield

SURFACE CONSIDERATIONS

The best snow to travel on is snow that will support climbers' weight and provide easy step-kicking, as well as being stable enough not to avalanche. The location of the best snow varies from day to day, even from hour to hour. If the snow in one spot is slushy, too hard, or too crusty, look around: There may be better snow a few feet away. Here are some tips for making the best use of the snow surface:

- **On a slushy slope,** walk in shade or use suncups as stairs to find patches of firmer snow.
- **On a slope that is too firm for good step-kicking,** try to find patches of softer snow.
- **When the going is difficult,** detour toward any surface that has a different appearance.
- **To find the best snow on a descent,** use a different route if necessary.
- **To find a firmer surface,** look for dirty snow. It absorbs more heat and therefore consolidates more quickly than does clean snow.
- **South and west slopes in the northern hemisphere** catch the heat of afternoon sun and consolidate earlier in the season and more quickly after storms. They offer hard surfaces when east and north slopes are still soft and unstable.
- **Take advantage of strong crusts on open slopes** before they melt. Get an early start after a clear, cold night that follows a hot day.
- **Beware of hidden holes** next to logs, trees, and rocks, where the snow has melted away from these warmer surfaces.
- **If the conditions are unfavorable on one side** of a ridge, gully, clump of trees, or large boulder, try the other side. The difference may be considerable.

VISIBILITY CONSIDERATIONS

The creative use of several routefinding methods becomes especially important when visibility is poor. In a whiteout, it is possible to lose all orientation. Distinguishing between uphill and downhill is difficult, as is distinguishing between solid snow and dense clouds. A whiteout can be caused by a temporary cloud cover or blowing snow that limits visibility and makes navigation difficult and hazardous. Care must be taken to avoid going off route. If a whiteout seems to be approaching, place wands in order to find the way out. This is the time to get out map, compass, and altimeter to navigate. An option includes waiting it out a while before proceeding; another is turning back. If possible, retrace the wanded route.

TERRAIN CONSIDERATIONS AND FEATURES

Major terrain features present obstacles as well as opportunities (fig. 16-40). Know which ones to use and which ones to avoid.

Ridges

A ridge (fig. 16-40b) may be the route of choice if it is not too steep or craggy. Ridges are generally free of rockfall and avalanche hazard. However, ridge routes take the full brunt of wind and bad weather, and climbers must be alert to the hazard of cornices, which form on ridge crests (see below).

Cornices

Cornices form when windblown snow accumulates horizontally on ridge crests and the sides of gullies, hanging suspended out past the supporting rock. The shape of a ridge determines the extent of the cornice that can develop (fig. 16-40d). A ridge that slopes on one side and breaks into an abrupt cliff on the other is a good candidate for a gigantic cornice. A knife-edge ridge (where snow cannot accumulate) or a ridge that is gentle on both sides (where snow can disperse) typically has only a small cornice, if any at all—although exceptions do exist.

When the physical features are right for building cornices, wind direction decides the exact location of the cornice. Because storm winds have definite patterns in each mountain range, most cornices in the same area face the same way. In the Pacific Northwest region of the United States, for example, most snowstorms come from the west or southwest, so the majority of cornices form on the north and east sides. These same northern and eastern exposures were made steep by past glaciation, creating ridges ideally shaped for cornice formation.

There are exceptions. Temporary or local wind deflection can contradict the general pattern. In rare instances, cornices are even built one atop the other, facing opposite directions, the lower one partially destroyed and hidden by later formations.

Cornices are a hazard. If climbers are traveling on a cornice, it could collapse spontaneously or under the added load of their weight, or the climbers could break through the cornice. Collapsing cornices can trigger avalanches. Cornices can fracture, falling into gullies or along the slopes below, or they can separate slightly from their host ridge, forming a crack or cornice crevasse. (See Figure 26-3 in Chapter 26, The Cycle of Snow.)

The safest course along a corniced crest is well behind the probable fracture line. Do not be misled by appearances. On a mature cornice, the probable line of fracture could be 30 feet (9 meters) or more back from the lip—farther back than might be expected upon examination. Usually the fracture line is not visible. Look for any crack or indentation in the snow, which might indicate a cornice that has partially collapsed and recently been covered with new snow.

The colder the weather, the more secure the cornice. A late-season cornice that is almost completely broken down also is not a problem. The safest strategy with cornices is to avoid them. Do not travel on them, under them, or through them.

Approaching from windward. The back side of a cornice appears to be a smooth snow slope that runs out to meet the sky.

Look at nearby ridges for an idea of the frequency, size, and location of cornices in the area. Try to view the lee side of the ridge from a safe vantage point, such as a rock or tree jutting through the crest.

Although rocks and trees projecting from the snow are safe, they do not indicate a stable route across the entire ridge. These can easily be on the tops of buttresses that randomly jut out perpendicularly to the ridge. The area directly in front of and behind these outcroppings may be all cornice. Many climbers have had the enlightening experience of looking back along a ridge and discovering that their tracks pass above a chasm.

When approaching from windward, stay well back from the crest if a cornice is suspected. If the crest must be approached, consider belaying the lead climber, who should probe carefully while advancing. The belayer also assumes a risk. If the cornice collapses, the belayer may have to bear the weight of the falling snow in addition to that of the climber.

Approaching from leeward. A cornice cannot be missed from the leeward side. Resembling a wave frozen as it is breaking, a large cornice close above a climber is an awesome sight. If a cornice's stability is doubtful, stay among trees or on the crest of a spur ridge while traveling below it.

Occasionally it may be necessary to climb directly through a cornice to force a way to a ridge crest or pass. Penetrate at an overhang, a rock spur, or a point where the cornice has partially collapsed. The lead climber cuts straight uphill at the point of least overhang, carefully tunneling and upsetting as little of the mass as possible.

Couloirs

Couloirs—steeply angled gullies (fig. 16-40t)—can provide a main avenue to the summit. Their overall angle is often less than that of the cliffs they breach, offering technically easier climbing. Couloirs are also the deadly debris chutes of mountains: Snow, rocks, and ice blocks that are loosened by the sun often pour down couloirs (fig. 16-40ee). Here are some tips for using couloirs:

- **Try to be out of couloirs before the sun hits them.** They can be safer in early morning when the snow is solid and when rocks and ice are frozen in place.
- **Keep to the sides,** because most of the debris comes down the center.
- **Listen for suspicious sounds from above;** keep an eye out for quiet slides and silently falling rock.
- **Examine a gully carefully before ascending it.** Couloirs can become increasingly nasty higher up, with extreme steepness, moats (see below), rubble strewn loosely over smooth rock slabs, thin layers of ice over rock, and cornices.
- **Bring crampons.** Deeply shaded couloirs may retain a layer of ice year-round. Early in the season, they are covered by hard snow and ice caused by freezing or avalanche scouring. Later in the season, the remaining hard snow and ice is encountered, sometimes with steep moats lining its edges.
- **Observe snow and avalanche conditions above steep gullies and on their floors.** Avalanches scour deep ruts in the floors of many steep couloirs. Cornices can hang above. Early in the year, the floors of the ruts offer the soundest snow available, and in cold weather they may be quite safe, particularly for a fast descent. If these conditions do not exist, cross the ruts rapidly or avoid them altogether.
- **During the ascent, look for alternative descent routes,** just in case time or changing snow conditions prevent descending the couloir on the return.
- **Research the area beforehand.** Finding the

correct couloir on a particular route can be challenging. They often look alike, and there may be several in the area. Rely on route information and knowledge of the terrain in order to choose the couloir that gives access to the summit rather than leading to a dead end.

- **Beware of meltwater streams running above or underneath the snow.** Listen for water. Look for sagging or holes in the snow where the stream may be. Walk on the sides of the gully and avoid any water; it may be slick with ice.

Bergschrunds

A bergschrund is the giant crevasse found at the upper limit of glacier movement, formed where the moving glacier breaks away from the permanent snow or ice cap above (fig. 16-40v). The downhill lip of the bergschrund can be considerably lower than the uphill edge, which may be overhanging. Sometimes the bergschrund is the final problem of the ascent. (See Chapter 17, Glacier Travel and Crevasse Rescue, for more information.)

Moats

Moats occur when snow partially melts and settles away from warmer rocks or trees. Moats are encountered on snowfields, around rock outcroppings and trees on ridges and along slopes, and in couloirs. Crossing a moat at the top of a snowfield where it separates from its rocky border can be as tough as getting past a bergschrund, with the main difference being that the uphill wall of a moat is rock, whereas the uphill wall of a bergschrund is ice.

Moats around trees and rocks may not be visible, appearing as merely an unstable layer of snow but actually covering an unseen large hole underneath. Stay away from treetops poking through the snow, and probe uncertain areas with an ice ax before stepping onto them. If a wide moat borders both sides of a slope along a steep couloir, it may indicate an equally wide moat at the head of the gully. Climbers may have to cross it or, worse yet, retreat and find an alternate ascent.

Rockfall

Snowfields and glaciers are subject to rockfall from bordering walls and ridges. Wear helmets in hazardous areas. Try to schedule climbs for less-dangerous periods. Early-season outings face less rockfall than summer climbs because snow still cements loose rock in place. In the northern hemisphere, southern and eastern slopes get the sun first, so climb these slopes early. The shaded northern exposures offer less rockfall danger.

AVALANCHE SAFETY

Mountaineers seek the freedom of the hills, and no freedom is harder to earn than the freedom of the snowy hills. In North America, according to the International Commission on Alpine Rescue, avalanches kill more winter recreationists than any other natural hazard: 26 fatalities in 2006–2007, 52 fatalities in 2007–2008, and 54 fatalities in 2008–2009. Nearly all avalanches that involve people are triggered either by the victims themselves or by a member of their party; according to avalanche expert Bruce Tremper, about 85 percent of avalanche victims trigger their own slide.

Climbers, backcountry skiers, and snowshoers are prime victims of avalanches. Better mountain gear and changing trends in backcountry recreation are leading more and more people to have fun where there are avalanche-prone slopes. The high level of risk to climbers and backcountry skiers can be explained by two factors:

1. Climbers' and backcountry skiers' destinations may be in avalanche terrain; therefore they spend time in avalanche terrain exposed to the potential for random events—in a way, in the "line of fire." Increased time in avalanche terrain equals more risk of involvement in an avalanche.
2. Climbers' and backcountry skiers' routes to their destinations may be avalanche prone, so they travel in avalanche-prone areas where human triggering is possible or even likely.

Reaching a climbing objective often involves traveling on steep and exposed avalanche start zones (see below). In choosing among route options, climbers must contend with the challenges of evaluating avalanche hazard. Early start times, moving really fast, and brute ambition are not enough to evade all avalanches. Avalanche hazard, unlike high-mountain exposure and severe weather, is not always obvious.

However, avalanches are not a mysterious phenomenon. Avalanche education can help backcountry travelers make better decisions about safe snow travel. This section introduces the subject of avalanches and reviews some of the ways that snow travelers can evaluate hazards and minimize risk; the next section explains methods of searching for avalanche victims.

This material is not intended to be comprehensive. For a more complete understanding of the subject, consult specialized publications (see Appendix D, Supplementary Resources) and take advantage of courses in avalanche awareness. For an explanation of the formation of avalanches and an assessment of dangers associated with various forms of snow, see Chapter 26, The Cycle of Snow.

UNDERSTANDING AVALANCHES

Snow—which is part of the allure of a climbing, snowshoeing, or skiing trip—is the source of avalanche hazard. Natural avalanches occur when snow deposited by storm systems places too great a load on the snowpack. The imposed stress exceeds the strength of the snowpack, and an avalanche is the result. A skier or climber may add sufficient stress to set off a slide.

The two principal types of avalanches that climbers encounter in a typical spring and summer climbing season are loose-snow avalanches and slab avalanches. Slab avalanches, also common in winter, can be very dangerous to skiers, snowshoers, and winter climbers and scramblers.

Loose-snow avalanches, which can consist of wet or dry snow, originate from a point source. They often look like an inverted V as they spread out and move downslope. They often move relatively slowly compared to slab avalanches. Wet loose-snow avalanches (common in spring) can overload a slope and cause failure in an underlying slab, resulting in a large and dangerous slab avalanche.

Slab avalanches are formed by a cohesive stronger snowpack layer forming over a weaker layer, often due to wind loading (see "Terrain," below). A slab avalanche occurs when the slope fails first in compression (the *whumph* sound that climbers sometime hear) and then in tension (the breaking of the slab that allows the slab to begin moving). A large area of snow (the slab) begins to move simultaneously and often breaks up into large plates and blocks of snow. Slab avalanches can strip snow all the way to the ground or can involve only the top layer(s) of poorly bonded snow. Wet springtime slab avalanches occur because of the layers in the existing snowpack that formed during the winter; this means that wet slab avalanche conditions are very sensitive to the slope aspect, time of day, and temperature.

Most avalanche victims are involved in small to medium-sized slides. Imagine a snowfield the size of a couple of tennis courts; it is poised on a slope, with weak layers hidden beneath the surface. A climber or skier enters the scene, and the additional load causes a failure: *crack!* The slab is off and away. The snow breaks and shears along the bed surface (the ground, ice, or hard snow layer that forms the sliding surface) between the weak layers, and across the top a fracture line marks the point where the tension holding the snow to the slope failed. Below the avalanche start zone (typically a 25- to 50-degree slope), the slab breaks up, and the churning snow accelerates down the avalanche track and into the runout zone, where the dense deposit accumulates and buries victims, on average, nearly 3 feet (about 1 meter) deep. Because the motion is sudden, it has an unbalancing effect; the suddenness, speed, and power of the avalanche typically sweep victims off their feet or skis, sometimes hurtling them into bad terrain or forcing them through confined tracks and burying them deeply in a cementlike medium tightly packed in a terrain trap.

Many avalanches create a destructive force capable of breaking trees, crushing a car, or wiping out a small cluster of buildings. Avalanche movement is varied; imagine slow lava, flowing white water, or 220-mile-per-hour (350-kilometer-per-hour) airborne turbulent masses.

EVALUATING AVALANCHE HAZARD

The interaction of three crucial variables—terrain, snowpack, and weather—determines whether or not an avalanche is possible (fig. 16-41). Is the terrain capable of producing an avalanche? Could the snowpack slide? Is the weather contributing to instability? However, to determine whether an avalanche hazard exists, another variable must be added: the backcountry traveler.

All of the information needed to evaluate avalanche hazards is generally available through observations and tests. A climber's decisions about avalanche hazard will be based on the results of these observations and tests. The results, if interpreted correctly, can reduce the risk of being caught in an avalanche. It is critical to learn the observations and tests, and then go to the backcountry to practice them in a safe area.

Terrain

Avalanches can occur only on slopes steeper than about 25 degrees, and they occur most often on slopes of between 35 and 45 degrees. The most common slope angle for an avalanche to occur is the "magic angle" of 38 degrees.

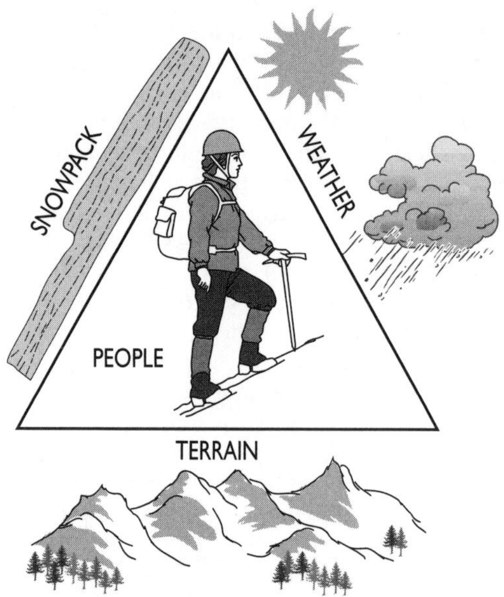

Fig. 16-41. Avalanche hazard triangle: terrain, snowpack, and weather—with the added variable of backcountry travelers.

Learning to recognize avalanche terrain is the first step in the process of evaluating avalanche hazard. The steepness of a slope, its aspect (which direction it faces), and the slope's shape and natural features (its configuration) are all important factors in determining whether a slide can occur on a particular slope.

Slope angle. Of all of these factors, the steepness, or slope angle, is the most important (fig. 16-42). Slab avalanches commonly occur on slopes with starting-zone angles between about 30 and 45 degrees, but slab avalanches occasionally occur on slopes of less than 30 and greater than 45 to 55 degrees. Slopes steeper than about 50 to 60 degrees tend to slough snow constantly, and slopes of about 25 degrees or less are generally not steep enough. It is difficult to estimate the angle of a slope just by looking at it. Use a clinometer. Simple plastic models are available, and many compasses have clinometers built into them (see Chapter 5, Navigation, for a discussion of clinometers).

The slope the climbers are on is not the only concern, because an avalanche could start from an adjacent slope. A party does not have to be climbing or skiing on a slope for it to avalanche. This is a very important concept: All of the snow is connected. Climbers can be traveling on a gentle slope or snow-covered road, and if the snowpack is unstable enough, they can trigger a slide on the steeper slope above them, even though they are not on a steep slope. All of the snow is connected, remember? It is critical to know what is above you as you travel.

Slope aspect. The direction a slope faces—its slope aspect—determines how much sun and wind the slope gets, which indicates a great deal about its avalanche potential. Here is how it works in the northern hemisphere (it is just the opposite on mountains south of the equator).

South-facing slopes receive more sun; therefore, snow settles and stabilizes faster on them than on north-facing slopes. In general (with plenty of local exceptions), this may make south-facing slopes somewhat safer in winter. They tend to release avalanches sooner after a storm, so if they are avalanching, it is an indication that slopes facing in other directions may soon follow their lead. As warmer spring and summer days arrive, south slopes become prone to wet-snow avalanches, and north-facing slopes may be safer.

North-facing slopes receive little or no sun in the winter, so consolidation of the snowpack takes longer. Colder temperatures within the snowpack create weak layers. Therefore, in general (again, with local exceptions), north slopes are more likely to slide in midwinter. In spring and summer, as south slopes become dangerously wet, look to the north side for firmer, safer snow.

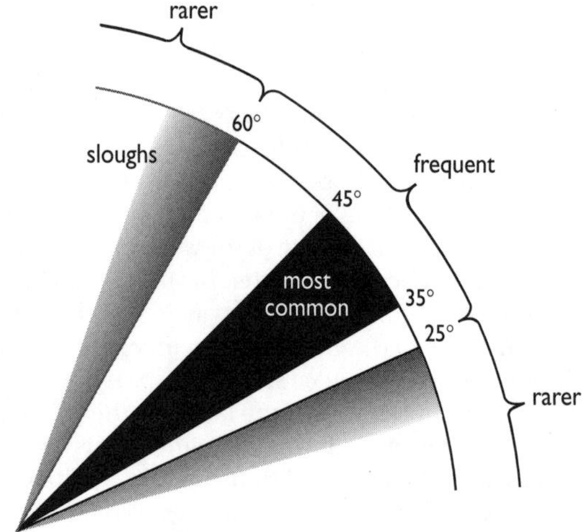

Fig. 16-42. Frequency of avalanches on slopes of various angles.

Windward slopes—those that face into the wind—tend to be safer than leeward slopes. Windward slopes may be blown clear of snow, or the remaining snow may be compacted by the force of the wind.

Leeward slopes—those that face away from the wind—are particularly dangerous because of wind loading, which happens when the wind transports snow from a wind-exposed area of the slope to a less wind-exposed leeward area of the slope. The snow is deposited in layers, making the snow deeper and therefore "loaded." A slope can become "top-loaded" by wind blowing snow over the top of a ridge crest and depositing it on the lee side, or it can become "cross-loaded" by the wind blowing along the ridges and depositing the snow in gullies between ridges. Leeward slopes collect snow rapidly when even moderate winds move snow from windward slopes onto the leeward side. The result is cornices on the lee side of ridges, snow that is deeper and less consolidated, and the formation of wind slabs ready to avalanche.

Be especially aware that in some areas, such as the passes in Washington State's North Cascades, the wind very often shifts direction with the onset of a storm, and what a climber thought was the windward slope may then be actually the leeward slope. It is quite common to have the wind blow the snow that was deposited by the last storm on the north and east aspects onto the south and west aspects as the storm approaches these mountains from the southwest. This makes the west and southwest aspects temporarily the leeward slopes and avalanche conditions dangerous on those slopes. As the storm moves onshore from the Pacific and into the Cascades, the wind then shifts to blowing from the west and southwest and begins to redeposit the snow on the now leeward north and northeast aspects, the "traditional" dangerous leeward slopes.

Slope configuration. Smooth slopes—those that, beneath the snow, are covered with grass or smooth rock slabs—generally have a poor bond with the snow and provide a slick surface for triggering a slide. Trees and rocks may serve as anchors that tend to stabilize the snow—at least until the snow covers them. But, in general, to act as effective anchors, the trees and rocks need to be so close together that it can be difficult or impossible for a climbing party to move through them. After these trees and rocks are buried by snowfall, they can actually become a source of weakness in the snowpack: As foreign bodies, the trees and rocks can inhibit or interfere with the bonding of the snow layers. Slides are not likely to originate in a dense forest, but they can run through dense forest from above.

The shape of a slope affects the hazard level. Snow on a slope that is straight, open, and moderately steep presents the most obvious danger. Snow on a convex slope, under tension as it stretches tightly over the curve of the hill, is more prone to avalanche than snow on a concave slope (fig. 16-43). Fracture lines frequently occur at or just below a convex area.

Snowpack

Slab configuration. The typical snowpack is composed of a series of discrete layers characterized by relative strength, hardness, and thickness. The depth and distribution of weak layers within the snowpack are significant factors in determining the stability of the snowpack. Climbers must determine what the composition of the snowpack is, its configuration.

Bonding ability. Throughout the winter, the snowpack accumulates layer by layer with each new precipitation, temperature, and wind event. A snowpack has both strong and weak layers. Strong layers tend to be cohesive—denser layers composed of small, round snow grains packed closely together and well bonded to each other. Weak layers tend to be less-dense layers composed of poorly bonded or cohesionless grains. These weak layers often appear loose or "sugary." Because weak layers prevent strong layers from bonding with one another, it is important for the backcountry traveler to know the relationship of these layers.

Sensitivity to stress. The snowpack exists in a balance between its strength and the stresses placed upon it. When the snow's strength is greater than the stresses, the snow is stable. Fortunately, this is most

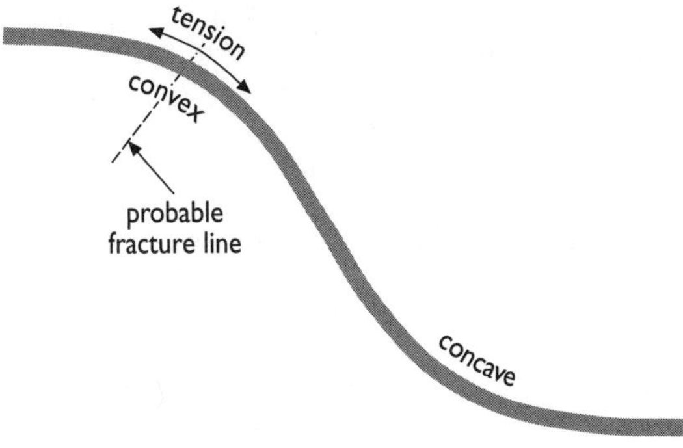

Fig. 16-43. Convex and concave slope configurations.

16

often the case; otherwise, snow would never stay on a hillside. But sometimes the balance between strength and stress is almost equal, and then the snowpack is unstable. Avalanches occur only when and if the snowpack is unstable. For an avalanche to occur, something must disturb the balance so that the stress on or within the snowpack exceeds its strength. The snowpack can adjust to only a limited amount of stress and only at a certain rate of speed. Add another stress such as a rapid load of precipitation, a sudden increase in temperature, windblown snow, or the weight of a climber or skier, and an avalanche could be triggered.

Weather

Before and during any backcountry trip, study the weather closely. Heavy precipitation, high winds, or extreme temperatures mean changes in the snowpack. Be prepared to look critically at the snow to see how the snowpack has been affected by recent weather. The snowpack adapts poorly to sudden changes, so rapid turns in the weather contribute to instability of the snowpack. The snowpack can bend and adapt when forces are applied slowly, but sudden stress can cause it to break. (See "The Formation of Snow Avalanches" in Chapter 26, The Cycle of Snow.)

Precipitation. Both forms of precipitation—either solid (snow and hail) or liquid (rain)—add to stress on the snowpack. Avalanche danger increases rapidly with snowfall of 1 inch (2.5 centimeters) or more per hour. The threshold of 12 inches (30 centimeters) or more in a day is critical. If a heavy load of new snow accumulates too quickly for the strength of the existing snowpack, an avalanche may result.

Rain can percolate into the snow, weakening bonds between layers. Rain tends to lubricate the layers, making it easier for a slide to start. Rain adds significant weight, and it may also rapidly warm the snowpack. Avalanches can be triggered very quickly after rainfall begins.

With either rain or new snow, consider these questions: How well does it bond with the snowpack? How big a load does it represent? The weight of the water in the new snow is the primary contributor of stress on the snowpack.

Wind. The high winds that transport snow from windward slopes and deposit it on leeward slopes break the interlocking bonds between snow crystals. These particles, once they are made smaller, pack closely together, forming cohesive slabs that fracture efficiently, resulting in avalanches. High winds also shape the cornices that overhang lee slopes. Cornices can break and fall, sometimes triggering an avalanche.

Temperature. Significant differences in temperature between the ground and the snow surface promote growth of highly faceted snow crystals (depth hoar, or "sugar snow") that cannot support much load. This temperature differential and the resulting sugar snow especially appear early in the season, notably in interior, snowy climates such as that in the Rocky Mountains or in the drier and colder parts of the North Cascades like the Washington Pass area. Less-severe temperature gradients and a deeper snowpack act as insulation that may allow this snow to stabilize. But highly faceted snow can persist as a dangerous underlying layer well into the snow season or until avalanches release it.

Another type of weak crystal growth, similar to dew, is surface hoar. It is common in all areas. The conditions that encourage its growth are cool, cloudless nights that are calm or nearly calm at the snow surface. When the thin, feathered crystals of surface hoar are covered by subsequent snowfall, they can form weak layers that—like sugar snow—increase avalanche hazard.

Temperature affects snow stability, especially that of new snow, in complicated ways. Warm temperatures accelerate settling, causing the snowpack to become denser and stronger and, thus, over the long term, more stable. But rapid, prolonged warming, particularly after a cold spell, initially weakens the snow cover, making it less stable and more susceptible to human-triggered failure. The snowpack remains unstable until temperatures cool down. Cold temperatures make dense snow layers stronger but are unlikely to strengthen weak layers of new, low-density snow.

KNOW BEFORE YOU GO

It is up to all climbers to gather important data before they head into avalanche terrain. There are many ways to minimize the risk of avalanches and to increase the chances of survival if one hits. In addition to evaluating avalanche hazard during a trip, climbers can also reduce avalanche risk by the things they do before they head into the mountains.

Take a class. Avalanche awareness and education are critical to making good decisions. Reading this chapter provides an introduction to decision making in avalanche terrain. After taking an avalanche course, however, climbers should be able to identify avalanche terrain; to identify basic snow grain types, weak layers, and strong layers; to perform field tests to determine snowpack stability and instability; to recognize weather and terrain factors contributing to instability; to perform rescue through fast and efficient transceiver use; and to apply safe travel techniques. There is no such thing as too much avalanche education.

Climbers can also improve their safety margin by taking the normal precautions called for on any climbing trip or ski tour: studying maps and photos of the area, researching alternative routes, preparing for an emergency bivouac, and identifying possible retreat routes. Determine the route—including its slope aspects, elevations, slope sizes and shapes, and exposure—and identify the probable locations of hazards. See the "Tips for Selecting a Safe Route" sidebar.

Finally, be sure the people in the climbing party have adequate training and equipment for heading into areas of possible avalanche risk. Be prepared to recognize, evaluate, avoid, and mitigate avalanche risk.

Check Weather and Avalanche Forecasts

It is obvious advice, but check the weather and avalanche forecasts before a trip. In many mountain areas, detailed avalanche reports are available by telephone and through the Internet from local avalanche forecast centers. Most local avalanche centers issue avalanche warnings (see Table 16-1) throughout the winter. Before heading out, check the avalanche hazard rating for the area the party plans to visit, and use this forecast to make decisions. If possible, follow the weather trends and snowfall history of the area, which provide information about the snowpack. Talk to people with local knowledge of the intended route, including any ranger who may be responsible for that area. Do not be afraid to rethink well-laid plans if crucial pretrip information is uncovered.

Consider Human Factors

In evaluating avalanche hazard, a prime component is the human factor. The judgments that mountaineers make affect the level of risk they face. The Avalanche Hazard Evaluation Checklist in Table 16-2 asks all members of a mountaineering party to ask questions of themselves and to reach a judgment on several points.

Attitude. What is the general attitude of the party toward its goals, toward risk, and toward the hazard data each member has been collecting? Consider the party's tolerance for risk and its degree of commitment to a climbing objective even in the face of hazard. Decide how willing the group is to look objectively at information on terrain, the snowpack, and weather. Many parties allow their desires to cloud the hard facts. Most avalanche victims were aware of the hazard but chose to interpret the information in such a way that an accident occurred. An unsafe attitude can be fatal.

Technical skill level. How skilled are members of the party at snow travel and at evaluating avalanche hazard? Are the party's overall mountaineering skills

TIPS FOR SELECTING A SAFE ROUTE

Travel safely in the backcountry by seeking routes that limit the party's exposure to danger. The following guidelines are based on some of the important considerations discussed in this chapter:

- Favor windward slopes, which tend to be more stable.
- Avoid leeward slopes where winds have deposited snow slabs.
- Choose the least-steep slopes that will get the party to its objective.
- Favor the edges of slopes, where avalanches are less likely and safer terrain is closer in case one does occur.
- Be particularly cautious of slopes of 35 to 45 degrees; use a clinometer to identify them. The majority of avalanches occur on slopes of 38 degrees.
- Be suspicious of the convex rollover at the top of a slope—a point of stress that can trigger an avalanche.
- Be careful of shaded slopes in winter and the very warm, sunny slopes of spring.
- Avoid gullies, which can be chutes for large quantities of snow that can deeply bury climbers or sweep them away.
- Keep aware of the runout zone below snow slopes and gullies, especially avoiding areas with cliffs below.
- Avoid camping in valleys that can be exposed to avalanche danger from above.
- Develop "avalanche eyeballs" by continually evaluating avalanche danger and its potential consequences.

TABLE 16-1. U.S. AVALANCHE DANGER SCALE

Danger Level (and Color)	*Avalanche Probability and Avalanche Trigger*	*Degree and Distribution of Avalanche Danger*	*Recommended Action in the Backcountry*
Low (green)	Natural avalanches very *unlikely*. Human-triggered avalanches *unlikely*.	Generally stable snow. Isolated areas of instability.	Travel is generally safe. Normal caution advised.
Moderate (yellow)	Natural avalanches *unlikely*. Human-triggered avalanches *possible*.	Unstable slabs *possible* on steep terrain.	Use caution in steeper terrain.
Considerable (orange)	Natural avalanches *possible*. Human-triggered avalanches *probable*.	Unstable slabs *probable* on steep terrain.	Be increasingly cautious in steeper terrain.
High (red)	Natural and human-triggered avalanches *likely*.	Unstable slabs *likely* on a variety of aspects and slope angles.	Travel in avalanche terrain is not recommended. Safest travel is on windward ridges of lower-angle slopes without steeper terrain above.
Extreme (black)	Widespread natural or human-triggered avalanches *certain*.	Extremely unstable slabs *certain* on most aspects and slope angles. Large, destructive avalanches *possible*.	Travel in avalanche terrain should be avoided. Confine travel to low-angle terrain well away from avalanche path runouts.

high? Just average? Low? A balanced party of able, experienced mountaineers can be expected to do well at avoiding avalanches and at responding efficiently if one strikes. A relatively untested party, or one whose members have a great difference in experience and skill levels, may need to be more conservative in its decisions.

Strength and equipment. What shape is the party in? Decide whether members of the group are strong and healthy enough to go on a demanding and possibly hazardous trip. How well equipped is the party to deal with an avalanche? Determine whether the party is adequately prepared, with shovels, rescue transceivers, first-aid supplies, and other gear that would be needed in case all precautions fail and the party is involved in an avalanche.

Deciding "Go" or "No Go" Before Leaving Home

After all the avalanche hazard information has been collected and evaluated, the climbing party must make the go or no go decision.

Every member of the party needs to give their opinion freely. Groups that take each person's thinking into account usually make better decisions than individuals. All climbers in the party have an obligation to express their concerns clearly, even in the face of differing opinions. When the party faces the risk of fatalities, prudent reservations, based on sound information, are essential. It is particularly important to avoid the group or "herd" mentality that so often takes over on the first blue-sky day after several days of storm and couple of feet of new snow. This "just go for it" thinking has caught many a climber or backcountry skier—even very experienced ones—in an avalanche.

Each person must understand the possible consequences of the decision and any alternatives to it. Everyone should understand any assumptions underlying the go or no go decision, including the thinking that resulted in assessments of the party's risk tolerance or its ability to deal with an avalanche. The party's decision-making process should proceed in this manner:

1. Identify potential hazards.
2. Continuously collect, evaluate, and integrate information.

TABLE 16-2. AVALANCHE HAZARD EVALUATION CHECKLIST

CRITICAL DATA		HAZARD RATING		
Parameters:	***Key Information***	***Green Light*** *(go/OK)*	***Yellow Light*** *(caution/ potentially dangerous)*	***Red Light*** *(stop/ dangerous)*
TERRAIN: Is the terrain capable of producing an avalanche?				
▪ Slope Angle (steep enough to slide? prime time?)		☐	☐	☐
▪ Slope Aspect (leeward, shadowed, extremely sunny?)		☐	☐	☐
▪ Slope Configuration (anchoring? shape?)		☐	☐	☐
Overall Terrain Rating:		☐	☐	☐
SNOWPACK: Could the snow fail?				
▪ Slab Configuration (slab? depth and distribution?)		☐	☐	☐
▪ Bonding Ability (weak layer? tender spots?)		☐	☐	☐
▪ Sensitivity (how much force to fail? shear tests? clues?)		☐	☐	☐
Overall Snowpack Rating:		☐	☐	☐
WEATHER: Is the weather contributing to instability?				
▪ Precipitation (type, amount, intensity? added weight?)		☐	☐	☐
▪ Wind (snow transport? amount and rate of deposition?)		☐	☐	☐
▪ Temperature (storm trends? effects on snowpack?)		☐	☐	☐
Overall Weather Rating:		☐	☐	☐
HUMAN FACTORS: What are the alternatives and their possible consequences?				
▪ Attitude (toward life? risk? goals? assumptions?)		☐	☐	☐
▪ Technical Skill Level (traveling? evaluating avalanche hazard?)		☐	☐	☐
▪ Strength/Equipment (strength? prepared for the worst?)		☐	☐	☐
Overall Human Factors Rating:		☐	☐	☐
DECISION/ACTION:				
Overall Hazard Rating/Go or No Go?:		***GO*** ☐	***or NO GO*** ☐	

Source: © Fredston and Fesler, Alaska Mountain Safety Center, Inc. (reproduced by permission)

3. Consciously explore assumptions, the consequences of a particular decision, and alternatives to that decision.
4. Make a decision—but be willing to reevaluate based on new information.

The information in this chapter can help simplify the decision-making process. Using the Avalanche Hazard Evaluation Checklist in Table 16-2, the party will assign each step of the evaluation with a green go-ahead light, a yellow caution light, or a red stop signal. The completed checklist then points the way to a sound decision.

USE THESE SKILLS IN THE FIELD

Once climbers have learned (and practiced) the fundamentals of avalanche safety, they must use these skills in the backcountry. Identifying avalanche terrain or suspect weather patterns is not enough; climbers must know how to put it all together. This section helps prepare climbers for making decisions and taking action in the backcountry. As with other aspects of avalanche safety, practice the techniques before ending up in hazardous terrain or involved in an avalanche rescue.

Observing Snow Conditions

Climbers need to know where they are going and, before they get there, what actions they are going to take. Look at conditions on similar terrain as soon and as often as possible. Observe the big picture first: on the road, up the trail, at camp, out on the terrain. Then fit the party's plans and situation into that picture. Use this perspective to decide where the party will test the snow for its stability and what tests will be used, and also use this perspective to aid the party in avoiding avalanche hazard.

To travel safely in the backcountry, climbers must be able to recognize unstable conditions. Generally, when unstable snow conditions exist, the majority of results from observations and tests will confirm that conditions are unstable on certain slope aspects, at certain elevations, and within a certain range of slope angles. Because there will be some uncertainty, particularly when the weather is changing, an extra margin of safety is required. Always make observations, looking for obvious signs of instability. Use the major clues shown in Table 16-3.

Testing Snow Stability

Climbers can get a lot of information on possible avalanche danger simply by paying close attention to the obvious signs of instability outlined in this section. Climbers can also test for snow stability. The Rutschblock test has received a high degree of acceptability among the backcountry ski community, though several other methods can also secure information on snow stability. These other methods are briefly introduced below, but climbers must refer to specialized publications and expert instruction to learn how to carry them out and evaluate them correctly. Use the information gained from personal observations and the results of the following tests to help the party make its go or no go decision.

Rutschblock (glide block) test. The Rutschblock test is reliable and considered to be a particularly good indicator of how likely a slope is to slide if traveled upon, since it uses an actual human being's weight to do the test. The Rutschblock test puts stress on a large block, or column, of snow (fig. 16-44), which provides better results than other tests, such as the shovel shear test (see below). In the Rutschblock test, a person on skis

TABLE 16-3. CLUES TO SNOWPACK STABILITY

Clue	Message
Recent avalanche activity	Best clue to instability. Slopes of similar elevation and aspect should be considered suspect.
Whumphing noises	Sounds caused by a sudden collapse of a weak subsurface layer; indicates extreme instability in the area. Pick routes across gentle slopes (slopes with angles of less than 25 degrees) and avoid runout zones of steeper slopes.
Shooting cracks	A form of brittle failure caused by the sudden release of stored elastic energy (in other words, extreme instability is present). As a rule, the longer or deeper the crack, the more serious the instability. Avoid avalanche terrain, including the runout zones of steeper slopes above.
Pluming and wind transport	A major clue that conditions have changed for the worse on leeward slopes. Wind pluming (wind-generated snow clouds) results from snow being eroded from the windward slopes and new snow being rapidly deposited on leeward slopes. If wind loading persists, the period of instability is usually followed by repeated cycles of avalanche activity and reloading. Avoid these leeward slopes and terrain below them.
Storm activity	Tends to make conditions more unstable. These periods of instability are generally of shorter duration in warmer snow climates, but persist for long periods of time in colder climates. Avoid travel in the backcountry.

Source: © Fredston and Fesler, Alaska Mountain Safety Center, Inc. (reproduced by permission)

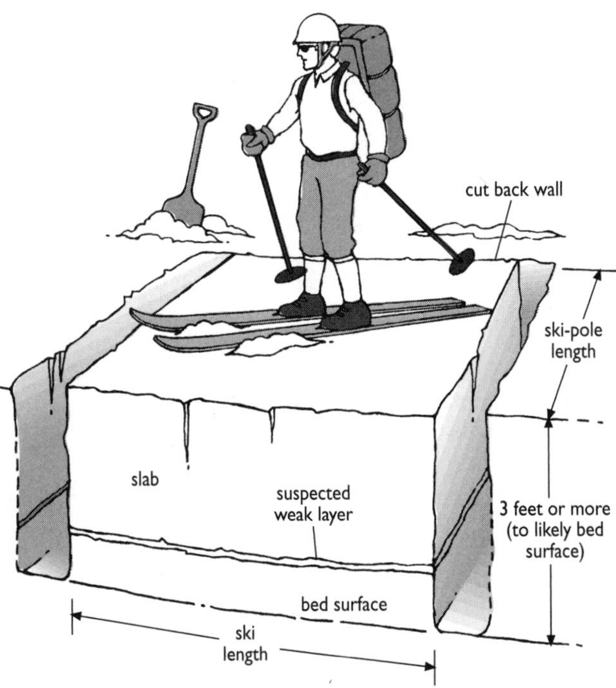

Fig. 16-44. Rutschblock test for snow stability.

stands atop the block. Follow these steps to conduct the Rutschblock test:

1. Find a spot that is representative of the slope aspect and angle that the party expects to encounter. The best information is usually garnered from an area that is not near trees or a ridge.
2. Using a shovel, a snow saw, or a ski, excavate to create three sides of a rectangular snow block: front (downslope) and two sides. Dig down at least 3 feet (1 meter), or deeper if necessary, to reach suspected weak layers. The length of the block in the cross-slope direction should be about the same as the length of a ski; the width of the block in the downslope direction should be about the same as the length of a ski pole. Make clean, vertical sides on the snow block; do not disturb the snow on top.
3. Cut the fourth side of the rectangle—the back wall of the block—free of the slope, using a saw, ski, or rope. It may be difficult to cut through hard or icy layers without a snow saw.
4. Have a person on skis step onto the center of the block from the slope above. If the block supports the skier, that person then stresses the block with a series of jumps, leaping up with both skis initially and then without skis. The amount of stress required to cause the block to shear (fail) at a weak layer indicates the relative stability of the slope only on that particular aspect and at that elevation and at that time of day.
5. Use the criteria in Table 16-4 to interpret the Rutschblock test results. Keep in mind that the result of the Rutschblock test is just one piece of information among many that must be collected to assess avalanche danger. After conducting the test, fill in the hole so that it is not a hazard for other travelers.

TABLE 16-4. INTERPRETING THE RUTSCHBLOCK TEST RESULTS

Results	Stability
Fails while excavating the site	Extremely unstable
Fails while approaching the test site after excavation	Extremely unstable
Fails while standing on the block	Extremely unstable
Fails while flexing for a jump	Unstable
Fails (to a questionable degree) with a jump	Unstable
Fails after repeated hard jumps	Relatively stable
Does not fail with repeated jumps	Stable

Shovel shear test. The shovel shear test can detect the presence of snow layers that are likely to slide. The procedure involves excavating a column of snow that is freestanding on the front and sides and has a cut at the back that is deep enough to allow you to insert a shovel. The column should be approximately as wide as the shovel, about 12 inches by 12 inches (30 centimeters by 30 centimeters). The tester stands in front of the column, inserts the shovel in the cut at the back, and pulls forward on the shovel handle with both hands. If the snow has a pronounced sliding layer, the column will shear off evenly at that point.

This test has been criticized for not providing reliable information on the amount of force needed to cause shearing. Although the shovel shear test may provide information about layering and stability, multiple test sites may be required. The Rutschblock and tap or compression test (described below) have proven to be much more reliable indicators of snow stability.

Tap or compression test. The tap or compression test has largely replaced the shovel shear test. It is quick and easy to interpret, and it works well with most weak layers of snow.

As in the shovel shear test, dig out and isolate a column of snow roughly as wide as the shovel, about 12 inches by 12 inches (30 centimeters by 30 centimeters). Unlike the shovel shear test, the column should be isolated on all sides. The column usually is not more than about 5 feet (1.5 meters) deep, since it is difficult for a human being's weight to trigger an avalanche at a depth greater than 5 feet (1.5 meters); beyond that depth, the forces an average-weight person exerts on the snowpack are essentially dissipated.

Lay the shovel blade face down on the surface of the column and tap the back of the shovel with the palm of one hand. Tap progressively harder, bending your hand at the wrist for 10 equal taps, then bending your arm at the elbow for 10 equal taps, and finally bending your entire arm from the shoulder for 10 equal taps.

If the column fails when you are tapping by articulating from the wrist, it is a red light—no go. If the column fails when you are tapping by bending your arm from the elbow, it is a yellow light—caution. Finally, if the column fails when you are tapping by articulating from your shoulder, or if the column does not break at all, it is a green light—a sign of bonded layers in the snow sample that you tested and on the slope aspect you chose. As with any snow stability test, elevation, time of day, and slope aspect are critical variables.

The quality of the break between the snowpack layers at the failure point is an important part of evaluating the tap test. Observing how the layer breaks and looking at how cleanly it breaks gives an indication of how much energy is stored in the snow and how likely the snow is to slide. The shear quality of a snowpack layer is described using a Q scale (where "Q" stands for quality). If the surface of the fracture is smooth and clean and the sheared snow pops off as though it is loaded, the shear is a Q1. A Q2 shear can be clean like a Q1, but a Q2 shear does not break or pop off as easily as a Q1. A Q3 shear breaks on a rough, often uneven plane. A Q1 shear is a significant sign of instability; Q2 and Q3 shears are associated with respectively less instability.

Stuff-block test. The stuff-block test is a more quantifiable variation of the tap test. The same principles apply, but instead of using a hand and arm to tap a shovel against an excavated column of snow, you use a stuff sack filled with 10 pounds (4.5 kilograms) of snow.

Progressing from lower to higher heights, drop the stuff sack onto the shovel blade placed on top of the column: start at 8 inches (20 centimeters) or less above the shovel, then 8–12 inches (20–30 centimeters), and finally 16–18 inches (40–45 centimeters). If the column fails at 8 inches or less, it is a red light warning. Failure at 8–12 inches means a yellow caution light. And no failure, or failure at 16–18 inches, means a green light for the slope and aspect tested.

Snow-pit observations. Observe the pattern of layering in a snow pit (perhaps the one dug for the Rutschblock, tap, or stuff-block test). The snow pit should be in a safe location that has a slope angle, slope aspect, and elevation similar to the nearby slopes that the party plans to cross. It should be in a spot away from trees. It is not difficult to identify the various snow layers and determine their relative hardness and strength by pushing against each one with a fist or jabbing them with a finger, pencil, or knife. Very hard layers or very soft layers may not bond well with other layers. Snow pits may not yield as much useful information as the Rutschblock test.

Ski-pole probe. Use a ski pole to puncture the snow surface and get an indication of what is below. If the snow is very soft, push the basket end of the pole smoothly into the snow; then pull it slowly out, trying to feel any hard or soft layers. It may be possible to reach down into the ski-pole hole and feel the snow layers with your fingers. In most other snow, use the handle end of the ski pole, or remove the basket to penetrate the snow. Regularly making these observations and discussing them with party members reinforces an awareness of avalanche hazard and preparedness. This informal test will not give information on the bonding of snow layers and it will miss thin shear planes, but it can reveal gross discontinuities in the snowpack structure that suggest instability.

Deciding "Go" or "No Go" During the Approach

Snow travelers facing possible avalanche hazard want the answer to one basic question: Is it a "go" or a "no go"? That is, can the party proceed, or must they turn back or find another route? Table 16-2 provides a checklist of critical data that snow travelers can use both at home in preparation and in the field en route to evaluate avalanche hazard and reach a go or no go decision. The checklist can guide the party in responding to four principal questions:

1. Is the terrain capable of producing an avalanche?
2. Could the snow fail?
3. Is the weather contributing to instability?
4. What are the alternatives and their possible consequences?

To respond effectively to these overall questions, the party needs to come up with answers to a series of secondary queries about the terrain, snowpack, weather, and the climbing party itself. Using the checklist in Table 16-2, answer each question with an assessment of relative hazard, expressed as a green light (OK), a yellow light (caution), or a red light (danger). *Be aware that most avalanche incidents occur on days when yellow signals are noted.* A review of the completed checklist should give the party enough input to reach a "go" or "no go" decision at each encounter with possible avalanche hazard.

Crossing a Questionable Slope Safely

Nobody likes it, but sometimes there is no way to avoid questionable avalanche terrain. The task then is to make the passage with the least danger of disturbing the slope and to minimize the consequences of a possible avalanche.

Before heading out onto a questionable slope, put on a hat, mittens, and warm clothing, and zip up clothing. Undo ski-pole straps. If on skis or snowshoes, use releasable bindings and remove the safety straps that connect the boots to the bindings. (Skis and snowshoes spread a person's weight over a relatively large area, putting less strain on the slope than boots do.)

When the route lies up a slope (and the party is walking, not skiing), head straight up the fall line instead of switchbacking, which can undercut the snow.

On a traverse, only one person moves at a time, and everyone else watches from safe places, ready to shout if a slide starts. Cross with long, smooth strides, being careful not to cut a trench across the slope. Each climber follows in turn, stepping in the leader's footprints. Everyone listens and watches for an avalanche. The route should follow a line as high on the slope as practical. It may be possible to hug cliff bands at the top of the slope.

Move from one position of safety to another, minimizing the potential exposure period. Do not fall; falling puts a sudden load on the snowpack. On an avalanche-ready slope, the impact of a falling body can be like the detonation of a little bomb.

Think twice before roping up on questionable slopes. Decide whether the risk of the slope avalanching is greater than the risk of a climber falling. If the party chooses to use a rope, belay directly off the anchor. The belayer should not tie in to the rope, because this would risk the belayer being pulled into an avalanche. If there are no solid anchors from which to belay, go unroped.

Surviving an Avalanche

Climbers must think ahead about what they would do in the event of an avalanche, because after one starts, there is no time.

While traveling, keep an eye out for escape paths. If you are caught in an avalanche, do not give up. Fight to survive. Try to get off the moving snow. Yell to your climbing partners. Jettison any gear you want to get rid of, including skis and ski poles. It might be a good idea to keep your pack to protect your back and neck. Larger objects tend to be transported to the surface of avalanche debris; the pack may help keep you near the surface, and it may help protect you from trauma. If you survive the traumatic forces of the avalanche, the clothing and equipment in the pack will certainly be needed.

At the start of an avalanche, try to stop before being swept away. Grab a rock or tree, or dig the ice ax or a ski pole into the snow, and hold on. If that does not work, try to stay on the surface by using swimming motions, flailing your arms and legs, or by rolling. Try to move to the side of the slide.

If your head goes below the surface, close your mouth to avoid being suffocated by snow. As the avalanche slows, thrust upward. If you are buried, try to make a breathing space by putting an elbow or hand in front of your face. Inhale deeply before the snow stops, in order to expand your ribs; as the snow closes around you, it will become impossible to move. Do not shout or struggle. Relax. Try to conserve oxygen and energy. Your climbing partners should know what to do, and they will begin immediate rescue efforts.

AVALANCHE RESCUE

The mountaineer's primary emphasis should be on avalanche evaluation and safe travel. Every party needs avalanche rescue skills and equipment, but these are no substitute for the ability to make sound judgments that promote safe travel in avalanche terrain. But if an avalanche does occur, this section covers what to do.

Appendix D, Supplementary Resources, lists several widely available books about avalanche rescue, as well as online resources. Avalanche.org is a comprehensive website run by several avalanche research organizations, providing international statistics, links to avalanche courses, and links to avalanche information centers.

THE WELL-PREPARED PARTY

A climbing party's level of preparedness is an important factor in minimizing avalanche hazard. A well-prepared party has the training and practice, conditioning, equipment, and critical judgment to evaluate avalanche hazard and to respond effectively to an avalanche if one occurs. Members of the party must have electronic avalanche rescue transceivers, shovels, and probe tools to perform a rescue, and they must have developed the skills to use them. They know that seconds—not minutes—do count in the safety of their party.

The well-equipped party may carry other tools to evaluate the snowpack and aid in avoiding an avalanche. A snow-study kit with a snow crystal card, a clinometer, and a snow saw help in analysis of slopes and the snowpack. New products to help avalanche victims survive include the Black Diamond Avalung II, avalanche air bags, and avalanche balls. Research and try out any avalanche safety item before relying on it in the backcountry.

USING AVALANCHE RESCUE TRANSCEIVERS

The electronic avalanche rescue transceiver is the principal tool for finding buried victims. A rescue transceiver can be switched to either transmit or receive signals. The international standard frequency for avalanche transceivers is 457 kilohertz. Transceivers that work at 2,275 hertz are obsolete and should not be used. Some rescue groups may still use dual-frequency transceivers, but the recommended transceivers for backcountry travelers and climbers operate exclusively at 457 kilohertz. The new standard transceivers have a greater range.

Continued progress in the avalanche safety field has produced transceivers with increasingly sophisticated digital processor capabilities. Older analog and newer digital transceivers are compatible, and both types utilize the 457 kilohertz standard frequency. The two types of transceivers have different features, so before investing money and time in one, read product reviews, talk to experienced users, and try out different units. Older analog units, while dated, may still be found at used-equipment stores, but digital transceivers are the new standard, and their features are rapidly evolving, making them very easy to use.

Digital transceivers convert the analog signal to a digital readout, and they typically provide both audible and visible signals in the search (receive) mode. Among the significant advantages of digital transceivers is that almost all users experience a shorter learning curve with a digital transceiver than with an analog transceiver. An especially valuable feature of newer digital transceivers is their ability to quickly separate and isolate signals in a multiple burial scenario in which two or more victims have been buried.

Rescue depends on each member of the party carrying a transceiver. All members of a party must know how to use the transceivers correctly. This skill requires regular practice, so practice before and during every season.

At the trailhead and at the beginning of each day, the group should verify that all transceivers can transmit and receive signals properly. Fresh batteries usually last for about 300 hours, but carry extras in case the signal from any transceiver weakens.

Strap the transceiver around your neck and torso. Carry it under a shirt or jacket to keep it from being lost in an avalanche. Do not carry it in your pack. During the climb, transceivers are left on, set to the transmit mode. If staying overnight in a snow cave or in an avalanche-prone area, consider leaving the transceiver on, set to transmit, even at night.

Once a search begins, unstrap the device and bring it out for rescue work; all rescuers switch their transceivers to the receive mode to locate the transmission from a victim. It is critically important that every searcher switch to receive; if a searcher's transceiver is left in the transmit mode, searchers will waste valuable time receiving this signal rather than the signal from the victim.

Each searcher listens for beeps and/or watches an optical display to detect the buried victim. A rescuer should be able to locate the buried victim in less than five minutes. It is essential to practice using rescue transceivers to ensure that searchers have the best chance of locating victims before they suffocate.

It is usually easier to move downhill while searching. Work rapidly but efficiently. Climbers may need to consciously control their feelings of shock and anxiety in order to be effective at trying to find the missing persons.

FIRST STEPS IN A RESCUE

Identify the Last Seen Area. The rescue effort starts even before the avalanche has stopped. In the shock of the moment, the first step in a successful rescue is a tough one: Someone must pay attention to the point where a victim is last seen. Identify the area to be searched based on the Last Seen Area.

Do not go for help. A critical principle of avalanche rescue is this: Do not send anyone for help. Stay and search. Survival depends almost certainly on locating the victim quickly. A person located in the first 15 minutes has an approximately 90 percent chance of survival if he or she initially survived the avalanche by not hitting rocks or trees or suffering trauma. The probability of survival drops off rapidly after that time. After 90 minutes, the probability of survival is approximately 25 percent. After the victim is unburied or after search efforts turn out to be futile, then send someone for help.

Select a search leader. The search leader directs a thorough and methodical rescue effort. Before entering the search area, consider the safety of the search party. Evaluate the potential for other slides in the area, choose a safe approach to the search area, and designate an escape path in case of another avalanche.

Do a scuff search. Start the search with an initial rapid "scuff search" of the snow surface. Rescuers look for someone partially buried, any castoff equipment, or any logical spot where the victim might have come to a stop against a tree or rock. Use anything to mark the location of any clues as an aid to further searching, and probe the likely catchment areas. The missing climber could turn up in this fast and immediate search. If not, then move quickly into the transceiver search.

THREE PHASES OF A TRANSCEIVER SEARCH—DIGITAL TRANSCEIVER

Those who grew up using the old analog transceivers and the grid search method can oftentimes be outperformed by near novices using a digital transceiver. Comparing the search steps used with a digital transceiver to those required when using an analog transceiver will quickly show why. Note that digital transceiver technology is rapidly evolving, with improvements announced almost yearly. Some of the newer transceivers can actually be updated regularly and can download newly developed software to improve their performance.

The digital transceiver search for a victim or victims occurs in three phases—coarse, fine, and pinpoint—just like the search using an older analog transceiver (described in the next section).

Coarse Search

In the coarse search phase, a signal has not yet been detected. The searchers start from the victim's last seen point and fan out no more than 65 feet (20 meters) apart—about the effective range of a modern digital transceiver—across the slope, moving straight down the fall line with their transceivers in receive mode until a signal is picked up. If there was no last seen point, then the entire slope must be searched. *Note:* A lone searcher must switchback down the slope with no more than 65 feet (20 meters), the effective range of the transceiver, between switchbacks.

Once a signal is detected, some searchers can move to the fine search while other rescuers prepare to dig out the victim. If there is more than one victim, the rest of the rescuers continue the coarse search. As each victim is found, turn off that person's transceiver so that searchers will not continue to pick up those signals.

Fine Search

The fine search phase begins when the searchers detect a signal. Use the directional lights and distance meter on the transceiver to follow the signal to roughly where the victim is buried. This will often be a curved path, as the transceiver is following the induction line. The induction line follows a curved path because the signal transmissions from the victim's transceiver are propagated outward in a curved path. Move as quickly as is practical during this phase.

Pinpoint Search

Once a searcher is within roughly 9 feet (3 meters) of the victim, the pinpoint search begins, and the searcher slows and moves the transceiver close to the surface of the snow. Search along the perpendicular axis to try to pinpoint the victim more closely. Pay more attention to the distance indicator lights than to the direction lights at this point of the search. It is critically important to practice with your beacon, since there are subtle differences in operation and sensitivity. Once searchers are this close, begin probing to locate the victim (see "Recovery," below).

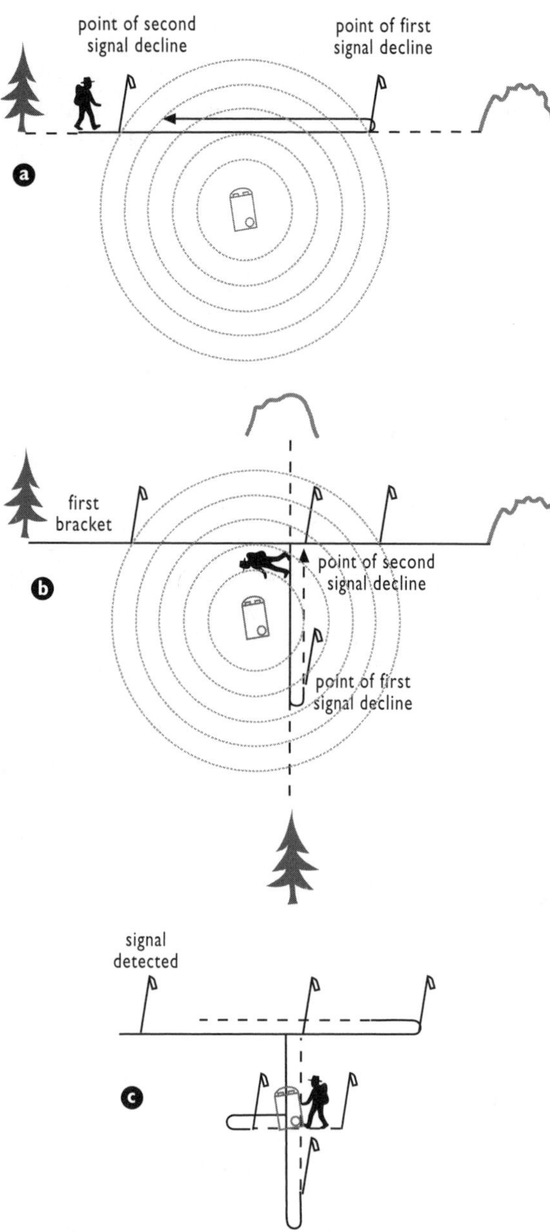

Fig. 16-45. Fine search, using the bracket method: a, first bracket; b, second bracket; c, summary of transceiver search bracketing. (Illustrations by Ray Smutek in "Avalanche Beacons," Summit *[March-April 1984], reprinted by permission.)*

THREE PHASES OF A TRANSCEIVER SEARCH—ANALOG TRANSCEIVER

Many analog units are still in use, and the search for an avalanche victim proceeds through the same three phases: coarse, fine, and pinpoint. With an analog transceiver, the coarse and pinpoint phases rely on a traditional technique called the bracket or grid method. But for the fine search phase, a newer method—the tangential or induction method—is up to 50 percent quicker when used by trained individuals. It is essential that climbers master the bracket method. However, they should also learn the tangential method because of the critical time it can save during the fine-search phase.

Coarse Search

Put the volume control or signal level all the way up on every transceiver. Searchers, spaced no more than 65 feet (20 meters) apart, should move in a clearly defined pattern over the search area (as a rule of thumb, don't space searchers farther apart than you know the range of the beacons to be).

Because a transceiver's wire-wrap antenna has directional characteristics (which are compensated for in a digital beacon, not so in an analog one), signals may be stronger or weaker depending on the position in which searchers hold their search transceiver, relative to the victim's transmitting transceiver. For this reason, it is important to rotate the transceiver left and right, forward and back, trying to find the strongest signal position.

When a signal is picked up, one or two searchers start to track down the signal with a fine transceiver search while other rescuers get ready to dig out the victim. If there is more than one victim, the rest of the rescuers continue the coarse search. As each victim is found, turn off that person's transceiver so that searchers will not continue to pick up those signals.

Fine Search

Bracket method. Using a single rescue transceiver, searchers employing the bracket method follow a series of steps to find their way to a spot very near the buried victim.

1. Orient the transceiver for maximum signal strength, moving the unit vertically and horizontally to find the best signal position. The transceiver is now oriented toward the strongest sound. (Some transceivers provide a visual display to show the strongest signal.) This ori-

entation must be maintained throughout the search.

2. Reduce the volume to be as low as possible while still allowing you to hear the signal. (Your ear is better able to distinguish changes in volume for low-volume sounds.)
3. Keep the transceiver in the same orientation while you walk in any straight line. As soon as the signal reaches a peak and begins to drop, again reduce the volume to be as low as possible.
4. Still holding the transceiver in the same orientation, continue on the same path. When the signal fades out, mark the spot.
5. Without changing orientation of the transceiver, turn around 180 degrees and retrace the same pathway. When the signal fades out again, mark that spot. There is now a straight line bracketed at the end by points where the signal disappears (fig. 16-45a).
6. Return to the center of this first bracketed line

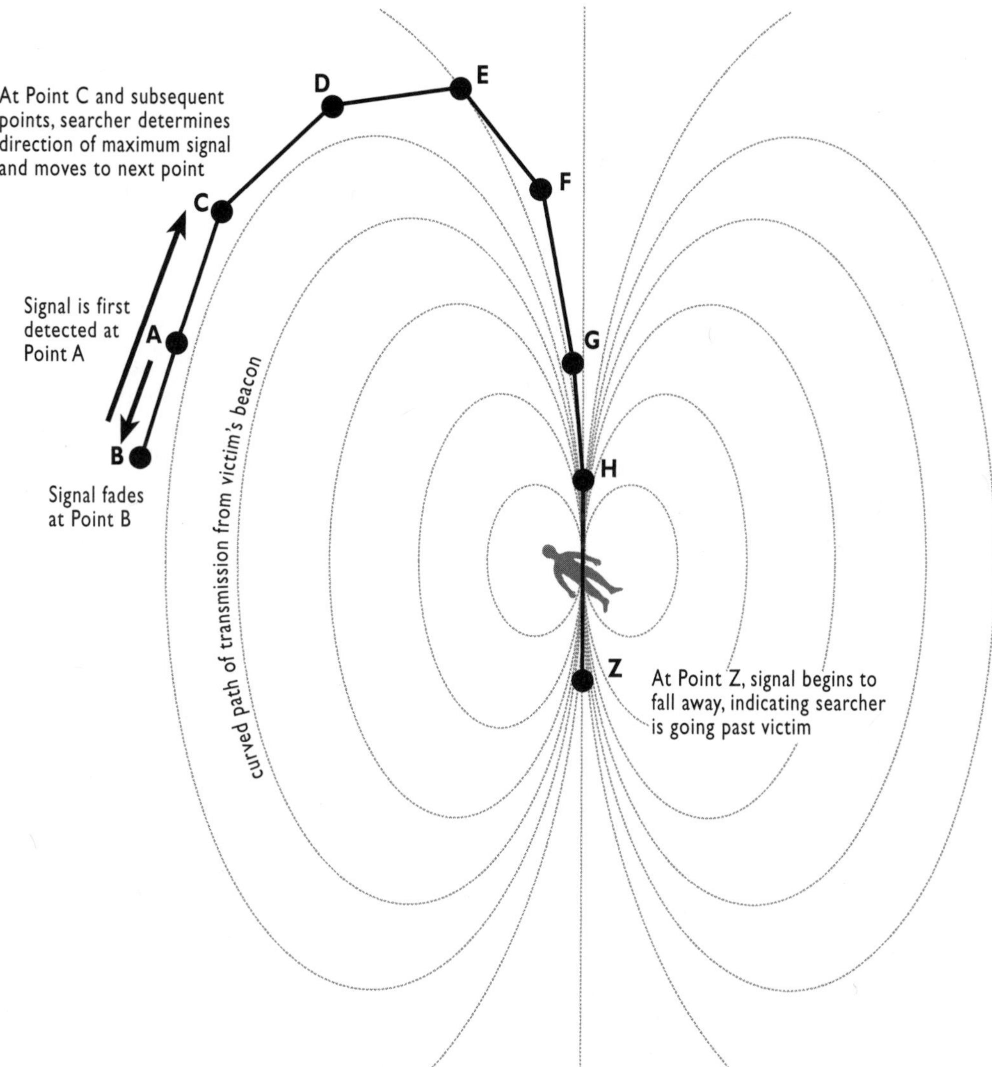

Fig. 16-46. Fine search, using the tangential (induction) method.

and make a 90-degree turn. Now repeat the process: Reduce the volume to a minimum, and walk in a straight line until the signal fades out. Mark the spot, turn around 180 degrees without disturbing the orientation of the transceiver, and retrace your steps until the signal again fades; mark that spot. There is now another straight line bracketed by two fade-out points (fig. 16-45b).

7. Return to the center of this new line and again make a 90-degree turn in the direction of the signal. Work fast and efficiently, without worrying too much about precision. Continue this process of making bracketed lines until the distance between fade-out points on a line is less than 6 feet (1.8 meters). Searchers can usually reach this stage within the first three brackets. You are now very close to the victim (fig. 16-45c) and ready to move into a pinpoint search.

Tangential method. The tangential method is an alternative to the bracket method for the fine search that became popular before the newer digital transceivers became widely available. The tangential method is faster when performed by a trained rescuer, but it takes more effort to learn and is not always successful. (In a sense, the operator is providing the "digital" input by following an induction line, just as the new digital beacons do.) Be prepared to switch back to the bracket method if the tangential method does not give the needed results. Following are the steps to follow for the tangential method (fig. 16-46). The first two steps are identical to the bracket method.

1. Orient the transceiver for maximum signal strength, moving the unit vertically and horizontally to find the best position. The transceiver is now oriented toward the strongest sound. (Some transceivers provide a visual display to show the strongest signal.) This orientation must be maintained throughout the search.
2. Reduce the volume to be as low as possible while still allowing you to hear the signal. (Your ear is better able to distinguish changes in volume for low-volume sounds.)
3. Head off in the direction of the strongest sound. If the volume drops before you have traveled about 15 feet (about 4.5 meters) on this first leg of the fine search, turn and walk in the opposite direction.
4. After walking about 15 feet (4.5 meters), again adjust the orientation of the transceiver for maximum signal, reduce signal volume to the minimum, and head in the direction of the strongest signal.
5. After walking another 15 feet (4.5 meters), again adjust orientation and signal volume. Continue with a series of these 15-foot walks and signal adjustments, each time setting off toward the strongest signal. On each leg, signal volume should increase as you walk.

These repeated procedures are designed to lead the searcher progressively closer to an area very near the victim. Because transmissions from the victim's transceiver follow a curved path, searchers will be following a curved arc to the buried person. Searchers know they are near the person when signal volume fades rather than increasing as they walk—the signal will fade as searchers pass the victim's location. They are now very close to the victim and ready to move into a pinpoint search.

Pinpoint Search

With the transceiver close to the snow surface, begin to pinpoint the victim by moving the transceiver from side to side and front to back in a small crisscross. When the volume is set very low, a loud signal means the searcher is very close to the victim. If the transceiver can identify only a fairly large space—perhaps several feet across—mark the four corners of this area of maximum signal. Using an avalanche probe, very carefully probe to determine the exact location of the person and proceed with recovery (see below).

PROBING

The older formal probe searches for avalanche victims that were used before the advent of transceivers are not very effective because they take so much time, even for small areas. However, spot-probing is necessary for checking likely burial spots, especially the area identified by the pinpoint search with the rescue transceiver.

Probing is a slow and uncertain mechanical process, but it may be the only alternative if rescue transceivers fail to locate a victim or if the party is traveling without transceivers. Probe first at likely areas: near pieces of the victim's equipment, at the points of disappearance, and around trees and rocks. Probing in a group is a skill that must be practiced before it is needed. It is hard work involving discipline and concentration. In the backcountry, there may not be enough people to carry out formal probe procedures.

Commercial avalanche probes work far better than any other alternative. However, to find one buried victim, use whatever is at hand as a probe, including commercial avalanche probes, ski poles, ice axes, or wands.

If a climber's ski poles can be joined together to create an avalanche probe, test them to verify whether they really work. They may not. It may be difficult to remove the baskets, screw in the adapter piece, or assemble the parts. Furthermore, the poles may not be strong enough to penetrate hard avalanche debris. Remember, these poles are only a poor substitute for a commercial avalanche probe.

RECOVERY

After locating the victim using the pinpoint search, very carefully probe to determine the exact location of the victim. Take care to avoid injuring the victim with shovels or probes or otherwise endangering the person being rescued. Some victims report that the most terrifying part of their avalanche experience was having their air space trampled on as they were being rescued.

Probe in a spiral pattern around the point of highest signal intensity, moving in 10-inch (25-centimeter) increments out from where the distance was least (digital transceiver) or the signal was strongest (analog transceiver). Probe gently to avoid injuring the victim. As soon as the person is located, begin digging. Leave the probe pole in place to guide the digging.

Start shoveling on the downhill side, away from the victim at an approximate distance of one and a half times the estimated depth of the probe to the victim. Move snow downhill. Excavate either in steps or at an angle to the victim (fig. 16-47). Expect to work very hard: Snow in an avalanche undergoes a transition as it slides, and it sets up like concrete when it finally comes

Fig. 16-47. Digging out a fully buried avalanche victim, shoveling in steps on the downhill side away from the victim's estimated location.

to a stop and settles. The goal in any recovery effort is to first uncover the victim's face and chest to get an airway established.

As the victim is uncovered, check to see that the person's mouth is not filled with snow and that there are no other obvious obstructions to breathing. Clear snow away from the victim's chest to allow room for it to expand and take in air. Be prepared to start cardiopulmonary resuscitation (CPR); the person need not be fully extracted from the snow before CPR begins. Be aware that suddenly moving a burial victim may cause cardiac failure as cold blood from the extremities moves to the heart. Make the person as warm and comfortable as possible, and be prepared to treat for hypothermia and injuries (see Chapter 23, First Aid).

If the avalanche buried more than one person, remember to switch off the transceiver carried by the rescued individual so that its transmissions will not interfere with the ongoing search for other victims. Once it is determined that the rescued individual does not need urgent care, continue to search for the other buried victims.

SAFE SNOW TRAVEL

Snow is a constantly changing medium. Safe snow travel requires alertness, preparation, and a constant reassessment of conditions. Here are some points to remember:

- **Continually assess the stability of the snow.** What is the relative level of avalanche hazard? Start with pretrip research and continually reassess throughout the climb.
- **Practice safe travel techniques in avalanche-prone areas.** Always choose the safest path of travel and cross avalanche-prone slopes one person at a time.
- **When in avalanche terrain, carry the necessary rescue gear:** avalanche transceivers, probes, shovels, and first-aid kit.
- **Continually assess the runout and snow conditions.**
- **Do not rely on self-arrest if the runout is dangerous or unknown.** If climbers are uncomfortable using a self-belay, use a running belay or an anchored belay, or turn back and find another route.
- **Bring crampons on snow climbs,** even in warm weather. Crampons are not just for glacier travel. Climbers may encounter a shady couloir or slope with ice or hard snow.
- **Anchor the climbing party** if it has to adjust equipment such as crampons on an exposed slope.
- **Wear gloves whenever on snow,** even when the weather is warm and it would be more comfortable to take them off. A climber can fall at any time.
- **Yell "Falling!" whenever anyone, including you, falls.** Follow up with "Arrest! Arrest!" until the fallen climber has safely come to a stop.
- **Continually observe the party's overall condition and climbing ability.** Late in the day, exhaustion may diminish reaction time in the event of a fall.

GLACIERS AND CREVASSES • EQUIPMENT FOR GLACIER TRAVEL • FUNDAMENTALS OF GLACIER TRAVEL • CREVASSE RESCUE RESPONSE • INSIDE THE CREVASSE • RESCUE METHODS • SPECIAL RESCUE SITUATIONS • PATHS TO THE SUMMIT

Chapter 17
GLACIER TRAVEL AND CREVASSE RESCUE

Glaciers can offer a convenient route to alpine summits. However, glaciers hold many hazards. Glacier travelers should learn about crevasses—the chasms that split a glacier as its great mass of consolidated snow flows slowly downhill—and other glacier hazards. Although glacier travel is a specialized skill, it is very necessary to mountaineering; therefore, climbers must learn how to contend with crevasses.

To travel safely on a glacier, climbers first need all the basic snow travel skills outlined in Chapter 16, Snow Travel and Climbing. To that must be added the ability to detect and avoid crevasses and other glacier hazards. If climbers regard crevasses with a healthy respect, they may never fall into one. If a fall does occur, it is imperative that climbers know the techniques that provide the best chance of safe recovery and escape from a crevasse. Before stepping onto a glacier, climbers must have a clear appreciation of the dangers as well as confidence in their ability to deal with those dangers.

GLACIERS AND CREVASSES

Glaciers constantly change as snow supply and temperature influence their advance and retreat. In classic form, glaciers are like a frozen river creeping down a mountain (as shown in Figure 17-1), yet they differ from a river in many ways. Some glaciers are small, relatively stagnant pockets of frozen snow. Others are ice fields of immense proportions, full of teetering forms and dramatic releases of ice. (See Chapter 26, The Cycle of Snow, for information on the formation of glaciers.)

Glacial flow patterns can be very complex, but a

Fig. 17-1. Aerial view of a glacier showing principal features.

typical mountain glacier may flow between 150 and 1,300 feet (roughly 45 to 400 meters) per year. Most glaciers flow faster in the warmth of summer than in winter because they are lubricated by increased meltwater. Glacial flow breaks the surface of the ice into those elemental mountaineering obstacles known as crevasses.

Crevasses often form where the angle of the slope increases significantly, putting tension on the snow and ice, which then split open (fig. 17-1e). Crevasses also commonly form where a glacier makes a turn, with the outside edge usually crevassing more (fig. 17-1f); where the distance between valley walls either narrows or expands; or where two glaciers meet. Crevasses may also develop around a bedrock feature that obstructs the glacial flow, such as a rock formation protruding through the ice—a *nunatak* (fig. 17-1d). At the point where a moving glacier breaks away from the permanent snow or ice cap above, the large crevasse called a bergschrund is formed (fig. 17-1b). The middle of a glacier tends to have fewer crevasses than the sides, and a gently sloping glacier usually has fewer crevasses than a steep, fast-moving one.

Crevasses are most dangerous in the accumulation zone (Figure 17-1h), that portion of a glacier that receives more snow every year than it loses to melting. Here, crevasses (Figure 17-2a and b) are frequently covered with snow bridges that may be too weak to support a climber. Below the accumulation zone is the area of the glacier where annual melting matches or exceeds the yearly snowfall. Between the two zones is

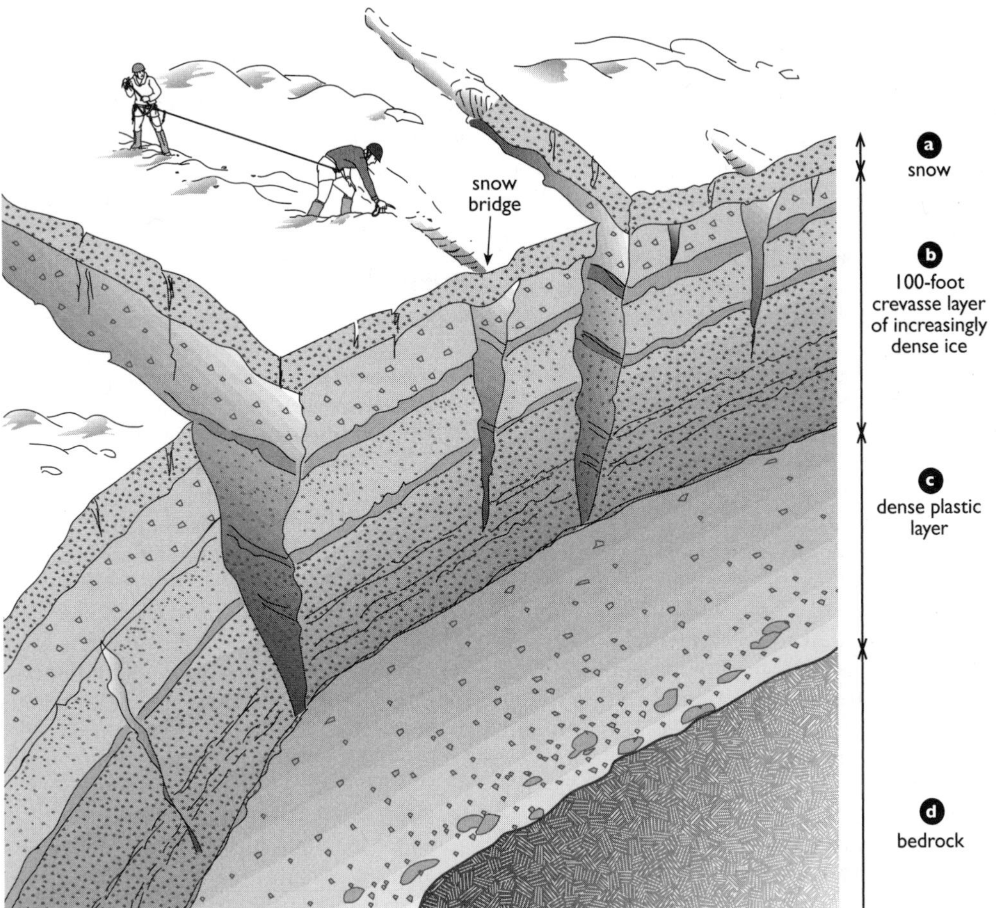

Fig. 17-2. Crevasse formation: a and b, crevasses open up in the upper snow and ice layers as glacier angle increases; c, denser lower area moves without splitting; d, bedrock.

17

the firn line, also known as the névé line (fig. 17-1c), both words for "old snow."

The deeper layers of a glacier, denser and more plastic than the upper section, can move and deform without cracking (Figure 17-2c). If this deeper, older ice becomes exposed, the glacier takes on a folded, seamless appearance, often without any true open crevasses. Travel on such a glacier can be relatively simple and safe. These glaciers are usually fairly flat, with narrow, shallow crevasses that are not difficult to cross.

OTHER COMMON GLACIER HAZARDS

Ice avalanches. Ice avalanches can pour from the steep, jumbled glacial sections known as icefalls (see Figure 16-40h in Chapter 16, Snow Travel and Climbing) when seracs (towers of ice) come crashing down (see Figure 16-40f and g). The inexorable movement of a glacier means that ice avalanches can occur anytime; their activity is only partly related to season, temperature, or snowfall. Serac collapse does seem to happen frequently during the day when the temperature rises above freezing and at night when it drops below freezing. Travel through these areas should be prudently swift if it cannot be avoided.

Moats. Big gaps that appear when winter snows melt back from a rock face, called moats (fig. 17-1a), can present major barriers to glacier travelers who need to regain the rock in order to stay on route. Belayed mountaineers may be able to cross a snow bridge over a moat or climb into the moat and back up onto the rock on the other side.

Glacial moraines. Mounds of rocky debris carried and then deposited by the glacier, called glacial moraines (fig. 17-1i, j, k, n, and o), make rugged venues indeed for mountain travel, impeding efficient movement by a climbing party. Moraines are typically steep-sided, narrow ridges with partly buried boulders ready to dislodge at the slightest touch. The moraine surface is often as hard as cement. As climbers approach the fringe where the glacier begins, there may be a soupy mix of ice and moraine gravel, or rocks skating around like ball bearings on hard ice.

Meltwater. The runoff flowing from a glacier (fig. 17-1m) can be a chilling challenge to cross. During warm weather, consider waiting to cross until the cooler hours of the next morning, when flow should be at its lowest. (See Chapter 6, Wilderness Travel, for more advice on crossing rivers.)

Whiteouts. In a whiteout on a glacier, sky and snow merge into a seamless blend of white—with no apparent up or down, east or west—taxing routefinding skills to the utmost. Climbers can defend against a whiteout by taking such precautions as placing route-marking wands and noting compass bearings and altimeter readings during the ascent—even when it looks as though clear weather will prevail. If snow or clouds close in and leave the climbing party in a whiteout, these simple precautions will pay off on the descent.

Rockfall. Glaciers are subject to rockfall from bordering walls and ridges. For glacier climbs, whatever the season, the general rule is "early on and early off." The nighttime cold freezes rock in place and prevents most rockfall, whereas direct sun melts the bonds. The greatest hazard comes in the late morning, when sun melts the ice, and in the evening, when meltwater expands as it refreezes, breaking rocks loose.

EQUIPMENT FOR GLACIER TRAVEL

Take a look at climbing gear with glaciers and crevasses in mind. Here are some considerations in getting ready for glacier travel.

ROPES

Ropes with "dry" treatment, although more expensive, absorb much less water from melting snow and pick up less grit from a glacier. This makes them lighter and easier to work with following an overnight freeze. The type of rope needed depends on the glacier.

For general glacier use, a single 8.5- to 9-millimeter rope will handle crevasse falls and reduce pack weight. A 9-millimeter rope that is 50 meters (165 feet) long weighs only two-thirds as much as an 11-millimeter rope—about 6 pounds (2.7 kilograms) compared to about 9 pounds (4 kilograms). The lighter, thinner rope is more than adequate for general glacier use, because crevasse falls put a relatively gradual impact on the rope due to rope friction on the snow and over the lip of the crevasse.

Steep technical climbing, however, which has the possibility of severe leader falls, requires a standard 10- to 11-millimeter climbing rope or two smaller ropes used in the double-rope or twin-rope technique (see Chapter 14, Leading on Rock).

A rope team traveling alone should also carry a lightweight 100-foot (30-meter) accessory line as a precaution for rescue situations.

HARNESSES

For glacier travel, be sure the waist belt and leg loops of the seat harness can adjust to fit over several layers of cold-weather clothing. Glacier travelers also wear a chest harness, which can be made from a piece of 1-inch (2.5-centimeter) webbing. Commercial full-body harnesses, which are more expensive, heavy, and cumbersome, are not commonly used. See "Harnesses" in Chapter 9, Basic Safety System.

ICE AX AND CRAMPONS

An ice ax and crampons are as important for safe glacier travel as they are for travel on any firm, sloped surface of snow or ice. The ice ax aids with balance and provides a means for self-belay and self-arrest. If a rope mate drops into a crevasse, other climbers on the rope use their ice axes to go into self-arrest, controlling and stopping the fall. Choose an ice ax with a uniform taper from the spike to the shaft, because a blunt spike or jutting ferrule (metal cap or ring on the shaft) makes it hard to feel the snow when climbers are probing for crevasses.

Crampons provide secure footing and enable efficient travel on refrozen snow, which is typically very hard in the early morning. A word of warning about using crampons for descending steep glacial terrain: A number of accidents and falls have resulted from crampon points getting caught on climbers' clothing, gaiters, or gear hanging low from gear loops. It is important to develop good habits of foot placement and to avoid having anything hang below thigh level (see the "Crampon Safety Rules" sidebar in Chapter 16, Snow Travel and Climbing).

ASCENDERS

Climbers traveling on glaciers also carry prusik slings, aiders, and/or ascenders, depending on the route.

Prusik Slings

For personal safety, one of the most important pieces of gear a glacier traveler can carry is a set of prusik slings for ascending the rope after a crevasse fall. The slings are two loops of 5- to 7-millimeter Perlon accessory cord attached to the climbing rope with friction hitches. When a climber puts weight on a prusik sling, the hitch grips the rope firmly; when the climber's weight is removed, the hitch can be loosened and moved up or down the rope.

Figure 17-3 shows details on how to make the Texas prusik slings, using 6-millimeter accessory cord. As with all prusik systems, sizing the slings correctly for each individual's height is critical (see Table 17-1). Figure 17-4 shows a way to approximately gauge the correct sizing. When a climber is standing in the sling (as shown in Figure 17-20c in "The Texas Prusik," later in this chapter), the top of the foot sling (fig. 17-4a) should be at about waist level and the top of the seat-harness sling (fig. 17-4b) should be at about eye level. The distance between the two friction hitches is the distance that the climber will move up for each movement cycle made using the Texas prusik.

Before taking the slings out onto a glacier, check their sizing at home. Dangle in the slings from a rope thrown over a garage rafter or a tree limb to find out what adjustments are needed in the sling lengths.

The two slings are commonly attached to the rope with prusik hitches. Some climbers prefer the bachmann friction hitch because it incorporates a carabiner, which makes a good handle to use while loosening and sliding the slings because it can be gripped easily with a gloved hand. If webbing must be used rather than accessory cord, the klemheist is the best friction hitch to use. (See "Knots, Bends, and Hitches" in Chapter 9, Basic Safety System.)

Etriers (Aiders)

Some climbers attach etriers (also called aiders) rather than conventional slings. The steps in these webbing ladders can help a person climb up and over a crevasse lip if the rope is entrenched in the snow. (See "Etriers" in Chapter 15, Aid and Big Wall Climbing.)

Mechanical Ascenders

Some glacier travelers carry mechanical ascenders, which attach to the rope more easily than friction

TABLE 17-1. SIZING PRUSIK SLINGS

Climber's Height	Foot Sling Length	Seat-Harness Sling Length
5 feet (1.5 meters)	11 feet (3.4 meters)	5 feet (1.5 meters)
5 feet 6 inches (1.7 meters)	11 feet 6 inches (3.5 meters)	5 feet 6 inches (1.7 meters)
6 feet (1.8 meters)	12 feet (3.6 meters)	6 feet (1.8 meters)
6 feet 6 inches (2 meters)	13 feet (3.9 meters)	6 feet 6 inches (2 meters)

17

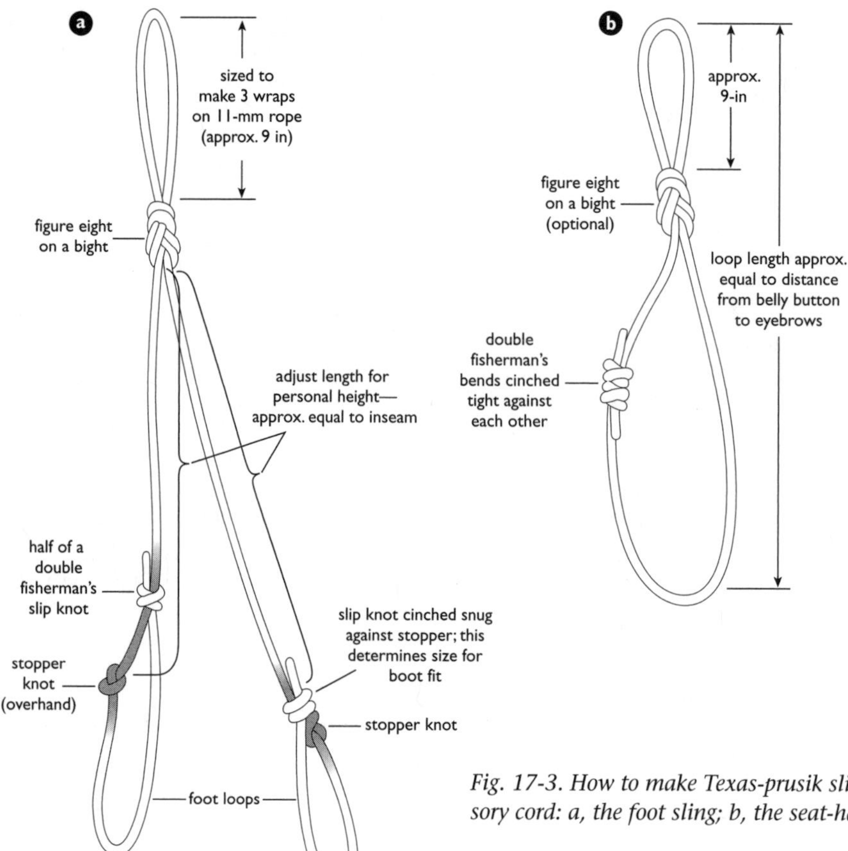

Fig. 17-3. How to make Texas-prusik slings using accessory cord: a, the foot sling; b, the seat-harness sling.

knots. On icy ropes, the ascenders work better and can be operated more readily with gloved hands. A disadvantage is that ascenders traditionally have been heavy and expensive, though a number of cheaper, lightweight devices are now available. Titanium models (made by Ushba) have smooth, rather than toothed, cams. These ascenders grip the rope by pure camming action, and so they may be safer to use in situations wherein high fall forces may occur, such as in a crevasse fall. (See "Mechanical Ascenders" in Chapter 15, Aid and Big Wall Climbing.)

OTHER STANDARD GLACIER GEAR

Often each climbing party carries a shovel, which is useful in flattening camping places and in rescue situations. Each party member should also carry the following gear:

Rescue pulley. Many models of pulley have been designed for use in climbing. Pulleys for use in rescue hauling systems should be compatible with a friction hitch (that is, the pulley should not get jammed when used with a prusik or bachmann hitch). If no pulley is available, a carabiner can be used in the rescue hauling system, but it adds considerable friction.

Anchor. If conditions warrant, carry a snow or ice anchor such as a snow picket, a snow fluke, or an ice screw. (See "Snow Anchors" in Chapter 16, Snow Travel and Climbing, and "Ice Screws" in Chapter 18, Alpine Ice Climbing.)

Runners. Bring at least two single-length and one double-length runner for attaching to anchors. Tied runners, rather than sewn runners, work better for crevasse rescue, because their length can be more easily adjusted.

Belay device. See "Using Belay Devices" in Chapter 10, Belaying.

Carabiners. Carry one locking carabiner and at least four regular carabiners.

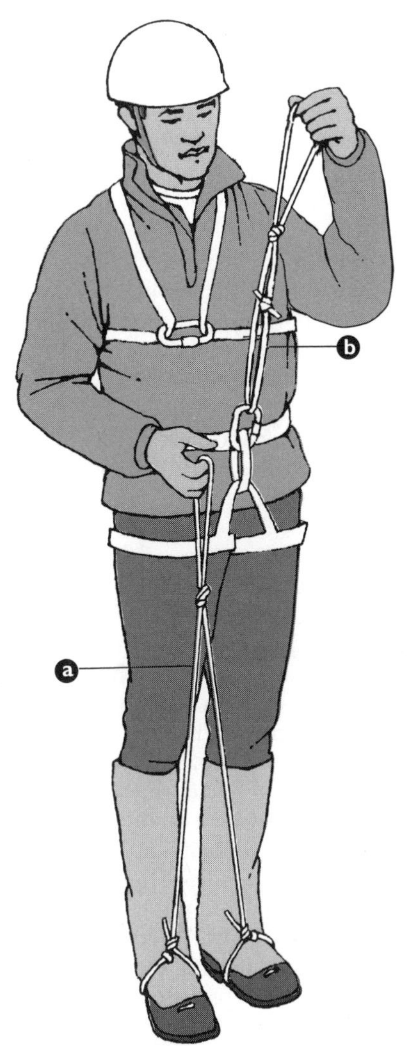

Fig. 17-4. Texas prusik dimensions: a, foot sling should extend from boots to belly button; b, seat-harness sling should extend from belly button to eyebrows.

CLOTHING

To be ready for a fall into a crevasse, climbers need to dress for the frigid interior of the glacier even when it is a hot day on top. Priorities collide here, because climbers are preparing for the cold but at the same time trying to minimize sweating and to keep well hydrated.

Select outer garments that can be ventilated easily, such as pants with side zippers and a wind parka with armpit zippers. Zip these closed if you end up in a crevasse. Consider strapping a jacket to the outside of the pack, where it can be easily reached. Stash a hat and gloves in the pockets.

On a warm day, the insulating layer will be a climber's outer layer. For the layer next to the skin, wear light-colored garments that may reflect the heat of the sun but still provide warmth if you end up inside a crevasse. To thwart the cold dampness in a crevasse, wear a synthetic-fiber shirt and long-underwear bottoms for optimal comfort over a wide range of temperatures.

SKIS AND SNOWSHOES

Skis or snowshoes are essential for winter or arctic mountaineering because they distribute climbers' weight over a larger area, thus keeping them from sinking too deeply into the snow. Skis or snowshoes also reduce the chance of breaking through snow bridges over hidden crevasses, which is helpful on some glacier climbs. Snowshoes are usually more practical than skis for roped glacier travel unless all members of the rope team are highly skilled skiers (for further information on ski mountaineering, see Appendix D, Supplementary Resources).

WANDS

Wands mark the location of crevasses, identify turning points, and show the climbing route in case a whiteout occurs on the return (see "Wands" in Chapter 16, Snow Travel and Climbing). Space between wands should be a distance equal to the total length of the climbing party when roped and moving in single file. A party of nine (three rope teams) will use 10 to 12 wands for each mile (1.6 kilometers) of glacier walking; smaller teams will need more.

FUNDAMENTALS OF GLACIER TRAVEL

Climbers need to be moving well before the sun rises and begins weakening snow bridges and loosening avalanche slopes. For glacier climbs, climbers grow to appreciate alpine starts: the brilliance of stars at higher altitudes, perhaps the glow of moonlight on snow, the distinctive sounds of crampons on ice, the tinkling of carabiners in the still night. Sometimes the climbing party is alone on the glacier; other times, distant trains of lights show that other parties are also on the route. The magic of watching a sunrise from high on a mountain above a sea of clouds remains with a climber long after memories of the trip's exertion have faded.

USING THE ROPE

The first rule of safe glacier travel is very simple: Rope up. This rule holds whether or not climbers are familiar with the glacier and whether or not they believe they can see and avoid all of its crevasses. Roping up is especially important in areas above the firn line, where every year the glacier gets more snow than it loses to melting, making it likely that snow covers some crevasses.

It is tempting to walk unroped onto a glacier that looks like a benign snowfield, especially if climbers have gone up similar routes time after time without mishap. Avoid the temptation. Like wearing a seat belt in a car, taking the extra time and trouble to deal with the rope greatly increases a climber's chances of surviving the most likely accident on a glacier: falling into a crevasse. Some climbers travel unroped on certain glaciers in the area below the firn line if crevasses are stable and easily seen, but this kind of unroped travel is best left to people with a great deal of glacier travel experience.

On bare ice, as in the late season, it is dangerous to rope up, because crevasse falls are almost impossible to arrest on hard ice, and likely consequences are broken ankles and more climbers in crevasses. However, consider the conditions and determine if using a running belay would be prudent (see "Running Belays" in Chapter 16, Snow Travel and Climbing).

Rope Teams

Rope teams of three climbers each are ideal for travel on glaciers where no technical climbing will be encountered. With a rope team of three, two people are available to arrest a rope mate's fall into a crevasse. A minimum party size of two rope teams is recommended so that a team involved in an accident will have backup help. In some instances, a party of four may climb on a single rope; for example, if one of the climbers may not be able to arrest a crevasse fall, or if just one of the party is experienced in crevasse rescue.

Glacier travelers usually put three people on a 37-meter (120-foot) rope, and three or four people on a 50- or 60-meter (165- to 200-foot) rope. These configurations space the climbers far enough apart so that as the rope team crosses a typical crevasse, only one person at a time is at risk. Where there are truly humongous crevasses—in the Himalaya or the Alaska Range, for example—greater spacing may be necessary.

On technical glacier terrain—with slopes steeper than 40 degrees or with severe crevassing—belaying may be necessary, making it more efficient to travel in two-person rope teams. In this situation, having a second rope team as rescue backup becomes even more important. While the person who is on the same rope as the fallen climber holds the rope fast, the second team can set up a snow anchor and initiate the rescue (see "Crevasse Rescue Response" later in this chapter).

Tying In

It is best to tie the rope directly in to the tie-in loops on the seat harness—rather than tying a butterfly knot or a figure eight on a bight in the rope, and clipping the loop in to a locking carabiner at the harness—because the direct tie-in does not require using a carabiner (a potential weak link) to connect climber and rope. Of course, a clip-in connection makes it easy to disconnect and reconnect to the rope, but this is not normally done repeatedly over the course of a day on a glacier. Following are some general glacier tie-in procedures, depending on the size of the rope team.

Three-person rope. The standard size for a rope team on a nontechnical glacier is three people. Two of the climbers tie in at the very ends of the rope, usually with a rewoven figure eight through the tie-in loops of their seat harnesses (fig. 17-5). The middle climber ties in to the very center of the rope, most commonly with a double bowline knot (fig. 17-6a). The small loop that remains at the end of the bowline should be clipped to the harness with a carabiner to ensure that the knot cannot come untied. A butterfly knot is also useful as the middle-person tie-in (fig. 17-6b); it has the advantage of being easier to untie after having been weighted, but as noted above, it adds a carabiner to the tie-in. Use a dedicated locking carabiner to clip it to the harness' tie-in loop, separate from the carabiner for the seat-harness sling (because the butterfly knot would be loaded with a fallen climber's weight, if the harness sling is on the same carabiner, it could be difficult to remove the sling should it need to be moved to the other rope strand).

Four-person rope. Divide the rope into thirds. Two climbers tie in at the ends, as just described above; the other two tie in at the one-third points, as just described above.

Two-person rope. Although a three-person rope is the standard for glacier travel, sometimes it is more efficient to have rope teams of only two climbers—for instance, on technical glacier terrain where belaying may be necessary. The most convenient procedure is to have only a portion of the rope stretched between

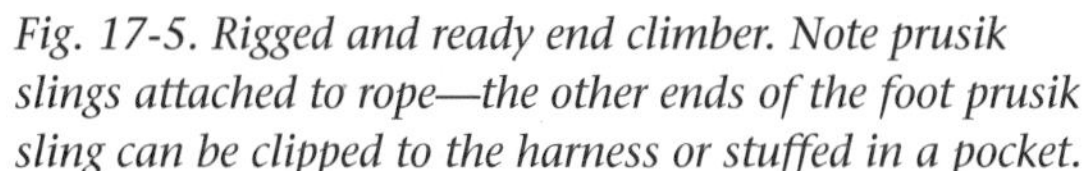
Fig. 17-5. Rigged and ready end climber. Note prusik slings attached to rope—the other ends of the foot prusik sling can be clipped to the harness or stuffed in a pocket.

Fig. 17-6. Rigged and ready middle climber: a, double bowline and locking carabiner; b, butterfly knot and two locking carabiners (one for the butterfly knot, the other for the seat-harness sling).

the climbers, because a full rope length can have too much slack as the climbers weave through a maze of crevasses. Using only part of the rope also leaves some rope free for rescue use. The adapted Kiwi coil system is the preferred method for tying in to a shortened rope. This is illustrated and explained in "Special Rescue Situations" later in this chapter.

Chest Harness

Put the chest harness on over the layer of clothing next to your skin before heading out onto the glacier. Whether the rope is clipped through the chest harness at this point depends on the situation. In expedition travel when climbers are carrying heavy packs, clipping the chest harness will help them stay upright in case of a fall; not clipping the chest harness may make it very difficult to regain an upright stance inside a crevasse. Traveling with the chest harness clipped to the rope hampers the ability to perform self-arrest in case of a teammate's fall, though, because the tension on the rope comes high on a climber's body.

Here is a good compromise: Clip the climbing rope in to the chest harness any time you cross a snow bridge or otherwise face obvious immediate danger of a crevasse fall; otherwise, travel with the chest harness unclipped (as shown in Figures 17-5 and 17-6).

Prusik Slings

Attach prusik slings to the climbing rope immediately after roping up to begin glacier travel, so that the slings are ready for use in an emergency (see Figure 17-5). The middle person on the rope will not know which end of the rope might have to be climbed after a fall; therefore, the middle climber should attach one prusik to the section of rope that goes to the climber in front and the other prusik to the section that goes to the climber behind (see Figure 17-6). After any fall, only one of the prusik slings will have to be moved to the side of the rope that must be climbed. Regardless of how the prusik slings are attached, stuff both foot loops into pockets, so they are ready to be pulled out and slipped onto the feet when needed, or clip them to the seat harness.

If using mechanical ascenders, do not attach them to the rope until after a crevasse fall; if an ascender receives a shock load, it can damage the rope.

Some climbers girth-hitch a sling and carabiner to their pack haul loop and clip them to a shoulder strap, so that if they fall into a crevasse, the pack is easier to secure and take off. This also makes it easier to anchor a pack on steep sections of the glacier.

Rope Management

No slack. The first rule of rope management on a glacier is to keep the rope extended—not taut, but without undue slack. A rope that is fully extended between climbers is insurance against a long plunge into a hidden crevasse. Increasing slack in the climbing rope puts additional force on the next climber (because the first climber is falling deeper in the crevasse), making it more and more difficult to arrest promptly. The falling climber therefore drops farther, increasing the chance of hitting something or becoming wedged if the crevasse narrows. For the climber(s) holding the fall, a slack rope can also pose the danger of causing them to be dragged into the hole too.

To keep slack out of the rope, a rope leader needs to set a pace the others can follow for a long time. For their part, the second and third climbers must try to closely match the pace of the leader so the rope stays extended. Be alert going downhill, when it becomes easy to walk too fast.

At sharp turns, the rope tends to go slack when the climber in front of you heads in a new direction and then tightens when you near the turn yourself. Throughout the turn, adjust your pace to keep the slack out of the rope. At sharp turns, it is usually necessary to make new tracks, outside the leader's footsteps, in order to keep the rope fully extended (although at other times, second and third climbers normally follow the leader's path for safety and ease of travel).

To keep the right amount of tension in the rope, travel with a small loop of the climbing rope 6 to 12 inches (15 to 30 centimeters) long, held in the downhill hand. Gripping this makes it easier to feel the progress of rope mates and adjust your pace as needed. Keeping the rope on the downhill side of a glacier keeps the rope out from under your feet and helps avoid entangling the rope in crampons.

Do not forget safety when reaching a rest stop or campsite. Always belay climbers into and out of all rest and camp areas. The rope must stay extended and slack free until the area has been thoroughly probed for crevasses. If a party must camp on a glacier, probe and then mark the boundaries of the safe area with wands.

Right angle to crevasses. The second important rule of rope management on a glacier is to run the rope at right angles to a crevasse whenever possible. A rope team that travels more or less parallel to a crevasse is risking a lengthy pendulum fall for a climber who falls in (fig. 17-7). Although it is not always possible to keep the rope at right angles to a crevasse, keeping this in mind helps climbers choose the best possible route (fig. 17-8).

DETECTING CREVASSES

The first step in safe glacier travel is figuring out where the crevasses are and picking a route through them. On many glaciers, routefinding is part planning, part experience, and part luck. See the "Tips for Detecting Crevasses" sidebar.

Sometimes climbers can get a head start on planning by studying photographs of the glacier before the trip, because some crevasse patterns remain fairly constant from year to year. Seek out recent reports from parties who have visited the area, though in summer, reports older than a week are generally not too helpful, due to melting.

On the approach hike, try to get a good up-valley or cross-valley look at the glacier before it is reached. Climbers may see an obvious route that would be impossible to discover once they are there. Make notes or sketches to help remember major crevasses, landmarks, and routes.

Though looking at guidebook photographs and getting distant views of a glacier are useful, prepare to be surprised when you actually get there. What appeared to be small cracks may be gaping chasms, and major crevasses may not have been visible from your angle of view. Plan alternative routes.

Once the climbing party is on the glacier, they play a continuous game of "Find the Crevasse." Just because a crevasse cannot be seen does not mean it is not there. After setting up base camp, have an advance party spend a little time scouting out the first portion of the

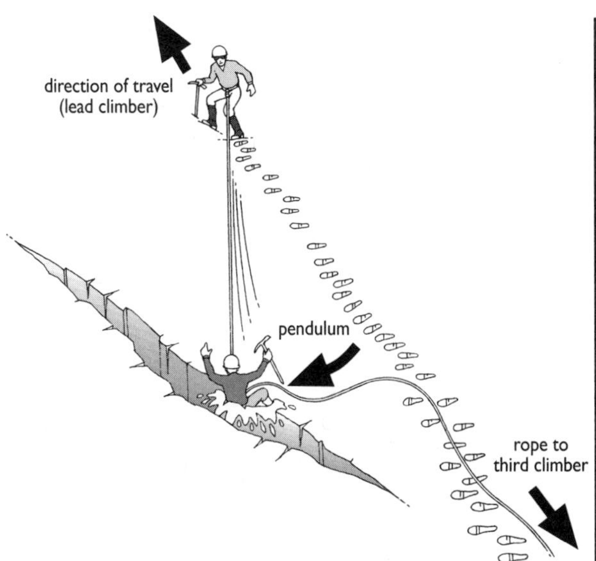

Fig. 17-7. Where rope runs more or less parallel to crevasse, a fall is worsened by pendulum.

route in daylight; this can sometimes save many hours of predawn routefinding.

Snow Probing

Snow probing is the technique to use if a suspicious-looking area has been found and the party wants to search it for crevasses. If a probe locates a crevasse, continue probing in all directions around this area to find the crevasse's true lip.

Probe with the ice ax, thrusting the shaft into the snow a couple of feet ahead. Keep the ax perpendicular to the slope and thrust it in with a smooth motion. If resistance to the thrust is uniform, the snow is consistent to at least the depth of the ax. If resistance lessens abruptly, you have probably found a hole. If the route must continue in the direction of this hole, use further ax thrusts to establish the extent of the hole. The leader should open up the hole and mark it with wands.

The value of probing depends on climbers' skill and experience at interpreting the changes they feel in the snow layers. An inexperienced prober may think the shaft has broken through into a hole when all it has done is hit a softer layer of snow.

The ice ax is a limited probe because it is relatively short. The lead climber can also use a ski pole (with the basket removed), which is lighter, longer, and thinner than an ax, for easier, deeper probes.

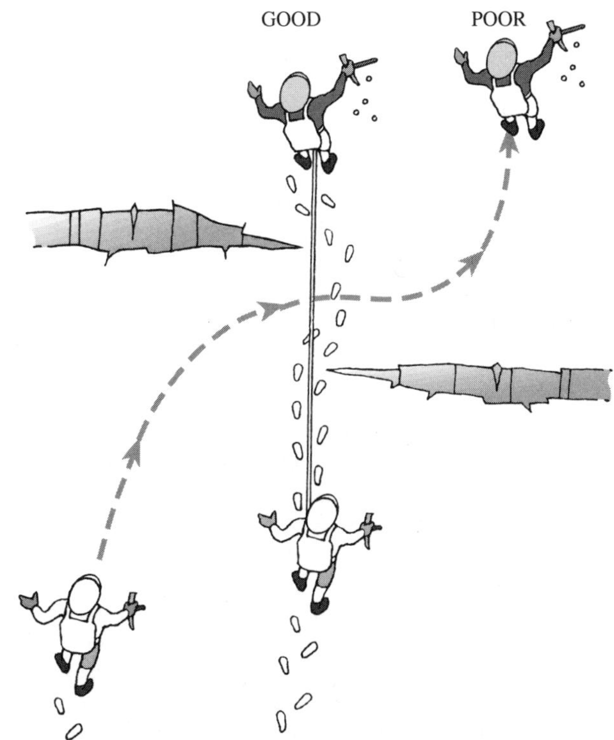

Fig. 17-8. Be aware of your rope partner's position in order to keep the rope as perpendicular to crevasses as possible.

17

CROSSING A CREVASSE FIELD

Climbers have a number of ways to get safely across a field of crevasses. The techniques described here are typical, but they will have to be adapted as needed in the field. Routefinding on a glacier involves finding a path around or over all the visible crevasses, guarding all the time against hidden crevasses. The crossing is seldom without its detours as climbers carefully pick their way over the glacier.

The End Run

Crossing directly over a crevasse is rarely a preferred choice. Where a crevasse narrows in width, often near its end, the safest and most dependable technique is to go around it, in an end run. A 0.25-mile (600-meter) walk may gain the rope team only 20 or 30 feet (7 to 10 meters) of forward progress, but it is often better than a direct confrontation with the crevasse. In late summer, when the winter snow has melted down to the ice, it may be possible to see the true end of the crevasse, but

TIPS FOR DETECTING CREVASSES

- **Keep an eye out for sagging trenches in the snow** that mark where gravity has pulled down on snow over a crevasse's opening. This is a prime characteristic of a hidden crevasse. The sags are visible by their slight difference in sheen, texture, or color. The low-angle light of early morning and late afternoon tends to accentuate this feature. (The sags may be impossible to detect in the flat light of a fog or in the glare of the midafternoon sun, and it takes additional information to distinguish them from certain wind-created forms.)
- **Be wary after storms.** New snow can fill a sagging trench and make it blend into the surrounding surface. (At other times, however, the new snow can actually make the sagging trench more apparent by creating a hollow of new snow that contrasts with surrounding areas of old snow.)
- **Be especially alert in areas where crevasses are known to form**—for example, where a glacier makes an outside turn or where slope angle increases.
- **Regularly sweep your eyes to the sides of the route to check for open cracks to the left or right.** Cracks could hint at crevasses that extend beneath your path.
- **Remember that where there is one crevasse, there are often many.**

Fig. 17-9. End run around a crevasse, keeping the rope fully extended by not following in the leader's footsteps.

if seasonal snows still blanket the glacier, the visible end of the crack may not be its true end. Make a wide swing around the corner, probing carefully (fig. 17-9). Look closely at adjacent crevasses to judge whether one of them could be an extension of your crevasse; you might actually be crossing a snow bridge.

Snow Bridges

If an end run is impractical, the next choice is to cross a crevasse on a snow bridge. Deep winter snow hardened by wind can create a crevasse bridge that lasts into the summer climbing season. Other, sturdier bridges are actually thin isthmuses between two crevasses, with foundations that extend deep into the body of the glacier.

Study a snow bridge carefully—try for a side view—before putting any faith in it. If in doubt, the leader can approach it to probe and get a close-up look while the second climber stays braced against the taut rope to help guard against possibly breaking through, being prepared to drop into self-arrest if needed (fig. 17-10). After the leader gets across, the rest of the party follows exactly in the leader's steps, also receiving a degree of protection from a taut rope held by a braced climber.

A snow bridge's strength varies tremendously with temperature. A bridge that might support a truck in the cold of winter or early morning may collapse under its own weight during an afternoon thaw. Use caution every time you cross a snow bridge. Do not assume that a bridge that held in the morning during the ascent will still be safe during the descent in the afternoon. In cases of dubious snow bridges, setting up a belay may save having to execute a time-consuming crevasse rescue.

Jumping

Jumping is one of the least-common tactics for crossing a crevasse (fig. 17-11). Most jumps across crevasses are short, simple leaps. Before planning a desperate lunge, be sure you have ruled out all the alternatives and see that you are well belayed.

While well supported by a taut rope or by a belay, probe to find the true edge of the crevasse. If a running start is needed for the jump, tramp down the snow for better footing. Put on a parka, mittens, and hat; check prusiks and harness; and spool out the amount of rope slack needed from the belayer. Then jump—with your ice ax in the self-arrest position, ready to help you claw over the edge if you fall shy of a clean landing on the other side.

Once the leader is safely on the other side, the rope is now linked to the landing side, so the other climbers have a less-dangerous jump ahead: The belay rope can help pull up any jumper who falls just short of the target.

Use caution and common sense if the leap is from the high lip of a crevasse over to a lower side. (Bergschrunds, for example, often have an overhanging high wall on the uphill side.) Injuries are possible in a long, hard leap. If such a leap must be made, keep feet slightly apart for balance, knees bent to absorb shock, and ice ax held ready for a quick self-arrest. Beware of getting crampons caught on gaiters.

Fig. 17-11. Jumping a crevasse (belay not shown).

Fig. 17-10. Crossing a snow bridge with caution.

Into the Crevasse

On rare occasions, it may be practical to get to the other side of a shallow crevasse by climbing down into the crevasse, crossing it at the bottom, and climbing up on the other side. This tactic should be attempted only by a strong, highly trained, well-equipped party that is ready to provide a good belay. One further caution: Often what appears to be a solid bottom is not; if the crevasse bottom collapses and leaves a climber hanging, the party must be able to provide assistance.

Echelon Formation

Certain crevasse patterns preclude the rule of keeping the rope at right angles to the crevasses. If the route demands travel that is parallel to crevasses, it sometimes helps to use the echelon formation: climbers somewhat to the side of and behind the leader, as in a series of stair steps (fig. 17-12). This formation is safest on stable, heavily crevassed glaciers on which the location of crevasses is known and the risk of hidden holes is small. The formation offers an alternative to following in the leader's footsteps through a maze of crevasses where single-file travel is impractical. Avoid moving in echelon formation where hidden crevasses are likely.

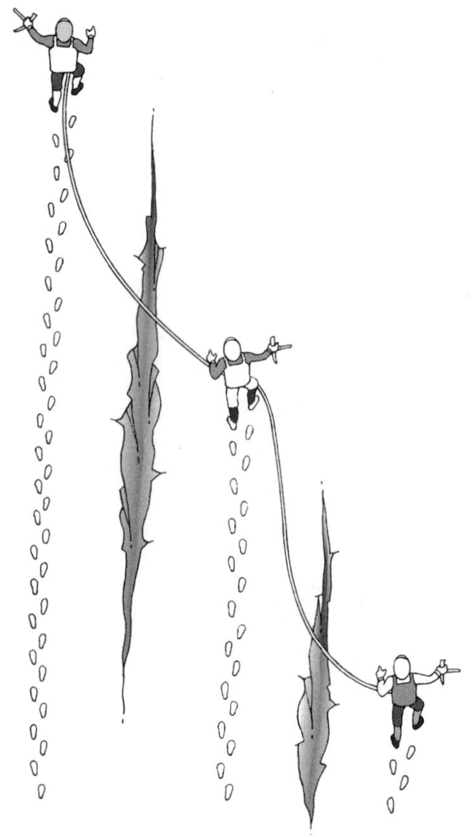

Fig. 17-12. Echelon formation, with a rope team in a stair-step–like position.

CREVASSE RESCUE RESPONSE

The depths of a great crevasse exhibit an awful beauty, both enticing and repellent. On a fine day, the walls are a sheen of soft blue ice in the filtered light from high above, and the cavern is cool and still as a church—or a tomb. It is a place every climber should visit occasionally—for crevasse rescue practice. But if you end up in a crevasse at another time, hopefully it will be in the company of climbers who know the rescue techniques described in this section. See the "Crevasse Rescue Safety Precautions" sidebar.

It is typically the first person on the rope who falls in when a rope team crosses a hidden crevasse. Here is the scene: You are the middle person on a three-person rope team traveling up a moderately angled glacier. The leader walking 50 feet (15 meters) in front of you suddenly disappears beneath the snow. What do you do? (A middle-climber fall is discussed in "Special Rescue Situations," later in this chapter.)

Stop the fall immediately! Drop into self-arrest (facing away from the direction of pull) and hold the fall. The other rope partner (the end climber) will do the same thing. (Chapter 16, Snow Travel and Climbing, has details on ice ax self-arrest.)

Once the fall is stopped (fig. 17-13), the critical steps in crevasse rescue begin. Learning these procedures well requires training in the field, augmented with annual practice. The principal steps in a successful crevasse rescue, beginning the instant the fall is stopped, are listed briefly here and discussed in detail in the sections that follow. (The more-involved seven steps in accident response are discussed in Chapters 23, First Aid, and 24, Alpine Search and Rescue.)

Step 1. Set up a secure anchor system.

Step 2. Communicate with the fallen climber.

Step 3. Devise a rescue plan. There are two basic choices:

Option 1. Self-rescue—the fallen climber ascends the rope with prusik slings.

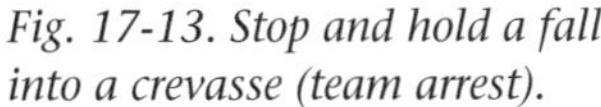

Fig. 17-13. Stop and hold a fall into a crevasse (team arrest).

- ***Option 2.*** Team rescue—team members use a hauling system to pull the climber out.

Step 4. Carry out the plan:

- ***Option 1.*** For a self-rescue, assist the fallen climber as needed.
- ***Option 2.*** For a team rescue, set up the chosen hauling system, then haul the climber out.

STEP 1: SET UP A SECURE ANCHOR SYSTEM

The goal in the first step is to anchor the climber in the crevasse and allow the rescuers safe access to communicate with the fallen climber.

The Initial Anchor

The end climber has responsibility for setting up the initial secure anchor. To free up the end climber, the middle climber on the three-person rope team stays in self-arrest to support the weight of the fallen climber, usually an easy task because rope friction across the snow does much of the work.

The end climber slowly gets out of self-arrest, making sure the middle climber can hold the weight alone, and then sets to work establishing an anchor (fig. 17-14). Of course, if another trained rope team is on hand, it is all right for both climbers to stay in self-arrest while the other team sets up the initial anchor.

In snow, a picket is often a good choice for the initial anchor because it can be placed quickly; failing that, an ice ax may also be used. (See "Snow Anchors" in Chapter 16, Snow Travel and Climbing.) Place the anchor 5 to 10 feet (1.5 to 3 meters) down-rope from the middle climber, toward the lip of the crevasse, and angled back 20 degrees from vertical, away from the victim. (If the anchor is placed instead up-rope from the middle climber, tension on the rope that eventually builds up could make it impossible for that person to untie.)

Attaching the Rope to the Anchor

The person who has set up the anchor now attaches a short sling to the climbing rope with a prusik hitch; a bachmann friction hitch may also be used (see "Knots, Bends, and Hitches" in Chapter 9, Basic Safety System). This person then attaches a runner to the sling with a carabiner and then clips the other end of the runner to the anchor with a locking carabiner (see Figure 17-14).

CREVASSE RESCUE SAFETY PRECAUTIONS

While working to rescue a fallen climber, observe these primary safety considerations:

- All anchor systems must be absolutely reliable, with backup anchors to guard against failure.
- All rescuers must be connected to anchors at all times.
- The rescue must proceed as quickly as possible using efficient, thorough execution of every essential step.

Fig. 17-14. End climber sets up the initial anchor.

The next move is to slide the friction hitch down the rope, toward the crevasse, until the sling assembly is tight, ready to take a load. Now anyone who is still in self-arrest can ease the load onto the anchor (but still remains in self-arrest, to back up the initial anchor). Confirm that the anchor is solid and that the hitch is gripping the climbing rope tightly. (Keep in mind that if a prusik hitch is used, one rescuer will have to tend the hitch later, whenever the fallen climber is being pulled up. The bachmann friction hitch, on the other hand, usually requires less tending.)

Just as soon as the load is transferred to the initial anchor, back up the friction hitch. Tie a figure eight loop in the climbing rope 12 inches or so (about 30 centimeters) up-rope from the friction hitch (fig. 17-15). At the same time, use a locking carabiner to clip a rescue pulley to the carabiner already on the sling, running the climbing rope through the pulley. Clip the figure eight loop in to this new carabiner. With the pulley in place, the beginnings of a 3:1 (Z) pulley hauling system are now created (see "Step 3," below), saving time later if such a system needs to be set up to haul the climber from the crevasse.

The Second Anchor

Never trust a single anchor that is certain to be fully weighted. Back it up. With a single anchor now in place, set up a second anchor. Meanwhile, the middle climber remains in self-arrest position as a temporary backup to the existing anchor.

The second anchor makes the anchor system as fail-safe as possible. This anchor needs to be good, so take the time to do it right. As with the initial anchor, use a picket or a deadman for snow or an ice screw for ice. In snow, a good combination is a picket for the first anchor and a deadman (such as a buried picket) for the second anchor (fig. 17-16).

Link the second anchor to the sling tied to the climbing rope with a prusik hitch in the same way that the initial anchor was linked to the sling: Attach a runner to the sling with a carabiner (also clipping through the pulley carabiner at the same time), and then clip the other end of the runner to the second anchor with a carabiner. Try to make a taut connection from anchor

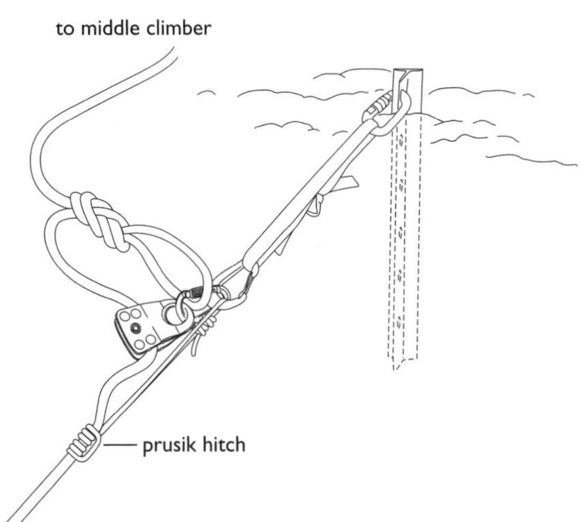

Fig. 17-15. Pulley and figure eight loop installed in the initial anchor.

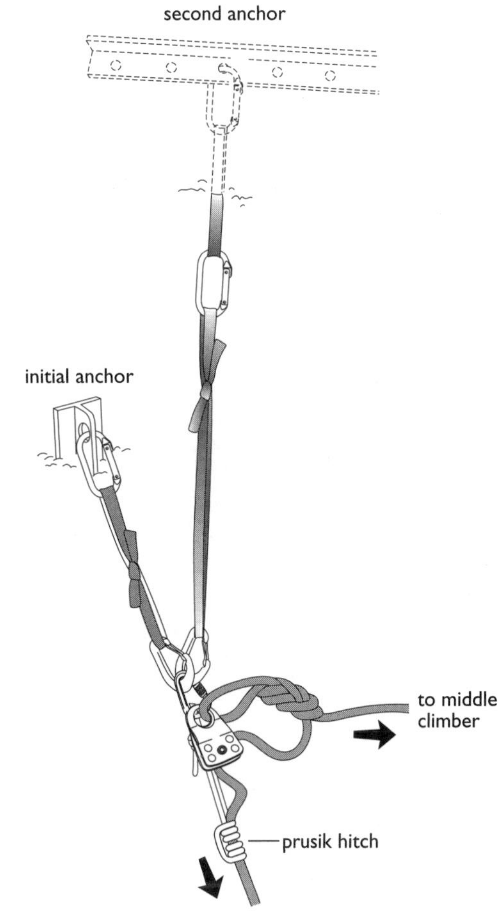

Fig. 17-16. Install a second anchor to make a tight and well-aligned connection.

to sling, and remember the principles of equalization: Keep the angle between the two anchor slings small (see "Equalizing Anchors" in Chapter 10, Belaying).

STEP 2: COMMUNICATE WITH THE FALLEN CLIMBER

To develop a complete understanding of the fallen climber's situation so the rescue plan can be devised, someone now needs to check the fallen climber's situation closely.

A rescuer can be belayed from the anchor by a teammate or, better yet, a rescuer can move to the lip of the crevasse with a self-belay. Use a prusik hitch to connect a sling to a rope that is attached to the anchor (this can be the climbing rope or a separate rope that is anchored), then clip the sling to the harness with a locking carabiner. By sliding this prusik hitch along the rope, a rescuer can move toward the crevasse edge on an anchored self-belay (fig. 17-17).

Probe with the ice ax when approaching the crevasse lip to discover where the snow surface may be undercut by the crevasse. Approach the lip somewhat to the side of where the fall occurred so snow is not knocked down onto the fallen climber.

Try to talk with the fallen climber. If there is no answer, the fallen climber may simply be out of earshot, or a noisy wind on the glacier may be masking the response. If further attempts still bring no response, a rescuer can rappel or be lowered on belay into the crevasse to help the climber. (See the information on an unconscious fallen climber in "Special Rescue Situations" later in this chapter.)

If the fallen climber responds to the rescuer's voice, ask questions to find out the full situation. Is the climber wedged in? Injured? In need of more clothing? Is the climber now standing in prusik slings? Most importantly, assure the climber that things are progressing topside but that the rescuers need help in deciding the best way to carry out the rescue.

The fallen climber should be able to tell the rescuer whether self-rescue—by climbing up the side of the crevasse or by prusiking out—is a good possibility

Fig. 17-17. Anchor system complete; self-belayed rescuer communicating with fallen climber. Note anchored ice ax protecting rope from entrenchment at crevasse edge.

or whether a hoist from above will be needed. There may even be the option of lowering the climber farther down, to a ramp or ledge from where self-rescue or hauling might be easier. Because the rescuer perched at the lip of the crevasse will gain the most complete picture of the situation above and below, that climber will have the most important input in the decision on a rescue method.

Minimize Entrenching of the Rope

Regardless of the rescue method that will be chosen, it is essential to pad the lip of the crevasse to minimize further entrenching of the rope. An entrenched rope will hinder the rescuers' efforts to hoist the climber up over the lip and will confound a fallen climber's own attempts to prusik over it. It may take some excavation to properly prepare the lip. In fact, the extent to which the rope has been entrenched by the climber's fall may force rescuers to consider setting up a different rescue rope from the one the climber is on.

For padding, slide the shaft of an ice ax, a ski (watch the sharp edges), a foam pad, or even a pack under the rescue rope as close to the edge of the crevasse as can safely be reached. Anchor the padding so it cannot fall into the crevasse (see Figure 17-17).

STEP 3: DEVISE A RESCUE PLAN

Choose a method for getting the fallen climber safely out of the crevasse. Will the climber attempt self-rescue? Or will the team members topside set up a hauling system to pull the climber out? After choosing between self-rescue or team rescue, the party must choose among the various methods of either self-rescue or team rescue. Factors that affect these decisions include the condition of the climber, the number of rescuers, the equipment available (ice climbing tools, additional ropes, pulleys, and so forth), weather conditions, topography of the crevasse area, and any other variables that will affect the safety of victim and rescuers.

Option 1: Self-Rescue

Self-rescue is often the easiest and fastest form of crevasse rescue, regardless of party size. It has the added advantage of keeping the fallen climber active and warm. Of course, it requires that the fallen climber is basically uninjured and able to maneuver in the crevasse.

For small parties that lack the muscle power to hoist the fallen climber or that are pinned down holding the rope, self-rescue may be the only practical option. This is especially true for a two-person party traveling alone.

A good self-rescue method for ascending the rope is the Texas prusik (see "Rescue Methods," later in this chapter).

Option 2: Team Rescue

Climbers have several choices among team-rescue methods, each with its own particular advantages. These methods are described and illustrated in "Rescue Methods," later in this chapter; here, they are summarized as part of the decision-making process.

Brute force. For a large party with an unentrenched rope, direct pull using brute force works excellently. It is fast and uncomplicated, uses minimal equipment, and requires little or no help from the fallen climber. It works best when perhaps a half dozen strong rescuers can haul on the rope and when the pullers are on flat ground or downhill from the fallen climber.

2:1 (single) pulley method. When the rope is badly entrenched or when there are few haulers, the 2:1 pulley method may be best. An entrenched rope will not matter because this method requires a separate length of rope—either the unused end of the accident rope or another rope entirely. The length of available rope must be at least twice as long as the distance from the initial anchor to the fallen climber. The mechanical advantage of the pulley makes hoisting this way a lot easier than by using brute force alone, though it still usually takes a minimum of three or four people to do the pulling. The fallen climber must be able to contribute to the rescue, with at least one good hand for clipping in to the rescue pulley and for maintaining balance.

3:1 (Z) pulley method. When a fallen climber is unable to help in the rescue or when few haulers are available, the 3:1 pulley is likely the best method. The pull force is on the accident rope, which may be partially entrenched in the snow, but the high mechanical advantage of the system gives haulers the power to overcome some entrenchment.

Piggyback pulleys. Even more power can be gained by piggybacking two systems together, such as a single-pulley setup hauling on a 3:1 pulley system.

Alternatives

A climber who falls into a crevasse does not necessarily have to come back out at the same spot. Check the possibility of lowering or swinging the fallen climber to a ledge. It might be a good spot for the victim to rest, as well as perhaps a gateway to a different part of the crevasse where rescue will be easier. Consider whether the bottom of the crevasse looks solid. This could offer another resting spot and a possible path to a climbing route or a snow ramp back to the surface.

STEP 4: CARRY OUT THE PLAN

Now the fallen climber must be gotten safely out of the crevasse. If self-rescue is the chosen plan, climbers topside assist as needed. If it will be a team rescue, the climbers topside set up the selected hauling system and pull the fallen climber out. See "Rescue Methods" later in this chapter.

A party with enough people should assign one climber as the communicator at the lip of the crevasse throughout the rescue. Good communication is especially important as the fallen climber approaches the lip.

In cases wherein the fallen climber has trouble climbing out over the crevasse lip due to an entrenched rope, consider lowering gear (ideally, linked to a different anchor) such as slings tied together, carabiner chains, etc., to provide additional support points away from the embedded rope.

INSIDE THE CREVASSE

While the climbers on top are taking the steps for rescue, the fallen climber has work to do down below, beginning with the moment of recovery from the fall. Below are the immediate actions the fallen climber should take.

Get Pack and Ice Ax Out of the Way

If possible, send your pack and ice ax up on a rope lowered by the rescuers. If this is not possible, clip the ax to your seat harness, letting it hang so it does not interfere with your movement. If at the beginning of the climb you did not rig a runner to the pack's haul loop (see "Using the Rope," earlier in this chapter), do this now: Girth-hitch a short sling through the pack's haul loop, then clip the sling with a carabiner in to the climbing rope between your seat harness and prusik attachments. The pack will then hang below you; as you prusik up the rope, the hanging pack will slide freely along the bottom of the loop of climbing rope and weight the rope, making it easier for you to climb (fig. 17-18).

Attain an Upright Position

If you did not do so automatically, work yourself into an upright position. Normally you do this by clipping the climbing rope through the carabiner at your chest harness. (This may be difficult or impossible to do until you have hung your pack, as described above.)

Get into Prusik Slings

Remove the prusik slings' foot loops from your pocket and slip one of the two adjustable loops over each boot (see "Using the Rope," earlier in this chapter). If you are wearing crampons, it will not be easy. Cinch the slipknot to tighten the slings around your boots. Getting into your prusik slings that are attached to the climbing rope permits you to alternate between standing in the foot sling and sitting from the seat-harness sling as you dangle (fig. 17-19). You will be a lot more comfortable and will be ready to climb up the rope using the slings.

As soon as you have gotten yourself upright, clipped in to your chest harness, moved your pack and ice ax out of the way, and caught your breath, it is usually advisable to begin prusiking partway to the top if you are just dangling free in the crevasse (see "Rescue Methods," below, for a description of the Texas prusik). If possible, let the other climbers know what you are doing. Move carefully and deliberately so that you do not put sharp or sudden tugs on the rope that could interfere with their work in holding your weight and setting up an anchor. Normally, though, the snow provides enough friction to help to hold the rope, especially at the lip of the crevasse, that your prusiking will not hamper your rescuers.

This preliminary prusiking gets you closer to the glacier surface, where it is easier to communicate with

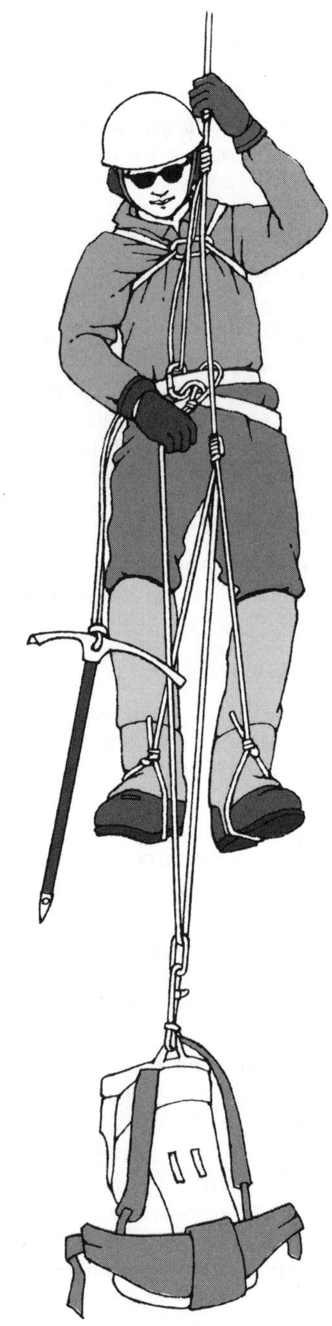

Fig. 17-18. Self-rescue using the Texas-prusik system.

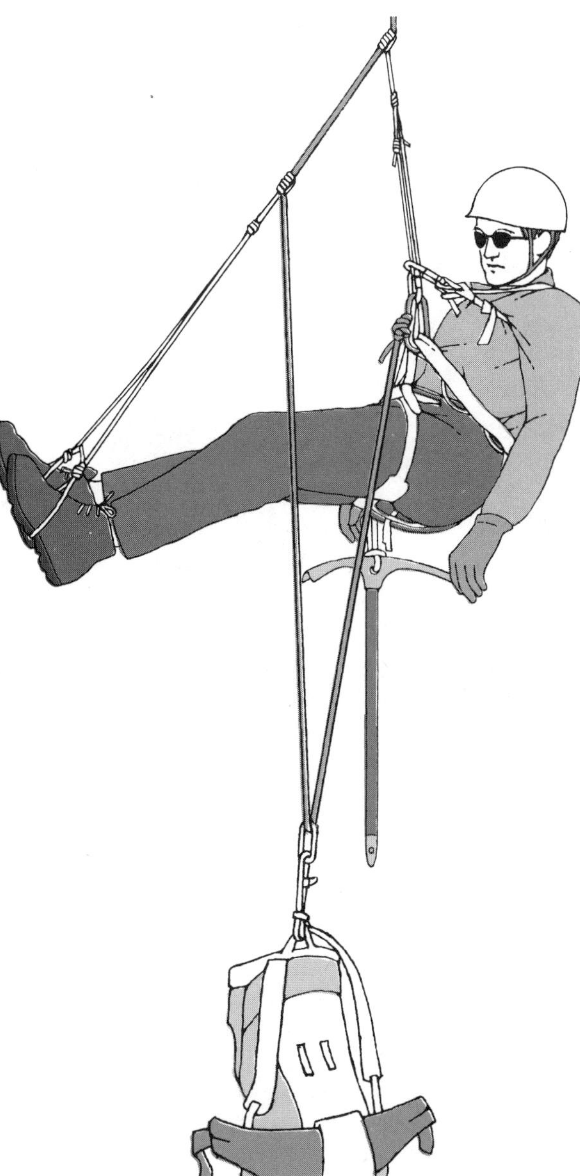

Fig. 17-19. Using the Texas-prusik system for a rest.

rescuers. You and the other climbers can then decide together on the best rescue plan. If the final plan is to use a hauling system, your initial prusiking will have helped by making the haul shorter. Even if the final plan is self-rescue by prusiking, you will probably need their help in getting over the crevasse lip.

If the fall did not leave you dangling free but, instead, dropped you onto a ledge, where most of your weight is off the rope, a different approach to prusiking is required. In this case, go ahead and get into the prusik slings, but wait to begin prusiking until you have talked it over with your rescuers. If you were to start prusiking without an OK from topside, your full weight coming suddenly onto the rope could unbalance and endanger the whole team.

Keep Warm

Close your parka, put on the hat and gloves you stuffed in its pockets earlier, and try to put on additional layers of clothing.

RESCUE METHODS

This section describes the principal prusiking method for self-rescue and the hauling methods for team rescue.

OPTION 1: SELF-RESCUE

The Texas prusik is a simple system that permits more progress per cycle and more comfortable rests than other methods such as the stair-step prusik. A climber with an injured leg can still ascend the rope with the Texas prusik by using just one of the foot loops. Unlike the stair-step prusik, the Texas prusik is easy to learn and execute. It will keep the climber upright without having to be connected to a chest harness. In fact, it may be easier to move the upper prusik when the climber is unclipped from the chest harness.

The Texas Prusik

This method of ascending the rope, developed by spelunkers (cavers), uses one prusik sling for the feet and a separate sling for the seat harness (which is clipped with a locking carabiner to your seat harness). The foot sling has two loops, one for each foot, tied so that they will adjust and cinch down on the boots. These are the steps for using the Texas prusik after recovering from a fall into a crevasse:

1. Stand up in the foot loops. You are now ready to move upward.
2. Unclip from the chest harness.
3. Loosen the friction hitch attached to the seat-harness sling and slide it up the rope until it is taut.
4. Sit down in the seat harness, putting all your weight on the seat-harness sling, which releases your weight from the foot sling (fig. 17-20a).

Fig. 17-20. Ascending a rope using the Texas-prusik system (pack and ice ax omitted for clarity): a, sitting or resting and moving foot prusik sling up; b, sitting on heels, ready to stand; c, standing and moving seat-harness prusik sling up.

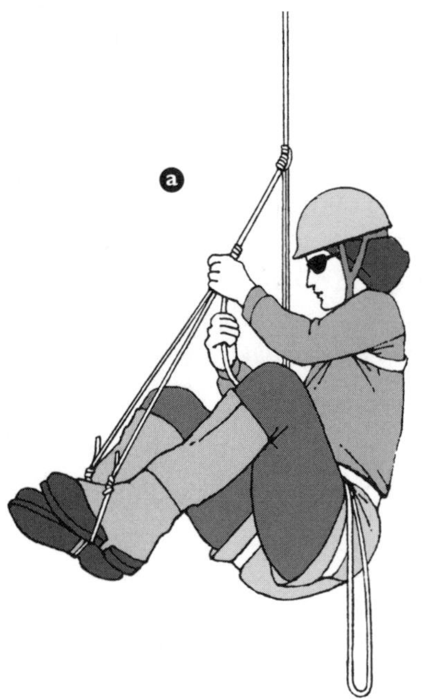

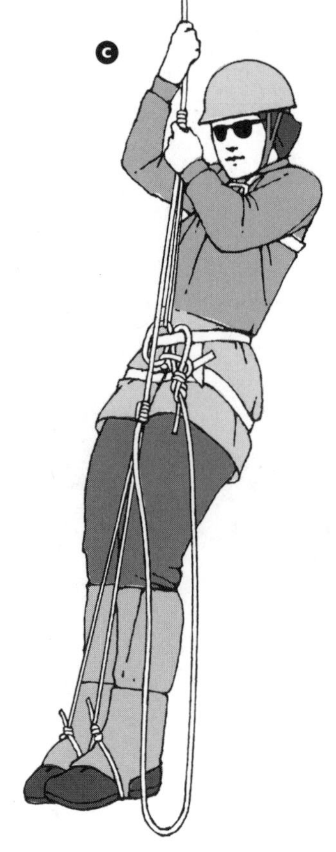

5. Loosen the friction hitch attached to the foot sling and slide it up the rope—18 to 24 inches (50 to 75 centimeters), if the sling is properly adjusted. Raise your feet with it (fig. 17-20b).
6. Stand up again in the foot loops (fig. 17-20c).
7. Keep repeating steps 3 through 6.

OPTION 2: TEAM RESCUE

All rescues are team rescues to some degree, because even in a self-rescue, the fallen climber usually needs some help getting over the crevasse lip. A full team rescue usually involves hauling the fallen climber to safety. The principal hauling methods—brute force, 2:1 (single) pulley, 3:1 (Z) pulley, and piggyback systems—are described in the sections that follow. In any rescue system calling for pulleys, carabiners can be substituted if necessary. However, carabiners create far more friction and make the rope harder to pull, and the load on the anchor system is correspondingly increased.

Brute Force

A half dozen or so strong haulers line up along the accident rope and grasp it. They position themselves up-rope beyond the point where the initial anchor is attached to the climbing rope with a prusik hitch or bachmann friction hitch. The hitch is then in the right place to hold the rope if the haulers slip or need a rest. Before hauling begins, unclip the backup figure eight loop from the anchor system (as shown in Figures 17-15, 17-16, and 17-17). Then the haulers go to work, pulling hand over hand on the rope or moving step by step away from the crevasse.

One rescuer tends the hitch, making sure the rope moves smoothly through it, and also keeps an eye on the anchor system. If there are enough people, another person can be stationed at the lip of the crevasse to stay in communication with the fallen climber.

The haulers should pull the rope at a slow, steady pace, especially when the fallen climber reaches the

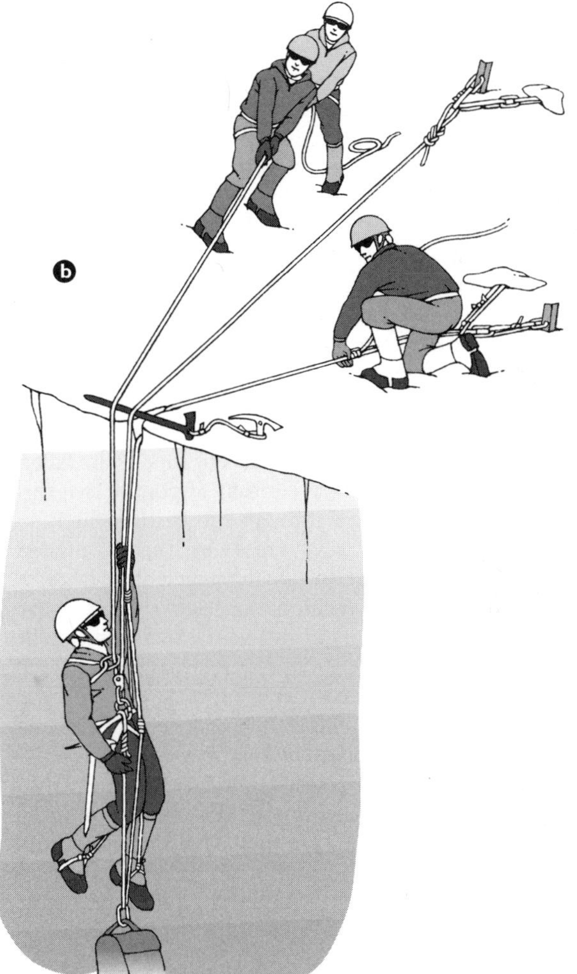

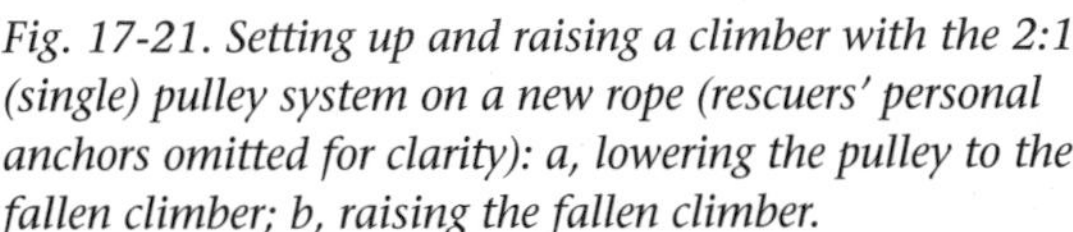

Fig. 17-21. Setting up and raising a climber with the 2:1 (single) pulley system on a new rope (rescuers' personal anchors omitted for clarity): a, lowering the pulley to the fallen climber; b, raising the fallen climber.

crevasse lip. If the rope has cut into the lip, the fallen climber could be hurt by being pulled into the crevasse wall. At this point, rescuers may ask the fallen climber to scramble over the lip (with the help of an ice ax) while they hoist.

2:1 (Single) Pulley System

The 2:1 pulley system theoretically doubles the amount of weight that each hauler could raise without a pulley, though friction lowers this ratio somewhat. Because this method uses a length of rope that is separate from the rope going to the fallen climber, this is the method of choice if the accident rope is entrenched into the edge of the crevasse. However, it also requires the assistance of the fallen climber, and so it cannot be performed when the fallen climber is unconscious. To carry out a rescue using the 2:1 pulley system, follow these steps:

1. Use a rescue rope (the unused end of the accident rope or a separate rope altogether) that is at least twice as long as the distance from the initial anchor down to the fallen climber. Attach the rope to either the existing anchor system or a new rescue anchor.
2. At the point where the rescue rope will go over the lip of the crevasse, prepare the lip with padding, such as an ice ax or pack, to prevent the rescue rope from entrenching itself in the snow.
3. Double the rescue rope into a big loop. Affix a

pulley to the loop and attach a locking carabiner to the pulley. Leave the carabiner unlocked.

4. Lower the pulley and carabiner dangling from the loop down to the fallen climber (fig. 17-21a). Have the climber clip and lock the carabiner in to the seat harness. Confirm that this has been done. Check that all the climber's equipment is secure and ready for hauling to begin. Have the climber clip the rescue rope—the portion that is between the pulley and the pulling rescuers above (not the portion that is between the pulley and the anchors above)—in to the chest harness, to help the climber stay upright.
5. Assign a rescuer to attend to the slack that will develop in the original accident rope as the fallen climber is raised. It is critically important that this person pull slack through the friction hitch so that the rope is always ready to accept the fallen climber's weight, in case the pullers slip or need a rest. If the fallen climber's pack is clipped to the accident rope, there will be considerable weight on the rope, and it may require two people to take in the slack. Keep the existing backup figure eight loop tied to the initial anchor in the system while the slack is taken in; do not remove the knot.
6. With everything ready, the haulers start pulling on the unanchored end of the rescue rope (fig. 17-21b). To ease their task somewhat, the fallen climber can pull up on the anchored side of the rescue rope while the hauling proceeds; this unweights the unanchored end of the rescue rope somewhat.

3:1 (Z) Pulley System

The 3:1 pulley system magnifies the muscle power of small climbing parties by offering a three-to-one theoretical mechanical advantage through the use of two pulleys. It can be set up and operated with no help from the fallen climber, making it valuable for rescuing an unconscious person. The 3:1 pulley system normally uses the accident rope. It requires more equipment and is more complicated than the other hauling methods described above.

First, confirm the solidity of the initial anchor system, because the 3:1 pulley system puts considerable stress on it. Take the loose end—the end that extends unweighted beyond the anchor—of the climbing rope attached to the fallen climber and lay out a long loop on the snow. This loop and the rest of the rope going from the anchor to the fallen climber should form a giant flat S in the snow, somewhat like a Z or a backward Z with the sharp edges worn off (fig. 17-22).

At the first bend in the Z (by the initial anchor system), the first pulley for hauling is already in place; this is the pulley attached to the initial anchor system with a locking carabiner when the system was first set up. Also clipped in to the locking carabiner are the prusik sling (also called the ratchet prusik) and the backup figure eight loop (see Figures 17-15 and 17-16).

At the second bend in the Z (the slack bend, closer to the crevasse lip), install a second pulley on the rope. Use a friction hitch to attach a short sling to the taut section of rope going from the anchor's first pulley to the fallen climber, and clip this sling with a carabiner in to the second pulley (this is called the traveling sling or prusik). Drag the friction hitch (traveling prusik) and traveling pulley as far down the taut rope as possible toward the crevasse. It may have to be seen to be believed, but this is now a 3:1 pulley system, ready for use. Here's how to haul using the 3:1 pulley system:

1. Unclip the backup figure eight loop from the initial anchor system and untie the knot as soon as the haulers and fallen climber are ready for pulling.
2. If the ratchet or keeper sling used a prusik hitch to attach the accident rope to the initial anchor system, assign a rescuer to tend the hitch so that the rope slips freely through it as the rope is pulled in. If a bachmann friction hitch was used instead, the attachment should tend itself, and the front hauler can simply keep an eye on it to see that all is well.
3. Start pulling at a steady rate, either hand over hand or by holding tight and walking backward.
4. The hauling will soon bring the second (traveling) pulley in close to the first (stationary or ratchet) pulley at the initial anchor. Stop hauling when the pulleys are about 2 feet (0.5 meter) apart. If they are pulled too close, the figure Z is collapsed and the mechanical advantage is lost.
5. Once hauling has stopped, relax the pull on the rope enough to transfer the fallen climber's weight back onto the ratchet or keeper sling at the initial anchor.
6. Reset the traveling pulley by loosening the traveling sling that is linked to the traveling pulley and sliding it back down the taut accident line toward the crevasse lip once again.
7. Keep repeating steps 3 through 6.

Fig. 17-22. Raising a climber with the 3:1 (Z) pulley system.

As the fallen climber nears the lip of the crevasse, use a friction hitch (for example, a prusik hitch) to attach a webbing chain to the taut accident line and lower it to the fallen climber (fig. 17-23a), who can use it to assist the rescuers helping the climber scramble over the lip of the crevasse (fig. 17-23b). Beware of the pulling power of the 3:1 (Z) pulley system. If care is not used, the climber can be injured by being pulled forcefully up into the lip.

Piggyback Pulleys

To get even more mechanical advantage out of a rescue hauling setup, combine, or "piggyback" two systems. For example, establish a separate 2:1 pulley setup to haul on the rope coming from a 3:1 pulley system. This gives a six-to-one theoretical mechanical advantage.

A 5:1 pulley system can be constructed in different ways. One method is to add a carabiner and a triple runner or cordelette 15 to 25 feet (5 to 8 meters) long clipped to the traveling prusik (see Figure 24-5b in Chapter 24, Alpine Search and Rescue). Another method is to add a second traveling prusik and pulley (or carabiner) to a 3:1 pulley system (see Figure 24-5c in Chapter 24).

For a 4:1 advantage, set up a 2:1 single-pulley system to haul on another 2:1 pulley system.

One note of caution: Beware of using piggyback systems to overcome the resistance of pulling the victim over the crevasse lip; serious injuries have resulted.

SPECIAL RESCUE SITUATIONS

A crevasse rescue can be complicated by any number of unusual twists. This section describes some special situations that could be encountered and ideas on how to deal with them. The situations can become complicated, and the rescuers' response will have to be adapted to the conditions of the moment. Anything that works safely is fine. (See Chapter 24, Alpine Search and Rescue, for more details on accident response and additional rescue techniques.)

WHEN THE MIDDLE PERSON FALLS IN

It is awkward at best when the middle person on a three-person rope team falls into a crevasse, especially if no

Fig. 17-23. Helping fallen climber over the lip of the crevasse: a, webbing chain prusiked to taut accident line is lowered so climber can put right foot into it; b, as climber steps up in the webbing, rescuers help in the scramble over the crevasse lip.

other climbers are around to set up the rescue anchor. With no second team, the only two people who can help are separated by a crevasse, each in self-arrest. Here is a general procedure for getting out of this fix.

The climbers begin by deciding which side of the crevasse will be the rescue side—that is, which side the fallen climber should come out on. Usually, one of the two rescuers in self-arrest is holding more weight than the other. The one holding the least weight usually has the best chance to get up and establish an anchor while the rescuer on the other side stays in self-arrest to hold the fall.

After the climber on the rescue side sets up the rescue anchor (see "Step 1: Set Up a Secure Anchor System," above), the climber in self-arrest on the other side of the crevasse can slowly release tension on the climbing rope and ease the fallen climber's weight onto the anchor.

If the climber who was in self-arrest is needed to help in the rescue operation, the climber on the rescue side now tries to belay the climber on the self-arrest side over to the rescue side. The rope on the rescue side can be used for belaying, if it is long enough, or a lightweight 100-foot (30-meter) accessory line—a precaution for a rope team traveling alone—can provide the belay. If no belay or safe route across the crevasse is available, however, the climber on the self-arrest side could be stuck there. This climber would then set up an anchor and stay put.

The most advantageous rescue plan now is for the fallen climber to self-rescue by ascending the rope on prusik slings, coming out on the rescue side, where the anchor has been placed. If a self-rescue by prusiking is not possible, then a 3:1 pulley or a piggyback system could be tried. This all takes plenty of time, competence, equipment, and resourcefulness. Learn to use the bachmann friction hitch for times when you might have to haul alone, because the hitch requires less tending than a standard prusik hitch in a hauling system.

In the case of a four-person rope team, the situation is a little simpler in the event that one of the two middle members falls into a crevasse. Conduct the rescue in a routine manner from the side that has two climbers topside.

WHEN A TWO-PERSON TEAM IS ALONE

For a party of two people with no other rope team nearby, glacier travel is risky indeed. Both climbers absolutely need to know their rescue techniques, period. The climber who stops a fall must set up an anchor alone while in self-arrest and then create a hauling system if one is needed. Therefore, each climber needs to carry at least two pieces of snow or ice protection for an anchor appropriate to the conditions, plus the equipment (pulleys, carabiners, slings) to set up a hauling system. And all of this must be readily at hand, clanking from seat harness or pack straps.

Rope teams of two should use the tie-in method known as the adapted Kiwi coil (see below), which automatically makes available an extra length of rope for rescue use. Packing along a 100-foot (30-meter) accessory line is also good precaution. The climbers should not have the rope clipped in to their chest harnesses, because this makes rescue very difficult. And with only two people, it is even more important than usual to travel with a personal prusiking system ready for use.

If you end up as the sole rescuer in a two-person rope team, holding your partner's fall with your self-arrest, begin your rescue efforts by augmenting the security of your arrest position by digging in your feet and pressing the ice ax more firmly into the snow. Imagine that you are establishing a belay stance while lying down.

Try to free one hand by rotating the upper half of your body—but keep leaning on the ax and bracing yourself with at least one stiff leg. If the rope is clipped in to your chest harness, unclip it now.

When you get one hand free, place a fluke, picket, ice screw, second ice tool—anything secure enough to hold and allow you to get up and create a main anchor. At this point, you will see the value of keeping the appropriate anchors easily accessible.

Now follow the steps described in "Crevasse Rescue Response" earlier in this chapter, though you will probably experience more difficulty than would a larger rope team or group of teams: Set up a secure main anchor, communicate with your fallen partner, settle on a rescue plan, and carry it out. Ideally, your partner will be able to handle self-rescue, prusiking out. If not, try a 3:1 pulley or piggyback hauling system. Of course, if you are unable to set up an anchor in the first place, the climber in the crevasse has no choice but to try self-rescue while you remain in self-arrest.

The Adapted Kiwi Coil

The Kiwi coil was developed by alpine glacier guides in New Zealand, and an adaptation of it is the preferred tie-in method for two-person glacier travel teams. The technique results in closer spacing between rope partners for more efficient, comfortable travel, and it provides some free rope for a hauling system or other rescue use.

The adapted Kiwi coil also is valuable in providing a means of quick transition between the closer spacing of roped glacier travel and the full rope-length requirements of belayed climbing. This transition is important on an alpine climb wherein a glacier approach is followed by belayed rock or ice climbing. To create an adapted Kiwi coil, take these steps:

1. Tie in to the rope at your seat harness, as you would normally.
2. Take a series of coils of rope into your hand (usually five, but no more than nine) until you have the desired spacing between you and your rope partner. Secure the coils together by tying an overhand knot around them, using a loop of the rope (fig. 17-24a).
3. Get the coils out of the way for travel, stowing them securely anywhere, such as in the top of your pack or over one shoulder, where they are easily accessible (fig. 17-24b).
4. Tie the shortened length of climbing rope to your seat harness with a double bowline. The rope is now tied twice to the seat harness, and any force coming onto the rope will be taken by this second knot.

Variation

A variation of the adapted Kiwi coil is often used in Europe; climbers put overhand knots on a bight in the rope (leaving a small loop) at 5-foot (1.5-meter) intervals between the two climbers, beginning with an initial 10-foot (3-meter) space between the climber and the first

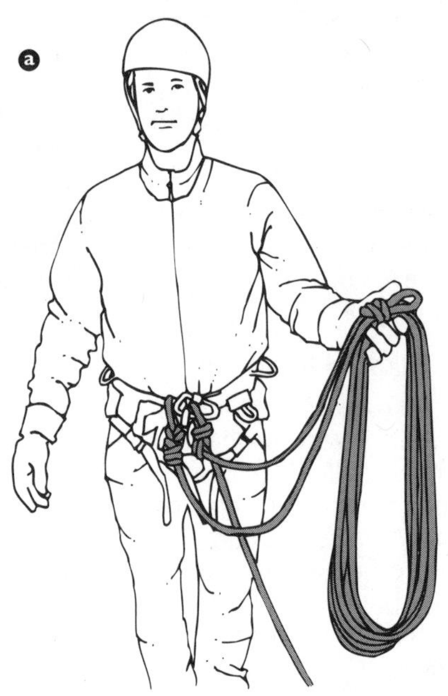
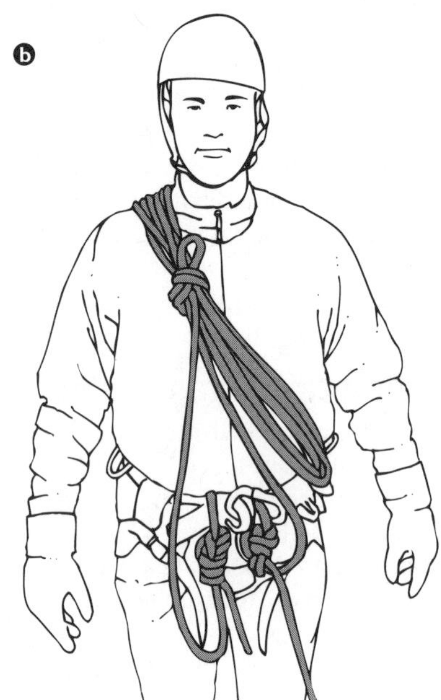

Fig. 17-24. Adapted Kiwi coil: a, tying in and creating the coil; b, draping the coil out of the way (prusik slings omitted for clarity).

knot (fig. 17-25). This method works on the principle that in the event of a fall into a crevasse, the rope will entrench and the knots will catch in the crevasse lip. This takes most of the weight off the arresting climber, which makes it considerably easier to set up the initial rescue anchor.

To use this rope to extract the fallen climber from the crevasse, the other climber must untie the knots in the rope before hauling. This may be possible because most of the load should be taken by the knot wedged in the lip of the crevasse. If the rescuer cannot do this, then rescue must be performed using either a 2:1 pulley system using the loose end of the rope or using another rope.

WHEN THE FALLEN CLIMBER IS UNCONSCIOUS

To help an unconscious climber, a rescuer should descend by rappeling or being lowered on belay. This rescuer can administer first aid and also get the fallen climber right-side up if necessary. The rescuers can then consider using any of the standard hauling methods. To help get the fallen climber over the lip of the crevasse, a rescuer may have to work right at the edge of or from inside the crevasse. Monitor the condition of the unconscious person, taking care to cause no further injury.

WHEN THERE IS MORE THAN ONE VICTIM

If more than one person has fallen into a crevasse, assess each person's condition and the best method for getting each one out, and then decide the order of rescue. Practicality usually determines the order of rescue, unless there is ample backup for rescuers and equipment. Be sure that each fallen climber is given warm clothing, if needed, and keep everyone informed of rescue plans as they develop.

WHEN THE WORKING SPACE IS CRAMPED

The climber who drops into self-arrest position to stop a rope mate's fall could be lying so close to the lip of the crevasse that there is very little room to place an anchor or pulley system. A solution to this situation is to set up the main anchor where there is enough room—on the up-rope side of the climber in self-arrest (instead of the usual place between the rescuer and the crevasse). Leave 24 inches or so (60 centimeters) of slack between the main anchor and this rescuer, so that this person is not trapped in the system by tension on the rope.

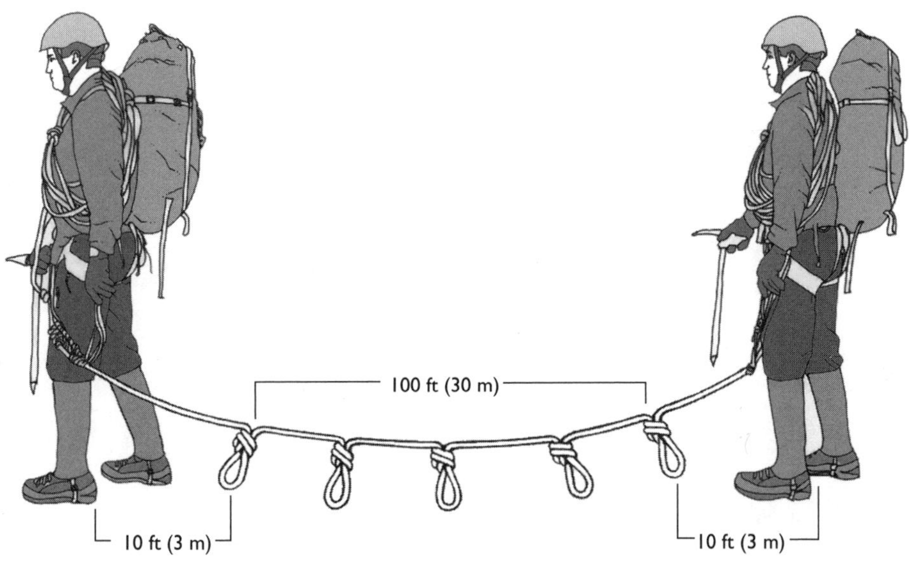

Fig. 17-25. Two-person glacier travel with knots in rope, which aid in arresting a crevasse fall by catching in the crevasse lip.

Then set up a temporary anchor, between the rescuer and the crevasse, that will take the weight of the fallen climber long enough to enable the rescuer to get up from self-arrest position and untie from the rope. Once hauling begins, untie the prusik sling attached to the temporary anchor.

WHEN THE WORKING SPACE IS BETWEEN TWO CREVASSES

Rescuers trying to work in a very narrow area between two crevasses can consider moving the operation. The rescue might proceed better if it is run from the opposite side of the crevasse that holds the fallen climber.

Another option is to change the direction of pull on a 3:1 pulley system. Hook a third pulley to the anchor and run the hauling end of the rope through it (fig. 17-26). Now the rescuers can pull in a direction more parallel to the crevasse.

WHEN THE ROPES ARE ENTRENCHED

The upward progress of a person climbing out or being pulled out of a crevasse can be stopped cold by a rope that has dug itself into the lip. This situation calls for some improvisation. For instance, a rescuer can attach prusik slings or etriers (aiders) above the entrenched portion of the rope and drop them down for the climber to step into.

Another option is to switch to a new rescue rope. A rescuer can lower a new rope to the fallen climber (as shown in Figure 17-21). Or the fallen climber can, in effect, provide a new rope by tossing the loose end of the climbing rope up to the rescuers. This is done by prusiking up to the lip, tying in higher up on the climbing rope, untying from the loose end of the climbing rope, and throwing the loose end up to the rescuers.

A new rescue rope, carefully padded at the lip of the crevasse so it does not also get entrenched, opens up several rescue possibilities. The fallen climber can switch prusik slings from the original climbing rope to the new free rope. Or the rescuers can haul the fallen climber up and out on the new rope. Or the fallen climber can merely transfer all weight to the new rope to give rescuers a much better chance of freeing the entrenched line.

WHEN THE FALL IS INTO A ROOFED CREVASSE

Wide, roofed crevasses present special problems. The fallen climber may be hanging free, without a stabilizing wall for support, and the accident rope typically entrenches itself deeply into the snow of the crevasse roof. The fallen climber may be bombarded by snow and ice dislodged by the rescuers, who will be working in an area of proven instability.

17

Fig. 17-26. Adding another pulley to the 3:1 (Z) pulley system for a change of direction in a tight space, such as between two crevasses.

It may be necessary to have a well-belayed rescuer take a shovel or ice ax and enlarge the hole the climber fell through. Do your best to keep snow and ice from hitting the fallen climber.

Knowledge and preparation will minimize the hazards of roofed crevasses and the other problems of traveling near crevasses.

PATHS TO THE SUMMIT

Glaciers move slowly but inexorably downward under the influence of gravity. Like rivers flowing to the sea, they follow the path of least resistance. Glaciers can appear to be obvious, rather convenient routes to alpine summits, but in reality they are massive, dynamic systems that hold many hazards. Climbers who seek the freedom of the glaciated peaks must learn how to safely negotiate crevasses and other dangers. Clearly, the best strategy for travel on a glacier is to minimize exposure to such hazards; take precautions to avoid falling into crevasses. Even when precautions are taken, however, falls and other accidents can occur. Anyone planning to travel on a glacier must master the techniques for dealing with the hazards and effecting a successful recovery if necessary. With these skills, climbers can safely take advantage of these paths up the glaciated summits.

EQUIPMENT • TECHNIQUES OF ALPINE ICE CLIMBING • ROPED CLIMBING TECHNIQUES • PRACTICE FOR THE FREEDOM OF THE HILLS

Chapter 18
ALPINE ICE CLIMBING

Ice is found on or around the summits of many alpine peaks, and developing ice climbing skills increases climbers' opportunities for safe exploration of those summits. With proper skills, they will be able to use ice as yet another avenue to the alpine realm.

To climb ice, mountaineers use much of what they have learned about rock and snow climbing, adding the special tools and techniques needed for climbing ice. Ice climbers experience the same joys as do snow climbers and face the same perils: avalanches, hazardous couloirs and unstable cornices, ice blocks, and icefalls. Ice climbing opportunities can be found year-round, from climbing waterfall ice on the short, dark days of winter to ascending alpine ice on long, warm summer days.

Ice can appear in a variety of forms. Under the combined effects of pressure, heat, and time, snow and other forms of frozen precipitation metamorphose into the alpine ice of glaciers, ice fields, and couloirs. There is no clear distinction between alpine ice and hard snow. Alpine ice sometimes appears as blue ice; this hue means that the ice is relatively pure. Black alpine ice—old, hard ice mixed with dirt, pebbles, or other debris—is another common variation. Liquid water freezes to form water ice. Water-ice formations can be as dramatic as a frozen waterfall or as common as *verglas,* the thin, clear coating of ice that forms when rainfall or melting snow freezes on a surface, such as rock. *Verglas* is difficult to climb because the thin, weak layer provides scant purchase for crampons and ice tools. Water ice is usually harder, steeper, and more brittle than alpine ice, but under some conditions—for example, high altitudes and low temperatures—the two may be indistinguishable.

Ice is as changeable and ephemeral as snow. A rock route is likely to be there for years or decades, but what was an ice route in the morning may by that afternoon be nothing but a jumbled pile of ice blocks or a wet spot on the rock. Climbers must learn to anticipate the changeability of ice. Ice can exhibit a wide range of characteristics. At one extreme, it can seem as hard as steel; ice tools bounce off it, barely scratching the surface. Hard ice can also be as brittle as glass, requiring climbers to expend time and energy chopping away at the surface until they can plant an ice tool without the placement shattering. At other times, ice can be soft and plastic, allowing climbers to make secure placements effortlessly with a single swing—an ice climber's dream. However, ice can be too soft and weak to provide good protection placements or to support your weight. It takes experience to assess the relative condition of ice.

As is true of all types of climbing, the steepness of the slope greatly affects which ice climbing technique is appropriate. On flat ice, such as level areas on a glacier or a frozen stream, it is usually possible to walk without crampons, especially if rocks and dirt are embedded in the surface. On short slopes, an ice ax can be used to chop steps, but longer sections call for crampons. As the slope angle increases, climbers can use French technique—"flat-footing"—but only up to a point. The very steepest routes require front-pointing, also called German technique.

This chapter uses the descriptive terms in Table 18-1 in referring to the approximate steepness of slopes.

TABLE 18-1. STEEPNESS OF SLOPES

Descriptive Term	Approximate Angle of Steepness
Gentle	0° to 30°
Moderate	30° to 45°
Steep	45° to 60°
Extremely steep	60° to 80°
Vertical	80° to 90°
Overhanging	Greater than 90°

EQUIPMENT

Continuing refinements in equipment have helped ice climbers improve and expand their techniques and use them to undertake greater climbing challenges. Manufacturers are producing a steady stream of specialized and innovative clothing, boots, crampons, ice tools, and ice protection. (See Chapter 16, Snow Travel and Climbing, for a general description of gear such as crampons and ice axes.) This section describes the equipment that is specific to alpine ice climbing.

CLOTHING

Clothes for ice climbing should offer a combination of comfort and function. Employ a layered system, with layers appropriate to the conditions. Some climbers wear bibs or a one-piece suit as an alternative to the conventional outfit of jacket and pants. A one-piece suit of windproof, waterproof synthetic material retains warmth and repels debris. The suit should provide a convenient means of ventilation—for example, an armpit zipper that opens from elbow to midriff and a second zipper that opens from front to back via the crotch. The one-piece suit should not be confused with the expedition suit (a heavily insulated one-piece suit designed for the extreme conditions of high-altitude or arctic environments).

Waterproof. Ice climbing is a wet activity, so the clothing system must be designed to keep you dry.

Unrestrictive. Freedom of movement is essential, so in choosing a jacket, make sure you can reach your arms high overhead without having the garment hem rise above waist level. Otherwise, your torso will be exposed to the elements when you reach high to make a tool placement.

Windproof. The chilling effect of wind means that a complete layer of windproof clothing should always be packed. The windproof layer must fit over all the insulating layers that are likely to be worn, and they should overlap or tuck together to provide a solid shield. Fabrics vary in their relative level of wind resistance, so get recommendations from other climbers and from staff at outdoor stores. Laminated fabrics such as Gore-Tex are among the most windproof.

Gloves and Mittens

Ice climbers' hands need protection from cold and abrasion. Climbing alpine ice on a summer day may require nothing more than a pair of lightweight gloves, but other conditions usually require much more elaborate layered systems. Many glove and mitten systems are available. Features to look for include waterproof shells (sealed Gore-Tex shells are good), articulated designs, removable liners, and retainer loops. Mittens are warmer than gloves but more cumbersome; as a compromise, some manufacturers offer mittens with a separate index finger compartment, which can be used in opposition with the thumb.

Ease of use. It should be possible to adjust straps hands-free, using your teeth. Check to see whether any straps or buckles interfere with the leashes of ice climbing tools. The components of the layered system protecting your hands must be compatible and should be easy to remove and replace, because it may be necessary to remove a glove or mitten to manipulate climbing gear.

Materials. Gloves or mittens should have high-friction material on the palms to help the climber grip ice tools; some fabrics, especially nylons, tend to be rather slippery. Leather is the best material for standing up to the rigors of rope handling. High density, boiled-wool mittens or gloves have one rather esoteric advantage: A mittened or gloved hand can temporarily be frozen to the ice, which can help a climber work through a move.

BOOTS

When selecting boots, it is essential to get a precise fit: room for the toes to wiggle but snug in the instep and heel, with minimal lift at the heel while walking. Be sure to fit boots to accommodate the stocking system you will wear. Most modern mountaineering boots have molded toe and heel grooves, so they are compatible with clip-on crampons.

Leather. For alpine ice climbing in moderate conditions, modern leather mountaineering boots are a good choice. However, if leather boots will be used for extensive front-pointing, they must be stiff-soled. Insulated leather boots are available that are specifically designed for technical ice climbing. In French technique (flat-footing), ankle rotation is very important, so boots must permit good range of motion; leather boots are usually better in this regard.

Plastic. In extreme cold, ice climbers use plastic boots more commonly than leather boots. Plastic boots are warm and dry, and they also provide a rigid platform for crampons, which is especially important for front-pointing. However, stiff plastic boots limit ankle flexibility.

GAITERS

Ice climbers need full-length gaiters that come up to just below the knee. Make sure the gaiters fit your boots and can accommodate any layers of insulation you wear on your legs. If you will wear insulated supergaiters for added warmth, check to see that they are compatible with your boot-crampon system.

TABLE 18-2. COMPARISON OF CRAMPON FRONT-POINT ANGLES

Orientation of Front Points	Advantages
Horizontal front points	Work well in warm ice, bad ice, alpine ice, and mixed climbing. If you own only one pair of crampons, then these are the ones to get.
Vertical mono front points	Work best on specific features, cold water-ice climbs, and mixed climbs.
Vertical dual front points	Work well for water ice that is in less than perfect condition.

CRAMPONS

Crampon points must be sharp, and the harder the ice, the sharper the points should be. Check the points before each climb and sharpen them if necessary. (See "Crampons" in Chapter 16, Snow Travel and Climbing.)

Hinged

Properly fitted, hinged, 12-point crampons are suitable for most alpine ice climbing. They work well with most types of climbing boots and are lighter and less expensive than rigid-frame designs.

Rigid and Semirigid

Climbers who do a lot of front-pointing prefer rigid or semirigid crampons, which vibrate less than hinged 18

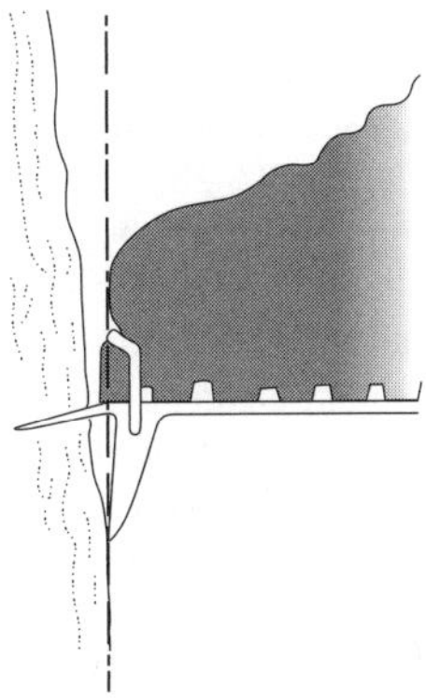

Fig. 18-1. Angle of front points for alpine ice is slightly downward; secondary points are angled slightly forward.

crampons when they are kicked into water ice, which is denser. Rigid crampons should be worn with stiff leather or plastic boots to prevent overstressing the crampon frame. Although some rigid crampons are strong enough to be worn with softer boots, a soft boot could twist out of a clip-on crampon binding.

Front and Secondary Points

The angles of the front points and the secondary points are critical in determining the best penetration into ice. For alpine ice, the front points are straight-shaped but bent slightly downward, and the secondary points are angled slightly forward (fig. 18-1). Chapter 19, Waterfall Ice and Mixed Climbing, discusses front-point angles preferred for waterfall ice climbing, including mono and dual front points. Table 18-2 compares advantages of various front-point angles.

ICE TOOLS

Ice tools have shorter shafts than the standard ice ax used for general mountaineering. The short shaft, commonly 50 centimeters (ice tool lengths are described only in metric units), is easier to control, increasing the accuracy of pick placement and reducing the shaft vibration that can fatigue arm muscles. Ice tools generally weigh 680 to 907 grams (24 to 32 ounces), and some feature removable head weights that allow climbers to fine-tune the tool's "swing weight." An ice tool with a relatively heavy head penetrates most readily, but it may be difficult to extract.

Ice tools, unlike ice axes, can have a hammerhead opposite the pick rather than an adze (fig. 18-2a). Ice climbers can use matched ice tools—both having a hammerhead—or can use one with a hammerhead and one with an adze. Many tools feature modular designs. Some models are semimodular; that is, only the pick is interchangeable (fig. 18-2b). Fully modular tools provide the option of interchangeable picks and adzes or hammerheads (fig. 18-2c). Being able to replace picks, adzes, and hammerheads as the need arises makes the tool more complex, and the additional parts can fail or become lost, but it also provides added flexibility because the tool can be assembled to accommodate prevailing conditions. Also, a broken pick can be replaced in the field—even in midpitch, theoretically, if the fastening system is not too complex.

There is no standard fastening system for interchangeable parts on modular ice tools. Components of one manufacturer's system are not compatible with those from another company, and some systems are easier to use than others. The trend has been to design fastening systems that require a minimum of tools. The components of some ice tools are designed to be changed with a simple wrench or using the pick or spike of another ice tool made by the same manufacturer.

What is the "perfect" ice tool? Most of the ice tools that are now available work quite well. The number of different designs and models is rapidly growing. Try out a variety of ice tools to determine which ones work best for you. See the "Questions to Consider When Selecting Ice Tools" sidebar.

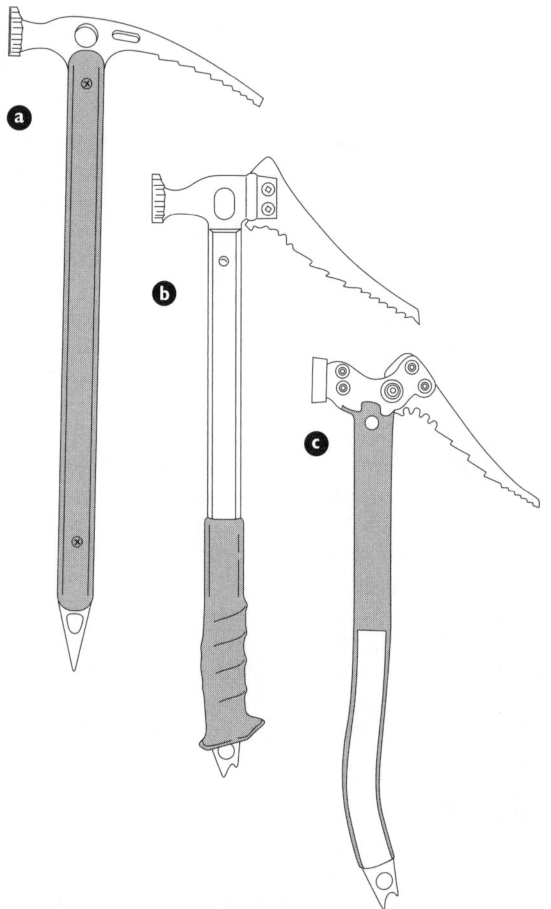

Fig. 18-2. Typical ice tools: a, north wall hammer; b, semimodular tool; c, fully modular tool.

QUESTIONS TO CONSIDER WHEN SELECTING ICE TOOLS

When selecting ice tools, ask the following questions:

1. Do the tools' length and weight fit me?
2. Can I comfortably grip the tools with gloves on?
3. Are they designed for the kind of climbing I intend to do?

On alpine ice, some climbers use a full-length general mountaineering ice ax and a shorter, straight-shafted ice tool such as a classic north wall hammer (as shown in Figure 18-2a). On more technical routes, many climbers use two short ice tools. A versatile combination is a pair of ice tools, one with an adze and one with a hammer. The adze is used to chop and scrape ice for steps, belay positions, ice protection, and ice bollards; the hammer is used to drive in pieces of protection. Some climbers prefer to hold the hammer in their dominant hand, making it easier to start ice screws or place pitons.

Some climbers carry a third tool, which can be used as a temporary personal anchor at belay points, placed as a piece of protection, or used to replace a lost or broken tool. The third tool can be a full-size ice tool, or it can be a shorter (35- to 40-centimeter) and lighter (454-gram/16-ounce) "third tool" model (as shown in Figure 18-2b). The spike of a holstered tool is a potential hazard, so some climbers carry a third tool that does not have a spike.

The styles of ice tools vary greatly. The following sections describe the principal design variations of the parts of the ice tool: shaft, pick, adze or hammerhead, spike, and leash.

Shafts

Ice tool shafts are manufactured from aluminum alloy, carbon fiber composites, and titanium alloy. A number of shaft designs are available, including a straight shaft (fig. 18-3a). Bent-grip models (fig. 18-3b) decrease strain in the wrist. Check to see that the curve of the bend and the swing weight complement your natural swing. A bent-grip design will not keep you from bashing knuckles; this is usually the result of poor technique. Bent-grip designs have some disadvantages: The bend may impede plunging the shaft into snow; the bend makes

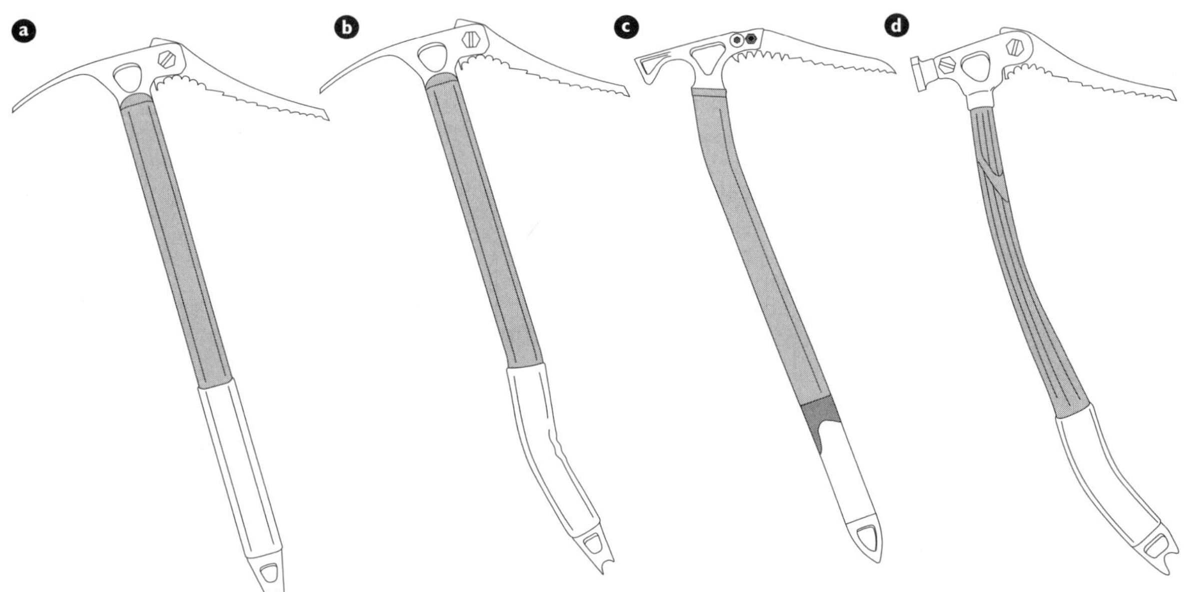

Fig. 18-3. Ice tools with various shaft designs: a, straight shaft; b, bent grip; c, bent shaft; d, compound-curve shaft.

18

hammering or chopping somewhat awkward; and a bent-grip tool may be difficult to remove from a holster. A bend high on the shaft near the head (fig. 18-3c) increases clearance around bulges or cauliflower ice (see Chapter 19, Waterfall Ice and Mixed Climbing). Some tools have both kinds of bends (fig. 18-3d)—that is, a bend at both top and bottom. Other tools feature shafts that have a continuous, long-radius curve. If the slope of the ice is less than 60 degrees, a bent-shaft tool is awkward to place.

The circumference and cross-sectional shape of the shaft affect your grip. A particular shaft might be too large or too small for your hand. A shaft that is too large in circumference is fatiguing to grip. A shaft that is too small in circumference is hard to control.

The array of grip styles—bumps, knobs, pommels, etc.—and shaft covering materials can be bewildering. Most ice tools have a shaft covering of high-friction material that facilitates grip. To further help you grip the ice tools, wear gloves or mittens with leather or rubberized palms. It should be comfortable to grip a tool while wearing the various glove and mitten combinations used when climbing.

Picks

The pick must penetrate the ice, hold against a downward pull, and release easily when its grip is no longer needed. The holding and releasing characteristics of a pick are determined by its geometry, thickness, and tooth configuration. Modular ice tools typically include a variety of pick designs, but not all manufacturers offer all types.

The steeper the droop of a pick and the sharper, deeper, and more numerous the teeth, the better the pick will hold; the smoother the pick, the easier it is to remove. The teeth should be shaped to bite into the ice as the end of the shaft is pulled on. In most cases, only the first few teeth provide any useful bite into the ice. Although thin picks penetrate and hold best, they are more vulnerable to damage. A thick-bladed pick, on the other hand, requires more force to place and is more likely to shatter the ice, but it is less prone to breaking.

Modular tools provide the option of choosing one of several types of interchangeable picks, so the right one can be chosen for a particular climb or a broken pick can be replaced instead of the tool having to be discarded.

Technically curved. The pick of a general mountaineering ice ax curves slightly downward, whereas the technically curved pick of an ice tool (fig. 18-4a) curves down more sharply and thus holds better in ice. It is most often used on alpine ice and glacial ice climbs. It is the most effective technical pick for self-arrest.

Reverse curved. The reverse-curved pick (fig. 18-4b) is both secure and easy to remove from the ice, making it overwhelmingly the most popular choice for extremely steep ice routes. During self-arrest, this pick grabs so well that climbers may not be able to hold on to the tool.

The shape of any pick can be easily changed with a hand file, but be judicious in removing metal. Consider beveling the top of the pick to aid in removing the tool from the ice (fig. 18-5). Be careful not to weaken the pick by overheating it or by removing too much material. The tooth pattern of a pick can also be changed if it either sticks too well or does not stick well enough. Modifying the pick clearance will affect its hooking ability; a more pronounced positive clearance should make the pick better for hooking with the tip. (See Figure 16-3 in Chapter 16, Snow Travel and Climbing, for positive and negative clearance.) Some picks are designed with a pounding surface or anvil. This permits a second tool to be used to drive in the tool for a

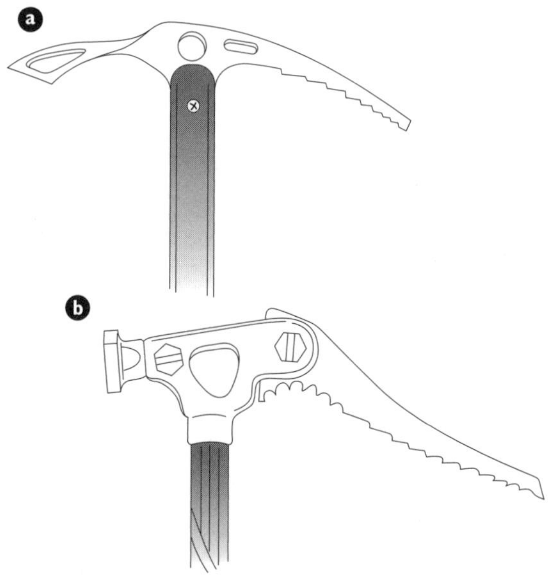

Fig. 18-4. Picks: a, technically curved; b, reverse-curved.

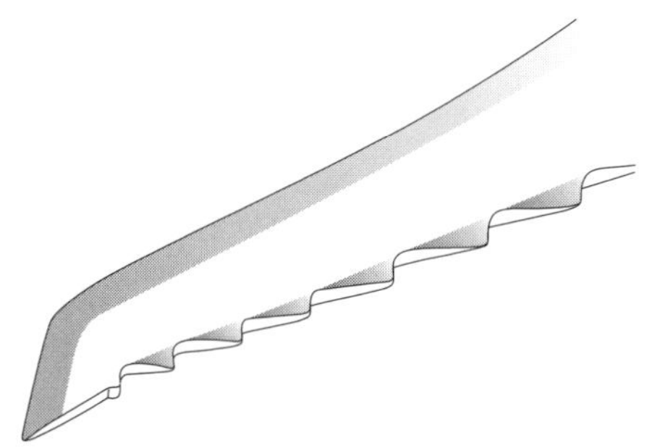

Fig. 18-5. Close-up view of a reverse-curved pick; note that the tip and top edge are sharp, and the sides of the teeth are beveled.

placement. This feature is useful if a tool will be used as a temporary personal anchor.

Adzes and Hammerheads

The adze of an ice tool can be used to chop steps, clear ice to make a good surface for a screw placement, or cut footholds at belay stances. Hammerheads are used to drive pickets or pitons or to pound in ice hooks.

As with picks, adzes come in an array of shapes and sizes. Modular ice tools provide the option of replacing a broken adze or changing adzes depending on ice conditions. An adze can even be exchanged for a hammerhead. Some climbers dislike having a sharp adze edge near their face, so they use two hammers. However, an adze is more convenient if it is necessary to chop a stance or clear rotten ice.

The most common adze is straight, extending more or less perpendicular to the shaft or drooping slightly downward (see Figure 18-4a). The straight adze's sharp corners are excellent for cutting steps. Some adzes curve downward like a technically curved pick (see Figure 18-3a and b). On some adzes, the very end of the working edge curves slightly inward, although this may impede cutting steps because it diffuses the full force of a swing. Drooped adzes can be used for climbing snow or rotten ice. The majority of adzes and hammerheads are now designed to be used for hooking or camming placements in rock.

Spikes

To penetrate ice, the spike on the bottom of an ice tool's shaft must be sharp, and the joint between spike and shaft must be smooth. Most spikes have carabiner holes (see Figures 18-2 and 18-3), to which a climber can clip when using the tool as a temporary personal anchor. This setup should not be used as part of a belay anchor.

Leashes

A wrist leash mounted on each ice tool serves several purposes. The leash secures a dropped tool, helps in the work of swinging the tool, and lets the climber rest her grip by hanging from it. In this last way, the wrist leash helps climbers conserve energy on steep or vertical ice.

A variety of leash features are available, designed to increase comfort and security. The leash can be attached through a hole or slot in the head of the tool (fig. 18-6) or in the tool shaft, and it should be adjusted so that it is just long enough to let the climber grasp the shaft above the spike. The wrist loop should be adjusted to snugly, but comfortably, fit a gloved hand.

An increasing number of quick-release leashes are available to allow climbers to quickly free their hand from the tool. These leashes are time- and energy-saving

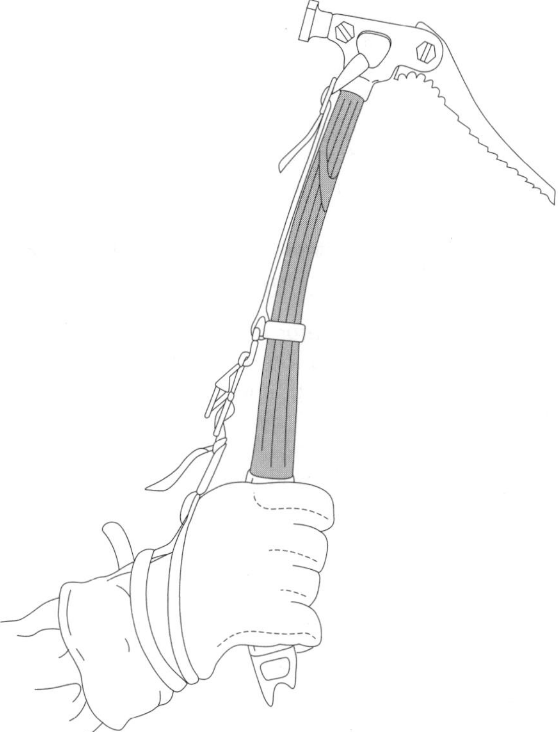

Fig. 18-6. Quick-release wrist leash for ice tools.

devices. When using a quick-release leash, be sure to take the time to practice releasing and securing it to the tool before starting the route. Quick-release leashes are not recommended for use in general mountaineering.

The leash can be adjusted to help hold the climber's hand in the desired spot and to direct a downward pull straight along the shaft. Used in this manner, the leash shares the work of holding and swinging the ax. The leash also makes it possible to hang from an ice tool without maintaining a forearm-killing grip.

Maintenance

Inspect ice tools before each outing, checking for cracks and other signs of wear or damage. Be sure that adzes, picks, and spikes are sharp. Keep these sharp edges covered with guards when they are not in use. If the tools are a modular design, also check to see that all fastening systems are secure.

ICE SCREWS

Modern tubular ice screws (fig. 18-7a) are made from steel, aluminum, or titanium alloy. Ice screws come in a variety of lengths ranging from 10 to 22 centimeters (ice screws are commonly measured in metric units). The length of an ice screw has a great bearing on its strength. A longer screw is stronger, but only if the length is not greater than the depth of the ice. The latest screw designs include integral spinning knobs or handles, which make placement and removal almost effortless compared to older pound-in screws (see the "History of Ice Screws" sidebar). The tubular design minimizes fracturing of the ice by allowing the displaced ice to work itself out through the hollow core of the screw.

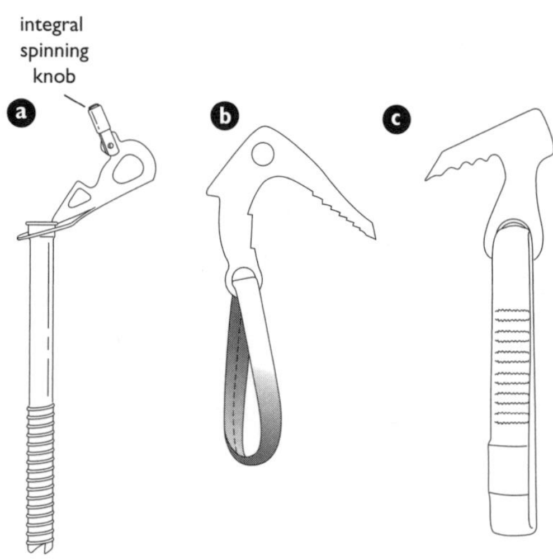

Fig. 18-7. Ice protection: a, tubular ice screw with knob; b and c, ice hooks.

The ice hook is a type of pound-in protection designed for thin ice (fig. 18-7b and c). The ice hook may be used to hook features in either ice or rock; driven into the ice as a piton using ice-tool or monopoint placements as starter holes; or pounded into ice-filled cracks. Typically, climbers use ice hooks in conjunction with a load-limiting runner. This type of protection usually needs to be chopped out by the second, an arduous task.

HISTORY OF ICE SCREWS

Until the mid-20th century, ice pitons were extra-long, blade-type rock pitons with holes, notches, or bulges to increase their grip in ice. After World War II, climbers experimented with new designs that featured a greater surface area (to decrease the load per square inch on the ice) and more holes (to help the shaft freeze into the slope). In the early 1960s, when ice pitons evolved into ice screws, enthusiasts claimed that they would revolutionize ice climbing, bringing security to the slopes. Critics countered that the screws were not much better than the older ice pitons. This was true of the lightweight, relatively weak "coat-hanger" ice screws, which are no longer in use. Ice screws have continued to improve and now provide reliable protection when placed in good ice.

OTHER GEAR

Ice climbers use other gear adapted specifically for ice, including specialized holsters, racking devices, eye protection, and V-thread tools.

Holsters

Use a holster, harness gear loop, or racking device (see below) to temporarily hold an ice tool. Two holsters or a double-size holster can be added to a seat harness or pack hip belt. Try out the tools in the holster before using it. The tools may be hard to remove if the holster was designed for rock climbing hammers, which have thinner and smoother shafts.

Racking Devices

A variety of devices are designed to facilitate the racking of ice screws and ice tools. Personal preference and compatibility with a particular harness or gear sling influence the selection. Some of these devices attach directly to the harness waist belt (fig. 18-8a); others rigidly hold a carabiner attached to the harness gear loops or gear sling (fig. 18-8b and c). These devices allow ice screws to be racked securely, yet provide easy, one-handed unclipping when the gear is needed. Racking devices can also be used for temporarily securing ice tools.

Ropes

Standard single ropes are most commonly used for ice climbing, though this depends on the type of climb and the climbers' preference (see Table 9-1 in Chapter 9, Basic Safety System). Using a rope longer than 50 meters (165 feet) permits longer pitches. Double-rope and twin-rope techniques (see Chapter 14, Leading on Rock) are an option for ice climbing. Some climbers feel more comfortable using a two-rope system for ice climbing because it provides redundancy amid the sharp tools, crampons, and falling ice debris, and it allows for full-length rappels on the descent.

Because ice climbing can be wet, water-repellent ("dry") ropes are worth the extra cost. In comparison with untreated ropes, dry ropes retain more strength and are less likely to freeze—though a dry rope can still become ice-coated and the water repellency may not last the lifetime of the rope.

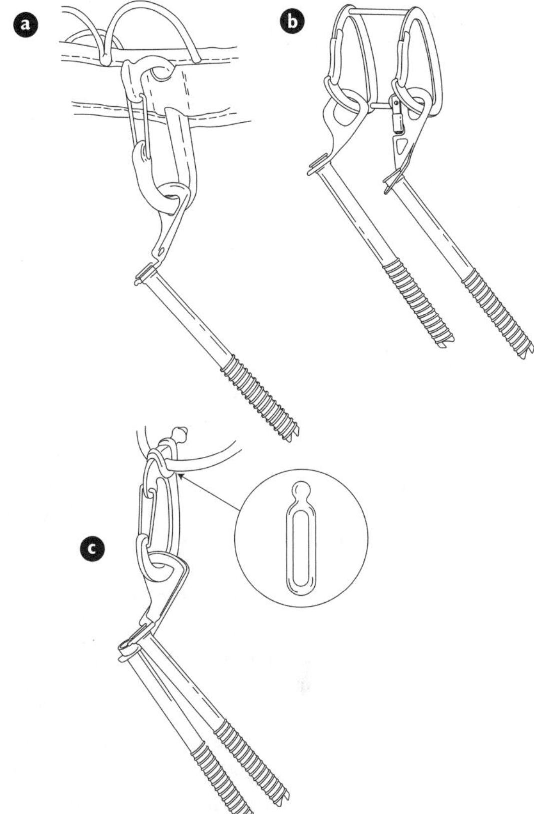

Fig. 18-8. Racking devices: a, attached directly to seat harness waist belt; b and c, carabiner(s) rigidly attached to seat harness gear loops or gear sling.

Head and Eye Protection

Prudent ice climbers wear helmets. The helmet should be fitted to accommodate a hat or balaclava. Ice climbers should also protect their eyes from flying debris and ultraviolet light by wearing either goggles or sunglasses. Goggles must fit when a helmet is worn and have adequate ventilation to minimize fogging, a constant problem.

Load-Limiting Runners

Consider using load-limiting runners, also known as energy-absorbing runners or slings (see Figure 9-35 in Chapter 9, Basic Safety System). It is advisable to use a load-limiting runner on the first piece of protection or when the protection placement is in ice of questionable quality. These runners can provide an extra margin of safety. Load-limiting runners can be placed in series, to increase the total energy absorption, or ganged, to increase the force required to activate the runner.

V-Thread Tools

The V-thread tool is a hooking device used to pull cord or webbing through the drilled tunnel of V-thread anchors (see "Setting Up Ice Anchors," later in this chapter). Two styles of V-thread tools are available commercially. One consists of a piece of wire cable with a hook swaged to one end (fig. 18-9a). The second type is a piece of stamped metal or plastic with a hook on one end (fig. 18-9b). Both types have advantages and disadvantages. The cable type is less likely to impale you but is less suited to pushing the cord or webbing into the hole. The rigid type is a better tool

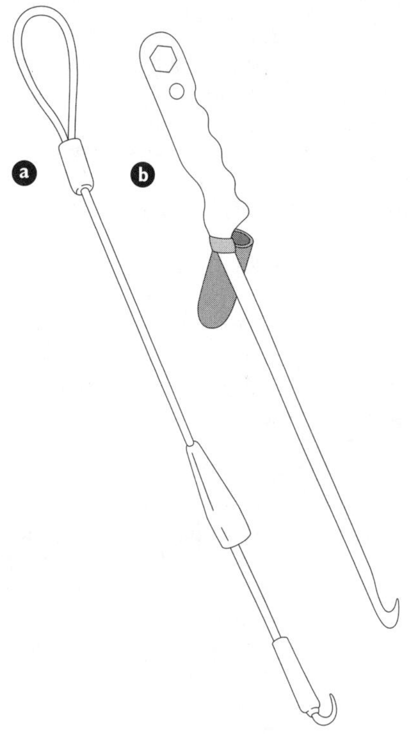

Fig. 18-9. V-thread tools with hook guards: a, cable; b, rigid.

for pushing the cord or webbing down into the hole but is also more likely to stab you. A V-thread tool can also be made from a piece of wire hanger. Remember to keep the hook sharp.

TECHNIQUES OF ALPINE ICE CLIMBING

Climbing the perennially shaded side of a mountain can be an exhilarating passage over an ever-changing medium in a steep and cold environment, all of which challenges both mind and body. An alpine ice climber must move quickly and efficiently up long and sometimes sparsely protected faces to reach the summit, and then safely descend within the allotted time. On alpine ice, climbers use surface features, seeking out depressions, pockets, and ledges for tool placements, crampon purchase, and belay points. Unlike rock climbers, ice climbers are not in direct contact with the surface of the mountain. The ice climber must rely on ice tools, axes, and crampons. They make do with anchors and protection placements that can be uncertain.

CLIMBING WITHOUT CRAMPONS

Alpine climbers often encounter short sections of ice or frozen snow. Sometimes they are not carrying crampons, or they may face short ice problems that do not merit taking the time to put on crampons. Negotiating these sections without crampons requires balance-climbing, moving up from one position of balance to the next. At each position of balance, the inside (uphill) foot is in front of and above the trailing outside (downhill) foot. The ax, in the uphill hand, moves only after body and feet are in balance, and the feet move only after the ax has been moved forward. Shift weight from one foot to the other smoothly as though friction climbing on rock. While climbing, look for irregularities in the surface of the ice such as suncups (small hollows that have been melted by the sun) or imbedded rocks to use as footholds.

If the slope is too steep for secure balance, consider taking another route or try cutting steps. Step-cutting is a good method if the steps can be cut quickly and efficiently.

Step-Cutting

For the earliest alpinists, chopping or cutting steps was the only technique available for climbing steep ice and hard snow. The invention of crampons reduced the need for step-cutting but never eliminated it. There are many good reasons for developing a working knowledge of the technique of cutting steps with the ice ax. A lost or broken crampon, or an injured or inexperienced climber, may be reason enough to cut steps. Even if wearing crampons, climbers might welcome a slight step for added security or to serve as a small platform on which to rest. Climbers should also be able to chop out a comfortable belay platform.

The adze of the ice ax can be used for cutting steps two ways. The adze can be used to slash the ice by swinging the tool in a motion nearly parallel to the surface of the ice to create a slash step (fig. 18-10), or it can be swung perpendicular to the ice to chop out a pigeonhole step (see below). For all step-cutting, use a wrist leash to help support the hard-working hand holding the ax and to keep from losing the ax if it is dropped.

Slash steps. The most frequently used step-cutting technique is cutting slash steps, for traversing up or down gentle to moderate slopes. To cut ascending slash

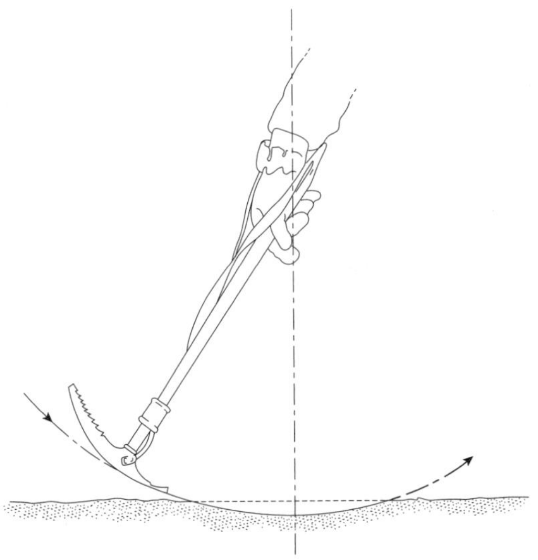

Fig. 18-10. The motion of the ice ax in cutting a slash step.

steps, stand in a position of balance, holding the ax in the inside (uphill) hand (fig. 18-11a). Cut two steps. Swing the adze parallel to the uphill foot and away from the body. Swing the ax from the shoulder, cutting with the adze and letting the weight of the ax do most of the work. With successive swings, slice ice out of the step, starting at the heel end of the new step and working toward the toe. Scoop out chunks of ice with the adze, and use the adze and pick to finish the step. The climber proceeds up the slope, moving in and out of a position of balance on the steps (fig. 18-11b).

Pigeonhole steps. For negotiating steeper slopes, cut pigeonhole steps. This is done by swinging the ax perpendicular to the ice and chopping out a hole with the adze. Each step should slope slightly inward to help keep boots from slipping out of the step. On gentler slopes, it is acceptable if the step holds only a small part of a boot, but the steps on steeper slopes should be large enough for the front half of a boot. Space the steps so they are convenient for all members of the party to use. Pigeonhole steps for the direct ascent of steep ice are placed about shoulder-width apart and within easy stepping distance of each other. Each step functions as both a handhold and foothold, so each should have a small lip to serve as a handhold.

Ladder steps. To chop steps down an ice slope, the easiest method is to cut a "ladder" of pigeonhole steps that descend almost straight down the hill. To cut two steps in sequence, start in a position of balance, facing down the slope. Chop two pigeonhole steps directly below. When the new steps are ready, step down with the outside (downhill) foot and then the inside (uphill) foot. To cut just one step at a time, again start in a position of balance. Cut the step for the outside (downhill) foot and move that foot down into the step. Then cut the step for the inside (uphill) foot and move that foot down into it. Some climbers may opt to rappel rather than cut steps down an icy incline.

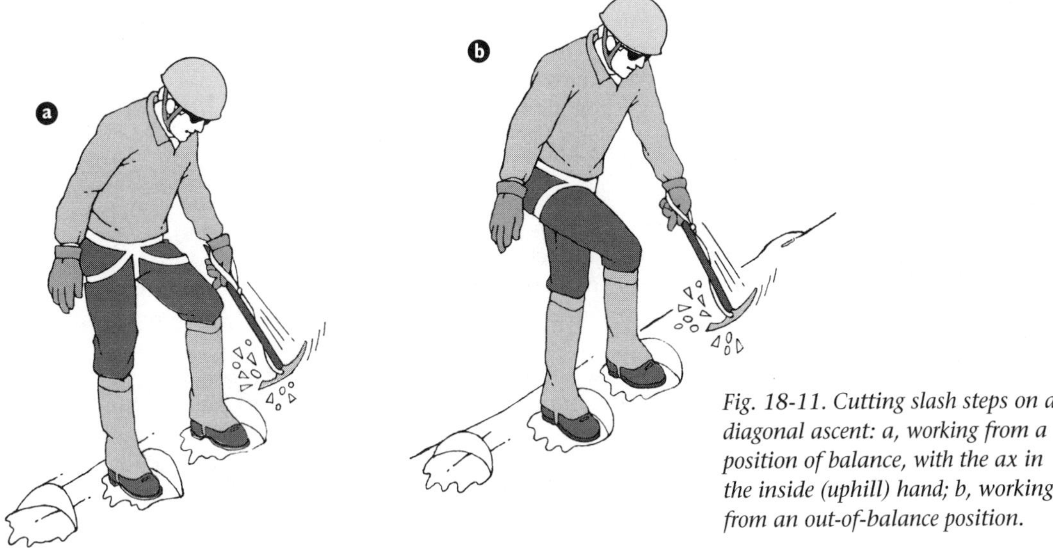

Fig. 18-11. Cutting slash steps on a diagonal ascent: a, working from a position of balance, with the ax in the inside (uphill) hand; b, working from an out-of-balance position.

CLIMBING WITH CRAMPONS

Ice climbers usually employ features of two basic techniques, depending on steepness of the slope, conditions of the ice, and their ability and confidence level. These are termed French technique and German technique. Although each technique has its own distinct benefits, modern ice climbing melds the two. Mastery of both French and German technique is essential for climbing in the changeable alpine environment. Below are brief descriptions of these methods, followed by sections that apply them to specific types of terrain.

French Technique (Flat-Footing)

French technique, also called flat-footing, is the easiest and most efficient method of climbing on gentle to steep ice and hard snow. Good French technique demands balance, rhythm, joint flexibility, and the confident use of crampons and ice ax. Specifics of this technique are described in the sections that follow.

German Technique (Front-Pointing)

Developed by Germans and Austrians for climbing the harder snow and ice of the eastern Alps, German technique, better known as front-pointing, allows an experienced ice climber to go up the steepest and most difficult ice slopes. With this technique, even average climbers can quickly overcome sections that would be difficult or impossible with French technique. The German technique is much like kicking steps straight up a snow slope, but instead of kicking a boot into the snow, kick that boot's front crampon points into the ice; step up with the other foot, directly supported by the placed boot's front points. Just as in French technique, good front-pointing is rhythmic and balanced, with the weight of the body balanced over the crampons. It is essential to move efficiently, whether planting front points, placing ice tools, or moving on the ice.

American Technique (Combination)

Modern crampon technique evolved from the French and German styles. As on rock, climbing on ice involves the efficient and confident use of footwork to maintain balance and minimize fatigue. Flat-footing is generally used on lower-angle slopes and where crampon point penetration is easy. Front-pointing is most commonly used on slopes steeper than 45 degrees and on very hard ice. In practice, most climbers blend them into a combination approach, sometimes called American technique.

In any technique, the most important element is confident use of the crampons. Practicing on gentle and moderate slopes helps develop skill, confidence, and the aggressive approach needed at steeper angles. A skilled ice climber, whether flat-footing or front-pointing, displays the same deliberate movement as a skilled rock climber. The crampon points must be carefully and deliberately placed into the ice, and the climber's weight transferred from one foot to the other smoothly and decisively. Boldness is essential to skillful crampon technique. Exposure must be disregarded and concentration focused solely on the climbing. But boldness is not blind bravado. It is confidence and skill born of experience and enthusiasm, nurtured in many practice sessions on glacial seracs and on ice bulges in frozen gullies, then matured by ascents of increasing length and difficulty.

ICE CLIMBING TERMS

Table 18-3 lists ice climbing techniques for crampons and ice ax, along with the approximate steepness of the slope on which each technique is used. French terms are sometimes used, given in parentheses. The French word *pied* (pronounced pee-EY) means "foot"; the French word *piolet* (pronounced pee-oh-LAY) means "ice ax." Terms including the word *pied* refer to footwork; terms including the word *piolet* refer to ice-ax positions.

None of these techniques are restricted to any particular set of conditions, and all can be useful in a wide range of snow and ice situations. When practicing these techniques, keep in mind that a sharp crampon is a happy crampon, requiring only body weight to set it securely in place.

CLIMBING ON GENTLE TO MODERATE SLOPES

On gently to moderately sloped ice, French technique dominates.

Using French Technique

French technique, or flat-footing, is an essential alpine ice climbing technique. Keep boot soles parallel to the ice surface and feet slightly farther apart than normal to avoid snagging a crampon point on clothing or on a crampon strap on the other foot. Firmly set all bottom points into the ice. Use the ice ax in the cane position (see Figures 18-12 and 18-13), holding the ax in the self-belay grasp (for ice ax positions and grasps, see Chapter 16, Snow Travel and Climbing). On gentle slopes, begin

TABLE 18-3. TECHNIQUES FOR CRAMPONS, ICE AXES, AND ICE TOOLS

Technique	Approximate Steepness of Slope
CRAMPONS	
Walking (French technique; *pied marche*)	Gentle, 0° to 15°
Duckwalk (French technique; *pied en canard*)	Gentle, 15° to 30°
Flat-footing (French technique; *pied à plat*)	Moderate to steep, 30° to 60° and higher
Rest position (French technique; *pied assis*)	Steep, 60° and higher
Three o'clock position (American technique; *pied troisième*)	Steep, 60° and higher
Front-pointing (German technique)	Steep through vertical and overhanging, 45° and higher
ICE AXES AND ICE TOOLS (FRENCH AND GERMAN TECHNIQUE)	
Cane position (*piolet canne*)	Gentle to moderate, 0° to 45°
Cross-body position (*piolet ramasse*)	Moderate, 30° to 45°
Anchor position (*piolet ancre*)	Steep to extremely steep, 45° and higher
Low-dagger position (*piolet panne*)	Steep, 45° to 55°
High-dagger position (*piolet poignard*)	Steep, 50° to 60°
Traction position (*piolet traction*)	Extremely steep through vertical and overhanging, 60° and higher

by simply walking. Flexible ankles are sometimes necessary in order to keep boot soles parallel to the surface. Boots that are flexible at the ankle facilitate flat-footing. Climbers with plastic boots can loosen their bootlaces at the cuff for more comfortable flat-footing. Ease ankle strain by rotating boots out, more and more downhill, as the slope steepens.

As the gentle slope steepens slightly, splay feet outward in duckwalk fashion (fig. 18-12). Keep knees bent and weight balanced over the feet. Continue to use the ax as a cane.

As the slope gets steeper still, no longer gentle but moderate, duckwalking straight upward causes severe ankle strain. Instead, turn sideways to the slope and ascend diagonally for a more relaxed, comfortable step. Be sure to use flat-footing, with all crampon points weighted into the ice (fig. 18-13). When using this technique for the first time, people have a tendency to edge with their crampons. The crampon points can skate off the ice, throwing the climber off balance. Fight this tendency, and keep the crampon points flat against the ice at all times. Start with feet pointed in the direction of travel. As the slope steepens, rotate both feet more and more downward in order to keep them flat. As the slope angle increases, ease ankle strain by pointing both boots downhill more and more, so that the flex needed to keep both feet flat comes from the more normal forward flex of the ankle and from the knees, which are bent away from the slope and spread well apart (see Figure 18-14). On the steepest slopes, both knees may be pointing straight downhill.

As the slope angle changes from gentle to moderate, using the ax in the cane position becomes awkward. Greater security can now be achieved by holding the ax in the cross-body position. Grip the shaft just above the spike with the inside (uphill) hand and hold the head of the ax in the self-belay grasp, pick pointing forward, with the outside (downhill) hand. Drive the spike into the ice, the shaft perpendicular to the slope. In the cross-body position, most of the force on the ax should be from the hand on the shaft. The hand on the head stabilizes the ax and is a reminder not to lean into the slope. To keep from leaning into the ice, a full-length ice ax is needed, rather than a shorter ice tool. Even experienced ice climbers have difficulty maintaining proper French technique with a short ax.

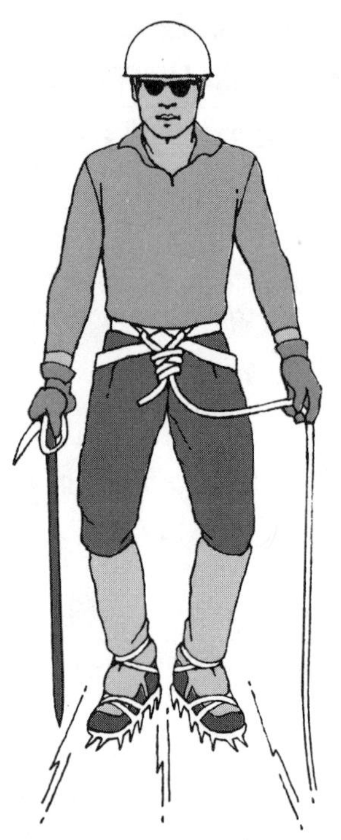

Fig. 18-12. French technique on a gentle slope, duckwalk combined with ice ax in cane position.

Fig. 18-13. French technique on a moderate slope, flat-footing in a diagonal ascent combined with ice ax in cane position.

Move diagonally upward in a two-step sequence, much the same as ascending a snow slope without crampons. Remember to keep feet flat at all times. Start from a position of balance, the inside (uphill) foot in front of and above the trailing outside (downhill) leg (fig. 18-14a). From this in-balance position, bring the outside foot in front of and above the inside foot, into the out-of-balance position (fig. 18-14b). Cross the outside leg over the knee of the inside leg; if the cross is made at the ankle, stability is compromised and the next step is difficult to make. To return to a position of balance, bring the inside foot up from behind and place it again in front of the outside foot (fig. 18-14c). Keep the body centered over the crampons. Avoid leaning into the slope and creating the danger of crampon points twisting out of the ice. Step on lower-angled spots and natural irregularities in the ice to ease ankle strain and conserve energy.

During this diagonal ascent, plant the ax about an arm's length ahead (as shown in Figure 18-14a) each time before moving another two steps. Whether using the ax in the cane or the cross-body position, plant it far enough forward so that it will be near the hip after you move up to the next in-balance position (as shown in Figure 18-14c).

To change direction (switchback) on a diagonal ascent of a moderate ice slope, use the same technique as on a snow slope where crampons would not be used, but keep both feet flat. From a position of balance, place the ax directly above this location. Move the outside (downhill) foot forward, into the out-of-balance position, to about the same elevation as the other foot and pointing slightly uphill (fig. 18-15a). Grasping the ax with both hands, turn into the slope, moving the inside (uphill) foot to point in the new direction and slightly uphill. You are now facing into the slope, standing with feet splayed outward in opposite directions (fig. 18-15b). If the splayed-foot position feels unstable, front-point. Return to the in-balance position by moving the foot that is still pointing in the original direction to above and in front of the other foot. Reposition your grasp on the ice ax, for either the cane or cross-body position. You are now back in balance and facing the new direction of travel (fig. 18-15c).

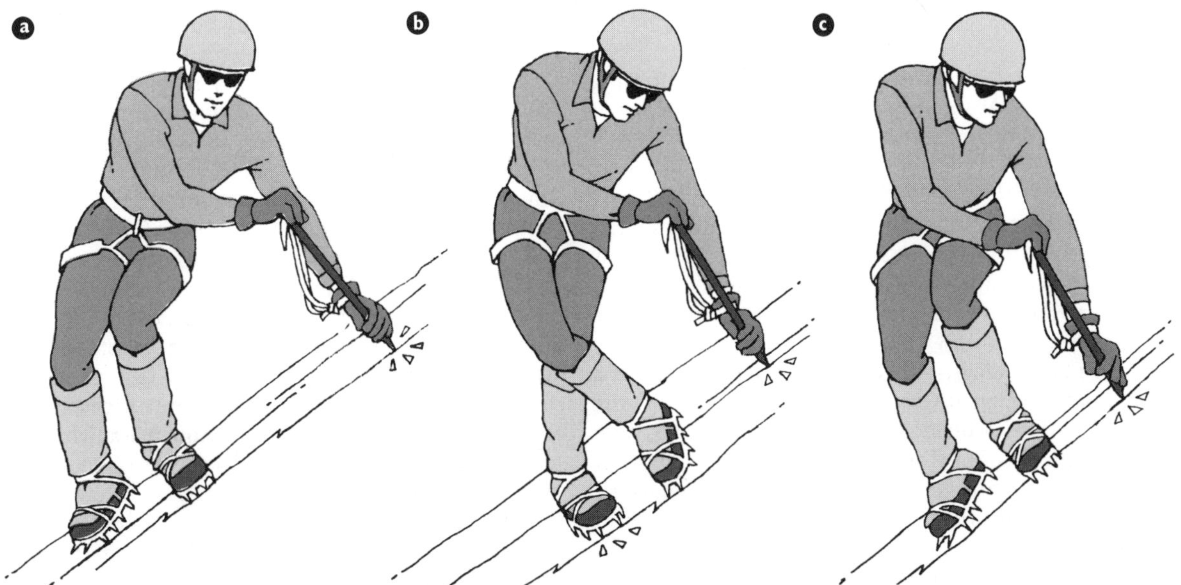

Fig. 18-14. French technique on a diagonal ascent of a moderate slope, flat-footing combined with ice ax in cross-body position (pick forward): a, in-balance position; b, out-of-balance position; c, back to in-balance position.

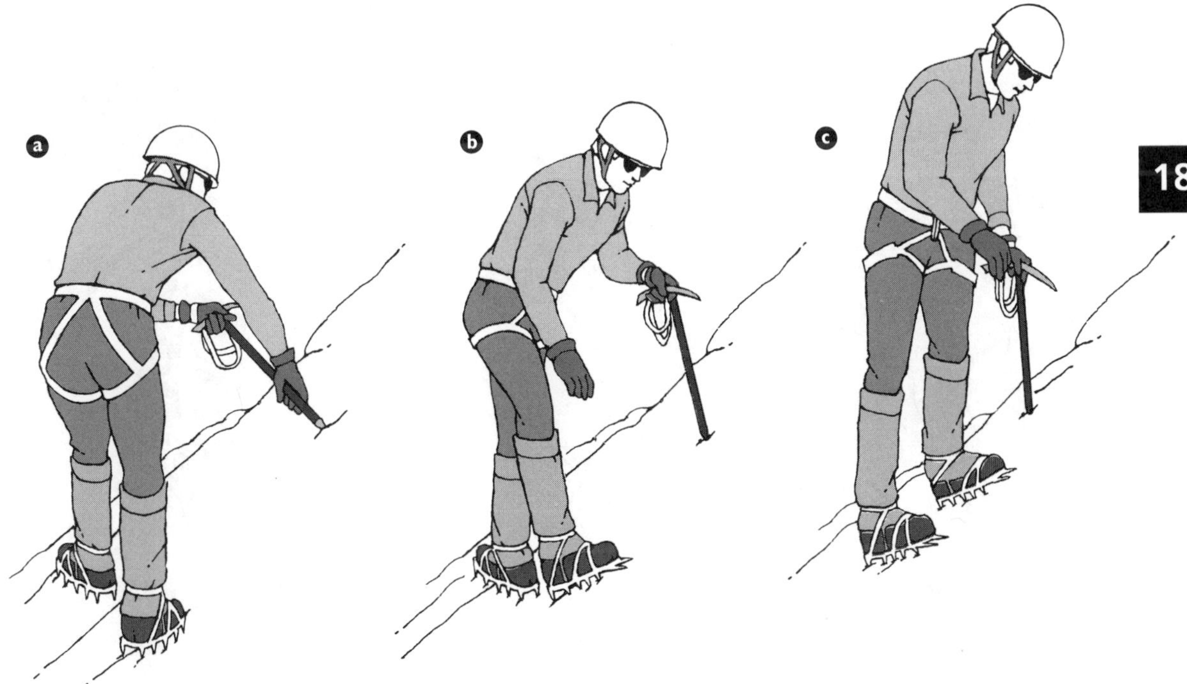

Fig. 18-15. French technique changing direction on a diagonal ascent of a moderate slope, flat-footing combined with ice ax in cross-body position: a, out-of-balance position; b, turning; c, in-balance position in new direction.

CLIMBING ON MODERATE TO STEEP SLOPES

On steeper ice, other variations of French technique are called for. At some point, the German technique of front-pointing comes into play.

Using French Technique

On moderate to steep slopes, for more security switch the ice ax from the cross-body position to what is known as the anchor position. Your feet remain flat, with all bottom crampon points weighted into the ice at each step.

To place the ax in the anchor position, begin in a position of balance. Grip the ice ax shaft just above the spike with the outside (downhill) hand (fig. 18-16a). Swing the ax so that the pick sticks into the ice in front of and above your head, with the shaft parallel to the slope; with the other hand, take hold of the ax head in the self-arrest grasp (fig. 18-16b). Now pull on the ax while moving two steps forward to a new position of balance (fig. 18-16c). Use a gentle and constant outward pull on the ice ax to set its teeth and keep it locked into the ice. When it is time to release it, push the bottom of the shaft toward the ice and lift the pick up and out.

To keep feet flat at these angles, your body must lean farther away from the slope, with knees and ankles flexed and the toes of your boots increasingly pointing downhill. Try to continue advancing upward in the standard sequence, moving two steps at a time. At the steepest angles, however, your feet point downhill and you must take increasingly smaller steps, essentially moving backward up the slope. But continue to plant and remove the pick from a position of balance. The foot that is on the same side as the direction of travel should be at least slightly higher than the other foot, allowing your upper body to rotate for a smooth, strong swing of the ax.

To change diagonal direction when the ice ax is in the anchor position, use the same sequence as with the cane or cross-body position, as in Figure 18-15. However, on the steepest slopes, where you are stepping backward, change direction simply by switching hands on the ax and planting it on the other side. There is not much diagonal movement at this point, because you are mainly moving backward straight up the slope.

The French also devised a rest position—called *pied assis*—that gives leg muscles a rest and provides more security for replanting the ax (fig. 18-17). From a

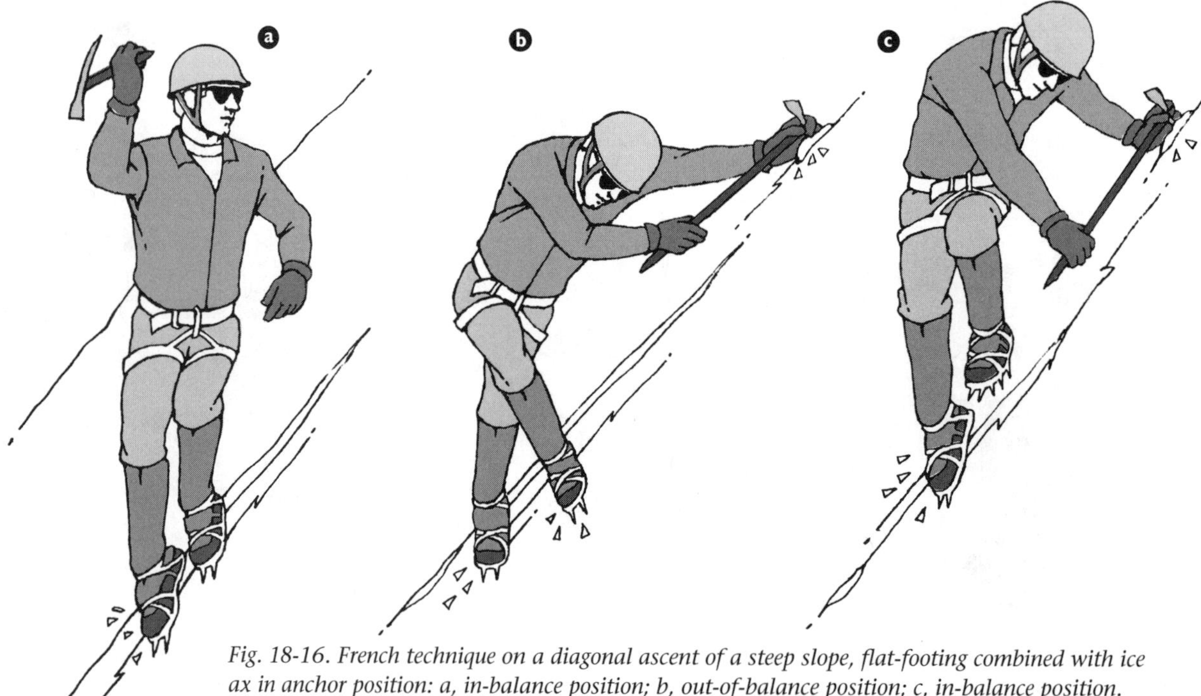

Fig. 18-16. French technique on a diagonal ascent of a steep slope, flat-footing combined with ice ax in anchor position: a, in-balance position; b, out-of-balance position; c, in-balance position.

Fig. 18-17. French technique of pied assis *for a balanced rest on a steep slope.*

position of balance, bring the outside (downhill) foot up and beneath your buttocks, with the boot—flat, as always—pointing straight downhill. Then sit down on the heel of that foot. This is a balanced position, a relatively comfortable one.

The invaluable technique of flat-footing, used with the ice ax in the cane or cross-body position, will serve an experienced climber for many alpine routes. For short stretches of steeper ice, flat-footing combined with the ice ax in anchor position will often work, but this marks the upper limit of French technique.

Using German Technique

On steep ice slopes, use of French technique and German technique begins to overlap. They both have a place on these slopes.

Most people pick up front-pointing quickly because it feels natural and secure. Unfortunately, this encourages its use on moderate slopes where flat-footing would be just as secure and more efficient. In flat-footing, most of the strain is on the large, powerful thigh muscles. Front-pointing, however, depends almost solely on the smaller calf muscles, which burn out much faster. Even climbers who strongly prefer front-pointing would benefit from alternating the techniques to give their calf muscles a rest.

Plastic boots provide a firm base for crampons and make front-pointing easiest. Very stiff-soled leather boots are also good. Less stiff-soled boots can be used in some cases but require more muscular effort. However, flexible-soled boots (fig. 18-18) just do not provide the necessary support for front-pointing. Pioneer ice climber Yvon Chouinard said it well in *Climbing Ice*: "You can't dance on hard ice with soft-soled shoes." (see Appendix D, Supplementary Resources).

Front-pointing uses not only the primary points of the crampons but also the secondary points immediately behind them. These points, attached to a rigid boot and properly placed in the ice, provide a platform

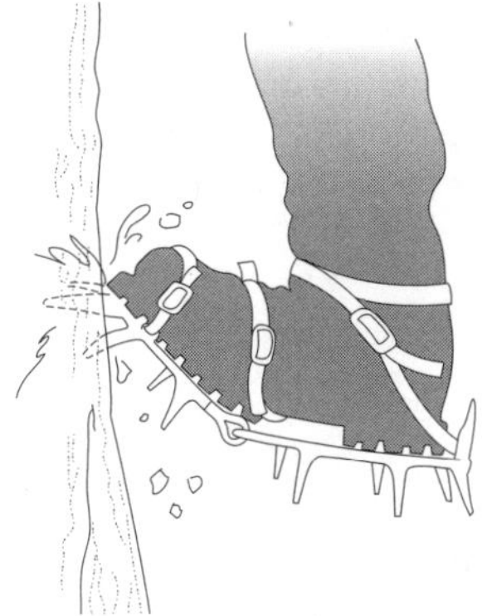

Fig. 18-18. Problems with trying to front-point in soft-soled boots.

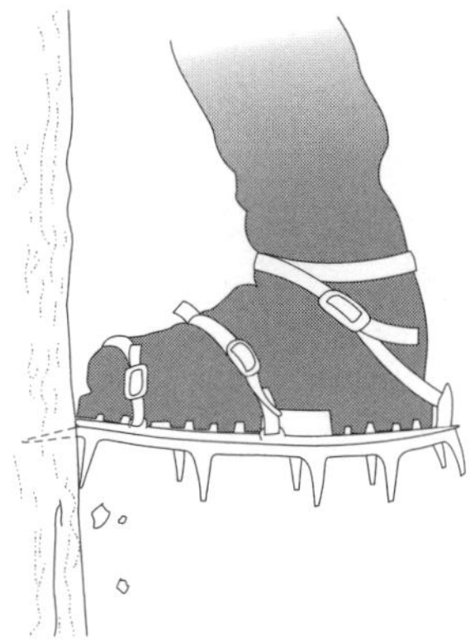

Fig. 18-19. Correct boot position in front-pointing is toes straight in, heels slightly down.

18

that can be stood upon. The most stable placement of the boot is straight into the ice, avoiding splayed feet, which tend to rotate the outside front points out of the ice. The boot soles should be perpendicular to the ice surface, with heels slightly down in order to engage the secondary points into the ice and complete the four-point platform for standing (fig. 18-19). Slightly bend at the knee to reduce the strain on calf muscles.

Resist the temptation to raise your heels. This pulls the secondary points from the ice, endangering placement of the front points, and accelerates calf muscle fatigue. Your heels will normally feel lower than they really are, so if it feels as though your heels are too low, the odds are that they are in the correct position, slightly lower than horizontal. This is especially important when a climber is coming over the top of steep ice onto a gentler slope, where the natural tendency is to raise the heels, relax the level of concentration, and hurry. This is a formula for trouble because it could cause the crampon points to shear from the ice. A good way to become comfortable with the essential skills of crampon placement and foot positioning is to practice on a top rope with an experienced ice climber who can critique your style.

In the initial crampon placements on a route, concentrate on determining the amount of force required to secure a foothold. After that, a single confident swing should be all that is needed. Watch out for two common mistakes: kicking too hard (which is fatiguing) and kicking too often in one place (which fractures the ice and makes it harder to get a good foothold). After making a crampon placement, avoid foot movement because it can make the points rotate out of the ice.

Front-pointing uses a variety of ice ax positions. Dagger positions are useful in hard snow and relatively soft ice. They do not work well in hard ice. The jabbing and stabbing motions of placing the pick are not very powerful, and poor pick penetration into the hard ice could mean an insecure placement. Attempts to force a deeper placement may result in nothing more than a bruised hand. For harder ice or a steeper slope, abandon the dagger positions for the anchor and traction positions, which are also used in flat-footing.

Low-dagger position. Hold the ax by the adze in

Fig. 18-20. Front-pointing with ax in low-dagger position, near waist level.

Fig. 18-21. Front-pointing with ax in high-dagger position, above shoulder height.

the self-belay grasp and push the pick into the ice near waist level, to aid balance (fig. 18-20). This position is helpful in tackling a short, relatively steep section that requires only a few quick front-pointing moves. It tends to hold you away from the slope and out over your feet, the correct stance for front-pointing.

High-dagger position. Hold the ax head in the self-arrest grasp and jab the pick into the ice above shoulder height (fig. 18-21). Use this position if the slope is a bit too steep to insert the pick effectively into the ice at waist level in the low-dagger position.

Anchor position. While standing on front points, hold the ax shaft near the spike and swing the pick in as high as possible without overreaching (fig. 18-22a). Front-point upward, holding onto the shaft higher and higher while progressing, adding a self-arrest grasp on the adze with your other hand when you are high enough (fig. 18-22b). Finally, switch hands on the adze, converting the anchor position to the low-dagger position (fig. 18-22c); when the adze is at waist level, remove it from the ice and replant it higher, again in the anchor position. Use the anchor position on harder ice or a steeper slope.

Piolet traction. Hold the ax near the spike and plant it high; then climb the ice by slightly pulling straight down on the ax while front-pointing up (fig. 18-23). Do not move your hand on the shaft. Use *piolet traction* on the steepest and hardest ice.

On very hard or extremely steep ice, when it becomes too difficult to balance on front points while replanting the ax, it is necessary to use a second ice tool. You can use two tools at the same time because, except for the anchor position, all ice-ax techniques used with front-pointing require only one hand.

Using two tools provides three points of support—for example, two crampons and one ice tool while you replant the second tool. The placements must be secure enough so that if one point of support fails, the other two will hold you until you replace the third point. Your legs carry most of the weight, but your arms help with both weight-bearing and balance.

In double-tool technique, you can use the same ice ax

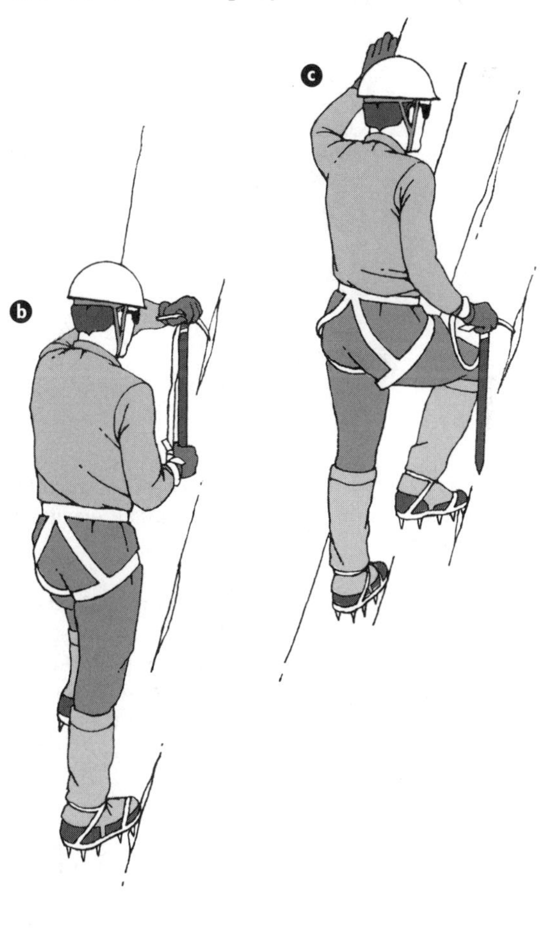

Fig. 18-22. Front-pointing using ax in anchor position: a, placing the ax high without overreaching; b, adding a self-arrest grasp on the ax while moving up; c, holding the ax in the low-dagger position before moving it up again.

Fig. 18-23. Front-pointing with ax overhead in traction position, pulling straight down on ax without moving the hand on shaft.

Fig. 18-24. Front-pointing using two tools, both in low-dagger position.

method for both hands or a different method for each. For instance, climb with both tools in low-dagger position (fig. 18-24). Or place one tool in high-dagger position and the other in *piolet traction* (fig. 18-25). (See "Climbing on Vertical Ice," later in this chapter, for details of double-tool technique using *piolet traction* with both tools.)

Using American Technique

One fast and powerful technique combines flat-footing and front-pointing. This is called the three o'clock position, *pied troisième* (fig. 18-26), because as one foot is front-pointing, the other is flat and points to the side (to three o'clock if it is the right foot or nine o'clock if it is the left). This combination is an example of American technique.

The three o'clock position is a potent resource for a direct line of ascent, much less tiring than front-pointing alone. The position lets climbers distribute the work over more muscle groups by alternating techniques with each leg. When climbing, seek out irregular flatter spots and any pockets or ledges for flat-footing, allowing calf muscles to rest. Use whatever ice-tool positions are appropriate for the situation.

Climbers alternate crampon techniques depending on ice conditions. Flat-footing is usually more secure on frozen snow, ice crust over snow, and soft or rotten ice, because more crampon points dig into the surface. When soft snow covers ice or hard snow, using front-pointing technique or the three o'clock position lets them blast through the surface to get points into the firmer layer beneath. Front-pointing is often the most secure technique for the average climber to use on very hard ice on all but gentle slopes. If you are having seri-

Fig. 18-25. Front-pointing using two tools, with the tool in the left hand in traction position and the tool in the right hand in high-dagger position.

Fig. 18-26. Three o'clock position for the feet, combining flat-footing (the right foot) and front-pointing (the left foot).

ous problems on a climb with flat-footing—perhaps due to fatigue, winds, high altitude, or fear—switch to front-pointing or the three o'clock position.

ICE-TOOL PLACEMENTS

The objective of placing any ice tool is to establish a solid placement with one swing. Each swing saved during a pitch means that much less fatigue at the top. It takes a lot of practice to learn pinpoint placement, especially when swinging the tool with the nondominant arm. But with a combination of proper technique and equipment, it should be possible to place a tool swiftly and precisely so that it is both secure and easy to remove.

At the base of the route, try a few tool placements to get a feel for the plasticity of the ice. Plasticity—which determines the ability of the ice to hold and release a tool—varies tremendously with temperature and age of the ice.

Study the ice for good placements. Ice holds the pick better in depressions than in bulges, which shatter or break off under the impact of an ice tool due to radiating fracture lines. Try to make placements in opaque ice, which is less brittle than clear ice because it has more air trapped inside. Minimize the number of placements needed by planting the pick as high as possible and by moving upward as far as possible with each placement. Placement techniques vary, depending on the type of pick.

Technically curved. Also known as alpine picks, technically curved picks are most like the pick of a standard ice ax (see Figure 18-4a). However, the picks are more acutely curved than that of a regular ax, so they hold better in ice. A tool with a technically curved pick is placed with a natural swing from the shoulder. This pick is used in conditions ranging from soft serac ice to hard water ice, though a harder swing is needed for good penetration in hard ice.

Reverse curved. The more acute angles of reverse-curved picks (see Figure 18-4b) require a somewhat different swing, with a definite wrist snap just prior to connecting. To plant the pick, bring your arm back, with your elbow bent about 90 degrees, then swing at the desired spot. At the end of the swing, snap your wrist toward the ice. The steeper the droop of the pick, the more wrist action is needed to set the pick.

The reverse-curved pick also works well for hooking holes in the ice. Large icicles often form in clusters on vertical sections, creating slots or gaps that are ideal for secure hooking placements.

Removing the Tool

In addition to learning the proper force to use in placing a tool, climbers must also learn the best way to remove it. Unless it is done correctly, removing a tool can be more tiring than placing it. Try to remove the tool in reverse of the motion used to set it. First, loosen the placement by rocking the shaft of the tool back and forth in the same plane as the pick (fig. 18-27a and b). Then try to remove the tool by pushing up with the shaft and then pulling the shaft out (fig. 18-27c and d). If this fails, release your grip on the tool and try to knock it loose by hitting up against the adze with the palm of your hand (fig. 18-27e).

Fig. 18-27. How to remove an ice tool: a and b, rock the shaft back and forth in the same plane as the pick; c and d, push up with the shaft and then pull the shaft out; e, strike up on the adze (or hammerhead).

Then grab the head and pull up and out. Never remove a tool by torquing it from side to side because the pick may break.

CLIMBING ON VERTICAL ICE

The most efficient and secure method of climbing vertical ice is front-pointing combined with use of two ice tools, vertically staggered, in *piolet traction*. This method of climbing ice is called tracking. The standard position for the feet is about shoulder width apart and level with each other, a stable and relatively comfortable stance. One tool is planted above your head so that your arm is straight. The other tool is locked off and weighted, at shoulder height. At this point your feet and upper tool form a triangle against the ice. Pull down and slightly outward on the tools to keep the picks' teeth set in the ice, and apply inward pressure on the crampon points. To conserve energy, hang from the wrist leashes rather than gripping the tools tightly.

To ascend, grasp the tools, walk both feet up taking small steps, then remove the lower tool and replant it above your head (fig. 18-28a). Maintain three points of contact at all times. Let your legs do most of the work; do not burn out your arms by doing pull-ups while climbing. Now repeat the sequence: Place one tool, move both feet, place the other tool (fig. 18-28b), move both feet, and so on. Be careful not to overreach for a tool placement because that motion may cause your front points to dislodge from the ice. Concentrate on efficient, methodical placement of crampon points and ice tools. Rhythm is as important as balance.

Climbers sometimes find themselves "barn-dooring"—swinging out of balance—as they remove one tool in order to place it higher. Avoid this by shifting your center of balance toward the tool that will remain in the ice. Once that new, higher placement is made, shift your center of balance to the higher tool and then remove the lower tool.

The monkey hang is a good technique to use for ascending ice bulges, small overhangs, and longer vertical sections (see Chapter 19, Waterfall Ice and Mixed Climbing).

From Vertical to a Horizontal Stretch

Oddly enough, one of the most challenging sequences involves climbing from a vertical face up onto a horizontal step or ledge. With a secure horizontal section of ice ahead, climbers may relax concentration and

Fig. 18-28. Staying in balance on vertical ice: a, center body weight on the right-hand tool and remove the left-hand tool for higher placement; b, then center body weight on the replanted left-hand tool and remove the right-hand tool.

forget about good foot placement. At the same time, they face the problem that it is virtually impossible to obtain a confident tool placement by blindly swinging over a ledge. They must move high enough to see onto the ledge.

To do this, make shorter tool and foot placements when approaching the lip of the ledge, then step up to a high-dagger position so you can see onto the ledge and look for a good spot to place an ice tool. You may need to remove snow or rotten ice, which often accumulates on ledges and moderate ice slopes. Place an ice tool securely into the ledge, well back from the lip, and then place the second ice tool; move your feet up until they are safely over the lip (fig. 18-29). Remember that it is especially important to keep the heels low.

TRAVERSING STEEP TO VERTICAL ICE

The principles for traversing are much the same as for front-pointing up steep ice. However, because the climber is moving to the side instead of straight up, it is

Fig. 18-29. Pulling onto a ledge.

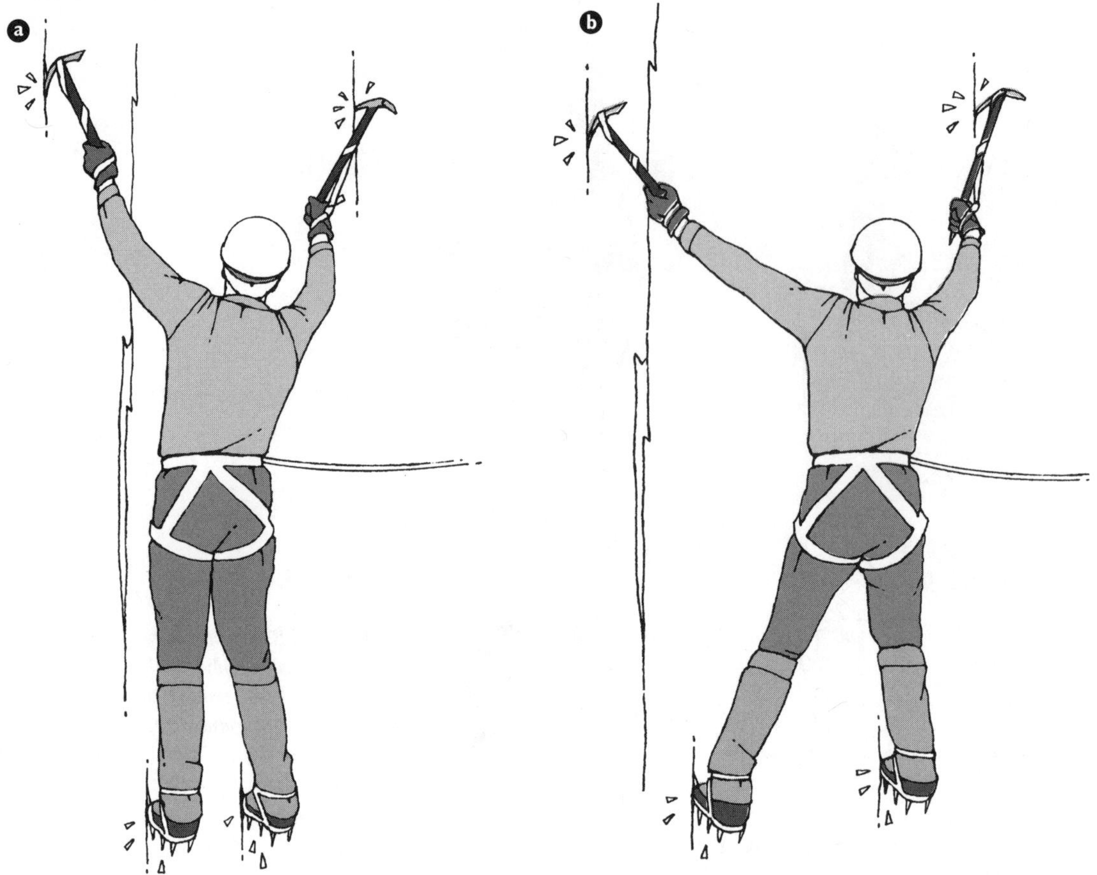

Fig. 18-30. Traversing to the right on vertical ice: a, planting the leading tool to the side to begin the traverse; b, moving the feet to the right.

more difficult to keep one foot perpendicular to the ice while replacing the front points of the other foot. If your heel rotates, the front points will also rotate and come out of the ice. Ice tools also tend to rotate out during sideways travel.

Start from a secure position with both feet at the same level. Lean in the direction of travel and plant the leading tool in the ice (fig. 18-30a). This places the leading tool lower than it would be if you were ascending, but not so far to the side that it causes your body to rotate out from the wall when the trailing tool is removed. This also puts the trailing tool in a position so that it can be pulled on in a modified lieback while you are traversing, without twisting the tool out of the ice.

Now shuffle sideways on front points (fig. 18-30b). It is also possible to make a two-step move, crossing the trailing foot over the leading foot, and then bringing the other foot back into the lead. Most climbers prefer the shuffle, which is less awkward and feels more secure. After moving your feet, replant the trailing tool closer to your body at a 45-degree angle (as in Figure 18-30a), replant the leading tool vertically, and repeat the process.

DESCENDING

Depending on the angle of the ice, French, German, or American technique may be used.

Using French Technique

Cane position. To descend gently sloping ice, simply face directly downhill, bend your knees slightly, and walk firmly downward. Plant all bottom crampon points into

Fig. 18-31. Flat-footing on descent with ice ax in cane position.

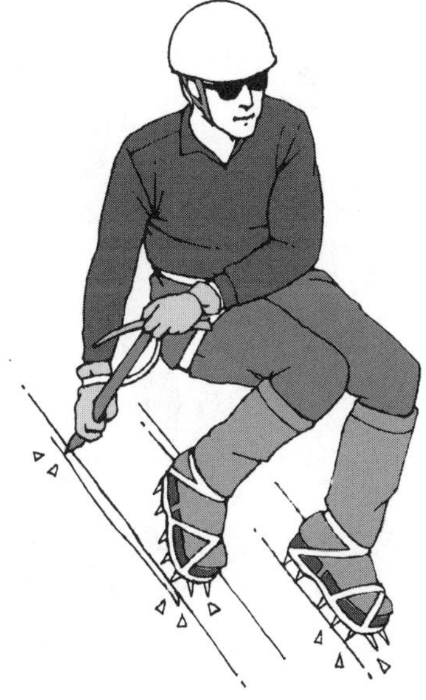

Fig. 18-32. Flat-footing on descent with ice ax in cross-body position.

the ice with each step. Hold the ax in the cane position. As the descent angle steepens, bend your knees more and spread them apart, with your body weight over your feet so that all crampon points bite securely (fig. 18-31). Thigh muscles do the bulk of the work.

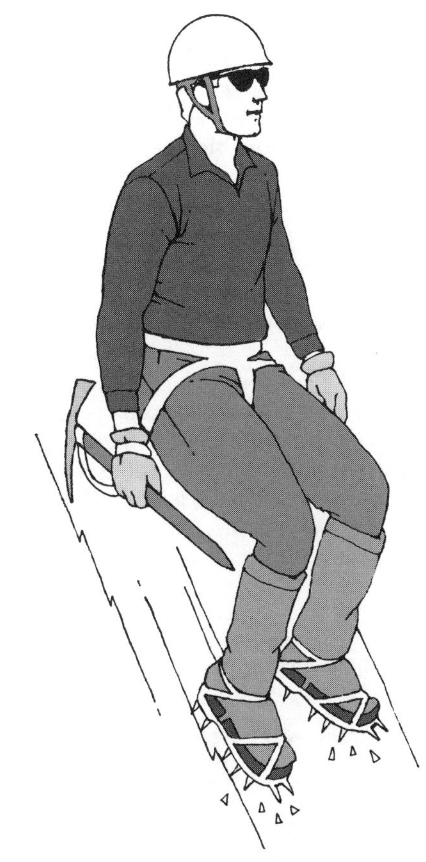

Fig. 18-33. Flat-footing on descent with ice ax in the support position.

Cross-body position. For greater security, plant the ax perpendicular to the slope in the cross-body position (fig. 18-32).

Support position. For the next level of security, use the ax in the support position (fig. 18-33). Grasp the ax near the middle of the shaft and hold it beside you while descending, with the ax head pointing uphill, pick down, and the spike pointing downhill.

Banister position. As the slope steepens, use the ax in the banister position. Grasp the ax near the spike and plant the pick as far below you as possible (fig. 18-34a). Walk downward, sliding your hand along the shaft toward the head of the ax (fig. 18-34b). Maintain a slight outward pull (away from the ice) on the shaft to keep the pick locked in the ice (fig. 18-34c). With a reverse-curved pick, this is less secure; you must pull parallel to the ice. Keep moving down until you are below the ax head (fig. 18-34d). Then release the pick (fig. 18-34e), and replant the ax farther down.

Anchor position. On a slope too steep to safely descend facing outward, turn sideways and descend diagonally. Your footwork changes to the same flat-footing technique used to ascend diagonally. Use the ax in the anchor position (fig. 18-35). With your outside arm, swing the ax out in front and plant the pick in the ice; take hold of the head with the other hand in the self-arrest grasp; and then flat-foot diagonally down below the ax. The shaft rotates as you pass below it.

Using German Technique

On steeper slopes, front-point and tool techniques are generally the same for going down as they are for going up. But, just as on rock, down-climbing is more difficult. The tendency is to step too low, which keeps your heels too high, so front points may fail to penetrate in the first place or may shear out. A good view of the route is not possible on a descent (although descending on a slight diagonal helps). It is awkward to plant the ice tools because they must be placed closer to your body, so the power of a good full swing is lost. On a descent, the only feasible way to get secure placements may be to plant the tools back in the holes that were made on the ascent.

Climbers do not often front-point to descend, but it is still a valuable skill for some occasions, such as retreating from a route. Down-climbing ability also builds confidence in ascending. Ice climbers usually rappel down steeper routes (see "Rappeling," later in this chapter).

ROPED CLIMBING TECHNIQUES

Climbers usually rope up on ice. Ice pitches can be climbed using a standard single rope or by using two

Fig. 18-34. Flat-footing on descent with ice ax in the banister position: a, planting the ax; b, slide hand along the shaft like a banister; c, pull outward slightly to keep ax locked in the ice (continued on facing page).

ropes (see "Double- and Twin-Rope Techniques" in Chapter 14, Leading on Rock). The principal exception comes when overall team safety is served best by climbing unroped. Late on a stormy day or while ascending a couloir threatened by rockfall, unroped travel might offer relatively more safety with its greater speed than would continuing on the rope. It may be sensible to travel unroped through a section so difficult to protect that a fall by one roped climber would sweep away the whole team. However, make no mistake: Unroped ice climbing is serious business.

PLACING PROTECTION ON ICE

Modern ice screws offer reliable protection in good ice. However, some safety is sacrificed because of the time and energy it takes to place them. Therefore leaders commonly place fewer points of protection on an ice pitch than they typically would on a rock pitch of the same

Fig. 18-35. Flat-footing on descent with ice ax in the anchor position.

Fig. 18-34. Continued from facing page; d, ready to replant the ax; e, remove and replant the ax.

length. Ice climbers also make some use of natural protection. Practice using either hand to place protection.

Natural Protection

Natural protection is often hard to come by on an alpine ice route. Good natural protection may be available not on the ice itself but in rock bordering the route or protruding through the ice. Shrubs and trees may be protection opportunities.

Ice Screws

For any given screw placement, there are dozens of variations. And climbers must ask some very serious questions: What is the quality of the ice? What is the depth of the ice? What is the projected amount of force on the piece? What is the projected direction of force? Which screws are still left on the rack? Which will be needed later? Observations, calculations, estimates, and experience will help you answer these questions and place gear accordingly.

Each screw placement is different—which is one of the great things about climbing ice. It is an ever-changing medium. In solid ice and under ideal conditions, ice screw placements are actually stronger if the screw is placed in the projected direction of force. In other cases, placements are stronger if the screws are oriented away from the direction of force. But the decision must be made at the time the placement is made. Practice. Set screws at various angles in different types of ice, and test them hard. Prove to yourself that they will hold you if you fall. Talk to people who have fallen on screws and had them hold. Talk to people who have ripped out every screw on a leader fall, and find out what went wrong.

A favorable location for an ice screw placement is the same as that for an ice tool. A good choice is a natural depression, where fracture lines caused by the screw are not as likely to reach the surface. A screw placed in a bulge in the ice, on the other hand, can cause serious fracturing that weakens the placement or makes it useless. In general, keep screw placements at least 2 feet (60 centimeters) apart to reduce danger that fracture lines from one placement will reach the other, weakening both.

The procedures for placing a screw vary somewhat with ice conditions, but the basic routine is much the same in any case:

1. For maximum leverage during placement, keep the screw placement at about waist level. Punch out a small starting hole with the pick or spike of the ice tool, to give the starting threads or teeth of the screw a good grip. Make the hole gently, with light taps, to avoid fracturing the ice. The starting hole can also be an old pick hole.
2. Start the screw in the hole set at the selected angle (fig. 18-36), press the screw firmly, and twist it into the ice at the same time. Drive the screw home. The screw hanger should be flush with the ice surface and pointed in the direction of anticipated force.
3. Clip a quickdraw or load-limiting runner in to the eye of the screw hanger, with the carabiner gate down and out. To slow the melt-out in soft summer ice or in ice exposed to direct sunlight, pack ice or snow over the screw. Clip the rope.

A screw with sharp teeth can easily be screwed in all the way by hand using the integral spinning knob. Even a screw without an integral knob, if its teeth are sharp, can usually be screwed in by hand. If not, drive it with the help of a lever through the screw eye; the pick of an ice tool works well (fig. 18-37).

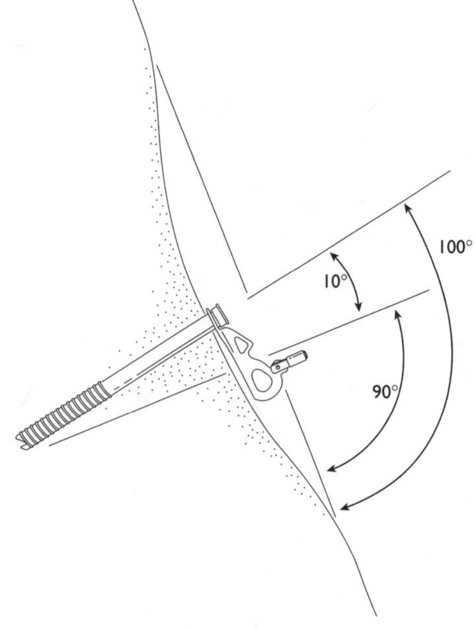

Fig. 18-36. Ice-screw placement in a solid surface, at a right angle to the surface of the flat ice surrounding a slight depression, with the screw head angled uphill about 10 degrees against the anticipated direction of pull and the screw eye facing the direction of pull.

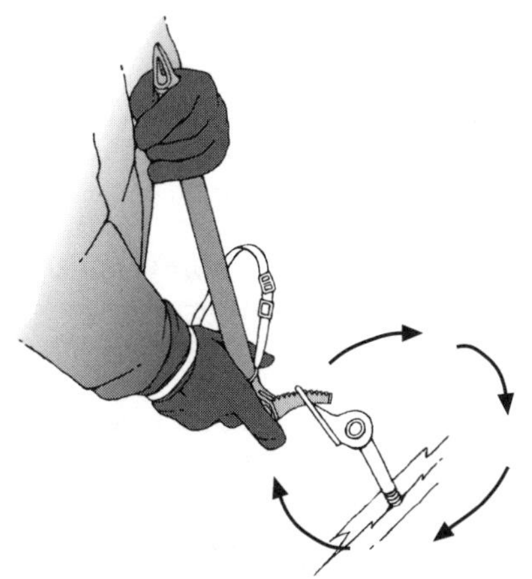

Fig. 18-37. Driving an ice screw with the pick of an ice tool.

On ice topped with a layer of soft snow or rotten ice, use the adze or pick to scrape down to a hard, trustworthy surface before you make the starting hole (fig. 18-38a). In extremely rotten ice, make a large horizontal step with an ice tool and place the screw vertically at the back of the step (fig. 18-38b). If the ice fractures and shatters at the surface, you may still get a secure placement by continuing to drive the screw and gently chopping out the shattered ice with sideways strokes of the pick.

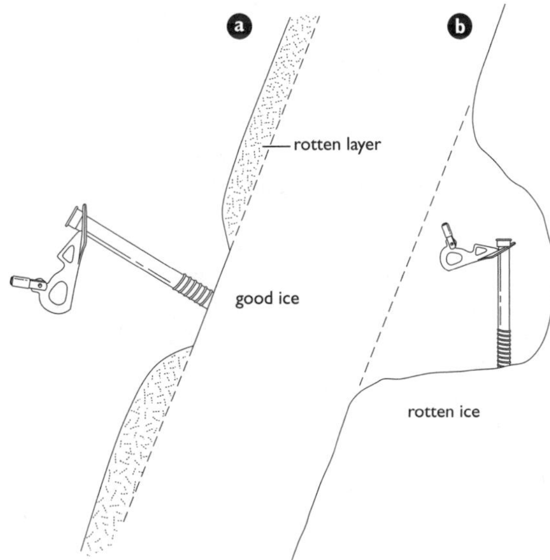

Fig. 18-38. Ice-screw placements: a, with soft or rotten surface layer; b, in extremely rotten ice.

Climbing extremely steep ice is fatiguing, both physically and mentally, so minimize the number of screw placements. If the ice is hard and solid or the slope not extremely steep, only one or two protection points may need to be placed on an entire pitch. Unless the ice is rotten, only one screw is placed at each protection point. Relying mainly on your tool and crampon placements and skills for safety (a concept known as "self-belayed" climbing) also affects the number of ice screws that need to be placed.

With practice, it should be possible to place an ice screw with one hand. On extremely steep ice, placing ice screws is exacting business. Try to place screws from natural resting spots on the route. Be sure to hang from your leashes; do not wear yourself out by gripping the shaft of the tool while placing screws. For extra support or when both hands are needed to place a screw, slip one arm through the wrist loop of a solidly planted ice tool (fig. 18-39).

On a moderate to steep slope, it may help to chop a step to stand in while placing the screw. On extremely steep ice, however, chopping steps is too difficult, so save your energy. When it is time to place an ice screw, do it efficiently and confidently from your front points, and then continue climbing.

After removing a screw, ice inside its core must be cleaned out immediately or it may freeze in place, rendering the screw useless until it is cleared. Before climbs, squirt a lubricating and penetrating oil inside the screws. The interiors of some screws are slightly tapered, facilitating ice removal. Shake the screw to remove the ice core; if this does not work, then tap the hanger end of the screw against the ice or the shaft of an ice tool. Do not bang the teeth or threads of the screw against anything hard. This will only pit the teeth and screw threads and make the screw harder to place, especially in cold conditions. If ice does freeze to the inside of the screw, try to melt it with your breath, with the warmth of your hand, or inside a jacket pocket. Be careful about cleaning a screw with your pick or a metal V-thread tool; this can damage the inner surface of the screw, making ice more likely to stick in the future.

SETTING UP ICE ANCHORS

For belaying or rappeling, ice climbers have several options for anchors, including the V-thread, an ice bollard, and multiple ice screws. This section discusses the V-thread and ice bollard, which are used mainly in

Fig. 18-39. Support from tools while placing an ice screw.

rappeling. The next section, "Belaying on Ice," explains the standard anchor setup using two ice screws.

The V-Thread

The V-thread anchor (see Figure 18-40) is popular because it is simple and easy to construct. Devised by Vitaly Abalakov, a premier Soviet alpinist in the 1930s, the V-thread anchor (also known as the Abalakov) is nothing more than a V-shaped tunnel bored into the ice, with accessory cord or webbing threaded through the tunnel and tied to form a sling. The V-thread anchor has held up well in testing and in use, but remember that it is only as strong as the ice in which it is constructed. Multiple V-thread placements can be constructed and rigged together to create an equalized anchor point. Here are the steps to construct a V-thread anchor:

1. Screw a 22-centimeter ice screw into the slope. Angle the screw uphill 10 degrees against the anticipated direction of pull; also tilt it about 60 degrees to one side (fig. 18-40a).
2. Back this screw out about halfway, but keep it there as a guide. Insert a second screw into the slope 6 to 8 inches (about 20 centimeters) from the first, angling it to intersect the first hole at its bottom (fig. 18-40b). Remove both screws.
3. Thread a length of 6- to 8-millimeter accessory cord into one side of the V-shaped tunnel. Use a V-thread tool to fish the end of the cord out through the other side of the tunnel (fig. 18-40c).
4. Holding both ends of the cord, saw it back and forth in the tunnel in order to smooth the sharp edge where the two screw holes intersect. Otherwise, the edge might cut the cord in a fall. Tie the cord so that it forms a sling (fig. 18-40d).
5. Place an ice screw 2 to 3 feet (0.6 to 1 meter) above the V-thread anchor. Clip this screw to the V-thread sling as a backup. The anchor is now complete.

For a rappel, the rope is threaded directly through the loop of cord or webbing and then pulled free when the rappel is completed.

Many abandoned V-threads are found on popular ice climbs at rappel and/or belay stations. As with any other fixed anchor, check it carefully before committing your life to it. Inspect the sling material for burn marks, wear, or other damage, and check that the knot is secure. Sometimes the free tails of the knot may be frozen in place, resembling a secure portion of the sling. Be sure that the rope is rigged through the sling and not through these frozen tails. Do not make that fatal error. Inspect the integrity of the V-shaped tunnel. See if it has melted out to an extent that it is too shallow for comfort and safety. If you have any doubt about the anchor, back it up or replace it.

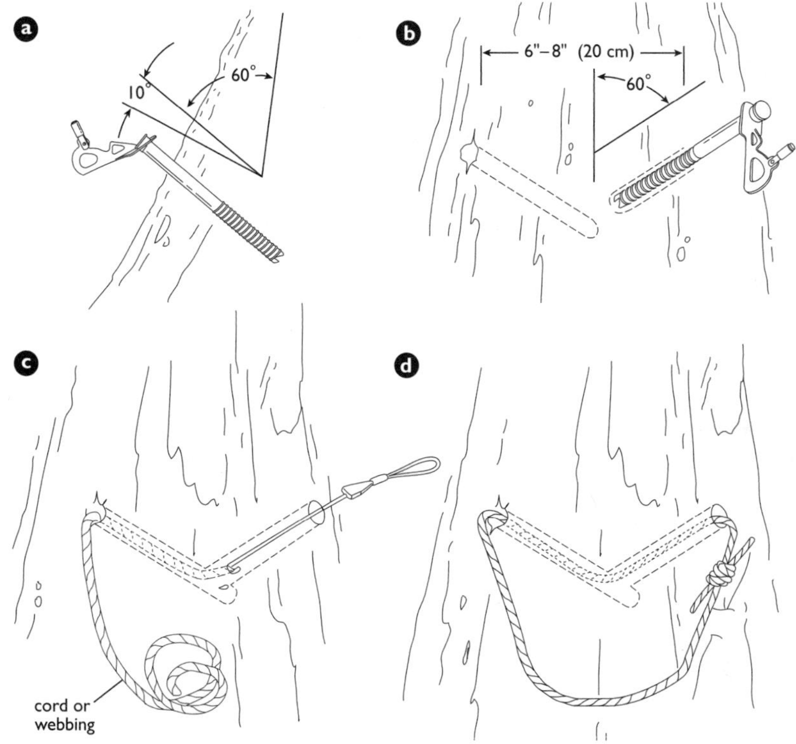

Fig. 18-40. The Abalakov, or V-thread anchor: a, bore first hole with ice screw tilted up 10 degrees and out to the side 60 degrees; b, bore an intersecting hole with another ice screw; c, thread a piece of accessory cord through the V-shaped tunnel, using a V-thread tool; d, tie cord to form a sling and complete the anchor.

Ice Bollard

A bollard can be among an ice climber's most useful anchors. Two bollards linked together, one cut for an upward pull and the other for a downward pull, form a multidirectional anchor. The strength of a bollard is proportional to its size and the quality of the ice. Made in hard, solid ice, a bollard can be stronger than the rope. The single largest disadvantage to a bollard is the long time it takes to construct one.

A completed ice bollard is teardrop-shaped when viewed from above (as in Figure 18-41a and c) and mushroom-shaped when viewed from the side (as in Figure 18-41b). All that is needed for a bollard is an ice ax and good ice, uniform and without cracks or holes.

Cut the outline of the bollard with the ax pick. In hard ice, give it a diameter of 12 to 18 inches (30 to 45 centimeters) across the wide end of the teardrop, and make it 24 inches (61 centimeters) long (fig. 18-41a). Cut a trench around the bollard at least 6 inches (15 centimeters) deep (fig. 18-41b), working outward

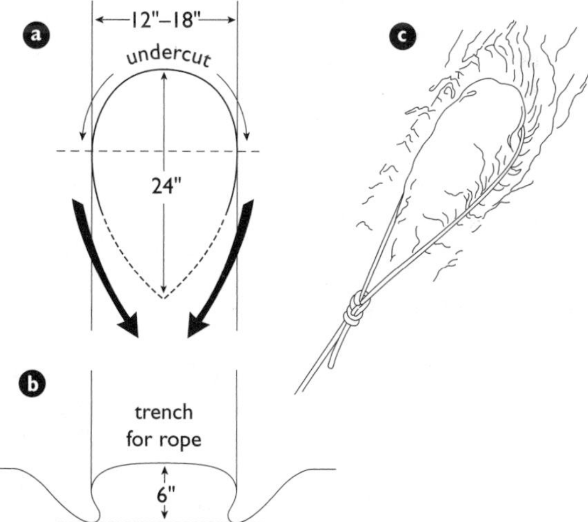

Fig. 18-41. Ice bollard: a, top view, showing width and length; b, side view, showing depth; c, top view, with rope in place.

18

from the outline with both the pick and the adze. Undercut the sides and top half of the bollard to form a horn that prevents the rope from popping off over the top (fig. 18-41c). This is the most sensitive part of the construction because the bollard is easily fractured or broken if you do not take care.

BELAYING ON ICE

Ice climbers have the options of using running belays or fixed belays, as in other types of roped climbing. They also have the use of boot–ice screw belay techniques.

Running Belays

By setting up a running belay, ice climbers can get a measure of protection that is somewhere between climbing on belay and climbing unroped. A running belay is another way for a team to move faster when storms or avalanches threaten—circumstances under which, more than ever, speed means safety. It can also be useful on gentle to moderate terrain where danger of falling is minimal and fixed belays would be too time-consuming.

A running belay on ice is created in very much the same way as a running belay on rock (see Chapter 14, Leading on Rock) or snow (see Chapter 16, Snow Travel and Climbing). The team members, usually just two climbers, move simultaneously. The leader places protection as they climb and clips the rope through it; the follower removes the protection. The idea is to keep at least two points of protection between them at all times to hold the rope in case of a fall. The protection is usually spaced so that as the leader makes each new placement, the follower is removing the bottom one.

Because the technique of running belays sacrifices much of the safety of true belaying, the decision to use it takes fine judgment, based on extensive experience.

Fixed Belays

Fixed belaying on ice requires a belayer, a belay anchor, and intermediate points of protection, just as it does on rock or snow. A belay anchor is set up; then the leader climbs the pitch on belay, sets up another anchor, and then belays the follower up the route. The climbers can either swing leads, or one climber can continue as the leader.

The leader should, when near the end of a pitch, keep an eye out for a good belay spot, perhaps at a slight depression, at a place where the ice is not so steep, or in an area where a platform can be chopped out quickly. Plant an ice tool off to one side and clip in for temporary protection while chopping a step large enough that you can stand facing the ice with both feet flat and splayed. On steep ice, it may be possible to chop only a simple ledge the width of your foot.

Belay Anchor

A standard anchor setup for an ice belay takes two ice screws. (Ice bollards and V-threads also can serve as belay anchors, but they are more time-consuming to set

Fig. 18-42. Anchor setup for an ice belay, using two ice screws 2 to 3 feet apart.

up and are used primarily for rappeling.) Place the first screw in the ice in front of you, a bit to one side, at about waist to chest level (fig. 18-42). Clip in a carabiner and tie yourself in to it with the climbing rope, using a clove hitch or figure eight knot. Then tell your belayer that you are off belay.

Now place the second ice screw, above you and about 2 or 3 feet (0.6 to 1 meter) higher than the first one and off to the other side. Ideally, place this screw on the side where the route will continue. Extend the climbing rope from the first screw to the second screw and tie it in with a clove hitch. There should be little or no slack in the rope between the two screws. Alternatively, use a runner: Clip the runner to both screws, then set up an equalized system (see "Equalizing Anchors" in Chapter 10, Belaying).

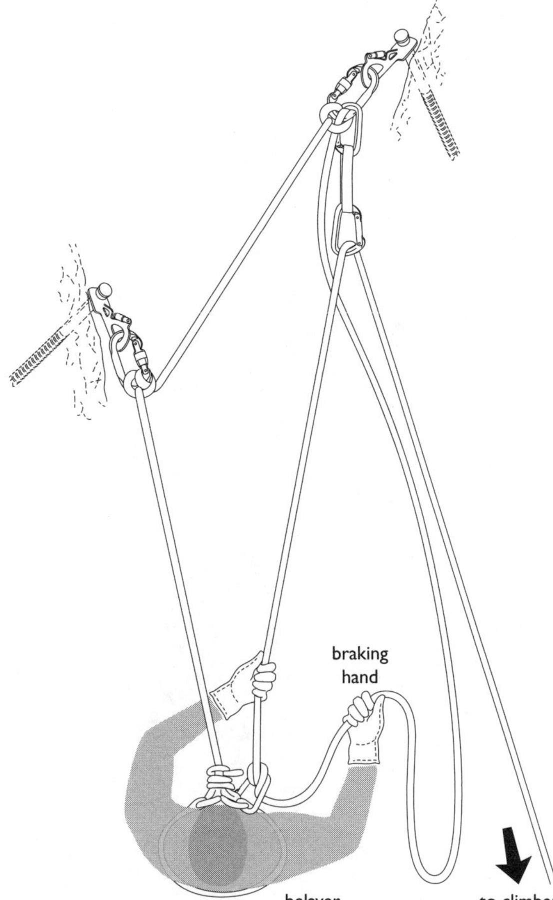

Fig. 18-43. Ice belay setup for a mechanical belay device or munter hitch at the climber's seat harness.

Clip a quickdraw or load-limiting runner to the carabiner on the second screw (or to the screw hanger eye, if it is large enough to accept two carabiners); clip the rope trailing down to the follower through the carabiner clipped to the quickdraw or load-limiting runner (see Figure 18-43). This completes the anchor setup.

Belay Methods

Choose between using a belay device, a munter hitch, or a hip belay. The anchor setup is the same in any case. The choice probably depends on what the climbers are accustomed to and on the degree of their confidence in the anchor. The hip belay tends to be somewhat dynamic, with a bit of movement at the belay—resulting in a slower stop to a fall but less force on the anchor and intermediate protection points. Belay devices and the munter hitch, on the other hand, tend to be less dynamic, stopping a fall faster but putting more force on the anchor and intermediate protection points. (See "Choosing a Method" in Chapter 10, Belaying.)

Belay device or munter hitch. A belay device or a munter hitch is easy to set up and efficient to use (fig. 18-43). Many ice climbers use such a method as standard procedure. The device is usually clipped to the seat harness, though you can also belay directly from the anchor. To belay a leader, the belayer usually faces into the ice; for belaying a follower, either face into the ice or face out.

If you face the ice to belay the follower (see Figure 18-43), the belay rope runs up through the top screw in the anchor setup, directing the pull from the second climber through this screw. After the follower ascends to the belay station and starts upward to take the lead, that screw becomes the first piece of protection on the new pitch. Remember that when the rope is clipped in to the belay anchor in this fashion, forces at the anchor can be multiplied. A fall from the follower will generate two times the force at the anchor because of the pulley effect.

If you face outward to belay the follower, the belay rope runs directly to the device at your harness, and you tie in to the anchor much as you would in a fixed belay in rock climbing.

Hip belay. The hip belay is especially favored when the rope is stiff and frozen and could jam in belay devices. Establish a hip belay as you stand facing the ice by running the belay rope through a control carabiner at your waist, around your back, through an extra carabiner on the first screw, and then into your braking hand (fig. 18-44). You can also face outward to belay a follower with a hip belay.

Boot–ice screw belay. On gentle ice slopes, the boot–ice screw belay can be useful. Place an ice screw, then clip in a carabiner and run the belay rope through the carabiner (fig. 18-45a). Plant your uphill boot over the screw, perpendicular to the direction of pull. Place your boot so that the inside point of the midboot row of crampons goes through the carabiner (fig. 18-45b). Do not jab the rope with your crampons. Bring the belay

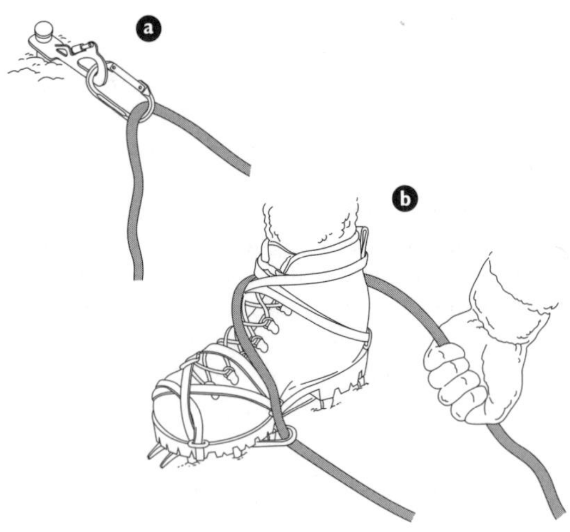

Fig. 18-45. Boot–ice screw belay: a, place an ice screw and clip the rope; b, plant a boot over the screw, with crampon point through carabiner, then bring rope over and around the back of the boot.

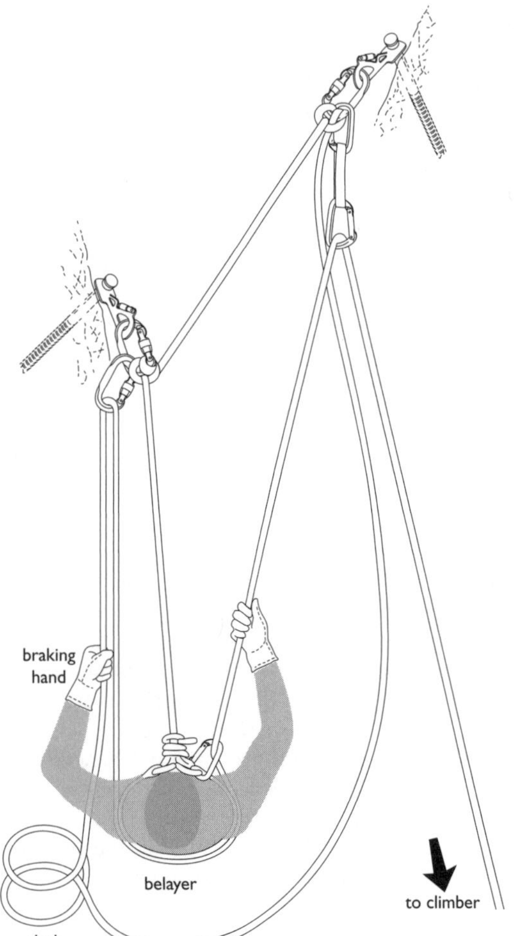

Fig. 18-44. Ice belay setup for a hip belay.

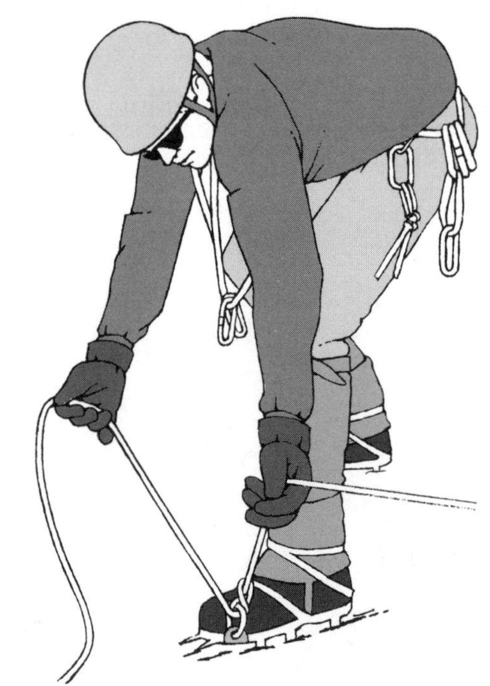

Fig. 18-46. Boot–ice screw belay using a munter hitch with a pear-shaped carabiner.

end of the rope over your instep, around the back of your boot ankle, and into your uphill hand.

Control friction on the rope by the amount of wrap on your ankle, much as in a boot-ax belay (see Chapter 16, Snow Travel and Climbing). The space between the edge of your boot and the outside edge of the carabiner can also be adjusted. If the climber you are belaying falls, slowly tighten the rope low against your ankle with your uphill hand.

Helpful variations of the boot–ice screw belay include two that use the munter hitch. Use a large pear-shaped carabiner, which has the correct radius for the munter hitch, instead of a standard carabiner. In one method, simply use a munter hitch at the carabiner instead of running the belay rope around your ankle (fig. 18-46). Another method permits you to operate the belay while standing. Use a munter hitch at a carabiner clipped to a runner that is clipped to the carabiner at the ice screw; stand on the runner, taking care not to stab it with your crampon points (fig. 18-47).

RAPPELING

For descending steep ice, rappeling is usually the method of choice. The principal considerations for rappeling on ice are the same as for rappeling on rock (see Chapter 11, Rappeling), but there is a big difference in anchor options. On rock, a natural anchor, such as a rock horn or a tree, can often be used. On ice, climbers frequently have to make their own anchors. The two most popular rappel anchors for ice are the V-thread and the ice bollard (see "Setting Up Ice Anchors," above). Ice screws are commonly used to back up an ice anchor until the last member of the party descends. The last person removes the screws and rappels on the anchor with no backup.

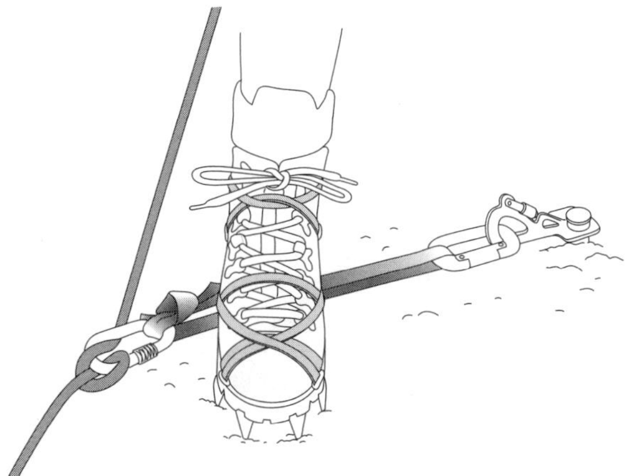

Fig. 18-47. Boot–ice screw belay using a munter hitch with two carabiners and a runner while standing.

PRACTICE FOR THE FREEDOM OF THE HILLS

Skill and confidence in ice climbing come with long practice. The ability to assess or read the ice comes with years of experience. Link up with a steady ice climbing partner if possible. Practice together often. Work on pinpoint ice-tool and crampon placement, which conserves energy. Also work to increase the speed and efficiency of your climbing, gearing it to the conditions of the ice and your body's current strength. It is up to each climber to decide when to rope up for protection—and when it is safer not to. Experienced ice climbers learn these skills, continue to hone them, and apply them with confidence and good judgment so they can meet the rigors of their chosen routes.

Chapter 19
WATERFALL ICE AND MIXED CLIMBING

As the temperature falls below the freezing point, liquid water changes to a solid. Even raging torrents can become spectacular, massive, hanging waterfall ice formations. Water ice is formed by gradual buildup. The usual formation is not a single, monolithic, crystalline structure. Typically, ice formations are the result of a series of freezes, and they have a laminated or layered structure. Water ice formations can display a broad spectrum of forms: smooth, broad slabs; flat runnels; cauliflower-textured walls; latticed sheets; chandeliered curtains; massive ice pillars; fantastic, free-hanging icicles.

Compared to the life cycle of glacial ice, the life spans of winter waterfall ice formations are all too brief. During a single winter season's freeze-thaw cycles, waterfall ice can form, collapse, then re-form, only to collapse again when the spring thaw arrives. When climbers visit the sites of winter ice climbs in warmer seasons, they may not be able to picture what is there in winter. Summer tourists traveling in Alberta, Canada, along the Icefields Parkway in Jasper National Park can easily miss the wet spot that marks the location that attracts waterfall ice climbers from around the world in winter: the Weeping Wall's spectacular ice curtain, an acre of vertical ice.

The technical difficulty of waterfall ice climbing continues to rise. The sport has transcended the traditional style—simple ascension of ice formations—and now includes dry tooling (climbing on technical rock with ice tools and crampons to link separate formations of ice). Climbing on mixed terrain (rock, thin ice, and ice) is not a new concept: It has long been part of ascending Scottish gullies in winter. In the classic sense, mixed climbing meant having one foot on rock and the other on ice—usually thin ice. However, the focus of the sport has shifted. On a modern mixed route, climbers may spend as much or more time on rock as on ice. Often the crux of a route consists of making an athletic transition from rock to an overhanging curtain or spear of ice.

Waterfall ice and mixed-route climbers must exercise caution on terrain that changes abruptly from ice to rock and back, but they must also act with concern for the environment. The hard steel of ice tools and crampons does scratch and can break the rock surface. When dry tooling, exercise care to minimize damage. When establishing mixed routes, give major consideration to the local ethics. Avoid climbing in culturally sensitive areas (for example, cliffs with pictographs) and popular rock climbing areas.

EQUIPMENT

This section includes a few considerations specific to waterfall ice and mixed climbing. For discussions of snow- and alpine ice–climbing equipment, see Chapters 16, Snow Travel and Climbing, and 18, Alpine Ice Climbing.

Crampons. For waterfall ice, the front points are curved or angled downward, and the secondary points are angled more forward. On extremely steep to overhanging waterfall ice or mixed terrain, the crampons of choice are rigid or semirigid with vertically oriented dual (fig. 19-1a) or mono (fig. 19-1b) front points. Monopoints are better for dry tooling. (See Table 18-2 in Chapter 18, Alpine Ice Climbing, for the advantages of various front-point angles.) Some crampons' front points are interchangeable.

Ice tools. The reverse-curved pick (see Figure 18-4b in Chapter 18, Alpine Ice Climbing) is overwhelmingly the most popular choice for waterfall ice and mixed climbing. Technical ice tools can be further broken down into traditional (leashed) and leashless tools. Traditional ice tools include wrist leashes; some clip on and off, whereas others are fixed to the head of the tool but can be slipped off as needed (fig. 19-2a and b). Leashless tools—more frequently used for mixed climbing—are designed to facilitate easy movement between low and high grip positions on the shaft (fig. 19-2c and d).

Ice hooks. The ice hook, a type of pound-in protection, is designed for thin ice and mixed climbing (see Figure 18-7b and c in Chapter 18, Alpine Ice Climbing). The ice hook may be used to hook features in either ice or rock.

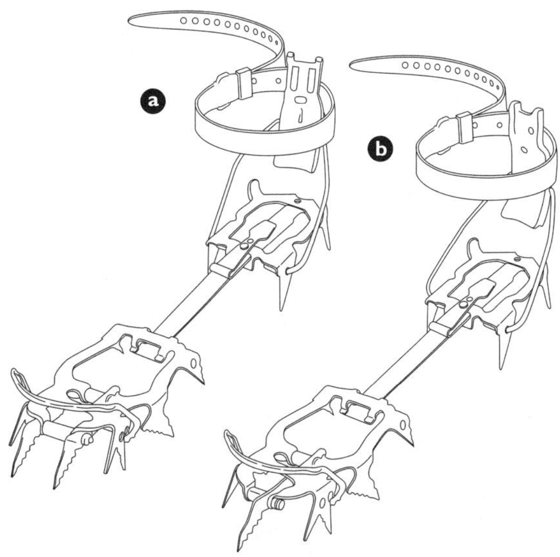

Fig. 19-1. Semirigid crampons with interchangeable front points: a, dual; b, mono.

WATERFALL ICE CLIMBING

Using crampons and ice tools, ice climbers move vertically on the varied ice found in frozen waterfalls.

CRAMPON TECHNIQUES

Footwork is the foundation of climbing techniques for steep waterfall ice. Good footwork allows climbers to keep most of their weight on their feet and the strong musculature of their legs, rather than on their arms, saving precious arm strength. Good footwork ensures smooth weight changes and greater efficiency. Poor footwork causes climbers to flail, burn out rapidly, and fall.

Front-pointing is the mainstay of footwork on vertical ice (see Chapter 18, Alpine Ice Climbing, for details on front-pointing). A good ice climber not only looks up for good tool placement opportunities but also continually looks down for front-point placements that ease the strain on the calves. As is true for tool placements, slight depressions make for ideal front-point placements. Similarly, a spot just above a small bulge can also be a nice placement.

After finding a likely spot, use a firm kick to set the front points in place. Except in rotten, chandelier, or extremely brittle ice (see "Unusual Conditions," later in this chapter), no more than one or two kicks should be necessary. Make sure that your feet are perpendicular

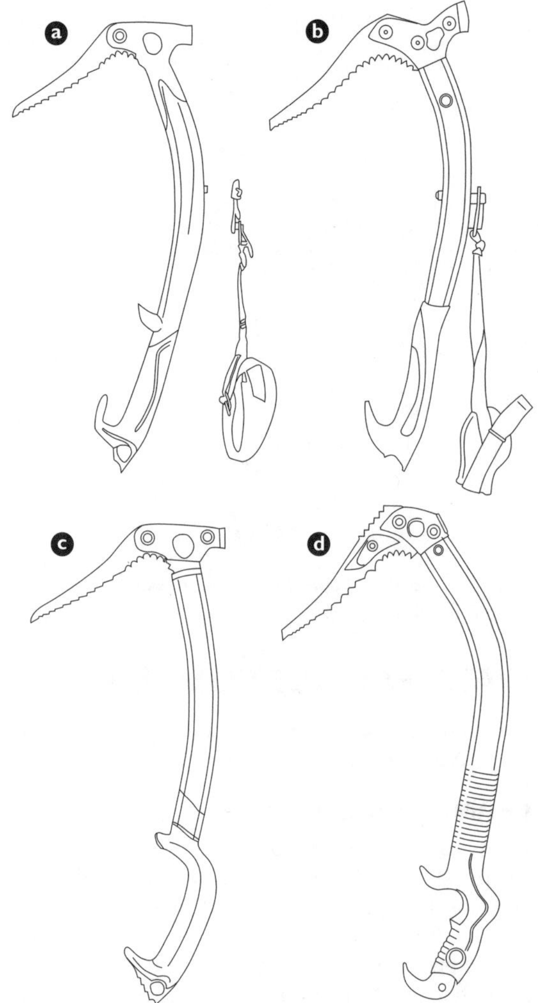

Fig. 19-2. Technical ice tools: a and b, traditional water ice tools with optional clip-on leashes; c and d, leashless.

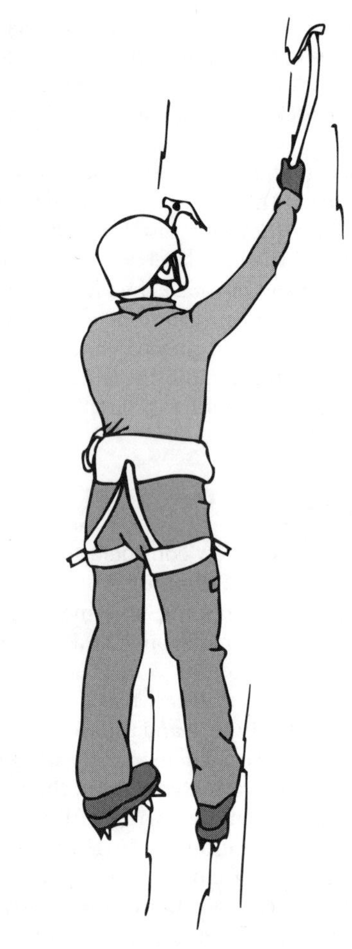

Fig. 19-3. A pigeon-toed stance is sometimes needed to plant front points squarely.

to the ice surface in both planes: Keep heels low so that the secondary points engage the surface, making for a much more stable placement, and make sure the toe of each boot is squarely facing the surface at that particular spot. A pigeon-toed stance (or its opposite, a duck-footed stance) may be necessary to plant the front points squarely (fig. 19-3). Monopoints can be slotted in old pick placements. Once your feet are placed, try to keep them steady until you are ready to move again. Nervous feet actually weaken the placement.

Keep feet shoulder-width apart, or slightly less, to reduce the tendency to "barn-door" to one side. Use several short steps, rather than high-stepping, to reduce the stress on your quadriceps—although high-stepping can be necessary occasionally to get past bulges.

Beyond straight-in front-pointing, footwork that is much more akin to rock climbing techniques is very useful for the variety of features found on many waterfall ice climbs. Stemming and flagging for counterbalance (see Chapter 12, Alpine Rock Climbing Technique) are also very useful on waterfall ice.

ICE-TOOL TECHNIQUES

Just as the mainstay of footwork on waterfall ice is front-pointing, the most frequent tool placement, by far, is *piolet traction* (see Chapter 18, Alpine Ice Climbing). Because it becomes very tiring to swing tools overhead, do everything possible to reduce the number of swings and placements you make.

When ice climbing using *piolet traction* placements, think of it as climbing on self-belay. Before trusting the integrity of each placement, test it by loading it with partial body weight. Do this test from the relative safety of a stable stance on the ice. This is a key concept: The goal is to create a position of strength and then to climb from that position. If each position is stable, you will climb with comfort and confidence. Do not fall into the trap of relying on a shaky placement, because this robs you of confidence and can lead to increasingly weak and unstable stances.

Selecting a placement and making the placement accurately are the keys to placing ice tools securely and quickly; strive to gain a secure placement with just one swing. One technique for hitting a precise spot is to tap the desired spot with the pick, then swing at that spot with force. The swing is more akin to a racquetball swing, with its wrist-snap just prior to connecting with the ball, than to a straight-wristed tennis swing. The steeper the droop of the pick, the more wrist action is needed to set the pick at the proper angle. (See "Ice-Tool Placements" in Chapter 18, Alpine Ice Climbing.)

Many beginning waterfall ice climbers tend to drive their tools in too hard; take care to avoid this, because it makes it much more difficult and tiring to remove the tool. (See "Removing the Tool" in Chapter 18.)

While climbing, look for secure placements that do not require you to swing the ice tool. Some old tool or monopoint placements may be deep enough that you can simply slot the pick in. Hooking opportunities abound on water ice. Large icicles often form in clusters on vertical sections, creating slots or gaps that are ideal for secure hooking placements; tools can be slotted into gaps between icicles. Larger columns can be hooked horizontally. Reverse-curved picks are best for hooking placements, a common technique in waterfall ice climbing. Many ice-tool picks have teeth where the pick attaches to the shaft; this provides more secure hooking.

In good ice, vertically stagger the tool placements using the tracking technique (see "Climbing on Vertical Ice" in Chapter 18, Alpine Ice Climbing). By staggering the tools (rather than planting them side by side) and by relying on a single tool at a time, climbers reduce the number of tool placements, thus decreasing the workload on the swinging and gripping muscles of their arms and hands. If the ice, and thus the placements, are suspect, plant both tools side by side, about 2 feet (0.6 meter) apart, before moving your feet up. This decreases the load on each placement and reduces the chance that a tool will shear out under the load.

Leashed Versus Leashless Tools

The development of leashless tools was primarily sparked by ice climbing competitions. To abide by the rules ("two ice tools that have no leash"), competitors removed the leashes from their tools but then added a variety of grip-aiding devices (for example, knobs, spurs, and handles) to the shafts of their tools. This freedom unexpectedly led to the development of a variety of new techniques and helped to raise standards of both ice and mixed climbing.

Leashless climbing has become increasingly common as more-specialized ice tools have been introduced, but debate continues regarding the use of leashes for waterfall ice climbing. Whereas climbing leashless may offer greater freedom of movement, using leashes has advantages. Leashes are a safety device; they allow climbers to efficiently rest their hands and arms on demanding routes (especially important when leading), and they can prevent climbers and their tools from becoming separated.

Whether or not to use leashes is a matter of personal choice and experience. For maximum flexibility, consider using a set of ice tools fitted with both the grips and rests of a true leashless tool (see Figure 19-2c and d), and clip-on leashes (see Figure 19-2a and b); fit the leash to your wrist and tuck the clip-on end into your jacket sleeve, or clip it back to the wrist strap. You can then take advantage of the freedom of leashless climbing, yet quickly convert to leashed climbing as needed.

VERTICAL PROGRESSION

Just as in climbing on rock, climbing on waterfall ice involves a coordinated combination of climbing techniques used by a leader and a belayer, who are connected by the rope, anchors, and protection points.

The Monkey Hang

The basic technique for ascending vertical and overhanging ice is the monkey hang. Rather than a single movement, the monkey hang is a series of movements for upward progress on steep ice that allows maximum rest for the gripping muscles of hands and forearms.

Follow these steps to perform the monkey hang:

1. While standing on front points and with one ice tool in *piolet traction*, place the other ice tool at full arm's length; immediately sag down, weighting that tool (fig. 19-4a).
2. With the tool still weighted (your arm fully extended), move your feet up until you are in a crouching position on your front points (fig. 19-4b).
3. Loosen, but do not yet remove, the lower of the two tools, and look above for the next placement for it.
4. In one motion, stand upright by pushing with your feet and pulling on the tools, remove the lower tool, and place it in the chosen spot, again preferably at full arm's length (fig. 19-4c).
5. Sag down, weight that tool, and loosen your grip on the tool just placed (fig. 19-4d).
6. Repeat steps 2 through 5.

Belaying

Setting up belay anchors and belaying on waterfall ice use the same procedures as those discussed in "Belaying on Ice" in Chapter 18, Alpine Ice Climbing. Take extra care in locating belays away from the fall line to avoid being showered with debris from the leader. In gullies, site the belay to one side of the route, seeking protection from the sidewall. On pillars or curtains, try placing the belay behind or to the side of the formation, but be aware that although this position provides greater protection from falling ice, it will make communication more difficult and rope drag a possibility. Look for a compromise between protection and convenience in belay stances.

Fig. 19-4. The monkey hang: a, place one tool at arm's length and weight it; b, move feet up to attain a crouching position; c, stand up and place the other tool at arm's length; d, weight the tool and move the feet to attain a crouching position.

Leading

Most waterfall ice climbs are led and followed in pitches, though many long climbs offer sections suitable for running belays. Ice pitches may be climbed with either a single rope or with two ropes, using either twin-rope or double-rope technique. (See Chapter 14, Leading on Rock.)

PROTECTION

Waterfall ice routes can be protected using both rock and ice gear, which affects racking and placements.

Rock Gear

Some waterfall ice climbs have options for using rock gear. On gully climbs, the rock sidewalls can provide protection opportunities. On freestanding columns or curtains, look behind the ice for placements in the back wall; these most likely will need to be extended by slings to prevent rope drag. In the winter, cracks tend to be filled by ice; as a result, pitons are used more frequently than on summer climbs, though the full variety of clean protection can be used as well.

Natural Protection

Waterfall ice offers more opportunities for natural protection than do the flows and steps of alpine ice, and many natural placements are quicker to set up than ice screws. Runners can be placed around small ice columns (fig. 19-5). A long ice screw tied off with webbing can be inserted between two columns or through a slot in an ice curtain, then rotated sideways and used as a deadman. In thin curtains, two holes can be punched in the curtain and then threaded with webbing or accessory cord as for a V-thread anchor (see Chapter 18, Alpine Ice Climbing). With all these placements, it is wise to use a load-limiting runner (described in Chapter 9, Basic Safety System).

Ice Screws and Pitons

Ice screws remain the most common type of protection used on waterfall ice. Although the methods for placing ice screws are the same as those discussed in Chapter 18, some considerations are specific to waterfall ice.

Significant testing has been done to determine the strength of ice screw placements in solid water ice at cold temperatures. Surprisingly, under those conditions the strongest screw placements are those with the long axis of the screw placed at a 10- to 20-degree upward angle, pointing toward the direction of anticipated force (fig. 19-6). This configuration can reduce fracturing of the ice when loaded by a leader fall.

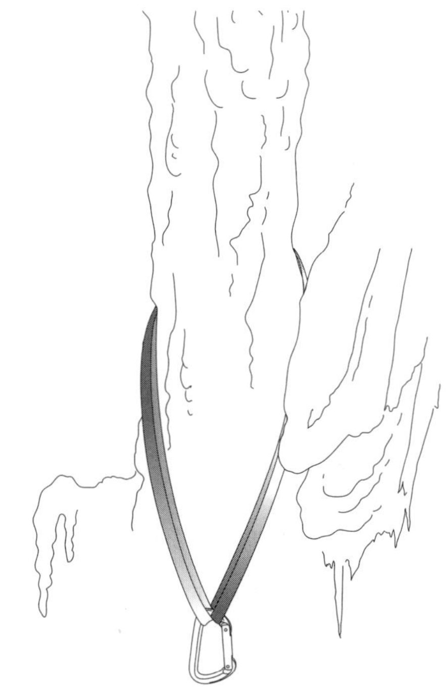

Fig. 19-5. Runner threaded around an ice pillar.

It is best to use a screw of a length that can be sunk to the hilt. If the ice is too shallow for a screw to be placed all the way in to its hanger, remove that screw and use a

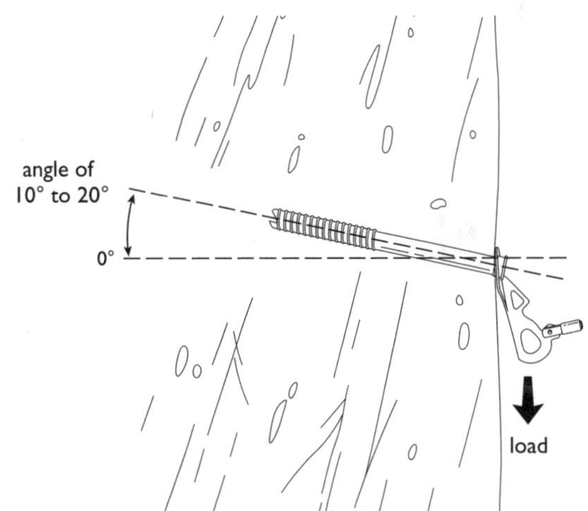

Fig. 19-6. Ice screw placement is strongest at an upward angle in cold, solid ice.

19

shorter one. Carry a variety of screw lengths to decrease the chances of needing to tie off a screw. Tie off a screw only as a last resort. When screws fail under loading, they do so by fracturing the ice below them and bending toward the direction of force. In the case of a tied-off screw, the webbing then slides to the hanger and is cut by its sharp edges.

If the screw protrudes no more than 2 inches (5 centimeters) from the surface of the ice, clip the hanger as you normally would (fig. 19-7a). If the screw protrudes more than 2 inches from the surface, the placement is highly suspect. Tie off the screw with a runner or a load-limiting runner (fig. 19-7b). In this situation, back up and equalize such a placement, climb confidently, and make better placements as soon as possible.

Another type of protection is the current crop of ice pitons, also called ice hooks (see Figure 18-7b and c in Chapter 18, Alpine Ice Climbing). An ice hook can be slotted into holes in ice curtains or between the laced-together icicles in chandelier ice and then set with a light tap. Ice hooks can also be driven into iced-up cracks.

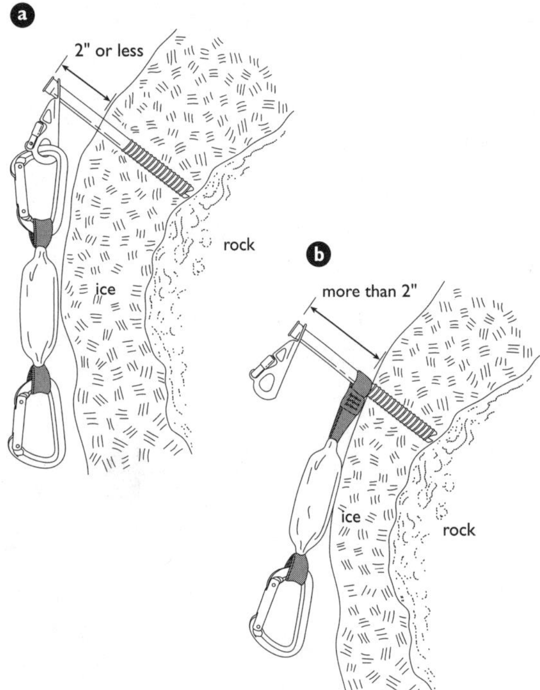

Fig. 19-7. Ice screw placement in thin ice over rock: a, clipped with a load-limiting runner; b, tied off with a load-limiting runner.

Protecting the Leader

Many more options for protecting the leader can be found on waterfall ice than on alpine ice. Alpine ice is limited to using ice screws, with occasional rock protection to the side or in rock "islands." On waterfall ice, frequently rock gear can be placed to the side of or even behind an ice column, or natural protection can be creatively used in the ice itself, in addition to ice screw and ice hook placements.

Racking

Although some ice climbers use gear slings to carry ice screws and other gear, many more use harness-mounted gear racking devices (see Chapter 18, Alpine Ice Climbing). It can be uncomfortable and inconvenient to carry long, sharp screws on a gear sling. Here is one suggested arrangement for racking gear on the harness (also see "The Rack for Ice Climbing" sidebar):

- **Rack most of the gear needed on lead on the same side as your dominant hand,** with a few pieces on your nondominant side. Place ice screws in front, arranged front to back by length, short to long, with teeth pointed to the rear. Next, rack quickdraws and load-limiting runners.
- **Use the rear gear loop of your dominant side as well as your non-dominant-side gear loops to rack gear that will not be needed immediately.** This includes longer screws for belay anchors, a belay device, free carabiners, a pulley, a V-thread tool, and cordelette.

Placing Gear on the Lead

Placing ice screws while leading on steep ice can be very physically demanding. To conserve energy, minimize the number of screw placements; typically, on a waterfall ice pitch far fewer protection placements are made than would be placed on a rock pitch of similar length. Similarly, climbers develop techniques for placing screws that minimize the effort expended.

For example, avoid the temptation to place a screw high (above shoulder height) to gain that momentary top-rope protection (having the rope above you). In this position, it is very difficult to put enough pressure on the screw so that its threads will bite into the ice. The most efficient placement is right at waist level. You have better leverage and can use your whole body weight to push the screw into the ice. Also, your arm remains below the level of your heart so blood flow remains constant.

Here is one technique for placing screws on lead (fig. 19-8):

1. Get a good stance for both feet and (if you are right-handed) plant the left tool high (at arm's length); weight the tool, hanging straight-armed.
2. At waist level, use the right tool to chip away any rotten or soft ice at the desired placement and make a starter hole for the screw. Secure that tool—holster it, clip it to your harness, or place it solidly in the ice out of the way.
3. Place the screw with your right hand; attach a quickdraw or load-limiting runner to the screw hanger; clip in the rope.
4. Retrieve the right tool; place the tool high and weight it; remove the left tool and shake that arm out as needed.

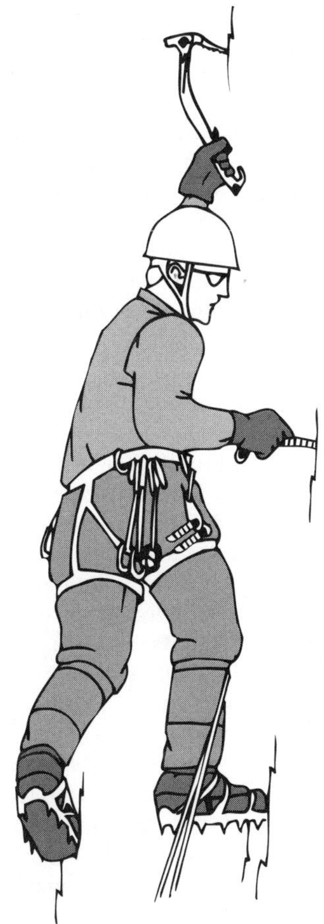

Fig. 19-8. Placing an ice screw on lead.

THE RACK FOR ICE CLIMBING

A typical ice climbing rack for a multipitch, pure ice climb might contain some or all of the following gear:

- Four long (19- to 22-centimeter) screws for anchors and/or constructing V-thread anchors
- Six to twelve ice screws of varying lengths appropriate for the thickness of the ice
- Six to twelve quickdraws and/or "alpine" draws (see Figure 14-7 in Chapter 14, Leading on Rock)
- A few long runners or cordelettes for threading gaps between the rock and the ice or ice columns
- Four (or more) load-limiting runners; four allows for one at each belay, one for the first protection screw above the anchor, and one for use elsewhere on the pitch
- An ice hook (as shown in Figure 18-7b and c in Chapter 18, Alpine Ice Climbing) for quick protection, frozen seams, and moss
- A V-thread tool (as shown in Figure 18-9 in Chapter 18)
- A few pieces of ½-inch tubular webbing or 6- to 8-millimeter accessory cord for constructing anchors
- A knife for cutting webbing and cord

UNUSUAL CONDITIONS

Unlike the more homogeneous ice of most alpine ice climbs, waterfall ice comes in an amazing and beautiful (and, many times, terrifying) array of formations, shapes, textures, features, and quality. These characteristics can make for difficult climbing with little opportunity for protection.

Pillars. Pillars are formed when meltwater drips off a free-hanging icicle until the resulting ice stalactite and stalagmite join. Climbable pillars can range in size from less than a body's width to many feet across. Although big pillars are climbed using the monkey hang, small pillars require much more varied technique. The tools must be vertically staggered so as not to weaken the pillar by having the two tools too close together. If placing screws in the pillar might weaken it, place protection in the adjacent rock. Both the tools and the front points might need to be placed in a pigeon-toed angle to keep the points and picks going straight into the ice, perpendicular to the ice in both planes. On really narrow pillars, a combination of front-pointing with one foot and heel-hooking with the other may need to be used (fig. 19-9).

Free-hanging ice. Free-hanging ice is formed when a pillar or curtain has not touched down onto ice or the ground or has broken off. Most of the climbing techniques are the same as for pillars. Use delicate tool and crampon placements. Place protection in the adjacent rock walls. Place screws in the ice only above its point of attachment to the rock. If screws are placed low in the formation and the formation fails, the climber, connected to the falling block, will be dragged down.

Chandelier ice. When thousands of small icicles melt and become laced together into a dense latticework, it is called chandelier ice. This ice formation is fairly common, beautiful to see, hard to climb, and difficult to protect. Belays must be located to avoid the constant rain of debris from the leader. Most of the time, there is little delicacy to climbing a chandelier. Kick your feet deep into the ice structure in hopes of finding secure purchase. Place the tools similarly, although you can be very creative with the tools. You might hook the slots between two larger icicles, stab the entire head of the tool directly into the ice and then rotate the tool 90 degrees so the hammer or adze and pick straddle the newly created slot, or thrust the entire tool (and your arm) through the lattice and grasp the tool midshaft, using it as a deadman. You may not be able to place a solid screw, but natural protection may exist.

Fig. 19-9. Combination footwork—front-pointing and heel-hooking.

Cauliflower ice. In *How to Ice Climb!* Craig Luebben described cauliflower ice as "looking like the out-turned scales of a pine cone," which forms at the "drip zone" of ice climbs (see Appendix D, Supplementary Resources). Ice domes at the bottom of pillars often sport cauliflower ice; it also forms above large ledges. The cauliflowers range in size from small (several inches) to very large (several feet wide and deep). Cauliflower ice offers many opportunities for hooking tools and often sports large footholds that can be flat-footed (see Chapter 18, Alpine Ice Climbing). Resist the temptation to place an entire foot into and onto a cauliflower. Your foot can get in so far that you are out of balance. Better to front-point it, or just set the front half of your boot on top of it. Protection can include screws in larger bulges as well as natural protection.

Brittle ice. The result of very cold temperatures, brittle ice usually appears only on the surface layers of ice formations. Work through the hard, brittle layers to get to the more plastic ice below, and in the process a cascade of falling ice will result, ranging in size from small chips to very large dinner plates. Be sure to stagger the placements of the tools far enough apart that the fracturing created by one tool does not reach the other, causing both placements to fail. Also, beware of falling dinner plates, which can dislodge front points. Place ice screws in better ice found beneath the brittle layers.

Rotten ice. Often the result of being baked by the sun or weakened by percolating water, rotten ice can run much deeper than brittle ice, even through an entire formation. Rotten ice is difficult to climb and harder to protect; a lengthy section of rotten ice may be all but unclimbable.

Thin ice. Thin ice ranges from just a glaze of ice over

the rock to ice a few inches thick. Thin ice can be very exciting and fun to climb. The thinnest ice is *verglas*: thick enough to obscure the underlying rock but not thick enough to gain purchase in with picks or points. Thicker ice is easier to climb, as long as temperatures are cold enough for cohesion to be maintained between the ice and the underlying rock. Make both tool and crampon placements with the gentlest of taps, swinging tools just from the wrist; sometimes placements can be scratched into place by chipping and hooking. Protection is usually found in the rock surrounding the ice. Extremely short screws may offer only psychological protection at best.

DESCENDING

Some waterfall ice climbs, especially gully routes, allow walk-off descents to one side or the other. Most, however, are descended by a combination of down-climbing and rappeling. The techniques of down-climbing ice are discussed fully in Chapter 18, Alpine Ice Climbing.

Rappeling

The principal techniques for rappeling on ice are the same as for rappeling on rock. Many rappels on popular waterfall ice climbs are done from fixed anchors, usually a combination of bolts and/or chains, slings on trees, or abandoned V-thread anchors. As with any fixed anchor, inspect these thoroughly before trusting them. Make sure the bolts are secure. Check the slings or accessory cord on the tree or the V-thread anchor for damage, wear, or burn marks, and check all knots. When in doubt, replace the material. Check found V-threads to ensure that they are still solid. If any found anchor is suspect in any way, or if there are none, place your own. The technique for building a V-thread is fully discussed in Chapter 18, Alpine Ice Climbing. Any V-thread should be backed up with a screw until the last climber removes the backup screw, then rappels.

MIXED CLIMBING

Mixed climbing combines climbing on rock, snow, and ice—and sometimes on frozen mud and moss as well. Usually climbers wear crampons. Perhaps mixed climbing means climbing a rock route in the winter, with ice-filled cracks and snow-covered ledges. Or maybe it involves making an alpine ascent that requires climbing an icy face broken by a rock band. Recently, mixed climbing has come to mean climbing sections of rock between discontinuous sections of ice. In its purest form, mixed climbing entails having one crampon on rock and the other on ice, one hand inserted into a crack and one ice tool placed in a frozen smear.

EQUIPMENT AND TECHNIQUES

The equipment used for mixed climbing most likely is whatever the climber was using right before the ice ran out. On a glacier climb, this means mountaineering crampons and a mountaineering ice ax. On a harder alpine ice climb, it most likely means a mountaineering ice ax used in combination with a shorter ice tool, likely a hammer, and rigid crampons. On a frozen waterfall with a mixed section, it is likely to be technical ice climbing tools and rigid crampons.

Crampons

When climbing a mixed route, climbers are most likely wearing crampons. Although considerable rock may be showing, it may be impractical to remove crampons only to put them back on when the route returns to the ice. Whichever crampons you choose, be sure that they are absolutely compatible with your boots. Their fit must be tight to withstand the tremendous stress of dancing on rock while wearing crampons.

Vertically oriented front points. Many mixed climbers prefer technical, rigid crampons with vertically oriented front points (see Figure 19-1a). Monopoint crampons (see Figure 19-1b) are particularly handy for precision accuracy on dime edges, vertical seams, and pick holes. Vertically oriented monopoints are also advantageous because the point mimics the pick of an ice tool. A monopoint can be delicately placed in the pick hole made just a few moves previously.

19

Horizontally oriented front points. Some mixed climbers prefer crampons with horizontally oriented front points (see Figure 16-5c in Chapter 16, Snow Travel and Climbing). Such crampons have greater stability because their horizontal alignment matches the features found in the sedimentary strata of many mountain ranges. They also are less prone to shearing because of their greater surface area.

Crampon Technique

Ultimately, crampon choice is secondary to proper technique. A good mixed climber selects a foothold and delicately places a crampon point or points in the spot. Smooth weight transfer is critical while gradually testing the foothold until it is completely weighted. Once that foot is weighted, it is important to keep it still, to prevent the points from rotating out of a crack or off a ledge. Careful footwork is the key to mixed climbing. With proper technique, climbers will not scratch the rock and their crampon points will remain sharp for any difficult ice climbing that may lie ahead.

Hands on Rock

Although it may be impractical to remove crampons for a rock section, it often makes sense to secure ice tools and grasp the rock directly with your hands. It may be next to impossible to find a pick placement on a downsloping rock ledge or fist-sized crack, but that same ledge or crack may easily yield a workable handhold.

Securing an ice tool may be as simple as releasing your grip on the shaft, as long as the leash is designed to remain snug around your wrist. This technique is particularly handy if the tool will be needed again after a few moves. Then it is readily available with a flick of the wrist.

For extensive climbing using your hands on rock, it may be more practical to holster the tool. Ice tool holsters can be mounted on your harness or pack hip belt. Or slide the shaft of the ice tool into a spare carabiner. But beware: An ice tool with high-friction material on the shaft to facilitate grip may not easily slide into a holster or carabiner, and a leash may get in the way. Be absolutely sure that there is no possibility of the ice tool coming out accidentally. Dropping a tool on a one-pitch sport-style mixed route may be merely annoying and embarrassing, but dropping a tool on a committing alpine route may have devastating consequences.

The surest method of securing an ice tool is to clip the ax-head hole in to a spare carabiner. To remove the tool, grasp the head of the tool and open the carabiner gate with a thumb.

Once one or both hands are free from the tools and leashes, use them as on any rock climb. Fist jams, cling and crimp holds, liebacks, and down-pressure can all be used to give your body the proper balance and positioning to support delicate footwork.

Keep in mind that while climbing with your hands on rock, you most likely will be wearing gloves. Technical mixed climbing, like technical rock climbing, requires dexterity. Handholds, carabiners, protection, and tool leashes must all be manipulated efficiently. It is therefore impractical to climb mixed terrain with a bulky glove system. Most mixed climbers wear one pair of midweight fleece gloves while climbing, keep a second pair warming in a clothing pocket, and have a third pair in the top lid of their pack.

Ice Tools on Rock

When the holds become too small for your hands and the cracks are filled with too much ice, it is time to use ice tools. When using an ice ax or ice tools on rock, employ every part of the tool and engage the different parts well. Be aggressive while being creative.

Hooking. The straightforward technique of hooking is the most common method for using the pick of the ice tool to climb rock. However, it is critical that, while pulling through the move, you hold the shaft of the tool steady against the rock (fig. 19-10a). If you pull outward on the shaft, the pick will skate off the hold (fig. 19-10b). You can also use the hammer or adze of the ice tool to hook rock holds, although you must exercise caution, because the pick will be pointing toward you.

While moving up, it is sometimes advantageous to turn a hook placement (fig. 19-11a) into a mantel by sliding your hand up the shaft (fig. 19-11b) and grasping the head of the tool (fig. 19-11c and d). This technique is especially handy if the next tool placement is far above you.

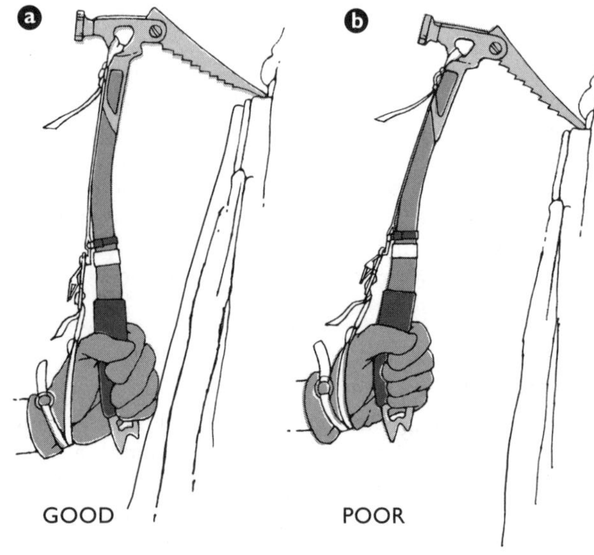

Fig. 19-10. Hooking technique: a, with downward force (good); b, with outward force (poor).

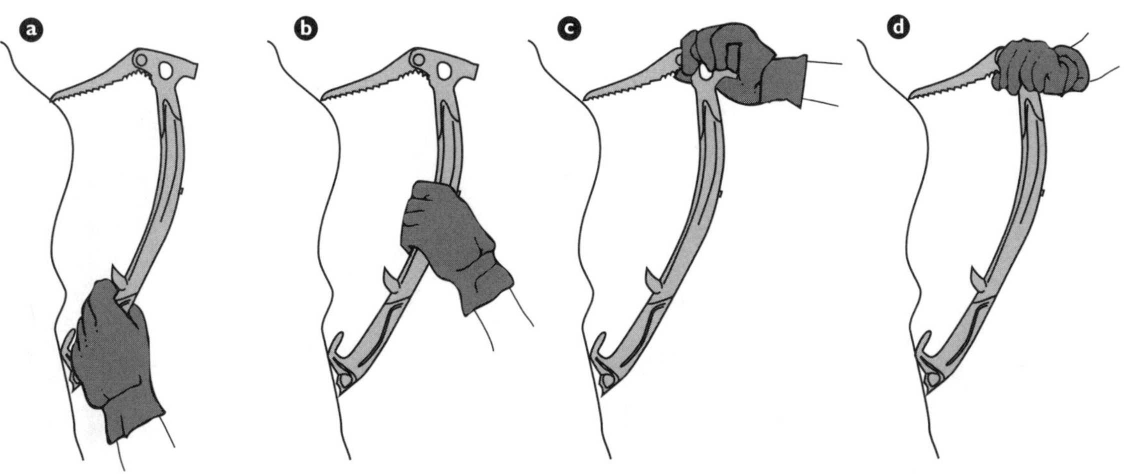

Fig. 19-11. Turning a hook into a mantel: a, hook the ledge; b, work your hand up the shaft; c, climb up, grasping the head of the tool; d, work your feet higher and mantel.

Torquing. Slide the pick into a crack that is a little too wide to be secure, and twist the shaft of the tool until the pick wedges itself securely (fig. 19-12). As long as adequate pressure is maintained, the placement will be secure. Or torque by using the hammer, adze, or even the shaft of the tool.

The stein puller. A very stable technique, the stein puller is most often performed by inserting the pick upside-down into a downward-facing seam or flake (fig. 19-13). Then, just as a bartender would pull down on a bar tap, pull down on the shaft of the tool, engaging the pick into the hold and forcing the head of the tool against the rock, creating opposing force. The

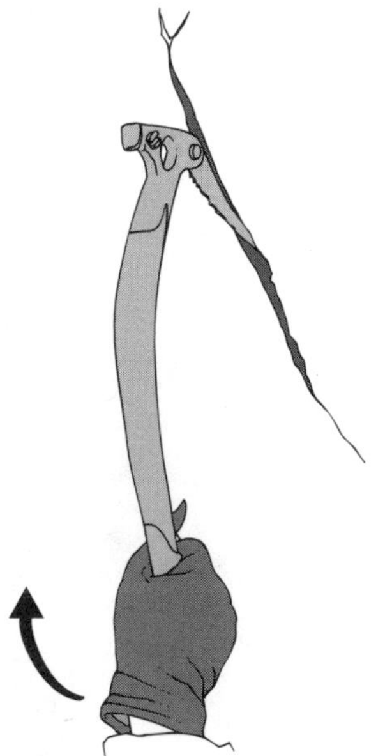

Fig. 19-12. Torquing.

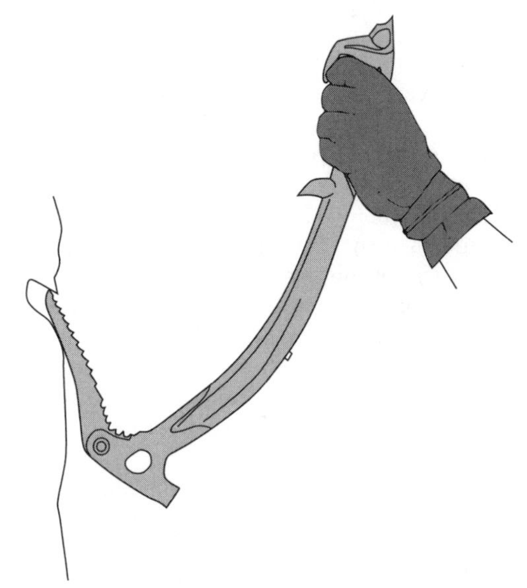

Fig. 19-13. Stein puller.

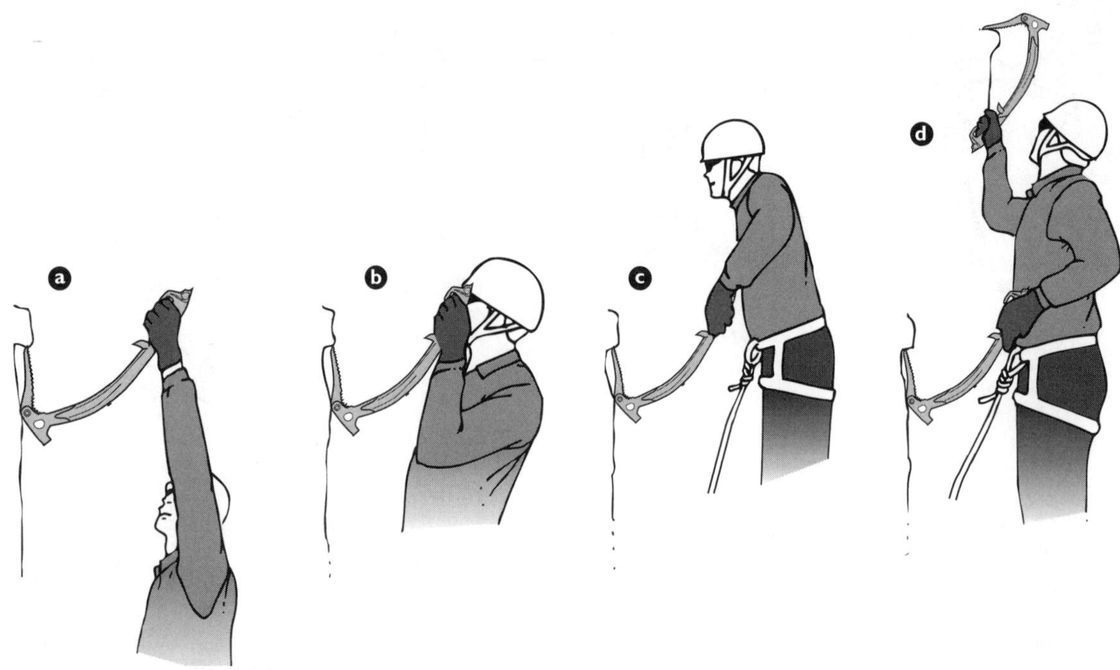

Fig. 19-14. Using a stein puller to mantel: a, place the stein puller; b, work your feet higher; c, mantel on the tool; d, reach up and place the other tool.

harder you pull down, the stronger the tool placement becomes.

A great advantage of the stein puller is that a hold above your head can be hooked (fig. 19-14a); then you can climb up (fig. 19-14b), turning the stein puller into a mantel without removing the tool from the rock (fig. 19-14c and d).

Matching. Another technique that is particularly useful while dry tooling is called matching. Just as on a rock climb when you place both hands on one hold, one hand on top of the other, one hold is used for both ice tools. One of the great things about the pick of the ice tool is that it is so narrow. Both tool picks can easily fit side by side on the same hold, as long as the hold is wider than about ¼ inch (6 to 7 millimeters). When matching, be sure that the hold is strong enough to withstand the tremendous force that can be generated by the two ice tools.

Stacking. Another technique used frequently in dry tooling is stacking. If there is one very good tool placement surrounded by bad ones, try hooking the pick of the well-placed tool with the other tool (fig. 19-15).

Fig. 19-15. Stacking.

When stacking, make sure once again that the hold is strong enough to withstand the tremendous force that can be generated by the two ice tools.

Body Positioning

In order to climb mixed terrain well, climbers must combine precision crampon and tool placements with calculated body positioning. Rarely do they simply pull down on hooked placements and walk their feet up the wall.

For instance, picture a ledge that slopes down to the right. In order to hook this ledge and keep the tool placement stable through a series of foot placements, pull down and to the left (fig. 19-16). Conversely, a right-leaning lieback is futile unless your crampons are in a position to allow you to push sideways to the right (fig. 19-17).

With a lot of practice on mixed terrain, climbers gain confidence in their crampon and tool technique. Climb as many mixed routes on top-rope as possible, no matter how hard the routes may look. If a certain move is elusive, examine your body positioning. A slight change in the way you are leaning may be the difference between frustration and exuberance.

Protection

Previous chapters contain detailed discussions of the various types of protection used on rock (Chapter 13, Rock Protection), snow (Chapter 16, Snow Travel and Climbing), and ice (Chapter 18, Alpine Ice Climbing). Also see "Protection" under "Waterfall Ice Climbing," earlier in this chapter, and "The Rack for Mixed Climbing" sidebar. Here is an additional consideration when combining the various types of protection for mixed climbing.

Fig. 19-16. Lieback to the left.

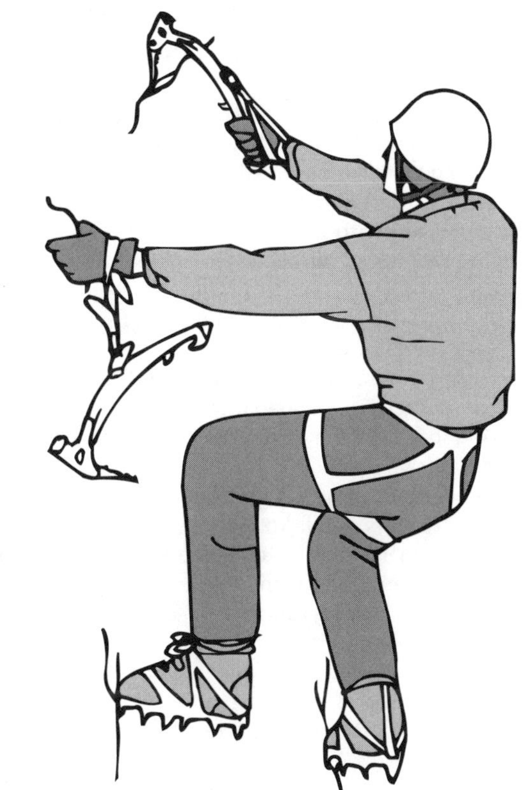

Fig. 19-17. Lieback to the right, pushing with feet.

19

If there is a choice between a rock anchor and a snow or ice anchor, use the rock anchor. It is relatively easy to evaluate the soundness of rock anchors, but this is not so with most snow or ice anchors. It might be necessary to do some digging and grooming to clear away snow, ice, and debris in order to place a piece of protection in the rock. Powdery snow can be knocked off with your hands, but an ice tool will probably be needed to clear hard snow or ice. If a crack is filled with ice, a piton or ice hook may be useful. Wired nuts can be pounded into cracks with the pick of the ice tool to create solid placements.

Belaying and Reducing Forces on the Climbing System

Because of the possibly dubious nature of mixed protection, a dynamic belay is required. As always, use a strong, multipoint, multidirectional belay anchor with well-placed screws or pitons. (See Chapter 10, Belaying, and "Belaying on Ice" in Chapter 18, Alpine Ice Climbing.)

A dynamic belay may be partially obtained by using a rope that has a relatively low impact force (4 to 7 kilonewtons). Several half-rope systems offer low impact forces. Keep in mind that low-impact-force ropes are stretchier than the more common larger-diameter rock climbing ropes. Therefore, if a fall occurs, the climber will fall a greater distance and so must watch out for any ledges.

It is also a good idea to use load-limiting runners on lead gear as well as incorporating them into the belay anchor. This further reduces forces on the climbing system.

Minimizing rope drag is also important when leading on shaky protection. If the rope zigzags up the route between points of protection and a fall occurs, the friction generated at the bends in the rope would prevent the rope from elongating as it should by design. If this occurs, a disproportionate amount of force is applied to the protection nearest to the fallen climber. Keep the rope running as straight as possible, use double-rope technique, and use long runners.

Leading

Leading on mixed terrain can be an exhilarating experience, but it is not for everyone. By its very nature, mixed leads tend to be bold and committing. Taking a leader fall while wearing crampons and holding ice tools is serious business. Before you decide to lead a mixed pitch on ice gear, be honest about your ability to climb it responsibly. If you decide that you can indeed climb and protect the pitch safely, here are a few tips to keep in mind:

- **Examine the crux(es) carefully.** Figure out the moves before you get there. Devise a plan and a backup plan for protecting and climbing through the crux.
- **Once on route, place gear at rests,** before the hard parts, instead of halfway through a crux sequence of moves.
- **Calculate your moves and climb with confidence.**
- **Relax and breathe deeply;** this will calm stressed nerves.
- **If you are stumped by a sequence of moves, down-climb to the last rest spot, reevaluate, and try again,** perhaps using a slightly different technique. If the sequence remains elusive, down-climb or lower off.

THE RACK FOR MIXED CLIMBING

A mixed climbing rack contains gear that is appropriate for the climb: Some modern mixed climbs are fully bolted, requiring only a set of quickdraws for protection. Longer classic mixed climbs require a full rock rack combined with a full ice rack. A typical mixed climbing rack might contain some or all of the following gear:

- Six to twelve ice screws of varying lengths appropriate for the thickness of the ice
- An assortment of nuts, Hexentrics, and Tricams that can be slotted or pounded into cracks
- Spring-loaded camming devices (SLCDs), both three- and four-cam units
- An assortment of pitons for ice-filled cracks
- Several runners or quickdraws
- A few long runners or cordelettes for threading gaps between the rock and the ice or ice columns
- Several load-limiting runners
- An ice hook (as shown in Figure 18-7b and c in Chapter 18, Alpine Ice Climbing) for quick protection, frozen seams, and moss
- A V-thread tool (as shown in Figure 18-9 in Chapter 18)
- A few pieces of ½-inch tubular webbing or 6- to 8-millimeter accessory cord for constructing rappel anchors
- A knife for cutting webbing and accessory cord

- **Be prepared to leave some gear behind.**
- **If a fall is imminent, check the landing zone.** Be sure that you will fall away from the trailing rope, which can be damaged by crampons or tools. Disengage your tools, then your crampons, and push away from the wall. Aim picks away from you and to the sides. Direct crampons toward the wall and keep your knees slightly bent to absorb the impact.

CLIMBING IN THE WINTER ENVIRONMENT

The extreme conditions of winter can create fantastic, almost surreal landscapes. On clear winter days, the bright blue sky is a perfect backdrop for the vivid blues of water ice formations. The ice glistens in the sunlight and leads skyward.

Waterfall ice and mixed climbing build on the skills of alpine mountaineering and can involve severe conditions that require specialized equipment, a high level of skill, and a tremendous will to succeed. Equipped for the winter environment, the waterfall ice and mixed climber combines the disciplines of rock climbing and ice climbing, is well schooled both in leading on rock and ice, and in avalanche assessment. But more importantly, waterfall ice and mixed climbers have an excellent understanding of their own abilities; they climb not for glory or recognition, but to fully experience the freedom of the hills.

PLANNING AND PREPARATION • EXPEDITIONARY CLIMBING TECHNIQUES • EXPEDITION WEATHER • HIGH-ALTITUDE HEALTH HAZARDS • AN EXPEDITION PHILOSOPHY

Chapter 20
EXPEDITION CLIMBING

Climbing the high and remote peaks of the world requires significant commitment of time and effort. Expedition mountain travel gives climbers the opportunity to explore faraway lands, immerse themselves in local mountain cultures, face the physical and mental challenges of greater mountaineering objectives, and build strong, lifelong relationships with climbing partners.

Many of the considerations for expeditions are similar to those for shorter climbing trips. However, there are some significant differences in planning, techniques, and health issues. Moreover, the required level of commitment is much higher.

Expedition climbing does not entail a different type or standard of climbing as much as an expansion of the time scale for a trip. A weekend trip may involve several hours to approach a peak, a day to climb it, and several hours to return home. An expedition may involve two or three days of air travel, followed by a day or two of land travel, and then a 10-day trek just to get to base camp. On an expedition, a rest break may be an entire day spent lounging and hydrating rather than a 15-minute sit-down during an approach hike.

The actual climbing is much the same as has been discussed in earlier chapters. The main differences between expedition climbing and other types of mountaineering are the logistics of tackling a remote peak, the more severe weather likely to be encountered, and the difficulties of climbing at high altitude—and often the challenge of dealing with local customs and the daunting red tape of climbing regulations in a foreign country. In addition, expeditions require special skills such as performing crevasse rescues while tied in to a sled, ascending and descending fixed lines, and functioning in extreme cold.

We've come this far. Let's make the last step together.
—Jim Wickwire to Lou Reichardt, as they put their arms around one another and together became the first Americans to reach the summit of K2, in 1978

PLANNING AND PREPARATION

Planning an expedition involves selecting a destination, choosing the climbing party, determining a climbing schedule, preparing supplies, and making sure the team members are in condition. The party might also need to decide whether to hire guides. Travel necessities such as passports, immunizations, and insurance cannot be overlooked either.

CHOOSING AN OBJECTIVE

In deciding what peak to try and which route to climb, mountaineers must consider a number of factors: the difficulty of the route, whether the expedition will tackle alpine- or expedition-style climbing, how long the expedition will last, what time of year it will take place, and its cost and location.

Difficulty of the Route

It is generally best to choose a route well within the climbing ability of the party because the added challenges of remoteness, altitude, changeable weather, and routefinding will add to the route's difficulties. Until climbers have gone on a few expeditions, they should think of the trip as an opportunity to apply well-practiced climbing skills in a new environment rather than to push the limits of their technical ability.

Choosing a Climbing Style

The route, the size and strength of the party, and the preferences of the climbers will help them choose a style of climbing—alpine style, expedition style, or somewhere in between. The choice will affect the length of the trip, the amount of risk involved, and the kinds of equipment and technical gear necessary, so it is an important decision that must be made early in the planning process.

Alpine style. An alpine-style expedition means moving camps up the mountain in a continuous push, so that the climbers ascend the route only once. All equipment and supplies are carried with the team at all times. There is less margin of safety on alpine-style trips because climbers cannot bring as much equipment and supplies as a team on an expedition-style trip can. However, because the team moves faster, there is also less exposure to objective hazards such as storms and avalanches.

Expedition style. An expedition-style climb involves multiple trips between camps, during which food, fuel, and supplies are carried to higher camps. Total group sizes are larger because more supplies and equipment must be carried. Technically difficult sections of the route are often protected with fixed lines—ropes anchored in place to minimize danger during repeated trips up and down the route. For these reasons, expedition-style climbing takes longer. This can be an advantage because climbers have more time to acclimatize to high altitude when they are ascending slowly in stages.

Duration of the Climb

Again, the party should be realistic. Do not try to cram a 25-day route into three weeks of annual leave. Remember that the time it takes to get to the mountain and then to return home can be a significant part of the expedition's schedule. Each individual climber's schedule should include extra time.

Time of Year

Study information on seasonal temperatures, winds, storms, precipitation, and amount of daylight in the area the party is considering for its expedition. These will affect the expedition's duration and needed gear.

20

Costs

Expeditions are costly because of the large amounts of time, equipment, and food required. Major costs include purchasing and/or renting equipment for the climb, purchasing transportation and other incidentals on the way to the peak, and hiring porters or pack animals to haul gear to base camp. In many cases, expenses incurred within a country are minor compared to the cost of getting there. Estimate costs based on the party's research about the peak and the area.

Some climbers try to save a few dollars by not using porters or pack animals to haul their gear to base camp. Do not scrimp in this regard only to waste extra days and exhaust the party just getting to the mountain. Be sure to budget adequate compensation for porters and other support staff, as well as supplies they will need for their own safety and comfort. The climbing party should be prepared to provide essential equipment, such as sunglasses and extra stove fuel, which many porters may not have. Know the going rates for support staff services and be sure to pay them accordingly. It is always best to set rates for their services before you head out on the expedition.

Location

There are so many choices for an expedition. Alaska, Mexico, South America, New Zealand, China, Nepal, Pakistan, India, Europe, Russia, Kazakhstan, and Africa all boast difficult, remote peaks. The experience of traveling in a new country is often one of the most enjoyable and rewarding aspects of an expedition.

After a peak is chosen, research the mountain and its routes. Talk to climbers who have been there; look for descriptions in the journals of the Alpine Club, American Alpine Club, the Alpine Club of Canada, and other climbing organizations. Seek out guidebooks, videos, and articles in climbing magazines, and research online sources. Note that in some countries, maps are considered restricted military information. Consider whether anyone in the party speaks the local language. Get all possible details on logistics, potential problems, where to buy fuel, what foods are available, objective hazards on the mountain, and so forth.

Select and research a backup route in case the original objective must be scratched because of avalanche hazard, bad weather, inability of some party members to continue, or any other reasons. If a highly technical route up the mountain has been chosen, consider acclimatizing by climbing the standard route first and then taking on the tougher challenge.

Find out what climbing and communication-device permits and approvals are necessary, and determine how long in advance an application must be made. It helps to have copies of itineraries, climbing résumés of party members, equipment lists, and medical information prepared ahead of time and available while traveling to the peak. Evidence of good organization impresses bureaucrats around the world.

CHOOSING THE TEAM

Choosing a compatible climbing team is the first and most essential step toward an enjoyable experience. Expedition climbing is full of stress, and climbers can be taxed to their physical and mental limits. Climbing literature abounds with "climb and tell" accounts of expeditions in which, it seems, team members came to despise their fellow climbers. Do not let your expedition end up being another such example. Make it a goal to head out as friends and return as even better friends.

The skill of the team must, of course, be equal to the demands of the climb. Climbing with people of similar technical ability may improve compatibility. Personalities also need to be compatible, and team members must be able to live harmoniously with others in close quarters under stressful conditions. The climbers should agree on the philosophy of the trip in terms of climbing style, climbing goals, environmental impact, and degree of acceptable risk.

It is important to agree on leadership before the trip gets under way. If all climbers are of roughly equal experience, democratic decision making usually works well. If one climber is clearly more experienced, that person can be given the leadership role. Even if democratic decision making works for the majority of situations on the climb, a designated leader who will step in when necessary, especially in urgent situations, is needed. Even if a single leader is designated, areas such as finances, food, medicine, and equipment should be delegated to others to lessen the leader's load and to keep everyone involved and informed. This also helps build expedition leaders for the future. (See Chapter 21, Leadership.)

The number of climbers in the expedition depends on the route and on the climbing style chosen. A party of two or four climbers may be best on technically difficult routes because of the efficiency of two-person rope teams and the limited space at bivouac sites. However, climbing with a very small team means that if even only one person becomes ill or cannot continue, the entire team may have to abandon the climb.

When the route itself does not determine the optimum party size, logistics become the deciding factor. As the number of climbers increases, issues of transportation, food, lodging, and equipment become more complicated. Climbing parties of six or eight have the advantage of strength and reserve capacity: If one climber is unable to continue, the rest of the party still has a chance to go on with the expedition. Larger parties are also better able to carry out self-rescue than smaller teams. However, an expedition with more than eight members can become logistically burdensome.

THE CLIMBING ITINERARY

Once climbers have researched their mountain and assembled a team, they must set up an itinerary that includes a good estimate of the number of days needed for the journey. Allow for the approach to the peak, carrying loads up the mountain, climbing, sitting out storms, and resting. An average elevation gain of 1,000 feet (300 meters) per day allows for acclimatization to high altitude, and this figure should be correlated, where possible, with good campsites. Rest days built into the schedule provide time for mental and physical recuperation, equipment sorting, and a time buffer for unplanned delays caused by storms, illness, or other problems. If a storm hits, try to adjust the itinerary to allow a rest period for the same time, making the best of a bad day.

GUIDED EXPEDITIONS

Guided climbs to just about any expedition destination are available. Climbers should consider hiring a guide if this is their first expedition, if they lack capable partners, or if the prospect of organizing such a major adventure is overwhelming. Using a guide on an expedition allows climbers to spend more time enjoying the experience and less time organizing it. They will be able to concentrate on mental and physical preparation. See the "Questions to Consider When Selecting a Guide Service" sidebar.

Conversely, a guided climb costs more than a privately organized venture. Climbers lose control over the selection of party members and other decisions that may affect individual safety or prospects for the summit. Also, there may not be the same unity of purpose and team spirit that characterize the best expedition experiences.

SUPPLIES

On expeditions to the remote mountains of the world, climbers either bring it with them or they do without it. Having the necessary equipment—and having it in working order—is much more critical than on a weekend climb where home is a short drive away. An expedition needs a complete equipment list, including both group and personal gear, agreed upon by all team members. See Table 20-2, later in this section.

Food

Food is the heaviest supply carried on an expedition. Climbers will, however, be grateful for every ounce of it. Food provides the necessary fuel for your body to carry loads and climb the route. It can also serve as one of the great pleasures of the trip.

Every climber has preferences in food, so conduct a team survey of strong food likes and dislikes before planning menus. Try out all the food ahead of time, preferably on training climbs with the team. Combat the danger of carrying unpopular foods by providing a lot of variety. This ensures that if some team members do not like one item, there should be several others they will find tasty, or at least palatable. A condiment and seasoning kit with hot sauce, spices, soy sauce, margarine, and mustard adds interest to bland packaged foods and perhaps will salvage the unpopular foods.

Although fats have the highest caloric density—at 9 calories per gram (calories are uniformly measured in metric units)—carbohydrates (4 calories per gram) are easiest to digest, providing the quickest energy. Proteins have about the same caloric density as carbohydrates but are not as easy to digest and are usually accompanied by substantially more fat. For a reasonable expeditionary diet, try to consume total calories in the ranges shown in Table 20-1 (compare with Table 3-3 in Chapter 3, Camping and Food).

QUESTIONS TO CONSIDER WHEN SELECTING A GUIDE SERVICE

If a climbing party decides to hire a guide, research the guide service it has in mind.

- Is the guide service licensed and insured as required by the governing authority of the destination?
- What is its safety record and success rate?
- What are the qualifications of the guide and the other party members?
- What reputation does the service have among climbers? Personal references are very helpful.

TABLE 20-1. CALORIC PROPORTIONS FOR EXPEDITIONS

Food Source	Percentage of Daily Calories
Carbohydrates	50 to 65 percent
Fats	20 to 30 percent
Proteins	15 to 20 percent

Plan to provide about 35 ounces—roughly 2¼ pounds (1 kilogram)—of food per person per day. With no waste, 35 ounces would provide more than 5,000 calories. In reality—because of packaging, nonnutritive fiber, and the food's irreducible water content—the food will provide only about 3,900 calories per day. Experience will tell climbers whether this is just right, too much, or not enough. Too much food means carrying extra-heavy loads between camps and possibly a slower trip. Too little means climbers will begin losing weight or have to abandon the climb; on a trip of three or four weeks, weight loss should not cause a problem, but on longer expeditions, too much weight loss may affect the team's strength and endurance.

It is tempting to take plenty of extra food. Keep in mind, however, that someone has to carry it up the mountain. Do you want that extra weight in your pack? Plan carefully. Take enough to remain adequately nourished and comfortable, but do not take unneeded supplies.

Packaging and organizing food is an important element of expedition planning. Repackage food in appropriately sized portions (either individual portions or meal-size portions for the entire group) to get rid of unnecessary packaging. Add spices or other additional ingredients as desired to the repackaged food. Keep the preparation instructions with the repackaged foods. Measure the food into the correct portions (so much per person per day) and label it. Clear plastic bags help organize the food while keeping the contents visible.

Adequate hydration is the first line of defense against altitude sickness. Bring plenty of soups, hot drinks, and cold-drink mixes to keep climbers motivated to drink the necessary fluids. Contaminated water plagues nearly every part of the world. The expedition kitchen must be able to furnish adequate potable water for everyone through chemical decontamination, filtering, or boiling.

For early in the trip, plan foods that differ from those that will be eaten later when the party is up on the mountain. Foods for lower elevations and warmer climates include those that are more time-consuming to prepare, such as pancakes; items that cannot withstand freezing (such as cheese and peanut butter); and canned foods. Foods carried to higher altitudes should be very light and require minimum preparation, freeze-dried items, instant noodles, instant rice, and instant potatoes, for example. Try to eat local food on the approach and at base camp. Not only will this help prevent climbers from getting tired of expedition food, but it will also give them an opportunity to sample the local fare.

Vitamins are another important item to take on an expedition. Bring vitamin C, vitamin E, and multivitamins to bolster overall health. These vitamins may also decrease susceptibility to upper-respiratory illness, which is common on high-altitude expeditions.

Fuel

Regulations for transporting fuel vary from airline to airline and destination to destination. Research the regulations for the party's specific airline and destination well ahead of time. It is not likely that the party will be permitted to take fuel on the flight, so make sure the fuel needed is available at the destination.

Fuel containers are usually available in Alaska or Canada, but elsewhere climbers must provide their own. Aluminum containers (plastic bottles have a reputation for leaking) as small as 1 quart (liter) are fine if not much fuel needs to be carried. For larger quantities, bring empty 1-gallon (3.8-liter) gas cans or sturdy, approved plastic fuel containers. They must be new, because some airlines object to containers with residual vapors. All fuel containers should be kept separate from other gear, especially food.

Multifuel stoves are good insurance in countries where white gas is not readily available. Even with a multifuel stove, check the fuel's compatibility with the stove before heading into the mountains. If kerosene or a similar low-volatility fuel will be used, be sure to buy alcohol or white gas for priming the stove. It is preferable to prime with and burn the same fuel whenever possible. The cleanliness of fuel in some areas is questionable. Bring a fuel filter, and filter all fuel before it is used. Clean the stove often.

Plan on using between 4 and 8 ounces (0.1 to 0.2

liter) of fuel per person per day, depending on how much water must be boiled for purification or melted from snow or ice. Bring sufficient stoves and fuel for any porters or other local individuals who will be part of the expedition, so that no fires will be needed for cooking. Adequate cooking equipment will help reduce the entire team's impact on the environment.

Group Gear

Kitchen. For communal cooking, take pots large enough for group meals and for melting large amounts of snow. Water bottles will need to be filled daily, so pots must be easy to pour from; a 2-quart (2-liter) coffeepot works well. Bring at least one cook pot per stove. Bring a metal gripper to use on pots that lack handles or bails, or use wool gloves as potholders. Be careful using synthetic gloves, which will melt if they get too hot.

Shelter. Tents are another communal item. Decide beforehand how many and what kinds of tents are best. If necessary, also decide ahead of time who will stay in what tent, keeping in mind the importance of making everyone comfortable for a good night's rest.

Other group gear. Digital altimeters and compasses can be useful, but they depend on battery power. To save a bit of weight, the party can carry one analog altimeter and one compass as pieces of group equipment, rather than having each climber carry his or her own. Note that if the climb objective is in the southern hemisphere, the compass must be balanced for the southern hemisphere (see "Compass Dip" and "The Altimeter" in Chapter 5, Navigation).

Wands, which are used to mark routes, camp perimeters, gear caches, and snow shelters, are another group gear item. The number of wands needed varies according to the specifics of the climb, such as length, terrain, and route. (See "Wands" in Chapter 16, Snow Travel and Climbing.)

The party may carry communication devices to get weather information, call for emergency help, or allow communication between climbers at different locations. The main choices are cell (or mobile) or satellite telephones, amateur radios, citizen-band (CB) radios, and marine-band FM radios. Investigate these options to determine both the technical feasibility and the legality of their use where the party will be traveling.

Repair kit. Be prepared for critical equipment failure under the prolonged and rugged demands of an expedition. Put together a comprehensive repair kit, keeping in mind the relative importance of each piece of equipment to the progress of the group (see Table 20-2).

First-aid kit. An expedition should assemble a comprehensive first-aid kit after everyone in the party has had input on the contents. Consider how isolated the peak is, and keep in mind the specific medical conditions of team members and their medical knowledge. Discuss the group's medical needs with a doctor who is familiar with mountaineering.

The first-aid kit may include such specialized or prescription items as a strong painkiller, antibiotics, a dental repair kit, and a suture kit. Be sure to carry a first-aid manual. (See "First-Aid Supplies" in Chapter 2, Clothing and Equipment, as well as Chapter 23, First Aid.)

Check on any restrictions or cautions regarding transporting drugs and medical equipment to a particular destination. Find out whether different climates or altitudes adversely affect medications that will be taken on the expedition. Also, bear in mind that just because certain drugs are legal in your country of origin does not mean they will be legal everywhere in the world.

Climbing Gear: Communal or Personal?

The route and the chosen climbing style determine what climbing gear is needed. A route that involves only glacier travel may require just the basics—rope, ice ax, crampons, and crevasse rescue gear. Technical routes can take the whole gamut of equipment, from ice screws, snow flukes, and pickets to camming devices, nuts, and pitons.

Depending on the climbing style and organization of the trip, climbing gear can be personal or common. On a technical route, where climbers operate in self-sufficient pairs, climbing gear should be personal or left to each rope team to work out. In other cases, virtually all climbing gear—carabiners, runners, screws, and so forth—can be treated as group equipment. The choice is up to the party. Certain pieces of climbing gear, such as crampons and ice axes, are indispensable, and a large party may want to carry spares.

Ropes. Deciding what rope to take depends on the route and its difficulty. Keep in mind, however, that an expedition can put extraordinary wear and tear on ropes with daily use in bright sunlight. The team needs to decide how much rope to bring for fixed lines along the route. Fixed lines usually use nylon kernmantle rope due to its strength and abrasion resistance.

Backpacks. Every person on an expedition team

TABLE 20-2. SAMPLE EXPEDITION EQUIPMENT LIST

GROUP GEAR

Shelter

Expedition-quality tent(s)
Ground cloths
Snow stakes and/or tent flukes
Sponge and whisk broom
Snow-shelter construction tools: large snow shovel (for moving a lot of snow), small snow shovel (for delicate trimming), snow saw (for cutting blocks)

Group Climbing Gear

Ropes
Hardware: snow and ice gear (pickets, flukes, ice screws), rock gear (pitons, spring-loaded camming devices, chocks), carabiners, runners, daisy chains, fixed line, extra climbing equipment (spare ice ax or tool, spare crampons, spare rescue pulleys)

Kitchen

Stove gear: stove, windscreen and stove platform, fuel containers and fuel filter, matches and/or butane lighters, firestarter
Cooking gear: pots, pot cozy, pot gripper, sponge or scrubber, dip cup, cooking spoon, snow sack (for collecting clean snow to melt for water)
Food
Water treatment: filter, chemicals

Repair Kit

Tent repair kit: pole splices, spare pole
Stove repair kit
Crampon repair kit: extra screws, connecting bars, straps
Tape (duct, filament, fabric repair)
Adhesive-backed repair cloth
Seam repair compound
Tools: multitool (with slotted and Phillips screwdrivers, small pliers, small wire cutter, shears, file); Allen wrenches
Sewing kit: assorted needles and thread; awl; assorted buttons, snaps, buckles, and D-rings; Velcro (hook-and-loop fastener), fabric (Cordura, ripstop nylon), flat webbing
Other: wire, accessory cord, pack buckle, extra ski-pole basket, patch kit for inflatable foam pads

First-Aid Kit

Most expeditions carry a comprehensive group first-aid kit. In addition to normal first-aid items, the kit should include the following drugs, plus others recommended by a physician:

Prescription drugs vary with the destination, but should include antibiotics, strong analgesics, antidiarrhetics, laxatives, and altitude medications (acetazolamide, dexamethasone).
Nonprescription drugs vary with the destination, but should include cough suppressants, decongestants, mild analgesics (aspirin, ibuprofen).

Other Group Gear

Wands
Weather radio
Altimeter, map, compass
Satellite phone
Radio transceiver, extra batteries
GPS receiver
Two-way radios
Latrine equipment

PERSONAL GEAR

Clothing

Synthetic-fabric underwear
Plastic boots
Insulating layers
Supergaiters and/or overboots
Down clothing
Wind-protection and rain-protection garments (top and bottom)
Extremities: hands (liner gloves, insulating gloves, mittens), feet (liner socks, insulating socks, vapor-barrier socks), head (balaclava, sun hat, face mask, wool hat)
Other: bandannas, sun shirt, synthetic fill or down booties

Sleep System

Sleeping bag
Vapor-barrier liner
Bivouac sack
Inflatable foam pad or closed-cell foam pad

Climbing Gear

Ice ax
Rescue pulley
Second ice tool
Ascenders and/or prusiks
Seat harness with ice-tool holster
Helmet
Chest harness
Large-volume pack
Crampons
Pack cover
Personal carabiners and slings
Snowshoes or skis
Chock pick
Sled with associated hardware for pulling
Belay device
Duffel bag

Other Gear

Ski poles
Headlamp, extra batteries and bulbs
Avalanche transceiver
Watch with alarm
Avalanche probe
Wide-mouth water bottles
Sunglasses, goggles
Insulated mug, bowl, spoon
Spare prescription glasses
Passport
Pocketknife
Sit pad
Personal hygiene: toilet paper, pee bottle, toothbrush, comb, chemical wipes and/or waterless skin cleanser, sunscreen, lip balm, foot powder, earplugs
Personal recreation: camera and film, books, journal, pen or pencil, personal stereo, playing cards

needs a backpack with a capacity between 5,500 and 7,000 cubic inches (90 and 115 liters), because at times climbers will be called on to carry extremely large and heavy loads. The pack must be comfortable while worn with a climbing harness.

Ascenders. The cam of a mechanical ascender permits one-way movement, gripping or squeezing the rope when the ascender is pulled downward, but freely sliding upward. Ascenders make it easier to haul heavy, bulky expedition loads and handle crevasse rescues. Expedition climbers prefer ascenders over prusik slings, both for crevasse rescue and for self-belay while climbing with a fixed line—the extra weight is justified by the greater utility. A pair of handled ascenders is the norm, although one ascender plus a prusik sling or a mini-ascender can work if equipment weight needs to be reduced. Regardless of the choice, make sure you can operate the system while wearing bulky gloves or mittens.

Personal Gear

Clothing. Expedition climbers need clothing that can stand up to prolonged use under severe conditions. The suggestions on clothing and equipment in the preceding chapters of this book (see Chapters 2, Clothing and Equipment; 16, Snow Travel and Climbing; and 18, Alpine Ice Climbing) are generally applicable to expeditions.

Sleeping bag. Take into account each sleeping system's comfort rating based on the anticipated climate, season, and altitude of the area the party will be visiting.

Other personal gear. Each climber will likely want some or all of the following:

- **Contact lenses**—Climbers who wear contact lenses should carry an extra set.
- **Prescription sunglasses**—Climbers who require prescription glasses should carry an extra set of prescription sunglasses as well.
- **Journal**—An expedition can make climbers introspective. A field journal made of waterproof paper and some pencils help pass the time.
- **Books**—Catch up on reading while waiting for flights or during rest days and storm days in the field. Coordinate the selection of books among the team members to avoid repetition and provide variety. A thick book can be cut in half or thirds to expedite sharing.
- **Personal hygiene items**—On cold-weather trips where water is at a premium, chemical wipes and/or waterless skin cleansers can provide a refreshing sponge bath, and talcum powder can take the edge off the often strong odors that develop over the course of an expedition.
- **Pee bottle**—The pee bottle eliminates those unpleasant trips to the latrine during storms and cold nights. Be sure the bottle has a secure top and is clearly labeled. The pee bottle should be a unique shape or have some obvious tactile difference from your water bottles so you do not mistake one for the other in the middle of the night.

PHYSICAL AND MENTAL CONDITIONING

Training for an expedition involves both physical and mental preparation. For your body, emphasize both cardiovascular and strength training (see Chapter 4, Physical Conditioning). Cardiovascular conditioning is important for physical activity at high altitudes. Strong muscles are essential for carrying heavy loads up mountains, not to mention hoisting and climbing with a large expeditionary pack.

Climbing itself is the best training. Climb often and in all weather conditions, carrying a heavy pack. If climbers are able to go on a typical two- to three-day climb while carrying gear for camping and climbing, gaining 3,000 to 5,000 feet (900 to 1,500 meters) per day, and feel they still have plenty of physical reserves, they are probably sufficiently fit for an expedition. They need the endurance to carry 40 to 60 pounds (18 to 27 kilograms)—sometimes in addition to pulling a sled—for an elevation gain of 2,000 to 3,000 feet (600 to 900 meters) every day, day after day.

Your mind and spirit also need to get in shape for the rigors of an expedition. Learn about the special challenges of expedition travel and prepare to accept them. Otherwise, the size and remoteness of the climbing area may be overwhelming, or a long storm or a bout with the flu may dispel your good spirits.

Expedition success often is earned by the climbers who have the desire or will to succeed, even though they may be physically weaker than other climbers. It takes more than physical strength to deal with extreme cold, sickness, cramped quarters, poor food, conflict with teammates, the stress of technical climbing, and the lethargy brought on by high altitude.

Work on both physical and mental conditioning by seeking out experiences that come as close as possible to what can be expected on the expedition. Prepare for the expedition by going on winter climbs and on longer trips. Once the expedition is underway, it may not be possible to alter such objective factors as extreme cold or illness, but with preparation, climbers can learn to exercise a great deal of mental control over their attitude toward and actions about these factors.

BEFORE LEAVING HOME

Food and gear must be packed and repacked to accommodate the various transportation modes used to get to the mountain. Become familiar with the requirements that face the expedition, such as airline regulations on bag sizes and weights or muleteer requirements on load balancing. Develop, and carry along on the expedition, detailed equipment lists, including what items are in what containers so that any item can be retrieved readily. Research what documentation is required for importing equipment to the destination (for example, a packing list or bill of lading).

Before leaving home, plan travel arrangements for each leg of the journey, making reservations where possible. Try to work with a travel agent who has booked trips to the region before.

Well before the departure, secure the following: passport, visa, medical insurance coverage, and required or suggested immunizations.

Climbers should be as healthy as possible when they leave home, because, in all likelihood, they will not get better while traveling. Have a dental exam, and have any dental work done before leaving. To stay healthy once the destination is reached, purify all water and be cautious about eating fresh vegetables or fruit, dairy products, and uncooked food (for proper precautions, see *The Pocket Doctor* by Stephen Bezruchka, listed in Appendix D, Supplementary Resources).

Finally, through all the complicated hurry and scurry of getting ready for a big expedition, remember that the goal is to get away from it all and climb a mountain.

EXPEDITIONARY CLIMBING TECHNIQUES

Expedition mountaineering calls for the rock, snow, ice, alpine, and winter climbing techniques covered throughout this book. An expedition also adds some new techniques to the climber's repertoire: hauling sleds and using fixed lines.

SLED HAULING

To move loads of gear and supplies on long glacier approaches, expedition members often pull sleds or haul bags behind them (fig. 20-1). Climbers may carry a normal load in a backpack and pull a sled with another pack's worth of gear. Before the expedition, practice on various types of terrain.

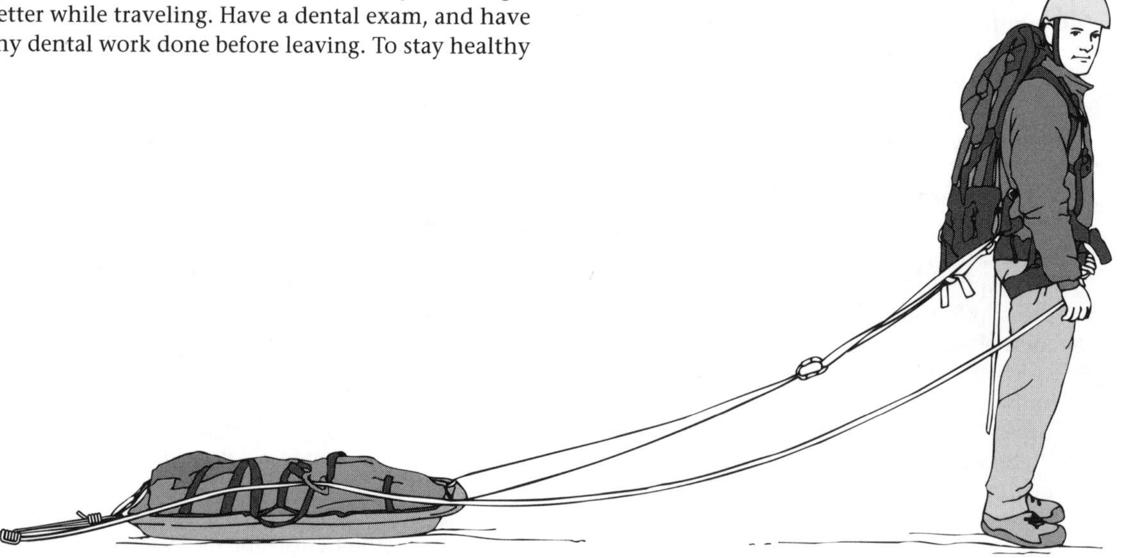

Fig. 20-1. Sled and climber rigged for glacier travel.

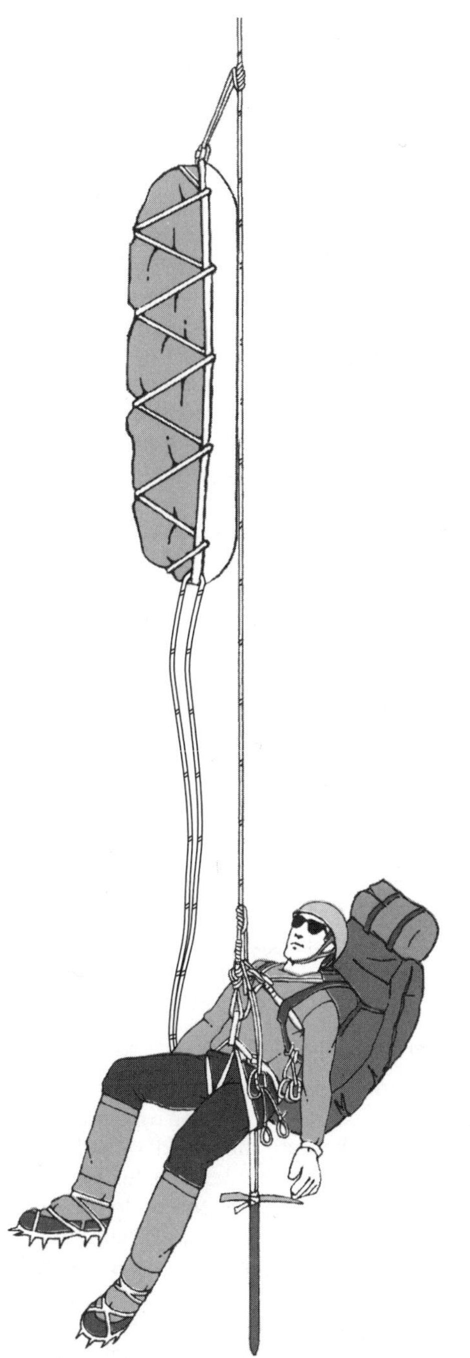

Fig. 20-2. Crevasse fall, with a sled hanging above fallen climber.

A commercial haul sled features zippered covers to hold the load, a waist harness, and rigid aluminum poles connecting the sled and harness. The poles help the climber control the sled when traversing or going downhill. An optional brake, typically a flat piece of aluminum, can be added to the rear of the sled, which will prevent backsliding on steeper terrain.

A cheaper but very workable alternative is a plastic children's sled with holes drilled in the sides for use as rope attachment points. Load gear into a duffel bag and tie it to the sled. Use 5- to 7-millimeter accessory cord to pull the sled. Most climbers find it more comfortable to attach the haul line to their pack rather than to their climbing harness.

Another alternative is to drag a haul bag, constructed of durable slick material to help it slide over the snow. A swivel connector that attaches the haul line to the haul bag keeps the bag's rolling from putting twists in the line.

As the route steepens, the amount of weight that can be pulled in a sled decreases. Sleds cannot be used at all on steep, technical climbing terrain. Haul bags may then be what is needed (see "Hauling" in Chapter 15, Aid and Big Wall Climbing).

Hauling a sled can get complicated during roped travel on glaciers. A fall into a crevasse is more treacherous with a sled plunging down behind the fallen climber. Even if the fallen climber is not injured by the plummeting sled, the sled's presence and added weight make rescue more difficult. Minimize the danger of getting hit by the sled during a crevasse fall by using this simple preventive technique:

Where the climbing rope runs past the sled, tie it snugly with a clove hitch or prusik hitch to a carabiner attached to the rear of the sled. Be sure to clip the duffel bag on the sled to the rope as well. In a crevasse fall, first the climber will drop into the crevasse, followed by the sled. The sled, however, will be stopped above the climber by the tie-in to the climbing rope (fig. 20-2). If the climber is using a hauling tether attached to the sled instead of rigid aluminum poles, be sure the tether is long enough so that the climber would be well below the sled as it would hang from the climbing rope in a crevasse fall.

This technique depends on having a team member on the rope behind the fallen climber, to arrest the fall of both the climber and the sled. Therefore, it will not work for the last climber on a rope. The last person either assumes the extra risk, or the team can decide to haul only two sleds for every three climbers on a three-person rope team.

Crevasse Rescue

There are special procedures for crevasse rescue involving a sled, beyond those discussed in Chapter 16, Snow Travel and Climbing. As you dangle in the crevasse, your weight may be on the sled haul line (or towing poles, if a commercial sled is used). First of all, transfer your weight to the climbing rope by standing in slings attached to your ascending system—whether that is mechanical ascenders, prusik slings, or a combination (see Chapter 17, Glacier Travel and Crevasse Rescue). Next, disconnect the attachment between you and the sled. If a haul line is attached to your pack, simply take off the pack and let it hang from the line.

Once you are free of the sled, try to rescue yourself or wait for your climbing mates to get you out. If you start up the climbing rope on your own, the sled will probably complicate matters. You may need to ascend around the knot in the rope holding the sled. In this case, remove your ascenders, one at a time, and reattach them above the knot. You may also need to untie from the climbing rope in order to move past the sled and reach the lip of the crevasse. To make it easier to disconnect from the climbing rope, some sled pullers travel with the rope clipped to a locking carabiner on their harness, rather than tying the rope directly to the harness itself. If you need to untie from the climbing rope, use extreme caution to ensure that your ascenders are secure.

A fall into a crevasse with a sled can also mean extra effort for topside teammates if they must pull out the fallen climber and the sled. If the fallen climber cannot disconnect from the sled, or if no extra rescue rope is available, topside teammates must haul both climber and sled at the same time. Using a 3:1 pulley system will give the most mechanical advantage pulling on the climbing rope (see Chapter 17, Glacier Travel and Crevasse Rescue). It is far preferable to use a spare rope to pull out a fallen climber and then use the climbing rope to haul out the sled.

FIXED LINES

A fixed line is a rope that is anchored and left in place on the route. It allows safe, quick travel up and down a difficult stretch. Climbers protect themselves by tying in to a mechanical ascender on the fixed line, eliminating the need for time-consuming belays. If a climber falls while climbing next to the fixed line, the ascender cam locks onto the fixed line to hold that person (see "Using Ascenders" and "Fixing Pitches" in Chapter 15, Aid and Big Wall Climbing).

The fixed line simplifies the movement of people and equipment, especially when numerous trips are required, and permits less-experienced climbers to follow a route. Fixed lines are common on large expeditions to major peaks to provide protection on long stretches of exposed climbing or to protect porters while they make carries from camp to camp in the face of such obstacles as icefalls, glaciers, and steep rock or ice. The lines make it possible for climbers and porters to carry heavier loads than they could safely carry without them.

Fixed lines are sometimes used as a siege tactic on difficult rock and ice faces, with climbers retreating down the lines each night to a base camp and then ascending again the next day to push the route a little farther.

Exercise extreme caution in deciding whether to make use of a fixed line already in place on a route. It is hard to determine the integrity of an existing line and its anchors. Age, exposure to weather, and the ice tools or crampons of climbers who used the line before your party may have damaged the rope.

Some climbers argue that fixing ropes is an outdated technique, no longer required to climb any established route. This is not the majority view, but the technique should not be abused. Fixed lines should not be used to supplement the climbing ability of an expedition team. Fixed lines should not be added on popular routes or in violation of the local climbing ethic.

Equipment for Fixed Lines

To set up and use fixed lines, the party needs rope, anchors, and ascenders. Climbing ropes do not make good fixed lines because they are designed to stretch when weighted, which is undesirable for a fixed line. A more static rope—that is, one with low elongation under load—is best. Nylon rope is the most common type for fixed lines. Kernmantle construction is best, though braided ropes can be used.

The diameter of fixed lines usually varies between 7 and 10 millimeters. The ideal size depends on the terrain and the amount of use the line is expected to get. Try to carry long sections of fixed line. They are usually manufactured in lengths ranging from 90 to 300 meters (300 to 1,000 feet), depending on diameter.

Anchoring Fixed Lines

Every fixed line needs an anchor at the bottom and a bombproof (secure) anchor at the top. To anchor the fixed line to the mountain, employ attachment points that are normally used in belaying and climbing on rock, snow, or ice—pitons, chocks, natural outcrops, ice screws, pickets, and snow flukes or other deadman anchors. Mark the location of the bottom and top anchors with wands, making it easier to find them during or after a snowstorm.

Place a series of intermediate anchors between the bottom and top of the fixed line. Tie off the fixed line at each anchor (intermediate as well as top and bottom) so that every section of line is independent of the others. This permits more than one climber at a time on the line. Be sure that a fall by any climber would not cause rope movement, rockfall, or anything else that could endanger a team member. Passing should be done at an anchor.

There are several rules of thumb when deciding where to place anchors: Place them to change the direction of the line where necessary or to prevent pendulum falls. An anchor at the top of a difficult section of the route is helpful. If possible, place the intermediate anchors at natural resting spots, making it easier for climbers to stand and move their ascenders past them.

Always bury or cover snow and ice anchors, and inspect them regularly for possible failure from creep or melting. Keep a close eye on any rock anchors capable of creeping or loosening. Place anchors at locations that will keep the line from rubbing on rough or sharp surfaces, or pad the line at points of abrasion. Even small amounts of wear can multiply into dangerous weak spots on fixed lines, which are typically lighter-weight rope. Falls will also damage the line. After any fall on the line, inspect it for damage and check the anchors for indications of possible failure.

Setting Up Fixed Lines

A variety of methods can be used to set a fixed line, each appropriate for certain conditions, climber preferences, and types of line. The key is to think through the chosen system prior to starting out and, if possible, to test and refine it before it is actually needed. It is a big job. Here are three possible approaches:

- The most common way is for two or three climbers to ascend the route, using a standard climbing rope to belay one another or to establish a running belay, and to set a fixed line as they climb. The climbers carry the whole spool of fixed line with them, letting it out as they ascend and tying off at each intermediate anchor along the way. Carrying a spool of rope is difficult.
- Another option is for the climbers to pull the end of the fixed line up as they ascend, clipping the fixed line in to each anchor with carabiners. After anchoring the top of the fixed line, the climbers go back down, tying off the fixed line at each anchor along the way. It is difficult to pull up on the end of the line and overcome the tremendous friction that develops as the line travels through the carabiners and over the route.

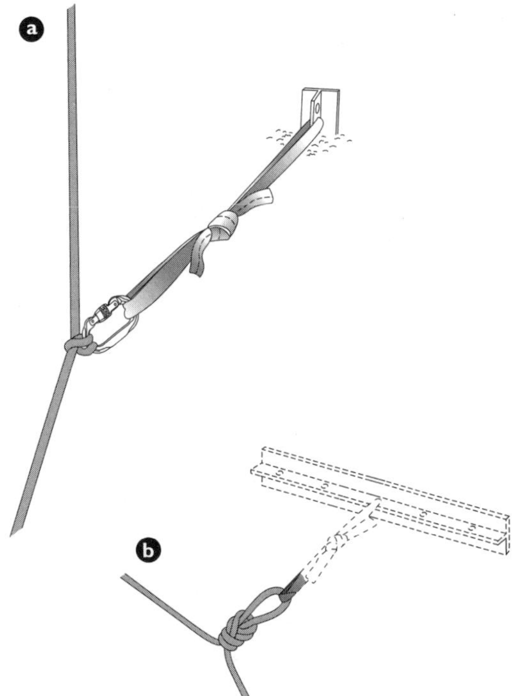

Fig. 20-3. Intermediate anchors on a fixed line: a, anchor with carabiner clove-hitched to fixed line; b, anchor without carabiner, using a sling tied through a figure eight loop of fixed line.

20

- Another option is to set the fixed line on the descent. This means, of course, that the material for the fixed line first must be carried to the top of the route. Tie the line in to a bombproof anchor at the top, then rappel or down-climb to tie the line off at intermediate anchors. These can be anchors that were placed on the earlier ascent of the route, although new ones may be added just for the fixed line.

To tie off the fixed line at each intermediate anchor, use a figure eight knot (the preferred method) or a clove hitch in the line. Tie a sling directly to the anchor, and clip the figure eight loop or clove hitch in to a carabiner attached to that sling (fig. 20-3a). Or better yet, minimize the use of carabiners and have one less link in the system by tying the sling directly through the figure eight loop (fig. 20-3b).

Ascending Fixed Lines

Ascending with a fixed line is just like regular climbing, except your harness is attached by a sling to a mechanical ascender, which is placed on the fixed line and used as a self-belay in case of a fall.

Tie the sling to the seat harness where you normally tie in with the climbing rope, or clip the sling into a locking carabiner attached to the harness. Make the sling short so the ascender is not out of reach if you fall. If you are climbing a near-vertical section or climbing with a heavy pack, pass the sling through your chest harness as well to prevent tipping upside down in a fall.

Attach the ascender to the fixed line, following the specific directions for that brand of ascender. The ascender should be oriented so that a fall will cause it to clamp the rope. It should slide easily up the line but lock tight when pulled down the line. Test it, and check the fittings on your seat harness, before starting upward.

Attach a carabiner clipped to the ascender sling, or clipped to a separate sling attached to your seat harness (fig. 20-4a), to the fixed line to serve as a backup safety link. If you fall and the ascender fails, the safety carabiner will slide down the fixed line, stopping at the next anchor below to arrest the fall.

At each intermediate anchor, the knot or hitch in the fixed line must be passed. This is the most dangerous moment in fixed-line travel, particularly if conditions are severe and you are exhausted. It is best to move the safety carabiner first (fig. 20-4b). Unclip the carabiner, then reclip it above the knot or hitch. Then

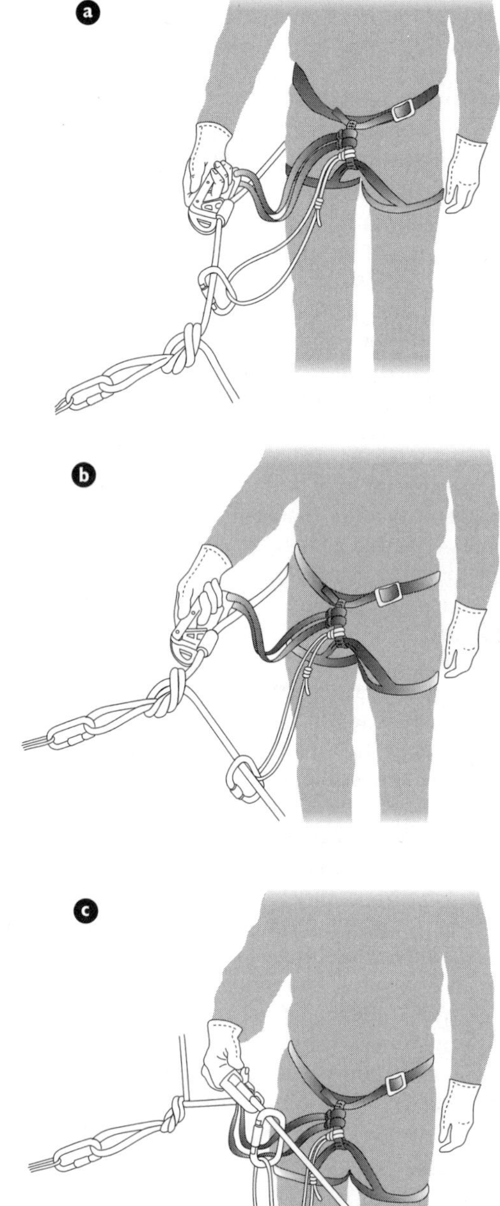

Fig. 20-4. Mechanical ascender attachment to fixed line: a, set up for ascending, with carabiner-sling backup; b, passing an anchor, move the safety carabiner first; c, move the ascender past the knot second.

move the ascender (fig. 20-4c). This sequence offers more security than moving the ascender first. Another option is to briefly clip in to the anchor while relocating the ascender. Be sure that the safety carabiner stays on the line when the ascender is detached. Think the procedure through in advance and practice it often so you can perform it reliably under the worst possible conditions.

Descending Fixed Lines

Climbing down with a fixed line is similar to climbing up. Attach the ascender sling to your seat harness. Attach the ascender to the fixed line in the same way as on the ascent. Double-check that the ascender locks onto the rope when you pull down on it and that it will be within reach if you end up hanging from it after a fall. Attach the safety carabiner.

Begin the descent. While climbing downward, move the ascender down the rope, keeping it with you. Use a light grip on the ascender release, which allows you to let go of it instantly in a fall so the ascender will grab the rope. It is natural to try to hang onto something if you lose your balance, but the last thing you should grab is the ascender release!

Be very careful in removing and reattaching the ascender while descending past anchors. Move the ascender, then move the safety carabiner (the opposite order from ascending a fixed line). Remember: Never detach the ascender and the safety carabiner at the same time. Keep in mind that you can temporarily clip in to the anchor while relocating the ascender. On steep sections of fixed line, rappeling the fixed line may be a good alternative to down-climbing.

Removing Fixed Lines

Climbing rope of any type is not a natural or biodegradable material. It must be packed out. Teams are responsible for removing any fixed lines that they have placed and then hauling them out. When setting them up, always bear in mind that they will need to be removed. In some cases it may be possible to use a "moving" fixed line, removing it and moving it higher as the party ascends the mountain, then descending via a safer route. If the party is leaving the mountain and thus going down a fixed route for the last time, plan a strategy (down-climbing or rappeling, or a combination) that will permit the party to remove the fixed line. Practice Leave No Trace guidelines (see Chapter 7), and respect the importance of taking everything with you when you leave.

EXPEDITION WEATHER

On an expedition, climbers need to become amateur weather forecasters because their safety and success are so closely bound to nature's moods. When the climbing area is reached, talk to other climbers and to people who live there about local weather patterns. Find out the direction of the prevailing winds. Ask about rain and storms. On the mountain, make note of weather patterns. The altimeter can serve as a barometer to signal weather changes.

Take clues from the clouds. Cirrus clouds (such as mare's tails) warn of a front bringing precipitation within the next 24 hours. Lenticular clouds (cloud caps) mean high winds. A rapidly descending cloud cap is a sign that bad weather is coming. If the party climbs into a cloud cap, expect high winds and poor visibility. (See Chapter 27, Mountain Weather for more about weather.) Be prepared for the fact that big mountains typically have big storms, strong winds, and rapidly changing weather. Wait out a storm, if possible, because there is risk inherent in descending under bad conditions. If the party expects to be stuck for some time, start rationing food and conserving fuel.

Fair weather poses problems too. If it is hot and sunny, glaciers intensify solar radiation. The result can be collapsing snow bridges, crevasse movement, and increased icefall. In such conditions, it is best to climb at night, when temperatures are lowest and snow and ice are most stable.

HIGH-ALTITUDE HEALTH HAZARDS

Expedition climbing is physically taxing. Inadequate levels of oxygen, extreme cold, and dehydration, among other things, are all potential health hazards. Learn to recognize, prevent, and treat potential health hazards when they occur (see Chapter 23, First Aid). Consult a first-aid manual, specialized texts, or physicians familiar with mountaineering for detailed information.

On high peaks, temperatures drop well below zero. Although this is good for keeping snow stable, it can have a detrimental effect on a climber's body. Everyone in the expedition party must be aware of the dangers of frostbite, as well as wind- and sunburn.

Expedition climbing, like any mountaineering, takes climbers to altitudes where the human body no longer feels at home. Every climber is affected to one degree or other by reduced oxygen at higher elevations, often leading to acute mountain sickness (altitude sickness). This can lead to the life-threatening conditions of high-altitude pulmonary edema (HAPE) and high-altitude cerebral edema (HACE). These illnesses are generally avoidable, however, through proper acclimatization and hydration.

ACCLIMATIZATION

The best way to combat altitude illness is to prevent it in the first place. The best way to do this is to ascend slowly. The human body needs time to acclimatize to higher altitude, though how much time it takes varies from person to person.

Ascend at a moderate rate, averaging 1,000 feet (300 meters) a day in net elevation gain. If suitable campsites are 3,000 feet (900 meters) apart, carry one day to the next camp (3,000-foot gain), move camp the next day, and rest the third day at the new camp, for a net gain of 3,000 feet every three days. Try not to push your limits until you have become well acclimatized. Schedule rest days after big pushes.

Above 18,000 feet (5,400 meters), most people begin to deteriorate physically regardless of acclimatization. Minimize time at high altitudes, and periodically return to lower altitudes to recover. The old advice is good: Climb high, sleep low. The body acclimatizes faster during exertion than during rest and recovers more quickly at a lower altitude. Expedition-style climbing takes advantage of these concepts by carrying loads to a high camp, returning to lower altitude to recover, and then ascending again.

HYDRATION

Hydration is critical in avoiding altitude illness. Everyone should drink 5 to 7 quarts (5 to 7 liters) of water a day and avoid alcohol and caffeine, which have a dehydrating effect. To supply that much water for everyone, several hours each day must be dedicated to melting snow. This is time well spent, however, because adequate hydration is an important key to the success of an expedition.

In addition to using the above recommendations for daily liquid intake, monitor your urine output and color. Urine should be copious and clear. Dark urine indicates that you are not drinking enough water.

Climbers usually lose their appetite at high altitudes. Everyone tends to eat and drink less than they should. This is why a varied menu—one that includes foods and drinks that are appealing to each member of the party—is so important.

AN EXPEDITION PHILOSOPHY

Members of an expedition need a common code to live by during their weeks of traveling and climbing together. One good code can be summed up in three promises that you and your teammates can make to one another: to respect the land, to take care of yourselves, and to come home again.

Respect the land. Every day, the expedition party has the chance to put the health and beauty of the land ahead of its own immediate comfort. The easy way out might be to burn wood fires, set up camp in a virgin meadow, or leave garbage and human waste on the ground. But if all the climbers have promised to respect the land, they will be aware of their impact and be responsible. Leave no trace.

Those who follow your trail will not want to see the wrappers from your snacks or other signs that your group passed through the area. If you pack it in, pack it out. Be sensitive to local customs. Local land managers may have specific wishes about the treatment of their areas. Learn what their expectations are ahead of time and be respectful. If local practices are laxer than Leave No Trace, however, do not follow local customs; instead, follow Leave No Trace practices.

Take care of yourselves. If you and your climbing partners have promised to take care of yourselves, you have made a commitment to group self-reliance. There may be no choice in the matter, because the party will likely be a long way from rescuers, helicopters, hospitals, or even other climbers. Prepare by thinking through the possible emergencies that the party could face and by making plans for responding to those. You will feel reassured that plans are ready if you have to use them and grateful if you do not.

In addition, foster team spirit by checking on one another throughout the day regarding adequate fluid intake, use of sunscreen, and other necessities that will keep team members healthy and in good spirits. After all, as the late renowned climber Alex Lowe said, "The best climber in the world is the one having the most fun!"

Come home again. The third promise might be the hardest to keep, because it can conflict with that burning desire for the summit. It is really a promise to climb safely and to be willing to sacrifice dreams of the summit in favor of survival. Expedition climbing is, all things considered, about pushing limits and testing yourself in a very tough arena.

Each person and each team must decide what level of risk they are willing to accept. Keep the third promise by first being sure that the team agrees upon what is safe and what is unsafe. Out of that discussion, decisions flow daily regarding how fast to ascend, what gear to carry, when to change routes, and when to retreat.

Most climbers would rather return home safely than push for the summit under unsafe conditions. Having the freedom of the hills does not just mean reaching the summit; the success of an expedition can be measured in many ways.

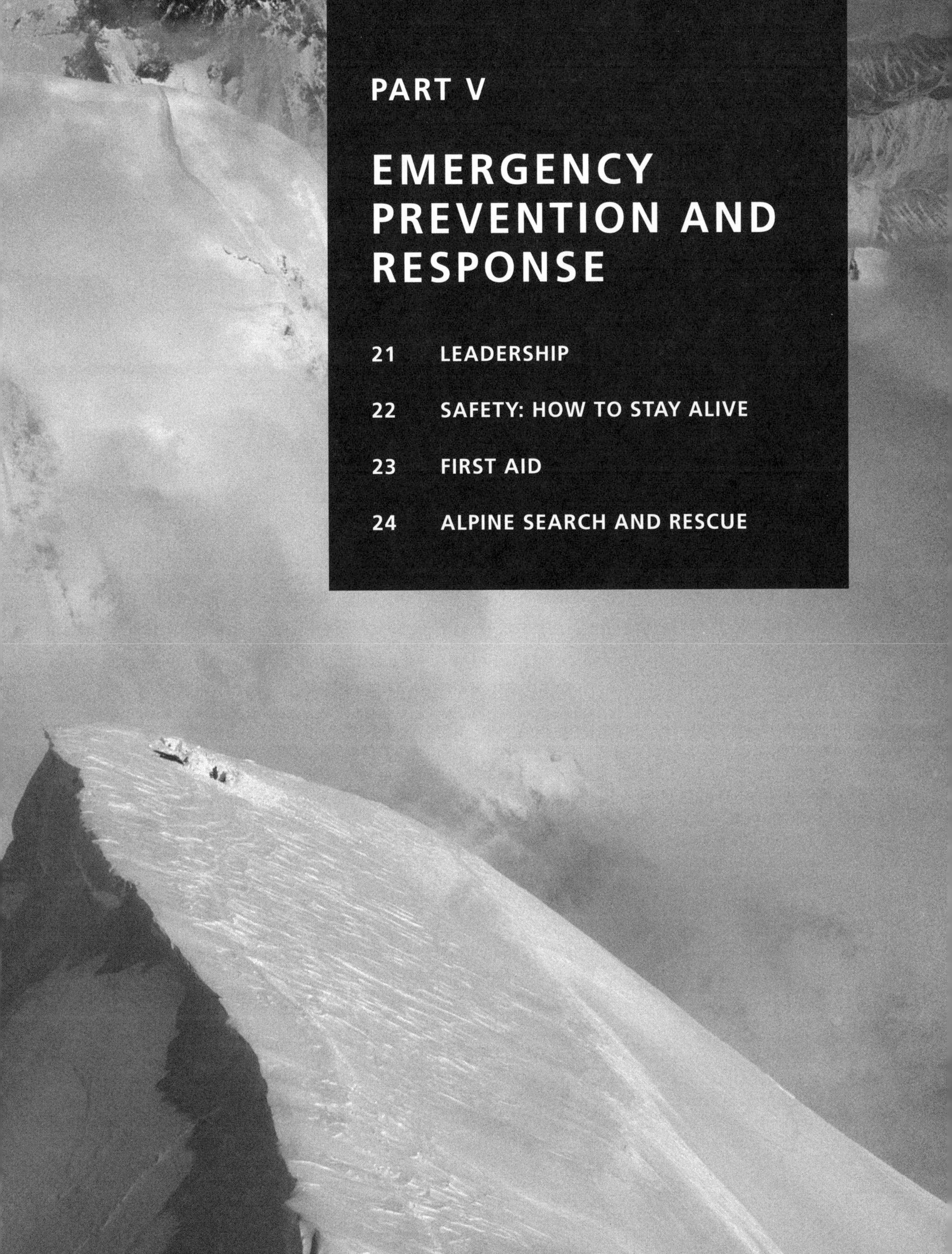

PART V

EMERGENCY PREVENTION AND RESPONSE

THE CLIMB LEADER • ORGANIZING THE CLIMB • BECOMING A LEADER

Chapter 21
LEADERSHIP

Just as every climbing party needs a map and compass, every climb needs good leadership—but the style and form of that guidance varies with the venture. It is one thing to head out with some longtime climbing companions for a sunny weekend of peak bagging, but it is entirely another to mount an extended technical climb with mountaineers who do not know one another to a peak none of them has ever seen.

Climbers who know one another well achieve good leadership very informally, probably without even knowing it. An expedition of climbers less familiar with one another requires a more formal, structured organization. But in both cases, leadership provides the same things: a way to put a climb together and make it a safe and enjoyable experience.

THE CLIMB LEADER

A climb leader is someone who has special responsibility for organizing the climb and for making decisions en route. Depending on the nature of the party, the degree of formal organization may vary from highly structured to virtually nonexistent. Nevertheless, certain necessary functions of the group are performed one way or another. The position of leader may be conferred by a sponsoring organization or may develop informally and spontaneously, but the fact is that most climbs have a leader.

Small, informal parties often do not select a leader. Everyone feels responsible for organizing, sharing work, and team building. It is easy for each member to know what the others are doing, so coordination is not much of an issue. The climb organizer or most experienced party member may be tacitly recognized as leader of such a group, but that type of leader should try not to be autocratic.

Large groups, on the other hand, do not lead themselves and usually do better with a designated leader. Members of the climbing party cannot know what every other person is doing, so someone needs to be chief organizer if only to make sure no critical details are overlooked. Large groups may also need more focus on team building, because it is likely that the members will not all know one another.

The leadership structure of most climbing parties tends to fit into one of the following categories.

Peers. A group of acquaintances that decide to go climbing together are peers. Usually there is no designated leader, but members informally allocate key functions. One climber may take responsibility for organizing equipment, another for transportation and food, and so forth. Most decisions are made by consensus. Even in this least-formal type of organization, one member will usually emerge as "first among equals" and be regarded as leader. It will be the person who displays initiative, good judgment, and concern for the group, and who generally inspires the most confidence.

Climb organizer. The person who organizes the climb is the one who has the original idea for the venture and then recruits others. The organizer is usually recognized as de facto leader, even if the position is never formalized.

Most experienced. A group tends to bestow leadership upon, and to defer to the judgment of, a climber who is clearly the most experienced in the party.

Climbing clubs and schools. Leadership is formally conferred by the sponsoring group when a climb is part of an organized program. Often, leaders must go through an accreditation process to ensure a certain level of experience and competence. There may even be a hierarchy among the leadership, with an overall leader and assistant instructors to help. There is no doubt who is leader, and it is not up to the party to select one. The leader is expected to research the climb and to take charge of equipment, transportation, and other logistical matters. Such climbs are often teaching situations; students are expected to follow the leader's guidance, but they are also supposed to be learning and gaining self-sufficiency.

Guided climbs. Climbers pay guide services to provide competent leadership. Professional guides are often outstanding climbers and are completely in charge of their groups. Guides make the decisions for their clients and assume responsibility for their safety.

Fail to honor people,
They fail to honor you;
But of a good leader, who talks little,
When his work is done, his aim fulfilled,
They will say, "We did this ourselves."
—Lao-tzu

ROLES OF THE LEADER

The leader's role is to help the party achieve the team's objectives in a safe, enjoyable manner, with minimum impact on the alpine environment. A leader must be experienced, with technical skills appropriate for the climb, but is not necessarily the most experienced in the group or the best climber. A leader should be in good enough shape to keep up, but need not be the strongest in the party. A leader does need an abundance of good judgment, common sense, and a sincere interest in the welfare of the entire party. Along the way, a leader simultaneously adopts many roles, such as the following:

Guardian of safety. The paramount concern of any party is safety, starting in the planning stage. A leader should ensure that everyone has appropriate equipment, experience, and stamina and that the route chosen is reasonable for the party and in safe condition. En route, when climbers become tired, impatient, or excited, they get careless. This can also happen if they are inexperienced. A leader learns to see these conditions as warnings and become more alert, watching, gently reminding, and even nagging when necessary. When tough decisions have to be made, such as turning back due to weather changes or time constraints, it is often up to the leader to initiate the unpleasant discussion before the situation becomes critical. (See Chapter 22, Safety: How to Stay Alive.)

Planner. Many details need attention if a group of people is to be at the right place at the right time with the right equipment to mount a successful summit attempt. A leader does not have to do all the planning personally, but does bear responsibility for seeing that all necessary preparations are being attended to by someone in the group.

Expert. Giving advice when asked or when needed is an important leadership role. Training, experience, and judgment are the prerequisites for this role. A person does not have to be the party's best climber to be an effective leader but certainly needs enough experience to have developed "mountain sense." A range of skills is needed in addition to technical climbing knowledge. Leaders should know something about equipment, navigation, first aid, rescue techniques, weather—in fact, all the topics addressed in the various chapters of this book.

Teacher. When less-experienced climbers are along, teaching becomes part of the leadership role. Usually this involves nothing more than occasional advice and demonstrations. However, if some members lack techniques required for safe progress, it may be wise to halt and conduct a little hands-on learning right then and there. Many seasoned mountaineers find that passing along their hard-won knowledge is a fulfilling experience—but it should be done with a careful touch. Novices may be embarrassed by their relative lack of skill or intimidated by the physical danger. This is no time for bullying. Instead of using the approach that says someone else is wrong, try saying, "Let me show you what works for me." The exception is when a student is doing something dangerous; then a more direct approach is needed.

Coach. This is a little different from the role of teacher. The coach helps people get past difficulties by adding encouragement and support to a base of knowledge. Often the real obstacle is lack of self-confidence. Assisting a companion through some difficulty helps that person and also keeps the entire party moving forward. Coaching effectively, helping people do their best and emerge smiling, can be one of the particular delights of leadership.

Initiator. A climb progresses by the party making a series of decisions: Where shall we make camp? Which route should we take? What time should we get up? When should we rope up? Often the decisions themselves are not hard to make, but they need to be made in a timely fashion. The function of leadership is not necessarily to dictate answers but to get the right issues on the table at the appropriate time.

Arbiter. Once a discussion is under way, differences of opinion will arise. It is good to collect opinions and get all viewpoints out into the open, but this can lead to indecision ("Which course do we select?") or argument ("You are wrong!"). Anyone in a position of leadership, whether or not formally conferred, has some leverage that can be used to advantage in these instances. If the party seems to be making a technically incorrect or dangerous decision, if tempers are rising, or if the discussion is aimlessly wandering, the weight of the leader's opinion will often settle matters and get the climb moving again.

Guardian of the environment. Climbers must do their best to leave the alpine environment undisturbed so that future generations may sample the same pleasures. Leaders should set the example by always practicing minimum-impact techniques (see Chapters 3, Camping and Food, and 7, Leave No Trace). If others fail to follow this example, they should be reminded, gently at first, insistently if necessary.

A leader's responsibility is to get things done, but not necessarily to do them. Delegating tasks has a host of benefits. It allows the leader to maintain an overview of the entire trip, rather than being tied down by every little problem and decision. It builds team spirit by giving people a chance to get involved and be useful. Also, delegation fosters individual responsibility by clearly demonstrating that doing and deciding are not the tasks of the leader alone. If someone is having difficulty and needs special help, a strong, experienced climber might be delegated the role of personal coach. In a larger group, especially in a teaching situation, the leader should appoint an assistant who can help keep things moving and who can take over if the leader is incapacitated.

STYLES OF LEADERSHIP

Two broad categories characterize the style in which leaders perform their roles. Also see the "Tips for Becoming a Leader" sidebar.

Goal-oriented style. A goal-oriented leadership style has to do with process and structure—what to do, who will do it, and how. Goal-oriented leaders concentrate on making decisions and directing others.

Relationship-oriented style. A relationship-oriented leadership style has to do with showing consideration and helping a group of people become a supportive, cooperative team. Relationship-oriented leaders take a personal interest in people and their views, consulting with them on decisions and thereby building group cohesion and morale.

Most people lean toward one style or the other, but it is not an either-or choice. Neither style should be neglected, and effective leaders balance both styles. The proper balance depends on the nature of the party and the needs of the moment.

Each leader must develop a personal style through the process of learning the craft of mountaineering and discovering effective ways of relating to climbing companions to help them become a happy, effective team.

Beyond that, leaders should be themselves. Some people are jolly and talkative; some are more reserved. Successful leaders are found among all types of people. It is more important to be genuine than to try copying some idealized style.

LEADING IN A CRISIS

Everyone hopes it will never happen, but sometimes things go wrong. Perhaps conditions turn dangerous or

TIPS FOR BECOMING A LEADER

There is no simple formula for becoming a leader, but there are guidelines:

- A leader cannot be self-centered; decisions are made for the good of the party, not the leader.
- A leader's genuine interest in every party member influences the degree to which they care about each other and strengthens the group.
- A leader cannot pretend and cannot show off; the leader should be honest about personal limitations. Leaders should admit it when there is something they do not know—and get the group to help them figure it out.
- A sense of humor helps.

someone is injured. Then the group focus shifts from recreation to safety and survival. The leader's role also changes. If the group has a designated leader, this is the time for that person to switch to a decisive style. A small, informal group may find that a leader emerges. When a clear need for coordination arises, people tend to look to the most-experienced person or the one who, for whatever reason, inspires the most confidence.

When an accident occurs, there is no time for lengthy debate. Prompt, effective action is needed, and it should be directed by someone with training and experience. Nevertheless, the leader should stay hands-off as much as possible, instead directing others, maintaining an overview, and thinking ahead to the next steps.

The party should be guided by the three rules of rescue (see Chapter 24, Alpine Search and Rescue) in managing a crisis:

- The safety of the rescuers comes first—even before that of the victim.
- Act promptly, but deliberately and calmly.
- Use procedures that have been learned and practiced; this is no time to experiment.

It is easy to think of all climbing mishaps as life-and-death situations in which the outcome depends solely on what the rescuers do. In fact, neither is usually the case.

First, most accidents result in cuts and bruises, sprains, sometimes broken bones, but only occasionally anything worse.

Second, the outcome is usually determined by factors beyond the rescuers' control. All that can reasonably be expected is that the climb leader will draw upon training and experience to devise an appropriate plan and then carry it out as safely and effectively as conditions permit.

Avoid trouble by anticipating it. Leaders should always be thinking ahead, asking "What if?" In camp, they think of the climb; on the ascent, of the descent; in summiting, of retreat. They look for early signs of fatigue in companions, mentally record bivouac sites, keep track of the time, and note any changes in weather. They consider who could take over the leadership role if circumstances demanded it. Everywhere on trips, leaders mentally cross bridges before reaching them; they borrow trouble. By staying a step ahead, they hope to avoid problems or to catch burgeoning ones before they become crises.

Accidents are unexpected, but climbers can prepare for them by taking courses, reading on the subject, and mentally rehearsing accident scenarios. Take note of the information in Chapter 24, Alpine Search and Rescue. First-aid training is a must. Chapter 23, First Aid, describes the prevention and treatment of medical conditions commonly experienced by mountaineers, but it is not a substitute for hands-on training. Public and private agencies offer first-aid courses, and some climbing clubs give mountain rescue training.

Also, climbers can benefit from studying the experiences of other climbers. The American Alpine Club and the Alpine Club of Canada jointly publish *Accidents in North American Mountaineering* (see Appendix D, Supplementary Resources). This informative annual publication contains detailed descriptions and analyses of mountaineering accidents.

ORGANIZING THE CLIMB

21

Even a simple climb is a complex undertaking. Once an objective is chosen, the leader has many tasks to complete before the climb. On the way to the trailhead and at the trailhead, last-minute checks and updates keep the outing organized. During the approach, the climb, the descent, and the way out, the leader helps keep the party organized until the outing is over. The checklist in Table 21-1 is a useful guide to this process.

BEFORE THE CLIMB

Once an objective is chosen, the leader needs to gather information on the approach and the climbing route itself. The party must be selected, and decisions must be made regarding what equipment is needed and

TABLE 21-1. CHECKLIST FOR ORGANIZING AND LEADING A CLIMB

BEFORE THE CLIMB

Research the route.

- Review guidebooks and maps.
- Talk with others who have done the route.
- Determine the technical level and any special problems of the route.
- Check weather forecast and avalanche conditions.
- Determine whether wilderness permits or reservations are required, and obtain these if necessary.

Form the party.

- Estimate the levels of climbing skill and physical condition required.
- Determine optimum party size.

Determine equipment needs, and make arrangements for sharing equipment as needed.

- Personal equipment: clothing, boots, food, camping equipment, crampons, ice ax, helmet, other technical gear.
- Shared equipment: tents, stoves, ropes, hardware.

Research the approach.

- Driving route: check to be sure backcountry roads are open.
- Hiking route: check trail conditions.

Develop a trip itinerary.

- Estimate miles/hours of driving.
- Estimate miles/hours of hiking to high camp or start of climb.
- Estimate hours to summit.
- Estimate hours back to cars.
- Leave trip itinerary with a responsible person.

ON THE WAY

- Make a final check of weather forecast and avalanche conditions.
- Register with park or forest agencies if required.

AT THE TRAILHEAD

Check equipment and discuss plan.

- Personal equipment: make sure everyone has enough food, clothing, and essential equipment; inadequately equipped climbers should not continue.
- Shared equipment: make an inventory of tents, stoves, ropes, and hardware.
- Redistribute group equipment, if necessary, to equalize loads.
- Discuss the plan: route, campsites, time schedule, expected hazards.

ON THE APPROACH

- Keep the party together. Agree to regroup at specified times or places—especially at trail junctions.
- Decide on formation of rope teams.

ON THE CLIMB

- Establish a turnaround time. Continuously evaluate, and adjust the turnaround time based on actual conditions encountered, if appropriate.
- Keep rope teams close enough to be in communication with each other.

ON THE WAY OUT

- Assign a "trail sweep."
- Regroup periodically.
- Be sure that no one leaves the trailhead until everyone is out and all cars have been started.

who will bring it. A schedule should be made to assure that there is enough time to complete the climb with a margin for contingencies. Everyone needs transportation to the trailhead. And in the days leading up to the climb, weather trends (and snow conditions, if applicable) should be monitored.

Research the Route and the Approach

Typically, climbers research the trip so they will know what to expect and can prepare accordingly. Guidebooks are available covering most popular climbing areas. They usually have written descriptions of approaches and routes, maps, drawings, and sometimes photos. Topographic maps are invaluable—be sure to know how to read them (see Chapter 5, Navigation). Check road and trail conditions for the approach as well.

Some climbing clubs keep files of trip reports from their outings; these can be valuable both in themselves and because they often give the names of those who went on the climb. Firsthand information from someone who has recently done the route can add significantly to information found in guidebooks. For peaks on public land, government agencies such as those in charge of national parks or forests can be good sources of information. Be sure to check for permit requirements, access restrictions, and fees (see "Determine and Obtain Necessary Permits and Fees," below).

For a full discussion of researching a route, see "Gather Route Information" in Chapter 6, Wilderness Travel.

Check Weather and Avalanche Conditions

The understanding of current and anticipated route conditions and weather remains as much an art as it is a science. However, mountaineers have ever-increasing access to weather and current route conditions, primarily via the Internet. The amount of information available for a given area, mountain, or specific route will vary greatly, and for many ranges and mountains, little or no current information is readily available.

Useful Internet sites include those of local and regional governments, national or regional parks, and private recreation areas, as well as those sites that detail weather and road conditions. Some of these sites include real-time weather and web cams for an up-to-the-minute view of conditions. Local climbing sites can also be useful for current route conditions, or the leader may be able to post a question.

However, the best source of information concerning current route conditions will be from a reliable individual who has recently been on the mountain and route the party is considering; a phone call to a park office, climbing shop, bush pilot, or friend in the area is a good idea. This is especially true if the climb involves a long drive or approach.

The "art" portion of understanding conditions and weather forecasting involves knowing how a change in weather will affect the route and the party's climbing objectives. In many areas, the only certainty about the weather is that it will change. How will specific changes in temperature, wind, humidity, and precipitation affect your climb? Having alternate objectives in mind is a good idea and will help you to avoid "forcing" a climb—nearly always a bad decision.

Determine and Obtain Necessary Permits and Fees

Permit, registration, and recreational fee requirements vary greatly from region to region. Many publicly owned parks, forests, and wilderness areas have some form of governmental regulation. Some may limit where the party can camp, which can affect the logistics of a climb. Typically, regulations are designed to preserve the ecology of an area or to increase the value of the wilderness experience. Some are created for the safety of visitors; others are in place to gather fees for rescue or for maintaining an area's infrastructure.

For popular climbing areas or specific climbing routes, it may be necessary to obtain a reservation a year or more in advance. Some areas, on the other hand, have a first-come, first-served approach to permitting. In either case, the time required to get a permit, and the hours in which the permit will be issued, should be calculated as part of the overall climb logistics. If there is any question about regulations, it is best to call ahead to get the latest information. As with the case of changeable weather and route conditions, the lack of permit availability will require a change in plans.

Form the Party

Party strength. A climbing party must have adequate strength in order to have a safe, enjoyable, and successful trip. Strength refers to the group's ability to accomplish the climb and to cope with situations that may arise. The party's strength is determined by the mountaineering proficiency of the members, their physical condition, the size of the party, and their equipment. Intangibles such as morale, the members' degree of commitment to the climb, and the quality of leadership also affect party strength.

A strong party consists of several experienced, proficient climbers who are in good condition and well equipped. What constitutes weakness is not as easy to define because a party is strong or weak only in relation to its goals. On a very challenging climb, the addition of a single ineffective member would make a party too weak. On easier trips, a party may be strong enough if it has only two strong climbers and several weaker ones; in fact, this is common on guided climbs. A party with no experienced members is weak in any situation.

Researching the route helps determine what party strength is needed for a particular climb. Is the route or the approach physically arduous? What level of technical challenge does it pose? Is the place so remote that the party will be completely on its own, or are there likely to be many other people in the vicinity?

Who should go? Every member of a climbing party must be up to the challenge, both physically and technically. Some climbers will go with only proven companions when they are attempting routes near the limit of their abilities. When a leader is considering inclusion of a climber whom the leader does not know, some questions should be asked.

Experience is the surest indicator of ability; someone who has climbed several times at a given level is probably capable of doing so again. Climbing skills should match the chosen route's requirements. For instance, experience gained from an indoor climbing gym will not necessarily translate to an alpine environment. Expedition leaders sometimes even request written résumés, but for a weekend climb, a bit of probing conversation is probably enough to ascertain a person's fitness. However, leaders should be aware that inexperienced people may not realize they are unprepared for the planned climb.

A party that includes novices, or even experienced people who have never before climbed at the route's required level of skill, will need veteran climbers who are willing and able to coach. The climb almost surely will take longer, and the chance of success will be reduced. Be sure everyone in the party understands this situation and accepts it.

Often the group is formed before the objective is selected. Several climbers may decide to "get together and do something." Then the selection process is reversed, and it becomes a matter of picking a climb to fit the group. It is important to gauge everyone's skill and stamina and to choose a peak that the party can realistically attempt safely. Usually the weakest member is the limiting factor.

A leader must also consider *compatibility* when forming a climbing party, especially for a long or arduous trip. Fortunately, most people seem to be on their best behavior while they are on climbs. The unspoken knowledge that climbing companions will soon be literally holding one another's lives in their hands does much to promote accommodation. Nevertheless, expedition literature is filled with engaging tales of squabbling parties. To say the least, dissension in a climbing party is no fun. It may reduce the party's chance of success; it is guaranteed to eliminate much of the enjoyment; and it can even compromise safety.

People who are known to dislike each other should not be on the same climb. The tensions and close proximity of the climb situation will only exacerbate any animosity. If two people are not getting along during the climb, other party members should do their best to keep the situation from erupting into open conflict, which might possibly threaten the safety and well-being of the group.

How many should go? The size of the party must be appropriate to the objective. Both strength and speed should be considered—and sometimes these two factors are at odds.

The Climbing Code given in Chapter 1, First Steps, recommends that the *minimum party size* for safety is three climbers: If one climber is hurt, the second can go for help while the third stays with the injured person. Another good conservative rule recommends at least two rope teams for safe travel on a glacier: If one team is pinned down holding a colleague who has fallen into a crevasse, the second team is there to effect the rescue.

These rules are general guidelines for minimum party size, but the specifics of the proposed trip may introduce other considerations. A prolonged wilderness venture may require a larger group to carry equipment and supplies, as well as to provide better backup in case of emergency. Some rock climbs require double-rope rappels on the descent; this dictates a minimum of two rope teams unless a single team wants to carry two ropes. Technical rock and ice climbs are best done with just two climbers on each rope; for these climbs, whatever the size of the party, there should always be an even number of climbers.

Maximum party size is also determined by considerations of speed and efficiency, as well as by concerns about environmental impact and by land-use regulations. A large group can carry more gear and offer more helpers in case of emergency, but a bigger party is not necessarily a safer one. Sometimes speed is safety, and experienced alpinists know that a larger group always moves more slowly. On certain routes, for example, climbers must move quickly to ensure finishing before dark. A larger party tends to get more spread out, can start bigger avalanches, and may kick down more loose rock.

As a general rule, the more difficult the route, the smaller the group should be. In the extreme case, some long technical climbs are done by parties of just two fast, experienced people, despite the general rule that three is the minimum safe party size.

Large groups have the potential of damaging the fragile alpine environment. They also erode the wilderness experience. Park and wilderness areas typically have party size limits (often 12 people maximum) to reduce impact and preserve aesthetic values. At the very least, these limits must be respected. Responsible mountaineers may even choose to impose tighter restrictions on themselves in particularly fragile places.

Determine Equipment Needs

The party needs to make decisions about equipment, both personal and shared.

Personal equipment is what each climber must bring—ice ax, pack, and clothing, for example. Some personal items, such as crampons or avalanche transceivers, are useful only if everybody brings them, so coordination is essential. In a large party, someone should take the lead in coordinating equipment.

Group equipment is shared: Tents, stoves and pots, food, ropes, racks, and snow shovels are examples. Someone needs to determine what is needed, survey the climbers to see who owns what, and then decide who will bring which items.

The party can give itself a margin of safety by planning to arrive at the trailhead with a little extra equipment. Surplus gear can be left out of view in vehicles, but if conditions are more severe than anticipated, or if someone forgets an item or fails to show up, then the party may still be adequately equipped.

Leaders should double-check their own gear before they leave home. It is embarrassing for the leader to forget some critical piece of equipment.

Develop a Trip Itinerary and Manage Time

Mountaineers can never be more than visitors to the alpine world. On every trip, there comes a time when climbers run out of daylight, supplies, or good weather; then it is time to return to lowland homes. Time has to be carefully rationed on a climb, and the important thing is not how fast to go but how wisely and well to use the time the party has.

Establish a schedule before the climb. Estimate the length of each segment—driving time, approach time, ascent time, and descent/return time—and allow some extra time for the unexpected. A typical estimate might be what is shown in Table 21-2.

In the estimate shown in Table 21-2, if it gets dark at 9:00 PM and the climbers want to be back at the trailhead by 8:00 PM, they must start at 3:30 AM.

Setting a turnaround time is a good practice. In the example just given, the party estimates four and a half hours from summit to trailhead for the descent, with no margin for the unexpected. They might decide it is reasonable to allow five and a half hours. This means they must start descending by 3:30 PM or risk walking out in the dark.

Most guidebooks give times for popular climbs and sometimes for the approaches as well. Keep in mind, though, that times vary greatly from party to party.

TABLE 21-2. ESTIMATING TRIP TIME

Trip Segment	Estimated Time
Drive to the trailhead	2.0 hours
Hike up the trail	2.0 hours
Cross-country approach	1.0 hour
The climb itself	4.0 hours
Time on the summit	1.0 hour
Descent time	2.0 hours
Return to the trail	1.0 hour
Hike out	1.5 hours
Total time estimate	14.5 hours
Contingencies	2.0 hours
Total time allowance	16.5 hours

Experience with a particular guidebook will indicate whether its estimates tend to be faster or slower than your personal times; adjust accordingly. Another good source for time estimates is someone who has done the climb.

If no information is available, use rules of thumb based on experience. For example, many climbers have found that they can average 2 miles (3-plus kilometers) per hour on an easy trail and 1,000 vertical feet (300 vertical meters) per hour on a nontechnical approach with light packs.

Avoid scheduling important business meetings, airplane flights, or social events for several hours after the scheduled end of a trip. Climbs frequently take significantly longer than expected. Climbing companions will not be happy if they have to turn back short of the summit or stumble out in the dark because someone in the party has a plane to catch.

Plan for Self-Reliance and Develop Contingency Options

When should climb organizers allow themselves to feel that their preparation is adequate? When is it enough? A good way to gauge is to ask whether the party has the people, proficiency, and equipment it needs to be self-reliant under normal circumstances. In the event of a serious accident, the party should call upon nearby climbers, and when needed, the party should request assistance from mountain rescue groups (see Chapter 24, Alpine Search and Rescue).

Have "a little extra." Any climbing party should be prepared to take care of itself in case of a minor mishap or downturn in the weather. In practice, this means having "a little extra" to provide a margin of safety: extra time, extra clothing, extra food, extra flashlight batteries, extra climbing hardware, and, above all, extra reserves of strength. As a general rule, climbers should plan to be self-sufficient for 24 hours in excess of the planned trip and understand that if help is needed, it may be delayed by weather and/or terrain. Balancing the benefit of extra supplies against the drag of their weight is an art every climber must develop.

Leave the trip itinerary with a responsible person. Leave a copy of the climb itinerary with a responsible person at home, specifying when the party expects to return and how long the person should wait before notifying authorities if the party is overdue. Be realistic when estimating how long the climb will take. Specify which authorities are to be notified if the party is overdue. For example, in the United States, the National Park Service has responsibility for mountain rescue in national parks; in most other areas of the United States, it is the county sheriff.

Carry cell (or mobile) phones. Cell phones are becoming more popular among mountaineers as the technology improves and their weight and cost decline. Using these tools can dramatically shorten the time it takes to summon rescuers. The devices are also useful for telling people back home that the party will be late but is not in trouble and, thus, can be used to avoid unnecessary rescue efforts.

Understanding the limits of cell phones is as important as understanding their usefulness. Batteries can be depleted, and cell phones are unable to transmit or receive in many mountain locations. They should be viewed as an adjunct to, not a substitute for, self-reliance. No party should set out ill prepared or inadequately equipped, or attempt a route beyond the ability of its members, with the notion that they will just call for help if necessary (see Chapter 24, Alpine Search and Rescue). Such an attitude imperils both the climbing party and the rescuers who may have to help them out.

AT THE TRAILHEAD AND ON THE APPROACH, THE CLIMB, AND THE DESCENT

Before the party leaves the trailhead, take a few minutes to check that all necessary equipment and supplies are in the climbers' packs. Anyone who has been climbing very long has had a weekend ruined by a missing critical item. Some climbers even use a written inventory checklist as a memory aid while they are packing. Redistribute group equipment, if necessary, to equalize loads. Go over the itinerary one last time to make sure everyone is on the same timetable.

On the approach and on the climb, set a steady pace, not necessarily a fast one. In the long run, the party cannot move faster than its slowest member; progress may even be slowed if that person is reduced to exhaustion. The important thing is to keep moving steadily. Rest stops for the whole party, taken at specific intervals, are more efficient than random halts whenever someone decides to stop.

A climbing party should stay together—not necessarily in a tight knot, but at least close enough to be in communication with one another. After all, mountaineers climb in groups partly because there is some safety in numbers. That safety is compromised when the party splits. Typically the stronger members forge ahead, leaving those most likely to need help isolated from those best able to give it. The danger of getting separated is greatest on the technical portions of a climb, where the more-skilled climbers move much faster, or on the descent, where some want to sprint while others may be dragging due to fatigue.

A small party of friends will naturally tend to stick together. Problems are more likely with larger groups. A large party usually benefits from having a designated leader, and one reason is that the leader can coordinate its movement. Climbers should be free to hike up the trail at their own pace but ought to regroup at designated rendezvous points, especially these:

- **Trail junctions**—to make sure everyone goes the right way
- **Danger spots** (such as hazardous stream crossings)—in case anyone needs help
- **The bottom of glissades**—because they naturally tend to split the party

A leader need not be at the front of the party. In fact, many prefer to lead from the middle, to better keep an eye on the whole group. However, the leader should be ready to swing into the forefront when a difficulty arises, such as a routefinding puzzle or a patch of demanding technical terrain. It may be wise to appoint a strong member as trail sweep, especially on the descent, to ensure there are no stragglers. A leader's a primary goal for any outing is to have the whole party return home safely.

BECOMING A LEADER

The responsibility of leadership is a burden, but the task can have great rewards. It gives the experienced alpinist an opportunity to pass along knowledge gained over the years: how to set a measured pace, how to read terrain and pick a route, how to deal with difficulties of many sorts. Mountaineers do not climb because they must; they climb because they love the mountains. Climb leaders help others enjoy the sport, and that can be deeply satisfying.

Some climbers may never want to take on the role of leader, but they will find that possessing a certain degree of leadership is almost inevitable as they gain experience. A party naturally tends to look to its more seasoned members for guidance, especially in a crisis. Therefore, all climbers should give some forethought to what they would do if they were suddenly called upon to take charge.

Climbers who do aspire to leadership should make it their business to climb with people they regard as capable leaders. Study them; observe how they organize the trip, make decisions, and work with people. Offer to help in order to participate in some of these activities. Veteran leaders report that they think ahead, anticipating problems that might arise and concocting possible solutions. This type of mental rehearsal is excellent training for future leaders. Climbers should develop the habit of thinking about the entire climb and the whole party, not just their part of it.

Studying respected leaders is always worthwhile, but it may be a mistake to copy anyone too closely. A group must believe that its leader is genuine, and therefore all leaders must develop their own style. Exercising leadership is not always easy, but it should be done in a way that is natural for each person. For example, a reserved person should not strain to act outgoing. Anyone who has technical skill, confidence, and a sincere interest in the party's welfare can succeed as a leader.

On your first time out as a leader, choose a climb comfortably within your abilities. Perhaps invite a proficient friend, someone to rely on. Spend some extra time organizing, and seek input from the more experienced members of the party. Be sure to delegate in order to take advantage of their skills. Do not make an issue of the fact that this is your debut as a leader; that will only undermine the group's confidence.

The Climbing Code in Chapter 1, First Steps, is a sound set of guidelines for making leadership decisions. It is deliberately conservative. Following the code may cost you some summits, but it is unlikely to cost a life. Seasoned leaders may draw on experience to safely modify some of the rules, but they are not likely to depart from it radically because the code embodies a commonsense approach to safe mountaineering.

EVERYONE A LEADER

Everyone on a climb needs to be a full partner in the twin tasks of moving the group safely toward its goal and of building group cohesion. In other words, each individual must share leadership responsibility. Individual leadership means, for example, being aware of the group and its progress: Is someone lagging behind? Ask whether there is a problem, offer encouragement, and look for ways to help. A group of climbers is weakened whenever the climbers become separated from each other. Work at being aware of where climbing companions are at all times, and help to keep the party together. When you are out front and moving fast, remember to look behind you from time to time. When you are too far ahead, stop and let the group catch up—then let them have a breather before you start off again.

Take part in routefinding. Study guidebooks and maps to become familiar with the approach and the climbing route. The climbing party is much less likely to get lost if everyone is actively involved in navigation. Use the map, compass, and route description frequently so you are always oriented and know where the party is.

Everyone should participate in the group decision making. Each person's experience is a resource for the party, but that resource goes untapped if that person fails to speak up.

Establishing a supportive atmosphere is one very important role of leadership. People need to know that their companions care about them and will help them. Be part of this effort: Help set up a tent, fetch water, carry the rope, share a cookie. Morale is intangible, but it makes a party stronger. Morale is often the deciding factor in party success, and it is always the deciding factor in making the climb enjoyable. Morale is everybody's job.

Assume responsibility also for your own knowledge, skill, and preparedness. Research the climb before committing yourself to it; make sure it is within your abilities. Be properly supplied and equipped. If you have questions about whether the climb is appropriate for you, or about what gear to take, ask your companions in advance. If you ever think that you are getting in over your head, speak up. Better to get some help over a rough spot or even quit the climb than to create an emergency. Thinking about the party, its welfare, and how you can contribute is in itself preparation—perhaps the very best preparation—for leadership.

INCREASE SAFETY BY ASSESSING HAZARDS • UNDERSTAND YOUR SPHERE OF ACCEPTABLE RISK • MAKE A PLAN • BE ALERT TO CHANGES THAT AFFECT RISK • MAKE GOOD DECISIONS • STAY ALIVE AND RETURN HOME SAFELY

Chapter 22
SAFETY: HOW TO STAY ALIVE

A good strategy for a safe climb has the number-one objective of returning home safely. Climbers make a plan that considers objectives, hazards, and the acceptable level of risk; they carry out their plan, remaining adaptable to changes in what was anticipated; and by being alert to changes and warnings, they make good decisions that get them home safely.

For most climbers, a bit of risk is a welcome challenge. But a trip ceases to be fun when it exceeds a person's acceptable level of risk. No mountaineer begins a climb intending to get hurt, yet every year, climbing accidents affect the lives of novice and experienced climbers alike. Safety must be a state of mind—this is far more important than consideration of mountain hazards (sometimes called objective hazards). Bad things happen to good people when warnings are missed or disregarded by poor decisions. It is critical to understand the importance of good decision making as conditions change during a climb.

As an alpinist who carries a long list of dead friends and partners, I approach the mountains differently than most. I go to them intending to survive, which I define as a success. A new route or the summit is a bonus.

—*Mark Twight,* Extreme Alpinism

INCREASE SAFETY BY ASSESSING HAZARDS

A common misunderstanding is that climbing is unsafe because of mountain hazards. Use of the word "accident" implies that the victim had no control over the mishap (see the "Terminology in Safety and Rescue" sidebar). Cavalier comments such as "Stuff happens" enhance that false view. In reality, a climber's worst enemy is not the mountain environment but his own poor decision making. In accident after accident, injuries and deaths have been primarily due to poor decision making by the climbers themselves. The key is to make good decisions to prevent injury so that you can return home safely.

"Safety" and "hazards" are relative terms. No climb is as safe as staying home, yet even a bathtub can be hazardous if someone slips and falls in it. The first thing to consider when assessing risk is the level of risk you are willing to tolerate. Then during the climb, make good decisions to keep the level of risk under control. Making good decisions requires that climbers maintain perspective in the heat of the moment, which is not easy. You might have one last day of vacation to achieve a long-desired summit, but it has been snowing all night—do you try for the summit anyway, even though you know this would be foolish?

TERMINOLOGY IN SAFETY AND RESCUE

- **Incident**—National parks, rescue organizations, and safety professionals generally use "incident" to describe any unplanned event. If hazards were present, a "near-miss incident" or "injury incident" (accident) could result. Normally, "accident" is not used because it suggests that an incident was unavoidable, which is almost never the case.
- **Exposure time**—The amount of time spent in hazardous conditions, called exposure time, is often a critical factor in incidents. An hour of roped climbing is far riskier than a few seconds spent on an occasional technical move, assuming both are of the same difficulty.
- **Margin of safety**—The term "margin of safety" describes how far from injury a person is operating. For example, just a few degrees difference in temperature could cause a snow slope to avalanche, or a slightly thinner snow bridge might fail under a person's weight.
- **Prevention and mitigation**—Anything that is done to prevent or minimize injury in an incident involves forethought. Ropes, helmets, and belays mitigate climbing injuries, for example.

Figure 22-1 shows the elements of a safe climb in three phases: inputs to the plan, the plan itself, and the climb. A critical element is the number-one objective of every climb: to return home safely. The inputs to the plan are the party's objectives (for example, returning home safely and staying within acceptable risk), plus assessment of possible mountain and human hazards. The plan itself consists of actions the party will take to achieve its objectives despite the hazards it will face; the plan must include adaptability to change once the true hazards are observed. During the climb, the party must be alert and observe deviation from what was expected. These observations should trigger warnings, which in turn should get your attention and, with good decision making, will force changes to the plan so the party will be able to return home safely.

LEARN FROM EXPERIENCE

Learning from your mistakes in the mountains can help you develop better decision-making skills, but the mountains are often unforgiving of even small mistakes. It is far less painful to learn from the mistakes and mishaps of others. For the novice mountaineer, this means seeking qualified instruction and skilled climbing partners before heading out with other novices. For mountaineers at all levels, this means studying reports of climbing accidents to learn what can go wrong and to apply the lessons others have learned.

As exposure to hazards increases, the probability of an incident (any unplanned event) increases, as does the probability of an injury. Incidents of all types, even those that do not result in an injury, are warnings. It behooves the safety-minded climber to recognize these warnings, adjust preemptively, and seek to avoid *all* incidents.

CAUSES OF MOUNTAINEERING ACCIDENTS

One of the best sources of mountaineering accident information is *Accidents in North American Mountaineering (ANAM)*, published annually by the American Alpine Club and the Alpine Club of Canada (see Resources).

Studying the *ANAM* reports can help climbers learn from the misfortunes of others and continue their personal education in the proper use of equipment, technique, and decision making. These reports influence climbers' attitudes toward safety, because they vividly

ANAM STATISTICS FOR UNITED STATES AND CANADA 1999–2008

- 100–200 major accidents occurred each year.
- 30–40 fatalities occurred each year.
- All ages and experience levels were involved.

demonstrate how injuries result from poor decision making in the mountains (see the "*ANAM* Statistics for United States and Canada 1999–2008" sidebar).

Table 22-1 shows the most common causes of mountaineering accidents and their relative frequency. Though this data is from more than 50 years of accident reporting, it is typical of recent history. An immediate cause is one that directly precipitates the incident, such as a fall. A contributing cause is one that sets up the incident and/or increases its harm. According to *ANAM* 2009, falls and slips dominated immediate causes, while many contributing causes were roughly equally likely.

A typical incident results from one immediate cause and multiple contributing causes. In one specific example, a novice was on steep snow when she slipped, lost her ice ax, was unable to self-arrest, and broke her leg after sliding 150 feet (45 meters). The slip was the immediate cause; contributing causes were climbing unroped, not having an ice-ax leash, and exceeding one's abilities. An immediate cause is generally a surprise, but contributing causes often precede an incident, and often the climbing party has missed or dismissed them. An alert climber sees potential contributing causes as warnings, which helps the climber in making good decisions in order to prevent an incident.

Though poor decisions themselves are not included

TABLE 22-1. REPORTED CAUSES OF MOUNTAINEERING ACCIDENTS

Most Frequent *Immediate* Causes	
Fall or slip on rock	3,879
Slip on snow or ice	1,230
Falling rock, ice, or object	763
Exceeding abilities	582
Most Frequent *Contributing* Causes	
Climbing unroped	1,178
Exceeding abilities	1,117
Placing no or inadequate protection	858
Inadequate equipment or clothing	760
Weather	546
Climbing alone	473
No helmet (hard hat)	419

Source: ANAM *2009*

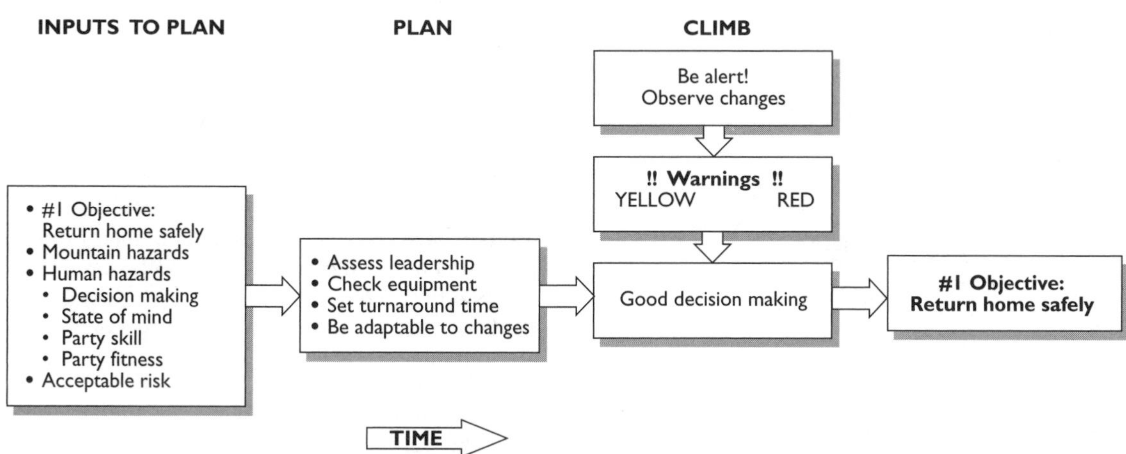

Fig. 22-1. A safe climb has three parts: Critical inputs must be known; the plan must address the hazards; the party must stay alert for changes during the climb so good decisions bring them home safely.

22

in *ANAM*'s list of accident causes, the *ANAM* reports do discuss poor decision making—it is the overwhelming reason for injuries, much more so than mountain hazards, just as in the workplace. The lesson is that climbing is not intrinsically dangerous—rather, the decisions climbers make are what bring them home safely.

MOUNTAINEERING INCIDENT PYRAMID

An incident (or accident) pyramid shows the number of injuries (major and minor), near misses, and unsafe acts relative to one fatality for an activity, such as mountaineering. The mountaineering incident pyramid in Figure 22-2 shows that for every 200,000 unsafe acts in mountaineering, approximately 1 fatality, 20 major injuries, 200 minor injuries, and 2,000 near misses can be expected. An example of an unsafe act is taking a step while using a poor self-belay that would not stop a fall. An example of a near miss is when a self-belay catches a slip.

Determining these numbers involves reviewing statistics from *ANAM* and from organizations such as The Mountaineers, then estimating and extrapolating. Using Figure 22-2, if your decision-making skills are similar to the climbers for whom the statistics were collected, your risk while mountaineering is one fatality for every 200,000 unsafe acts. But if you make much better (or worse) decisions, then the inevitable unsafe acts would cause injuries and fatalities far less (or more) often.

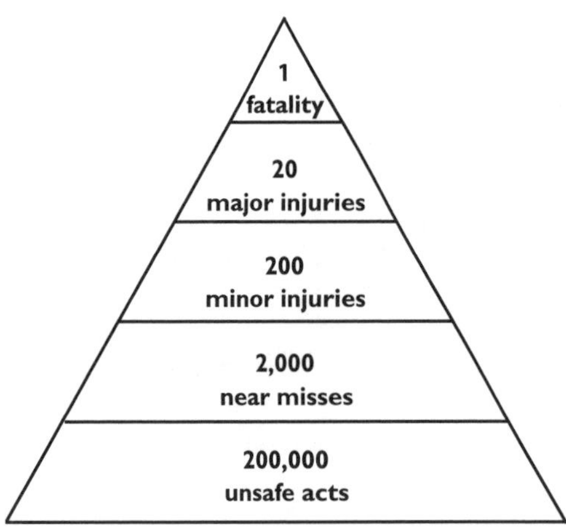

Fig. 22-2. Mountaineering incident pyramid: 200,000 unsafe acts result in near misses, injuries, and fatality.

H. W. Heinrich, a pioneer in industrial accident prevention, first proposed the incident pyramid for industry, arguing that if hazards were reduced (for example, by adding guards on machinery), then unsafe acts and all injuries would also be reduced. Industries have employed this reasoning for many years. However, one problem with this approach is that it is fatalistic and does not account for human behavior (for example, people remove guards).

Similarly, mountaineering safety originally focused on avoiding mountain hazards; prevailing wisdom said that accidents were random events that could not be avoided. But over the years, studies of both industrial and mountaineering safety have determined that human behavior (state of mind and decision making, for instance) is much more important to safety than the existence of hazards. Every climbing party commits many minor unsafe acts—none of us is perfect. To be safe, climbers must be alert, heed warnings, and make good decisions so that unsafe acts do not cause injuries. Safety is a choice that is each climber's to make.

HAZARDS

Hazards encountered while climbing are generally considered to be one of two kinds: objective (or mountain) hazards and subjective (or human) hazards.

Mountain hazards. Hazardous mountain conditions include the following:

- Crevasses, icefalls, moats, cornices, unstable snow
- Loose rock (permits natural or climber-induced rockfall)
- Exposure (affects distance climbers could fall)
- Weather
- High altitude (affects climbers' health)

Human hazards. The hazards that climbers bring to the mountain include, in order of importance:

- Poor decision making
- Poor state of mind (fosters poor decision making) due to:
  - Ignorance
  - Casualness
  - Distraction
- Inadequate skill
- Inadequate fitness

As discussed in "Causes of Mountaineering

Accidents," above, climbing injuries are predominantly due to human hazards, especially poor decision making. Some mountain hazards are visible, such as loose rock in a gully or obvious crevasses in a glacier. Other mountain hazards may be invisible, such as glacier crevasses hidden by fresh snow. Decisions regarding how, when, and where to cross such a mountain hazard—or whether to cross it at all—determine the amount of risk a party takes. This is especially true for difficult climbs at high altitude, where the margin of safety is slim and the seductive summit often affects the party's decision making.

Some high-altitude climbers strongly embrace the objective of returning home safely. Ed Viesturs, the first American to climb the world's 14 highest peaks—whose summits are all above 8,000 meters (26,000 feet)—without supplemental oxygen, has spoken extensively about turning back on many climbs because he insisted on safe conditions.

> *Reaching the summit is optional. Getting down is mandatory.*
>
> —*Ed Viesturs,* No Shortcuts to the Top: Climbing the World's 14 Highest Peaks

At all levels of climbing, if a climber's common practice is to do unsafe things, that climber will eventually lose because the odds will catch up with him. This applies as much at the local crag as on some faraway mountain.

UNDERSTAND YOUR SPHERE OF ACCEPTABLE RISK

Acceptable risk is difficult to assess. Climbing involves risk, and the level of risk an individual climber is willing to accept is a personal decision. Some climbers are happy to limit their mountaineering adventures to an occasional snowfield traverse or rock scramble. Others seek out the most challenging peaks that require serious commitment, the best gear, advanced technique, and top physical conditioning.

A useful model for visualizing risk is a sphere or bubble, with the climber at the center (fig. 22-3). Anything within the sphere is what that person considers an acceptable risk. Outside the sphere are risks the climber chooses not to accept. Keep in mind that climbers often think they know what risks are acceptable to them, but their perceptions of risk may be very optimistic. Year after year, climbers are injured or killed because they were ignorant of the hazards they faced.

Once a climber rationally understand risks—knowing what could go wrong on a climb, knowing how to prevent things from going wrong or dealing with them if they do, knowing the proper function of equipment and that good decision making is the key to staying safe—the diameter of the climber's sphere of acceptable risk depends on skill level, individual goals, and, most importantly, personal comfort level with the hazards encountered while climbing. With experience, each climber's sphere grows as he or she becomes more confident (as for the aspiring summiter in Figure 22-3). Most climbers will reach a point when they are satisfied with the level of risk they are taking and wish to take no more. The spheres of some climbers may also get smaller if they scale back their climbing goals because of, for instance, family responsibilities or an accident involving themselves or friends—or because they are finally beginning to understand that risks and probabilities apply to *everyone*, not just to "the other guy."

MAKE A PLAN

Choose routes that are within the climbing party's sphere of acceptable risk. This can be done at home by consulting guidebooks and people who have tried the route of interest. Figure 22-1 lists the things to be considered when planning a trip (see the "Inputs to Plan" and "Plan" boxes). Good questions to ask are these:

- What are the hazards?
- How can they be avoided?
- Does everyone in the party have the skills needed to safely deal with the hazards?
- How can climbers protect themselves from the hazards?
- How can exposure time to them be minimized?
- How can an incident be mitigated so it does not become an accident?
- How should the party adjust its plans to respond to new hazards?

If not everyone in the party possesses the necessary skill level, plan a different route. On some trips, it may be appropriate to pick an alternate route or retreat if the original route proves to be outside the party's sphere of acceptable risk.

A risk-savvy climber doing good research while planning can predict (and plan ahead for) the likely events to occur during a climb; other climbers will see them only as "surprises" when they occur.

Once the party is on the route, continue to ask these questions and make decisions accordingly. Consider how the climbing party is performing—both mentally and physically—and how changes in the weather and party strength may affect the risks posed by the hazards. Be ready to adjust plans if necessary.

BE ALERT TO CHANGES THAT AFFECT RISK

During a climb, the climbing party starts with its plan and then carefully observes changes in conditions. These

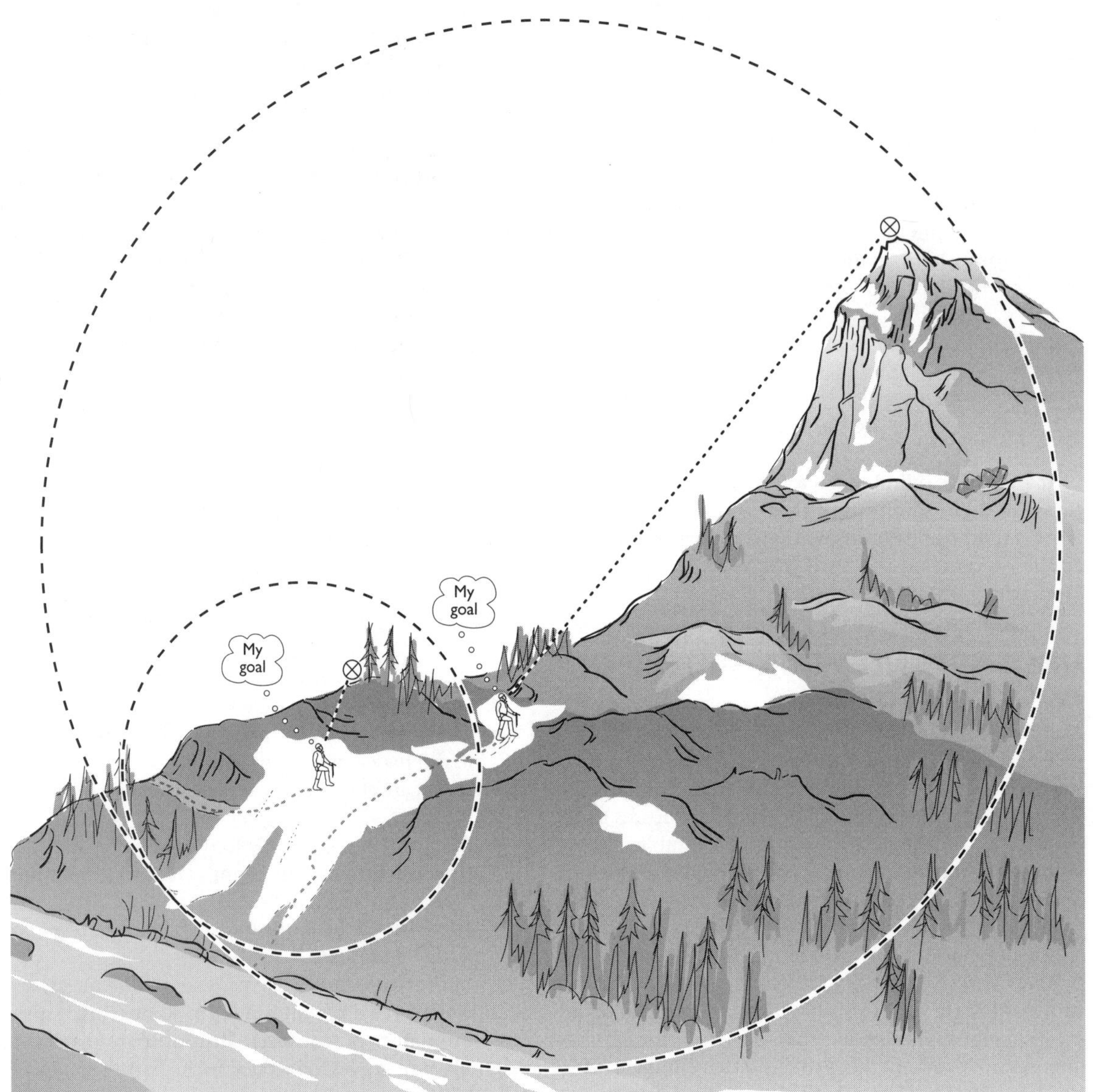

Fig. 22-3. Climbers have different spheres of acceptable risk; they must understand how this relates to the objective.

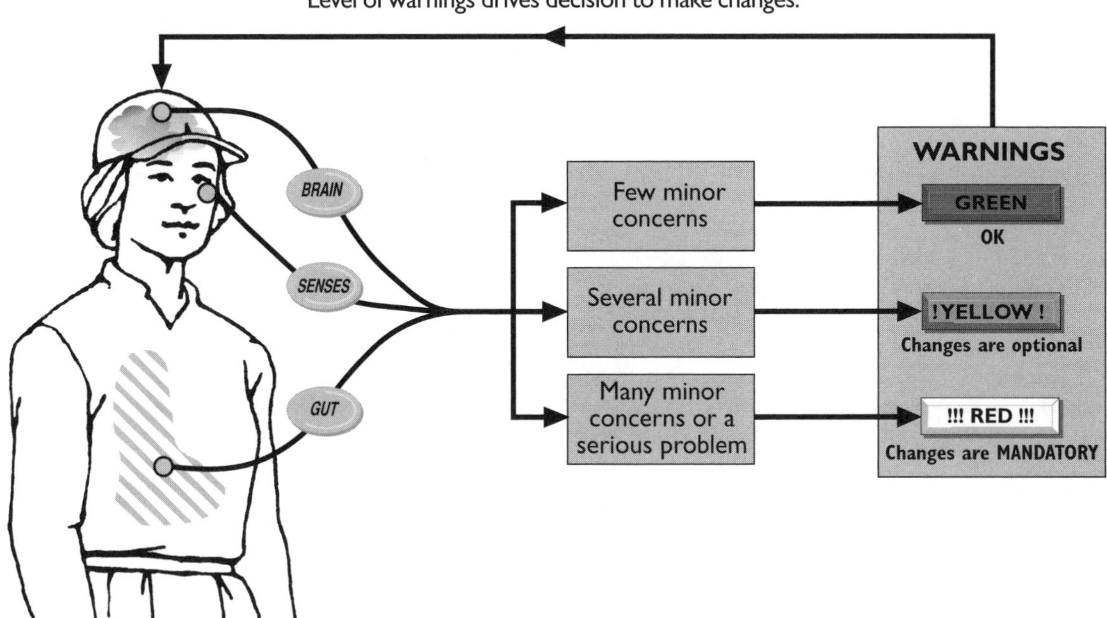

Fig. 22-4. Climbers must keep their senses alert for warnings and then make changes to stay safe.

changes can involve everything from blisters and light rain to loss of equipment, getting off route, bad weather, darkness, an exhausted or injured party member, and shortage of food or water—anything that increases risk to the party.

All observed changes must be evaluated for increased risk. Figure 22-4 illustrates that concerns about changing conditions can come from a climber's brain—that is, deductive reasoning (for example, determining that the party is off route by comparing the landscape to the map), senses (primarily sight—bad weather looming—and hearing, but perhaps touch as well—a blister forming—or smell and taste, too), or a bad feeling—that is, a premonition that disaster is about to strike (for instance, an intuition that you are about to slip).

Pay attention to all the messages you are getting, from every source. Many of these concerns become apparent if the party is moving more slowly than planned—for example, reaching an initial objective such as base camp later than anticipated. The problem could be due to weather or terrain, which affects everyone; or the problem could be due to the fitness, skill, or equipment of only one party member. Both situations usually require changes in the group's plan, for safety.

If there are a few minor concerns, the party can usually adapt; this is a **green** (OK) light. If there are several minor concerns, and making changes to the climbing party's plan is optional, this is a **yellow** (caution) light. When there are many minor concerns or when a serious concern arises, changes to the climbing plan are *mandatory*; this is a **red** light (danger). A traffic signal is a good mental image to have, especially its yellow and red blinking lights. When a climber perceives a yellow or red warning, this should feed into decision making and force changes in the plan (as shown in Figure 22-1)—good decisions will reduce risk and get the party home safely. For example, at a yellow or red signal, the party might decide to turn around, to set up a belay, or to bivouac.

Advance thinking is key. At any point during your most recent climb, did **yellow** or **red** lights flash? Were you moving outside your sphere of acceptable risk? Did you heed the warnings? Climbers often read accident accounts and think, "I would have had bells and flashing lights all over the place—that would never happen to me." The essence of making good decisions is to have this perspective during the climb *before* an accident occurs.

MAKE GOOD DECISIONS

Climbers rarely have all the information they want; this means they are often unable to grasp the entire complexity of a given problem, and their assumptions are often incorrect. Climbers must make decisions with incomplete information, sometimes when saddled with fatigue, hunger, dehydration, discomfort, or injury. With hindsight, it is usually easy to see what went wrong on a climb. But in the middle of the climb, making good decisions is rarely easy. Desire to reach the summit is the most common factor causing poor decisions on climbs (as the Climbing Code in Chapter 1, First Steps, says, "Never let judgment be overruled by desire when choosing the route or deciding whether to turn back."). This is especially true for expeditions and climbing vacations, in which considerable time and effort have been invested toward that goal.

Many things contribute to a successful climb: research, careful planning, party selection, good routefinding, technical skills, favorable weather, stamina, efficient use of time. Problems with any one of these can put party members at risk. When problems arise, party members need to evaluate the difficulties they encounter, discuss alternatives for overcoming them, and assess how these possible solutions fit within their collective sphere of acceptable risk. Often a climbing party finds a solution that allows them to attain their climbing goal, but sometimes the only safe solution is to retreat and try again another day. Reflecting on the number-one objective—that everyone wants to return home safely—might make that decision easier for all.

National Park Service search-and-rescue ranger John Dill gives a sobering overview of Yosemite climbing accidents in an article titled "Climb Safely: Staying Alive" that is particularly insightful about climbers' states of mind: "It's impossible to know how many climbers were killed by haste or overconfidence, but many survivors will tell you that they somehow lost their good judgment long enough to get hurt. It's a complex subject and sometimes a touchy one. Nevertheless, at least three states of mind frequently contribute to accidents: ignorance, casualness, and distraction."

DON'T BE IGNORANT

Lack of experience, training, or information about potential mountain hazards influences decision making, especially for newer climbers. For example, a climbing party may not realize the seriousness of a route's mountain hazards—this constitutes poor planning. Over time, even experienced climbers may forget some of the things they learned as novice climbers and develop complacency or dangerous habits. Even if rain may not be a common weather pattern in the region of your climb, do not fail to be prepared for inclement weather.

While learning to climb, develop safe procedures and habits by noting how experienced climbers evaluate hazards and make decisions. Follow the Climbing Code (see Chapter 1, First Steps). Be selective—evaluate what you hear from other climbers and be alert for advice that may not provide the level of safety you desire; it may be offered by climbers who lack sufficient experience. Keep in mind that guidebooks cannot mention every potential hazard on a route. Be alert—the route may need to be altered if what you find is not what was expected.

DON'T BE CASUAL

Casualness, complacency, and overconfidence are other human hazards to consider. Table 22-1 lists climbing beyond ("exceeding") one's abilities as the second most-frequent contributing cause of mountaineering accidents.

Until climbers have some experience, they will not know their limits. They also will not yet know all the ways that things can go wrong. It takes years to develop the knowledge and decision-making skills needed for safe climbing, but many new climbers have difficulty containing their enthusiasm for the sport. As a result, they may get into situations that are beyond their capabilities and be hurt in the process. Images of experts leading or soloing sheer rock and ice couloirs are inspiring, but beginning climbers may not appreciate the years of training and experience that prepared those climbers for those routes. Nor do pictures reveal the detailed process of risk evaluation that the climbers undoubtedly undertook. The technical portion of a route is only one of many hazardous parts of the climb. Choose climbs that are less difficult than your skill level.

If a climber is "lucky" and survives a poor decision, casualness in interpreting what actually happened can lead to accidents in the future:

- **The real risk may remain hidden.** A dangerous practice then becomes habit. For example, you may cross a loaded avalanche slope without releasing the snowpack, or your method of rigging a belay anchor may be weak but has never been tested by a fall. The difference between safe travel and an accident may be just a few degrees in temperature or one leader fall. Be sure your technique and decision-making habits are not setting you up for an accident. Do not rely on luck, because when it runs out, the consequences may be serious.

- **You realize you have survived a near miss, but you pass it off as "luck."** You will be jubilant in the moment, but the close call's lesson must be heeded, especially because you may have been operating with no margin of safety. You won the roll of the dice *this* time. What about next time? Will you act differently, or will one condition change slightly and lead to a devastating conclusion?

DON'T BE DISTRACTED

Yosemite Ranger John Dill says that "distraction is caused by whatever takes your mind off your work—anxiety, sore feet, skinny-dippers below—the list is endless. Being in a hurry is one of the most common causes." Many experienced climbers, he says, are hurt on easy pitches because they were thinking of a cold beer or a good bivy and made "beginner's errors" by taking shortcuts to get to these goals. One particular climber Dill writes about was distracted by darkness, which led the climber to hurry—he died after rappeling off the end of his rope.

BREAK THE CHAIN OF POOR DECISIONS

Climbing accidents usually result from a series of problems or errors, mostly visible, which combine to put the party in peril. One more poor decision or a mild problem such as a simple slip then precipitates disaster. The following example describes an accident in the United States in which three experienced climbers died:

It began with a routefinding error when the party ascended the wrong gully. They continued on, trying to make sense out of the route description. They realized their error and attempted to traverse to the correct route. Rockfall injured the party leader and so key leadership was lost; then the weather deteriorated.

The party decided to descend to the glacier. The climbers chose a huge boulder for a rappel anchor, not noticing it was resting on a downsloping slab with soil and loose rocks. Two of the climbers successfully completed single-person rappels, but when two other climbers assisted the injured leader in a three-person rappel, their combined weight pulled the boulder off the downsloping slab. They all fell, as did a fourth climber who was tied to the anchor, resulting in three deaths plus a severe head injury.

The immediate cause of the incident was failure of a rappel anchor. The terrain was not conducive to redundancy in the rescue anchor, but there were options that were not utilized. For instance, instead of self-rescue, another option would have been to send two of the climbers to get help, with the rest of the party securing and caring for the injured leader until help arrived. The party may have chosen to rappel because of perceived urgency, an established habit of using huge boulders that had made good rappel anchors in the past, and not noticing the downslope. Each individual contributing cause (poor routefinding, rockfall injury, leadership loss, nonredundant anchor, limited redundancy options, deteriorating weather) was probably manageable by itself, but together they overwhelmed the party's ability to function safely, despite the presence of four experienced climbers.

Most climbing incidents have a similar string of warnings (the contributing causes) that should flash bright warning lights in every climber's brain. Sometimes these warnings are ignored and injuries happen. Sometimes people shrug and say, "Stuff happens"—but often this phrase is an excuse for poor decisions.

All injury incidents have their "reversible moments," when a better decision would have prevented the injury. Climbing parties should constantly evaluate their situation, especially after any event, to assure their safety. Sadly, as people become increasingly stressed, they tend to hurry and make decisions that in retrospect can be seen to be poor. The people on the climb described above did not deliberately choose to roll the safety dice. They planned to return home safely. Would you have acted differently on that trip? How?

A chain of poor decisions tends to happen without being noticed: One poor decision increases the chance of another. For example, climbing beyond a party's turnaround time increases the chance that they will rush their climbing, just when they are most tired. Each error can provide false information that can lead to more errors. For example, when off route, if climbers erroneously match a feature to the route description, they may continue the wrong way. As the chain of poor decisions grows, the alternatives that may lead to a safe outcome decrease. Climbers may find themselves in a desperate situation.

Heed Kurt Diemberger's message in *The Endless Knot*:

> *It was diabolic machinery, into the cogwheels of which all of us were imperceptibly but irretrievably being sucked—the mechanism being so complicated that it was not recognizable to the individual: every way that might have led us out eventually became blocked by the taking of single decisions, which by themselves would never have been so critical, but in their conjunction opened the death trap for seven people up at 8,000 meters.*

Learn to recognize the poor-decision chain. Watch for these signs that the party may not be fully aware of its situation:

- **Failure to meet planned schedule.** Why? Is this due to poor party strength or routefinding problems?
- **Preoccupation with a hard section of the climb.** Is the party losing track of other factors, such as changing weather or impending darkness?
- **Violating the sphere of acceptable risk.** Are conditions or the route now beyond the party's capabilities?
- **Unresolved discrepancies.** Are the features encountered on the route consistent with the route description?
- **Gut feeling that something is wrong.** Could your body be conveying something that your mind has not yet processed?

The following steps can help break the poor-decision chain:

1. **Be willing to recognize your own poor decisions.** A way to gut-check your decisions is the so-called headline test—"If I had an accident now, how would it look in the next *ANAM*?" Ask your climbing partners for their honest opinions.
2. **Avoid very low or high levels of stress or focus.** Complacency results from the former, panic from the latter. Instead, respect your vulnerability and use this to sharpen your ability to make good decisions.

A little fear is healthy while climbing.
—Stu, longtime climber

3. **Be alert for a chain of poor decisions.** If you recognize one poor decision, its underpinnings are likely to cause others—and may already have.
4. **Review what happened as soon as you have recognized and broken the poor-decision chain.** This analysis can help you avoid beginning a poor-decision chain in the future.

STAY ALIVE AND RETURN HOME SAFELY

Knowledge of mountain hazards, human hazards, and your sphere of acceptable risk, plus a good state of mind, all assist you in making good decisions. And all decisions should be reexamined throughout the climb. A good climb is a climb you return from—a safe climb makes this happen.

- Know the **hazards** (mountain and human).
- Know your **acceptable risk.**
- Have a good **state of mind.**
  - Be **prepared** for surprises.
  - Be alert to **changes** in conditions.
- Use **good decision making** to manage risk.
  - Heed **warnings.**
  - **Reexamine** your decisions as you go.
- Return home safely.

PLANNING AND PREPARATION • THE SEVEN STEPS IN ACCIDENT RESPONSE • MOUNTAIN MALADIES • INJURIES • FIRST-AID KIT

Chapter 23 FIRST AID

Accidents and illness can strike mountaineers, just as they can hit anyone at home. However, mountaineers are far away from expert help and must be able to manage the situation, providing first aid when needed. The mountain environment and the physical demands of wilderness travel not only can encompass everyday injuries and ailments, but also may introduce new hazards to a climber's well-being.

The most artful mountaineers grow adept at minimizing the hazards of travel in the mountains, preventing exposure to risk whenever possible. It is vastly preferable for the members of a mountaineering party to prevent injuries to themselves rather than to be experts at treating injuries after they occur.

Even if you are aware of accident prevention, however, you could become the individual who requires first-aid help: The first-aid expert of the group could become the victim. Therefore, all members of the party should be trained in first aid through a mountaineering-oriented first-aid course or other wilderness medical educational programs offered by many respected organizations.

The fun part of learning to climb certainly is not the first-aid training. It is tempting to assume that reading first-aid texts carefully is sufficient training. Unfortunately, first aid is very much like any other skill: You can read, even memorize, all of the greatest texts on skiing, and yet if you do not practice, you simply will not be a good skier. The same is true with first aid; to be truly competent in first aid, you must practice and refresh your skills periodically. This is because of two elements of serious first-aid situations: uncertainty and alarm.

In most serious first-aid situations, there is a large element of uncertainty: uncertainty about what happened; uncertainty about the nature, extent, or seriousness of injuries; uncertainty about what should be done; uncertainty about what the outcome will be. An injured person does not wear a big sign that says precisely what is injured and how to care for it. Sometimes it is obvious, but more often it is not.

A second fundamental element of first-aid situations is that people react to them with alarm. Serious accidents are frightening and tend to flood people's minds with a spectrum of emotions, which can interfere with a calm, thoughtful, rational response. Although alarm is perhaps the most difficult challenge to overcome, practicing first-aid scenarios such as those included in many outdoor first-aid classes can help a person respond well even when the situation is overwhelmingly stressful.

There are essentially two categories of first-aid skills: the framework for responding to an accident and the techniques for treating specific conditions. This chapter first presents the framework, in the form of seven simple steps that are appropriate responses to most backcountry accidents. Following that is a brief discussion of medical conditions that are more frequently encountered in the backcountry. However, many of the essential first-aid skills, such as cardiopulmonary resuscitation (CPR), splinting, and wound care are omitted or limited in scope, because this book is not intended to be a comprehensive first-aid text. As noted above, these skills are best learned if practiced through outdoor first-aid classes.

PLANNING AND PREPARATION

Before leaving the trailhead, a mountaineering party should have a designated first-aid leader, as well as a clearly identified climb leader. The climb leader is responsible for the welfare of the entire party; the first-aid leader assumes leadership of any first-aid incident in the field. If evacuation of a patient becomes necessary, the climb leader—not the first-aid leader—orchestrates the evacuation.

The climb leader and first-aid leader should check with party members to learn of any relevant medical conditions (such as an allergy to bee stings) or use of medications (such as insulin for diabetes). Opinions differ on the best format for gathering this information. Some climb leaders like to ask for medical information individually from each party member in advance of the trip. The information is then shared with any assistant leader and with the first-aid leader. This approach protects individual privacy, but it has the disadvantage of not giving other party members the information they might need to be most helpful to a stricken person. Thus another approach is to ask for this information from the group as a whole, at the trailhead.

Before departing, the leaders should confirm that the party has sufficient first-aid supplies. See "First-Aid Kit" at the end of this chapter.

THE SEVEN STEPS IN ACCIDENT RESPONSE

An orderly reaction to an emergency can make all the difference in how party members translate their first-aid knowledge into effective action. The effective response to an accident in the mountains can be simplified into seven steps, as shown in Table 23-1. The rest of this section covers these seven steps in detail.

STEP 1: TAKE CHARGE OF THE SITUATION

Establish the leadership roles that were planned at the trailhead. The climb leader is responsible for decisions that involve the welfare of the entire party, such as surveying the accident scene to determine objective hazards, and the first-aid leader directs all first-aid-related actions.

Survey the accident scene, noting all victims, current objective hazards, and the likely cause of the accident. See whether anyone can provide an account of what happened and when.

If there are several patients, triage decisions are needed to direct the party's limited resources toward actions likely to have the most benefit and away from actions that are either trivial or hopeless. Triage decisions are modified as each patient's condition and triage status change. In a serious accident with numerous patients, triage consists of sorting patients into groups, based on priority in receiving assistance.

First priority goes to seriously injured people who have a good chance of survival if they are given immediate help; second priority is seriously injured people whose conditions are stable and who can wait perhaps an hour or two for first aid; third priority is people with minor injuries who can wait for simple first aid or can administer it themselves with a little help; the final group consists of critically injured people with very little chance of survival no matter what treatment is attempted.

Making decisions about who receives care first is a wrenching task, but it is essential if the party's efforts are to be used to best effect. A triage viewpoint also helps in evaluating which patients are most in need of evacuation to outside medical help.

STEP 2: APPROACH THE PATIENT SAFELY

Do not endanger uninjured party members in the effort to reach an injured person; such action might increase the severity of the disaster. If avalanche or rockfall is a danger, the climb leader can designate a lookout to keep watch while the first-aid effort proceeds, but everyone needs to be alert to physical limits and dangers, both present and potential. Discuss before acting.

Approaching the patient safely also means protecting the patient and the rescuers from blood and body fluids that might transmit communicable, infectious diseases. Protective measures create a barrier between the skin and mucous membranes and include disposable gloves

TABLE 23-1. THE SEVEN STEPS IN ACCIDENT RESPONSE

Step	Action to Take
1. Take charge of the situation.	The climb leader is in charge of the entire group's welfare and any evacuation efforts; the first-aid leader is in charge of the first-aid effort.
2. Approach the patient safely.	Protect the patient from further injury, and protect the party by choosing a safe approach to the patient.
3. Perform emergency rescue and urgent first aid.	The first-aid leader directs moving the injured person to a safer location if necessary and conducts a primary examination to identify and treat potentially fatal conditions. The first-aid leader checks ABCD—**A**irway + **B**reathing + **C**irculation + **D**eadly bleeding—and administers CPR if needed.
4. Protect the patient.	The first-aid leader is alert for the signs and symptoms of shock and provides insulation, dry clothing, pain management, and psychological support, including reassurance and sensitive care.
5. Check for other injuries.	The first-aid leader conducts a thorough secondary examination and records findings on an accident report form (see Figure 23-1).
6. Make a plan.	The climb leader decides how best to evacuate the injured person.
7. Carry out the plan.	Keep the needs of the patient in mind and constantly monitor the patient's condition and the progress of the plan.

(made of latex or nitrile), protective eyewear such as sunglasses, and a facial mask such as a bandanna. In some situations with considerable bleeding or vomiting, wearing raingear will offer additional protection.

STEP 3: PERFORM EMERGENCY RESCUE AND URGENT FIRST AID

At this point, the first-aid leader should move a patient only if one of two conditions is present:

1. The rescuer is in imminent danger in the present location.
2. The patient is in danger of further harm in the present location.

Absent one of these two conditions, do not move the patient. Patients do not have to be lying on their back to be treated, and the risk of harm from prematurely moving the patient can be significant.

If the patient must be moved out of a danger zone, do so swiftly, safely, and without causing further injury. Note the patient's body position, and decide whether it is likely that a back or neck injury has occurred. If so, support and immobilize the injured area as further measures are carried out.

Conduct a primary survey to recognize and treat any potentially fatal conditions. Quickly note the victim's level of consciousness. The four levels of consciousness, in decreasing order of responsiveness, are:

1. Alert
2. Responsive to vocal stimuli
3. Responsive to painful stimuli
4. Unresponsive

Next check the patient's ABCD indicators to assess the patient's vital functions:

Airway is clear of obstruction.

Breathing is spontaneous and adequate.

Circulation of blood is adequate, indicated by a beating heart and enough blood pressure to supply a pulse.

Deadly bleeding is absent. "D" also refers to neurological disability (brain, spinal cord, or peripheral nerve function).

If any of the patient's ABCD indicators do not check out, take the following actions:

Airway. If the airway is blocked, clear it.

Breathing. If the patient is not breathing, start rescue breathing.

Circulation of blood. If circulation is absent (no pulse), start CPR (see "Wilderness CPR," below).

Deadly bleeding. Put on gloves. If there is deadly bleeding, control dangerous blood loss with direct pressure over the site of hemorrhage. Use sterile gauze or clean clothing. If the injury is to a limb, elevate the bleeding extremity. Direct pressure is almost always effective. If it is not, a second-level effort to stop serious bleeding is to compress the artery supplying blood to the injury site. If bleeding persists after 20 minutes and/or some other emergent problem needs to be addressed, a pressure dressing can be applied. Limb tourniquets should be used only after neither direct pressure nor compression of the relevant arterial pressure point have stemmed a life-threatening hemorrhage and only when the party is prepared for the likelihood that the affected limb will be lost. See the "Management of Bleeding" sidebar.

MANAGEMENT OF BLEEDING

- Recognize that risk of shock may exist.
- Take precautions (gloves, sunglasses) to protect accident responders from potential contamination from the injured person's blood and/or other body fluids.
- Apply direct pressure to control bleeding.
- Elevate a bleeding extremity.
- Use pressure dressings (add dressings on top of existing ones).
- Apply pressure at pressure points (for extremities).
- Immobilize a bleeding extremity when possible (using fixation splints, air splints).
- Apply a tourniquet 4 inches wide (an absolute last resort, when all else fails).

Wilderness CPR

Performing CPR in the wilderness is different from performing CPR minutes away from a hospital, and it requires special consideration of injuries and circumstances specific to wilderness settings.

***Do not* perform CPR if any of the following conditions exist:**

- The patient is in cardiac arrest caused by trauma.
- The patient is a drowning victim who has been immersed for more than an hour.
- The cardiac arrest was unwitnessed and the time of onset is unknown.
- The patient is hypothermic with an incompressible chest.
- The patient appears to be dead, based on rigor mortis (stiffening) or livor mortis (discoloration of the body parts next to the ground), lethal injuries, or a body core (rectal) temperature below 60 degrees Fahrenheit (16 degrees Celsius).
- Giving CPR would be hazardous to rescuers.

Discontinue CPR when any of the following occur:

- Successful resuscitation is achieved.
- Rescuers are exhausted.
- Rescuers are placed in danger.
- The patient is turned over to professional care.
- The patient does not respond to prolonged (approximately 30 minutes) resuscitative efforts.

Follow these steps to perform CPR in hypothermia patients:

- If respirations are absent or ineffective, initiate rescue breathing immediately.
- If there is evidence of organized cardiac activity by electrocardiogram (ECG), Doppler ultrasound, or physical exam, do not initiate CPR.
- If CPR is commenced, it must be continued without interruption until the patient is in a hospital emergency department.

Follow these steps to perform CPR in avalanche victims:

Triage avalanche victims without vital signs at the scene according to the criteria of the International Commission for Alpine Rescue (ICAR) Medical Commission:

1. If there is no pulse and core temperature is 90 degrees Fahrenheit (32 degrees Celsius) or above, or burial was less than 30 minutes, continue CPR for 30 minutes. If successful with CPR, transfer victim to a hospital with an intensive care unit. If unsuccessful, stop CPR.
2. If the core temperature is below 90 degrees Fahrenheit or burial was more than 30 minutes, treatment depends upon the presence of an air pocket (any space around the nose or mouth, no matter how small):
   - If an air pocket is present, continue CPR and transfer to a hospital with cardiopulmonary bypass capability.
   - If no air pocket is present, stop CPR.
   - If an air pocket is possible, but not certain, continue CPR and transfer to a hospital with cardiopulmonary bypass capability or to a closer hospital where potassium can be measured. Patients with serum potassium greater than 10 millimoles per liter have no chance of survival and are declared dead by asphyxiation.

Follow these steps to perform CPR in lightning victims:

- If there are multiple victims, institute reverse triage principles (in other words, treat seemingly dead victims first).
- Initiate CPR immediately on all pulseless, nonbreathing victims of lightning strike.
- Following a severe electrical shock, respiratory paralysis may persist long after cardiac activity returns. Rescuers must be prepared to provide prolonged rescue breathing, but no more than 30 minutes of chest compressions.

STEP 4: PROTECT THE PATIENT

The first-aid leader should protect the patient from the environment (heat, cold, rain, etc.) and make every effort to maintain the patient's body temperature. Initial protection from the elements can be done quickly and usually without moving the patient. As in step 3, the patient should not be moved unless it is absolutely necessary to prevent further injury, particularly of the head, neck, and spine.

One of the key goals of step 4—along with maintaining adequate breathing and blood circulation and controlling blood loss—is to prevent or limit shock. Shock is a medical emergency in which the organs and tissues of the body are not receiving an adequate flow of blood. Uncontrolled shock is often progressive and potentially fatal. Be aware of the symptoms and signs of shock (see the "Symptoms and Signs of Shock" sidebar).

Shock can be limited by insulating the patient—replacing wet garments with dry ones to prevent body-heat loss—and by providing pain management. Provide the patient with as much reassurance and psychological support as possible, and orient the patient to her circumstances and surroundings if the patient is confused. Provide fluids if the patient is able to swallow. Remain vigilant because shock may emerge later in the course of care; a patient who becomes more withdrawn and less responsive could well be drifting into shock.

At this stage, psychological support becomes important for the patient, anyone involved in helping the patient (accident responders), and any bystanders. Responders should keep an eye out for anyone behaving irrationally or in an agitated or dazed fashion. Often such individuals can be assigned a simple task that will refocus them on the work of the group. Members of the accident response party should learn the names of each patient, use their names when talking to them, and tell them the names of the accident response party members. Give the patients reasonable updates about how each person is doing and about the overall plan in progress. It is not reassuring to keep a patient in the dark, and empty statements such as "everything's going to be fine" tend to be alienating and unsettling. Keep in mind the vantage point of each patient: While maneuvering around the first-aid scene, avoid stepping over injured persons as if they were pieces of wood.

SYMPTOMS AND SIGNS OF SHOCK

The patient may experience these symptoms:

- Nausea
- Thirst
- Weakness
- Fear and/or restlessness
- Sweating
- Shortness of breath

Observers may note these signs:

- Pulse rapid but weak
- Breathing rapid and shallow
- Skin cool and clammy
- Lips and nail beds blue
- Restlessness
- Face pale
- Eyes dull
- Pupils dilated
- Unresponsiveness (a late sign)

STEP 5: CHECK FOR OTHER INJURIES

Once the patient has been stabilized and treated initially for life-threatening conditions, the first-aid leader checks for other injuries. Conduct a systematic head-to-toe secondary survey, so that no injury goes undiscovered. The secondary survey can bring into view less-severe injuries and problems that could turn critical if left untreated. Only one person should perform the examination, because more than one set of hands on a patient may result in misleading findings, as well as anxiety for the injured person. (When two people attempt to do an examination, it is not uncommon for a portion of the patient to be left unexamined when each examiner assumes that the other checked it. A discussion between the examiners right there,

FIRST AID/ACCIDENT REPORT FORM (begin here)

FINDINGS			ASSESMENT OF PROBLEMS
Airway, Breathing, Circulation Initial Rapid Check (Chest Wounds, Severe Bleeding)			
ASK WHAT HAPPENED: ASK WHERE IT HURTS:			
ALLERGIES	MEDICATIONS		
TAKE PULSE & RESPIRATIONS	PULSE	RESPIRATIONS	
SKIN: Color Temperature Moisture			
PUPILS: Regular in size Equally reactive			PLAN/FIRST AID GIVEN
STATE OF CONSCIOUSNESS:			
HEAD: Scalp – Wounds Ears, Nose – Fluids Jaw – Stability Mouth – Wounds			
NECK: Wounds, Deformity			
CHEST: Movement, Symmetry			
ABDOMEN: Wounds, Rigidity			
PELVIS: Stability			
EXTREMETIES: Wounds, Deformity Sensations & Movement Pulses Below Injury			
BACK: Wounds, Deformity			
PAIN (Location)			
MEDICAL PROBLEMS			
LOOK FOR MEDICAL ID TAG			
VICTIM'S NAME			AGE
COMPLETED BY			DATE TIME

DETACH HERE – SEND OUT WITH REQUEST FOR FIRST AID

TEAR HERE – KEEP THIS SECTION WITH VICTIM

RESCUE REQUEST

Fill Out One Form Per Victim

TIME OF INCIDENT AM PM	DATE

NATURE OF INCIDENT

EXCESSIVE ☐ HEAT ☐ COLD

FALL ON ☐ ROCK ☐ SNOW ☐ CREVASSE ☐ AVALANCHE

☐ FALLING ROCK ☐ ILLNESS

BRIEF DESCRIPTION OF INCIDENT

INJURIES (List Most Severe First)	FIRST AID GIVEN
SKIN TEMP/COLOR:	
STATE OF CONSCIOUSNESSS:	
PAIN (Location)	

RECORD:

Time	Initial					When leave scene
Pulse						
Respiration						

VICTIM'S NAME AGE

ADDRESS

NOTIFY (Name)

RELATIONSHIP PHONE

OTHER COMMENTS:

SIDE 2 RESCUE REPORT

EXACT LOCATION (Include Marked Map if Possible)

QUADRANGLE: SECTION:

GPS Coordinates: DATUM:

TERRAIN: ☐ GLACIER ☐ SNOW ☐ ROCK
☐ BRUSH ☐ TIMBER ☐ TRAIL
☐ FLAT ☐ MODERATE ☐ STEEP
☐ OTHER (Describe)

ON-SITE PLANS:
☐ Will Stay Put
☐ Will Evacuate To: ____________________

Can Stay Overnight Safely ☐ Yes ☐ No

ON-SITE EQUIPMENT: ☐ Tent ☐ Sleeping Bags ☐ Ground Insulation
☐ Flares ☐ Saw ☐ Hardware
☐ Ropes ☐ Stoves ☐ Fuel
☐ Other:

Cell Phone: ____________________

LOCAL WEATHER

SUGGESTED EVACUATION: ☐ Carry-Out ☐ Helicopter
☐ Lowering ☐ Raising

EQUIPMENT NEEDED: ☐ Rigid Litter ☐ Food ☐ Water
☐ Other:____________________

PARTY MEMBERS REMAINING (Indicate Numbers)

_______Scrambling Students _______Basic Students _______Basic Grads
_______Intermediate Students _______Intermediate Grads _______Others

ATTACH THE PRE-TRIP LIST OF PARTY MEMBERS, including names, addresses, and phone numbers. Update the list to accurately reflect party membership and persons to notify in case of delays.

PARTY LEADERS:

NAMES OF MESSENGERS SENT FOR HELP:

WHOM TO NOTIFY TO INITIATE THE RESCUE:
IN NATIONAL PARK: Notify the Park Ranger
OUTSIDE NATIONAL PARK: Sheriff/County Police (Call 911)
IN CANADA: RCMP

VITAL SIGNS RECORD

Record TIME	BREATHS		PULSE		PULSES BELOW INJURY	PUPILS	SKIN	STATE OF CON-SCIOUS-NESS	OTHER
	Rate	Character	Rate	Character					
		Deep Shallow, Noisy, Labored		Strong Weak Regular Irregular	Strong Weak Absent	Equal size React to light Round	Color Temp Moist-ness	Alert Confused Unre-sponsive	Pain Anxiety Thirst Etc.

Other Observations:

Fig. 23-1. Accident report form and rescue request form.

over the patient, often ensues, leaving the patient unsure if the examiners know what they are doing.) It is important to examine bare skin while making thorough observations for possible injuries. Protect the patient from exposure to the elements, and replace clothing after examining any area of the body. Specific clues of injury that may be noted during this examination include the following:

- Deformity compared with another body part (for example, one arm is different from the other)
- Discoloration or bruising
- Bleeding or loss of other fluids
- Swelling
- Pain or tenderness
- Limited range of motion
- Guarding of a particular body part
- Numbness

The person conducting the examination should use an accident report form, such as the one shown in Figure 23-1, to guide the exam. All findings must be recorded in detail on the form. The report provides essential information in the event of a change in the patient's condition or in case evacuation becomes necessary and the injured person is turned over to others for treatment. Frequent reassessments are needed to detect changes or deterioration in the patient's condition.

STEP 6: MAKE A PLAN

Essentially, three plans need to be made:

1. The first-aid leader makes a plan for further first aid for the patient.
2. The climb leader makes a plan for the evacuation of the patient.
3. The climb leader makes a plan for the rest of the party.

Up until this point, the steps primarily have included urgent first aid and thorough assessment. Additional first aid may be required, such as splinting an injured limb, treating hypothermia, or wound care. The first-aid leader makes this first part of the plan.

Next, the climb leader must make a decision about whether the patient can self-evacuate or an outside evacuation is needed. Take time and think the decision through. A patient who is not ambulatory nearly always requires an outside evacuation. Carrying a patient requires proper equipment and a large number of people to assist, which is generally beyond the capabilities of most climbing parties. Self-evacuation should not be attempted if there are any indications of serious head, neck, or back injuries (see "Injuries," later in this chapter). Factors to consider in deciding whether to attempt a self-evacuation (in addition to the patient's condition) include the terrain, the weather, the strength and skills of other party members, and the practicality of stopping en route if an outside evacuation clearly becomes the preferred option.

Finally, the climb leader makes a plan for the rest of the climbing party. If self-evacuation is the plan, party members will have to organize and plan that. On the other hand, if the climb leader decides to seek outside help, the party will need a plan for getting that done and taking care of all members remaining in the field. If the party has a cell phone, consider that it is better to call 911 and request rescue assistance early, rather than to find the party with a deteriorating climbing partner in the middle of a rainy night and unable to continue self-evacuation. Rescue agencies appreciate early notification as well. See Chapter 24, Alpine Search and Rescue, for more details.

STEP 7: CARRY OUT THE PLAN

The climb leader is in charge of carrying out the plan. Party members may need to prepare to spend time where they are: setting up a shelter, heating water, and perhaps getting ready for a night in the wilderness. In all the preparations, keep the needs of the patient in mind. When dispatching people to find help, try to send at least two of the party's stronger and more competent members, along with the completed accident report form with information on the patient's condition, the condition of the rest of the party, adequacy of survival supplies, and the party's specific location. (See Chapter 24, Alpine Search and Rescue, for details on rescue and evacuation methods.) The most essential elements of step 7 are for the first-aid leader to constantly monitor the condition of the patient and for the climb leader to monitor the progress of the plan.

MOUNTAIN MALADIES

The mountain environment presents hazards that are, for the most part, predictable. One study of the National Outdoor Leadership School courses over a five-year period showed that 80 percent of the injuries were sprains, strains, and soft-tissue injuries. Sixty percent of the illnesses were nonspecific viral illnesses or diarrhea; hygiene appeared to have a significant impact on these illnesses (see "Intestinal Disorders," later in this chapter). Table 23-2 lists some of the conditions that can arise from the stress these hazards apply to the human body.

DEHYDRATION

Maintaining good hydration reduces the risk of heat-related illness, cold-related illness (including frostbite), and altitude illness. Your overall physical performance is improved dramatically as well.

Individuals vary in the rate at which their bodies lose water. Water loss occurs through sweating, respiratory loss, urination, and diarrhea. Climbers may not be aware how much water their body is losing; for instance, in winter climbers can experience substantial "insensible" fluid loss from respiration and perspiration that they cannot feel. Conditioning can play a minor role in the body's efficient maintenance of water balance by aiding the body in maintaining water balance more effectively. Various medications can influence the body's ability to maintain water balance, by changing how much you sweat or feel thirst or by increasing or decreasing your urine output.

Always begin mountaineering outings well hydrated. Drink a cup of water or its equivalent 15 minutes before starting out. Once under way, continue drinking fluids at a rate of 1 to 1½ cups (0.2 to 0.3 liter) every 20 to 30 minutes. This rate of drinking helps maintain hydration without making your stomach distended from the volume taken in. Do not rely on your sense of thirst as a gauge of when to drink; drink before you feel thirsty. If you do not need to urinate periodically during the day, or if your urine color becomes unusually dark, you are not drinking enough fluids.

Commercial sports drinks are not usually necessary in a mountaineering setting, although they can help to make fluid replacement more palatable. Juices, if used, should be diluted by at least 50 percent in order to prevent diarrhea. Electrolytes—body salts—lost through sweating can be replaced by eating snacks that have some salt content.

HEAT-RELATED CONDITIONS

If a person builds up more heat than the body can lose, heat-related illness can result. Heat builds up by extreme exertion or by exposure to a hot environment. High humidity also impairs heat dissipation because it slows evaporation by perspiration. Humans lose heat largely through their skin. (See Appendix C, Heat Index.)

Heat Cramps

Muscle cramps can develop if a climber becomes dehydrated or electrolyte-imbalanced during sustained exertion. Rest, massage, and gentle, slow stretching of the affected muscles usually help. Replacing water and electrolytes is the most important treatment. Heat cramps are avoidable if fluids and electrolytes are replenished

TABLE 23-2. ENVIRONMENTALLY RELATED CONDITIONS AND INJURIES

Environmental Stressor	Generalized Conditions (Potentially Affecting Entire Body)	Localized Conditions (Affecting Only Portion of Body)
Heat	Heat exhaustion, heatstroke ✚	Heat cramps
Cold	Hypothermia ✚	Frostbite, immersion foot
Ultraviolet radiation		Sunburn, snow blindness
High altitude	Acute mountain sickness, high-altitude pulmonary edema ✚, high-altitude cerebral edema ✚	
Lightning	Cardiopulmonary arrest ✚, shock ✚, coma ✚	Burns, eye or ear injuries, nerve damage
Insect bites or stings	Sting-induced allergic response ✚, tick-introduced illness	Localized pain and swelling
Snake bites	Generalized envenomization reaction ✚	Localized tissue damage

✚ Indicates urgent or life-threatening condition

throughout the climb. Heat cramps are often associated with heat exhaustion.

Heat Exhaustion

Of the two major kinds of heat illness, heat exhaustion is the milder affliction compared to heatstroke (see below). In the effort to reduce body temperature, blood vessels in the skin become so dilated (and sweating-related moisture loss is so pronounced) that circulation to the brain and other vital organs is reduced to inadequate levels. The result is an effect similar to fainting. All or some of the following symptoms may be present:

- Headache
- Cool and clammy skin
- Dizziness
- Fatigue
- Nausea
- Thirst
- Rapid pulse and respiratory rate

Treatment consists of resting (feet up, head down a bit), preferably in the shade, removing excess clothing, and drinking plenty of liquids and electrolytes. Pouring water over the head, skin, and clothing can promote evaporative cooling. On average, it takes one hour to get 1 quart (1 liter) of fluid into the circulatory system.

The following people appear particularly susceptible to heat exhaustion: the elderly, individuals on medications that interfere with sweating, people inadequately acclimatized to a hot climate, and individuals who are dehydrated or salt-depleted.

Heatstroke

Heatstroke, also called sunstroke, is a life-threatening emergency. In heatstroke, the body's heat gain is so substantial that body core temperature rises to dangerous levels—105 degrees Fahrenheit (41 degrees Celsius) or more. Symptoms of heatstroke include the following:

- Altered mental state (confusion or uncooperativeness, advancing toward unconsciousness)
- Rapid pulse and respiratory rate
- Headache
- Weakness
- Flushed, hot skin (wet with sweat or sometimes dry)
- Seizures
- Loss of coordination

The most reliable symptom is altered mental state, which might manifest as irritability, combativeness, delusions, or incoherent speech.

Treatment must be immediate, despite the patient's potential inability to cooperate. Get the patient into the shade. Cool the head and body by packing them in snow or through evaporative cooling by splashing on water and vigorously fanning them. Remove clothing that retains heat. Add ice packs (snow) to the neck, groin, and armpits. Once body temperature has dropped to 102 degrees Fahrenheit (39 degrees Celsius), the cooling efforts can be stopped. However, continue to monitor the patient's temperature, mental status, and general condition, because temperature instability may continue for some time, and body temperature could climb again, necessitating recooling. If the patient's gag reflex and swallowing ability are intact, cold drinks may be provided, since rehydration is critical.

A heatstroke patient must be evaluated by competent medical personnel and should not resume activity until after such an evaluation.

COLD-INDUCED CONDITIONS

Cold-related illness can strike if a person loses more body heat than the body can restore. Body heat is lost to the environment through evaporation, radiation, convection, and conduction. (See Appendix B, Windchill Temperature Index, for the effects of wind on temperature and body-heat loss.)

A cold-related illness that affects the entire body is hypothermia. Like heatstroke, hypothermia is a life-threatening condition that must be treated immediately to prevent the patient's death. In contrast, the other cold-related illnesses—frostbite and immersion foot—are localized in their effects. In triage (deciding which condition to treat first) of a patient with hypothermia and frostbite, the potentially deadly generalized condition of hypothermia must be treated and adequately stabilized before energy is devoted to treating the localized injury of frostbite.

Hypothermia

Hypothermia results when the body's core temperature drops to 95 degrees Fahrenheit (35 degrees Celsius) or less. Hypothermia occurs as blood is diverted away from the skin surface and from extremities in an attempt to preserve the core temperature. Hypothermia is more likely to occur with dehydration, inadequate nutritional intake, and fatigue.

Wet clothing and exposure to wind greatly increase the risk of excessive heat loss. Dehydration also can be a risk factor. (In cold conditions, the body may jettison some of its fluids by sending more water out than usual through urination, resulting in dehydration.) Usually hypothermia occurs after prolonged exposure to chilly environs rather than exposure to extreme cold. A drizzly day with the temperature around 50 degrees Fahrenheit (10 degrees Celsius) and a strong breeze is a more typical setting for hypothermia than a minus-30-degree-Fahrenheit (minus-34-degree-Celsius) cold snap at the ice cliffs.

Hypothermia symptoms vary dynamically depending on the severity of the loss in body core temperature. For example, shivering appears in mild hypothermia—body temperatures of 90 to 95 degrees Fahrenheit (32 to 35 degrees Celsius)—as the body attempts to rewarm itself through the muscular work involved in shivering. In mild hypothermia, symptoms include intense shivering, fumbling hand movements, stumbling, dulling of mental functions, and uncooperative or isolative behavior. Typically, the hypothermia patient does not notice these early signs. If in doubt about the presence of mild hypothermia in someone, have the person walk an imaginary tightrope for 15 feet (5 meters), heel to toe. Loss of coordination tends to become apparent during this test.

As hypothermia progresses to a more severe level, shivering ceases. In severe hypothermia—body temperatures below 90 degrees Fahrenheit (32 degrees Celsius)—shivering stops, but muscle and nervous system functioning obviously decline. The patient may not be able to walk but may still be able to maintain posture. Muscles are stiff and movements uncoordinated. Behavior is confused or irrational; stupor or actual unconsciousness may occur. As hypothermia progresses, it may be extremely difficult to observe a pulse or respiration. The patient's pupils may dilate.

Hypothermia is an emergency condition that unless treated immediately will lead to the patient's death. Treatment of hypothermia begins with ending further heat loss by stopping the patient's exposure to the elements. Get the patient out of the wind and wet; remove wet clothing. In mild hypothermia cases, it may suffice to supply dry clothing, add insulation under and around the patient, and shelter the patient from the wind and elements. If the patient's gag reflex and swallowing ability are intact, offer liquids and, later, sugar-based foods. Contrary to mountain lore, supplying warm drinks is not as important in mild hypothermia as is simply replenishing fluids. (Consider this: Pouring a teaspoonful of warm water into a cupful of ice water would not be an effective way to warm up the cup.) Dehydration should be treated until urine output is restored.

TIPS FOR PREVENTING HYPOTHERMIA

Follow these bits of common sense:

- Avoid being wet by layering your clothing; if you do get wet, get out of the weather and into dry clothes.
- Avoid being exposed to the wind; if exposure is impossible to avoid, at least get out of the wind as soon as possible.
- Avoid dehydration; if you do become dehydrated, replenish fluids.
- Have adequate insulation.
- Stay well fed.
- Pace yourself to avoid excessive sweating and fatigue.

In some cases, these measures alone may not be enough to rewarm the patient. Direct body contact with a (warm) party member may be needed, though studies suggest this is less effective than using heat packs or hot water bottles.

In severe hypothermia, gentle rewarming is necessary. If possible, evacuate the patient promptly for rewarming at a hospital. The hypothermia patient must be handled very gently, to avoid inadvertently sending a spurt of cold blood from the surface circulation back to the heart; this could cause heart rhythm abnormalities. Rewarming shock also is a danger.

If field rewarming is necessary, hot water bottles wrapped in mittens or socks can be placed at the patient's chest, neck, armpits, and groin, where large blood vessels are located near the body surface. Laying the patient in a wrap of sleeping pads and sleeping bags, enclosed in a tarp, can protect against heat loss effectively. Do not offer oral liquids to a semiconscious patient. As in heatstroke, once the severe hypothermia patient is back to normal core temperature, the patient must still be monitored because temperature-regulating mechanisms may not be stable for a considerable period.

Because a severely hypothermic person may appear dead, it is essential not to give up on resuscitation efforts until the patient is warm, has received adequately performed CPR, and still shows no signs of life. Keep in mind the saying that "no one is dead until warm and dead." Accompany or follow careful rewarming by CPR or rescue breathing, as circumstances dictate.

The party members must know when to call off the summit quest. Shivering must never be ignored. Because hypothermia interferes with a mountaineer's judgment and perception, typically climbing partners must be annoyingly persistent to get a shivering party member to don warmer gear. Forestall exhaustion by keeping tabs on the condition of one another (see the "Tips for Preventing Hypothermia" sidebar). When a party member becomes exhausted, that person is often "too tired" to bother adding clothing, to eat, or to drink, making hypothermia more likely to occur.

Frostbite

Frostbite is the actual freezing of the blood vessels and surrounding tissues of a body part. Blood vessels can be severely and even permanently damaged. In the small vessels that nourish the skin, blood cells clump in a reversible fashion early in the freezing process, but after prolonged freezing, these clumps may become permanent plugs. Skin injury is common, with the epidermis separating from deeper dermis, causing blisters. Frostbitten tissue is cold, hard, and pale or darkly discolored. Frostbitten tissue is fragile and never should be massaged.

Treatment for frostbite starts with treatment of any hypothermia. Following that, the party must assess whether field rewarming is appropriate or desirable. Usually it is not. If there is any chance that a frostbitten body part, once thawed, might refreeze during the trip, the patient should be evacuated instead so that rewarming can be done in a medical setting. If the body part is thawed and then refreezes, the line of tissue death will probably extend to the refreeze line. More tissue damage occurs during the thawing phase.

If a person has a frostbitten foot, the foot must be kept frozen. Once the foot has thawed, it will be impossible to walk on, and the patient will have to be carried out.

In the rare instance that field rewarming is considered advisable, the frostbitten part should be rewarmed in a water bath that is 104 to 108 degrees Fahrenheit (40 to 42 degrees Celsius), never warmer. Do not use hot water; the frostbitten part is extremely susceptible to thermal injury. The frostbite patient should lie down with the injured part elevated. Skin-to-skin thawing is acceptable in the wilderness, such as placing a cold finger against a warm belly.

Blisters often emerge during rewarming. In the wilderness, leave these blisters alone in order to reduce the risk of infection. Any open wounds or blisters should be washed gently with a skin antiseptic and covered with sterile dressings. Aspirin or ibuprofen may be administered, if the patient is not allergic to these, to relieve pain. More definitive treatment of frostbite should be reserved for competent medical care.

Avoid frostbite by wearing appropriate clothing. Mittens can be warmer than gloves. Dry feet are important, and avoid constricting boots. Avoid skin contact with cold metal or stove gasoline, which can cause frostbite on contact. Stop and warm your fingers and toes while they are still causing tingling and pain, before they go numb.

Immersion Foot

Immersion foot, also called trench foot, occurs when a person's feet have been wet and cool—but not freezing cold—for long periods. Climbers on Mount McKinley (Denali) who wear vapor-barrier socks but neglect to dry and warm their feet each night are prime targets for this condition. Similarly, tundra hikers who clamber through the muskeg day after day but never dry their feet at night can be affected. The injury appears to be a kind of trauma to nerves and muscles caused by diminished oxygen distribution (hypoxia), rather than an injury to blood vessels and skin as in frostbite.

Immersion foot reveals its presence in pale, pulseless, tingling feet. Typically, the unhappy mountaineer discovers these symptoms in the tent at night. Very careful rewarming is needed—in a water bath just slightly warmer than body temperature—or gangrene can occur. During rewarming, the affected feet shift to a painful hyperemic phase (congested with blood): They become reddened and swollen, with a bounding pulse. It may be necessary to slightly cool the feet in order to tone down the intensity of this phase. During the subsequent days of the recovery period, the patient may be at risk for recurrence of immersion foot.

UV RADIATION–RELATED CONDITIONS

Intense ultraviolet (UV) radiation from the sun, particularly when it is reflected off snow and ice, can burn an unprepared mountaineer at high altitudes. For every 1,000 feet (305 meters) above sea level, UV radiation increases about 5 to 6 percent. Burn injuries from overexposure to UV radiation are potentially serious but preventable.

Sunburn

Cloud cover does not filter out UV radiation effectively, so skin can burn even on an overcast day. Certain medications (such as tetracycline, sulfa drugs, and diuretics) can increase the skin's sensitivity to sun and thus to the danger of its burning.

Sunburn should be treated like any other burn: Cool the burned area, cover it, and treat for pain. Blistered areas in particular should be covered with sterile dressings to minimize the risk of infection. Drink plenty of fluids.

To prevent sunburn, climbers must be aware of the risk of getting burned and maintain skin protection. The most effective prevention is to cover exposed skin with clothing. Clothing's ability to screen UV radiation depends on its weave and fiber. A tighter weave works better, though it is hotter to wear. Lightweight garments have been specifically developed for their sunscreening capability and have an ultraviolet protection factor (UPF) rating. Hats should include a wide brim to protect the back of the neck as well as face and ears.

When skin must be exposed, sunscreen products extend the time that can be spent in the sun without getting burned. Properly applied, sunscreens can work remarkably well. Chapter 2, Clothing and Equipment, discusses sunscreens and UPF-rated clothing. Be sure to use sunscreen with an SPF rating that is appropriate for the conditions. Some sunscreens can be difficult to extract from their containers in cold weather, so assess this potential problem with a favorite sunscreen before your next chilly glacier morning.

Snow Blindness

Snow blindness is a potentially serious problem that results when the outer layers of the eyes are burned by UV radiation. The cornea (the clear layer at the front of the eye) is most easily burned. Its surface can become roughened and blistered. With further radiation, the lenses of the eyes can become burned as well. Snow blindness sets in 6 to 12 hours after the radiation exposure. The first symptoms, therefore, do not appear until after the damage is done. Dry, sandy-feeling eyes become light sensitive, then reddened and teary, and then extremely painful. Recovery takes from one to several days.

Treatment of snow blindness includes providing pain relief and preventing further injury. Remove contact lenses, and protect the eyes from bright light. Advise the snow-blindness patient to avoid rubbing the eyes and to try to rest. Cool compresses may reduce pain. To prevent irritation from eyelid movement, cover the eyes with sterile dressings and padding. Recheck for light sensitivity at half-day intervals. When the eyes are no longer extremely light sensitive, dressings can be removed, but the patient should wear protective sunglasses.

Prevention of snow blindness is straightforward. In high-UV environs, climbers must wear either goggles or glacier sunglasses with side shields to block UV radiation bouncing off the snow. This eyewear needs to filter out 90 percent of the UV wavelength that burns. Glare can be filtered out with a darkly tinted lens, but the tint itself will not filter out the burning UV light. Polarizing layers on the lenses can help in settings where reflection is especially intense. If climbers lose their eye protection, emergency goggles can be fashioned out of duct tape or cardboard by cutting narrow, horizontal slits for each eye. (See "Sun Protection" in Chapter 2, Clothing and Equipment.)

HIGH-ALTITUDE CONDITIONS

As climbers reach higher elevations, the altitude begins to change the way their body functions. As the air gets thinner, the amount of available oxygen in each breath decreases. Just as important, the mechanism that is instrumental in permitting the body to absorb oxygen from the lungs also decreases. The body's tissues have a harder time getting the oxygen they need for metabolism, and climbers enter the state of reduced oxygen called hypoxia.

The body attempts to adapt to this drastic environmental change, but adaptation (acclimatization) takes time (see the "Tips for Acclimatization" sidebar). How rapidly and how completely each individual acclimatizes varies greatly. The single most critical reason people get sick at high altitude is that they ascend too high too fast. The single most important way to prevent altitude illness is to undertake a slow ascent to high elevation.

Physiological Adaptations to Altitude

Increased breathing rate. One adaptation to high-altitude hypoxia is an increase in the rate of breathing. After ascending to high altitude, a climber's breathing rate continues to increase for several days. As this occurs, dissolved carbon dioxide in the bloodstream decreases (as carbon dioxide is exhaled).

Diuresis. Another normal adaptation to high-altitude hypoxia is that the kidneys send more water on to the bladder as urine, ridding the body of more fluid. This diuresis makes the blood slightly thicker. This change begins promptly upon ascent and continues for several weeks. Eventually the body produces a greater number of red blood cells in an effort to increase oxygen-carrying capacity.

Insomnia. The ability to sleep soundly deteriorates at high altitude. Most mountaineers have insomnia at altitude, waking up more often during the night and getting less deep sleep. Commonly, an irregular breathing rhythm appears during sleep and sometimes during wakefulness, too. There are periods of apnea (no breathing) interspersed with periods of hyperventilation (this alternating rhythm is known as Cheyne-Stokes respiration). The low carbon dioxide content of the blood appears to drive this odd change in breathing. A small dose (one-quarter tablet) of acetazolamide (Diamox) at bedtime decreases Cheyne-Stokes respiration and may aid your sleep. New evidence suggests that prescription sleeping pills help with insomnia at altitude; despite concerns that they depress respiration, they have been used at altitude without adverse consequences.

It is difficult to work as efficiently or powerfully at high altitude as at lower elevations, due to the effect of hypoxia and the related changes in how the body functions. For good acclimatization, it is critical to maintain adequate fluid intake amid these physiologic changes. Three high-altitude-related conditions—acute mountain sickness (AMS), high-altitude cerebral edema (HACE), and high-altitude pulmonary edema (HAPE)—still have unknown causes. It is important to differentiate AMS from the more ominous, related conditions of HACE and HAPE.

Acute Mountain Sickness

At least half of the sea-level residents who travel rapidly to moderate altitude—8,000 to 14,000 feet (2,400 to 4,300 meters)—experience some degree of acute mountain sickness (AMS). This is a collection of nonspecific symptoms that can resemble a case of flu, carbon monoxide poisoning from stove use inside an inadequately ventilated shelter, or a hangover. AMS can vary widely in severity. Signs of acute mountain sickness are headache plus one or two of several other symptoms:

- Insomnia
- Listlessness and/or lassitude
- Loss of appetite
- Nausea
- Vomiting
- Lightheadedness or dizziness made worse when in an upright position

AMS settles in within a day of the initial ascent, and if it is mild, it lasts only a day or so; however, it can progress in severity. In cases wherein symptoms (such as headache and nausea) progress, a descent of 2,000 to 3,000 feet (600 to 900 meters) in elevation is the best treatment. The diagnosis of AMS is confirmed if the condition improves upon descent.

Some medicines can be used to deal with altitude-related health problems; ask your physician about the appropriateness of such drugs for your situation. For example, some mountaineers use acetazolamide the night before or morning of the ascent and through the first 48 hours at high altitude in order to prevent AMS or block its recurrence. Potential problems caused by this medication are tingling of the extremities, ringing in the ears, nausea, frequent urination, and a change in the sense of taste. Individuals with sulfa allergies must be careful, as 6 to 8 percent will have an allergic reaction to acetazolamide. It is better to test this possibility at home rather than in the mountains. Acetazolamide does appear to be effective in preventing and treating AMS as well as the breathing changes brought on by high altitude.

TIPS FOR ACCLIMATIZATION

These are rough guidelines for controlling the rate of ascent to allow your body to acclimatize:

- Above 10,000 feet (about 3,000 meters), limit increases in sleeping elevation to about 1,000 to 1,500 feet (300 to about 460 meters) per night.
- Two or three times a week, allow an additional night at the same elevation as the night before.

High-Altitude Cerebral Edema

High-altitude cerebral edema (HACE) usually develops in unacclimatized climbers above 10,000 feet (about 3,000 meters), although it can occur as low as 8,500 feet (2,600 meters). HACE may just be the severe manifestation of AMS. HACE rarely occurs out of the blue and more often occurs in people who have had AMS that is worsening. Generally, it takes from one to three days at altitude for HACE to develop. Vessels in the brain respond to the stress of high altitude by becoming leaky, resulting in the brain swelling with increased fluid. Ultimately, the brain swells inside its rigid container of cranial bones.

Early signs of this deadly condition include deteriorating coordination (ataxia), headache, loss of energy, and altered mental status, ranging from confusion or signs of not thinking clearly to hallucinating. Use the coordination test in which you ask a person to walk an imaginary tightrope for 15 feet (5 meters), heel to toe, to check for ataxia. Nausea and forceful vomiting may be present.

Once HACE develops, it may advance rapidly. The patient may become somnolent and lapse into a coma. Descent is critical to survival. On some expeditions, portable hyperbaric chambers (such as the Gamow bag) are used to create a temporary artificial "descent" environment in the effort to stabilize the patient for a few hours. Supplemental oxygen can also be helpful for temporary stabilization. Drugs such as the steroid dexamethasone are beneficial, and acetazolamide might be an additional part of the treatment.

High-Altitude Pulmonary Edema

In high-altitude pulmonary edema (HAPE), body fluids leak into the lungs to a degree that interferes with respiratory function. HAPE is a potentially fatal condition and survival depends on a rapid response. HAPE appears to be a different disease from AMS or HACE and can occur quite suddenly in climbers who were otherwise performing well. Occasionally, HAPE and HACE do occur together.

Early signs of HAPE may overlap with more benign problems, such as a persistent cough caused by simple bronchial irritation from dry, high-mountain air. Decreasing ability to exercise, needing to take more frequent rest breaks, or falling behind companions might be more subtle signs of HAPE. Breathlessness and a hacking cough appear as HAPE develops. Rates of breathing and pulse increase.

If HAPE is allowed to advance, breathing will require effort and will include bubbling noises. Lips and nail beds may appear dusky or tinged with blue, reflecting the body's inability to transfer oxygen into arterial blood due to the water barrier in the lungs. Some affected people also develop a low-grade fever, making it difficult to distinguish HAPE from pneumonia; one indicator of HAPE is how rapidly it worsens with continued ascent.

The key to treating HAPE is to descend. A descent of 3,000 feet (900 meters) will resolve nearly all HAPE cases that are caught early. If descent is impossible, oxygen and a Gamow bag are useful. Ultimately, however, real descent must occur. Some mountaineers use the drug nifedipine to help prevent or treat HAPE (the drug widens blood vessels). Studies suggest that drugs for erectile dysfunction (tadalafil and sildenafil) also can be used for treatment (of both men and women), particularly when descent is not feasible.

LIGHTNING-CAUSED INJURIES

The high-mountain environment receives many more thunderstorms each year than coastal areas do, as the weather systems mass against the mountains before rising over them. Summer afternoons are the most likely time for thunderstorms, and therefore lightning, to endanger the mountaineer. Most lightning ground strikes occur directly below a cloud and hit the nearest high point. But lightning strikes can emanate from several miles away toward high points ahead of (or, less frequently, behind) the main thunderhead cloud formation—"out of a clear blue sky." Therefore, mountaineers can be in danger of a lightning strike at times even when the storm is not directly overhead.

Lightning can strike a climber in various ways:

- Direct strike of a mountaineer in the open who could not find shelter
- Splash strike, in which the lightning current jumps from an object it initially hit onto a mountaineer who sought shelter nearby
- Contact injury, from holding an object that lightning hits
- Step voltage, transmitted along the ground or through an object near a climber (even a wet rope)
- Blunt trauma or blast effect, created by the shock wave from a nearby strike

Lightning-caused injuries include cardiac arrest, burns, and internal injuries.

Cardiac arrest. The most immediate danger from being struck by lightning is cardiac arrest.

Burns. Lightning burns often take several hours to develop after the strike. These burns are usually superficial (similar to first-degree burns) and do not usually require treatment, although serious internal injuries can also occur.

Neurological injuries. The patient may be knocked unconscious or have temporary paralysis.

Internal injuries. The eyes, a vulnerable port of entry for electrical current, can be damaged in a lightning strike. Ear damage also may occur; a patient might not respond to your questions because of a loss of hearing caused by the strike.

After the lightning strike, the patient does not present an electrical hazard to rescuers. Proceed promptly with first aid, assessing the ABCD indicators: Airway, Breathing, Circulation, and Deadly bleeding and/or disability. It is important to get the lightning patient to a medical facility, because vital body functions may remain unstable for a considerable time after resuscitation.

For information on how to avoid being struck by lightning, see "Thunder and Lightning" in Chapter 27, Mountain Weather.

INTESTINAL DISORDERS

On mountaineering trips, the most common cause of gastrointestinal infections that entail diarrhea and abdominal cramping is fecal-oral contamination. Most often, the source of the feces is mountaineers themselves. Climbers may not realize that their hands have become contaminated. Some rock climbing routes may be contaminated with feces from previous parties. On glacier routes, handling ropes that have dragged through soiled snow and ice can lead to contamination. Water bottles as well as food can become contaminated from soiled hands. Animal wastes also present a risk. Many small rodents live in the same crags that mountaineers climb, and your hands may rest on mouse scat on the way up a cliff.

For most intestinal infections associated with diarrhea, treatment during a trip consists of adequately replacing fluids and electrolytes. This can be challenging if the climber is also nauseated. Mix a packet of replacement electrolytes into drinking water; a packet usually contains 1 teaspoon of salt and 8 teaspoons of sugar and is added to 1 quart (liter) of water. If electrolyte replacements are not available, simply replace fluids. Eat palatable foods and broths with a substantial salt content.

To prevent contaminating your hands, use biodegradable soap and water; when they are not available, use hand cleansers and towelettes. Simply washing hands before eating and especially after defecation can help a climber avoid many intestinal disorders. Climbers often are gregarious at rest stops—but think twice before offering your snack bag for each person to plunge a hand into; pouring some contents into each person's hands is less risky. Avoid camping near rodent burrows. Cover food and water so that they are secure from rodent invasion during the night.

Giardiasis

Giardiasis, caused by a waterborne protozoan (*Giardia lamblia*) traveling in cyst form from an infected animal host's feces, is prevalent in the United States, particularly in the West. *Giardia* infection has a long incubation period, ranging from one to three weeks (averaging a week and a half) after the organism is swallowed. Usually symptoms do not develop until after the climber has returned from the wilderness outing. Watery, explosive diarrhea may erupt, accompanied by abdominal cramps, flatus, bloating, nausea, and vomiting. After three or four days, the condition simmers down into an unpleasant subacute phase marked by greasy, mushy stools; mild abdominal cramping; belching; etc.

Before giardiasis can be treated, it must be diagnosed by laboratory tests. Tinidazole or metronidazole is the treatment of choice in the United States.

To protect against giardiasis and other waterborne diarrheas, always sanitize drinking water. All ingested water, including that used in dishwashing and tooth brushing, must be purified. (See "Water Purification" in Chapter 3, Camping and Food.)

If heading into regions with questionable hygiene and water disinfection practices, seek medical advice about antibiotics that can be taken to help ward off infection, and also ask about antimotility ("antidiarrheal") drugs. However, taking drugs is not a substitute for dietary discretion. Avoid eating raw fruits or vegetables, raw meat, raw seafood, tap water, and ice. Instead, stick to boiled water, properly cooked meat and vegetables, bottled beverages, and reputable eating establishments.

WOUND CARE, BURNS, AND BLISTERS

Wound care. Wounds such as scrapes, cuts, and punctures are very common. The goals of wound care are to prevent infection, avoid further trauma, and optimize healing. When providing first aid to someone else, put on protective gloves to prevent exposure to any possible blood-borne pathogens. All wounds should be thoroughly irrigated with sanitized (filtered, chemically treated, or boiled) water. High-pressure irrigation using a syringe is more painful but will dislodge dirt and other contaminants more effectively. Scrubbing gently may be needed to clean the wound better. Topical antimicrobial agents reduce the risk of infection and can be applied before dressing with a bandage or gauze. Larger wounds can be covered with a nonadherent dressing. Smaller lacerations can be closed with butterfly bandages if the wound is clean.

Burns. Cooling a burn within 30 minutes reduces pain and the depth of injury. Burns can also be covered with a topical antimicrobial agent and a nonadherent dressing.

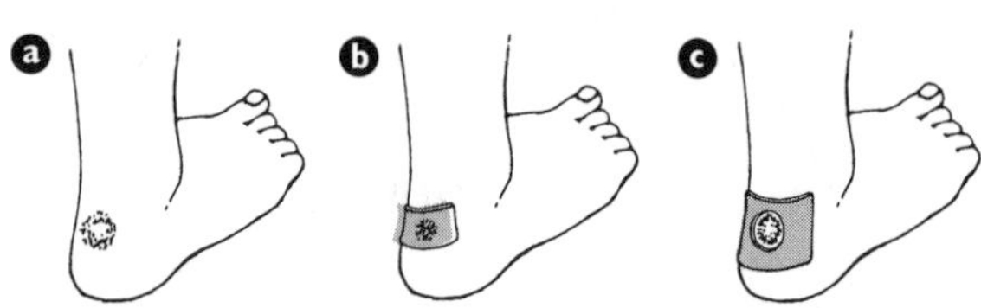

Fig. 23-2. Blisters: a, starting out as a hot spot; b, tape the hot spot to prevent blister formation; c, doughnut-cushion a blister once it forms.

Blisters. All wilderness travelers dread blisters. These bubbles under the skin, filled with clear or blood-tinged fluid, probably represent the most common health-related reason for ending outings. Small blisters generally are a source of minor irritation and discomfort. Larger blisters can cause significant pain and, if ruptured, can lead to serious infection and ulceration.

A blister usually becomes noticeable first as a hot spot (fig. 23-2a), a localized sensation of heat that increases in size and intensity over time. Inspect such spots immediately, and take preventive measures. Place a generous strip of waterproof, plastic adhesive tape or moleskin over the spot (fig. 23-2b). Other suitable products include 2nd Skin and Dr. Scholl's Molefoam; some sufferers are successful with duct tape or waterproof first-aid tape. Avoid using adhesive bandage strips (such as Band-Aids) for covering hot spots; these strips seem to promote blister formation when the nonadhesive dressing pad balls up and rubs against the already sensitive skin.

Once a blister has formed, avoid opening it unless absolutely necessary; opening a blister may introduce infection to the area. Your body will reabsorb the blister fluid after several days, and it will heal. If the hike or whatever activity caused the blister must be continued, pad the blister and protect it from rupture (fig. 23-2c). Layer a "doughnut" of padding until it reaches the proper depth so that the blister itself does not receive pressure. The padding doughnut must be deeper and wider than the blister. Tape the padding well to prevent it from becoming displaced.

If a blister breaks open, wash and dress it with sterile dressings, as with any open wound. Infection is a concern, and further tissue damage should be avoided if at all possible.

Often blisters are caused by new or poorly fitted boots. Blisters result from the skin rubbing against socks and the inner lining of the boot. This happens when boots are too large or too loosely laced or when socks are lumpy or wrinkled. Moisture tends to soften the skin, so wet boots or socks promote blister formation.

To prevent blisters, fit your boots properly. Break them in slowly and thoroughly before launching into any extended hikes. The areas most prone to blistering are over the heel or Achilles tendon at the back of the ankle and on the toes. If you tend to blister easily, pad the blister-prone areas with Moleskin or other adhesive foam, but do not pad them so much that a new pressure point is created around the edge of the Moleskin. Keep your feet dry, and wear adequate, well-fitting socks.

PANIC AND/OR ANXIETY

Mountaineering outings can be refreshing and rejuvenating experiences. They also can induce stress in climbers. In extreme situations, such as a serious accident, nearly all climbers have to deal with their own and one another's anxiety or even panic. A challenging situation or a difficult climbing move may evoke a more intense anxiety response than anticipated. This is unpleasant, especially if it occurs when a climber is halfway up a cliff. It is important to be able to manage these responses without becoming disabled by them.

Some people have a tendency toward intense anxiety in response to certain physical situations in climbing, such as exposure to heights or to enclosed spaces. This tendency can erupt in a panic response during a step-across move on a cliff face or while squeezing up a rock chimney. If affected, a climber may freeze and refuse to go on. The climber may hyperventilate (breathe rapidly) or be unable to recognize that there are safe movements available. The person's ability to fully assess the situation will be blocked temporarily; physical movements will be clumsy and fearful, raising the risk of a mishap.

Self-calming techniques are helpful in such situations. One approach involves a five-step process:

1. Identify the panic response for what it is (simply a physical adrenaline reaction to perceived risk).
2. Decide to deal with the panic response effectively.
3. Refocus on slow, steady, deep breathing (perhaps enhanced with a mental image of exhaling the worry out with each breath).
4. Identify, systematically, the options for safe movement.
5. Carry out one of these options.

If hyperventilation is a problem, try the old trick of breathing into a paper bag to increase the concentration of carbon dioxide in the inhaled air, which can slow down the hyperventilation trend. Redirecting your focus onto a useful physical task can be an excellent strategy for interrupting the snowballing effect of panic.

Fellow climbers can be most helpful by calmly and matter-of-factly prompting a panicked climber to use the self-calming techniques, by maintaining an atmosphere of confident acceptance and support, and by pointing out an option for retreat if appropriate.

INJURIES

To minimize injuries from a mountaineering accident, it is critical to immediately apply skillful and caring first aid. Specific treatments for serious injuries are beyond the scope of this book. Hands-on instruction in mountaineering first aid is essential. (See Appendix D, Supplementary Resources, for the titles of detailed first-aid texts.)

HEAD, NECK, AND BACK INJURIES

Head and spine injuries are common causes of death in alpine wilderness accidents. Any injury to the head or spine is potentially life threatening. Such injuries often are caused by falling objects, such as rock or ice, or by a fall in which the climber's head or back strikes a hard object. The spine can also be injured by deceleration, such as coming to an abrupt stop at the end of a rope while still suspended in air, even if the climber does not actually strike anything during the fall.

For all head injuries, assume that there is a cervical spine (neck) injury until a thorough examination proves otherwise. For all cervical spine injuries, the patient must be monitored for potential head and brain injury. Indicators of possible head injuries include the following:

- Unconsciousness
- Drainage of blood or clear fluid from the ears, nose, or eyes
- Unequal eye pupil size or unequal constricting response of the pupils to light
- A very slow pulse or noticeable fluctuations in respiratory (breathing) rate
- A headache generalized over the entire head
- Disorientation and confusion
- Seizure

The head and spine are so delicate that the slightest mistake in first-aid response may cause further injury or death, yet symptoms of injury are often so nonspecific that it can be difficult to choose a course of action. It is usually a question of whether the patient can be moved safely or requires essential treatment on the spot. As noted above, specific treatment for serious injuries such as head injuries requires skills that are beyond the scope of this book except for basic emergency stabilization, which is briefly covered in the next section. Hands-on practice is essential.

Avoid head injuries . . . wear a helmet!

FRACTURE MANAGEMENT

- Take precautions (gloves, sunglasses) to protect accident responders from potential contamination from the injured person's blood.
- Assess limb and/or joint for circulation, sensation, and function.
- Expose the injury site, and control bleeding if present.
- Apply dressings to wounds as needed.
- Prepare splint.
- Stabilize injured extremity and apply splint without excessive movement of extremity.
- Use padding to fill any large gaps between limb and splint.
- Immobilize fracture site and joints above and below.
- Reassess circulation, bleeding, and sensation frequently.

FRACTURES AND SPLINTING

While this chapter cannot adequately cover the details of fractures, several principles apply in splinting. Also see the "Fracture Management" sidebar.

Splints should be well padded to avoid damage to skin and superficial tissues. This is often accomplished by wrapping elastic bandages around the splint material or by using a soft material to cover the injured limb. A structural aluminum malleable (SAM) splint is a highly recommended addition to a climber's first-aid kit (fig. 23-3). A SAM splint is a highly versatile, lightweight and reusable splint. Because it can be rolled, flat, curved, cut or folded, it is adaptable to splinting many types of injuries, even the neck.

A victim with a head or neck injury may have sustained a fracture to the spinal column; for that reason, immobilization is necessary. A SAM splint can be wrapped around the neck to stabilize the head and neck, usually in the position the victim was found.

For extremity splinting, when possible, the joints above and below the injury should be immobilized with the splint. Splint the injury in a position that is comfortable and natural. For an upper-extremity injury, the patient will generally hold the injured arm in toward the chest, cradling it with the uninjured arm; splint the arm in this position. For a lower-extremity injury, strive to make the splint as comfortable as possible and in line with the patient's body.

Improvising a splint is often necessary (as shown

TABLE 23-3. BASIC PERSONAL FIRST-AID KIT

Item	Quantity/Size	Use
Adhesive bandages	Six 1-inch	To cover small minor wounds
Butterfly bandages or Steri-Strips	Three, in various sizes	To close minor lacerations
Sterile gauze pads	Four 4-inch by 4-inch	To cover larger wounds
Carlisle bandage or sanitary napkin	One 4-inch	To absorb and control severe bleeding
Nonadherent dressings	Two 4-inch by 4-inch	To cover abrasions and burns
Self-adhering roller bandages	Two rolls, 2-inch width by 5 yards	To hold dressings in place
SAM splint (malleable)	One	To splint sprains and fractures
Athletic tape	One roll, 2-inch width	Multiple uses
Triangular bandages	Two 36-inch by 36-inch by 52-inch	To use as a sling or cravat (for splinting)
Moleskin or Molefoam	4-inch to 6-inch square	To cushion blister areas
Tincture of benzoin	One 0.5-ounce bottle	To aid in adherence of adhesive tape; to protect skin
Povidone-iodine swabs	Two packages	To treat surface wounds with antiseptic
Alcohol or soap pads	Three packages	To cleanse skin
Thermometer	Range of 90° to 105° Fahrenheit (30° to 41° Celsius)	To measure body temperature
Sugar packets	Four packets	To treat diabetes; for hypoglycemia intervention
Aspirin	Six tablets	To treat headache, pain; if the party includes children, bring acetaminophen tablets instead of aspirin
Anaphylaxis (epinephrine) kit (EpiPen)	One	To treat severe allergic reaction. Climbers should carry if known to have severe allergy.
Antihistamine (diphenhydramine)	Six tablets	To treat allergic reactions
Elastic bandage	One 2-inch width	To wrap sprains; for compression of injured area
Gloves, latex or nitrile	Two pairs	To serve as an infection barrier
Safety pins	Two	Multiple uses
Tweezers	One pair	To remove splinters, ticks, wound debris
Plastic bag	One 12-inch by 18-inch	To hold contaminated materials
Breathing barrier, disposable	One	To administer CPR, rescue breathing
Pen, paper, accident report form	One each	To record accident response

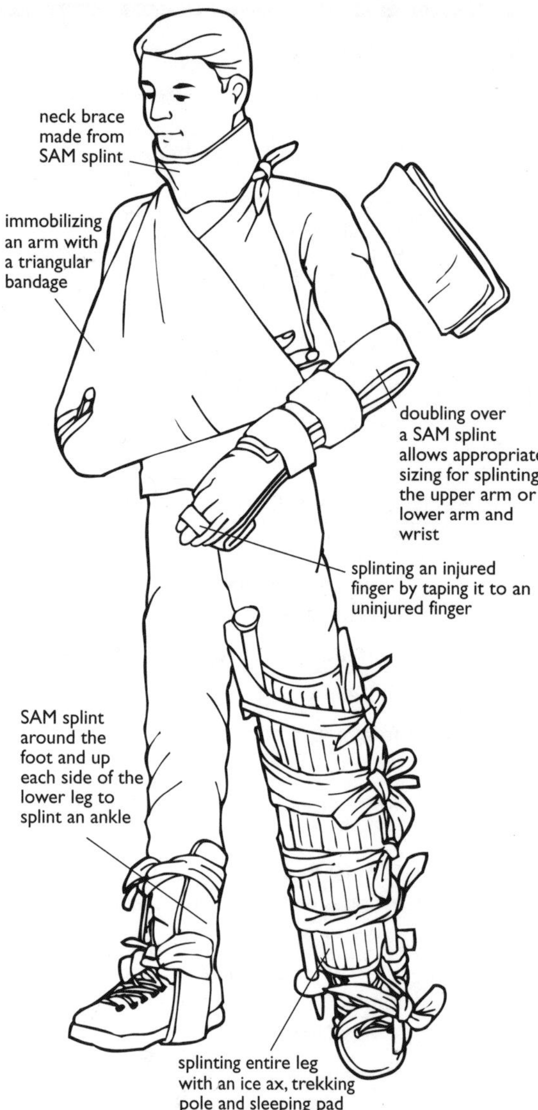

Fig. 23-3. Splinting can be done with a SAM splint (doubled for a neck brace, doubled over to an appropriate length to splint all of a forearm or wrist injury, or wrapped around a foot to splint an ankle and secured with bandannas) or improvised with available materials (injured finger taped to adjacent finger, injured hand immobilized with a triangular bandage, entire injured leg splinted with ice ax, trekking pole, and sleeping pad).

in Figure 23-3). For example, if no appropriate material is readily available, a lower-leg injury can often be protected by "buddy taping" the leg to the uninjured leg. Similarly, an injured finger can be secured to the adjacent finger for temporary protection. Splints can be fashioned from a wide variety of materials, including sticks and mountaineering equipment such as metal stays in a backpack, sleeping pads, trekking poles, or an ice ax. Spare webbing, twisted duct tape, bandannas, or athletic tape can be used to secure a splint.

Care must be taken to avoid applying splints too tightly and thus impairing circulation to the affected limb. After applying a splint, reassess the patient's neurovascular status by checking pulse, skin temperature, and sensation below the injury; make these assessments periodically while awaiting definitive care.

To minimize swelling of the injured extremity, a bag of snow or ice can be incorporated into the splint by wrapping the bag in the elastic bandage that secures the splint. Care must be taken to remove the bag periodically to avoid cold injury to soft tissue. In general, the snow or ice should be applied for no more than 10 minutes at a time. The injured extremity should also be elevated to minimize swelling.

FIRST-AID KIT

In a mountaineering party, each member must carry a basic personal first-aid kit. Suggested contents of a basic personal first-aid kit are given in Table 23-3. On trips where dampness is a possibility, it is wise to put the kit in a plastic bag to keep the bandaging materials dry.

In addition, the party often brings group first-aid supplies, depending on the nature and duration of the outing. Many parties carry a compact splint (such as a SAM splint), an oral antihistamine, and a pair of bandage scissors. Note that pharmaceuticals should be used only by the person to whom they were prescribed, and then only as directed. Giving medications to others runs the risk of serious drug reactions or drug interactions.

Be aware that the longer and more remote the adventure, the more supplies are appropriate, yet typically the more weight-conscious the party needs to be. Avoid the temptation to strip a first-aid kit below the bare minimum simply to reduce weight. On most trips, the first-aid kit will not be needed, but that does not make it less essential.

LEARNING RESCUE TECHNIQUES • THE SEVEN STEPS IN ACCIDENT RESPONSE • RESCUE • PUTTING IT ALL TOGETHER • EVACUATION • SEARCHES • GOING FORWARD

Chapter 24
ALPINE SEARCH AND RESCUE

Climbing instruction emphasizes strategies for preventing and mitigating accidents. However, even the best-prepared climbers may eventually encounter a situation requiring first-aid and rescue skills. With outside assistance hours or days away, a climbing party needs to be able to perform first aid and to initiate search and rescue (SAR) efforts.

It is possible for a small party of climbers to carry out many kinds of rescues using typical climbing gear. This chapter introduces some techniques for small-party rescues from steep alpine terrain, as well as techniques for searching and interacting with SAR agencies. In the event of an accident sustained by another party, prepare to forgo your planned climb. Offer assistance; donate gear, time, and expertise to help.

LEARNING RESCUE TECHNIQUES

First aid and alpine rescue are the two components of responding to an accident or serious illness.

The first-aid skills taught in most urban and workplace classes are designed to help a severely injured subject survive for the short time—typically less than 15 minutes—it takes for emergency medical services to arrive. Wilderness or mountaineering-oriented first aid helps a subject survive a much longer time, possibly days, in an often hostile outdoor environment. (See Chapter 23, First Aid, for first-aid references throughout this chapter.)

Alpine rescue describes actions a party can take to rescue an injured climber from difficult terrain and evacuate an ill or injured climber from the wilderness.

The challenges of rescue and evacuation of an ill climber can be just as difficult as those for an injured climber. The early identification of a serious illness is the best strategy for treatment or evacuation before it becomes disabling. Share suspicious signs and behaviors with other party members; the discussion of these clues can facilitate a prompt diagnosis and faster response. Many more rescue options are available for the ill climber who can still walk without assistance.

As climbing skills build and broaden, climbers should also be adding to their personal knowledge of rescue systems and techniques. Due to the wide variety of rescue situations and available techniques, consider taking courses from the many organizations that offer classes in rescue. Practice setting up and running the systems to keep your skills fresh.

THE SEVEN STEPS IN ACCIDENT RESPONSE

Accidents are not inevitable. Planning and preparing beforehand, practicing sound climbing strategies and techniques, and recognizing and reacting appropriately to unexpected hazards all but eliminate risk. (See Chapter 22, Safety.)

Accidents occur unexpectedly. An accident can stimulate an intense reaction and lead to an adrenaline response. This "fight or flight" response can compromise a climber's ability to think clearly. Inappropriate action during the accident may cause even more injuries. If there is nothing specific that can be done immediately to lessen the accident event, the smartest course is to focus on personal safety until calm, deliberate action can be taken.

Devastating accidents have the potential to overwhelm and emotionally paralyze people just when concentration and reason are needed. Should this happen, briefly acknowledge what occurred, tell yourself there will be time to address that aspect later, then focus attention on what needs to be done right now and get busy. If necessary, start with something small.

The seven steps in accident response outlined in Chapter 23, First Aid, serve as guidance for both first aid and rescue. The seven steps help the party focus on the tasks to be accomplished (see "The Seven Steps in Accident Response" sidebar). This chapter elaborates on these steps as they relate to rescue. In search and rescue, the person being rescued is most often referred to as the "subject," so this terminology is used in this chapter. Once it is known that the person has injuries, the first-aid and/or medical terminology is "patient," as is used in Chapter 23, First Aid. To prevent added emotional distress, it is best to avoid calling the subject a "victim."

THE SEVEN STEPS IN ACCIDENT RESPONSE

1. Take charge of the situation.
2. Approach the subject safely.
3. Perform emergency rescue and urgent first aid.
4. Protect the subject.
5. Check for other injuries.
6. Make a plan.
7. Carry out the plan.

STEP 1. TAKE CHARGE OF THE SITUATION

The climb leader has overall responsibility for accident response. If the climb leader is incapacitated, however, then an experienced party member must step forward. The immediate priority is to exert control to assure the party's safety.

Leading a party in an emergency can be the hardest thing a climb leader ever does. While experiencing the stress of the emergency situation, like all other members of the party, the leader must keep the big picture in perspective. The leader maintains this broad focus by delegating specific tasks to be accomplished and avoiding undue involvement with details.

STEP 2. APPROACH THE SUBJECT SAFELY

The first-aid caregiver needs access to the injured climber. This may require climbing, rappeling, or being lowered to the subject.

The party is likely to want to hurry to reach the injured climber. Acting hastily or in an unsafe manner increases the probability of additional injuries. Actions must be deliberate rather than simply reactive. Rescuer safety comes first. The time it takes to assure rescuer safety will not make a difference in the outcome of the subject's situation.

STEP 3. PERFORM EMERGENCY RESCUE AND URGENT FIRST AID

The subject should not be moved unless there is a danger at the current location, such as from rockfall, icefall, or water immersion, or unless the subject is in need of urgent first aid that cannot be administered at the current location.

If the injured climber is hanging in the seat harness, lower the subject to a level, or relatively level, location if possible.

STEP 4. PROTECT THE SUBJECT

The subject may be exposed to harsh environmental conditions and may experience shock and emotional stress. Be reassuring and communicate that the team is doing all it can to help. As appropriate to the situation, anticipate and treat the subject for dehydration, excessive heat or cold, and shock as soon as possible.

STEP 5. CHECK FOR OTHER INJURIES

Make a thorough (that is, as thorough as possible) examination of the subject to determine if there are any injuries, illnesses, or medical conditions and their extent. This may be very difficult in steep terrain and may need to be repeated as soon as the subject can be moved to a more suitable location.

STEP 6. MAKE A PLAN

Input from other party members can ensure that the climb leader takes all crucial factors into account. The climb leader should consider the following in preparing the rescue plan:

Terrain. Is roped climbing required to reach the subject? Will a rope system be needed to raise or lower the subject?

Subject. What continued care, if any, is required? Can the subject be moved without significant aggravation of injuries?

Evacuation. If the subject is unable to walk, then outside assistance will likely be needed. How far is the trailhead? How physically demanding is the route to the trailhead? Can the patient tolerate the rigors of party evacuation? Is there helicopter access to the accident site?

Weather. Temperature, wind, and precipitation affect both the subject and the rescue team.

Party. How many climbers are available? Are they able to remain on-site for several hours or overnight? Are other members of the group injured or traumatized and unable to contribute? Some traumatized climbers may even need to be secured to an anchor or relocated to a safe location, to assure they do not inadvertently endanger themselves or wander off.

Equipment. What equipment was lost or damaged in the accident? What equipment is available?

Assistance. Are climbing parties nearby that can help? Unless it is obvious that the injured climber can self-evacuate, seek outside assistance. It is better to have outside assistance on the way, even if it turns out later that it is not needed, than to delay the request until need is a certainty. It typically takes several hours, days in some situations, for rescuers to mobilize and reach the site.

With the assessment completed, the climb leader draws together a plan of action. Initially, it may be difficult to anticipate all the details. The plan is not rigid and should be expected to evolve. The narrow focus of individual climbers carrying out the specific tasks of the rescue plan may lead to insights that improve upon the original rescue plan.

STEP 7. CARRY OUT THE PLAN

Carry out the plan organized in step 6, remembering to continually assess the subject, team, and situation so that appropriate adjustments to the plan may be made.

RESCUE

When an injured climber or stranded hiker is on steep terrain (for example, rock cliffs, icefalls, or steep boulder fields), a team may need to use ropes to lower or raise the subject. Figure 24-1 gives an overall picture of what this might look like: a lowering and raising system (fig. 24-1a) with a high directional (fig. 24-1b), backed up by a belayer (fig. 24-1c); one climber is anchored near the edge (fig. 24-1d) to communicate with the rescuer and subject below (fig. 24-1e).

EQUIPMENT CONSIDERATIONS

When climbing, the protection and belay systems are designed to absorb or safely transfer the forces generated by the fall of a one-person load. Rescue systems may necessitate having two people supported by the rope and gear. Typical climbing gear and placements may not be strong enough to withstand the fall of a two-person load. To safely use recreational climbing gear in a rescue, the lowering and raising systems must be designed and rigged to withstand higher forces.

Anchors. Strong anchors are the foundation of rescue systems. Follow the principles of building anchors that are SRENE—Strong, Redundant, and Equalized, with No Extension—just as you would when climbing, until you are confident the anchor system will not fail (see "Anchors" in Chapter 10, Belaying). When trees are available, they usually make very strong anchors. A good method for using a tree as an anchor is the wrap-three–pull-two made using roughly 17 feet (5 meters) of 9⁄16- or 1-inch webbing: wrap the webbing three times around the tree (fig. 24-2a) and tie it, then clip two of the strands (fig. 24-2b). Snow and ice anchors are typically weaker than rock anchors, and so a larger number of snow anchor points are used when doing rescues from steep snow and ice. See "Snow Anchors"

Fig. 24-1. Small-party rescue: a, lowering system on the rescue rope; b, high directional on the rescue rope; c, belay rope; d, rescuer anchored when near edge; e, rescuer stabilizing subject in front of her.

in Chapter 16, Snow Travel and Climbing, and "Equipment" in Chapter 18, Alpine Ice Climbing.

Ropes. Dynamic climbing ropes are designed for a single climber. They typically stretch approximately 8 percent under the suspended weight of one climber; when 100 feet (30 meters) of a dynamic rope is extended, it will stretch nearly 8 feet (2.5 meters). The amount of stretch increases considerably with a two-person load. On a steep face, this stretch translates into a rubber-band-like effect. Each time the subject and rescuer hang freely, the rope will stretch. Each time they transfer weight to a feature or ledge, the rope will contract. For example, during a two-person lower, after stepping onto a small ledge and then stepping back onto the face, the pair could drop a considerable distance until the rope stretches fully again. This drop can be unnerving and may result in injuries if they hit something.

The mantle (sheath) on climbing ropes is thin and subject to much more abrasion with a two-person load than with a one-person load. The rubber-band effect accentuates this abrasion. Pad edges and points where the rope contacts the rock. It may be useful to raise the rope off the rock using a high directional to lift the rope off the ground. Trees make for the best high directionals. Place a wrap-three–pull-two anchor as

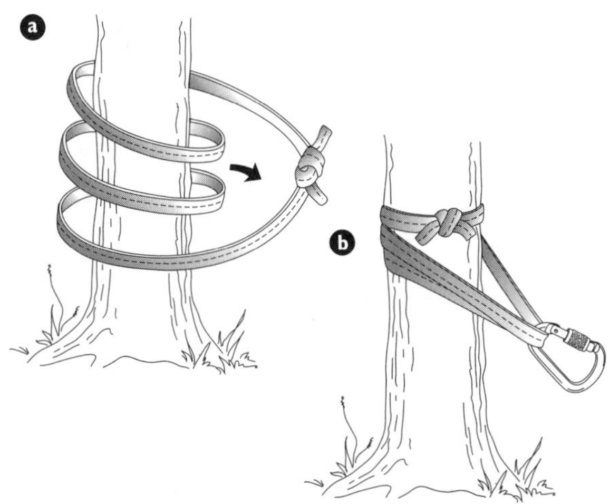

Fig. 24-2. Wrap-three–pull-two anchor around a tree: a, wrap webbing three times around a natural feature like a tree and join ends with water knot on load side of tree; b, attach a locking carabiner to two strands of the webbing.

high in the tree as can be done safely, climbing the tree a few feet if possible. Connect a locking carabiner to the anchor with the rescue rope running through the carabiner, since typical climbing pulleys are not strong enough (see Figure 24-1b).

Note that the original climbing rope may have been damaged in the fall. Prudence normally calls for transferring the subject to a different rope—the rescue rope—if available. If a low-stretch rope is available, it is better suited for a rescue rope since it does not stretch; however, this lack of stretch makes such ropes unsuitable for catching any fall, and systems must be built to handle large forces. Low-stretch ropes are used by mountain rescue teams and often by big wall climbers for hauling gear.

When performing a rescue, it is helpful to name the rope used by its function. A climbing rope is a rope used for typical climbing. The rescue rope is whatever rope is used to raise or lower a subject and/or a rescuer. A belay rope is a backup rope to the rescue rope and should be used whenever two people are raised or lowered.

Belay-rappel devices for lowering. Most belay and rappel devices lack the friction necessary to lower, stop, or hold a two-person load on a single strand. The munter hitch, double munter hitch, and double carabiner brake provide sufficient friction to do this. If the munter hitch (fig. 24-3a) does not provide sufficient

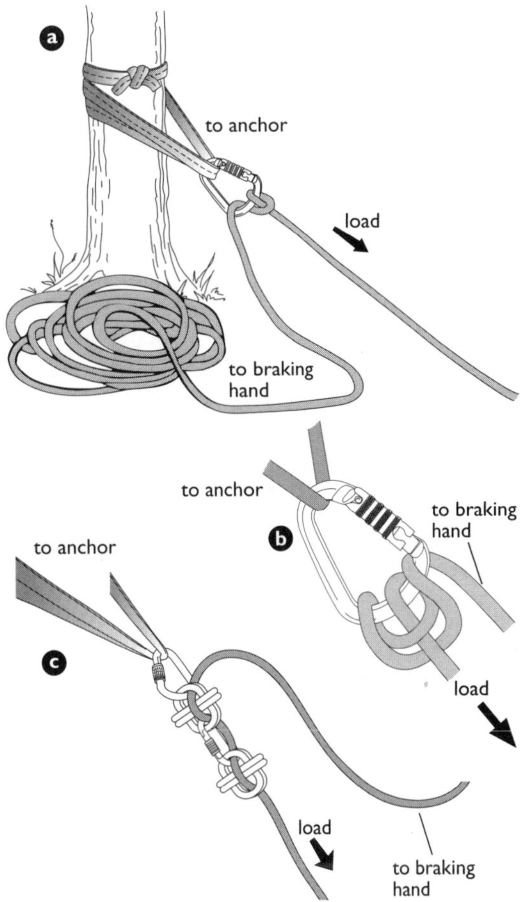

Fig. 24-3. Lowering systems: a, using a munter hitch; b, using a double munter hitch; c, using a double carabiner brake.

friction to safely and easily control the lower, use the double munter hitch by adding a wrap around the loaded rope strand and then through the munter-hitch carabiner (fig. 24-3b). The double-carabiner–brake lowering system consists of two carabiner brakes connected by a locking carabiner (fig. 24-3c; see also Chapter 11, Rappeling). Place the single-strand lowering system directly on the anchor.

Most belay and rappel devices, as well as the munter hitch and carabiner brake, do provide enough friction for a tandem rappel. In a tandem rappel, two climbers rappel together by attaching themselves to the same rappel device with a rappel extension made from a double runner (fig. 24-4a; see also "Rappel Extension" in Chapter 11, Rappeling). The rescuer should back up the rappel with an autoblock attached to the harness (as shown in Figure 24-4a; see also "Safety Backups" in Chapter 11). The rappel system may use an aperture-belay device (as shown in Figure 24-4a), a munter hitch (fig. 24-4b), or a carabiner brake (fig. 24-4c).

Pulleys. Not all pulleys work as well with the increased weight of two-person loads. Mountain rescue teams use pulleys that are larger and heavier than typical climbing pulleys. They are triangle-shaped so that they prevent the prusik hitch from being pulled into and trapped in the pulley. This type of pulley is generally called a prusik-minding pulley (PMP). They also have bearings that reduce friction when pulling. Small, lightweight pulleys, similar to those used by mountain rescue teams, are available to climbers. Several have the PMP shape and some have bearings. In a pinch, placing the rope through one or two carabiners may serve as a substitute for a pulley. Place the best-quality pulley (one with PMP shape and bearings) closest to the load for greatest efficiency.

RAISING AND LOWERING SYSTEMS

Safety. In a rescue situation, safety is paramount. Everyone is responsible for party safety. Everyone must continually be observing and analyzing the systems, activity, and environment for hazards. Before a raise or lower, every item in the system must be carefully inspected by more than one person.

Utilizing climbing ropes, which are designed for one person, with two-person loads is risky. Where resources are sufficient, use a belay rope to back up the rescue rope. The belay rope is an independent system that uses a munter hitch and is placed parallel to the rescue rope. During a raise or lower, this belay rope normally bears only a small percent of the load. If a problem should arise or the main rescue rope fails, this rope can help safeguard the rescuer and subject. When practicing these rope techniques, use a belay rope (see Figure 24-1c).

Commands. In addition to the climbing commands outlined in Table 10-2 of Chapter 10, Belaying, a couple of other ones are helpful. At any time, if anything appears unsafe or amiss, shout "Stop!" immediately. Only when the issue is resolved does the rescue resume. Calling out "Stop" dozens of times can be expected. "Up" or "Down" are commands used to direct those operating the raising or lowering system. "Reset" is used

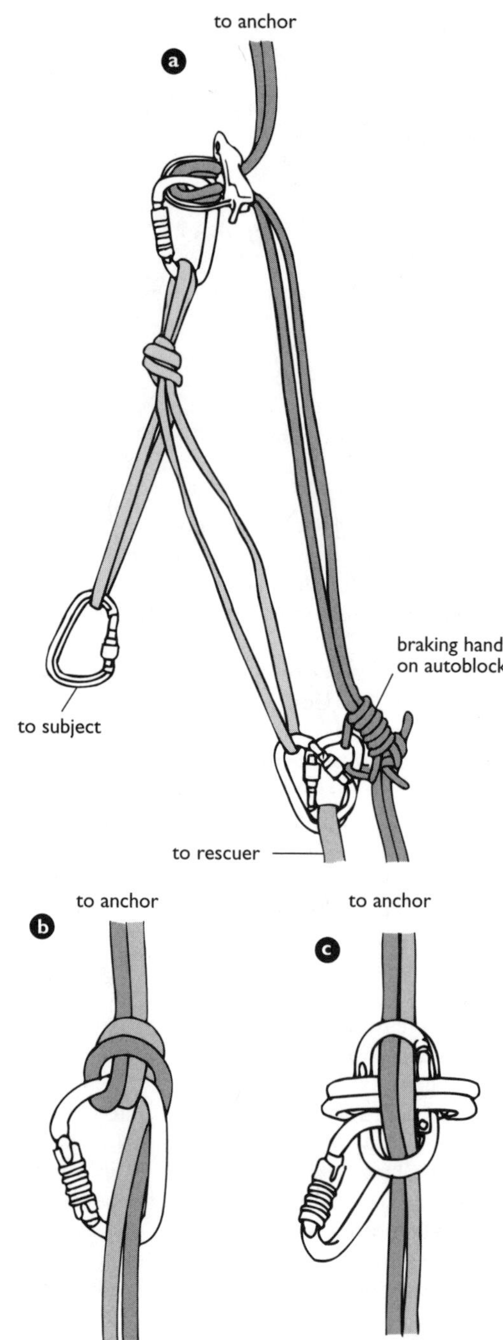

Fig. 24-4. Tandem rappels: a, using an aperture device; b, using a munter hitch; c, using a carabiner brake.

when the pullers need to reset the traveling prusiks and pulleys in a raising system. Pass the commands from person to person, as needed, to assure that everyone has heard them. Repeat the commands to acknowledge receiving them.

Lowering systems. It is much easier and faster to lower a subject than to raise one. When the subject needs some help descending, lowering the rescuer and subject together is better than tandem rappeling, because other climbers perform the lowering, which allows the rescuer to focus on negotiating the route and helping the subject.

Raising systems. The 3:1 (Z) pulley system (fig. 24-5a) is usually the most efficient of the simple raising systems. Chapter 17, Glacier Travel and Crevasse Rescue, describes setting up a 3:1 system.

If more mechanical advantage is needed, a 5:1 pulley system can be constructed in one of two ways: by adding a carabiner and a triple runner or cordelette that is 15 to 25 feet (5 to 8 meters) long (fig. 24-5b); or by adding a second traveling prusik and carabiner instead of a second pulley (fig. 24-5c). Where there is a very heavy load or only a few haulers, a second 3:1 system can be added to the pulling end of the first 3:1 pulley system to create a 9:1 (Z-on-Z) raising system (fig. 24-5d).

Be careful that haulers do not pull too zealously on the rope. A fast, jerky raise makes it difficult for the rescuer and subject to negotiate broken terrain and maintain a stable position. If the rope jams and the haulers keep pulling, the system then applies its powerful mechanical advantage to the anchors instead of to raising the climbers; this may pull out the anchors or break the rope.

Combining systems and using tension release hitches. If a short lower will be followed by a raise, set up a raising system and use it in reverse to lower the rescuer to the subject. Then it is instantly ready to begin a raise. If a long lower will be followed by a raise, or if a knot in the rope (most likely a butterfly knot used to isolate a damaged section) must be passed through a lowering system or high directional, a tension release hitch is invaluable: options include a prusik hitch with a munter-mule backed up with an overhand knot (fig. 24-6a), a mariner's hitch on a double runner (fig. 24-6b), and a classic load-releasing hitch on cordelette (fig. 24-6c). Tension release hitches are also invaluable for escaping a belay (see "Escaping the Belay" in Chapter 10, Belaying).

The combination of a prusik hitch and a tension release hitch allows the rope behind the prusik hitch to be slacked and manipulated; two examples are moving a knot ahead of a lowering system or converting a lowering system to a raising system. Once the manipulation is complete, the tension release hitch is used to transfer the load back to the raising or lowering system.

Subject and rescuer. If the subject is uninjured or has minor upper-body injuries, the rescuers may decide to raise or lower the subject without a rescuer attached to the rope too. A single person puts less stress on the rope system than two people do. The subject ties in to the rescue rope and is then raised or lowered off the steep terrain.

For injuries that do not allow the subject to fully assist in being lowered or raised, an accompanying rescuer is required. Both the subject and rescuer are secured to the rescue rope. The rescuer ties in at the very end of the rescue rope. Upon reaching the subject, the rescuer clips a double sling between the rescuer's harness and the subject's harness using locking carabiners. The subject is attached to the rescue rope with a friction hitch that is connected to the subject's seat harness with a carabiner. The two most common ways of creating this connection are to use the seat-harness prusik sling from the Texas-prusik system (see Chapter 17, Glacier Travel and Crevasse Rescue) or to use a short prusik and single runner joined by a girth hitch.

Slide the friction hitch up or down the rescue rope as needed to place the subject alongside the rescuer (as shown in Figure 24-1e), in the rescuer's lap, below the rescuer, or on the back of the rescuer with the subject's chest even with the rescuer's upper back. In this position, on steeper angle faces, the subject's weight hangs from the rescue rope and not on the rescuer, and the rescuer can support and stabilize the subject. If the rescuer cannot manage the subject's weight on low-angle terrain, it may be helpful to have another rescuer rappel on a separate anchor and rope to assist. The rappeling rescuer should use an appropriate rappel backup like the autoblock (see "Safety Backups" in Chapter 11, Rappeling).

PUTTING IT ALL TOGETHER

No definitive step-by-step "recipe" will work for all rescues. Far too many variables must be considered. There are countless accident scenarios and possible ways to use rescue techniques to solve the problems that arise. Following the seven steps in accident response and using the party's technical climbing, rescue, and first-aid skills

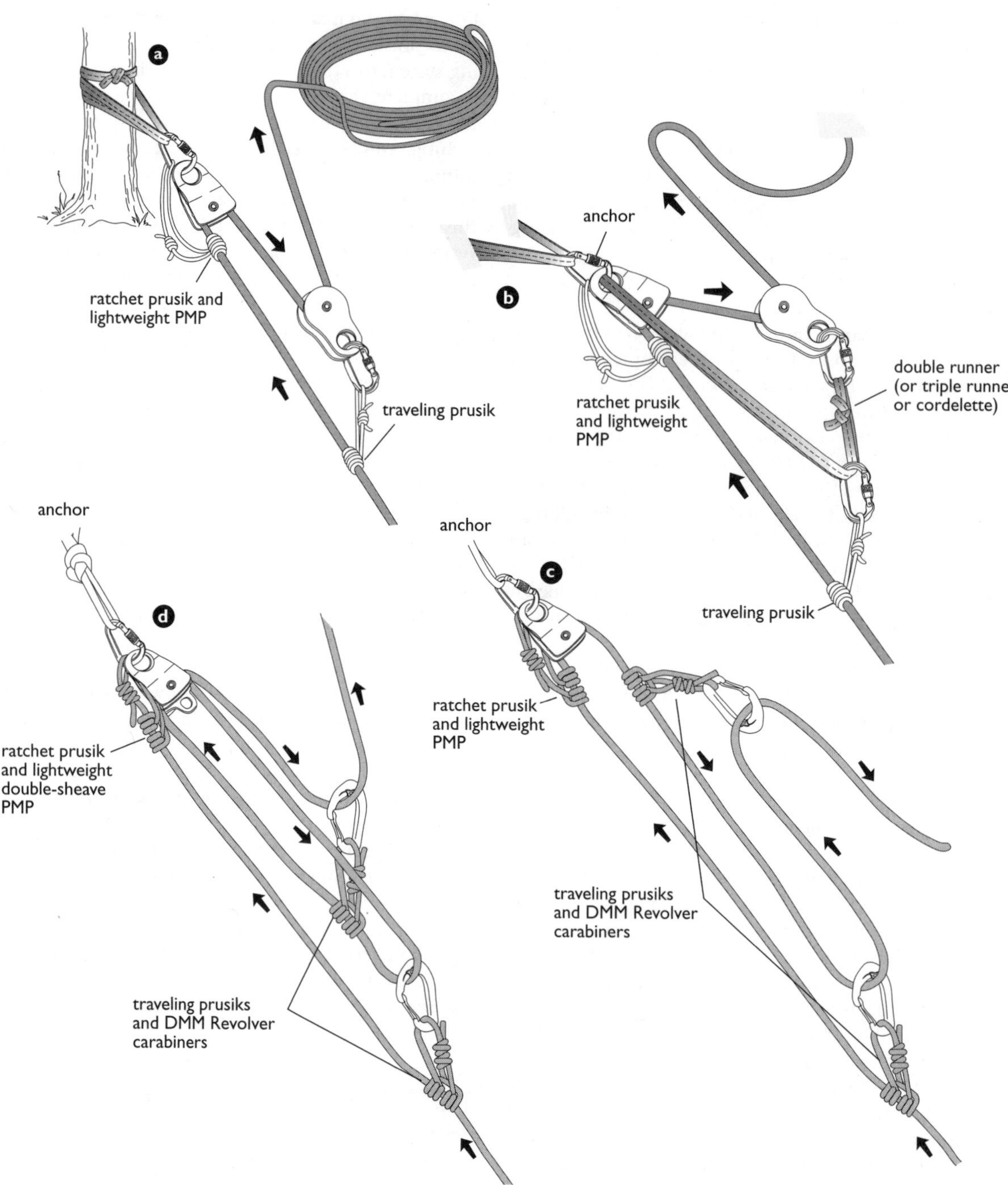

Fig. 24-5. Raising systems: a, 3:1 (Z) pulley; b, 5:1 pulley with a second carabiner and long runner (or cord); c, 5:1 pulley with two traveling prusiks and one pulley; d, 9:1 pulley (Z-on-Z). Note that the pulley shown is a double-sheave PMP. Two single-sheave pulleys could be substituted; ideally the ratchet pulley would be a PMP.

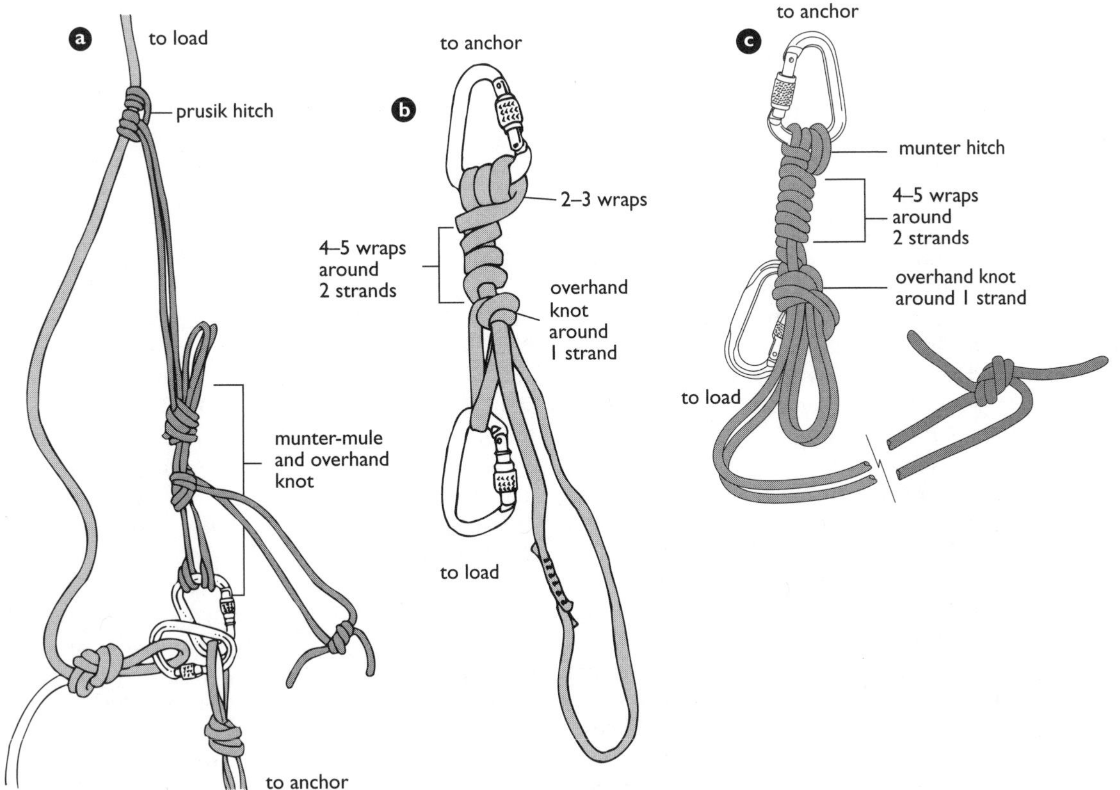

Fig. 24-6. Tension release hitches: a, prusik hitch with munter-mule; b, mariner's hitch using a double runner; c, classic load-releasing hitch using a cordelette.

will guide everyone through what needs to be done to respond to an accident in steep terrain.

The scenario of a lead climber falling on steep terrain illustrates how to use the seven steps, interwoven with many climbing, rescue, and first-aid skills. In this scenario, the climbing party is made up of two rope teams of two climbers each. Each team has a rope and a rack. The lead climber has fallen on a steep face, halfway through the last pitch of a multipitch climb, and is incapacitated. The climbing rope has been damaged. The other team has already completed the climb. There is an easy walk-off trail on the other side of the mountain.

Step 1. Take charge of the situation. The lead climber's belayer stops the fall and establishes communication with the two other climbers on the summit (either by voice or radio) when the fallen lead climber does not respond. The belayer takes charge.

Step 2. Approach the subject safely. One of the two climbers on the summit rappels on a single-rope strand to assess the unresponsive, fallen lead climber, taking down first-aid supplies, a warm jacket, and the rack.

Step 3. Perform emergency rescue and urgent first aid. The rescuer who rappeled determines that the fallen lead climber is breathing, has a pulse, is not bleeding, but is unconscious.

Step 4. Protect the subject. While rappeling, the rescuer noticed that the fallen climber's rope is damaged (the core is showing through the sheath), so the rescuer builds an intermediate anchor and attaches the fallen climber to it with a mariner's hitch. He also attaches the fallen climber's personal anchor to the anchor he just built. The belayer then slowly and gently transfers the fallen climber from the climbing rope to the newly established anchor. The rescuer places a warm jacket on the fallen climber to help prevent shock.

Step 5. Check for other injuries. The rescuer does a head-to-toe examination of the fallen climber but, without verbal feedback from her, can find no obvious injuries aside from a few abrasions.

Step 6. Make a plan. The three climbers discuss their options and decide the best course of action is to raise the fallen climber to the summit and then for two of them to go for help via the walk-off trail (they have no cell phone reception).

Step 7. Carry out the plan. The rescuer at the fallen climber ties the end of the rope on which he rappeled, now designated the rescue rope, to the fallen climber, unties the fallen climber's rope from her, and ties it to himself. He isolates the damage in this rope with a butterfly knot; it is now the belay rope. Then he ascends the rescue rope back to the summit, taking the belay rope with him. On the summit, he attaches the belay rope to another anchor.

The lead climber's belayer ascends the belay rope, removing protection the leader had placed as she ascended, until he reaches the fallen climber. The two climbers on the summit pull up slack and set up a 3:1 (Z) pulley raising system and high directional on the rescue rope. The two climbers on the summit then raise the fallen climber until her weight is transferred from the intermediate anchor, to which she is attached, to the raising system. The belayer connects his harness to the fallen climber's harness using a single runner with a locking carabiner at each end. The belayer then disconnects the mariner's hitch and fallen climber's personal anchor and removes the intermediate anchor.

The belayer ascends the belay rope, managing the fallen climber as best he can, while the two climbers on the summit raise the fallen climber using the rescue rope. Once all are on the summit, the fallen climber's condition is reassessed and a camp is established in the shelter of some trees. The two strongest climbers go for help while the remaining climber continues to care for the subject.

EVACUATION

Once a rescue party is off steep terrain of ice or rock, the hard work of evacuation back to the trailhead begins. There may be miles of ground, both on and off trail, to cover. The subject's condition, the distance to be traveled, and the rescue party's strength determine the feasibility of evacuation to the trailhead. The rescue party may also decide to evacuate the subject a short distance to a better location to wait or to an area suitable for helicopter pickup, or they may remain in place until outside assistance arrives.

For a time after an injury, the subject's pain may be lessened by endorphins in the bloodstream. Additionally, as time goes on, swelling tissues may add to pain or limit range of motion. If the subject must be moved, or must move under her own power, sooner is less painful than later.

Snow evacuations. The party may be able to improvise a sled with typical gear carried by the group (fig. 24-7). Spread out a tarp, bivy sack, tent, or rain fly. Place two skis flat on top of the tarp, with the tips and the tails tied approximately two to three ski widths apart; the skis provide support for the subject's head, torso, and pelvis, so the final spacing between the skis should be adjusted to maximize this support. Next, place layers of sleeping pads, packs, clothing, and sleeping bags on the skis to protect the subject from heat loss and bumps by isolating the subject from the ground. Now place the subject on top of the padding. Wrap and secure the tarp around the subject. At the top of the subject's head, gather the tarp material together and tie a rope or sling around this point; an overhand knot in the tarp material will keep the cord or webbing from slipping off.

Place a loop in the hauling rope to go around the pullers' waists. Following the fall line of a modest slope provides the easiest snow evacuation. Traversing on a firm slope is difficult. A trailing line, attached to the rear of the sled, may be used as a brake on steeper downhill slopes to keep the sled from overrunning the pulling climbers. On steep slopes, lower the subject with a lowering system as described in "Raising and Lowering Systems," above.

Cross-country versus trail evacuations. It takes considerable effort to move a nonambulatory subject a short distance on a trail. It is almost impossible without a trail.

Assisted walk. If the subject is able, she walks, and one or more rescuers walk alongside the subject, providing physical support. A rescuer close behind can help in difficult terrain. Have party members ahead selecting the easiest route and removing obstacles. Along some stretches, such as in boulder fields or crossing logs, the subject may choose to scoot across on her own.

Back carries. A strong climber may be able to carry the subject on his back for a short distance if the weight is distributed properly. Either the coil carry (fig. 24-8) or the nylon-webbing carry (fig. 24-9) is helpful. For the nylon-webbing carry, use two strands of webbing, and

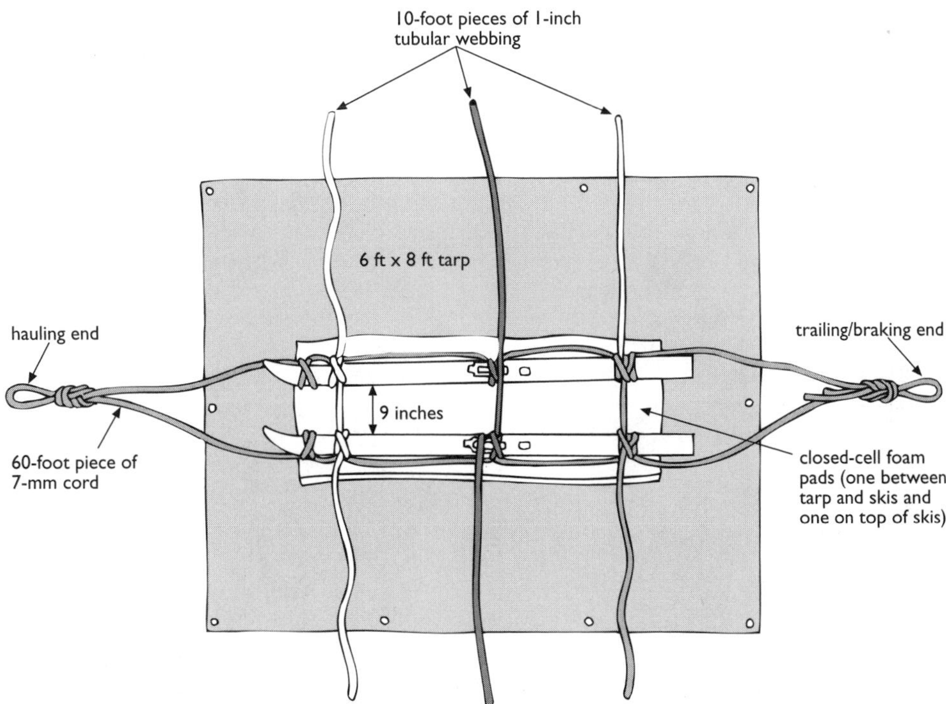

Fig. 24-7. Improvised sled for snow evacuation using a tarp, a pair of skis, and sleeping pads.

pad pressure points for greater comfort. The rucksack carry is another method of back carry. Make slits in the sides of a large backpack so the subject can step into it as though it were a pair of shorts, then the carrier wears the backpack as usual, with the subject as the load. Use of any of these techniques off trail can be difficult. Rescuers should take turns acting as carriers and choose a pace that will not exhaust the party.

Stream and boulder-field crossings. A rescue party may need to cross swift-running streams or jumbled boulder fields. Loss of footing could prove disastrous to both the subject and a rescuer who is doing a carry.

To cross either a modest stream or a boulder field, form two lines of rescuers across the obstacle: in the stream from shore to shore, or across the boulder field from one end to the other. These rescuers can act as handholds and supports for the rescuer who is carrying the subject.

With swift water, it is easy to underestimate the water's hydraulic forces. Some key points include these: Stay on the downstream side of ropes. Ropes must be angled downstream. Do not clip in to the rope—a loss of footing would likely entrap a person underwater. A Tyrolean traverse may be possible if it can be rigged high enough above the water to ensure that the subject will not sag down into the water.

RESCUES INVOLVING OUTSIDE RESOURCES

Outside rescue assistance is needed when the party lacks the resources to deal with the injuries, rescue, or evacuation. Organized search and rescue (SAR) groups bring to the scene the benefits of extensive training and experience, combined with specialized equipment and techniques.

Worldwide, a variety of approaches to SAR are found. In urban North America, the local fire department is responsible for rescue. In the backcountry, responsibility most frequently rests with the county sheriff's department. In some parts of the country, the state, the National Park Service, the military, or the coast guard may be responsible for search and rescue. Other countries may have nationalized SAR services. SAR may be very localized in remote regions.

Most of the field SAR personnel in North America are volunteers. Mountain rescue teams are volunteer

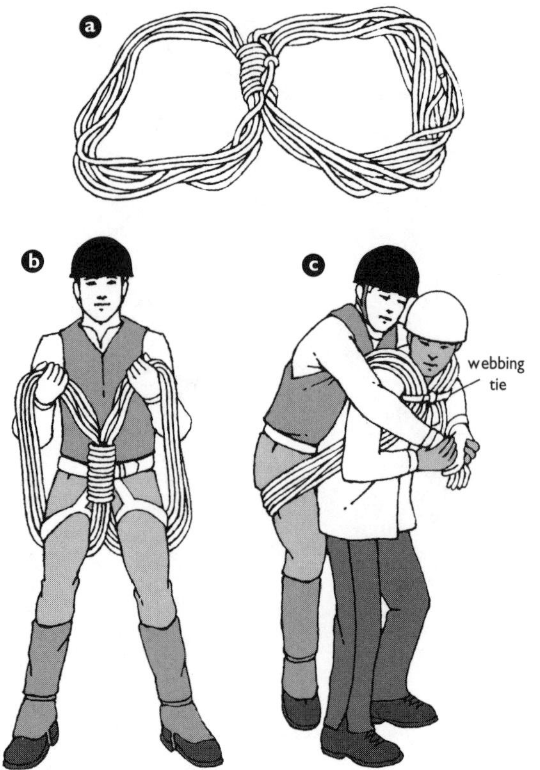

Fig. 24-8. Coil carry: a, coil the rope, sizing the loops to fit from the subject's armpits to crotch, then separate the coil in half to form a pair of loops; b, place subject's legs through loops; c, slip upper part of loops over carrier's shoulders and tie these loops together at the chest with short piece of webbing.

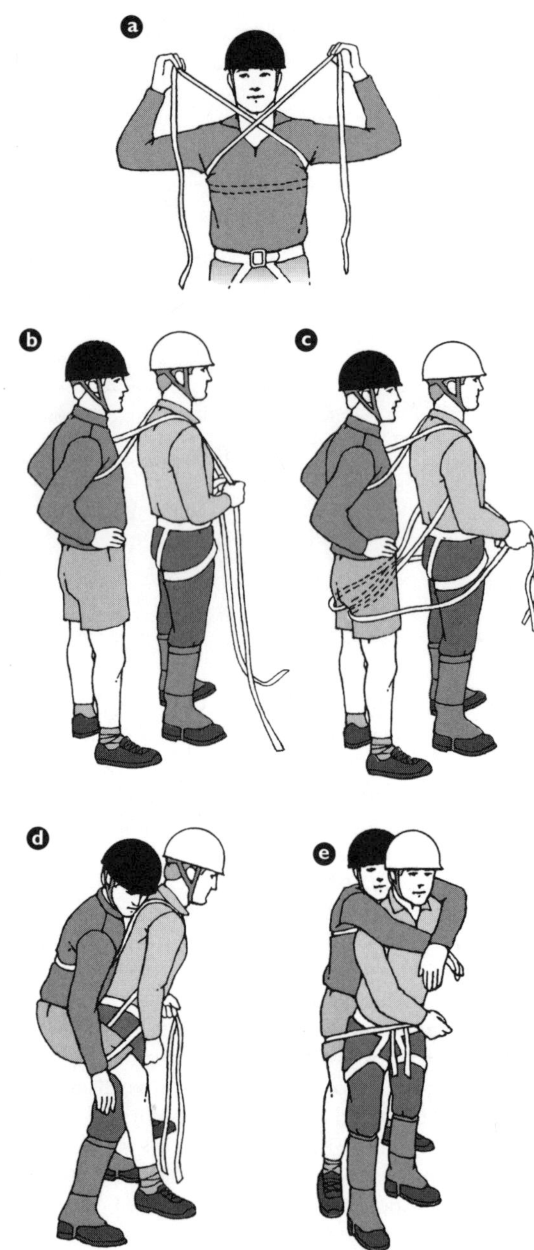

Fig. 24-9. Nylon-webbing carry: a, place webbing around subject's back and cross in front of chest; b, place ends over carrier's shoulders; c, bring ends under carrier's arms, through subject's crotch, and around outside of subject's thighs; d, carrier ties ends of webbing together around waist; e, subject puts arms around carrier's neck, if able.

organizations, consisting of local climbers who receive training in wilderness-oriented first aid, search, rescue, and helicopter operations.

In North America, it is rare to be charged for SAR costs. In Europe and many other parts of the world, climbers must expect to be charged. Usually, inexpensive insurance policies for climbing are available in many of these regions for this purpose.

Prepare a report. It is essential to communicate clearly with the outside agency. From an outside rescuer perspective, information on the injury, the location, and the route condition is critical to carrying out the rescue. The accident report in Figure 23-1, in Chapter 23, First Aid, is a suitable report format.

Deliver the report. Outside rescuers can be contacted

using various methods: via radio, cell phone, locator beacon, or in-person messengers.

Radios and cell phones. Climbing parties will save hours if they can get through with a radio or cell phone, but in the mountains and wilderness, cell phones and radios tend to be unreliable. Radios require line-of-sight communications with another radio or repeater station. Amateur radios, together with amateur repeaters, are generally the most reliable method of communication. These radios are regulated by the federal government, and operation requires a license. Citizens band (CB), family radio service (FRS), and general mobile radio service (GMRS) radios have range and propagation limitations. With all devices, sometimes moving a bit, reorienting the antenna, or transmitting from a higher elevation will improve service.

Where cell phones work, they are invaluable for communicating with outside rescuers. During a remote climb, cell phone batteries are likely to be rapidly depleted due to the phones' intensified attempts to stay on the network where coverage is poor. Cell phones should be turned off at the trailhead. Take along an extra battery or a cell phone battery charger that will run off a headlamp, a GPS, or other batteries that are being carried. When battery life becomes an issue, tell the SAR authorities; it may be best to shut the phone off for a period of time and schedule a turn-on time. Inform the outside rescuers if the phone has texting capabilities, which will help preserve instructions without having to write them down and also save battery life.

Satellite phones, due to their greater bulk and expense, have not seen widespread acceptance except in remote climbing areas.

If the party is able to make contact by radio or phone, read from the accident report instead of relying on memory.

Locator beacons. Personal locator beacons (PLBs) that send signals to government satellites are increasing in popularity; they are similar to those used in aircraft and ships. Their signal's location will be routed to the local government authority. These robust devices will send signals for at least 24 hours in extreme environments.

Businesses have developed somewhat similar devices using commercial satellites. Confusingly, they may also be called personal locator beacons. Some of these allow ongoing location tracking and sending a notification that help is needed.

In-person messengers. In many situations, sending someone from the climbing party may be the only means of communicating with outside help. If an adequate number of climbers is available, send two messengers. Messengers need to pace themselves and travel safely. They must avoid the natural tendency to rush. It is more important to be certain the messengers reach assistance than to worry about the time they will take to reach assistance.

Working (Interacting) with SAR

When planning a climbing trip, make sure to find out and include in the itinerary what outside agency will be contacted should outside assistance be required. The initial call for outside assistance should use the normal local procedure for fire, police, or medical emergencies, such as dialing 911 in the United States. The dispatcher will connect the party to the appropriate SAR authority.

Determine the party's location and communicate that clearly. Because emergency dispatch centers handle wilderness search-and-rescue requests infrequently, there is potential for miscommunication. For example, the jurisdiction where the accident is reported, or where the emergency dispatch center is located, may be different from where the accident occurred. Geographical names may vary and may even be used for different places in the same region. The dispatcher is not likely to be familiar with climbing terminology.

The location of the accident must be communicated unmistakably. Start with simple information such as the state, county, closest city or town, and road access. This may seem too basic, but heart-rending stories abound of rescuers being sent to the wrong side of a mountain or of a stranded climbing party watching a helicopter search an adjacent peak. A messenger should carry a map showing the precise location of the subject. If communicating by radio or phone, give information such as map coordinates; the type of map and its name, along with a description of the location; and the route name, including a guidebook that describes it. Use more than one way to describe the location. The party's elevation can be an extraordinarily useful piece of information for establishing location. If using a coordinate system, specify the datum and format, especially when using latitude and longitude. Specify whether any compass bearings are true or magnetic.

Speak to and help the rescue team. Make every effort to speak with the rescue team that will be entering the field. Mountain rescuers will have specific questions about route conditions and subject access that are unlikely to be asked by dispatcher or SAR mission leaders. This information will assist the mountain rescuers in formulating their strategy and selecting equipment. Be prepared to escort rescuers back to the accident scene if that is requested.

Do everything possible to help the arriving SAR team. This could range from having water available to fixing ropes. When a mountain rescue team arrives, they will assume responsibility for first-aid treatment and completing the rescue and evacuation. The SAR leader will look to members of the arriving teams to perform most of the vital tasks.

The climbing party can help by cooperating closely with the new team. The original climb leader remains in charge of the remaining climbing party and is responsible for its safety. The climbing party may be escorted out at this point. However, the climbing party should be prepared to lend a hand in the rescue if the SAR leader asks for help. If this happens, the SAR leader assumes authority over everyone at the scene.

HELICOPTER RESCUE

Helicopters have revolutionized mountain rescue. They can deliver rescue teams to remote areas and pluck injured climbers from cliffs and glaciers. Helicopters can deliver an injured climber to the hospital in hours, whereas ground evacuation can take days.

Do not base rescue plans on an immediate helicopter rescue just because helicopters are used in the area. Bad weather, darkness, hot temperatures, or high altitude may limit helicopter operation. A helicopter also may not be available due to another assignment or maintenance.

Safety. Safety concerns are of the utmost importance when dealing with helicopters. Many things pose a danger, including static electricity buildup on the helicopter, blowing dust and debris, and loss of visibility from blowing snow. The downwash and noise of the helicopter are overwhelming; wear eye protection and climbing helmets. Anything not secured *will* blow away!

Make the party visible. In many types of terrain, it is surprisingly difficult to see people from a helicopter. Help the crew by waving brightly colored items, using mirrors (for example, watch faces, stove windscreens, and shiny pots), making tracks in snow, or moving around on a contrasting background, such as snow, forest clearings, ridges, and stream- or riverbeds. New devices, similar to laser presentation pointers, are intended for this purpose. Effectively sized flares and smoke bombs are too large for climbing parties to carry. Once the helicopter has positively identified the party, it may fly off to prepare for the rescue or to land rescuers a short distance away.

If a helicopter approaches at night, it is reasonable to presume the pilot is using night vision goggles. If so, too much light can be disruptive to such vision. A single small light directed at the ground is sufficient.

Prepare the area. A rescue helicopter loads an injured person in one of three ways: It lands (or hovers) and takes the subject aboard, it hovers while hoisting the subject aboard, or it flies with the subject suspended from a cable.

Clear a level area for the helicopter. Move all loose objects, including natural vegetation such as fallen branches, well away from the landing zone. Stay out of the immediate landing area and behind protection from windblown debris. Expect a crew member, upon landing, to come to you; approach only when instructed to do so. If you must approach, do so from the front or sides of the helicopter, as long as you can stay well below the main rotor. Do not approach from behind, to avoid the low and nearly invisible tail rotors.

Alternatively, a member of the helicopter crew might be lowered to the ground. Prepare to assist this crew member. This person will not necessarily be a climber and may be unfamiliar with glaciers, steep terrain, and safe climbing practices. Do not touch any cables and baskets from the helicopter until they touch the ground, which discharges static electricity.

Finally, in the event a bare hook is lowered, the subject will need both a seat harness and a chest harness to remain upright when hoisted. The attachment point should be a single-length sling girth-hitched to the belay loop and passed through the chest harness. Allow the helicopter cable's hook to touch the ground to discharge static electricity before touching it! Do not anchor the hook to the ground, and ensure that it does not snag on anything. Expect the hook and cable to move about as the helicopter attempts to hold its hover. Disengage the hook's safety latch and place the attaching sling in the hook. If a pack must accompany the subject, girth-hitch a double-length sling through both shoulder straps (the pack's haul loop may not be strong enough) and place it into the same hook; the pack will hang below the subject. Once the attaching sling is secured in the hook and the subject is no longer attached to any anchor, make eye contact with the hoist operator and raise your hand overhead pointing to the sky. Be sure to send the written accident report out with the subject.

SEARCHES

The Climbing Code described in Chapter 1, First Steps, instructs climbers to stay together. Generally, the smaller the group, the higher the risk for becoming lost. Solo travelers are at greatest risk. Do not allow a single person to descend on his own, and do not spread out the party in unfamiliar terrain and on poorly marked trails.

When a climber becomes separated from the climbing party, there is always the risk that an accident has injured that individual, who will now be in need of help. If bad weather, difficult terrain, or medical considerations suggest that the missing climber might need help, start the search without delay.

Prepare a search plan. Give consideration to the lost person's skill level, resources, and remaining stamina. Review the route and examine the topographical map for possible alternate paths the climber may have taken. Lost people tend to head downhill and to take the path of least resistance. In preparing the search plan, look for inviting pathways, choke points that limit travel options, and barriers that block travel altogether.

Start the search. Before sending out party members, the climb leader should set meeting times and return times. If radios or cell phones are available, the teams should agree on scheduled call-in times.

The most effective search strategy is to return to the point where the missing person was last seen and retrace the party's route, looking for places where the climber might have left the path. Try to visualize errors the person might have made. Look for clues, such as footprints in mud, sand, or snow.

Request outside help. If, after a reasonable period of searching, the members find no sign of the missing climber, it is time to request outside help. The longer a lost person is on the move, the farther he can travel and the harder it is to find the person. Prominently mark and identify all physical points you want outside searchers to be able to locate.

SEARCHES INVOLVING OUTSIDE RESOURCES

The science of searching has advanced over the years. Search leaders from the responsible government agency now use models to predict the behavior of lost subjects and determine search areas.

A number of SAR groups may work with the search leaders. Search dogs follow scents and disturbances; human trackers can spot signs of passage; helicopters cover large areas quickly; horse and ground teams search less difficult terrain; four-wheel-drive and all-terrain vehicles travel rough roads and wait at exit trailheads; mountain rescue teams cover steep terrain. SAR teams usually consist of volunteers with skills appropriate for the local terrain.

Each search has different needs. Once the authorities have been notified, the best action for the original climbing team is to meet with the SAR leader. The SAR leader will want specific information that only the climbing team can provide. Information transfer is always better in person. The party will be directed where to meet the SAR leader, which usually means waiting at the trailhead. After an initial debriefing, the search leader may ask the climbing team to remain at the SAR base to answer questions that come up or assist in the search effort, or the search leader may release the party to go home. When leaving the SAR base, always leave contact information. The climb leader should call the emergency contact of the missing climber. Friends of the missing person and other untrained volunteers are not likely to be used during a search.

GOING FORWARD

Good leadership and climbing skills can help climbers to avoid situations wherein first-aid and rescue skills are needed. Yet circumstances that require these skills do arise, so being prepared to perform rescues is essential. Learn leadership, first-aid, and rescue skills, and keep current through regular practice and review. Make sure to practice the rescue techniques outlined in this chapter—reading by itself does not provide the necessary skills. Consider contributing your mountaineering skills to the community by joining your local mountain rescue group.

Become one of those climbers—confident of leadership, first-aid, and rescue skills—who has the ability to safely rescue and evacuate an injured person in treacherous terrain. Then you will be more fully prepared to pursue the freedom of the hills.

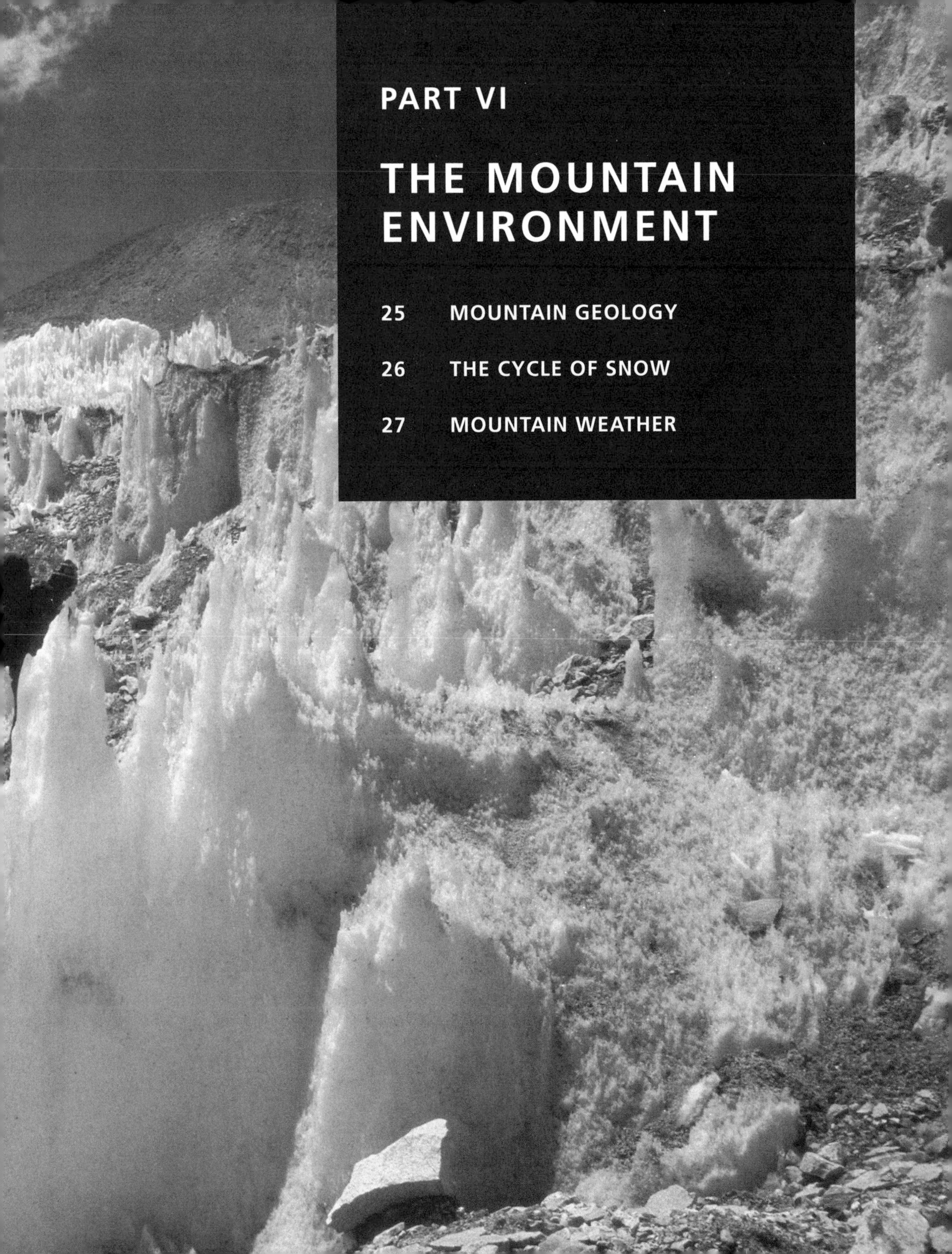

PART VI

THE MOUNTAIN ENVIRONMENT

GEOLOGIC PERSPECTIVES • HOW MOUNTAINS ARE FORMED • MOUNTAIN STRUCTURES • MOUNTAIN MATERIALS • WHERE TO GET GEOLOGIC INFORMATION

Chapter 25
MOUNTAIN GEOLOGY

Geology is the basis for understanding the form and substance of mountains. Climbers learn from experience that different types of rock affect what different routes are like, ranging from sheer walls to those having cracks and ledges galore. Climbers also discover that some kinds of rocks are very durable, whereas others crumble under pressure. Geology is essential knowledge; climbing success—or even your life—can depend on that knowledge.

GEOLOGIC PERSPECTIVES

Climbers can gain a better understanding of mountains by examining them on three scales: as an overall landscape, as a single outcrop, and as a close-up view of a single specimen of rock. Each perspective contributes to an overall comprehension of the mountain environment.

Landscape. The wide-angle landscape view examines the mountain as a whole, sometimes from miles away. Observing geology at this scale helps climbers find a viable route to the summit. Using photos or binoculars, look for routes with strong, supportive rock, or identify areas where rock may be weak and unreliable—in other words, places to trust and places to treat with caution. Ridges may follow a layer of resistant rock. Sets of fractures may offer a zigzag route to the summit. Sudden changes in slope may indicate a fault (a fracture along which movement has occurred) or an abrupt change in rock type.

Outcrop. The midrange perspective focuses on specific outcrops from 10 to 100 feet (3 to 30 meters) away. Here climbers can see features that could help—or hinder—an ascent. For example, a regular pattern of cracks is probably a good bet for chock placements, and a resistant dike may provide a reliable avenue upward (a resistant dike forms when the intrusive magma that has filled a fracture has cooled to form rock harder than the host rock).

Rock. At arm's length from the outcrop or closer, the details of the rock are more apparent. At this scale, climbers can identify rock types and recognize textures that might be difficult to climb or provide advantageous holds.

HOW MOUNTAINS ARE FORMED

The ultimate landscape view is the whole earth. When looking at mountain ranges on a global scale, a clear pattern of their occurrence can be seen, and this pattern can be explained by plate tectonic processes. According to the theory of plate tectonics, the outermost layer of the earth (called the lithosphere) is composed of plates that are slowly but constantly moving.

Most mountain ranges are formed by immense forces that squeeze rock masses together or pull them apart. Where tectonic plates move toward each other, their edges (margins) are called convergent. Where tectonic plates pull away from each other, their margins are called divergent. Along what are called transform margins, blocks of lithosphere move side by side and mountains rarely form. This section describes the two types of mountain-forming plate margins.

CONVERGENT PLATE MARGINS

Three varieties of convergent margins each produce a somewhat different type of mountain.

Ocean–ocean margins. Where two plates of oceanic lithosphere converge is called an ocean–ocean margin (fig. 25-1a). The older, colder slab forms a subduction zone by sinking beneath the younger, warmer slab. Deep within the subduction zone, 55 to 60 miles (90 to 100 kilometers) below the earth's surface, abundant magma (molten rock beneath the surface of the earth) is formed and rises buoyantly. Over time, much of the magma makes its way to the surface, where a chain of oceanic island volcanoes grows. The island mountains of the Aleutians and Indonesia are two examples.

Ocean–continent margins. Subduction can also occur where oceanic lithosphere is subducted beneath the edge of a continent (fig. 25-1b). This produces a chain of volcanic mountains on land. Three types of volcanoes can be formed. *Shield volcanoes,* great conical stacks of basalt flows with gentle slopes, such as Belknap Crater in the Cascades Range of central Oregon, are uncommon. Most of the climbing destinations along ocean–continent convergent margins are *stratovolcanoes* (also known as *composite volcanoes*), composed mainly of andesite and having steep slopes, such as Washington State's Mount Rainier and Mount Baker or Japan's Mount Fuji. Cinder cones, composed of pyroclastic fragments, are generally only a few hundred feet high. Examples include the Black Buttes near Bend, Oregon, and Wizard Island in Oregon's Crater Lake.

As tectonic plates move, they cause various stresses—faulting, folding, and uplift—that create mountain structures (see "Mountain Structures," later in this chapter). These movements, as well as erosion, expose deeper layers of the earth's crust. For example, the schist and gneiss exposed in Washington's North Cascades originated as clay and silt on the seafloor 250 million years ago. During plate convergence, this material was buried as much as 100,000 feet (30,000 meters) beneath the earth's surface, where it was metamorphosed by heat and pressure into schist and gneiss. Continued plate convergence has now moved these rocks back to the surface in the northern part of the North Cascades range. To the south, volcanism has buried the metamorphic basement yet again and has built a chain of large stratovolcanoes that extends from British Columbia to northern California. Mountain ranges of similar origin include the Andes of South America and the Japanese Alps.

Suture zones. Many of the major mountain ranges of the earth are found where continental plates or island arcs have smashed together as they have converged (fig. 25-1c). For example, the Himalayan range has been uplifted by the collision of India and Asia, Europe's Alps were created by Africa's northward push into Europe, and the Rocky Mountains were uplifted by the collision of numerous microplates that extended the edge of North America hundreds of miles westward over the past 170 million years. In these mountain ranges, faulting may thrust one part of the range over another. These huge thrust-faulted structures are well exposed in the Alps, the Canadian Rockies, and the North Cascades (see Figure 25-2).

DIVERGENT PLATE MARGINS

Where lithospheric plates diverge, the lithosphere is stretched and ultimately breaks apart, as when taffy is pulled too quickly. The most extensive divergent margins are the submarine mountain ranges of the

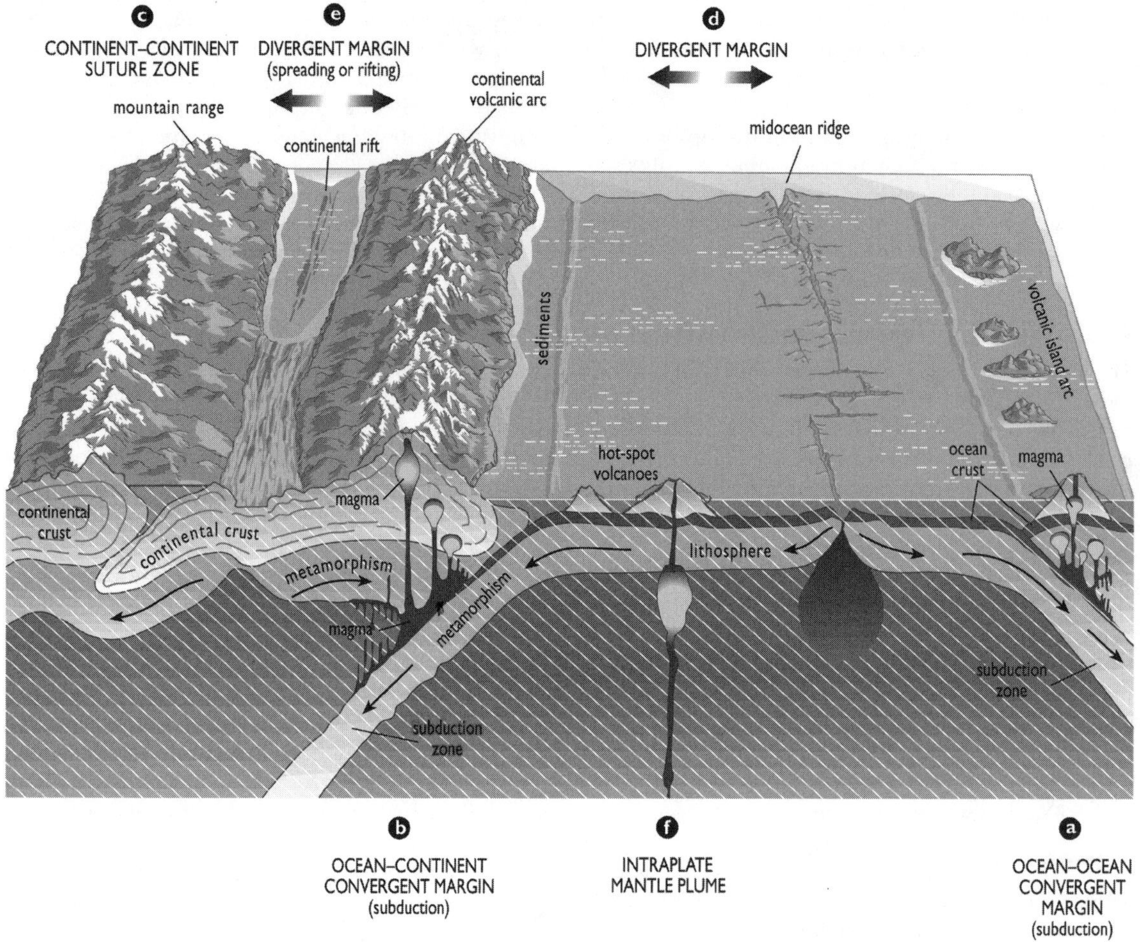

Fig. 25-1. Characteristic features of various types of convergent and divergent plate margins: a, ocean–ocean convergent margin producing a volcanic island arc; b, ocean-continent convergent margin producing a continental volcanic arc; c, continent–continent convergent zone producing a suture zone mountain range; d, oceanic divergent margin producing a midocean ridge; e, continental divergent margin producing a continental rift; f, intraplate mantle plume producing a chain of seafloor hot-spot volcanoes.

midocean ridges (fig. 25-1d), but these are obviously inaccessible to climbers. Divergent margins also develop within continents (fig. 25-1e), and these definitely produce terrain of interest to mountaineers.

Continental rifts. As the lithospheric plates move apart along continental rifts, vertical faults break the crust into huge block-shaped mountains with nearly vertical faces on one side and gentler slopes on the other. These form great escarpments, such as East Africa's Great Rift Valley. Some mountains of the western United States, including Utah's Wasatch Range and California's Sierra Nevada, are fault-block ranges associated with stretching (extension) within the North American Plate rather than along its margin (see Figure 25-3).

Mountains created by extension generally have less relief (contrasting elevations) than those created by convergent margins, but not always. Mount Whitney, part of the Sierra Nevada, is the highest peak in the contiguous United States, at 14,494 feet (4,400 meters); Wheeler Peak of the Snake Range in eastern Nevada rises above 13,000 feet (4,000 meters).

Volcanism also affects the topography of rifted margins. Magma from the upwelling mantle beneath the rift can rise through faults to the surface, where over time it builds up both shield volcanoes and composite volcanoes, such as Africa's Kilimanjaro.

INTRAPLATE HOT-SPOT VOLCANOES

The tallest mountain on Earth is not Mount Everest but, rather, the island of Hawaii, where the summit of Mauna Kea is 30,000 feet (9,000 meters) above the seafloor. Hawaii is part of a chain of volcanic islands and underwater seamounts that extend from the mid-Pacific nearly to Japan. These gigantic islands of basalt are the surface expression of thermal plumes, called hot spots (fig. 25-1f), that rise from the lower mantle toward the overlying lithosphere like a cumulus cloud building toward the stratosphere on a warm summer day. These plumes burn through the moving lithosphere, creating a chain of volcanoes built upward from the seafloor.

Hot spots are also located within the continents—an example is the chain of volcanoes and lava flows (lava is rock that is molten at the surface of the earth) that extend across the Snake River Plain from near Boise, Idaho, northeast to Yellowstone National Park, where the plume is currently located. Because hot spots produce mainly shield volcanoes with gentle slopes, technical climbing is rarely required to ascend them. However, one of the most interesting traverses in the world is the trail to the summit of Mauna Loa on the island of Hawaii.

MOUNTAIN STRUCTURES

The slowest tectonic plates move at about the same velocity as fingernails grow, and the fastest move at about the same velocity as hair grows: a range of about 2 to 7 inches (5 to 17 centimeters) per year. Such slow movements cannot be seen, but the effect on the surface of the earth can be profound. Slow as it is, this movement of the tectonic plates stresses rocks, and the results are the varying structures known as mountains. These stresses move mountains up, down, or from side to side and break them up into pieces. Near the earth's surface the rock layers are brittle, so they fracture into joints or move along faults. At greater depth, where the temperature and pressure are higher, the rocks tend to bend into folds rather than breaking.

FOLDS

Most sedimentary rocks are originally deposited in horizontal layers known as beds. However, in mountains such as the Front Range of Colorado, it is common to see beds that dip steeply or are even vertical. These rocks have been compressed into folds. This movement can be simulated by laying a napkin flat on a table and pushing its sides together, producing a series of archlike *anticlines*

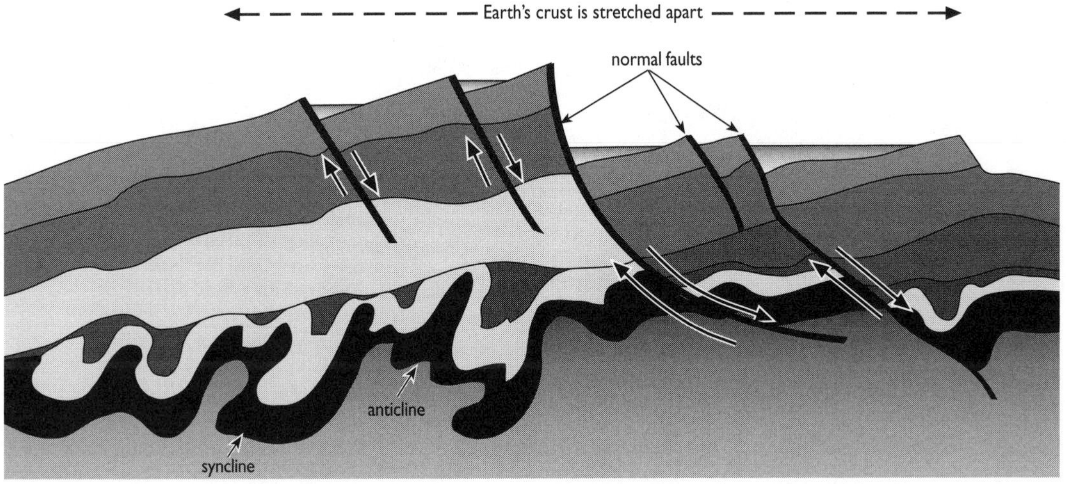

Fig. 25-2. Typical structures of a continental divergent plate margin, such as the Basin and Range of the western United States or the East African Great Rift Valley; note steep escarpment formed due to normal faulting.

25

and troughlike *synclines* (fig. 25-2). Folds range in size from microscopic to a mile or more high. In some cases, such as the Ridge and Valley Province of the United States' Appalachians, the shape of the range is dictated by the underlying fold structure. The patterns of folds create ramps, overhangs, and resistant ridges that can be crucial factors in planning a route to a summit.

JOINTS AND VEINS

Joints are cracks that develop when rock masses expand or contract. Contraction joints are formed when hot rock shrinks during cooling. The only common kind of pure contraction jointing is the columnar structure of lava flows. The result is an array of roughly hexagonal columns that are typically 10 feet (3 meters) in height. Exceptionally high columns such as Devils Tower in Wyoming provide spectacular climbing opportunities.

Joints also develop when erosion exposes rocks that were once buried deeply within the earth, and as the overlying rocks are stripped away, fracturing can result from the once-buried rocks expanding upward. If the expansion joints develop parallel to the exposed surface (as at Half Dome in California's Yosemite National Park), rocks peel off in layers that are called *exfoliation joints* (as shown in Figure 25-3). Sets of joints commonly occur at angles of 30, 60, or 90 degrees to each other—and these joint angles tend to be persistent as long as the rock type is the same. Recognition of joint patterns is essential for routefinding, especially on vertical faces in granitic rocks, where joints could be the only path to the summit without aid climbing.

Veins are fractures that have been filled by minerals, most commonly quartz or calcite. Veins can have an important effect on the texture of weathered rock surfaces. Quartz veins tend to project out as resistant ridges, whereas softer calcite veins are recessed. On some sheer faces, these can provide the only holds available, so the pattern of fractures determines where climbers should look for the next hand- or foothold.

FAULTS

Faults are fractures along which movement has occurred. The discernible movement may be only a fraction of an inch, or the movement can uplift a whole mountain range, such as Wyoming's Teton Range. Climbers need to know about faults because they can bring blocks of very different rock together. Fault zones also can consist of very weak, ground-up rock called *gouge* that may present a hazard to climbers.

Faults are classified according to their relative movement. *Normal faults* involve vertical movement that occurs when the earth's crust is stretched to the point of breaking (fig. 25-2), as in the Basin and Range region of Nevada, Utah, and California. Vertical movement also occurs along *reverse faults* and along *thrust faults*, which are reverse faults with an angle of less than 20 degrees (as shown in Figure 25-3). Here the fault is caused by compression due to the collision of lithospheric plates; examples are Europe's Alps and the Himalaya.

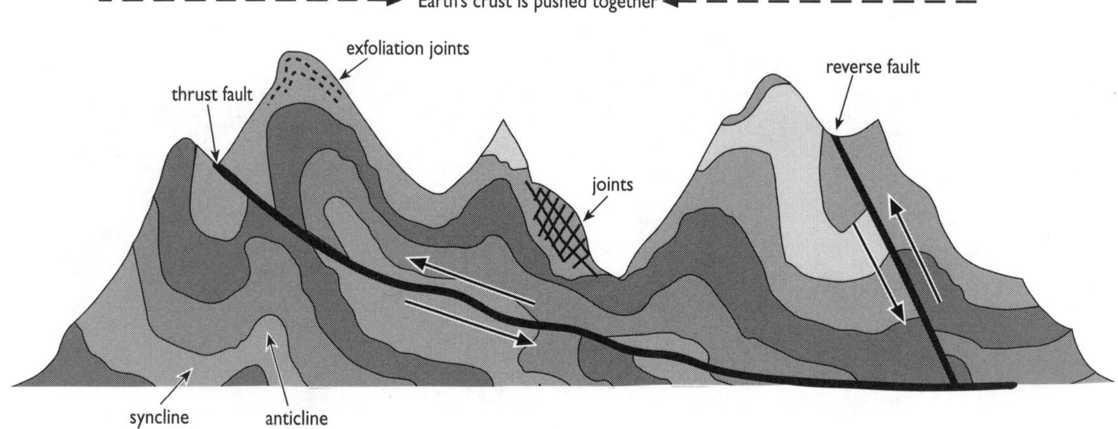

Fig. 25-3. Typical structures of a continental convergent margin, such as Europe's Alps, the Himalaya, and North America's Rocky Mountains.

Strike-slip faults (for example, the San Andreas Fault in California) move the lithosphere in a horizontal plane, rather than up and down. This can move mountains from place to place but generally does not cause uplift.

MOUNTAIN MATERIALS

The rocks that compose mountains are the foundation of the climbing experience. Each type of rock has a different fracture pattern, surface texture, and durability. The strength of rocks, as well as their resistance to erosion and weathering, depends on the minerals of which they are composed. This in turn determines the reliability of holds and the overall climbing strategy for different rock types.

MINERALS

Minerals are crystals that are solid and inorganic; they have unique properties by which they can be identified: color, hardness, cleavage (the tendency to split along definite crystalline planes), luster, and crystal shape. Only seven minerals compose most rocks of the earth's crust. Six of these are silicate minerals: feldspar, quartz, olivine, pyroxene, amphibole, and biotite. Except for biotite, these silicates are generally hard, durable materials. Only one common mineral, calcite, is soft and soluble. Calcite is composed of calcium carbonate (the major ingredient in many antacid tablets). It is resistant and stable in arid climates but dissolves readily in humid climates—and in acid rain.

Feldspar and quartz are the most resistant to breakdown under the constant assault of weathering. They are also the most abundant rock-forming minerals, composing most granites and sandstones. The other silicates (olivine, pyroxene, amphibole, and biotite) are dark, iron-rich minerals. Pyroxene is commonly found in basalt and gabbro. Amphibole and biotite are familiar as the black crystals in granite, granodiorite, and diorite, as well as in many schists and gneisses.

ROCKS

Rocks are subdivided into three categories: igneous (crystallized from a melt), sedimentary (deposited as particles, precipitates, or organic matter), and metamorphic (recrystallized by heat and/or pressure).

A mountain climber does not need to be an expert in classifying rocks. However, it is very useful to be able to recognize a few general categories, because different rock types call for very different climbing strategies.

The first thing climbers need to know is that rocks are like a box of chocolates: You cannot tell what flavor they are until you look inside each one. Weathering or lichens obscure the surface of many rock outcrops. To identify a rock's true color and appearance, look for a fresh surface that has recently broken open. Beneath a brown exterior there may be a black basalt, a white rhyolite, or even a glassy obsidian.

The following sections contain a few glittering generalities about what kinds of climbing are effective on some of the most common rock types.

Igneous Rocks

Igneous rocks (from the Latin *ignis*, meaning "fire") crystallize from magma or lava. Volcanic rocks (named for Vulcan, the Roman god of fire) form from lava that is

TABLE 25-1. CLASSIFICATION OF VOLCANIC AND PLUTONIC ROCKS

Color/Mineral Content	**Volcanic (Extrusive)** fine-grained rock erupted as lava or ash; cools quickly; may contain small holes or crystals	**Plutonic (Intrusive)** coarse-grained rock that cools and crystallizes slowly underground
Light-colored; very little iron content	Rhyolite or dacite (black, glassy = obsidian)	Granite or granodiorite
Usually gray; moderate iron content	Andesite	Diorite
Dark (black to green-black); high iron content	Basalt	Gabbro or peridotite (rare)

extruded at the surface; plutonic rocks (named for Pluto, the Roman god of the underworld) form underground from magma (see Table 25-1).

Volcanic rock. The two types of volcanic rock are lava flows and pyroclastics. Most lavas crystallize rapidly under conditions of supercooling, so they commonly consist mainly of very tiny mineral grains that are invisible without magnification. However, they often include large crystals that formed in magma chambers underground before eruption. The composition of lava flows is essentially the same as their plutonic counterparts, the granitoids—in others words, rhyolite has the same chemical composition and minerals as granite, andesite matches diorite, and basalt matches gabbro (see Table 25-1). Most lava flows make very good climbing rock. Exceptions are lavas that are full of small cavities formed by gas bubbles and flows that have been chemically altered (alteration zones) by corrosive volcanic gases. This type of lava flow, which is composed of crumbly rock that is hazardous to climb, can be found on most volcanoes.

Pyroclastics are deposits of volcanic rock fragments produced by explosive eruptions. These include outcrops of ash and pumice that tend to fail unpredictably and therefore should be avoided on climbing routes if possible. Many pyroclastics also show some degree of chemical alteration. Anyone climbing stratovolcanoes from the Aleutians to the Andes should be aware of this potential hazard.

Plutonic rocks. The most common plutonic rocks are the coarse-grained granitoids—granite, granodiorite, and diorite. Granitoids are very durable unless highly weathered. They tend to have multiple fracture planes that define crack systems toward the summit or chimneys if accentuated by weathering. A good way to check the reliability of protection in granitoid rock is to hit it with a hammer. If it rings, it is good rock; if it makes a dull thud, be careful.

Sedimentary Rocks

Most sedimentary rocks are made of three types of material: fragments (clastics) of preexisting rocks, precipitates from solution (chemical), or organic material. Clastic rocks are classified according to the size of fragments in the rock. Fine-grained rocks, including thinly bedded shales, are the products of deposition in quiet, low-energy environments such as lakes or the seafloor (fig. 25-4). Coarse-grained clastic rocks, including sandstones and conglomerates, are transported and deposited in higher-energy regimes such as stream channels and beaches washed by waves crashing onshore.

Sandstone with silica cement (gritstone) is, for many, the most desirable rock to climb. It has continuous fracture systems, as do granitoids, coupled with high friction from its sandpaper-like surface formed of quartz and feldspar grains. Sandstone outcrops are commonly slabby with many reliable hand- and footholds. Sandstone provides good protection unless it is highly weathered or poorly cemented. Note that sandstone can be weak when wet.

Shale is also slabby, but because it is composed chiefly of soft clay, it crumbles just as easily as do altered pyroclastics. The best protection is probably a long, thin blade driven between layers, but nothing should be trusted. Avoid shale if possible, but be aware that it is commonly found in layers between sandstones.

Limestones, composed of chemical precipitates or organic material, are deposited in warm equatorial seas. Routefinding on limestone can be challenging because crack systems are far less continuous than on granitoid rocks. Also, limestone is composed of the soft mineral calcite, so if protection points are stressed during an ascent, as in the event of a leader fall, they can degrade and fail. Where limestone has been below the water table before uplift, it can have many solution cavities, caves, and overhangs that make climbing interesting.

Metamorphic Rocks

Metamorphic rocks are igneous or sedimentary rocks that have been recrystallized by heat and pressure. The most distinctive change is foliation, wherein minerals are aligned like the grain in wood; foliation is found in slates, phyllites, schists, and gneisses. Foliation is a plane of weakness in the rock, from a rock climber's viewpoint. This weakness dominates in slate, which is fine-grained. If you try to drive a piton parallel to the foliation, a slab of rock will easily split off that looks like a piece of blackboard. Schist, which has mineral grains coarse enough to be visible, has more resistance to splitting, but protection is still poor if it is placed parallel to the foliation. Most gneisses are similar to granitoids in strength, but climbers should still be aware of the foliation plane.

There are also several nonfoliated metamorphic rock types, including quartzite, marble, and hornfels. Quartzite, like sandstone, is a climber's favorite. It is slabby with continuous fractures and forms very solid outcrops, but it lacks the friction of sandstone, espe-

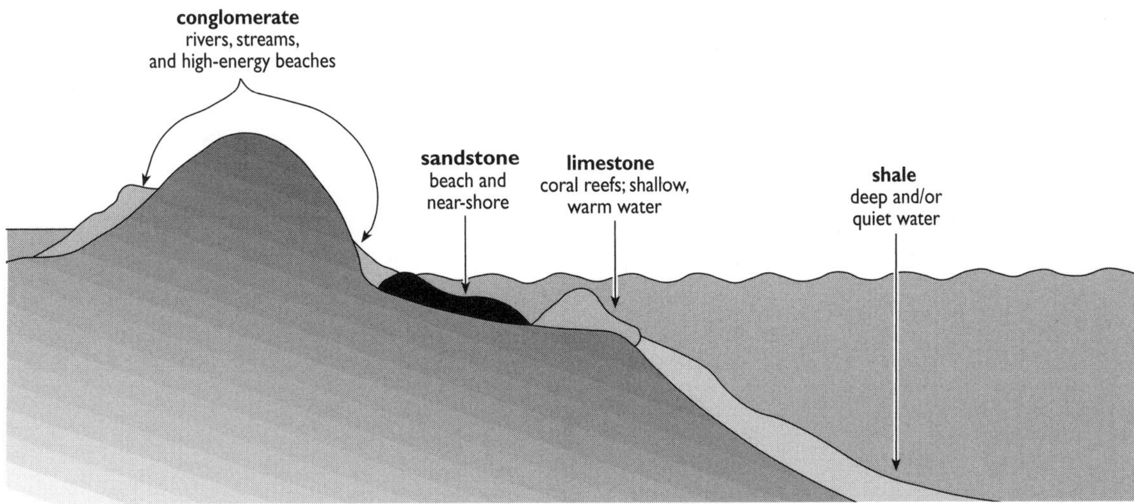

Fig. 25-4. Environments of deposition of various kinds of sedimentary rocks.

cially when wet. Note that in the alpine zone, where extensive freezing and thawing occur, quartzite slabs can slough off, but not as easily as sandstone does. Marble is similar to limestone in that it is composed of soft calcite that is easily degraded and soluble in humid climates. It tends to have more continuous fractures than limestone, but expect unusual topography. Hornfels is a baked rock that is formed along the margin of granitoid plutons. It is very hard and brittle. Chocks and cams work well in this rock, but driving pitons and placing bolts tend to create splinters.

Climbers should be aware of metamorphic changes along fault zones. In the shallow part of faults, movement shatters or grinds rock into gouge. Decomposition can also occur if hot fluids circulate through the fractured rock. Both the gouge and decomposed rock are very weak and are unreliable for protection. Deeper in the fault zone, rocks tend to flow rather than break. This produces mylonites, which have an intense foliation and are generally as unreliable as schist for protection points.

WHERE TO GET GEOLOGIC INFORMATION

The primary provider of geologic maps and information in the United States is the U.S. Geological Survey (USGS); its website is the gateway to a cornucopia of geologic data for the entire world (see Appendix D, Supplementary Resources, for all websites mentioned here). Check out links to the USGS map finder—a clickable set of maps showing the name and location of all available 7.5-minute topographic maps. The USGS also has a cooperative arrangement with the Microsoft TerraServer-USA that can provide online maps and aerial photos of nearly every part of the United States. Another useful service of the USGS is the national geologic map database. A new venture of the USGS is the Geology in the Parks program, which provides information via a website and brochures in cooperation with the National Park Service. The USGS Cascades Volcano Observatory's "Big List of Volcano and Earth Science–Oriented Websites" is also a good resource.

Other federal agencies that dispense geologic data are the U.S. Forest Service and the U.S. Bureau of Land Management.

Nearly all of the state geological surveys also maintain websites with abundant geologic information; links to state geological surveys are listed online.

The Google Earth software is another useful tool for planning climbing trips. It is a virtual map and geographic information system that can be downloaded from the Internet for free. Most of the satellite images displayed are two-dimensional, but three-dimensional images are increasingly available. Usually the images have a resolution of 49 feet (15 meters), but some are as high as about 6 inches (15 centimeters). Ground-level and standard aerial photos are also available through Google's Panoramio service. Both of these products enable climbers to easily see outcrop-scale geologic features for almost any mountain on Earth on a home computer, facilitating route planning before leaving home.

To get a site-specific geologic map or details on the geology of a chosen climbing route, there is no better place than the nearest college geology department. Many have websites with a lot of local geologic information, and all have faculty and students who are avid climbers and know exactly what rocks and structures they have seen on different routes.

Better still, start looking carefully and making detailed notes on the geologic features of the routes that you climb. Climbers are in effect practicing geologists, interpreting rock types and structures as they ascend. Personal observations are the best way to learn how to read the rocks for future climbs.

SURFACE FORMS OF SNOW COVER • AGING OF THE SNOW COVER • THE FORMATION OF GLACIERS • THE FORMATION OF SNOW AVALANCHES • UNDERSTANDING THE CYCLE OF SNOW

Chapter 26
THE CYCLE OF SNOW

Understanding the cycle of snow helps climbers anticipate changes in traveling conditions from the bottom of the mountain to the top, from morning to evening, and from day to day. While dramatic changes occur during storms, often more subtle changes, caused by different exposures to sun and wind or gradual aging processes, create significant impediments or enhancements to travel.

Snow crystals form in the atmosphere when water vapor condenses at temperatures below freezing. They form around centers of foreign matter, such as microscopic dust particles, and grow as more atmospheric water vapor condenses onto them. Tiny water droplets also may contribute to snow-crystal growth. The crystals generally are hexagonal, but variations in size and shape are almost limitless, including plates (fig. 26-1a), dendrites (fig. 26-1b and e), columns (fig. 26-1c and f), and needles (fig. 26-1d). The particular shape depends on the air temperature and the amount of water vapor available.

When a snow crystal falls through air masses of different temperatures and with different water-vapor contents, snow crystals may become more complex or combine. In air that has a temperature near freezing, snow crystals stick together to become snowflakes: aggregates of individual crystals. When snow crystals fall through air that contains water droplets, the droplets freeze to the crystals, forming the rounded snow particles called graupel (fig. 26-1g)—soft hail. When snow crystals ascend and descend into alternating layers of above- and below-freezing clouds, layers of glaze and rime build up to form hailstones (fig. 26-1h). Sleet (fig. 26-1i) is a refrozen raindrop or melted snowflakes that have refrozen.

The density of new-fallen snow depends on weather conditions. The general rule is that the higher the temperature, the denser (heavier and wetter) the snow. However, density varies widely in the range of 20 to 32 degrees Fahrenheit (minus 6 to 0 degrees Celsius).

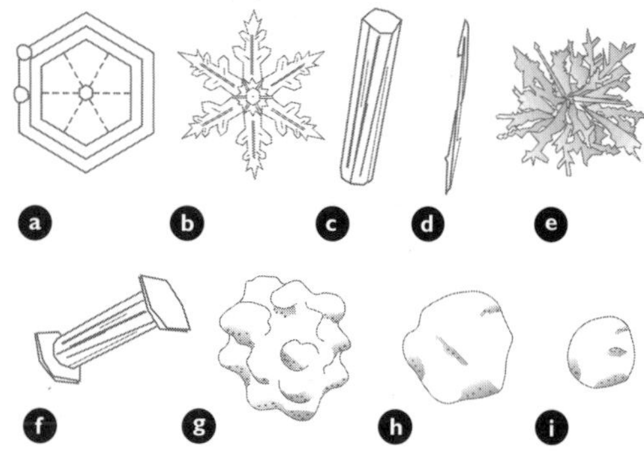

Fig. 26-1. Snow-crystal forms: a, plate, b, dendrite (stellar crystal); c, column; d, needle; e, spatial dendrite (combination of feathery crystals); f, capped column; g, graupel (soft hail); h, hail (solid ice); i, sleet (icy shell, inside wet).

Wind affects snow density, because high winds break up falling crystals into fragments that pack together to form dense, fine-grained snow. The stronger the wind, the denser the snow. The lowest-density (lightest and driest) snow falls under moderately cold and very calm conditions. At extremely low temperatures, new snow is fine and granular, with somewhat higher densities. The very highest densities are associated with graupel or needle crystals falling at temperatures near freezing.

The amount of water (solid or liquid) in layers of snow can indicate its density. Higher water content means that more space is occupied by ice or water and less air is present, causing higher density. In new-fallen snow, water content ranges from 1 to 30 percent, sometimes even higher, with the average for mountain snowfall being 7 to 10 percent.

SURFACE FORMS OF SNOW COVER

Snow and ice undergo endless surface changes as they are affected by wind, air temperature, solar radiation, freeze-thaw cycles, and rain. This section describes most of the surface permutations that mountaineers typically encounter. Table 26-1 summarizes the dangers and travel considerations associated with these various forms of snow.

Rime. Formed right at ground level, rime is the dense, dull white deposit formed by water droplets freezing on trees, rocks, and other objects exposed to the wind. Rime deposits build into the oncoming wind. Rime may form large, feathery flakes or a solid incrustation, but it lacks regular crystalline patterns. Typically it is easy to break, forming a weak, crusty surface when it is on top of snow and a poor, unreliable anchor when it is on rock or ice faces.

Hoarfrost. Another type of snow that forms at ground level, hoarfrost, forms on solid objects by the process of sublimation—the direct conversion of atmospheric water vapor to a solid. Unlike rime, hoarfrost displays distinct crystalline shapes: blades, cups, and scrolls. The crystals appear fragile and feathery, sparkling brilliantly in sunlight. Deposited on top of snow, hoarfrost is known as surface hoar, generally produced during a cold, clear night. A heavy deposit of surface hoar makes for fast, excellent skiing with fun, crinkly sounds. (For depth hoar, see "Aging of the Snow Cover," later in this chapter.)

Powder snow. A popular term for light, fluffy, new-fallen snow, powder snow is more specifically defined as new snow that has lost some of its cohesion because large temperature differences between the pits and peaks of its feathery dendrite (branching) crystals have caused recrystallization. The changed snow is loose (uncohesive) and powdery (mostly air). It commonly affords good downhill skiing and may form dry, loose-snow avalanches. Climbing or walking through powder is difficult, and any weight on it readily sinks.

Corn snow. After the advent of melting in early spring, a period of fair weather may lead to the formation of coarse, rounded crystals on the snow surface. The crystals, often called corn snow, are formed when the same surface layer of snow melts and refreezes for several days. When corn snow thaws each morning after the nighttime freeze, it is great for skiing and step kicking. Later in the day, after thawing has continued, corn snow can become too thick and gooey for easy travel. During the afternoon, the associated meltwater also may lubricate the underlying snow and promote wet, loose-snow avalanches, especially if the snow is stressed by people glissading on it or by the sliding and turning actions of skis, snowboards, and snowmobiles.

Rotten snow. Rotten snow is a spring condition characterized by soft, wet lower layers that offer little support to the firmer layers above. Rotten snow forms when lower layers of depth hoar (see "Aging of the Snow Cover," later in this chapter) become wet and lose what little strength they have. It is a condition that often leads to wet, loose-snow or slab avalanches running clear to the bare ground. Continental climates, such as that of the North American Rockies, often produce rotten snow. Maritime climates, such as that of the Pacific coastal ranges, which usually have deep, dense snow covers, are less likely to produce rotten snow conditions. In its worst forms, rotten snow will not support the weight of even a skier. Snow that promises good spring skiing in the morning, when there is some strength in the crust, may deteriorate to rotten snow later in the day.

Meltwater crust. A snow crust that forms when water that melted on the snow's surface refreezes and bonds snow crystals into a cohesive layer is called a meltwater crust. Sources of heat that cause meltwater crusts include warm air, condensation at the snow surface, direct sunlight, and rain.

Sun crust is a common variety of meltwater crust that derives its name from the main source of heat for melting. In winter and early spring, the thickness of a sun crust over dry snow usually is determined by the depth of solar heating. Often it is thin enough that skiers and hikers break through, which is very uncomfortable. In later spring and summer, when free water is found throughout the snow cover, the thickness—usually less than about 2 inches (5 centimeters)—depends on how cold it becomes at night.

Rain crust is another type of meltwater crust; it forms after rainwater has percolated into the surface layers of snow. The rainwater often follows preferred paths as it percolates through the snow, creating fingerlike features that act as pinning points, holding the crust to the underlying snow after it refreezes. The pinning action of many rain crusts helps to stabilize the snow against avalanching and makes for strong walking surfaces, especially in the Pacific's coastal ranges where heavy winter rainfall is common, even at high elevations. Glazed rain crusts can be extremely slippery and dangerous. Rain nearly always freezes on top of glacier ice, even during summer. This makes travel on glaciers following a fresh rain particularly hazardous.

Wind slab. After surface snow layers are disturbed by the wind, age-hardening takes place. When fragments of snow crystals broken by the wind come to rest, they are compacted together. Then the wind provides heat, particularly through water-vapor condensation, which causes melting. Even when there is not enough heat to cause melting, the disturbed surface layer warms and then cools when the wind dies, providing additional metamorphic hardening. Traveling usually is fast and easy on hard wind slabs, but the slabs can break in long-running fractures, and if they overlie a weak layer or form a cornice, added stress causes avalanching.

Firnspiegel. The thin layer of clear ice sometimes seen on snow surfaces in spring or summer is called *firnspiegel* (a German word meaning "snow mirror," pronounced FEARN-spee-gull). Under the right conditions of sunlight and slope angle, the reflecting of sunlight on *firnspiegel* produces the brilliant sheen called glacier fire. *Firnspiegel* forms when solar radiation penetrates the snow and causes melting just below the surface at the same time that freezing conditions prevail at the surface. Once *firnspiegel* is formed, it acts like a greenhouse, allowing snow beneath to melt while the transparent ice layer at the surface remains frozen. *Firnspiegel* usually is paper thin and quite breakable. Breaking through *firnspiegel* while traveling causes little discomfort, unlike sun crusts.

Verglas. A layer of thin, clear ice formed by water, from either rainfall or snowmelt, freezing on rock is called *verglas*. It is most commonly encountered at higher elevations in the spring or summer when a freeze follows a thaw. *Verglas* (a French word meaning "glazed frost" or "glass ice," pronounced vair-GLAH) also may be formed by supercooled raindrops freezing directly as they fall onto exposed objects (freezing rain, also sometimes inaccurately called silver thaw). *Verglas* forms a very slippery surface and, like black ice on a roadway, it can be difficult to anticipate.

Suncups. Also called ablation hollows, suncups can vary in depth from 1 inch to 3 feet (2.5 centimeters to 1 meter) or more (fig. 26-2a). Where sunshine is intense and the air is relatively dry, suncup depths usually increase with increasing elevation and decreasing latitude. On the ridges of each cup, sun-heated water molecules evaporate from the snow surface. In the hollows, water molecules released by solar heating are trapped near the snow surface, forming a liquid layer that promotes further melt. Because melting can occur with only one-seventh of the heat that is required for evaporation, the hollows melt and deepen faster than the ridges evaporate. The hollows are further deepened by differential melting when dirt in the hollows absorbs solar radiation. The suncups melt faster on the south (sunny) side in the northern hemisphere, so the whole suncup pattern gradually migrates northward across a snowfield.

Warm, moist winds tend to destroy suncups by causing faster melt at the high points and edges. A

TABLE 26-1. SNOW CONDITIONS AND THEIR RELATED TRAVEL CONSIDERATIONS AND DANGERS

Snow Condition	Effects on Travel	Effects on Protection	Dangers
Rime	Breakable; can trap feet or skis	—	—
Hoarfrost	Fun skiing	—	If hoarfrost is buried, potential avalanche danger
Powder snow	Difficult walking, good skiing	Ropes cut through it; ice axes do not hold in it; clogs crampons; deadmen need reinforcing with buried packs, etc.	Potential avalanche danger
Corn snow	Walking on it best in morning; skiing on it best in afternoon	Bollards must be large to hold stability depends on	When frozen, avalanche potential low; when melted, water content and underlying layer strengths
Rotten snow	Difficult traveling	Ropes cut through it; ice axes do not hold in it; deadmen need reinforcing with buried packs, etc.	Potential avalanche danger
Meltwater crust	Breakable; can trap feet if crust thin; good walking if crust thick; skis require edges	May require crampons	Slippery
Wind slab	Good walking	—	Potential avalanche danger, especially on leeward slopes
Firnspiegel	Breakable	—	—
Verglas	Breakable; impedes rock travel	—	Slippery
Suncups	Uneven but solid walking or skiing	—	Low danger because usually form in old, stable snow
Nieves penitentes	Difficult to negotiate	Ropes catch on them	Low danger because usually form in old, stable snow
Drain channels	Uneven but solid walking or skiing	—	Low danger because usually form in old, stable snow
Sastrugi and barchans	Uneven but solid walking or skiing	Ropes catch on them	A sign of wind transport and potential slab formation; ski edges may catch on them.
Cornices	Difficult to negotiate; best to avoid	Ropes cut through them	Can break away underneath or above traveler
Crevasses	Difficult to negotiate; may be hidden by snow: best to avoid	Require rope protection	Easy to fall into, especially if hidden
Seracs	Difficult to negotiate; best to avoid	Ropes catch on them	Very unstable; can break catastrophically
Avalanche paths	Hard surface, good walking	—	Slippery; relatively free from avalanche danger unless portion of slab remains or is recharged by new snow
Avalanche debris	Difficult to negotiate	—	Relatively free from avalanche danger unless portion of slab remains or is recharged by new snow

prolonged summer storm accompanied by fog, wind, and rain often will erase a suncup pattern completely, but the cups start to form again as soon as dry, fair weather returns. While skiing over suncups, it is easy to catch an edge, especially if the cups are hard and frozen from nighttime cooling. The unevenness of suncupped surfaces makes walking uphill tedious, but traveling downhill is made a little easier by "skating" into each hollow.

Nieves penitentes. When suncups grow up, they become *nieves penitentes* (pronounced nee-EH-vays pen-ih-TEN-tays, from the Spanish for "snow penitents," derived from the forms' similarity to the shape of a penitent's cowl). *Nieves penitentes* are the pillars produced when suncup hollows become very deep, accentuating the ridges into columns of snow that look like praying statues (fig. 26-2b). They are peculiar to snowfields at high altitudes and low latitudes, where solar radiation and atmospheric conditions conducive to suncups are intense. The columns often slant toward the midday sun. *Nieves penitentes* reach their most striking development among the higher peaks of South America's Andes and the Himalaya, where they may become several feet high and make mountain travel very difficult.

Drain channels. After melting has begun in spring, water runoff forms drainage patterns on snowfields. The actual flow takes place within the snowpack, not on the surface. As snow melts at the surface, the water that is formed percolates downward until it encounters either impervious layers that deflect its course or highly permeable layers that it can easily follow. Much of the water also reaches the ground beneath. Water that flows within the snow often causes a branching pattern of channels that appear on the surface. This happens because the flowing water accelerates the snow settlement around its channels, which are soon outlined by depressions at the surface. The dirt that collects in these depressions absorbs solar radiation, causing differential melting that further deepens them.

On a sloping surface, drain channels flow downhill and form a parallel ridge pattern that can make it a little difficult to turn while glissading or skiing. On flat surfaces, drain fields create a dimpled-looking surface, similar to suncups but more rounded. The appearance of dimples or drain channels suggests that a significant amount of water has percolated into the snow cover. If these dimples or channels are frozen, it can be a good sign of stability against avalanches. However, if they are newly formed and still soft with liquid water, snow stability may be compromised by meltwater that has percolated into a susceptible buried layer and weakened it.

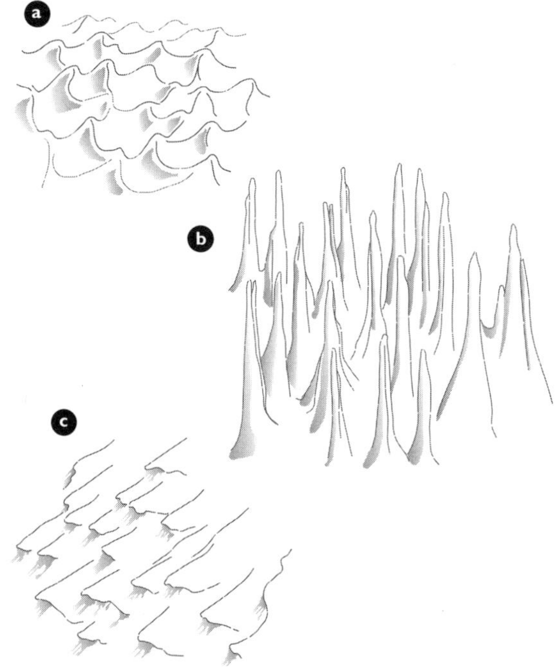

Fig. 26-2. Surface features on snow: a, suncups; b, nieves penitentes*; c,* sastrugi.

***Sastrugi* and barchans.** When it is scoured by wind, the surface of dry snow develops a variety of erosional forms, such as small ripples and irregularities. On flat, treeless territory and high ridges, both of which are under the full sweep of the wind, these features attain considerable size. Most characteristic are *sastrugi* (pronounced sass-TRUE-gee, a Russian word meaning "grooves"), the wavelike forms with sharp prows directed into the prevailing wind (fig. 26-2c). A field of *sastrugi*—hard, unyielding, and as much as several feet high—can make for tough going.

High winds over featureless snow plains also produce dunes similar to those found in desert sand, with the crescent-shaped dune, or *barchan*, being most common. These stiff, uneven features cause difficult traveling, especially when ice or rocky ground is exposed between each one.

Cornices. Deposits of snow on the lee edge of a ridge top, pinnacle, or cliff are called cornices (fig. 26-3a).

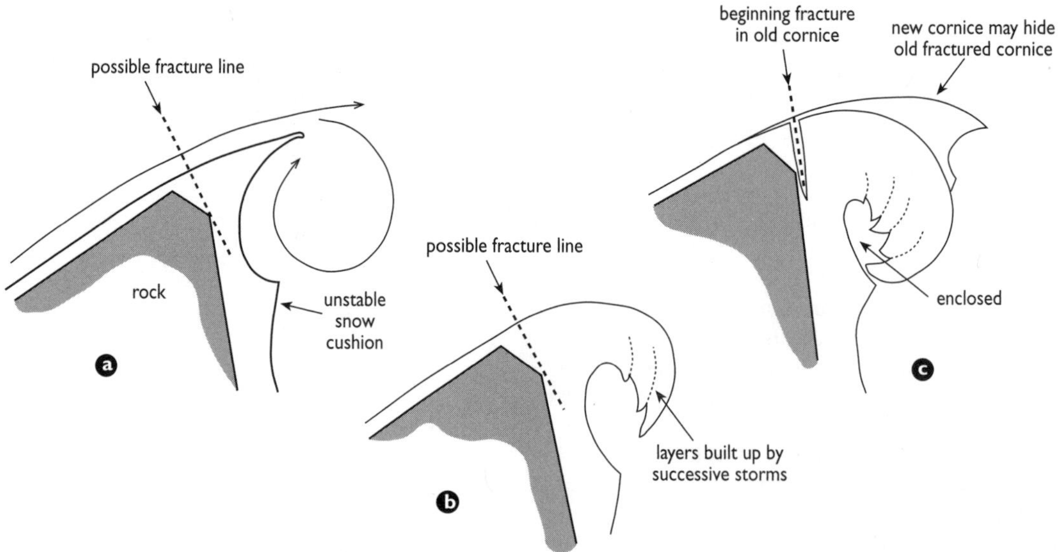

Fig. 26-3. Formation of cornices: a, wind blows snow into a cornice formation; b, successive storms build up layers; c, cornice becomes fully enclosed and a new cornice begins on top of the first.

Snow that falls during storms furnishes material for cornice formation. Cornices also are formed or enlarged by snow blown from snowfields that lie to the windward side of the ridge or feature (fig. 26-3b and c). As a general rule, cornices formed during snowstorms are softer than those produced by wind drift alone. Cornices present a particular hazard because they overhang, forming an unsupported, unstable mass that can break off due to natural causes or human disturbance. It is dangerous to walk on a cornice. In addition, falling cornices are dangerous to those below and also can set off avalanches.

AGING OF THE SNOW COVER

Snow that remains on the ground changes with time. The crystals undergo a process of change—metamorphism—that usually results in smaller, simpler forms and a snowpack that shrinks and settles. Metamorphism begins the moment that snow falls and lasts until it completely melts away. Because the snowpack continually changes over time, mountaineers find it useful to know the recent history of weather and snow conditions in an area, in order to calculate what the snow cover will be like.

One type of metamorphism, the equilibrium growth process, gradually converts the varied original forms of the snow crystals into old snow—homogeneous, rounded grains of ice (fig. 26-4). Both temperature and pressure affect the rate of change. When temperature within the snow is near the freezing point—32 degrees Fahrenheit (0 degrees Celsius)—change is rapid. The colder it gets, the slower the change; it virtually stops below minus 40 degrees Fahrenheit (minus 40 degrees Celsius). Pressure from the weight of new snowfall speeds changes within older layers. Snow that has reached old age—surviving at least one year and with all original snow crystals now converted into grains of ice—is called *firn* or *névé*. Any further changes to firn snow lead to formation of glacier ice.

Another type of metamorphism, the kinetic growth process, takes place when water vapor moves from one part of the snowpack to another by vapor diffusion, which deposits ice crystals that are different from those of the original snow. This kinetic growth produces faceted crystals (fig. 26-5). When the process is completed, the crystals often have a scroll or cup shape, appear to be layered, and may grow to considerable size—up to 1 inch (2.5 centimeters) or so. They form a fragile structure known as *depth hoar* that loses all strength when crushed and becomes very soft and weak when wet. This weak, unstable snow form is popularly referred to as "sugar snow" when dry and "rotten snow" when wet. The conditions necessary for its formation are a

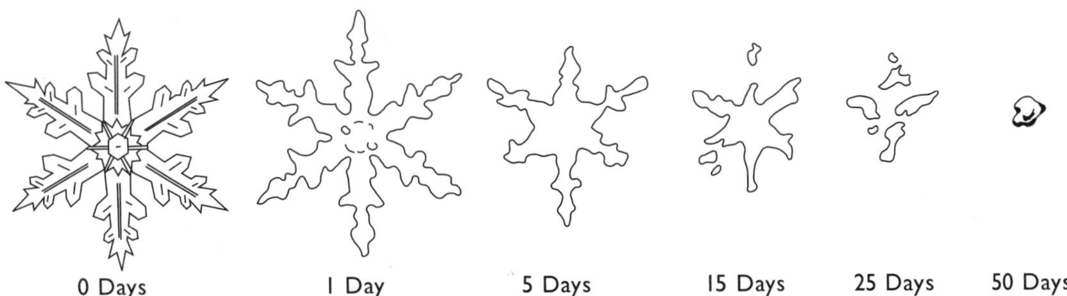

Fig. 26-4. Metamorphism of a snow crystal in the equilibrium growth process; days indicate time required for shapes to change under average temperature and pressure conditions in a typical seasonal snow cover.

large difference in temperature at different depths in the snow and sufficient air space so that water vapor can diffuse freely. The conditions are most common early in winter when the snowpack is shallow and unconsolidated.

In addition to undergoing metamorphic changes caused by variations in temperature and pressure, snow can age by mechanical means, such as wind. Snow particles broken by wind or other mechanical disturbances undergo a process known as age-hardening for several hours after they are disturbed. This age-hardening is the reason why it is easier to travel in snow if you follow tracks previously set by feet, skis, snowshoes, or snowmobiles.

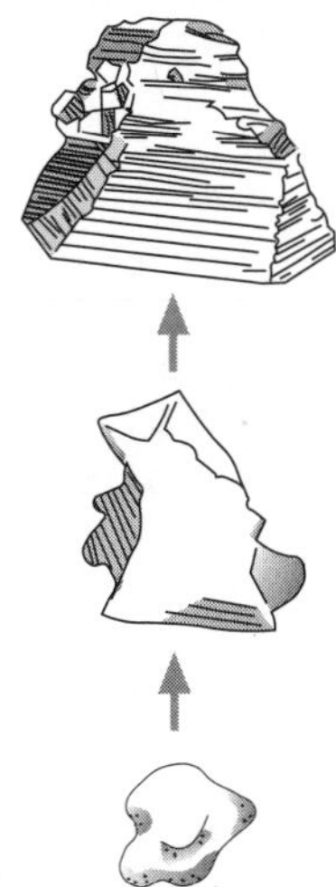

Fig. 26-5. Metamorphism of a snow crystal in the kinetic growth process results in a scroll or cup shape that appears layered and may become relatively large.

Snow's variations in strength are among the widest strength variations found in nature: New snow is about 90 percent air, and the individual, unconnected grains make it a fluffy, weak material that is easy to break apart. In contrast, wind-packed old snow may contain less than 30 percent air, with the small, broken particles forming strong interconnected bonds that can create layers 50,000 times harder than fluffy new snow. The variations between these two extremes and the continual changes in strength caused by changes in temperature, pressure, and wind make for highly variable conditions from place to place and hour to hour.

THE FORMATION OF GLACIERS

Glaciers form for a rather simple reason. Snow that does not melt or evaporate during the course of a year is carried over to the next winter. If snow continues to accumulate year after year, eventually consolidating and beginning a slow downhill movement, it has become a glacier.

Within the old snow—the firn or névé—the metamorphic conversion of snow crystals into grains of ice has been completed. Now the grains of ice are changed into glacier ice in a process called *firnification*. Firn turns into glacier ice when the air spaces between the grains become sealed off from each other so that the mass becomes airtight (fig. 26-6).

Each spring when the lower snow layers are still at temperatures below freezing, percolating meltwater refreezes when it reaches these lower layers. This refrozen meltwater forms ice layers within the firn. Therefore, by the time compaction and metamorphism have prepared an entire area of firn for conversion to glacier ice, the firn may already contain irregular bodies of ice.

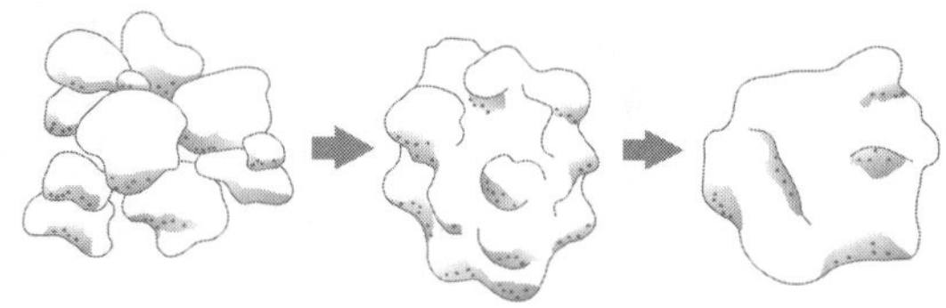

Fig. 26-6. Rounded snow grains that are pressed and squeezed together form a large glacier ice crystal.

Once glacier ice has formed, metamorphism does not cease. Some of the ice grains continue to grow at the expense of their neighbors, and the average size of the ice crystals increases with age (fig. 26-7). Large glaciers, in which the ice takes centuries to reach the glacier's foot, may produce crystals more than 12 inches (30 centimeters) in diameter, gigantic specimens grown from minute snow particles.

To understand how a simple, valley-type alpine glacier is born, picture a mountain in the northern hemisphere that has no glaciers. Now suppose climatic changes occur that cause snow to persist from year to year in a sheltered spot with northern exposure. From the beginning, snow starts to flow toward the valley in the very slow motion called *creep*. New layers are added each year, the patch of firn snow grows deeper and bigger, and the amount of snow in motion increases. The creeping

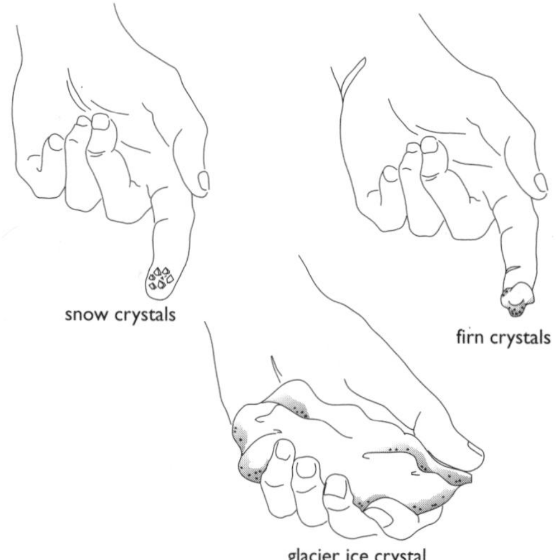

Fig. 26-7. Ice crystals increase greatly in size as they transform from snowflakes and firn into glacier ice.

snow, while melting and refreezing, dislodges soil and rock, and the flow of water around and under the snow patch additionally influences the surroundings. This small-scale process of erosion eventually leads to formation of a hollow where the winter snows are deposited in deeper drifts. After the snow deepens beyond 100 feet (30 meters) or so, the increasing pressure of the many upper layers of firn causes the lower layers to begin turning to glacier ice. A glacier is born.

With continued nourishment from heavy winter snows, the glacier flows toward the valley as a stream of ice. At some point in its descent, the glacier reaches an elevation low enough and warm enough that no new snow accumulates. The glacier ice begins to melt. Eventually the glacier reaches a point, even lower and warmer, at which all ice carried down from above melts each year. This is the lower limit of the glacier.

Glaciers vary from stagnant masses with little motion to vigorously flowing rivers of ice that transport large masses each year from higher to lower elevations. Glaciers in relatively temperate climates flow both by internal deformation and by sliding on their beds. Differences in speed within the glacier are somewhat like those in a river: fastest at the center and surface and slower at the sides and bottom where bedrock creates drag. Small polar glaciers present a striking difference in appearance from their temperate cousins, for they are frozen to their beds and can flow only by internal deformation. The polar glaciers look much like flowing molasses, whereas temperate glaciers are rivers of broken ice.

CREVASSES

Crevasses are important features of glaciers. Crevasses are fractures that occur when ice encounters a force greater than it can bear. Near the surface of a glacier, where ice is just beginning to form, the ice is full of tiny flaws and weakly bonded crystals. When it stretches or bends too fast, it can break apart in a brittle manner, like glass. The result is a crevasse.

Crevasses typically are 80 to 100 feet (25 to 30 meters) deep. At depths greater than that, ice layers become stronger, with increasingly large and well-bonded crystals. When stresses try to pull this deeply buried ice apart, overlying pressure further squeezes it together, causing it to flow and deform like thick, gooey honey. In colder glaciers—at high elevations or in polar climates—crevasses can penetrate somewhat deeper because colder ice is more brittle and tends to break more easily.

Temperate glaciers normally have more, and shallower, crevasses than polar glaciers because temperate glaciers usually move faster. When glaciers move very fast, such as over a very precipitous drop, icefall—extensive fracturing—occurs. The numerous crevasses link together, isolating columns of ice called seracs.

ICE AVALANCHES

Ice avalanches can pour from hanging glaciers, icefalls, and any serac-covered portion of a glacier. Ice avalanches are caused by a combination of glacier movement, temperature, and serac configuration. On warm, low-elevation glaciers, ice avalanches are most common during late summer and early fall when meltwater has accumulated enough to flow underneath the glacier and increase its movement. The avalanche activity of high-elevation glaciers and cold glaciers that are frozen to the bedrock has no such seasonal cycle.

Reports differ on what time of day ice avalanches are most active. Field observers suggest that they are most common during the afternoon. This may be possible in a snow-covered serac field if daytime heating loosens snow enough to avalanche into seracs and cause them to fall, creating an ice avalanche. However, scientists have discovered an increase in activity during the early morning hours when the ice is cold and most brittle. Ice avalanches can occur any time of year and any time of day or night.

THE FORMATION OF SNOW AVALANCHES

Numerous combinations of snow patterns cause avalanches. Every snowstorm deposits a new layer of snow. Even during the same storm, a different type of layer may be deposited each time the wind shifts or the temperature changes. After snow layers are deposited, their character is continually altered by the forces of wind, temperature, sun, and gravity. Each layer is composed of a set of snow crystals that are similar in shape to each other and that are bonded together in similar ways. Because each layer—each set of crystals—is different, each reacts differently to the various forces. Knowing something about these differences can help climbers understand and avoid avalanches.

Snow avalanches usually are categorized by their release mechanism: loose-snow avalanches start at a point; slab avalanches begin in blocks. Slab avalanches usually are much larger and involve deeper layers of snow. Loose-snow avalanches can be equally dangerous, however—especially if they are wet and heavy, if they catch victims who are above cliffs or crevasses, or if they trigger slab avalanches or serac falls.

LOOSE-SNOW AVALANCHES

Loose-snow avalanches can occur when new snow builds up on steep slopes and loses its ability to remain on the slope. The snow rolls off the slope, drawing more snow along as it descends. Sun and rain also can weaken the bonds between snow crystals, especially if they are newly deposited, causing individual grains to roll and slide into loose-snow avalanches. Skiing, glissading, and other human activities also can set off loose-snow avalanches by disturbing the snow. Loose-snow avalanches can easily sweep climbers into crevasses and over cliffs, destroy tents, and bury or carry away vital equipment.

SLAB AVALANCHES

Slab avalanches are more difficult to anticipate than loose-snow avalanches because they involve buried layers of snow that often cannot be detected from the surface. Usually a buried weak layer or weak interface is sandwiched between a slab layer and a bed layer or the ground (fig. 26-8). The buried weakness is disturbed in a way that causes it to reduce its frictional hold on the overlying slab.

Slab avalanches create an equal or greater amount of havoc to climbers than loose-snow avalanches. Not only can slab avalanches fling people and equipment off slopes or bury them, but the tremendous speed of a slab avalanche and the force of impact have been known to move entire buildings and transport objects and people hundreds of yards downslope. It is difficult to survive an avalanche that is hurtling downslope, and once a person is buried, the snow hardens, rapidly making it difficult to breathe and hampering rescue.

The Buried Weak Layer

Depth hoar and buried surface hoar (hoarfrost) are the most notorious weak layers. They can withstand a significant amount of vertical load but have little or no shear strength; that is, they slide easily along their horizontal interface. They may collapse like a house of cards, or their structure may give way like a row of dominoes. In

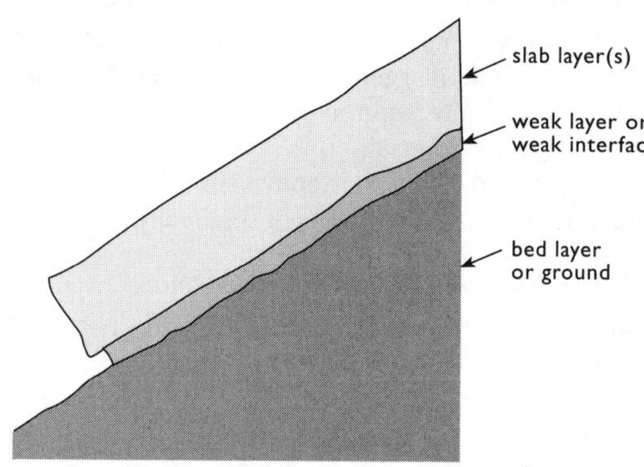

Fig. 26-8. Typical snow layering in a slab avalanche, with a weak layer between the slab and bed layers.

addition, depth hoar and buried surface hoar can survive weeks to months with little change in their fragile structure.

Surface hoar can form all across the snow cover, persisting most in shaded places that are protected from wind. Buried by subsequent snowfall, it becomes a weak layer that can promote avalanching. It becomes most dangerous if the first storm following hoarfrost formation begins with cool, calm conditions.

Depth hoar matures fastest in the shallow snow of early winter, when the ground is still warm and the air is cold (common in continental regions), but it can develop anytime or anyplace where there are large differences in temperature at different depths of snow. Weakness begins as soon as temperature and associated vapor-pressure differences cause molecules of water vapor to move onto facets of individual ice crystals instead of into bonds between crystals. This causes a loose, sugarlike collection of ice grains. Therefore, immature depth hoar (solid, faceted shapes) may be just as weak as mature depth hoar (open, cup, and scroll shapes).

Buried graupel (soft hail; see Figure 26-1g) is another classic weakness within the snowpack because it can act like ball bearings if disrupted. Other weaknesses that can make it easier for slabs to avalanche include plate-shaped crystals (see Figure 26-1a).

Buried weak layers may persist longer over glacier ice than over bare ground. The glacier reduces the amount of geothermal heating available to the snow from the ground, keeping temperatures somewhat cooler and slowing metamorphism. This means that buried weaknesses in seasonal snow underlain by glaciers can persist following storms and well into the summer long after adjacent snowy slopes have stabilized.

The Slab Layer

Once the underpinning of a snowpack is sufficiently weakened, the overlying snow (either a single layer or group of layers) begins to slide. If the overlying snow is cohesive enough to develop some tension as sliding begins—that is, if it sticks together enough to form a slab—it may break in long fractures that propagate across the slope. Lengthy fractures can result in large, heavy blocks that easily pull away from the rest of the slope, such as along the side and bottom of a slope where more stable snow may exist.

Slabs commonly are formed by brittle, wind-deposited snow layers. Wind often deposits snow in pillowlike patterns on the leeward side of ridges, thickest in the middle of the slope (where most of the weight of the slab, and thus the greatest avalanche danger, exists) and thinner on the edges. Wind slabs can maintain their blocky integrity throughout a slide, thrusting powerful masses downslope.

Slabs also are commonly formed by layers of needle-shaped crystals (see Figure 26-1d) deposited like a pile of pickup sticks, and by layers of branching crystals with many interlocking arms (see Figure 26-1b and e), which often pulverize immediately after release to form fast-moving powder avalanches.

Thick rain crusts often bridge over weakened surfaces and are rarely involved in avalanches until they begin to melt in spring. Sun crusts, on the other hand, usually are thinner and weaker than rain crusts and can be incorporated in a group of slab layers.

If the overlying snow is too warm or too wet compared to the underlying weakness, it may not break, instead just deforming slightly in response to the change in basal friction, and stay on the slope. However, if the underlying weak layer fails quickly and initial movement is significant, even this wet and pliable slab can avalanche. This scenario occurs commonly during spring when thick layers of old depth hoar are weakened by percolating meltwater. The resulting collapse of the depth hoar can cause a bending motion, like a whip, that overstresses the slab and causes it to fracture and slide. This whiplike effect also can occur in dry snow.

If the overlying snow is fragile and noncohesive—technically not a slab—the failure of a weak layer may simply result in snow grains in the overlying snow collapsing over each other but remaining in place. However, if the weak layer is buried surface hoar or slightly rounded branching or plate crystals, the failure can be so rapid that even the most fragile snow layers can turn into slab avalanches.

The Bed Layer

A bed layer provides the initial sliding surface of avalanches. Common bed layers are the smooth surfaces of old snow, meltwater crust, glaciers, bedrock, or grass. The interface of these smooth surfaces and the snow above can be further weakened if temperature changes promote the formation of depth hoar or if the interface is lubricated by meltwater or percolating rainwater. The bed layer also can be the collapsed fragments of old depth hoar.

AVALANCHE TRIGGERS

Humans are efficient trigger mechanisms for avalanches. Stomping snowshoers and ascending skiers, especially when executing kick turns, disturb layers of depth hoar or buried surface hoar. The sweeping turns and traversing motions of downhill skiers and snowboarders are effective at releasing loose-snow avalanches and fragile but fast-moving soft-slab avalanches. Skiers doing snowplow turns or sliding downhill, snowboarders, and glissaders may release wet loose-snow and wet slab avalanches. It is even possible to initiate an avalanche by traveling below a slope, especially if the buried weakness is surface or depth hoar, because a domino effect can occur as the delicate crystal structure collapses, propagating the failure uphill. The weight and vibration of snowmobiles can set off avalanches in places where nonmotorized travel would not.

Storms also trigger avalanches. Many types of buried layers (such as thin layers of slightly rounded branches and platelike crystals) fail when a force is applied evenly over a broad surface, as occurs when storms deposit layers of new snow. Earthquakes, cornice and serac falls, and other internal and external effects on the snow can cause avalanches at unpredictable times and places.

UNDERSTANDING THE CYCLE OF SNOW

Learning about the terrain and weather preceding a trip can help climbers anticipate snow conditions before leaving home. During a trip, understanding how wind, sun, and precipitation affect snow at different elevations and on different slope aspects will help determine choice of route and use of equipment.

Dense snow can provide good walking surfaces and sound bollards for rope belays, but if the snow is dense enough to have transformed to ice, then the walking can be slippery and carving bollards can be difficult. Fluffy new snow is fun for skiing downhill but makes uphill travel arduous and provides little or no support for belaying. Combinations of snow layering can promote avalanching.

The cycle of snow, from the first falling flake to glacier ice to meltwater, creates a dramatic and ever-evolving environment for climbers.

FORCES THAT CREATE WEATHER • THUNDER AND LIGHTNING • LOCALIZED WINDS • FIELD FORECASTING IN THE MOUNTAINS • FREEZING LEVEL AND SNOW LEVEL • CREATING CUSTOM WEATHER BRIEFINGS • APPLYING THE INFORMATION

Chapter 27 MOUNTAIN WEATHER

It is no accident that many of the world's grandest monuments and temples—the pyramids of Egypt and Mexico, for example—mimic mountains. Mountains exude massive strength and permanence, their summits frequently assailed by storms that the ancients believed were signals of divine presence and power. Approaching the summit of such a peak was an act thought to risk the disfavor of the gods.

Today most climbers believe that a disastrous encounter with severe weather is the result of insufficient respect for the elements or bad luck, rather than the work of an angry god. There is no question that a trip into the mountains can expose people to more dangerous weather than most other environments on Earth. Refuge can be harder to find, and major peaks can manufacture their own weather. Despite improvements in weather forecasting, knowledge of exactly how the atmosphere works, particularly in mountainous regions, is still incomplete. The wise climber not only carefully checks weather forecasts and reports before a trip but also develops an ability to assess the weather in the field.

FORCES THAT CREATE WEATHER

Understanding weather forecasts and reports requires a basic understanding of the forces that create weather. Such knowledge will not only help the mountaineer better digest such information before leaving home, it will also aid in detecting important changes on the trail or climbing route.

THE SUN

The sun does far more than simply illuminate planet Earth. It is the engine that drives the earth's atmosphere, providing the heat that, along with other factors, creates the temperature variations that are ultimately responsible for wind, rain, snow, thunder, and lightning—everything known as weather.

The key to the sun's impact is that the intensity of the sun's radiation varies across the earth's surface. Closer to the equator, the sun's heat is more intense. The extremes in temperature between the equator and the poles come as little surprise; those differences in air temperature also lead to air movement, which moderates those temperature extremes.

AIR MOVEMENT

The horizontal movement of air (what is called wind) is all too familiar to anyone who has pitched a tent in the mountains. However, air also rises and descends. When air cools, it becomes denser and sinks; the air pressure increases. But when air warms, it becomes less dense and rises; the air pressure decreases. These pressure differences, the result of temperature differences, produce moving air—called wind. Air generally moves from an area of high pressure to one of low pressure (fig. 27-1).

Air moving from high to low pressure carries moisture with it. As that air moves into the zone of lower pressure, then rises and then cools, the moisture condenses into clouds or fog. This occurs because, as the air cools, its capacity to hold water vapor is reduced. This is why you can "see" your breath when the air temperature becomes cold; the water vapor in your mouth condenses into liquid water droplets as you breathe out. The process of cooling and condensation operates on a large scale in the earth's atmosphere as air moves from high-pressure systems into low-pressure systems, where it rises.

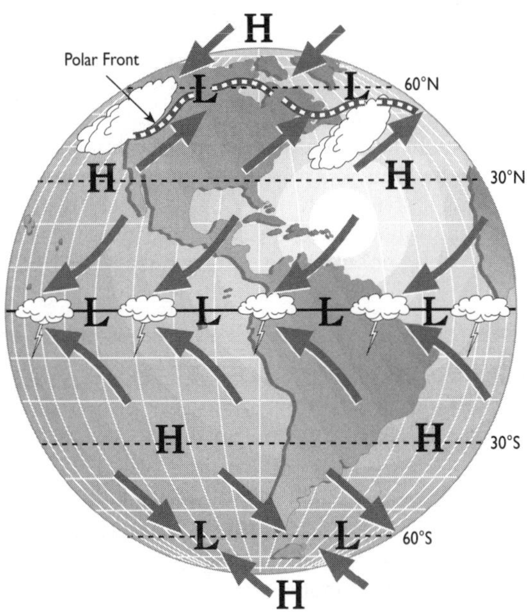

Fig. 27-1. The earth's air circulation patterns: movement from areas of high pressure at the poles toward areas of low pressure at the equator, deflected in the middle latitudes by the earth's rotation.

Because polar and arctic air is colder and therefore more dense than air farther south, it sinks. The zone where it sinks and piles up is a region of high pressure. As the air sinks and its pressure increases, its temperature warms a bit. The effect is similar to what happens to football or rugby players caught at the bottom of a pile: they get squeezed the most, and their temperature (and possibly temperament) heats up. In the atmosphere, this warming within a high-pressure area tends to evaporate some of the moisture present. That is why the Arctic receives very little precipitation. Although this sinking motion heats the air enough to evaporate much of the moisture present, it does not heat up enough to transform the poles into the tropics!

THE EARTH'S ROTATION

If the earth did not rotate, the cold polar air would just continue to slide southward to the equator. However, the air sinking and moving south from the poles and the air rising from the equator do not form a simple loop moving from north to south and back again. The rotation of the earth around its axis deflects this air. Some of the air rising from the equator descends over the subtropics, creating a region of high pressure. In turn, part of the air moving from these subtropical highs moves north into the air moving south from the poles. The boundary between these two very different air masses is called the polar front (see Figure 27-1). When this boundary does not move, it is called a stationary front. It often serves as a nursery for the development of storms.

COLD FRONTS AND WARM FRONTS

Because of the great contrast in temperatures across the polar front, together with imbalances caused by the rotation of the earth and differing influences of land, sea, ice, and mountains, some of the cold, dry air from the north slides south. That forces some of the warm air to rise. The zone where cold air is replacing warm air is

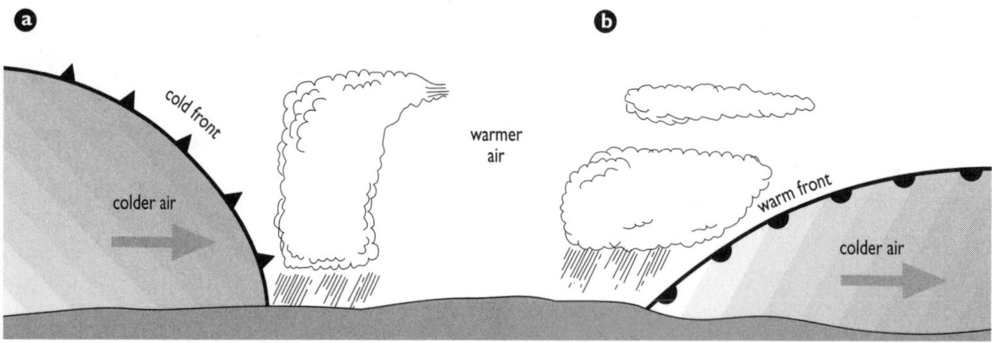

Fig. 27-2. Fronts: a, cold front displaces warmer air; b, warm front displaces colder air.

referred to as a cold front (fig. 27-2a), and the zone where warm air is gradually replacing cooler air is referred to as a warm front (fig. 27-2b); both types of fronts appear as a "wave" or bend on the stationary front. An occluded front combines characteristics of warm and cold fronts and is typically found near the center of a mature low-pressure system.

Both cold and warm fronts are marked by unique clouds, which help the mountaineer distinguish one type of front from the other. Clouds seen ahead of, along, or just behind a cold front include cumulus (fig. 27-3a), altocumulus (fig. 27-3b), cumulonimbus (fig. 27-3c), and stratocumulus (fig. 27-3d). These clouds are puffy, resembling cotton candy. The name cumulus refers to their "pile" or "heap" shape. Stratocumulus clouds are sheetlike layers of cumulus clouds; the name stratus refers to the "sheetlike" or "layered" characteristics of these clouds.

Clouds seen ahead of or along a warm front include a halo (fig. 27-3e), lenticular (fig. 27-3f), stratus (fig. 27-3g), cirrocumulus (fig. 27-3h), cirrostratus (fig. 27-3i), altostratus (fig. 27-3j), and nimbostratus (fig. 27-3k).

The "wave" or bend that develops along what started out as a stationary front may develop into a low-pressure system, with air circulating counterclockwise around the low (the opposite direction of air moving around a high)—again, a consequence of the earth's rotation and friction.

THUNDER AND LIGHTNING

Thunderstorms can be set off by the collision of different air masses when fronts move through, or by the rapid heating of air when it comes in contact with sun-warmed mountain slopes. Once this air is warmed, it becomes buoyant and tends to rise. If the atmosphere above is cold enough, the air tends to keep rising, producing what are called air-mass thunderstorms. A single lightning bolt can heat the surrounding air up to 50,000 degrees Fahrenheit (approximately 25,000 degrees Celsius). That heating causes the air to expand explosively, generating earsplitting thunder.

Thunderstorms in the mountains can and do kill (fig. 27-4)—and not just from lightning strikes, although lightning is the biggest killer, claiming an average of 200 lives in the United States alone each year. Lightning can also spark dangerous wildfires, and even a moderate thunderstorm may release up to 125 million gallons (473 million liters) of rainwater. The resulting flash floods can quickly inundate streambeds and small valleys, sweeping away entire campgrounds. The growing popularity of canyoneering, particularly

TIPS IF THUNDERSTORMS ARE FORECAST

- Obtain updated weather reports and forecasts before hitting the trail.
- Do not camp or climb in a narrow valley or gully.
- Do not climb or hike in high, exposed areas.
- Climb high early and descend by the afternoon.
- Watch small cumulus clouds for strong, upward growth; this may signal a developing thunderstorm.
- Watch for cumulus clouds changing from white to dark gray or black.

rappeling in deep slot canyons, increases climbers' exposure to flash floods and drowning. Thunderstorms can also produce winds of lethal intensity, capable of leveling entire stretches of forest.

By taking a few precautions, climbers can avoid most accidents caused by mountain thunderstorms (see the "Tips If Thunderstorms Are Forecast" sidebar). Begin by obtaining updated weather reports and forecasts before hitting the trail.

GAUGE THE MOVEMENT OF A THUNDERSTORM

How is it possible to gauge the movement of a thunderstorm? It is easy with a watch. Use the "flash to bang" principle. The moment lightning flashes, start counting the seconds. Stop timing once the bang of thunder is heard. Divide the number of seconds by five; the result is the thunderstorm's distance away in miles. Continue to time lightning and thunder discharges to judge whether the thunderstorm is approaching, remaining in one place, or receding. If the time interval between the lightning and thunder is decreasing, the thunderstorm is approaching; if the interval is increasing, it is moving away.

This technique works because the light from the lightning moves much faster than the sound from the thunder. Although the thunder occurs at virtually the same instant as the lightning, its sound travels only about 1 mile (1.6 kilometers) every five seconds, whereas the lightning flash, traveling at 186,000 miles (300,000 kilometers) per second, arrives essentially instantaneously. That is why the lightning is seen before the thunder is heard, unless the thunderstorm is very close—too close.

IF A THUNDERSTORM APPROACHES

If climbers are caught out in the open during a thunderstorm, they should try to seek shelter. Tents are poor protection: metal tent poles may function as lightning rods; stay away from poles and wet items inside the tent. Take the following precautions to avoid being struck by lightning.

- **Get away from water,** which readily conducts electricity.
- **Seek low ground** if the party is in an open valley or meadow.
- **Move immediately** if your hair stands on end.
- **Avoid standing on ridge tops,** at lookout structures, or near or under lone tall trees, especially isolated or diseased trees.
- **Look for a stand of even-sized trees** if in a wooded area.
- **Do not remain near or on rocky pinnacles or peaks.**
- **Do not remain near, touch, or wear metal or graphite equipment,** such as ice axes, crampons, climbing devices, and frame packs.
- **Insulate yourself from the ground** if possible. Place a soft pack or foam pad beneath you to protect against step-voltage transfer of the lightning strike through the ground—though ground currents may move through such insulation.
- **Crouch to minimize your profile,** and cover your head and ears.
- **Do not lie down**—lying down puts more of your body in contact with the ground, which can conduct more electrical current.

LOCALIZED WINDS

Understanding large-scale wind patterns, both at the earth's surface and in the upper atmosphere, is important for being able to gauge the weather. However, because mountains, by their very nature, alter wind considerably, understanding localized patterns is crucial to the mountaineer. It can mean the difference between successfully reaching the summit, being tent-bound, or getting blown off the mountain.

GAP WINDS

Winds are often channeled through gaps in the terrain, such as major passes or even between two peaks. Wind speeds can easily double as they move through such gaps (fig. 27-5).

Climbers can use this knowledge to their advantage. If possible, gauge the surface wind speeds upwind of a gap or pass before traveling into the vicinity of these terrain features. Knowing the upwind velocities can prepare a climber for gap winds that may be twice as strong. Avoid camping near the downwind portion of the gap, and consider selecting climbing routes not exposed to such winds. A major peak can block or slow winds for a few miles downwind.

VALLEY AND GRAVITY WINDS

Sparsely vegetated ground is typically found closer to ridges. Because it heats more rapidly than forest-covered

CLOUD TYPES SEEN AHEAD OF, ALONG, OR JUST BEHIND A COLD FRONT

a. **cumulus**—with continued upward growth, these suggest showers later in the day

b. **altocumulus**—high-based clouds often indicating potential for thunder, rain showers

c. **cumulonimbus**—cumulus producing rain, snow, or thunder and lightning

d. **stratocumulus**—lumpy, layered clouds often following a cold front, suggesting showers

CLOUD TYPES SEEN AHEAD OF OR ALONG A WARM FRONT

e. **halo**—commonly seen 24–48 hours ahead of precipitation

f. **lenticular**—lens-like clouds over mountains often suggesting precipitation within 48 hours

CLOUD TYPES SEEN AHEAD OF OR ALONG A WARM FRONT

g. stratus—layerlike clouds associated with widespread precipitation or ocean air

h. cirrocumulus

i. cirrostratus

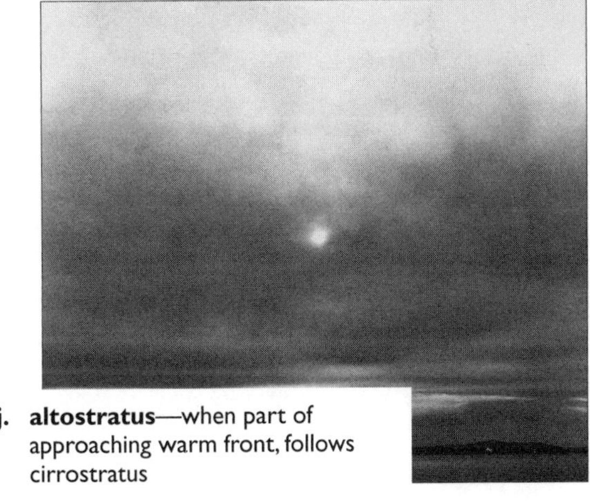

j. altostratus—when part of approaching warm front, follows cirrostratus

k. nimbostratus—stratus clouds producing widespread precipitation and low stability

Fig. 27-3. Identifying cloud types: a, b, c, and d, cloud types seen ahead of, along, or just behind a cold front; e, f, g, h, i, j, and k, cloud types seen ahead of or along a warm front.

land near valley floors, and because heated air rises, wind is generated that moves up either side of a valley, spilling over adjoining ridge tops. Such uphill breezes, called valley winds, can reach 10 to 15 miles (16 to 24 kilometers) per hour, attaining peak speed during the early afternoon and dying out shortly before sunset.

At night the land cools, and the cool air flows downslope in what is called a gravity wind. Such downslope breezes reach their maximum after midnight, dying out just before sunrise. Camping at the base of a cliff may result in an uncomfortably breezy evening. The more open the slopes between a campsite and the ridge above, the faster the winds will be.

FOEHN WINDS (CHINOOKS)

When winds descend a slope, air temperatures may increase dramatically in what is called a foehn wind or, in the western United States, a chinook. The air heats as it sinks and compresses on the leeward side of the crest, sometimes warming 30 degrees Fahrenheit (17 degrees

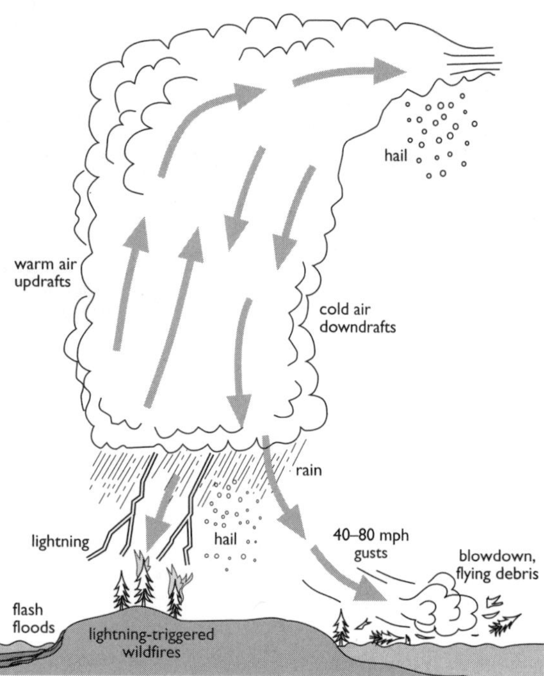

Fig. 27-4. Thunderstorm hazards include lightning, flash floods, and high winds.

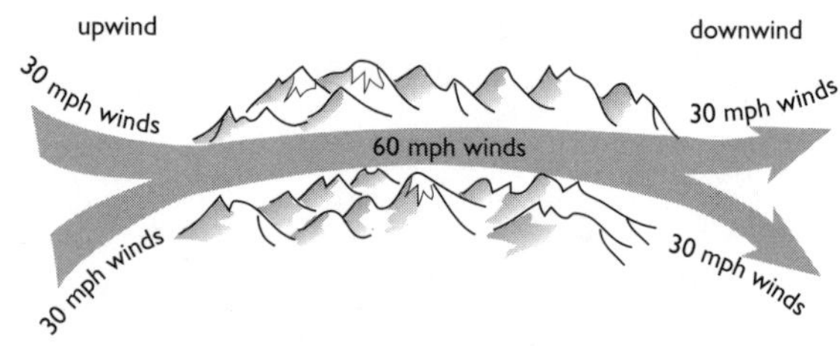

Fig. 27-5. Wind accelerates through gaps and passes.

Celsius) in minutes, melting as much as a foot of snow in a few hours (fig. 27-6). These winds are significant because of their potential speed, the rapid rise in air temperature associated with them, and the potential they create for both rapid melting of snow and flooding. Such winds can increase the risk of avalanches, weaken snow bridges, and lead to sudden rises in stream levels.

Warning signs make it possible to anticipate a potentially dangerous foehn wind or chinook. Expect such a wind, with temperatures warming as much as 6 degrees Fahrenheit per 1,000 feet (3 degrees Celsius per 300 meters) of descent, if these three conditions are met:

1. You are downwind of a major ridge or crest, primarily to the east of mountains.
2. Wind speeds across the crest or ridge exceed 30 miles (48 kilometers) per hour.
3. You observe precipitation above the crest.

BORA WINDS

The opposite of a chinook is a bora or, as it is called in Greenland, a *piteraq*. A bora is simply wind consisting of air so cold that its sinking, compressing motion as it flows downslope fails to warm it significantly. Such subzero winds are most common downslope of large

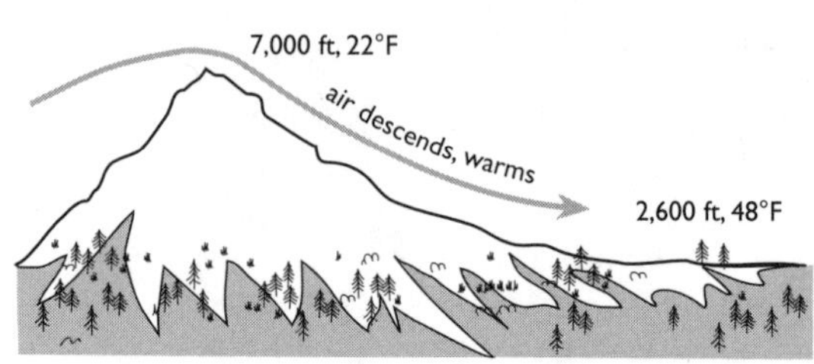

Fig. 27-6. Foehn winds (chinooks) descend and warm quickly.

TABLE 27-1. CLOUD-COVER CLUES (REFER TO FIGURE 27-3)

If	Then	Check for
High cirrus clouds, halo around sun or moon	Precipitation possible within 24–48 hours	Lowering, thickening clouds
High cirrus clouds forming tight ring or corona around sun or moon	Precipitation possible within 24 hours	Lowering, thickening clouds
"Cap" or lenticular clouds forming over peaks	Precipitation possible within 24 to more than 48 hours; strong winds possible near summits or leeward slopes	Lowering, thickening clouds
Thickening, lowering, layered flat clouds	Warm or occluded front likely within 12–24 hours	Wind shifts; pressure drops
Breaks in cloud cover closing up	Cold front likely within 12 hours	Wind shifts; pressure drops

TABLE 27-2. AIR PRESSURE AND/OR ALTIMETER CHANGE OVER 3 HOURS

Pressure Decrease	Altimeter Increase	Advised Action
0.02–0.04 inch (0.6–1.2 millibars)	20–40 feet (6–12 meters)	None. Continue to monitor.
0.04–0.06 inch (1.2–1.8 millibars)	40–60 feet (12–18 meters)	Clouds lowering hourly or thickening? If so, begin checking pressure changes hourly.
0.06–0.08 inch (1.8-2.4 millibars)	60–80 feet (18–24 meters)	Winds ranging from 18 to 33 knots (21 to 38 miles per hour) are likely. Consider less-exposed locations; continue monitoring conditions.
More than 0.08 inch (more than 2.4 millibars)	More than 80 feet (more than 24 meters)	Winds of 34 knots (40 miles per hour) or greater are likely. Immediate movement to protected area advised.

TABLE 27-3. WIND DIRECTION AND SPEED CLUES (NORTHERN HEMISPHERE)

If	And If	Then
Winds shift to E or SE	Air pressure drops; low-pressure system approaching	Clouds lower, thicken; precipitation possible
Winds shift from SW to NW	Air pressure rises	Drying and clearing likely; showers on windward slopes, especially along the U.S. or Canadian west coast
Increasing winds from E to SE	Continued air pressure drop; low-pressure system approaching	Winds likely to increase
Winds shift from SW to W	Air pressure rises; high-pressure system approaching	Showers possible along windward slopes, especially along U.S. or Canadian west coast

glaciers. Their speeds can easily exceed 50 miles (80 kilometers) per hour. A bora can blow away tents, throw climbers off balance, lower the windchill to dangerous levels (see Appendix B, Windchill Temperature Index), and obscure visibility by blowing snow.

FIELD FORECASTING IN THE MOUNTAINS

The process of gathering and evaluating weather data should not end at the trailhead or at the beginning of the climbing route. Changes in weather—which can cause weather-related accidents in the mountains—rarely occur without warning. At times the clues can be subtle, and sometimes they are as broad as daylight (see the "Major Indicators of an Approaching Storm" sidebar).

No single one of the four factors shown in the sidebar will tell you all you need to know; examine each carefully. The rest of this section gives some guidelines for evaluating these elements, which can enhance the weather reports and forecasts obtained before leaving home. For changes in cloud cover, see Table 27-1; for changes in wind direction and speed, see Table 27-3.

AIR-PRESSURE CLUES

A barometer or barometer-altimeter can give excellent warning of an approaching weather system. A barometer measures air pressure directly; a barometer-altimeter measures air pressure and reports elevation. A decrease in air pressure shows on an altimeter as an increase in elevation even when there has not been a change in elevation; an increase in air pressure shows on an altimeter as a decrease in elevation, again, even when there has not been a change in elevation. (See "The Altimeter" in Chapter 5, Navigation.)

Table 27-2 evaluates a developing low-pressure system, but rapidly building high pressure also can have its troublesome effects: principally, strong winds.

FREEZING LEVEL AND SNOW LEVEL

It can be useful to estimate the freezing level and snow level. Such estimates are subject to error because they are based on the average decrease in temperature as altitude increases: 3.5 degrees Fahrenheit per 1,000 feet (2 degrees Celsius per 304 meters) of elevation gain. Still, such estimates are usually better than the alternative: no estimate.

Once the freezing level has been estimated, use the guidelines in Table 27-4 to estimate the snow level.

MAJOR INDICATORS OF AN APPROACHING STORM

- Changes in cloud cover
- Changes in air pressure
- Changes in wind direction
- Changes in wind speed

CREATING CUSTOM WEATHER BRIEFINGS

Consider gathering weather information at least one day, and preferably two days, before a planned departure. That gives the party a chance to verify the forecasts by observing conditions. If the forecasts are pretty close to what is actually seen, proceed with planning with more confidence than if the forecast and observed weather conditions are 180 degrees apart.

TWO DAYS BEFORE THE TRIP

- **Check the overall weather pattern:** the positions of highs, lows, and fronts.
- **Check the projected weather forecast** for the next two days.

ONE DAY BEFORE THE TRIP

- **Check the current weather** to evaluate the accuracy of the previous day's forecasts.
- **Check the overall weather pattern again:** the positions of highs, lows, and fronts.
- **Check the projected weather** for the next two days.
- **Check for updates every six to eight hours** if the possibility of strong winds, thunderstorms, or significant snow or rain is mentioned. The lead time on such forecasts is short because of the rapid changes that sometimes occur.

ON THE FIRST DAY OF THE TRIP

- **Check the current weather** to evaluate the accuracy of the previous day's forecasts.

ESTIMATING THE FREEZING LEVEL

To estimate the elevation at which the temperature drops to 32 degrees Fahrenheit, climbers simply need to know their elevation and the temperature in degrees Fahrenheit:

$$\text{your elevation in feet} + \frac{(\text{Fahrenheit temperature} - 32) \times 1{,}000}{3.5} = \text{estimated freezing level}$$

For example:

$$1{,}000 \text{ feet elevation} + \frac{(39 \text{ degrees F} - 32) \times 1{,}000}{3.5} = 1{,}000 \text{ feet} + \frac{7{,}000}{3.5} = 1{,}000 \text{ feet} + 2{,}000 = 3{,}000 \text{ feet}$$

To estimate the elevation at which the temperature drops to 0 degrees Celsius, climbers simply need to know their elevation and the temperature in degrees Celsius:

$$\text{your elevation in meters} + \frac{(\text{camp temperature degrees Celsius}) \times 304}{2} = \text{estimated freezing level}$$

TABLE 27-4. ESTIMATING THE SNOW LEVEL

If	And If	Then
Stratus clouds or fog present	Steady, widespread precipitation	Expect to find the snow level 1,000 feet (304 meters) below the freezing level
Cumulus clouds present or a cold front is approaching	Locally heavy precipitation	Expect to find the snow level as much as 2,000 feet (608 meters) below the freezing level; snow will stick 1,000 feet (304 meters) below the freezing level

- **Check the projected weather** for the trip's duration.
- **Make a go or no-go decision** based on current forecasts, the track record of earlier forecasts, personal experience, and the demands of the trip.

APPLYING THE INFORMATION

Mountaineers have a rich supply of weather information sources available to them before they depart on a trip. Although information by itself is of limited use, information gathered with a purpose is of great value. That begins with the vital step of obtaining current forecasts for the locale of the climb, followed by careful observation during the outing. Continue to analyze changes in cloud cover, pressure, and wind speed and direction. Consider all such weather information thoroughly when selecting approach and climbing routes, camp locations, and start and turnaround times. Constant awareness of the environment and its impact on the party's plans will create a greater margin of safety during your pursuit of the freedom of the hills.

APPENDIX A
RATING SYSTEMS

A rating system is a tool that helps a climber choose a climb that is both challenging and within his or her ability. In some circumstances, a rating will indicate the amount and type of equipment needed.

The development of rating systems for climbing began in the late 19th and early 20th centuries in Britain and Germany. In the 1920s, Willo Welzenbach created a rating system, using roman numerals and the British adjectival system, to compare and describe routes in the Alps. This system was used as the basis of the Union Internationale des Associations d'Alpinisme (UIAA) system of rating. Rating systems have since proliferated. Ratings used internationally today include no fewer than seven systems for rock, four for alpine climbing, four for ice, and two for aid climbing.

Rating climbs is a subjective task, which makes consistency between climbing areas elusive. The rating of climbs assumes fair weather and availability of the best possible equipment. Variables that affect the rating include the size, strength, and flexibility of the climber, as well as the type of climb (for instance, face, crack, or friction climbing).

Ideally, a route is rated by consensus in order to reduce personal bias, though climbs often are rated by the first-ascent party. A guidebook author typically does not climb every route in the guidebook and therefore has to rely on the opinions of others. In some cases, a route may have been completed only once.

Ratings described as "stiff" indicate that the climb is harder than it is rated, whereas a description of a "soft" rating indicates the climb is easier than it is rated. Of course, evaluation of a rating system is no more precise than the rating system itself. Whenever you climb in an area for the first time, it's a good idea to start out on recommended or "starred" routes at a level lower than your usual ability until you can evaluate the local ratings and the nature of the rock.

ALPINE CLIMBING

The National Climbing Classification System (NCCS), developed in the United States, assigns grades to describe the overall difficulty of a multipitch alpine climb or long rock climb in terms of time and technical rock difficulty. It takes the following factors into account: length of climb, number of difficult pitches, difficulty of hardest pitch, average pitch difficulty, commitment, routefinding problems, and ascent time. The approach and remoteness of a climb might or might not affect the grade given, depending on the guidebook and area. It should be emphasized that with increasing grade, an increasing level of psychological preparation and commitment is necessary. This system assumes a party that is competent for the expected level of climbing.

GRADE I. Normally requires several hours; can be of any technical difficulty.

GRADE II. Requires half a day; any technical difficulty.

GRADE III. Requires a day to do the technical portion; any technical difficulty.

GRADE IV. Requires a full day for the technical portion; the hardest pitch is usually no less than 5.7 (in the Yosemite Decimal System for rating rock climbs; see below).

GRADE V. Requires a day and a half; the hardest pitch is at least 5.8.

GRADE VI. A multiday excursion with difficult free climbing and/or aid climbing.

Like other rating systems, the grade is subjective. For example, the Nose on El Capitan in California's Yosemite National Park is rated Grade VI. Warren Harding and companions took 45 days for the first ascent, in 1958. John Long, Billy Westbay, and Jim Bridwell made the first one-day ascent in 1975. Hans Florine and Peter Croft cut the time to under four and a half hours in 1992, and Lynn Hill (accompanied by a belayer) led the first free ascent in 1993 and the first one-day free ascent in 1994. The time needed for a climb is as relative as the abilities and technologies of the climbers. The type of climb affects what factors of the given grade are emphasized. Proper planning, including study of a route description, are more valuable in estimating a party's climbing time than the given grade.

ROCK CLIMBING

Rating systems have been created for free climbing, aid climbing, and bouldering.

FREE CLIMBING

In 1937, a modified Welzenbach rating system was introduced in the United States as the Sierra Club System. In the 1950s, this system was modified to more accurately describe rock climbing being done at Tahquitz Rock in California by adding a decimal to the Class 5 rating. This is now known as the Yosemite Decimal System (YDS). This system categorizes terrain according to the techniques and physical difficulties encountered when rock climbing. Figure A-1 compares the YDS with other international rating systems.

CLASS 1. Hiking.

CLASS 2. Simple scrambling, with possible occasional use of the hands.

CLASS 3. Scrambling; hands are used for balance; a rope might be carried.

CLASS 4. Simple climbing, often with exposure. A rope is often used. A fall could be fatal. Typically, natural protection can be easily found.

CLASS 5. Where rock climbing begins in earnest. Climbing involves the use of a rope, belaying, and protection (natural or artificial) to protect the leader from a long fall.

The decimal extension of Class 5 climbing originally was meant to be a closed-end scale; that is, ranging from 5.0 to 5.9. Up until 1960 or so, a climb that was the hardest of that era would be rated 5.9. The rising standards in the 1960s, however, led to a need for an open-ended scale. Strict decimal protocol was abandoned, and 5.10 (pronounced "five-ten") was adopted as the next highest level. As the open-ended system let the decimal numbers go up to 5.11, 5.12, and ever higher, not all climbs were rerated, leaving a disparity between the "old-school ratings" and the new ratings.

The YDS numbers reached 5.15 in the first few years of the 21st century. The ratings from 5.10 to 5.15 are subdivided into a, b, c, and d levels to more precisely state the difficulty. The most difficult 5.12 climb, for instance, is rated 5.12d. A plus sign or a minus sign is occasionally used as a more approximate way to refine a classification. Sometimes a plus sign will be added to indicate that the pitch is sustained at its particular rating, while a minus sign might indicate that the pitch has only a single move at that level.

The extended numbers of the fifth-class rating system can't be defined precisely, but the following descriptions offer general guidelines:

5.0–5.7. Easy for experienced climbers; where most novices begin.

5.8–5.9. Where most weekend climbers become comfortable; employs the specific skills of rock climbing, such as jamming, liebacks, and mantels.

5.10–5-11. A committed recreational climber can reach this level.

5.12–5.15. The realm of true experts; demands much training and natural ability, as well as, often, repeated working of a route.

The YDS rates only the hardest move on a pitch and, for multipitch climbs, the hardest pitch on a climb. The YDS gives no indication of overall difficulty, protection, exposure, run-out, or strenuousness. Some guidebooks, however, will rate a pitch higher than the hardest move if the pitch is very sustained at a lower level. A guidebook's introduction should explain any variations on the YDS that may be used.

Because the YDS does not calculate the potential of a fall, but only the difficulty of a move or pitch, a seriousness rating has been developed. This seriousness rating (introduced by James Erickson in 1980) appears in guidebooks in a variety of forms; read the introduction to any guidebook for an explanation of its particular version.

PG-13. Protection is adequate, and if it is properly placed, a fall would not be long.

R. Protection is considered inadequate; there is potential for a long fall, and a falling leader would take a real "whipper," suffering serious injuries.

X. Inadequate or no protection; a fall would be very long with serious, perhaps fatal, consequences.

Ratings of the quality of routes are common in guidebooks. If anything, they are even more subjective than the basic climb ratings because they attempt to indicate aesthetics. The number of stars given for a route indicates the quality of the route in the eyes of the guidebook writer. A standard number of stars for the very

UIAA	FRENCH	YOSEMITE DECIMAL SYSTEM	AUSTRALIAN	BRAZILIAN	UNITED KINGDOM
I	1	5.2			3a, VD
II	2	5.3	11		3b
III	3	5.4	12	II	3c, HVD, MS
IV	4	5.5		IIsup	4a, S, HS
V-	5	5.6	13	III	4b
V		5.7	14	IIIsup	VS
V+			15		4c
VI-		5.8	16	IV	HVS
VI	6a	5.9	17, 18	IVsup	5a, E1
VI+	6a+	5.10a	19	V	5b
VII-	6b	5.10b, 5.10c	20	Vsup, VI	E2
VII	6b+	5.10d	21, 22	VIsup	5c, E3
VII+	6c, 6c+	5.11a, 5.11b	23	7a	6a
VIII-	7a	5.11c	24	7b	E4
VIII	7a+, 7b	5.11d, 5.12a	25	7c, 8a	6b, E5
VIII+	7b+	5.12b	26	8b	6c
IX-	7c	5.12c, 5.12d	27	8c, 9a	E6
IX	7c+	5.13a	28	9b	
IX+	8a	5.13b	29	9c	
X-	8a+	5.13c	30, 31	10a	7a, E7
X	8b, 8b+	5.13d	32	10b	E8
X+	8c	5.14a	33	10c	
XI-	8c+	5.14b		11a	7b
XI	9a	5.14c, 5.14d	34, 35	11b, 11c	E9
XI+	9a+	5.15a	36	12a	
XII-	9b	5.15b	37	12b	7c
XII	9b+	5.15c	38	12c	

Fig. A-1. Six of the world's seventeen climbing rating systems.

best climbs has not been established. A climb with no stars does not mean the climb isn't worth doing, nor does a star-spangled listing mean that everyone will like the route.

AID CLIMBING

Rating aid moves or aid climbs is different from rating free climbs in that the rating system is not open-ended like the YDS. An aid climbing rating primarily indicates the severity of a possible fall, based on the quality of protection available. To some extent, an aid rating indicates the difficulty of the climbing, but only in that there is a loose correlation between easy-to-place protection and its ability to arrest a fall. However, following a series of "easy" hook moves for a distance of 40 feet (12 meters) with no protection left to arrest a fall might garner a rating of A3, while conversely some A1 pitches might accommodate high-quality protection at regular intervals but could be extremely difficult to climb if the crack is a deep, awkward flare with protection available only at its very back.

The scale is from A0 to A5 or from C0 to C5. The "A" refers to aid climbs in general, which may utilize pitons, bolts, or chocks. The "C" refers to clean aid climbing, meaning that a hammer is not used to make placements. A rating such as C2F, with the "F" indicating "fixed," indicates that the pitch can be climbed clean only if critical gear normally placed with a hammer has been left in place by other parties. It is sometimes possible to climb a pitch clean that is rated with the A0–A5 system, and some pitches have two ratings, one A rating and one C rating, which indicates the grade with or without a hammer.

The following rating system is used worldwide except in Australia (which uses M0 to M8; the "M" stands for mechanical):

A0 or C0. No aiders are required. Fixed gear such as bolts may be in place, or the climber may be able to simply pull on a piece of gear to get through the section, a technique sometimes called "French free."

A1 or C1. Good aid placements; virtually every placement is capable of holding a fall. Aiders are generally required.

A2 or C2. Placements are fairly good but may be tricky to place. There may be a couple of bad placements between good placements.

A2+ or C2+. Same as A2, though with increased fall potential—perhaps 20 to 30 feet (6 to 10 meters).

A3 or C3. Hard aid. Several hours to lead a pitch, with the potential of 60- to 80-foot (18- to 24-meter) falls, but without danger of grounding (hitting the ground) or serious injury.

A3+ or C3+. Same as A3, but with the potential of serious injury in a fall. Tenuous placements.

A4 or C4. Serious aid. Fall potential of 80 to 100 feet (24 to 30 meters), with very bad landings. Placements hold only body weight.

A4+ or C4+. More serious than A4. More time on the route, with increased danger.

A5 or C5. Placements hold only body weight for an entire pitch, with no solid protection such as bolts. A leader fall at the top of a 150-foot (45-meter) A5 pitch means a 300-foot (90-meter) fall or a fall that would cause a serious impact on a rock feature, the latter of which may be equivalent to hitting the ground.

A5+. A theoretical grade; A5, but with bad belay anchors. A fall means falling to the ground (anchor failure).

Aid ratings are always subject to change. What was once a difficult A4 seam may have been beaten out with pitons to the point that it will accept large chocks, rendering it C1. Camming devices and other examples of newer technology can sometimes turn difficult climbs into easy ones. Some climbs once considered A5 might now be rated A2 or A3 after repeated traffic and with the use of modern equipment.

Big wall climbs are rated like this:

The Nose, El Capitan: VI, 5.8, C2

This means that the Nose route on Yosemite's El Capitan is a Grade VI (a "multiday excursion"); the most difficult moves that you must free-climb (with no option to aid) are YDS 5.8; and the most difficult aid is C2.

BOULDERING

Bouldering—climbing on large rocks, fairly close to the ground—has gained popularity. Though once a game played by alpinists in mountain boots on days too rainy for climbing, bouldering has become an all-out pursuit of its own. John Gill created his B-scale to rate boulder problems:

B1. Requires moves at a high level of skill—moves that would be rated 5.12 or 5.13.

B2. Moves as hard as the hardest climbs being done in standard rock climbing (5.15 currently).

B3. A successful B2 climb that has yet to be repeated.

Once repeated, the boulder rating automatically drops to B2.

John Sherman created the open-ended V-scale, which gives permanent ratings to boulder problems (unlike Gill's scale, with its floating ratings). As shown in Figure A-2, Sherman's scale starts at V0– (comparable to 5.8 YDS); it moves up through V0, V0+, V1, V2, and so on, with V16 being comparable to 5.15c YDS. Neither the B- nor V-scale takes into account the consequences of a rough landing on uneven terrain.

YOSEMITE DECIMAL SYSTEM	SHERMAN V-SCALE (BOULDERING)
5.8	V0-
5.9	V0
5.10a–b	V0+
5.10c–d	V1
5.11a–b	V2
5.11c–d	V3
5.12-	V4
5.12	V5
5.12+	V6
5.13-	V7
5.13	V8
5.13+	V9
5.14a	V10
5.14b	V11
5.14c	V12
5.14d	V13
5.15a	V14
5.15b	V15
5.15c	V16

Fig. A-2. The Sherman V-scale for rating boulder problems, compared with the Yosemite Decimal System for rating rock climbs.

ICE CLIMBING

The variable conditions of snow and ice climbing make rating those climbs difficult. The only factors that usually do not vary throughout the season and from year to year are length and steepness. Snow depth, ice thickness, and temperature affect the conditions of the route; these factors plus the nature of the ice and its protection possibilities determine a route's difficulty. These rating systems apply mainly to waterfall ice and other ice formed by meltwater (rather than from consolidating snow, as on glaciers).

COMMITMENT RATING

The important factors in this ice climbing rating system are length of the approach and descent, the length of the climb itself, objective hazards, and the nature of the climbing. (The roman numeral ratings used in this system have no correlation to the numerals used in the grading system for alpine climbs.)

- **I.** A short, easy climb near the road, with no avalanche hazard and a straightforward descent.
- **II.** A route of one or two pitches within a short distance of rescue assistance, with very little objective hazard.
- **III.** A multipitch route at low elevation, or a one-pitch climb with an approach that takes an hour or so. The route requires from a few hours to a long day to complete. Descent may require building rappel anchors, and the route might be prone to avalanche.
- **IV.** A multipitch route at higher elevations; may require several hours of approach on skis or foot. Subject to objective hazards; possibly with a hazardous descent.
- **V.** A long climb in a remote setting, requiring all day to complete the climb itself. Requires many rappels off anchors for the descent. Sustained exposure to avalanche or other objective hazard.
- **VI.** A long ice climb in an alpine setting, with sustained technical climbing. Only elite climbers will complete it in a day. A difficult and involved approach and descent, with objective hazards ever-present, all in a remote area far from the road.

VII. Everything a grade VI has, and more of it. Possibly requires days to approach the climb, and objective hazards render survival as certain as a coin toss. Needless to say, difficult physically and mentally.

TECHNICAL RATING

The technical grade rates the single most difficult pitch, taking into account the sustained nature of the climbing, ice thickness, and natural ice features such as chandeliers, mushrooms, or overhanging bulges. These ratings have been further subdivided, with a plus added to grades of 4 and above if the route is usually more difficult than its stated numerical grade.

1. A frozen lake or streambed (the equivalent of an ice rink).
2. A pitch with short sections of ice up to 80 degrees; lots of opportunity for protection and good anchors.
3. Sustained ice up to 80 degrees; the ice is usually good, with places to rest, but it requires skill at placing protection and setting anchors.
4. A sustained pitch that is vertical or slightly less than vertical; may have special features such as chandeliers and runouts between protection.
5. A long, strenuous pitch—possibly 165 feet (50 meters) of 85- to 90-degree ice with few if any rests between anchors. Or the pitch may be shorter but on featureless ice. Good skills at placing protection are required.
6. A full 165-foot pitch of dead-vertical ice, possibly of poor quality; requires efficiency of movement and ability to place protection from awkward stances.
7. A full pitch of thin, vertical or overhanging ice of dubious adhesion. An extremely tough pitch, physically and mentally, requiring agility and creativity.
8. Thin, gymnastic, overhanging, and bold. Pure ice climbs at this level are extremely rare.

These ratings typically describe a route in its first-ascent condition. Therefore a route that was rated a 5 on its first ascent might be a 6– in a lean year for ice, but only a 4+ in a year with thick ice. The numerical ice ratings are often prefaced with WI (water ice, or frozen waterfalls), AI (alpine ice), or M (mixed rock and ice; historically, mixed climbs were described with the Yosemite Decimal System).

NEW ENGLAND ICE RATING SYSTEM

A system developed for the water ice found in New England applies to normal winter ascent of a route in moderate weather conditions:

NEI 1. Low-angle water ice of 40 to 50 degrees, or a long, moderate snow climb requiring a basic level of technical expertise for safety.

NEI 2. Low-angle water ice with short bulges up to 60 degrees.

NEI 3. Steeper water ice of 50 to 60 degrees, with bulges of 70 to 90 degrees.

NEI 4. Short vertical columns, interspersed with rests, on 50- to 60-degree ice; fairly sustained climbing.

NEI 5. Generally multipitch ice climbing with sustained difficulties and/or strenuous vertical columns, with little rest possible.

NEI 5+. Multipitch routes with a heightened degree of seriousness, long vertical sections, and extremely sustained difficulties; the hardest ice climbing in New England to date.

MIXED CLIMBING

Jeff Lowe introduced the Modern Mixed Climbing Grade to simplify the rating of the crux on mixed ice and rock routes. It is an open-ended scale with routes rated M1 to M13. A plus sign or a minus sign is added to broaden the range and to prevent grade compression. It is the consensus of top climbers that the M ratings in Europe are inflated by one grade. See Figure A-3 for a comparison of the M grades to YDS ratings.

OTHER MAJOR RATING SYSTEMS

A variety of rating systems are used throughout the world. Figure A-1 compares the principal systems. Apart from the main rating systems described here, other rating systems are used around the world, which are unique to their own treatment of seriousness and local weather and conditional phenomena. The Alaska Grade, for example, is a grading system unique to Alaska that takes into account severe storms, cold, altitude, and cornicing; it extends from Grade 1 to 6 (instead of overall commitment ratings I to VII).

When climbing in a new area, be sure to check with local authorities and/or guidebooks and become knowledgeable about any possible local grading systems and their peculiarities.

MODERN MIXED GRADE	YOSEMITE DECIMAL SYSTEM
M4	5.8
M5	5.9
M6	5.10
M7	5.11
M8	5.11+/5.12–
M9	5.12+/5.13–
M10	5.13+/5.14–
M11	5.14+/5.15–
M12	5.15
M13	5.15+

Fig. A-3. The Modern Mixed Climbing Grades for mixed rock and ice climbs, compared with the Yosemite Decimal System for rating rock climbs.

ROCK CLIMBING

Australian. The Australian system uses an open-ended number series. The Australian number 38, for example, is equivalent to 5.15c in the Yosemite Decimal System.

Brazilian. The rating of climbs in Brazil is composed of two parts. The first part gives the general level of difficulty of the route as a whole, ranging from first to eighth grade (or degree). The second part gives the difficulty of the hardest free move (or sequence of moves without a natural rest). Figure A-1 shows only the second part of the Brazilian system, the part that is most comparable to the other systems shown. The lower range is expressed in roman numerals; the designation "sup" (for superior) is added to refine the accuracy of the rating. The upper range is expressed in Arabic numerals with letter modifiers.

British. The British system is composed of two elements: an adjectival grade and a technical grade.

The adjectival grade—such as Very Difficult (VD) or Hard Severe (HS)—describes the overall difficulty of a route, including such factors as exposure, seriousness, strenuousness, protection, and runouts. The list of adjectives to describe increasingly difficult routes became so cumbersome that the British finally ended it at Extremely Severe (ES) and now simply advance the listing with numbers: E1 for Extremely Severe 1, E2 for Extremely Severe 2, and so forth:

E. Easy.
M. Moderate.
D. Difficult.
VD. Very difficult.
HVD. Hard very difficult.
MS. Mild severe.
S. Severe.
HS. Hard severe.
VS. Very severe.
HVS. Hard very severe.
ES. Extremely severe.
E1. Extremely severe 1.
E2. Extremely severe 2.
E3. Extremely severe 3.

The technical grade is defined as the hardest move on a particular route. This numeric component of the British system is also open-ended and is subdivided into a, b, and c.

The two grades are linked to each other. For example, the standard adjectival grade for a well-protected 6a, which is not particularly sustained, is E3 (and the combined rating would be expressed as E3 6a). If the route is a bit run-out, it would be E4; if it is really run-out, it would be E5. See Figure A-1.

French. In the French open-ended system, ratings of 6 and above are subdivided into a, a+, b, b+, c, and c+. The French rating of 9b+ is comparable to 5.15c in the Yosemite Decimal System.

UIAA. The UIAA open-ended rating system uses roman numerals. Beginning with the fifth level (V), the ratings also include pluses and minuses. The UIAA rating of XII is comparable to 5.15c in the YDS. German climbers use the UIAA system.

ALPINE CLIMBING AND ICE CLIMBING

The International French Adjectival System (IFAS) is an overall rating of alpine and ice climbs used primarily in the Alps. The system is used by several countries, including France, Britain, Germany, Italy, and Spain. It expresses the seriousness of the route, including factors such as length, objective danger, commitment, altitude, runouts, descent, and technical difficulty in terms of terrain.

The system has six categories that are symbolized by the initials of the French adjectives used. It is further refined with the use of plus or minus signs, or the terms "sup" (superior) or "inf" (inferior). The ratings end with an adjective readily understood in English:

- **F.** *Facile* ("easy"). Steep walking routes, rock scrambling, and easy snow slopes. Crevasses possible on glaciers. Rope not always necessary.
- **PD.** *Peu difficile* ("a little difficult"). Rock climbing with some technical difficulty, snow and ice slopes, serious glaciers, and narrow ridges.
- **AD.** *Assez difficile* ("fairly difficult"). Fairly hard climbs, steep rock climbing, and long snow and/or ice slopes steeper than 50 degrees.
- **D.** *Difficile* ("difficult"). Sustained hard rock and snow and/or ice climbing.
- **TD.** *Très difficile* ("very difficult"). Serious technical climbing on all kinds of terrain.
- **ED.** *Extrêmement difficile* ("extremely difficult"). Extremely serious climbs with long, sustained difficulties of the highest order.
- **ABO.** *Abominable.* Translation—and difficulty—obvious.

APPENDIX B
WINDCHILL TEMPERATURE INDEX

The windchill temperature index provides a measure of how wind can accelerate the rate of heat loss from exposed skin. The calculation of windchill is based on heat-transfer theory, and a model of a human face was used to derive this index.

The index defines "calm" as wind speed equal to or less than 3 miles per hour (5 kilometers per hour). As wind speed increases, it draws heat from exposed skin, speeding up relative cooling time. Therefore, the wind cools exposed skin at a faster rate than if there were no wind. For example, if the air temperature is minus 10 degrees Fahrenheit (minus 23 degrees Celsius) and the wind is blowing at 25 miles per hour (40 kilometers per hour), then the windchill temperature is minus 37 degrees Fahrenheit (minus 38 degrees Celsius), as shown in Figure B-1. At this temperature and at this wind speed, exposed skin can freeze in 10 minutes.

By definition the windchill temperature is lower than the air temperature, but windchill cannot cause skin temperature to go below the ambient air temperature. Windchill is of greater significance when the air temperature is relatively cool (that is, when there is risk of frostbite or hypothermia). Keep in mind that windchill affects only exposed skin. If a climber is properly dressed for the conditions of the mountain environment, then the windchill effect can be negated.

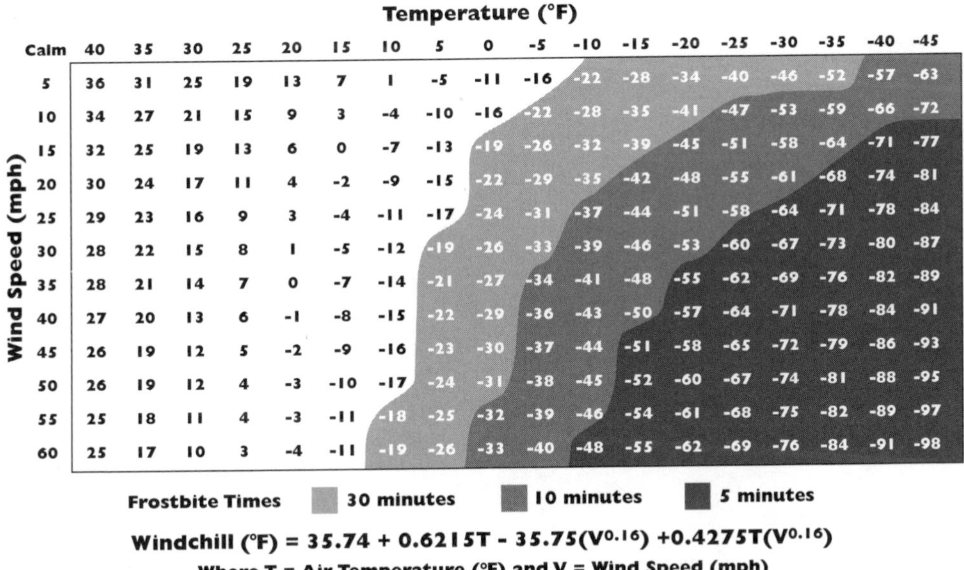

Temperature (°F)

Wind Speed (mph) / Calm	40	35	30	25	20	15	10	5	0	-5	-10	-15	-20	-25	-30	-35	-40	-45
5	36	31	25	19	13	7	1	-5	-11	-16	-22	-28	-34	-40	-46	-52	-57	-63
10	34	27	21	15	9	3	-4	-10	-16	-22	-28	-35	-41	-47	-53	-59	-66	-72
15	32	25	19	13	6	0	-7	-13	-19	-26	-32	-39	-45	-51	-58	-64	-71	-77
20	30	24	17	11	4	-2	-9	-15	-22	-29	-35	-42	-48	-55	-61	-68	-74	-81
25	29	23	16	9	3	-4	-11	-17	-24	-31	-37	-44	-51	-58	-64	-71	-78	-84
30	28	22	15	8	1	-5	-12	-19	-26	-33	-39	-46	-53	-60	-67	-73	-80	-87
35	28	21	14	7	0	-7	-14	-21	-27	-34	-41	-48	-55	-62	-69	-76	-82	-89
40	27	20	13	6	-1	-8	-15	-22	-29	-36	-43	-50	-57	-64	-71	-78	-84	-91
45	26	19	12	5	-2	-9	-16	-23	-30	-37	-44	-51	-58	-65	-72	-79	-86	-93
50	26	19	12	4	-3	-10	-17	-24	-31	-38	-45	-52	-60	-67	-74	-81	-88	-95
55	25	18	11	4	-3	-11	-18	-25	-32	-39	-46	-54	-61	-68	-75	-82	-89	-97
60	25	17	10	3	-4	-11	-19	-26	-33	-40	-48	-55	-62	-69	-76	-84	-91	-98

Frostbite Times: 30 minutes; 10 minutes; 5 minutes

$$\text{Windchill (°F)} = 35.74 + 0.6215T - 35.75(V^{0.16}) + 0.4275T(V^{0.16})$$

Where T = Air Temperature (°F) and V = Wind Speed (mph)

Fig. B-1. Windchill temperature index. (Source: National Oceanographic and Atmospheric Administration, National Weather Service)

APPENDIX C
HEAT INDEX

The evaporation of perspiration is one of the principal mechanisms for cooling the human body. Relative humidity affects the rate of evaporation. High humidity slows the rate of evaporation, inhibiting this cooling effect. The heat index in Figure C-1 provides a measure of the apparent temperature increase due to the effect of increasing humidity. For example, if the ambient air temperature is 90 degrees Fahrenheit (32 degrees Celsius), at a relative humidity of 40 percent, the perceived temperature will be 91 degrees Fahrenheit (33 degrees Celsius); at a relative humidity of 90 percent, the perceived temperature will be 122 degrees Fahrenheit (50 degrees Celsius).

High temperature combined with high humidity and strenuous exertion can lead to overheating. This can cause a range of problems, from the physical discomfort of heat cramps to heat exhaustion to heatstroke (see Chapter 23, First Aid).

(Opposite) Fig. C-1. Heat index: Find temperature on left and move to right to find what the temperature feels like at different percentages of relative humidity. Add up to 15 degrees Fahrenheit to this temperature if in direct sun. (Source: Lans Rothfusz, National Weather Service Central Region Headquarters, National Oceanographic and Atmospheric Administration)

HEAT INDEX °F (°C)													
The heat index is an accurate measurement of how hot it really feels when the effects of humidity are added to high temperature.													
	RELATIVE HUMIDITY (%)												
Temp.	**40**	**45**	**50**	**55**	**60**	**65**	**70**	**75**	**80**	**85**	**90**	**95**	**100**
110 (47)	136 (58)												
108 (43)	130 (54)	137 (58)											
106 (41)	124 (51)	130 (54)	137 (58)										
104 (40)	119 (48	124 (51)	131 (55)	137 (58)									
102 (39)	114 (46)	119 (48)	124 (51)	130 (54)	137 (58)								
100 (38)	109 (43)	114 (46)	118 (48)	124 (51)	128 (54)	136 (58)							
98 (37)	105 (41)	109 (43)	113 (46)	117 (47)	123 (51)	128 (53)	134 (57)						
96 (36)	101 (38)	104 (40)	108 (42)	112 (44)	116 (47)	121 (49)	126 (52)	132 (56)					
94 (34)	97 (36)	100 (38)	103 (39)	106 (41)	110 (43)	114 (46)	119 (48)	124 (51)	129 (54)	135 (57)			
92 (33)	94 (34)	96 (36)	99 (37)	101 (38)	105 (41)	108 (42)	112 (44)	116 (47)	121 (49)	126 (52)	131 (55)		
90 (32)	91 (33)	93 (34)	95 (35)	97 (36)	100 (38)	103 (39)	106 (41)	109 (43)	113 (45)	117 (47)	122 (50)	127 (53)	132 (56)
88 (31)	88 (31)	89 (32)	91 (33)	93 (34)	95 (35)	98 (37)	100 (38)	103 (39)	106 (41)	110 (43)	113 (45)	117 (47)	121 (49)
86 (30)	85 (29)	87 (31)	88 (31)	89 (32)	91 (33)	93 (34)	95 (35)	97 (36)	100 (38)	102 (39)	105 (41)	108 (42)	112 (44)
84 (29)	83 (28)	84 (29)	85 (29)	86 (30)	88 (31)	89 (32)	90 (32)	92 (33)	94 (34)	96 (36)	98 (37)	100 (38)	103 (39)
82 (28)	81 (27)	82 (28)	83 (28)	84 (29)	84 (29)	85 (29)	86 (30)	88 (31)	89 (32)	90 (32)	91 (33)	93 (34)	95 (35)
80 (27)	80 (27)	80 (27)	81 (27)	81 (27)	82 (28)	82 (28)	83 (28)	84 (29)	84 (29)	85 (29)	86 (30)	86 (30)	87 (31)

Category	**Heat Index**	**Possible heat disorders of people in high-risk groups**
Extreme Danger	130°F or higher (54°C or higher)	Heatstroke or sunstroke likely.
Danger	105–129°F (41–54°C)	Sunstroke, muscle cramps, and/or heat exhaustion likely. Heatstroke possible with prolonged exposure and/or physical activity.
Extreme Caution	90–105°F (32–41°C)	Sunstroke, muscle cramps, and/or heat exhaustion possible with prolonged exposure and/or physical activity.
Caution	80–90°F (27–32°C)	Fatigue possible with prolonged exposure and/or physical activity

APPENDIX D
SUPPLEMENTARY RESOURCES

Chapter 1. First Steps

Barcott, Bruce. *The Measure of a Mountain: Beauty and Terror on Mount Rainier.* Seattle: Sasquatch Books, 1997.

Blum, Arlene. *Annapurna: A Woman's Place.* San Francisco: Sierra Club Books, 1980.

Bonatti, Walter. *The Mountains of My Life.* Translated and edited by Robert Marshall. New York: Modern Library, 2001.

Gillman, Peter. *The Wildest Dream: The Biography of George Mallory.* Seattle: The Mountaineers Books, 2000.

Hertzog, Maurice. *Annapurna: First Conquest of an 8000-Meter Peak.* Translated by Nea Morin and Janet Adam Smith. New York: Dutton, 1953.

Krakauer, Jon. *Eiger Dreams: Adventures Among Men and Mountains.* Guilford, CT: Lyons Press, 2009.

Molenaar, Dee. *The Challenge of Rainier: A Record of the Explorations and Ascents, Triumphs and Tragedies.* Seattle: The Mountaineers Books, 1971.

Muir, John. *Nature Writings; The Story of My Boyhood and Youth; My First Summer in the Sierra; The Mountains of California; Stickeen; Selected Essays.* Edited by William Cronon. New York: Library of America, 1997.

—. *The Wild Muir: Twenty-two of John Muir's Greatest Adventures.* Selected and introduced by Lee Stetson. Yosemite National Park, CA: Yosemite Association, 1994.

Nash, Roderick Frazier. *Wilderness and the American Mind.* 4th ed. New Haven, CT: Yale University Press, 2001.

Roberts, David. *The Mountain of My Fear: Deborah: A Wilderness Narrative.* Seattle: The Mountaineers Books, 1991.

Simpson, Joe. *Touching the Void.* New York: Perennial, 2004.

Turner, Jack. *Teewinot: A Year in the Teton Range.* New York: St. Martin's Press, 2000.

Washburn, Bradford, and David Roberts. *Mount McKinley: The Conquest of Denali.* New York: Abrams, 1991.

Chapter 2. Clothing and Equipment

Carline, Jan D., Martha J. Lentz, and Steven C. MacDonald. *Mountaineering First Aid: A Guide to Accident Response and First Aid Care.* 5th ed. Seattle: The Mountaineers Books, 2004.

Manning, Harvey. *Backpacking One Step at a Time.* New York: Random House, 1986.

Soles, Clyde. *Rock and Ice Gear: Equipment for the Vertical World.* Seattle: The Mountaineers Books, 2000.

Weiss, Hal. *Secrets of Warmth: For Comfort or Survival.* Seattle: The Mountaineers Books, 1998.

Wilkerson, James A., ed. *Medicine for Mountaineering and Other Wilderness Activities.* 6th ed. Seattle: The Mountaineers Books, 2009.

Chapter 3. Camping and Food

Backer, Howard. "In Search of the Perfect Water Treatment Method." *Wilderness and Environmental Medicine* 11 (2000): 1–4.

Curtis, Rick. *The Backpacker's Field Manual: A Comprehensive Guide to Mastering Backcountry Skills.* New York: Three Rivers Press, 1998.

Fleming, June. *The Well-Fed Backpacker.* New York: Vintage Books, 1986.

Gorman, Stephen. *Winter Camping.* 2nd ed. Lebanon, NH: Appalachian Mountain Club, 1999.

Howe, Steve, Alan Kesselheim, and Dennis Coello. *Making Camp: A Complete Guide for Hikers, Mountain Bikers, Paddlers, and Skiers.* Seattle: The Mountaineers Books, 1997.

Keyes, Linda E., Robert S. Hamilton, and John S. Rose. "Carbon Monoxide Exposure from Cooking in Snow Caves at High Altitude." *Wilderness and Environmental Medicine* 12 (2001): 208–212.

Miller, Dorcas. *Backcountry Cooking: From Pack to Plate in 10 Minutes.* Seattle: The Mountaineers Books, 1998.

Prater, Yvonne, and Ruth D. Mendenhall. *Gorp, Glop, and Glue Stew: Favorite Foods from 165 Outdoor Experts.* Seattle: The Mountaineers Books, 1982.

Prichard, Nancy. "Buying a Camp Stove." www.gorp.com.

—. "Buying a Camp Stove: Before You Buy." www.gorp.com.

—. "Buying a Camp Stove: Cartridge Stoves." www.gorp.com.

—. "Buying a Camp Stove: Liquid Gas." www.gorp.com.

Tilton, Buck, and Rick Bennett. *Don't Get Sick: The Hidden Dangers of Camping and Hiking.* Seattle: The Mountaineers Books, 2002.

Townsend, Chris. *The Backpacker's Handbook.* 2nd ed. New York: McGraw-Hill, 1996.

Chapter 4. Physical Conditioning

Haskell, W. L., I. Lee, R. R. Pate, K. E. Powell, S. N. Blair, B. A. Franklin, C. A. Maera, G. W. Heath, P. D. Thompson, and A. Bauman. "Physical Activity and Public Health: Updated Recommendation for Adults from the American College of Sports Medicine and the American Heart Association." *Medicine and Science in Sports and Exercise* 39, no. 8 (2007): 1423–1434.

Hörst, Eric J. *How to Climb 5.12.* 2nd ed. Guilford, CT: Globe Pequot / Falcon, 2003.

—. *Training for Climbing.* 2nd ed. Guilford, CT: Globe Pequot / Falcon, 2008.

Schurman, Courtenay W., and Doug G. Schurman. *The Outdoor Athlete.* Champaign, IL: Human Kinetics, 2009.

—. *Train to Climb Mount Rainier or Any High Peak.* Video. Seattle: Body Results, 2002. www.bodyresults.com.

Soles, Clyde. *Climbing: Training for Peak Performance,* 2nd ed. Seattle: The Mountaineers Books, 2008.

Chapter 5. Navigation

Burns, Bob, and Mike Burns. *Wilderness Navigation.* 2nd ed. Seattle: The Mountaineers Books, 2004.

DeLorme. Topographic maps. www.delorme.com/topousa.

Geological Survey of Canada, National Resources Canada. Declination information. http://geomag.nrcan.gc.ca/apps/mdcal-eng.php.

Global Positioning Systems Resource Library. www.gpsy.com/gpsinfo.

Google Earth. Aerial photographs. http://earth.google.com.

Letham, Lawrence. *GPS Made Easy.* 5th ed. Seattle: The Mountaineers Books, 2008.

National Geographic. Topographic maps. www.natgeomaps.com/topo.html.

National Oceanographic and Atmospheric Administration, National Geophysical Data Center. Declination information. www.ngdc.noaa.gov/geomag/declination.shtml.

Renner, Jeff. *Mountain Weather: Backcountry Forecasting and Weather Safety for Hikers, Campers, Climbers, Skiers, and Snowboarders.* Seattle: The Mountaineers Books, 2005.

TerraServer-USA. Aerial photographs; topographic maps. http://terraserver-usa.com.

Trails.com. Topographic maps. www.trails.com.

U.S. Coast Guard, Navigation Center. GPS information. www.gps.gov.

Chapter 6. Wilderness Travel

Allen, Dan. *Don't Die on the Mountain.* 2nd ed. New London, NH: Diapensia Press, 1998.

Berger, Karen. *Everyday Wisdom.* Seattle: The Mountaineers Books, 1997.

Fletcher, Colin, and Chip Rawlins. *The Complete Walker IV.* New York: Alfred A. Knopf, 2002.

Herrero, Stephen. *Bear Attacks: Their Causes and Avoidance.* Guilford, CT: The Lyons Press, 2002.

Nelson, Dan. *Predators at Risk in the Pacific Northwest.* Seattle: The Mountaineers Books, 2000.

Petzoldt, Paul. *The New Wilderness Handbook.* New York: W. W. Norton, 1984.

Schrad, Jerry, and David Moser, eds. *Wilderness Basics.* 3rd ed. Seattle: The Mountaineers Books, 2004.

Smith, Dave. *Backcountry Bear Basics.* 2nd ed. Seattle: The Mountaineers Books, 2006.

Chapter 7. Leave No Trace

Hampton, Bruce, and David Cole. *Soft Paths: How to Enjoy the Wilderness Without Harming It.* Mechanicsburg, PA: Stackpole Books, 2003.

Leave No Trace Center for Outdoor Ethics. *Outdoor Skills and Ethics.* Boulder, CO: Leave No Trace Center for Outdoor Ethics, n.d. Booklet series covering regions of the United States and a variety of outdoor activities applicable anywhere. www.lnt.org.

Chapter 8. Stewardship and Access

Access Fund, The. *Climbing Management: A Guide to Climbing Issues and the Production of a Climbing Management Plan.* Boulder, CO: The Access Fund, 2001. www.accessfund.org.

Attarian, Aram, and Kath Pyke, comps. *Climbing and Natural Resources Management: An Annotated Bibliography.* Raleigh: North Carolina State University; Boulder, CO: The Access Fund, 2001.

Chouinard, Yvon. "Coonyard Mouths Off." *Ascent* 1 (June 1972): 50–52.

Leave No Trace Center for Outdoor Ethics. *Skills and Ethics: Rock Climbing.* Boulder, CO: Leave No Trace Center for Outdoor Ethics, 2001. www.lnt.org.

Pritchard, Paul. *Deep Play: A Climber's Odyssey from Llanberis to the Big Walls.* Seattle: The Mountaineers Books, 1998.

Chapter 9. Basic Safety System

Lewis, S. Peter, and Dan Cauthorn. *Climbing: From Gym to Crag.* Seattle: The Mountaineers Books, 2000.

Lipke, Rick. *Technical Rescue Riggers Guide.* 2nd ed. Bellingham, WA: Conterra, 2009.

Luebben, Craig. *Knots for Climbers.* Guilford, CT: Globe Pequot / Falcon, 2001.

Owen, Peter. *The Book of Climbing Knots.* Guilford, CT: The Lyons Press, 2000.

Soles, Clyde. *The Outdoor Knots Book.* Seattle: The Mountaineers Books, 2004.

—. *Rock and Ice Gear: Equipment for the Vertical World.* Seattle: The Mountaineers Books, 2000.

Chapter 10. Belaying

Lewis, S. Peter, and Dan Cauthorn. *Climbing: From Gym to Crag.* Seattle: The Mountaineers Books, 2000.

Long, John. *Climbing Anchors.* Guilford, CT: Globe Pequot / Falcon, 1993.

Long, John, and Bob Gaines. *More Climbing Anchors.* Guilford, CT: Globe Pequot / Falcon, 1998.

Chapter 11. Rappeling

Lewis, S. Peter, and Dan Cauthorn. *Climbing: From Gym to Crag.* Seattle: The Mountaineers Books, 2000.

Luebben, Craig. *How to Rappel.* Guilford, CT: Globe Pequot / Falcon, 2000.

—. *Knots for Climbers.* Guilford, CT: Globe Pequot / Falcon, 2001.

Chapter 12. Alpine Rock Climbing Technique

Goodard, D., and U. Neumann. *Performance Rock Climbing.* Mechanicsburg, PA: Stackpole Books, 1993.

Hörst, Eric J. *How to Climb 5.12.* 2nd ed. Guilford, CT: Globe Pequot / Falcon, 2003.

Ilgner, Arno. *The Rock Warrior's Way: Mental Training for Climbers.* 2nd ed. La Vergne, TN: Desiderata Institute, 2006.

Layton, Michael A. *Climbing Stronger, Faster, Healthier: Beyond the Basics.* Charleston, SC: BookSurge Publishing, 2009.

Leavitt, Randy. "Leavittation: The Off-Width Rennaissance." *Mountain Magazine,* no. 106 (November-December 1985): 25–29. www.widefetish.com/pages/how_to.html#leavittation.

Lewis, S. Peter, and Dan Cauthorn. *Climbing: From Gym to Crag*. Seattle: The Mountaineers Books, 2000.

Long, John. *How to Rock Climb!* 3rd ed. Guilford, CT: Globe Pequot / Falcon, 2000.

—. *Sport and Face Climbing*. Evergreen, CO: Chockstone Press, 1994.

Long, John, and John Middendorf. *Big Walls*. Guilford, CT: Globe Pequot / Falcon, 1994.

Loughman, Michael. *Learning to Rock Climb*. San Francisco: Sierra Club Books, 1981.

Wide Fetish. Off-width cracks. www.widefetish.com.

Chapter 13. Rock Protection and Chapter 14. Leading on Rock

Long, John. *Climbing Anchors*. Guilford, CT: Globe Pequot / Falcon, 1993.

Long, John, and Bob Gaines. *More Climbing Anchors*. Guilford, CT: Globe Pequot / Falcon, 1998.

Long, John, and Craig Luebben. *Advanced Rock Climbing*. Guilford, CT: Globe Pequot / Falcon, 1997.

Chapter 15. Aid and Big Wall Climbing

Long, John, and John Middendorf. *Big Walls*. Guilford, CT: Globe Pequot / Falcon, 1994.

Lowe, Jeff, and Ron Olevsky. *Clean Walls*. Video. Ogden, UT: Adaptable Man Productions, 2004.

McNamara, Chris, and Erik Sloan. *Yosemite Big Walls*. 2nd ed. San Francisco: SuperTopo, 2005.

Ogden, Jared. *Big Wall Climbing: Elite Technique*. Seattle: The Mountaineers Books, 2005.

Robbins, Royal. *Advanced Rock Craft*. Glendale, CA: La Siesta Press, 1973.

Chapter 16. Snow Travel and Climbing

Armstrong, Betsy R., and Knox Williams. *The Avalanche Book*. Golden, CO: Fulcrum Publishing, 1992.

Atkins, Dale. *Avalanche Rescue Beacons: A Race against Time*. Video. Boulder, CO: People Productions, 1995.

Avalanche.org. Avalanche information. www.avalanche.org.

Cliff, Peter. *Ski Mountaineering*. Seattle: Pacific Search Press, 1987.

Daffern, Tony. *Avalanche Safety for Skiers and Climbers*. 2nd ed. Seattle: The Mountaineers Books, 2000.

Dostie, Craig. "Ooops on the Range: Beacon Basics for the Primary Search." *Couloir* (November 2001): 84–87.

Ferguson, Sue, and Edward R. LaChapelle. *The ABCs of Avalanche Safety*. 3rd ed. Seattle: The Mountaineers Books, 2003.

Fredston, Jill A., and Doug Fesler. *Snow Sense: A Guide to Evaluating Snow Avalanche Hazard*. 5th ed. Anchorage: Alaska Mountain Safety Center, 1999.

Fyffe, Allen, and Iain Peter. *The Handbook of Climbing*. London: Pelham Books, 1997.

LaChapelle, Edward R. *Secrets of Snow: Visual Clues to Avalanche and Ski Conditions*. Seattle: University of Washington Press, 2001.

McClung, David, and Peter Schaerer. *The Avalanche Handbook*. 2nd ed. Seattle: The Mountaineers Books, 2006.

Parker, Paul. *Free-Heel Skiing: Telemark and Parallel Techniques for All Conditions*. 3rd ed. Seattle: The Mountaineers Books, 2001.

Prater, Gene, and Dave Felkley. *Snowshoeing: From Novice to Master*. 5th ed. Seattle: The Mountaineers Books, 2002.

Soles, Clyde. *Rock and Ice Gear: Equipment for the Vertical World*. Seattle: The Mountaineers Books, 2000.

Tremper, Bruce. *Staying Alive in Avalanche Terrain*. 2nd ed. Seattle: The Mountaineers Books, 2008.

Twight, Mark, and James Martin. *Extreme Alpinism: Climbing Light, Fast, and High*. Seattle: The Mountaineers Books, 1999.

Wasatch Interpretive Association. *Winning the Avalanche Game*. Video. Salt Lake City, UT: Wasatch Interpretive Association, 1993.

Chapter 17. Glacier Travel and Crevasse Rescue

Barry, John. *Snow and Ice Climbing*. Seattle: Cloudcap Press, 1987.

Cinnamon, Jerry. *Climbing Rock and Ice: Learning the Vertical Dance*. Camden, ME: Ragged Mountain Press, 1994.

Cliff, Peter. *Ski Mountaineering.* Seattle: Pacific Search Press, 1987.

Fawcett, Ron, Jeff Lowe, Paul Nunn, and Alan Rouse. *The Climber's Handbook.* San Francisco: Sierra Club Books, 1987.

Ferguson, Sue. *Glaciers of North America.* Golden, CO: Fulcrum Publishing, 1992.

Fyffe, Allen, and Iain Peter. *The Handbook of Climbing.* London: Pelham Books, 1997.

Hambrey, Michael, and Jurg Alean. *Glaciers.* Cambridge, England: Cambridge University Press, 1992.

March, Bill. *Modern Snow and Ice Techniques.* Milnthorpe, Cumbria, England: Cicerone Press, 1984.

McMullen, John. *The Basic Essentials of Climbing Ice.* Merrillville, IN: ICS Books, 1992.

Powers, Phil. *NOLS Wilderness Mountaineering.* Mechanicsburg, PA: Stackpole Books, 1993.

Schubert, Pit. *Modern Alpine Climbing, Equipment, and Techniques.* Translated by G. Steele and M. Vapenikova. Milnthorpe, Cumbria, England: Cicerone Press, 1991.

Selters, Andy. *Glacier Travel and Crevasse Rescue.* 2nd ed., rev. Seattle: The Mountaineers Books, 2006.

Shirahata, Shiro. *The Karakoram: Mountains of Pakistan.* Seattle: Cloudcap Press, 1990.

Soles, Clyde. *Rock and Ice Gear: Equipment for the Vertical World.* Seattle: The Mountaineers Books, 2000.

Chapter 18. Alpine Ice Climbing and Chapter 19. Waterfall Ice and Mixed Climbing

Barry, John. *Alpine Climbing.* Seattle: Cloudcap Press, 1988.

Chouinard, Yvon. *Climbing Ice.* San Francisco: Sierra Club Books, 1978.

Cliff, Peter. *Ski Mountaineering.* Seattle: Pacific Search Press, 1987.

Fawcett, Ron, Jeff Lowe, Paul Nunn, and Alan Rouse. *The Climber's Handbook.* San Francisco: Sierra Club Books, 1987.

Fyffe, Allen, and Iain Peter. *The Handbook of Climbing.* London: Pelham Books, 1997.

Gadd, Will. *Ice and Mixed Climbing: Modern Technique.* Seattle: The Mountaineers Books, 2003.

Harmston, Chris. "Myths, Cautions and Techniques of Ice Screw Placement." Paper presented at 1999 International Technical Rescue Symposium, Fort Collins, CO, November 5–7, 1999.

Lowe, Jeff. *The Ice Experience.* Chicago: Contemporary Books, 1979.

—. *Ice World: Techniques and Experiences of Modern Ice Climbing.* Seattle: The Mountaineers Books, 1996.

Luebben, Craig. *How to Ice Climb!* Guilford, CT: Globe Pequot / Falcon, 2001.

March, Bill. *Modern Snow and Ice Techniques.* Milnthorpe, Cumbria, England: Cicerone Press, 1984.

Raleigh, Duane. *Ice Tools and Techniques.* Carbondale, CO: Primedia, 1995.

Soles, Clyde. *Rock and Ice Gear: Equipment for the Vertical World.* Seattle: The Mountaineers Books, 2000.

Twight, Mark, and James Martin. *Extreme Alpinism: Climbing Light, Fast, and High.* Seattle: The Mountaineers Books, 1999.

Chapter 20. Expedition Climbing

Bearzi, Michael. "Doing the Mixed Thing." *Climbing,* no. 130 (February-March 1992): 101–103.

Bezruchka, Stephen. *Altitude Illness: Prevention and Treatment.* 2nd ed. Seattle: The Mountaineers Books, 2005.

—. *The Pocket Doctor.* 3rd ed. Seattle: The Mountaineers Books, 1999.

Fyffe, Allen, and Iain Peter. *The Handbook of Climbing.* London: Pelham Books, 1997.

Houston, Charles. *Going Higher: Oxygen, Man, and Mountains.* 5th ed. Seattle: The Mountaineers Books, 2005.

Jenkins, Mark, and Dan Moe. "Adventures in the Refrigerator Zone: 30 Tips for Successful Winter Camping." *Backpacker* (October 1993): 42–43.

Powers, Phil, and Clyde Soles. *Climbing: Expedition Planning.* Seattle: The Mountaineers Books, 2003.

Soles, Clyde. *Rock and Ice Gear: Equipment for the Vertical World.* Seattle: The Mountaineers Books, 2000.

Warrell, David, and Sarah Anderson, eds. *The Royal Geographic Society Expedition Medicine.* London: Profile Books, 1998.

Wilkerson, James A., ed. *Medicine for Mountaineering and Other Wilderness Activities.* 6th ed. Seattle: The Mountaineers Books, 2009.

Chapter 21. Leadership

American Alpine Club and Alpine Club of Canada. *Accidents in North American Mountaineering.* Annual publication. Distributed by The Mountaineers Books, Seattle.

Bass, Bernard M., and Ralph Melvin Stogdill. *Bass and Stogdill's Handbook of Leadership.* 3rd ed. New York: Free Press, 1990.

Graham, John. *Outdoor Leadership: Technique, Common Sense, and Self-Confidence.* Seattle: The Mountaineers Books, 1997.

Petzoldt, Paul. *The New Wilderness Handbook.* New York: W. W. Norton, 1984.

Roskelley, John. *Nanda Devi: The Tragic Expedition.* Seattle: The Mountaineers Books, 2000.

Chapter 22. Safety: How to Stay Alive

American Alpine Club and Alpine Club of Canada. *Accidents in North American Mountaineering.* Annual publication. Distributed by The Mountaineers Books, Seattle.

Diemberger, Kurt. *The Endless Knot: K2, Mountain of Dreams and Destiny.* Seattle: The Mountaineers Books, 1991.

Dill, John. "Climb Safely: Staying Alive." Yosemite National Park: U.S. Department of the Interior, National Park Service, Yosemite National Park Search and Rescue, 2004. www.nps.gov/archive/yose/sar/climbsafe.htm.

Twight, Mark, and James Martin. *Extreme Alpinism: Climbing Light, Fast, and High.* Seattle: The Mountaineers Books, 1999.

Viesturs, Ed, with Dave Roberts. *No Shortcuts to the Top: Climbing the World's 14 Highest Peaks.* New York: Broadway, 2006.

Chapter 23. First Aid

Bergeron, J. David, and Gloria Bizjak. *First Responder.* 6th ed. Englewood Cliffs, NJ: Brady / Prentice Hall, 2000.

Bezruchka, Stephen. *Altitude Illness: Prevention and Treatment.* 2nd ed. Seattle: The Mountaineers Books, 2005.

Bowman, Warren D., American Academy of Orthopaedic Surgeons, and National Ski Patrol. *Outdoor Emergency Care: Comprehensive Prehospital Care for Nonurban Settings.* 4th ed. Boston: Jones and Bartlett, 2003.

Carline, Jan D., Martha J. Lentz, and Steven C. MacDonald. *Mountaineering First Aid: A Guide to Accident Response and First Aid Care.* 5th ed. Seattle: The Mountaineers Books, 2004.

Darville, Fred T. Jr. *Mountaineering Medicine: A Wilderness Medical Guide.* 12th ed. Berkeley, CA: Wilderness Press, 1989.

Drummond, Roger. *Ticks and What You Can Do about Them.* rev. ed. Berkeley, CA: Wilderness Press, 1998.

Dubas, Frédéric, and Jacques Valloton, eds. *Color Atlas of Mountain Medicine.* St. Louis, MO: Mosby, 1991.

Fitch, A.M., B.A. Nicks, et al. "Basic Splinting Techniques." *New England Journal of Medicine* 359:26. (2008).

Forgey, William W. *Wilderness Medicine: Beyond First Aid.* 4th ed. Merrillville, IN: ICS Books, 1994.

—, ed. *Wilderness Medical Society Practice Guidelines for Wilderness Emergency Care.* 5th ed. Guilford, CT: Globe Pequot / Falcon, 2006.

Fritz, Robert L., and David H. Perrin. "Cold-Exposure Injuries: Prevention and Treatment." *Clinics in Sports Medicine* 8, no. 1 (January 1989): 111–128.

Gentile, Douglas A., John A. Morris, Tod Schimelpfenig, Sue M. Bass, and Paul S. Auerbach. "Wilderness Injuries and Illnesses." *Annals of Emergency Medicine* 21, no. 7 (July 1992): 853–861.

Hackett, Peter H. *Mountain Sickness: Prevention, Recognition, and Treatment.* 2nd ed. Golden, CO: American Alpine Club, 1995.

Hackett, Peter H., and Robert C. Roach. "High-Altitude Illness." *New England Journal of Medicine* 345, no. 2 (July 12, 2001): 107–114.

Houston, Charles. *High Altitude: Illness and Wellness.* Merrillville, IN: ICS Books, 1993.

Isaac, Jeff, and Peter Goth. *The Outward Bound Wilderness First-Aid Handbook.* New York: Lyons & Burford, 1991.

Luks, A.M. and E.R. Swenson. "High-Altitude Pulmonary Edema: Prevention and Treatment." *American College of Chest Physicians* 21 (2007): Lesson 22.

Schimelpfenig, Tod, Linda Lindsey, and National Outdoor Leadership School. *Wilderness First Aid.* 3rd ed. Mechanicsburg, PA: Stackpole Books, 2002.

Singer, A.J. and A.B Dagum. "Current Management of Acute Cutaneous Wounds." *New England Journal of Medicine* 359:10 (2008).

Steele, Peter. *Backcountry Medical Guide.* 2nd ed. Seattle: The Mountaineers Books, 1999.

Tilton, Buck, and Tom Burke. *The Wilderness First Responder.* Guilford, CT: Globe Pequot / Falcon, 1998.

Tilton, Buck, and Frank Hubbell. *Medicine for the Backcountry.* 3rd ed. Guilford, CT: Globe Pequot / Falcon, 1999.

Van Tilburg, Christopher, ed. *First Aid: A Pocket Guide. Quick Information for Mountaineering and Backcountry Use.* 4th ed. Seattle: The Mountaineers Books, 2001.

Ward, Michael P., James S. Milledge, and John B. West. *High-Altitude Medicine and Physiology.* 3rd ed. London: Edward Arnold, 2000.

Warrell, David, and Sarah Anderson, eds. *Expedition Medicine.* 6th ed. New York: Fitzroy Dearborn Publishers, 2003.

Weiss, Eric A. *A Comprehensive Guide to Wilderness and Travel Medicine.* 2nd ed. Berkeley, CA: Adventure Medical Kits, 1998.

—. *Wilderness 911: A Step-by-Step Guide for Medical Emergencies and Improvised Care in the Backcountry.* Seattle: The Mountaineers Books, 1998.

Wilkerson, James A., ed. *Medicine for Mountaineering and Other Wilderness Activities.* 6th ed. Seattle: The Mountaineers Books, 2009.

Wilkerson, James A., ed., with Cameron C. Bangs and John S. Hayward. *Hypothermia, Frostbite, and Other Cold Injuries: Prevention, Recognition, and Prehospital Treatment.* 2nd ed. Seattle: The Mountaineers Books, 2006.

Chapter 24. Alpine Search and Rescue

Fasulo, David. *Self-Rescue.* Guilford, CT: Globe Pequot / Chockstone, 1997.

Lipke, Rick. *Technical Rescue Riggers Guide.* Bellingham, WA: Conterra Technical Systems, 1997.

Long, John. *Climbing Anchors.* Guilford, CT: Globe Pequot / Falcon, 1993.

Long, John, and Bob Gaines. *More Climbing Anchors.* Guilford, CT: Globe Pequot / Falcon, 1998.

May, W. G. *Mountain Search and Rescue Techniques.* Boulder, CO: Rocky Mountain Rescue Group, 1973.

Padgett, Allen, and Bruce Smith. *On Rope.* Huntsville, AL: National Speleological Society, 1987.

Setnicka, Tim J. *Wilderness Search and Rescue.* Boston: Appalachian Mountain Club, 1980.

Tyson, Andy, and Molly Loomis. *Climbing Self-Rescue: Improvising Solutions for Serious Situations.* Seattle: The Mountaineers Books, 2006.

Chapter 25. Mountain Geology

Association of American State Geologists. www.stategeologists.org.

Google Panoramio. www.panoramio.com.

Hiking the Geology series (various states). Seattle: The Mountaineers Books, various dates.

McPhee, John. *Assembling California.* New York: Farrar, Straus and Giroux, 1993.

—. *Basin and Range.* New York: Farrar, Straus and Giroux, 1981.

Roadside Geology series (various states). Missoula, MT: Mountain Press, various dates.

U.S. Bureau of Land Management. www.blm.gov.

U.S. Forest Service. www.fs.fed.us.

U.S. Geological Survey. www.usgs.gov.

—. Geology in the Parks program. http://3dparks.wr.usgs.gov.

—. National geologic map database. http://ngmdb.usgs.gov.

U.S. Geological Survey, Cascades Volcano Observatory. "Big List of Volcano and Earth Science–Oriented Websites." http://vulcan.wr.usgs.gov/Servers/earth_servers.html.

Chapter 26. The Cycle of Snow

Benn, Douglas I., and David J. A. Evans. *Glaciers and Glaciation.* New York: John Wiley and Sons, 1998.

Colbeck, S., E. Akitaya, R. Armstrong, H. Gubler, J. Lafeuille, K. Lied, D. McClung, and E. Morris. *The International Classification for Seasonal Snow on the Ground.* Cambridge, England: International Glaciological Society and International Association of Scientific Hydrology, 1992.

Ferguson, Sue. *Glaciers of North America: A Field Guide.* Golden, CO: Fulcrum Publishing, 1992.

Gray, D. M., and D. H. Male, eds. *Handbook of Snow.* New York: Pergamon Press, 1981.

Hobbs, P. V. *Ice Physics.* Oxford: Claredon Press, 1974.

LaChapelle, Edward R. *Field Guide to Snow Crystals.* Cambridge, England: International Glaciological Society, 1992.

—. *Secrets of Snow: Visual Clues to Avalanche and Ski Conditions.* Seattle: University of Washington Press; Cambridge, England: International Glaciological Society, 2001.

Paterson, W. S. B. *The Physics of Glaciers.* 3rd ed. New York: Pergamon Press, 1994.

Post, Austin, and Edward R. LaChapelle. *Glacier Ice.* Seattle: University of Washington Press; Cambridge, England: International Glaciological Society, 2000.

Chapter 27. Mountain Weather

Renner, Jeff. *Lightning Strikes: Staying Safe under Stormy Skies.* Seattle: The Mountaineers Books, 2002.

—. *Mountain Weather: Backcountry Forecasting for Hikers, Campers, Climbers, Skiers, Snowboarders.* Seattle: The Mountaineers Books, 2005.

—. *Northwest Mountain Weather.* Seattle: The Mountaineers Books, 1992.

Schaefer, Vincent J., and John A. Day. *A Field Guide to the Atmosphere.* Boston: Houghton Mifflin Company, 1991.

Whiteman, David C. *Mountain Meteorology: Fundamentals and Applications.* New York: Oxford University Press, 2000.

Williams, Jack. *The Weather Book.* McLean, VA: USA Today, 1992.

GLOSSARY

A

accessory cord. Core-and-sheath constructed cord of diameters ranging from 2 to 8 millimeters, fabricated from aramid (Kevlar), nylon, Perlon, polyester and polyethylene (Dyneema or Spectra) fibers.

accumulation zone. That portion of a glacier that receives more snow every year than it loses to melting.

acute mountain sickness (AMS). An altitude-related illness.

aid climbing. The technique of using gear to support a climber's weight while climbing.

aiders. Webbing ladders that allow an aid climber to step up; also called *etriers*.

alpine rock climbing. Rock climbing that requires mountaineering skills.

alpine start. Starting before daybreak.

alpine touring. *See* **randonée skiing.**

American technique. Cramponing technique that combines flat-footing (French) and front-pointing (German) techniques on steep snow or ice; also called *combination technique*.

AMS. *See* **acute mountain sickness.**

anchor. The point on the mountain to which the climbing system is securely attached; there are belay anchors, rappel anchors, and protection in rock, snow, and ice.

approach shoes. Lightweight, sticky-soled shoes designed for both trails and moderate rock climbing.

ascender. Mechanical device used to ascend a rope; also called *jug, jumar*.

autoblock. A self-belay backup used while rappeling.

B

back-cleaning. A procedure in which the leader cleans some protection while ascending the route.

balance-climbing. Moving up from one position of balance to the next.

bashies. Old name for heads. *See* **heads.**

bearing. Line between two points measured in degrees.

belay anchor. *See* **anchor.**

belay device. A piece of equipment that applies friction to the rope to arrest a fall.

belaying. Fundamental technique of using a rope to stop a fall if one should occur while climbing.

bergschrund. Giant crevasse found at the upper limit of glacier movement, formed where the moving glacier breaks away from the ice cap or snowfield above.

bight. A 180-degree turn in a rope.

big wall climbing. Climbing on a large, sheer wall, which usually requires bivouacs and extensive aid climbing.

bivy. From the French *bivouac*, meaning "temporary encampment."

bivy sack. No-frills, weatherproof tube shelter.

body belay. *See* **hip belay.**

bollard. A mound carved out of snow or ice and rigged with rope, webbing, or accessory cord to provide an anchor.

bolt. Permanent piece of artificial protection consisting of a threaded bolt that is placed into a hole drilled into rock.

boot. *See* **mountaineering boot.**

braking hand. The belayer's hand that secures the belay; must be kept in contact with the rope at all times.

bridging. *See* **stemming.**

C

cairn. A pile of rocks used as a route marker.

cam. *See* **spring-loaded camming device, Tricam.**

camming. Application of torquing or counterpressure with climbing gear.

carabiner. Metal snap-links of various shapes and sizes; indispensable and versatile tool of climbing used for belaying, rappeling, clipping in to safety anchors, securing the rope to points of protection, and numerous other tasks.

CE. A marking that signifies that a product meets all applicable European legislation.

CEN. Comité Européen de Normalisation, the European nonprofit organization responsible for creating and maintaining climbing equipment standards. *See also* **UIAA.**

chimney. A crack wide enough to fit a climber's body and narrow enough to allow for opposing force to be applied to both walls.

chock. Climbers' hardware comprising removable protection; also called *stopper, wired nut.*

chock pick. Tool used for removing protection; also known as *nut tool.*

chockstone. A rock firmly lodged in a crack or between gully walls.

circlehead. *See* **copperhead.**

clean climbing. Climbing without permanently marring the rock.

cleaning. Removing protection.

combination technique. *See* **American technique.**

contour lines. Lines on topographic maps that represent constant elevations.

copperhead. Malleable hardware used in aid climbing; also called *head, circlehead.*

cord. *See* **accessory cord.**

cordelette. A long runner usually made of 7- to 8-millimeter nylon or small-diameter, high-strength accessory cord.

C-pulley system. *See* **2:1 pulley system.**

crag climbing. Technical rock climbing that is close to roads and civilization, and does not require alpine skills.

crampons. A set of metal spikes that attach to boots in order to penetrate hard snow and ice.

crevasse. A chasm that splits a glacier.

crux. The most significant, committing, or difficult section of a pitch or climb.

D

daisy chain. Sewn sling with sewn loops.

deadman. Any object buried in the snow to serve as an anchor.

dihedral. Where two walls meet in approximately a right-angled inside corner; also called *open book.*

dry rope. Rope treated to make it more water-repellent.

dry tooling. Climbing on rock with ice tools and crampons.

dynamic rope. A rope that stretches under loads.

Dyneema. Ultra-high-molecular-weight polyethylene or high-modulus polyethylene synthetic fiber. *See* **accessory cord.**

dyno. A dynamic move; a lunge or quick move.

E

edging. Climbing technique using either the inside or outside edge of the foot so that the edge of the sole is weighted over the hold.

equalette. A cordelette with pretied knots used to rig anchors. *See* **cordelette.**

equalization. Equalizing forces on a multipoint anchor.

etriers. *See* **aiders.**

F

fall factor. The length of a fall divided by the length of the rope between belay device and fallen climber.

fall line. The line of travel of a freely falling object.

feeling hand. The belayer's hand that pays the rope in and out.

fixed line. Rope anchored in place.

fixed pin. Permanent piton.

flagging. Climbing technique that involves extending a limb for counterbalance, to prevent pivoting or "barn-door" effect.

flaking. Uncoiling the rope, one loop at a time, into a neat pile.

flat-footing. *See* **French technique.**

fluke. Metal-plate anchor used in snow and sand.

follower. *See* **second.**

free climbing. Climbing using only physical ability to move over the rock via handholds and footholds, without weighting protection.

French technique. Cramponing technique used on moderately steep snow and ice in which the feet are placed flat against the surface of the snow or ice; also called *flat-footing.*

frictioning. *See* **smearing.**

front-pointing. Kicking front crampon points into hard snow or ice; also known as *German technique.*

G

German technique. *See* **front-pointing.**

glissade. A controlled slide on snow.

H

HACE. *See* **high-altitude cerebral edema.**

***halbmastwurf sicherung* (HMS).** German for "half clove-hitch belay"; another term for the munter hitch. Carabiners stamped "HMS" accommodate the munter hitch.
HAPE. *See* **high-altitude pulmonary edema.**
heads. Malleable hardware used in aid climbing; also called circleheads, copperheads.
hero loop. *See* **tie-off loop.**
hex. Hexagonally shaped removable protection.
high-altitude cerebral edema (HACE). An altitude-related illness affecting the brain.
high-altitude pulmonary edema (HAPE). An altitude-related illness affecting the lungs.
hip belay. A method of applying friction to the rope with the belayer's body that does not require a mechanical device; also known as *body belay*.
HMS. *See* ***halbmastwurf sicherung*.**

I

ice ax. Specialized ax used by climbers, generally for snow and ice travel.
ice screw. Ice protection that is a tubular, hollow screw.
ice tool. Short ice ax or hammer used for technical ice climbing.
icefall. Steep, jumbled section of a glacier.

J

jamming. A basic technique of crack climbing in which a hand or foot is jammed into a crack, then turned or flexed so that it is snugly in contact with both sides of the crack and it will not come out when weighted.
jugging. Ascending the climbing rope with mechanical ascenders in aid climbing; also called *jumaring*.
jumaring. *See* **jugging.**

K

kernmantle rope. Rope composed of a core of braided or parallel nylon filaments encased in a smooth, woven sheath of nylon; designed specifically for climbing.
Kevlar. Aramid synthetic fiber trademarked by DuPont; used in accessory cord, among other things.
Kiwi coil. The preferred tie-in method for two-person glacier travel teams, for closer spacing between rope partners and more efficient travel.

L

leader. The climber who takes the lead on a roped pitch.
leashless tool. Ice tools specifically designed to be used without leashes.
Leave No Trace. Principles of minimum impact developed by the organization of the same name.
lieback. A rock climbing technique that uses hands in opposition to feet to create a counterforce.
load-limiting runner. A presewn runner with a series of weaker bar tacks that fail at lower impact forces and absorb high loads; also called *energy-absorbing sling*.

M

mantel. A climbing technique that uses hand down-pressure to permit raising of the feet.
matching. Climbing technique in which both hands or both feet are placed on the same hold.
moat. Gap between snow and rock.
moraine. Mounds of rock and debris deposited by a glacier.
mountaineering boot. Crampon-compatible, stiff-soled footwear.
munter hitch. A friction knot used for belaying; also called the *HMS*, the *Italian half hitch*.

N

***nieves penitentes*.** Snow pillars produced when suncup hollows become very deep, accentuating the ridges into columns of snow that look like a person wearing a penitent's cowl.
nut. Passive removable protection that is a wedging-type chock.
nut tool. *See* **chock pick.**
nylon cord. *See* **accessory cord.**

O

objective hazard. Physical hazard associated with a climbing route, such as rockfall, exposure, and high altitude.
off-width. A crack that is too wide for a hand jam but too narrow for chimney technique.
open book. *See* **dihedral.**

P

Perlon. A fiber similar to nylon. *See* **accessory cord.**
picket. An aluminum stake used for an anchor in snow.
pitch. The distance between belays on a climb.
piton. A metal spike used as protection.
plunge-stepping. A technique for walking down a snow slope that involves assertively stepping away from

the slope and landing solidly on the heel with the leg vertical (but not with the knee locked), transferring weight to the new position.

posthole. To sink deeply with each step in snow.

protection. Point of attachment that links climbing rope to the terrain; also known as *pro*.

prusik. A friction hitch. Also a technique for ascending a climbing rope using friction hitches.

Q

quickdraw. A presewn runner, typically 4 to 8 inches (10 to 20 centimeters) long, with a carabiner loop sewn into each end.

R

randonée skiing. Ski technique used by climbers that employs hybrid equipment allowing free-heel ascent and alpine descent and that accommodates climbing boots; also known as *alpine touring, ski mountaineering*.

rappel anchor. *See* **anchor**.

rappeling. The technique of descending a rope by using friction to safely control the rate of descent.

rest step. Ascent technique that ends every step with a momentary stop relying on skeletal structure to give muscles a rest.

rock shoe. Specialized rock climbing footwear with a sticky rubber sole.

rope drag. Friction that impedes the rope's travel.

runner. Length of webbing or accessory cord used to connect components of the climbing safety system; also called a *sling*.

running belay. Climbing technique in which all members of the rope team climb at the same time, relying on immediate protection rather than a fixed belay; also called *simul-climbing*.

S

scrambling. Unroped, off-trail travel that requires some use of hands.

scree. Loose slope of rock fragments smaller than talus.

second. The climber who follows the leader on a roped pitch; also known as a *follower*.

self-arrest. Ice-ax technique used to stop a fall on snow.

self-belay. Ice-ax technique in which the ice ax is jammed straight down into the snow and held by the head or head and shaft.

serac. Tower of ice on a glacier.

simul-climbing. *See* **running belay**.

single-pulley system. *See* **2:1 pulley system**.

ski mountaineering. *See* **randonée skiing**.

skins. Strips of textured material attached to the bottom of skis for traction.

SLCD. *See* **spring-loaded camming device**.

sling. *See* **runner**.

smearing. Rock climbing technique in which the foot points uphill and the climber maximizes contact between the rock and the sole of the shoe for friction; also called *frictioning*.

snow pit. Pit dug into snow in order to observe snow conditions.

soft shells. Stretch-woven shell garments designed to maximize wind and water resistance, plus breathability.

Spectra. Ultra-high-molecular-weight polyethylene or high-modulus polyethylene synthetic fiber. *See* **accessory cord**.

SPF. Sun protection factor, the rating system that quantifies the degree of sun protection provided by a sunscreen product.

sport climbing. Technical rock climbing that relies on fixed protection or a top rope and does not require mountaineering skills; compare *trad climbing*.

spring-loaded camming device (SLCD). Active removable protection that uses spring-loaded cams to create opposing force in a crack. Also called a *cam*.

spring-loaded wedge. A chock that uses a small sliding piece to expand the profile of the chock after it is placed in a crack.

static rope. A rope that does not stretch; used for fixed lines and hauling.

stemming. Climbing technique using counterforce in which one foot presses against one feature while the other foot or an opposing hand pushes against another feature; commonly used to climb chimneys or dihedrals. Also called *bridging*.

step-kicking. Climbing technique that creates ascending steps in snow.

stopper. *See* **wired nut**.

suncup. Small hollow in snow or ice that is created by melting and evaporation.

T

talus. Rock fragments large enough to step on individually. *See also* **scree**.

team arrest. Arrest effected by several members of a rope team on a snow slope.

technical climbing. Climbing in which belays or protection should be used for safety.

3:1 pulley system. Rescue system that theoretically triples the amount of weight a rescue team could haul without a pulley; also called *Z-pulley system.*

tie-off loop. Short runner commonly used for tying off belays, for self-belay during a rappel, in aid climbing, and in rescue. Also called *hero loop.*

topos. Topographic maps or route sketches.

top-roping. A technique used in sport climbing in which the climber is belayed using a rope that runs up from the belayer, through a preplaced top anchor, and back down to the climber.

trad climbing. Technical rock climbing in which climbers place and remove protection; compare *sport climbing.*

Tricam. Removable protection with a lobe-shaped camming wedge; can be set actively or passively.

tube chock. Telescoping protection used for off-width cracks.

2:1 pulley system. Rescue system that theoretically doubles the amount of weight that a rescue team could haul without a pulley; also called *single-pulley system, C-pulley system.*

U

UIAA. Union Internationale des Associations d'Alpinisme, the internationally recognized authority in setting standards for climbing equipment. *See also* **CEN.**

UPF. Ultraviolet protection factor, the rating system that quantifies the degree of sun protection provided by a garment.

V

verglas. The thin, clear coating of ice that forms when rainfall or melting snow freezes on a rock surface.

V-thread anchor. A V-shaped tunnel bored into the ice, with accessory cord or webbing threaded through the tunnel and tied to form a sling.

V-thread tool. A hooking device used to pull accessory cord or webbing through the drilled tunnel of a V-thread ice anchor.

W

webbing. *See* **runner.**

Web-o-lette. Cordelette made of ½-inch (12-millimeter) nylon-Dyneema webbing with a carabiner loop sewn into each end.

wired nut. Passive removable protection; also known as *chock, stopper.*

Z

Z-pulley system. *See* **3:1 pulley system.**

INDEX

Page numbers in **boldface** indicate illustrations

D

E

THE MOUNTAINEERS, founded in 1906, is a nonprofit outdoor activity and conservation organization based in Seattle, Washington. The Mountaineers' mission is "To enrich the community by helping people explore, conserve, learn about, and enjoy the lands and waters of the Pacific Northwest."

The Mountaineers sponsors classes and year-round outdoor activities, including hiking, mountain climbing, backpacking, skiing, snowboarding, snowshoeing, bicycling, camping, kayaking and canoeing, nature study, photography, sailing, and adventure travel; these classes and activities are open to both members and the general public. The Mountaineers' conservation efforts support environmental causes through educational activities and programming, and through its publishing division. All activities are led by skilled, experienced volunteers, who are dedicated to promoting safe and responsible enjoyment and preservation of the outdoors.

If you would like more information on programs or membership, please write to The Mountaineers Program Center, 7700 Sand Point Way NE, Seattle, WA 98115-3996; phone 206-521-6001; visit www.mountaineers.org; or e-mail clubmail@mountaineers.org.

THE MOUNTAINEERS BOOKS, the nonprofit publishing division of The Mountaineers, produces guidebooks, instructional texts, historical works, natural history guides, and, through partnership with Braided River, works on environmental conservation. Books are aimed at fulfilling the mission of The Mountaineers. For more information please visit www.mountaineersbooks.org and www.BraidedRiver.org.

Send or call for our catalog of more than 500 outdoor titles:

The Mountaineers Books
1001 SW Klickitat Way, Suite 201
Seattle, WA 98134
800-553-4453
mbooks@mountaineersbooks.org
www.mountaineersbooks.org

THE MOUNTAINEERS FOUNDATION is a public foundation established in 1968 to promote the study of mountains, forests, and streams, and to contribute to the preservation of natural beauty and ecological integrity. The Mountaineers Foundation fulfills its mission by stewardship of important preserves and by awarding grants. Grants are targeted for startup activities, important small-scale studies, and innovative initiatives. Flexible cooperation with the Trust for Public Lands, The Nature Conservancy of Washington, and other conservation agencies greatly extends the foundation's ability to preserve habitats, protect wilderness areas, and remove the threat of development from other significant lands. The Mountaineers Foundation is a 501(c)(3) charitable organization and contributions to The Mountaineers Foundation are tax deductible to the extent allowed by the United States Internal Revenue Code. More information is available at www.mountaineersfoundation.org or through The Mountaineers.

The Mountaineers Books is proud to be a corporate sponsor of The Leave No Trace Center for Outdoor Ethics, whose mission is to promote and inspire responsible outdoor recreation through education, research, and partnerships. The Leave No Trace program is focused specifically on human-powered (nonmotorized) recreation.

Leave No Trace strives to educate visitors about the nature of their recreational impacts, as well as offer techniques to prevent and minimize such impacts. Leave No Trace is best understood as an educational and ethical program, not as a set of rules and regulations.

For more information, visit www.LNT.org, or call 800-332-4100.